See what students love about LearningCurve.

 Macmillan Education **LearningCurve** learningcurveworks.com

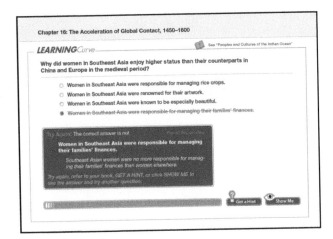

"With LearningCurve, students engage with the content and retain it better."

— Melissa Walker,
Converse College

Students using LaunchPad receive access to LearningCurve for *Understanding World Societies*.

Each chapter-based LearningCurve activity gives students multiple chances to understand key concepts, return to the narrative textbook if they need to reread, and answer questions correctly.

Over 90% of students report satisfaction with LearningCurve's fun and accessible game-like interface.

Assigning LearningCurve in place of reading quizzes is easy for instructors, and the reporting features help instructors track overall class trends and spot topics that are giving students trouble so that they can adjust lectures and class activities.

To learn more about LearningCurve, visit learningcurveworks.com.

LearningCurve: Everyone's got a learning curve — what's yours?

Each section has tools that help you focus on what's important.

The **question in red** asks about the specific topic being discussed in this section. Pause to answer each one after you read the section.

> ## How was the era of global contact shaped by new commodities, commercial empires, and forced migrations?

A New World Sugar Refinery in Brazil

Sugar was the most important and most profitable plantation crop in the New World. This image shows the processing and refinement of sugar on a Brazilian plantation. Sugarcane was grown, harvested, and processed by African slaves who labored under brutal and ruthless conditions to generate enormous profits for plantation owners. (The Bridgeman Art Library/Getty Images)

THE CENTURIES-OLD AFROEURASIAN trade world was forever changed by the European voyages of discovery and their aftermath. For the first time, a truly global economy emerged in the sixteenth and seventeenth centuries, and it forged new links among far-flung peoples, cultures, and societies.

The Columbian Exchange

Key terms in the margins give you background on important people, ideas, and events. Use these for reference while you read, but also think about which terms are emphasized and why they matter.

Columbian exchange
▶ The exchange of animals, plants, and diseases between the Old and the New Worlds.

The travel of people and goods between the Old and New Worlds led to an exchange of animals, plants, and diseases, a complex process known as the Columbian exchange. As we have seen, the introduction of new diseases to the Americas had devastating consequences. But other results of the exchange brought benefits not only to the Europeans but also to native peoples.

Everywhere they settled, the Spanish and Portuguese brought and raised wheat. Grapes and olives brought over from Spain did well in parts of Peru and Chile. Perhaps the most significant introduction to the diet of Native Americans

Memorizing facts and dates for a history class won't get you very far. That's because history isn't just about "facts." This textbook is designed to help you focus on what's truly significant in the history of world societies and to give you practice thinking like a historian.

Nezahualpilli At the time of the arrival of Europeans, Nezahualpilli was ruler of the city-state of Texcoco, the second most important city in the Aztec Empire after Tenochtitlan. (Nezahualpilli, portrait from *Codex Ixtlilxochitl*, 1582, pigment on European paper/Bibliothèque Nationale, Paris, France/De Agostini Picture Library/akg-images)

> What was the Afroeurasian trade world like prior to the éra of European exploration?

> Why and how did Europeans undertake ambitious voyages of expansion?

> What was the impact of Iberian conquest and settlement on the peoples and ecologies of the Americas?

> How was the era of global contact shaped by new commodities, commercial empires, and forced migrations?

> How did new encounters shape cultural attitudes and beliefs in Europe and the New World?

The **chapter-opening questions** are also the questions that open the new sections of the chapter and will be addressed in turn on the following pages. You should think about answers to them as you read.

How to use this book to figure out what's really important

> The **chapter title** tells you the subject of the chapter and identifies the time span that will be covered.

> The **opening question** and **chapter introduction** identify the most important themes, events, and people that will be explored in the chapter.

16
THE ACCELERATION OF GLOBAL CONTACT
1450–1600

> **What new global connections were forged in the fifteenth and sixteenth centuries?** Chapter 16 examines the causes, course, and effects of European expansion in the fifteenth and sixteenth centuries. Before 1500 Europeans were relatively marginal players in a centuries-old trading system that linked Africa, Asia, and Europe. By 1550 the European search for better access to Asian trade goods had led to a new overseas empire in the Indian Ocean and the accidental discovery of the Western Hemisphere. With this discovery South and North America were drawn into an international network of trade centers and political empires, which Europeans came to dominate. The era of globalization had begun, creating new political systems and forms of economic exchange as well as cultural assimilation, conversion, and resistance.

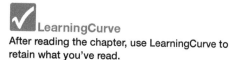
LearningCurve
After reading the chapter, use LearningCurve to retain what you've read.

Understanding
World Societies

A HISTORY

For Bedford / St. Martin's

Vice President, Editorial, Macmillan Higher Education Humanities: Edwin Hill
Publisher for History: Michael Rosenberg
Director of Development for History: Jane Knetzger
Associate Editor for History: Robin Soule
Production Editor: Annette Pagliaro Sweeney
Senior Production Supervisor: Dennis Conroy
Executive Marketing Manager: Sandra McGuire
Project Manager: Katrina Ostler, Jouve
Editorial Assistant: Arrin Kaplan
Cartography: Mapping Specialists, Ltd.
Photo Researcher: Bruce Carson
Director of Rights and Permissions: Hilary Newman
Senior Art Director: Anna Palchik
Cover Design: William Boardman
Cover Art: Woman meeting with a Yogini (detail)
Indian, early to mid-18th century
Object Place: possibly Golconda, Deccan, southern India
Opaque watercolor and gold on paper
23.2 × 18.9 cm (9 1/8 × 7 7/16 in.)
Museum of Fine Arts, Boston
Marshall H. Gould Fund
64.2024
Photograph © 2014 Museum of Fine Arts, Boston.
All rights reserved/Bridgeman Images.
Composition: Jouve
Printing and Binding: King Printing Co., Inc.

9 8 7
f e d

For information, write: Bedford/St. Martin's, 75 Arlington Street, Boston, MA 02116
(617-399-4000)

ISBN 978-1-4576-9992-4 (Combined Edition)
ISBN 978-1-319-00837-6 (Volume 1)
ISBN 978-1-319-00838-3 (Volume 2)

Acknowledgments

Understanding
World Societies

A HISTORY   SECOND EDITION

John P. McKay
University of Illinois at Urbana-Champaign

Bennett D. Hill
Late of Georgetown University

John Buckler
Late of University of Illinois at Urbana-Champaign

Patricia Buckley Ebrey
University of Washington

Roger B. Beck
Eastern Illinois University

Clare Haru Crowston
University of Illinois at Urbana-Champaign

Merry E. Wiesner-Hanks
University of Wisconsin–Milwaukee

Jerry Dávila
University of Illinois at Urbana-Champaign

Bedford/St. Martin's
Boston • New York

20°E 40°E 60°E 80°E 100°E 120°E 140°E 160°E 80°N

60°N

40°N

EUROPE

ALPS

URAL MTS.

Volga R.

Ob R.

ASIA

GOBI

Yellow R. (Huang He)

HIMALAYA MTS.

Yangzi R.

Mediterranean Sea

Tropic of Cancer

ARABIAN DESERT

20°N

SAHARA

AFRICA

Nile

Arabian Sea

Bay of Bengal

South China Sea

PACIFIC OCEAN

Congo R.

Equator 0°

INDIAN OCEAN

Zambezi R.

20°S

Tropic of Capricorn

KALAHARI DESERT

AUSTRALIA

Arctic Circle

Vegetation zones

Tundra
Northern forest
Temperate forest
Temperate grassland
Desert and dry shrub
Mediterranean shrub
Mountain grassland
Tropical grassland and savanna
Tropical forest
Permanent ice cover

40°S

60°S

Antarctic Circle

80°S

ARCTIC OCEAN

NORWAY
SWEDEN
FINLAND
DEN.
ESTONIA
LATVIA
LITHUANIA
GERMANY POLAND BELARUS
LUX. CZ.
SLK. UKRAINE
AUS. HUNG. MOLDOVA
SLN. ROMANIA
SWITZ. CR. SE.
ITALY MO. KO. BULGARIA
B.H.
ALB. MAC. GEORGIA
GREECE
TUNISIA
MALTA
CYPRUS
ISRAEL
Gaza Strip
West Bank
TURKEY
ARMENIA
AZERBAIJAN
SYRIA LEBANON
IRAQ
JORDAN
KUWAIT

RUSSIAN FEDERATION

KAZAKHSTAN
MONGOLIA
UZBEKISTAN KYRGYZSTAN
TURKMENISTAN TAJIKISTAN
AFGHANISTAN
IRAN
BAHRAIN
SAUDI ARABIA
QATAR
UNITED ARAB
EMIRATES
OMAN

N. KOREA
S. KOREA
JAPAN

CHINA

PACIFIC OCEAN

PAKISTAN
NEPAL
BHUTAN
BANGLADESH
INDIA
MYANMAR
(BURMA)
VIETNAM
LAOS
THAILAND
CAMBODIA

Taiwan

Mariana Is.
(U.S.)

Guam
(U.S.)

MARSHALL
IS.

ALGERIA
LIBYA
EGYPT

NIGER
CHAD
SUDAN
ERITREA
YEMEN
DJIBOUTI

NIGERIA
BENIN
TOGO
CENTRAL
AFRICAN REP.
SOUTH
SUDAN
ETHIOPIA
SOMALIA

CAMEROON
EQ.
GUINEA
GABON
CONGO
RWANDA
UGANDA
KENYA
DEM. REP. OF
THE CONGO
SÃO
TOMÉ
& PRÍNCIPE
BURUNDI
TANZANIA
COMOROS
SEYCHELLES

MALDIVES
SRI
LANKA

BRUNEI
MALAYSIA
PALAU

SINGAPORE

PHILIPPINES

FEDERATED STATES
OF MICRONESIA

NAURU
KIRIBATI

TUVALU

INDONESIA

PAPUA
NEW
GUINEA

SOLOMON
IS.

ANGOLA
ZAMBIA
MALAWI

INDIAN OCEAN

TIMOR
LESTE

VANUATU
FIJI

NAMIBIA
ZIMBABWE
BOTSWANA
MADAGASCAR

MAURITIUS

New Caledonia
(Fr.)

MOZAMBIQUE
SWAZILAND
SOUTH
AFRICA
LESOTHO

AUSTRALIA

NEW
ZEALAND

Tasmania
(Aust.)

ANTARCTICA

ABBREVIATIONS

ALB.	ALBANIA
AUS.	AUSTRIA
BEL.	BELGIUM
B.H.	BOSNIA AND HERZEGOVINA
CR.	CROATIA
CZ.	CZECH REPUBLIC
DEN.	DENMARK
HUNG.	HUNGARY
KO.	KOSOVO
LUX.	LUXEMBOURG
MAC.	MACEDONIA
MO.	MONTENEGRO
NETH.	NETHERLANDS
SE.	SERBIA
SLK.	SLOVAKIA
SLN.	SLOVENIA
SWITZ.	SWITZERLAND

THE CONTEMPORARY WORLD

Understanding
World Societies

A HISTORY

to pay tributes in cash, rather than in labor. To respond to a shortage of indigenous workers, royal officials established a new government-run system of forced labor, called *repartimiento* in New Spain and *mita* in Peru. Administrators assigned a certain percentage of the inhabitants of native communities to labor for a set period each year in public works, mining, agriculture, and other tasks.

Spanish systems for exploiting the labor of indigenous peoples were both a cause of and a response to the disastrous decline in the numbers of such peoples that began soon after the arrival of Europeans. Some indigenous people died as a direct result of the violence of conquest and the disruption of agriculture and trade caused by warfare. The most important cause of death, however, was infectious disease. Having little or no resistance to diseases brought from the Old World, the inhabitants of the New World fell victim to smallpox, typhus, influenza, and other illnesses.

The pattern of devastating disease and population loss established in the Spanish colonies was repeated everywhere Europeans settled. Overall, population declined by as much as 90 percent or more but with important regional variations. In general, densely populated urban centers were worse hit than rural areas and tropical, low-lying regions suffered more than cooler, higher-altitude ones.

Colonial administrators responded to native population decline by forcibly combining dwindling indigenous communities into new settlements and imposing the rigors of the encomienda and the repartimiento. By the end of the sixteenth century the search for fresh sources of labor had given birth to the new tragedy of the Atlantic slave trade (see page 598).

Patterns of Settlement

The century after the discovery of silver in 1545 marked the high point of Iberian immigration to the Americas. Although the first migrants were men, soon whole families began to cross the Atlantic, and the European population began to increase through natural reproduction. By 1600 American-born Europeans, called *Creoles*, outnumbered immigrants.

Iberian settlement was predominantly urban in nature. Spaniards settled into the cities and towns of the former Aztec and Inca Empires as the native population dwindled through death and flight. They also established new cities in which settlers were quick to establish urban institutions familiar to them from home: city squares, churches, schools, and universities.

Despite the growing number of Europeans and the rapid decline of the native population, Europeans remained a small minority of the total inhabitants of the Americas. Iberians formed sexual relationships with native women leading to a substantial population of mixed Iberian and Indian descent known as *mestizos* (meh-STEE-zohz). The large-scale arrival of enslaved Africans, starting in Brazil in the mid-sixteenth century, added new ethnic and racial dimensions to the population (see pages 598–603).

QUICK REVIEW <

What factors help explain the conquest of the mighty Inca and Aztec Empires by the Spanish?

| What was the impact of Iberian conquest and settlement on the peoples of the Americas? | How was the era of global contact shaped by new commodities and forced migrations? | How did new encounters shape cultural attitudes and beliefs in Europe and the New World? | LearningCurve Check what you know. |

473

The **quick review** helps you check your recall of the section before you resume reading.

The **chapter locator** at the bottom of the page puts this section in the context of the chapter as a whole so you can see how this section relates to what's coming next.

The Chapter Study Guide provides a process that will build your understanding and your historical skills.

STEP 1 Go to LaunchPad to complete the chapter's LearningCurve activity.

STEP 2 Identify the key terms and **explain** their significance.

STEP 3 Analyze differences and similarities among ideas, events, people, or societies discussed in the chapter.

> CHAPTER 16 STUDY GUIDE

STEP 1 **GET STARTED ONLINE**

✓ LearningCurve

Now that you've read the chapter, make it stick by completing the LearningCurve activity.

STEP 2 **EXPLAIN WHY IT MATTERS**

Put your reading into practice. Identify each term below, and then explain why it matters in world history.

TERM	WHO OR WHAT & WHEN	WHY IT MATTERS
bride wealth (p. 459)		
caravel (p. 462)		
Ptolemy's *Geography* (p. 462)		
Treaty of Tordesillas (p. 466)		
conquistador (p. 468)		
Aztec Empire (p. 469)		
Inca Empire (p. 469)		
viceroyalties (p. 472)		
captaincies (p. 472)		
encomienda system (p. 472)		
Columbian exchange (p. 474)		
Valladolid debate (p. 479)		
Black Legend (p. 479)		

STEP 3 **MOVE BEYOND THE BASICS**

To demonstrate a more advanced understanding of the nature and impact of Spanish exploration and conquest in the Americas, fill in the chart below with descriptions of the motives behind Spanish expansion across the Atlantic. Next, identify key Spanish conquests and discoveries and the institutions of Spanish rule in the Americas. Finally, describe the impact of Spanish conquest in the New World and Europe. How do the motives you listed help explain the course of Spanish expansion in the New World?

Motives	Conquests and Discoveries	Institutions of Spanish Rule	Impact in the New World and Europe

482

PUT IT ALL TOGETHER Now, take a step back and try to explain the big picture. Remember to use specific examples from the chapter in your answers.

THE AFROEURASIAN TRADE WORLD BEFORE COLUMBUS

▶ Which states were at the center of global trade prior to 1492? Why?

▶ Why were Europeans at a trading disadvantage prior to 1492? How did geography limit European participation in world trade? What role did Europe's economy and material culture play in this context?

DISCOVERY AND CONQUEST

▶ In your opinion, what was the most important motive behind European expansion? What evidence can you provide to support your position?

▶ What was the Columbian exchange? How did it transform both Europe and the Americas?

CHANGING VALUES AND BELIEFS

▶ How did European expansion give rise to new ideas about race?

▶ How did expansion complicate European's understanding of themselves and their place in the world?

LOOKING BACK, LOOKING AHEAD

▶ If Europe was at the periphery of the global trading system prior to 1492, where was it situated by the middle of the sixteenth century? What had changed? What had not?

▶ What connections can you make between our own experience of globalization in the twenty-first century and the experience of globalization in the sixteenth century? In what ways are the experiences similar? In what ways do they differ?

Imagine that you must give an oral report to the class answering the following question: What new global connections were forged in the fifteenth and sixteenth centuries? What would be the most important points and why?

STEP 4 Answer the big-picture questions using specific examples or evidence from the chapter.

ACTIVE RECITATION Explain how you would answer the chapter-opening question in your own words to make sure you have a firm grasp of the most important themes and events of the chapter.

PREFACE: Why This Book This Way

Understanding World Societies grew out of many conversations we have had among ourselves and with other instructors about the teaching and learning of history. We knew that instructors wanted a world history text that introduced students to the broad sweep of history but that also re-created the lives of ordinary men and women in appealing human terms. We knew that instructors wanted a text that presented cutting-edge scholarship in new fields of historical inquiry. We also knew that many instructors wanted a text that would help students focus as they read, keep their interest in the material, and encourage them to learn historical thinking skills. It is our hope that *Understanding World Societies* addresses all of these concerns.

The second edition of *Understanding World Societies* continues to provide the social and cultural focus, comprehensive regional organization, and global perspective that have long been hallmarks of the book. All three of these qualities have been greatly enhanced by the addition of a new member to the author team, Jerry Dávila from the University of Illinois, who brings expertise in Latin America and the twentieth century. A renowned scholar of Brazil whose work focuses on race and social policy, Jerry offers a fresh perspective to our coverage of Latin America and to the final chapters in the book, which he has completely reconceptualized. Not only do we thus continue to benefit from a collaborative team of regional experts with deep experience in the world history classroom, but we are also pleased to introduce a suite of digital tools designed to save you time and help students gain confidence and learn historical thinking skills.

New Tools for the Digital Age

Because we know that your classroom needs are changing rapidly, we are excited to announce that *Understanding World Societies* is available with **LaunchPad**. Free when packaged with the book, or heavily discounted as a stand-alone product, LaunchPad's course space and interactive e-book is ready to use as is or can be edited and customized with your own material and assigned right away. Developed with extensive feedback from history instructors and students, LaunchPad includes the complete narrative e-book, as well as abundant primary documents, maps, images, assignments, and activities. The aims of key learning outcomes are addressed via formative and summative assessment, short-answer and essay questions, multiple-choice quizzing, and **LearningCurve**, an adaptive learning tool designed to get students to read before they come to class. Available with training and support, LaunchPad can help you take your teaching into a new era. To learn more about the benefits of LearningCurve and LaunchPad, see the "Versions and Supplements" section on page xxix and see below on how specific skills-based features of *Understanding World Societies* benefit from the ability to assign and track student work in LaunchPad.

Understanding World Societies: Bringing the Past to Life for Students

In this age of global connections, with its influence on the global economy, global migration patterns, popular culture, and global warming, among other things, the study of world history is more vital and urgent than ever before. An understanding of the broad sweep of the human past helps us comprehend today's dramatic changes and enduring continuities. People now migrate enormous distances and establish new lives far from their places of birth, yet migration has been a constant in history since the first humans walked out of Africa. Satellite and cell phones now link nearly every inch of the planet, yet the expansion of communication networks is a process that is thousands of years old. Children who speak different languages at home now sit side by side in schools and learn from one another, yet intercultural encounters have long been a source of innovation, transformation, and at times, unfortunately, conflict.

This book is designed for twenty-first-century students who will spend their lives on this small interconnected planet and for whom an understanding of only local or national history will no longer be sufficient. We believe that the study of world history in a broad and comparative context is an exciting, important, and highly practical pursuit. It is our conviction, based on considerable experience in introducing large numbers of students to world history, that a book reflecting current trends in scholarship can excite readers and inspire an enduring interest in the long human experience.

Our strategy has been twofold. First, we have made social and cultural history the core elements of our narrative. We seek to re-create the lives of ordinary people in appealing human terms and also to highlight the interplay between men's and women's lived experiences and the ways they reflect on these to create meaning. Thus, in addition to foundational works of philosophy and literature, we include popular songs and stories. We present objects along with texts as important sources for studying history, and this has allowed us to incorporate the growing emphasis on material culture in the work of many historians. At the same time, we have been mindful of the need to give great economic, political, and intellectual developments the attention they deserve. We want to give individual students and instructors an integrated perspective so that they can pursue—on their own or in the classroom—the themes and questions that they find particularly exciting and significant.

Second, we have made every effort to strike an effective global and regional balance. The whole world interacts today, and to understand the interactions and what they mean for today's citizens, we must study the whole world's history. Thus we have adopted a comprehensive regional organization with a global perspective that is clear and manageable for students. For example, Chapter 7 introduces students in depth to East Asia, and at the same time the chapter highlights the cultural connections that occurred via the Silk Road and the spread of Buddhism. We study all geographical areas, conscious of the separate histories of many parts of the world, particularly in the earliest millennia of human development. We also stress the links among cultures, political units, and economic systems, for these connections have made the world what it is today. We make comparisons and connections across time as well as space, for understanding the unfolding of the human story in time is the central task of history.

An Inquiry-Based Model Designed for Understanding

By employing innovative pedagogy, we believe that *Understanding World Societies* helps students not only understand the book's major developments but also begin to grasp the question-driven methodology that is at the heart of the historian's craft. Each chapter opens with a **new chapter-opening question** that drives students toward the overarching themes of the chapter, followed by a **brief chapter introduction** that identifies the most important events and people to be discussed. **Section-opening headings** expressed as questions and **section-ending quick review questions** further model the kinds of questions historians ask and help students engage in inquiry-based reading and understanding.

Chapter Study Guides Designed for Active Learning

At the core of the unique pedagogical features of *Understanding World Societies* are the revised **Chapter Study Guides** that provide a carefully structured four-step process to help students build deep understanding of the chapter material. In **Step 1**, students go to LaunchPad to complete the LearningCurve activity to ensure that they have a grasp of the basic content and concepts of the chapter. In **Step 2**, students not only identify the chapter's key terms but also explain why each matters. In **Step 3**, they begin to apply their understanding of the chapter material through activities that ask them to consider comparison, change over time, or cause and effect. In **Step 4**, analytical and synthetic questions require students to engage in higher-order historical thinking. And, finally, in an active recitation exercise, students **answer the chapter-opening question** to fully realize their understanding of the chapter. In LaunchPad, instructors can assign the NEW **Guided Reading Exercise** for each chapter, which prompts students to read actively to collect information that answers a broad analytic question central to the chapter as a whole.

Primary Sources for Teaching Critical Thinking and Analysis

Understanding World Societies offers an extensive program of primary source assignments to help students master a number of key learning outcomes, among them **critical thinking**, **historical thinking**, **analytical thinking**, **argumentation**, and learning about the **diversity of world cultures**. When assigned in LaunchPad, all primary source features are accompanied by multiple-choice quizzes that help you ensure that students come to class prepared.

New assignable **Online Document Projects** in LaunchPad offer students more practice in interpreting primary sources. Each project, based on the Individuals in Society feature described below, prompts students to explore a key question through analysis of multiple sources. Chapter 22, for example, asks students to analyze documents on the complexities of the Haitian Revolution and the conditions that made Toussaint L'Ouverture's story possible. Auto-graded multiple-choice questions based on the documents help students analyze the sources.

Finally, we have revised our **primary source documents collection**, *Sources for World Societies*, to add more visual sources and to closely align the readings with the chapter topics and themes of the second edition. The documents are now available in a fully assignable and assessable electronic format within each LaunchPad unit, and the accompanying multiple-choice questions measure comprehension and hold students accountable for their reading.

Student Engagement with Biography

In our years of teaching world history, we have often noted that students come alive when they encounter stories about real people in the past. To give students a chance to see the past through ordinary people's lives, each chapter includes one of the popular **Individuals in Society** biographical essays, each of which offers a brief study of an individual or a group, informing students about the societies in which the individuals lived. This feature grew out of our long-standing focus on people's lives and the varieties of historical experience, and we believe that readers will empathize with these human beings who themselves were seeking to define their own identities. The spotlighting of individuals, both famous and obscure, perpetuates the book's continued attention to cultural and intellectual developments, highlights human agency, and reflects changing interests within the historical profession as well as the development of "micro-history." As mentioned previously, the majority of these features are tied to **NEW Online Document Projects**, available in LaunchPad, that allow students to explore further the historical conditions in which these individuals lived. **NEW** features include essays on Sudatta, a lay follower of the Buddha; Cosimo and Lorenzo de' Medici; Malintzin; and Sieng, a Mnong refugee living in the United States.

Geographical and Visual Literacy

We recognize students' difficulties with geography and visual analysis, and the new edition retains our **Mapping the Past map activities** and **Picturing the Past visual activities**. Included in each chapter, these activities ask students to analyze the map or visual and make connections to the larger processes discussed in the narrative, giving them valuable practice in reading and interpreting maps and images. In LaunchPad, they are assignable, and students can submit their work. Throughout the textbook and online in LaunchPad, more than **92 full-size maps** illustrate major developments in the chapter. In addition, **74 spot maps** are embedded in the narrative to show specific areas under discussion.

Chronological Reasoning

To help students make comparisons, understand change over time, and see relationships among contemporaneous events, each chapter begins with a **chapter chronology** that reviews major developments discussed in the chapter. This chronology, available from every page in LaunchPad, allows students to compare developments over the centuries.

Better-Prepared Students

To help students fully understand their reading and come to class prepared, instructors who adopt LaunchPad for *Understanding World Societies* can assign the **LearningCurve** formative assessment activities. This online learning tool is popular with students because it helps them rehearse content at their own pace in a nonthreatening, game-like environment. LearningCurve is also popular with instructors because the reporting features allow them to track overall class trends and spot topics that are giving students trouble so they can adjust their lectures and class activities. When LearningCurve is assigned, students come to class better prepared, and instructors can better evaluate and adjust their classes.

To further encourage students to read and fully assimilate the text as well as measure how well they do this, instructors can assign the **new multiple-choice summative quizzes** in LaunchPad, where they are automatically graded. These secure tests not only encourage students to study the book, they can be assigned at specific intervals as high-stakes testing and thus provide another means for analyzing class performance.

Organizational and Textual Changes

To meet the demands of the evolving course, we have made several major changes in the organization of chapters to reflect the way the course is taught today. The most dramatic changes are the reordering of Chapter 17: "The Islamic World Powers, 1300–1800" (formerly Chapter 20) and a complete overhaul of the final section of the book, covering the postwar era. This new placement for our coverage of Islam reflects a growing interest among instructors and students in the Islamic world and highlights early Islamic cultural contributions.

To address the concerns of instructors who teach from the second volume of the text, we have added a new section on the Reformation to Chapter 18 so that students whose courses begin with Chapters 15 or 16 will now receive that coverage in Volume 2. The new section includes the Protestant and Catholic Reformations, as well as religious violence and witch-hunts.

In its examination of the age of revolution in the Atlantic world, Chapter 22 now incorporates revolutions in Latin America. In order to provide a more global perspective on European politics, culture, and economics in the early modern period, Chapter 23 on the Industrial Revolution considers industrialization more broadly as a global phenomenon with a new section titled "The Global Picture." Together, the enhanced global perspectives of these chapters help connect the different regions of the globe and, in particular, help explain the crucial period when Europe began to dominate the rest of the globe.

The final section of the text covering the post-1945 period has also been completely reworked. In addition to updating all of the postwar chapters through 2014, Jerry Dávila substantially rewrote and streamlined the last four chapters into three to create a more tightly focused and accessible section that now divides the period chronologically as follows: *Chapter 31: Decolonization, Revolution, and the Cold War, 1945–1968*; *Chapter 32: Liberalization, 1968–2000s*; *Chapter 33: The Contemporary World in Historical Perspective*. The last three chapters are now organized around two dominant themes of the postwar world: liberation movements that challenged power structures such as colonialism and racial supremacism and the spread of liberalization that characterized the end of the Cold War in particular, marking the rise of free markets and liberal political systems. The final chapter examines the significance of social movements in shaping a contemporary world that continues to struggle with historic conflicts and inequalities.

In terms of specific textual changes, we have worked hard to keep the book up to date and to strengthen our comprehensive, comparative, and connective approach. Moreover, we revised every chapter with the goal of readability and accessibility. Highlights of the new edition include:

- Chapter 1 includes new information on the recent archaeological find at Göbekli Tepe in present-day Turkey that suggests that cultural factors may have played a role in the development of agriculture.
- Chapter 2 has new coverage on Egyptian society and a discussion of gender distinctions in Sumerian society.
- In Chapter 6, the section on the founding of Rome has been completely rewritten.
- Chapter 8 contains a new section on Christian missionaries and conversion, and it explains the process of the Christianization of barbarian Europe.
- Chapter 11 now centers on the ways in which systems of religious belief shaped ancient societies of the Americas and provided tools that people used to understand and adapt their world. It also looks at the role of sources produced after the European encounter in shaping our understanding of the histories of indigenous American empires.
- An expanded discussion of witchcraft in Chapter 15 now discusses practices of indigenous peoples in the New World.
- Chapter 18 has expanded coverage of Russian imperial expansion as well as a new section called "Peoples Beyond Borders" that includes piracy and gives students a feeling for the ways in which imperial borders were often more real on the map than in real life.
- In Chapter 19, a new section called "The Early Enlightenment" clarifies the mixture of religious, political, and scientific thought that characterized the early period of the Enlightenment.
- Chapter 22 emphasizes the indigenous origins of the Haitian revolution by highlighting the African backgrounds of slaves and the considerable military experience many of them had, which helps explain how they could defeat the French and British.
- Chapter 23 has been heavily revised to reflect new scholarship on industrialization and to provide a broader, more comparative perspective.
- A new section in Chapter 24 on social and economic conflict connects the industrialization of continental Europe with the political coverage of the revolutions of 1848.
- Chapter 27 now focuses on the Americas within the framework of liberalism and examines connections between the experiences with settlement, state formation, and economic integration in the United States and Latin America.
- Chapter 29 contains more detail on the reforms of emir Amanullah Khan in the section on the modernization of Afghanistan.
- As noted previously, the final three chapters of the book have been entirely rewritten by new author Jerry Dávila.

In sum, we have tried to bring new research and interpretation into our global history, believing it essential to keep our book stimulating, accurate, and current for students and instructors.

Acknowledgments

It is a pleasure to thank the many instructors who critiqued the parent textbook, *A History of World Societies*, Tenth Edition. Their feedback helped inform the shape this book has taken.

Stewart Anderson, *Brigham Young University*

Brian Arendt, *Lindenwood University*

Stephen Auerbach, *Georgia College*

Michael Bardot, *Lincoln University*

Natalie Bayer, *Drake University*

Michael Bazemore, *William Peace University*

Brian Becker, *Delta State University*

Rosemary Bell, *Skyline College*

Chris Benedetto, *Granite State College*

Wesley L. Bishop, *Pitt Community College*

Robert Blackey, *California State University–San Bernardino*

Edward Bond, *Alabama A&M University*

Nathan Brooks, *New Mexico State University*

Jurgen Buchenau, *The University of North Carolina at Charlotte*

Paul Buckingham, *Morrisville State College*

Steven B. Bunker, *University of Alabama*

Kate Burlingham, *California State University, Fullerton*

David Bush, *The College of the Siskiyous*

Laura M. Calkins, *Texas Tech University*

Robert Caputi, *Erie Community College–North Campus*

Lucia Carter, *Mars Hill College*

Lesley Chapel, *Saginaw Valley State University*

Nevin Crouse, *Chesapeake College*

Everett Dague, *Benedictine College*

Peter de Rosa, *Bridgewater State University*

Jeffrey Demsky, *San Bernardino Valley College*

Nicholas Di Liberto, *Newberry College*

Randall Dills, *University of Louisville*

Shawn Dry, *Oakland Community College*

Roxanne Easley, *Central Washington University*

John Fielding, *Mount Wachusett Community College*

Barbara Fuller, *Indian River State College*

Dolores Grapsas, *New River Community College*

Emily Fisher Gray, *Norwich University*

Gayle Greene-Aguirre, *Mississippi Gulf Coast Community College*

Neil Greenwood, *Cleveland State Community College*

Christian Griggs, *Dalton State College*

W. Scott Haine, *Cañada College*

Irwin Halfond, *McKendree University*

Alicia Harding, *Southern Maine Community College*

Jillian Hartley, *Arkansas Northeastern College*

Robert Haug, *University of Cincinnati*

John Hunt, *Utah Valley University*

Fatima Imam, *Lake Forest College*
Rashi Jackman, *De Anza College*
Jackie Jay, *Eastern Kentucky University*
Timothy Jenks, *East Carolina University*
Andrew Kellett, *Harford Community College*
Christine Kern, *Edinboro University*
Christopher Killmer, *St. Johns River State College*
Mark Klobas, *Scottsdale Community College*
Chris Laney, *Berkshire Community College*
Erick D. Langer, *Georgetown University*
Mary Jean Lavery, *Delaware County Community College*
Mark Lentz, *University of Louisiana, Lafayette*
Darin Lenz, *Fresno Pacific University*
Yi Li, *Tacoma Community College*
Jonas Liliequist, *Umeå University*
Ron Lowe, *University of Tennessee at Chattanooga*
Mary Lyons-Carmona, *University of Nebraska at Omaha*
Elizabeth S. Manley, *Xavier University of Louisiana*
Brandon D. Marsh, *Bridgewater College*
Sean F. McEnroe, *Southern Oregon University*
John McLeod, *University of Louisville*
Brendan McManus, *Bemidji State University*
Christina Mehrtens, *University of Massachusetts-Dartmouth*
Charlotte Miller, *Middle Georgia State College*
Robert Montgomery, *Baldwin Wallace University*
Curtis Morgan, *Lord Fairfax Community College*
Richard Moss, *Harrisburg Area Community College*
Larry Myers, *Butler Community College*
Erik Lars Myrup, *University of Kentucky*
April Najjaj, *Mount Olive College*
Katie Nelson, *Weber State University*
Lily Rhodes Novicki, *Virginia Western Community College*
Monica Orozco, *Westmont College*
Neal Palmer, *Christian Brothers University*
Jenifer Parks, *Rocky Mountain College*
Melinda Pash, *Fayetteville Technical Community College*
Tao Peng, *Minnesota State University–Mankato*
Patricia Perry, *St. Edward's University*
William Plants, *University of Rio Grande/Rio Grande Community College*
Joshua Pollock, *Modesto Junior College*
Fabrizio Prado, *College of William & Mary*
Daniel Prosterman, *Salem College*
Tracie Provost, *Middle Georgia College*
Melissa Redd, *Pulaski Technical College*
Charles Reed, *Elizabeth City State University*
Leah Renold, *Texas State University*
Kim Richardson, *Front Range Community College*
David Ruffley, *Colorado Mountain College*
Martina Saltalamacchia, *University of Nebraska at Omaha*

Karl Schmidt, *South Dakota State University*
Kimberly Schutte, *SUNY–The College at Brockport*
Eva Seraphin, *Irvine Valley College*
Courtney Shah, *Lower Columbia College*
Jeffrey Shumway, *Brigham Young University*
David Simonelli, *Youngstown State University*
James Smith, *Southwest Baptist University*
Kara D. Smith, *Georgia Perimeter College*
Ilicia Sprey, *Saint Joseph's College*
Rachel Standish, *San Joaquin Delta College*
Kate Staples, *West Virginia University*
Brian Strayer, *Andrews University*
Sonia Chandarana Tandon, *Forsyth Technical Community College*
James Todesca, *Armstrong Atlantic State University*
Elisaveta Todorova, *University of Cincinnati*
Dianne Walker, *Baton Rouge Community College*
Kenneth Wilburn, *East Carolina University*
Carol Woodfin, *Hardin-Simmons University*
Laura Zeeman, *Red Rocks Community College*

It is also a pleasure to thank the many editors who have assisted us over the years, first at Houghton Mifflin and now at Bedford/St. Martin's. At Bedford/St. Martin's, these include associate editor Robin Soule; senior development editors Sara Wise and Laura Arcari; editorial assistant Arrin Kaplan; former executive editor Traci Mueller Crowell; director of development Jane Knetzger; former publisher for history Mary Dougherty; map editor Charlotte Miller; photo researcher Bruce Carson; text permissions editor Eve Lehmann; and production editor Annette Pagliaro Sweeney, with the assistance of Erica Zhang and the guidance of Sue Brown, director of editing, design, and media production, and managing editor Michael Granger. We would also like to thank former vice president for editorial humanities Denise Wydra and former president Joan E. Feinberg.

VERSIONS AND SUPPLEMENTS

Adopters of *Understanding World Societies* and their students have access to abundant print and digital resources and tools, including documents, assessment and presentation materials, the acclaimed Bedford Series in History and Culture volumes, and much more. And for the first time, the full-featured LaunchPad course space provides access to the narrative with all assignment and assessment opportunities at the ready. See below for more information, visit the book's catalog site at **bedfordstmartins.com/mckayworldunderstanding/catalog**, or contact your local Bedford/St. Martin's sales representative.

Get the Right Version for Your Class

To accommodate different course lengths and course budgets, *Understanding World Societies* is available in several different formats, including 3-hole-punched loose-leaf Budget Books versions and low-priced PDF e-books, such as the *Bedford e-Book to Go* from our Web site and other PDF e-books from other commercial sources. And for the best value of all, package a new print book with LaunchPad at no additional charge to get the best each format offers—a print version for easy portability and reading with a LaunchPad interactive e-book and course space with loads of additional assignment and assessment options.

- **Combined Volume** (Chapters 1–33): available in paperback, loose-leaf, and e-book formats and in LaunchPad
- **Volume 1, To 1600** (Chapters 1–16): available in paperback, loose-leaf, and e-book formats and in LaunchPad
- **Volume 2, Since 1450** (Chapters 16–33): available in paperback, loose-leaf, and e-book formats and in LaunchPad

As noted below, any of these volumes can be packaged with additional titles for a discount. To get ISBNs for discount packages, see the online catalog at **bedfordstmartins.com/mckayworldunderstanding/catalog** or contact your Bedford/St. Martin's representative.

NEW Assign LaunchPad — A Content-Rich and Assessment-Ready Interactive e-book and Course Space

Available for discount purchase on its own or for packaging with new books at no additional charge, LaunchPad is a breakthrough solution for today's courses. Intuitive and easy-to-use for students and instructors alike, LaunchPad is ready to use as is, but it can be edited, customized with your own material, and assigned in seconds. *LaunchPad for Understanding World Societies* includes Bedford/St.

Martin's high-quality content all in one place, including the full interactive e-book and the *Sources of World Societies* documents collection plus LearningCurve formative quizzing, guided reading activities designed to help students read actively for key concepts, additional primary sources, images, videos, chapter summative quizzes, and more.

Through a wealth of formative and summative assessments, including short-answer questions, essay questions, multiple-choice quizzing, and the adaptive learning program of LearningCurve (see the full description below), students gain confidence and get into their reading *before* class. Map and visual activities engage students with visual analysis and critical thinking as they work through each unit, while special boxed features become more meaningful through automatically graded multiple-choice exercises and short-answer questions that prompt students to analyze their reading.

LaunchPad easily integrates with course management systems, and with fast ways to build assignments, rearrange chapters, and add new pages, sections, or links, it lets teachers build the courses they want to teach and hold students accountable. For more information, visit **launchpadworks.com** or contact us at **history@bedfordstmartins.com** to arrange a demo.

✅ NEW Assign LearningCurve So Your Students Come to Class Prepared

Students using LaunchPad receive access to LearningCurve for *Understanding World Societies*. Assigning LearningCurve in place of reading quizzes is easy for instructors, and the reporting features help instructors track overall class trends and spot topics that are giving students trouble so they can adjust their lectures and class activities. This online learning tool is popular with students because it was designed to help them rehearse content at their own pace, in a nonthreatening, game-like environment. The feedback for wrong answers provides instructional coaching and sends students back to the book for review. Students answer as many questions as necessary to reach a target score, with repeated chances to revisit material they haven't mastered. When LearningCurve is assigned, students come to class better prepared.

Take Advantage of Instructor Resources

Bedford/St. Martin's has developed a rich array of teaching resources for this book and for this course. They range from lecture and presentation materials and assessment tools to course management options. Most can be found in LaunchPad or can be downloaded or ordered at **bedfordstmartins.com/mckayworldunderstanding /catalog**.

▶ **Instructor's Resource Manual.** The instructor's manual offers both experienced and first-time instructors tools for preparing lectures and running discussions. It includes chapter content learning objectives, teaching strategies, and a guide to chapter-specific supplements available for the text, plus suggestions on how to get the most out of LearningCurve and a survival guide for first-time teaching assistants.

▶ **Guide to Changing Editions.** Designed to facilitate an instructor's transition from the previous edition of *Understanding World Societies* to the second edition, this guide presents an overview of major changes as well as of changes in each chapter.

▶ **Computerized Test Bank.** The test bank includes a mix of fresh, carefully crafted multiple-choice, short-answer, and essay questions for each chapter. All questions appear in Microsoft Word format and in easy-to-use test bank software that allows instructors to add, edit, re-sequence, and print questions and answers. Instructors can also export questions into a variety of formats, including Blackboard, Desire2Learn, and Moodle.

▶ *The Bedford Lecture Kit:* **PowerPoint Maps and Images.** Look good and save time with ***The Bedford Lecture Kit***. These presentation materials are downloadable individually from the Instructor Resources tab at **bedfordstmartins .com/mckayworldunderstanding/catalog**. They include all maps, figures, and images from the textbook in JPEG and PowerPoint formats.

Package and Save Your Students Money

For information on free packages and discounts up to 50%, visit **bedfordstmartins .com/mckayworldunderstanding/catalog** or contact your local Bedford/St. Martin's sales representative. The products that follow all qualify for discount packaging.

▶ **The Bedford Series in History and Culture.** More than 100 titles in this highly praised series combine first-rate scholarship, historical narrative, and important primary documents for undergraduate courses. Each book is brief, inexpensive, and focused on a specific topic or period. For a complete list of titles, visit **bedfordstmartins.com/history/series**.

▶ *Rand McNally Atlas of World History.* This collection of almost 70 full-color maps illustrates the eras and civilizations in world history from the emergence of human societies to the present.

▶ *The Bedford Glossary for World History.* This handy supplement for the survey course gives students historically contextualized definitions for hundreds of terms—from *abolitionism* to *Zoroastrianism*—that they will encounter in lectures, reading, and exams.

▶ *World History Matters: A Student Guide to World History Online.* Based on the popular "World History Matters" Web site produced by the Center for History and New Media, this unique resource, edited by Kristin Lehner (The Johns Hopkins University), Kelly Schrum (George Mason University), and T. Mills Kelly (George Mason University), combines reviews of 150 of the most useful and reliable world history Web sites, with an introduction that guides students in locating, evaluating, and correctly citing online sources.

▶ **Trade Books.** Titles published by sister companies Hill and Wang; Farrar, Straus and Giroux; Henry Holt and Company; St. Martin's Press; Picador; and Palgrave Macmillan are available at a 50% discount when packaged with Bedford/St. Martin's textbooks. For more information, visit **bedfordstmartins.com /tradeup**.

▶ *A Pocket Guide to Writing in History.* This portable and affordable reference tool by Mary Lynn Rampolla provides reading, writing, and research advice useful to students in all history courses. Concise yet comprehensive advice on approaching typical history assignments, developing critical reading skills, writing effective history papers, conducting research, using and documenting sources, and avoiding plagiarism—enhanced with practical tips and examples throughout—has made this slim reference a best-seller.

▶ *A Student's Guide to History.* This complete guide to success in any history course provides the practical help students need to be successful. In addition to introducing students to the nature of the discipline, author Jules Benjamin teaches a wide range of skills, from preparing for exams to approaching common writing assignments, and explains the research and documentation process with plentiful examples.

BRIEF CONTENTS

CONTENTS

1

THE EARLIEST HUMAN SOCIETIES

TO 2500 B.C.E.   *2*

4

CHINA'S CLASSICAL AGE

TO 221 B.C.E. *88*

5

THE GREEK EXPERIENCE

3500–30 B.C.E. *114*

6

THE WORLD OF ROME

7

EAST ASIA AND THE SPREAD OF BUDDHISM

8

CONTINUITY AND CHANGE IN EUROPE AND WESTERN ASIA

250–850 *202*

9

THE ISLAMIC WORLD

600–1400 *232*

10

AFRICAN SOCIETIES AND KINGDOMS

1000 B.C.E.–1500 C.E. *266*

11

THE AMERICAS

2500 B.C.E.–1500 C.E. *296*

12

CULTURAL EXCHANGE IN CENTRAL AND SOUTHERN ASIA

300–1400 *328*

13

STATES AND CULTURES IN EAST ASIA

800–1400 *360*

16
THE ACCELERATION OF GLOBAL CONTACT

1450–1600 *454*

17
THE ISLAMIC WORLD POWERS

1300–1800 *484*

18
EUROPEAN POWER AND EXPANSION

1500–1750 *512*

19
NEW WORLDVIEWS AND WAYS OF LIFE

1540–1790 *548*

26

ASIA AND THE PACIFIC IN THE ERA OF IMPERIALISM

1800–1914 *780*

27

THE AMERICAS IN THE AGE OF LIBERALISM

1810–1910 *812*

32
LIBERALIZATION

1968–2000s *990*

33
THE CONTEMPORARY WORLD IN HISTORICAL PERSPECTIVE

1028

MAPS, FIGURES, AND TABLES

SPECIAL FEATURES

Understanding
World Societies

A HISTORY

1
THE EARLIEST HUMAN SOCIETIES

TO 2500 B.C.E.

> How did human societies change and develop in the Paleolithic and Neolithic Eras? Chapter 1 examines early human history, tracing developments from the first humans through the emergence of settled agriculture. Human history began in Africa, where millions of years ago humans evolved from a primate ancestor. They migrated out of Africa in several waves, walking along coasts and over land, eventually spreading across much of the earth. Their tools were initially multipurpose sharpened stones and sticks, but gradually they invented more specialized tools. Environmental changes, such as the advance and retreat of the glaciers, shaped life dramatically and may have led to the most significant change in all of human history, the domestication of plants and animals.

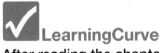**LearningCurve**
After reading the chapter, use LearningCurve to retain what you've read.

> How did humans evolve, and where did they migrate?

> What were the key features of Paleolithic society?

> How did plant and animal domestication develop, and what effects did it have on human society?

> How did growing social and gender hierarchies and expanding networks of trade increase the complexity of human society in the Neolithic period?

West African Man Humans began to portray themselves on the surfaces of places where they lived and traveled as early as 50,000 B.C.E. This rock painting from the region of Niger in Africa shows a person, perhaps a shaman, wearing a large headdress. (© David Coulson/Robert Estall photo agency/Alamy)

> How did humans evolve, and where did they migrate?

Fossil Footprints from Laetoli in Tanzania

About 3.5 million years ago, several australopithecines walked in wet ash from a volcanic eruption. Their footprints, discovered by the archaeologist Mary Leakey, indicate that they walked fully upright and suggest that they were not solitary creatures, for they walked close together. (John Reader/Science Source)

STUDYING THE EARLIEST ERA OF HUMAN HISTORY involves methods that seem simple—looking carefully at an object—as well as new high-tech procedures, such as DNA analysis. Through such research, scholars have examined early human evolution, traced the expansion of the human brain, and studied migration out of Africa and across the planet. Combined with spoken language, that larger brain enabled humans to adapt to many different environments and to be flexible in their responses to new challenges.

Understanding the Early Human Past

People throughout the world have developed systems of classification that help them understand things: earth and sky; seen and unseen; animal, vegetable, and mineral; past, present, and future. Among these systems of classification was

CHAPTER LOCATOR | How did humans evolve, and where did they migrate? | What were the key features of Paleolithic society?

CHAPTER 1
4   THE EARLIEST HUMAN SOCIETIES

ca. 4.4 million years ago
Ardipithecus evolve in Africa

ca. 2.5–4 million years ago
Australopithecus evolve in Africa

ca. 500,000–2 million years ago
Homo erectus evolve and spread out of Africa

ca. 250,000–9000 B.C.E.
Paleolithic era

ca. 250,000 years ago
Homo sapiens evolve in Africa

ca. 30,000–150,000 years ago
Neanderthals flourish in Europe and western Asia

ca. 120,000 years ago
Homo sapiens migrate out of Africa to Eurasia

ca. 50,000 years ago
Human migration to Australia

ca. 20,000–30,000 years ago
Possible human migration from Asia to the Americas

ca. 25,000 B.C.E.
Earliest evidence of woven cloth and baskets

ca. 15,000 B.C.E.
Earliest evidence of bows and atlatls; humans cross the Bering Strait land bridge to the Americas

ca. 15,000–10,000 B.C.E.
Final retreat of glaciers; megafaunal extinctions

ca. 9000 B.C.E.
Beginning of the Neolithic; horticulture; domestication of sheep and goats

ca. 7000 B.C.E.
Domestication of cattle; plow agriculture

ca. 5500 B.C.E.
Smelting of copper

ca. 5000 B.C.E.
Invention of pottery wheel

ca. 3200 B.C.E.
Earliest known invention of writing

ca. 3000 B.C.E.
Development of wheeled transport; beginning of bronze technology

ca. 2500 B.C.E.
Bronze technology becomes common in many areas; beginning of the Bronze Age

A note on dates: This book generally uses B.C.E. (Before the Common Era) and C.E. (Common Era) when giving dates, a system of chronology based on the Christian calendar and now used widely around the world. Scholars who study the very earliest periods of hominid and human history usually use the phrase "years ago" to date their subjects, as do astrophysicists and geologists; this is often abbreviated as B.P. (Before the Present). Because the scale of time covered in Chapter 1 is so vast, a mere 2,000 years does not make much difference, and so B.C.E. and "years ago" have similar meaning.

one invented in eighteenth-century Europe that divided all living things on earth into groups. Each of these divisions—such as that between plants and animals—is further subdivided into smaller and smaller groups, such as class, order, family, and genus. The final important division is the species, which is generally defined as a group of organisms that can interbreed with one another and produce fertile offspring of both sexes.

In their natural state, members of a species resemble one another, but over time they can become increasingly dissimilar. (Think of Chihuahuas and Great Danes, both members of the same species.) Ever since humans began shaping the world around them, this process has often been the result of human action. But in the long era before humans, the increasing dissimilarity resulted, in the opinion of most scientists, from the process of natural selection. Small variations within individuals in one species enabled them to acquire more food and better living conditions and made them more successful in breeding, thus allowing them to pass their genetic material on to the next generation. When a number of individuals within a species became distinct enough that they could no longer interbreed

How did plant and animal domestication develop, and what effects did it have on human society?

How did social hierarchies and trade increase complexity?

☑ LearningCurve
Check what you know.

successfully with others, they became a new species. Species also become extinct, particularly during periods of mass extinctions such as the one that killed the dinosaurs about 65 million years ago. Natural processes of species formation and extinction continue, although today changes in the biosphere—the living matter in the world—result far more from human action than from natural selection.

The scientists who developed this system of organizing the world placed humans within it, using the same means of classification that they used for all other living things. Humans were in the animal kingdom, the order of Primates, the family Hominidae, and the genus *Homo*. Like all classifications, this was originally based on externally visible phenomena: humans were placed in the Primates order because, like other primates, they have hands that can grasp, eyes facing forward to allow better depth perception, and relatively large brains; they were placed in the hominid family along with chimpanzees, gorillas, and orangutans because they shared even more features with these great apes. Over 98 percent of human DNA is the same as that of chimpanzees, which indicates to most scientists that humans and chimpanzees share a common ancestor. That common ancestor probably lived between 5 million and 7 million years ago.

Physical remains were the earliest type of evidence studied to learn about the distant human past, and scholars used them to develop another system of classification, one that distinguished between periods of time rather than types of living creatures. (Constructing models of time is called "periodization.") They gave labels to eras according to the primary materials out of which tools that survived were made. Thus the earliest human era became the Stone Age, the next era the Bronze Age, and the next the Iron Age. They further divided the Stone Age into the Old Stone Age, or Paleolithic era, during which people used stone, bone, and other natural products to make tools and gained food largely by foraging—that is, by gathering plant products, trapping or catching small animals and birds, and hunting larger prey. This was followed by the New Stone Age, or Neolithic era, which saw the beginning of agricultural and animal domestication. People around the world adopted agriculture at various times, and some never did, but the transition between the Paleolithic and the Neolithic is usually set at about 9000 B.C.E., the point at which agriculture was first developed.

Geologists refer to the last twelve thousand years as the Holocene (meaning very recent) epoch. The entire history of the human species fits well within the Holocene and the previous geologic epoch, the Pleistocene (PLIGH-stuh-seen), which began about 2.5 million years ago.

The Pleistocene was marked by repeated advances in glaciers and continental ice sheets. Glaciers tied up huge quantities of the earth's water, leading to lower sea levels, making it possible for animals and eventually humans to walk between places that were separated by oceans during interglacial times. Animals and humans were also prevented from migrating to other places by the ice sheets themselves, however, and the colder climate made large areas unfit to live in. Climate thus dramatically shaped human cultures.

Hominid Evolution

Using many different pieces of evidence from all over the world, archaeologists, paleontologists, and other scholars have developed a view of human evolution whose basic outline is widely shared, though there are disagreements about

---

hominids

▶ Members of the family Hominidae that contains humans, chimpanzees, gorillas, and orangutans.

Paleolithic era

▶ Period during which humans used tools of stone, bone, and wood and obtained food by gathering and hunting. Roughly 250,000–9,000 B.C.E.

foraging

▶ A style of life in which people gain food by gathering plant products, trapping or catching small animals and birds, and hunting larger prey.

Neolithic era

▶ Period beginning in 9000 B.C.E. during which humans obtained food by raising crops and animals and continued to use tools primarily of stone, bone, and wood.

CHAPTER LOCATOR | How did humans evolve, and where did they migrate? | What were the key features of Paleolithic society?

6 CHAPTER 1 THE EARLIEST HUMAN SOCIETIES

details. Most primates, including other hominids such as chimpanzees and gorillas, have lived primarily in trees, but at some point a group of hominids in East Africa began to spend more time on the ground, and between 6 and 7 million years ago they began to walk upright at least some of the time.

Over many generations, the skeletal and muscular structure of some hominids evolved to make upright walking easier, and they gradually became fully bipedal. The earliest fully bipedal hominids, whom paleontologists place in the genus *Australopithecus*, lived in southern and eastern Africa between 2.5 and 4 million years ago. Walking upright allowed australopithecines to carry and use things, which allowed them to survive better and may have also spurred brain development.

About 3.4 million years ago, some hominids began to use naturally occurring objects as tools, and sometime around 2.5 million years ago, one group of australopithecines in East Africa began to make and use simple tools, evolving into a different type of hominid that later paleontologists judged to be the first in the genus *Homo*. Called *Homo habilis* ("handy human"), they made sharpened stone pieces, which archaeologists call hand axes, and used them for various tasks. This suggests greater intelligence, and the skeletal remains support this, for *Homo habilis* had a larger brain than did the australopithecines.

About 2 million years ago, another species, called *Homo erectus* ("upright human"), evolved in East Africa. *Homo erectus* had still larger brains and made tools that were slightly specialized for various tasks, such as handheld axes, cleavers, and scrapers. Archaeological remains indicate that *Homo erectus* lived in larger groups than had earlier hominids and engaged in cooperative gathering, hunting, and food preparation. The location and shape of the larynx suggests that members of this species were able to make a wider range of sounds than were earlier hominids, so they may have relied more on vocal sounds than on gestures to communicate ideas to one another.

One of the activities that *Homo erectus* carried out most successfully was moving (Map 1.1). Gradually small groups migrated out of East Africa onto the open plains of central Africa, and from there into northern Africa. From 1 million to 2 million years ago, the earth's climate was in a warming phase, and these hominids ranged still farther, moving into western Asia by as early as 1.8 million years ago. Bones and other materials from China and the island of Java in Indonesia indicate that *Homo erectus* had reached there by about 1.5 million years ago, migrating over large landmasses as well as along the coasts. (Sea levels were lower than they are today, and Java could be reached by walking.) *Homo erectus* also walked north, reaching what is now Spain by at least 800,000 years ago and what is now Germany by 500,000 years ago. In each of these places, *Homo erectus* adapted gathering and hunting techniques to the local environment, learning how to find new sources of plant food and how to best catch local animals.

The Great Rift Valley

Homo Sapiens, "Thinking Humans"

Homo erectus was remarkably adaptable, but another hominid proved still more so: *Homo sapiens* ("thinking humans"). A few scientists think that *Homo sapiens* evolved from *Homo erectus* in a number of places in Afroeurasia, but the majority think that, like hominid evolution from earlier primates, this occurred only in East Africa. The evidence is partly archaeological, but also genetic. One type of DNA,

How did plant and animal domestication develop, and what effects did it have on human society?

How did social hierarchies and trade increase complexity?

LearningCurve
Check what you know.

7

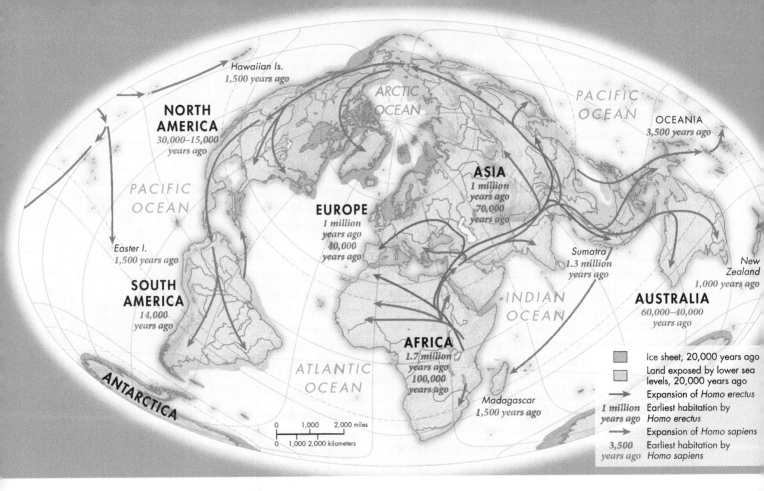

MAP 1.1 ■ Human Migration in the Paleolithic and Neolithic Eras

> MAPPING THE PAST

ANALYZING THE MAP: What were the major similarities and differences between the migrations of *Homo erectus* and those of *Homo sapiens*? How did environmental factors shape human migration?

CONNECTIONS: What types of technology were required for the migration patterns seen here? What do these migration patterns suggest about the social organization of early people?

called mitochondrial DNA, indicates that modern humans are so similar genetically that they cannot have been evolving for the last 1 million or 2 million years. This evidence suggests that the evolution of *Homo sapiens* has instead taken place for only about 250,000 years. Because there is greater human genetic variety today in Africa than in other parts of the world, the evidence also suggests that *Homo sapiens* have lived there the longest, so that Africa is where they first emerged.

Although there is some debate about where and when *Homo sapiens* emerged, there is little debate about what distinguished these humans from earlier hominids: a bigger brain, in particular a bigger forebrain, the site of conscious thought. The ability to think reflectively allowed for the creation of symbolic language, that is, for language that follows certain rules and that can refer to things or states of

CHAPTER LOCATOR | How did humans evolve, and where did they migrate? | What were the key features of Paleolithic society?

8 CHAPTER 1 THE EARLIEST HUMAN SOCIETIES

being that are not necessarily present. Greater intelligence allowed *Homo sapiens* to better understand and manipulate the world around them, and symbolic language allowed this understanding to be communicated within a group and passed from one generation to the next. Through spoken language *Homo sapiens* began to develop collective explanations for the world around them that we would now call religion, science, and philosophy. Spoken language also enabled *Homo sapiens* to organize socially into larger groups, thus further enhancing their ability to affect the natural world.

The advantages of a larger brain seem evident to us, so we may not think to ask why hominids evolved this way. Large brains also bring disadvantages, however. They take more energy to run than other parts of the body, so that large-brained animals have to eat more than small-brained ones. Large brains create particular problems for bipedal mammals, for the narrow pelvic structure that works best for upright walking makes giving birth to a large-headed infant difficult and painful.

The question of why hominids developed ever-larger brains might best be answered by looking at how paleontologists think it happened. As *Homo habilis*, *Homo erectus*, and *Homo sapiens* made and used tools, the individuals whose mental and physical abilities allowed them to do so best were able to obtain more food and were more likely to mate and have children who survived. Thus bigger brains led to better tools, but the challenges of using and inventing better tools also created selective pressure that led to bigger brains.

The same thing may have happened with symbolic language and thought. A slightly bigger brain allowed for more complex thought and better language skills. These thinking and speaking skills enabled individuals to better attract mates and fend off rivals, which meant a greater likelihood of passing on the enhanced brain to the next generation.

The growth in brain size and complexity may also have been linked to social organization. Individuals who had better social skills were more likely to mate than those who did not — this has been observed in chimpanzees and, of course, in modern humans — and thus to pass on their genetic material. Social skills were particularly important for females, because the combination of bipedalism and growing brain size led to selective pressure for hominid infants to be born at an even earlier stage in their development than other primate infants. Thus the period when human infants are dependent on others is very long, and mothers with good social networks to assist them were more likely to have infants who survived.

All these factors operated together in processes that promoted bigger and better brains. In the Paleolithic period, *Homo sapiens'* brains invented highly specialized tools made out of a variety of materials that replaced the more general-purpose stone tools made by *Homo erectus*: barbed fishhooks and harpoons, snares and traps for catching small animals, bone needles for sewing clothing, awls for punching holes in leather, nets for catching fish, sharpened flint pieces bound to wooden or bone handles for hunting or cutting, and slings for carrying infants. By 25,000 years ago, and perhaps earlier, humans in some parts of the world were weaving cloth and baskets, and by 17,000 years ago they were using bows and atlatls (AHT-lah-tuhlz) — notched throwing sticks made of bone, wood, or antler — to launch arrows and barbs with flint points bound to wooden shafts.

How did plant and animal domestication develop, and what effects did it have on human society?

How did social hierarchies and trade increase complexity?

☑ LearningCurve
Check what you know.

The archaeological evidence for increasingly sophisticated language and social organization is less direct than that for tool use, but it is hard to imagine how humans could have made the tools they did—or would have chosen to decorate so many of them—without both of these.

Migration and Differentiation

Like *Homo erectus* had earlier, groups of *Homo sapiens* moved. By 200,000 years ago they had begun to spread across Africa, and by 120,000 years ago they had begun to migrate out of Africa to Eurasia (see Map 1.1). They most likely walked along the coasts of India and Southeast Asia, and then migrated inland. At the same time, further small evolutionary changes led to our own subspecies of anatomically modern humans, *Homo sapiens sapiens* (which literally translates as "thinking thinking humans"). *Homo sapiens sapiens* moved into areas where there were already *Homo erectus* populations, eventually replacing them, leaving *Homo sapiens* as the only survivors and the ancestors of all modern humans.

The best-known example of interaction between *Homo erectus* and *Homo sapiens sapiens* is that between Neanderthals (named after the Neander Valley in Germany, where their remains were first discovered) and a group of anatomically modern humans called Cro-Magnons. **Neanderthals** lived throughout Europe and western Asia beginning about 150,000 years ago, had brains as large as those of modern humans, and used tools, including spears and scrapers for animal skins, that enabled them to survive in the cold climate of Ice Age central Europe and Russia. They built freestanding houses and decorated objects and themselves with red ochre, a form of colored clay. They sometimes buried their dead carefully with tools, animal bones, and perhaps flowers, which suggests that they understood death to have a symbolic meaning.

Cro-Magnon peoples moved into parts of western Asia where Neanderthals lived by about 70,000 years ago, and into Europe by about 45,000 years ago. The two peoples appear to have lived side by side for millennia, hunting the same types of animals and gathering the same types of plants. The last evidence of Neanderthals as a separate species comes from about 30,000 years ago, and it is not clear exactly how they died out. They may have been killed by Cro-Magnon peoples, or they simply may have lost the competition for food as the climate worsened around 30,000 years ago and the glaciers expanded.

Homo erectus migrated great distances, but *Homo sapiens sapiens* made use of greater intelligence and better toolmaking capabilities to migrate still farther. They used simple rafts to reach Australia by at least 50,000 years ago, and by 35,000 years ago had reached New Guinea. By at least 15,000 years ago, humans had walked across the land bridges then linking Siberia and North America at the Bering Strait and had crossed into the Americas. Because by 14,000 years ago humans were already in southern South America, ten thousand miles from the land bridges, many scholars now think that people came to the Americas much earlier. They think humans came from Asia to the Americas perhaps as early as 20,000 or even 30,000 years ago, walking or using rafts along the coasts. (See Chapter 11 for a longer discussion of this issue.)

With the melting of glaciers sea levels rose, and parts of the world that had been linked by land bridges, including North America and Asia as well as many parts of Southeast Asia, became separated by water. This cut off migratory paths

Neanderthals
▶ Group of *Homo erectus* with brains as large as those of modern humans that flourished in Europe and western Asia between 150,000 and 30,000 years ago.

Land Bridge Across the Bering Strait, ca. 15,000 B.C.E.

but also spurred innovation. Humans designed and built ever more sophisticated boats and learned how to navigate by studying wind and current patterns, bird flights, and the position of the stars. They sailed to increasingly remote islands, including those in the Pacific, the last parts of the globe to be settled. The western Pacific islands were inhabited by about 2000 B.C.E., Hawaii by about 500 C.E., and New Zealand by about 1000 C.E. (For more on the settlement of the Pacific islands, see page 355.)

Once humans had spread out over much of the globe, groups often became isolated from one another, and people mated only with other members of their own group or those who lived nearby, a practice anthropologists call endogamy. Thus, over thousands of generations, although humans remained one species, *Homo sapiens sapiens* came to develop differences in physical features, including skin and hair color, eye and body shape, and amount of body hair. Language also changed over generations, so that thousands of different languages were eventually spoken. Groups created widely varying cultures and passed them on to their children, further increasing diversity among humans.

QUICK REVIEW

In what ways was *Homo sapiens* different from other hominids?

How did plant and animal domestication develop, and what effects did it have on human society?

How did social hierarchies and trade increase complexity?

LearningCurve
Check what you know.

> What were the key features of Paleolithic society?

Paleolithic Hand Axes

Like most Paleolithic stone tools, these two hand axes from Libya in northern Africa were made by chipping flakes off stone to form a sharpened edge. Although they are traditionally called axes, they were used for a variety of purposes, including skinning, cutting, and chopping. (Robert Harding Images/Masterfile)

EVENTUALLY HUMAN CULTURES BECAME WIDELY DIVERSE, but in the Paleolithic period people throughout the world lived in ways that were similar to one another. Archaeological evidence and studies of modern foragers suggest that people lived in small groups of related individuals and moved throughout the landscape in search of food. Most had few material possessions, only what they could carry, although in areas where food resources were especially rich, such as along seacoasts, they built structures and lived more permanently in one place. In the later Paleolithic, people in many parts of the world created art and music and developed religious ideas that linked the natural world to a world beyond.

Foraging for Food

Paleolithic peoples have often been called hunter-gatherers, but recent archaeological and anthropological research indicates that both historical and contemporary hunter-gatherers have depended much more on gathered foods than on hunted meat. Thus most scholars now call them foragers, a term that highlights

CHAPTER LOCATOR | How did humans evolve, and where did they migrate? | What were the key features of Paleolithic society?

the flexibility and adaptability in their search for food. Most of what foragers ate were plants, and much of the animal protein in their diet came from foods gathered or scavenged rather than hunted directly: insects, shellfish, small animals caught in traps, fish and other sea creatures caught in weirs and nets, and animals killed by other predators.

Paleolithic peoples did hunt large game. Groups working together forced animals over cliffs, threw spears, and, beginning about 15,000 B.C.E., used bows and atlatls to shoot projectiles so that they could stand farther away from their prey while hunting. The final retreat of the glaciers also occurred between 10,000 and 15,000 years ago, and the warming climate was less favorable to the very large mammals that had roamed the open spaces of many parts of the world. Wooly mammoths, mastodons, and wooly rhinos all died out in Eurasia in this **megafaunal extinction**, as did camels, horses, and sloths in the Americas and giant kangaroos and wombats in Australia. In many places, these extinctions occurred just about the time that modern humans appeared, and increasing numbers of scientists think that they were at least in part caused by human hunting.

Most foraging societies that exist today or did so until recently have some type of **division of labor** by sex, and also by age, with children and older people responsible for different tasks than adult men and women. Men are more often responsible for hunting and women for gathering plant and animal products. This has led scholars to assume that in Paleolithic society men were also responsible for hunting, and women for gathering.

Obtaining food was a constant preoccupation, but it was not a constant job. Studies of recent foragers indicate that, other than in times of environmental disasters such as prolonged droughts, people need only about ten to twenty hours a week to gather food and carry out the other tasks needed to survive, such as locating water and building shelters. Moreover, the diet of foragers is varied and nutritious. The slow pace of life and healthy diet did not mean that Paleolithic life spans approached those of the modern world, however. People avoided such contemporary killers as heart disease and diabetes, but they often died at young ages from injuries, infections, animal attacks, and interpersonal violence. Mothers and infants died in childbirth, and many children died before they reached adulthood.

Total human population thus grew very slowly during the Paleolithic. Moreover, the population was widely scattered, with small bands of people occupying very large territories. The low population density meant that human impact on the environment was relatively small, although still significant. In addition to contributing to the extinction of some large animals, Paleolithic people may have also shaped their environments by setting fires, which encouraged the growth of new

megafaunal extinction
▶ Die-off of large animals in many parts of the world about 15,000–10,000 B.C.E., caused by climate change and perhaps human hunting.

division of labor
▶ Differentiation of tasks by gender, age, training, status, or other social distinction.

> **Human Population Growth in the Paleolithic and Present Eras:**

30,000 years ago: 500,000

10,000 years ago: 5 million

300 years ago: 1 billion

Today: 7 billion

How did plant and animal domestication develop, and what effects did it have on human society?

How did social hierarchies and trade increase complexity?

 LearningCurve
Check what you know.

plants and attracted animals that fed on them, making hunting or snaring game easier. This practice was a factor in the spread of plants that thrived best with occasional burning, such as the eucalyptus in Australia.

Family and Kinship Relationships

Small bands of humans—twenty or thirty people was a standard size for foragers in harsh environments—were scattered across broad areas, but this did not mean that each group lived in isolation. Their travels in search of food brought them into contact with one another, not simply for talking and celebrating, but also for providing opportunities for the exchange of sexual partners, which was essential to group survival. Mating arrangements varied in their permanence, but many groups seem to have developed a somewhat permanent arrangement whereby a man or woman left his or her original group and joined the group of his or her mate, what would later be termed marriage.

Within each band, and within the larger kin groups, individuals had a variety of identities; they were simultaneously fathers, sons, husbands, and brothers, or mothers, daughters, wives, and sisters. Each of these identities was relational (parent to child, sibling to sibling, spouse to spouse), and some of them, especially parent to child, gave one power over others. Paleolithic people were not differentiated by wealth, for in a foraging society accumulating material goods was not advantageous. But they were differentiated by such factors as age, gender, and position in a family, and no doubt by personal qualities such as intelligence, courage, and charisma.

Stereotypical representations of Paleolithic people often portray men going off to hunt while women and children crouched around a fire, waiting for the men to bring back meat. Studies of the relative importance of gathering to hunting, women's participation in hunting, and gender relations among contemporary foraging peoples have led some analysts to turn these stereotypes on their heads. They see Paleolithic bands as egalitarian groups in which the contributions of men and women to survival were recognized and valued, and in which both men and women had equal access to the limited amount of resources held by the group. Other scholars argue that this is also a stereotype, overly romanticizing Paleolithic society. They note that, although social relations among foragers were not as hierarchical as they were in other types of societies, many foraging groups had one person who held more power than others, and that person was almost always a man. This debate about gender relations is often part of larger discussions about whether Paleolithic society—and by implication, "human nature"—was primarily peaceful and nurturing or violent and brutal, and whether these qualities are gender related. Like much else about the Paleolithic, sources about gender and about violence are fragmentary and difficult to interpret; there may simply have been a diversity of patterns, as there is among more modern foragers.

Whether peaceful and egalitarian or violent and hierarchical, heterosexual relations produced children, who were cared for as infants by their mothers or other women who had recently given birth. Breast milk was the only food available that infants could easily digest, so mothers nursed their children for several years. Other than for feeding, children were most likely cared for by other male and female members of the group as well as by their mothers during the long period of human childhood.

CHAPTER LOCATOR | How did humans evolve, and where did they migrate? | What were the key features of Paleolithic society?

14 CHAPTER 1
THE EARLIEST HUMAN SOCIETIES

Cultural Creations and Spirituality

Beginning in the Paleolithic, human beings expressed themselves through what we would now term the arts or culture: painting and decorating walls and objects, making music with their voices and a variety of instruments, imagining and telling stories, dancing alone or in groups. Evidence from the Paleolithic, particularly from after about 50,000 years ago, includes flutes, carvings, jewelry, and paintings done on cave walls and rock outcroppings that depict animals, people, and symbols.

At the same time that people marked and depicted the world around them, they also appear to have developed ideas about supernatural forces that controlled some aspects of the natural world and the place of humans in it, what we now term spirituality or religion. Paleolithic burials, paintings, and objects suggest that people may have thought of their world as extending beyond the visible. People, animals, plants, natural occurrences, and other things around them had spirits, an idea called animism. The only evidence of Paleolithic animism that survives is physical, of course, but more recent animist traditions carry on this understanding of the spiritual nature and interdependence of all things.

animism
▶ Idea that people, animals, plants, natural occurrences, and other parts of the physical world have spirits.

Cave Paintings of Horses and a Horned Aurochs from Lascaux Cave, Southern France, ca. 15,000 B.C.E.

The artist who made these amazing animals in charcoal and red ochre first smoothed the surface, just as a contemporary artist might. This cave includes paintings of hundreds of animals, including predators such as lions, as well as abstract symbols. (JM Labat/Photo Researchers, Inc.)

> PICTURING THE PAST
ANALYZING THE IMAGE: The artist painted the animals so close together that they overlap. What might this arrangement have been trying to depict or convey?
CONNECTIONS: Why might Paleolithic people have made cave paintings? What do these paintings suggest about Stone Age culture and society?

How did plant and animal domestication develop, and what effects did it have on human society?

How did social hierarchies and trade increase complexity?

☑ LearningCurve
Check what you know.

This flute, carved from the wing bone of a griffon vulture, was unearthed in a cave in Germany along with pieces of other flutes made from mammoth ivory and stone tools. Dating from at least 33,000 B.C.E., it is the oldest musical instrument ever found and suggests that music has long been an important part of human culture. (H. Jensen/University of Tübingen)

Death took people from the realm of the living, but for Paleolithic groups people continued to inhabit an unseen world, along with spirits and deities, after death; thus kin groups included deceased as well as living members of a family. The unseen world regularly intervened in the visible world, for good and ill, and the actions of dead ancestors, spirits, and gods could be shaped by living people. Concepts of the supernatural pervaded all aspects of life; hunting, birth, death, and natural occurrences such as eclipses, comets, and rainbows all had religious meaning. Supernatural forces were understood to determine the basic rules for human existence, and upsetting these rules could lead to chaos.

Ordinary people learned about the unseen world through dreams and portents, and messages and revelations were also sent more regularly to shamans, spiritually adept men and women who communicated with the unseen world. Shamans created complex rituals through which they sought to ensure the health and prosperity of an individual, family, or group. Objects understood to have special power, such as carvings or masks in the form of an animal or person, could give additional protection, as could certain plants or mixtures eaten, sniffed, or rubbed on the skin. Shamans thus also operated as healers, with cures that included what we would term natural medicines and religious healing.

shamans

▶ Spiritually adept men and women who communicated with the unseen world.

> **QUICK REVIEW**

What social relationships shaped and defined Paleolithic bands?

CHAPTER LOCATOR | How did humans evolve, and where did they migrate? | What were the key features of Paleolithic society?

16   CHAPTER 1
THE EARLIEST HUMAN SOCIETIES

Neolithic Pot, from China, ca. 2600–2300 B.C.E.

This two-handled pot, made in the Yellow River Valley of baked ceramics, is painted in a swirling red and black geometric design. Neolithic agricultural communities produced a wide array of storage containers for keeping food and other commodities from one season to the next. (Museum purchase, Fowler McCormack, Class of 1921. Fund. y1979-94. Photo: Bruce M. White/Princeton University Art Museum/Art Resource, NY)

FORAGING REMAINED THE BASIC WAY OF LIFE for most of human history. In a few especially fertile areas, however, the natural environment provided enough food that people could become more settled. As they remained in one place, they began to plant seeds as well as gather wild crops, to raise certain animals instead of hunting them, and to selectively breed both plants and animals to make them more useful to humans. This seemingly small alteration was the most important change in human history; because of its impact it is often termed the **Agricultural Revolution**. Plant and animal domestication marked the transition from the Paleolithic to the Neolithic. It allowed the human population to grow far more quickly than did foraging, but it also required more labor, which became increasingly specialized.

Agricultural Revolution

▶ Dramatic transformation in human history resulting from the change from foraging to raising crops and animals.

The Development of Horticulture

Areas of the world differed in the food resources available to foragers. In some, acquiring enough food to sustain a group was difficult, and groups had to move constantly. In others, moderate temperatures and abundant rainfall allowed for verdant plant growth; or seas, rivers, and lakes provided substantial amounts of fish and shellfish. Groups in such areas were able to become more settled. About

How did plant and animal domestication develop, and what effects did it have on human society?

How did social hierarchies and trade increase complexity?

 LearningCurve
Check what you know.

The following labels appear on the map:

NORTH AMERICA

ATLANTIC OCEAN

EURASIA

Central Asia
Bactrian camel

Southwest Steppes
Horse

Eastern North America
Gourd
Squash
Sunflower

Sahara
Cattle

AFRICA

Fertile Crescent
Barley
Lentils
Peas
Wheat
Flax
Cattle
Dog
Donkey
Goat
Pig
Sheep

Mesoamerica
Avocado
Beans
Gourd
Maize (Corn)
Pepper
Pumpkin
Squash
Tomato
Cotton
Dog
Turkey

PACIFIC OCEAN

Amazon River Valley
Manioc
Yam

West Africa
African rice
Oil palm
Pearl millet
Sorghum
Yam?

Andean region
Beans
Chili pepper
Gourd
Manioc
Potato
Quinoa
Alpaca
Guinea pig
Llama

SOUTH AMERICA

Sudanic Africa
Finger millet
Peanut
Sesame
Sorghum
Tef
Cattle

0   1,000   2,000 miles
0   1,000   2,000 kilometers

Independent development of agriculture
Early pastoralism
Limit of early agriculture
→ Spread of agriculture
Beans Domesticated plant or animal

15,000 years ago, the earth's climate entered a warming phase, and the glaciers began to retreat. As the earth became warmer, the climate became wetter, and more parts of the world were able to support sedentary or semi-sedentary groups of foragers.

In several of these places, foragers began planting seeds in the ground along with gathering wild grains, roots, and other foodstuffs. By observation, they learned the optimum times and places for planting. They removed unwanted plants through weeding and selected the seeds they planted in order to get crops that had favorable characteristics, such as larger edible parts. Through this human intervention, certain crops became domesticated, that is, modified by selective breeding so as to serve human needs, in this case to provide a more reliable source of food.

This early crop planting was done by individuals using hoes and digging sticks, and it is often termed horticulture to distinguish it from the later agriculture using plows. Intentional crop planting developed first in the area archaeologists call the Fertile Crescent, which runs from present-day Lebanon, Israel, and Jordan north to Turkey and then south to the Iran-Iraq border (Map 1.2). About 9000 B.C.E. people there began to plant seeds of the wild wheat and barley they had already been harvesting, along with seeds of legume crops, such as peas and lentils, and

domesticated
▶ Plants and animals modified by selective breeding so as to serve human needs; domesticated animals will behave in specific ways and breed in captivity.

horticulture
▶ Crop raising done with hand tools and human power.

How did humans evolve, and where did they migrate?

What were the key features of Paleolithic society?

East Asia
Millet
Rice
Soybean
Silkworm
Pig

Southeast Asia
Banana
Yam
Chicken
Water buffalo
Zebu cattle

New Guinea
Sugar cane
Taro
Yam

PACIFIC OCEAN

AUSTRALIA

MAP 1.2 ■ **The Spread of Agriculture and Pastoralism**

Local plants and animals were domesticated in many different places. Agriculturalists and pastoralists spread the knowledge of how to raise them, and spread the plants and animals themselves through migration, trade, and conquest.

The Fertile Crescent

of the flax with which they made linen cloth. By about 8000 B.C.E. people were growing sorghum and millet in parts of the Nile River Valley, and perhaps yams in western Africa. By about 7000 B.C.E. they were growing domesticated rice, millet, and legumes in China; yams and taro in Papua New Guinea; and perhaps squash in Mesoamerica. In each of these places, the development of horticulture occurred independently, and it may have happened in other parts of the world as well.

Why, after living successfully as foragers for tens of thousands of years, did humans in so many parts of the world all begin raising crops at about the same time? The answer to this question is not clear, but crop raising may have resulted from population pressures in those parts of the world where the warming climate provided more food. More food meant lower child mortality and longer life spans, which allowed communities to grow. When population growth outstripped the local food supply, people had a choice: they could move to a new area—the solution that foragers had relied on when faced with the problem of food scarcity—or they could develop ways to increase the food supply to keep up with population growth, a solution that the warming climate was making possible. They chose the latter and began to plant more intensively, beginning cycles of expanding population and intensification of land use that have continued to today.

How did plant and animal domestication develop, and what effects did it have on human society?

How did social hierarchies and trade increase complexity?

LearningCurve
Check what you know.

A recent archaeological find at Göbekli Tepe in present-day Turkey, at the northern edge of the Fertile Crescent, suggests that cultural factors may have played a role in the development of agriculture. Here, around 9000 B.C.E. hundreds of people came together to build rings of massive, multiton, elaborately carved limestone pillars and then covered them with dirt and built more. The people who created this site lived some distance away, where archaeological evidence indicates they first carved the pillars. The evidence also reveals that they ate wild game and plants, not crops. The project may have unintentionally spurred the development of new methods of food production that would allow the many workers to be fed efficiently. Indeed, it is very near here that evidence of the world's oldest domesticated wheat has been discovered.

Whatever the reasons for the move from foraging to crop raising, within several centuries of initial crop planting, people in the Fertile Crescent, parts of China, and the Nile Valley were relying on domesticated food products alone. They built permanent houses near one another in villages surrounded by fields, and they invented new ways of storing foods, such as in pottery made from clay. Villages were closer together than were the camps of foragers, so population density as well as total population grew.

A field of planted and weeded crops yields ten to one hundred times as much food—measured in calories—as the same area of naturally occurring plants. It also requires much more labor, however, which was provided both by the greater number of people in the community and by those people working longer hours. Farming peoples were often in the fields from dawn to dusk. Early farmers were also less healthy than foragers were. Their narrower range of foodstuffs made them more susceptible to disease and nutritional deficiencies such as anemia.

Foragers who lived at the edge of horticultural communities appear to have recognized the negative aspects of crop raising, for they did not immediately

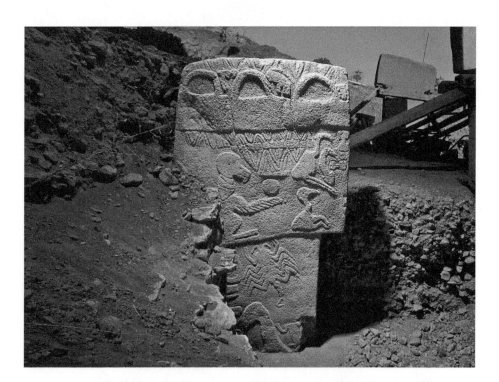

Pillar at Göbekli Tepe

The huge limestone pillars arranged in rings at the Paleolithic site Göbekli Tepe are somewhat humanoid in shape, and the carvings are of dangerous animals, including lions, boars, foxes, snakes, vultures, and scorpions. The structure required enormous skill and effort of the people who built it, and clearly had great importance to them. (Vincent J. Musi/National Geographic Creative)

CHAPTER LOCATOR | How did humans evolve, and where did they migrate? | What were the key features of Paleolithic society?

20   CHAPTER 1
THE EARLIEST HUMAN SOCIETIES

adopt this new way of life. Instead farming spread when a village became too large and some residents moved to a new area. Because the population of farming communities grew so much faster than that of foragers, however, horticulture quickly spread into fertile areas. By about 6500 B.C.E. farming had spread northward from the Fertile Crescent into Greece, and by 4000 B.C.E. farther northward all the way to Britain; by 4500 B.C.E. it had spread southward into Ethiopia. At the same time, crop raising spread out from others areas in which it was first developed, and slowly larger and larger parts of China, South and Southeast Asia, and East Africa became home to horticultural villages.

People adapted crops to their local environments, choosing seeds that had qualities that were beneficial, such as drought resistance. They also domesticated new kinds of crops. In the Americas, for example, by about 3000 B.C.E. corn was domesticated in southern Mexico and potatoes and quinoa in the Andes region of South America, and by about 2500 B.C.E. squash and beans in eastern North America. These crops then spread, so that by about 1000 B.C.E. people in much of what is now the western United States were raising corn, beans, and squash. In the Indus Valley of South Asia, people were growing dates, mangoes, sesame seeds, and cotton along with grains and legumes by 4000 B.C.E. Accordingly, crop raising led to dramatic human alteration of the environment.

Certain planted crops eventually came to be grown over huge areas of land, so that some scientists describe the Agricultural Revolution as a revolution of codependent domestication: humans domesticated crops, but crops also "domesticated" humans so that they worked long hours spreading particular crops around the world. Of these, corn has probably been the most successful; more than half a million square miles around the world are now planted in corn.

In some parts of the world horticulture led to a dramatic change in the way of life, but in others it did not. Horticulture can be easily combined with gathering and hunting, as plots of land are usually small; many cultures, including some in Papua New Guinea and North America, remained mixed foragers and horticulturists for thousands of years. Especially in deeply wooded areas, people cleared small plots by chopping and burning the natural vegetation, and planted crops in successive years until the soil eroded or lost its fertility, a method termed "slash and burn." They then moved to another area and began the process again, perhaps returning to the first plot many years later, after the soil had rejuvenated itself. Groups using shifting slash-and-burn cultivation remained small and continued to rely on the surrounding forest for much of their food.

Animal Domestication and the Rise of Pastoralism

At roughly the same time that they domesticated certain plants, people also domesticated animals. The earliest animal to be domesticated was the dog, which separated genetically as a subspecies from wolves at least 15,000 years ago and perhaps much earlier. The relationship provided both humans and dogs with benefits: humans gained dogs' better senses of smell and hearing and their body warmth, and dogs gained new food sources and safer surroundings.

Dogs fit easily into a foraging lifestyle, but humans also domesticated animals that led them to completely alter their way of life. In about 9000 B.C.E., at the same

| How did plant and animal domestication develop, and what effects did it have on human society? | How did social hierarchies and trade increase complexity? | ✔ LearningCurve Check what you know. |

21

Sheep Herders in Western China

Pastoral economies thrive in many parts of the world today, particularly in areas that are too dry for agriculture, including central Australia, Central Asia, northern and western Africa, and much of the U.S. West. As in early pastoralism, contemporary herders choose and breed their animals for qualities that will allow them to prosper in the local environment.
(Yvan Travert/akg-images)

pastoralism

▶ An economic system based on herding flocks of goats, sheep, cattle, or other animals.

time they began to raise crops, people in the Fertile Crescent domesticated wild goats and sheep, probably using them first for meat, and then for milk, skins, and eventually fleece (see Map 1.2). They learned from observation and experimentation that traits are passed down from generation to generation, and they began to breed the goats and sheep selectively for qualities that they wanted. Sometimes they trained dogs to assist them in herding, and then selectively bred the dogs for qualities that were advantageous for this task.

Sometime after goats and sheep, pigs were domesticated in both the Fertile Crescent and China, as were chickens in southern Asia. Like domesticated crops, domesticated animals eventually far outnumbered their wild counterparts. Animal domestication also shaped human evolution; groups that relied on animal milk and milk products for a significant part of their diet tended to develop the ability to digest milk as adults, while those that did not remained lactose intolerant as adults, the normal condition for mammals.

Sheep and goats allow themselves to be herded, and people developed a new form of living, pastoralism, based on herding and raising livestock. In areas with sufficient rainfall and fertile soil, pastoralism can be relatively sedentary and thus is easily combined with horticulture; people built pens for animals, or in colder climates constructed special buildings or took them into their houses. They learned that animal manure increases crop yields, so they gathered the manure from enclosures and used it as fertilizer.

Increased contact with animals and their feces also increased human contact with various sorts of disease-causing pathogens. This was particularly the case where humans and animals lived in tight quarters. Thus pastoralists and agriculturalists developed illnesses that had not plagued foragers, and the diseases became endemic, that is, widely found within a region without being deadly. Ultimately people who lived with animals developed resistance to some of these illnesses, but foragers' lack of resistance to many illnesses meant that they died more readily after coming into contact with new endemic diseases, as was the case when Europeans brought smallpox to the Americas in the sixteenth century.

In drier areas, flocks need to travel long distances from season to season to obtain enough food, so some pastoralists became nomadic. Nomadic pastoralists often gather wild plant foods as well, but they tend to rely primarily on their flocks of animals for food. Pastoralism was well suited to areas where the terrain or climate made crop planting difficult, such as mountains, deserts, dry grasslands, and tundras. Eventually other grazing animals, including cattle, camels, horses, yak, and reindeer, also became the basis of pastoral economies in Central and West Asia, many parts of Africa, and far northern Europe.

Plow Agriculture

Horticulture and pastoralism brought significant changes to human ways of life, but the domestication of certain large animals had an even bigger impact. Cattle and water buffalo were domesticated in some parts of Asia and North Africa in which they occurred naturally by at least 7000 B.C.E., and horses, donkeys, and camels by about 4000 B.C.E. All these animals can be trained to carry people or burdens on their backs and to pull loads dragged behind them. The domestication of large animals dramatically increased the power available to humans to carry out their tasks, which had both an immediate effect in the societies in which this happened and a long-term effect when these societies later encountered societies in which human labor remained the only source of power.

The pulling power of animals came to matter most, because it could be applied to food production. Sometime in the seventh millennium B.C.E., people attached wooden sticks to frames that animals dragged through the soil, thus breaking it up and allowing seeds to sprout more easily. Using plows, Neolithic people produced a significant amount of surplus food, which meant that some people in the community could spend their days performing other tasks, increasing the division of labor. Surplus food had to be stored, and some began to specialize in making products for storage, such as pots, baskets, and other kinds of containers. Others specialized in making tools, houses, and other items needed in village life, or for producing specific types of food. Families and households became increasingly interdependent, trading food for other commodities or services.

Stored food was also valuable and could become a source of conflict, as could other issues in villages where people lived close together. Villagers needed more complex rules than did foragers about how food was to be distributed and how different types of work were to be valued. Certain individuals began to specialize in the determination and enforcement of these rules, and informal structures of power gradually became more formalized as elites developed. These elites then distributed resources to their own advantage, often using force to attain and maintain their power.

QUICK REVIEW

Why was the invention of the plow such a profound turning point in human history?

| How did plant and animal domestication develop, and what effects did it have on human society? | How did social hierarchies and trade increase complexity? | ✅ LearningCurve Check what you know. |

How did growing social and gender hierarchies and expanding networks of trade increase the complexity of human society in the Neolithic period?

Stone Circle at Nabta Playa, Egypt, ca. 4800 B.C.E.

This circle of stones, erected when the Egyptian desert received much more rainfall than it does today, may have been a type of calendar marking the summer solstice. Circular arrangements of stones or ditches were constructed in many places during the Neolithic era, and most no doubt had calendrical, astronomical, and/or religious purposes. (Courtesy of Raymond Betz)

social hierarchies

▶ Divisions between rich and poor, elites and common people that have been a central feature of human society since the Neolithic era.

THE DIVISION OF LABOR THAT PLOW AGRICULTURE ALLOWED LED TO THE creation of social hierarchies, the divisions between rich and poor, elites and common people that have been a central feature of human society since the Neolithic era. Plow agriculture also strengthened differentiation based on gender, with men becoming more associated with the world beyond the household and women with the domestic realm. Social hierarchies were reinforced over generations as children inherited goods and status from their parents. People increasingly communicated ideas within local and regional networks of exchange, just as they traded foodstuffs, tools, and other products.

Social Hierarchies and Slavery

Within foraging groups, some individuals already had more authority because of their links with the world of gods and spirits, positions as heads of kin groups, or personal characteristics. These three factors gave individuals advantages in agricultural societies, and the advantages became more significant over time as there

CHAPTER LOCATOR | How did humans evolve, and where did they migrate? | What were the key features of Paleolithic society?

24 CHAPTER 1 THE EARLIEST HUMAN SOCIETIES

were more resources to control. Priests and shamans became full-time religious specialists, exchanging their services in interceding with the gods for food. In many communities, religious specialists were the first to work out formal rules of conduct that later became oral and written codes of law. The codes often required people to accord deference to priests as the representatives of the gods, so that they became an elite group with special privileges.

Individuals who were the heads of large families or kin groups had control over the labor of others, and this power became more significant when that labor brought material goods that could be stored. Material goods—plows, sheep, cattle, sheds, pots, carts—gave one the ability to amass still more material goods, and the gap between those who had them and those who did not widened. Storage also allowed wealth to be retained over long periods of time and handed down from one family member to another, so that over generations small differences in wealth grew larger. The ability to control the labor of others could also come from physical strength, a charismatic personality, or leadership talents, and such traits may have also led to greater wealth.

Wealth itself could command labor, as individuals or families could buy the services of others to work for them or impose their wishes through force, hiring soldiers to threaten or carry out violence. Eventually some individuals bought others outright. Like animals, slaves were a source of physical power for their owners, providing them an opportunity to amass still more wealth and influence.

Gender Hierarchies and Inheritance

Along with hierarchies based on wealth and power, the development of agriculture was intertwined with a hierarchy based on gender. The system in which men have more power and access to resources than women and some men are dominant over other men is called patriarchy.

Plow agriculture heightened patriarchy. Although farming with a hoe was often done by women, plow agriculture came to be a male task, perhaps because of men's upper-body strength or because plow agriculture was more difficult to combine with care for infants and small children than was horticulture. At the same time that cattle began to be raised for pulling plows and carts rather than for meat, sheep began to be raised primarily for wool. Spinning thread and weaving cloth became primarily women's work. Spinning and weaving were generally done indoors and involved simpler and cheaper tools than plowing; they could also be taken up and put down easily, and so could be done at the same time as other tasks.

Though in some ways this arrangement seems complementary, with each sex doing some of the necessary labor, plow agriculture increased gender hierarchy. Men's responsibility for plowing and other agricultural tasks took them outside the household more often than women's duties did, enlarging their opportunities for leadership. This role may have led to their being favored as inheritors of family land and the right to farm communally held land. Accordingly, over generations, women's independent access to resources decreased, and it became increasingly difficult for women to survive without male support.

As inherited wealth became more important, men wanted to make sure that their sons were theirs, so they restricted their wives' movements and activities. This was especially the case among elite families. Among foragers and

patriarchy
▶ Social system in which men have more power and access to resources than women and some men are dominant over other men.

How did plant and animal domestication develop, and what effects did it have on human society?

How did social hierarchies and trade increase complexity?

✔️ LearningCurve
Check what you know.

25

horticulturalists, women needed to be mobile for the group to survive; their labor outdoors was essential. Among agriculturalists, the labor of animals, slaves, and hired workers could substitute for that of women in families that could afford them. Thus in some Neolithic societies, there is evidence that women spent more and more of their time within the household.

Social and gender hierarchies were enhanced over generations as wealth was passed down unequally, and they were also enhanced by rules and norms that shaped sexual relationships, particularly heterosexual ones. However their power originated, elites began to think of themselves as a group set apart from the rest by some element that made them distinctive — such as military prowess, natural superiority, or connections with a deity. They increasingly understood this distinctive quality to be hereditary and developed traditions — later codified as written laws — that stipulated which heterosexual relationships would pass this quality on, along with passing on wealth. Relationships between men and women from elite families were formalized as marriage, through which both status and wealth were generally passed down. Relationships between elite men and non-elite women generally did not function in this way, or did so to a lesser degree; the women were defined as concubines or mistresses, or simply as sexual outlets for powerful men. Relations between an elite woman and a non-elite man generally brought shame and dishonor to the woman's family and sometimes death to the man.

No elite can be completely closed to newcomers, however, because the accidents of life and death, along with the genetic problems caused by repeated close intermarriage, make it difficult for any small group to survive over generations. Thus mechanisms were developed in many cultures to adopt boys into elite families, to legitimate the children of concubines and slave women, or to allow elite girls to marry men lower on the social hierarchy. All systems of inheritance also need some flexibility. The inheritance patterns in some cultures favored male heirs exclusively, but in others close relatives were favored over those more distant, even if this meant allowing daughters to inherit. The drive to keep wealth and property within a family or kin group often resulted in women inheriting, owning, and in some cases managing significant amounts of wealth, a pattern that continues today.

Trade and Cross-Cultural Connections

The increase in food production brought by the development of plow agriculture allowed Neolithic villages to grow ever larger. By 7000 B.C.E. or so, some villages in the Fertile Crescent may have had as many as ten thousand residents. One of the best known of these, Çatal Hüyük in what is now modern Turkey, shows evidence of trade as well as of the specialization of labor. Çatal Hüyük's residents lived in mud-brick houses whose walls were covered in white plaster. The men and women of the town grew wheat, barley, peas, and almonds and raised sheep and perhaps cattle, though they also seem to have hunted. They made textiles, pots, figurines, baskets, carpets, copper and lead beads, and other goods. They gathered, sharpened, and polished obsidian, a volcanic rock that could be used for knives, blades, and mirrors, and then traded it with neighboring towns. From here the obsidian was exchanged still farther away, for Neolithic societies slowly developed local and then regional networks of exchange and communication.

CHAPTER LOCATOR | How did humans evolve, and where did they migrate? | What were the key features of Paleolithic society?

CHAPTER 1
26 THE EARLIEST HUMAN SOCIETIES

INDIVIDUALS IN SOCIETY
The Iceman

On September 19, 1991, two German vacationers climbing in the Italian Alps came upon a corpse lying facedown and covered in ice. Scientists determined that the Iceman, as the corpse is generally known, died 5,300 years ago. He was between twenty-five and thirty-five years old at the time of his death, and he stood about five feet two inches tall. An autopsy revealed much about the man and his culture. The bluish tinge of his teeth showed a diet of milled grain, which proves that he came from an environment where crops were grown. The Iceman hunted as well as farmed: he was found with a bow and arrows and shoes of straw, and he wore a furry cap and a robe of animal skins that had been stitched together with thread made from grass.

The equipment discovered with the Iceman demonstrates that his people mastered several technologies. He carried a hefty copper ax, made by someone with a knowledge of metallurgy. In his quiver were numerous wooden arrow shafts and two finished arrows. The arrows had sharpened flint heads and feathers attached to the ends of the shafts with resin-like glue. Apparently the people of his culture knew the value of feathers to direct the arrow and thus had mastered the basics of ballistics. His bow was made of yew, a relatively rare wood in central Europe that is among the best for archers.

Yet a mystery still surrounds the Iceman. When his body was first discovered, scholars assumed that he was a hapless traveler overtaken in a fierce snowstorm. But the autopsy found an arrowhead lodged under his left shoulder. The Iceman was not alone on his last day. Someone was with him, and that someone had shot him from below and behind. The Iceman is the victim in the first murder mystery in Europe, and the case will never be solved.

The artifacts found with the body tell scientists much about how the Iceman lived. The Iceman's shoes, made with a twine framework stuffed with straw and covered with skin, indicate that he used all parts of the animals he hunted. (discovery: Courtesy, Roger Teissl; shoes: South Tyrol Museum of Archaeology, http://www.iceman.it)

QUESTIONS FOR ANALYSIS

1. What does the autopsy of the corpse indicate about the society in which the Iceman lived?
2. How do the objects found with the Iceman support the generalizations about Neolithic society in this chapter?

LaunchPad

ONLINE DOCUMENT PROJECT

What can artifacts tell us about Neolithic society?
Examine the objects found with the Iceman, and then complete a quiz and writing assignment based on the evidence and details from this chapter. *See inside front cover to learn more.*

Among the goods traded in some parts of the world was copper. Pure copper occurs close to the surface in some areas, and people, including those at Çatal Hüyük, hammered it into shapes for jewelry and tools. More often, copper, like most metals, occurs mixed with other materials in a type of rock called ore, and by about 5500 B.C.E. people in the Balkans had learned that copper could be extracted from ore by heating it in a smelting process. (See "Individuals in Society: The Iceman," page 27.) Smelting techniques were discovered independently in many places around the world, including China, Southeast Asia, West Africa, and the Andes region. Pure copper is soft, but through experimentation artisans learned that it would become harder if they mixed it with other metals such as arsenic, zinc, or tin during heating, creating an alloy called bronze.

Because it was stronger than copper, bronze had a far wider range of uses, so much so that later historians decided that its adoption marked a new period in human history, the Bronze Age. It began about 3000 B.C.E. in some places, and by about 2500 B.C.E. bronze technology was having an impact in many parts of the world, especially in weaponry. The end of the Bronze Age came with the adoption of iron technology, which also varied in its beginnings from 1200 B.C.E. to 300 B.C.E.

Objects were not the only things traded over increasingly long distances during the Neolithic period, for people also carried ideas as they traveled. Knowledge about the seasons and the weather was vitally important for those who depended on crop raising, and agricultural peoples in many parts of the world began to calculate recurring patterns in the world around them, slowly developing calendars. Scholars have demonstrated that people built circular structures of mounded earth or huge upright stones to help them predict the movements of the sun and stars.

The rhythms of the agricultural cycle and patterns of exchange also shaped religious beliefs and practices. Shamans and priests developed ever more elaborate rituals designed to assure fertility, in which the gods were often given something from a community's goods in exchange for their favor. In many places gods came to be associated with patterns of birth, growth, death, and regeneration. Like humans, the gods came to have a division of labor and a social hierarchy. Thus, as human society was becoming more complex, so was the unseen world.

> ## QUICK REVIEW

What connections can you make between the advent of agriculture and the intensification of gender hierarchies?

CHAPTER SUMMARY

Through studying the physical remains of the past, sometimes with very new high-tech procedures such as DNA analysis, scholars have determined that human evolution involved a combination of factors, including bipedalism, larger brain size, spoken symbolic language, and longer periods of infancy. Humans invented ever more complex tools, many of which were made of stone, from which later scholars derived the name for this earliest period of human history,

CHAPTER LOCATOR | How did humans evolve, and where did they migrate? | What were the key features of Paleolithic society?

28 CHAPTER 1 THE EARLIEST HUMAN SOCIETIES

the Paleolithic era. These tools allowed Paleolithic peoples to shape the world around them. During this era, humans migrated out of Africa, adapting to many different environments and developing diverse cultures. Early humans lived in small groups of related individuals, moving through the landscape as foragers in the search for food.

Beginning about 9000 B.C.E. people living in southwest Asia, and then elsewhere, began to plant seeds as well as gather wild crops, raise certain animals, and selectively breed both plants and animals to make them more useful to humans. This domestication of plants and animals was the most important change in human history and marked the beginning of the Neolithic Era. The domestication of large animals led to plow agriculture, through which humans could raise much more food, and the world's population grew. Plow agriculture allowed for a greater division of labor, which strengthened social hierarchies based on wealth and gender. Neolithic agricultural communities developed technologies to meet their needs and often traded with one another for products that they could not obtain locally. Religious ideas came to reflect the new agricultural society.

 CONNECTIONS The human story is often told as a narrative of unstoppable progress toward greater complexity. The small kin groups of the Paleolithic gave way to Neolithic villages that grew ever larger until they became cities. Egalitarian foragers became stratified by divisions of wealth and power that were formalized as aristocracies, castes, and social classes. Oral rituals of worship, healing, and celebration in which everyone participated grew into a dizzying array of religions, philosophies, and branches of knowledge presided over by specialists. The rest of this book traces this story and explores the changes over time that are the central thread of history.

As you examine what can seem to be a staggering number of developments, it is also important to remember that many things were slow to change and that some aspects of human life in the Neolithic, or even the Paleolithic, continued. Foraging, horticulture, pastoralism, and agriculture have been the primary economic activities of most people throughout the entire history of the world. The social patterns set in early agricultural societies—with most of the population farming the land and a small number of elite who lived off their labor—lasted for millennia. You have no doubt recognized other similarities between the early peoples discussed in this chapter and the people you see around you, and it is important to keep these continuities in mind as you embark on your examination of human history.

 LaunchPad

ONLINE DOCUMENT PROJECT
The Iceman's World
What can artifacts tell us about Neolithic society?

Examine the objects found with the Iceman, and then complete a quiz and writing assignment based on the evidence and details from this chapter. *See inside front cover to learn more.*

How did plant and animal domestication develop, and what effects did it have on human society?

How did social hierarchies and trade increase complexity?

✔ LearningCurve
Check what you know.

CHAPTER 1 STUDY GUIDE

STEP 1

GET STARTED ONLINE

 LearningCurve

Now that you've read the chapter, make it stick by completing the LearningCurve activity.

STEP 2

EXPLAIN WHY IT MATTERS

Put your reading into practice. Identify each term below, and then explain why it matters in world history.

TERM	WHO OR WHAT & WHEN	WHY IT MATTERS
hominids (p. 6)		
Paleolithic era (p. 6)		
foraging (p. 6)		
Neolithic era (p. 6)		
Neanderthals (p. 10)		
megafaunal extinction (p. 13)		
division of labor (p. 13)		
animism (p. 15)		
shamans (p. 16)		
Agricultural Revolution (p. 17)		
domesticated (p. 18)		
horticulture (p. 18)		
pastoralism (p. 22)		
social hierarchies (p. 24)		
patriarchy (p. 25)		

STEP 3

MOVE BEYOND THE BASICS

To demonstrate a more advanced understanding of the similarities and differences between Paleolithic and Neolithic society, fill in the chart below with descriptions of each society in four key areas: social organization and hierarchy, gender relations, technology and trade, and religion and spirituality. In what ways were Paleolithic and Neolithic societies the most similar? How would you explain these instances of continuity?

	Social Organization and Hierarchy	Gender Relations	Technology and Trade	Religion and Spirituality
Paleolithic Society				
Neolithic Society				

STEP 4 · PUT IT ALL TOGETHER

Now, take a step back and try to explain the big picture. Remember to use specific examples from the chapter in your answers.

HUMAN EVOLUTION AND MIGRATION

▶ What explains the evolution of ever larger brains in successive hominid species?

▶ How did geography and climate shape the migration and distribution of early human communities?

PALEOLITHIC SOCIETY

▶ What role did family, kinship, and gender relations play in Paleolithic society?

▶ What do we know about the culture and spirituality of Paleolithic peoples? How do we know it?

THE AGRICULTURAL REVOLUTION AND THE DEVELOPMENT OF NEOLITHIC SOCIETY

▶ Why did some human communities make the transition from foraging to settled agriculture while others did not?

▶ How did agriculture contribute to the development of new social, political, and economic institutions in Neolithic communities?

LOOKING BACK, LOOKING AHEAD

▶ In your opinion, at what point did human history begin? With the first bipedal hominids? Later? Why did you choose the point in the past you did?

▶ Argue for or against the following statement. "The Agricultural Revolution should be considered the fundamental turning point in human history, the moment when the foundations of all future social, economic, and political institutions were laid down."

> IN YOUR OWN WORDS

Imagine that you must give an oral report to the class answering the following question: **How did human societies change and develop in the Paleolithic and Neolithic Eras?** What would be the most important points and why?

2

THE RISE OF THE STATE IN SOUTHWEST ASIA AND THE NILE VALLEY

3200–500 B.C.E.

> **Where, how, and why did the first states emerge?** Chapter 2 examines the emergence of new and more complex societies in Southwest Asia and the Nile Valley. As small villages grew into cities, people continued to develop technologies and systems to handle new issues. To control their more complex structures, people created governments, militaries, and taxation systems. In some places they invented writing to record taxes, inventories, and payments, and they later put writing to other uses. The first places where these new technologies and systems were introduced were the Tigris and Euphrates River Valleys of southwest Asia and the Nile Valley of northeast Africa, areas whose histories became linked through trade, military conquests, and migrations.

Persian Archers In this colorful decorative frieze made of glazed brick, men wearing long Persian robes and laced ankle boots carry spears, bows, and quivers. This reconstruction in the Louvre Museum in Paris was made from material found in the palace of King Darius I of Persia in Susa, built about 510 B.C.E. Enough bricks were found there to suggest that there were originally many archers, perhaps representing Darius's royal guards or symbolizing the entire Persian people. (Louvre, Paris, France/Erich Lessing/Art Resource, NY)

> How does writing shape what we can know about the past, and how did writing develop to meet the needs of cities and states?

> How did the peoples of Mesopotamia form states and develop new technologies and institutions?

> How did the Egyptians create a prosperous and long-lasting society?

> How did the Hebrews create an enduring written religious tradition?

> How did the Assyrians and the Persians consolidate their power and control the subjects of their empires?

LearningCurve

After reading the chapter, use LearningCurve to retain what you've read.

How does writing shape what we can know about the past, and how did writing develop to meet the needs of cities and states?

Clay Letter Written in Cuneiform and Its Envelope, ca. 1850 B.C.E.

In this letter from a city in Anatolia, located on the northern edge of the Fertile Crescent in what is now southern Turkey, a Mesopotamian merchant complains to his brother at home, hundreds of miles away, that life is hard and comments on the trade in silver, gold, tin, and textiles. Correspondents often enclosed letters in clay envelopes and sealed them by rolling a cylinder seal across the clay, leaving the impression of a scene, just as you might use a stamped wax seal today. Here the very faint impression of the sender's seal at the bottom shows a person, probably the owner of the seal, being led in a procession toward a king or god. (© The Trustees of the British Museum/Art Resource, NY)

Beginning about 5,000 years ago, people in some parts of the world developed a new technology, writing. Writing developed to meet the needs of more complex urban societies that are often referred to as "civilizations." In particular, writing met the needs of the state, a new political form that developed during the time covered in this chapter.

Written Sources and the Human Past

Historians who study human societies that developed systems of writing continue to use many of the same types of physical evidence as do those who study societies without writing. For some cultures, the writing or record-keeping systems have not yet been deciphered, so our knowledge of these people also depends largely on physical evidence. Scholars can read the writing of a great many societies, however, adding greatly to what we can learn about them.

Much ancient writing survives only because it was copied and recopied, sometimes years after it was first produced. The survival of a work means that someone from a later period — and often a long chain of someones — judged it

CHAPTER LOCATOR | How does writing shape what we can know about the past, and how did writing develop? | How did the peoples of Mesopotamia form states and develop new technologies?

34 CHAPTER 2
THE RISE OF THE STATE IN SOUTHWEST ASIA AND THE NILE VALLEY

ca. 3800 B.C.E.
Establishment of first cities in Sumer

ca. 3200 B.C.E.
Earliest surviving cuneiform writing

2660–2180 B.C.E.
Period of the Old Kingdom in Egypt

2500 B.C.E.
Bronze weaponry becomes common in Mesopotamia

ca. 2300 B.C.E.
Establishment of Akkadian empire

1792–1750 B.C.E.
Hammurabi rules Babylon

ca. 1600 B.C.E.
Hittites begin to expand their empire

ca. 1570–1070 B.C.E.
Period of the New Kingdom in Egypt

ca. 1200 B.C.E.
Bronze Age Collapse; destruction and drought

ca. 1100 B.C.E.
Iron technology improves; beginning of the Iron Age; Phoenicians begin to trade in the Mediterranean

ca. 965–925 B.C.E.
Hebrew kingdom ruled by Solomon

ca. 900–612 B.C.E.
Assyrian Empire

722 B.C.E.
Kingdom of Israel destroyed by the Assyrians

587 B.C.E.
Kingdom of Judah destroyed by the Babylonians

550 B.C.E.
Cyrus the Great consolidates the Persian Empire

worthy of the time, effort, and resources needed to produce copies. The copies may not be completely accurate. Historians studying ancient works thus often try to find as many early copies as they can and compare them to arrive at the version they think is closest to the original.

The works considered worthy of copying tend to be those that are about the political and military events involving major powers, those that record religious traditions, or those that come from authors who were later regarded as important. By contrast, written sources dealing with the daily life of ordinary men and women were few to begin with and were rarely saved or copied because they were not considered significant.

Some early written texts survive in their original form because people inscribed them in stone, shells, bone, or other hard materials, intending them to be permanent. Stones with inscriptions were often erected in the open in public places for all to see, so they include text that leaders felt had enduring importance, such as laws, religious proclamations, decrees, and treaties. Sometimes this permanence was accidental: in ancient Mesopotamia (in the area of modern Iraq), all writing was initially made up of indentations on soft clay tablets, which then hardened. Hundreds of thousands of these tablets have survived, the oldest dating to about 3200 B.C.E., and from them historians have learned about many aspects of everyday life. By contrast, writing in Egypt at the same time was often done in ink on papyrus sheets, made from a plant that grows abundantly in Egypt. Some of these papyrus sheets have survived, but papyrus is much more fragile than hardened clay, so most have disintegrated. In China, the oldest surviving writing is on bones and turtle shells from about 1200 B.C.E., but it is clear that writing was done much earlier on less permanent materials such as silk and bamboo. (For more on the origins of Chinese writing, see page 95.)

| How did the Egyptians create a prosperous and long-lasting society? | How did the Hebrews create an enduring written religious tradition? | How did the Assyrians and the Persians consolidate their power and control the subjects? | ✓ LearningCurve Check what you know. |

Cities and the Idea of Civilization

Along with writing, the growth of cities has often been a way that scholars mark the increasing complexity of human societies. In the ancient world, residents of cities generally viewed themselves as more advanced and sophisticated than rural folk. They saw themselves as more "civilized," a word that comes from the Latin adjective *civilis*, which refers to either a citizen of a town or of a larger political unit such as an empire.

This depiction of people as either civilized or uncivilized was gradually extended to whole societies. Beginning in the eighteenth century European scholars described those societies in which political, economic, and social organizations operated on a large scale as "civilizations." Civilizations had cities; laws that governed human relationships; codes of manners and social conduct that regulated how people were to behave; and scientific, philosophical, and theological ideas that explained the larger world. Generally only societies that used writing were judged to be civilizations.

Until the middle of the twentieth century, historians often referred to the earliest places where writing and cities developed as the "cradles of civilization," proposing a model of development for all humanity patterned on that of an individual person. However, the idea that all human societies developed (or should develop) in a uniform process from a "cradle" to a "mature" civilization has now been largely discredited, and some world historians choose not to use the word *civilization* at all because it could imply that some societies are superior to others.

The Rise of States, Laws, and Social Hierarchies

Cities concentrated people and power, and they required more elaborate mechanisms to make them work than had small agricultural villages and foraging groups. These mechanisms were part of what political scientists call "the state," an organization in which a small share of the population is able to coerce resources out of everyone else in order to gain and then maintain power. In a state, the interest that gains power might be one particular family, a set of religious leaders, or even a charismatic or talented individual able to handle the problems of dense urban communities.

However they are established, states coerce people through violence, or the threat of violence, and develop permanent armies for this purpose. Using armed force every time they need food or other resources is not very efficient, however, so states also establish bureaucracies and systems of taxation. States also need to keep track of people and goods, so they sometimes develop systems of recording information and accounting. These systems allow for the creation of more elaborate rules of behavior, often written down in the form of law codes, which facilitate further growth in state power, or in the form of religious traditions, which specify what sort of behavior is pleasing to the gods or other supernatural forces.

Written laws and traditions generally create more elaborate social hierarchies, in which divisions between elite groups and common people are established more firmly. They also generally heighten gender hierarchies. Those who

CHAPTER LOCATOR | How does writing shape what we can know about the past, and how did writing develop? | How did the peoples of Mesopotamia form states and develop new technologies?

36   CHAPTER 2
THE RISE OF THE STATE IN SOUTHWEST ASIA AND THE NILE VALLEY

gain power in states are most often men, so they tend to establish laws and norms that favor males in marriage, property rights, and other areas.

Whether we choose to call the process "the birth of civilization" or "the growth of the state," in the fourth millennium B.C.E., Neolithic agricultural villages expanded into cities that depended largely on food produced by the surrounding countryside while people living in cities carried out other tasks. The organization of a more complex division of labor was undertaken by an elite group, which enforced its will through laws, taxes, and bureaucracies backed up by armed force or the threat of it. Social and gender hierarchies became more complex and rigid. All this happened first in Mesopotamia, then in Egypt, and then in India and China.

QUICK REVIEW <

What connections can you make between the invention of writing and the emergence and growth of cities?

How did the Egyptians create a prosperous and long-lasting society?

How did the Hebrews create an enduring written religious tradition?

How did the Assyrians and the Persians consolidate their power and control the subjects?

☑ LearningCurve
Check what you know.

How did the peoples of Mesopotamia form states and develop new technologies and institutions?

States first developed in Mesopotamia, where sustained agriculture reliant on irrigation from the Euphrates and Tigris Rivers resulted in larger populations, a division of labor, and the growth of cities. Priests and rulers developed ways to control and organize these complex societies. Conquerors from the north unified Mesopotamian city-states into larger empires and spread Mesopotamian culture over a large area.

Environmental Challenges, Irrigation, and Religion

Mesopotamia was part of the Fertile Crescent, where settled agriculture first developed (see pages 17–21). The earliest agricultural villages in Mesopotamia were in the northern, hilly parts of the river valleys, where there is abundant rainfall for crops. Farmers had brought techniques of crop raising southward by about

CHAPTER LOCATOR | How does writing shape what we can know about the past, and how did writing develop? | **How did the peoples of Mesopotamia form states and develop new technologies?**

CHAPTER 2
38 THE RISE OF THE STATE IN SOUTHWEST ASIA AND THE NILE VALLEY

5000 B.C.E., to the southern part of Mesopotamia known as Sumer (soo-MAIR). In this arid climate farmers developed large-scale irrigation, which required organized group effort but allowed the population to grow. By about 3800 B.C.E. one of these agricultural villages, Uruk (OO-rook), had expanded significantly, becoming what many historians view as the world's first city. Over the next thousand years, other cities emerged in Sumer. These cities built defensive walls, marketplaces, and large public buildings; each came to dominate the surrounding countryside, becoming city-states independent from one another, though not very far apart.

The city-states of Sumer relied on irrigation systems that required cooperation and at least some level of social and political cohesion. The authority to run this system was, it seems, initially assumed by Sumerian priests. Encouraged and directed by their religious leaders, people built temples on tall platforms in the center of their cities. Temples grew into elaborate complexes of buildings with storage space for grain and other products and housing for animals. Surrounding the temple and other large buildings were the houses of ordinary citizens, each constructed around a central courtyard.

To Sumerians, and to later peoples in Mesopotamia as well, many different gods and goddesses controlled the world, a religious idea later scholars called **polytheism**. Each deity represented cosmic forces such as the sun, moon, water, and storms. The gods judged good and evil and would punish humans who lied or cheated. People believed that humans had been created to serve the gods and generally anticipated being well treated by the gods if they served them well.

polytheism
▶ The worship of many gods and goddesses.

Sumerian Politics and Society

Exactly how kings emerged in Sumerian society is not clear. Scholars have suggested that during times of crisis, a chief priest or sometimes a military leader assumed what was supposed to be temporary authority over a city. He established an army, trained it, and led it into battle. Temporary power gradually became permanent kingship, and kings in some Sumerian city-states began to hand down the kingship to their sons, establishing patriarchal hereditary dynasties in which power was handed down through the male line. The symbol of royal status was the palace, which came to rival the temple in its grandeur.

Kings made alliances with other powerful individuals, often through marriage. Royal family members were responsible for many aspects of government. Kings worked closely with religious authorities and relied on ideas about their connections with the gods, as well as the kings' military might, for their power. Acting together, priests, nobles, and kings in Sumerian cities used force, persuasion, and threats of higher taxes to maintain order, keep the irrigation systems working, and keep food and other goods flowing.

The king and the nobles held extensive tracts of land, as did the temple; these lands were worked by the palace's or the temple's clients—free men and women who were dependent on the palace or the temple. They received crops and other goods in return for their labor. Although this arrangement assured the clients of a livelihood, the land they worked remained the possession of the palace or the temple. Some individuals and families owned land outright and paid their taxes in the form of agricultural products or items they made. At the bottom rung of society were slaves. Like animals, slaves were a source of physical power for their owners, providing them an opportunity to amass more wealth and influence.

How did the Egyptians create a prosperous and long-lasting society?

How did the Hebrews create an enduring written religious tradition?

How did the Assyrians and the Persians consolidate their power and control the subjects?

☑ LearningCurve
Check what you know.

39

Each of these social categories included both men and women, but their experiences were not the same, for Sumerian society made distinctions based on gender. Most elite landowners were male, but women who held positions as priestesses or as queens ran their own estates independently of their husbands and fathers. Some women owned businesses and took care of their own accounts. They could own property and distribute it to their offspring. Sons and daughters inherited from their parents, although a daughter received her inheritance in the form of a dowry, which technically remained hers but was managed by her husband or husband's family after marriage. The Sumerians established the basic social, economic, and intellectual patterns of Mesopotamia and influenced their neighbors to the north and east.

Writing, Mathematics, and Poetry

The origins of writing probably date back to the ninth millennium B.C.E., when people in southwest Asia used clay tokens as counters for record keeping. By the fourth millennium people had realized that impressing the tokens on soft clay, or drawing pictures of the tokens on clay, was simpler than making tokens. This breakthrough in turn suggested that more information could be conveyed by adding pictures of other objects, and slowly the new technology of writing developed. The result was a complex system of pictographs in which each sign pictured an object, such as "star" (line A of Figure 2.1). These pictographs were the forerunners of the Sumerian form of writing known as cuneiform (kyou-NEE-uh-form).

Pictographs were initially limited in that they could not represent abstract ideas, but the development of ideograms—signs that represented ideas—made writing more versatile. Thus the sign for "star" could also be used to indicate "heaven," "sky," or even "god." The real breakthrough came when scribes started using signs to represent sounds.

cuneiform

▶ Sumerian form of writing; the term describes the wedge-shaped marks made by a stylus.

The development of the Sumerian system of writing was piecemeal, with scribes making changes and additions as they were needed. The system became so complicated that the Sumerians established scribal schools, which by 2500 B.C.E. flourished throughout the region. Students at the schools were all male, and most came from families in the middle range of urban society. Scribal schools were primarily intended to produce individuals who could keep records of the property of temple officials, kings, and nobles. Thus writing first developed as a way to enhance the growing power of elites, not to record speech.

Sumerians wrote numbers as well as words on clay tablets, and some surviving tablets show multiplication and division problems. The Sumerians and later Mesopotamians made significant advances in mathematics using a numerical system based on units of sixty, ten, and six, from which we derive our division of hours into sixty minutes and minutes into sixty seconds. They also developed the concept of place value—that the value of a number depends on where it stands in relation to other numbers.

MEANING	PICTOGRAPH	IDEOGRAM	PHONETIC SIGN
A Star			
B Woman			
C Mountain			
D Slave woman			
E Water In			

FIGURE 2.1 ■ Sumerian Writing

(Source: Excerpted from S. N. Kramer, *The Sumerians: Their History, Culture, and Character.* Copyright © 1963 by the University of Chicago Press. Used by permission of The University of Chicago Press.)

CHAPTER LOCATOR | How does writing shape what we can know about the past, and how did writing develop? | **How did the peoples of Mesopotamia form states and develop new technologies?**

CHAPTER 2
40 THE RISE OF THE STATE IN SOUTHWEST ASIA AND THE NILE VALLEY

Written texts were not an important part of Sumerian religious life, nor were they central to the religious practices of most of the other peoples in this region. Stories about the gods circulated orally and traveled with people when they moved up and down the rivers. Sumerians also told stories about heroes and kings, many of which were eventually reworked into the world's first epic poem, the *Epic of Gilgamesh* (GIL-guh-mesh), which was later written down.

epic poem
▶ An oral or written narration of the achievements and sometimes the failures of heroes that embodies peoples' ideas about themselves.

Empires in Mesopotamia

The wealth of Sumerian cities also attracted conquerors from the north. Around 2300 B.C.E. Sargon, the king of a region to the north of Sumer, conquered a number of Sumerian cities with what was probably the world's first permanent army and created a large state. The symbol of his triumph was a new capital, the city of Akkad (AH-kahd). Sargon also expanded the Akkadian empire westward to northern Syria, which became the breadbasket of the empire. He encouraged trading networks that brought in goods from as far away as the Indus River in South Asia and what is now Turkey (Map 2.1). Sargon spoke a different language than did the Sumerians, one of the many languages that scholars identify as belonging to the Semitic language family, which includes modern-day Hebrew and Arabic.

MAP 2.1 ■ Spread of Cultures in Southwest Asia and the Nile Valley, ca. 3000–1640 B.C.E.

This map illustrates the spread of the Mesopotamian and Egyptian cultures through the semicircular stretch of land often called the Fertile Crescent. From this area, the knowledge and use of agriculture spread throughout western Asia, northern Africa, and Europe.

How did the Egyptians create a prosperous and long-lasting society?

How did the Hebrews create an enduring written religious tradition?

How did the Assyrians and the Persians consolidate their power and control the subjects?

✓ LearningCurve
Check what you know.

Akkadians adapted cuneiform writing to their own language, and Akkadian became the diplomatic language used over a wide area.

Sargon tore down the defensive walls of Sumerian cities and appointed his own sons as their rulers to help him cement his power. He also appointed his daughter, Enheduana (2285–2250 B.C.E.), as high priestess in the city of Ur. Here she wrote a number of hymns, becoming the world's first author to put her name to a literary composition.

Sargon's dynasty appears to have ruled Mesopotamia for about 150 years, and then collapsed, in part because of a period of extended drought. Various city-states then rose to power, one of which was centered on the city of Babylon. Babylon was in an excellent position to dominate trade on both the Tigris and Euphrates Rivers, and it was fortunate in having a very able ruler in Hammurabi (hahm-moo-RAH-bee) (r. 1792–1750 B.C.E.). Initially a typical king of his era, he unified Mesopotamia later in his reign by using military force, strategic alliances with the rulers of smaller territories, and religious ideas. As had earlier rulers, Hammurabi linked his success with the will of the gods. He connected himself with the sun-god Shamash, the god of law and justice, and encouraged the spread of myths that explained how Marduk, the primary god of Babylon, had been elected king of the gods by the other deities in Mesopotamia. Babylonian ideas and beliefs thus became part of the cultural mixture of Mesopotamia.

Life Under Hammurabi

Hammurabi's most memorable accomplishment was the proclamation of an extensive law code, introduced about 1755 B.C.E. **Hammurabi's law code** set a variety of punishments for breaking the law, including fines and physical punishment such as mutilation, whipping, and burning. It demanded that the punishment fit the crime, calling for "an eye for an eye and a tooth for a tooth," at least among social equals, although higher-ranking people could pay a fine to lower-ranking victims instead of having an arm broken or losing an eye.

Hammurabi's law code
▶ A proclamation issued by Babylonian king Hammurabi to establish laws regulating many aspects of life.

Law Code of Hammurabi

Hammurabi ordered his code to be inscribed on stone pillars and set up in public throughout the Babylonian empire. At the top of the pillar Hammurabi (left) is depicted receiving the rod and ring of authority from Shamash, the god of law and justice. (© RMN-Grand Palais/Art Resource, NY)

CHAPTER LOCATOR | How does writing shape what we can know about the past, and how did writing develop? | **How did the peoples of Mesopotamia form states and develop new technologies?**

CHAPTER 2
42 THE RISE OF THE STATE IN SOUTHWEST ASIA AND THE NILE VALLEY

Hammurabi's code provides a wealth of information about daily life in Meso-potamia. Because of farming's fundamental importance, the code dealt exten-sively with agriculture. Tenants faced severe penalties for neglecting the land or not working it at all. The code also regulated other trades, and artisans had to guarantee the quality of their goods and services to consumers. Hammurabi gave careful attention to marriage and the family. As elsewhere in the area, marriage had aspects of a business agreement. The groom or his father offered the prospec-tive bride's father a gift, and if this was acceptable, the bride's father provided his daughter with a dowry, which technically remained hers. A father could not disinherit a son without just cause, and the code ordered the courts to forgive a son for his first offense. On family matters and other issues, Hammurabi's code influenced other law codes, including those later written down in Hebrew Scrip-ture (see page 53).

QUICK REVIEW <

What role did kings play in Mesopotamian society?
What about priests?

How did the Egyptians create a prosperous and long-lasting society?

How did the Hebrews create an enduring written religious tradition?

How did the Assyrians and the Persians consolidate their power and control the subjects?

LearningCurve
Check what you know.

How did the Egyptians create a prosperous and long-lasting society?

Egyptian Home Life

This grave painting depicts an intimate moment in the life of an aristocratic family, with the father and mother in the center and their children around them. (Gianni Dagli Orti/The Art Archive at Art Resource, NY)

> **PICTURING THE PAST**

ANALYZING THE IMAGE: What evidence do you find in the painting that Egyptian artists based the size of figures on people's status in the household?

CONNECTIONS: Based on your reading, how might an image of a poor family differ from this depiction?

At about the same time that Sumerian city-states expanded and fought with one another in the Tigris and Euphrates Valleys, a more cohesive state under a single ruler grew in the valley of the Nile River in North Africa. This was Egypt, which for long stretches of history was prosperous and secure. At various times groups invaded and conquered Egypt or migrated into Egypt seeking better lives. Often these newcomers adopted aspects of Egyptian culture, and Egyptians also carried their traditions with them when they established an empire and engaged in trade.

The Nile and the God-King

No other single geographical factor had such a fundamental and profound impact on Egyptian life, society, and history as the Nile River (see Map 2.2, page 47). The Nile flooded once a year for a period of several months, bringing fertile soil

CHAPTER LOCATOR | How does writing shape what we can know about the past, and how did writing develop? | How did the peoples of Mesopotamia form states and develop new technologies?

44 CHAPTER 2 THE RISE OF THE STATE IN SOUTHWEST ASIA AND THE NILE VALLEY

and moisture for farming. Through the fertility of the Nile and their own hard work, Egyptians produced an annual agricultural surplus, which in turn sustained a growing and prosperous population. The Nile also unified Egypt, serving as a highway that promoted easy communication.

The political power structures that developed in Egypt came to be linked with the Nile. Somehow the idea developed that a single individual, a king, was responsible for the rise and fall of the Nile. The king came to be viewed as a descendant of the gods and thus a god himself. Political unification most likely proceeded slowly, but stories told about early kings highlighted one who had united Upper Egypt—the upstream valley in the south—and Lower Egypt—the delta area of the Nile that empties into the Mediterranean Sea—into a single kingdom around 3100 B.C.E. The political unification of Egypt in the Archaic Period (3100–2660 B.C.E.) ushered in the period known as the Old Kingdom (2660–2180 B.C.E.).

The focal point of religious and political life in the Old Kingdom was the king, who commanded the wealth, resources, and people of Egypt. The king's surroundings had to be worthy of a god, and only a magnificent palace was suitable for his home; in fact, the word **pharaoh**, which during the New Kingdom (1570–1070 B.C.E.) came to be used for the king, originally meant "great house." Just as the kings occupied a great house in life, so they reposed in great pyramids after death. Built during the Old Kingdom, these massive stone tombs contained all the things needed by the king in his afterlife and also symbolized the king's power and his connection with the sun-god.

Like the Mesopotamians, the Egyptians were polytheistic, worshipping many gods of all types, some mightier than others. They developed complex ideas of their gods that reflected the world around them, and these views changed over the many centuries of Egyptian history as gods took on new attributes and often merged with one another. During the Old Kingdom, Egyptians considered the sun-god Ra the creator of life. Much later, during the New Kingdom (see page 46), the pharaohs of a new dynasty favored the worship of a different sun-god, Amon. As his cult grew, Amon came to be identified with Ra, and eventually the Egyptians combined them into one sun-god, Amon-Ra.

The Egyptians likewise developed views of an afterlife that reflected the world around them and that changed over time. During the later part of the Old Kingdom, the walls of kings' tombs were carved with religious texts that provided spells that would bring the king back to life and help him ascend to heaven. Toward the end of the Old Kingdom, the tombs of powerful nobles also contained such inscriptions, an indication that more people expected to gain everlasting life. In the Middle Kingdom (2080–1640 B.C.E.), new types of spells appeared on the coffins of even more people, a further expansion in admissions to the afterlife.

PERIODS OF EGYPTIAN HISTORY

Period	Dates	Significant Events
Archaic	3100–2660 B.C.E.	Unification of Egypt
Old Kingdom	2660–2180 B.C.E.	Construction of the pyramids
First Intermediate	2180–2080 B.C.E.	Political chaos
Middle Kingdom	2080–1640 B.C.E.	Recovery and political stability
Second Intermediate	1640–1570 B.C.E.	Hyksos migrations; struggles for power
New Kingdom	1570–1070 B.C.E.	Creation of an Egyptian empire; growth in wealth
Third Intermediate	1100–653 B.C.E.	Political fragmentation and conquest by outsiders

pharaoh
▶ The title given to the king of Egypt in the New Kingdom, from a word that meant "great house."

How did the Egyptians create a prosperous and long-lasting society? | How did the Hebrews create an enduring written religious tradition? | How did the Assyrians and the Persians consolidate their power and control the subjects? | ✓ LearningCurve Check what you know.

45

During the New Kingdom, a time when Egypt came into greater contact with the cultures of the Fertile Crescent, Egyptians developed even more complex ideas about the afterlife, recording these in written funerary manuscripts that have come to be known as the *Book of the Dead*. These texts explained that the soul left the body to become part of the divine after death and told of the god Osiris (oh-SIGH-ruhs), who died each year and was then brought back to life by his wife Isis (IGH-suhs) when the Nile flooded. Osiris eventually became king of the dead, weighing dead humans' hearts to determine whether they had lived justly enough to deserve everlasting life.

Egyptian Society and Work

Egyptian society reflected the pyramids that it built. At the top stood the pharaoh, who relied on a circle of nobles, officials, and priests to administer his kingdom. All of them were assisted by scribes, who used a writing system perhaps adapted from Mesopotamia or perhaps developed independently. Egyptian scribes actually created two writing systems: one called hieroglyphics for engraving important religious or political texts on stone or writing them on papyrus made from reeds growing in the Nile Delta, and a much simpler system called hieratic that allowed scribes to write more quickly and was used for the documents of daily life. The cities of the Nile Valley were also home to artisans of all types, along with merchants and other tradespeople. A large group of farmers made up the broad base of the social pyramid.

For Egyptians, the Nile formed an essential part of daily life. During the flooding season—from June to October—farmers worked on the pharaoh's building programs and other tasks away from their fields. When the water began to recede, they diverted some of it into ponds for future irrigation and began planting wheat and barley, using plows pulled by oxen or people. From October to February, farmers planted and tended crops, and from February until the next flood, they harvested them. As in Mesopotamia, common people paid their obligations to their superiors in products and in labor. Some young men were drafted into the pharaoh's army, which served as both a fighting force and a labor corps.

The lives of all Egyptians centered around the family. Just as in Mesopotamia, marriage was a business arrangement. A couple's parents arranged the marriage, which seems to have taken place at a young age. Once couples were married, having children, especially sons, was a high priority. Most Egyptian men had only one wife, but among the wealthy some had several wives or concubines. Ordinary women were expected to obey their fathers, husbands, and other men, but they possessed considerable economic and legal rights. They could own land in their own names, operate businesses, and testify in court. Literature and art depict a world in which ordinary husbands and wives enjoyed each other's company.

Migrations, Revivals, and Collapse

While Egyptian civilization flourished in the Nile Valley, various groups migrated throughout the Fertile Crescent and then accommodated themselves to local cultures (Map 2.2). Some settled in the Nile Delta, including a group the Egyptians called Hyksos. Although they were later portrayed as a conquering horde, the

Hittite homeland, ca. 1500 B.C.E.
Hittite Empire, ca. 1300 B.C.E.
Old Kingdom (2660–2180 B.C.E.)
and Middle Kingdom (2080–1640 B.C.E.)
of Egypt
New Kingdom of Egypt, ca. 1300 B.C.E.
Babylonian Empire, ca. 1300 B.C.E.
Mycenaean Greece, ca. 1300 B.C.E.
Migration of Hyksos, ca. 1640 B.C.E.
Late Bronze Age migrations, ca. 1200 B.C.E.

MAP 2.2 ■ **Empires and Migrations in the Eastern Mediterranean**

The rise and fall of empires in the eastern Mediterranean were shaped by internal developments, military conflicts, and the migration of peoples to new areas.

> **MAPPING THE PAST**

ANALYZING THE MAP: At what point was the Egyptian Empire at its largest? The Hittite Empire? What were the other major powers in the eastern Mediterranean at this time?

CONNECTIONS: What were the major effects of the migrations of the Hyksos? Of the late Bronze Age migrations? What clues does the map provide as to why the late Bronze Age migrations had a more powerful impact than those of the Hyksos?

Hyksos were actually migrants looking for good land, and their entry into the delta, which began around 1800 B.C.E., was probably gradual and generally peaceful. The newcomers began to worship Egyptian deities and modeled their political structures on those of the Egyptians.

The Hyksos brought with them methods of making bronze (see Chapter 1) and casting it into weapons that became standard in Egypt. They thereby brought Egypt fully into the Bronze Age culture of the Mediterranean world. The Hyksos also introduced horse-drawn chariots and the composite bow, made of multiple materials for greater strength, which along with bronze weaponry revolutionized Egyptian warfare. The migration of the Hyksos, combined with a series of famines and internal struggles for power, led Egypt to fragment politically.

How did the Egyptians create a prosperous and long-lasting society?	How did the Hebrews create an enduring written religious tradition?	How did the Assyrians and the Persians consolidate their power and control the subjects?	☑ LearningCurve Check what you know.

In about 1570 B.C.E. a new dynasty of pharaohs arose, pushing the Hyksos out of the delta and conquering territory to the south and northeast. These warrior-pharaohs inaugurated what scholars refer to as the New Kingdom, a period characterized not only by enormous wealth and conscious imperialism but also by a greater sense of insecurity because of new contacts and military engagements. By expanding Egyptian power beyond the Nile Valley, the pharaohs created the first Egyptian empire.

The New Kingdom pharaohs include a number of remarkable figures. Among these was Hatshepsut (haht-SHEP-soot) (r. ca. 1479–ca. 1458 B.C.E.), one of the few female pharaohs in Egypt's long history. (See "Individuals in Society: Hatshepsut and Nefertiti," page 49.) Amenhotep III (ah-men-HOE-tep) (r. ca. 1388–ca. 1350 B.C.E.) corresponded with other powerful kings in Babylonia and other kingdoms in the Fertile Crescent. Amenhotep III was succeeded by his son, who took the name Akhenaten (ah-keh-NAH-tuhn) (r. 1351–1334 B.C.E.). He renamed himself as a mark of his changing religious ideas, choosing to worship a new sun-god, Aten, instead of the traditional Amon or Ra. Akhenaten's wife Nefertiti (nehf-uhr-TEE-tee) supported his religious ideas, but this new religion, imposed from above, failed to find a place among the people, and after his death traditional religious practices returned.

One of the key challenges facing the pharaohs after Akhenaten was the expansion of the kingdom of the Hittites. At about the same time that the Sumerians were establishing city-states, speakers of Indo-European languages migrated into Anatolia, modern-day Turkey. Indo-European is a large family of languages that includes English, most of the languages of modern Europe, ancient Greek, Latin, Persian, Hindi, Bengali, and Sanskrit (for more on Sanskrit, see page 67). It also includes Hittite, the language of one of the peoples who migrated into this area. Beginning about 1600 B.C.E., Hittite kings began to conquer more territory (see Map 2.2). As the Hittites expanded southward, they came into conflict with the Egyptians, who were establishing their own larger empire. There were a number of battles, but both sides seem to have recognized the impossibility of defeating the other, and in 1258 the Egyptian king Ramesses II (r. ca. 1290–1224 B.C.E.) and the Hittite king Hattusili III (r. ca. 1267–1237 B.C.E.) concluded a peace treaty.

The treaty brought peace between the Egyptians and the Hittites for a time, but this stability did not last. Within several decades of the treaty, groups of seafaring peoples whom the Egyptians called "Sea Peoples" raided, migrated, and marauded in the eastern Mediterranean, disrupting trade and in some cases looting and destroying cities. These raids, combined with the expansion of the Assyrians (see page 55), led to the collapse of the Hittite Empire and the fragmentation of the Egyptian empire. There is evidence of drought, and some scholars have suggested that a major volcanic explosion in Iceland cooled the climate for several years, leading to a series of poor harvests. All of these developments are part of a general "Bronze Age Collapse" in the period around 1200 B.C.E. that historians see as a major turning point.

The Emergence of New States

The Bronze Age Collapse was a time of massive political and economic disruption, but it was also a period of the spread of new technologies, especially iron. The

Indo-European languages

▶ A large family of languages that includes English, most of the languages of modern Europe, ancient Greek, Latin, Persian, Hindi, Bengali, and Sanskrit, the sacred tongue of ancient India.

CHAPTER LOCATOR | How does writing shape what we can know about the past, and how did writing develop? | How did the peoples of Mesopotamia form states and develop new technologies?

48 CHAPTER 2 THE RISE OF THE STATE IN SOUTHWEST ASIA AND THE NILE VALLEY

INDIVIDUALS IN SOCIETY
Hatshepsut and Nefertiti

Egyptians understood the pharaoh to be the living embodiment of the god Horus, the source of law and morality, and the mediator between gods and humans. His connection with the divine stretched to members of his family, so his siblings and children were also viewed as in some ways divine. Because of this, a pharaoh often took his sister or half-sister as one of his wives. This concentrated divine blood set the pharaonic family apart from other Egyptians (who did not marry close relatives) and allowed the pharaohs to imitate the gods, who in Egyptian mythology often married their siblings. A pharaoh chose one of his wives to be the "Great Royal Wife," or principal queen. Often this was a relative, though sometimes it was one of the foreign princesses who married pharaohs to establish political alliances.

The familial connection with the divine allowed a handful of women to rule in their own right in Egypt's long history. We know the names of four female pharaohs, of whom the most famous was Hatshepsut. She was the sister and wife of Thutmose II and, after he died, served as regent — as adviser and co-ruler — for her young stepson Thutmose III, who was the son of another woman. Hatshepsut sent trading expeditions and sponsored artists and architects, ushering in a period of artistic creativity and economic prosperity. She built one of the world's great buildings, an elaborate terraced temple at Deir el Bahri, which eventually served as her tomb. Hatshepsut's status as a powerful female ruler was difficult for Egyptians to conceptualize, and she is often depicted in male dress or with a false beard, thus looking more like the male rulers who were the norm. After her death, Thutmose III tried to destroy all evidence that she had ever ruled, smashing statues and scratching her name off inscriptions, perhaps because of personal animosity and perhaps because he wanted to erase the fact that a woman had once been pharaoh. Only within recent decades have historians and archaeologists begun to (literally) piece together her story.

Though female pharaohs were very rare, many royal women had power through their position as Great Royal Wives. The most famous was Nefertiti (ca. 1370–1330 B.C.E.), the wife of Akhenaten. Her name means "the perfect (or beautiful) woman has come," and inscriptions give her many other titles.

Nefertiti used her position to spread the new religion of the sun-god Aten. Together she and Akhenaten built a new palace at Akhetaten, the present-day Amarna, away from the old centers of power. There they developed the cult of Aten to the exclusion of the traditional deities. Nearly the only literary survivor of their religious belief is the "Hymn to Aten," which declares Aten to be the only god. It describes Nefertiti as "the great royal consort whom

Painted limestone bust of Nefertiti. (bpk, Berlin/Aegyptisches Museum, Staaliche Museen, Berlin, Germany/Photo: Margarete Buesing/Art Resource, NY)

Granite head of Hatshepsut. (bpk, Berlin/Aegyptisches Museum, Staaliche Museen, Berlin, Germany/Photo: Margarete Buesing/Art Resource, NY)

he, Akhenaten, loves. The mistress of the Two Lands, Upper and Lower Egypt."

Nefertiti is often shown as being the same size as her husband, and in some inscriptions she is performing religious rituals that would normally have been carried out only by the pharaoh. The exact details of her power are hard to determine, however. An older theory held that her husband removed her from power, though there is also speculation that she may have ruled secretly in her own right after his death. Her tomb has long since disappeared, though some scholars believe that an unidentified mummy discovered in 2003 in Egypt's Valley of the Kings may be Nefertiti's.

QUESTIONS FOR ANALYSIS

1. Why might it have been difficult for Egyptians to accept a female ruler?
2. What opportunities do hereditary monarchies such as that of ancient Egypt provide for women? How does this fit with gender hierarchies in which men are understood as superior?

▷LaunchPad

ONLINE DOCUMENT PROJECT

Considering Egyptian views of gender roles, what complexities did Egyptian writers and artists face in depicting Hatshepsut? Analyze written and visual representations of Hatshepsut, and then complete a quiz and writing assignment based on the evidence and details from this chapter. *See inside front cover to learn more.*

Iron Age

▶ Period beginning about 1100 B.C.E. when iron became the most important material for weapons and tools in some parts of the world.

Iron Age began in about 1100 B.C.E. Iron weapons became important items of trade around the Mediterranean and throughout the Tigris and Euphrates Valleys, and the technology for making them traveled as well.

The decline of Egypt allowed new powers to emerge. South of Egypt along the Nile was a region called Nubia, which as early as 2000 B.C.E. served as a conduit of trade through which a variety of products flowed north from sub-Saharan Africa. As Egypt expanded during the New Kingdom, it took over northern Nubia, incorporating it into the growing Egyptian empire. The Nubians adopted many features of Egyptian culture, including Egyptian gods, the use of hieroglyphs, and the building of pyramids. Many Nubians became officials in the Egyptian bureaucracy and officers in the army, and there was significant intermarriage between the two groups.

With the contraction of the Egyptian empire, an independent kingdom, Kush, rose to power in Nubia, with its capital at Napata in what is now Sudan. The Kushites conquered southern Egypt, and in 727 B.C.E. the Kushite king Piye (r. ca. 747–716 B.C.E.) swept through the entire Nile Valley to the delta in the north. United once again, Egypt enjoyed a brief period of peace during which the Egyptian culture continued to influence that of its conquerors. In the seventh century B.C.E. invading Assyrians pushed the Kushites out of Egypt, and the Kushite rulers moved their capital farther up the Nile to Meroë, where they built hundreds of pyramids. Meroë became a center of iron production, exporting iron goods to much of Africa and across the Red Sea and the Indian Ocean to India. Gold and cotton textiles also provided wealth to the Kushite kingdom, which in the third century B.C.E. developed its own alphabet.

While Kush expanded in the southern Nile Valley, another group rose to prominence along the Mediterranean coast of modern Lebanon. These people established the prosperous commercial centers of Tyre, Sidon, and Byblos. These peoples were master shipbuilders, and from about 1100 B.C.E. to 700 B.C.E. many of the residents of these cities became the seaborne merchants of the Mediterranean. Their most valued products were purple and blue textiles, from which originated their Greek name, **Phoenicians**, meaning "Purple People."

The variety and quality of the Phoenicians' trade goods generally made them welcome visitors. They established colonies and trading posts throughout the Mediterranean and as far west as the Atlantic coast of modern-day Portugal. The Phoenicians' voyages brought them into contact with the Greeks, to whom they introduced many aspects of the older and more urbanized cultures of Mesopotamia and Egypt.

Phoenicians

▶ People of the prosperous city-states in what is now Lebanon who traded and founded colonies throughout the Mediterranean and spread the phonetic alphabet.

> **Phoenician Trade Goods:**

- Dyed textiles
- Bronze
- Iron
- Wine
- Hunting dogs
- Gold
- Ivory

CHAPTER LOCATOR | How does writing shape what we can know about the past, and how did writing develop? | How did the peoples of Mesopotamia form states and develop new technologies?

CHAPTER 2
50 THE RISE OF THE STATE IN SOUTHWEST ASIA AND THE NILE VALLEY

FIGURE 2.2 ■ Origins of the Alphabet

List of hieroglyphic, Ugaritic, Phoenician, Greek, and Roman sign forms. (Source: A. B. Knapp, *The History and Culture of Ancient Western Asia and Egypt.* © 1988 Wadsworth, a division of Cengage Learning, Inc. Reproduced by permission, www.cengage.com/permissions.)

HIEROGLYPHIC	REPRESENTS	UGARITIC	PHOENICIAN	GREEK	ROMAN
	Throw stick	T		Γ	G
	Man with raised arms			E	E
	Basket with handle			K	K
	Water			M	M
	Snake			N	N
	Eye		O	O	O
	Mouth		?	Π	P
	Head			P	R
	Pool with lotus flowers		W	Σ	S
	House			B	B
	Ox-head		K	A	A

The Phoenicians' overwhelming cultural achievement was the spread of a completely phonetic system of writing—that is, an alphabet (see Figure 2.2). Writers of cuneiform and hieroglyphics had developed signs that were used to represent sounds, but these were always used with a much larger number of ideograms. Sometime around 1800 B.C.E., workers in the Sinai Peninsula, which was under Egyptian control, began to use only phonetic signs to write, with each sign designating one sound. The Greeks modified this alphabet for their own language, and the Romans later based their alphabet—the script we use to write English today—on Greek. Alphabets based on the Phoenician alphabet were also created in the Persian Empire and formed the basis of Hebrew, Arabic, and various alphabets of South and Central Asia.

Phoenician Settlements in the Mediterranean

QUICK REVIEW <

How did the Nile shape the society and culture of ancient Egypt?

How did the Egyptians create a prosperous and long-lasting society?	How did the Hebrews create an enduring written religious tradition?	How did the Assyrians and the Persians consolidate their power and control the subjects?	✓ LearningCurve Check what you know.

How did the Hebrews create an enduring written religious tradition?

Hebrew Seal

Archaeologists found this stone seal in 2012 while unearthing an ancient drainage channel in central Jerusalem. Dating from the seventh or sixth century B.C.E., the tiny seal would have been set in a ring and used for signing letters. The inscription reads, "Belonging to Matanyahu . . . ," a name that is found in Hebrew Scripture and is very close to the name of the current prime minister of Israel, Benjamin Netanyahu. (Bible Land Pictures/akg-images)

Yahweh

▶ All-powerful god of the Hebrew people and the basis for the enduring religious traditions of Judaism.

The legacy of another people who took advantage of Egypt's collapse to found an independent state may have been even more far-reaching than that of the Phoenicians. For a period of several centuries, the Hebrews controlled first one and then two small states on the western end of the Fertile Crescent. The Hebrews created a new form of religious belief, a monotheism based on the worship of an all-powerful god they called **Yahweh** (YAH-way). Beginning in the late seventh century B.C.E. the Hebrews began to write down their religious ideas, traditions, laws, advice literature, prayers, hymns, history, and prophecies in a series of books. These were gathered together centuries later to form the Hebrew Bible. These writings later became the core of the Hebrews' religion, Judaism. Jews today revere these texts, as do many Christians, and Muslims respect them, all of which gives them particular importance.

The Hebrew State

The Hebrews were nomadic pastoralists who may have migrated into the Nile Delta from the east seeking good land for their herds of sheep and goats. According to the Hebrew Bible, they were enslaved by the Egyptians but were led out of Egypt by a charismatic leader named Moses. The Hebrews settled in the area between the Mediterranean and the Jordan River known as Canaan and were organized into tribes, each tribe consisting of numerous families who thought of themselves as related to one another. They slowly adopted agriculture and, not surprisingly, at times worshipped the agricultural gods of their neighbors. In this they followed the common historical pattern of newcomers by adapting the culture of an older, well-established people.

The Bible reports that the greatest danger to the Hebrews came from a group known as the Philistines (FIH-luh-steenz), who migrated to and established a kingdom in Canaan. The Hebrews found a leader in Saul, who with his men fought the Philistines. Saul subsequently established a monarchy over the Hebrew tribes, an event conventionally dated to about 1025 B.C.E. Saul's work was carried on by David of Bethlehem, who captured the city of Jerusalem, which he made the religious and political center of the realm. David's son Solomon (r. ca. 965–925 B.C.E.) launched a building program that the biblical narrative describes as including cities, palaces, fortresses, and roads. The most symbolic of these projects was the Temple of Jerusalem. The Temple of Jerusalem was intended to be the religious heart of the kingdom, a symbol of Hebrew unity and of Yahweh's approval of the Hebrew state.

This state did not last long. At Solomon's death his kingdom broke into political halves. The northern part became Israel, with its capital at Samaria, and the southern half was Judah, with Jerusalem remaining its center. War broke out between the northern and southern halves, and the Assyrians wiped out the northern kingdom in 722 B.C.E. Judah survived numerous invasions until the Babylonians crushed it in 587 B.C.E. The survivors were sent into exile in Babylonia, a period commonly known as the Babylonian Captivity. In 538 B.C.E. the Persian king Cyrus the Great conquered the Babylonians and permitted some forty thousand exiles to return to Jerusalem (see page 56).

Possible route of the Exodus, ca. 1250 B.C.E.
Solomon's kingdom, ca. 950 B.C.E.
Israel, ca. 800 B.C.E.
Judah, ca. 800 B.C.E.

The Hebrew Exodus and State, ca. 1250–800 B.C.E.

The Jewish Religion

During and especially after the Babylonian Captivity, the most important Hebrew texts of history, law, and ethics were edited and brought together in the Torah, the first five books of the Hebrew Bible. Fundamental to an understanding of the Jewish religion is the concept of the Covenant, an agreement that people believed to exist between themselves and Yahweh. According to the Bible, Yahweh appeared to the tribal leader Abraham, promising him that he would be blessed, as would his descendants, if they followed Yahweh. Yahweh next appeared to Moses when he was leading the Hebrews out of Egypt, and Yahweh made a covenant with the Hebrews: if they worshipped Yahweh as their only god, he would consider them his chosen people and protect them from their enemies. Individuals such as Abraham and Moses who acted as intermediaries between Yahweh and the Hebrew people were known as "prophets." Much of the Hebrew Bible consists of writings in the prophets' voices, understood as messages from Yahweh to the Hebrews.

Worship was embodied in a series of rules of behavior, the Ten Commandments, which Yahweh gave to Moses; these required certain kinds of religious observances and forbade the Hebrews to steal, kill, lie, or commit adultery, thus

How did the Egyptians create a prosperous and long-lasting society?

How did the Hebrews create an enduring written religious tradition?

How did the Assyrians and the Persians consolidate their power and control the subjects?

✓ LearningCurve
Check what you know.

53

creating a system of ethical absolutes. From the Ten Commandments a complex system of rules of conduct was created and later written down as Hebrew law. The later prophets such as Isaiah created a system of ethical monotheism, in which goodness was understood to come from a single transcendent god, and in which religious obligations included fair and just behavior toward other people as well as rituals.

Like Mesopotamian deities, Yahweh punished people, but the Hebrews also believed he would protect them all, not simply kings and powerful priests, and make them prosper if they obeyed his commandments. The religion of the Hebrews was thus addressed to not only the elites but also the individual. Because kings or other political leaders were not essential to its practice, the rise or fall of a kingdom was not crucial to the religion's continued existence. Religious leaders were important in Judaism, but personally following the instructions of Yahweh was the central task for observant Jews in the ancient world.

Hebrew Society

The Hebrews were originally nomadic, but they adopted settled agriculture in Canaan, and some lived in cities. Over time, communal use of land gave way to family or private ownership, and devotions to the traditions of Judaism replaced tribal identity.

Family relationships reflected evolving circumstances. Marriage and the family were fundamentally important in Jewish life. Celibacy was frowned upon, and almost all major Jewish thinkers and priests were married. As in Mesopotamia and Egypt, marriage was a family matter, too important to be left solely to the whims of young people. The bearing of children was seen in some ways as a religious function. Sons were especially desired because they maintained the family bloodline while keeping ancestral property in the family. A firstborn son became the head of the household upon his father's death. Mothers oversaw the early education of the children, but as boys grew older, their fathers provided more of their education.

The development of urban life among Jews created new economic opportunities, especially in crafts and trade. People specialized in certain occupations, and, as in most ancient societies, these crafts were family trades.

> **QUICK REVIEW**

How did the religion of the Hebrews differ from that of their Near Eastern neighbors?

CHAPTER LOCATOR | How does writing shape what we can know about the past, and how did writing develop? | How did the peoples of Mesopotamia form states and develop new technologies?

CHAPTER 2

54 THE RISE OF THE STATE IN SOUTHWEST ASIA AND THE NILE VALLEY

How did the Assyrians and the Persians consolidate their power and control the subjects of their empires?

Assyrian Warriors Attack a City

In this Assyrian carving from a royal throne room made about 865 B.C.E., warriors cross a river on inflated skins, which both support them and provide air for breathing underwater. Such innovative techniques, combined with a large army and effective military organization, allowed the Assyrians to establish a large empire. (Werner Forman Archive/British Museum, London. Location: 10. © 2004 Werner Forman/TopFoto/The Image Works)

Small kingdoms like those of the Phoenicians and the Jews could exist only in the absence of a major power. In the ninth century B.C.E. one major power arose in the form of the Assyrians, who starting in northern Mesopotamia created an empire through often-brutal military conquests. And from a base in what is now southern Iran, the Persians established an even larger empire, developing effective institutions of government.

Assyria, the Military Monarchy

Starting from a base in northern Mesopotamia around 900 B.C.E., the Assyrians began a campaign of expansion and domination, conquering, exacting tribute, and building new fortified towns, palaces, and temples. By means of almost constant warfare, the Assyrians created an empire that stretched from their capital of Nineveh on the Tigris River to central Egypt. Revolt against the Assyrians inevitably promised the rebels bloody battles and cruel sieges followed by surrender, accompanied by systematic torture and slaughter, and sometimes deportations.

Assyrian methods were certainly harsh, but in practical terms Assyria's success was due primarily to the size of its army and to the army's sophisticated and effective military organization. In addition, the Assyrians developed a wide variety of siege machinery and techniques. Never before in this area had anyone

How did the Egyptians create a prosperous and long-lasting society?

How did the Hebrews create an enduring written religious tradition?

How did the Assyrians and the Persians consolidate their power and control the subjects?

✓ LearningCurve
Check what you know.

55

applied such technical knowledge to warfare. The Assyrians also knew how to coordinate their efforts, both in open battle and in siege warfare. Not only did the Assyrians know how to win battles, but they also knew how to take advantage of their victories. As early as the eighth century B.C.E., the Assyrian kings began to organize their conquered territories into an empire. The lands closest to Assyria became provinces governed directly by Assyrian officials. Kingdoms beyond the provinces were not annexed but became dependent states.

By the seventh century B.C.E. Assyrian power seemed firmly established. Yet the downfall of Assyria was swift and complete. Babylon won its independence in 626 B.C.E. and joined forces with a new group, the Medes, an Indo-European-speaking people from Persia. Together the Babylonians and the Medes destroyed the Assyrian Empire in 612 B.C.E., paving the way for the rise of the Persians.

The Rise and Expansion of the Persian Empire

As we have seen, Assyria rose to power from a base in the Tigris and Euphrates River Valleys of Mesopotamia, which had seen many earlier empires. The Assyrians were defeated by a coalition that included not only a Mesopotamian power—

MAP 2.3 ■ The Assyrian and Persian Empires, ca. 1000–500 B.C.E.

The Assyrian Empire at its height around 650 B.C.E. included almost all of the old centers of power in the ancient Near East. By 500 B.C.E., however, the Persian Empire was far larger, extending from the Mediterranean Sea to the Indus River.

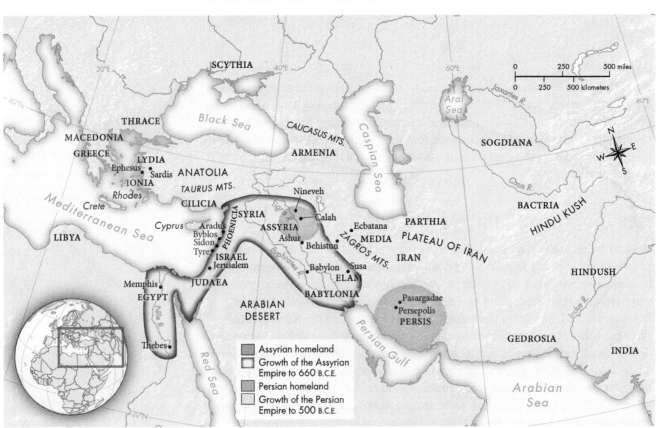

CHAPTER LOCATOR | How does writing shape what we can know about the past, and how did writing develop? | How did the peoples of Mesopotamia form states and develop new technologies?

56 CHAPTER 2 THE RISE OF THE STATE IN SOUTHWEST ASIA AND THE NILE VALLEY

Babylon—but also a people with a base of power in a part of the world that had not been the site of earlier urbanized states: Persia (modern-day Iran) (Map 2.3).

Iran's geographical position and topography explain its traditional role as the highway between western and eastern Asia. Nomadic peoples migrating south from the broad steppes of Russia and Central Asia have streamed into Iran throughout much of history. (For an in-depth discussion of these groups, see Chapter 12.) Confronting the uncrossable salt deserts, most have turned either westward or eastward, moving on until they reached the advanced and wealthy urban centers of Mesopotamia and India. Cities did emerge along these routes, however, and Iran became the area where nomads met urban dwellers.

Among these nomads were Indo-European-speaking peoples who migrated into this area about 1000 B.C.E. with their flocks and herds. They were also horse breeders, and the horse gave them a decisive military advantage over those who already lived in the area. One of these groups was the Medes, who settled in northern Iran. With the rise of the Medes, the balance of power in western Asia shifted east of Mesopotamia for the first time.

In 550 B.C.E. Cyrus the Great (r. 559–530 B.C.E.), king of the Persians (another Indo-European-speaking group) and one of the most remarkable statesmen of antiquity, conquered the Medes. Cyrus then set out to win control of the shore of the Mediterranean and thus of the terminal ports of the great trade routes that crossed Iran and Anatolia and to secure eastern Iran from the threats of nomadic invasions. In a series of major campaigns Cyrus achieved both goals.

After his victories, Cyrus made sure the Persians were portrayed as liberators, and in some cases he was more benevolent than most conquerors. According to his own account, he freed all the captive peoples, including the Hebrews, who were living in forced exile in Babylon.

Cyrus's successors continued the Persian conquests, creating the largest empire the world had yet seen. Darius (r. 521–486 B.C.E.) conquered Scythia in Central Asia, along with much of Thrace and Macedonia, areas north of the Aegean Sea (see Map 2.3, page 56). Darius began to call himself "King of Kings." Invasions of Greece by Darius and his son Xerxes were unsuccessful, but the Persian Empire lasted another two hundred years, until it became part of the empire of Alexander the Great (see page 131).

The Persians also knew how to preserve the peace they had won on the battlefield. To govern the empire, they created an efficient administrative system based in their newly built capital city of Persepolis. Under Darius, they divided the empire into districts and appointed either Persian or local nobles as administrators called satraps to head each one. The satrap controlled local government, collected taxes, heard legal cases, and maintained order. He was assisted by a council and also by officials and army leaders sent from Persepolis who made sure that he knew the will of the king and that the king knew what was going on in the provinces.

Scythian Saddlecloth

This red felt saddlecloth, dating from the fifth century B.C.E., is decorated with appliqués showing a winged griffon vulture with its claws in the back of a horned ibex. It was made by one of the nomadic peoples of western Asia, an area the Greeks called Scythia, some of which was conquered by the Persians. Items of daily use decorated with animals may have been thought to offer protection or assist in a hunt; this cloth was placed in a tomb, where it was preserved through the millennia by being frozen. (Hermitage, St. Petersburg, Russia/Photo © Boltin Picture Library/The Bridgeman Art Library)

How did the Egyptians create a prosperous and long-lasting society?

How did the Hebrews create an enduring written religious tradition?

How did the Assyrians and the Persians consolidate their power and control the subjects?

✓ LearningCurve
Check what you know.

The Persians allowed the peoples they conquered to maintain their own customs and beliefs as long as they paid the proper amount of taxes and did not rebel.

Communication and trade were eased by a sophisticated system of roads linking the empire from the coast of Asia Minor to the valley of the Indus River. These roads meant that the king was usually in close touch with officials and subjects, and they simplified the defense of the empire by making it easier to move Persian armies. The roads also aided the flow of trade, which Persian rulers further encouraged by building canals, including one that linked the Red Sea and the Nile.

The Religion of Zoroaster

Persian religion was originally polytheistic and tied to nature, with Ahuramazda (ah-HOOR-uh-MAZ-duh) as the chief god. Around 600 B.C.E. the ideas of Zoroaster (zoh-roh-ASS-tuhr), a thinker and preacher whose dates are uncertain, began to gain prominence. Zoroaster is regarded as the author of key religious texts, which were later gathered together in a collection of sacred texts called the Avesta. He introduced new spiritual concepts, stressing devotion to Ahuramazda alone and emphasizing the individual's responsibility to choose between the forces of creation, truth, and order and those of nothingness, chaos, falsehood, and disorder. At the end of time, the forces of order would win, and the victorious Ahuramazda, like the Egyptian god Osiris, would preside over a last judgment to determine each person's eternal fate.

Zoroaster's writings were communicated by teachers, and King Darius began to use Zoroastrian language and images. Under the protection of the Persian kings, Zoroastrian ideas spread throughout Iran and the rest of the Persian Empire, and then into central China. Zoroastrianism survived the fall of the Persian Empire to influence Christianity, Islam, and Buddhism, largely because of its belief in a just life on earth and a happy afterlife. Good behavior in the world, even though unrecognized at the time, would receive ample reward in the hereafter. Evil, no matter how powerful a person had been in life, would be punished after death. In some form or another, Zoroastrian concepts still pervade many modern religions and Zoroastrianism still exists as a religion.

Zoroastrianism
▶ Religion based on the teachings of Zoroaster that emphasized the individual's responsibility to choose between good and evil.

> QUICK REVIEW

How did the Assyrians treat subject peoples?
What about the Persians?

CHAPTER SUMMARY

Beginning about 5,000 years ago, people in some parts of the world invented writing, in large part to meet the needs of the state. States first developed in the southern part of Mesopotamia known as Sumer, where priests and rulers invented ways to control and organize people who lived in cities reliant on irrigation. Conquerors from the north unified Mesopotamian city-states into larger empires and spread Mesopotamian culture over a large area.

CHAPTER LOCATOR | How does writing shape what we can know about the past, and how did writing develop? | How did the peoples of Mesopotamia form states and develop new technologies?

58   CHAPTER 2   THE RISE OF THE STATE IN SOUTHWEST ASIA AND THE NILE VALLEY

During the third millennium B.C.E. Egypt grew into a cohesive state under a single ruler. For long stretches of history, Egypt was prosperous and secure in the Nile Valley, although at times various groups migrated in or invaded and conquered this kingdom. During the period known as the New Kingdom, warrior-kings created a large Egyptian empire. After the collapse of the New Kingdom, the Nubian rulers of Kush conquered Egypt, and another group, the Phoenicians, came to dominate trade in the Mediterranean, spreading a letter alphabet. Another group, the Hebrews, created a new form of religious belief based on the worship of a single all-powerful god.

In the ninth century B.C.E. the Assyrians used a huge army and sophisticated military tactics to create an empire from a base in northern Mesopotamia. The Persians established an even larger empire, developing effective institutions of government and building roads. The Persians generally allowed their subjects to continue their own customs, traditions, and religions. Around 600 B.C.E. a new religion grew in Persia based on the teachings of the prophet Zoroaster.

 CONNECTIONS Writing was invented to serve the needs of people who lived close to one another in cities and states, and almost everyone who could write lived in states. Because most history, including this book, concentrates on areas with states, the next two chapters examine the states that were developing in India and China during the period discussed in this chapter. In Chapter 5 we pick up on developments in the Mediterranean that link to those in Mesopotamia, Egypt, and Persia discussed in this chapter.

It is important to remember that, as was the spread of agriculture, the growth of the state was a slow process. States became the most powerful and most densely populated forms of human society, and today almost everyone on the planet is at least hypothetically a citizen of a state. In 500 B.C.E. perhaps only a little over 5 percent of the world's population lived in states. In his *Histories*, Herodotus pays primary attention to the Persians and the Greeks, both of whom had writing and states, but he also discusses many peoples who had neither. In their attempts to provide a balanced account of all the world's peoples, historians today are also looking beyond written sources.

How did the Egyptians create a prosperous and long-lasting society? | How did the Hebrews create an enduring written religious tradition? | How did the Assyrians and the Persians consolidate their power and control the subjects? | ✓ **LearningCurve** Check what you know.

CHAPTER 2 STUDY GUIDE

STEP 1

GET STARTED ONLINE

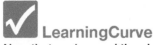 LearningCurve

Now that you've read the chapter, make it stick by completing the LearningCurve activity.

STEP 2

EXPLAIN WHY IT MATTERS

Put your reading into practice. Identify each term below, and then explain why it matters in World history.

TERM	WHO OR WHAT & WHEN	WHY IT MATTERS
polytheism (p. 39)		
cuneiform (p. 40)		
epic poems (p. 41)		
Hammurabi's law code (p. 42)		
pharaoh (p. 45)		
Indo-European languages (p. 48)		
Iron Age (p. 50)		
Phoenicians (p. 50)		
Yahweh (p. 52)		
Zoroastrianism (p. 58)		

STEP 3

MOVE BEYOND THE BASICS

To demonstrate a more advanced understanding of the development of regional powers in Mesopotamia, Egypt, Assyria, and Persia, fill in the chart below with descriptions of the factors contributing to the emergence of a powerful state in each region, focusing on four key areas: government, method of expansion, role of religion, and role of trade. How would you characterize the relationship between each state and the other cultures and societies that came under its control?

	Government	Methods of Expansion	Role of Religion	Role of Trade
Mesopotamia				
Egypt				
Assyria				
Persia				

PUT IT ALL TOGETHER

Now, take a step back and try to explain the big picture. Remember to use specific examples from the chapter in your answers.

GOVERNMENT AND SOCIETY IN ANCIENT MESOPOTAMIA AND EGYPT

▶ What role did religion play in legitimizing the power of Mesopotamian and Egyptian rulers?

▶ What similarities and differences do you note in the structure of Mesopotamian and Egyptian society? How would you explain these similarities and differences?

HEBREW RELIGION AND SOCIETY

▶ How did the experience of subjugation and exile shape Hebrew religion and culture?

▶ How did the Hebrew's relationship with Yahweh differ from that of their neighbors' relationships with their deities?

IMPERIAL POWERS: ASSYRIA AND PERSIA

▶ How did the brutality of Assyrian rule contribute both to the rise and fall of their empire?

▶ How did the Persians build and maintain their empire? What explains its long-term stability?

LOOKING BACK, LOOKING AHEAD

▶ How did the states of Mesopotamia, Egypt, Assyria, and the Persian Empire differ from earlier forms of social and political organization?

▶ How would you explain the fact that, over time, the state became the dominant form of political organization in societies around the world?

> ## IN YOUR OWN WORDS

Imagine that you must give an oral report to the class answering the following question: **Where, how, and why did the first states emerge?** What would be the most important points and why?

3
THE FOUNDATION OF INDIAN SOCIETY

TO 300 C.E.

> **What were the defining social and cultural characteristics of ancient India?** Chapter 3 examines the development of ancient India from its first civilization to the collapse of its first empire. From about 2800 B.C.E. to 1800 B.C.E., the Indus Valley, or Harappan culture, thrived and expanded over a huge area. A very different Indian society emerged after the decline of this civilization. It was dominated by the Aryans, warriors who spoke an early version of Sanskrit. It was in this period that Buddhism and Jainism were founded and the early Brahmanic religion of the Aryans developed into Hinduism. The Mauryan Dynasty emerged in the wake of the Greek invasion of north India in 326 B.C.E. The empire proved short-lived, however, and for several centuries India was politically divided. Nonetheless, cultural elements dating back to the ancient period spread through trade and other contact.

Female Spirit from an Indian Stupa Royal patronage aided the spread of Buddhism in India, especially the patronage of King Ashoka, who sponsored the construction of numerous Buddhist monuments. This head of a female spirit (called a *yakshini*) is from the stupa that Ashoka had built at Bharhut in central India. (Sudarsana Yakshini, relief from Stupa of Bharhut, Madhya Pradesh, India/De Agostini Picture Library/G. Nimatallah/The Bridgeman Art Library)

> What does archaeology tell us about the Harappan civilization in India?

> What kind of society and culture did the Indo-European Aryans create?

> What ideas and practices were taught by the founders of Jainism, Buddhism, and Hinduism?

> What was the result of Indian contact with the Persians and Greeks, and what were the consequences of unification under the Mauryan Empire?

> How was India shaped by political disunity and contacts with other cultures during the five centuries from 185 B.C.E. to 300 C.E.?

✓ **LearningCurve**
After reading the chapter, use LearningCurve to retain what you've read.

> What does archaeology tell us about the Harappan civilization in India?

Mohenjo-daro

Mohenjo-daro was a planned city built of fired mud brick. Its streets were straight, and covered drainpipes were installed to carry away waste. From sites like this, we know that the early Indian political elite had the power and technical expertise to organize large, coordinated building projects. Found in Mohenjo-daro, this small ceramic figurine (right) shows a woman adorned with necklaces and an elaborate headdress. (site: © M. Kenoyer/Harrapa.com. Courtesy, Department of Archeology and Museums, Government of Pakistan; figurine: © Angelo Hornak/Alamy)

In India, as elsewhere, the possibilities for both agriculture and communication have always been shaped by geography. Monsoon rains sweep northward from the Indian Ocean each summer. The lower reaches of the Himalaya Mountains in the northeast are covered by dense forests. Immediately to the south are the fertile valleys of the Indus and Ganges Rivers. These lowland plains, which stretch all the way across the subcontinent, were tamed for agriculture over time, and India's great empires were centered there. To their west are the deserts of Rajasthan and southeastern Pakistan, historically important in part because their flat terrain enabled invaders to sweep into India from the northwest. South of the great river valleys rise the Vindhya Mountains and the dry, hilly Deccan Plateau. Only along the western coast of this part of India do the hills give way to narrow plains where crop agriculture flourished (Map 3.1). India's long coastlines and predictable winds fostered maritime trade with other countries bordering the Indian Ocean.

Agriculture was well established in India by about 7000 B.C.E. Wheat and barley were the early crops, probably having spread in their domesticated form from what is today the Middle East. Farmers also domesticated cattle, sheep, and goats and learned to make pottery.

CHAPTER LOCATOR | What does archaeology tell us about the Harappan civilization in India? | What kind of society and culture did the Indo-European Aryans create?

CHAPTER 3
64 THE FOUNDATION OF INDIAN SOCIETY

2800–2000 B.C.E. Height of Harappan civilization	**326 B.C.E.** Alexander the Great enters Indus Valley
ca. 1500–500 B.C.E. Vedic Age; flourishing of Aryan civilization; *Rig Veda*	**ca. 322–185 B.C.E.** Mauryan Empire
ca. 1000 B.C.E. Introduction of iron	**ca. 300 B.C.E.** Jain religion splits into two sects
750–500 B.C.E. *Upanishads*	**ca. 269–232 B.C.E.** Reign of Ashoka
ca. 513 B.C.E. Persians conquer the Indus Valley and Kashmir	**ca. 150 B.C.E.–250 C.E.** Classical period of Tamil culture
ca. 500 B.C.E. Founding of Buddhism and Jainism	**ca. 100 C.E.** More inclusive Mahayana form of Buddhism emerges
ca. 400 B.C.E.–200 C.E. Gradual evolution of the Brahmanic religion into Hinduism	**ca. 200 C.E.** *Code of Manu*

India's first civilization is known today as the Indus Valley or the **Harappan** (huh-RAH-puhn) civilization, from the modern names of the river and city near where the first ruins were discovered. Archaeologists have discovered some three hundred Harappan cities and many more towns and villages in both Pakistan and India (see Map 3.1). It was a literate civilization, but no one has been able to decipher the more than four hundred symbols inscribed on stone seals and copper tablets. The civilization flourished most from 2500 B.C.E. to 2000 B.C.E.

The Harappan civilization extended over nearly five hundred thousand square miles in the Indus Valley, making it more than twice as large as ancient Egypt or Sumer. Yet Harappan civilization was marked by striking uniformity. Throughout the region, for instance, even in small villages, bricks were made to the same standard proportion (4:2:1). Figurines of pregnant women have been found throughout the area, suggesting common religious ideas and practices.

Like Mesopotamian cities, Harappan cities were centers for crafts and trade and were surrounded by extensive farmland. The Harappans were the earliest known manufacturers of cotton cloth. Trade was extensive. As early as the reign of Sargon of Akkad in the third millennium B.C.E. (see page 41), trade between India and Mesopotamia carried goods and ideas between the two cultures, probably by way of the Persian Gulf.

Harappan

▶ The first Indian civilization; also known as the Indus Valley civilization.

MAP 3.1 ■ Harappan Civilization, ca. 2500 B.C.E.

The earliest civilization in India developed in the Indus River Valley in the west of the subcontinent.

What ideas were taught by the founders of Jainism, Buddhism, and Hinduism?	What was the result of Indian contact with the Persians and Greeks?	How was India shaped by political disunity and contacts with other cultures?	✓ LearningCurve Check what you know.

The cities of Mohenjo-daro in southern Pakistan, and Harappa, some 400 miles to the north, were huge for this period, more than 3 miles in circumference, with populations estimated at 35,000 to 40,000. Both were defended by great citadels that were 40 to 50 feet high. The cities had obviously been planned and built before being settled. Streets were straight and varied from 9 to 34 feet in width. The houses were substantial, many two stories tall, some perhaps three. The focal point of a house was a central courtyard onto which the rooms opened.

Perhaps the most surprising aspect of the elaborate planning of these cities was their complex system of drainage. Each house had a bathroom with a drain connected to brick-lined sewers located under the major streets. Openings allowed the refuse to be collected, probably to be used as fertilizer on nearby fields. No other ancient city had such an advanced sanitation system.

Both Mohenjo-daro and Harappa also contained numerous large structures, which archaeologists think were public buildings. One of the most important was the large ventilated storehouse for the community's grain. Mohenjo-daro also had a marketplace or place of assembly, a palace, and a huge pool some 39 feet long by 23 feet wide by 8 feet deep. Like the later Roman baths, it had spacious dressing rooms for the bathers.

The prosperity of the Indus civilization depended on constant and intensive cultivation of the rich river valley. Although rainfall seems to have been greater then than in recent times, the Indus, like the Nile, flowed through a relatively dry region made fertile by annual floods and irrigation. And as in Egypt, agriculture was aided by a long, hot growing season and near-constant sunshine.

Because no one has yet deciphered the written language of the Harappan people, their political, intellectual, and religious life is largely unknown. There clearly was a political structure with the authority to organize city planning and facilitate trade, but we do not even know whether there were hereditary kings.

Soon after 2000 B.C.E., the Harappan civilization mysteriously declined. The decline cannot be attributed to the arrival of powerful invaders, as was once thought. Rather it was internally generated. Environmental theories include an earthquake that led to a shift in the course of the river, or a severe drought. Some scholars speculate that long-distance commerce collapsed, leading to an economic depression. Others theorize that the population fell prey to diseases, such as malaria, that caused people to flee the cities.

> **QUICK REVIEW**

What do the archeological remains of the great cities of Harappa and Mohenjo-daro suggest about Harappan society and government?

CHAPTER LOCATOR | What does archaeology tell us about the Harappan civilization in India? | What kind of society and culture did the Indo-European Aryans create?

66 CHAPTER 3
THE FOUNDATION OF INDIAN SOCIETY

What kind of society and culture did the Indo-European Aryans create?

Bronze Sword

This bronze sword, with a rib in the middle of the blade for strength, is a striking example of the quality of Aryan arms. Superior weapons gave the Aryans military advantage. (© The Trustees of the British Museum/Art Resource, NY)

After the decline of the Harappan civilization, a people who called themselves Aryans became dominant in north India. They were speakers of an early form of Sanskrit, an Indo-European language closely related to ancient Persian and more distantly related to Latin, Greek, Celtic, and their modern descendants, such as English. The Aryans flourished during the Vedic Age (ca. 1500–500 B.C.E.). Named for the Vedas, a large and significant body of ancient sacred works written in Sanskrit, this period witnessed the Indo-Aryan development of the caste system and the Brahmanic religion and the writing of the great epics that represent the earliest form of Indian literature.

Aryans

▶ The dominant people in north India after the decline of the Indus Valley civilization; they spoke an early form of Sanskrit.

Aryan Dominance in North India

Until relatively recently, the dominant theory was that the Aryans came into India from outside, perhaps as part of the same movements of people that led to the Hittites

> **Links Between English and Sanskrit:**

Sanskrit Word:	Meaning:	Related English Word:
nava	ship	naval
deva	god	divine
raja	ruler	regal

| What ideas were taught by the founders of Jainism, Buddhism, and Hinduism? | What was the result of Indian contact with the Persians and Greeks? | How was India shaped by political disunity and contacts with other cultures? | LearningCurve Check what you know. |

occupying parts of Anatolia, the Achaeans entering Greece, and the Kassites conquering Sumer—all in the period from about 1900 B.C.E. to 1750 B.C.E. Some scholars, however, have proposed that the Indo-European languages spread to this area much earlier; to them it seems possible that the Harappan people were speakers of an early Indo-European language. If that was the case, the Aryans would be one of the groups descended from this early population.

The central source of information on the early Aryans is the *Rig Veda*, the earliest of the Vedas, originally an oral collection of hymns, ritual texts, and philosophical treatises composed in Sanskrit between 1500 B.C.E. and 500 B.C.E. The *Rig Veda* portrays the Aryans as warrior tribes who glorified military skill and heroism; loved to drink, hunt, race, and dance; and counted their wealth in cattle. The Aryans did not sweep across India in a quick campaign, nor were they a disciplined army led by one conqueror. Rather they were a collection of tribes that frequently fought with each other and only over the course of several centuries came to dominate north India.

The key to the Aryans' success probably lay in their superior military technology, including two-wheeled chariots, horses, and bronze swords and spears. Their epics present the struggle for north India in religious terms, describing their chiefs as godlike heroes and their opponents as irreligious savages who did not perform the proper sacrifices. In time, however, the Aryans clearly absorbed much from those they conquered, such as agricultural techniques and foods.

At the head of each Aryan tribe was a chief, or raja (RAH-juh), who led his followers in battle and ruled them in peacetime. The warriors in the tribe elected the chief for his military skills. Next in importance to the chief was the priest. In time, priests evolved into a distinct class possessing precise knowledge of the complex rituals and of the invocations and formulas that accompanied them. Below them in the pecking order was a warrior nobility who rode into battle in chariots and perhaps on horseback. The warrior class met at assemblies to reach decisions and advise the raja. The common tribesmen tended herds and worked the land. To the conquered non-Aryans fell the drudgery of menial tasks. It is difficult to define precisely their social status. Though probably not slaves, they were certainly subordinate to the Aryans and worked for them in return for protection.

Over the course of several centuries, the Aryans pushed farther east into the valley of the Ganges River, at that time a land of thick jungle populated by aboriginal forest peoples. The tremendous challenge of clearing the jungle was made somewhat easier by the introduction of iron around 1000 B.C.E., probably by diffusion from Mesopotamia.

As Aryan rulers came to dominate large settled populations, the style of political organization changed from tribal chieftainship to territorial kingship. In other words, the ruler now controlled an area with people living in permanent settlements, not a nomadic tribe that moved as a group. Moreover, kings no longer needed to be elected by the tribe; it was enough to be invested by priests and to perform the royal ceremonies they designed. The priests, or Brahmins, supported the growth of royal power in return for confirmation of their own power and status. The Brahmins also served as advisers to the kings. In the face of this royal-priestly alliance, the old tribal assemblies of warriors withered away. By the time Persian armies reached the Indus around 513 B.C.E., there were sixteen major Aryan kingdoms in north India.

Rig Veda

▶ The earliest collection of Indian hymns, ritual texts, and philosophical treatises, it is the central source of information on early Aryans.

Indo-European Migrations and the Vedic Age

Possible Indo-European homeland

Spread of Indo-European speakers

Extent of Indo-European speakers

Aryan settlement, ca. 900 B.C.E.

Brahmins

▶ Priests of the Aryans; they supported the growth of royal power in return for royal confirmation of their own religious rights, power, and status.

CHAPTER LOCATOR | What does archaeology tell us about the Harappan civilization in India? | **What kind of society and culture did the Indo-European Aryans create?**

68 CHAPTER 3 THE FOUNDATION OF INDIAN SOCIETY

Life in Early India

Caste was central to the social life of these north Indian kingdoms. Early Aryan society had distinguished among the warrior elite, the priests, ordinary tribesmen, and conquered subjects. These distinctions gradually evolved into the caste system, which divided society into strictly defined hereditary groups. Society was conceived of as four hierarchical strata whose members did not eat with or marry each other. These strata, or varnas, were Brahmin (priests), Kshatriya (warriors and officials), Vaishya (merchants), and Shudra (peasants and laborers). The caste system thus allowed the numerically outnumbered Aryans to maintain dominance over their subjects and not be culturally absorbed by them.

caste system
▶ The Indian system of dividing society into hereditary groups whose members interacted primarily within the group, and especially married within the group.

Social and religious attitudes supported the caste system. Aryans considered the work of artisans impure. They left all such work to the local people, who were probably superior to them in these arts anyway. Trade, by contrast, was not viewed as demeaning. Brahmanic texts of the period refer to trade as equal in value to farming, serving the king, or being a priest.

As priests, the Brahmins were expected to memorize every syllable and tone of the Vedas so that their rituals would please the gods. They not only conducted the traditional ceremonies but also developed new ones for new circumstances. As agriculture became more important to the Aryans, for example, Brahmins acted as agents of Agni, the god of fire, to purify the land for crops. The Brahmins also knew the formulas and spells that were effective against diseases and calamities.

Those without places in the four varnas—that is, newly conquered peoples and those who had lost their caste status through violations of ritual—were outcastes. That simply meant that they belonged to no caste. In time, some of them became "untouchables" because they were "impure." They were scorned because they earned their living by performing such "polluting" jobs as slaughtering animals and dressing skins.

Slavery was a feature of early social life in India. People captured in battle often became slaves, but captives could also be ransomed by their families. Later, slavery was less connected with warfare and became more of an economic and social institution. At birth, slave children automatically became the slaves of their parents' masters. Indian slaves could be bought, used as collateral, or given away.

Like most nomadic tribes, the Aryans were patrilineal and patriarchal (tracing descent through males and placing power in the senior men of the family). Thus the roles of women in Aryan society probably were more subordinate than were the roles of women in local Dravidian groups, many of which were matrilineal (tracing descent through females). But even in Aryan society women were treated somewhat more favorably than in later Indian society. In epics such as the *Ramayana*, women are often portrayed as forceful personalities, able to achieve their goals both by using feminine ploys to cajole men and by direct action.

Brahmanism

The Aryans recognized a multitude of gods who shared some features with the gods of other early Indo-European societies such as the Persians and Greeks. Ordinary people dealt with these gods through priests who made animal sacrifices to them. By giving valued things to the gods, people strengthened both the power of the gods and their own relationships with them. Gradually, under the

What ideas were taught by the founders of Jainism, Buddhism, and Hinduism? | What was the result of Indian contact with the Persians and Greeks? | How was India shaped by political disunity and contacts with other cultures? | ✔ LearningCurve Check what you know.

priestly monopoly of the Brahmins, correct sacrifice and proper ritual became so important that most Brahmins believed that a properly performed ritual would force a god to grant a worshipper's wish. Ordinary people could watch a ceremony, but could not perform the key steps in the ritual.

The *Upanishads* (oo-PAH-nih-shadz), composed between 750 B.C.E. and 500 B.C.E., record speculations about the mystical meaning of sacrificial rites and about cosmological questions of man's relationship to the universe. They document a gradual shift from the mythical worldview of the early Vedic Age to a deeply philosophical one. Associated with this shift was a movement toward asceticism (uh-SEH-tuh-sihz-uhm)—severe self-discipline and self-denial.

Ancient Indian cosmology (theories of the universe) focused not on a creator who made the universe out of nothing, but rather on endlessly repeating cycles. Key ideas were samsara, the reincarnation of souls by a continual process of rebirth, and karma, the tally of good and bad deeds that determined the status of an individual's next life. Good deeds led to better future lives, evil deeds to worse future lives. Reward and punishment worked automatically; there was no all-knowing god who judged people and could be petitioned to forgive a sin, and each individual was responsible for his or her own destiny in a just and impartial world.

To most people, especially those on the low end of the economic and social scale, these ideas were attractive. By living righteously and doing good deeds, people could improve their lot in the next life. Yet there was another side to these ideas: the wheel of life could be seen as a treadmill, giving rise to a yearning for release from the relentless cycle of birth and death. One solution offered in the *Upanishads* was moksha, or release from the wheel of life. Brahmanic mystics claimed that life in the world was actually an illusion and that the only way to escape the wheel of life was to realize that ultimate reality was unchanging.

The unchanging ultimate reality was called brahman. Brahman was contrasted to the multitude of fleeting phenomena that people consider important in their daily lives. The individual soul or self was ultimately the same substance as the universal brahman, in the same way that each spark is in substance the same as a large fire.

The *Upanishads* gave the Brahmins a high status to which the poor and lowly could aspire in a future life. Consequently, the Brahmins greeted the concepts presented in these works and those who taught them with tolerance and understanding and made a place for them in traditional religious practice. The rulers of Indian society also encouraged the new trends, since the doctrines of samsara and karma encouraged the poor and oppressed to labor peacefully and dutifully. Thus, although the new doctrines were intellectually revolutionary, in social and political terms they supported the existing power structure.

samsara
▶ The transmigration of souls by a continual process of rebirth.

karma
▶ The tally of good and bad deeds that determines the status of an individual's next life.

brahman
▶ The unchanging ultimate reality, according to the *Upanishads*.

> **QUICK REVIEW**

How did religion reinforce social hierarchy in Aryan society?

CHAPTER LOCATOR | What does archaeology tell us about the Harappan civilization in India?
What kind of society and culture did the Indo-European Aryans create?

CHAPTER 3
70 THE FOUNDATION OF INDIAN SOCIETY

The God Vishnu

Vishnu is depicted here coming to the rescue of an elephant in the clutches of a crocodile. It comes from the fifth-century-C.E. Dasavatara Temple in Uttar Pradesh. (© akg-images/Jean-Louis Nou/The Image Works)

What ideas and practices were taught by the founders of Jainism, Buddhism, and Hinduism?

By the sixth and fifth centuries B.C.E., cities had reappeared in India, and merchants and trade were thriving. Bricks were again baked in kilns and used to build ramparts around cities. One particular kingdom, Magadha, had become much more powerful than any of the other states in the Ganges plain. Written language had also reappeared.

This was a period of intellectual ferment throughout Eurasia—the period of the early Greek philosophers, the Hebrew prophets, Zoroaster in Persia, and Confucius and the early Daoists in China. In India it led to numerous sects that rejected various elements of Brahmanic teachings. The two most influential were Jainism and Buddhism. Hinduism emerged in response to these new religions but at the same time was the most direct descendant of the old Brahmanic religion.

What ideas were taught by the founders of Jainism, Buddhism, and Hinduism?	What was the result of Indian contact with the Persians and Greeks?	How was India shaped by political disunity and contacts with other cultures?	✔️ LearningCurve Check what you know.

The most extreme Jain ascetics not only endured the elements without the help of clothes, but also were generally indifferent to bodily comfort. The Jain saint depicted in this eighth-century-C.E. cave temple has maintained his posture for so long that vines have grown up around him. (Courtesy, Robert Fisher)

Jainism

The key figure of Jainism, Vardhamana Mahavira (fl. ca. 520 B.C.E.), was the son of the chief of a small state and a member of the warrior class. Like many ascetics of the period, he left home to become a wandering holy man. For twelve years he traveled through the Ganges Valley until he found enlightenment and became a "completed soul." Mahavira taught his doctrines for about thirty years, founding a disciplined order of monks and gaining the support of many lay followers, male and female.

Mahavira accepted the Brahmanic doctrines of karma and rebirth but developed these ideas in new directions, founding the religion referred to as Jainism. He asserted that human beings, animals, plants, and even inanimate objects all have living souls enmeshed in matter, accumulated through the workings of karma. The ascetic, who willingly undertakes suffering, can dissipate some of the accumulated karma and make progress toward liberation. If a soul at last escapes from all the matter weighing it down, it becomes lighter than ordinary objects and floats to the top of the universe, where it remains forever in bliss.

Mahavira's followers pursued such liberation by living ascetic lives and avoiding evil thoughts and actions. The Jains considered all life sacred and tried to live without destroying other life. A Jain who wished to avoid violence to life became a vegetarian and took pains not to kill any creature, even tiny insects in the air and soil. Among the most conservative Jains, priests practiced nudity, for clinging to clothes, even a loincloth, was a form of attachment. Lay Jains could pursue Jain teachings by practicing nonviolence and not eating meat.

Although Jainism never took hold as widely as Hinduism and Buddhism (discussed below), it has been an influential strand in Indian thought and has several million adherents in India today. Fasting and nonviolence as spiritual practices in

Jainism

▶ Indian religion whose followers consider all life sacred and avoid destroying other life.

CHAPTER LOCATOR | What does archaeology tell us about the Harappan civilization in India? | What kind of society and culture did the Indo-European Aryans create?

CHAPTER 3
72 THE FOUNDATION OF INDIAN SOCIETY

India owe much to Jain teachings. In the twentieth century Mohandas Gandhi, leader of the Indian independence movement, was influenced by these ideas through his mother, and the American civil rights leader Dr. Martin Luther King, Jr., was influenced by Gandhi.

Siddhartha Gautama and Buddhism

Siddhartha Gautama (fl. ca. 500 B.C.E.), also called Shakyamuni ("sage of the Shakya tribe"), is best known as the Buddha ("enlightened one"). He was a contemporary of Mahavira and came from the same warrior social class. At age twenty-nine, unsatisfied with his life of comfort and troubled by the suffering he saw around him, he left home to become a wandering ascetic. He traveled south to the kingdom of Magadha, where he studied with yoga masters, but later took up extreme asceticism. According to tradition, while meditating under a bo tree at Bodh Gaya, he reached enlightenment. After several weeks of meditation, he preached his first sermon, urging a "middle way" between asceticism and worldly life. For the next forty-five years, the Buddha traveled through the Ganges Valley,

Gandharan Frieze Depicting the Buddha

This carved stone from ca. 200 C.E. is one in a series portraying scenes from the life of the Buddha. From the Gandharan kingdom (located in modern Pakistan), this frieze depicts the Buddha seated below the bo tree, where he was first enlightened. (Scenes from the life of the Buddha, Kushan Dynasty (stone)/Freer Gallery, Smithsonian Institution, Washington, D.C., U.S.A./The Bridgeman Art Library)

> PICTURING THE PAST

ANALYZING THE IMAGE: What are the people around the Buddha doing? What animals are portrayed?
CONNECTIONS: Does this frieze effectively convey any Buddhist principles? If so, which ones?

| What ideas were taught by the founders of Jainism, Buddhism, and Hinduism? | What was the result of Indian contact with the Persians and Greeks? | How was India shaped by political disunity and contacts with other cultures? | ☑ LearningCurve Check what you know. |

73

propounding his ideas, refuting his adversaries, and attracting followers. Probably because he refused to recognize the divine authority of the Vedas and dismissed sacrifices, he attracted followers mostly from among merchants, artisans, and farmers, rather than Brahmins.

In his first sermon the Buddha outlined his main message, summed up in the **Four Noble Truths** and the **Eightfold Path**. The Four Noble Truths are as follows: (1) pain and suffering, frustration, and anxiety are ugly but inescapable parts of human life; (2) suffering and anxiety are caused by human desires and attachments; (3) people can understand these weaknesses and triumph over them; and (4) this triumph is made possible by following a simple code of conduct, the Eightfold Path. The basic insight of Buddhism is thus psychological. The deepest human longings can never be satisfied, and even those things that seem to give pleasure cause anxiety because we are afraid of losing them. Attachment to people and things causes sorrow at their loss.

Buddhism differed from Brahmanism and later Hinduism in that it ignored the caste system. Everyone, noble and peasant, educated and ignorant, male and female, could follow the Eightfold Path. Moreover, the Buddha was extraordinarily nondogmatic. In his view, there was no harm in honoring local gods or observing traditional ceremonies, as long as one remembered the goal of enlightenment and did not let sacrifices become snares or attachments. The willingness of Buddhists to tolerate a wide variety of practices aided the spread of the religion.

The Buddha's followers transmitted his teachings orally until they were written down in the second or first century B.C.E. These scriptures are called sutras. The form of monasticism that developed among the Buddhists was less strict than that of the Jains. Buddhist monks moved about for eight months of the year (except the rainy season), begging for their one meal a day, but they could bathe and wear clothes. Within a few centuries Buddhist monks began to overlook the rule that they should travel. They set up permanent monasteries, generally on land donated by kings or other patrons. Orders of nuns also appeared, giving women the opportunity to seek truth in ways men had traditionally used. The main ritual that monks and nuns performed in their monastic establishments was the communal recitation of the sutras. Lay Buddhists could aid the spread of the Buddhist teachings by providing food for monks and support for their monasteries, and they could pursue their own spiritual progress by adopting practices such as abstaining from meat and alcohol. (See "Individuals in Society: Sudatta, Lay Follower of the Buddha," page 76.)

Because Buddhism had no central ecclesiastical authority, early Buddhist communities developed several divergent traditions and came to stress different sutras. One of the most important of these, associated with the monk-philosopher Nagarjuna (fl. ca. 100 C.E.), is called **Mahayana**, or "Great Vehicle," because it was a more inclusive form of the religion. One branch of Mahayana taught that reality is empty (that is, nothing exists independently of itself). Another branch held that ultimate reality is consciousness, that everything is produced by the mind.

Just as important as the metaphysical literature of Mahayana Buddhism was its devotional side, influenced by the religions then prevalent in Central Asia, such as Zoroastrianism (see page 58). The Buddha became deified and was placed at the head of an expanding pantheon of other Buddhas and **bodhisattvas** (boh-dih-SUHT-vuhz). Bodhisattvas were Buddhas-to-be who had stayed in the world after enlightenment to help others on the path to salvation. The Buddhas and

Four Noble Truths

▶ The Buddha's message that pain and suffering are inescapable parts of life; suffering and anxiety are caused by human desires and attachments; people can understand and triumph over these weaknesses; and the triumph is made possible by following a simple code of conduct.

Eightfold Path

▶ The code of conduct set forth by the Buddha in his first sermon, beginning with "right conduct" and ending with "right contemplation."

Mahayana

▶ The "Great Vehicle," a tradition of Buddhism that aspires to be more inclusive.

bodhisattvas

▶ Buddhas-to-be who stayed in the world after enlightenment to help others on the path to salvation.

CHAPTER LOCATOR | What does archaeology tell us about the Harappan civilization in India? | What kind of society and culture did the Indo-European Aryans create?

bodhisattvas became objects of veneration. With the growth of Mahayana, Buddhism attracted more and more laypeople.

Buddhism remained an important religion in India until about 1200 C.E. By that time it had spread widely through East, Central, and Southeast Asia. After 1200 C.E. Buddhism declined in India, losing out to both Hinduism and Islam, and the number of Buddhists in India today is small. Buddhism never lost its hold in Nepal and Sri Lanka, however, and today it is also a major religion in Southeast Asia, Tibet, China, Korea, and Japan.

Hinduism

Both Buddhism and Jainism were direct challenges to the old Brahmanic religion. Both rejected animal sacrifice, which by then was a central element in the rituals performed by Brahmin priests. Even more important, both religions tacitly rejected the caste system, accepting people of any caste into their ranks. Over the next several centuries (ca. 400 B.C.E.–200 C.E.), in response to this challenge, the Brahmanic religion evolved in a more devotional direction, developing into the religion commonly called Hinduism. In Hinduism Brahmins retained their high social status, but it became possible for individual worshippers to have more direct contact with the gods, showing their devotion without using priests as intermediaries.

The bedrock of Hinduism is the belief that the Vedas are sacred revelations and that a specific caste system is implicitly prescribed in them. Hinduism is a guide to life, the goal of which is to reach union with brahman, the unchanging ultimate reality. There are four steps in this search, progressing from study of the Vedas in youth to complete asceticism in old age. In their quest for brahman, people are to observe **dharma** (DAHR-muh), the moral law.

Hinduism assumes that there are innumerable legitimate ways of worshipping brahman, including devotion to personal gods. After the third century B.C.E. Hinduism began to emphasize the roles and personalities of thousands of powerful gods. These gods were usually represented by images, either small ones in homes or larger ones in temples. People could show devotion to their personal gods by reciting hymns or scriptures and by making offerings of food or flowers before these images. Hinduism's embrace of a large pantheon of gods enabled it to incorporate new sects, doctrines, beliefs, rites, and deities.

A central ethical text of Hinduism is the *Bhagavad Gita* (BAH-guh-vahd GEE-tuh), a part of the world's longest ancient epic, the *Mahabharata*. The *Bhagavad Gita* offers guidance on the most serious problem facing a Hindu—how to live in the world and yet honor dharma and thus achieve release from the wheel of life. The heart of the *Bhagavad Gita* is the spiritual conflict confronting Arjuna, a human hero about to ride into battle against his kinsmen. As he surveys the battlefield, struggling with the grim notion of killing his relatives, Arjuna voices his doubts to his charioteer, none other than the god Krishna. When at last Arjuna refuses to spill his family's blood, Krishna explains compassionately to Arjuna the duty to act—to live in the world and carry out his duties as a warrior. Indeed, the *Bhagavad Gita* emphasizes the necessity of action, which is essential for the welfare of the world. For Arjuna the warrior's duty is to wage war in compliance with his dharma. Only those who live within the divine law without complaint will be

dharma

▶ The Sanskrit word for moral law, central to both Buddhist and Hindu teachings.

| What ideas were taught by the founders of Jainism, Buddhism, and Hinduism? | What was the result of Indian contact with the Persians and Greeks? | How was India shaped by political disunity and contacts with other cultures? | ✓ LearningCurve Check what you know. |

Sudatta, Lay Follower of the Buddha

During the decades when the Buddha traveled around north India spreading his teachings, he attracted both disciples and lay followers. Stories of the Buddha's interactions with them were passed down orally for centuries, and undoubtedly were elaborated over time. Still, these accounts give us a sense of what life was like in early India. The wealthy banker or merchant Sudatta is a good example of an ardent lay follower. He was so generous to others that he is normally referred to by his epithet, Anathapindada, which means "benefactor of the needy."

Sudatta met the Buddha in the first year after his enlightenment. In one early conversation with him, Sudatta asks if he must leave the world to attain nirvana:

The people depicted here are performing the Buddhist ritual of circumambulating a stupa (a mound containing the ashes or other relics of a monk). (British Museum, London/Erich Lessing/Art Resource, NY)

> Now, I have heard thy disciples praise the bliss of the hermit and denounce the unrest of the world. "The Holy One," they say, "has given up his kingdom and his inheritance, and has found the path of righteousness, thus setting an example to all the world how to attain Nirvana." My heart yearns to do what is right and to be a blessing unto my fellows. Let me then ask you, Must I give up my wealth, my home, and my business enterprises, and, like you, go into homelessness in order to attain the bliss of a religious life?

The Buddha replied that the crucial issue was the way an individual looked on wealth. Anyone who cleaves to wealth needs to cast it aside, but anyone who "possessing riches, uses them rightly, will be a blessing unto his fellows." It is cleaving to wealth and power that enslaves people, not the mere possession of wealth. Artisans, merchants, or officers of the king who stay in the world should concentrate on performing their duties well. "If they live in the world not a life of self but a life of truth, then surely joy, peace, and bliss will dwell in their minds."*

Sudatta purchased a large park to provide a place where the Buddha and his disciples could live during the rainy season and had many buildings built there. The Buddha returned to this Jetavana Monastery many times and frequently gave sermons there. Sudatta also provided food for monks and gave generously to the poor and needy. As a result of his generosity, Sudatta was gradually reduced to poverty himself. Then, through divine intervention, those who owed him money returned it, making him wealthy once again.

Stories recounted that Sudatta's family, including his three daughters, became pious followers. Although Sudatta's son initially resisted the Buddha, he eventually became a generous patron himself. The Buddha himself helped convert Sudatta's unpleasant daughter-in-law. Once when the Buddha was preaching at Sudatta's home, he was disrupted by the sounds of Sudatta's son's wife scolding the servants. The Buddha asked to have her brought to him, and he instructed her on the proper conduct of wives. There were three types of bad wives, he told her: the destructive wife, who is pitiless, fond of other men, and contemptuous of her husband; the thievish wife, who squanders the family wealth; and the mistress wife, who is rude, lazy, and domineering. These he contrasted with the four kinds of good wives: the motherly wife, who cares for her husband as a mother for her son; the sisterly wife, who defers to her husband in the same affectionate way that a younger sister defers to her older brother; the friend wife, who loves her husband as if he were her best friend; and the handmaiden wife, who is calm, patient,

*Paul Carus, *The Gospel of Buddha* (Chicago: Open Court, 1894/1915), pp. 61–63, slightly modified.

and obedient. Deeply moved by these teachings, the daughter-in-law determined to be a handmaiden wife.

Sudatta died before the Buddha. A sutra that survives purports to be the sermon two of the Buddha's chief disciples preached to him on his deathbed. They counseled Sudatta on how to face his situation by training himself to decide not to cling to what is seen, heard, sensed, thought, attained, sought after, or pondered by the intellect.

QUESTIONS FOR ANALYSIS

1. What can you infer about the circumstances of the early followers of the Buddha from the life of Sudatta?
2. What insights does the life of Sudatta provide into the ways faith in Buddhism was spread?

ONLINE DOCUMENT PROJECT

What made Buddhism accessible to everyone? Read a selection of Buddhist parables, and then complete a quiz and writing assignment based on the evidence and details from this chapter. *See inside front cover to learn more.*

released from rebirth. One person's dharma may be different from another's, but both individuals must follow their own dharmas.

Hinduism provided a complex and sophisticated philosophy of life and a religion of enormous emotional appeal that was attractive to ordinary Indians. Over time it grew to be the most common religion in India. Hinduism validated the caste system, adding to the stability of everyday village life, since people all knew where they stood in society. Hinduism also inspired the preservation of literary masterpieces in Sanskrit and the major regional languages of India. Among these are the *Puranas*, which are stories of the gods and great warrior clans, and the *Mahabharata* and *Ramayana*, which are verse epics of India's early kings.

QUICK REVIEW

What elements of Buddhism and Jainism were incorporated into Hinduism?

What was the result of Indian contact with the Persians and Greeks, and what were the consequences of unification under the Mauryan Empire?

Hellenistic Influences in Gandharan Art

Because Alexander the Great's army had reached Gandhara and Hellenistic states and subsequently controlled it for more than a century, the art of this region was strongly influenced by Greek artistic styles. This stucco figure was excavated from a site in eastern Afghanistan where some twenty-three thousand Greco-Buddhist sculptures were found. Hellenistic influence, as evidenced by the drape of the clothing and the modeling of the head, is particularly easy to recognize in this piece. (Erich Lessing/Art Resource, NY)

In the late sixth century B.C.E., with the creation of the Persian Empire that stretched from the west coast of Anatolia to the Indus River (see pages 56–58), west India was swept up in events that were changing the face of the ancient Near East. A couple of centuries later, by 322 B.C.E., the Greeks had supplanted the Persians in northwest India. Chandragupta saw this as an opportunity to expand his territories, and he successfully unified all of north India. The Mauryan (MAWR-ee-uhn) Empire that he founded flourished under the reign of his grandson, Ashoka, but after Ashoka's death the empire declined.

CHAPTER LOCATOR | What does archaeology tell us about the Harappan civilization in India? | What kind of society and culture did the Indo-European Aryans create?

Encounters with the West

India became involved in the turmoil of the sixth century B.C.E. when the Persian emperor Darius conquered the Indus Valley and Kashmir about 513 B.C.E. Persian control did not reach eastward beyond the Punjab, but even so it fostered increased contact between India and the Near East and led to the introduction of new ideas, techniques, and materials into India.

The Persian Empire in turn succumbed to Alexander the Great, and in 326 B.C.E. Alexander led his Macedonian and Greek troops through the Khyber Pass into the Indus Valley (discussed in Chapter 5 on page 131). The India that Alexander encountered was composed of many rival states. He defeated some of these states in the northwest and heard reports of others.

The Greeks were intrigued by the Indian culture they encountered. Alexander had heard of the sophistication of Indian philosophers and summoned some to instruct him or debate with him. The Greeks were also impressed with Indian cities, most notably Taxila, a major center of trade in the Punjab. From Taxila, Alexander followed the Indus River south, hoping to find the end of the world. His men, however, mutinied and refused to continue. When Alexander turned back, he left his general Seleucus (suh-LOO-kuhs) in charge of his easternmost region.

Chandragupta and the Founding of the Mauryan Empire

The one to benefit most from Alexander's invasion was Chandragupta, the ruler of a growing state in the Ganges Valley. He took advantage of the crisis caused by Alexander's invasion to expand his territories, and by 322 B.C.E. he had made himself sole master of north India (Map 3.2). In 304 B.C.E. he defeated the forces of Seleucus.

With stunning effectiveness, Chandragupta applied the lessons learned from Persian rule. He adopted the Persian practice of dividing the area into provinces. Each province was assigned a governor, usually drawn from Chandragupta's own family. He established a complex bureaucracy to see to the operation of the state and a bureaucratic taxation system that financed public services through taxes on agriculture. He also built a regular army, complete with departments for everything from naval matters to the collection of supplies.

For the first time in Indian history, one man governed most of the subcontinent, exercising control through delegated power. From his capital at Pataliputra in the Ganges Valley, Chandragupta sent agents to the provinces to oversee the workings of government and to keep him informed of conditions in his realm. In designing his bureaucratic system, Chandragupta enjoyed the able assistance of his great minister Kautilya, who wrote a treatise called the *Arthashastra* on how a king should seize, hold, and manipulate power.

Megasthenes, a Greek ambassador sent by Seleucus, spent fourteen years in Chandragupta's court. He left a lively description of life there. He described the city as square and surrounded by wooden walls, twenty-two miles on each side, with 570 towers and 64 gates. It had a university, a library, and magnificent palaces, temples, gardens, and parks. The king personally presided over court

| What ideas were taught by the founders of Jainism, Buddhism, and Hinduism? | **What was the result of Indian contact with the Persians and Greeks?** | How was India shaped by political disunity and contacts with other cultures? | ✓ LearningCurve Check what you know. |

79

MAP 3.2 ■ The Mauryan Empire, ca. 250 B.C.E.

The Ganges River Valley was the heart of the Mauryan Empire. Although India is protected from the cold by mountains in the north, mountain passes in the northwest allowed both migration and invasion.

Map legend:
- Farthest extent of the Persian Empire, ca. 500 B.C.E.
- Farthest extent of Alexander's conquests, 326 B.C.E.
- The Mauryan Empire, ca. 250 B.C.E.
- → Ashoka's travels

> **MAPPING THE PAST**

ANALYZING THE MAP: Where are the major rivers of India? How close are they to mountains?

CONNECTIONS: Can you think of any reasons that the Persian Empire and Alexander's conquests both reached into the same region of northwest India?

sessions where legal cases were heard and petitions received. The king claimed for the state all mines and forests, and there were large state farms, granaries, shipyards, and spinning and weaving factories. Even prostitution was controlled by the state. Only a portion of the empire was ruled so directly, according to Megasthenes. In outlying areas, local kings were left in place if they pledged loyalty.

According to Jain tradition, Chandragupta became a Jain ascetic and died a peaceful death in 298 B.C.E. Although he personally adopted a nonviolent philosophy, he left behind a kingdom with the military might to maintain order and defend India from invasion.

The Reign of Ashoka, ca. 269–232 B.C.E.

Chandragupta's grandson Ashoka proved to be one of India's most remarkable figures. The era of Ashoka was enormously important in the religious history of the world, because Ashoka embraced Buddhism and promoted its spread beyond India.

As a young prince, Ashoka served as governor of two prosperous provinces where Buddhism flourished. At the death of his father about 274 B.C.E., Ashoka rebelled against his older brother, who had succeeded as king, and after four years of fighting won his bid for the throne. Crowned king, Ashoka ruled intelligently and energetically.

In the ninth year of his reign, 261 B.C.E., Ashoka conquered Kalinga, on the east coast of India. In a grim and savage campaign, Ashoka reduced Kalinga by wholesale slaughter. Instead of exulting like a conqueror, however, Ashoka was consumed with remorse and revulsion at the horror of war. He embraced Buddhism and used the machinery of his empire to spread Buddhist teachings throughout India. He supported the doctrine of not hurting humans or animals that was then spreading among religious people of all sects in India. Two years after his conversion, he undertook a 256-day pilgrimage to all the holy sites of Buddhism, and on his return he sent missionaries to all known countries. Ashoka's remarkable crisis of conscience changed the way he ruled. He emphasized compassion, nonviolence, and adherence to dharma. He appointed officials to oversee the moral welfare of the realm and required local officials to govern humanely. He may have perceived dharma as a kind of civic virtue, a universal ethical model capable of uniting the diverse peoples of his extensive empire.

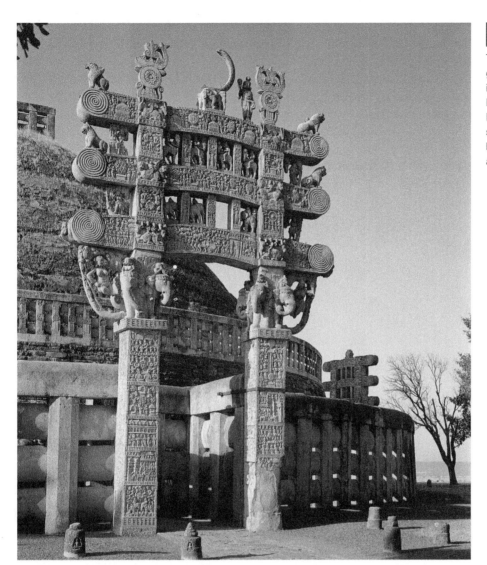

The North Gate at Sanchi

This is one of four ornately carved gates guarding the stupa at Sanchi in the state of Madhya Pradesh in India. Containing the relics of the Buddha, this Buddhist memorial shrine was originally commissioned by Ashoka, but the gateways were added later. (Jean-Louis Nou/akg-images)

Ashoka felt the need to protect his new religion and to keep it pure. He warned Buddhist monks that he would not tolerate schism—divisions based on differences of opinion about doctrine or ritual. According to Buddhist tradition, a great council of Buddhist monks was held at Pataliputra, where the earliest canon of Buddhist texts was codified. At the same time, Ashoka honored India's other religions, even building shrines for Hindu and Jain worshippers.

Despite his devotion to Buddhism, Ashoka never neglected his duties as emperor. He tightened the central government of the empire and kept a close check on local officials. He built roads and rest spots to improve communication within the realm. These measures also facilitated the march of armies and the armed enforcement of Ashoka's authority.

Ashoka directly administered the central part of the **Mauryan Empire**, focusing on Magadha. Beyond it were four large provinces under princes who served as viceroys, each with its own sets of smaller districts and officials. The interior of south India was described as inhabited by undefeated forest tribes. Farther south,

Mauryan Empire
▶ The first Indian empire founded by Chandragupta.

What ideas were taught by the founders of Jainism, Buddhism, and Hinduism?

What was the result of Indian contact with the Persians and Greeks?

How was India shaped by political disunity and contacts with other cultures?

✓ LearningCurve
Check what you know.

81

along the coasts, were peoples that Ashoka maintained friendly relations with but did not rule, such as the Cholas and Pandyas. Relations with Sri Lanka were especially close under Ashoka.

Ashoka ruled for thirty-seven years. After he died in about 232 B.C.E., the Mauryan Dynasty went into decline, and India broke up into smaller units, much like those in existence before Alexander's invasion. Even though Chandragupta had instituted bureaucratic methods of centralized political control and Ashoka had vigorously pursued the political and cultural integration of the empire, the institutions they created were not entrenched enough to survive periods with weaker kings.

> **QUICK REVIEW**

What steps did Ashoka take to strengthen and consolidate Mauryan rule?

CHAPTER LOCATOR | What does archaeology tell us about the Harappan civilization in India? | What kind of society and culture did the Indo-European Aryans create?

CHAPTER 3
82 THE FOUNDATION OF INDIAN SOCIETY

How was India shaped by political disunity and contacts with other cultures during the five centuries from 185 B.C.E. to 300 C.E.?

After the Mauryan Dynasty collapsed in 185 B.C.E., and for much of subsequent Indian history, political unity would be the exception rather than the rule. By this time, however, key elements of Indian culture—the caste system; the religious traditions of Hinduism, Buddhism, and Jainism; and the great epics and legends—had given India a cultural unity strong enough to endure even without political unity.

In the years after the fall of the Mauryan Dynasty, a series of foreign powers dominated the Indus Valley and adjoining regions. The first were hybrid Indo-Greek states ruled by the inheritors of Alexander's defunct empire stationed in what is now Afghanistan. The city of Taxila became a major center of trade, culture, and education, fusing elements of Greek and Indian culture.

The great, slow movement of nomadic peoples out of East Asia that brought the Scythians to the Near East brought the Shakas to northwest India. They controlled the region from about 94 B.C.E. to 20 B.C.E., when they were displaced by a new nomadic invader, the Kushans, who ruled the region of today's Afghanistan, Pakistan, and west India as far south as Gujarat.

During the Kushan period, Greek culture had a considerable impact on Indian art. Indo-Greek artists and sculptors working in India adorned Buddhist shrines, modeling the earliest representation of the Buddha on Hellenistic statues of Apollo. Another contribution from the Indo-Greek states was coin cast with images of the king, which came to be widely adopted by Indian rulers, aiding commerce and adding evidence of rulers' names and sequence to the historical record. Places where coins are found also show patterns of trade.

Cultural exchange also went in the other direction. Old Indian animal folktales were translated into Syriac and Greek and these translated versions eventually made their way to Europe. South India in this period was also the center of active seaborne trade, with networks reaching all the way to Rome. Indian sailing technology was highly advanced, and much of this trade was in the hands of Indian merchants. In the first century C.E. a Greek merchant involved in this trade reported that the traders sold coins, topaz, coral, crude glass, copper, tin, and lead

The Kushan Empire, ca. 200 B.C.E.

What ideas were taught by the founders of Jainism, Buddhism, and Hinduism? | What was the result of Indian contact with the Persians and Greeks? | **How was India shaped by political disunity and contacts with other cultures?** | ✓ LearningCurve Check what you know.

83

and bought pearls, ivory, silk (probably originally from China), jewels of many sorts (probably many from Southeast Asia), and above all cinnamon and pepper.

During these centuries there were significant advances in science, mathematics, and philosophy. Indian astronomers charted the movements of stars and planets and recognized that the earth was spherical. In the realm of physics, Indian scientists, like their Greek counterparts, conceived of matter in terms of five elements: earth, air, fire, water, and ether. This was also the period when Indian law was codified. The *Code of Manu*, which lays down family, caste, and commercial law, was compiled in the second or third century C.E., drawing on older texts.

Regional cultures tend to flourish when there is no dominant unifying state, and the Tamils of south India were one of the major beneficiaries of the collapse of the Mauryan Dynasty. The period from 200 B.C.E. to 200 C.E. is considered the classical period of Tamil culture, when many great works of literature were written under the patronage of the regional kings. Some of the poems written then provide evidence of lively commerce, mentioning bulging warehouses, ships from many lands, and complex import-export procedures. From contact of this sort, the south came to absorb many cultural elements from the north, but also retained differences. Castes were present in the south before contact with the Sanskrit north, but they took distinct forms, as the Kshatriya (warrior) and Vaishya (merchant) varnas were hardly known in the far south.

Code of Manu

▶ The codification of early Indian law that lays down family, caste, and commercial law.

> **QUICK REVIEW**

What impact did the Kushans have on Indian society and culture?

CHAPTER SUMMARY

Civilization first emerged in the Indus River Valley of India in the third millennium B.C.E. The large cities of this Harappan civilization were carefully planned, with straight streets and sewers; buildings were of kiln-dried brick. Harappan cities were largely abandoned by 1800 B.C.E. for unknown reasons.

A few centuries later, the Aryans, speakers of an early form of the Indo-European language Sanskrit, rose to prominence in north India, marking the beginning of the Vedic Age. Aryan warrior tribes fought using chariots and bronze swords and spears, gradually expanding into the Ganges River Valley. The first stages of the Indian caste system date to this period, when warriors and priests were ranked above merchants, artisans, and farmers. The Vedas document the religious ideas of this age, such as the importance of sacrifice and the notions of karma and rebirth.

Beginning around 500 B.C.E. three of India's major religions emerged. Mahavira, the founder of the Jain religion, taught his followers to live ascetic lives, avoid harming any living thing, and renounce evil thoughts and actions. The founder of Buddhism, Siddhartha Gautama, or the Buddha, similarly taught his followers a path to liberation that involved freeing themselves from desires, avoiding violence, and gaining insight. Hinduism developed in response to the popularity of

CHAPTER LOCATOR | What does archaeology tell us about the Harappan civilization in India? | What kind of society and culture did the Indo-European Aryans create?

CHAPTER 3
84 THE FOUNDATION OF INDIAN SOCIETY

Jainism and Buddhism. Hindu traditions validated sacrifice and caste and developed devotional practice, giving individuals a more personal relationship with the gods they worshipped.

From contact with the Persians and Greeks in the sixth century B.C.E. and fourth century B.C.E., respectively, new political techniques, ideas, and art styles and the use of money entered the Indian repertoire. Shortly after the arrival of the Greeks, much of north India was politically unified by the Mauryan Empire under Chandragupta. His grandson Ashoka converted to Buddhism, promoted its spread inside and outside of India.

After the decline of the Mauryan Empire, India was politically fragmented for several centuries. Indian cultural identity remained strong, however, because of shared literature and religious ideas. In the northwest, new monadic groups, the Shakas and the Kushans, emerged. Cultural interchange was facilitated through trade both overland and by sea.

 CONNECTIONS India was a very different place in the third century C.E. than it had been in the early phase of Harappan civilization more than two thousand years earlier. The region was still divided into many different polities, but people living there in 300 shared much more in the way of ideas and traditions. The great epics such as the *Mahabharata* and the *Ramayana* provided a cultural vocabulary for groups that spoke different languages and had rival rulers. New religions had emerged, notably Buddhism and Jainism, and Hinduism was much more a devotional religion. Contact with ancient Mesopotamia, Persia, Greece, and Rome had brought new ideas, practices, and products.

During this same time period, civilization in China underwent similar expansion and diversification. China was farther away than India from other Eurasian centers of civilization, and its developments were consequently not as closely linked. Logographic writing appeared with the Bronze Age Shang civilization and was preserved into modern times, in striking contrast to India and lands to its west, which developed alphabetical writing systems. Still, some developments affected both India and China, such as the appearance of chariots and horseback riding. The next chapter takes up the story of these developments in early China. In Chapter 12, after considering early developments in Europe, Asia, Africa, and the Americas, we return to the story of India.

ONLINE DOCUMENT PROJECT

Accessible Enlightenment

What made Buddhism accessible to everyone?

Read a selection of Buddhist parables, and then complete a quiz and writing assignment based on the evidence and details from this chapter. *See inside front cover to learn more.*

What ideas were taught by the founders of Jainism, Buddhism, and Hinduism?	What was the result of Indian contact with the Persians and Greeks?	How was India shaped by political disunity and contacts with other cultures?	✓ LearningCurve Check what you know.

STEP 1

GET STARTED ONLINE

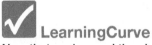

LearningCurve

Now that you've read the chapter, make it stick by completing the LearningCurve activity.

STEP 2

EXPLAIN WHY IT MATTERS

Put your reading into practice. Identify each term below, and then explain why it matters in world history.

TERM	WHO OR WHAT & WHEN	WHY IT MATTERS
Harappan (p. 65)		
Aryans (p. 67)		
Rig Veda (p. 68)		
Brahmins (p. 69)		
caste system (p. 70)		
samsara (p. 70)		
karma (p. 70)		
brahman (p. 70)		
Jainism (p. 72)		
Four Noble Truths (p. 74)		
Eightfold Path (p. 74)		
Mahayana (p. 74)		
bodhisattva (p. 74)		
dharma (p. 75)		
Mauryan Empire (p. 81)		
Code of Manu (p. 84)		

STEP 3

MOVE BEYOND THE BASICS

To demonstrate a more advanced understanding of India's great indigenous religious traditions, fill in the chart below with descriptions of three key aspects of these religions: core beliefs, social and ethical implications, appeal and spread. What aspects of Brahmanic belief and practice did Jainism and Buddhism reject? What core Brahmanic beliefs remained a part of Hinduism?

	Core Beliefs	Social and Ethical Implications	Appeal and Spread
Jainism			
Buddhism			
Hinduism			

PUT IT ALL TOGETHER

Now, take a step back and try to explain the big picture. Remember to use specific examples from the chapter in your answers.

EARLY INDIAN CIVILIZATIONS

▶ What similarities were there between Harappan civilization and the civilizations of Mesopotamia and Egypt?

▶ How did Brahmanism shape early Indian society and politics?

INDIA'S GREAT RELIGIONS

▶ What beliefs do Jainism, Buddhism, and Hinduism have in common?

▶ How would you explain the fact that Hinduism eventually grew to be the most common religion in India?

THE RISE AND FALL OF THE MAURYAN EMPIRE

▶ What were the keys to Mauryan political success?

▶ How did encounters with outsiders contribute to both the rise of the Mauryan Empire and to Indian development in the centuries after the empire's fall?

LOOKING BACK, LOOKING AHEAD

▶ How did geography and climate shape the development of commercial connections both within India and between India and the larger world?

▶ How would you explain the fact that, up until the establishment of the Mughal Empire in the sixteenth century, periods of political unification of the Indian subcontinent have been the exception and not the rule? What light does the early history of India shed on this question?

> **IN YOUR OWN WORDS**

Imagine that you must give an oral report to the class answering the following question: **What were the defining social and cultural characteristics of ancient India?** What would be the most important points and why?

4

CHINA'S CLASSICAL AGE

TO 221 B.C.E.

> How did war and conquest shape China's development in the Classical Age? Chapter 4 examines the development of the central features of Chinese society in the Classical Age. Chinese history is commonly discussed in terms of a succession of dynasties. The Shang Dynasty (ca. 1500–1050 B.C.E.) was the first to have writing, metalworking, cities, and chariots. The Shang were overthrown by one of their vassal states, which founded the Zhou Dynasty (ca. 1050–256 B.C.E.). The Zhou rulers set up a decentralized feudal governmental structure that evolved over centuries into a multistate system. As warfare between the states intensified in the sixth century B.C.E., social and cultural change quickened. It was in this period that the philosophies of Confucianism, Daoism, and Legalism were developed.

LearningCurve

After reading the chapter, use LearningCurve to retain what you've read.

Bronze Head from China Archaeological discoveries continue to expand our knowledge of the cultures and civilizations of early China. This large bronze mask was found among a large set of sacrificial offerings in the modern province of Sichuan. These unusual objects, which were found only there, suggest a distinct culture. (Sanxingdui Three Star Mound Museum, Guanghan Chengdu Sichuan, China/© William Perry/Alamy)

> What was the impact of China's geography on the development of Chinese societies?

> What was life like during the Shang Dynasty, and what effect did writing have on Chinese culture and government?

> How was China governed, and what was life like during the Zhou Dynasty?

> How did advances in military technology contribute to the rise of independent states?

> What ideas did Confucius teach, and how were they spread after his death?

> How did the teachings of Daoism, Legalism, and other schools of thought differ from Confucianism?

What was the impact of China's geography on the development of Chinese societies?

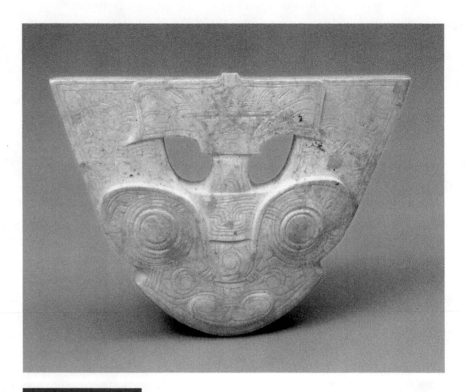

Neolithic Jade Plaque

This small plaque (2½ inches by 3¼ inches), dating from about 2000 B.C.E., is similar to others of the Liangzhu area near modern Shanghai. It is incised to depict a human figure that merges into a monster mask. The lower part could be interpreted as his arms and legs but at the same time resembles a monster mask with bulging eyes, prominent nostrils, and a large mouth. (Zhejiang Provincial Institute of Cultural Relics and Archeology/Uniphoto Press, Japan/Ancient Art & Architecture Collection, Ltd.)

The term *China*, like the term *India*, does not refer to the same geographical entity at all points in history. The historical China, also called China proper, was smaller than present-day China. The contemporary People's Republic of China includes Tibet, Inner Mongolia, Turkestan, Manchuria, and other territories that in premodern times were neither inhabited by Chinese nor ruled directly by Chinese states.

The Impact of Geography

China proper, about a thousand miles north to south and east to west, occupies much of the temperate zone of East Asia (Map 4.1). The northern part, drained by the Yellow River, is colder, flatter, and more arid than the south. Wheat and millet were the region's most important crops. The dominant soil is loess—fine wind-driven earth that is fertile and easy to work even with simple tools. Because so much of the loess ends up as silt in the Yellow River, the riverbed rises and easily

loess

▶ Soil deposited by wind; it is fertile and easy to work.

CHAPTER LOCATOR | What was the impact of China's geography on the development of Chinese societies? | What was life like during the Shang Dynasty, and how did writing affect Chinese culture?

CHAPTER 4
90 CHINA'S CLASSICAL AGE

ca. 5000 B.C.E. Emergence of regional Neolithic settlements	**500–200** B.C.E. Golden age of Chinese philosophy
ca. 1500–1050 B.C.E. Shang Dynasty	**453–403** B.C.E. *The Art of War*
ca. 1200 B.C.E. Evidence of writing found in royal tombs; chariots come into use	**403–221** B.C.E. Warring States Period; decline of the Zhou Dynasty
ca. 1050–256 B.C.E. Zhou Dynasty	**ca. 370–300** B.C.E. Mencius
ca. 900 B.C.E. *Book of Songs*, *Book of Changes*, *Book of Documents*	**ca. 350** B.C.E. Infantry armed with crossbows
551–479 B.C.E. Confucius	**ca. 310–215** B.C.E. Xunzi
ca. 500 B.C.E. Iron technology in wide use; cities spread across the central Zhou states	**ca. 300–200** B.C.E. Early Daoist teachings outlined in *Laozi* and the *Zhuangzi*

floods unless diked. Drought is another perennial problem for farmers in the north. The Yangzi (YANG-zuh) River is the dominant feature of the warmer, wetter, and more lush south, a region well suited to rice cultivation. The Yangzi and its many tributaries are navigable, so boats were traditionally the preferred means of transportation in the south.

Mountains, deserts, and grasslands separated China proper from other early civilizations. Between China and India lay Tibet, with its vast mountain ranges and high plateaus. North of Tibet are great expanses of desert, and north of the desert, grasslands stretch from Ukraine to eastern Siberia. Chinese civilization did not spread into any of these Inner Asian regions, above all because they were not suited to growing crops. Inner Asia, where raising animals is a more productive use of land than planting crops, became the heartland of China's traditional enemies, such as the nomadic tribes of the Xiongnu (SHUHNG-noo) and Mongols.

Early Agricultural Societies of the Neolithic Age

From about 10,000 B.C.E. agriculture was practiced in China. It apparently originated independently of somewhat earlier developments in Egypt and Mesopotamia but was perhaps influenced by developments in Southeast Asia, where rice was also cultivated very early. By 5000 B.C.E. there were Neolithic village settlements in several regions of China. The primary Neolithic crops were drought-resistant millet, grown in the loess soils of the north, and rice, grown in the wetlands of the lower reaches of the Yangzi River. In both areas pigs, dogs, and cattle were domesticated, and by 3000 B.C.E. sheep had become important in the north and water buffalo in the south. Silk production can also be traced back to this period.

How was China governed, and what was life like during the Zhou Dynasty?	How did advances in military technology contribute to the rise of independent states?	What ideas did Confucius teach, and how were they spread after his death?	How did the teachings of Daoism, Legalism, and other schools differ from Confucianism?	✓ LearningCurve Check what you know.

MAP 4.1 ■ **The Geography of Historical China**

Chinese civilization developed in the temperate regions drained by the Yellow and Yangzi Rivers.

> **MAPPING THE PAST**

ANALYZING THE MAP: Trace the routes of the Yellow and Yangzi Rivers. Where are the areas of loess soil? Where are the Neolithic sites concentrated?

CONNECTIONS: Does China's geography explain much about its history? (See also Map 4.2.) What geographical features had the greatest impact in the Neolithic Age? How might the fact that the Yellow and Yangzi Rivers flow west to east, rather than north to south, have influenced the development of Chinese society?

Over the course of the fifth to third millennia B.C.E., many distinct regional Neolithic cultures emerged. These Neolithic societies left no written records, but we know from the material record that over time they came to share more social and cultural practices. Many practices related to the treatment of the dead spread to other groups from their original area. Fortified walls made of rammed earth were built around settlements in many places, suggesting not only increased contact between Neolithic societies but also increased conflict. (For more on life in Neolithic societies, see Chapter 1.)

> ## QUICK REVIEW

What were the most important differences between the region around the Yellow River and the region around the Yangzi River?

CHAPTER LOCATOR | What was the impact of China's geography on the development of Chinese societies? | What was life like during the Shang Dynasty, and how did writing affect Chinese culture?

92 CHAPTER 4 CHINA'S CLASSICAL AGE

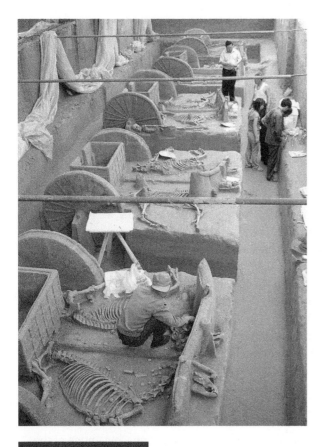

Eleven large tombs and more than a thousand small graves have been excavated at the royal burial ground at Anyang. In 2005 seven pits were discovered in which horses and chariots had been buried to accompany a king in the afterlife. (© CHINA NEWSPHOTO/Reuters/Corbis)

What was life like during the Shang Dynasty, and what effect did writing have on Chinese culture and government?

Archaeological evidence indicates that after 2000 B.C.E. a Bronze Age civilization appeared in north China that shared traits with Bronze Age civilizations elsewhere in Eurasia, such as Mesopotamia, Egypt, and Greece. These traits included writing, metalworking, domestication of the horse, class stratification, and cult centers. The archaeological findings are linked to the Shang Dynasty, long known from early texts.

Shang Society

Shang civilization was not as densely urban as that of Mesopotamia, but Shang kings ruled from large settlements (Map 4.2). The best excavated is **Anyang**, from which the Shang kings ruled for more than two centuries. At the center of Anyang were large palaces, temples, and altars. Outside the central core were industrial

Anyang

▶ One of the Shang Dynasty capitals from which the Shang kings ruled for more than two centuries.

| How was China governed, and what was life like during the Zhou Dynasty? | How did advances in military technology contribute to the rise of independent states? | What ideas did Confucius teach, and how were they spread after his death? | How did the teachings of Daoism, Legalism, and other schools differ from Confucianism? | ☑ LearningCurve Check what you know. |

Shang Dynasty, ca. 1500 B.C.E.
Early Zhou Dynasty, ca. 550 B.C.E.

MAP 4.2 ■ **The Shang and Early Zhou Dynasties, ca. 1500–400 B.C.E.**

The early Zhou government controlled larger areas than the Shang did, but the independent states of the Warring States Period were more aggressive about pushing out their frontiers, greatly extending the geographical boundaries of Chinese civilization.

areas where bronzeworkers, potters, stone carvers, and other artisans lived and worked. Beyond these urban settlements were farming areas and large forests.

Texts found in the Shang royal tombs at Anyang show that Shang kings were military chieftains. They fought rebellious vassals and foreign tribes, but the situation constantly changed as vassals became enemies and enemies accepted offers of alliance. War booty was an important source of the king's revenue, especially the war captives who could be made into slaves.

Bronze-tipped spears and battle axes were widely used by Shang warriors, giving them an advantage over less technologically advanced groups. Bronze was also used for the fittings of the chariots that came into use around 1200 B.C.E. Chariot technology apparently spread by diffusion across Asia, passing from one society to the next.

Shang power did not rest solely on military supremacy. The Shang king was also the high priest, the one best qualified to offer sacrifices to the royal ancestors and the high god Di. Royal ancestors were viewed as able to intervene with Di, send curses, produce dreams, assist the king in battle, and so on. The king divined his ancestors' wishes by interpreting the cracks made in heated cattle bones or tortoise shells prepared for him by professional diviners.

Shang palaces were undoubtedly splendid but were constructed of perishable material like wood, and nothing of them remains today, giving China none of the ancient stone buildings and monuments so characteristic of the West. What has survived are the lavish underground tombs built for Shang kings and their consorts.

The one royal tomb not robbed before it was excavated was for Lady Hao, one of the many wives of the king Wu Ding (ca. 1200 B.C.E.). The tomb was filled with almost 500 bronze vessels and weapons, over 700 jade and ivory ornaments, and 16 people who would tend to Lady Hao in the afterlife. Human sacrifice did not occur only at funerals. Inscribed bones report sacrifices of war captives in the dozens and hundreds.

Shang society was marked by sharp status distinctions. The king and other noble families had family and clan names transmitted along patrilineal lines, from father to son. Kingship similarly passed along patrilineal lines. The kings and the aristocrats owned slaves, many of whom had been captured in war. In the urban centers there were substantial numbers of craftsmen who worked in stone, bone, and bronze.

Shang farmers were obligated to work for their lords (making them essentially serfs). Their lives were not that different from the lives of their Neolithic ancestors, and they worked the fields with similar stone tools. They usually lived in small, compact villages surrounded by fields.

Bronze Metalworking

As in Egypt, Mesopotamia, and India, the development of more complex forms of social organization in Shang China coincided with the mastery of metalworking, specifically bronze. The bronze industry required the coordination of a large labor

CHAPTER LOCATOR | What was the impact of China's geography on the development of Chinese societies? | **What was life like during the Shang Dynasty, and how did writing affect Chinese culture?**

CHAPTER 4
94 CHINA'S CLASSICAL AGE

force and skilled artisans. Bronze was used more for ritual than for war in Shang times. Most surviving Shang bronze objects are vessels that would have originally been used during sacrificial ceremonies.

The decoration on Shang bronzes seems to say something interesting about Shang culture, but scholars do not agree about what that is. In the art of ancient Egypt, Assyria, and Babylonia, representations of agriculture and of social hierarchy are very common, matching our understandings of the social, political, and economic development of those societies. In Shang China, by contrast, images of wild animals predominate. Some animal images readily suggest possible meanings. Birds, for example, suggest to many the idea of messengers that can communicate with other realms, especially realms in the sky. More problematic is the most common image, the stylized animal face called the taotie (taow-tyeh). To some it is a monster—a fearsome image that would scare away evil forces. Others imagine a dragon—an animal whose vast powers had more positive associations. Some hypothesize that it reflects masks used in rituals. Others associate it with animal sacrifices, totemism, or shamanism. Still others see these images as hardly more than designs. Without new evidence, scholars can only speculate.

taotie
▶ A stylized animal face commonly seen in Chinese bronzes.

The Development of Writing

The survival of divination texts inscribed on bones from Shang tombs demonstrates that writing was already a major element in Chinese culture by 1200 B.C.E. Writing must have been developed earlier, but the early stages cannot be traced, probably because writing was done on wood, bamboo, silk, or other perishable materials.

The invention of writing had profound effects on China's culture and government. A written language made possible a bureaucracy capable of keeping records and corresponding with commanders and governors far from the palace. Hence literacy became the ally of royal rule, facilitating control over a wide realm. Literacy also preserved the learning, lore, and experience of early Chinese society and facilitated the development of abstract thought.

Like ancient Egyptian and Sumerian scripts, the Chinese script was logographic: each word was represented by a single symbol (Figure 4.1). In western Eurasia

logographic
▶ A system of writing in which each word is represented by a single symbol, such as the Chinese script.

FIGURE 4.1 ■ The Origins of Chinese Writing

The modern Chinese writing system (bottom row) evolved from the script employed by diviners in the Shang period (top row). (Source: Adapted from Patricia Buckley Ebrey, *The Cambridge Illustrated History of China* [Cambridge: Cambridge University Press, 1996], p. 26. Reprinted by permission of Cambridge University Press.)

WORD	ox	goat, sheep	tree	moon	earth	water	to show, declare	then (men and bowl)	heaven	to pray
SHANG SYMBOL	屮	⼲	朩	D	ꝺ	巛	朮	釻	呆	瓧
MODERN CHARACTER	牛	羊	木	月	土	水	示	就	天	祝

How was China governed, and what was life like during the Zhou Dynasty?

How did advances in military technology contribute to the rise of independent states?

What ideas did Confucius teach, and how were they spread after his death?

How did the teachings of Daoism, Legalism, and other schools differ from Confucianism?

✓ LearningCurve
Check what you know.

logographic scripts were eventually modified or replaced by phonetic scripts, but that never happened in China. Because China retained its logographic writing system, many years were required to gain full mastery of reading and writing, which added to the prestige of education.

Why did China retain a logographic writing system even after encounters with phonetic ones? Although phonetic systems have many real advantages, especially with respect to ease of learning to read, there are some costs to dropping a logographic system. Since characters did not change when the pronunciation changed, educated Chinese could read texts written centuries earlier without the need for translation. Moreover, as the Chinese language developed regional variants, readers of Chinese could read books and letters by contemporaries whose oral language they could not comprehend. Thus the Chinese script played a large role in holding China together and fostering a sense of connection with the past. In addition, many of China's neighbors (Japan, Korea, and Vietnam, in particular) adopted the Chinese script, allowing communication through writing between people whose languages were totally unrelated. In this regard, Chinese characters were like Arabic numerals, which have the same meaning however they are pronounced (Table 4.1).

TABLE 4.1 ■ Pronouncing Chinese Words

Letter	Phonetic Equivalent in Chinese

Phonetic equivalents for the vowels and especially perplexing consonants are given here.

a	ah
e	uh
i	ee; except after *z*, *c*, and *ch*, when the sound is closer to *i* in *it*
u	oo; as in English *food*
c	ts (*ch*, however, is like English *ch*)
q	ch
z	dz
zh	j
x	sh

> **QUICK REVIEW**

What were the sources of Shang power and wealth?

CHAPTER LOCATOR

CHAPTER LOCATOR | What was the impact of China's geography on the development of Chinese societies? | What was life like during the Shang Dynasty, and how did writing affect Chinese culture?

How was China governed, and what was life like during the Zhou Dynasty?

Winged Immortal

Less than 8 inches tall, this bronze candelabra is in the shape of an immortal. Those who mastered the secrets of not dying were thought to be able to fly through the heavens. (Werner Forman/akg-images)

The Shang campaigned constantly against enemies in all directions. To the west of the Shang were the fierce Qiang (chyang). Between the Shang capital and the Qiang were the Zhou (joe). In about 1050 B.C.E. the Zhou rose against the Shang and defeated them in battle. Their successors maintained the cultural and political advances that the Shang rulers had introduced.

Zhou Politics

The early Zhou period is the first one for which transmitted texts exist in some abundance. The *Book of Documents* (ca. 900 B.C.E.) describes the Zhou conquest of the Shang as the victory of just and noble warriors over decadent courtiers led by an irresponsible and sadistic king.

Book of Documents

▶ One of the earliest Chinese books, containing documents, speeches, and historical accounts about early Zhou rule.

How was China governed, and what was life like during the Zhou Dynasty?	How did advances in military technology contribute to the rise of independent states?	What ideas did Confucius teach, and how were they spread after his death?	How did the teachings of Daoism, Legalism, and other schools differ from Confucianism?	✓ LearningCurve Check what you know.

Like the Shang kings, the Zhou kings sacrificed to their ancestors, but they also sacrificed to Heaven. The *Book of Documents* assumes a close relationship between Heaven and the king, who was called the Son of Heaven. According to the documents, Heaven gives the king a mandate to rule only as long as he rules in the interests of the people. Because the last king of the Shang had been decadent and cruel, Heaven took the mandate away from him and entrusted it to the virtuous Zhou kings. This theory of the **Mandate of Heaven** remained a central feature of Chinese political ideology from the early Zhou period on.

Rather than attempt to rule all their territories directly, the early Zhou rulers set up a decentralized feudal system. They sent relatives and trusted subordinates with troops to establish walled garrisons in the conquered territories. Such a vassal was generally able to pass his position on to a son, so that in time the domains became hereditary. By 800 B.C.E. there were about two hundred lords with domains large and small.

As generations passed and ties of loyalty and kinship grew more distant, the regional lords became so powerful that they no longer obeyed the commands of the king. In 771 B.C.E. the Zhou king was killed by an alliance of non-Chinese tribesmen and Zhou vassals. One of his sons was put on the throne, and then for safety's sake the capital was moved east to modern Luoyang, just south of the Yellow River in the heart of the central plains (see Map 4.2, page 94). However, the revived Zhou Dynasty never fully regained control over its vassals, and China entered a prolonged period without a strong central authority.

Life During the Zhou Dynasty

During the early Zhou period, aristocratic attitudes and privileges were strong. Inherited ranks placed people in a hierarchy ranging downward from the king to the rulers of states with titles like duke and marquis, to the hereditary great officials of the states, to the lower ranks of the aristocracy—known as shi—and finally to the ordinary people (farmers, craftsmen, and traders). Patrilineal family ties were very important in this society, and at the upper reaches, at least, sacrifices to ancestors were one of the key rituals used to forge social ties.

Glimpses of what life was like at various social levels in the early Zhou Dynasty can be found in the *Book of Songs* (ca. 900 B.C.E.), which contains the earliest Chinese poetry. Some of the songs are hymns used in court religious ceremonies, such as offerings to ancestors. Others clearly had their origins in folk songs. The seasons set the pace for rural life, and the songs contain many references to seasonal changes. Some of these songs depict farmers clearing fields, plowing and planting, gathering mulberry leaves for silkworms, and spinning and weaving.

Social and economic change quickened after 500 B.C.E. Cities began appearing all over north China. Thick earthen walls were built around the palaces and ancestral temples of the ruler and other aristocrats, and often an outer wall was added to protect the artisans, merchants, and farmers who lived outside the inner wall. Accounts of sieges launched against these walled citadels are central to descriptions of military confrontations in this period.

The development of iron technology in the early Zhou Dynasty promoted economic expansion and allowed some people to become very rich. By the fifth

Mandate of Heaven
▶ The theory that Heaven gives the king a mandate to rule only as long as he rules in the interests of the people.

shi
▶ The lower ranks of Chinese aristocracy; these men could serve in either military or civil capacities.

Book of Songs
▶ The earliest collection of Chinese poetry; it provides glimpses of what life was like in the early Zhou Dynasty.

CHAPTER LOCATOR | What was the impact of China's geography on the development of Chinese societies? | What was life like during the Shang Dynasty, and how did writing affect Chinese culture?

98   CHAPTER 4
CHINA'S CLASSICAL AGE

Bells of the Marquis of Zeng

Music played a central role in court life in ancient China, and bells are among the most impressive bronze objects of the period. The tomb of a minor ruler who died about 400 B.C.E. contained 124 musical instruments, including drums, flutes, mouth organs, pan pipes, zithers, a set of 32 chime stones, and this 64-piece bell set. The bells bear inscriptions that name the two tones each bell could make, depending on where it was struck. Five men, using poles and mallets and standing on either side of the set of bells, would have played the bells by hitting them from outside. (Hubei Provincial Museum/Uniphoto Press, Japan/Ancient Art & Architecture Collection, Ltd.)

century B.C.E. iron was being widely used for both farm tools and weapons. In the early Zhou, inherited status and political favor had been the main reasons some people had more power than others. Beginning in the fifth century wealth alone was also an important basis for social inequality. Late Zhou texts frequently mention trade across state borders. People who grew wealthy from trade or industry began to rival rulers for influence. Rulers who wanted trade to bring prosperity to their states welcomed traders and began making coins to facilitate trade.

Social mobility increased over the course of the Zhou period. Rulers often sent out their own officials rather than delegate authority to hereditary lesser lords. This trend toward centralized bureaucratic control created opportunities for social advancement for the shi on the lower end of the old aristocracy. Competition among such men guaranteed rulers a ready supply of able and willing subordinates, and competition among rulers for talent meant that ambitious men could be selective in deciding where to offer their services. (See "Individuals in Society: Lord Mengchang," page 100.)

Religion in Zhou times was not simply a continuation of Shang practices. The practice of burying the living with the dead—so prominent in the royal tombs of the Shang—steadily declined in the middle Zhou period. New deities and cults also appeared, especially in the southern state of Chu, where areas that had

How was China governed, and what was life like during the Zhou Dynasty?

How did advances in military technology contribute to the rise of independent states?

What ideas did Confucius teach, and how were they spread after his death?

How did the teachings of Daoism, Legalism, and other schools differ from Confucianism?

☑ LearningCurve
Check what you know.

99

INDIVIDUALS IN SOCIETY
Lord Mengchang

During the Warring States Period, men could rise to high rank on the basis of talent. Lord Mengchang rose on the basis of his people skills: he treated his retainers so well that he attracted thousands of talented men to his service, enabling him to rise to prime minister of his native state of Qi (chee) in the early third century B.C.E.

Lord Mengchang's beginnings were not promising. His father, a member of the Qi royal family, already had more than forty sons when Mengchang was born, and he ordered the mother, one of his many concubines, to leave the baby to die. She, however, secretly reared him, and while still a child he was able to win his father's approval through his cleverness.

At his father's death Mengchang succeeded him. Because Mengchang would provide room and board to men who sought to serve him, he soon attracted a few thousand retainers, many of humble background, some fleeing justice. Every night, we are told, he ate with them all in his hall, treating them equally no matter what their social origins.

Most of the stories about Mengchang revolve around retainers who solved his problems in clever ways. Once, when Mengchang had been sent as an envoy to Qin, the king of Qin was persuaded not to let so talented a minister return to help Qi. Under house arrest, Mengchang was able to ask one of the king's consorts to help him, but in exchange she wanted a fur coat kept in the king's treasury. A former thief among Mengchang's retainers stole it for him, and Mengchang was soon on his way. By the time he reached the barrier gate, Qin soldiers were pursuing him, and he knew that he had to get through quickly. One of his retainers imitated the crowing of a cock, which got the other cocks to crow, making the guards think it was dawn, so they opened the gates and let his party through.

When Mengchang served as prime minister of Qi, his retainers came up with many clever stratagems that convinced the nearby states of Wei and Han to join Qi in resisting Qin. Several times, one of his retainers of modest origins, Feng Xuan (schwan), helped Mengchang withstand the political vicissitudes of the day. When sent to collect debts owed to Mengchang in his fief of Xue, Feng Xuan instead forgave all the debts of those too poor to repay their loans. Later, when Lord Mengchang lost his post at court and returned to his fief, most of his retainers deserted him, but he found himself well loved by the local residents, all because of Feng Xuan's generosity in his name. After Mengchang reattained his court post and was traveling back to Qi, he complained to Feng Xuan about those who had deserted him. Feng Xuan, we are told, got down from the carriage and bowed to Lord Mengchang, and when pressed said that the lord should accept the retainers' departures as part of the natural order of things:

Mengchang promoted trade by issuing bronze coins. Some Zhou coins, like the one shown here with the mold used to cast it, were shaped like miniature knives. (© The Trustees of the British Museum/Art Resource, NY)

Wealth and honor attract while poverty and lowliness repel; such is the nature of things. Think of it like the market. In the morning it is crowded and in the evening it is deserted. This is not because people prefer the morning to the evening, but rather because what they want can not be found there [in the evening]. Do not let the fact that your retainers left when you lost your position lead you to bar them from returning. I hope that you will treat them just the way you did before.*

QUESTIONS FOR ANALYSIS

1. How did Mengchang attract his many retainers, and how did their service benefit him?
2. Who in this story benefited from hereditary privilege, and who advanced because of ability? What does this suggest about social mobility during the Warring States Period?
3. Many of the stories about Mengchang are included in *Intrigues of the Warring States*, a book that Confucians disapproved of. What do you think they found objectionable?

*Shi ji 75.2362. Translated by Patricia Ebrey.

ONLINE DOCUMENT PROJECT

How did rulers and their subordinates interact during the Warring States Period? Read a selection of stories from the Warring States Period, and then complete a quiz and writing assignment based on the evidence and details from this chapter. *See inside front cover to learn more.*

earlier been considered barbarian were being incorporated into the cultural sphere of the Central States, as the core region of China was called. The state of Chu expanded rapidly in the Yangzi Valley, defeating and absorbing fifty or more small states as it extended its reach north to the heartland of Zhou and east to absorb the old states of Wu and Yue. By the late Zhou period, Chu was on the forefront of cultural innovation and produced the greatest literary masterpiece of the era, the *Songs of Chu*, a collection of fantastical poems full of images of elusive deities and shamans who can fly through the spirit world.

QUICK REVIEW <

What were the most important differences between Shang and Zhou society and culture?

| **How was China governed, and what was life like during the Zhou Dynasty?** | How did advances in military technology contribute to the rise of independent states? | What ideas did Confucius teach, and how were they spread after his death? | How did the teachings of Daoism, Legalism, and other schools differ from Confucianism? | ✅ LearningCurve Check what you know. |

101

How did advances in military technology contribute to the rise of independent states?

Mounted Swordsman

This depiction of a warrior fighting a leopard decorates a bronze mirror inlaid with gold and silver dating from the Warring States Period. (From *Gugong wenwu yuekan*, 91 [1990])

By 400 B.C.E. advances in military technology were undermining the old aristocratic social structure of the Zhou. Large, well-drilled infantry armies able to withstand and defeat chariot-led forces became potent military forces in the **Warring States Period**, which lasted from 403 B.C.E. to 221 B.C.E. Fueled by the development of new weaponry and war tactics, the Chinese states destroyed each other one by one until only one state was left standing—the state of Qin (chin).

New Technologies for War

By 300 B.C.E. states were sending out armies of a few hundred thousand drafted foot soldiers, usually accompanied by horsemen. Adding to their effectiveness was the development of the **crossbow** around 350 B.C.E. The intricate bronze trigger of the crossbow allowed a foot soldier to shoot farther than could a horseman carrying a light bow. To defend against crossbows, soldiers began wearing armor and helmets. Most of the armor was made of leather strips tied with cords. Helmets were sometimes made of iron.

Warring States Period

▶ The period of Chinese history between 403 B.C.E. and 221 B.C.E. when states fought each other and one state after another was destroyed.

crossbow

▶ A powerful mechanical bow developed during the Warring States Period.

CHAPTER LOCATOR | What was the impact of China's geography on the development of Chinese societies? | What was life like during the Shang Dynasty, and how did writing affect Chinese culture?

The introduction of cavalry in this period further reduced the need for a chariot-riding aristocracy. Shooting bows and arrows from horseback was first perfected by non-Chinese peoples to the north of China proper, who at that time were making the transition to a nomadic pastoral economy. The northern state of Jin developed its own cavalry to defend itself from the attacks of these horsemen. Once it started using cavalry against other Chinese states, they too had to master the new technology. From this time on, acquiring and pasturing horses was a key component of military preparedness.

Because of these developments, rulers wanted to increase their populations, to have more commoners to serve as foot soldiers and more craftsmen to supply more weapons. To increase agricultural output, they brought new land into cultivation, drained marshes, and dug irrigation channels. Rulers began surveying their land and taxing farmers. They wanted to undermine the power of lords over their subjects in order to get direct access to the peasants' labor power. Serfdom thus gradually declined.

The development of infantry armies also created the need for a new type of general, and rulers became less willing to let men lead troops merely because of aristocratic birth. In *The Art of War* (453–403 B.C.E.), Sun Wu described the ideal general as a master of maneuver, illusion, and deception. He argued that heroism is a useless virtue that leads to needless deaths. Discipline, however, is essential, and he insisted that the entire army had to be trained to follow the orders of its commanders without questioning them.

The Warring States, 403–221 B.C.E.

The Victorious States

During the Warring States Period, states on the periphery of the Zhou realm had more room to expand than states in the center. With access to more resources, they were able to pick off their neighbors, one after the other. Still, for two centuries the final outcome was far from clear, as alliances among states were regularly made and nearly as regularly broken.

By the third century B.C.E. there were only seven important states remaining. These states were much more centralized than their early Zhou predecessors. Their kings had eliminated indirect control through vassals and in their place dispatched royal officials to remote cities. Before the end of the third century B.C.E. one state, Qin, conquered all of the others, a development discussed in Chapter 7.

QUICK REVIEW

What connections can you make between military and social developments in the Warring States Period?

How was China governed, and what was life like during the Zhou Dynasty?

How did advances in military technology contribute to the rise of independent states?

What ideas did Confucius teach, and how were they spread after his death?

How did the teachings of Daoism, Legalism, and other schools differ from Confucianism?

 LearningCurve
Check what you know.

103

What ideas did Confucius teach, and how were they spread after his death?

Serving Parents with Filial Piety

This twelfth-century-C.E. illustration of a passage in the *Classic of Filial Piety* shows how commoners should serve their parents: by working hard at productive jobs such as farming and tending to their parents' daily needs. The married son and daughter-in-law offer food or drink to the older couple as their own children look on, thus learning how they should treat their own parents after they become aged. (National Palace Museum, Taiwan/The Art Archive at Art Resource, NY)

The Warring States Period was the golden age of Chinese philosophy, the era when the "Hundred Schools of Thought" contended. During the same period in which Indian sages and mystics were developing religious speculation about karma, souls, and ultimate reality (see Chapter 3), Chinese thinkers were arguing about the ideal forms of social and political organization and man's connections to nature.

Confucius

As a young man, Confucius (traditional dates: 551–479 B.C.E.) served in the court of his home state of Lu without gaining much influence. After leaving Lu, he set out with a small band of students and wandered through neighboring states in search of a ruler who would take his advice. We know what he taught from the *Analects*, a collection of his sayings put together by his followers after his death.

The thrust of Confucius's thought was ethical rather than theoretical or metaphysical. He talked repeatedly of an ideal age in the early Zhou Dynasty when

CHAPTER LOCATOR | What was the impact of China's geography on the development of Chinese societies? | What was life like during the Shang Dynasty, and how did writing affect Chinese culture?

everyone was devoted to fulfilling his or her role: superiors looked after those dependent on them; inferiors devoted themselves to the service of their superiors; parents and children, husbands and wives all wholeheartedly embraced what was expected of them. Confucius saw five relationships as the basis of society: between ruler and subject; between father and son; between husband and wife; between elder brother and younger brother; and between friend and friend. Mutual obligations of a hierarchical sort underlay the first four of these relationships—the senior leads and protects; the junior supports and obeys. The exception was the relationship between friends, which was conceived in terms of mutual obligations between equals.

A man of moderation, Confucius was an earnest advocate of gentlemanly conduct. He redefined the term *gentleman* (*junzi*) to mean a man of moral cultivation rather than a man of noble birth. He repeatedly urged his followers to aspire to be gentlemen rather than petty men intent on personal gain. Confucius did not advocate social equality, but his teachings minimized the importance of class distinctions and opened the way for intelligent and talented people to rise in the social scale. The Confucian gentleman found his calling in service to the ruler. Loyal advisers should encourage their rulers to govern through ritual, virtue, and concern for the welfare of their subjects, and much of the *Analects* concerns the way to govern well. To Confucius the ultimate virtue was **ren** (humanity). A person of humanity cares about others and acts accordingly.

In the Confucian tradition, studying texts came to be valued over speculation, meditation, and mystical identification with deities. Confucius encouraged the men who came to study with him to master the poetry, rituals, and historical traditions that we know today as Confucian classics.

ren
▶ The ultimate Confucian virtue; it is translated as perfect goodness, benevolence, humanity, human-heartedness, and nobility.

The Spread of Confucian Ideas

The eventual success of Confucian ideas owes much to Confucius's followers in the three centuries following his death. The most important of them were Mencius (ca. 370–300 B.C.E.) and Xunzi (ca. 310–215 B.C.E.).

Mencius, like Confucius, traveled around offering advice to rulers of various states. Over and over he tried to convert them to the view that the ruler able to win over the people through benevolent government would succeed in unifying "all under Heaven." Mencius proposed concrete political and financial measures to ease tax burdens and otherwise improve the people's lot. Men willing to serve an unworthy ruler earned his contempt, especially when they worked hard to fill the ruler's coffers or expand his territory.

With his disciples and fellow philosophers, Mencius also discussed other issues in moral philosophy, arguing strongly, for instance, that human nature is fundamentally good, as everyone is born with the capacity to recognize what is right and act on it. Xunzi, a half century later, took the opposite view of human nature, arguing that people are born selfish and that only through education and ritual do they learn to put moral principle above their own interest. In his view, much of what is desirable is not inborn but must be taught.

Neither Confucius nor Mencius had had much actual political or administrative experience, but Xunzi had worked for many years in the court of his home state. Not surprisingly, he showed more consideration than either Confucius or

How was China governed, and what was life like during the Zhou Dynasty?

How did advances in military technology contribute to the rise of independent states?

What ideas did Confucius teach, and how were they spread after his death?

How did the teachings of Daoism, Legalism, and other schools differ from Confucianism?

✓ LearningCurve
Check what you know.

105

Mencius for the difficulties a ruler might face in trying to rule through ritual and virtue. Xunzi was also a more rigorous thinker than his predecessors and developed the philosophical foundations of many ideas merely outlined by Confucius and Mencius. Confucius, for instance, had declined to discuss gods, portents, and anomalies and had spoken of sacrificing as if the spirits were present. Xunzi went further and explicitly argued that Heaven does not intervene in human affairs.

Still, Xunzi did not propose abandoning traditional rituals. In his view, rulers and educated men should continue traditional ritual practices such as complex funeral protocols because the rites themselves have positive effects on performers and observers. Not only do they let people express feelings and satisfy desires in an orderly way, but because they specify graduated ways to perform the rites according to social rank, ritual traditions sustain the social hierarchy.

The Confucian vision of personal ethics and public service found a small but ardent following during the Warring States Period. In later centuries rulers came to see men educated in Confucian virtues as ideal advisers and officials. Neither revolutionaries nor flatterers, Confucian scholar-officials opposed bad government and upheld the best ideals of statecraft. Confucian political ideals shaped Chinese society into the twentieth century.

The Confucian vision also provided a moral basis for the Chinese family that continues into modern times. Repaying parents and ancestors came to be seen as a sacred duty. Because people owe their very existence to their parents, they should reciprocate by respecting their parents, making efforts to please them, honoring their memories, and placing the interests of the family line above personal preferences, all of which were aspects of **filial piety**. Since the family line is a patrilineal line from father to son to grandson, placing great importance on it has had the effect of devaluing women.

filial piety
▶ Reverent attitude of children to their parents extolled by Confucius.

> **QUICK REVIEW**

How did ideas about the family shape Confucian philosophy?

CHAPTER LOCATOR | What was the impact of China's geography on the development of Chinese societies? | What was life like during the Shang Dynasty, and how did writing affect Chinese culture?

CHAPTER 4
106 CHINA'S CLASSICAL AGE

How did the teachings of Daoism, Legalism, and other schools of thought differ from Confucianism?

Inscribed Bamboo Slips

In 1993 Chinese archaeologists discovered a late-fourth-century-B.C.E. tomb in Hubei province that contained 804 bamboo slips bearing some 12,000 Chinese characters. Scholars have been able to reconstruct more than a dozen books from them, many of them previously unknown. (Private Collection/Archives Charmet/The Bridgeman Art Library)

> PICTURING THE PAST

ANALYZING THE IMAGE: Can you spot any repeated characters? Can you see any very simple characters?

CONNECTIONS: What were the consequences of recording texts on bamboo or wooden strips? How might doing so have shaped reading and writing in Zhou times? For modern archaeologists who discover these texts in tombs, would the medium used pose any challenges?

During the Warring States Period, rulers took advantage of the destruction of states to recruit newly unemployed men to serve as their advisers and court assistants. Lively debate often resulted as these strategists proposed policies and refuted opponents, and new schools of thought emerged. Many of these schools directly opposed the ideas of Confucius and his followers. Most notable were the Daoists, who believed that the act of striving to improve society only made it worse, and the Legalists, who argued that a strong government depended not so much on moral leadership as on effective laws and procedures.

Daoism

Confucius and his followers believed in moral action. They thought men of virtue should devote themselves to making the government work to the benefit of the people. Those who came to be labeled Daoists disagreed. They thought striving to make things better generally made them worse. They sought to go beyond

How was China governed, and what was life like during the Zhou Dynasty?

How did advances in military technology contribute to the rise of independent states?

What ideas did Confucius teach, and how were they spread after his death?

How did the teachings of Daoism, Legalism, and other schools differ from Confucianism?

☑ LearningCurve
Check what you know.

107

Dao

▶ The Way, a term used by Daoists to refer to the natural order and by Confucians to refer to the moral order.

everyday concerns and to let their minds wander freely. Rather than making human beings and human actions the center of concern, they focused on the larger scheme of things, the whole natural order identified as the Way, or Dao.

Early Daoist teachings are known from two surviving books, the *Laozi* and the *Zhuangzi*, both dating to the third century B.C.E. Laozi, the putative author of the *Laozi*, may not be a historical figure, but the text ascribed to him has been of enduring importance. A recurrent theme in this brief, aphoristic text is the mystical superiority of yielding over assertion and silence over words. Because purposeful action is counterproductive, the ruler should let people return to a natural state of ignorance and contentment. In the philosophy of the *Laozi*, the people would be better off if they knew less, gave up tools, renounced writing, stopped envying their neighbors, and lost their desire to travel or engage in war.

Zhuangzi (369–286 B.C.E.), the author of the book of the same name, shared many of the central ideas of the *Laozi*. The *Zhuangzi* is filled with parables, flights of fancy, and fictional encounters between historical figures, including Confucius and his disciples. A more serious strain of Zhuangzi's thought concerned death. He questioned whether we can be sure life is better than death. People fear what they do not know, the same way a captive girl will be terrified when she learns she is to become the king's concubine. Perhaps people will discover that death has as many delights as life in the palace.

Zhuangzi was similarly iconoclastic in his political philosophy. In one parable a wheelwright insolently tells a duke that books are useless because all they contain are the dregs of men long dead. The duke, offended, threatens execution unless the wheelwright can explain his remark. The wheelwright responds by arguing that truly skilled craftsmen respond to situations spontaneously; they do not analyze or reason or even keep in mind the rules they have mastered. The most important truths they know cannot be written down or even explained to others. They are simply the result of experience. This strain of Daoist thought denies the validity of verbal reasoning and the sorts of knowledge conveyed through words.

Daoism can be seen as a response to Confucianism, a rejection of many of its basic premises. Nevertheless, over the course of Chinese history, many people felt the pull of both Confucian and Daoist ideas and studied the writings of both schools. Even Confucian scholars who had devoted much of their lives to public service might find that the teachings of the *Laozi* or *Zhuangzi* helped to put their frustrations in perspective.

Legalism

Legalists

▶ Political theorists who emphasized the need for rigorous laws and laid the basis for China's later bureaucratic government.

Over the course of the fourth and third centuries B.C.E., one small state after another was conquered, and the number of surviving states dwindled. Rulers fearful that their states might be next were ready to listen to political theorists who claimed expertise in the accumulation of power. These theorists, labeled Legalists because of their emphasis on the need for rigorous laws, argued that strong government depended not on the moral qualities of the ruler and his officials, as Confucians claimed, but on establishing effective laws and procedures. Legalism, though eventually discredited, laid the basis for China's later bureaucratic government.

CHAPTER LOCATOR | What was the impact of China's geography on the development of Chinese societies? | What was life like during the Shang Dynasty, and how did writing affect Chinese culture?

In the fourth century B.C.E. the state of Qin radically reformed itself along Legalist lines. The king of Qin abolished the aristocracy. Social distinctions were to be based on military ranks determined by the objective criterion of the number of enemy heads cut off in battle. In place of the old fiefs, the Qin king created counties and appointed officials to govern them according to the laws he decreed at court. To increase the population, Qin recruited migrants from other states. To encourage farmers to work hard and improve their land, they were allowed to buy and sell it. Ordinary farmers were thus freed from serf-like obligations to the local nobility, but direct control by the state could be even more onerous. Taxes and labor service obligations were heavy. Travel required a permit, and vagrants could be forced into penal labor service. All families were grouped into mutual responsibility groups of five and ten families; whenever anyone in the group committed a crime, all the others were equally liable unless they reported it.

Legalism found its greatest exponent in Han Feizi (ca. 280–233 B.C.E.). In his writings he warned rulers of the political pitfalls awaiting them. They had to be careful where they placed their trust, for "when the ruler trusts someone, he falls under that person's control." Given subordinates' propensities to pursue their own selfish interests, the ruler should keep them ignorant of his intentions and control them by manipulating competition among them. Warmth, affection, or candor should have no place in his relationships with others.

In Han Feizi's view, the Confucian notion that government could be based on virtue was naïve. If rulers would make the laws and prohibitions clear and the rewards and punishments automatic, then the officials and common people would be easy to govern. Uniform laws get people to do things they would not otherwise be inclined to do, such as work hard and fight wars; such laws are thus essential to the goal of establishing hegemony over all the other states.

The laws of the Legalists were designed as much to constrain officials as to regulate the common people. The third-century-B.C.E. tomb of a Qin official has yielded statutes detailing the rules for keeping accounts, supervising subordinates, managing penal labor, conducting investigations, and many other responsibilities of officials. Infractions were generally punishable through the imposition of fines.

Legalism saw no value in intellectual debate or private opinion. Divergent views of right and wrong lead to weakness and disorder. The ruler should not allow others to undermine his laws by questioning them. In Legalism, there were no laws above or independent of the wishes of the rulers, no laws that might set limits on rulers' actions.

Yin and Yang

Confucians, Daoists, and Legalists had the greatest long-term impact on Chinese civilization, but the Hundred Schools of Thought also included everyone from logicians, hedonists, and utopians to natural philosophers who analyzed the workings of nature.

A key idea developed by the natural philosophers was the concept of **yin and yang**, first described in the divination manual called the *Book of Changes* (ca. 900 B.C.E.), and developed into much more elaborate theories by late Zhou theorists. Yin is the feminine, dark, receptive, yielding, negative, and weak; yang is the masculine, bright, assertive, creative, positive, and strong. Yin and yang are

yin and yang
▶ A concept of complementary poles, one of which represents the feminine, dark, and receptive, and the other the masculine, bright, and assertive.

How was China governed, and what was life like during the Zhou Dynasty?

How did advances in military technology contribute to the rise of independent states?

What ideas did Confucius teach, and how were they spread after his death?

How did the teachings of Daoism, Legalism, and other schools differ from Confucianism?

LearningCurve
Check what you know.

109

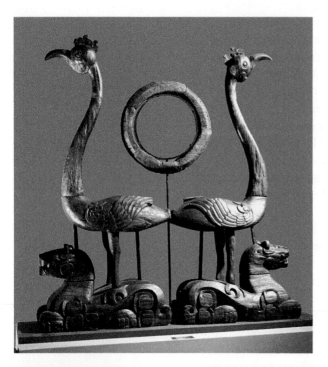

complementary poles rather than distinct entities or opposing forces. The movement of yin and yang accounts for the transition from day to night and from summer to winter. These models based on observation of nature were extended to explain not only phenomena we might classify as natural, but also social phenomena, such as the rise and fall of states and conflict in families. In all these realms, unwanted things happen when the balance between yin and yang gets disturbed.

In recent decades archaeologists have further complicated our understanding of early Chinese thought by unearthing records of the popular religion of the time—astrological manuals, handbooks of lucky and unlucky days, medical prescriptions, exercises, and ghost stories. The tomb of an official who died in 316 B.C.E., for example, has records of divinations showing that illness was seen as the result of unsatisfied spirits or malevolent demons, best dealt with through performing exorcisms or offering sacrifices to the astral god Taiyi (Grand One).

Phoenix and Tigers

Divine animals, such as dragons and phoenixes, are often portrayed in the art of the Warring States Period, especially in the south, where the art of lacquered wood was perfected. (Werner Forman/akg-images)

> **Competing Views of Politics and Government in Chinese Philosophy:**

Confucianism:	Men of virtue should devote themselves to making government work to the benefit of all people.
Daoism:	Political reforms generally made things worse and individuals should avoid participation in government.
Legalism:	Strong government did not depend on the moral qualities of rulers and officials, but on clear, effective laws and procedures.

> **QUICK REVIEW**

How did ideas about human nature shape Daoism and Legalism?

CHAPTER SUMMARY

After several thousand years of Neolithic cultures, beginning after 2000 B.C.E., Bronze Age civilization developed in China, with cities, writing, and sharp social distinctions. Shang kings led armies and presided at sacrifices to the high god Di and the imperial ancestors. The Shang armies' bronze-tipped weapons and chariots gave them technological superiority over their neighbors.

The Zhou Dynasty, which overthrew the Shang in about 1050 B.C.E., parceled out its territory to hereditary lords. The earliest Chinese books date to this period. The *Book of Documents* provides evidence of the belief in the Mandate of Heaven,

CHAPTER LOCATOR | What was the impact of China's geography on the development of Chinese societies? | What was life like during the Shang Dynasty, and how did writing affect Chinese culture?

CHAPTER 4
110 CHINA'S CLASSICAL AGE

which justified Zhou rule. The *Book of Songs* offers glimpses into what life was like for elites and ordinary people alike in the early Zhou.

By the Warring States Period, which began in 403 B.C.E., the old domains had become independent states. As states destroyed each other, military technology made many advances, including the introduction of cavalry, infantry armies, and the crossbow. Despite its name, the Warring States Period was the golden age of Chinese philosophy. Confucius and his followers promoted the virtues of sincerity, loyalty, benevolence, filial piety, and duty. Mencius urged rulers to rule through goodness and argued that human nature is good. Xunzi stressed the power of ritual and argued that human nature is selfish and must be curbed through education. Daoists and Legalists rejected all these ideas. The Daoists Laozi and Zhuangzi looked beyond the human realm to the entire cosmos and spoke of the relativity of concepts such as good and bad and life and death. Legalists heaped ridicule on the Confucian idea that a ruler could get his people to be good by being good himself and proposed instead rigorous laws with strict rewards and punishments. Natural philosophers explained the changes of seasons and health and illness in terms of the complementary forces of yin and yang.

 CONNECTIONS China's transition from Neolithic farming villages to a much more advanced civilization occurred centuries later than in Mesopotamia or India, but by the Warring States Period China was at much the same stage of development as other advanced societies in Eurasia. Although many elements of China's civilization were clearly invented in China—such as its writing system, its method of casting bronze, and its Confucian philosophy—it also adopted elements that diffused across Asia, such as the cultivation of wheat, the horse-driven chariot, and riding horseback.

Greece, the subject of the next chapter, is located very close to the ancient Near Eastern civilizations, so its trajectory was quite different from China's. It was also much smaller than China, yet in time had enormous impact on the wider world. With India and China in mind, the originality of the political forms and ideas of early Greece will stand out more clearly. We return to China's history in Chapter 7, after looking at Greece and Rome.

> LaunchPad

ONLINE DOCUMENT PROJECT
The Limits of Loyalty

How did rulers and their subordinates interact during the Warring States Period?

Read a selection of stories from the Warring States Period, and then complete a quiz and writing assignment based on the evidence and details from this chapter. *See inside front cover to learn more.*

How was China governed, and what was life like during the Zhou Dynasty? | How did advances in military technology contribute to the rise of independent states? | What ideas did Confucius teach, and how were they spread after his death? | How did the teachings of Daoism, Legalism, and other schools differ from Confucianism? | ✓ **LearningCurve** Check what you know.

111

CHAPTER 4 STUDY GUIDE

STEP 1 — GET STARTED ONLINE

 LearningCurve

Now that you've read the chapter, make it stick by completing the LearningCurve activity.

STEP 2 — EXPLAIN WHY IT MATTERS

Put your reading into practice. Identify each term below, and then explain why it matters in world history.

TERM	WHO OR WHAT & WHEN	WHY IT MATTERS
loess (p. 90)		
Anyang (p. 93)		
taotie (p. 95)		
logographic (p. 95)		
Book of Documents (p. 97)		
Mandate of Heaven (p. 98)		
shi (p. 98)		
Book of Songs (p. 98)		
Warring States Period (p. 102)		
crossbow (p. 102)		
ren (p. 105)		
filial piety (p. 106)		
Dao (p. 108)		
Legalists (p. 108)		
yin and yang (p. 109)		

STEP 3 — MOVE BEYOND THE BASICS

To demonstrate a more advanced understanding of the three philosophical traditions that originated during China's Classical Age, fill in the chart below with descriptions of three key aspects of these philosophies: core beliefs, social and ethical teachings, and vision of politics and public life. What problems and tensions in Chinese society did each of these philosophies attempt to remedy?

	Core Beliefs	Social and Ethical Teachings	Vision of Politics and Public Life
Confucianism			
Daoism			
Legalism			

PUT IT ALL TOGETHER Now, take a step back and try to explain the big picture. Remember to use specific examples from the chapter in your answers.

DEVELOPMENT OF EARLY CHINESE SOCIETY

▶ How did geography shape the way Chinese culture spread and developed?

▶ What role did the Shang king play in Shang society? What was the source of his power and legitimacy?

ZHOU DYNASTY AND THE WARRING STATES PERIOD

▶ What innovations did the Zhou introduce into Chinese society and politics? What were there consequences?

▶ What were the social and cultural consequences of political decentralization during the Warring States Period?

CHINESE PHILOSOPHY IN THE CLASSICAL AGE

▶ What role do hierarchical relationships play in Confucian's philosophy? What light does this shed on Chinese beliefs and values in the Classical Age?

▶ How would you explain the fact that the Warring States period, a time of unrest and conflict, was also the golden age of Chinese philosophy?

LOOKING BACK, LOOKING AHEAD

▶ What similarities and differences do you see between Chinese society and government under the Shang and society and government in the early kingdoms of Mesopotamia? How would you explain the similarities and differences you note?

▶ How would you explain the long-term influence of Confucianism on Chinese society and culture? What elements of Confucianism might explain its enduring appeal?

> **IN YOUR OWN WORDS**

Imagine that you must give an oral report to the class answering the following question: **How did war and conquest shape China's development in the Classical Age?** What would be the most important points and why?

5
THE GREEK EXPERIENCE

3500–30 B.C.E.

> **What unique contributions did the Greeks make to global culture?** Chapter 5 examines the development of ancient Greek civilization. The history of the Greeks can be divided into three broad periods: the Helladic period, which covered the Bronze Age, roughly 3000 B.C.E. to 1200 B.C.E.; the Hellenic period, from the Bronze Age Collapse to the conquest of Greece by Macedonia in 338 B.C.E.; and the Hellenistic period, stretching from the death of Alexander the Great in 323 B.C.E. to the Roman conquest of Egypt in 30 B.C.E. During the Hellenic period, Greeks developed a distinctive form of city-state known as the polis and made lasting cultural and intellectual achievements. During the Hellenistic period, Macedonian and Greek armies defeated the Persian Empire and built new cities and kingdoms, spreading Greek ideas as far as India (see Chapter 3).

Greek Boy with Goose In the Hellenistic culture that developed across a huge area after Alexander the Great's conquests, wealthy urban residents wanted art that showed real people rather than gods. This statue of a little boy wrestling a goose, originally carved about 200 B.C.E., no doubt found an eager buyer. (© Vanni Archive/Art Resource, NY)

> How did the geography of Greece shape its earliest history?

> What was the role of the polis in Greek society?

> In the classical period, how did war influence Greece, and how did the arts, religion, and philosophy develop?

> How did Alexander the Great's conquests shape society in the Hellenistic period?

> How did religion, philosophy, and science develop in the Hellenistic world?

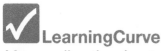**LearningCurve**

After reading the chapter, use LearningCurve to retain what you've read.

How did the geography of Greece shape its earliest history?

Mycenaean Dagger Blade

This scene in gold and silver on the blade of an iron dagger depicts hunters armed with spears and protected by shields defending themselves against charging lions. The Mycenaeans were a robust, warlike people who enjoyed the thrill and the danger of hunting. (From the Royal Tomb IV, Mycenae, found by H. Schliemann. National Archeological Museum, Athens/Ancient Art & Architecture Collection, Ltd./The Bridgeman Art Library)

Hellas, as the Greeks call their land, encompasses the Greek peninsula with its southern peninsular extension, known as the Peloponnesus (peh-luh-puh-NEE-suhs), and the islands surrounding it, an area known as the Aegean (ah-JEE-uhn) basin (Map 5.1). During the Bronze Age, which for Greek history is called the "Helladic period," early settlers in Greece began establishing small communities contoured by the mountains and small plains that shaped the land. The geographical fragmentation of Greece encouraged political fragmentation. Early in Greek history several kingdoms did emerge—the Minoan on the island of Crete and the Mycenaean on the mainland—but the rugged terrain prohibited the growth of a great empire like those of Mesopotamia or Egypt.

The Minoans and Mycenaeans

On the large island of Crete, Bronze Age farmers and fishermen began to trade their surpluses with their neighbors, and cities grew, housing artisans and merchants. Beginning about 2000 B.C.E. Cretans voyaged throughout the eastern Mediterranean and the Aegean, carrying the copper and tin needed to make bronze as well as many other goods. Social hierarchies developed, and in many cities certain individuals came to hold power. The Cretans began to use writing about 1900 B.C.E., in a form later scholars called Linear A. At about the same time that writing began, rulers in several cities of Crete began to build large structures with hundreds of interconnected rooms. The archaeologists who discovered these huge structures called them palaces, and they named the flourishing and vibrant culture of this era Minoan, after the mythical king of Crete, Minos.

CHAPTER LOCATOR | **How did the geography of Greece shape its earliest history?** | What was the role of the polis in Greek society?

116 CHAPTER 5 THE GREEK EXPERIENCE

ca. 3000–1200 B.C.E.
Helladic period

ca. 2000–1100 B.C.E.
Minoan and Mycenaean civilizations

ca. 1200–323 B.C.E.
Hellenic period

ca. 1100–800 B.C.E.
Greece's Dark Age; population declines, trade decreases, writing disappears

ca. 800–500 B.C.E.
Archaic age; rise of the polis; Greek colonization of the Mediterranean

ca. 700–500 B.C.E.
Sparta and Athens develop distinctive political institutions

ca. 500–338 B.C.E.
Classical period; development of drama, philosophy, and major building projects in Athens

499–404 B.C.E.
Persian and Peloponnesian wars

323–30 B.C.E.
Hellenistic period

336–324 B.C.E.
Alexander the Great's military campaigns

323–ca. 300 B.C.E.
Civil wars lead to the establishment of the Ptolemaic, Antigonid, and Seleucid dynasties

168 B.C.E.
Roman overthrow of the Antigonid dynasty

30 B.C.E.
Roman conquest of Egypt; Ptolemaic dynasty ends

Few specifics are known about Minoan political life except that a king and a group of nobles stood at its head. Minoan society was long thought to have been relatively peaceful, but new excavations are revealing more and more walls around cities, which has called the peaceful nature of Minoan society into question. In terms of their religious life, Minoans appear to have worshipped goddesses far more than gods. Whether this translated into more egalitarian gender roles for real people is unclear, but surviving Minoan art suggests that it might have.

As Minoan culture was flourishing on Crete, a different type of society developed on the mainland. This society was founded by groups who had migrated in during the period after 2000 B.C.E. By about 1650 B.C.E. one group of these immigrants had raised palaces and established cities at Thebes, Athens, Mycenae (migh-SEE-nee) and elsewhere. These palace-centers ruled by local kings formed a loose hegemony under the authority of the king of Mycenae, and the archaeologists who first discovered traces of this culture called it the Mycenaean (migh-see-NEE-ahn).

As in Crete, the political unit was the kingdom, and the king and his warrior aristocracy stood at the top of society. The seat and symbol of the king's power was his palace, which was also the economic center of the kingdom. Palace scribes kept records with a script known as Linear B.

The available evidence suggests a society in which war was common. Mycenaean cities were all fortified by thick stone walls, and graves contain spears, javelins, swords, helmets, and the first examples of metal armor known in the world.

How did war influence Greece, and how did the arts, religion, and philosophy develop?	How did Alexander the Great's conquests shape society in the Hellenistic period?	How did religion, philosophy, and science develop in the Hellenistic world?	✔️ LearningCurve Check what you know.

MAP 5.1 ◼ Classical Greece, ca. 450 B.C.E.

In antiquity the home of the Greeks included the islands of the Aegean and the western shore of Turkey as well as the Greek peninsula itself. Crete, the home of Minoan civilization, is the large island at the bottom of the map. The Peloponnesian peninsula, where Sparta is located, is connected to the rest of mainland Greece by a very narrow isthmus at Corinth.

Contacts between the Minoans and Mycenaeans were originally peaceful, and Minoan culture and trade goods flooded the Greek mainland. But most scholars think that around 1450 B.C.E., possibly in the wake of an earthquake that left Crete vulnerable, the Mycenaeans attacked Crete, destroying many towns and occupying Knossos, Crete's leading city. For about the next fifty years, the Mycenaeans ruled much of the island. Then, between about 1300 B.C.E. and 1000 B.C.E., various kingdoms in and beyond Greece ravaged one another in a savage series of wars that destroyed both the Minoan and Mycenaean civilizations.

The fall of the Minoans and Mycenaeans was part of what some scholars see as a general collapse of Bronze Age civilizations in the eastern Mediterranean, including the end of the Egyptian New Kingdom and the fall of the Hittite Empire (see Chapter 2). This collapse appears to have had a number of causes: internal economic and social problems; invasions and migrations by outsiders; changes in warfare and weaponry, particularly the adoption of iron weapons, which made foot soldiers the most important factor in battles and reduced the power of kings and wealthy nobles fighting from chariots; and natural disasters such as volcanic eruptions, earthquakes, and droughts.

CHAPTER LOCATOR | How did the geography of Greece shape its earliest history? | What was the role of the polis in Greek society?

CHAPTER 5
118 THE GREEK EXPERIENCE

The "Dark Age"

In Greece these invasions, migrations, disasters, and social problems worked together to usher in a period of poverty and disruption that historians have traditionally called the "Dark Age" of Greece (ca. 1100–800 B.C.E.). Cities were destroyed, population declined, villages were abandoned, and trade decreased. Even writing, which was not widespread before this period, was a casualty of the chaos.

The Bronze Age Collapse led to the widespread and prolonged movement of Greek peoples, both within Greece itself and beyond. They dispersed beyond mainland Greece farther south to the islands of the Aegean Sea and in greater strength across the Aegean to the shores of Anatolia (see Map 5.1). By the conclusion of the Dark Age, the Greeks had spread their culture throughout the Aegean basin, and like many other cultures around the Mediterranean and the Near East, they had adopted iron.

Archaeological sources from the Dark Age are less rich than those from the periods that came after, so they are often used in conjunction with literary sources written in later centuries to give us a more complete picture of the era. These included tales of the heroic deeds of legendary heroes similar to the epic poems of Mesopotamia and the *Ramayana* in India. Sometime in the eighth or seventh century B.C.E. many of these were gathered together in two long epic poems: the *Iliad*, which tells the story of the Trojan War, a war similar to those fought by Mycenaean kings, and the *Odyssey*, which records the adventures of one of the heroes of that war. These poems were recited orally, and once writing was reintroduced to Greece, they were written down and attributed to a poet named Homer, though scholars debate whether Homer was an actual historical individual. The two poems present human and divine characters who are larger than life but also petty, vindictive, pouting, and deceitful, flaws that drive the action forward, usually with tragic results.

QUICK REVIEW <

What role did trade play in Minoan and Mycenaean society?

How did war influence Greece, and how did the arts, religion, and philosophy develop?

How did Alexander the Great's conquests shape society in the Hellenistic period?

How did religion, philosophy, and science develop in the Hellenistic world?

 LearningCurve
Check what you know.

What was the role of the polis in Greek society?

Spartan Hoplite

This bronze figurine portrays an armed foot soldier about to strike an enemy. His massive helmet with its full crest gives his head nearly complete protection, while a metal corselet covers his chest and back, and greaves (similar to today's shin guards) protect his shins. In his right hand he carries a thrusting spear (now broken off), and in his left a large round shield. (bpk, Berlin/Antikensammlung, Staaliche Museen, Berlin, Germany/Photo: Johannes Laurentius/Art Resource, NY)

polis

▶ Generally translated as "city-state," it was the basic political and institutional unit of ancient Greece.

Homer lived in the era after the Dark Age, which later historians have termed the Archaic age (800–500 B.C.E.). The most important political change in this period was the development of the **polis** (PAH-luhs; plural *poleis*), a word generally translated as "city-state." During the Archaic period, poleis established colonies throughout much of the Mediterranean, spreading Greek culture, and two particular poleis rose to prominence on the Greek mainland: Sparta and Athens.

Organization of the Polis

The Greek polis was not the first form of city-state to emerge. The earliest states in Sumer were also city-states, as were many of the small Mycenaean kingdoms. What differentiated the new Greek model from older city-states was that the polis was more than a political institution—it was a community of citizens with their own customs and laws. With one exception, the poleis that emerged after 800 B.C.E. did not have kings but instead were self-governing. The physical, religious, and political forms of the polis varied from place to place, but everywhere it was relatively small, reflecting the fragmented geography of Greece. The very smallness of the polis enabled Greeks to see how they fit individually into the overall system, and thus how the individual parts made up the social whole.

The polis included a city and its surrounding countryside. The countryside was essential to the economy of the polis and provided food to sustain the entire population. The people of the polis typically lived in a compact group of houses within the city, which by the fifth century B.C.E. was generally surrounded by a wall. Another feature was a usually elevated area called the acropolis, where the people erected temples, altars, and public monuments. The polis also contained a public square or marketplace, the agora, where there were porticoes, shops, public buildings, and courts. The agora was the political center of the polis.

All poleis, with one exception, did not have standing armies. Instead they relied on their citizens for protection. Very rich citizens often served as cavalry, which was, however, never as important as the heavily armed infantrymen known as hoplites. These commoners were the backbone of the army, just as foot soldiers were in China during the Warring States Period (see Chapter 4).

Greek poleis had several different types of government. Sporadic periods of violent political and social upheaval often led to the seizure of power by one man, a type of government the Greeks called tyranny. Tyrants were not always oppressive rulers, however, and sometimes used their power to benefit average citizens.

Democracy was rule by citizens, not the people as a whole. Almost all Greek cities defined a citizen as an adult man with at least one citizen parent. Thus citizens shared ancestry as well as a place of residence. Women were citizens for religious and reproductive purposes, but their citizenship did not give them the right to participate in government. Free men who were not children of a citizen, known as resident foreigners, and slaves were not citizens and had no political voice.

Oligarchy was government by a small group of wealthy citizens. Many Greeks preferred oligarchy because it provided more political stability than did democracy. Although oligarchy was the government of the prosperous, it left the door open for political and social advancement. If members of the polis could meet property or money qualifications, they could enter the governing circle.

hoplites
▶ Heavily armed citizens who served as infantrymen and fought to defend the polis.

democracy
▶ A type of Greek government in which all citizens administered the workings of government.

oligarchy
▶ A type of Greek government in which citizens who owned a certain amount of property ruled.

Overseas Expansion

The development of the polis coincided with the growth of the Greek world in both wealth and numbers, bringing new problems. The increase in population created more demand for food than the land could supply. The resulting social and political tensions drove many people to seek new homes outside of Greece (Map 5.2).

Greeks traveled throughout the Mediterranean, sailing in great numbers to Sicily and southern Italy, where there was ample space for expansion. Some adventurous Greeks sailed farther west to Sardinia, France, Spain, and perhaps even the Canary Islands. From these new outposts Greek influence extended to southern France.

In contrast to earlier military invasions and migrations of peoples, these were very often intentional colonizing ventures, organized and planned by a specific polis seeking new land for its residents, or by the losers in a political conflict within a polis who were forced to leave. Colonization changed the entire Greek world, both at home and abroad. In economic terms the expansion of the Greeks created a much larger market for agricultural and manufactured goods.

How did war influence Greece, and how did the arts, religion, and philosophy develop?

How did Alexander the Great's conquests shape society in the Hellenistic period?

How did religion, philosophy, and science develop in the Hellenistic world?

☑ LearningCurve
Check what you know.

121

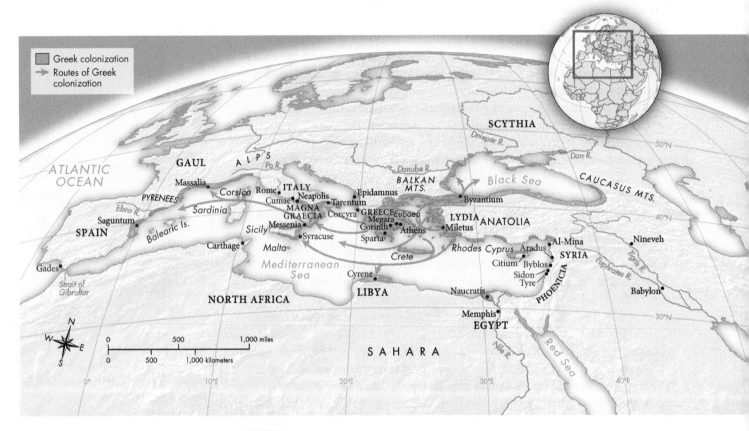

MAP 5.2 ■ Greek Colonization, ca. 750–550 B.C.E.

The Greeks established colonies along the shores of the Mediterranean and Black Seas, spreading Greek culture and creating a large trading network.

The Growth of Sparta

During the Archaic period Sparta became the leading military power in Greece. To expand their polis, the Spartans did not establish colonies but instead conquered Messenia (muh-SEE-nee-uh), a region in the southwestern Peloponnesus. They turned the Messenians into helots (HEH-luhts), unfree residents forced to work state lands. The helots soon rose in a revolt that took the Spartans thirty years to crush. Afterward, non-nobles who had shared in the fighting as foot soldiers appear to have demanded rights equal to those of the nobility and a voice in the government. Under intense pressure the aristocrats agreed to remodel the state into a new system.

The plan for the new system in Sparta was attributed to the lawgiver Lycurgus (ligh-KUHR-guhs), who may or may not have been an actual person. Political distinctions among Spartan men were eliminated, and all citizens became legally equal. Two kings, who were primarily military leaders, and a council of nobles shared executive power with five ephors (EH-fuhrs), overseers elected by the citizens. Helots worked the land, while Spartan citizens devoted their time to military training, and Sparta became extremely powerful.

In the system attributed to Lycurgus, every citizen owed primary allegiance to Sparta. Suppression of the individual along with an emphasis on military prowess led to a barracks state. Even family life was sacrificed to the polis. After long,

CHAPTER LOCATOR | How did the geography of Greece shape its earliest history? | What was the role of the polis in Greek society?

CHAPTER 5
THE GREEK EXPERIENCE

122

hard military training that began at age seven, citizens became lifelong soldiers. Because men often did not see their wives or other women for long periods, not only in times of war but also in times of peace, their most meaningful relations were same-sex ones.

Spartans expected women in citizen families to be good wives and strict mothers of future soldiers. With men in military service much of their lives, women in citizen families ran the estates and owned land in their own right, and they were not physically restricted or secluded.

The Evolution of Athens

Like Sparta, Athens faced pressing social and economic problems during the Archaic period, but instead of creating a state devoted to the military, the Athenians created a state that became a democracy. For Athens, the late seventh century B.C.E. was a time of turmoil. In 621 B.C.E. Draco (DRAY-koh), an Athenian aristocrat, under pressure from small landholders and with the consent of the nobles, published the first law code of the Athenian polis. His code was harsh, but it embodied the ideal that the law belonged to all citizens. Yet the aristocracy still governed Athens oppressively, and the social and economic situation remained dire. Noble landholders continued to force small farmers and artisans into economic dependence. Many families were sold into slavery as settlement for debts, while others were exiled and their land mortgaged to the rich.

One person who recognized these problems was the aristocrat Solon (SOH-luhn). Solon condemned his fellow aristocrats for their greed and dishonesty. According to later sources, Solon's sincerity and good sense convinced other aristocrats that he was no crazed revolutionary. Moreover, he gained the trust of the common people. Around 594 B.C.E. the nobles elected him *archon* (AHR-kahn), chief magistrate of the polis, and gave him extraordinary power to reform the state.

Solon immediately freed all people enslaved for debt, recalled all exiles, canceled all debts on land, and made enslavement for debt illegal. Solon allowed non-nobles into the old aristocratic assembly, where they could vote in the election of magistrates. Later sixth-century-B.C.E. leaders further broadened the opportunities for commoners to take part in government, transforming Athens into a democracy.

The democracy functioned on the ideal that all full citizens should play a role in government. In 487 B.C.E. the election of the city's nine archons was replaced by reappointment by lot, which meant that any citizen with a certain amount of property had a chance of becoming an archon. Making laws was the responsibility of two bodies, the *boule* (BOO-lee), or council, composed of five hundred members, and the *ecclesia* (ee-KLEE-zhee-uh), the assembly of all citizens.

QUICK REVIEW <

How did the Greek polis differ from Near Eastern city-states?

How did war influence Greece, and how did the arts, religion, and philosophy develop?

How did Alexander the Great's conquests shape society in the Hellenistic period?

How did religion, philosophy, and science develop in the Hellenistic world?

☑ LearningCurve
Check what you know.

123

In the classical period, how did war influence Greece, and how did the arts, religion, and philosophy develop?

Religious Procession in Hellenic Greece

This painted wooden slab from about 540 B.C.E., found in a cave near Corinth, shows adults and children about to sacrifice a sheep to the deities worshipped in this area. The participants are dressed in their finest clothes and crowned with garlands. Music adds to the festivities. Rituals such as this were a common part of religious life throughout Greece. The boys are shown with tanned skin and women with white, reflecting the ideal that men's lives took place largely outside in the sun-filled public squares, and women's in the shaded interiors of homes. The woman at the front of the procession has her hair up, indicating her married status, while the women at the rear have the long uncovered hair of unmarried women. (Pitsa/National Archeological Museum, Athens, Greece/Gianni Dagli Orti/De Agostini Picture Library/The Bridgeman Art Library)

From the time of the Mycenaeans, violent conflict was common in Greek society, and this did not change in the fifth century B.C.E., the beginning of what scholars later called the classical period of Greek history. First, the Greeks beat back the armies of the Persian Empire. Then, turning their spears against one another, they destroyed their own political system in a century of warfare that began with the Peloponnesian War. Although warfare was one of the hallmarks of the classical period, intellectual and artistic accomplishments were as well.

The Deadly Conflicts, 499–404 B.C.E.

In 499 B.C.E. the Greeks who lived in Ionia unsuccessfully rebelled against the Persian Empire, which had ruled the area for fifty years (see Chapter 2). The Athenians provided halfhearted help to the Ionians, and in retaliation the Persians struck at Athens, only to be surprisingly defeated by the Athenian hoplites at the Battle of Marathon. In 480 B.C.E. the Persian king Xerxes (ZUHRK-seez) personally led a massive invasion of Greece. Under the leadership of Sparta, many

CHAPTER LOCATOR | How did the geography of Greece shape its earliest history? | What was the role of the polis in Greek society?

Greek poleis, though not all, united to fight the Persians. The larger Persian army enjoyed early success, but the tide quickly turned and the invasion ended in failure.

The victorious Athenians and their allies then formed the Delian League, a military alliance intended to liberate Ionia from Persian rule and keep the Persians out of Greece. The Athenians, however, turned the league into an Athenian empire. They reduced their allies to the status of subjects. Athenian ideas of freedom and democracy did not extend to the citizens of other cities, and cities that objected to or revolted over Athenian actions were put down.

Under their great leader Pericles (PEHR-uh-kleez) (ca. 494–429 B.C.E.), the Athenians grew so powerful and aggressive that they alarmed Sparta and its allies. In 431 B.C.E. Athenian imperialism finally drove Sparta into the conflict known as the Peloponnesian War. The Peloponnesian War lasted a generation (431–404 B.C.E.) and brought in its wake disease, widespread civil wars, destruction, famine, and huge loss of life. In 404 B.C.E. the Athenians finally surrendered to Sparta and its allies, and Sparta stripped it of its empire. Conflicts among the states of Greece continued, however.

The Persian Wars, 499–479 B.C.E.

Athenian Arts in the Age of Pericles

In the midst of the warfare of the fifth century B.C.E., Pericles turned Athens into the showplace of Greece. He appropriated Delian League money to pay for a huge building program to rebuild the city that had been destroyed during the Persian occupation in 480 B.C.E. and to display to all Greeks the glory of the Athenian polis. The Acropolis in the center of the city was crowned by the Parthenon, a temple that celebrated the greatness of Athens and its patron goddess, Athena, who was represented by a huge statue.

Other aspects of Athenian culture were also rooted in the life of the polis. The polis sponsored plays as part of the city's religious festivals and required wealthy citizens to pay the expenses of their production. Many plays were highly controversial, with overt political and social commentary, but they were neither suppressed nor censored. Not surprisingly, given the incessant warfare, conflict was a constant element in Athenian drama, and playwrights used their art in attempts to portray, understand, and resolve life's basic conflicts.

Aeschylus (EHS-kuh-luhs) (525–456 B.C.E.) was the first dramatist to explore such basic questions as the rights of the individual, the conflict between the individual and society, and the nature of good and evil. In his trilogy of plays, *The Oresteia*, he treats the themes of betrayal, murder, and reconciliation, urging the use of reason and justice to reconcile fundamental conflicts.

The plays of Sophocles (SAH-fuh-kleez) (496–406 B.C.E.) also deal with matters personal, political, and divine. In *Antigone*—which tells of how a king's mistakes in judgment lead to the suicides of his son, his son's fiancée, and his wife—Sophocles emphasizes the precedence of divine law over political law and family custom. In *Oedipus the King*, Sophocles tells the story of a good man doomed by the gods to kill his father and marry his mother. When Oedipus fails to avoid his fate, he blinds himself in despair and flees into exile. In *Oedipus at Colonus*, Sophocles treats the last days of the broken man, whose patient suffering and uncomplaining piety ultimately win the blessings and honor of the gods.

The Delian League, ca. 478–431 B.C.E.

How did war influence Greece, and how did the arts, religion, and philosophy develop?

How did Alexander the Great's conquests shape society in the Hellenistic period?

How did religion, philosophy, and science develop in the Hellenistic world?

LearningCurve
Check what you know.

125

The Acropolis of Athens

The natural rock formation of the Acropolis probably had a palace on top as early as the Mycenaean period, when it was also surrounded by a defensive wall. Temples were constructed beginning in the sixth century B.C.E., and after the Persian wars Pericles ordered the reconstruction and expansion of many of these, as well as the building of new and more magnificent temples and an extension of the defensive walls. The largest building is the Parthenon, a temple dedicated to the goddess Athena, which originally housed a 40-foot-tall statue of Athena made of ivory and gold sheets attached to a wooden frame. Much of the Parthenon was damaged when it was shelled during a war between Venice and the Ottoman Empire in the seventeenth century, and air pollution continues to eat away at the marble. (Marie Mauzy/Art Resource, NY)

> PICTURING THE PAST
ANALYZING THE IMAGE: Imagine yourself as an Athenian walking up the hill toward the Parthenon. What impression would the setting and the building itself convey?
CONNECTIONS: What were the various functions of the Acropolis?

Euripides (yoo-RIH-puh-deez) (ca. 480–406 B.C.E.) likewise explored the theme of personal conflict within the polis and sounded the depths of the individual. With Euripides drama entered a new and more personal phase. To him the gods mattered far less than people.

Athens also produced writers of comedies, who used humor as political commentary in an effort to suggest and support the best policies for the polis. Best known of the comedians is Aristophanes (eh-ruh-STAH-fuh-neez) (ca. 445–386 B.C.E.), a merciless critic of cranks, quacks, and fools. He used his art of sarcasm to dramatize his ideas on the right conduct of citizens and their leaders for the good of the polis.

Families and Sexual Relations

The Athenians, like other Greeks, lived with comparatively few material possessions in houses that were rather simple. A typical Athenian house consisted of a series of rooms opening onto a central courtyard that contained a well, an altar,

CHAPTER LOCATOR | How did the geography of Greece shape its earliest history? | What was the role of the polis in Greek society?

126 CHAPTER 5
THE GREEK EXPERIENCE

and a washbasin. Meals consisted primarily of various grains, especially wheat and barley, as well as lentils, olives, figs, grapes, fish, and a little meat.

In the city a man might support himself as a craftsman, or he could contract with the polis to work on public buildings. Certain crafts, including spinning and weaving, were generally done by women. Men and women without skills worked as paid laborers. Slavery was commonplace in Greece. Slaves, who were paid for their work, were usually foreigners.

The available sources suggest that women rarely played notable roles in public affairs. The status of a free woman was strictly protected by law. Only her sons could be citizens. Only she was in charge of the household and the family's possessions, yet the law gave her these rights primarily to protect her husband's interests. Women in Athens and elsewhere in Greece, like those in Mesopotamia, brought dowries to their husbands upon marriage, which went back to their fathers in cases of divorce.

In ancient Athens the main function of women from citizen families was to bear and raise children. Women in citizen families probably spent most of their time at home, leaving the house only to attend religious festivals, and perhaps occasionally plays, although this is debated. In their quarters of the house they oversaw domestic slaves and hired labor, and together with servants and friends worked wool into cloth. Women from noncitizen families lived freer lives, although they worked harder and had fewer material comforts. They performed manual labor in the fields or sold goods and services in the agora, going about their affairs much as men did.

Same-sex relations were generally accepted in all of ancient Greece. In classical Athens part of a male adolescent citizen's training might entail a hierarchical sexual and tutorial relationship with an older man, who most likely was married and may have had female sexual partners as well. A small number of sources refer to female-female sexual desire, the most famous of which are a few of the poems of Sappho (SEH-FOH), a female poet of the sixth century B.C.E.

Same-sex relations did not mean that people did not marry, for Athenians saw the continuation of the family line as essential. Sappho, for example, appears to have been married and had a daughter. Sexual desire and procreation were both important aspects of life, but ancient Greeks did not necessarily link them.

Hetaera and Young Man

In this scene painted on the inside of a drinking cup, a hetaera holds the head of a young man who has clearly had too much to drink. Sexual and comic scenes were common on Greek pottery, particularly on objects that would have been used at a private dinner party hosted by a citizen, known as a symposium. Wives did not attend symposia, but hetaerae and entertainers were often hired to perform for the male guests. (© Martin Von Wagner Museum der Universitat Wurzburg. Foto: P. Neckermann, respectively E. Oehrlein)

How did war influence Greece, and how did the arts, religion, and philosophy develop?

How did Alexander the Great's conquests shape society in the Hellenistic period?

How did religion, philosophy, and science develop in the Hellenistic world?

✔ LearningCurve
Check what you know.

Public and Personal Religion

Like most peoples of the ancient world, the Greeks were polytheists, worshipping a variety of gods and goddesses who were immortal but otherwise acted just like people. As elsewhere, Greek religion was primarily a matter of ritual, with rituals designed to appease the divinities believed to control the forces of the natural world. Processions, festivals, and sacrifices offered to the gods were frequently occasions for people to meet together socially. Migration, invasion, and colonization brought the Greeks into contact with other peoples and caused their religious beliefs to evolve.

By the classical era, the primary gods were understood to live metaphorically on Mount Olympus, the highest mountain in Greece. Besides these Olympian gods, each polis had its own minor deities, each with his or her own local group of worshippers. The polis administered the cults and religious festivals, and everyone was expected to participate in these civic rituals. In contrast to Mesopotamia, Egypt, and Vedic India, priests held little power in Greece; their purpose was to care for temples and sacred property and to conduct the proper rituals, but not to make religious or political rules or doctrines. Much religion was local and domestic, and individual families honored various deities privately in their homes. Many people also believed that magic rituals and spells were effective and sought the assistance of individuals reputed to have special knowledge or powers.

> The Olympian Gods:

Zeus	King of the gods
Hera	Wife and sister of Zeus
Ares	God of war
Apollo	Patron god of music and poetry
Athena	Goddess of wisdom and patron goddess of Athens

mystery religions

▶ Belief systems that were characterized by secret doctrines, rituals of initiation, and sometimes the promise of rebirth or an afterlife.

Along with public and family forms of honoring the gods, some Greeks also participated in what later historians have termed **mystery religions**, in which participants underwent an initiation ritual and gained secret knowledge that they were forbidden to reveal to the uninitiated. Many of these religions promised rebirth or an afterlife to adherents.

The Greeks also shared some Pan-Hellenic festivals, the chief of which were held at Olympia to honor the god Zeus and at Delphi to honor the god Apollo. The festivities at Olympia included athletic contests that inspired the modern Olympic games. Held every four years after they started in 776 B.C.E., the contests attracted visitors from all over the Greek world. The Pythian games at Delphi were also held every four years, and these contests included musical and literary competitions.

The Flowering of Philosophy

Just as the Greeks developed rituals to honor gods, they spun myths and epics to explain the origins of the universe. Over time, however, some Greeks began to question their old gods and myths, and they sought rational rather than super-

CHAPTER LOCATOR | How did the geography of Greece shape its earliest history? | What was the role of the polis in Greek society?

128 CHAPTER 5
THE GREEK EXPERIENCE

natural explanations for natural phenomena. These Greek thinkers, based in Ionia, are called the Pre-Socratics because their rational efforts preceded those of the better-known Socrates. Taking individual facts, they wove them into general theories that led them to conclude that, despite appearances, the universe is actually simple and subject to natural laws.

Drawing on their observations, the Pre-Socratics speculated about the basic building blocks of the universe, and most decided that all things were made of four simple substances: fire, air, earth, and water. Democritus (dih-MAW-kruh-tuhs) (ca. 460 B.C.E.) broke this down further and created the atomic theory that the universe is made up of invisible, indestructible particles. The stream of thought started by the Pre-Socratics branched into several directions. Hippocrates (hih-PAW-kruh-teez) (ca. 470–400 B.C.E.) became the most prominent physician and teacher of medicine of his time. He sought natural explanations for diseases and natural means to treat them. Illness was caused not by evil spirits, he asserted, but by physical problems in the body, particularly by imbalances in what he saw as four basic bodily fluids: blood, phlegm, black bile, and yellow bile.

The Sophists (SOFF-ihsts), a group of thinkers in fifth-century-B.C.E. Athens, applied philosophical speculation to politics and language, questioning the beliefs and laws of the polis to understand their origin. They believed that excellence in both politics and language could be taught, and they provided lessons for the young men of Athens who wished to learn how to persuade others.

Socrates (SOK-ruh-teez) (ca. 470–399 B.C.E.), whose ideas are known only through the works of others, also applied philosophy to politics and to people. His approach when exploring ethical issues and defining concepts was to start with a general topic or problem and to narrow the matter to its essentials. He did so by continuously questioning participants in a discussion or argument rather than lecturing, a process known as the Socratic method. Many Athenians viewed Socrates with suspicion because he challenged the traditional beliefs and values of Athens. His views brought him into conflict with the government. The leaders of Athens tried him for corrupting the youth of the city, and for impiety, that is, for not believing in the gods honored in the city. In 399 B.C.E. they executed him.

Most of what we know about Socrates comes from his student Plato (427–347 B.C.E.), who wrote dialogues in which Socrates asks questions and who also founded the Academy, a school dedicated to philosophy. Plato developed the theory that there are two worlds: the impermanent, changing world that we know through our senses, and the eternal, unchanging realm of "forms" that constitute the essence of true reality. According to Plato, true knowledge and the possibility of living a virtuous life come from contemplating ideal forms — what later came to be called Platonic ideals — not from observing the visible world.

Plato's student Aristotle (384–322 B.C.E.) believed that true knowledge came from observation of the world, analysis of natural phenomena, and logical reasoning, not contemplation. Aristotle thought that everything had a purpose, so that to know something, one also had to know its function. The range of Aristotle's thought is staggering. His interests embraced logic, ethics, natural science, physics, politics, poetry, and art. He studied the heavens as well as earth and judged the earth to be the center of the universe, with the stars and planets revolving around it.

Platonic ideals
▶ In Plato's thought, the eternal unchanging ideal forms that are the essence of true reality.

How did war influence Greece, and how did the arts, religion, and philosophy develop?

How did Alexander the Great's conquests shape society in the Hellenistic period?

How did religion, philosophy, and science develop in the Hellenistic world?

LearningCurve
Check what you know.

The philosophers of ancient Athens lived at roughly the same time as major thinkers in religious and philosophical movements in other parts of the world, including Mahavira (the founder of Jainism), the Buddha, Confucius, and several prophets in Hebrew Scripture. All of these individuals thought deeply about how to live a moral life, and all had tremendous influence on later intellectual, religious, and social developments. There is no evidence that they had any contact with one another, but the parallels among them are strong enough that some historians describe the period from about 800 B.C.E. to 200 B.C.E. as the "Axial Age," by which they mean that this was a pivotal period of intellectual and spiritual transformation.

> ## QUICK REVIEW

How did Athenian art, drama, and religion reflect Athenian values and beliefs?

CHAPTER LOCATOR | How did the geography of Greece shape its earliest history? | What was the role of the polis in Greek society?

130 CHAPTER 5
THE GREEK EXPERIENCE

Harbor and Marketplace at Delos

During the Hellenistic period, the tiny island of Delos in the Aegean became a thriving trading center, with a paved marketplace filled with shops and stands, as well as temples paid for by merchants and ship captains. From Delos cargoes were shipped to virtually every part of the Mediterranean. Liquids such as wine and oil were generally shipped in amphoras (inset) made of baked clay. Amphoras were easy and cheap to make and surprisingly durable. (harbor: age fotostock/SuperStock; amphora: Alexis Rosenfeld/Photo Researchers, Inc.)

The Greek city-states wore themselves out fighting one another, and Philip II, the ruler of Macedonia, a kingdom in the north of Greece, gradually conquered one after another and took over their lands. He then turned against the Persian Empire but was killed by an assassin. His son Alexander continued the fight. Alexander conquered the entire Persian Empire from Libya in the west to Bactria in the east (see Map 5.3, page 133). He also founded new cities in which Greek and local populations mixed, although he died while planning his next campaign. Alexander left behind an empire that quickly broke into smaller kingdoms, but more important, his death in 323 B.C.E. ushered in an era, the Hellenistic, in which Greek culture, the Greek language, and Greek thought spread as far as India, blending with local traditions.

Hellenistic

▶ Literally means "like the Greek"; describes the period from the death of Alexander the Great in 323 B.C.E. to the Roman conquest of Egypt in 30 B.C.E., when Greek culture spread.

How did war influence Greece, and how did the arts, religion, and philosophy develop?	**How did Alexander the Great's conquests shape society in the Hellenistic period?**	How did religion, philosophy, and science develop in the Hellenistic world?	LearningCurve Check what you know.

From Polis to Monarchy, 404–200 B.C.E.

Immediately after the Peloponnesian War, Sparta began striving for empire over all of the Greeks but could not maintain its hold. In 371 B.C.E. an army from the polis of Thebes destroyed the Spartan army, but the Thebans were unable to bring peace to Greece. Philip II, ruler of the kingdom of Macedonia on the northern border of Greece (r. 359–336 B.C.E.), turned the situation to his advantage. By clever use of his wealth and superb army, Philip won control of the northern Aegean, and in 338 B.C.E. he defeated a combined Theban-Athenian army, conquering Greece.

After his victory, Philip united the Greek states with his Macedonian kingdom and got the states to cooperate in a crusade to liberate the Ionian Greeks from Persian rule. Before he could launch his crusade, Philip fell to an assassin's dagger in 336 B.C.E. His son Alexander vowed to carry on Philip's mission and led an army of Macedonians and Greeks into western Asia. He won major battles against the Persians and seized Egypt from them without a fight.

By 330 B.C.E. the Persian Empire had fallen, but Alexander had no intention of stopping, and he set out to conquer much of the rest of Asia. After four years of fighting his soldiers crossed the Indus River (in the area that is now Pakistan), and finally, at the Hyphasis River, the troops refused to go farther. Alexander was enraged by the mutiny, but the army stood firm. Still eager to explore the limits of the world, Alexander turned south to the Arabian Sea and then back west (Map 5.3).

Alexander died in Babylon in 323 B.C.E. from fever, wounds, and excessive drinking. In just thirteen years he had created an empire that stretched from his homeland of Macedonia to India. His campaign swept away the Persian Empire, and in its place he established a Macedonian monarchy, although this fell apart with his death. Several of the chief Macedonian generals aspired to become sole ruler, which led to a civil war that lasted for decades and tore Alexander's empire apart. By the end of this conflict, the most successful generals had carved out their own smaller monarchies, although these continued to be threatened by internal splits and external attacks.

Ptolemy (TAH-luh-mee) seized Egypt, and his descendants, the Ptolemies, ruled Egypt for nearly three hundred years, until the death of the last Ptolemaic ruler, Cleopatra VII, in 30 B.C.E. Antigonus and his descendants, the Antigonids (an-TIH-guh-nuhds), gained control of the Macedonian kingdom in Europe, which they held until they were overthrown by the Romans in 168 B.C.E. (see Chapter 6). Seleucus won the bulk of Alexander's empire, his monarchy extending from western Asia to India (see page 133), gradually broke into smaller states. In terms of political stability and peace, these monarchies were no improvement on the Greek polis.

To encourage obedience, Hellenistic kings often created ruler cults that linked the king's authority with that of the gods, or they adopted ruler cults that already existed. This created a symbol of unity within kingdoms ruling different peoples who at first had little in common. Kings sometimes gave the cities in their territory all the external trappings of a polis, such as a council or an assembly of citizens, but these had no power. The city was not autonomous, as the polis had been, but had to follow royal orders. Hellenistic rulers generally relied on paid professionals to staff their bureaucracies and on trained, paid, full-time soldiers rather than citizen hoplites to fight their wars.

MAP 5.3 ■ Alexander's Conquests, 336–324 B.C.E.

Alexander's campaign of conquest was extensive and speedy. More important than the great success of his military campaigns was his founding of Hellenistic cities.

> MAPPING THE PAST

ANALYZING THE MAP: Where are most of the cities founded by Alexander located in relation to Greece? What does this suggest about his aims?

CONNECTIONS: Compare this map with Map 5.2, which shows Greek colonization in the Hellenic period (page 122). What are the major differences between the two processes of expansion?

Building a Hellenized Society

Alexander's most important legacy was the spread of Greek ideas and traditions across a wide area, a process scholars later called **Hellenization**. To maintain contact with the Greek world as he moved farther eastward, Alexander founded new cities and military colonies and settled Greek and Macedonian troops and veterans in them. This practice continued after his death. These cities and colonies became powerful instruments in the spread of Hellenism and in the blending of Greek and other cultures. Wherever it was established, the Hellenistic city resembled a modern city. It was a cultural center with theaters, temples, and libraries—a seat of learning and a place for amusement. The Hellenistic city was also an economic center—a marketplace and a scene of trade and manufacturing.

Hellenization

▶ The spread of Greek ideas, culture, and traditions to non-Greek groups across a wide area.

| How did war influence Greece, and how did the arts, religion, and philosophy develop? | **How did Alexander the Great's conquests shape society in the Hellenistic period?** | How did religion, philosophy, and science develop in the Hellenistic world? | ✓ LearningCurve Check what you know. |

133

The ruling dynasties of the Hellenistic world were Macedonian in origin, and Greeks and Macedonians initially filled all important political, military, and diplomatic positions. The prevailing institutions and laws were Greek, and Greek became the common spoken language of the entire eastern Mediterranean. Everyone who wanted to find an official position or compete in business had to learn it. Those who did gained an avenue of social mobility, and as early as the third century B.C.E. local people in some Greek cities began to rise in power and prominence. Cultural influences in the other direction occurred less frequently because they brought fewer advantages. Few Greeks learned a non-Greek language unless they were required to because of their official position. Greeks did begin to worship local deities, but often these were somewhat Hellenized and their qualities blended with those of an existing Greek god or goddess.

In the booming city of Alexandria, the Ptolemies generally promoted Greek culture over that of the local Egyptians. This favoritism eventually led to civil unrest, but it also led the Ptolemies to support anything that enhanced Greek learning or traditions. Ptolemaic kings established what became the largest library in the ancient world. Alexandria was also home to the largest Jewish community in the ancient world, and here Jewish scholars translated the Hebrew Bible into Greek for the first time.

The kings of Bactria and Parthia spread Greek culture far to the east, and their kingdoms became outposts of Hellenism. Some Bactrian and Parthian rulers converted to Buddhism, and the Buddhist ruler of the Mauryan Empire in northern India, Ashoka, may have ordered translations of his laws into Greek for the Greek-speaking residents of Bactria and Parthia. In the second century B.C.E., after the collapse of the Mauryan Empire, Bactrian armies conquered part of northern India, establishing several small Indo-Greek states where the mixing of religious and artistic traditions was particularly pronounced (see Chapter 3).

Yet the spread of Greek culture was wider than it was deep, as it generally did not extend far beyond the reaches of the cities. Many urban residents adopted the aspects of Hellenism that they found useful, but people in the countryside generally did not embrace it, nor were they encouraged to.

The Growth of Trade and Commerce

Not only did Alexander's conquests change the political face of the ancient world, but the spread of Greeks eastward also created new markets, causing trade to flourish. The economic connections of the Hellenistic world later proved valuable to the Romans, allowing them to trade products and ideas more easily over a broad area.

Alexander used the wealth of the Persian Empire to finance the building of roads, the development of harbors, and especially, as noted earlier, the founding of new cities. These cities opened whole new markets to merchants. Whenever possible, merchants sent their goods by water, but overland trade also became more prominent in the Hellenistic era. This period also saw the development of standardized business customs, so that merchants of different nationalities communicated in a way understandable to them all. Trade was further facilitated by the coining of money, which provided merchants with a standard way to value goods as well as a convenient method of payment.

CHAPTER LOCATOR | How did the geography of Greece shape its earliest history? | What was the role of the polis in Greek society?

CHAPTER 5
134 THE GREEK EXPERIENCE

The increased volume of trade helped create prosperity that made luxury goods affordable to more people. As a result, overland traders brought easily transportable luxuries such as gold, silver, and precious stones to market. They extended their networks into China, from which the most prominent good in terms of volume was silk. The trade in silk later gave the major east-west route its name: the Great Silk Road. In return the peoples of the eastern Mediterranean sent east manufactured or extracted goods, especially metal weapons, cloth, wine, and olive oil. (For more on the Silk Road in East Asia, see Chapter 7.)

More economically important than trade in exotic goods were commercial dealings in essential commodities like raw materials and grain and industrial products such as pottery. Most trade in bulk commodities like grain and wood was seaborne.

For the cities of Greece and the Aegean the trade in grain was essential, because many of them could not grow enough in their mountainous terrain. Fortunately for them, abundant wheat supplies were available nearby in Egypt and in the area north of the Black Sea. The Greek cities often paid for their grain by exporting olive oil, wine, honey, dried fruit, nuts, and vegetables. Another significant commodity supplied by the Greeks was fish, which for export was salted, pickled, or dried.

Slaves were a staple of Hellenistic trade, traveling in all directions on both land and sea routes. War provided prisoners for the slave market; to a lesser extent, so did kidnapping and capture by pirates, although the origin of most slaves is unknown. Both old Greek states and new Hellenistic kingdoms were ready slave markets, and throughout the Mediterranean world slaves were almost always in demand.

Despite the increase in trade, the Hellenistic period did not see widespread improvements in the way most people lived and worked. Cities flourished, but many people who lived in rural areas were actually worse off than they had been before, because of higher levels of rents and taxes. Technology was applied to military needs, but not to the production of food or other goods. Manual labor, not machinery, continued to turn out the agricultural produce, raw materials, and manufactured goods the Hellenistic world used.

QUICK REVIEW

How did the Hellenistic city differ from the Hellenic polis?

How did war influence Greece, and how did the arts, religion, and philosophy develop?

How did Alexander the Great's conquests shape society in the Hellenistic period?

How did religion, philosophy, and science develop in the Hellenistic world?

☑ LearningCurve
Check what you know.

> How did religion, philosophy, and science develop in the Hellenistic world?

Hellenistic Married Life

This small terra-cotta figurine from Myrina in what is now Turkey, made in the second century B.C.E., shows a newly married couple sitting on a bridal bed. The groom is drawing back the bride's veil, and she is exhibiting the modesty that was a desired quality in young women. Figurines representing every stage of life became popular in the Hellenistic period and were used for religious offerings in temples and sacred places. This one was found in a tomb. (Louvre, Paris, France/Erich Lessing/Art Resource, NY)

The mixing of peoples in the Hellenistic era influenced religion, philosophy, and science. The Hellenistic kings built temples to the old Olympian gods and promoted rituals and ceremonies like those in earlier Greek cities, but new deities also gained prominence. More people turned to mystery religions that blended Greek and non-Greek elements. Others turned to practical philosophies that provided advice on how to live a good life. In the scholarly realm, Hellenistic thinkers made advances in mathematics, astronomy, and mechanical design. Additionally, physicians used observation and dissection to better understand the way the human body works.

Religion in the Hellenistic World

When Hellenistic kings founded cities, they also built temples for the old Olympian gods. In this way they spread Greek religious beliefs throughout the Hellenistic world. Greeks and non-Greeks in the Hellenistic world also honored and worshipped deities that had not been important in the Hellenic period or that were a blend of imported Greek and indigenous gods and goddesses. Tyche (TIGH-kee), for example, was a new deity, the goddess and personification of luck, fate, chance, and fortune.

Increasingly, many people were attracted to mystery religions, which in the Hellenic period had been linked to specific gods in particular places, so that people who wished to become members had to travel. But new mystery religions, like Hellenistic culture in general, were not tied to a particular place; instead they were spread throughout the Hellenistic world, and temples of the new deities sprang up wherever Greeks lived.

Mystery religions incorporated aspects of both Greek and non-Greek religions and claimed to save their adherents from the worst that fate could do. Most taught that by the rites of initiation, in which the secrets of the religion were shared, devotees became united with a deity who had also died and risen from the dead. The sacrifice of the god and his victory over death saved the devotee from eternal death. Similarly, mystery religions demanded a period of preparation in which the converts strove to become pure and holy, that is, to live by the religion's precepts. Once aspirants had prepared themselves, they went through the initiation, usually a ritual of great emotional intensity symbolizing the entry into a new life.

Among the mystery religions the Egyptian cult of Isis took the Hellenistic world by storm. In Egyptian mythology Isis brought her husband, Osiris, back to life (see page 44), and during the Hellenistic era this power came to be understood by her followers as extending to them as well. She promised to save any mortal who came to her, and her priests asserted that she had bestowed on humanity the gift of civilization and founded law and literature. Isis was understood to be a devoted mother as well as a devoted wife, and she became the goddess of marriage, conception, and childbirth. She became the most important goddess of the Hellenistic world.

Philosophy and Its Guidance for Life

While some people turned to mystery religions to overcome Tyche and provide something permanent in a world that seemed unstable, others turned to philosophy. Several new schools of philosophical thought emerged in the Hellenistic period. One of these was Epicureanism, a practical philosophy of serenity in an often-tumultuous world. Epicurus (340–270 B.C.E.) decided that the principal goods of human life were contentment and pleasure, which he defined as the absence of pain, fear, and suffering. By encouraging the pursuit of pleasure, he was not advocating drunken revels or sexual excess, which he thought caused pain, but promoting moderation. Epicurus also taught that individuals could most easily attain peace and serenity by ignoring the outside world and looking instead into their personal feelings. His followers ignored politics because it led to tumult, which would disturb the soul.

Zeno (335–262 B.C.E.), a philosopher from Cyprus, advanced a different concept of human beings and the universe. Zeno first came to Athens to form his own school, the Stoa. His philosophy, Stoicism (STOH-uh-sih-zuhm), in turn, came to be named for his school. Zeno and his followers considered nature an expression

Epicureanism

▶ A system of philosophy based on the teachings of Epicurus, who viewed a life of contentment, free from fear and suffering, as the greatest good.

Stoicism

▶ A philosophy, based on the ideas of Zeno, that held that people could only be happy when living in accordance with nature and accepting whatever happened.

How did war influence Greece, and how did the arts, religion, and philosophy develop?

How did Alexander the Great's conquests shape society in the Hellenistic period?

How did religion, philosophy, and science develop in the Hellenistic world?

☑ LearningCurve
Check what you know.

137

INDIVIDUALS IN SOCIETY
Archimedes, Scientist and Inventor

Archimedes was born in the Greek city of Syracuse in Sicily, an intellectual center in which he pursued scientific interests. He was the most original thinker of his time and a practical inventor. In his book *On Plane Equilibriums*, he dealt for the first time with the basic principles of mathematics, including the principle of the lever. He once said that if he were given a lever and a suitable place to stand, he could move the world. He also demonstrated how easily his compound pulley could move huge weights with little effort:

> A three-masted merchant ship of the royal fleet had been hauled on land by hard work and many hands. Archimedes put aboard her many men and the usual freight. He sat far away from her; and without haste, but gently working a compound pulley with his hand, he drew her towards him smoothly and without faltering, just as though she were running on the surface.*

He likewise invented the Archimedian screw, a pump to bring subterranean water up to irrigate fields, which quickly came into common use. In his treatise *On Floating Bodies*, Archimedes founded the science of hydrostatics. He concluded that an object will float if it weighs less than the water it displaces, and that whenever a solid floats in a liquid, the weight of the solid equals the weight of the liquid displaced. This discovery and his reaction to it has become famous:

> When he was devoting his attention to this problem, he happened to go to a public bath. When he climbed down into the bathtub there, he noticed that water in the tub equal to the bulk of his body flowed out. Thus, when he observed this method of solving the problem, he did not wait. Instead, moved with joy, he sprang out of the tub, and rushing home naked he kept indicating in a loud voice that he had indeed discovered what he was seeking. For while running he was shouting repeatedly in Greek, "Eureka, eureka" ("I have found it, I have found it").†

*Plutarch, *Life of Marcellus*.
†Vitruvius, *On Architecture*, 9 Preface, 10.

Several of Archimedes's treatises were found on a palimpsest, a manuscript that has been scraped and washed so that another text can be written over it, thus reusing the expensive parchment. Reusing parchment was a common practice in the Middle Ages, but the original text can sometimes be reconstructed. Using digital processing with several types of light and X-rays to study this thirteenth-century-C.E. prayer book, scientists were slowly able to decipher the texts by Archimedes that were underneath, including one that had been completely lost. (Image by the Rochester Institute of Technology. Copyright resides with the owner of the Archimedes Palimpsest, but digital images of the entire manuscript can be found at www.archimedespalimpsest.org.)

War between Rome and Syracuse unfortunately interrupted Archimedes's scientific life. In 213 B.C.E., during the Second Punic War, the Romans besieged the city. Hiero, its king and Archimedes's friend, asked the scientist for help in repulsing Roman attacks. Archimedes began to build remarkable devices that served as artillery. One weapon shot missiles to break up infantry attacks. Others threw huge masses of stones that fell on the enemy with incredible speed and noise. They tore gaping holes in the Roman lines and broke up attacks. For use against Roman warships he is said to have designed a machine with beams from which large claws dropped onto the hulls of enemy warships, hoisted them into the air, and dropped them back into the sea. Later Greek authors reported that he destroyed Roman ships with a series of polished mirrors that focused sunlight and caused the ships to catch fire. Modern experiments recreating Archimedes's weapons have found that the claw may have been workable, but the mirrors probably were not, as they required a ship to remain stationary for the fire to ignite. It is not certain whether his war machines were actually effective, but later people recounted tales that the Romans became so fearful that whenever they saw a bit of rope or a stick of timber projecting over one of the walls protecting Syracuse, they shouted, "There it is. Archimedes is trying some engine on us" and fled. After many months the Roman siege was successful, however, and Archimedes was killed by a Roman soldier.

QUESTIONS FOR ANALYSIS

1. How did Archimedes combine theoretical mathematics and practical issues in his work?
2. What applications do you see in the world around you of the devices Archimedes improved or invented, such as the lever, the pulley, and artillery?

ONLINE DOCUMENT PROJECT

What advances in technological warfare occurred during the Hellenistic period? Read accounts of the siege of Syracuse, and then complete a quiz and writing assignment based on the evidence and details from this chapter. *See inside front cover to learn more.*

of divine will; in their view, people could be happy only when living in accordance with nature. They stressed the unity of humans and the universe, stating that all people were obliged to help one another.

The Stoics' most lasting practical achievement was the creation of the concept of natural law. They concluded that as all people were kindred, partook of divine reason, and were in harmony with the universe, one natural law governed them all.

Hellenistic Science and Medicine

Hellenistic thinkers made advances in mathematics, astronomy, and mechanical design. The most notable of the Hellenistic astronomers was Aristarchus of Samos (ca. 310–230 B.C.E.). Aristarchus rightly concluded that the sun is far larger than the earth and that the stars are enormously distant from the earth. He also argued against Aristotle's view that the earth is the center of the universe, instead propounding the heliocentric theory—that the earth and planets revolve around the sun.

In geometry Euclid (YOO-kluhd) (fl. ca. 300 B.C.E.), a mathematician living in Alexandria, compiled a valuable textbook of existing knowledge. His *The Elements of Geometry* became the standard introduction to the subject.

The greatest thinker of the Hellenistic period was Archimedes (ahr-kuh-MEE-deez) (ca. 287–212 B.C.E.). A clever inventor, he devised new artillery for military purposes. In peacetime he created the water screw to draw water from a lower to a higher level. (See "Individuals in Society: Archimedes, Scientist and Inventor," page 138.) He also invented the compound pulley to lift heavy weights. His chief interest, however, lay in pure mathematics. He founded the science of hydrostatics (the study of fluids at rest) and discovered the principle that the weight of a solid floating in a liquid is equal to the weight of the liquid displaced by the solid.

Eratosthenes (ehr-uh-TOSS-thuh-neez) (285–ca. 204 B.C.E.), who was the librarian of the vast Ptolemaic royal library in Alexandria, used mathematics to further the geographical studies for which he is most famous. He concluded that the earth is a spherical globe and calculated the circumference of the earth geometrically with remarkable accuracy.

As the new artillery devised by Archimedes indicates, Hellenistic science was used for purposes of war as well as peace. Theories of mechanics were applied to build military machines. The catapult became the most widely used artillery piece. As the Assyrians had earlier, engineers built siege towers, large wooden structures that served as artillery platforms, and put them on wheels so that soldiers could roll them up to a town's walls. Generals added battering rams to bring down large portions of walls. If these new engines made warfare more efficient, they also added to the misery of the people, as war often directly involved the populations of cities. War and illness fed the need for medical advances, and doctors as well as scientists combined observation with theory during the Hellenistic period. Herophilus, who lived in the first half of the third century B.C.E., worked in Alexandria and studied the writings attributed to Hippocrates. He approached the study of medicine in a systematic, scientific fashion: he dissected dead bodies and measured what he observed. His students carried on his work, searching for the causes and nature of illness and pain.

> ## QUICK REVIEW

What connections can you make between political turmoil and cultural trends during the Hellenistic period?

CHAPTER SUMMARY

Greece's mountainous terrain encouraged the development of small, independent communities and political fragmentation. Sometime after 2000 B.C.E. two kingdoms—the Minoan on Crete and the Mycenaean on the mainland—did emerge, but these remained smaller than the great empires of Mesopotamia, India, and China. The fall of these kingdoms led to a period of disruption and decline known as the Greek Dark Age (ca. 1100–800 B.C.E.). However, Greek culture survived, and Greeks developed the independent city-state, known as the polis. Greeks also established colonies and traveled and traded as far east as the Black Sea and as far west as the Atlantic Ocean. Two poleis became especially powerful: Sparta, which created a military state in which men remained in the army most of their lives, and Athens, which created a democracy in which male citizens had a direct voice. In the classical period, between 500 B.C.E. and 338 B.C.E., Greeks engaged in war with the Persians and with one another, but they also created drama, philosophy, and magnificent art and architecture.

In the middle of the fourth century B.C.E. the Greek city-states were conquered by the Macedonians under King Philip II and his son Alexander. Alexander conquered the entire Persian Empire and founded new cities in which Greek and local populations mixed. His successors continued to build cities and colonies, which were centers of trade and spread Greek culture over a broad area, extend-

CHAPTER LOCATOR | How did the geography of Greece shape its earliest history? | What was the role of the polis in Greek society?

140   CHAPTER 5
THE GREEK EXPERIENCE

ing as far east as India. The mixing of peoples in the Hellenistic era influenced religion, philosophy, and science. New deities gained prominence, and many people turned to mystery religions that blended Greek and non-Greek elements as they offered followers secret knowledge and eternal life. Others turned to practical philosophies that provided advice on how to live a good life. Advances were made in technology, mathematics, science, and medicine, but these were applied primarily to military purposes, not to improving the way ordinary people lived and worked.

 CONNECTIONS The Greek world was largely conquered by the Romans, as you will learn in the following chapter, and the various Hellenistic monarchies became part of the Roman Empire. In cultural terms the lines of conquest were reversed: the Romans derived their alphabet from the Greek alphabet, though they changed the letters somewhat. Roman statuary was modeled on Greek and was often, in fact, made by Greek sculptors, who found ready customers among wealthy Romans. Furthermore, the major Roman gods and goddesses were largely the same as Greek ones, though they had different names. Although the Romans did not seem to have been particularly interested in the speculative philosophy of Socrates and Plato, they were drawn to the more practical philosophies of the Epicureans and Stoics. And like the Hellenistic Greeks, many Romans turned to mystery religions that offered secret knowledge and promised eternal life.

The influence of the ancient Greeks was not limited to the Romans, of course. As discussed in Chapter 3, art and thought in northern India was shaped by the blending of Greek and Buddhist traditions. And as you will see in Chapter 15, European thinkers and writers made conscious attempts to return to classical ideals in art, literature, and philosophy during the Renaissance. In America political leaders from the Revolutionary era on decided that important government buildings should be modeled on the Parthenon or other temples. In some ways, capitol buildings in the United States are good symbols of the legacy of Greece—gleaming ideals of harmony, freedom, democracy, and beauty that (as with all ideals) do not always correspond with realities.

ONLINE DOCUMENT PROJECT
Technological Warfare

What advances in technological warfare occurred during the Hellenistic period?

Read accounts of the siege of Syracuse, and then complete a quiz and writing assignment based on the evidence and details from this chapter. *See inside front cover to learn more.*

How did war influence Greece, and how did the arts, religion, and philosophy develop?

How did Alexander the Great's conquests shape society in the Hellenistic period?

How did religion, philosophy, and science develop in the Hellenistic world?

✔ LearningCurve
Check what you know.

141

CHAPTER 5 STUDY GUIDE

 STEP 1

GET STARTED ONLINE

 LearningCurve

Now that you've read the chapter, make it stick by completing the LearningCurve activity.

 STEP 2

EXPLAIN WHY IT MATTERS

Put your reading into practice. Identify each term below, and then explain why it matters in world history.

TERM	WHO OR WHAT & WHEN	WHY IT MATTERS
polis (p. 120)		
hoplites (p. 121)		
democracy (p. 121)		
oligarchy (p. 121)		
mystery religions (p. 128)		
Platonic ideals (p. 129)		
Hellenistic (p. 131)		
Hellenization (p. 133)		
Epicureanism (p. 137)		
Stoicism (p. 137)		

STEP 3

MOVE BEYOND THE BASICS

To demonstrate a more advanced understanding of Greek identity in the Hellenic and Hellenistic worlds, fill in the chart below with descriptions of key aspects of Hellenic Greece and the Hellenistic world. How did the Greek sense of identity change after Alexander's conquests?

	Government	Economy	Religion and Philosophy	Cultural Diversity and Exchange
Hellenic Greece				
The Hellenistic World				

PUT IT ALL TOGETHER

Now, take a step back and try to explain the big picture. Remember to use specific examples from the chapter in your answers.

THE ORIGINS AND EARLY DEVELOPMENT OF HELLENIC GREECE

► How did the polis embody key aspects of Greek society and culture? Is it fair to say that, in a sense, the polis was the essence of Greek civilization? Why or why not?

► Compare and contrast Sparta and Athens. To what extent do these two city-states represent different solutions to the same basic challenges?

THE CLASSICAL PERIOD

► What were the causes and consequences of the Peloponnesian War?

► How was Athens's emergence as an imperial power reflected in Athenian thought and culture?

THE HELLENISTIC WORLD

► Why did Alexander's empire split apart shortly after his death? What impact did this political fragmentation have on the development of the Hellenistic world?

► What characterized the relationship between Greeks and Easterners in the Hellenistic period? To what extent were Easterners "Hellenized"?

LOOKING BACK, LOOKING AHEAD

► Classical Greece was a period of almost constant warfare. With this in mind, compare and contrast classical Greece with earlier periods of endemic warfare in the Near East. What factors seem to have been conducive to peace in the ancient world? What conditions tended to produce war?

► How would you explain the enduring influence of Greek ideas and ideals? What examples of the continuing influence of Greek culture can you identify in the contemporary world?

> **IN YOUR OWN WORDS**

Imagine that you must give an oral report to the class answering the following question: **What unique contributions did the Greeks make to global culture?** What would be the most important points and why?

6

THE WORLD OF ROME

CA. 1000 B.C.E.–400 C.E.

> **How did the Romans build and control an empire that spanned the Mediterranean world?**
Chapter 6 examines the Roman Empire. With a republican government under the leadership of the Senate, the Romans conquered Italy, then the western Mediterranean basin, and then areas in the East that had been part of Alexander the Great's empire. The wars of conquest led, however, to serious problems that the Senate proved unable to handle. After a period of civil war that ended in 31 B.C.E., the emperor Augustus restored peace and expanded Roman power and law as far east as the Euphrates River. Later emperors extended Roman authority farther still, so that at its largest the Roman Empire stretched from England to Egypt and from Portugal to Persia.

LearningCurve
After reading the chapter, use LearningCurve to retain what you've read.

Woman from Pompeii This brightly painted fresco from a villa in Pompeii shows a young woman carrying a tray in a religious ritual. Pompeii was completely buried in ash in a volcanic explosion in 79 C.E., and excavations have revealed life in what was a vacation spot for wealthy Romans. (Detail of the Initiate, from the Catechism Scene, North Wall fresco/Villa dei Misteri, Pompeii/The Bridgeman Art Library)

> How did the Romans come to dominate Italy, and what political institutions did they create?

> How did Rome expand its power beyond Italy, and what were the effects of this expansion?

> What was life like in Rome, and what was it like in the provinces?

> What was Christianity, and how did it affect life in the Roman Empire?

> How did the emperors respond to political, economic, and religious issues in the third and fourth centuries?

How did the Romans come to dominate Italy, and what political institutions did they create?

Sarcophagus of Seianti Hanunia Tlesnasa

The woman portrayed on this lavish sarcophagus is the wealthy Etruscan Seianti Hanunia Tlesnasa. Although she is portrayed as a lovely young woman, analysis of the teeth on the body indicate that she was about fifty when she died. The influence of Hellenistic Greek art on Etruscan art is apparent in almost every feature of the sarcophagus. (© The Trustees of the British Museum/Art Resource, NY)

The colonies established by Greek poleis (city-states) in the Hellenic era included a number along the coast of southern Italy and Sicily. So many Greek settlers came to this area that it later became known as Magna Graecia—Greater Greece. These Greek colonies transmitted much of their culture to people who lived farther north in the Italian peninsula. These included the Etruscans (ih-TRUHS-kuhns), who built the first cities north of Magna Graecia, and then the Romans, who eventually came to dominate the peninsula. In addition to allying with conquered peoples and granting them citizenship, the Romans established a republic ruled by a Senate. However, social conflicts over the rights to power eventually erupted and had to be resolved.

> Major Periods of Roman History:

- The monarchical period (753 B.C.E.–509 B.C.E.) in which Rome was ruled by kings
- The republic (509 B.C.E.–27 B.C.E.) in which Rome was ruled by the Senate
- The empire (27 B.C.E. to 476 C.E.) in which Roman territories were ruled by an emperor

CHAPTER LOCATOR | **How did the Romans dominate Italy, and what political institutions did they create?** | How did Rome expand its power beyond Italy, and what were the effects of this expansion?

CHAPTER 6
146 THE WORLD OF ROME

753 B.C.E.
Traditional founding of the city of Rome

509 B.C.E.
Traditional date of the establishment of the Roman Republic

451–449 B.C.E.
Laws of the Twelve Tables written and issued

ca. 265 B.C.E.
Romans control most of Italy

264–241 B.C.E.; 218–201 B.C.E.;
149–146 B.C.E.
Punic Wars

53–31 B.C.E.
Civil wars among rival claimants to power

44 B.C.E.
Assassination of Julius Caesar

31 B.C.E.
Octavian (Augustus) defeats Antony and Cleopatra

27 B.C.E.
Senate grants Octavian the title "Augustus"; date marks the beginning of the Roman Empire

27 B.C.E.–68 C.E.
Julio-Claudian emperors; expansion into northern and western Europe

ca. 3 B.C.E.–29 C.E.
Life of Jesus

69–96 C.E.
Flavian emperors; restoration of order after civil wars

96–192 C.E.
Antonine emperors; prosperity and the height of the pax Romana

235–284 C.E.
Third-century crisis; civil war; invasions; economic decline

284–337 C.E.
Diocletian and Constantine attempt to reconstruct the empire

313 C.E.
Emperor Constantine issues Edict of Milan, allowing practice of all religions in the Roman Empire

380 C.E.
Emperor Theodosius makes Christianity the official religion of the empire

476 C.E.
Odoacer deposes the last Roman emperor in the West

The Etruscans

The culture that is now called Etruscan developed in north-central Italy about 800 B.C.E. The Etruscans most likely originated in Turkey or elsewhere in southwest Asia, although when they migrated to Italy is not clear. The Etruscans spoke a language that was very different from Greek and Latin, but they adopted the Greek alphabet to write their language.

The Etruscans established permanent settlements that evolved into cities resembling the Greek city-states (see page 120). They spread their influence over the surrounding countryside, which they farmed and mined for its rich mineral resources. From an early period the Etruscans began to trade natural products, especially iron, with their Greek neighbors to the south and with other peoples throughout the Mediterranean in exchange for luxury goods. Etruscan cities appear to have been organized in leagues, and beginning about 750 B.C.E. the Etruscans expanded southward into central Italy through military actions and through the establishment of colony cities. In the process they encountered a small collection of villages subsequently called Rome.

The Etruscans,
ca. 500 B.C.E.

What was life like in Rome, and what was it like in the provinces?

What was Christianity, and how did it affect life in the Roman Empire?

How did emperors respond to political and religious issues?

 LearningCurve
Check what you know.

The Founding of Rome

Archaeological evidence indicates that the ancestors of the Romans began to settle on the hills east of the Tiber during the early Iron Age, around 1000 B.C.E. to 800 B.C.E. Later Romans told a number of stories about the founding of Rome. These mix legend and history, but they illustrate the traditional ethics, morals, and ideals of Rome.

According to legend, Romulus and Remus founded the city of Rome, an event later Roman authors dated precisely to 753 B.C.E. These twin brothers were the sons of the war god Mars, and their mother, Rhea Silvia, was a descendant of Aeneas, a brave and pious Trojan who left Troy after it was destroyed by the Greeks in the Trojan War. The brothers, who were left to die by a jealous uncle, were raised by a female wolf. When they were grown they decided to build a city, but quarreled over its location; Romulus killed Remus and named the city after himself. He also established a council of advisers later called the Senate. He and his mostly male followers expanded their power over neighboring peoples, in part by abducting and marrying their women. The women then arranged a peace by throwing themselves between their brothers and their husbands, convincing them that killing kin would make the men cursed. The Romans, favored by the gods, continued their rise to power. This founding myth ascribes positive traits to the Romans: they are descended from gods and heroes, can thrive in wild and tough settings, will defend their boundaries at all costs, and mix with other peoples rather than simply conquering them. Also, the story portrays women who were ancestors of Rome as virtuous and brave.

Later Roman historians continued the story by describing a series of kings after Romulus, each elected by the Senate. According to tradition, the last three kings were Etruscan, and another tale about female virtue was told to explain why the Etruscan kings were overthrown. In this story, the son of King Tarquin, the Etruscan king who ruled Rome, raped Lucretia, a virtuous Roman wife, in her own home. She demanded that her husband and father seek vengeance and then committed suicide in front of them. Her father and husband and the other Roman nobles swore to avenge Lucretia's death by throwing out the Etruscan kings, and they did. The Romans generally accepted this story as historical fact and dated the expulsion of the Etruscan kings to 509 B.C.E. They thus saw this year as marking the end of the monarchical period and the dawn of the republic, which had come about because of a wronged woman and her demands.

Most historians today view the idea that Etruscan kings ruled the city of Rome as legendary, but they stress the influence of the Etruscans on Rome. The Etruscans transformed Rome into a real city with walls, temples, a drainage system, and other urban structures. The Romans adopted the Etruscan alphabet, which the Etruscans themselves had adopted from the Greeks. Even the toga came from the Etruscans, as did gladiatorial combat honoring the dead. In engineering and architecture the Romans adopted some design elements and the basic plan of their temples, along with paved roads, from the Etruscans.

In this early period the city of Rome does appear to have been ruled by kings. A hereditary aristocracy also developed which advised the kings and may have played a role in choosing them. And sometime in the sixth century B.C.E. a group of aristocrats revolted against these kings and established a government in which the main institution of power would be the Senate, an assembly of aristocrats, rather than a single monarch. Executive power was in the hands of leaders called

Senate

► The assembly that was the main institution of power in the Roman Republic, originally composed only of aristocrats.

CHAPTER LOCATOR | How did the Romans dominate Italy, and what political institutions did they create? | How did Rome expand its power beyond Italy, and what were the effects of this expansion?

148   CHAPTER 6   THE WORLD OF ROME

consuls, but there were always two of them and they were elected for one-year terms only, not for life. Rome thereby became a republic, not a monarchy.

consuls
▶ Primary executives in the Roman Republic, elected for one-year terms, who commanded the army in battle, administered state business, and supervised financial affairs.

The Roman Conquest of Italy

In the years following the establishment of the republic, the Romans fought numerous wars with their neighbors on the Italian peninsula. The Roman army was made up primarily of citizens of Rome, who were organized for military campaigns into legions. War also involved diplomacy, at which the Romans became masters.

In 387 B.C.E. the Romans suffered a major setback when the Celts—or Gauls, as the Romans called them—invaded the Italian peninsula from the north and sacked the city of Rome. The Celts agreed to abandon Rome in return for a thousand pounds of gold. In the century that followed, the Romans rebuilt their city and recouped their losses. They brought Latium and their Latin allies fully under their control and conquered Etruria. In a series of bitter wars the Romans also subdued southern Italy and then turned north. Their superior military institutions, organization, and manpower allowed them to conquer or bring under their influence most of Italy by about 265 B.C.E. (Map 6.1).

As they expanded their territory, the Romans spread their religious traditions throughout Italy, blending them with local beliefs and practices. Religion for the Romans was largely a matter of honoring the state and the family. The main goal of religion was to secure the peace of the gods and to harness divine power for public and private enterprises. Religious rituals were an important way of expressing common values, which for Romans meant those evident in their foundation myths: bravery, morality, seriousness, family, and home. Victorious generals made sure to honor the gods of people they had conquered and by doing so transformed them into gods they could also call on for assistance in their future campaigns. As the Romans conquered the cities of Magna Graecia, the Greek deities were absorbed into the Roman pantheon.

Once they had conquered an area, the Romans did what the Persians had earlier done to help cement their new territory: they built roads. Roman roads facilitated the flow of communication, trade, and armies from the capital to outlying areas.

In politics the Romans shared full Roman citizenship with many of their oldest allies, particularly the inhabitants of the cities of Latium. In other instances they granted citizenship without the franchise, that is, without the right to vote or hold Roman office. These allies were subject to Roman taxes and calls for military service but ran their own local affairs.

The Roman State

Along with citizenship, the republican government was another important institution of Roman political life. In the early republic, social divisions determined the shape of politics. Political power was in the hands of a hereditary aristocracy—the **patricians**, whose privileged legal status was determined by their birth as members of certain families. The common people of Rome, the **plebeians** (plih-BEE-uhns), were free citizens with a voice in politics, but they had few of the patricians' political and social advantages. While some plebeian merchants rivaled the patricians in wealth, most plebeians were poor artisans, small farmers, and landless urban dwellers.

patricians
▶ The Roman hereditary aristocracy, who held most of the political power in the republic.

plebeians
▶ The common people of Rome, who were free but had few of the patricians' advantages.

What was life like in Rome, and what was it like in the provinces?

What was Christianity, and how did it affect life in the Roman Empire?

How did emperors respond to political and religious issues?

✓ LearningCurve
Check what you know.

149

MAP 6.1 ■ Roman Italy and the City of Rome, ca. 218 B.C.E.

As Rome expanded, it built roads linking major cities and offered various degrees of citizenship to the territories it conquered or with which it made alliances. The territories outlined in green that are separate from the Italian peninsula were added by 218 B.C.E., largely as a result of the Punic Wars.

The Romans created several assemblies through which men elected high officials and passed ordinances. The most important of these was the Senate. During the republic, the Senate advised the consuls and other officials about military and political matters and handled government finances. Because the Senate sat year after year with the same members, while the consuls changed annually, it provided stability, and its advice came to have the force of law. Another responsibility of the Senate was to handle relations between Rome and other powers.

CHAPTER LOCATOR | **How did the Romans dominate Italy, and what political institutions did they create?** | How did Rome expand its power beyond Italy, and what were the effects of this expansion?

The highest officials of the republic were the two consuls, positions initially open only to patrician men. The consuls commanded the army in battle, administered state business, and supervised financial affairs. When the consuls were away from Rome, praetors (PREE-tuhrz) could act in their place. After the age of overseas conquests (see below), the Romans divided their lands in the Mediterranean into provinces governed by ex-consuls and ex-praetors.

A lasting achievement of the Romans was their development of law. Roman civil law, the *ius civile*, consisted of statutes, customs, and forms of procedure that regulated the lives of citizens. As the Romans came into more frequent contact with foreigners, the praetors applied a broader *ius gentium*, the "law of the peoples," to such matters as peace treaties, the treatment of prisoners of war, and the exchange of diplomats. In the ius gentium, all sides were to be treated the same regardless of their nationality. By the late republic, Roman jurists had widened this still further into the concept of *ius naturale*, "natural law" based in part on Stoic beliefs (see page 137). Natural law, according to these thinkers, is made up of rules that govern human behavior that come from applying reason rather than customs or traditions, and so apply to all societies.

Social Conflict in Rome

Inequality between plebeians and patricians led to a conflict known as the Struggle of the Orders. In this conflict the plebeians sought to increase their power by taking advantage of the fact that Rome's survival depended on its army, which needed plebeians to fill the ranks of the infantry. According to tradition, in 494 B.C.E. the plebeians literally walked out of Rome and refused to serve in the army. Their general strike worked, and the patricians made important concessions. They allowed the plebeians to elect their own officials, the tribunes, who could bring plebeian grievances to the Senate for resolution and could also veto the decisions of the consuls.

The law itself was the plebeians' primary target. Only the patricians knew what the law was, and only they could argue cases in court. All too often they used the law for their own benefit. The plebeians wanted the law codified and published. After much struggle, in 449 B.C.E. the patricians surrendered their legal monopoly and codified and published the Laws of the Twelve Tables. The patricians also made legal procedures public so that plebeians could argue cases in court. Several years later the patricians passed a law that for the first time allowed patricians and plebeians to marry one another.

After a ten-year battle, the Licinian-Sextian laws passed in 367 B.C.E. gave wealthy plebeians access to all the offices of Rome, including the right to hold one of the two consulships. Once plebeians could hold the consulship, they could also sit in the Senate and advise on policy. Though decisive, this victory did not automatically end the Struggle of the Orders. That happened only in 287 B.C.E. with the passage of the *lex Hortensia*, which gave the resolutions of the *concilium plebis*, the plebeian assembly, the force of law for patricians and plebeians alike.

QUICK REVIEW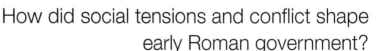

How did social tensions and conflict shape
early Roman government?

What was life like in Rome, and what was it like in the provinces?

What was Christianity, and how did it affect life in the Roman Empire?

How did emperors respond to political and religious issues?

 LearningCurve
Check what you know.

How did Rome expand its power beyond Italy, and what were the effects of this expansion?

Two Triremes Race

In this fresco painting from the temple of Isis in Pompeii, two triremes — narrow warships powered by several banks of long oars — race in what was most likely a festival celebrating the goddess. Greeks, Carthaginians, and Romans all used triremes, which had bronze front pieces designed to smash into enemy ships. The one hundred to two hundred oarsmen had to row in time to achieve the necessary speed, which took long practice, so this religious celebration also served a military purpose. (© Ministero per i Beni le Attivita Culturali — Soprintendenza archeologia de Napoli/ Scala/Art Resource, NY)

As the republican government was developing, Roman territory continued to expand. The Romans conquered lands all around the Mediterranean, bringing them unheard-of power and wealth. As a result, many Romans became more cosmopolitan and comfortable, and they were especially influenced by the culture of one conquered land: Greece. Yet social unrest also came in the wake of the wars, opening unprecedented opportunities for ambitious generals who wanted to rule Rome like an empire. A series of civil wars ensued, wars which republican government did not survive.

Overseas Conquests and the Punic Wars, 264–133 B.C.E.

The Romans did not map out grandiose strategies to conquer the world. Rather they responded to situations as they arose. This meant that they sought to eliminate any state they saw as a military threat.

Their presence in southern Italy brought the Romans to the island of Sicily, where they confronted another great power in the western Mediterranean, Carthage (CAHR-thij). The city of Carthage had been founded by Phoenicians as a trading colony in the eighth century B.C.E. (see page 50). By the fourth century

B.C.E. the Carthaginians began to expand their holdings. At the end of a long string of wars, the Carthaginians had created a mercantile empire that stretched from western Sicily to beyond Gibraltar.

The conflicting ambitions of the Romans and Carthaginians led to the first of the three Punic Wars. During the course of the first war, which lasted from 264 B.C.E. to 241 B.C.E., Rome built a navy and defeated Carthage in a series of sea battles. Sicily became Rome's first province, but despite a peace treaty, the conflict was not over.

Punic Wars

▶ A series of three wars between Rome and Carthage in which Rome emerged the victor.

Carthaginian armies moved into Spain, where Rome was also claiming territory. The brilliant Carthaginian general Hannibal (ca. 247–183 B.C.E.) marched an army of tens of thousands of troops from Spain across what is now France and over the Alps into Italy, beginning the Second Punic (PYOO-nik) War (218–201 B.C.E.). Hannibal won three major victories, including a devastating blow at Cannae in southeastern Italy in 216 B.C.E. He then spread devastation throughout Italy. Yet Hannibal was not able to win areas near Rome in central Italy.

The Roman general Scipio Africanus (ca. 236–ca. 183 B.C.E.) took Spain from the Carthaginians and then struck directly at Carthage itself, prompting the Carthaginians to recall Hannibal from Italy to defend the homeland. In 202 B.C.E., near the town of Zama, Scipio defeated Hannibal in one of the world's truly decisive battles. Scipio's victory meant that the world of the western Mediterranean would henceforth be Roman.

The Second Punic War contained the seeds of still other wars. Unabated fear of Carthage led to the Third Punic War (149–146 B.C.E.), a needless, unjust, and savage conflict that ended with obliteration of the city of Carthage itself.

The Carthaginian Empire and the Roman Republic, 264 B.C.E.

After the Second Punic War, the Romans turned east. Roman victory in Macedonia turned Antigonid Macedonia into a Roman province. Then they moved farther east and defeated the Seleucid monarchy. In 133 B.C.E. the king of Pergamum in Asia Minor willed his kingdom to Rome when he died. The Ptolemies of Egypt retained formal control of their kingdom, but they obeyed Roman wishes in terms of trade policy. Declaring the Mediterranean *mare nostrum*, "our sea," the Romans began to create a political and administrative machinery to hold the Mediterranean together under a system of provinces ruled by governors sent from Rome.

New Influences and Old Values in Roman Culture

With the conquest of the Mediterranean world, Rome became a great city. The spoils of war went to build theaters, stadiums, and other places of amusement, and Romans and Italian townspeople began to spend more of their time in leisure pursuits. This new urban culture reflected Hellenistic influences. Romans developed a liking for Greek literature and art, and it became common for an educated Roman to speak both Latin and Greek.

What was life like in Rome, and what was it like in the provinces? | What was Christianity, and how did it affect life in the Roman Empire? | How did emperors respond to political and religious issues? | ☑ LearningCurve Check what you know.

The Greek custom of bathing also gained popularity in the Roman world. Increasingly, Romans built large public buildings containing pools supplied by intricate systems of aqueducts. These structures were more than just places to bathe. Baths included gymnasia where men exercised, snack bars and halls where people chatted and read, and even libraries and lecture halls. Women had opportunities to bathe, generally in separate facilities or at separate times, and both women and men went to the baths to see and be seen.

New customs did not change the core Roman social structures. The male head of the household was called the **paterfamilias**, and he had great power over his children. Fathers had the power to decide how family resources should be spent, and sons did not inherit until after their fathers had died. Women could inherit and own property, though they generally received a smaller portion of any family inheritance than their brothers. Very young children were under their mother's care, and most children learned the skills they needed from their own parents. For children from wealthier urban families, opportunities for formal education increased in the late republic. Boys and girls might be educated in their homes by tutors, and boys also might go to a school, paid for by their parents.

An influx of slaves from Rome's conquests provided labor for the fields, mines, and cities. To the Romans slavery was a misfortune that befell some people, but it did not entail any racial theories. For loyal slaves the Romans always held out the possibility of freedom, and manumission—the freeing of individual slaves by their masters—became common. Nonetheless, slaves rebelled from time to time in large-scale revolts put down by Roman armies.

Membership in a family did not end with death, as the spirits of the family's ancestors were understood to remain with the family. They and other gods regarded as protectors of the household were represented by small statues that stood in a special cupboard, were honored at family celebrations, and were taken with the family when they moved.

The Late Republic and the Rise of Augustus, 133–27 B.C.E.

The wars of conquest eventually created serious political problems for the Romans. When the soldiers returned home, they found their farms practically in ruins. Many were forced to sell their land to ready buyers who had grown rich from the wars. These wealthy men created huge estates called latifundia. Now landless, veterans moved to the cities, especially Rome, but could not find work. These developments not only created unrest in the city but also threatened Rome's army by reducing its ranks, because landless men, even if they were Romans and lived in Rome, were forbidden to serve in the Roman army. The landless veterans found a leader in Tiberius Gracchus (163–133 B.C.E.), an aristocrat who was appalled by the situation. He proposed dividing public land among the poor. But a group of wealthy senators murdered him, launching a long era of political violence that would destroy the republic. Still, Tiberius's brother Gaius Gracchus (153–121 B.C.E.) passed a law providing the urban poor with cheap grain and urged practical reforms. Once again senators tried to stem the tide of reform by murdering him.

The next reformer, Gaius Marius (ca. 157–86 B.C.E.), recruited landless men into the army to put down a rebel king in Africa. He promised them land for their service. But after his victory, the Senate refused to honor his promise. From then

paterfamilias

▶ The oldest dominant male of the family, who held great power over the lives of family members.

CHAPTER LOCATOR | How did the Romans dominate Italy, and what political institutions did they create? | How did Rome expand its power beyond Italy, and what were the effects of this expansion?

on, Roman soldiers looked to their commanders, not to the Senate or the state, to protect their interests. Rome was also dividing into two political factions, both of which wanted political power. Both factions named individuals as supreme military commander and each led Roman troops against an external enemy but also against each other. One of these generals, Sulla, gained power in Rome, and in 81 B.C.E. the Senate made him dictator, an official office in the Roman Republic given to a man who was granted absolute power temporarily to handle emergencies such as war. Dictators were supposed to step down after six months, but Sulla held this position for nine years, and after that it was too late to restore the republican constitution.

The history of the late republic is the story of power struggles among many famous Roman figures against a background of unrest at home and military campaigns abroad. Pompey (PAHM-pee) used military victories in Spain to force the Senate to allow him to run for consul. In 59 B.C.E. he was joined in a political alliance called the First Triumvirate by Crassus, another ambitious politician and the wealthiest man in Rome, and by Julius Caesar (100–44 B.C.E.). Recognizing that military success led to power, Caesar led his troops to victory in Spain and Gaul, modern France. The First Triumvirate fell apart after Crassus was killed in battle in 53 B.C.E. while trying to conquer Parthia, leaving Caesar and Pompey in competition with each other for power. The result was civil war. The Ptolemaic rulers of Egypt became mixed up in this war, particularly Cleopatra VII, who allied herself with Caesar and had a son by him. (See "Individuals in Society: Queen Cleopatra," page 156.) Caesar emerged victorious, and he began to make a number of legal and economic reforms, acting on his own authority, though often with the approval of the Senate, which he packed with his supporters. He issued laws about debt, the collection of taxes, and the distribution of grain and land. Roman allies in Italy were to have full citizenship. He founded new colonies, which were to be populated by veterans and the poor.

Caesar was wildly popular with most people in Rome, but some senators opposed his rise to what was becoming absolute power. In 44 B.C.E. a group of conspirators assassinated him and set off another round of civil war. His grandnephew, the eighteen-year-old Octavian (63 B.C.E.–14 C.E.), joined with two of Caesar's followers, Marc Antony and Lepidus, in the Second Triumvirate. After defeating Caesar's murderers, they had a falling-out. Octavian forced Lepidus out of office and waged war against Antony, who had now also become allied with Cleopatra. In 31 B.C.E. Octavian defeated the combined forces of Antony and Cleopatra at the Battle of Actium in Greece. His victory ended the age of civil war.

The Successes of Augustus

After Augustus ended the civil wars, he faced the monumental problems of reconstruction. He had to rebuild effective government, pay his army for its services, care for the welfare of the provinces, and address the danger of various groups on Rome's frontiers. Augustus was highly successful in meeting these challenges.

Augustus claimed that he was restoring the republic, but he was actually transforming the government into one in which all power was held by a single ruler. Augustus fit his own position into the republican constitution not by creating a new office for himself but by gradually taking over many of the offices that traditionally had been held by separate people.

Augustus as Imperator

In this marble statue, found in the villa of Augustus's widow, Augustus is dressed in a military uniform and in a pose usually used to show leaders addressing their troops. This emphasizes his role as imperator, the head of the army. The figures on his breastplate show various peoples the Romans had defeated or with whom they had made treaties, along with assorted deities. Although Augustus did not declare himself a god — as later Roman emperors would — this statue shows him barefoot, just as gods and heroes were in classical Greek statuary, and accompanied by Cupid riding a dolphin, both symbols of the goddess Venus, whom he claimed as an ancestor. (Scala/Art Resource, NY)

What was life like in Rome, and what was it like in the provinces?

What was Christianity, and how did it affect life in the Roman Empire?

How did emperors respond to political and religious issues?

☑ LearningCurve
Check what you know.

Cleopatra VII (69–30 B.C.E.) was a Ptolemy, a member of the dynasty of Hellenistic rulers of Egypt who had established power in the third century B.C.E. Although she was a Greek, she was passionately devoted to her Egyptian subjects and was the first in her dynasty who could speak Egyptian as well as Greek. Just as ancient pharaohs had linked themselves with the gods, she had herself portrayed as the goddess Isis and may have seen herself as a reincarnation of Isis (see page 44).

At the same time that civil war was raging in the late Roman Republic, Cleopatra and her brother Ptolemy XIII were in a dispute over who would be supreme ruler in Egypt. Julius Caesar captured the Egyptian capital of Alexandria, Cleopatra arranged to meet him, and the two became lovers, although Cleopatra was much younger and Caesar was married. The two apparently had a son, Caesarion, and Caesar's army defeated Ptolemy's army, ending the power struggle. In 46 B.C.E. Cleopatra arrived in Rome, where Caesar put up a statue of her as Isis in one of the city's temples. The Romans hated her because they saw her as a decadent Eastern queen and a threat to what were considered traditional Roman values.

After Caesar's assassination, Cleopatra returned to Alexandria. There she became involved in the continuing Roman civil war that now pitted Octavian, Caesar's heir, against Marc Antony, who commanded the Roman army in the East. When Antony visited Alexandria in 41 B.C.E. he met Cleopatra, and though he was already married to Octavian's sister, he became her lover. He abandoned (and later divorced) his Roman wife, married Cleopatra in 37 B.C.E., and changed his will to favor his children by Cleopatra. Antony's wedding present to Cleopatra was a huge grant of territory, much of it Roman, that greatly increased her power and that of all her children, including Caesarion. Antony also declared Caesarion to be Julius Caesar's rightful heir.

Octavian used the wedding gift as the reason to declare Antony a traitor. He and other Roman leaders described Antony as a romantic fool captivated by the seductive Cleopatra. Roman troops turned against Antony and joined with Octavian, and at the Battle of Actium in 31 B.C.E. Octavian defeated the army and navy of Antony and Cleopatra. Antony committed suicide, as did Cleopatra shortly afterward. Octavian ordered the teenage Caesarion killed, but the young children of Antony and Cleopatra were allowed to go back to Rome, where they were raised by Antony's widow. In another consequence of Octavian's victory, Egypt became a Roman province.

Roman sources are viciously hostile to Cleopatra, and she became the model of the alluring woman

The only portraits of Cleopatra that date from her own lifetime are on the coins that she issued. This one, made at the mint of Alexandria, shows her as quite plain, reinforcing the point made by Cicero that her attractiveness was based more on intelligence and wit than physical beauty. The reverse of the coin shows an eagle, a symbol of rule. (© The Trustees of the British Museum/Art Resource, NY)

whose sexual attraction led men to their doom. Stories about her beauty, sophistication, lavish spending, desire for power, and ruthlessness abounded and were retold for centuries. The most dramatic story was that she committed suicide through the bite of a poisonous snake, which may have been true and which has been the subject of countless paintings. Her tumultuous relationships with Caesar and Antony have been portrayed in plays, novels, movies, and television programs.

QUESTIONS FOR ANALYSIS

1. How did Cleopatra benefit from her relationships with Caesar and Antony? How did they benefit from their relationships with her?
2. How did ideas about gender and Roman suspicion of the more sophisticated Greek culture combine to shape Cleopatra's fate and the way she is remembered?
3. "Individuals in Society: Hatshepsut and Nefertiti" in Chapter 2 (see page 49) also focuses on leading female figures in Egypt, but these two women lived more than a thousand years before Cleopatra. How would you compare their situation with hers?

LaunchPad

ONLINE DOCUMENT PROJECT

What do Roman depictions of Cleopatra reveal about the attitudes and values of her time? Explore Roman accounts of Cleopatra to see what light they shed on political, social, and cultural values in the late republic and early empire, and then complete a quiz and writing assignment based on the evidence and details from this chapter. *See inside front cover to learn more.*

The Senate named him often as both consul and tribune. He was also named imperator (ihm-puh-RAH-tuhr), a title given to victorious commanders, and held control of the army, which he made a permanent standing organization. Furthermore, recognizing the importance of religion, he had himself named *pontifex maximus*, or chief priest. The Senate also gave him the honorary title *princeps civitatis*, "first citizen of the state."

Considering what had happened to Julius Caesar, Augustus wisely wielded all this power in the background, and his period of rule is officially called the "principate." The Senate continued to exist as a court of law and deliberative body. Without specifically saying so, however, Augustus created the office of emperor. In other reforms, Augustus made provincial administration more orderly and improved its functioning. He further professionalized the army and awarded grants of land in the frontier provinces to veterans. He encouraged local self-government and the development of cities. As a spiritual bond between the provinces and Rome, Augustus encouraged the cult of *Roma et Augustus* (Rome and Augustus) as the guardian of the state. In addition, he had temples, stadiums, marketplaces, and public buildings constructed in Rome and other cities.

In the social realm, Augustus promoted marriage and childbearing through legal changes that released free women and freedwomen (female slaves who had been freed) from male guardianship if they had given birth to a certain number of

---

Ara Pacis

In the middle years of Augustus's reign, the Roman Senate ordered a huge altar, the Ara Pacis, built to honor him and the peace he had brought to the empire. This was decorated with life-size reliefs of Augustus and members of his family, prominent Romans, and other people and deities. One side, shown here, depicts a goddess figure, most likely the goddess Peace herself, with twin babies on her lap, flanked by nymphs representing land and sea, and surrounded by plants and animals. (Scala/Art Resource, NY)

> PICTURING THE PAST

ANALYZING THE IMAGE: What do the elements depicted here most likely symbolize?

CONNECTIONS: The Ara Pacis was a work of public art designed to commemorate the deeds of Augustus. Why might the Senate have commissioned such a work? Can you think of contemporary parallels?

| What was life like in Rome, and what was it like in the provinces? | What was Christianity, and how did it affect life in the Roman Empire? | How did emperors respond to political and religious issues? | ✔ LearningCurve Check what you know. |

children. Men and women who were unmarried or had no children were restricted in the inheritance of property.

Aside from addressing legal issues and matters of state, Augustus actively encouraged poets and writers. For this reason the period of his rule is known as the "golden age" of Latin literature. Roman poets and prose writers celebrated human accomplishments in works that were highly polished, elegant in style, and intellectual in conception.

Rome's greatest poet was Virgil (70–19 B.C.E.), whose masterpiece is the *Aeneid* (uh-NEE-id), an epic poem that is the Latin equivalent of the Greek *Iliad* and *Odyssey* (see page 119). Virgil's account of the founding of Rome and the early years of the city gave final form to the legend of Aeneas, the Trojan hero (and ancestor of Romulus and Remus; see page 149) who escaped to Italy at the fall of Troy.

One of the most significant aspects of Augustus's reign was Roman expansion into northern and western Europe (Map 6.2). Augustus completed the conquest of Spain, founded twelve new towns in Gaul, and saw that the Roman road system linked new settlements with one another and with Italy. After hard fighting, he made the Rhine River the Roman frontier in Germania (Germany). Meanwhile, generals conquered areas as far as the Danube River, and Roman legions penetrated the areas of modern Austria, southern Bavaria, and western Hungary. The regions of modern Serbia, Bulgaria, and Romania also fell. Within this area the legionaries built fortified camps. Roads linked these camps with one another, and settlements grew up around the camps, eventually becoming towns. Traders began to frequent the frontier and to do business with the people who lived there; as a result, for the first time, central and northern Europe came into direct and continuous contact with Mediterranean culture.

Romans did not force their culture on native people in Roman territories. However, just as earlier ambitious people in the Hellenistic world knew that the surest path to political and social advancement lay in embracing Greek culture and learning to speak Greek (see page 133), those determined to get ahead now learned Latin and adopted aspects of Roman culture.

CHAPTER LOCATOR | How did the Romans dominate Italy, and what political institutions did they create? | **How did Rome expand its power beyond Italy, and what were the effects of this expansion?**

CHAPTER 6
158   THE WORLD OF ROME

Modern place names of Roman cities

Roman name	Modern name
Aquincum	Budapest
Colonia Claudia Agrippinensis	Cologne
Corduba	Córdoba
Eburacum	York
Londinium	London
Lugdunum	Lyons
Lutetia Parisiorum	Paris
Massilia	Marseilles
Singidunum	Belgrade
Vindobona	Vienna

Roman territory

- At outset of Punic Wars, 264 B.C.E.
- Added by death of Tiberius Gracchus, 133 B.C.E.
- Added by death of Julius Caesar, 44 B.C.E.
- Added by death of Augustus, 14 C.E.
- Added by death of Hadrian, 138 C.E.
- Territory gained and lost, with dates held
- Parthian Empire, ca. 200 C.E.
- — Principal land trade route

MAP 6.2 ■ Roman Expansion, 262 B.C.E.–180 C.E.

Rome expanded in all directions, eventually controlling every shore of the Mediterranean and vast amounts of land.

> MAPPING THE PAST

ANALYZING THE MAP: How would you summarize the pattern of Roman expansion — that is, which areas were conquered first and which later? How long was Rome able to hold on to territories at the outermost boundaries of its empire?

CONNECTIONS: Many of today's major cities in these areas were founded as Roman colonies. Why do you think so many of these cities were founded along the northern border of Roman territory?

QUICK REVIEW

Why did military commanders grow increasingly powerful in Late Republican Rome?

| What was life like in Rome, and what was it like in the provinces? | What was Christianity, and how did it affect life in the Roman Empire? | How did emperors respond to political and religious issues? | ✓ LearningCurve Check what you know. |

What was life like in Rome, and what was it like in the provinces?

Roman Architecture

These three structures demonstrate the beauty and utility of Roman architecture. The Coliseum in Rome (below), a sports arena that could seat fifty thousand spectators, built between 70 C.E. and 80 C.E., was the site of gladiatorial games, animal spectacles, and executions. The Pantheon in Rome (right), a temple dedicated to all the gods, was built in its present form about 130 C.E., after earlier temples on the site had burned down. Its dome, 140 feet in diameter, remains the largest unreinforced concrete dome in the world. Romans also used concrete for more everyday purposes. The Pont du Gard at Nîmes in France (above) is a bridge over a river that carried an aqueduct supplying millions of gallons of water per day to the Roman city of Nîmes in Gaul; the water flowed in a channel at the very top. Although this bridge was built largely without mortar or concrete, many Roman aqueducts and bridges relied on concrete and sometimes iron rods for their strength.

(Pont du Gard: © Vanni Archive/Art Resource, NY; Pantheon: Gianni Dagli Orti/The Art Archive at Art Resource, NY; Coliseum: Scala/Art Resource, NY)

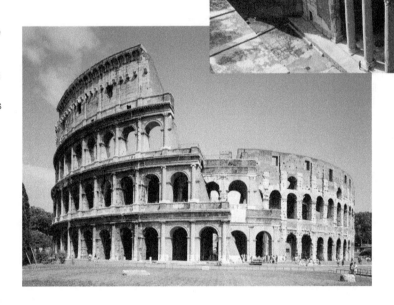

pax Romana
▶ The "Roman peace," a period during the first and second centuries C.E. of political stability and relative peace.

In the late eighteenth century the English historian Edward Gibbon dubbed the stability and relative peace within the empire that Augustus created the **pax Romana**, the "Roman peace," which he saw as lasting about two hundred years. During this time the growing city of Rome saw great improvements, and trade and production flourished in the provinces. Rome also expanded eastward and came into indirect contact with China.

CHAPTER LOCATOR | How did the Romans dominate Italy, and what political institutions did they create? | How did Rome expand its power beyond Italy, and what were the effects of this expansion?

160 CHAPTER 6
THE WORLD OF ROME

Political and Military Changes in the Empire

For fifty years after Augustus's death in 14 C.E. the dynasty that he established—known as the Julio-Claudians because all were members of the Julian and Claudian clans—provided the emperors of Rome. Some of the Julio-Claudians, such as Tiberius and Claudius, were sound rulers and created a bureaucracy of able administrators to help them govern. Others, including Caligula and Nero, were weak and frivolous.

In 68 C.E. Nero's inept rule led to military rebellion and widespread disruption. Two years later Vespasian (r. 69–79 C.E.), who established the Flavian dynasty, restored order. He also turned Augustus's principate into a hereditary monarchy and expanded the emperor's powers. During the brief reign of Vespasian's son Titus, Mount Vesuvius in southern Italy erupted, destroying Pompeii and other cities and killing thousands of people. The Flavians (69–96 C.E.) paved the way for the Antonines (96–192 C.E.), a dynasty of emperors under whose leadership the Roman Empire experienced a long period of prosperity and the height of the pax Romana. Wars generally ended victoriously and were confined to the frontiers. Second-century emperors made further changes in government that helped the empire run more efficiently while increasing the authority of the emperor.

The Roman army also saw changes, transforming from a mobile unit to a much larger defensive force, with more and more troops who were noncitizens. Because army service could lead to citizenship, non-Romans joined the army willingly to gain citizenship, receive a salary, and learn a trade. The frontiers became firmly fixed and were defended by a system of forts and walls. Behind these walls, the network of roads was expanded and improved, both to supply the forts and to reinforce them in times of trouble.

Life in Imperial Rome

The expansion and stabilization of the empire created great wealth, much of which flowed into Rome. The city, with a population of over a million, may have been the largest city in the world at that time. Fire and crime were perennial problems even in Augustus's day, and sanitation was poor. In the second century urban planning and new construction greatly improved the situation. For example, engineers built an elaborate system that collected sewage from public baths, the ground floors of buildings, and public latrines. They also built hundreds of miles of aqueducts, most of them underground, to bring fresh water into the city from the surrounding hills.

Rome grew so large that it became ever more difficult to feed its residents. Emperors solved the problem by providing citizens with free oil, wine, and grain for bread. By doing so, they also stayed in favor with the people. They and other sponsors also entertained the people with gladiatorial contests in which participants fought using swords and other weapons. Some gladiators were criminals or prisoners of war, but by the imperial period increasing numbers were volunteers, often poor immigrants who saw gladiatorial combat as a way to support themselves. All gladiators were trained in gladiatorial schools and were legally slaves, although they could keep their winnings and a few became quite wealthy. The Romans were even more addicted to chariot racing than to gladiatorial shows. Winning charioteers were idolized just as sports stars are today.

| What was life like in Rome, and what was it like in the provinces? | What was Christianity, and how did it affect life in the Roman Empire? | How did emperors respond to political and religious issues? | ✓ LearningCurve Check what you know. |

161

Prosperity in the Roman Provinces

As the empire grew and stabilized, many Roman provinces grew prosperous through the growth of agriculture, trade, and industry, among other factors. Peace and security opened Britain, Gaul, and the lands of the Danube to settlers from other parts of the Roman Empire. Veterans were given small parcels of land in the provinces, becoming tenant farmers. The garrison towns that grew up around provincial military camps became the centers of organized political life, and some grew into major cities,

The rural population throughout the empire left few records, but the inscriptions that remain point to a melding of cultures. Latin blended with the original language of an area and with languages spoken by those who came into the area later. Slowly what would become the Romance languages of Spanish, Italian, French, Portuguese, and Romanian evolved. Religion was another site of cultural exchange and mixture. Romans moving into an area learned about and began to venerate local gods, and local people learned about Roman ones. Gradually hybrid deities and rituals developed.

The Romans were the first to build cities in northern Europe, but in the eastern Mediterranean they ruled cities that had existed before Rome itself was even a village. Here there was much continuity in urban life from the Hellenistic period. There was less construction than in the Roman cities of northern and western Europe because existing buildings could simply be put to new uses.

The expansion of trade during the pax Romana made the Roman Empire an economic as well as a political force. Britain and Belgium became prime grain producers, and Britain's wool industry probably got its start under the Romans. Italy and southern Gaul produced huge quantities of wine. Roman colonists introduced the olive to southern Spain and northern Africa, which soon produced most of the oil consumed in the western part of the empire. In the East the olive oil production of Syrian farmers reached an all-time high, and Egypt produced tons of wheat that fed the Roman populace.

The growth of industry in the provinces was another striking development of this period. Cities in Gaul and Germany eclipsed the old Mediterranean manufacturing centers, and in the second century C.E. Gaul and Germany took over the pottery market. Lyons in Gaul and later Cologne in Germany became the new centers of the glassmaking industry, and the cities of Gaul were nearly unrivaled in the manufacture of bronze and brass. Aided by all this growth in trade and industry, Europe and western Asia were linked in ways they had not been before.

Eastward Expansion and Contacts Between Rome and China

As the Romans drove farther eastward, they encountered the Parthians, who had established a kingdom in what is now Afghanistan and Iran in the Hellenistic period (see page 133). In the second century the Romans tried unsuccessfully to drive out the Parthians, who came to act as a link between Roman and Chinese merchants. Chinese merchants sold their wares to the Parthians, who then carried the goods overland to Mesopotamia or Egypt, from which they were shipped throughout the Roman Empire.

CHAPTER LOCATOR | How did the Romans dominate Italy, and what political institutions did they create? | How did Rome expand its power beyond Italy, and what were the effects of this expansion?

CHAPTER 6
162 THE WORLD OF ROME

Although warfare disrupted parts of western Asia, it did not stop trade that had prospered from Hellenistic times (see pages 134–135). Silk was still a major commodity from east to west, along with other luxury goods. In return the Romans traded glassware, precious gems, and slaves. The Parthians added exotic fruits, rare birds, rugs, and other products.

The pax Romana was also an era of maritime trade, and Roman ships sailed from Egyptian ports to the mouth of the Indus River, where they purchased local merchandise and wares imported by the Parthians. Some hardy mariners pushed down the African coast and into the Indian Ocean. Roman coins have been found in Sri Lanka and Vietnam, clear evidence of trade connections.

The period of this contact coincided with the era of Han greatness in China (see page 178). During the reign of the Roman emperor Nerva (r. 96–98 c.e.), a Han emperor sent an ambassador, Gan Ying, to make contact with the Roman Empire. Gan Ying made it as far as the Persian Gulf ports, where he heard about the Romans from Parthian sailors and reported back to his emperor that the Romans were wealthy, tall, and strikingly similar to the Chinese. His report became part of a group of accounts about the Romans and other "western" peoples that circulated widely among scholars and officials in Han China.

QUICK REVIEW <

What were the economic consequences of Roman expansion?

| What was life like in Rome, and what was it like in the provinces? | What was Christianity, and how did it affect life in the Roman Empire? | How did emperors respond to political and religious issues? | ✔ LearningCurve Check what you know. |

163

> # What was Christianity, and how did it affect life in the Roman Empire?

Depiction of Jesus

This mural, from a Roman camp at Dura-Europos on the Euphrates River, may be the earliest known depiction of Jesus. Dating to 235 C.E., it depicts Jesus healing a paralytic man, an incident described in the New Testament. Early Christians used art to spread their message. (Yale University Art Gallery, Dura-Europos Collection)

During the reign of the emperor Tiberius (r. 14–37 C.E.), in the Roman province of Judaea a Jewish man named Jesus of Nazareth preached, attracted a following, and was executed on the order of the Roman prefect Pontius Pilate. Christianity, the religion created by Jesus's followers, came to have an enormous impact first in the Roman Empire and later throughout the world.

Factors Behind the Rise of Christianity

The civil wars that destroyed the Roman Republic left their mark on Judaea, where Jewish leaders had taken sides in the conflict. The turmoil created a climate of violence throughout the area, and among the Jews movements in opposition to the Romans spread. Many Jews came to believe that a final struggle was near and that it would lead to the coming of a savior, or **Messiah**, who would destroy the Roman legions and inaugurate a period of happiness and

Messiah

▶ In Jewish belief, a savior who would bring a period of peace and happiness for Jews; many Christians came to believe that Jesus was that Messiah.

CHAPTER LOCATOR | How did the Romans dominate Italy, and what political institutions did they create? | How did Rome expand its power beyond Italy, and what were the effects of this expansion?

164 CHAPTER 6 THE WORLD OF ROME

plenty for Jews. This apocalyptic belief was an old one among Jews, but by the first century C.E. it had become more widespread than ever.

The pagan world also played its part in the story of early Christianity. The term pagan, which originally referred to those who lived in the countryside, came to refer to those who practiced religions other than Judaism or Christianity. This included religions devoted to the traditional Roman gods of the hearth, home, and countryside. Known as syncretistic religions, these religions blended Roman and indigenous deities. The cult of the emperor spread through the erection of statues, temples, and monuments, and mystery religions offered the promise of life after death (see Chapter 5). Many people in the Roman Empire practiced all of these religions, combining them in whatever way seemed most beneficial or satisfying to them.

The Life and Teachings of Jesus

Into this climate of Messianic hope and Roman religious blending came Jesus of Nazareth (ca. 3 B.C.E.–29 C.E.). According to Christian Scripture, he was born to deeply religious Jewish parents and raised in Galilee. His ministry began when he was about thirty, and he taught by preaching and telling stories.

Like Socrates and the Buddha, Jesus left no writings. Accounts of his sayings and teachings first circulated orally among his followers and were later written down. The principal evidence for his life and deeds are the four Gospels of the Bible (Matthew, Mark, Luke, and John). These Gospels are records of Jesus's teachings, written sometime in the late first century to build a community of faith. Their authors had probably heard many different people talk about what Jesus said and did, and there are discrepancies among the four accounts. These differences indicate that early followers had a diversity of beliefs about Jesus's nature and purpose.

However, almost all the early sources agree on certain aspects of Jesus's teachings: he preached of a heavenly kingdom of eternal happiness in a life after death and of the importance of devotion to God and love of others. His teachings were based on Hebrew Scripture and reflected a conception of God and morality that came from Jewish tradition. The Greek translation of the Hebrew word *Messiah* is *Christus*, the origin of the English word *Christ*. Was Jesus the Messiah, the Christ? A small band of followers thought so, and Jesus claimed that he was. Yet Jesus had his own conception of the Messiah. He would establish a spiritual kingdom, not an earthly one.

The Roman official Pontius Pilate knew little about Jesus's teachings. He was concerned with maintaining peace and order. According to the New Testament, crowds followed Jesus into Jerusalem at the time of Passover, a highly emotional point in the Jewish year that marked the Jewish people's departure from Egypt under the leadership of Moses (see page 52). The prospect that these crowds would spark violence alarmed Pilate. Some Jews believed that Jesus was the long-awaited Messiah. Others hated and feared him because they thought him religiously dangerous. To avert riot and bloodshed, Pilate condemned Jesus to death, and his soldiers carried out the sentence. On the third day after Jesus's crucifixion, some of his followers claimed that he had risen from the dead. For his earliest followers and for generations to come, the resurrection of Jesus became a central element of faith.

pagan
▶ Originally referring to those who lived in the countryside, the term came to mean those who practiced religions other than Judaism or Christianity.

What was life like in Rome, and what was it like in the provinces? | **What was Christianity, and how did it affect life in the Roman Empire?** | How did emperors respond to political and religious issues? | ✔ LearningCurve Check what you know.

165

The Spread of Christianity

Believers in Jesus's divinity met in small assemblies or congregations, often in one another's homes, to discuss the meaning of Jesus's message and to celebrate a ritual (later called the Eucharist or Lord's Supper) commemorating his last meal with his disciples before his arrest. Because they expected Jesus to return to the world very soon, they regarded earthly life and institutions as unimportant. Only later did these congregations evolve into what came to be called the religion of Christianity, with a formal organization and set of beliefs.

The catalyst in the spread of Jesus's teachings and the formation of the Christian Church was Paul of Tarsus, a well-educated Hellenized Jew. Paul traveled all over the Roman Empire and wrote letters of advice to many groups. These letters were copied and widely circulated, transforming Jesus's ideas into more specific moral teachings. As a result of his efforts, Paul became the most important figure in changing Christianity from a Jewish sect into a separate religion.

Though most of the earliest converts seem to have been Jews, Paul urged that Gentiles, or non-Jews, be accepted on an equal basis. The earliest Christian converts included people from all social classes. These people were reached by missionaries and others who spread the Christian message through family contacts, friendships, and business networks. Many women were active in spreading Christianity. Paul greeted male and female converts by name in his letters and noted that women often provided financial support for his activities. The growing Christian communities differed over the extent to which women should participate in the workings of the religion; some favored giving women a larger role in church affairs, while others were more restrictive.

People were attracted to Christian teachings for a variety of reasons. It was in many ways a mystery religion, offering its adherents special teachings that would give them immortality. But in contrast to traditional mystery religions, Christianity promised this immortality widely, not only to a select few. Christianity also offered the possibility of forgiveness, for believers accepted that human nature is weak and that even the best Christians could fall into sin. But Jesus loved sinners and forgave those who repented. Christianity was also attractive to many because it gave the Roman world a cause. By spreading the word of Christ, Christians played their part in God's plan for the triumph of Christianity on earth. Christianity likewise gave its devotees a sense of identity and community. To stress the spiritual kinship of this new type of community, Christians often called one another brother and sister. Also, many Christians took Jesus's commandment to love one another as a guide and provided support for widows, orphans, and the poor, just as they would for family members.

The Growing Acceptance and Evolution of Christianity

At first, most Roman officials largely ignored the followers of Jesus, viewing them simply as one of the many splinter groups within Judaism, but slowly some came to oppose Christian practices and beliefs. They considered Christians to be subversive dissidents because they stopped practicing traditional rituals and they objected to the cult of the emperor. Some Romans thought that Christianity was

CHAPTER LOCATOR | How did the Romans dominate Italy, and what political institutions did they create? | How did Rome expand its power beyond Italy, and what were the effects of this expansion?

one of the worst of the mystery cults, with immoral and indecent rituals. Pagans also feared that the Greco-Roman gods would withdraw their favor from the Roman Empire because of the Christian insistence that the pagan gods either did not exist or were evil spirits. And many worried that Christians were trying to destroy the Roman family with their insistence on a new type of kinship.

Persecutions of Christians, including torture and executions, were organized by governors of Roman provinces and sometimes by the emperor, beginning with Nero. Most persecutions were, however, local and sporadic in nature. Responses to Christianity on the part of Roman emperors varied. Some left Christians in peace, while others ordered them to sacrifice to the emperor and the Roman gods or risk death.

By the second century Christianity was changing. The belief that Jesus was soon coming again gradually waned, and as the number of converts increased, permanent institutions were established. These included buildings and a hierarchy of officials often modeled on those of the Roman Empire. Bishops, officials with jurisdiction over a certain area, became especially important. They began to assert that they had the right to determine the correct interpretation of Christian teachings and to choose their successors.

Christianity also began to attract more highly educated individuals who developed complex theological interpretations of issues that were not clear in scripture. Bishops and theologians often modified teachings that seemed upsetting to Romans, such as Jesus's harsh words about wealth and family ties. Given all these changes, Christianity became more formal in the second century, with power more centralized.

bishop
▶ A Christian Church official with jurisdiction over a certain area and the power to determine the correct interpretation of Christian teachings.

QUICK REVIEW

How did Christianity change in the centuries following the death of Jesus?

| What was life like in Rome, and what was it like in the provinces? | **What was Christianity, and how did it affect life in the Roman Empire?** | How did emperors respond to political and religious issues? | ✓ LearningCurve Check what you know. |

167

How did the emperors respond to political, economic, and religious issues in the third and fourth centuries?

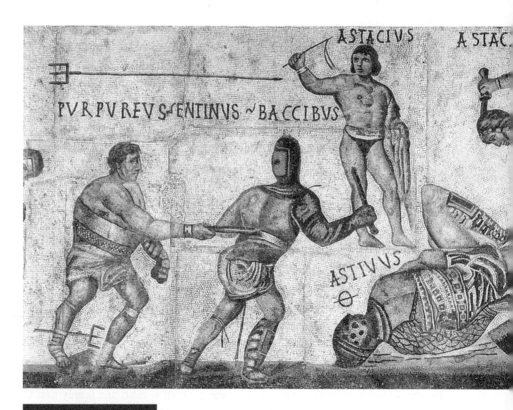

Gladiator Mosaic

Made in the first half of the fourth century c.e., this mosaic from an estate outside Rome includes the name of each gladiator next to the figure. At the top a gladiator stands in a victory pose, while the fallen gladiator at the bottom is marked with the symbol Ø, indicating that he has died in combat. Many of the gladiators in this mosaic, such as those at the left, appear less fit and fearsome than the gladiators depicted in movies, more closely reflecting the reality that gladiatorial combat was a job undertaken by a variety of people. (Galleria Borghese, Rome, Italy/Scala/Art Resource, NY)

The prosperity and stability of the second century gave way to a period of domestic upheaval and foreign invasion in the Roman Empire that historians have termed the "crisis of the third century." Trying to repair the damage was the major work of the emperors Diocletian (r. 284–305) and Constantine (r. 306–337).

Political Measures

During the crisis of the third century the Roman Empire was stunned by civil war, as different individuals, generally military commanders from the border provinces, claimed rights to leadership of the empire. Beginning in 235, emperors often ruled for only a few years or even months. Non-Roman groups on the frontiers took advantage of the chaos to invade Roman-held territory along the Rhine and Danube, occasionally even crossing the Alps to maraud in Italy. In the East, Sassanid armies advanced all the way to the Mediterranean. By the time peace was

CHAPTER LOCATOR | How did the Romans dominate Italy, and what political institutions did they create? | How did Rome expand its power beyond Italy, and what were the effects of this expansion?

168 CHAPTER 6 THE WORLD OF ROME

restored, the empire's economy was shattered, cities had shrunk in size, and many farmers had left their lands.

Diocletian, who had risen through the ranks of the military to become emperor in 284, ended the period of chaos. Under Diocletian the princeps became *dominus*, "lord," reflecting the emperor's claim that he was "the elect of god." To underscore the emperor's exalted position, Diocletian and his successor, Constantine, adopted the court ceremonies and trappings of the Persian Empire.

Diocletian recognized that the empire had become too large for one man to handle and so in 293 divided it into a western and an eastern half. He assumed direct control of the eastern part, giving a colleague the rule of the western part along with the title *augustus*. Diocletian and his fellow augustus further delegated power by appointing two men to assist them. Each man was given the title *caesar* to indicate his exalted rank.

After a brief civil war following Diocletian's death, Constantine eventually gained authority over the entire empire but ruled from the East. Here he established a new capital for the empire at Byzantium, an old Greek city on the Bosporus, a strait on the boundary between Europe and Asia. He named it "New Rome," though it was soon called Constantinople. In addition, he built defensive works along the borders of the empire, trying hard to keep it together, as did his successors. Despite their efforts, however, the eastern and the western halves drifted apart.

The emperors ruling from Constantinople could not provide enough military assistance to repel invaders in the western half of the Roman Empire, and Roman authority there slowly disintegrated. In 476 a Germanic chieftain, Odoacer, deposed the Roman emperor in the West. This date thus marks the official end of the Roman Empire in the West, although the Roman Empire in the East, later called the Byzantine Empire, would last for nearly another thousand years.

The Division of the Roman World, 293 C.E.

Economic Issues

Along with political challenges, major economic problems also confronted Diocletian and Constantine, including inflation and declining tax revenues. In an attempt to curb inflation, Diocletian issued an edict that fixed maximum prices and wages throughout the empire. He and his successors dealt with the tax system just as strictly and inflexibly. Taxes became payable in kind, that is, in goods and services instead of money. All those involved in the growing, preparation, and transportation of food and other essentials were locked into their professions, as the emperors tried to assure a steady supply of these goods. In this period of severe depression, many localities could not pay their taxes. In such cases local tax collectors, who were themselves locked into service, had to make up the difference from their own funds. This system soon wiped out a whole class of moderately wealthy people and set the stage for the lack of social mobility that was a key characteristic of European society for many centuries to follow.

The emperors' measures did not really address Rome's central economic problems. During the turmoil of the third and fourth centuries, many free farmers and their families were killed by invaders or renegade soldiers, or abandoned farms ravaged in the fighting. Consequently, large tracts of land lay untended. Landlords with ample resources began at once to claim as much of this land as they

What was life like in Rome, and what was it like in the provinces?

What was Christianity, and how did it affect life in the Roman Empire?

How did emperors respond to political and religious issues?

✓ LearningCurve
Check what you know.

169

could. The huge estates that resulted, called villas, were self-sufficient and became islands of stability in an unsettled world. In return for the protection and security landlords could offer, many small landholders gave over their lands and their freedom. To guarantee a supply of labor, landlords denied them the freedom to move elsewhere. Free men and women were becoming tenant farmers bound to the land, what would later be called serfs.

The Acceptance of Christianity

By the late third century most Romans tolerated Christianity, even if they did not practice it. Constantine ordered toleration of all religions in the Edict of Milan, issued in 313. He supported the church throughout his reign, expecting in return the support of church officials in maintaining order, and late in his life he was baptized as a Christian. Constantine also freed the clergy from imperial taxation and endowed the building of Christian churches.

Helped in part by its favored position in the empire, Christianity slowly became the leading religion, and emperors after Constantine continued to promote it. In 380 the emperor Theodosius (r. 379–395) made Christianity the official religion of the empire. He allowed the church to establish its own courts and to use its own body of law, called "canon law." With this he laid the foundation for later growth in church power (see Chapter 8).

> **QUICK REVIEW**

What challenges did Roman emperors face in the third and fourth centuries?

CHAPTER SUMMARY

The Italian peninsula was settled by many different groups, including Greeks in the south and Etruscans in the north. The Etruscans expanded southward into central Italy, where they influenced the culture of the small town that was growing into the city of Rome. Rome prospered and expanded its own territories, establishing a republican government led by the Senate. In a series of wars the Romans conquered the Mediterranean, creating an overseas empire that brought them unheard-of power and wealth, but also social unrest and civil war. The meteoric rise to power of Julius Caesar in the first century B.C.E. led to his assassination, but his grandnephew Augustus finally restored peace and order to Rome. Under Augustus, the republic became an empire.

Augustus and his successors further expanded Roman territories. The city of Rome became the magnificent capital of the empire. The Roman provinces and frontiers also saw extensive prosperity through the growth of agriculture, industry, and trade connections. Christianity, a religion created by the followers of Jesus of Nazareth, spread across the empire, beginning in the first century C.E.

CHAPTER LOCATOR | How did the Romans dominate Italy, and what political institutions did they create? | How did Rome expand its power beyond Italy, and what were the effects of this expansion?

CHAPTER 6
170   THE WORLD OF ROME

Initially some Roman officials and emperors persecuted Christians, but gradually hostility decreased. Emperors in the fourth century first allowed Christianity and then made it the official religion of the empire, one of many measures through which they attempted to solve the problems created by invasions and political turmoil. Their measures were successful in the East, where the Roman Empire lasted for another thousand years, but not in the West, where the Roman Empire ended in the fifth century.

 CONNECTIONS Despite the efforts of emperors and other leaders, the Western Roman Empire slowly broke apart and by the fifth century C.E. no longer existed. By the fourteenth century European scholars were beginning to see the fall of the Roman Empire as one of the great turning points in Western history, the end of the classical era. That began the practice of dividing Western history into different periods—eventually, the ancient, medieval, and modern eras. Those categories still shape the way that Western history is taught and learned.

This three-part conceptualization also shapes the periodization of world history. As you saw in Chapter 4 and will see in Chapter 7, China is also understood to have had a classical age, and, as you will read in Chapter 11, the Maya of Mesoamerica did as well. The dates of these ages are different from those of the classical period in the Mediterranean, but there are striking similarities among all three places: successful large-scale administrative bureaucracies were established, trade flourished, cities grew, roads were built, and new cultural forms developed. In all three places this period was followed by an era of less prosperity and more warfare and destruction.

ONLINE DOCUMENT PROJECT

Queen Cleopatra

What do Roman depictions of Cleopatra reveal about the attitudes and values of her time?

Explore Roman accounts of Cleopatra to see what light they shed on political, social, and cultural values in the late republic and early empire, and then complete a quiz and writing assignment based on the evidence and details from this chapter. *See inside front cover to learn more.*

What was life like in Rome, and what was it like in the provinces?　What was Christianity, and how did it affect life in the Roman Empire?　How did emperors respond to political and religious issues?　✓ LearningCurve Check what you know.

171

CHAPTER 6 STUDY GUIDE

STEP 1

GET STARTED ONLINE

LearningCurve

Now that you've read the chapter, make it stick by completing the LearningCurve activity.

STEP 2

EXPLAIN WHY IT MATTERS

Put your reading into practice. Identify each term below, and then explain why it matters in world history.

TERM	WHO OR WHAT & WHEN	WHY IT MATTERS
Senate (p. 148)		
consuls (p. 149)		
patricians (p. 149)		
plebeians (p. 149)		
Punic Wars (p. 153)		
paterfamilias (p. 154)		
pax Romana (p. 160)		
Messiah (p. 164)		
pagan (p. 165)		
bishop (p. 167)		

STEP 3

MOVE BEYOND THE BASICS

To demonstrate a more advanced understanding of the impact of expansion on Roman identity, fill in the chart below with descriptions of the social, cultural, and political consequences of Roman expansion. What steps did the Romans take to "Romanize" subject peoples? How was Roman life, in turn, altered by contact and connections with diverse peoples?

Social Consequences of Roman Expansion	Political Consequences of Roman Expansion	Cultural Consequences of Roman Expansion

PUT IT ALL TOGETHER Now, take a step back and try to explain the big picture. Remember to use specific examples from the chapter in your answers.

THE ORIGINS AND DEVELOPMENT OF THE ROMAN REPUBLIC

▶ How did the Romans integrate conquered Italian territories into their state? How did their policies in this regard create a foundation for further expansion?

▶ How did the evolution of Roman political institutions reflect the evolution of Roman society?

ROMAN IMPERIALISM AND ITS CONSEQUENCES

▶ What explains the instability that characterized Roman politics in the century following the Punic Wars? Why did republican institutions fail to produce the kinds of reforms and compromises that had resolved earlier political conflicts?

▶ How did Rome help connect greater Europe to the economic and cultural life of the Mediterranean world?

ROMAN DECLINE AND THE RISE OF CHRISTIANITY

▶ What factors facilitated the spread of Christianity throughout the Roman Empire? Why did many Romans initially fear Christianity? Why did such fears diminish over time?

▶ How and why did the political, cultural, and economic center of the Roman Empire shift from west to east starting in the third century C.E.?

LOOKING BACK, LOOKING AHEAD

▶ How was Roman society and culture shaped by Greek ideas and ideals? Why was Greek civilization so appealing to so many Romans?

▶ What are the implications of the claim that, together, Greek and Roman civilization represent the "classical era" in Western history? What does this claim suggest about the connections between these two civilizations and the contemporary Western world?

> **IN YOUR OWN WORDS**

Imagine that you must give an oral report to the class answering the following question: **How did the Romans build and control an empire that spanned the Mediterranean world?** What would be the most important points and why?

7

EAST ASIA AND THE SPREAD OF BUDDHISM

221 B.C.E.–800 C.E.

> **How did China come to play a dominant role in the development of East Asia?** Chapter 7 examines major developments in East Asia between 221 B.C.E. and 800 C.E. At the beginning of this era, China had just been unified into a single state. War, trade, diplomacy, missionary activity, and the pursuit of learning led the Chinese to travel to distant lands and people from distant lands to go to China. Among the results were the spread of Buddhism from India and Central Asia to China and the adaptation of many elements of Chinese culture by near neighbors, especially Korea and Japan. Increased communication also stimulated state formation among China's neighbors: Tibet, Korea, Manchuria, Vietnam, and Japan.

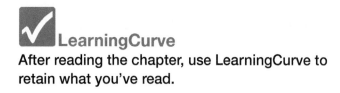

LearningCurve
After reading the chapter, use LearningCurve to retain what you've read.

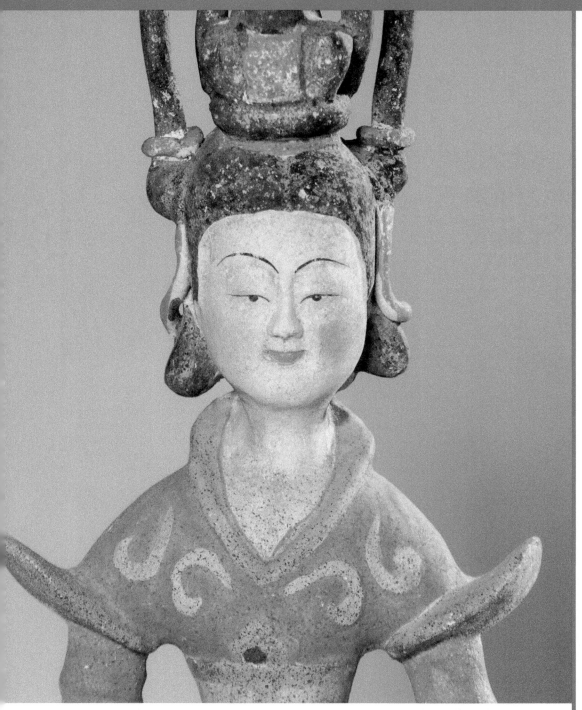

Palace Maid Ceramic models of attractive young women were often placed in Chinese tombs, reflecting hopes for the afterlife. (© Panorama/The Image Works)

> What were the social, cultural, and political consequences of the unification of China under the strong centralized governments of the Qin and Han empires?

> How did Buddhism find its way into East Asia, and what was its appeal and impact?

> What were the lasting accomplishments of the Sui and Tang Dynasties?

> What elements of Chinese culture were adopted by Koreans, Vietnamese, and Japanese, and how did they adapt them to their own circumstances?

What were the social, cultural, and political consequences of the unification of China under the strong centralized governments of the Qin and Han empires?

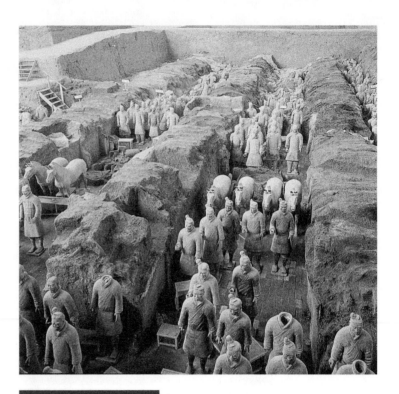

Army of the First Emperor

The thousands of life-size ceramic soldiers buried in pits about a half mile from the First Emperor's tomb help us imagine the Qin military machine. It was the Qin emperor's concern with the afterlife that led him to construct such a lifelike guard. The soldiers were originally painted in bright colors, and they held real bronze weapons. (Robert Harding World Imagery)

Like the Roman Empire (see Chapter 6), the Chinese empire was put together through force of arms and held in place by sophisticated centralized administrative machinery. The governments created by the Qin and Han Dynasties affected many facets of Chinese social, cultural, and intellectual life.

The Qin Unification, 221–206 B.C.E.

In 221 B.C.E., after decades of constant warfare, Qin (chin), the state that had adopted Legalist policies during the Warring States Period (see page 108), succeeded in defeating the last of its rivals, and China was unified for the first time in many centuries. The king of Qin decided to call himself the First Emperor (*Shihuangdi*) in anticipation of a long line of successors. His state, however, did not long outlast him.

Once he ruled all of China, the First Emperor and his shrewd Legalist minister Li Si embarked on a sweeping program of centralization that touched the

CHAPTER LOCATOR | What were the social, cultural, and political consequences of the unification of China? | How did Buddhism find its way into East Asia, and what was its appeal and impact?

176 CHAPTER 7 EAST ASIA AND THE SPREAD OF BUDDHISM

ca. 230–208 B.C.E.
Construction of Great Wall

221 B.C.E.
China unified under Qin Dynasty

206 B.C.E.–220 C.E.
Han Dynasty

145–ca. 85 B.C.E.
Sima Qian, Chinese historian

114 B.C.E.
Han government gains control over Silk Road trade routes across Central Asia

111 B.C.E.
Emperor Wu conquers Nam Viet

108 B.C.E.
Han government establishes colonies in Korea

105 C.E.
Chinese invention of paper

ca. 200 C.E.
Buddhism begins rapid growth in China

220–589 C.E.
Age of Division in China

313–668 C.E.
Three Kingdoms Period in Korea

372 C.E.
Buddhism introduced in Korea

538 C.E.
Buddhism introduced in Japan

581–618 C.E.
Sui Dynasty

604 C.E.
Prince Shōtoku introduces Chinese-style government in Japan

605 C.E.
Introduction of merit-based examination system for the selection of officials in China

618–907 C.E.
Tang Dynasty; great age of Chinese poetry

668 C.E.
First political unification of Korea under Silla

690 C.E.
Empress Wu declares herself emperor, becoming the only Chinese woman emperor

710 C.E.
Nara made the capital of Japan

735–737 C.E.
Smallpox epidemic in Japan

845 C.E.
Tang emperor begins persecution of Buddhism

---

lives of nearly everyone in China. To cripple the nobility of the defunct states, the First Emperor ordered the nobles to leave their lands and move to the capital. The private possession of arms was outlawed to make it more difficult for subjects to rebel. The First Emperor dispatched officials to administer the territory that had been conquered and controlled the officials through a long list of regulations, reporting requirements, and penalties for inadequate performance.

To harness the enormous human resources of his people, the First Emperor ordered a census of the population. To make it easier to administer all regions uniformly, the Chinese script was standardized, outlawing regional variations in the ways words were written. The First Emperor also standardized weights, measures, coinage, and even the axle lengths of carts. To make it easier for Qin armies to move rapidly, thousands of miles of roads were built. Good roads indirectly facilitated trade.

Hundreds of thousands of subjects were drafted to build the **Great Wall** (ca. 230–208 B.C.E.), a rammed-earth fortification along the northern border between the Qin realm and the land controlled by the nomadic Xiongnu.

Great Wall

▶ A rammed-earth fortification built along the northern border of China during the reign of the First Emperor.

| What were the lasting accomplishments of the Sui and Tang Dynasties? | What elements of Chinese culture were adopted by Koreans, Vietnamese, and Japanese? | ✓ LearningCurve Check what you know. |

After Li Si complained that scholars (especially Confucians) used records of the past to denigrate the emperor's achievements and undermine popular support, the emperor had all writings other than useful manuals on topics such as agriculture, medicine, and divination collected and burned. As a result of this massive book burning, many ancient texts were lost.

After the First Emperor died in 210 B.C.E., the Qin state unraveled. The Legalist institutions designed to concentrate power in the hands of the ruler made the stability of the government dependent on his strength and character, and his heir proved ineffective. The heir was murdered by his younger brother, and uprisings soon followed.

The Han Dynasty, 206 B.C.E.–220 C.E.

The eventual victor in the struggle for power that ensued in the wake of the collapse of the Qin Dynasty was Liu Bang, known in history as Emperor Gaozu (r. 202–195 B.C.E.). The First Emperor of Qin was from the Zhou aristocracy. Gaozu was, by contrast, from a modest family of commoners, so his elevation to emperor is evidence of how thoroughly the Qin Dynasty had destroyed the old order.

Gaozu did not disband the centralized government created by the Qin, but he did remove its most unpopular features. Harsh laws were canceled, taxes were sharply reduced, and a policy of noninterference was adopted in an effort to promote economic recovery. With policies of this sort, relative peace, and the extension of China's frontiers, the Chinese population grew rapidly (Map 7.1).

The Han government was largely supported by the taxes and forced labor demanded of farmers, but this revenue regularly fell short of the government's needs. To pay for his military campaigns, Emperor Wu, the "Martial Emperor" (r. 141–87 B.C.E.), took over the minting of coins, confiscated the land of nobles, sold offices and titles, and increased taxes on private businesses. A widespread suspicion of commerce made it easy to levy especially heavy assessments on merchants. The worst blow to businessmen, however, was the government's decision to enter into market competition with them by selling the commodities that had been collected as taxes. In 119 B.C.E. government monopolies were established in the production of iron, salt, and liquor. These enterprises had previously been sources of great profit for private entrepreneurs. Large-scale grain dealing also had been a profitable business, and the government now took that over as well.

Han Intellectual and Cultural Life

In contrast to the Qin Dynasty, which favored Legalism, the Han came to promote Confucianism. The Han government's efforts to recruit men trained in the Confucian classics marked the beginning of the Confucian scholar-official system, one of the most distinctive features of imperial China.

However, the Confucianism that made a comeback during the Han Dynasty was a changed Confucianism. Although Confucian texts had fed the First Emperor's bonfires, some dedicated scholars had hidden their books, and others had memorized whole works. The ancient books recovered in this way — called the Confucian classics — were revered as repositories of the wisdom of the past. Confucian scholars treated these classics with piety and attempted to make them more useful as sources of moral guidance by writing commentaries on them.

Confucian classics

▶ The ancient texts recovered during the Han Dynasty that Confucian scholars treated as sacred scriptures.

CHAPTER LOCATOR | What were the social, cultural, and political consequences of the unification of China?   How did Buddhism find its way into East Asia, and what was its appeal and impact?

CHAPTER 7
178   EAST ASIA AND THE SPREAD OF BUDDHISM

MAP 7.1 ▪ The Han Empire, 206 B.C.E.–220 C.E.

The Han Dynasty asserted sovereignty over vast regions from Korea in the east to Central Asia in the west and Vietnam in the south. Once garrisons were established, traders were quick to follow, leading to considerable spread of Chinese material culture in East Asia. Chinese goods, especially silk, were in demand far beyond East Asia, promoting long-distance trade across Eurasia.

A major intellectual accomplishment of the Han Dynasty was history writing. Sima Qian (145–ca. 85 B.C.E.) wrote a comprehensive history of China from the time of the mythical sage-kings of high antiquity to his own day, dividing his account into a chronology recounting political events; biographies of key individuals; and treatises on subjects such as geography, taxation, and court rituals. As an

What were the lasting accomplishments of the Sui and Tang Dynasties?	What elements of Chinese culture were adopted by Koreans, Vietnamese, and Japanese?	✓ LearningCurve Check what you know.

official of the emperor, he had access to important people and documents and to the imperial library. Sima Qian believed fervently in visiting the sites where history was made, examining artifacts, and questioning people about events. He was also interested in China's geography and local history. The result of his research, ten years or more in the making, was *Records of the Grand Historian*, a massive work of literary and historical genius.

For centuries to come, Sima Qian's work set the standard for Chinese historical writing, although most of the histories modeled after it covered only a single dynasty. The first of these was the work of three members of the Ban family in the first century C.E. (See "Individuals in Society: The Ban Family," page 181.)

The circulation of books like Sima Qian's was made easier by the invention of paper, which the Chinese traditionally date to 105 C.E. Scribes had previously written on strips of bamboo and wood or rolls of silk. Cai Lun, to whom the Chinese attribute the invention of paper, worked the fibers of rags, hemp, bark, and other scraps into sheets of paper. Paper, thus, was somewhat similar to the papyrus made from pounded reeds in ancient Egypt. Though much less durable than wood, paper was far cheaper than silk and became a convenient means of conveying the written word.

Inner Asia and the Silk Road

The difficulty of defending against the nomadic pastoral peoples to the north in the region known as Inner Asia is a major reason China came to favor a centralized bureaucratic form of government. Resources from the entire subcontinent were needed to maintain control of the northern border.

Chinese civilization did not spread easily to the grasslands north of China proper because those lands were too dry and cold to make good farmland. Herding sheep, horses, camels, and other animals made better economic use of those lands. By the third century B.C.E. several different peoples practicing nomadic pastoralism lived in those regions. Chinese farmers and Inner Asian herders had such different modes of life that it is not surprising that they had little respect for each other. For most of the imperial period, Chinese farmers looked on the northern non-Chinese horsemen as gangs of bullies who thought robbing was easier than working for a living. The nomads identified glory with military might and viewed farmers as contemptible weaklings.

In the late third century B.C.E. the Xiongnu (possibly the same group that was known in the West as the Huns) formed the first great confederation of nomadic tribes (see Map 7.1). The Qin's Great Wall was built to defend against the Xiongnu, and the Qin sent out huge armies in pursuit of them. The early Han emperors tried to make peace with them, offering generous gifts of silk, rice, cash, and even imperial princesses as brides. Xiongnu power did not wane, and in 166 B.C.E. 140,000 Xiongnu raided to within a hundred miles of the Chinese capital.

Emperor Wu then decided that China had to push the Xiongnu back. He sent several enormous armies deep into Xiongnu territory. These costly campaigns were of limited value because the Xiongnu were a moving target. If the Xiongnu

Records of the Grand Historian

▶ A comprehensive history of China written by Sima Qian.

Bronze Mirror

The backs of bronze mirrors were frequently decorated with images of deities and animals and with auspicious words. As viewers turned the mirrors, they saw different scenes. This Han mirror features an outer border with semicircles decorated with cloud patterns and squares with words written on them. In the center are deities. (Mirror Featuring Deities and Kings in Three Sections Surrounded by Rings of Squares and Semicircles [bronze]. Eastern Han Dynasty [25-220]/Cleveland Museum of Art, Ohio, U.S.A./Gift of Drs. Thomas and Martha Carter in Honor of Sherman E. Lee/The Bridgeman Art Library)

CHAPTER LOCATOR | What were the social, cultural, and political consequences of the unification of China? | How did Buddhism find its way into East Asia, and what was its appeal and impact?

CHAPTER 7
180 EAST ASIA AND THE SPREAD OF BUDDHISM

The Ban Family

Ban Biao (3–54 C.E.), a successful official from a family with an envied library, had three highly accomplished children: his twin sons, the general Ban Chao (32–102) and the historian Ban Gu (32–92); and his daughter, Ban Zhao (ca. 45–120). After distinguishing himself as a junior officer in campaigns against the Xiongnu, Ban Chao was sent in 73 C.E. to the western regions to see about the possibility of restoring Chinese overlordship there, which had been lost several decades earlier. Ban Chao spent most of the next three decades in Central Asia. Through patient diplomacy and a show of force, he re-established Chinese control over the oasis cities of Central Asia, and in 92 he was appointed protector general of the area.

His twin brother, Ban Gu, was one of the most accomplished writers of his age, excelling in a distinctive literary form known as the rhapsody *(fu)*. His "Rhapsody on the Two Capitals" is in the form of a dialogue between a guest from Chang'an and his host in Luoyang. It describes the palaces, spectacles, scenic spots, local products, and customs of the two great cities. Emperor Zhang (r. 76–88) was fond of literature and often had Ban Gu accompany him on hunts or travels. He also had him edit a record of the court debates he held on issues concerning the Confucian classics.

Ban Biao was working on the *History of the Former Han Dynasty* when he died in 54. Ban Gu took over this project, modeling it on Sima Qian's *Records of the Grand Historian*. He added treatises on law, geography, and bibliography, the last a classified list of books in the imperial library.

Because of his connection to a general out of favor, Ban Gu was sent to prison in 92, where he soon died. At that time the *History of the Former Han Dynasty* was still incomplete. The emperor called on Ban Gu's widowed sister, Ban Zhao, to finish it. She came to the palace, where she not only worked on the history but also became a teacher of the women of the palace. According to the *History of the Later Han*, she taught them the classics, history, astronomy, and mathematics. In 106 an infant succeeded to the throne, and the widow of an earlier emperor became regent. This empress frequently turned to Ban Zhao for advice on government policies.

Ban Zhao credited her own education to her learned father and cultured mother and became an advocate of the education of girls. In her *Admonitions for Women,* Ban Zhao objected that many families taught their sons to read but not their daughters. She did not claim girls should have the same education as boys; after all, "just as yin and yang differ, men and women have different characteristics." Women, she

Ban Zhao, Han Dynasty historian. (© Fotoe/Uniphoto Press, Japan/Ancient Art & Architecture Collection, Ltd.)

wrote, will do well if they cultivate womanly virtues such as humility. "Humility means yielding and acting respectful, putting others first and oneself last, never mentioning one's own good deeds or denying one's own faults, enduring insults and bearing with mistreatment, all with due trepidation."* In subsequent centuries Ban Zhao's *Admonitions* became one of the most commonly used texts for the education of Chinese girls.

QUESTIONS FOR ANALYSIS

1. What inferences can you draw from the fact that a leading general had a brother who was a literary man?
2. What does Ban Zhao's life tell us about women in her society? How do you reconcile her personal accomplishments with the advice she gave for women's education?

*Patricia Buckley Ebrey, ed., *Chinese Civilization: A Sourcebook*, 2d ed., revised and expanded (New York: Free Press, 1993), p. 75.

ONLINE DOCUMENT PROJECT

What do Ban Zhao's writings reveal about attitudes toward women during her time? Read sources by and about Ban Zhao, and then complete a quiz and writing assignment based on the evidence and details from this chapter. *See the inside front cover to learn more.*

Xiongnu Metalwork

The metal ornaments of the Xiongnu provide convincing evidence that they were in contact with nomadic pastoralists farther west in Asia, such as the Scythians, who also fashioned metal plaques and buckles in animal designs. This buckle or ornament is made of gold and is about 3 inches tall. (Image copyright © The Metropolitan Museum of Art/ Image source: Art Resource, NY)

Silk Road

▶ The trade routes across Central Asia linking China to western Eurasia.

tributary system

▶ A system first established during the Han Dynasty to regulate contact with foreign powers. States and tribes beyond its borders sent envoys bearing gifts and received gifts in return.

did not want to fight the Chinese troops, they simply moved their camps. To try to find allies and horses, Emperor Wu turned his attention west, toward Central Asia. From an envoy he sent into Bactria, Parthia, and Ferghana in 139 B.C.E., the Chinese learned for the first time of other civilized states comparable to China.

In 114 B.C.E. Emperor Wu sent an army into Ferghana and gained recognition of Chinese overlordship in the area, thus obtaining control over the trade routes across Central Asia commonly called the **Silk Road** (see Map 7.1). The city-states along this route could carry out the trade on which they depended more conveniently with Chinese garrisons to protect them.

At the same time, Emperor Wu sent troops into northern Korea to establish military districts that would flank the Xiongnu on their eastern border. By 111 B.C.E. the Han government also had extended its rule south into Nam Viet, which extended from south China into what is now northern Vietnam.

During the Han Dynasty, China developed a **tributary system** to regulate contact with foreign powers. States and tribes beyond its borders sent envoys bearing gifts and received gifts in return. Over the course of the dynasty, the Han government's outlay on these gifts was huge, perhaps as much as 10 percent of state revenue. Although the tributary system was a financial burden to the Chinese, it reduced the cost of defense and offered China confirmation that it was the center of the civilized world.

Silk given to the Xiongnu and other northern tributaries as part of the tributary system often entered the trading networks of Persian, Parthian, and Indian merchants, who carried it by caravans across Asia. There was a market both for skeins of silk thread and for silk cloth woven in Chinese or Syrian workshops. Caravans returning to China carried gold, horses, and occasionally handicrafts of West Asian origin, such as glass beads and cups. Through the trade along the Silk Road, the Chinese learned of new foodstuffs, including walnuts, pomegranates, sesame, and coriander, all of which came to be grown in China.

Maintaining a military presence so far from the center of China was expensive. To cut costs, the government set up self-supporting military colonies, recruited Xiongnu tribes to serve as auxiliary forces, and established vast government horse farms. Still, military expenses threatened to bankrupt the Han government.

CHAPTER LOCATOR | What were the social, cultural, and political consequences of the unification of China? | How did Buddhism find its way into East Asia, and what was its appeal and impact?

CHAPTER 7
182 EAST ASIA AND THE SPREAD OF BUDDHISM

Life in Han China

How were ordinary people's lives affected by the creation of a huge Han bureaucratic empire? The lucky ones who lived in Chang'an or Luoyang, the great cities of the empire, got to enjoy the material benefits of increased long-distance trade and a boom in the production of luxury goods.

The government did not promote trade per se. The Confucian elite, like ancient Hebrew wise men, considered trade necessary but lowly. Agriculture and crafts were more honorable because they produced something, but merchants merely took advantage of others' shortages to make profits as middlemen. This attitude justified the government's takeover of the grain, iron, and salt businesses. Still, the government indirectly promoted commerce by building roads and defending cities.

Markets were the liveliest places in the cities. Besides stalls selling goods of all kinds, markets offered fortune-tellers and entertainers. The markets were also used for the execution of criminals, to serve as a warning to onlookers.

Government patronage helped maintain the quality of craftsmanship in the cities. By the beginning of the first century C.E. China also had about fifty state-run ironworking factories. Chinese metalworking was the most advanced in the world at the time. In contrast to Roman blacksmiths, who hammered heated iron to make wrought iron tools, the Chinese knew how to liquefy iron and pour it into molds, producing tools with a higher carbon content that were harder and more durable.

Iron was replacing bronze in tools, but bronzeworkers still turned out a host of goods. Bronze was prized for jewelry, mirrors, and dishes. Bronze was also used for minting coins and for precision tools such as carpenters' rules and adjustable wrenches. Han metal-smiths were mass-producing superb crossbows long before the crossbow was dreamed of in Europe.

The bulk of the population consisted of peasants living in villages of a few hundred households. Because the Han empire, much like the contemporaneous Roman Empire, drew its strength from a large population of free peasants who contributed both taxes and labor services to the state, the government had to try to keep peasants independent and productive.

To fight peasant poverty, the government kept land taxes low (one-thirtieth of the harvest), provided relief in time of famine, and promoted up-to-date agricultural methods. Still, many hard-pressed peasants were left to choose between migration to areas where new lands could be opened and quasi-servile status as the dependents of a magnate. Throughout the Han period, Chinese farmers in search of land to till pushed into frontier areas, expanding Chinese domination at the expense of other ethnic groups, especially in central and south China.

The Chinese family in Han times was much like Roman (see page 153) and Indian (see page 69) families. In all three societies senior males had great authority, parents arranged their children's marriages, and brides normally joined their husbands' families. Other practices were more distinctive to China, such as the universality of patrilineal family names, the practice of dividing land equally among the sons in a family, and the great emphasis placed on the virtue of filial piety. One of the most commonly used texts for the education of women is Ban Zhao's *Admonitions for Women*, in which she extols the feminine virtues, such as humility. (See "Individuals in Society: The Ban Family," page 181.)

What were the lasting accomplishments of the Sui and Tang Dynasties?

What elements of Chinese culture were adopted by Koreans, Vietnamese, and Japanese?

✓ LearningCurve
Check what you know.

China and Rome

The empires of China and Rome (discussed in Chapter 6) were large, complex states governed by monarchs, bureaucracies, and standing armies. Both reached the people directly through taxation and conscription policies, and both invested in infrastructure such as roads and waterworks. The empires faced the similar challenge of having to work hard to keep land from becoming too concentrated in the hands of hard-to-tax wealthy magnates. In both empires people in neighboring areas that came under political domination were attracted to the conquerors' material goods, productive techniques, and other cultural products, resulting in gradual cultural assimilation. China and Rome also had similar frontier problems and tried similar solutions, such as recruiting "barbarian" soldiers and settling soldier-colonists.

Nevertheless, the differences between Rome and Han China are worth as much notice as the similarities. The Roman Empire was linguistically and culturally more diverse than China. In China there was only one written language; people in the Roman Empire still wrote in Greek and several other languages, and people in the eastern Mediterranean could claim more ancient civilizations. Politically the dynastic principle was stronger in China than in Rome, nor were there republican ideals in China. In contrast to the graduated forms of citizenship in Rome, Han China drew no distinctions between original and added territories. The social and economic structures also differed in the two empires. Slavery was much more important in Rome than in China, and merchants were more favored.

The Fall of the Han and the Age of Division

In the second century C.E. the Han government suffered a series of blows. A succession of child emperors required regents to rule in their place until they reached maturity, allowing the families of empresses to dominate the court. Emperors, once grown, turned to **eunuchs** (castrated palace servants) for help in ousting the empresses' families, only to find that the eunuchs were just as difficult to control. In 166 and 169 scholars who had denounced the eunuchs were arrested, killed, or banished from the capital and official life. Then in 184 a millenarian religious sect rose in massive revolt. The armies raised to suppress the rebels soon took to fighting among themselves. After years of fighting, a stalemate was reached, with three warlords each controlling distinct territories in the north, the southeast, and the southwest. In 220 one of them forced the last of the Han emperors to abdicate, formally ending the Han Dynasty.

The period after the fall of the Han Dynasty is often referred to as the **Age of Division** (220–589). A brief reunification from 280 to 316 came to an end when non-Chinese who had been settling in north China since Han times seized the opportunity afforded by the political turmoil to take power. For the next two and a half centuries, north China was ruled by one or more non-Chinese dynasties (the Northern Dynasties), and the south was ruled by a sequence of four short-lived Chinese dynasties (the Southern Dynasties) centered in the area of the present-day city of Nanjing.

In the south a hereditary aristocracy entrenched itself in the higher reaches of officialdom. They saw themselves as maintaining the high culture of the Han and looked on the emperors of the successive dynasties as upstarts. In this aristocratic

eunuchs
▶ Castrated males who played an important role as palace servants.

Age of Division
▶ The period after the fall of the Han Dynasty, when China was politically divided.

CHAPTER LOCATOR | What were the social, cultural, and political consequences of the unification of China? | How did Buddhism find its way into East Asia, and what was its appeal and impact?

184 CHAPTER 7 EAST ASIA AND THE SPREAD OF BUDDHISM

culture the arts of poetry and calligraphy flourished, and people began collecting writings by famous calligraphers.

Establishing the capital at Nanjing, south of the Yangzi River, had a beneficial effect on the economic development of the south. To pay for an army and to support the imperial court and aristocracy in a style that matched their pretensions, the government had to expand the area of taxable agricultural land. The south, with its temperate climate and ample supply of water, offered nearly unlimited possibilities for such development.

The Northern Dynasties are interesting as the first case of alien rule in China. Ethnic tensions flared from time to time. In the late fifth century the Northern Wei (way) Dynasty (386–534) moved the capital from near the Great Wall to the ancient city of Luoyang, adopted Chinese-style clothing, and made Chinese the official language. But the armies remained in the hands of the non-Chinese Xianbei tribesmen. Soldiers who saw themselves as marginalized by the pro-Chinese reforms rebelled in 524. For the next fifty years north China was torn apart by struggles for power.

QUICK REVIEW

How did the Han emperors respond to the challenges presented by nomadic peoples?

| What were the lasting accomplishments of the Sui and Tang Dynasties? | What elements of Chinese culture were adopted by Koreans, Vietnamese, and Japanese? | ☑ LearningCurve Check what you know. |

How did Buddhism find its way into East Asia, and what was its appeal and impact?

Meditating Monk

This monk, wearing the traditional patchwork robe, sits in the crossed-legged meditation position. His small niche is to the left of the main image of the Buddha in cave 285 at Dunhuang, a cave completed in 539 C.E. under the patronage of a prince of the Northern Wei imperial house who was then the local governor. (Photo: Lois Conner. Courtesy, Dunhuang Academy)

In much the same period that Christianity was spreading out of its original home in ancient Israel, Buddhism was spreading beyond India. Buddhism came to Central, East, and Southeast Asia with merchants and missionaries along the overland Silk Road, by sea from India and Sri Lanka, and also through Tibet. Like Christianity, Buddhism was shaped by its contact with cultures in the different areas into which it spread, leading to several distinct forms.

Buddhism's Path Through Central Asia

Under Ashoka in India (see pages 80–82), Buddhism began to spread to Central Asia. This continued under the Kushan empire (ca. 50–250 C.E.). Over the next several centuries most of the city-states of Central Asia became centers of Buddhism, from Bamiyan northwest of Kabul, to Kucha, Khotan, Loulan, Turfan, and Dunhuang (Map 7.2).

CHAPTER LOCATOR | What were the social, cultural, and political consequences of the unification of China? | **How did Buddhism find its way into East Asia, and what was its appeal and impact?**

186 CHAPTER 7
EAST ASIA AND THE SPREAD OF BUDDHISM

Expansion of Buddhism
- ■ Area of origin
- ■ 5th to 2d century B.C.E.
- ■ 2d century B.C.E. to 3d century C.E.
- ■ 3d to 8th century C.E.
- → Spread of Buddhism
- — Silk Road
- — Indian Ocean trade routes

MAP 7.2 ■ **The Spread of Buddhism, ca. 500 B.C.E.–800 C.E.**

Buddhism spread throughout India in Ashoka's time and beyond India in later centuries. The different forms of Buddhism found in Asia today reflect this history. The Mahayana Buddhism of Japan came via Central Asia, China, and Korea, with a secondary later route through Tibet. The Theravada Buddhism of Southeast Asia came directly from India and indirectly through Sri Lanka.

> MAPPING THE PAST

ANALYZING THE MAP: Trace the routes of the spread of Buddhism by time period. How fast did Buddhism spread?
CONNECTIONS: Why do you think Buddhism spread more to the east of India than to the west?

The form of Buddhism that spread from Central Asia to China, Japan, and Korea was called Mahayana, which means "Great Vehicle" (see page 73), reflecting the claims of its adherents to a more inclusive form of the religion. Influenced by the Iranian religions then prevalent in Central Asia, Buddhism became more devotional. The Buddha came to be treated as a god, the head of an expanding pantheon of other Buddhas and bodhisattvas (Buddhas-to-be). With the growth of this pantheon, Buddhism became as much a religion for laypeople as for monks and nuns.

What were the lasting accomplishments of the Sui and Tang Dynasties?

What elements of Chinese culture were adopted by Koreans, Vietnamese, and Japanese?

✓ LearningCurve
Check what you know.

The Appeal and Impact of Buddhism in China

Why did Buddhism find so many adherents in China during the three centuries after the fall of the Han Dynasty in 220? There were no forced conversions, but still the religion spread rapidly. In the unstable political environment, many people were open to new ideas. To Chinese scholars the Buddhist concepts of the reincarnation of souls, karma, and nirvana posed a stimulating intellectual challenge. To rulers the Buddhist religion offered a source of magical power and a political tool to unite Chinese and non-Chinese. In a tumultuous age Buddhism's emphasis on kindness, charity, and eternal bliss was deeply comforting. As in India, Buddhism posed no threat to the social order, and the elite who were drawn to Buddhism encouraged its spread to people of all classes.

The monastic establishment grew rapidly in China. Like their Christian counterparts in medieval Europe, Buddhist monasteries played an active role in social, economic, and political life. Given the importance of family lines in China, becoming a monk was a major decision, since a man had to give up his surname and take a vow of celibacy, thus cutting himself off from the ancestral cult. Those not ready to become monks or nuns could pursue Buddhist goals as pious laypeople.

In China women turned to Buddhism as readily as men. Joining a nunnery became an alternative for a woman who did not want to marry or did not want to stay with her husband's family in widowhood. Later, the only woman ruler of China, Empress Wu, invoked Buddhist principles to justify her role (see page 190), further evidence of how Buddhism brought new understandings of gender.

Buddhism had an enormous impact on the visual arts in China, especially sculpture and painting. Before Buddhism, Chinese had not set up statues of gods in temples, but now they decorated temples with a profusion of images. Inspired by the cave temples of India and Central Asia, in China, too, Buddhists carved caves into rock faces to make temples.

Not everyone was won over by Buddhist teachings. Critics of Buddhism labeled it immoral, unsuited to China, and a threat to the state since monastery land was not taxed and monks did not perform labor service.

> **QUICK REVIEW**

To which groups in Chinese society did Buddhism appeal? Why?

CHAPTER LOCATOR | What were the social, cultural, and political consequences of the unification of China? | How did Buddhism find its way into East Asia, and what was its appeal and impact?

188   CHAPTER 7   EAST ASIA AND THE SPREAD OF BUDDHISM

Chang'an

Urban Planning

Chang'an in Tang times attracted merchants, pilgrims, and students from all over East Asia. The city was laid out on a square grid (left) and divided into walled wards, the gates to which were closed at night. Temples were found throughout the city, but trade was limited to two government-supervised markets. In the eighth and ninth centuries the Japanese copied the general plan of Chang'an in designing their capitals — first at Nara, then at Heian, shown on the right. (Cradles of Civilization/Visual Connection Archive)

Heian (Kyoto)

Political division was finally overcome when the Sui Dynasty conquered its rivals to reunify China in 581. Although the dynasty lasted only thirty-seven years, it left a lasting legacy in the form of political reform, the construction of roads and canals, and the institution of written merit-based exams for the appointment of officials. The Tang Dynasty that followed would build upon the Sui's accomplishments to create an era of impressive cultural creativity and political power.

The Sui Dynasty, 581–618

In the 570s and 580s the long period of division in China was brought to an end under the leadership of the Sui (sway) Dynasty. In addition to reunifying China, the Sui reasserted Chinese control over northern Vietnam and campaigned into Korea and against the new force on the steppe, the Turks. The Sui strengthened

| What were the lasting accomplishments of the Sui and Tang Dynasties? | What elements of Chinese culture were adopted by Koreans, Vietnamese, and Japanese? | LearningCurve Check what you know. |

189

central control of the government by curtailing the power of local officials to appoint their own subordinates and by instituting in 605 C.E. competitive written examinations for the selection of officials.

The crowning achievement of the Sui Dynasty was the construction of the **Grand Canal**, which connected the Yellow and Yangzi River regions. Henceforth the rice-growing Yangzi Valley and south China played an ever more influential role in the country's economic and political life, strengthening China's internal cohesion and facilitating maritime trade with Southeast Asia, India, and areas farther west.

Despite these accomplishments, the Sui Dynasty lasted for only two reigns. The ambitious projects of the two Sui emperors led to exhaustion and unrest, and in the ensuing warfare Li Yuan seized the throne.

Grand Canal

▶ A canal, built during the Sui Dynasty, that connected the Yellow and Yangzi Rivers, notable for strengthening China's internal cohesion and economic development.

The Tang Dynasty, 618–907

The dynasty founded by Li Yuan, the Tang, was one of the high points of traditional Chinese civilization. Especially during this dynasty's first century, its capital, Chang'an, was the cultural center of East Asia. This position of strength gave the Chinese the confidence to be open to learning from the outside world, leading to a more cosmopolitan culture than in any other period before the twentieth century.

The first two Tang rulers, Gaozu (Li Yuan, r. 618–626) and Taizong (r. 626–649), were able monarchs. Adding to their armies auxiliary troops composed of Turks, Tanguts, Khitans, and other non-Chinese led by their own chieftains, they campaigned into Korea, Vietnam, and Central Asia. In 630 the Chinese turned against their former allies, the Turks, gaining territory from them and winning for Taizong the title of Great Khan.

In the civil sphere Tang emperors subdivided the administration of the empire into departments, much like the numerous agencies of modern governments. They built on the Sui precedent of using written examinations to select officials. Candidates had to master the Confucian classics and the rules of poetry, and they had to be able to analyze practical administrative and political matters. Government schools were founded to prepare the sons of officials and other young men for service as officials.

The mid-Tang Dynasty saw two women—Empress Wu and Consort Yang Guifei—rise to positions of great political power. Empress Wu was the consort of Emperor Gaozong. After Gaozong suffered a stroke in 660, she took charge. She continued to rule after Gaozong's death, summarily deposing her own two sons and dealing harshly with all opponents. In 690 she proclaimed herself emperor, the only woman who took that title in Chinese history. Although despised by later Chinese historians as an evil usurper, Empress Wu was an effective leader. It was not until she was over eighty that members of the court were able to force her out in favor of her son.

Her grandson, the emperor Xuanzong (r. 713–756), presided over a brilliant court in his early years. In his later years, however, after he became enamored of his consort Yang Guifei, he did not want to be bothered by the details of government. The emperor allowed her to place friends and relatives in important posi-

Tang China, ca. 750 C.E.

tions in the government. One of her favorites was the general An Lushan, who rebelled in 755. Xuanzong had to flee the capital, and the troops that accompanied him forced him to have Yang Guifei executed.

The rebellion of An Lushan was devastating to the Tang Dynasty. Peace was restored only by calling on the Uighurs (WEE-gurz), a Turkish people allied with the Tang, who looted the capital after taking it from the rebels. After the rebellion was finally suppressed in 763, the central government had to keep meeting the extortionate demands of the Uighurs. Many military governors came to treat their provinces as hereditary kingdoms. In addition, eunuchs gained increasing power at court.

Tang Culture

The reunification of north and south led to cultural flowering. The Tang capital cities of Chang'an and Luoyang became great metropolises. The cities were laid out in rectangular grids and contained a hundred-odd walled "blocks" inside their walls. Like the gates of the city, the gates of each block were locked at night.

In these cosmopolitan cities, knowledge of the outside world was stimulated by the presence of envoys, merchants, pilgrims, and students who came from neighboring states in Central Asia, Japan, Korea, Tibet, and Southeast Asia. Because of the presence of foreign merchants, many religions were practiced. Foreign fashions in hair and clothing were often copied, and foreign amusements such as the Persian game of polo found followings among the well-to-do. The introduction of new musical instruments and tunes from India, Iran, and Central Asia brought about a major transformation in Chinese music.

The Tang Dynasty was the great age of Chinese poetry. Skill in composing poetry was tested in the civil service examinations, and educated men had to be able to compose poems at social gatherings. The pain of parting, the joys of nature, and the pleasures of wine and friendship were all common poetic topics.

In Tang times Buddhism fully penetrated Chinese daily life. Stories of Buddhist origin became widely known, and Buddhist festivals became among the most popular holidays. Buddhist monasteries became an important part of everyday life. They ran schools for children. In remote areas they provided lodging for travelers. Merchants entrusted their money and wares to monasteries for safekeeping, in effect transforming the monasteries into banks and warehouses. The wealthy often donated money or land to support temples and monasteries, making monasteries among the largest landlords.

At the intellectual and religious level, Buddhism was developing in distinctly Chinese directions. Two schools that thrived were Pure Land and Chan. **Pure Land** appealed to laypeople because its simple act of calling on the Buddha Amitabha and his chief helper, the compassionate bodhisattva Guanyin, could lead to rebirth in Amitabha's paradise, the Pure Land. Among the educated elite the **Chan** school (known in Japan as Zen) also gained popularity. Chan teachings rejected the authority of the sutras and claimed the superiority of mind-to-mind transmission of Buddhist truths.

Opposition to Buddhism re-emerged in the late Tang period. In addition to concerns about the fiscal impact of removing so much land from the tax rolls and

Pure Land
▶ A school of Buddhism that taught that by calling on the Buddha Amitabha, one could achieve rebirth in Amitabha's Pure Land paradise.

Chan
▶ A school of Buddhism (known in Japan as Zen) that rejected the authority of the sutras and claimed the superiority of mind-to-mind transmission of Buddhist truths.

What were the lasting accomplishments of the Sui and Tang Dynasties?

What elements of Chinese culture were adopted by Koreans, Vietnamese, and Japanese?

✓ LearningCurve
Check what you know.

so many men from government labor service, there were concerns about Buddhism's foreign origins. As China's international position weakened, xenophobia surfaced. During the persecution of 845, more than 4,600 monasteries and 40,000 temples and shrines were destroyed, and more than 260,000 Buddhist monks and nuns were forced to return to secular life. Although this ban was lifted after a few years, the monastic establishment never fully recovered.

> **QUICK REVIEW**

How did Chinese Buddhism develop under the Tang?

CHAPTER LOCATOR | What were the social, cultural, and political consequences of the unification of China? | How did Buddhism find its way into East Asia, and what was its appeal and impact?

CHAPTER 7
192   EAST ASIA AND THE SPREAD OF BUDDHISM

What elements of Chinese culture were adopted by Koreans, Vietnamese, and Japanese, and how did they adapt them to their own circumstances?

During the millennium from 200 B.C.E. to 800 C.E., China exerted a powerful influence on its immediate neighbors, who began forming states of their own. By Tang times China was surrounded by independent states in Korea, Manchuria, Tibet, the area that is now Yunnan province, Vietnam, and Japan. All of these states were much smaller than China in area and population, making China by far the dominant force politically and culturally. Nevertheless, each of these separate states developed a strong sense of its independent identity.

The earliest information about each of these countries is found in Chinese sources. Han armies brought Chinese culture to Korea and Vietnam, but even in those cases much cultural borrowing was entirely voluntary as the elite, merchants, and craftsmen adopted the techniques, ideas, and practices they found appealing. In Japan much of the process of absorbing elements of Chinese culture was mediated via Korea. In Korea, Japan, and Vietnam the fine arts—painting, architecture, and ceramics in particular—were all strongly influenced by Chinese models. Tibet was as much in the Indian sphere of influence as in the Chinese and thus followed a somewhat different trajectory. Most significantly, it never

What were the lasting accomplishments of the Sui and Tang Dynasties?

What elements of Chinese culture were adopted by Koreans, Vietnamese, and Japanese?

 LearningCurve
Check what you know.

adopted Chinese characters as its written language, nor was it as influenced by Chinese artistic styles as were other areas. Moreover, the form of Buddhism that became dominant in Tibet came directly from India, not through Central Asia and China.

In each area Chinese-style culture was at first adopted by elites, but in time many Chinese products and ideas became incorporated into everyday life. By the eighth century the written Chinese language was used by educated people throughout East Asia. The books that educated people read included the Chinese classics, histories, and poetry, as well as Buddhist sutras translated into Chinese. The great appeal of Buddhism known primarily through Chinese translation was a powerful force promoting cultural borrowing.

Vietnam

Vietnam's climate is much like that of southernmost China—subtropical, with abundant rain and rivers. The Vietnamese first appear in Chinese sources as a people of south China called the Yue, who gradually migrated farther south as the Chinese state expanded. The people of the Red River Valley in northern Vietnam had achieved a relatively advanced level of Bronze Age civilization by the first century B.C.E. Power was held by hereditary tribal chiefs who served as civil, religious, and military leaders, with the king as the most powerful chief.

The collapse of the Qin Dynasty in 206 B.C.E. had an impact on this area because a former Qin general, Zhao Tuo (Trieu Da in Vietnamese), finding himself in the far south, set up his own kingdom of Nam Viet (Nan Yue in Chinese). This kingdom covered much of south China and was ruled by Trieu Da from his capital near the present site of Guangzhou. Its population consisted chiefly of the Viet people. After killing all officials loyal to the Chinese emperor, Trieu Da adopted the customs of the Viet and made himself the ruler of a vast state that extended as far south as modern-day Da Nang.

After almost a hundred years of diplomatic and military duels between the Han Dynasty and Trieu Da and his successors, Nam Viet was conquered in 111 B.C.E. by Chinese armies. Chinese administrators were assigned to replace the local nobility. Chinese political institutions were imposed, and Confucianism was treated as the official ideology. The Chinese language was introduced as the medium of official and literary expression, and Chinese characters were adopted as the written form for the Vietnamese spoken language. The Chinese built roads, waterways, and harbors to facilitate communication within the region and to ensure that they maintained administrative and military control over it. Chinese art, architecture, and music had a powerful impact on their Vietnamese counterparts.

Chinese innovations that were beneficial to the Vietnamese were readily integrated into the indigenous culture, but the local elite were not reconciled to Chinese political domination. The most famous early revolt took place in 39 C.E., when two widows of local aristocrats, the Trung sisters, led an uprising against foreign rule. After overwhelming Chinese strongholds, they declared themselves queens of an independent Vietnamese kingdom. Three years later a powerful army sent by the Han emperor re-established Chinese rule.

China retained at least nominal control over northern Vietnam through the Tang Dynasty. The local elite became culturally dual, serving as brokers between the Chinese governors and the native people.

The Kingdom of Nam Viet, ca. 200 B.C.E.

Korea

Korea is a mountainous peninsula some 600 miles long extending south from Manchuria and Siberia (Map 7.3). Archaeological, linguistic, and anthropological evidence indicates that the Korean people share a common ethnic origin with other peoples of North Asia, including those of Manchuria, Siberia, and Japan. Linguistically, Korean is not related to Chinese.

Korea began adopting elements of technology from China in the first millennium B.C.E., including bronze and iron technology. Chinese-Korean contact expanded during the Warring States Period, when the state of Yan extended into part of Korea. In about 194 B.C.E. Wiman, an unsuccessful rebel against the Han Dynasty, fled to Korea and set up a state called Choson in what is now northwest Korea and southern Manchuria. In 108 B.C.E. this state was overthrown by Han armies and four prefectures were established there.

The impact of the Chinese prefectures in Korea was similar to that of the contemporaneous Roman colonies in Britain in encouraging the spread of culture and political forms. The prefectures survived not only through the Han Dynasty, but also for nearly a century after the fall of the dynasty, until 313 C.E. The Chinese never controlled the entire Korean peninsula, however. The Han commanderies coexisted with the native Korean kingdom of Koguryŏ, founded in the first century B.C.E. After the Chinese colonies were finally overthrown, the kingdoms of Paekche and Silla emerged farther south on the peninsula in the third and fourth centuries C.E., leading to what is called the Three Kingdoms Period (313–668 C.E.).

MAP 7.3 ■ Korea and Japan, ca. 600 C.E.

Korea and Japan are of similar latitude, but Korea's climate is more continental, with harsher winters. Of Japan's four islands, Kyushu is closest to Korea and mainland Asia.

Iron Artifacts from Korean Tomb

In the third and second centuries B.C.E. iron and bronze was being used in Korea to make mirrors, bells, and practical tools.
(National Museum of Gwangju, Korea/EuroCreon/ Ancient Art & Architecture Collection, Ltd.)

What were the lasting accomplishments of the Sui and Tang Dynasties?

What elements of Chinese culture were adopted by Koreans, Vietnamese, and Japanese?

LearningCurve
Check what you know.

In all three Korean kingdoms Chinese was used as the language of government and learning. Each of the three kingdoms had hereditary kings, but their power was curbed by the existence of very strong hereditary elites.

Buddhism was officially introduced in Koguryŏ from China in 372 and in the other states not long after. Buddhism connected Korea to societies across Asia. Buddhist monks went back and forth between China and Korea.

When the Sui Dynasty finally reunified China in 589, it tried, unsuccessfully, to establish control of at least a part of Korea. The Tang government then tried allying itself with one state, Silla, to fight the others. Silla and Tang jointly destroyed Paekche in 660 and Koguryŏ in 668. With its new resources Silla was able to repel Tang efforts to make Korea a colony but agreed to vassal status. The unification under Silla marked the first political unification of Korea. For the next century Silla embarked on a policy of wholesale borrowing of Chinese culture and institutions.

Japan

The heart of Japan is four mountainous islands off the coast of Korea (see Map 7.3). Since the land is rugged and lacking in navigable waterways, the Inland Sea, like the Aegean in Greece, was the easiest avenue of communication in early times. Hence the land bordering the Inland Sea—Kyushu, Shikoku, and Honshu— developed as the political and cultural center of early Japan. Geography also blessed Japan with a moat to protect it against external interference—the Korea Strait and the Sea of Japan.

Japan's early development was closely tied to that of the mainland, especially to Korea. Anthropologists have discerned several major waves of immigrants into Japan. People of the Jōmon culture, established by about 10,000 B.C.E., after an influx of people from Southeast Asia, practiced hunting and fishing and fashioned clay pots. New arrivals from northeast Asia brought agriculture and a distinct culture called Yayoi (ca. 300 B.C.E.–300 C.E.). During the Han Dynasty, objects of Chinese and Korean manufacture found their way into Japan, an indication that people were traveling back and forth as well. In the third century C.E. Chinese histories begin to report on the land called Wa made up of mountainous islands. It had numerous communities with markets, granaries, tax collection, and class distinctions.

During the fourth through sixth centuries new waves of migrants from Korea brought the language that evolved into Japanese. They also brought sericulture (silkmaking), bronze swords, crossbows, iron plows, and the Chinese written language. In this period a social order similar to Korea's emerged, dominated by a warrior aristocracy organized into clans. Each clan had its own chieftain, who marshaled clansmen for battle and served as chief priest. Over time the clans fought with each other, and their numbers were gradually reduced through conquest and alliance. By the fifth century the chief of the clan that claimed descent from the sun-goddess, located in the Yamato plain around modern Osaka, had come to occupy the position of Great King—or Queen, as female rulers were not uncommon in this period.

The Yamato rulers used their religion to subordinate the gods of their rivals, much as Hammurabi had used Marduk in Babylonia (see page 41). This native religion was later termed **Shinto**, the Way of the Gods. Buddhism was formally

Shinto

▶ The Way of the Gods, Japan's native religion.

CHAPTER LOCATOR | What were the social, cultural, and political consequences of the unification of China? | How did Buddhism find its way into East Asia, and what was its appeal and impact?

196 CHAPTER 7 EAST ASIA AND THE SPREAD OF BUDDHISM

introduced in 538 c.e. and coexisted with the Shinto reverence for the spirits of ancestors and all living things.

In the sixth century Prince Shōtoku (574–622) undertook a sweeping reform of the state designed to strengthen Yamato rule by adopting Chinese-style bureaucratic practices. Near his seat of government, Prince Shōtoku built the magnificent Hōryūji Temple and staffed it with Buddhist monks from Korea. He also opened direct relations with China, sending four missions during the brief Sui Dynasty.

State-building efforts continued through the seventh century and culminated in the establishment in 710 of Japan's first long-term true city, the capital at Nara, north of modern Osaka. Nara, which was modeled on the Tang capital of Chang'an, gave its name to an era that lasted until 794 and was characterized by the avid importation of Chinese ideas and methods. As Buddhism developed a stronghold in Japan, it inspired many trips to China to acquire sources and to study at Chinese monasteries. Chinese and Korean craftsmen were often brought back to Japan. Musical instruments and tunes were imported as well, many originally from Central Asia. Chinese practices were instituted, such as the compilation of histories and law codes, the creation of provinces, and the appointment of governors to

> **Prince Shōtoku's Reforms: The Seventeen Principles of 604**

- Drew from both Confucian and Buddhist teachings
- Likened the ruler to Heaven
- Instructed officials to put their duty to the ruler above the interest of their families
- Instituted a ladder of official ranks similar to China's
- Admonished the nobility to avoid strife and opposition
- Urged adherence to Buddhist precepts

Nara

▶ Japan's capital and first true city; it was established in 710 and modeled on the Tang capital of Chang'an.

Hōryūji Temple

Japanese Buddhist temples, like those in China and Korea, consisted of several buildings within a walled compound. The buildings of the Hōryūji Temple (built between 670 and 711, after Prince Shōtoku's original temple burned down) include the oldest wooden structures in the world and house some of the best early Buddhist sculpture in Japan. The three main buildings depicted here are the pagoda, housing relics; the main hall, with the temple's principal images; and the lecture hall, for sermons. The five-story pagoda could be seen from far away, much like the steeples of cathedrals in medieval Europe. (Michael Hitoshi/The Image Bank/Getty Images)

> **PICTURING THE PAST**

ANALYZING THE IMAGE: How are the buildings arranged? How large is the compound? What is interesting about the roofs?

CONNECTIONS: Was this temple laid out primarily for the convenience of monks who resided there or more for lay believers coming to worship? How would their needs differ?

What were the lasting accomplishments of the Sui and Tang Dynasties?	**What elements of Chinese culture were adopted by Koreans, Vietnamese, and Japanese?**	✓ LearningCurve Check what you know.

collect taxes from them. By 750 some seven thousand men staffed the central government.

Increased contact with the mainland had unwanted effects as well. In contrast to China and Korea, Japan had been relatively isolated from many deadly diseases, so when diseases arrived with travelers, people did not have immunity. The great smallpox epidemic of 735–737 is thought to have reduced the population of about 5 million by 30 percent.

The Buddhist monasteries that ringed Nara were both religious centers and wealthy landlords, and the monks were active in the political life of the capital. Copying the policy of the Tang Dynasty in China, the government ordered every province to establish a Buddhist temple with twenty monks and ten nuns to chant sutras and perform other ceremonies on behalf of the emperor and the state. When an emperor abdicated in 749 in favor of his daughter, he became a Buddhist monk, a practice many of his successors would later follow.

> **QUICK REVIEW**

Why did elites in Korea, Vietnam, and Japan find aspects of Chinese culture and government so appealing?

CHAPTER SUMMARY

After unifying China in 221 B.C.E., the Qin Dynasty created a strongly centralized government that did away with noble privilege. The First Emperor standardized script, coinage, weights, and measures. He also built roads, the Great Wall, and a huge tomb for himself. During the four centuries of the subsequent Han Dynasty, the harsher laws of the Qin were lifted, but the strong centralized government remained. The Han government promoted internal peace by providing relief in cases of floods, droughts, and famines and by keeping land taxes low for the peasantry. The Han government sent huge armies against the nomadic Xiongnu, whose confederation threatened them in the north, but the Xiongnu remained a potent foe. Still, Han armies expanded Chinese territory in many directions. For nearly four centuries after the fall of the Han Dynasty, China was divided among contending states. After 316 the north was in the hands of non-Chinese rulers, while the south had Chinese rulers.

In the first and second centuries C.E. merchants and missionaries brought Buddhism to China. Many elements of Buddhism were new to China—a huge body of scriptures, celibate monks and nuns, traditions of depicting Buddhas and bodhisattvas in statues and paintings, and a strong proselytizing tradition. Rulers became major patrons in both north and south.

Unlike the Roman Empire, China was successfully reunified in 589 C.E. The short Sui Dynasty was followed by the longer Tang Dynasty. Tang China regained overlordship of the Silk Road cities in Central Asia. The Tang period was one of cultural flowering. Tang power declined after 755, when a powerful general

CHAPTER LOCATOR | What were the social, cultural, and political consequences of the unification of China? | How did Buddhism find its way into East Asia, and what was its appeal and impact?

CHAPTER 7
198 EAST ASIA AND THE SPREAD OF BUDDHISM

turned his army against the government. Although the rebellion was suppressed, the government was not able to regain its strong central control. Moreover, powerful states were formed along Tang's borders.

Over the ten centuries covered in Chapter 7, Korea, Japan, and Vietnam developed distinct cultures while adopting elements of China's material, political, and religious culture, including the Chinese writing system. During the Tang era, ambitious Korean and Japanese rulers sought Chinese expertise and Chinese products, including Chinese-style centralized governments and the Chinese written language.

 CONNECTIONS East Asia was transformed in the millennium between the Qin unification in 221 B.C.E. and the end of the eighth century C.E. The Han Dynasty and four centuries later the Tang Dynasty proved that a centralized, bureaucratic monarchy could bring peace and prosperity. By 800 C.E. neighboring societies along China's borders, from Korea and Japan on the east to the Uighurs and Tibetans to the west, had followed China's lead, forming states and building cities. Buddhism had transformed the lives of all of these societies, bringing new ways of thinking about life and death and new ways of pursuing spiritual goals.

In the same centuries that Buddhism was adapting to and simultaneously transforming the culture of much of eastern Eurasia, comparable processes were at work in western Eurasia, where Christianity continued to spread. The spread of these religions was aided by increased contact among different cultures, facilitated in Eurasia by the merchants traveling the Silk Road or sailing the Indian Ocean. Where contact among cultures wasn't as extensive, as in Africa (discussed in Chapter 10), religious beliefs were more localized. The collapse of the Roman Empire in the West during this period was not unlike the collapse of the Han Dynasty, but in Europe the empire was never put back together at the level that it was in China. The story of these centuries in western Eurasia is taken up in the next two chapters, which trace the rise of Christianity and Islam and the movement of peoples throughout Europe and Asia. Before returning to the story of East Asia after 800 in Chapter 13, we will also examine the empires in Africa (Chapter 10) and the Americas (Chapter 11).

ONLINE DOCUMENT PROJECT

Ban Zhao Offers Advice to Elite Women

What do Ban Zhao's writings reveal about attitudes toward women during her time?

Read sources by and about Ban Zhao, and then complete a quiz and writing assignment based on the evidence and details from this chapter. *See the inside front cover to learn more.*

What were the lasting accomplishments of the Sui and Tang Dynasties?	What elements of Chinese culture were adopted by Koreans, Vietnamese, and Japanese?	✔ LearningCurve Check what you know.

CHAPTER 7 STUDY GUIDE

STEP 1

GET STARTED ONLINE

 LearningCurve

Now that you've read the chapter, make it stick by completing the LearningCurve activity.

STEP 2

EXPLAIN WHY IT MATTERS

Put your reading into practice. Identify each term below, and then explain why it matters in world history.

TERM	WHO OR WHAT & WHEN	WHY IT MATTERS
Great Wall (p. 177)		
Confucian classics (p. 178)		
Records of the Grand Historian (p. 180)		
Silk Road (p. 182)		
tributary system (p. 182)		
eunuchs (p. 184)		
Age of Division (p. 184)		
Grand Canal (p. 190)		
Pure Land (p. 191)		
Chan (p. 191)		
Shinto (p. 196)		
Nara (p. 197)		

STEP 3

MOVE BEYOND THE BASICS

To demonstrate a more advanced understanding of the similarities and differences between the Han and Roman Empires, fill in the chart below with descriptions of the society, economy, and government of the Han and Roman Empires (you may want to review Chapter 6 for this exercise). Based on your comparison of these two empires, what generalizations might you make about the emergence, expansion, and decline of empires?

	Society	Economy	Government
Han Empire			
Roman Empire			

PUT IT ALL TOGETHER

Now, take a step back and try to explain the big picture. Remember to use specific examples from the chapter in your answers.

IMPERIAL CHINA

▶ What role did political philosophy play in Chinese imperial government? How did Legalism shape Qin government? How did Confucianism shape Han government?

▶ What common aspirations and challenges linked the Qin, Han, Sui, and Tang Dynasties?

THE SPREAD OF BUDDHISM

▶ How did Buddhism change as it spread throughout East Asia? How did the malleability of Buddhism aid its spread?

▶ What role did monasticism play in the promotion and spread of Buddhism?

CHINA AND ITS NEIGHBORS

▶ Compare and contrast the adoption of Chinese culture in Korea, Vietnam, and Japan. How would you explain the similarities and differences you note?

▶ What role did Chinese military expansion play in the spread of Chinese culture? What role did commerce and trade play?

LOOKING BACK, LOOKING AHEAD

▶ Compare and contrast China under the Han and Tang with China under the Shang and Zhou. How did unification during the later period differ from unification during the earlier period?

▶ What role did Buddhism play in facilitating the emergence of shared culture in East Asia? In your opinion, does Christianity continue to play a similar role in contemporary Western societies? Why or why not?

> IN YOUR OWN WORDS

Imagine that you must give an oral report to the class answering the following question: **How did China come to play a dominant role in the development of East Asia?** What would be the most important points and why?

8

CONTINUITY AND CHANGE IN EUROPE AND WESTERN ASIA

250–850

> **What role did Christianity play in the development of Europe and Western Asia in the centuries following the collapse of the Western Roman Empire?** Chapter 8 examines developments in Europe and western Asia in the centuries following the collapse of the Western Roman Empire. Scholars have long seen this era as one of the great turning points in Western history, but during the last several decades focus has shifted to continuities as well as changes. What is now usually termed "late antiquity" has been recognized as a period of creativity and adaptation in Europe and western Asia, not simply of decline and fall. The two main agents of continuity were the Eastern Roman (or Byzantine) Empire and the Christian Church. The main agent of change in late antiquity was the migration of barbarian groups throughout much of Europe and western Asia.

Orthodox Icon of Jesus In this painted icon, made for the monastery of Saint Catherine in Egypt in the eighth century, Jesus is shown on the cross, with two angels above him. Icons were important objects of veneration in the Eastern Christian, or Orthodox, Church, although they were also a source of controversy, as some church leaders thought that people were not simply using them as an aide to piety, but worshipping the image. (Kharbine-Tapabor/The Art Archive at Art Resource, NY)

> How did the Byzantine Empire preserve the legacy of Rome?

> How did the Christian Church become a major force in Europe?

> How did Christian thinkers adapt classical ideas to Christian teachings, and what new religious concepts and practices did they develop?

> How did the barbarians shape social, economic, and political structures in Europe and western Asia?

> How did the church convert barbarian peoples to Christianity?

> How did the Franks build and govern a European empire?

LearningCurve
After reading the chapter, use LearningCurve to retain what you've read.

How did the Byzantine Empire preserve the legacy of Rome?

Greek Fire

In this illustration from a twelfth-century manuscript, sailors shoot Greek fire toward an attacking ship from a pressurized tube that looks strikingly similar to a modern flamethrower. The exact formula for Greek fire has been lost, but it was probably made from a petroleum product because it continued burning on water. Greek fire was particularly important in Byzantine defenses of Constantinople from Muslim forces in the late seventh century. (Prado, Madrid, Spain/The Bridgeman Art Library)

The Byzantine (or Eastern Roman) Empire (Map 8.1) preserved the forms, institutions, and traditions of the old Roman Empire, and its people even called themselves Romans. Most important, however, is how Byzantium protected the intellectual heritage of Greco-Roman civilization and then passed it on.

Sources of Byzantine Strength

While the western parts of the Roman Empire gradually succumbed to barbarian invaders, the Byzantine Empire survived Germanic, Persian, and Arab attacks. In 540 a force of Xiongnu and Bulgars reached the gates of Constantinople. In 583 the Avars, a mounted Mongol people who had swept across Russia and the Balkans, seized Byzantine forts along the Danube and also reached the walls of Constantinople. Between 572 and 630 the Greeks were repeatedly at war with the Sassanid Persians (see page 206). Beginning in 632 Muslim forces pressured the Byzantine Empire (see Chapter 9).

Why didn't one or a combination of these enemies capture Constantinople? The answer lies in strong military leadership and even more in the city's location and excellent fortifications. During the long reign of the emperor Justinian (r. 527–565), Byzantine generals were able to reconquer much of Italy and North Africa. The Byzantines ruled most of Italy from 535 to 572 and the southern part of the peninsula until the eleventh century. They ruled North Africa until it was con-

CHAPTER LOCATOR | **How did the Byzantine Empire preserve the legacy of Rome?** | How did the Christian Church become a major force in Europe?

204 CHAPTER 8 CONTINUITY AND CHANGE IN EUROPE AND WESTERN ASIA

224–651 Sassanid dynasty	**ca. 481–511** Reign of Clovis
325 Nicene Creed produced	**527–565** Reign of Justinian
340–419 Life of Saint Jerome	**529** Writing of *The Rule of Saint Benedict*
354–430 Life of Saint Augustine	**535–572** Byzantines reconquer and rule Italy
380 Theodosius makes Christianity official religion of Roman Empire	**730–843** Iconoclastic controversy
ca. 385–461 Life of Saint Patrick	**768–814** Reign of Charlemagne
476 Odoacer deposes the last Roman emperor in the West	**843** Treaty of Verdun divides Carolingian kingdom

quered by Muslim forces in the late seventh century. Massive triple walls, built by the emperors Constantine and Theodosius II (408–450) and kept in good repair by later emperors, protected Constantinople from sea invasion. Within the walls huge cisterns provided water, and vast gardens and grazing areas supplied food so the defending people could hold out far longer than the besieging army. Attacking Constantinople by land posed greater geographical and logistical problems

MAP 8.1 ■ The Byzantine and Sassanid Empires, ca. 600

Both the Byzantine and Sassanid Empires included territory that had earlier been part of the Roman Empire. The Sassanid Persians fought Roman armies before the founding of the Byzantine Empire. Later Byzantium and the Sassanids engaged in a series of wars that weakened both and brought neither lasting territorial acquisitions.

How did Christian thinkers adapt classical ideas to Christian teachings, and develop new practices?	How did the barbarians shape social, economic, and political structures in Europe and west Asia?	How did the church convert barbarian peoples to Christianity?	How did the Franks build and govern a European empire?	✓ LearningCurve Check what you know.

than a seventh- or eighth-century government could solve. Because the city survived, the empire, though reduced in territory, endured.

The Sassanid Empire and Conflicts with Byzantium

For several centuries the Sassanid empire of Persia was Byzantium's most regular foe. Ardashir I (r. 224–243), the ruler of a small state and the first of the Sassanid dynasty, conquered the Parthian empire in 226 (see Map 6.2, page 158). Ardashir kept expanding his holdings to the east and northwest. Like all empires, the Sassanid depended on agriculture for its economic prosperity, but its location also proved well suited for commerce (see Map 8.1). A lucrative caravan trade linked the Sassanid empire to the Silk Road and China. This trade brought about considerable cultural contact between the Sassanids and the Chinese.

Whereas the Parthians had tolerated many religions, the Sassanid Persians made Zoroastrianism the official state religion. The king's power rested on the support of nobles and Zoroastrian priests who monopolized positions in the court and in the imperial bureaucracy. A highly elaborate court ceremonial and ritual exalted the status of the king and emphasized his semidivine pre-eminence over his subjects. Adherents to religions other than Zoroastrianism, such as Jews and Christians, faced discrimination.

An expansionist foreign policy brought Persia into frequent conflict with Rome and then with Byzantium. Neither side was able to achieve a clear-cut victory until the early seventh century, when the Sassanids advanced all the way to the Mediterranean and even took Egypt in 621. Their victory would be very short-lived, however, as the taxes required to finance the wars and conflicts over the succession to the throne had weakened the Persians. The Byzantines crushed the Persians in a series of battles ending with one at Nineveh in 627. Just five years later, the first Arabic forces inspired by Islam entered Persian territories, and by 651 the Sassanid dynasty had collapsed (see page 238).

Sassanid Cameo

In this cameo — a type of jewelry made by carving into a multicolored piece of rock — the Sassanid king Shapur and the Byzantine emperor Valerian fight on horseback, each identifiable by his distinctive clothing and headgear. This does not record an actual hand-to-hand battle, but uses the well-muscled rulers as symbols of their empires. (Erich Lessing/Art Resource, NY)

Justinian's Code of Law

Byzantine emperors organized and preserved Roman law, making a lasting contribution to the medieval and modern worlds. By the fourth century Roman law had become a huge, bewildering mass. Its sheer bulk made it almost unusable.

The emperor Justinian appointed a committee of eminent jurists to sort through and organize the laws. The result was the *Corpus Juris Civilis* (Body of Civil Law), a multipart collection of laws and legal commentary issued from 529 to 534 that is often simply termed Justinian's *Code*. Like so much of classical culture, Justinian's *Code* was lost in western Europe with the end of the Roman Empire, but it was rediscovered in the eleventh century and came to form the foundation of law for nearly every modern European nation.

Justinian's *Code*
▶ Multipart collection of laws and legal commentary issued in the sixth century by the emperor Justinian.

CHAPTER LOCATOR | How did the Byzantine Empire preserve the legacy of Rome? | How did the Christian Church become a major force in Europe?

CHAPTER 8
206 CONTINUITY AND CHANGE IN EUROPE AND WESTERN ASIA

- The *Codex*: brought together all the existing imperial laws into a coherent whole, eliminated outmoded laws and contradictions, and clarified the law itself
- The *Digest*: a collection of the opinions of the foremost Roman jurists on complex legal problems
- The *Institutes*: a handbook of civil law designed for students and beginning jurists

Byzantine Intellectual Life

Just as they valued the law, the Byzantines prized education. As a result, many masterpieces of ancient Greek literature survived to influence the intellectual life of the modern world. Among members of the large reading public, history was a favorite subject. The most remarkable Byzantine historian was Procopius (ca. 500–ca. 562), who wrote the *Secret History*, a vicious and uproarious attack on Justinian and his wife, the empress Theodora. (See "Individuals in Society: Theodora of Constantinople," page 208.)

Although the Byzantines discovered little that was new in mathematics and geometry, they made advances in military applications. For example, they invented an explosive liquid that came to be known as "Greek fire." The liquid was heated and propelled by a pump through a bronze tube, and as the jet left the tube, it was ignited—somewhat like a modern flamethrower.

The Byzantines devoted a great deal of attention to medicine, and their general level of medical competence was far higher than that of western Europeans. Yet their physicians could not cope with the terrible disease, often called "the Justinian plague," that swept through the Byzantine Empire and parts of western Europe between 542 and 560. Probably originating in northwestern India and carried to the Mediterranean region by ships, the disease was similar to the bubonic plague. The epidemic had profound political as well as social consequences. It weakened Justinian's military resources, thus hampering his efforts to restore unity to the Mediterranean world.

Life in Constantinople

By the seventh century Constantinople was the greatest city in the Christian world: a large population center, the seat of the imperial court and administration, and the pivot of a large volume of international trade. Given that the city was a natural geographical connecting point between East and West, its markets offered goods from many parts of the world. At the end of the eleventh century Constantinople may have been the world's third-largest city, with only Córdoba in Spain and Kaifeng in China larger.

Although merchants could become fabulously wealthy, the landed aristocracy always held the dominant social position, as in western Europe and China. Aristocrats and monasteries usually invested their wealth in real estate, which involved little risk but brought little gain.

Constantinople did not enjoy constant political stability. Between the accession of Emperor Heraclius in 610 and the fall of the city to Western Crusaders in 1204 (see page 401), four separate dynasties ruled at Constantinople. Imperial

How did Christian thinkers adapt classical ideas to Christian teachings, and develop new practices?	How did the barbarians shape social, economic, and political structures in Europe and west Asia?	How did the church convert barbarian peoples to Christianity?	How did the Franks build and govern a European empire?	☑ LearningCurve Check what you know.

The most powerful woman in Byzantine history was the daughter of a bear trainer for the circus. Theodora (ca. 497–548) grew up in what her contemporaries regarded as an undignified and morally suspect atmosphere, and she worked as a dancer and actress, both dishonorable occupations in the Roman world. Despite her background, she caught the eye of Justinian, who was then a military leader and whose uncle (and adoptive father) Justin had himself risen from obscurity to become the ruler of the Byzantine Empire. Under Justinian's influence, Justin changed the law to allow an actress who had left her disreputable life to marry whom she liked, and Justinian and Theodora married in 525. When Justinian was proclaimed co-emperor with his uncle Justin on April 1, 527, Theodora received the rare title of *augusta*, empress. Thereafter her name was linked with Justinian's in the exercise of imperial power.

Most of our knowledge of Theodora's early life comes from the *Secret History*, a tell-all description of the vices of Justinian and his court written by Procopius around 550. Procopius was the official court historian and thus spent his days praising those same people. In the *Secret History*, however, he portrays Theodora and Justinian as demonic, greedy, and vicious, killing courtiers to steal their property. In scene after detailed scene, Procopius portrays Theodora as particularly evil, sexually insatiable, and cruel, a temptress who used sorcery to attract men, including the hapless Justinian.

In one of his official histories, *The History of the Wars of Justinian*, Procopius presents a very different Theodora. Riots between the supporters of two teams in chariot races had turned deadly, and Justinian wavered in his handling of the perpetrators. Both sides turned against the emperor, besieging the palace while Justinian was inside it. Shouting "*Nika!*" (Victory), the rioters swept through the city, burning and looting. Justinian's counselors urged flight, but, according to Procopius, Theodora rose and declared:

> For one who has reigned, it is intolerable to be an exile. . . . If you wish, O Emperor, to save yourself, there is no difficulty: we have ample funds and there are the ships. Yet reflect whether, when you have once escaped to a place of security, you will not prefer death to safety. I agree with an old saying that the purple [that is, the color worn only by emperors] is a fair winding sheet [to be buried in].

Justinian rallied, ordered more than thirty thousand men and women executed, and crushed the revolt.

A sixth-century mosaic of the empress Theodora, made of thousands of tiny cubes of glass, shows her with a halo — a symbol of power — and surrounded by officials, priests, and court ladies. (Scala/Art Resource, NY)

Other sources describe or suggest Theodora's influence on imperial policy. Justinian passed a number of laws that improved the legal status of women, such as allowing women to own property and to be guardians over their own children. He forbade the exposure of unwanted infants, which happened more often to girls than to boys because boys were valued more highly. Theodora presided at imperial receptions for Arab sheiks, Persian ambassadors, Germanic princesses from the West, and barbarian chieftains from southern Russia. When Justinian fell ill from the bubonic plague in 542, Theodora took over his duties. Justinian is reputed to have consulted her every day about all aspects of state policy, including religious policy regarding the doctrinal disputes that continued throughout his reign.

Theodora's influence over her husband and her power in the Byzantine state continued until she died, perhaps of cancer, twenty years before Justinian. Her influence may have even continued after death, for Justinian continued to pass reforms favoring women and, at the end of his life, accepted an interpretation of Christian doctrine she had favored. Institutions that she established, including hospitals and churches, continued to be reminders of her charity and piety.

Theodora has been viewed as a symbol of the use of beauty and cleverness to attain position and power, and also as a strong and capable co-ruler who held the empire together during riots, revolts, and deadly epidemics. Just as she fascinated Procopius, she continues to intrigue writers today, who make her a character not only in historical works, but also in science fiction and fantasy.

QUESTIONS FOR ANALYSIS

1. How would you assess the complex legacy of Theodora?
2. Since Procopius's public and private views of the empress are so different, should he be trusted at all as a historical source? Why or why not?

ONLINE DOCUMENT PROJECT

What do Procopius's descriptions of Theodora and Justinian tell us about the problems and challenges his society faced? Examine sources that reveal the connections Procopius saw between Byzantium's rulers and the rapid decline he perceived in Byzantine society, and then complete a quiz and writing assignment based on the evidence and details from this chapter. *See the inside front cover to learn more.*

government involved such intricate court intrigue, assassination plots, and military revolts that the word *byzantine* is sometimes used in English to mean extremely entangled and complicated politics.

The typical household in the city included family members and servants, some of whom were slaves. Artisans lived and worked in their shops, while clerks, civil servants, minor officials, and business people commonly dwelled in multistory buildings perhaps comparable to the apartment complexes of modern American cities. Wealthy aristocrats resided in freestanding mansions.

In the homes of the upper classes, the segregation of women seems to have been the first principle of interior design. As in ancient Athens, private houses contained a *gynaeceum* (jihn-uh-SEE-uhm), or women's apartment, where women were kept strictly separated from the outside world. The fundamental reason for this segregation was the family's honor.

As it was throughout the world, marriage was part of a family's strategy for social advancement. Both the immediate family and the larger kinship group participated in the selection of a bride or a groom, choosing a spouse who might enhance the family's wealth or prestige.

QUICK REVIEW

Why did Roman government in the east survive long after it collapsed in the west?

How did the Christian Church become a major force in Europe?

Sarcophagus of Helena

This marble sarcophagus was made for Helena, the mother of Emperor Constantine, at her death. Its detailed carvings show victorious Roman horsemen and barbarian prisoners. Like her son, Helena became a Christian, and she was sent by Constantine on a journey to bring sacred relics from Jerusalem to Constantinople as part of his efforts to promote Christianity in the empire. (© Vanni Archive/Art Resource, NY)

A As the Western Roman Empire disintegrated, the Christian Church survived and grew. The church developed permanent institutions that drew on the Greco-Roman tradition but also expressed Christian values.

The Evolution of Church Leadership and Orthodoxy

Believers in early Christian communities chose their own leaders, but over time appointment by existing church leaders or secular rulers became the common practice. During the reign of Diocletian (r. 284–305), the Roman Empire had been divided for administrative purposes into geographical units called **dioceses**, and Christianity adopted this pattern. Each diocese was headed by a bishop. The center of a bishop's authority was his cathedral, a word deriving from the Latin *cathedra*, meaning "chair."

The early Christian Church benefited from the administrative abilities of church leaders. Bishop Ambrose of Milan (339–397) was typical of the Roman

dioceses

▶ Geographic administrative districts of the church, each under the authority of a bishop and centered around a cathedral.

CHAPTER LOCATOR | How did the Byzantine Empire preserve the legacy of Rome?

How did the Christian Church become a major force in Europe?

aristocrats who held high public office, converted to Christianity, and subsequently became bishops. Like many bishops, Ambrose had a solid education in classical law and rhetoric, which he used to become an eloquent preacher. He had a strong sense of his authority and even successfully resisted Emperor Theodosius's (r. 379–395) efforts to take control of church property. Ambrose's assertion that the church was supreme in spiritual matters and the state in secular issues was to serve as the cornerstone of the church's position on church-state relations for centuries.

Although conflicts between religious and secular leaders were frequent, the church also received support from the emperors. In 380 Theodosius made Christianity the official religion of the empire, and later in his reign he authorized the closure or destruction of temples and holy sites dedicated to the traditional Roman and Greek gods. In return for such support, the emperors expected the Christian Church's assistance in maintaining order and unity.

Christians disagreed with one another about many issues. In the fourth and fifth centuries disputes arose over the nature of Christ. For example, Arianism, developed by Arius (ca. 250–336), a priest of Alexandria, held that Jesus was created by the will of God the Father and thus was not co-eternal with him. Emperor Constantine, who legalized Christianity in 312, rejected the Arian interpretation. In 325 he summoned a council of church leaders to Nicaea in Asia Minor and presided over it personally. The council produced the Nicene (nigh-SEEN) Creed, which defined the position that Christ is "eternally begotten of the Father" and of the same substance as the Father. Arius and those who refused to accept Nicene Christianity were banished. Their interpretation of the nature of Christ was declared a heresy, that is, a belief that contradicted the interpretation the church leaders declared was correct, which was termed orthodoxy. These actions did not end Arianism, however. Several later emperors were Arian Christian, and Arian missionaries converted many barbarian tribes. The Nicene interpretation eventually became the most widely held understanding of the nature of Christ.

heresy
▶ A religious practice or belief judged unacceptable by church officials.

Nonetheless, disputes about the nature of Christ also continued, with factions establishing themselves as separate Christian groups. The Nestorians, for example, regarded the divine and human natures in Jesus as distinct from one another, whereas the orthodox opinion was that they were united. The Nestorians split from the rest of the church in the fifth century after their position was outlawed and settled in Persia. Nestorian Christian missionaries later founded churches in Central Asia, India, and China (see Chapter 12).

The Western Church and the Eastern Church

The leader of the church in the West, the bishop of Rome, became more powerful than his counterpart in the Byzantine East for a variety of reasons. Most significantly, bishops of Rome asserted that Rome had a special place in Christian history. According to tradition, Saint Peter, chief of Jesus's disciples, had lived in Rome and been its first bishop. Thus, as successors of Peter, the bishops of Rome—known as popes, claimed a privileged position in the church hierarchy, an idea called the Petrine Doctrine. They urged other churches to appeal to Rome for the resolution of disputed issues and sent letters of guidance to other bishops. (The Christian Church headed by the pope in Rome was generally called the Roman Church in this era, and later the Roman Catholic Church.)

popes
▶ Heads of the Roman Catholic Church, who became political as well as religious authorities. The period of a pope's term in office is called a pontificate.

| How did Christian thinkers adapt classical ideas to Christian teachings, and develop new practices? | How did the barbarians shape social, economic, and political structures in Europe and west Asia? | How did the church convert barbarian peoples to Christianity? | How did the Franks build and govern a European empire? | ✔ LearningCurve Check what you know. |

211

This wood carving shows Saint Ambrose and Saint Jerome, two of the most important early church fathers, hard at work writing. Divine inspiration appears in the form of an angel and a dove. (Duomo, Modena, Italy/Alinari/Art Resource, NY)

The popes also expanded the church's secular authority. They made treaties with barbarian leaders, charged taxes, enforced laws, and organized armies. The Western Christian Church headed by the pope in Rome would become the most enduring nongovernmental institution in world history.

By contrast, in the East the emperor's jurisdiction over the church was fully acknowledged. As in Rome, there was a head of the church in Constantinople, called the patriarch, but he did not develop the same powers that the pope did in the West because there was never a similar power vacuum into which he needed to step. He and other high church officials were appointed by the emperor. The Eastern emperors looked on religion as a branch of the state, and they considered it their duty to protect the faith not only against heathen outsiders but also against heretics within the empire. Following the pattern set by Constantine, the emperors summoned councils of bishops and theologians to settle doctrinal disputes. They and the Eastern bishops did not accept Rome's claim to primacy, and gradually the Byzantine Christian Church, generally called the Orthodox Church, and the Roman Church began to diverge.

Orthodox Church

▶ Another name for the Eastern Christian Church, over which emperors continued to have power.

Christian Monasticism

Christianity began and spread as a city religion. With time, however, some especially pious Christians started to feel that a life of asceticism (extreme material sacrifice, including fasting and the renunciation of sex) was a better way to show their devotion to Christ's teachings, just as followers of Mahavira or the Buddha had centuries earlier in South Asia (see Chapter 3).

Ascetics often separate themselves from their families and normal social life, and this is what Christian ascetics did. Individuals and small groups withdrew from cities and moved to the Egyptian desert, where they sought God through prayer in caves and shelters in the desert or mountains. These individuals were called hermits or monks. Gradually, large groups of monks emerged in the deserts of Upper Egypt, creating a style of life known as monasticism. Many devout women were also attracted to this eremitical type of monasticism, becoming nuns. Although monks and nuns led isolated lives, ordinary people soon recognized them as holy people and sought them as spiritual guides.

CHAPTER LOCATOR | How did the Byzantine Empire preserve the legacy of Rome? | **How did the Christian Church become a major force in Europe?**

Church leaders did not really approve of eremitical life. Hermits sometimes claimed to have mystical experiences—direct communications with God. If hermits could communicate directly with the Lord, what need had they for priests, bishops, and the institutional church? The church hierarchy instead encouraged those who wanted to live ascetic lives of devotion to do so in communities. Consequently, in the fourth, fifth, and sixth centuries many different kinds of communal monasticism developed in Gaul, Italy, Spain, Anglo-Saxon England, and Ireland.

In 529 Benedict of Nursia (ca. 480–547) wrote a brief set of regulations for the monks who had gathered around him at Monte Cassino, between Rome and Naples. Benedict's guide for monastic life, known as *The Rule of Saint Benedict*, slowly replaced all others, and it has influenced all forms of organized religious life in the Roman Church. The guide outlined a monastic life of regularity, discipline, and moderation in an atmosphere of silence. Under Benedict's regulations, monks spent part of each day in formal prayer, chanting psalms and other prayers from the Bible. The rest of the day was passed in manual labor, study, and private prayer. The monastic life as conceived by Saint Benedict provided opportunities for men of different abilities and talents—from mechanics to gardeners to literary scholars. The Benedictine form of religious life also appealed to women, because it allowed them to show their devotion and engage in study. Benedict's twin sister, Scholastica (480–543), adapted the *Rule* for use by her community of nuns.

Benedictine monasticism also succeeded partly because it was so materially successful. In the seventh and eighth centuries Benedictine monasteries pushed back forests and wastelands, drained swamps, and experimented with crop rotation, making a significant contribution to the agricultural development of Europe. Monasteries also conducted schools for local young people. Some learned about prescriptions and herbal remedies and went on to provide medical treatment for their localities. Others copied manuscripts and wrote books. Local and royal governments drew on the services of the literate men and able administrators the monasteries produced.

Monasticism in the Orthodox world differed in fundamental ways from the monasticism that evolved in western Europe. First, while *The Rule of Saint Benedict* gradually became the universal guide for all western European monasteries, each monastic house in the Byzantine world developed its own set of rules for organization and behavior. Second, education never became a central feature of the Orthodox houses. Since bishops and patriarchs of the Orthodox Church were recruited only from the monasteries, however, these institutions did exercise cultural influence.

QUICK REVIEW

What were the most important differences
between the Roman and Orthodox Churches?
How would you explain these differences?

| How did Christian thinkers adapt classical ideas to Christian teachings, and develop new practices? | How did the barbarians shape social, economic, and political structures in Europe and west Asia? | How did the church convert barbarian peoples to Christianity? | How did the Franks build and govern a European empire? | ☑ LearningCurve Check what you know. |

213

> How did Christian thinkers adapt classical ideas to Christian teachings, and what new religious concepts and practices did they develop?

The Marys at Jesus's Tomb

This late-fourth-century ivory panel tells the biblical story of Mary Magdalene and another Mary who went to Jesus's tomb to anoint the body (Matthew 28:1–7). At the top guards collapse when an angel descends from Heaven, and at the bottom the Marys listen to the angel telling them that Jesus has risen. Here the artist uses Roman artistic styles to convey Christian subject matter, synthesizing classical form and Christian teaching. (Castello Sforzesco Milan, Italy/Scala/Art Resource, NY)

The growth of Christianity was tied not just to institutions such as the papacy and monasteries but also to ideas. Initially, Christians rejected Greco-Roman culture. Gradually, however, Christian leaders and thinkers developed ideas that drew on classical influences, though there were also areas of controversy that differed in the Western and Eastern Churches.

Christianity and Classical Culture

In the first century Christians believed that Christ would soon fulfill his promise to return and that the end of the world was near; therefore, they saw no point in

CHAPTER LOCATOR | How did the Byzantine Empire preserve the legacy of Rome? | How did the Christian Church become a major force in Europe?

CHAPTER 8
214 CONTINUITY AND CHANGE IN EUROPE AND WESTERN ASIA

devoting time to learning. By the second century, however, these apocalyptic expectations were diminishing, and church leaders began to incorporate elements of Greek and Roman philosophy and learning into Christian teachings (see page 166). They found support for this incorporation in the written texts that circulated among Christians. In the third and fourth centuries these texts were brought together as the New Testament of the Bible, with general agreement about most of what should be included but sharp disputes about some books. Although some of Jesus's sermons as recorded in the Gospels (see page 165) urged followers to avoid worldly attachments, other parts of the Bible advocated acceptance of existing social, economic, and political structures. Christian thinkers built on these, adapting Christian teachings to fit with Roman realities and Roman ideas to fit with Christian aims, just as Buddhist thinkers adapted Buddhist teachings when they spread them to Central Asia, China, Korea, and Japan (see Chapter 7).

Saint Jerome (340–419) translated the Old Testament and New Testament from Hebrew and Greek, respectively, into vernacular Latin. Called the Vulgate, his edition of the Bible served as the official translation until the sixteenth century. Familiar with the writings of classical authors such as Cicero and Virgil, Saint Jerome believed that Christians should study the best of ancient thought because it would direct their minds to God. He maintained that the best ancient literature should be interpreted in light of the Christian faith.

Christian attitudes toward gender and sexuality provide a good example of the ways early Christians first challenged and then largely adopted the views of their contemporary world. In his plan of salvation Jesus considered women the equal of men. Women were among the earliest converts to Christianity and took an active role in its spread, preaching, acting as missionaries, being martyred alongside men, and perhaps even baptizing believers. Some women embraced the ideal of virginity and either singly or in monastic communities declared themselves "virgins in the service of Christ." All this initially made Christianity seem dangerous to many Romans who viewed marriage as the foundation of society and the proper patriarchal order.

Not all Christian teachings about gender were radical, however. In the first century male church leaders began to place restrictions on female believers. Women were forbidden to preach and were gradually excluded from holding official positions in Christianity other than in women's monasteries. In so limiting the activities of female believers, Christianity was following well-established social patterns, just as it modeled its official hierarchy after that of the Roman Empire.

Christian teachings about sexuality also built on and challenged classical models. The rejection of sexual activity involved an affirmation of the importance of a spiritual life, but it also incorporated hostility toward the body found in some Hellenistic philosophies. Just as spirit was superior to matter, the thinking went, the mind was superior to the body. Though Christian teachings affirmed that God had created the material world and sanctioned marriage, most Christian thinkers also taught that celibacy was the better life and that anything that distracted one's attention from the spiritual world performed an evil function. For most clerical writers (who were themselves male), this temptation came from women, and in some of their writings women themselves are portrayed as evil, the "devil's gateway."

| How did Christian thinkers adapt classical ideas to Christian teachings, and develop new practices? | How did the barbarians shape social, economic, and political structures in Europe and west Asia? | How did the church convert barbarian peoples to Christianity? | How did the Franks build and govern a European empire? | LearningCurve Check what you know. |

215

Saint Augustine on Sin, Grace, and Redemption

One thinker had an especially strong role in shaping Christian views about sexual activity and many other issues: Saint Augustine of Hippo (354–430). Augustine was born into an urban family in what is now Algeria in North Africa. His father was a pagan; his mother, Monica, was a devout Christian. He gained an excellent education, fathered a son, and experimented with various religious ideas. In adulthood he converted to his mother's religion, eventually becoming bishop of the city of Hippo Regius.

Written in the rhetorical style and language of late Roman antiquity, Augustine's autobiography, *The Confessions*, marks a synthesis of Greco-Roman forms and Christian thought. *The Confessions* describes Augustine's moral struggle, the conflict between his spiritual aspirations and his sensual self. Many Greek and Roman philosophers had taught that knowledge would lead to virtue. Augustine came to reject this idea, claiming that people do not always act on the basis of rational knowledge. Instead the basic or dynamic force in any individual is the will. When Adam ate the fruit forbidden by God in the Garden of Eden (Genesis 3:6), he committed the "original sin" and corrupted the will, wrote Augustine. Adam's sin did not simply remain his own but was passed on to all later humans through sexual intercourse. Original sin thus became a common social stain, in Augustine's opinion, transmitted by sexual desire. According to Augustine, because Adam disobeyed God, all human beings have an innate tendency to sin: their will is weak. But Augustine held that God restores the strength of the will through grace, which is transmitted in certain rituals that the church defined as sacraments. Augustine's ideas on sin, grace, and redemption became the foundation of all subsequent Western Christian theology, Protestant as well as Catholic.

sacraments
▶ Certain rituals of the church believed to act as a conduit of God's grace, such as the Eucharist and baptism.

The Iconoclastic Controversy

In the centuries after Constantine, the most serious dispute within the Orthodox Church concerned icons—images or representations of God the Father, Jesus, and the saints in painting, bas-relief, or mosaic. Since the third century the church had allowed people to venerate icons. Although all prayer was to be directed to God the Father, Christian teaching held that icons representing the saints fostered reverence and that Jesus and the saints could most effectively plead a cause to God the Father. (For more about the role of saints, see page 223.) Iconoclasts, those who favored the destruction of icons, argued that people were worshipping the image itself rather than what it signified. This, they claimed, constituted idolatry, a violation of one of the Ten Commandments, the religious and moral code found in Hebrew Scripture that was also sacred to Christians.

The result of this dispute was a terrible theological conflict, the iconoclastic controversy, that split the Byzantine world for a century. In 730 the emperor Leo III (r. 717–741) ordered the destruction of icons. The removal of these images from Byzantine churches provoked a violent reaction: entire provinces revolted, and the Byzantine Empire and the Roman papacy severed relations. Since Eastern monasteries were the fiercest defenders of icons, Leo's son Constantine V (r. 741–775) seized their property, executed some of the monks, and forced other monks

iconoclastic controversy
▶ The conflict over the veneration of religious images in the Byzantine Empire.

CHAPTER LOCATOR | How did the Byzantine Empire preserve the legacy of Rome? | How did the Christian Church become a major force in Europe?

CHAPTER 8
216 CONTINUITY AND CHANGE IN EUROPE AND WESTERN ASIA

into the army. Theological disputes and civil disorder over the icons continued intermittently until 843, when the icons were restored.

The implications of the iconoclastic controversy extended far beyond strictly theological issues. Iconoclasm raised the question of the right of the emperor to intervene in religious disputes. Iconoclasm antagonized the pope and served to encourage him in his quest for an alliance with the Frankish monarchy (see page 226). This further divided the two parts of Christendom, and in 1054 a theological disagreement led the pope in Rome and the patriarch of Constantinople to declare each other a heretic. The outcome was a continuing schism between the Roman Catholic and the Orthodox Churches.

QUICK REVIEW

How did the works of Saint Augustine both embrace and challenge Greco-Roman ideas?

| How did Christian thinkers adapt classical ideas to Christian teachings, and develop new practices? | How did the barbarians shape social, economic, and political structures in Europe and west Asia? | How did the church convert barbarian peoples to Christianity? | How did the Franks build and govern a European empire? | ✓ LearningCurve Check what you know. |

> How did the barbarians shape social, economic, and political structures in Europe and western Asia?

Visigothic Work and Play

This page comes from one of the very few manuscripts from the time of the barbarian invasions to have survived, a copy of the first five books of the Old Testament — the Pentateuch — made around 600, perhaps in Visigothic Spain or North Africa. The top shows biblical scenes, while the bottom shows people engaged in everyday activities: building a wall, drawing water from a well, and trading punches.
(Bibliothèque Nationale, Paris, France/The Art Archive at Art Resource, NY)

The word *barbarian* comes from the Greek *barbaros*, meaning someone who did not speak Greek. The Greeks used this word to include people such as the Egyptians, whom the Greeks respected. The Romans usually used the Latin version of *barbarian* to mean the peoples who lived beyond the northeastern boundary of Roman territory, whom they regarded as unruly, savage, and primitive. That value judgment is generally also present when we use *barbarian* in English, but there really is no other word to describe the many different peoples who lived to the north of the Roman Empire. Thus historians of late antiquity use the word *barbarian* to designate these peoples, who spoke a variety of languages but had similarities in their basic social, economic, and political structures.

Barbarians included many different ethnic groups with social and political structures, languages, laws, and beliefs developed in central and northern Europe and western Asia over many centuries. Among the largest barbarian groups were the Celts and Germans; Germans were further subdivided into various tribes, such as Ostrogoths, Visigoths, Burgundians, and Franks. *Celt* and *German* are

CHAPTER LOCATOR | How did the Byzantine Empire preserve the legacy of Rome? | How did the Christian Church become a major force in Europe?

MAP 8.2 ■ The Barbarian Migrations, ca. 340–500

Various barbarian groups migrated throughout Europe and western Asia in late antiquity, pushed and pulled by a number of factors. Many of them formed loosely structured states, of which the Frankish kingdom would become the most significant.

often used as ethnic terms, but they are better understood as linguistic terms, a Celt being a person who spoke a Celtic language and a German one who spoke a Germanic language. Celts, Germans, and other barbarians brought their customs and traditions with them when they moved south and west, and these gradually combined with classical and Christian customs and beliefs to form new types of societies. From this cultural mix the Franks emerged as an especially strong and influential force, and they built a lasting empire (see page 226).

Social and Economic Structures

Barbarian groups usually resided in small villages, and climate and geography determined the basic patterns of agricultural and pastoral life. Many groups settled on the edges of clearings where they raised barley, wheat, oats, peas, and beans. Men and women tilled their fields with simple scratch plows and harvested their grain with small iron sickles. Most of people's caloric intake came from grain in some form.

| How did Christian thinkers adapt classical ideas to Christian teachings, and develop new practices? | **How did the barbarians shape social, economic, and political structures in Europe and west Asia?** | How did the church convert barbarian peoples to Christianity? | How did the Franks build and govern a European empire? | LearningCurve Check what you know. |

Within the villages, there were great differences in wealth and status. Free men and their families constituted the largest class, and the number of cattle these men possessed indicated their wealth and determined their social status. Free men also took part in tribal warfare. Slaves acquired through warfare worked as farm laborers, herdsmen, and household servants. Barbarian society was patriarchal. Some wealthy and powerful men had more than one wife, a pattern that continued even after they became Christian, but polygamy was not widespread among ordinary people. Once women were widowed, they sometimes assumed their husbands' rights over family property and took guardianship of their children.

Tribes, Warriors, and Laws

The basic social and political unit among barbarian groups was the tribe or confederation, made up of kin groups whose members believed they were all descended from a common ancestor. Tribes were led by chieftains, who were elected from among the male members of the most powerful family. The chief led the tribe in war, settled disputes among its members, conducted negotiations with outside powers, and offered sacrifices to the gods. As barbarian groups migrated into and conquered parts of the Western Roman Empire, their chiefs became even more powerful. Often chiefs adopted the title of king.

Closely associated with the chief in some tribes was the comitatus (kuhm-ee-TAH-tuhs), or war band. The warriors swore loyalty to the chief and fought alongside him in battle. Warriors may originally have been relatively equal to one another, but during the migrations and warfare of the second through the fourth centuries, the war band was transformed into a system of stratified ranks. When tribes settled down, warriors also began to acquire land as both a mark of prestige and a means to power. Social inequalities emerged and gradually grew stronger. These inequalities help explain the origins of the European noble class.

Beginning in the late fifth century some chieftains began to collect, write, and publish lists of their customs and laws. Barbarian law codes often included clauses designed to reduce interpersonal violence. Any crime that involved a personal injury, such as assault, rape, and murder, was given a particular monetary value, called the **wergeld** (WUHR-gehld) that was to be paid by a person accused of a crime to the victim or the victim's family. The wergeld varied according to the severity of the crime and also the social status and gender of the victim.

Like most people of the ancient world, barbarians worshipped hundreds of gods and goddesses with specialized functions. They regarded certain mountains, lakes, rivers, or groves of trees as sacred because these were linked to deities. Among the Celts, religious leaders called druids had legal and educational as well as religious functions, orally passing down laws and traditions from generation to generation. Bards singing poems and ballads also passed down myths and stories of heroes and gods, which were written down much later.

Migrations and Political Change

Migrating groups that the Romans labeled barbarians had moved southward and eastward off and on since about 100 C.E. (see page 168). Why did the barbarians migrate? In part, they were searching for more regular supplies of food, better

wergeld

▶ Compensatory payment for death or injury set in many barbarian law codes.

CHAPTER LOCATOR | How did the Byzantine Empire preserve the legacy of Rome? | How did the Christian Church become a major force in Europe?

CHAPTER 8
220 CONTINUITY AND CHANGE IN EUROPE AND WESTERN ASIA

farmland, and a warmer climate. Conflicts within and among barbarian groups also led to war and disruption, which motivated groups to move. Roman expansion led to further movement of barbarian groups but also to the blending of cultures.

The spread of the Celts presents a good example of both conflict and assimilation. Celtic-speaking peoples had lived in central Europe since at least the fifth century B.C.E. and had spread out from there to the Iberian Peninsula in the west, Hungary in the east, and the British Isles in the north. As Julius Caesar advanced northward into what he termed Gaul (present-day France), he defeated many Celtic tribes (see page 154). Celtic peoples conquered by the Romans often assimilated to Roman ways, intermarrying with Romans, adopting the Latin language and many aspects of Roman culture. By the fourth century C.E., however, Gaul and Britain were under pressure from Germanic groups moving westward. Roman troops withdrew from Britain, and Celtic-speaking peoples clashed with Germanic-speaking invaders, of whom the largest tribes were the Angles and the Saxons. Some Celtic-speakers moved farther west. Others remained and intermarried with Germanic peoples, their descendants forming a number of small Anglo-Saxon kingdoms.

In eastern Europe, a significant factor in barbarian migration and the merging of various Germanic groups was pressure from nomadic steppe peoples from central Asia, most prominently the Huns, who attacked the Black Sea area and the Eastern Roman Empire beginning in the fourth century. Under the leadership of their warrior-king Attila, the Huns attacked the Byzantine Empire in 447 and then turned westward, allying with some Germanic groups and moving into what is now France. After Attila turned his army southward and crossed the Alps into Italy. Though papal diplomacy was later credited with stopping the advance of the Huns, their dwindling food supplies and a plague that spread among their troops were probably much more important factors. The Huns retreated from Italy, and within a year Attila was dead. The Huns never again played a significant role in European history. Their conquests had pushed many Germanic groups together, however, which transformed smaller bands of people into larger, more unified peoples who could more easily pick the Western Roman Empire apart.

After they conquered an area, barbarians generally established states ruled by kings. However, the kingdoms did not have definite geographical borders, and their locations shifted as tribes moved. Eventually, barbarian kingdoms came to include Italy itself. From Constantinople, Eastern Roman emperors such as Justinian (see page 206) worked to reconquer at least some of the West from barbarian tribes. They were occasionally successful but could not hold the empire together for long.

Anglo-Saxon Helmet

This ceremonial bronze helmet from seventh-century England was found inside a ship buried at Sutton Hoo. The nearly 100-foot-long ship was dragged overland before being buried completely. It held one body and many grave goods, including swords, gold buckles, and silver bowls made in Byzantium. The unidentified person who was buried here was clearly wealthy and powerful, and so was very likely a chief. (© The Trustees of the British Museum/Art Resource, NY)

QUICK REVIEW <

How were barbarian societies organized?

How did Christian thinkers adapt classical ideas to Christian teachings, and develop new practices?

How did the barbarians shape social, economic, and political structures in Europe and west Asia?

How did the church convert barbarian peoples to Christianity?

How did the Franks build and govern a European empire?

✓ LearningCurve
Check what you know.

How did the church convert barbarian peoples to Christianity?

The Mediterranean served as the highway over which Christianity spread to the cities of the Roman Empire. Christian teachings were often spread into the countryside and into areas beyond the borders of the empire by those who had dedicated their lives to the church, such as monks. Such missionaries were often sent by popes specifically to convert certain groups.

Missionaries' Actions

Throughout barbarian Europe, religion was not a private or individual matter; it was a social affair, and the religion of the chieftain or king determined the religion of the people. Thus missionaries concentrated their initial efforts not on ordinary people but on kings or tribal chieftains and the members of their families. Because they had more opportunity to spend time with missionaries, queens and other female members of the royal family were often the first converts in an area, and they influenced their husbands and brothers.

Many barbarian groups were converted by Arian missionaries, who also founded dioceses. Bishop Ulfilas (ca. 310–383), for example, an Ostrogoth himself, translated the Bible from Greek into the Gothic language even before Jerome wrote the Latin Vulgate, creating a new Gothic script in order to write it down. In the sixth and seventh centuries most Goths and other Germanic tribes converted to Roman Christianity, sometimes peacefully and sometimes as a result of conquest. Ulfilas's Bible—and the Gothic script he invented—were forgotten and rediscovered only a thousand years later.

Tradition identifies the conversion of Ireland with Saint Patrick (ca. 385–461). After a vision urged him to Christianize Ireland, Patrick studied in Gaul and in 432 was consecrated a bishop. He then returned to Ireland, where he converted the Irish tribe by tribe, first baptizing the king.

The Christianization of the English began in earnest in 597, when Pope Gregory I (pontificate 590–604) sent a delegation of monks to England. The conversion of the English had far-reaching consequences because Britain later served as a base for the Christianization of Germany and other parts of northern Europe (Map 8.3). Between the fifth and tenth centuries the majority of people living on the European continent and the nearby islands accepted the Christian religion.

In eastern Europe missionaries traveled far beyond the boundaries of the Byzantine Empire. In 863 the emperor Michael III (r. 842–867) sent the brothers

MAP 8.3 ■ The Spread of Christianity, ca. 300–800

Originating in the area near Jerusalem, Christianity spread throughout and then beyond the Roman world.

> MAPPING THE PAST

ANALYZING THE MAP: Based on the map, how did the roads and sea-lanes of the Roman Empire influence the spread of Christianity?

CONNECTIONS: How does the map support the conclusion that Christianity began as an urban religion and then spread into more rural areas?

Cyril (826–869) and Methodius (815–885) to preach Christianity in Moravia (an eastern region of the modern Czech Republic). Cyril invented a Slavic alphabet using Greek characters, later called the Cyrillic alphabet. In the tenth century other missionaries spread Christianity, the Cyrillic alphabet, and Byzantine art and architecture to Russia.

The Process of Conversion

How did missionaries and priests get masses of pagan and illiterate peoples to understand Christian ideals and teachings? They did it through preaching, assimilation of pagan customs, the ritual of penance, and veneration of the saints. Those

| How did Christian thinkers adapt classical ideas to Christian teachings, and develop new practices? | How did the barbarians shape social, economic, and political structures in Europe and west Asia? | **How did the church convert barbarian peoples to Christianity?** | How did the Franks build and govern a European empire? | ✓ LearningCurve Check what you know. |

who preached aimed to present the basic teachings of Christianity and strengthen the newly baptized in their faith through stories about the lives of Christ and the saints.

Deeply ingrained pagan customs and practices, however, could not be stamped out by words alone. Thus Christian missionaries often pursued a policy of assimilation, easing the conversion of pagan men and women by stressing similarities between their customs and beliefs and those of Christianity and by mixing barbarian pagan ideas and practices with Christian ones. For example, bogs and lakes sacred to Germanic gods became associated with saints, as did various aspects of ordinary life, such as traveling, planting crops, and worrying about a sick child. Aspects of existing midwinter celebrations were assimilated into celebrations of Christmas. Spring rituals involving eggs and rabbits (both symbols of fertility) were added to celebrations of Easter.

penance
▶ Ritual in which Christians asked a priest for forgiveness for sins and the priest set certain actions to atone for the sins.

The ritual of penance was also instrumental in teaching people Christian ideas. Christianity taught that certain actions and thoughts were sins. Only by confessing sins and asking forgiveness could a sinning believer be reconciled with God. Confession was initially a public ritual, but by the fifth century individual confession to a parish priest was more common. During this ritual the individual knelt before the priest, who questioned him or her about sins he or she might have committed. The priest then set a penance such as fasting or saying specific prayers to allow the person to atone for the sin. Penance gave new converts a sense of the behavior expected of Christians, encouraged the private examination of conscience, and offered relief from the burden of sinful deeds.

saints
▶ People who were venerated for having lived or died in a way that was spiritually heroic or noteworthy.

Veneration of saints, people who had lived (or died) in a way that was spiritually heroic or noteworthy, was another way that Christians formed stronger connections with their religion. Saints were understood to provide protection and assistance to worshippers, and parish churches often housed saints' relics, that is, bones, articles of clothing, or other objects associated with them. The relics served as links between the material world and the spiritual, and miracle stories about saints and their relics were an important part of Christian preaching and writing.

Christians came to venerate the saints as powerful and holy. They prayed to saints or to the Virgin Mary to intercede with God, or they simply asked the saints to assist and bless them. The entire village participated in processions marking saints' days or important points in the agricultural year, often carrying images of saints or their relics around the houses and fields. The decision to adopt Christianity was often made first by an emperor or king, but actual conversion was a local matter, as people came to feel that the parish priest and the saints provided them with benefits in this world and the world to come.

> **QUICK REVIEW**

What role did kings and other elites play in the conversion of barbarian peoples to Christianity?

Charlemagne and His Wife

This illumination from a ninth-century manuscript portrays Charlemagne with one of his wives. Marriage was an important tool of diplomacy for Charlemagne, and he had a number of wives and concubines. (Erich Lessing/Art Resource, NY)

> PICTURING THE PAST

ANALYZING THE IMAGE: What does Charlemagne appear to be doing? How would you characterize his wife's reaction?
CONNECTIONS: Does this depiction of a Frankish queen match what you've read about female rulers in this era, such as Theodora and Clotild?

How did the Franks build and govern a European empire?

Most barbarian kingdoms did not last very long, but one that did—and that came to have a decisive role in history—was that of the confederation of Germanic peoples known as the Franks. In the fourth and fifth centuries the Franks settled within the empire and allied with the Romans, some attaining high military and civil positions. Though at that time the Frankish kingdom was simply one barbarian kingdom among many, rulers after the influential Clovis used a variety of tactics to expand their holdings, enhance their authority, and create a stable system. Charles the Great (r. 768–814), generally known by the French version of his name, Charlemagne (SHAHR-luh-mayne), created the largest state in western Europe since the Roman Empire.

How did Christian thinkers adapt classical ideas to Christian teachings, and develop new practices?

How did the barbarians shape social, economic, and political structures in Europe and west Asia?

How did the church convert barbarian peoples to Christianity?

How did the Franks build and govern a European empire?

☑ LearningCurve
Check what you know.

225

The Merovingians and Carolingians

The Franks believed that Merovech, a semi-legendary figure, founded their ruling dynasty, which was thus called Merovingian (mehr-uh-VIHN-jee-uhn). The reign of Clovis (r. ca. 481–511) was decisive in the development of the Franks as a unified people. Through military campaigns, Clovis acquired the central provinces of Roman Gaul and began to conquer southern Gaul from other Germanic tribes. His wife, Clotild, a Roman Christian, pressured him to convert, but he refused. His later biographer Gregory of Tours, a bishop in the Frankish kingdom in the sixth century, attributed his conversion to a battlefield vision, just as Emperor Constantine's biographers had reported about his conversion.

Most historians today conclude that Clovis's conversion to Roman Christianity was a pragmatic choice: it brought him the crucial support of the bishops of Gaul in his campaigns against tribes that were still pagan or had accepted the Arian version of Christianity. As the defender of Roman Christianity against heretical tribes, Clovis went on to conquer the Visigoths, extending his domain to include much of what is now France and southwestern Germany.

Following Frankish traditions in which property was divided among male heirs, at Clovis's death his kingdom was divided among his four sons. For the next two centuries rulers of the various kingdoms fought one another in civil wars, and other military leaders challenged their authority.

Merovingian kings based some aspects of their government on Roman principles. For example, they adopted the Roman concept of the *civitas*—Latin for a city and its surrounding territory. A count presided over the civitas, raising troops, collecting royal revenues, and providing justice. Within the royal household, Merovingian politics provided women with opportunities, and some queens not only influenced but occasionally also dominated events. Because the finances of the kingdom were merged with those of the royal family, queens often had control of the royal treasury just as more ordinary women controlled household expenditures.

At the king's court an official called the mayor of the palace supervised legal, financial, and household officials; the mayor of the palace also governed in the king's absence. In the seventh century the position as mayor was held by members of an increasingly powerful family, the **Carolingians** (ka-ruh-LIHN-jee-uhns), who advanced themselves through advantageous marriages, a well-earned reputation for military strength, and the help of the church.

Eventually the Carolingians replaced the Merovingians as rulers of the Frankish kingdom, cementing their authority when the Carolingian Charles Martel defeated Muslim invaders in 732 at the Battle of Poitiers (pwah-tee-AY) in central France. The Battle of Poitiers helped the Carolingians acquire more support from the church, perhaps their most important asset. They further strengthened their ties to the church by supporting the work of missionaries who preached Christian principles—including the duty to obey secular authorities—to pagan peoples and by allying themselves with the papacy against other Germanic tribes.

Carolingian

▶ A dynasty of rulers that took over the Frankish kingdom from the Merovingians in the seventh century; *Carolingian* derives from the Latin word for "Charles," the name of several members of this dynasty.

The Warrior-Ruler Charlemagne

The most powerful of the Carolingians was Charlemagne. Through brutal military expeditions that brought wealth and by peaceful travel, personal appearances, shrewd marital alliances, and the sheer force of his personality, Charlemagne

CHAPTER LOCATOR | How did the Byzantine Empire preserve the legacy of Rome? | How did the Christian Church become a major force in Europe?

CHAPTER 8

226 CONTINUITY AND CHANGE IN EUROPE AND WESTERN ASIA

sought to awe newly conquered peoples and rebellious domestic enemies. By around 805 the Frankish kingdom included all of continental Europe except Spain, Scandinavia, southern Italy, and the Slavic fringes of the East.

For administrative purposes, Charlemagne divided his entire kingdom into counties. Each of the approximately six hundred counties was governed by a count. As a link between local authorities and the central government, Charlemagne appointed officials called *missi dominici*, "agents of the lord king." Each year beginning in 802 two missi, usually a count and a bishop or abbot, visited assigned districts. They checked up on the counts and their districts' judicial, financial, and clerical activities.

In the autumn of the year 800 Charlemagne visited Rome, where on Christmas Day Pope Leo III crowned him emperor. The event had momentous consequences. In taking as his motto *Renovatio romani imperi* (Revival of the Roman Empire), Charlemagne was deliberately perpetuating old Roman imperial ideas while identifying with the new Rome of the Christian Church. The Byzantines regarded his papal coronation as rebellious and Charlemagne as a usurper. His crowning as emperor thus marked a decisive break between Rome and Constantinople and gave church authorities in the West proof that the imperial title could only be granted by the pope.

As he built an empire through conquest and strategic alliances, Charlemagne also set in motion a cultural revival that later historians called the "Carolingian Renaissance." The Carolingian Renaissance was a rebirth of interest in, study of, and preservation of the language, ideas, and achievements of classical Greece and Rome. Scholars at Charlemagne's capital of Aachen copied Greco-Roman and Christian books and manuscripts and created libraries housed in churches and monasteries. Furthermore, Charlemagne urged monasteries to promote Christian learning.

Charlemagne left his vast empire to his sole surviving son, Louis the Pious (r. 814–840), who attempted to keep the empire intact. This proved to be impossible. Members of the nobility engaged in plots and open warfare against the emperor, often allying themselves with one of Louis's three sons. In 843, shortly after Louis's death, those sons agreed to the Treaty of Verdun, which divided the empire into three parts: Charles the Bald received the western part, Lothair the middle and the title of emperor, and Louis the eastern part, from which he acquired the title "the German."

The weakening of central power was hastened by invasions and migrations from the north, south, and east. Thus Charlemagne's empire ended in much the same way that the Roman Empire had earlier, from a combination of internal weakness and external pressure.

Charlemagne's Conquests, ca. 768–814

- ■ Frankish Kingdom, 768
- ■ Areas conquered by Charlemagne
- ■ Tributary peoples
- ■ Byzantine Empire

The Treaty of Verdun, 843

Treaty of Verdun

▶ A treaty ratified in 843 that divided Charlemagne's territories among his three surviving grandsons; their kingdoms set the pattern for the modern states of Germany, France, and Italy.

QUICK REVIEW

What role did the Roman Church play in the rise of the Carolingians to power?

| How did Christian thinkers adapt classical ideas to Christian teachings, and develop new practices? | How did the barbarians shape social, economic, and political structures in Europe and west Asia? | How did the church convert barbarian peoples to Christianity? | **How did the Franks build and govern a European empire?** | ✔ LearningCurve Check what you know. |

227

CHAPTER SUMMARY

During the sixth and seventh centuries the Byzantine Empire survived waves of attacks, owing to effective military leadership and to fortifications around Constantinople. Byzantine emperors organized and preserved Roman institutions, and the Byzantine Empire survived until 1453. The emperor Justinian oversaw creation of a new uniform code of Roman law. The Byzantines prized education, and because of them many aspects of ancient Greek thought survived to influence the intellectual life of the Muslim world and eventually that of western Europe.

Christianity gained the support of the fourth-century emperors, and the church gradually adopted the Roman system of hierarchical organization. The church possessed able administrators and leaders. Bishops expanded their activities, and in the fifth century the bishops of Rome, taking the title "pope," began to stress their supremacy over other Christian communities. Monasteries offered opportunities for individuals to develop deeper spiritual devotion and also provided a model of Christian living and places for education and learning. Christian thinkers reinterpreted the classics in a Christian sense, incorporating elements of Greek and Roman philosophy into Christian teachings.

Barbarian groups migrated throughout Europe and Central Asia beginning in the second century. Among barbarians, the basic social unit was the tribe, made up of kin groups and led by a tribal chieftain. Missionaries and priests persuaded pagan and illiterate peoples to accept Christianity. Most barbarian kingdoms were weak and short-lived, though the kingdom of the Franks was relatively more unified and powerful. Rulers first in the Merovingian dynasty, and then in the Carolingian, used military victories, carefully calculated marriage alliances, and the help of the church to enhance their authority. Carolingian government reached the peak of its power under Charlemagne, who brought much of Europe under his authority through military conquest and strategic alliances.

 CONNECTIONS For centuries the end of the Roman Empire in the West was seen as a major turning point in history, the fall of the sophisticated and educated classical world to uncouth and illiterate tribes. Over the last several decades, however, many historians have put a greater emphasis on continuities. Barbarian kings relied on officials trained in Roman law, and Latin remained the language of scholarly communication and the Christian Church. Greco-Roman art and architecture still adorned the land, and people continued to use Roman roads, aqueducts, and buildings. In eastern Europe and western Asia, the Byzantine Empire preserved the traditions of the Roman Empire and protected the intellectual heritage of Greco-Roman culture for another millennium.

In the middle of the era covered in this chapter, a new force emerged that had a dramatic impact on much of Europe and western Asia—Islam. In the seventh and eighth centuries Sassanid Persia, much of the Byzantine Empire, and the barbarian kingdoms in the Iberian Peninsula fell to Arab forces carrying this new religion. As

CHAPTER LOCATOR | How did the Byzantine Empire preserve the legacy of Rome? | How did the Christian Church become a major force in Europe?

CHAPTER 8
228 CONTINUITY AND CHANGE IN EUROPE AND WESTERN ASIA

we have seen in this chapter, a reputation as victors over Islam helped the Franks establish the most powerful state in Europe. As we will see when we pick up the story of Europe again in Chapter 14, Islam continued to shape European culture and politics in subsequent centuries. In terms of world history, the expansion of Islam may have been an even more dramatic turning point than the fall of the Roman Empire. Here, too, however, there were continuities, as the Muslims adopted and adapted Greek, Byzantine, and Persian political and cultural institutions.

ONLINE DOCUMENT PROJECT
Theodora of Constantinople

What do Procopius's descriptions of Theodora and Justinian tell us about the problems and challenges his society faced?

Examine sources that reveal the connections Procopius saw between Byzantium's rulers and the rapid decline he perceived in Byzantine society, and then complete a quiz and writing assignment based on the evidence and details from this chapter. *See the inside front cover to learn more.*

How did Christian thinkers adapt classical ideas to Christian teachings, and develop new practices? | How did the barbarians shape social, economic, and political structures in Europe and west Asia? | How did the church convert barbarian peoples to Christianity? | How did the Franks build and govern a European empire? | ✔️ LearningCurve Check what you know.

229

CHAPTER 8 STUDY GUIDE

STEP 1

GET STARTED ONLINE

 LearningCurve

Now that you've read the chapter, make it stick by completing the LearningCurve activity.

STEP 2

EXPLAIN WHY IT MATTERS

Put your reading into practice. Identify each term below, and then explain why it matters in world history.

TERM	WHO OR WHAT & WHEN	WHY IT MATTERS
Justinian's *Code* (p. 206)		
dioceses (p. 210)		
heresy (p. 211)		
popes (p. 211)		
Orthodox Church (p. 212)		
sacraments (p. 216)		
iconoclastic controversy (p. 216)		
wergeld (p. 220)		
penance (p. 224)		
saints (p. 224)		
Carolingian (p. 226)		
Treaty of Verdun (p. 227)		

STEP 3

MOVE BEYOND THE BASICS

To demonstrate a more advanced understanding of the role of the Byzantine Empire and the Christian Church in preserving the legacy of Greco-Roman civilization, fill in the chart below with descriptions of the contributions of the Byzantine Empire and the Christian Church in this context in two key areas: politics and government and culture and ideas. Why was the church so important to the preservation of the Greco-Roman legacy in the West? How did church and state work together to preserve the Greco-Roman legacy in the East?

	Politics and Government	Culture and Ideas
Byzantine Empire		
Christian Church		

PUT IT ALL TOGETHER

Now, take a step back and try to explain the big picture. Remember to use specific examples from the chapter in your answers.

THE BYZANTINE EMPIRE

▶ Compare and contrast the Western Roman Empire and the Eastern Roman Empire in the period just prior to the fall of the Western Roman Empire. Why was the Eastern Roman Empire able to withstand the pressure of barbarian migrations, while the Western Roman Empire was not?

▶ How did conflicts and connections with neighboring peoples shape the development of the Byzantine Empire?

THE SPREAD AND DEVELOPMENT OF CHRISTIANITY

▶ Is it more accurate to say that Rome was Christianized or that the Christian church was Romanized? What evidence can you present to support your position?

▶ Why did so many barbarian elites aid in the spread of Christianity in Europe? What does the receptivity of such elites to Christianity tell us about barbarian society and culture?

MIGRATING PEOPLES

▶ How did barbarian society and culture compare to Roman society and culture? Were there any areas of similarity?

▶ How were Germanic and Roman influences combined in the structure and institutions of the Frankish kingdom?

LOOKING BACK, LOOKING AHEAD

▶ Compare and contrast Europe and western Asia before and after the fall of the Roman Empire in the West. What were the most important areas of continuity?

▶ How did the Byzantine Empire and the Christian Church lay the foundation in late antiquity for the subsequent medieval European civilization? What contributions did barbarian peoples make in this context?

> IN YOUR OWN WORDS

Imagine that you must give an oral report to the class answering the following questions: **What role did Christianity play in the development of Europe and Western Asia in the centuries following the collapse of the Western Roman Empire?** What would be the most important points and why?

9
THE ISLAMIC WORLD
600–1400

> How did Islamic civilization both build on and transform earlier civilizations? Chapter 9 examines the emergence and development of Islamic civilization. Around 610 in the city of Mecca in what is now Saudi Arabia, a merchant called Muhammad had a religious vision that inspired him to preach God's revelations. By the time he died in 632, he had many followers in Arabia, and a century later his followers controlled what is now Syria, Palestine, Egypt, Iraq, Iran, northern India, northern Africa, Spain, and southern France. Within another century Muhammad's beliefs had been carried across Central Asia to the borders of China and India. The brilliant civilization that grew out of Muhammad's vision profoundly influenced the development of both Eastern and Western civilizations.

LearningCurve

After reading the chapter, use LearningCurve to retain what you've read.

Egyptian Man Life remained gracious in the great cities of North Africa and the Middle East even as Islam brought new traditions. This image of a man wearing a turban and holding a cup is from a wall painting. Found in Egypt, it dates to the eleventh century, during the Fatimid caliphate. (Museum of Islamic Art, Cairo, Egypt/Gianni Dagli Orti/The Art Archive at Art Resource, NY)

> From what kind of social and economic environment did Muhammad arise, and what did he teach?

> What made possible the spread of Islam, and what forms of government were established to rule Muslim lands?

> How were the Muslim lands governed from 900 to 1400, and what new challenges did rulers face?

> What social distinctions were important in Muslim society?

> Why did trade thrive in Muslim lands?

> What new ideas and practices emerged in the arts, sciences, education, and religion?

> How did Muslims and Christians come into contact with each other, and how did they view each other?

From what kind of social and economic environment did Muhammad arise, and what did he teach?

The aesthetic appeal of Arabic calligraphy is easy to recognize in this page from a fourteenth-century manuscript. (Or Ms 161 fol.88v Abraham Destroys the Idols of the Sabians, from *The Chronology of Ancient Nations* by Al-Biruni, 1307 [gouache on paper], Islamic School [14th century]/ Edinburgh University Library, Scotland/With kind permission of the University of Edinburgh/The Bridgeman Art Library)

Much of the Arabian peninsula is desert. By the seventh century C.E. farming prevailed in the southwestern mountain valleys with their ample rainfall. In other areas scattered throughout the peninsula, oasis towns sustained sizable populations. Outside the towns were Bedouin (BEH-duh-uhn) nomadic pastoralist tribe. Though always small in number, Bedouins were the most important political and military force in the region. Mecca became the economic and cultural center of western Arabia, in part because pilgrims came to visit the Ka'ba, a temple containing a black stone thought to be a god's dwelling place. Muhammad's roots were in this region.

Arabian Social and Economic Structure

The basic social unit of the Bedouins and other Arabs was the tribe. Consisting of people connected through kinship, tribes provided protection and support and in turn expected members' total loyalty. Like the Germanic peoples in the age of

CHAPTER LOCATOR | From what kind of environment did Muhammad arise, and what did he teach?

What made possible the spread of Islam and what government was established?

How were Muslim lands governed and what challenges did rulers face?

CHAPTER 9
234 THE ISLAMIC WORLD

622
Muhammad and his followers emigrate from Mecca to Medina

632
Muhammad dies; Abu Bakr becomes the first caliph

642
Muslim defeat of the Persians marks end of the Sassanid empire

651
Publication of the Qur'an

661
Ali assassinated; split between Shi'a and Sunnis

711
Muslims defeat Visigothic kingdom in Spain

722–1492
Progressive loss of most of Spain to the Christian reconquest (*reconquista*)

750–1258
Abbasid caliphate

762
Baghdad founded by Abbasids

800–1300
Height of Muslim learning and creativity

869–883
Zanj (slave) revolts

950–1100
Entry on a large scale of Turks into the Middle East

1055
Baghdad falls to Seljuk Turks

1099–1187
Christian Crusaders hold Jerusalem

1258
Mongols capture Baghdad and kill the last Abbasid caliph

their migrations (see pages 218–221), Arab tribes were not static entities but rather continually evolving groups. A particular tribe might include both nomadic and sedentary members.

In northern and central Arabia in the early seventh century, tribal confederations led by their warrior elite were dominant. In the southern parts of the peninsula, however, priestly aristocracies tended to hold political power.

The power of the northern warrior class rested on its fighting skills. The southern religious aristocracy, by contrast, depended on its religious and economic power. The political genius of Muhammad was to bind together these different tribal groups into a strong, unified state.

Muhammad's Rise as a Religious Leader

Much like the earliest sources for Jesus and the Buddha, the earliest account of the life of Muhammad (ca. 570–632) comes from oral traditions passed down among followers. According to these traditions, at about age forty, Muhammad had a vision of an angelic being who commanded him to preach the revelations that God would be sending him. Muhammad began to preach to the people of Mecca, urging them to give up their idols and to submit to the one indivisible God. After his death, scribes organized the revelations jotted down by followers or memorized into chapters. In 651 they published the version of them that Muslims consider authoritative, the **Qur'an** (kuh-RAHN).

For the first two or three centuries after the death of Muhammad, there was considerable debate about theological and political issues. Likewise, religious scholars had to sort out and assess the **hadith** (huh-DEETH), collections of the

Qur'an
▶ The sacred book of Islam.

hadith
▶ Collections of the sayings of and anecdotes about Muhammad.

What social distinctions were important in Muslim society?

Why did trade thrive in Muslim lands?

What new ideas and practices emerged in the arts, sciences, education, and religion?

How did Muslims and Christians come into contact with and view each other?

LearningCurve
Check what you know.

Sunna

► An Arabic term meaning "trodden path." The term refers to the deeds and sayings of Muhammad, which constitute the obligatory example for Muslim life.

sayings of or anecdotes about Muhammad. Muhammad's example as revealed in the hadith became the legal basis for the conduct of every Muslim. The life of Muhammad provides the "normative example," or **Sunna**, for the Muslim believer. Muhammad's example became central to the Muslim way of life.

The Tenets of Islam

Islam, the strict monotheistic faith that is based on the teachings of Muhammad, rests on the principle of the oneness and omnipotence of God (Allah). Muslims believe that Muhammad was the last of the prophets, completing the work begun by Abraham, Moses, and Jesus. The Qur'an holds that the holy writings of both Jews and Christians represent divine revelation, but it claims that both Jews and Christians tampered with the books of God.

Muslims believe that they worship the same God as Jews and Christians. Islam appropriates much of the Old and New Testaments of the Bible but often retells the narratives with significant shifts in meaning. Muhammad insisted that he was not preaching a new message; rather, he was calling people back to the one true God, urging his contemporaries to reform their lives, to return to the faith of Abraham, the first monotheist.

The Qur'an prescribes a strict code of moral behavior. A Muslim must recite the profession of faith in God and in Muhammad as his prophet: "There is no God but God, and Muhammad is his Prophet." A believer must also pray five times a day, fast and pray during the sacred month of Ramadan, make a pilgrimage (hajj) to the holy city of Mecca once during his or her lifetime, and give alms to the Muslim poor. These fundamental obligations are known as the **Five Pillars of Islam**.

Islam forbids alcoholic beverages and gambling. It condemns usury in business—that is, lending money and charging the borrower interest—and taking advantage of market demand for products by charging high prices. Muslim jurisprudence condemned licentious behavior by both men and women and specified the same punishments for both.

Like the Christian Judgment Day, on the Islamic Judgment Day God will separate the saved and the damned. The Qur'an describes in detail the frightful tortures with which God will punish the damned and the heavenly rewards of the saved and the blessed.

Five Pillars of Islam

► The basic tenets of the Islamic faith; they include reciting a profession of faith in God and in Muhammad as God's prophet, praying five times daily, fasting and praying during the month of Ramadan, making a pilgrimage to Mecca once in one's lifetime, and contributing alms to the poor.

> **QUICK REVIEW**

What connections did Muslims see between their own religion and Christianity and Judaism?

CHAPTER LOCATOR | From what kind of environment did Muhammad arise, and what did he teach? | **What made possible the spread of Islam and what government was established?** | How were Muslim lands governed and what challenges did rulers face?

236 CHAPTER 9 THE ISLAMIC WORLD

The court of the Spanish Umayyads prized small, intricately carved ivory chests, often made in a royal workshop and used to store precious perfumes. This exquisite side panel depicts an eleventh-century caliph flanked by two attendants. An inscription on the front translates as "In the Name of God. Blessings from God, goodwill, and happiness." (Museo Navarra, Pamplona, Spain/Institut Amatller d'Art Hispanic)

What made possible the spread of Islam, and what forms of government were established to rule Muslim lands?

According to Muslim tradition, Muhammad's preaching at first did not appeal to many people. In preaching a transformation of the social order and calling for the destruction of the idols in the Ka'ba, Muhammad challenged the power of the local elite and the pilgrimage-based economy. As a result, the townspeople of Mecca turned against him, and he and his followers were forced to flee to Medina. This *hijra* (hih-JIGH-ruh), or emigration, occurred in 622, and Muslims later dated the beginning of their era from it.

| What social distinctions were important in Muslim society? | Why did trade thrive in Muslim lands? | What new ideas and practices emerged in the arts, sciences, education, and religion? | How did Muslims and Christians come into contact with and view each other? | LearningCurve Check what you know. |

At Medina, Muhammad attracted increasing numbers of believers, many of whom were Bedouins who supported themselves by raiding caravans en route to Mecca, setting off a violent conflict between Mecca and Medina. After eight years of strife, Mecca capitulated. In this way, by the time Muhammad died in 632, he had welded together all the Bedouin tribes.

Muhammad displayed genius as both a political strategist and a religious teacher. He gave Arabs the idea of a unique and unified **umma** (UH-muh), or community, that consisted of all those whose primary identity and bond was a common religious faith. The umma was to be a religious and political community led by Muhammad for the achievement of God's will on earth. The Islamic notion of an absolute higher authority transcended the boundaries of individual tribal units and fostered political consolidation.

umma

▶ A community of people who share a religious faith and commitment rather than a tribal tie.

Islam's Spread Beyond Arabia

After the Prophet's death, Islam quickly spread far beyond Arabia. In the sixth century two powerful empires divided the Middle East: the Greek-Byzantine empire centered at Constantinople and the Persian-Sassanid empire concentrated at Ctesiphon (near Baghdad in present-day Iraq). From the fourth through sixth centuries the Byzantines and Sassanids fought each other fiercely, each trying to expand its territories at the expense of the other and to control and tax the rich trade coming from Arabia and the Indian Ocean region. Many peripheral societies were drawn into the conflict. The resulting disorder facilitated the growth of Muslim states.

The second and third successors of Muhammad, Umar (r. 634–644) and Uthman (r. 644–656), launched a two-pronged attack against the Byzantine and Sassanid Empires. One force moved north from Arabia against the Byzantine provinces of Syria and Palestine (see page 204). From Syria, the Muslims conquered the rich province of Egypt. Simultaneously, Arab armies swept into the Sassanid empire. The Muslim defeat of the Persians at Nihawand in 642 signaled the collapse of this empire (Map 9.1).

The Muslims continued their drive eastward and in the mid-seventh century occupied the province of Khurasan, where the city of Merv became the center of Muslim control over eastern Persia and the base for campaigns farther east. By 700 the Muslims had crossed the Oxus River and swept toward Kabul, today the capital of Afghanistan. They then penetrated Kazakhstan and seized Tashkent. From southern Persia, a Muslim force marched into the Indus Valley in northwest India and in 713 founded an Islamic community there. Beginning in the eleventh century Muslim dynasties from Ghazni in Afghanistan carried Islam deeper into the Indian subcontinent (see page 345).

To the west, Arab forces moved across North Africa and crossed the Strait of Gibraltar. In 711 at the Guadalete River they easily defeated the Visigothic kingdom of Spain. Muslims controlled most of Spain until the thirteenth century. Advances into France were stopped in 732 when the Franks defeated Arab armies in a battle near the city of Tours, and Muslim occupation of parts of southern France did not last long.

CHAPTER LOCATOR | From what kind of environment did Muhammad arise, and what did he teach? | **What made possible the spread of Islam and what government was established?** | How were Muslim lands governed and what challenges did rulers face?

CHAPTER 9

238 THE ISLAMIC WORLD

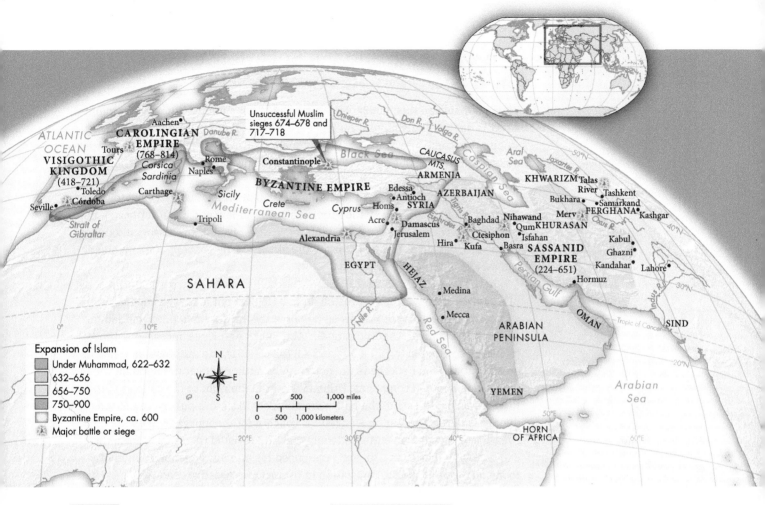

MAP 9.1 ■ The Expansion of Islam, 622–900

The rapid expansion of Islam in a relatively short span of time testifies to the Arabs' superior fighting skills, religious zeal, and economic ambition as well as to their enemies' weakness. Plague, famine, and political troubles in Sassanid Persia contributed to Muslim victory there.

> MAPPING THE PAST

ANALYZING THE MAP: Trace the routes of the spread of Islam by time period. How fast did it spread? How similar were the climates of the regions that became Muslim?

CONNECTIONS: Which were the most powerful and populous of the societies that were absorbed into the Muslim world? What regions or societies were more resistant?

Reasons for the Spread of Islam

By the beginning of the eleventh century the crescent of Islam had flown from the Iberian heartlands to northern India. How can this rapid and remarkable expansion be explained? Most historians point to a combination of the Arabs' military advantages and the political weaknesses of their opponents. The Byzantine and Sassanid Empires had just fought a grueling century-long war and had also been weakened by the plague. Equally important are the military strength and tactics of the Arabs. For example, rather than scattering as landlords of peasant farmers over conquered lands, Arab soldiers remained together in garrison cities, where their Arab ethnicity, tribal organization, religion, and military success set them apart. All soldiers were registered in the **diwān** (dih-WAHN), an administrative organ adopted from the Persians or Byzantines. Soldiers received a monthly ration of food for themselves and their families and an annual cash stipend. In return, they had to be available for military service.

diwān
▶ A unit of government.

| What social distinctions were important in Muslim society? | Why did trade thrive in Muslim lands? | What new ideas and practices emerged in the arts, sciences, education, and religion? | How did Muslims and Christians come into contact with and view each other? | ✔ LearningCurve Check what you know. |

The Caliphate and the Split Between Shi'a and Sunni Alliances

When Muhammad died in 632, he left a large Muslim umma, but this community stood in danger of disintegrating into separate tribal groups. How was the vast empire that came into existence within one hundred years of his death to be governed? Neither the Qur'an nor the Sunna offered guidance concerning the succession.

In this crisis, according to tradition, a group of Muhammad's ablest followers elected Abu Bakr (573–634), the Prophet's father-in-law and close supporter, and hailed him as caliph, a term combining the ideas of leader, successor, and deputy (of the Prophet). This election marked the victory of the concept of a universal community of Muslim believers.

In the two years of his rule (632–634), Abu Bakr governed on the basis of his personal prestige within the Muslim umma. He sent out military expeditions, collected taxes, dealt with tribes on behalf of the entire community, and led the community in prayer. Gradually, under Abu Bakr's first three successors, Umar (r. 634–644), Uthman (r. 644–656), and Ali (r. 656–661), the caliphate emerged as an institution. Umar succeeded in exerting his authority over the Bedouin tribes involved in ongoing conquests. Uthman asserted the right of the caliph to protect the economic interests of the entire umma. Also, Uthman's publication of the definitive text of the Qur'an showed his concern for the unity of the umma. However, Uthman was from a Mecca family that had resisted the Prophet until the capitulation of Mecca in 630, and he aroused resentment when he gave favors to members of his family. Opposition to Uthman coalesced around Ali, and when Uthman was assassinated in 656, Ali was chosen to succeed him.

Uthman's cousin Mu'awiya, a member of the Umayyad family who had built a power base as governor of Syria, refused to recognize Ali as caliph. In the ensuing civil war Ali was assassinated, and Mu'awiya (r. 661–680) assumed the caliphate. Mu'awiya founded the Umayyad Dynasty and shifted the capital of the Islamic state from Medina in Arabia to Damascus in Syria. Although electing caliphs remained the Islamic ideal, beginning with Mu'awiya, the office of caliph increasingly became hereditary. Two successive dynasties, the Umayyad (661–750) and the Abbasid (750–1258), held the caliphate.

From its inception the caliphate rested on the theoretical principle that Muslim political and religious unity transcended tribalism. Mu'awiya sought to enhance the power of the caliphate by making tribal leaders dependent on him for concessions and special benefits. At the same time, his control of a loyal and well-disciplined army enabled him to take the caliphate in an authoritarian direction. Through intimidation he forced the tribal leaders to accept his son Yazid as his heir, thereby establishing the dynastic principle of succession.

The assassination of Ali and the assumption of the caliphate by Mu'awiya had another profound consequence. It gave rise to a fundamental division in the umma and in Muslim theology. Ali had claimed the caliphate on the basis of family ties—he was Muhammad's cousin and son-in-law. When Ali was murdered, his followers argued that Ali had been the Prophet's designated successor—partly because of the blood tie, partly because Muhammad had designated Ali **imam** (ih-MAHM), or leader in community prayer. These supporters of Ali were called

imam

▶ The leader in community prayer.

CHAPTER LOCATOR | From what kind of environment did Muhammad arise, and what did he teach? | **What made possible the spread of Islam and what government was established?** | How were Muslim lands governed and what challenges did rulers face?

CHAPTER 9
240 THE ISLAMIC WORLD

Shi'a (SHEE-uh), meaning "supporters" or "partisans" of Ali (Shi'a are also known as Shi'ites). In succeeding generations, opponents of the Umayyad Dynasty emphasized their blood descent from Ali and claimed to possess divine knowledge that Muhammad had given them as his heirs.

Those who accepted Mu'awiya as caliph insisted that the central issue was adhering to the practices and beliefs of the umma based on the precedents of the Prophet. They came to be called Sunnis (SOO-neez), which derived from *Sunna* (examples from Muhammad's life). When a situation arose for which the Qur'an offered no solution, Sunni scholars searched for a precedent in the Sunna, which gained an authority comparable to the Qur'an itself.

Both Sunnis and Shi'a maintain that authority within Islam lies first in the Qur'an and then in the Sunna. Who interprets these sources? Shi'a claim that the imam does, for he is invested with divine grace and insight. Sunnis insist that interpretation comes from the consensus of the ulama, the group of religious scholars.

Throughout the Umayyad period, the Shi'a constituted a major source of discontent. They condemned the Umayyads as worldly and sensual rulers, in contrast to the pious true successors of Muhammad. A rival Sunni clan, the Abbasid (uh-BA-suhd), exploited the situation, agitating the Shi'a and encouraging dissension among tribal factions. The Abbasid contrasted their own piety with the pleasure-loving style of the Umayyads.

The Abbasid Caliphate

In 747 the Abbasid leader Abu' al-Abbas led a rebellion against the Umayyads, and in 750 he won general recognition as caliph. Damascus had served as the headquarters of Umayyad rule. Abu' al-Abbas's successor, al-Mansur (r. 754–775), founded the city of Baghdad in 762 and made it his capital. Thus the geographical center of the caliphate shifted eastward to former Sassanid territories. The first three Abbasid caliphs crushed their opponents, turned against many of their supporters, and created a new ruling elite drawn from newly converted Persian families. The Abbasid revolution established a basis for rule and citizenship more cosmopolitan and Islamic than the narrow, elitist, and Arab basis that had characterized Umayyad government.

The Abbasids worked to identify their rule with Islam. They patronized the ulama, built mosques, and supported the development of Islamic scholarship. Although at first Muslims represented only a small minority of the conquered peoples, Abbasid rule provided the religious-political milieu in which Islam gained, over time, the allegiance of the vast majority of the populations from Spain to Afghanistan.

The Abbasids also borrowed heavily from Persian culture. Following Persian tradition, the Abbasid caliphs claimed to rule by divine right. A majestic palace with hundreds of attendants and elaborate court ceremonies deliberately isolated the caliph from the people he ruled. Subjects had to bow before the caliph and kiss the ground, symbolizing his absolute power.

Under the third caliph, Harun al-Rashid (r. 786–809), Baghdad emerged as a flourishing commercial, artistic, and scientific center. Its population of about a million people created a huge demand for goods and services, and Baghdad became

Shi'a
▶ Arabic term meaning "supporters of Ali"; they make up one of the two main divisions of Islam.

Sunnis
▶ Members of the larger of the two main divisions of Islam; the division between Sunnis and Shi'a began in a dispute about succession to Muhammad, but over time many differences in theology developed.

ulama
▶ A group of religious scholars whom Sunnis trust to interpret the Qur'an and the Sunna.

| What social distinctions were important in Muslim society? | Why did trade thrive in Muslim lands? | What new ideas and practices emerged in the arts, sciences, education, and religion? | How did Muslims and Christians come into contact with and view each other? | ✓ LearningCurve Check what you know. |

241

Abbasid Wooden Doors

These ninth-century wooden doors are thought to come from Samarra, a city about 125 miles upstream from Baghdad, which briefly served as the capital in the ninth century. (Image copyright © The Metropolitan Museum of Art/Image source: Art Resource, NY)

an entrepôt (trading center) for textiles, slaves, and foodstuffs coming from Oman, East Africa, and India. The city also became intellectually influential. Harun al-Rashid organized the translation of Greek medical and philosophical texts. As part of this effort the Christian scholar Hunayn Ibn Ishaq (808–873) translated Galen's medical works into Arabic and made Baghdad a center for the study and practice of medicine. Likewise, impetus was given to the study of astronomy, and through a program of astronomical observations, Muslim astronomers sought to correct and complement Ptolemaic astronomy. Above all, studies in Qur'anic textual analysis, history, poetry, law, and philosophy—all in Arabic—reflected the development of a distinctly Islamic literary and scientific culture.

An important innovation of the Abbasids was the use of slaves as soldiers. The caliph al-Mu'taşim (r. 833–842) acquired several thousand Turkish slaves who were converted to Islam and employed in military service. Scholars have offered varied explanations for this practice: that the use of slave soldiers was a response to a manpower shortage; that as highly skilled horsemen, the Turks had military skills superior to those of the Arabs and other peoples; and that al-Mu'taşim felt he could trust the Turks more than other recruits. In any case, slave soldiers—later including Slavs, Indians, and sub-Saharan blacks—became a standard feature of Muslim armies in the Middle East until the twentieth century.

Administration of the Islamic Territories

The Islamic conquests brought into being a new imperial system. The Muslims adopted the patterns of administration used by the Byzantines in Egypt and Syria and by the Sassanids in Persia. Specifically, Arab **emirs**, or governors, were appointed and given overall responsibility for public order, maintenance of the armed forces, and tax collection. Below them, experienced native officials remained in office. Thus there was continuity with previous administrations.

The Umayyad caliphate witnessed the further development of the imperial administration. At the head stood the caliph. Theoretically, he had the ultimate

emirs
▶ Arab governors who were given overall responsibility for public order, maintenance of the armed forces, and tax collection.

CHAPTER LOCATOR | From what kind of environment did Muhammad arise, and what did he teach? | **What made possible the spread of Islam and what government was established?** | How were Muslim lands governed and what challenges did rulers face?

CHAPTER 9
242 THE ISLAMIC WORLD

responsibility for the interpretation of the sacred law. In practice, however, the ulama interpreted the law as revealed in the Qur'an and the Sunna. In the course of time, the ulama's interpretations constituted a rich body of law, the shari'a (shuh-REE-uh). The ulama enjoyed great prestige in the Muslim community and was consulted by the caliph on difficult legal and spiritual matters. The *qadis* (KAH-dees), or judges, who were well versed in the sacred law, carried out the judicial functions of the state.

The central administrative organ was the diwān, which collected the taxes that paid soldiers' salaries (see page 239) and financed charitable and public works. Another important undertaking was a relay network established to rapidly convey letters and intelligence reports between the capital and distant outposts.

The early Abbasid period witnessed considerable economic expansion and population growth, complicating the work of government. New and specialized departments emerged, each with a hierarchy of officials. The most important new official was the vizier (vuh-ZEER), a position that the Abbasids adopted from the Persians. The vizier was the caliph's chief assistant. Depending on the caliph's personality, viziers could acquire extensive power, and some used their offices for personal gain.

shari'a
▶ Muslim law, which covers social, criminal, political, commercial, and religious matters.

QUICK REVIEW <

How did Islamic government evolve in the two centuries following the death of Muhammad?

| What social distinctions were important in Muslim society? | Why did trade thrive in Muslim lands? | What new ideas and practices emerged in the arts, sciences, education, and religion? | How did Muslims and Christians come into contact with and view each other? | ✓ LearningCurve Check what you know. |

How were the Muslim lands governed from 900 to 1400, and what new challenges did rulers face?

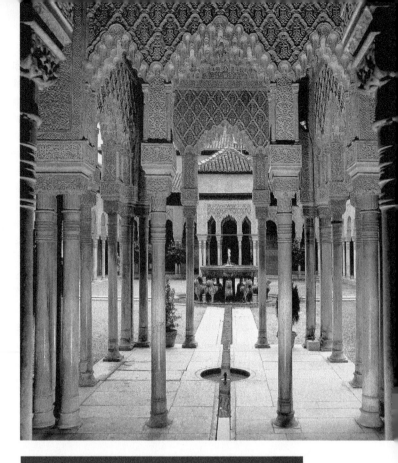

The Patio of the Lions at Alhambra, Fourteenth Century

The fortress that the Moorish rulers of Spain built at Granada is considered one of the masterpieces of Andalusian art, notable for the fine carving of geometrical designs and Arabic calligraphy. (George Holton/Photo Researchers, Inc.)

In theory, the caliph and his central administration governed the whole empire, but in practice, the many parts of the empire enjoyed considerable local independence. At the same time, the enormous distance between many provinces and the imperial capital made it difficult for the caliph to prevent provinces from breaking away. Consequently, regional dynasties emerged in much of the Islamic world, including Spain, Persia, Central Asia, northern India, and Egypt. None of these states repudiated Islam, but they did stop sending tax revenues to Baghdad. Moreover, states frequently fought costly wars against their neighbors in their attempts to expand. Sometimes these conflicts were worsened by Sunni-Shi'a antagonisms. All these developments, as well as invasions by Turks and Mongols, posed challenges to central Muslim authority.

Breakaway Territories and Shi'a Gains

One of the first territories to break away from the Baghdad-centered caliphate was Spain. In 755 an Umayyad prince who had escaped death at the hands of the Abbasids and fled to Spain set up an independent regime at Córdoba (see

CHAPTER LOCATOR | From what kind of environment did Muhammad arise, and what did he teach? | What made possible the spread of Islam and what government was established? | **How were Muslim lands governed and what challenges did rulers face?**

244 CHAPTER 9 THE ISLAMIC WORLD

Map 9.1). Other territories soon followed. In 800 the emir in Tunisia in North Africa set himself up as an independent ruler. And in 820 Tahir, the son of a slave, was rewarded with the governorship of Khurasan because he had supported the caliphate. Once he took office, however, Tahir ruled independently of Baghdad.

In 946 a Shi'a Iranian clan overran Iraq and occupied Baghdad. The caliph was forced to recognize the clan's leader as commander in chief and to allow the celebration of Shi'a festivals. A year later the caliph was accused of plotting against his new masters, snatched from his throne, dragged through the streets, and blinded. This incident marked the practical collapse of the Abbasid caliphate. Abbasid caliphs, however, remained as puppets of a series of military commanders and symbols of Muslim unity until the Mongols killed the last Abbasid caliph in 1258 (see page 246).

In another Shi'a advance, the Fatimids, a Shi'a dynasty that claimed descent from Muhammad's daughter Fatima, conquered North Africa and then expanded into the Abbasid province of Egypt, founding the city of Cairo as their capital in 969. For the next century or so, Shi'a were in ascendancy in much of the western Islamic world.

The Fatimid Caliphate, 909–1171

The Ascendancy of the Turks

In the mid-tenth century the Turks began to enter the Islamic world in large numbers. First appearing in Mongolia in the sixth century, groups of Turks, such as the Seljuks, gradually appeared across the grasslands of Eurasia. Skilled horsemen, they became prime targets for Muslim slave raids, as they made good slave soldiers. Once the Turks understood that Muslims could not be captured for slaves, more and more of them converted to Sunni Islam and often became *ghazi*, frontier raiders, who attacked unconverted Turks to capture slaves.

In the 1020s and 1030s Seljuk Turks overran Persia and then pushed into Iraq and Syria. Baghdad fell to them on December 18, 1055, and the caliph became a puppet of the Turkish sultan. The Turkic elite rapidly gave up pastoralism and took up the sedentary lifestyle of the people they governed.

The Turks brought badly needed military strength to the Islamic world. They played a major part in recovering Jerusalem after it was held for nearly a century, from 1099 to 1187, by the European Crusaders (who had fought to take Christian holy lands back from the Muslims; see page 401). They also were important in preventing the later Crusades from accomplishing much. Moreover, the Turks became staunch Sunnis and led a campaign against the Shi'a.

The influx of Turks from 950 to 1100 also helped provide a new expansive dynamic. At the Battle of Manzikert in 1071, Seljuk Turks broke through Byzantine border defenses, opening Anatolia to Turkish migration. Over the next couple of centuries, perhaps a million Turks entered the area—including bands of ghazis and dervishes (Sufi brotherhoods, see page 258).

The Seljuk Empire in 1000

What social distinctions were important in Muslim society?

Why did trade thrive in Muslim lands?

What new ideas and practices emerged in the arts, sciences, education, and religion?

How did Muslims and Christians come into contact with and view each other?

LearningCurve
Check what you know.

245

The Mongol Invasions

In the early thirteenth century the Mongols arrived in the Middle East. Originally from the grasslands of Mongolia, in 1206 they proclaimed Chinggis Khan (ca. 1162–1227) as their leader, and he welded Mongol, Tartar, and Turkish tribes into a strong confederation that rapidly subdued neighboring settled societies (see pages 335–340). After conquering much of north China, the Mongols swept westward.

In 1219–1221, when the Mongols first reached the Islamic lands, the areas from Persia through the Central Asian cities of Herat and Samarkand were part of the kingdom of Khwarizm. The ruler—the son of a Turkish slave who had risen to governor of a province—had the audacity to execute Chinggis's envoy, and Chinggis retaliated with a force of a hundred thousand soldiers that sacked city after city. Millions are said to have died.

Not many Mongol forces were left in Persia after the campaign of 1219–1221, and another army, sent in 1237, captured the Persian city of Isfahan. In 1251 the decision was taken to push farther west. Chinggis Khan's grandson Hülegü (1217–1265) led an attack on the Abbasids in Baghdad, sacking and burning the city and killing the last Abbasid caliph in 1258. The fall of Damascus followed in 1260. Mamluk soldiers from Egypt, however, were able to withstand the Mongols and win a major victory at Ayn Jalut in Syria, which has been credited with saving Egypt and the Muslim lands in North Africa and perhaps Spain. At any rate, the desert ecology of the region did not provide suitable support for the Mongol armies, which required five horses for each soldier. Moreover, in 1260 the Great Khan (ruler of Mongolia and China) died, and the top Mongol generals withdrew to Mongolia for the selection of the next Great Khan.

Hülegü and his descendants ruled the central Muslim lands (referred to as the Il-Khanate) for eighty years. In 1295 his descendant Ghazan embraced Islam and worked for the revival of Muslim culture. As the Turks had done earlier, the Mongols, once converted, injected new vigor into the faith and spirit of Islam. In the Il-Khanate the Mongols governed through Persian viziers and native financial officials.

> **QUICK REVIEW**

Why did the caliphate find it so difficult to maintain control over the Islamic empire?

CHAPTER LOCATOR | From what kind of environment did Muhammad arise, and what did he teach? | What made possible the spread of Islam and what government was established? | How were Muslim lands governed and what challenges did rulers face?

246 CHAPTER 9 THE ISLAMIC WORLD

What social distinctions were important in Muslim society?

When the Prophet appeared, Arab society consisted of independent Bedouin tribal groups loosely held together by loyalty to a strong leader and by the belief that all members of a tribe were descended from a common ancestor. Heads of families elected the sheik, or tribal chief. He was usually chosen from among elite warrior families who believed their bloodlines made them superior. According to the Qur'an, however, birth counted for nothing; piety was the only criterion for honor. The idea of social equality was a basic Muslim doctrine.

When Muhammad defined social equality, he was thinking about equality among Muslims alone. But even among Muslims, a sense of pride in ancestry could not be destroyed by a stroke of the pen. Claims based on birth remained strong among the first Muslims, and after Islam spread outside of Arabia, full-blooded Arab tribesmen regarded themselves as superior to foreign converts.

| What social distinctions were important in Muslim society? | Why did trade thrive in Muslim lands? | What new ideas and practices emerged in the arts, sciences, education, and religion? | How did Muslims and Christians come into contact with and view each other? | ✔ LearningCurve Check what you know. |

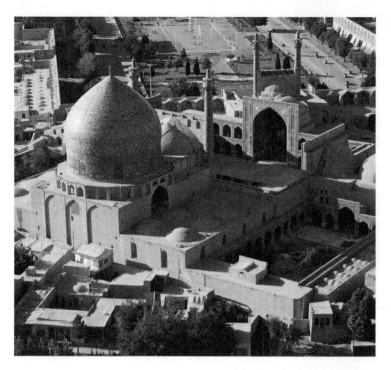

Great Mosque at Isfahan in Persia

Begun in the late eighth century and added to over the centuries, the Great Mosque in Isfahan is one of the masterpieces of Islamic architecture. The huge dome and the vaulted niches around the courtyard are covered with blue, turquoise, white, and yellow tile. (© Roger Wood/Corbis)

The Social Hierarchy

In the Umayyad period, Muslim society was distinctly hierarchical. At the top of the hierarchy were the caliph's household and the ruling Arab Muslims. Descended from Bedouin tribespeople, this class constituted the ruling elite. It was a relatively small group, greatly outnumbered by Muslim villagers and country people.

Converts constituted the second class in Islamic society, one that grew slowly over time. Converts to Islam had to attach themselves to one of the Arab tribes in a subordinate capacity. From the Muslim converts eventually came the members of the commercial and learned professions—merchants, traders, teachers, doctors, artists, and interpreters of the shari'a. Second-class citizenship led some Muslim converts to adopt Shi'ism (see page 240). Even so, over the centuries, converts to Islam intermarried with their Muslim conquerors. Gradually, assimilation united peoples of various ethnic backgrounds.

Dhimmis (zih-MEEZ)—including Jews, Christians, and Zoroastrians—formed the third stratum. Considered "protected peoples" because they worshipped only one God, they were allowed to practice their religions, maintain their houses of worship, and conduct their business affairs as long as they gave unequivocal recognition to Muslim political supremacy and paid a small tax. Because many Jews and Christians were well educated, they were often appointed to high positions in government. However, their social position deteriorated during the Crusades and the Mongol invasions, when there was a general rise of religious loyalties. At those times, Muslims suspected the dhimmis, often rightly, of collaborating with the enemies of Islam.

How did the experience of Jews under Islam compare with that of Jews living in Christian Europe? Recent scholarship shows that, in Europe, Jews were first marginalized in the Christian social order and then completely expelled from it. In Islam, Jews, though marginalized, participated fully in commercial and professional activities, some attaining economic equality with their Muslim counterparts.

dhimmis

▶ A term meaning "protected peoples"; they included Jews, Christians, and Zoroastrians.

Slavery

Slavery had long existed in the ancient Middle East, and Muslim expansion ensured a steady flow of slaves captured in war. Moreover, the Qur'an accepted slavery much the way the Old and New Testaments did. But the Qur'an prescribes

CHAPTER LOCATOR | From what kind of environment did Muhammad arise, and what did he teach? | What made possible the spread of Islam and what government was established? | How were Muslim lands governed and what challenges did rulers face?

248 CHAPTER 9
THE ISLAMIC WORLD

just and humane treatment of slaves, explicitly encourages the freeing of slaves, and urges owners whose slaves ask for their freedom to give them the opportunity to buy it.

Women slaves worked as cooks, cleaners, laundresses, and nursemaids. A few performed as singers, musicians, dancers, and reciters of poetry. Many female slaves also served as concubines. Not only rulers but also high officials and rich merchants owned many concubines. Down the economic ladder, artisans and tradesmen often had a few concubines who assumed domestic as well as sexual duties.

According to tradition, the seclusion of women in a harem protected their virtue (see below), and when men had the means the harem was secured by eunuch (castrated) guards. Muslims also employed eunuchs as secretaries, tutors, and commercial agents, possibly because eunuchs were said to be more manageable and dependable than men with ordinary desires. Male slaves, eunuchs or not, were also set to work as longshoremen on the docks, as oarsmen on ships, in construction crews, in workshops, and in gold and silver mines. Male slaves also fought as soldiers.

Slavery in the Islamic world differed in at least two fundamental ways from the slavery later practiced in the Americas. First, race had no particular connection to slavery among Muslims, who were as ready to take slaves from Europe as from Africa. Second, slavery in the Islamic world was not the basis for plantation agriculture, as it was in the southern United States, the Caribbean, and Brazil in the eighteenth and nineteenth centuries.

Slavery was rarely hereditary in the Muslim world. Most slaves who were taken from non-Muslim peoples later converted, which often led to emancipation. The children of female slaves by Muslim masters were by definition Muslim and thus free. To give Muslim slavery the most positive possible interpretation, one could say that it provided a means to fill certain socioeconomic and military needs and that it assimilated rather than segregated outsiders.

Slaves Dancing

A few women slaves performed as dancers, singers, and musicians, usually before an elite audience of rulers, officials, and wealthy merchants. This reconstructed wall painting from the ninth century adorned a harem in a royal palace in Samarra. (bpk, Berlin/Art Resource, NY)

Women in Classical Islamic Society

Before Islam, Arab tribal law gave women virtually no legal powers. Girls were sold into marriage by their guardians, and their husbands could terminate the union at will. Also, women had virtually no property or succession rights. Seen from this perspective, the Qur'an sought to improve the social position of women.

The Qur'an, like the religious writings of other traditions, represents moral precept rather than social practice, and the texts are open to different interpretations. Modern scholars tend to agree that the Islamic sacred book intended women to be the spiritual equals of men and gave them considerable economic

| What social distinctions were important in Muslim society? | Why did trade thrive in Muslim lands? | What new ideas and practices emerged in the arts, sciences, education, and religion? | How did Muslims and Christians come into contact with and view each other? | ✔ LearningCurve Check what you know. |

249

rights. In the early Umayyad period, moreover, women played active roles in the religious, economic, and political life of the community. They owned property, had freedom of movement and traveled widely, and participated with men in public religious rituals and observances. But this Islamic ideal of women and men having equal value to the community did not last, and, as Islamic society changed, the precepts of the Qur'an were interpreted in more patriarchal ways.

Although the hadith—records of what Muhammad said and did, and what believers in the first two centuries after his death believed he said and did (see page 235)—usually depict women in terms of moral virtue, domesticity, and saintly ideals, they also show some prominent women in political roles. For example, Aisha, daughter of the first caliph and probably Muhammad's favorite wife, played a leading role in rallying support for the movement opposing Ali, who succeeded Uthman in 656 (see page 240). However, by the Abbasid period the status of women had declined. The practices of the Byzantine and Persian lands that had been conquered, including seclusion of women, were absorbed. The supply of slave women increased substantially. Some scholars speculate that as wealth replaced ancestry as the main criterion of social status, men more and more viewed women as possessions, as a form of wealth.

Men were also seen as dominant in their marriages. The Qur'an states that "men are in charge of women because Allah hath made the one to excel the other, and because they (men) spend of their property (for the support of women). So good women are obedient, guarding in secret that which Allah hath guarded."[1] A thirteenth-century commentator on this passage argued from it that women are incapable of and unfit for any public duties. This view came to be accepted, and later interpreters further categorized the ways in which men were superior to women.

The practices of veiling and seclusion of women have their roots in pre-Islamic times, and they took firm hold in classical Islamic society. As Arab conquerors subjugated various peoples, they adopted some of the vanquished peoples' customs. Veiling was probably of Byzantine or Persian origin. The Qur'an contains no specific rule about the veil, but its few vague references have been interpreted as sanctioning the practice. An even greater restriction on women than veiling was the practice of seclusion, the harem system. The practice of secluding women also derives from Arabic contacts with Persia and other Eastern cultures. By 800 women in more prosperous households stayed out of sight.

Marriage, the Family, and Sexuality

As in medieval Europe and traditional India and China, marriage in Muslim society was considered too important an undertaking to be left to the romantic emotions of the young. Families or guardians, not the prospective bride and groom, identified suitable partners and finalized the contract. Because it was absolutely essential that the bride be a virgin, marriages were arranged shortly after the onset of the girl's menstrual period at age twelve or thirteen. Husbands were commonly ten to fifteen years older. Youthful marriages ensured a long period of fertility.

A wife's responsibilities depended on the wealth and occupation of her husband. A farmer's wife helped in the fields, ground the corn, carried water,

CHAPTER LOCATOR | From what kind of environment did Muhammad arise, and what did he teach? | What made possible the spread of Islam and what government was established? | How were Muslim lands governed and what challenges did rulers face?

CHAPTER 9
250 THE ISLAMIC WORLD

prepared food, and did the myriad tasks necessary in rural life. Shopkeepers' wives in the cities sometimes helped in business. In an upper-class household, the wife supervised servants, looked after all domestic arrangements, and did whatever was needed for her husband's comfort.

In every case, children were the wife's special domain. A mother exercised authority over her children and enjoyed their respect. Thus, as in Chinese culture, the prestige of the young wife depended on the production of children— especially sons—as rapidly as possible. A wife's failure to have children was one of the main reasons for a man to divorce his wife or take a second wife.

Like the Jewish tradition, Muslim law permits divorce. Although divorce is allowed, it is not encouraged. One commentator cited the Prophet as saying, "The lawful thing which God hates most is divorce."[2]

In contrast to the traditional Christian view of sexual activity as inherently shameful and only a cure for lust even within marriage, Islam maintains a healthy acceptance of sexual pleasure for both males and females. The Qur'an permits a man to have four wives, provided that all are treated justly. The vast majority of Muslim males, however, were monogamous because only the wealthy could afford to support more than one wife.

QUICK REVIEW <

How did ideas about gender roles shape life in classical Islamic society?

| What social distinctions were important in Muslim society? | Why did trade thrive in Muslim lands? | What new ideas and practices emerged in the arts, sciences, education, and religion? | How did Muslims and Christians come into contact with and view each other? | LearningCurve Check what you know. |

251

Why did trade thrive in Muslim lands?

Unlike the Christian West or the Confucian East, Islam looked favorably on profit-making enterprises. The Qur'an, moreover, has no prohibition against trade with Christians or other unbelievers. In fact, non-Muslims, including the Jews of Cairo and the Armenians in the central Islamic lands, were prominent in mercantile networks.

Waterways served as the main commercial routes of the Islamic world (Map 9.2). They included the Mediterranean and Black Seas; the Caspian Sea and the Volga River, which gave access deep into Russia; the Aral Sea, from which caravans departed for China; the Gulf of Aden; and the Arabian Sea and the Indian Ocean, which linked the Persian Gulf region with eastern Africa, the Indian subcontinent, and eventually Indonesia and the Philippines.

Cairo was a major Mediterranean entrepôt for intercontinental trade. Foreign merchants sailed up the Nile to the Aswan region, traveled east from Aswan by caravan to the Red Sea, and then sailed down the Red Sea to Aden, where they entered the Indian Ocean on their way to India. They exchanged textiles, glass, gold, silver, and copper for Asian spices, dyes, and drugs and for Chinese silks and porcelains. Muslim and Jewish merchants dominated the trade with India, and all spoke and wrote Arabic. Their commercial practices included the *sakk*, an order to a banker to pay money held on account to a third party. Muslims also developed other business innovations, such as the bill of exchange, a written order from one person to another to pay a specified sum of money to a designated person or party, and the idea of the joint stock company, an arrangement that lets a group of people invest in a venture and share its profits (and losses) in proportion to the amount each has invested.

Trade also benefited from improvements in technology. The adoption from the Chinese of the magnetic compass greatly helped navigation of the Arabian Sea and the Indian Ocean. The construction of larger ships led to a shift in long-distance cargoes from luxury goods such as pepper, spices, and drugs to bulk goods such as sugar, rice, and timber.

In this period Egypt became the center of Muslim trade, benefiting from the decline of Iraq caused by the Mongol capture of Baghdad and the fall of the Abbasid caliphate (see page 246). Beginning in the late twelfth century Persian and Arab seamen sailed down the east coast of Africa and established trading towns between Somalia and Sofala (see pages 288–290). These thirty to fifty urban centers linked Zimbabwe in southern Africa with the Indian Ocean trade and the Middle Eastern trade.

CHAPTER LOCATOR | From what kind of environment did Muhammad arise, and what did he teach? | What made possible the spread of Islam and what government was established? | How were Muslim lands governed and what challenges did rulers face?

CHAPTER 9
252 THE ISLAMIC WORLD

MAP 9.2 ■ The Expansion of Islam and Its Trading Networks in the Thirteenth and Fourteenth Centuries

By 1500 Islam had spread extensively in North and East Africa, and into the Balkans, the Caucasus, Central Asia, India, and the islands of Southeast Asia. Muslim merchants played a major role in bringing their religion as they extended their trade networks. They were active in the Indian Ocean long before the arrival of Europeans.

One byproduct of the extensive trade through Muslim lands was the spread of useful plants. Cotton, sugarcane, and rice spread from India to other places with suitable climates. Citrus fruits made their way to Muslim Spain from Southeast Asia and India. The value of this trade contributed to the prosperity of the Abbasid era.

QUICK REVIEW <

How did Islamic political and religious leaders view trade and commerce?

| What social distinctions were important in Muslim society? | **Why did trade thrive in Muslim lands?** | What new ideas and practices emerged in the arts, sciences, education, and religion? | How did Muslims and Christians come into contact with and view each other? | LearningCurve Check what you know. |

What new ideas and practices emerged in the arts, sciences, education, and religion?

Teachers Disputing in a Madrasa

Although Islamic education relied heavily on memorization of the Qur'an, religious scholars frequently debated the correct interpretation of a particular text. Listening to this lively disputation, the students illustrated in this 1222 book are learning to think critically and creatively. (From *The Schefer Maqamat*, Ms. Arabe 5847, fol. 118v/R. and S. Michaud/akg-images)

I

Long-distance trade provided the wealth that made possible a gracious and sophisticated culture in the cities of the Muslim world. (See "Individuals in Society: Ibn Battuta," page 255.) Education helped foster achievements in the arts and sciences, and Sufism brought a new spiritual and intellectual tradition.

The Cultural Centers of Baghdad and Córdoba

Although cities and mercantile centers dotted the entire Islamic world, the cities of Baghdad and Córdoba, at their peak in the tenth century, stand out as the finest examples of cosmopolitan Muslim civilization. On Baghdad's streets thronged representatives of a kaleidoscope of races, creeds, and cultures. Shops and marketplaces offered a dazzling and exotic array of goods from all over the world.

The caliph Harun al-Rashid presided over a glamorous court. He invited writers, dancers, musicians, poets, and artists to live in Baghdad. This brilliant era

CHAPTER LOCATOR | From what kind of environment did Muhammad arise, and what did he teach? | What made possible the spread of Islam and what government was established? | How were Muslim lands governed and what challenges did rulers face?

CHAPTER 9
254 THE ISLAMIC WORLD

INDIVIDUALS IN SOCIETY
Ibn Battuta

In 1354 the sultan of Morocco appointed a scribe to write an account of the travels of Abu 'Abdallah Ibn Battuta (1304–1368), who between 1325 and 1354 had traveled through most of the Islamic world. The two men collaborated. The result was a travel book written in Arabic and later hailed as the richest eyewitness account of fourteenth-century Islamic culture. It has often been compared to the slightly earlier *Travels* of the Venetian Marco Polo (see page 341).

Ibn Battuta was born in Tangiers to a family of legal scholars. As a youth, he studied Muslim law, gained fluency in Arabic, and acquired the qualities considered essential for a civilized Muslim gentleman: courtesy, manners, and the social polish that eases relations among people.

At age twenty-one he left Tangiers to make the hajj (pilgrimage) to Mecca. He crossed North Africa and visited Alexandria, Cairo, Damascus, and Medina. Reaching Mecca in October 1326, he immediately praised God for his safe journey, kissed the Holy Stone at the Ka'ba, and recited the ritual prayers. There he decided to see more of the world.

In the next four years Ibn Battuta traveled to Iraq and to Basra and Baghdad in Persia, then returned to Mecca before sailing down the coast of Africa as far as modern Tanzania. On the return voyage he visited Oman and the Persian Gulf region, then traveled by land across central Arabia to Mecca. Strengthened by his stay in the holy city, he decided to go to India by way of Egypt, Syria, and Anatolia; across the Black Sea to the plains of western Central Asia, detouring to see Constantinople; back to the Asian steppe; east to Khurasan and Afghanistan; and down to Delhi in northern India.

For eight years Ibn Battuta served as a judge in the service of the sultan of Delhi. In 1341 the sultan chose him to lead a diplomatic mission to China. After the expedition was shipwrecked off the southeastern coast of India, Ibn Battuta traveled through southern India, Sri Lanka, and the Maldive Islands. Then he went to China, stopping in Bengal and Sumatra before reaching the southern coast of China, then under Mongol rule. Returning to Mecca in 1346, he set off for home, getting to Morocco in 1349. After a brief trip across the Strait of Gibraltar to Granada, he undertook his last journey, by camel caravan across the Sahara to Mali in the West African Sudan (see page 281), returning home in 1354. Scholars estimate that he had traveled about seventy-five thousand miles.

Ibn Battuta had a driving intellectual curiosity to see and understand the world. At every stop, he sought the learned jurists and pious men at the mosques and madrasas. He marveled at the Lighthouse of Alexandria, then in ruins; at the vast harbor at Kaffa (in southern Ukraine on the Black Sea), whose two hundred Genoese ships were loaded with

Travelers to Baghdad would have seen slave markets like this one. (© BnF, Dist, RMN–Grand Palais/Art Resource, NY)

silks and slaves for the markets at Venice, Cairo, and Damascus; and at the elephants in the sultan's procession in Delhi, which carried machines that tossed gold and silver coins to the crowds.

Ibn Battuta must have had an iron constitution. Besides walking long distances on his land trips, he endured fevers, dysentery, malaria, the scorching heat of the Sahara, and the freezing cold of the steppe. His thirst for adventure was stronger than his fear of nomadic warriors and bandits on land and the dangers of storms and pirates at sea.

Source: R. E. Dunn, *The Adventures of Ibn Battuta: A Muslim Traveler of the Fourteenth Century* (Berkeley: University of California Press, 1986).

QUESTIONS FOR ANALYSIS

1. Trace the routes of Ibn Battuta's travels on Map 9.2 (page 253).
2. How did a common Muslim culture facilitate Ibn Battuta's travels?

LaunchPad

ONLINE DOCUMENT PROJECT

How did Ibn Battuta describe his travels? Read parts of Ibn Battuta's account of his travels, and then complete a quiz and writing assignment based on the evidence and details from this chapter. *See the inside front cover to learn more.*

- Population: 1 million
- Mosques: 1,600
- Public Baths: 900
- Houses and Mansions: 273,177
- Shops: 80,455
- Weavers: 13,000
- Free Schools: 27
- Volumes in Library: 400,000

provided the background for the tales that appear in *The Thousand and One Nights*.

Córdoba in southern Spain competed with Baghdad for the cultural leadership of the Islamic world. Córdoba's scholars made contributions in chemistry, medicine and surgery, music, philosophy, and mathematics. In the tenth century no city in Asia or Europe could equal dazzling Córdoba. It's streets were well paved and lighted, and the city had an abundant supply of fresh water. The contemporary Saxon nun Hrosthwita of Gandersheim (d. 1000) described Córdoba as the "ornament of the world."[3]

Education and Intellectual Life

Muslim culture valued learning, especially religious learning, because knowledge provided the guidelines by which men and women should live. Parents thus established elementary schools for the training of their children. From the eighth century onward, formal education for young men involved reading, writing, and the study of the Qur'an, believed essential for its religious message and for its training in proper grammar and syntax.

madrasa

▶ A school for the study of Muslim law and religion.

Islam is a religion of the law, taught at madrasas (muh-DRA-suhs), schools for the study of Muslim law and religion. Schools were urban phenomena. Wealthy merchants endowed them, providing salaries for teachers, stipends for students, and living accommodations for both. All Islamic higher education rested on a close relationship between teacher and students, so in selecting a teacher, the student (or his father) considered the character and intellectual reputation of the teacher, not that of the institution. Students built their subsequent careers on the reputation of their teachers.

Learning depended heavily on memorization. In primary school, which was often attached to an institution of higher learning, a boy began his education by memorizing the entire Qur'an. In adolescence a student learned by heart an introductory work in one of the branches of knowledge, such as jurisprudence or grammar. Later he analyzed the texts in detail. Every class day, the teacher examined the student on the previous day's learning and determined whether the student fully understood what he had memorized. Students, of course, learned to write, for they had to record the teacher's commentary on a particular text. But the overwhelming emphasis was on the oral transmission of knowledge.

Because Islamic education focused on particular books, when the student had mastered a text to his teacher's satisfaction, the teacher issued the student a certificate stating that he had studied the book or collection of traditions with his teacher. The certificate allowed the student to transmit a text to the next generation on the authority of his teacher.

As the importance of books suggests, the Muslim transmission and improvement of papermaking techniques had special significance to education. After Chinese papermaking techniques spread westward, Muslim papermakers improved on them by adding starch to fill the pores in the surfaces of the sheets. Muslims carried this new method to Baghdad in Iraq, Damascus in Syria, Cairo in Egypt, and the Maghrib (North Africa), from which it entered Spain. Even before the

CHAPTER LOCATOR | From what kind of environment did Muhammad arise, and what did he teach? | What made possible the spread of Islam and what government was established? | How were Muslim lands governed and what challenges did rulers face?

256 CHAPTER 9 THE ISLAMIC WORLD

invention of printing, papermaking had a revolutionary impact on the collection and diffusion of knowledge.

Muslim higher education, apart from its fundamental goal of preparing men to live wisely and in accordance with God's law, aimed at preparing them to perform religious and legal functions as Qur'an—or hadith—readers; as preachers in the mosques; as professors, educators, or copyists; and especially as judges. Judges issued fatwas, or legal opinions, in the public courts; their training was in the Qur'an, hadith, or some text forming part of the shari'a.

On the issue of female education, Islamic culture was ambivalent. Tradition holds that Muhammad said, "The seeking of knowledge is a duty of every Muslim," but, because of the basic Islamic principle that "men are the guardians of women, because God has set the one over the other," the law excluded women from participating in the legal, religious, or civic occupations for which the madrasa prepared young men. Moreover, educational theorists insisted that men should study in a sexually isolated environment. Nevertheless, many young women received substantial educations at home. According to one biographical dictionary covering the lives of 1,075 women, 411 of them had memorized the Qur'an, studied with a particular teacher, and received a certificate.

In comparing Islamic higher education during the twelfth through fourteenth centuries with that available in Europe or China at the same time (see pages 368, 407), there are some striking similarities and some major differences. In both Europe and the Islamic countries religious authorities ran most schools, while in China the government, local villages, and lineages ran schools, and private tutoring was very common. In the Islamic world, as in China, the personal relationship of teacher and student was seen as key to education. In Europe the reward for satisfactorily completing a course of study was a degree granted by the university. In China, at the very highest levels, the state ran a civil service examination system that rewarded achievement with appointments in the state bureaucracy. In Muslim culture, by contrast, it was not the school or the state but the individual teacher whose evaluation mattered and who granted certificates.

Still, there were also some striking similarities in the practice of education. Students in all three cultures had to master a sacred language. In all three cultures education rested heavily on the study of basic religious, legal, or philosophical texts. Also, in all three cultures memorization played a large role in the acquisition and transmission of learning. Furthermore, teachers in all three societies lectured on particular passages, and leading teachers might disagree fiercely about the correct interpretations of a particular text, forcing students to question, to think critically, and to choose among divergent opinions. All these similarities in educational practice contributed to cultural cohesion and ties among the educated living in scattered localities.

In the Muslim world the spread of the Arabic language, not only among the educated classes but also among all the people, was the decisive element in the creation of a common culture. Arabic became the official language of the state and its bureaucracies in former Byzantine and Sassanid territories, and Muslim conquerors forbade Persian-speaking people to use their native language. Islamic rulers required tribute from monotheistic peoples—the Persians and Greeks—but they did not force them to change their religions. Conquered peoples were, however, compelled to submit to a linguistic conversion—to adopt the Arabic language.

What social distinctions were important in Muslim society?

Why did trade thrive in Muslim lands?

What new ideas and practices emerged in the arts, sciences, education, and religion?

How did Muslims and Christians come into contact with and view each other?

☑ LearningCurve Check what you know.

257

In time Arabic produced a cohesive and "international" culture over a large part of the Eurasian world. Among those who wrote in Arabic was the erudite Gregory Bar-Hebraeus (1226–1286), a bishop of the Syrian Orthodox Church.

As a result of Muslim creativity and vitality, modern scholars consider the years from 800 to 1300 to be one of the most brilliant periods in the world's history. Near the beginning of this period the Persian scholar al-Khwarizmi (d. ca. 850) harmonized Greek and Indian findings to produce astronomical tables that formed the basis for later Eastern and Western research. Al-Khwarizmi's textbook on algebra (from the Arabic *al-Jabr*) was the first work in which the word *algebra* is used to mean the "transposing of negative terms in an equation to the opposite side."

Muslim medical knowledge far surpassed that of the West. Muslim medical science reached its peak in the work of Ibn Sina of Bukhara (980–1037), known in the West as Avicenna. His *al-Qanun* codified all Greco-Arabic medical thought, described the contagious nature of tuberculosis and the spreading of diseases, and listed 760 drugs.

Muslim scholars also wrote works on geography, jurisprudence, and philosophy. Al-Kindi (d. ca. 870) was the first Muslim thinker to try to harmonize Greek philosophy and the religious precepts of the Qur'an. Avicenna maintained that the truths found by human reason cannot conflict with the truths revealed in the Qur'an. Ibn Rushid, or Averroës (1126–1198), of Córdoba, paraphrased and commented on the works of Aristotle. He insisted on the right to subject all knowledge, except the dogmas of faith, to the test of reason and on the essential harmony of religion and philosophy.

The Mystical Tradition of Sufism

Like the world's other major religions — Buddhism, Hinduism, Judaism, and Christianity — Islam also developed a mystical tradition: Sufism (SOO-fih-zuhm). It arose in the ninth and tenth centuries as a popular reaction to the materialism and worldliness of the later Umayyad regime. Sufis sought a personal union with God — divine love and knowledge through intuition rather than through rational deduction and study of the shari'a. The earliest of the Sufis followed an ascetic routine (denial of physical desires to achieve a spiritual goal), dedicating themselves to fasting, prayer, meditation on the Qur'an, and the avoidance of sin.

The woman mystic Rabi'a (717–801) epitomized this combination of renunciation and devotion. An attractive woman who refused marriage so that nothing would distract her from a total commitment to God, Rabi'a attracted followers, for whom she served as a spiritual guide.

Between the tenth and the thirteenth centuries groups of Sufis gathered around prominent leaders called *shaykhs*; members of these groups were called *dervishes*. Dervishes entered hypnotic or ecstatic trances, either through the constant repetition of certain prayers or through physical exertions such as whirling or dancing.

Some Sufis acquired reputations as charismatic holy men to whom ordinary Muslims came seeking spiritual consolation, healing, charity, or political mediation between tribal and factional rivals. Other Sufis became known for their writings. Probably the most famous medieval Sufi was the Spanish mystic-philosopher Ibn al'Arabi (1165–1240). The author of a number of important works, he traveled widely in Spain, North Africa, and Arabia seeking masters of Sufism.

CHAPTER LOCATOR | From what kind of environment did Muhammad arise, and what did he teach? | What made possible the spread of Islam and what government was established? | How were Muslim lands governed and what challenges did rulers face?

CHAPTER 9
258 THE ISLAMIC WORLD

Sufi Collective Ritual

Collective or group rituals, in which Sufis tried through ecstatic experiences to come closer to God, have always fascinated outsiders, including non-Sufi Muslims. Here the sixteenth-century Persian painter Sultan Muhammad illustrates the writing of the fourteenth-century lyric poet Hafiz. Notice the various musical instruments and the delicate floral patterns so characteristic of Persian art. (Or. Ms. 104, from *The Kulliyyati-I Sa'di* [The Collected Works of Sa'di], 1556, vellum/Edinburgh University Library, Scotland/With kind permission of the University of Edinburgh/The Bridgeman Art Library)

> PICTURING THE PAST

ANALYZING THE IMAGE: What sort of architectural space is depicted here? What distinctions do you see among the people in terms of how they dress and what they are doing?

CONNECTIONS: How common are music and dance in religion? What do they provide?

QUICK REVIEW

How did Islamic education compare to education in Europe and China?

What social distinctions were important in Muslim society?

Why did trade thrive in Muslim lands?

What new ideas and practices emerged in the arts, sciences, education, and religion?

How did Muslims and Christians come into contact with and view each other?

✓ LearningCurve
Check what you know.

How did Muslims and Christians come into contact with each other, and how did they view each other?

Playing Chess

This page from a thirteenth-century book on chess and other games depicts a Moor and a Christian playing chess together. (Biblioteca Monasterio del Escorial, Madrid, Spain/Index/The Bridgeman Art Library)

During the early centuries of its development, Islam came into contact with the other major religions of Eurasia—Hinduism in India, Buddhism in Central Asia, Zoroastrianism in Persia, and Judaism and Christianity in western Asia and Europe. However, the relationship that did the most to define Muslim identity was the one with Christianity. The close physical proximity and the long history of military encounters undoubtedly contributed to making the Christian-Muslim encounter so important to both sides.

European Christians and Middle Eastern Muslims shared a common Judeo-Christian heritage. In the classical period of Islam, Muslims learned about Christianity from the Christians they met in conquered territories; from the Old and New Testaments; from Jews; and from Jews and Christians who converted to Islam.

In the Middle Ages, Christians and Muslims met frequently in business and trade. Commercial contacts, especially when European merchants resided for a

CHAPTER LOCATOR | From what kind of environment did Muhammad arise, and what did he teach? | What made possible the spread of Islam and what government was established? | How were Muslim lands governed and what challenges did rulers face?

CHAPTER 9
260 THE ISLAMIC WORLD

long time in the Muslim East, gave Europeans familiarity with Muslim art and architecture. Likewise, when in the fifteenth century Muslim artists in the Ottoman Empire and in Persia became acquainted with Western artists they admired and imitated them. Also, Christians very likely borrowed aspects of their higher education system from Islam.

In the Christian West, Islam had the greatest cultural impact in Andalusia in southern Spain. Between roughly the eighth and twelfth centuries Muslims, Christians, and Jews lived in close proximity in Andalusia, and some scholars believe the period represents a remarkable era of interfaith harmony. Many Christians adopted many aspects of Arabic culture. These assimilated Christians, called Mozarabs (moh-ZAR-uhbz), did not attach much importance to the doctrinal differences between the two religions.

However, Mozarabs soon faced the strong criticism of both Muslim scholars and Christian clerics. Muslim teachers feared that close contact between people of the two religions would lead to Muslim contamination and become a threat to the Islamic faith. Christian bishops worried that a knowledge of Islam would lead to confusion about essential Christian doctrines. Both Muslim scholars and Christian theologians argued that assimilation led to moral decline.

Thus, beginning in the late tenth century, Muslim regulations closely defined what Christians and Muslims could do. A Christian, however much assimilated, remained an unbeliever, a word that carried a pejorative connotation. Mozarabs had to live in special sections of cities; could not learn the Qur'an, employ Muslim workers or servants, or build new churches; and had to be buried in their own cemeteries. A Muslim who converted to Christianity was sentenced to death. By about 1250 the Christian reconquest of Muslim Spain had brought most of the Iberian Peninsula under Christian control. With their new authority, Christian kings set up schools that taught both Arabic and Latin to train missionaries.

Beyond Andalusian Spain, mutual animosity limited contact between people of the two religions. The Muslim assault on Christian Europe in the eighth and ninth centuries left a legacy of bitter hostility. Christians felt threatened by a faith that acknowledged God as creator of the universe but denied the Trinity and that accepted Jesus as a prophet but denied his divinity. Europeans' perception of Islam as a menace helped inspire the Crusades of the eleventh through thirteenth centuries (see page 401).

Despite the conflicts between the two religions, Muslim scholars often wrote sympathetically about Jesus. For example, the great historian al-Tabari (d. 923), relying on Arabic sources, wrote positively of Jesus's life, focusing on his birth and crucifixion. The prominent theologian and qadi (judge) of Teheran, Abd al-Jabbar (d. 1024), though not critical of Jesus, argued that Christians failed to observe the laws of Moses and Jesus and distorted Jesus's message.

In the Christian West, both positive and negative views of Islam appeared in literature. The Bavarian knight Wolfram von Eschenbach's *Parzival* and the Englishman William Langland's *Piers the Plowman* reveal broad-mindedness and tolerance toward Muslims. Some travelers in the Middle East were impressed by the kindness and generosity of Muslims and with the strictness and devotion with which Muslims observed their faith. Frequently, however, Christian literature portrayed Muslims as the most dreadful of Europe's enemies, guilty of every kind of crime.

Mozarabs
▶ Christians who adopted some Arabic customs but did not convert.

| What social distinctions were important in Muslim society? | Why did trade thrive in Muslim lands? | What new ideas and practices emerged in the arts, sciences, education, and religion? | **How did Muslims and Christians come into contact with and view each other?** | ☑ LearningCurve Check what you know. |

261

Even when they rejected each other most forcefully, the Christian and Muslim worlds had a significant impact on each other. Art styles, technology, and even institutional practices spread in both directions. During the Crusades Muslims adopted Frankish weapons and methods of fortification. Christians in contact with Muslim scholars recovered ancient Greek philosophical texts that survived only in Arabic translation.

> ## QUICK REVIEW

Why did Christian-Muslim relations deteriorate over the course of the Middle Ages?

CHAPTER SUMMARY

Muhammad, born in the Arabian peninsula, experienced a religious vision, after which he preached to the people to give up their idols and submit to the one indivisible God. He believed in the same God as the Christians and Jews and taught strict monotheism. After Muhammad's death, his followers gathered his revelations, eventually producing the Qur'an.

Within the span of a century, Muslims carried their faith from the Arabian peninsula through the Middle East, to North Africa and Spain, and to the borders of China and India. Successors to Muhammad established the caliphate, which through two successive dynasties coordinated rule over Muslim lands. A key challenge faced by the caliphate was a fundamental division in Muslim theology between the Sunnis and the Shi'a.

Over time, many parts of the Muslim empire gained considerable local independence. By the tenth century Turks played a more important role in the armies and came to be the effective rulers in much of the Middle East. They were succeeded by the Mongols, who invaded the Middle East in the thirteenth century.

Muslim society was distinctly hierarchical. In addition to a structure that privileged the ruling Arab Muslims over converts to Islam, then over Jews, Christians, and Zoroastrians, there were also a substantial number of slaves. Distinctions between men and women in Islamic society were strict. Over time, the seclusion and veiling of women became common practices.

Islam did not discourage trade and profitmaking. By land and sea Muslim merchants transported a rich variety of goods across Asia, the Middle East, Africa, and western Europe. As trade thrived, technical innovations aided the conduct of business.

Wealth from trade made possible a gracious and sophisticated culture in the cities of the Muslim world. During this period Muslim scholars produced important work in many disciplines, especially mathematics, medicine, and philosophy. A new spiritual and intellectual tradition arose in the mystical practices of Sufism. Muslims, Christians, and Jews interacted in many ways during this period. Many Christians converted in the early centuries of the spread of Islam. Others such as the Mozarabs assimilated into Muslim culture while retaining their religion.

CHAPTER LOCATOR | From what kind of environment did Muhammad arise, and what did he teach? | What made possible the spread of Islam and what government was established? | How were Muslim lands governed and what challenges did rulers face?

CHAPTER 9
262 THE ISLAMIC WORLD

CONNECTIONS During the five centuries that followed Muhammad's death, his teachings came to be revered in large parts of the world. Although in some ways similar to the earlier spread of Buddhism out of India and Christianity out of Palestine, the spread of Islam occurred largely through military conquests that extended Muslim lands.

Muslim civilization in these centuries drew from many sources, including Persia and Byzantium, and in turn had broad impact beyond its borders. Muslim scholars preserved much of early Greek philosophy and science through translation into Arabic. Trade connected the Muslim lands both to Europe and to India and China.

During the first and second centuries after Muhammad, Islam spread along the Mediterranean coast of North Africa. The next chapter explores other developments in Africa during this time. Many of the written sources that tell us about the African societies of these centuries were written in Arabic by visitors from elsewhere in the Muslim world. Africa's history is introduced in the next chapter.

ONLINE DOCUMENT PROJECT
Long-Distance Travel in the Fourteenth Century
How did Ibn Battuta describe his travels?

Read parts of Ibn Battuta's account of his travels, and then complete a quiz and writing assignment based on the evidence and details from this chapter. *See the inside front cover to learn more.*

What social distinctions were important in Muslim society?	Why did trade thrive in Muslim lands?	What new ideas and practices emerged in the arts, sciences, education, and religion?	How did Muslims and Christians come into contact with and view each other?	✔️ LearningCurve Check what you know.

CHAPTER 9 STUDY GUIDE

STEP 1

GET STARTED ONLINE

 LearningCurve

Now that you've read the chapter, make it stick by completing the LearningCurve activity.

STEP 2

EXPLAIN WHY IT MATTERS

Put your reading into practice. Identify each term below, and then explain why it matters in world history.

TERM	WHO OR WHAT & WHEN	WHY IT MATTERS
Qur'an (p. 235)		
hadith (p. 235)		
Sunna (p. 236)		
Five Pillars of Islam (p. 236)		
umma (p. 238)		
diwān (p. 239)		
imam (p. 240)		
Shi'a (p. 241)		
Sunnis (p. 241)		
ulama (p. 241)		
emirs (p. 242)		
shari'a (p. 243)		
dhimmis (p. 248)		
madrasa (p. 256)		
Mozarabs (p. 261)		

STEP 3

MOVE BEYOND THE BASICS

To demonstrate a more advanced understanding of the relationship between Islamic beliefs and social, economic, and cultural developments in the Islamic world, fill in the first column of the chart below with a description of the core Islamic beliefs. Then, fill in the remaining three columns with descriptions of the impact of those beliefs on social, economic, and cultural developments. How did the advent of Islam impact the status of women in Islamic lands?

Core Islamic Beliefs	Impact on Social Developments	Impact on Economic Developments	Impact on Cultural Developments

PUT IT ALL TOGETHER

Now, take a step back and try to explain the big picture. Remember to use specific examples from the chapter in your answers.

THE ORIGINS OF ISLAM

▶ What characterized the social and economic environment in which Muhammad lived and preached?

▶ What are the core teachings of Islam? How do they compare to the core teachings of Christianity and Judaism?

ISLAMIC EXPANSION

▶ Argue for or against the following proposition: "The single most important factor explaining the rapid expansion of Islamic territories was the religious fervor of Muslim leaders and their armies." What evidence can you present to support your position?

▶ What explains the fragmentation of the Islamic world after 900? How did internal factors contribute to this trend? What about external threats?

ISLAMIC SOCIETY, COMMERCE, AND CULTURE

▶ Compare and contrast Roman (Chapter 6) and Islamic slavery. What role did slaves play in each society? How would you explain the similarities and differences you note?

▶ Compare and contrast Islamic and Confucian ideas (Chapter 7) about merchants and trade. How did such attitudes shape the social and economic trajectories of the Islamic and Chinese civilizations?

LOOKING BACK, LOOKING AHEAD

▶ What older Persian and Byzantine institutions and ideas did Islamic states incorporate into their own governments? How were those ideas and institutions modified by Islamic beliefs and practices?

▶ What connections can you make between the history of Muslim-Christian interactions and the contemporary relationship between Western and Islamic societies? How do long-held beliefs shape each society's view of the other?

> IN YOUR OWN WORDS

Imagine that you must give an oral report to the class answering the following question: How did Islamic civilization both build on and transform earlier civilizations? What would be the most important points and why?

10

AFRICAN SOCIETIES AND KINGDOMS

1000 B.C.E.–1500 C.E.

> **What role did trade play in the development of African kingdoms and empires?** Chapter 10 examines Africa's history to 1500. Between about 400 and 1500 highly centralized, bureaucratized, and socially stratified civilizations developed in Africa alongside communities with looser forms of social organization that were often held together through common kinship bonds. In West Africa several large empires closely linked to the trans-Saharan trade arose during this period. After 700 this trade connected West Africa with Muslim societies in North Africa and the Middle East. Meanwhile, Bantu-speaking peoples spread ironworking and domesticated crops and animals from modern Cameroon to Africa's southern tip, and the Swahili established large and prosperous city-states along the Indian Ocean coast.

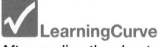 **LearningCurve**

After reading the chapter, use LearningCurve to retain what you've read.

Ife Ruler West African rulers, such as the one shown in this bronze head of a Yoruban king, or *Oni*, from the thirteenth or fourteenth century, were usually male.

> How did Africa's geography shape its history and contribute to its diverse population?

> How did agriculture affect life among the early societies in the western Sudan and among the Bantu-speaking societies of central and southern Africa?

> What characterized trans-Saharan trade, and how did it affect West African society?

> How were the East African city-states, Aksum, and Great Zimbabwe different from and similar to the kingdoms of the western Sudan?

How did Africa's geography shape its history and contribute to its diverse population?

Nok Woman

Hundreds of terra-cotta sculptures such as the head of this woman survive from the Nok culture, which originated in the central plateau of northern Nigeria in the first millennium B.C.E. (Werner Forman/Art Resource, NY)

Five main climatic zones roughly divide the African continent. Fertile land with unpredictable rainfall borders parts of the Mediterranean in the north and the southwestern coast of the Cape of Good Hope in the south. Inland from these areas are dry steppes with little plant life. These steppes gradually give way to Africa's great deserts: the Sahara in the north and the Namib (NAH-mihb) and Kalahari in the south. The Sahara's southern sub-desert fringe is called the Sahel (SA-hihl). The savannas—flat grasslands—extend in a swath across the continent's widest part—parts of south-central Africa and along the eastern coast. Dense, humid tropical rain forests stretch along coastal West Africa and on both sides of the equator in central Africa. Africa's climate is mostly tropical, with subtropical climates limited to the northern and southern coasts and the regions of high elevation. Rainfall is seasonal on most of the continent and is very sparse in desert and semidesert areas.

Geography and climate have significantly shaped African economic development. In the eastern African plains, the earliest humans hunted wild animals. The drier steppe regions favored herding. Wetter savanna regions, like the Nile Valley, encouraged grain-based agriculture. Tropical forests favored hunting and gathering and, later, root-based agriculture. Rivers and lakes supported economies based on fishing.

CHAPTER LOCATOR | **How did Africa's geography shape its history and contribute to its diverse population?** | How did agriculture affect life in the western Sudan and central and southern Africa?

268 CHAPTER 10 AFRICAN SOCIETIES AND KINGDOMS

ca. 1000 B.C.E.–1500 C.E.
Bantu-speakers expand across central and southern Africa

ca. 600 C.E.
Christian missionaries convert Nubian rulers

639–642 C.E.
Islam introduced to Africa

642 C.E.
Muslim conquest of Egypt

650–1500 C.E.
Slave trade from sub-Saharan Africa to the Mediterranean

700–900 C.E.
Berbers develop caravan routes

ca. 900–1100 C.E.
Kingdom of Ghana; bananas and plantains arrive in Africa from Asia

ca. 1100–1400 C.E.
Great Zimbabwe is built, flourishes

ca. 1200–1450 C.E.
Kingdom of Mali

ca. 1312–1337 C.E.
Reign of Mansa Musa in Mali

1314–1344 C.E.
Reign of Amda Siyon in Ethiopia

1324–1325 C.E.
Mansa Musa's pilgrimage to Mecca

Africa's peoples are as diverse as the continent's topography. In North Africa contacts with Asian and European civilizations date back to the ancient Phoenicians, Greeks, and Romans (see Chapters 5 and 6). Groups living on the coast or along trade routes had the greatest degree of contact with outside groups. The Berbers of North Africa, living along the Mediterranean, intermingled with many different peoples—with Muslim Arabs, who first conquered North Africa in the seventh and eighth centuries C.E. (see page 238); with Spanish Muslims and Jews, many of whom settled in North Africa after their expulsion from Spain in 1492 (see page 433); and with sub-Saharan peoples, with whom they traded across the Sahara Desert. The Swahili peoples along the East African coast developed a maritime civilization and had rich commercial contacts with southern Arabia, the Persian Gulf, India, China, and the Malay Archipelago.

South of the Sahara, short-statured peoples, sometimes inaccurately referred to as Pygmies, inhabited the equatorial rain forests. South of those forests, in the continent's southern third, lived the Khoisan (KOI-sahn), people who were primarily hunters but also had domesticated livestock.

Ancient Egypt, at the crossroads of three continents, was a melting pot of different cultures and peoples. Many diverse peoples contributed to the great achievements of Egyptian culture. Many scholars believe that Africans originating in the sub-Sahara resided in ancient Egypt, primarily in Upper Egypt (south of what is now Cairo), but that other ethnic groups constituted the majority of the population.

QUICK REVIEW

Which groups of Africans had the most contact with outside peoples? Why?

What characterized trans-Saharan trade, and how did it affect West African society?

How did the East African city-states compare to the kingdoms of the western Sudan?

LearningCurve
Check what you know.

How did agriculture affect life among the early societies in the western Sudan and among the Bantu-speaking societies of central and southern Africa?

Rock Painting at Tassili, Algeria

This scene of cattle grazing while a man stands guard over them was found on a rock face in Tassili n'Ajjer, a mountainous region in the Sahara where over fifteen thousand of these paintings have been catalogued. The oldest date back 9,000–12,000 years. Behind the man are perhaps his two children at play and his two wives working together in the compound. A cow stands in the enclosure to the right. (George Holton/Photo Researchers, Inc. Colorization by Robin Treadwell)

New crops introduced from Asia and the establishment of settled agriculture profoundly changed many African societies, although the range of possibilities largely depended on local variations in climate and geography. Bantu-speakers took the knowledge of domesticated livestock and agriculture, along with the ironworking skills that had developed in northern and western Africa, and spread them south across central and southern Africa. The most prominent feature of early West African society was a strong sense of community based on blood relationships and religion.

Agriculture and Its Impact

Agriculture began very early in Africa. Knowledge of plant cultivation moved west from the Levant (modern Israel and Lebanon), arriving in the Nile Delta in Egypt about the fifth millennium B.C.E. Settled agriculture then traveled down the Nile Valley and moved west across the Sahel to the central and western Sudan. West

CHAPTER LOCATOR | How did Africa's geography shape its history and contribute to its diverse population? | **How did agriculture affect life in the western Sudan and central and southern Africa?**

270 CHAPTER 10 AFRICAN SOCIETIES AND KINGDOMS

Africans were living in agricultural communities by the first century B.C.E. From there plant cultivation spread to the equatorial forests. Gradually most Africans evolved a sedentary way of life: living in villages, clearing fields, relying on root crops, and fishing. Hunting-and-gathering societies survived only in scattered parts of Africa, particularly in the central rain forest region and in southern Africa.

Between 1500 B.C.E. and 1000 B.C.E. agriculture also spread southward from Ethiopia along the Great Rift Valley of present-day Kenya and Tanzania. Archaeological evidence reveals that the peoples of East Africa grew cereals, raised cattle, and used wooden and stone tools.

Cereals such as millet and sorghum are indigenous to Africa. Scholars speculate that traders brought bananas, taros (a type of yam), sugarcane, and coconut palms to Africa from Southeast Asia. Because tropical forest conditions were ideal for banana plants, their cultivation spread rapidly. Throughout sub-Saharan Africa native peoples also domesticated donkeys, pigs, chickens, geese, and ducks, although all these came from outside Africa.

The evolution from a hunter-gatherer life to a settled life had profound effects. In contrast to nomadic societies, settled societies made shared or common needs more apparent, and those needs strengthened ties among extended families. Agricultural and pastoral populations also increased, though scholars speculate that this increase did not remain steady, but rather fluctuated over time. Nor is it clear that population growth was accompanied by a commensurate increase in agricultural output.

Early African societies were similarly influenced by the spread of ironworking, though scholars dispute the route by which this technology spread to sub-Saharan Africa. Some believe the Phoenicians brought the iron-smelting technique to northwestern Africa, from which it spread southward. Others insist it spread westward from the Meroë (MEHR-oh-ee) region of the Nile. The great trans-Saharan trade routes (see page 275) may have carried ironworking south from the Mediterranean coast. In any case, ancient iron tools found at the village of Nok on the Jos Plateau in present-day Nigeria seem to prove that ironworking industries existed in West Africa by at least 700 B.C.E.

Bantu Migrations

The spread of ironworking is linked to the migrations of Bantu-speaking peoples. Today the overwhelming majority of the 70 million people living south of the Congo River speak a Bantu language. Lacking written sources, modern scholars have tried to reconstruct the history of Bantu-speakers on the basis of linguistics, oral traditions, archaeology, and anthropology. Botanists and zoologists have played particularly critical roles in providing information about early diets and environments.

Bantu-speaking peoples originated in the Benue region, the borderlands of modern Cameroon and Nigeria. In the second millennium B.C.E. they began to spread south and east into the equatorial forest zone. Historians still debate why they began this movement. Some hold that rapid population growth sent people in search of land. Others believe that the evolution of centralized kingdoms allowed rulers to expand their authority, while causing newly subjugated peoples to flee in the hope of regaining their independence.

Bantu

▶ Speakers of a Bantu language living south and east of the Congo River.

What characterized trans-Saharan trade, and how did it affect West African society?

How did the East African city-states compare to the kingdoms of the western Sudan?

☑ LearningCurve
Check what you know.

**Bantu Migrations,
ca. 1000 B.C.E.–1500 C.E.**

During the next fifteen hundred years, Bantu-speakers migrated throughout the savanna, adopted mixed agriculture, and learned ironworking. Mixed agriculture (cultivating cereals and raising livestock) and ironworking were practiced in western East Africa (the region of modern Burundi) in the first century B.C.E. In the first millennium C.E. Bantu-speakers migrated into eastern and southern Africa. Here the Bantu-speakers, with their iron weapons, either killed, drove off, or assimilated the hunting-gathering peoples they met. Some of the assimilated inhabitants gradually adopted a Bantu language, contributing to the spread of Bantu culture.

The settled cultivation of cereals, the keeping of livestock, and the introduction of new crops such as the banana—together with Bantu-speakers' intermarriage with indigenous peoples—led over a long period to considerable population increases and the need to migrate farther. The so-called Bantu migrations should not be seen as a single movement sweeping across Africa from west to east to south and displacing all peoples in its path. Rather, those migrations were an extended series of group interactions between Bantu-speakers and pre-existing peoples in which bits of culture, languages, economies, and technologies were shared and exchanged to produce a wide range of cultural variation across central and southern Africa.[1]

The Bantu-speakers' expansion and subsequent land settlement that dominated eastern and southern African history in the first fifteen hundred years of the Common Era were uneven. Significant environmental differences determined settlement patterns. Some regions had plenty of water, while others were very arid. These differences resulted in very uneven population distribution. The greatest population density seems to have been in the region bounded on the west by the Congo River and on the north, south, and east by Lakes Edward and Victoria and Mount Kilimanjaro. The rapid growth of the Bantu-speaking population led to further migration southward and eastward. By the eighth century the Bantu-speaking people had crossed the Zambezi River and had begun settling in the region of present-day Zimbabwe. By the fifteenth century they had reached Africa's southeastern coast.

Life in the Kingdoms of the Western Sudan, ca. 1000 B.C.E.–800 C.E.

Sudan

▶ The African region surrounded by the Sahara, the Gulf of Guinea, the Atlantic Ocean, and the mountains of Ethiopia.

The **Sudan** is the region bounded by the Sahara to the north, the Gulf of Guinea to the south, the Atlantic Ocean to the west, and the mountains of Ethiopia to the east (see Map 10.1). In the western Sudan savanna a series of dynamic kingdoms emerged in the millennium before European intrusion began in the 1400s and 1500s.

Between 1000 B.C.E. and 200 C.E. the peoples of the western Sudan made the momentous shift from nomadic hunting to settled agriculture. The rich savanna proved ideally suited to cereal production, especially rice, millet, and sorghum. People situated near the Senegal River and Lake Chad supplemented their diet with fish. Food supply affects population, and the region's inhabitants increased dramatically in number. By 400 C.E. the entire savanna, particularly around Lake Chad, the Niger River bend, and present-day central Nigeria, had a large population.

Families and clans affiliated by blood kinship lived together in villages or small city-states. The extended family formed the basic social unit. A chief, in

MAP 10.1 ■ The Geography of Africa

Africa's climate zones have always played a critical role in the history of the continent and its peoples. These zones mirror each other north and south of the equator: tropical forest, savanna, sub-desert, desert, and Mediterranean climate.

Major climatic zones of Africa

- Wet equatorial
- Humid tropical and subtropical
- Tropical with long dry season (6–9 months)
- Sahelian or subdesert
- Desert
- Mediterranean
- Highland (climate moderated by altitude)
- Savanna

consultation with a council of elders, governed a village. Some villages seem to have formed kingdoms. In this case, village chiefs were responsible to regional heads, who answered to provincial governors, who in turn were responsible to a king. The kings and their families formed an aristocracy.

Kingship in the Sudan may have emerged from the priesthood. African kings always had religious sanction or support for their authority and were often considered divine. In this respect, early African kingship bears a strong resemblance to Germanic kingship of the same period (discussed in Chapter 14).

Women exercised significant power and autonomy in many African societies. Among the Asante in modern-day Ghana, one of the most prominent West African peoples, the king was considered divine but shared some royal power with the Queen Mother. Among the Yoruba in modern Nigeria, the Queen Mother held the royal insignia and could refuse it if the future king did not please her. The institutions of female chiefs, known as *iyalode* among the Yoruba and *omu* among the Igbo in modern Nigeria, were established to represent women in the political process. The *omu* was even considered a female co-ruler with the male chief.

What characterized trans-Saharan trade, and how did it affect West African society?

How did the East African city-states compare to the kingdoms of the western Sudan?

✓ LearningCurve
Check what you know.

Western Sudanese religious practices, like African religions elsewhere, were animistic and polytheistic. Most people believed that a supreme being had created the universe and was the source of all life. Most African religions also recognized ancestral spirits, which might seek God's blessings for families' and communities' prosperity and security as long as these groups behaved appropriately. Some African religions believed as well that nature spirits lived in such things as the sky, forests, rocks, and rivers. These spirits controlled natural forces and had to be appeased. Because special ceremonies were necessary to satisfy the spirits, special priests with the knowledge and power to communicate with them through sacred rituals were needed. Family and village heads were often priests. Each family head was responsible for ceremonies honoring the family's dead and living members.[2] In some West African societies, oracles who spoke for the gods were particularly important.

Kinship patterns and shared religious practices helped to bind together the early western Sudan kingdoms. Islam's spread across the Sahara by at least the ninth century C.E., however, created a north-south religious and cultural divide in the western Sudan. Islam advanced across the Sahel but halted when it reached the West African savanna and forest zones. Societies in these southern zones maintained their traditional animistic religious practices. Muslim empires along the Niger River's great northern bend evolved into formidable powers ruling over sizable territory as they seized control of the southern termini of the trans-Saharan trade. What made this long-distance trade possible was the "ship of the desert," the camel.

> **QUICK REVIEW**

How did the Bantu migrations shape early Africa?

CHAPTER LOCATOR | How did Africa's geography shape its history and contribute to its diverse population? | How did agriculture affect life in the western Sudan and central and southern Africa?

CHAPTER 10
274 AFRICAN SOCIETIES AND KINGDOMS

Copper Coin from Mogadishu, Twelfth Century

Islamic proscriptions against representation of the human form prevented the use of rulers' portraits on coinage, unlike the practice of the Romans, Byzantines, and Sassanids. Instead Islamic coins since the Umayyad period were decorated exclusively with writing. Sultan Haran Ibn Suleiman of Kilwa on the East African coast minted this coin, a symbol of the region's Muslim culture and of its rich maritime trade. (© The Trustees of the British Museum/Art Resource, NY)

What characterized trans-Saharan trade, and how did it affect West African society?

"Trans-Saharan trade" refers to the north-south trade across the Sahara (Map 10.2). The camel had an impact on this trade comparable to the very important impact of horses and oxen on European agriculture. Although scholars dispute exactly when the camel was introduced from Central Asia—first into North Africa, then into the Sahara and the Sudan—they agree that it was before 200 C.E. The trans-Saharan trade brought lasting economic and social change to Africa, facilitating the spread of Islam via Muslim Arab traders, and affected the development of world commerce.

The Berbers of North Africa

Sometime in the fifth century C.E. the North African **Berbers** fashioned a saddle for use on the camel. The saddle gave the Berbers and later the region's Arabian inhabitants maneuverability on the animal and thus a powerful political and military advantage: they came to dominate the desert and to create lucrative routes across it. The Berbers determined who could enter the desert, and they extracted large sums of protection money from merchant caravans in exchange for a safe trip.

Between 700 C.E. and 900 C.E. the Berbers developed a network of caravan routes between the Mediterranean coast and the Sudan (see Map 10.2). Ibn Battuta, an Arab traveler in the fourteenth century, when the trade was at its height, left one of the best descriptions of the trans-Saharan traffic. (See "Individuals in Society: Ibn Battuta," page 255.)

Berbers

▶ North African peoples who controlled the caravan trade between the Mediterranean and the Sudan.

| What characterized trans-Saharan trade, and how did it affect West African society? | How did the East African city-states compare to the kingdoms of the western Sudan? | LearningCurve Check what you know. |

MAP 10.2 ■ African Kingdoms and Trade, ca. 800–1500

Throughout world history powerful kingdoms have generally been closely connected to far-flung trade networks.

Ghana, ca. 900–1100
Mali, ca. 1450
Songhai, ca. 1500
Other state, ca. 1000–1500
→ Trans-Saharan trade route
→ Coastal trade route

> **MAPPING THE PAST**

ANALYZING THE MAP: Which kingdoms, empires, and city-states were linked to the trans-Saharan trade network? Which were connected to the Indian Ocean trade network? To the Portuguese route?

CONNECTIONS: How were the kingdoms, empires, and city-states shown on this map shaped by their proximity to trade routes?

CHAPTER LOCATOR | How did Africa's geography shape its history and contribute to its diverse population? | How did agriculture affect life in the western Sudan and central and southern Africa?

CHAPTER 10
276 AFRICAN SOCIETIES AND KINGDOMS

Nomadic raiders, the Tuareg (TWAH-rehg), posed a serious threat to trans-Saharan traders. The Tuareg were Berbers who lived in the desert uplands and preyed on the caravans as a way of life. To avoid being victimized, merchants made safe-conduct agreements with them and selected guides from among them. Large numbers of merchants crossed the desert together to discourage attack; caravans of twelve thousand camels were reported in the fourteenth century.

Berber merchants from North Africa controlled the caravan trade that carried dates, salt from the Saharan salt mines, and some manufactured goods—silk and cotton cloth, beads, mirrors—to the Sudan. These products were exchanged for the much-coveted commodities of the West African savanna—gold, ivory, gum, kola nuts (eaten as a stimulant), and enslaved West African men and women who were sold to Muslim slave markets in Morocco, Algiers, Tripoli, and Cairo.

Effects of Trade on West African Society

The steady growth of trans-Saharan trade had three important effects on West African society. First, trade stimulated gold mining. Parts of modern-day Senegal, Nigeria, and Ghana contained rich veins of gold, and scholars estimate that by the eleventh century nine tons of gold were exported to the Mediterranean coast and Europe annually. Some of this metal went to Egypt. From there it was transported down the Red Sea and eventually to India (see Map 9.2, page 253) to pay for the spices and silks demanded by Mediterranean commerce. In this way, African gold linked the entire world, exclusive of the Western Hemisphere.

Second, trade in gold and other goods created a desire for slaves. Slaves were West Africa's second-most valuable export (after gold). Slaves worked the gold and salt mines, and in Muslim North Africa, southern Europe, and southwestern Asia there was a high demand for household slaves among the elite. African slaves, like their early European and Asian counterparts, seem to have been peoples captured in war. Recent research suggests, moreover, that large numbers of black slaves were also recruited for Muslim military service through the trans-Saharan trade. Table 10.1 shows the scope of the trans-Saharan slave trade. The total number of blacks enslaved over an 850-year period may be tentatively estimated at more than 4 million.[3]

The third important effect of trans-Saharan trade on West African society was its role in stimulating the development of urban centers. Scholars date the growth of African cities from around the early ninth century. Families that had profited from trade tended to congregate in the border zones between the savanna and the Sahara. They acted as middlemen between the miners to the south and the Muslim merchants from the north. By the early thirteenth century these families had become powerful merchant dynasties. Muslim traders from the Mediterranean settled permanently in the trading depots, from which they organized the trans-Saharan caravans. The concentration of people stimulated agriculture and the craft industries. Gradually cities of sizable population emerged, including: Jenne, Gao, and Timbuktu, Sijilmasa, and Koumbi Saleh. Between 1100 and 1400 these cities played a dynamic role in West Africa's commercial life and became centers of intellectual creativity.

TABLE 10.1 ■ Estimated Magnitude of Trans-Saharan Slave Trade, 650–1500

Years	Annual Average of Slaves Traded	Total
650–800	1,000	150,000
800–900	3,000	300,000
900–1100	8,700	1,740,000
1100–1400	5,500	1,650,000
1400–1500	4,300	430,000

Source: R. A. Austen, "The Trans-Saharan Slave Trade: A Tentative Census," in *The Uncommon Market: Essays in the Economic History of the Atlantic Slave Trade*, ed. H. A. Gemery and J. S. Hogendorn (New York: Academic Press, 1979). Used with permission.

> **Major Effects of Trade on West African Society:**

- Stimulation of gold mining
- Increased demand for slaves
- Development of urban centers

What characterized trans-Saharan trade, and how did it affect West African society?

How did the East African city-states compare to the kingdoms of the western Sudan?

✓ LearningCurve
Check what you know.

The Spread of Islam in Africa

The Spread of Islam in Africa

Perhaps the most influential consequence of the trans-Saharan trade was the introduction of Islam to West Africa. In the eighth century Arab invaders overran all of coastal North Africa. They introduced the Berbers living there to Islam (see page 239), and gradually the Berbers became Muslims. As traders, these Berbers carried Islam to sub-Saharan West Africa. From the eleventh century onward militant Almoravids, a coalition of fundamentalist western Saharan Berbers, preached Islam to the rulers of Ghana, Mali, Songhai, and Kanem-Bornu. These rulers, admiring Muslim administrative techniques and wanting to protect their kingdoms from Muslim Berber attacks, converted to Islam. Some merchants also sought to preserve their elite mercantile status with the Berbers by adopting Islam. Muslims quickly became integral to West African government and society. Hence, from roughly 1000 to 1400, Islam in West Africa was a class-based religion with conversion inspired by political or economic motives. Rural people in the Sahel region and the savanna and forest peoples farther south, however, largely retained their traditional animism.

Conversion to Islam introduced West Africans to a rich and sophisticated culture. By the late eleventh century Muslims were guiding the ruler of Ghana in the operation of his administrative machinery. Because efficient government depends on keeping and preserving records, Islam's arrival in West Africa marked the advent of written documents there. Arab Muslims also taught Ghana's rulers how to manufacture bricks, and royal palaces and mosques began to be built of brick. African rulers corresponded with Arab and North African Muslim architects, theologians, and other intellectuals, who advised them on statecraft and religion. Islam accelerated the development of the West African empires of the ninth through fifteenth centuries.

After the Muslim conquest of Egypt in 642 (see page 238), Islam spread southward from Egypt up the Nile Valley and west to Darfur and Wadai. This Muslim penetration came not suddenly by military force but, as in the trans-Saharan trade routes in West Africa, gradually through commercial networks.

Muslim expansion from the Arabian peninsula across the Red Sea to the Horn of Africa, then southward along the coast of East Africa, represents a third direction of Islam's growth in Africa. From ports on the Red Sea and the Gulf of Aden, maritime trade carried Islam to East Africa and the Indian Ocean. Muslims founded the port city of Mogadishu between the eighth and tenth centuries, today Somalia's capital. In the twelfth century Mogadishu developed into a Muslim sultanate. Archaeological evidence, confirmed by Arabic sources, reveals a rapid Islamic expansion along Africa's east coast in the thirteenth century as far south as Kilwa, where Ibn Battuta visited a center for Islamic law in 1331.

Mogadishu

▶ A Muslim port city in East Africa founded between the eighth and tenth centuries; today it is the capital of Somalia.

> **QUICK REVIEW**

What connections were there between trade and the spread of Islam in Africa?

CHAPTER LOCATOR | How did Africa's geography shape its history and contribute to its diverse population? | How did agriculture affect life in the western Sudan and central and southern Africa?

278 CHAPTER 10 AFRICAN SOCIETIES AND KINGDOMS

Ruins of Great Zimbabwe

Considered the most impressive monument in the African interior south of the Ethiopian highlands, these ruins of Great Zimbabwe consist of two complexes of dry-stone buildings, some surrounded by a massive serpentine wall 32 feet high and 17 feet thick at its maximum. (Robert Harding World Imagery)

How were the East African city-states, Aksum, and Great Zimbabwe different from and similar to the kingdoms of the western Sudan?

All African societies shared one basic feature: a close relationship between political and social organization. Ethnic or blood ties bound clan members together. What scholars call **stateless societies** were culturally homogeneous ethnic societies, generally organized around kinship groups. These societies lacked a central authority figure, such as a king, capital city, or military. A village or group of villages might recognize a chief who held very limited powers and whose position was not hereditary, but more commonly they were governed by local councils, whose members were either elders or persons of merit. Although stateless societies functioned successfully, their weakness lay in their inability to organize and defend themselves against attack by the powerful armies of neighboring kingdoms or by the European powers of the colonial era.

While stateless societies were relatively common in Africa, the period from about 800 to 1500 is best known as the age of Africa's great empires (see Map 10.2). This period witnessed the flowering of several powerful African states. In the western Sudan the large empires of Ghana, Mali, and Songhai developed, complete with sizable royal bureaucracies. On the east coast emerged thriving city-states based on sophisticated mercantile activities and, like the western Sudan, heavily influenced by Islam. In Ethiopia, in central East Africa, kings relied

stateless societies
▶ African societies bound together by ethnic or blood ties rather than by being political states.

What characterized trans-Saharan trade, and how did it affect West African society?

How did the East African city-states compare to the kingdoms of the western Sudan?

✓ LearningCurve
Check what you know.

279

on their peoples' Christian faith to strengthen political authority. In southern Africa the empire of Great Zimbabwe, built on the gold trade with the east coast, flourished.

The Kingdom of Ghana, ca. 900–1100

So remarkable was the kingdom of Ghana during the age of Africa's great empires that Arab and North African visitors praised it as a model for other rulers. The Soninke people inhabited the nucleus of the territory that became the Ghanaian kingdom. They called their ruler *ghana*, or war chief. By the late eighth century Muslim traders and other foreigners applied the king's title to the region where the Soninke lived, the kingdom south of the Sahara. The Soninke themselves called their land Wagadou (WAH-guh-doo). Only the southern part of Wagadou received enough rainfall to be agriculturally productive, and it was here that the civilization of Ghana developed (see Map 10.2). Skillful farming and efficient irrigation systems led to abundant crop production, which eventually supported a population of as many as two hundred thousand.

In 992 Ghana captured the Berber town of Awdaghost, strategically situated on the trans-Saharan trade route. Thereafter Ghana controlled the southern portion of a major caravan route. Before the year 1000 Ghana's rulers had extended their influence almost to the Atlantic coast and had captured a number of small kingdoms in the south and east. By the early eleventh century the Ghanaian king exercised sway over a territory approximately the size of Texas. No other power in the western Sudan could successfully challenge him.

Throughout this vast West African territory, all authority sprang from the king. Religious ceremonies and court rituals emphasized the king's sacredness and were intended to strengthen his authority. The king's position was hereditary in the matrilineal line—that is, the ruling king's heir was one of the king's sister's sons (presumably the eldest or fittest for battle).

A council of ministers assisted the king in the work of government, and from the ninth century on most of these ministers were Muslims. The royal administration was well served by ideas, skills, and especially literacy brought from the North African and Arab Muslim worlds. The king and his people, however, clung to their ancestral religion and basic cultural institutions.

The Ghanaian king held court in the city of Koumbi Saleh, which was actually two towns, one inhabited by the king and the other by Muslims. Either to protect themselves or to preserve their special identity, the Muslims of Koumbi Saleh lived separately from the African artisans and tradespeople. Ghana's Muslim community was large and prosperous, and Muslim religious leaders exercised civil authority over their fellow Muslims. The presence of religious leaders and other learned Muslims suggests that Koumbi Saleh was a city of vigorous intellectual activity.

The king's elaborate court, the administrative machinery he built, and the extensive territories he governed were all expensive. To support the kingdom, the royal estates—some hereditary, others conquered in war—produced annual revenue, mostly in the form of foodstuffs for the royal household. The king also received tribute annually from subordinate chieftains. Customs duties on goods entering and leaving the country generated revenues as well. Salt was the largest import. Berber merchants paid a tax to the king on the cloth, metalwork, weapons,

Ghana

▶ From the word for "ruler," the name of a large and influential African kingdom inhabited by the Soninke people.

Koumbi Saleh

▶ The city in which the king of Ghana held his court.

CHAPTER LOCATOR | How did Africa's geography shape its history and contribute to its diverse population? | How did agriculture affect life in the western Sudan and central and southern Africa?

280 CHAPTER 10 AFRICAN SOCIETIES AND KINGDOMS

and other goods they brought into the country from North Africa; in return these traders received royal protection from bandits. African traders bringing gold into Ghana from the south also paid the customs duty. Finally, the royal treasury held a monopoly on the export of gold. The gold industry was undoubtedly the king's largest source of income.

The governing aristocracy—the king, his court, and Muslim administrators—occupied the highest rung on the Ghanaian social ladder. On the next rung stood the merchant class. Considerably below the merchants stood the farmers, cattle breeders, gold mine supervisors, and skilled craftsmen and weavers—what today might be called the middle class. Some merchants and miners must have enjoyed great wealth, but, as in all aristocratic societies, money alone did not grant prestige. High status was based on blood and royal service. On the social ladder's lowest rung were slaves, who worked in households, on farms, and in the mines. As in Asian and European societies of the time, slaves accounted for only a small percentage of the population.

Apart from these social classes stood the army. Ghana's king maintained at his palace a standing force of a thousand men, comparable to the bodyguards of the Roman emperors. These thoroughly disciplined, well-armed, totally loyal troops protected the king and the royal court. They lived in special compounds, enjoyed the king's favor, and sometimes acted as his personal ambassadors to subordinate rulers. In wartime this regular army was augmented by levies of soldiers from conquered peoples and by the use of slaves and free reserves.

The reasons for ancient Ghana's decline are still a matter of much debate. The most commonly accepted theory for Ghana's rapid decline is that the Berber Almoravid dynasty of North Africa invaded and conquered Ghana around 1100 and forced its rulers and people to convert to Islam. Some historians examining this issue have concluded that while Almoravid and Islamic pressures certainly disrupted the empire, weakening it enough for its incorporation into the rising Mali empire, there was no Almoravid military invasion and subsequent forced conversion to Islam.[4]

The Kingdom of Mali, ca. 1200–1450

Ghana and its capital of Koumbi Saleh were in decline between 1100 and 1200. The old empire split into several small kingdoms that feuded among themselves. One people, the Mandinka, from the kingdom of Kangaba on the upper Niger River, gradually asserted their dominance over these kingdoms. The Mandinka had long been part of the Ghanaian empire, and the Mandinka and Soninke belonged to the same language group. Kangaba formed the core of the new empire of Mali. Building on Ghanaian foundations, Mali developed into a better-organized and more powerful state than Ghana.

Mali owed its greatness to two fundamental assets. First, its strong agricultural and commercial base supported a large population and provided enormous wealth. Second, Mali had two rulers, Sundiata (soon-JAH-tuh) and Mansa Musa, who combined military success with exceptionally creative personalities.

The Expansion of Mali, ca. 1200–1450

Territory of Mali
- ca. 1100
- ca. 1350
- ca. 1500

What characterized trans-Saharan trade, and how did it affect West African society?

How did the East African city-states compare to the kingdoms of the western Sudan?

LearningCurve
Check what you know.

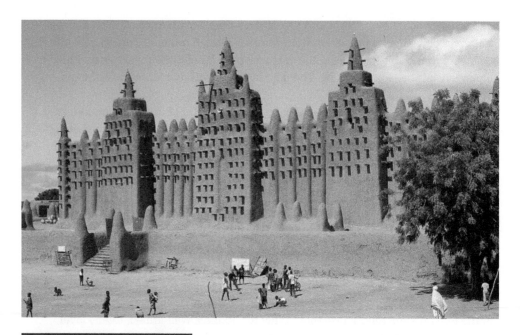

The Great Friday Mosque, Jenne

The mosque at Jenne was built in the form of a parallelogram. Inside, nine long rows of adobe columns run along a north-south axis and support a flat roof of palm logs. A pointed arch links each column to the next in its row, forming nine east-west archways facing the *mihrab*, the niche in the wall of the mosque indicating the direction of Mecca, and from which the imam speaks. This mosque (rebuilt in 1907 based on the original thirteenth-century structure) testifies to the considerable wealth, geometrical knowledge, and manpower of Mali. (Gerard Degeorge/akg-images)

The earliest surviving evidence about the Mandinka, dating from the early eleventh century, indicates that they were extremely successful at agriculture. Consistently large harvests throughout the twelfth and thirteenth centuries meant a plentiful food supply, which encouraged steady population growth. Kangaba's geographical location also ideally positioned the Mandinka in the heart of the West African trade networks. Earlier, during the period of Ghanaian hegemony, the Mandinka had acted as middlemen in the gold and salt traffic flowing north and south. In the thirteenth century Mandinka traders formed companies, traveled widely, and gradually became a major force in the entire West African trade.

Mali's founder, Sundiata (r. ca. 1230–1255) set up his capital at Niani, transforming the city into an important financial and trading center. He then embarked on a policy of imperial expansion. Through a series of military victories, Sundiata and his successors absorbed into Mali other territories of the former kingdom of Ghana and established hegemony over the trading cities of Gao, Jenne, and Walata.

These expansionist policies were continued in the fourteenth century by Sundiata's descendant Mansa Musa (r. ca. 1312–1337), early Africa's most famous ruler. Ultimately Mansa Musa's influence extended northward to several Berber cities in the Sahara, eastward to the trading cities of Timbuktu and Gao, and westward to the Atlantic Ocean. Throughout his territories, he maintained strict royal control over the flourishing trans-Saharan trade. Thus this empire, roughly

CHAPTER LOCATOR | How did Africa's geography shape its history and contribute to its diverse population? | How did agriculture affect life in the western Sudan and central and southern Africa?

282 CHAPTER 10 AFRICAN SOCIETIES AND KINGDOMS

twice the size of the Ghanaian kingdom and containing perhaps 8 million people, brought Mansa Musa fabulous wealth.

Mansa Musa built on the foundations of his predecessors. Malian society's stratified aristocratic structure perpetuated the pattern set in Ghana, as did the system of provincial administration and annual tribute. The emperor took responsibility for the territories that formed the heart of the empire and appointed governors to rule the outlying provinces and dependent kingdoms. But Mansa Musa made a significant innovation: in a practice strikingly similar to a system used in both China and France at the time, he appointed royal family members as provincial governors.

In another aspect of administration, Mansa Musa also differed from his predecessors. He became a devout Muslim. Although most of the Mandinka remained animists, Islamic practices and influences in Mali multiplied.

The most celebrated event of Mansa Musa's reign was his pilgrimage to Mecca in 1324–1325, during which he paid a state visit to the Egyptian sultan. Mansa Musa's entrance into Cairo was magnificent. Preceded by five hundred slaves, each carrying a six-pound staff of gold, he followed with a huge host of retainers, including one hundred elephants each bearing one hundred pounds of gold. The emperor lavished his wealth on the citizens of the Egyptian capital.

As a result of this pilgrimage, for the first time, the Mediterranean world learned firsthand of Mali's wealth and power, and the kingdom began to be known as one of the world's great empires. Mali retained this international reputation into the fifteenth century. Musa's pilgrimage also had significant consequences within Mali. He gained some understanding of the Mediterranean countries and opened diplomatic relations with the Muslim rulers of Morocco and Egypt. His zeal for the Muslim faith and Islamic culture increased. Musa brought back from Arabia the distinguished architect al-Saheli, whom he commissioned to build new mosques in Timbuktu and other cities. These mosques served as centers for African conversion to Islam.

Timbuktu began as a campsite for desert nomads, but under Mansa Musa it grew into a thriving entrepôt (trading center), attracting merchants and traders from North Africa and all parts of the Mediterranean world. In the fifteenth century Timbuktu developed into a great center for scholarship and learning. Architects, astronomers, poets, lawyers, mathematicians, and theologians flocked there. One hundred fifty schools, for men only, were devoted to Qur'anic studies. The school of Islamic law enjoyed a distinction comparable to the prestige of the Cairo school (see page 256). The vigorous traffic in books that flourished in Timbuktu made them the most common items of trade. Timbuktu's tradition and reputation for African scholarship lasted until the eighteenth century.

Moreover, in the fourteenth and fifteenth centuries many Arab and North African Muslim intellectuals and traders married native African women. The necessity of living together harmoniously, the traditional awareness of diverse cultures, and Timbuktu's cosmopolitan atmosphere contributed to a rare degree of racial tolerance and understanding.

The third great West African empire, Songhai, succeeded Mali in the fourteenth century. It encompassed the old empires of Ghana and Mali and extended its territory farther north and east to become one of the largest African empires in history (see Map 10.2).

Timbuktu
▶ Originally a campsite for desert nomads, it grew into a thriving city under Mansa Musa, king of Mali and Africa's most famous ruler.

What characterized trans-Saharan trade, and how did it affect West African society?

How did the East African city-states compare to the kingdoms of the western Sudan?

LearningCurve
Check what you know.

Ethiopia: The Christian Kingdom of Aksum

Just as the ancient West African empires were significantly affected by Islam and the Arab culture that accompanied it, the African kingdoms that arose in modern Sudan and Ethiopia in northeast Africa were heavily influenced by Egyptian culture, and they influenced it in return. This was particularly the case in ancient Nubia. Nubia's capital was at Meroë (see Map 10.2); thus the country is often referred to as the Nubian kingdom of Meroë.

As part of the Roman Empire, Egypt was subject to Hellenistic and Roman cultural forces, and it became an early center of Christianity. Nubia, however, was never part of the Roman Empire; its people retained ancient Egyptian religious ideas. Christian missionaries traveled to the Upper Nile region and successfully converted the Nubian rulers around 600 C.E. By that time, there were three separate Nubian states, of which the kingdom of Nobatia, centered at Dongola, was the strongest. The Christian rulers of Nobatia had close ties with the **Aksum** kingdom in Ethiopia, and through this relationship Egyptian culture spread to Ethiopia.

Two-thirds of Ethiopia consists of the Ethiopian highlands, the rugged plateau region of East Africa. The Great Rift Valley divides this territory into two massifs (mountain masses), of which the Ethiopian Plateau is the larger. Sloping away from each side of the Great Rift Valley are a series of mountains and valleys. Together with this mountainous environment, the three Middle Eastern religions—Judaism, Christianity, and Islam—have all influenced Ethiopian society.

By the first century C.E. the Aksum kingdom in northwestern Ethiopia was a sizable trading state. Merchants at Adulis, its main port on the Red Sea, sold ivory, gold, emeralds, rhinoceros horns, shells, and slaves to the Sudan, Arabia, Yemen, and various cities across the Indian Ocean in exchange for glass, ceramics, fabrics, sugar, oil, spices, and precious gems. Adulis contained temples, stone-built houses, and irrigated agriculture. Between the first and eighth centuries Aksum served as the capital of an empire extending over much of what is now northern Ethiopia. The empire's prosperity rested on trade.

Islam's expansion into northern Ethiopia in the eighth century (see page 278) weakened Aksum's commercial prosperity. The Arabs first ousted the Greek Byzantine merchants who traded on the Dahlak Archipelago (in the southern Red Sea) and converted the islands' inhabitants. Then Muslims attacked and destroyed Adulis. Some Aksumites converted to Islam; many others found refuge in the rugged mountains north of the kingdom, where they were isolated from outside contacts. Thus began the insularity that characterized later Ethiopian society.

Tradition ascribes to Frumentius (ca. 300–380 C.E.), a Syrian Christian trader, the introduction of Coptic Christianity, an Orthodox form of Christianity that originated in Egypt, into Ethiopia. Kidnapped as a young boy en route from India to Tyre (in southern Lebanon), Frumentius was taken to Aksum, given his freedom, and appointed tutor to the future king, Ezana. Upon Ezana's accession to the throne, Frumentius went to Alexandria, Egypt, where he was consecrated the first bishop of Aksum around 328 C.E. He then returned to Ethiopia with some priests to spread Christianity. Shortly after members of the royal court accepted Christianity, it became the Ethiopian state religion.

Ethiopia's acceptance of Christianity led to the production of ecclesiastical documents and royal chronicles, making Ethiopia the first sub-Saharan African

Aksum

▶ A kingdom in northwestern Ethiopia that was a sizable trading state and the center of Christian culture.

The Kingdom of Aksum, ca. 600

CHAPTER LOCATOR | How did Africa's geography shape its history and contribute to its diverse population? | How did agriculture affect life in the western Sudan and central and southern Africa?

284 CHAPTER 10
AFRICAN SOCIETIES AND KINGDOMS

society that can be studied from written records. The Scriptures were translated into Ge'ez (gee-EHZ), an ancient language and script used in Ethiopia and Aksum. Pagan temples were dedicated to Christian saints, and, as in early medieval Ireland and in the Orthodox Church of the Byzantine world, monasteries were the Christian faith's main cultural institutions in Ethiopia. As the Ethiopian state expanded, vibrant monasteries provided inspiration for the establishment of convents for nuns, as in medieval Europe (see page 396).

Monastic records provide fascinating information about early Ethiopian society. Settlements were formed on the warm and moist plateau lands. Farmers used a scratch plow (unique in sub-Saharan Africa) to cultivate wheat and barley, and they regularly rotated these cereals. Plentiful rainfall seems to have helped produce abundant crops, which in turn led to population growth. Because of ecclesiastical opposition to polygyny (the practice of having multiple wives), monogamy was the norm, other than for kings and the very rich. An abundance of land meant that young couples could establish independent households. Widely scattered farms, with the parish church as the central social unit, seem to have been the usual pattern of existence.

Above the broad class of peasant farmers stood warrior-nobles. Their wealth and status derived from their fighting skills. To acquire lands and to hold warriors' loyalty, Ethiopian kings pursued a policy of constant territorial expansion. (See "Individuals in Society: Amda Siyon," page 286.) Nobles maintained order in their regions, supplied kings with fighting men, and displayed their superior status by the size of their households and their generosity to the poor.

Sometime in the fourteenth century, six scribes in the Tigrayan highlands of Ethiopia combined oral tradition, Jewish and Islamic commentaries, apocryphal

Christianity and Islam in Ethiopia

The prolonged contest between the two religions in Ethiopia was periodically taken to the battlefield. This drawing from the eighteenth century by an Ethiopian artist shows his countrymen (left) advancing victoriously and celebrates national military success. (© The British Library Board/The Image Works)

What characterized trans-Saharan trade, and how did it affect West African society?

How did the East African city-states compare to the kingdoms of the western Sudan?

LearningCurve
Check what you know.

Scholars consider Amda Siyon (r. 1314–1344) the greatest ruler of Ethiopia's Solomonic dynasty. Yet we have no image or representation of him. We know nothing of his personal life, though if he followed the practice of most Ethiopian kings, he had many wives and children. Nor do we know anything about his youth and education. The evidence of what he did, however, suggests a tough military man who personified the heroic endurance and physical pain expected of warriors. According to a chronicle of Siyon's campaign against the Muslim leader of Ifat,

> [Siyon] clove the ranks of the rebels and struck so hard that he transfixed two men as one with the blow of his spear, through the strength of God. Thereupon the rebels scattered and took to flight, being unable to hold their ground in his presence.

Amda Siyon reinforced control over his kingdom's Christian areas. He then expanded into the neighboring regions of Shewa, Gojam, and Damot. Victorious there, he gradually absorbed the Muslim states of Ifat and Hedya to the east and southeast. These successes gave him effective control of the central highlands and also the Indian Ocean trade routes to the Red Sea (see Map 10.2). He governed in a quasi-feudal fashion. Theoretically the owner of all land, he assigned *gults*, or fiefs, to his ablest warriors. In return for nearly complete authority in their regions, these warrior-nobles conscripted soldiers for the king's army, required agricultural services from the farmers working on their land, and collected taxes in kind.

Ethiopian rulers received imperial coronation at Aksum, but their kingdom had no permanent capital. Rather, the ruler and court were peripatetic. They constantly traveled around the country to crush revolts, to check the warrior-nobles' management of the gults, and to impress ordinary people with royal dignity.

Territorial expansion had important economic and religious consequences. Amda Siyon concluded trade agreements with Muslims by which they were allowed to trade with his country in return for Muslim recognition of his authority and their promise to accept his administration and pay taxes. Economic growth followed. As a result of these agreements, the flow of Ethiopian gold, ivory, and slaves to Red Sea ports for export to the Islamic heartlands and to South Asia accelerated. Profits from commercial exchange improved people's lives, or at least the lives of the upper classes.

Colorful biblical scenes adorn the interior of the Urai Kidane Miharet Church, one of the many monasteries established by Amda Siyon. (De Agostini Picture Library/akg-images)

Monk-missionaries from traditional Christian areas flooded newly conquered regions, stressing that Ethiopia was a new Zion, or a second Israel — a Judeo-Christian nation defined by religion. Ethiopian Christianity focused on the divinity of the Old Testament Yahweh, rather than on the humanity of the New Testament Jesus. Jewish dietary restrictions, such as the avoidance of pork and shellfish, shaped behavior, and the holy Ark of the Covenant had a prominent place in the liturgy. But the monks also taught New Testament values, especially the importance of charity and spiritual reform. Following the Byzantine pattern, the Ethiopian priest-king claimed the right to summon church councils and to issue doctrinal degrees. Christianity's stress on monogamous marriage, however, proved hard to enforce. As in other parts of Africa (and in Islamic lands, China, and South Asia), polygyny remained common, at least among the upper classes.

Sources: G. W. B. Huntingford, ed., *The Glorious Victories of Amda Seyon* (Oxford: Oxford University Press, 1965), pp. 89–90; H. G. Marcus, *A History of Ethiopia*, updated ed. (Berkeley: University of California Press, 2002); J. Iliffe, *Africans: The History of a Continent*, 2d ed. (New York: Cambridge University Press, 2007).

QUESTIONS FOR ANALYSIS

1. What features mark Ethiopian culture as unique and distinctive among early African societies?
2. Referring to Solomonic Ethiopia, assess the role of legend in history.

ONLINE DOCUMENT PROJECT

What role did religion play in the formation of Ethiopian identity? Explore early Ethiopian chronicles, and then complete a quiz and writing assignment based on the evidence and details from this chapter. *See inside the front cover to learn more.*

(noncanonical) Christian texts, and the writings of the early Christian Church fathers to produce the *Kebra Nagast* (The Glory of Kings). This history served the authors' goals: it became an Ethiopian national epic, glorifying a line of rulers descended from the Hebrew king Solomon (see page 52), arousing patriotic feelings, and linking Ethiopia's identity to the Judeo-Christian tradition. The book mostly deals with the origins of Emperor Menilek I of Ethiopia in the tenth century B.C.E.

The *Kebra Nagast* asserts that Queen Makeda of Ethiopia (called Sheba in the Jewish tradition) had little governmental experience when she came to the throne. So she sought the advice and wise counsel of King Solomon (r. 965–925 B.C.E.) in Jerusalem. During this visit, Solomon tricked Makeda into allowing him into her bed. Their son, Menilek, was born some months later. When Menilek reached maturity, he visited Solomon in Jerusalem. There Solomon anointed him crown prince of Ethiopia and sent a retinue of young Jewish nobles to accompany him home as courtiers. Unable to face life without the Hebrews' Ark of the Covenant, the courtiers stole the cherished wooden chest, which the Hebrews believed contained the Ten Commandments. God apparently approved the theft, for he lifted the youths, pursued by Solomon's army, across the Red Sea and into Ethiopia. Thus, according to the *Kebra Nagast*, Menilek avenged his mother's shame, and God gave his legal covenant to Ethiopia, Israel's successor.[5] Although written around twenty-three hundred years after the events, the myths and legends contained in the *Kebra Nagast* effectively served the purpose of building nationalistic fervor.

Based on this lineage, from the tenth to the sixteenth centuries, and even in the Ethiopian constitution of 1955, Ethiopia's rulers claimed they belonged to the Solomonic line of succession. In the later thirteenth century the dynasty of the Solomonic kings witnessed a literary and artistic renaissance particularly notable for works of hagiography (biographies of saints), biblical exegesis (critical explanation or interpretation of the Bible), and manuscript illumination. The most striking feature of Ethiopian society from 500 to 1500 was the close relationship between the church and the state. Christianity inspired fierce devotion and equated doctrinal heresy with political rebellion, thus reinforcing central monarchical power.

RICO' TIMOR

MISTICAT·INDONIS·REGINA·FIDEM·SALEMONIS·

REGINA·SABA·

The Queen of Sheba and King Solomon

Sheba, Queen Makeda, figured prominently in European as well as Ethiopian art. Created in about 1180 by a French artist as part of a series of biblical scenes for an abbey in Austria, this image shows Solomon receiving gifts from Sheba's servants. The inscription surrounding the scene reads "Solomon joins himself to the Queen of Sheba and introduces her to his faith." (Erich Lessing/Art Resource, NY)

> PICTURING THE PAST
ANALYZING THE IMAGE: What are King Solomon and Queen Sheba wearing and holding? How are the other figures depicted, and what are they doing?
CONNECTIONS: What does the style of this image suggest about the background of the artist and about the audience for whom the image was intended?

The East African City-States

Like Ethiopia, the East African city-states were shaped by their proximity to the trade routes of the Red Sea and Indian Ocean. In the first century c.e. a merchant seaman from Alexandria in Egypt sailed down the Red Sea and out into the Indian Ocean, where he stopped at seaports along the coasts of East Africa, Arabia, and India. He took careful notes on all he observed, and the result, *Periplus of the Erythraean Sea*, is the earliest surviving literary evidence of the city-states of the East African coast. Although primarily preoccupied with geography and naviga-tion, the *Periplus* includes accounts of the local East African peoples and their

CHAPTER LOCATOR | How did Africa's geography shape its history and contribute to its diverse population? | How did agriculture affect life in the western Sudan and central and southern Africa?

CHAPTER 10
288 AFRICAN SOCIETIES AND KINGDOMS

commercial activities. Since the days of the Roman emperors, the *Periplus* testifies, the East African coast had strong commercial links with India and the Mediterranean.

Greco-Roman ships sailed from Adulis on the Red Sea around the tip of the Gulf of Aden and down the portion of the East African coast that the Greeks called Azania, in modern-day Kenya and Tanzania (see Map 10.2). These ships carried manufactured goods that were exchanged for spices, captive slaves, and animal byproducts such as ivory, rhinoceros horns, and tortoise shells. The ships then sailed to India, where ivory was in great demand.

In the early centuries of the Common Era many merchants and seamen from the Mediterranean settled in East African coastal towns. Succeeding centuries saw the arrival of more traders. The great emigration from Arabia after the death of Muhammad accelerated Muslim penetration of the area. Along the coast, Arabic Muslims established small trading colonies whose local peoples were ruled by kings and practiced various animistic religions. Eventually—whether through Muslim political hegemony or gradual assimilation—the coastal peoples slowly converted to Islam. Indigenous African religions, however, remained strong in the continent's interior.

Migrants from the Arabian peninsula and the Malay Archipelago had a profound influence on the lives of the East African coastal people. Beginning in the late twelfth century fresh waves of Arabs and of Persians from Shiraz poured down the coast, first settling at Mogadishu, then pressing southward to Kilwa. Everywhere they landed, they introduced Islamic culture to the indigenous population. Similarly, from the first to the fifteenth centuries Indonesians crossed the Indian Ocean and settled on the African coast and on the large island of Madagascar. All these immigrants intermarried with Africans, and the resulting society combined Asian, African, and especially Islamic traits. The East African coastal culture was called **Swahili**, after a Bantu language whose vocabulary and poetic forms exhibit a strong Arabic influence.

By the late thirteenth century **Kilwa** had become the most powerful coastal city, exercising political hegemony as far north as Pemba and as far south as Sofala (see Map 10.2). In the fourteenth and fifteenth centuries the coastal cities were great commercial empires, comparable to the Italian city-state of Venice (discussed in Chapter 14). Like Venice, Swahili cities such as Kilwa, Mombasa, and Pemba were situated on offshore islands. The tidal currents that isolated them from the mainland also protected them from landside attack.

Much current knowledge about life in the East African trading societies rests on the account of Ibn Battuta. He described Kilwa as "one of the finest and most substantially built towns; all the buildings are of wood, and the houses are roofed with al-dis [reeds]."[6] On the mainland were fields and orchards of rice, millet, oranges, mangoes, and bananas and pastures and yards for cattle, sheep, and poultry. Yields were apparently high; Ibn Battuta noted that the rich enjoyed three enormous meals a day and were very fat.

From among the rich mercantile families that controlled the coastal cities arose rulers who governed both the main city and surrounding territory. Such was the case with the island city of Kilwa and the nearby mainland. These rulers took various titles, including king, sultan, and sheik.

Approaching the East African coastal cities in the late fifteenth century, Portuguese traders were astounded at their enormous wealth and prosperity. This

Swahili
▶ The East African coastal culture, named after a Bantu language whose vocabulary and poetic forms exhibit strong Arabic influences.

Kilwa
▶ The most powerful city on the east coast of Africa by the late thirteenth century.

What characterized trans-Saharan trade, and how did it affect West African society?

How did the East African city-states compare to the kingdoms of the western Sudan?

☑ LearningCurve
Check what you know.

Great Mosque at Kilwa

Built between the thirteenth and fifteenth centuries to serve the Muslim commercial aristocracy of Kilwa on the Indian Ocean, the mosque attests to the wealth and power of the East African city-states. (© Ulrich Doering/Alamy)

wealth rested on the ruler's monopolistic control of all trade in the area. Some coastal cities manufactured goods for export, such as cloth and iron tools. The bulk of the cities' exports, however, consisted of animal products—leopard skins, tortoise shell, ambergris, ivory—and gold. The gold originated in the Mutapa region south of the Zambezi River, where the Bantu mined it. As in tenth-century Ghana, gold was a royal monopoly in the fourteenth-century coastal city-states. Kilwa's prosperity rested on its traffic in gold.

African goods satisfied the global aristocratic demand for luxury goods. In Arabia leopard skins were made into saddles, shells were made into combs, and ambergris was used in the manufacture of perfumes. Because African elephants' tusks were larger and more durable than those of Indian elephants, African ivory was in great demand in India. Wealthy Chinese also valued African ivory for use in sedan chair construction. In exchange for these natural products, the Swahili cities brought in, among many other items, incense, glassware, glass beads, and carpets from Arabia; textiles, spices, rice, and cotton from India; and grains, fine porcelain, silk, and jade from China.

Slaves were another export from the East African coast. Reports of East African slave trading began with the publication of the *Periplus*. The trade accelerated with the establishment of Muslim settlements in the eighth century and continued up through the arrival of the Portuguese in the late fifteenth century, which provided a market for African slaves in the New World (discussed in Chapter 15). In fact, the global slave market fueled the East African coastal slave trade until at least the beginning of the twentieth century.

As in West Africa, traders obtained slaves primarily through raids and kidnapping. The Arabs called the northern Somalia coast *Ras Assir* (Cape of Slaves). From there, Arab traders transported slaves northward up the Red Sea to the markets of Arabia and Persia. Muslim dealers also shipped blacks from the Zanzibar region across the Indian Ocean to markets in India.

As early as the tenth century sources mention persons with "lacquer-black bodies" in the possession of wealthy families in Song China.[7] In 1178 a Chinese official noted in a memorial to the emperor that Arab traders were shipping thousands of blacks from East Africa to the Chinese port of Guangzhou (Canton) by way of the Malay Archipelago.

CHAPTER LOCATOR | How did Africa's geography shape its history and contribute to its diverse population? | How did agriculture affect life in the western Sudan and central and southern Africa?

CHAPTER 10
290 AFRICAN SOCIETIES AND KINGDOMS

Southern Africa and Great Zimbabwe

Southern Africa, bordered on the northwest by the Kalahari Desert and on the northeast by the Zambezi River (see Map 10.2), enjoys a mild and temperate climate. Desert conditions prevail along the Atlantic coast. Eastward toward the Indian Ocean rainfall increases, amounting to fifty to ninety inches a year in some places. Temperate grasslands characterize the interior highlands. Considerable variations in climate occur throughout much of southern Africa from year to year.

Southern Africa has enormous mineral resources: gold, copper, diamonds, platinum, and uranium. Preindustrial peoples mined some of these deposits in open excavations down several feet, but fuller exploitation required modern technology.

Southern Africa has a history that is very different from those of West Africa, the Nile Valley, and the East African coast. Unlike the rest of coastal Africa, southern Africa remained far removed from the outside world until the Portuguese arrived in the late fifteenth century—with one important exception. Bantu-speaking people reached southern Africa in the eighth century. They brought skills in ironworking and mixed farming (settled crop production plus cattle and sheep raising) and immunity to the kinds of diseases that later decimated the Amerindians of South America (discussed in Chapter 16).

The earliest residents of southern Africa were hunters and gatherers. In the first millennium c.e. new farming techniques from the north arrived. Lack of water and timber slowed the spread of iron technology and tools and thus of crop production in southwestern Africa. These advances reached the western coastal region by 1500. By that date, Khoisan-speakers were tending livestock in the arid western regions. To the east, descendants of Bantu-speaking immigrants grew sorghum, raised cattle and sheep, and fought with iron-headed spears.

The nuclear family was the basic social unit among early southern African peoples, who practiced polygyny and traced descent in the male line. Several families formed bands numbering between twenty and eighty people. Such bands were not closed entities; people in neighboring territories identified with bands speaking the same language. As in most preindustrial societies, a division of labor existed whereby men hunted and women cared for children and raised edible plants. People lived in caves or in camps made of portable material, and they moved from one watering or hunting region to another as seasonal or environmental needs required.

In 1871 a German explorer came upon the ruined city of **Great Zimbabwe** southeast of what is now Masvingo in Zimbabwe. The ruins consist of two vast complexes of dry-stone buildings, a fortress, and an elliptically shaped enclosure commonly called the Temple. Stone carvings, gold and copper ornaments, and Asian ceramics once decorated the buildings. The ruins extend over sixty acres and are encircled by a massive wall. The entire city was built from local granite between the eleventh and fifteenth centuries without any outside influence.

These ruins tell a remarkable story. Great Zimbabwe was the political and religious capital of a vast empire. During the first millennium c.e. settled crop cultivation, cattle raising, and work in metal led to a steady buildup in population in the Zambezi-Limpopo region. The area also contained a rich gold-bearing belt. Gold ore lay near the surface; alluvial gold lay in the Zambezi River tributaries. In the tenth century the inhabitants collected the alluvial gold by panning and

Great Zimbabwe

▶ A ruined South African city discovered by a German explorer in 1871; it is considered the most powerful monument south of the Nile Valley and Ethiopian highlands.

What characterized trans-Saharan trade, and how did it affect West African society?

How did the East African city-states compare to the kingdoms of the western Sudan?

☑ LearningCurve
Check what you know.

washing; after the year 1000 the gold was worked in open mines with iron picks. Traders shipped the gold eastward to Sofala (see Map 10.2). Great Zimbabwe's wealth and power rested on this gold trade.

Great Zimbabwe declined in the fifteenth century, perhaps because the area had become agriculturally exhausted and could no longer support the large population. Some people migrated northward and settled in the Mazoe River Valley, a tributary of the Zambezi. This region also contained gold, and the settlers built a new empire in the tradition of Great Zimbabwe. This empire's rulers were called Mwene Mutapa, and their power was also based on the gold trade down the Zambezi River to Indian Ocean ports. It was this gold that the Portuguese sought when they arrived on the East African coast in the late fifteenth century.

> ## QUICK REVIEW

What connections were there among the kingdoms of West Africa, the city-states of East Africa, and the larger Islamic world?

CHAPTER SUMMARY

Africa is a huge continent with many different climatic zones and diverse geography. The African peoples are as varied as the topography. North African peoples were closely connected with the Middle Eastern and European civilizations of the Mediterranean basin. New crops introduced from Asia and the adoption of agriculture profoundly affected early societies across western and northeastern Africa as they transitioned from hunting and gathering in small bands to settled farming communities. Beginning in modern Cameroon and Nigeria, Bantu-speakers spread across central and southern Africa over a two-thousand-year period. Possessing iron tools and weapons, domesticated livestock, and a knowledge of agriculture, these Bantu-speakers assimilated, killed, or drove away the region's previous inhabitants.

Africans in the West African Sahel participated in the trans-Saharan trade, which affected West African society in three important ways: it stimulated gold mining; it increased the demand for West Africa's second-most important commodity, slaves; and it stimulated the development of large urban centers in West Africa.

Similarly, the Swahili peoples along the East African coast organized in city-states traded with Arabia, the Persian Gulf, India, China, and the Malay Archipelago. They depended on Indian Ocean commercial networks, which they used to trade African products for luxury items from Arabia, Southeast Asia, and East Asia. Great Zimbabwe, in southern Africa's interior, traded gold to the coast for the Indian Ocean trade.

The Swahili city-states and the Western Sudan kingdoms were both part of the Islamic world. Arabian merchants brought Islam with them as they settled

CHAPTER LOCATOR | How did Africa's geography shape its history and contribute to its diverse population? | How did agriculture affect life in the western Sudan and central and southern Africa?

CHAPTER 10
292 AFRICAN SOCIETIES AND KINGDOMS

along the East African coast, and Berber traders brought Islam to West Africa. Differing from its neighbors, Ethiopia formed a unique enclave of Christianity in the midst of Islamic societies. The Bantu-speaking peoples of Great Zimbabwe and central and southern Africa generally, were neither Islamic nor Christian.

 CONNECTIONS Africa was an integral part of the vast trans-Saharan and Indian Ocean trading networks that stretched from Europe to China. This trade brought wealth to African kingdoms, empires, and city-states that developed alongside the routes. But the trade in ideas more profoundly connected the growing African states to the wider world, most notably through Islam, which had arrived by the seventh century, and Christianity, which developed a foothold in Ethiopia.

Prior to the late fifteenth century Europeans had little knowledge about African societies. All this would change during the European Age of Discovery. Chapter 16 traces the expansion of Portugal from a small, poor European nation to an overseas empire, as it established trading posts and gained control of the African gold trade. Portuguese expansion led to competition, spurring Spain and then England to strike out for gold of their own in the Americas. The acceleration of this conquest would forever shape the history of Africa and the Americas (discussed in Chapters 11 and 15) and intertwine them via the African slave trade that fueled the labor needs of the colonies in the Americas.

ONLINE DOCUMENT PROJECT
Creating an Ethiopian National Identity

What role did religion play in the formation of Ethiopian identity?

Explore early Ethiopian chronicles, and then complete a quiz and writing assignment based on the evidence and details from this chapter. *See inside the front cover to learn more.*

| What characterized trans-Saharan trade, and how did it affect West African society? | How did the East African city-states compare to the kingdoms of the western Sudan? | ✓ LearningCurve Check what you know. |

CHAPTER 10 STUDY GUIDE

STEP 1 **GET STARTED ONLINE**

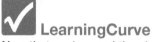 **LearningCurve**

Now that you've read the chapter, make it stick by completing the LearningCurve activity.

STEP 2 **EXPLAIN WHY IT MATTERS**

Put your reading into practice. Identify each term below, and then explain why it matters in world history.

TERM	WHO OR WHAT & WHEN	WHY IT MATTERS
Bantu (p. 272)		
Sudan (p. 273)		
Berbers (p. 275)		
Mogadishu (p. 278)		
stateless societies (p. 279)		
Ghana (p. 280)		
Koumbi Saleh (p. 280)		
Timbuktu (p. 283)		
Aksum (p. 284)		
Swahili (p. 289)		
Kilwa (p. 289)		
Great Zimbabwe (p. 291)		

STEP 3 **MOVE BEYOND THE BASICS**

To demonstrate a more advanced understanding of the role of geographic and climatic diversity in African history, fill in the chart below with descriptions of the society, government, and economy of each of Africa's five main climatic zones. In which regions did settled agriculture lead to population growth and urbanization? Which regions had the strongest economic and cultural connections to societies outside of Africa? Which regions were most isolated from the outside world?

	Society	Government	Economy
Fertile northern and southern coastal regions			
Steppe lands			
Deserts			
Savanna			
Tropical rain forests			

PUT IT ALL TOGETHER

Now, take a step back and try to explain the big picture. Remember to use specific examples from the chapter in your answers.

GEOGRAPHY AND AGRICULTURE

▶ How did geography and climate shape the spread of agriculture in Africa?

▶ What common characteristics were shared by settled agricultural societies across Africa? What role did Bantu-speaking peoples play in linking diverse African societies?

THE TRANS-SAHARAN TRADE

▶ What role did West Africa play in international commerce between 800 and 1500 C.E.?

▶ How did the growth of the Trans-Saharan trade stimulate political and religious change in West Africa?

KINGDOMS AND EMPIRES

▶ How did Islam shape the political development of West Africa?

▶ Compare and contrast Ethiopia and the East African city-states. How would you explain the differences you note?

LOOKING BACK, LOOKING AHEAD

▶ How has the paucity of indigenous written records shaped our understanding of early African history?

▶ How might the advent of the Atlantic slave trade in the sixteenth century and European imperialism in Africa in the nineteenth century have affected Western assumptions about conditions in Africa prior to 1500?

> ## IN YOUR OWN WORDS

Imagine that you must give an oral report to the class answering the following question: **What role did trade play in the development of African kingdoms and empires?** What would be the most important points and why?

11

THE AMERICAS

2500 B.C.E.–1500 C.E.

> ## What similarities and differences were there between the societies of the Americas and other premodern societies around the world?

Chapter 11 examines the development of American societies prior to contact with other world civilizations. Ancient America was home to diverse and sophisticated societies. At times these societies grew into vast empires. In **Mesoamerica** — the region stretching from present-day Nicaragua to California — the dense urban centers of Maya, Teotihuacan, Toltec, and Mexica city-states and empires featured great monuments, temples, and complex urban planning. Roadways and canals extended trade networks that reached from South America to the Great Lakes region of North America. These achievements were rivaled only in the Andes Mountains of South America. The technological, agricultural, and engineering innovations of ancient Andean civilizations allowed people to make their difficult mountain terrain a home rather than a boundary.

Mesoamerica
▶ The term used to designate the area of present-day Mexico and Central America.

Moche Portrait Vessel A Moche artist captured the commanding expression of a ruler in this ceramic vessel. The Moche were one of many cultures in Peru that developed technologies that were simultaneously useful and beautiful, including brightly colored cloth, hanging bridges made of fiber, and intricately fit stone walls. (Private Collection/Photo © Boltin Picture Library/ The Bridgeman Art Library)

> How did ancient peoples of the Americas adapt to, and adapt, their environment?

> What patterns established by early societies shaped civilization in Mesoamerica and the Andes?

> What were the sources of strength and prosperity, and of problems, for the Incas?

> How did the Maya and Teotihuacan develop prosperous and stable societies in the classical era?

> How did the Aztecs build on the achievements of earlier Mesoamerican cultures and develop new traditions to create their large empire?

> What did the European encounter mean for peoples of the major American empires?

✔ LearningCurve
After reading the chapter, use LearningCurve to retain what you've read.

How did ancient peoples of the Americas adapt to, and adapt, their environment?

Inca Khipu

Khipus like these (left) were used by communities and by Inca imperial officials to store and communicate data. The dyes, weaves, and knots made by their users recorded data much like contemporary binary computer storage, allowing users (like the seated person) to read information about populations, production, and tribute. (khipu: The Granger Collection, NYC — All rights reserved; illustration: from *Historia y Genealogia Real de los Reyes Incas del Peru, de sus hechos, constumbres, trajes y manera de Gobierno*, known as the *Codice Murua* [vellum], 16th century/Private Collection/The Bridgeman Art Library)

Like people everywhere, civilizations of the Americas interpreted the meaning of the world and their place in the cosmos. They organized societies stratified not just by gender, class, and ethnicity but also by professional roles and wealth, and they adapted to and reshaped their physical and natural world. But they did all this on their own, without outside influences and within a distinct environment.

If the differences between civilizations in the Americas and other world regions are remarkable, the similarities are even more so. By studying the peoples of the Americas before their encounters with other world societies, we gain a clearer view of universal aspects of the human experience.

Trade and Technology

The domestication of crops and animals created an abundance of food and live-stock, which allowed people to take on new social roles and to develop specialized occupations. As cities emerged, they became hubs of a universal human activity:

CHAPTER LOCATOR | **How did ancient peoples of the Americas adapt to, and adapt, their environment?** | What patterns shaped civilization in Mesoamerica and the Andes?

298 CHAPTER 11 THE AMERICAS

ca. 40,000–13,000 B.C.E. Initial human migration to the Americas	**ca. 300–650 C.E.** Peak of Teotihuacan's influence
ca. 5000 B.C.E. Intensification of agriculture	**ca. 600–900 C.E.** Peak of Maya culture
ca. 2000 B.C.E. Earliest mound building in North America	**ca. 1050–1250 C.E.** Construction of mounds at Cahokia
ca. 1500–300 B.C.E. Olmec culture	**ca. 1325 C.E.** Construction of Aztec city of Tenochtitlan begins
ca. 1200 B.C.E. Emergence of Chavín culture in the Andes	**ca. 1428–1521 C.E.** Aztec Empire dominates Mesoamerica
ca. 100–800 C.E. Moche culture	**ca. 1438–1532 C.E.** Inca Empire dominates the Andes

trade. These cities were home to priests who interpreted the nature of our world, as well as a nobility from which kings emerged.

The differences in the development and application of three different kinds of technologies—the wheel, writing and communications systems, and calendars—capture this essential nature of human adaptability.

Before their encounters with other world peoples that began in 1492, societies in Mesoamerica and the Andes did not use wheels. In Mesoamerica there were no large animals like horses or oxen to domesticate as beasts of burden, so there was no way to power wagons or chariots. In the Andes, domesticated llamas and alpacas served as pack animals and were a source of wool and meat. But in the most densely settled, cultivated, and developed areas, the terrain was too difficult for wheeled transportation. Instead Andean peoples developed extensive networks of roads that navigated steep changes in altitude, supported by elaborate suspension bridges made from woven vegetable fibers.

Peoples of the Americas also did not develop an alphabet or character-based writing systems, but this did not mean they did not communicate or record information. Peoples of the Americas spoke thousands of languages. Mesoamericans, beginning with the Olmecs (1500–400 B.C.E.), used pictographic glyphs similar to those of ancient Egyptian writing to record and communicate information. Later civilizations continued to adapt these systems. The Aztecs produced hieroglyphic books written on paper or deerskin.

The Andean innovation for recording information was particularly remarkable. The **khipu** (KEY-pooh) was an assemblage of colored and knotted strings. The differences in color, arrangement, and type of knot, as well as the knots' order and placement, served as a binary system akin to a contemporary computer database. Khipus were used to record demographic, economic, and political information that allowed imperial rulers and local leaders to understand and manage complex data.

Mesoamerican peoples used a sophisticated combination of calendars. These were based on a Calendar Round that combined a 365-day solar calendar with a

khipu

▶ An intricate system of knotted and colored strings used by early Andean cultures to store information such as census and tax records.

What were the sources of strength and prosperity, and of problems, for the Incas?

How did the Maya and Teotihuacan develop prosperous societies in the classical era?

How did the Aztecs build on earlier Mesoamerican cultures and develop new traditions?

What did the European encounter mean for peoples of the major American empires?

✓ LearningCurve
Check what you know.

260-day calendar based on the numbers thirteen and twenty, which were sacred to peoples of Mesoamerica. Annual cycles are completed when twenty 13-day bundles converge with thirteen 20-day bundles. Together with the solar calendar, these formed a fifty-two-year cycle whose precision was unsurpassed in the pre-modern world.

Settlement and Environment

The ancient settlers of the Americas migrated from Asia, though their timing and their route are debated. One possibility is that the first settlers migrated across the Bering Strait from what is now Russia to Alaska and gradually migrated southward sometime between 15,000 and 13,000 B.C.E. But archaeological excavations have identified much earlier settlements, perhaps dating to over 40,000 years ago, along the Andes in South America than they have for Mesoamerica or North America. These findings suggest that the original settlers in the Americas arrived instead (or also) as fishermen circulating the Pacific Ocean.

Like early settlers elsewhere in the world, populations of the Americas could be divided into three categories: nomadic peoples, semi-sedentary farming communities, and dense agricultural communities capable of sustaining cities. Urban settlement and empire formation centered around two major regions. The first area was Lake Titicaca, located at the present-day border between Peru and Bolivia. The second area was in the Valley of Mexico on the central plateau of Mesoamerica, where empires emerged from the cities around Lake Texcoco. Access to these large freshwater lakes allowed agriculture to expand through irrigation, which in turn supported large urban populations.

The earliest farming settlements emerged around 5000 B.C.E. These farming communities began the long process of domesticating and modifying plants, including maize (corn) and potatoes. The origins of maize in Mesoamerica are unclear, though it became a centerpiece of the Mesoamerican diet and spread across North and South America. Eaten together with beans, maize provided Mesoamerican peoples with a diet sufficient in protein despite the scarcity of meat. Mesoamericans processed kernels through nixtamalization, boiling the maize in a solution of water and mineral lime. The process broke down compounds in the kernels, increasing their nutritional value, while enriching the resulting *masa*, or paste, with dietary minerals including calcium, potassium, and iron.

This masa could be rolled flat on a stone called a *metate* and baked into tortillas. Tortillas played roles similar to bread in wheat-producing cultures: they could be stored, they were light and easy to transport, and they were used as the basic building block of meals. Aztec armies of the fifteenth century could travel long distances because they carried tortillas for sustenance.

Andean peoples cultivated another staple of the Americas, the potato. Potatoes first grew wild, but selective breeding produced many different varieties. For Andean peoples, potatoes became an integral part of a complex system of cultivation at varying altitudes. Communities created a system of "vertical archipelagos" through which they took advantage of the changes of climate along the steep escarpments of the Andes. Different crops could be cultivated at different altitudes, allowing communities to engage in intense and varied farming in what would otherwise have been inhospitable territory.

nixtamalization

▶ Boiling maize in a solution of water and mineral lime to break down compounds in the kernels, increasing their nutritional value.

CHAPTER LOCATOR | How did ancient peoples of the Americas adapt to, and adapt, their environment? | What patterns shaped civilization in Mesoamerica and the Andes?

300 CHAPTER 11 THE AMERICAS

- Highest Elevations: grazing of llamas and alpacas
- Higher Elevations: cultivation of potatoes
- Middle Elevations: terrace cultivation of corn
- Lowlands: cultivation of quinoa, beans, peppers, coca, and cotton
- Coastal Areas: Harvesting of fish and mussels

Communities raised multiple crops and engaged in year-round farming by working at different altitudes located within a day's journey from home. Some of these zones of cultivation were so distant—sometimes over a week's journey—that they were tended by temporary or permanent colonies, called *mitmaq*, of the main settlement.

At higher elevations, members of these communities cultivated potatoes. Arid conditions across much of the altiplano, or high-plains plateau, meant that crops of potatoes could sometimes be planted only every few years. But the climate—dry with daily extremes of heat and cold—could be used to freeze-dry potatoes that could be stored indefinitely. Above the potato-growing zone, shepherds tended animals such as llamas and alpacas.

At middle altitudes, communities used terraces edged by stone walls to extend cultivation along steep mountainsides to grow corn. In the lowlands, they cultivated the high-protein grain quinoa, as well as beans, peppers, and coca. In the lowlands communities also grew cotton, and in coastal areas they harvested fish and mussels. Fishermen built inflatable rafts made of sealskin.

QUICK REVIEW <

What were the most striking similarities between the early societies of the Americas and those of Eurasia?

| What were the sources of strength and prosperity, and of problems, for the Incas? | How did the Maya and Teotihuacan develop prosperous societies in the classical era? | How did the Aztecs build on earlier Mesoamerican cultures and develop new traditions? | What did the European encounter mean for peoples of the major American empires? | LearningCurve Check what you know. |

301

What patterns established by early societies shaped civilization in Mesoamerica and the Andes?

Gulf of Mexico

YUCATÁN PENINSULA

Olmecs

Tres Zapotes
Laguna de los Cerros
San Lorenzo
La Venta
El Manatí

PACIFIC OCEAN

0   100   200 miles
0   100   200 kilometers

■ Olmec site

MAP 11.1 ■ The Olmecs, ca. 1500–300 B.C.E.

Olmec civilization flourished in the coastal lowlands of southern Mexico along the Caribbean coast. Olmec patterns of settlement, culture, religion, organization, and trade are known almost solely through excavation of archaeological sites.

Between 1500 and 1200 B.C.E. emerging civilizations in Mesoamerica and the Andes established lasting patterns of production, culture, and social organization that would long influence societies of the Americas. In Mesoamerica, Olmec civilization laid the foundation for future empires. The imprint of Olmec civilization spread across long networks of trade that would one day extend from Central America to the Mississippi Valley and the Great Lakes of North America. In the Andes, Chavín and Moche civilizations formed the early part of a long cycle of centralization and decentralization. This political and economic centralization helped spread technology, culture, and religion.

Olmec Agriculture, Technology, and Religion

Olmecs

▶ The oldest of the early advanced Mesoamerican civilizations.

The Olmecs were an early civilization that shaped the religion, trade practices, and technology of later civilizations in Mesoamerica. They flourished in the coastal lowlands of Mexico from 1500 to 300 B.C.E. The Olmecs formed the first cities of Mesoamerica, and these cities served as centers of agriculture, trade, and religion (Map 11.1). Through long-distance trade, the Olmecs spread their culture and technology across Mesoamerica, establishing beliefs and practices that became common to the civilizations that followed.

The Olmecs cultivated maize, squash, beans, and other plants and supplemented their diet with wild game and fish. But they lacked many other resources. In particular, they carried stone for many miles for the construction of temples and for carving massive monuments, many in the shape of heads. Across far-flung networks the Olmecs traded rubber, cacao, pottery, clay figures, and jaguar pelts, as well as the services of artisans such as painters and sculptors, in exchange for

CHAPTER LOCATOR | How did ancient peoples of the Americas adapt to, and adapt, their environment? | **What patterns shaped civilization in Mesoamerica and the Andes?**

obsidian, a volcanic glass that could be carved to a razor-sharp edge and used for making knives, tools, spear tips, and other weapons.

These ties between the Olmecs and other communities spread religious practices, creating a shared framework of beliefs among later civilizations. These practices included the construction of large pyramid temples, as well as sacrificial rituals. In addition to the manner of worship, archaeologists can trace the nature of the deities common in Mesoamerica. Olmec deities, like those of their successors, were combinations of gods and humans, included merged animal and human forms, and had both male and female identities.

The Olmecs also used a Long Count solar calendar—a calendar based on a 365-day year. Archaeologists presume that the existence of the Long Count calendar meant that the Calendar Round combining the 260-day and 365-day years already existed as well. All the later Mesoamerican civilizations used at least one of these calendars, and most used both of them.

Hohokam, Hopewell, and Mississippian Societies

Mesoamerican trading networks extended into southwestern North America, where by 300 B.C.E. the Hohokam people and other groups were using irrigation canals, dams, and terraces to enhance their farming of arid lands (Map 11.2). Like the Olmecs and other Mesoamerican peoples, the Hohokam built ceremonial platforms and played games with rubber balls that were traded over a long distance in return for turquoise and other precious stones. Along with trade goods came religious ideas, including the belief in local divinities who created, preserved, and destroyed. Desert peoples planted crops such as agave, as well as cotton and maize that came from Mexico. Other groups, including the Anasazi (ah-nah-SAH-zee), the Yuma, and later the Pueblo and Hopi also built settlements in this area using large sandstone blocks and masonry to construct thick-walled houses that offered protection from the heat. Eventually drought, deforestation, and soil erosion led to decline in both the Hohokam and Anasazi cultures.

To the east, the Mississippian culture also engaged in monumental mound building beginning around 2000 B.C.E. One of the most important mound-building cultures was the Hopewell (200 B.C.E.–600 C.E.), named for a town in Ohio near the site of the most extensive mounds. Some mounds were burial chambers. Other mounds formed animal or geometric figures. Hopewell earthworks also included canals that enabled trading networks to expand, bringing products from the Caribbean far into the interior. Those trading networks also carried maize, allowing more intensive agriculture to spread throughout the eastern woodlands of North America.

At Cahokia (kuh-HOE-kee-uh), near the confluence of the Mississippi and Missouri Rivers in Illinois, archaeologists have uncovered the largest mound of all, part of a ceremonial center and city that housed perhaps thirty-eight thousand people. Work on this complex of mounds, plazas, and houses began about 1050 C.E. and was completed about 1250 C.E. The largest mound rose in four stages to a height of one hundred feet and was nearly one thousand feet long. On its top stood a large building, used perhaps as a temple.

Cahokia engaged in long-distance trade reaching far across North America and became a highly stratified society. Mississippian mound builders relied on

What were the sources of strength and prosperity, and of problems, for the Incas?

How did the Maya and Teotihuacan develop prosperous societies in the classical era?

How did the Aztecs build on earlier Mesoamerican cultures and develop new traditions?

What did the European encounter mean for peoples of the major American empires?

☑ LearningCurve
Check what you know.

303

MAP 11.2 ■ Major North American Agricultural Societies, ca. 600–1500 C.E.

Many North American groups used agriculture to increase the available food supply and allow greater population density and the development of urban centers. This map shows three of these cultures: the Mississippian, Anasazi, and Hohokam.

Approximate extent of mound-building cultures

Approximate extent of the Mississippian culture

Approximate extent of the Anasazi culture

Approximate extent of the Hohokam culture

agriculture to support their complex cultures, and by the time Cahokia was built, maize agriculture had spread to the Atlantic coast. Particularly along riverbanks and the coastline, fields of maize, beans, and squash surrounded large, permanent villages containing many houses, all encompassed by walls made of earth and timber.

Kinship and Ancestors in the Andes

As in Mesoamerica, in the Andes social organization and religion shaped ideas of spiritual kinship as well as patterns of production and trade. The *ayllu* (EYE-you), or clan, served as the fundamental social unit of Andean society. Kinship was based on a shared ancestor, or *huaca*, who could be a once-living person whose remains were mummified and preserved, but could also be an animal spirit or a combination of the two. Members of an ayllu considered their huaca as more than a spirit: it was an entity that owned lands the ally's farmers tended, and the huaca served as the center of community obligations such as the pooling of labor.

Ancestor worship provided the foundations of Andean religion and spirituality, served as the basis of authority, and guided food production. All members

CHAPTER LOCATOR | How did ancient peoples of the Americas adapt to, and adapt, their environment? | What patterns shaped civilization in Mesoamerica and the Andes?

304 CHAPTER 11 THE AMERICAS

of the ayllu owed allegiance to *kuracas*, or clan leaders, who typically traced the most direct lineage to the ancestor, or huaca. This lineage made them both temporal and spiritual leaders of their ayllu. An Andean family's identity came from membership in an ayllu's ancestral kinship, and its subsistence came from participation in the broader community's shared farming across vertical climate zones. People often labored collectively and reciprocally.

Andean history unfolded in a cycle of centralization and decentralization. There were three great periods of centralization, which archaeologists call the Early, Middle, and Late Horizon. The Late Horizon, which included the Inca Empire, was the briefest, cut short by the Spanish conquest (see page 323). The first period, the Early Horizon (ca. 1200–200 B.C.E.), centered on the people of Chavín, upland from present-day Lima. The Chavín spread their religion along with technologies for the weaving and dyeing of wool and cotton. Weaving became the most widespread means of recording and representing information in the Andes.

After the end of the Early Horizon, regional states emerged, including Moche (MOH-cheh) civilization, which flourished along a 250-mile stretch of Peru's northern coast between 100 and 800 C.E. The Moche people developed complex irrigation systems, with which they raised food crops and cotton. Each Moche valley contained a large ceremonial center with palaces and pyramids surrounded by settlements of up to ten thousand people. Moche artifacts reveal a remarkable skill in metalwork and pottery.

Politically, the Moche were organized into a series of small city-states rather than one unified state, and warfare was common among them. Beginning about 500 the Moche suffered several severe El Niños, changes in ocean current patterns in the Pacific that bring searing drought and flooding. They were not able to respond effectively to the devastation, and their urban population declined.

Pan-Andean cultures re-emerged during the Middle Horizon (500–1000 C.E.), centered to the south in Tiwanaku, near Lake Titicaca, and to the north at Wari, near present-day southern Peru. The city-state of Wari's dominion stretched from the altiplano north of Lake Titicaca to the Pacific coast, drawing on Moche cultural influences. Its reach between mountain and coastal regions led to extensive exchanges of goods and beliefs between ecologically different farming zones. The city-state of Tiwanaku extended its influence in the other direction, south of the lake.

Storms and climate shifts were central to Andean people's worldview because changes in climate, particularly abrupt changes brought by El Niño, could devastate whole civilizations. El Niño disrupted Moche culture and contributed to the decline of Wari and Tiwanaku. As the Middle Horizon ended, the cities of Tiwanaku and Wari endured on a smaller scale, but between 1000 and 1200 C.E. they lost their regional influence. The eras between the Early, Middle, and Late Horizon, known as Intermediate Periods, were times of decentralization in which local cultures and practices re-emerged. It was out of these local developments that new centralizing empires would over time emerge.

Moche

▶ A Native American culture that thrived along Peru's northern coast between 100 and 800 C.E. The culture existed as a series of city-states and was distinguished by an extraordinarily rich and diverse pottery industry.

QUICK REVIEW <

What role did trade play in cultural diffusion in the Americas?

What were the sources of strength and prosperity, and of problems, for the Incas?

How did the Maya and Teotihuacan develop prosperous societies in the classical era?

How did the Aztecs build on earlier Mesoamerican cultures and develop new traditions?

What did the European encounter mean for peoples of the major American empires?

☑ LearningCurve
Check what you know.

What were the sources of strength and prosperity, and of problems, for the Incas?

The Inca ruins of Machu Picchu rise spectacularly above the steep valley of the Urubamba River. The site was built around 1450 as a royal estate and abandoned after the Spanish conquest. (Tony Camacho/Photo Researchers, Inc.)

Inca

▶ The name of the dynasty of rulers who built a large empire across the Andes that was at its peak around 1500.

I nca was the name of a governing family of the largest and last Andean empire. The empire, whose people we will call the Incas, was called Tawantinsuyu (TAH-want-een-soo-you), meaning from "from the four parts, one," expressing the idea of a unified people stretching in all directions.

The Inca Model of Empire

In the Late Intermediate Period (1200–1470), the Pan-Andean influences of Wari and Tiwanaku waned. City-states around Lake Titicaca competed and fought with each other. The strongest ones again emerged. To the north, the Chimu claimed the legacy of the Moche and Wari. To the south, the city of Cuzco became the hub of a growing kingdom under the hereditary control of the Inca (Map 11.3). According to their religious, the Inca rulers invented civilization. In reality, they inherited it from the civilizations of the Titicaca basin and the Chimu in the northern coast.

From the 1420s until 1438 Viracocha Inca emerged as the first Inca leader to attempt permanent conquest. Unlike the *sinchis* (SEEN-cheese), or kings, of earlier and rival city-states, Viracocha Inca fashioned himself an emperor, and in adopting the name Viracocha, connected himself to the god of creation. In 1438 rivals invaded Viracocha Inca's territories and he fled. His son, Pachacuti, remained in Cuzco and fended off the invaders. He crowned himself emperor and embarked on a campaign of conquest. Pachacuti Inca (r. 1438–1471) conquered the Chimu near the end of his reign.

CHAPTER LOCATOR | How did ancient peoples of the Americas adapt to, and adapt, their environment? | What patterns shaped civilization in Mesoamerica and the Andes?

MAP 11.3 ■ The Inca Empire, 1532

Andean peoples turned their stark mountain landscape to their advantage by settling and farming in vertical archipelagos. Settlements were located at temperate altitudes, while farming and herding took place at higher and lower altitudes.

ANALYZING THE MAP: In what ways did Andean peoples turn their mountain landscape from an obstacle into a resource? **CONNECTIONS:** What types of geographic features did peoples of the Americas other than the Incas or peoples in other regions of the world adapt to their advantage? How did adaptation to their geography shape other societies?

Inca Empire, 1532
— Inca road

After conquering the Chimu, Pachacuti instituted practices that quickly expanded the empire across the Andes. He combined Andean ancestor worship with the Chimu system of a split inheritance, a combination that drove swift territorial expansion and transformed Tawantinsuyu into one of the largest empires in the world within less than fifty years. Under the system of ancestor worship, the Incas believed the dead emperor's spirit was still present, and they venerated him through his mummy. Split inheritance meant that the dead emperor retained all the lands he had conquered, commanded the loyalty of all his subjects, and continued to receive tribute. A *panaqa* (pan-AH-kah), a trust formed by his closest relatives, managed both the cult of his mummy and his temporal affairs.

When the ruler died, his corpse was preserved as a mummy in elaborate clothing and housed in a sacred and magnificent chamber. The panaqa of descendants of each dead ruler managed his lands and used his income to care for his mummy, maintain his cult, and support themselves, all at great expense. One of his sons was named the new Inca emperor. He received the title, but not the lands and tribute—nor, for that matter, the direct allegiance of the nobility, bound as it was to the deceased ruler. The new emperor built his own power and wealth by conquering new lands.

Inca Imperial Expansion

The combination of ancestor worship and split inheritance provided the logic and impulse for expanding Inca power. The desire for conquest provided incentives for courageous (or ambitious) nobles: those who succeeded in battle and gained new territories for the state could expect to be richly rewarded. Even common soldiers who distinguished themselves in battle could be rewarded with booty and raised to noble status. Under Pachacuti Inca and his successors, Inca domination was extended by warfare to the frontier of present-day Ecuador and Colombia in the north and to the Maule River in present-day Chile in the south, an area of about 350,000 square miles. Eighty provinces, scores of ethnic groups, and 16 million people came under Inca control.

The Incas pursued the integration of regions they conquered by imposing their language and their gods. Magnificent temples housed images of these gods. Priests led prayers and elaborate rituals, and during occasions such as terrible natural disasters or great military victories they sacrificed humans. The Incas

| **What were the sources of strength and prosperity, and of problems, for the Incas?** | How did the Maya and Teotihuacan develop prosperous societies in the classical era? | How did the Aztecs build on earlier Mesoamerican cultures and develop new traditions? | What did the European encounter mean for peoples of the major American empires? | ✓ LearningCurve Check what you know. |

Quechua

▶ First deemed the official language of the Incas under Pachacuti, it is still spoken by most Peruvians today.

forced conquered peoples to adopt Quechua (KEH-chuh-wuh), the official language of the empire, which extinguished many regional languages.

The pressure for growth strained the Inca Empire. Open lands became scarce, so the Incas tried to penetrate the tropical Amazon forest east of the Andes—an effort that led to repeated military disasters. Another source of stress came from revolts among subject peoples in conquered territories. Even the system of roads and message-carrying runners couldn't keep up with the administrative needs of the empire. The round trip from the capital at Cuzco to Quito in Ecuador, for example, took from ten to twelve days, so an emperor might have to base urgent decisions on incomplete or out-of-date information. The empire was overextended.

Imperial Needs and Obligations

At its height, the Inca Empire extended over 2,600 miles. The challenges of sustaining an empire with that reach, not to mention one built so fast, required extraordinary resourcefulness. The Inca Empire met these demands by adapting aspects of local culture to meet imperial needs. For instance, the empire demanded that the ayllus, the local communities with shared ancestors, include imperial tribute in the rotation of labor and the distribution of harvested foods.

As each new Inca emperor conquered new lands and built his domain, he mobilized people and resources by drawing on local systems of labor and organization. Much as ayllus had developed satellite communities called mitmaq, populated by settlers from the ayllu in order to take advantage of remote farming areas, the emperor relocated families or even whole villages over long distances to consolidate territorial control or quell unrest. What had been a community practice became a tool of imperial expansion. The emperor also consolidated the empire by regulating marriage, using maternal lines to build kinship among conquered peoples. Inca rulers and nobles married the daughters of elite families among the peoples they conquered.

The reciprocal labor carried out within ayllus expanded into a labor tax called the *mit'a* (MEE-tuh), which rotated among households in an ayllu throughout the year. Tribute paid in labor provided the means for building the infrastructure of empire. Rotations of laborers carried out impressive engineering feats, allowing the vast empire to extend over the most difficult and inhospitable terrain. An excellent system of roads facilitated the transportation of armies and the rapid communication of royal orders by runners. On these roads Inca officials, tax collectors, and accountants traveled throughout the empire, using elaborate khipus to record financial and labor obligations, the output of fields, population levels, land transfers, and other numerical records. Like Persian and Roman roads, these great feats of Inca engineering linked an empire. The government also made an ayllu responsible for maintaining state-owned granaries, which distributed grain in times of shortage and famine and supplied assistance in natural disasters.

> ## QUICK REVIEW

How did the Incas use existing local practices as tools of imperial expansion?

CHAPTER LOCATOR | How did ancient peoples of the Americas adapt to, and adapt, their environment? | What patterns shaped civilization in Mesoamerica and the Andes?

CHAPTER 11
308 THE AMERICAS

Lady Xoc, principal wife of King Shield-Jaguar, who holds a torch over her, pulls a thorn-lined rope through her tongue to sanctify with her blood the birth of a younger wife's child — reflecting the importance of blood sacrifice in Maya culture. The elaborate headdresses and clothes of the couple show their royal status. (© The Trustees of the British Museum/Art Resource, NY)

How did the Maya and Teotihuacan develop prosperous and stable societies in the classical era?

I In Mesoamerica the classical period (300 C.E. to 900 C.E.) saw major advances in religion, art, architecture, and farming, akin to those of the classical civilizations of the Mediterranean (see Chapters 5 and 6). It saw the rise of many city-states, and although the **Maya** city-states, which peaked between 600 C.E. and 900 C.E., were the longest lasting, others were significant as well. The city of **Teotihuacan** in the Valley of Mexico emerged as a major center of trade (300–650 C.E.). It was followed by the postclassical Toltec Empire (900–1200 C.E.), which adapted the cultural, ritual, and aesthetic practices that influenced later empires like the Aztecs.

Maya

▶ A highly developed Mesoamerican culture centered in the Yucatán peninsula of Mexico. The Maya created the most intricate writing system in the Western Hemisphere.

Teotihuacan

▶ The monumental city-state that dominated trade in classical era Mesoamerica.

Maya Agriculture and Trade

The Maya inhabited the highlands of Guatemala and the Yucatán peninsula in present-day Mexico and Belize. Their physical setting shaped two features of Maya society. First, the abundance of high-quality limestone allowed them to

What were the sources of strength and prosperity, and of problems, for the Incas?

How did the Maya and Teotihuacan develop prosperous societies in the classical era?

How did the Aztecs build on earlier Mesoamerican cultures and develop new traditions?

What did the European encounter mean for peoples of the major American empires?

☑ LearningCurve
Check what you know.

MAP 11.4 ■ The Maya World, 300–900 C.E.

The Maya built dozens of cities linked together in trading networks of roads and rivers. Only the largest of them are shown here.

build monumental architecture. Second, limestone formations created deep natural wells called *cenotes* (say-NOH-tehs), which became critical sources of water in an often-arid environment. The staple crop of the Maya was maize, often raised in small remote plots called *milpas* in combination with other foodstuffs, including beans, squash, chili peppers, some root crops, and fruit trees.

The entire Maya region may have had as many as 14 million inhabitants. Sites like Uxmal, Uaxactún, Copán, Piedras Negras, Tikal, Palenque, and Chichén Itzá (Map 11.4) emerged as independent city-states, each ruled by a hereditary king. These cities produced polychrome pottery and featured altars, engraved pillars, masonry temples, palaces for nobles, pyramids where nobles were buried, and courts for ball games. The largest site, Tikal, may have had forty thousand people and served as a religious and ceremonial center. A hereditary nobility owned land, waged war, traded, exercised political power, and directed religious rituals. Artisans and scribes made up the social level below. Other residents were farmers, laborers, and slaves, the latter including prisoners of war.

At Maya markets, jade, obsidian, beads of red spiny oyster shell, lengths of cloth, and cacao beans served as media of exchange. The extensive trade among Maya communities, plus a common language, promoted unity among the peoples of the region. Merchants traded beyond Maya regions, particularly with the Zapotecs of Monte Albán, in the Valley of Oaxaca, and with the Teotihuacanos of the central valley of Mexico. Since this long-distance trade played an important part in international relations, the merchants conducting it were high nobles or even members of the royal family.

Maya Science and Religion

The Maya developed the most complex writing system in the Americas, a script with nearly a thousand glyphs. They recorded important events and observations in books made of bark paper and deerskin, on pottery, on stone pillars called steles, and on temples and other buildings. Archaeologists and anthropologists have demonstrated that the inscriptions are historical documents that record major events in the lives of Maya kings and nobles.

Surviving Maya books offer a window into religious rituals and practices, as well as Maya astronomy. From observation of the earth's movements around the sun, the Maya used a calendar of eighteen 20-day months and one 5-day month, for a total of 365 days, along with the 260-day calendar based on 20 weeks of 13 days. When these calendars coincided every fifty-two years, the Maya celebrated with feasting, ball-game competitions, and religious observance. These and other observances included blood sacrifice by kings to honor the gods.

The Maya devised a form of mathematics based on the vigesimal (20) rather than the decimal (10) system. More unusual was their use of the number zero, which allows for more complex calculations than are possible in number systems

CHAPTER LOCATOR | How did ancient peoples of the Americas adapt to, and adapt, their environment? | What patterns shaped civilization in Mesoamerica and the Andes?

310 CHAPTER 11 THE AMERICAS

1	•	11	≡•
2	• •	12	≡••
3	• • •	13	≡•••
4	• • • •	14	≡••••
5	—	15	≡
6	—•	16	≡•
7	—••	17	≡••
8	—•••	18	≡•••
9	—••••	19	≡••••
10	≡		

without it. The Maya's proficiency with numbers made them masters of abstract knowledge—notably in astronomy and mathematics.

Between the eighth and tenth centuries the Maya abandoned their cultural and ceremonial centers. Archaeologists attribute their decline to a combination of agricultural failures due to drought, land exhaustion, overpopulation, disease, and constant wars fought for economic and political gain. Royalty also suffered from the decline in Maya civilization. When military, economic, and social conditions deteriorated, their subjects saw the kings as the cause and turned against them.

Decline did not mean disappearance. The Maya ceased building monumental architecture around 900 C.E., which likely marked the end of the era of rule by powerful kings who could mobilize the labor required to build it. The Maya persisted in farming communities, a pattern of settlement that helped preserve their culture and language in the face of external pressures. They resisted invasions from warring Aztec armies by dispersing from their towns and villages and residing in their milpas during invasions. When Aztec armies entered the Yucatán, communities dispersed, leaving Aztec armies with nothing to conquer. This tactic continued to serve the Maya under Spanish colonial rule, with many communities avoiding Spanish domination for generations.

Teotihuacan and the Toltecs

The most powerful city in classical Mesoamerica emerged at Teotihuacan, northwest of the lands of the Maya. By 100 C.E. it had a population of 60,000. At its height, between 300 and 600 C.E., its population reached as high as 250,000. The

| What were the sources of strength and prosperity, and of problems, for the Incas? | **How did the Maya and Teotihuacan develop prosperous societies in the classical era?** | How did the Aztecs build on earlier Mesoamerican cultures and develop new traditions? | What did the European encounter mean for peoples of the major American empires? | ✓ LearningCurve Check what you know. |

311

heart of Teotihuacan was a massive ceremonial center anchored by a colossal Pyramid of the Sun, 700 feet wide and 200 feet tall, and a Pyramid of the Moon. Connecting them was the Avenue of the Dead, 150 feet wide and 2 miles long, along which stood the homes of scores of priests and lords.

The monuments of the ceremonial district of Teotihuacan were matched in grandeur by the city's markets, which extended its influence across Mesoamerica. The city's trade empire lay in its control of a resource vital to Mesoamerican society and religion: obsidian, a glasslike volcanic rock that could be worked into objects with both material and spiritual uses. Obsidian knives were used for daily tasks and for important rituals such as the blood sacrifice practiced by the Maya.

Religion followed trade. Teotihuacan was a religious and cultural center whose influence extended over large distances. One factor in the city's success was its ethnic diversity. Teotihuacan grew through the migration of outsiders along trade networks, and these groups built separate ethnic neighborhoods. Two gods that were particularly important to classical period civilizations were Tlaloc (Chac in Maya), the god of rain, and Quetzalcoatl, the plumed serpent. The worship of these deities became an enduring aspect of Mesoamerican religion that the Toltecs and the Aztecs embraced.

Teotihuacan thrived because it controlled trade of the most valuable goods. This helped it grow, and in turn the trade networks it sustained helped other regions in Mesoamerica develop through intensified contact with other groups

The Pyramid of the Sun at Teotihuacan

Built in several stages beginning in about 100 C.E., the Pyramid of the Sun has sides measuring 700 feet long and 200 feet high. Originally it was covered with lime plaster decorated with brightly colored murals. Smaller pyramids surround it in what was the heart of the bustling city of Teotihuacan. (© age fotostock/SuperStock)

CHAPTER LOCATOR | How did ancient peoples of the Americas adapt to, and adapt, their environment? | What patterns shaped civilization in Mesoamerica and the Andes?

312 CHAPTER 11 THE AMERICAS

and the spread of technologies. Over time, improvements in other regions decreased Teotihuacan's comparative advantage, as its trading partners produced increasingly valuable goods, spurring competition. By 600 its influence had begun to decline, and in 650 the residents of the city seem to have burned its ceremonial center in what may have been a revolt against the city's leadership. The city had ceased to be a major trade center by 900 C.E.[1]

The Toltecs (900–1200 C.E.) filled the void created by Teotihuacan's decline. The Toltecs inaugurated a new era, the postclassical, which ended with the Spanish conquest of the Aztec Empire. The postclassical period saw fewer technological or artistic advances. Instead it was a time of intensified warfare in Mesoamerica and a time of rapid and bold imperial expansion through conquest. After the decline of Teotihuacan, the Toltecs entered the Valley of Mexico and settled in Tula. The Toltecs' legend of their origins held that in 968 C.E. their people were led into the valley by a charismatic leader who fused himself to the plumed serpent god and called himself Topiltzin-Quetzalcoatl. In 987, amid infighting, Topiltzin-Quetzalcoatl and his followers were expelled from Tula. They marched south, where they conquered and settled in a Maya region.

The Toltecs built a military empire and gradually absorbed the culture, practices, and religion of their neighbors in the Valley of Mexico. Their empire waned amid war, drought, and famine over the eleventh and twelfth centuries. After the demise of the Toltec Empire, city-states in the Valley of Mexico competed with each other militarily and to cast themselves as the legitimate descendants and heirs of the Toltecs.

QUICK REVIEW

What were the main sources of Maya wealth and power?
What about Teotihuacan?

| What were the sources of strength and prosperity, and of problems, for the Incas? | **How did the Maya and Teotihuacan develop prosperous societies in the classical era?** | How did the Aztecs build on earlier Mesoamerican cultures and develop new traditions? | What did the European encounter mean for peoples of the major American empires? | LearningCurve Check what you know. |

313

How did the Aztecs build on the achievements of earlier Mesoamerican cultures and develop new traditions to create their large empire?

Huitzilopochtli

This painting of the hummingbird god of war carrying a shield in one hand and a serpent-headed knife in the other was made by Aztec priests in a book written on bark paper about the time of the Spanish conquest. He is shown descending from a step-pyramid, perhaps a reference to the great pyramid in the center of Tenochtitlan, where he was worshipped.
(© Foundation for the Advancement of Mesoamerican Studies, Inc., www.famsi.org)

Nahuatl
▶ The language of both the Toltecs and the Aztecs.

Mexica
▶ The dominant ethnic group of what is now Mexico, who created an empire based on war and religion that reached its height in the mid-1400s; in the nineteenth century the people became known as Aztecs.

According to their oral tradition, between 1300 and 1345 a group of **Nahuatl**-speaking people, the **Mexica**, migrated southward from what is now northern Mexico, settling on the shores and islands of Lake Texcoco in the central valley of Mexico (Map 11.5). They formed a vast and rapidly expanding empire centered around the twin cities of Tenochtitlan (tay-nawch-TEET-lahn) and Tlatelolco, which by 1500 were probably larger than any city in Europe except Istanbul. This was the Aztec Empire, a network of alliances and tributary states with the Mexica at its core. Examining the means by which they formed and expanded their empire, as well as the vulnerabilities of that empire, can help us build a rich understanding of Mesoamerican society.

The Mexica: From Vassals to Masters

In the early fourteenth century, the Mexica, a migrant, seminomadic group, arrived in the Valley of Mexico. They found an environment that, since the collapse of the Toltec Empire in the twelfth century, had divided into small, fragile

CHAPTER LOCATOR | How did ancient peoples of the Americas adapt to, and adapt, their environment? | What patterns shaped civilization in Mesoamerica and the Andes?

314 CHAPTER 11 THE AMERICAS

MAP 11.5 ■ The Aztec (Mexica) Empire in 1519

The Mexica migrated into the central valley of what is now Mexico from the north, conquering other groups and establishing an empire, later called the Aztec Empire. The capital of the Aztec Empire was Tenochtitlan, built on islands in Lake Texcoco.

alliances that battled to claim the legacy of the Toltecs. At the moment of their arrival, control over much of the valley lay in the hands of the Tepanec Alliance. The Mexica negotiated the right to settle on a swampy island on Lake Texcoco in exchange for military service to the Tepanecs.

The Mexica adopted the customs of their new region, organizing clan-based communities called *calpolli*, incorporating the deities of their new neighbors, and serving the Tepanecs. They gradually reclaimed land around their island to form two urban centers, Tenochtitlan and Tlatelolco. They adopted a farming technique used in parts of Lake Texcoco called *chinampa* (chee-NAHM-pah) agriculture. Under this system, farmers built up reeds and mud along the margins of Lake Texcoco to gradually extend farming well into the lake.

At its peak, the chinampa farming system formed vast areas of tidy rectangular plots divided by canals that allowed for canoe transportation of people and crops. When the Spanish entered Tenochtitlan (which they called Mexico City) in November 1519, they were amazed at this city which seemed to rise straight out of the lake.

Over time, the Mexica improved their standing in the Valley of Mexico by asking a powerful neighboring city-state to name a prince considered to be of noble Toltec descent to rule them, forming a dynasty that would become the most powerful in Mesoamerica. The new ruler, or *tlatoani* (tlah-toh-annie), Acamapichtli (ah-camp-itch-lee), brought the Mexica higher social rank and the ability to form alliances.

Tenochtitlan

▶ A large and prosperous Aztec city that was built starting in 1325. The Spanish admired it when they entered in 1519.

| What were the sources of strength and prosperity, and of problems, for the Incas? | How did the Maya and Teotihuacan develop prosperous societies in the classical era? | **How did the Aztecs build on earlier Mesoamerican cultures and develop new traditions?** | What did the European encounter mean for peoples of the major American empires? | ✓ LearningCurve Check what you know. |

Chinampa Farming

This illustration shows farmers in the Aztec Empire building chinampa farming plots by reclaiming land from Lake Texcoco. Farmers created the plots by packing them with vegetation and mud from the lake, supporting their boundaries by planting willow trees. Chinampas allowed for intensive farming in a region that had limited rainfall, and the canals between them permitted easy transportation. (© Gianni Dagli Orti/Corbis)

By the end of Acamapichtli's reign (1372–1391), the Mexica had fully adapted to their new environment and had adopted the highly stratified social organization that would encourage the ambitions of their own warrior class. Under the rule of Acamapichtli's successors Huitzilihuitl (r. 1391–1417) and Chimalpopoca (r. 1417–1427), the Mexica remained subordinate to the Tepanec Alliance. But in 1427 a dispute over the succession of the Tepanec king created an opportunity for the Mexica.

Taking advantage of the fluid political situation, in 1428 the Mexica formed a coalition with other cities in the Valley of Mexico, besieged the Tepanec capital for nearly three months, and then defeated it. A powerful new coalition had emerged: the Triple Alliance, with the Mexica as its most powerful partner. The Aztec Empire was born.[2]

To consolidate the new political order, Tlatoani Itzcoatl, guided by his nephew Tlacaelel, burned his predecessors' books and drafted a new history. The new history placed the warrior cult and its religious pantheon at the center of Mexica history, making the god of war, Huitzilopochtli, the patron deity of the empire. Huitzilopochtli, "Hummingbird of the South," was a god unique to the Mexica who, according to the new official origin stories of the Mexica people, had ordered them to march south until they found an island where he gave them the sign of an eagle eating a serpent, which appeared to them in Tenochtitlan. (See "Individuals in Society: Tlacaelel," page 318.)

CHAPTER LOCATOR | How did ancient peoples of the Americas adapt to, and adapt, their environment? | What patterns shaped civilization in Mesoamerica and the Andes?

CHAPTER 11
316 THE AMERICAS

Under the new imperial order, government offices combined military, religious, and political functions. Eventually, tlatoanis formalized these functions into distinct noble and common classes. The Valley of Mexico had sustained itself through chinampa agriculture, but as the empire grew, crops provided as tribute from distant conquered peoples increasingly fed the valley's rapidly growing population. The Mexica sustained themselves through military conquest, imposing their rule over a vast part of modern Mexico.

Life in the Aztec Empire

Few sharp social distinctions existed among the Aztecs during their early migrations, but by the early sixteenth century Aztec society had changed. A stratified social structure had emerged, and the warrior aristocracy exercised great authority. Men who had distinguished themselves in war occupied the highest military and social positions in the state. Generals, judges, and governors of provinces were appointed by the emperor from among his servants who had earned reputations as war heroes. These great lords, or *tecuhtli* (teh-COOT-lee), dressed luxuriously and lived in palaces.

Beneath the great nobility of military leaders and imperial officials was the class of warriors. Theoretically, every free man could be a warrior, and parents dedicated their male children to war, burying a male child's umbilical cord with arrows and a shield on the day of his birth. In actuality, the sons of nobles were more likely to become warriors because of their fathers' positions and influence in the state. At the age of six, boys entered a school that trained them for war. They were taught to fight, learned to live on little food and sleep, and to accept pain without complaint. At about age eighteen, a warrior fought his first campaign. If he captured a prisoner for ritual sacrifice, he acquired the title *iyac*, or warrior. If in later campaigns he succeeded in killing or capturing four of the enemy, he became a *tequiua*—one who shared in the booty and was thus a member of the nobility. If a young man failed in several campaigns to capture the required four prisoners, he became a *macehualli* (plural *macehualtin*), a commoner.

The macehualtin were the ordinary citizens—the backbone of Aztec society and the vast majority of the population. Members of this class performed agricultural, military, and domestic services and carried heavy public burdens not required of noble warriors. Government officials assigned them to work on the temples, roads, and bridges. Unlike nobles, priests, orphans, and slaves, macehualtin paid taxes. Macehualtin in the capital, however, possessed certain rights: they held their plots of land for life, and they received a small share of the tribute paid by the provinces to the emperor.

Beneath the macehualtin were the *tlalmaitl*, the landless workers or serfs who provided agricultural labor, paid rents in kind, and were bound to the soil—they could not move off the land. In many ways the tlalmaitl resembled the serfs of western Europe, but unlike serfs they performed military service when called on to do so. Slaves were the lowest social class. Most were prisoners captured in war or kidnapped from enemy tribes. Mexica slaves differed fundamentally from European ones, for they could possess goods; save money; buy land, houses, and even slaves for their own service; and purchase their freedom. If a male slave

What were the sources of strength and prosperity, and of problems, for the Incas?

How did the Maya and Teotihuacan develop prosperous societies in the classical era?

How did the Aztecs build on earlier Mesoamerican cultures and develop new traditions?

What did the European encounter mean for peoples of the major American empires?

✓ LearningCurve Check what you know.

317

The hummingbird god Huitzilopochtli was originally a somewhat ordinary god of war and of young men, but in the fifteenth century he was elevated in status among the Mexica. He became increasingly associated with the sun and gradually became the most important Mexica deity. This change appears to have been primarily the work of Tlacaelel, the very long-lived chief adviser to the emperors Itzcóatl (r. 1427–1440), Moctezuma I (r. 1440–1469), and Axayacatl (r. 1469–1481). Tlacaelel first gained influence during wars in the 1420s in which the Mexica defeated the rival Tepanecs, after which he established new systems of dividing military spoils and enemy lands. At the same time, he advised the emperor that new histories were needed in which the destiny of the Mexica people was made clearer. Tlacaelel ordered the destruction of older historical texts, and under his direction the new chronicles connected Mexica fate directly to Huitzilopochtli. Mexica writing was primarily pictographic, drawn and then read by specially trained scribes who used written records as an aid to oral presentation, especially for legal issues, historical chronicles, religious and devotional poetry, and astronomical calculations.

Tlacaelel emphasized human sacrifice as one of the Aztecs' religious duties. (From the *Codex Magliabechiano* [vellum]/Biblioteca Nazionale Centrale, Florence, Italy/ The Bridgeman Art Library)

According to these new texts, the Mexica had been guided to Lake Texcoco by Huitzilopochtli; there they saw an eagle perched on a cactus, which a prophecy foretold would mark the site of their new city. Huitzilopochtli kept the world alive by bringing the sun's warmth, but to do this he required the Mexica, who increasingly saw themselves as the "people of the sun," to provide a steady offering of human blood.

The worship of Huitzilopochtli became linked to cosmic forces as well as daily survival. In Nahua tradition, the universe was understood to exist in a series of five suns, or five cosmic ages. Four ages had already passed, and their suns had been destroyed; the fifth sun, the age in which the Mexica were now living, would also be destroyed unless the Mexica fortified the sun with the energy found in blood. Warfare thus brought new territory under Mexica control and provided sacrificial victims to nourish the sun-god. With these ideas, Tlacaelel created what Miguel León-Portilla, a leading contemporary scholar of Nahua religion and philosophy, has termed a "mystico-militaristic" conception of Aztec destiny.

Human sacrifice was practiced in many cultures of Mesoamerica, including the Olmec and the Maya as well as the Mexica, before the changes introduced by Tlacaelel, but historians believe the number of victims increased dramatically during the last period of Mexica rule. A huge pyramid-shaped temple in the center of Tenochtitlan, dedicated to Huitzilopochtli and the god of rain Tlaloc, was renovated and expanded many times, the last in 1487. To dedicate each expansion, priests sacrificed war captives. Similar ceremonies were held regularly throughout the year on days dedicated to Huitzilopochtli and were attended by many observers, including representatives from neighboring states as well as masses of Mexica. According to many accounts, victims were placed on a stone slab, and their hearts were cut out with an obsidian knife; the officiating priest then held the heart up as an offering to the sun. Sacrifices were also made to other gods at temples elsewhere in Tenochtitlan, and perhaps in other cities controlled by the Mexica.

Estimates of the number of people sacrificed to Huitzilopochtli and other Mexica gods vary enormously and are impossible to verify. Both Mexica and later Spanish accounts clearly exaggerated the numbers, but most historians today assume that between several hundred and several thousand people were killed each year.

Sources: Miguel León-Portilla, *Pre-Columbian Literatures of Mexico* (Norman: University of Oklahoma Press, 1969); Inga Clendinnen, *Aztecs: An Interpretation* (Cambridge: Cambridge University Press, 1991).

QUESTIONS FOR ANALYSIS

1. How did the worship of Huitzilopochtli contribute to Aztec expansion? To hostility toward the Aztecs?
2. Why might Tlacaelel have believed it was important to destroy older texts as he created this new Aztec mythology?

ONLINE DOCUMENT PROJECT

Why did Tlacaelel believe the Aztec Empire needed a new history? Read documents that examine Aztec history and culture, and then complete a quiz and writing assignment based on the evidence and details from this chapter. *See inside the front cover to learn more.*

married a free woman, their offspring were free. Most slaves eventually gained their freedom.

Women of all social classes operated within the domestic sphere. As the little hands of the newborn male were closed around a tiny bow and arrow indicating his warrior destiny, so the infant female's hands were wrapped around miniature weaving instruments and a small broom. Save for the few women vowed to the service of the temple, marriage and the household were a woman's fate, and marriage represented social maturity for both sexes.

The Limits of the Aztec Empire

Mesoamerican empires like that of the Aztecs were not like modern nation-states that consolidate control of the territory within their borders. Instead the Aztec Empire was a syndicate in which the Mexica, their allies, and their subordinates thrived on trade and tribute backed by the threat of force.

When a city succumbed, its captive warriors were marched to Tenochtitlan to be sacrificed. The defeated city was obligated to provide tribute to be distributed within the empire. But conquest stopped short of assimilation. Rulers and nobles remained in place. Subjects were not required to adopt Mexica gods.

The death of a ruler is always a time of uncertainty, and this was especially true in Mesoamerica under the Aztec Empire. For peoples of the Valley of Mexico and beyond, this meant war was sure to arrive. The council of high nobles who served the deceased ruler chose the new tlatoani, who was often the commander of the army. Once the new tlatoani was named, he would embark on a military campaign in order to prove his worthiness.

A success in the tlatoani's inaugural military campaign provided new tribute-paying subjects, produced a long train of sacrificial victims captured in battle, maintained the stability of the empire's alliances, warned off potential foes, and kept conquered areas in subordination. After the successful campaign, the new tlatoani invited the rulers of allied, subject, and enemy city-states alike to his coronation ceremony.

But success was not always possible, as the troubled rule of Tizoc (r. 1481–1486) demonstrated. His wars sometimes resulted in a greater number of casualties among his own forces than of sacrificial victims for his altars. Five years after he was crowned, he was poisoned by his own subjects. His successor, Ahuitzotl (r. 1486–1502), faced the challenge of reinvigorating the empire through renewed displays of strength. To symbolize the restoration of Tenochtitlan's power, he waged wars of conquest that defied precedence in their scale, culminating in two coronation ceremonies, the second of which incorporated sacrificing over eighty thousand captive warriors.

Blood sacrifice was not new to the Aztecs. For centuries Mesoamerican peoples had honored their gods this way. The Aztecs elevated the warrior cult as the central observance. The Mexica believed the earth had been destroyed and re-created four times. The end of creation loomed after their age, the fifth sun. Since this apocalypse might be forestalled through divine intervention, their sacrifice could show that humans were worthy of divine intervention. If ancient deities had given their lives to save the sun, how could mortals refuse to do the same? Their service to the gods culminated on the altar of the temple to Huitzilopochtli, where priests cut into the chests of warriors with their obsidian knives to pull out their beating hearts and raise them in sacrifice to the sun.

Such sacrifice evoked the power of Aztec rulers, but the ceremony observing the end of each fifty-two-year bundle better reflected the Mexica worldview. Had humans sacrificed enough for the gods to intercede and ensure the sun would rise again? In preparation for the end, families broke their earthenware vessels, cleansed their homes, and extinguished all fires. As the new day came, priests made a fire on the chest of a living, powerful captive warrior. Noble warriors lit torches from this new fire, and relayed the noble flame of creation into each hearth in the empire. For the next fifty-two years, all would know the fire in their hearth, like the rising of the sun itself, was the fruit of a sacred warrior sacrifice.

The need for sacrifice, as well as the glorification of the warriors who provided it through battle, was a powerful rationale for the expansion of the Aztec Empire. The role of the Aztecs' sacrifice-based religious system is the subject of scholarly debate: Did the religious system guide imperial expansion? Or did imperial expansion guide the religious system? These views are by no means incompatible: for the Aztecs, the peoples who came under their rule, and the peoples who resisted them, the twin goals of empire building and service to the gods were inseparable.

> **QUICK REVIEW**

What role did warfare play in Mexica society?

CHAPTER LOCATOR | How did ancient peoples of the Americas adapt to, and adapt, their environment? | What patterns shaped civilization in Mesoamerica and the Andes?

320 CHAPTER 11
THE AMERICAS

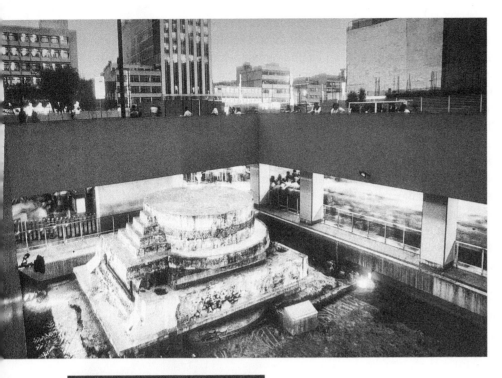

Past and Present Meet in Mexico City

Construction for the Pino Suárez metro station unearthed the Aztec ceremonial altar of Ehecatl, the Aztec god of wind. (David Hiser/National Geographic/SuperStock)

B By 1500 the Incas and Aztecs strained under the burdens of managing the largest empires the Americas had seen. Both faced the challenges of consolidating their gains, bearing the costs of empire and of the swelling nobility, and waging war in increasingly distant and difficult conditions.

The Fall of the Aztecs

In 1502 Moctezuma II, the last Mexica to rule before the arrival of the Spaniards, was named tlatoani. Moctezuma inherited a strained empire. His predecessors had expanded the empire's reach from the Caribbean coast to the Pacific. At the margins of the empire the Aztecs encountered peoples who were seminomadic or who, like the Maya, abandoned their cities to resist conquest. An empire that had expanded rapidly through conquest found itself with little room to grow.

What were the sources of strength and prosperity, and of problems, for the Incas?

How did the Maya and Teotihuacan develop prosperous societies in the classical era?

How did the Aztecs build on earlier Mesoamerican cultures and develop new traditions?

What did the European encounter mean for peoples of the major American empires?

✓ LearningCurve
Check what you know.

Aztec leaders had sought targets for conquest that were easy to overpower or were strategic for trade, or that possessed resources or produced goods that made for valuable tribute. This created an empire riddled with independent enclaves that had resisted conquest. The most powerful of these was Tlaxcala, at the edge of the Valley of Mexico. In addition, even those areas nominally under Aztec rule retained local leadership and saw themselves as subjected peoples, not as Aztecs.

Finally, the costs of expanding and sustaining the empire had become onerous. Generations of social mobility through distinction in combat had produced a bloated nobility both exempt from and sustained by tribute. Tenochtitlan became dependent on tributary maize in order to feed itself. Materially, the lack of new peoples to conquer meant the empire had little promise of increased prosperity. Spiritually, the dwindling flow of sacrificial victims meant the Mexica might be losing the great cosmic struggle to keep creation from ending.

Faced with these challenges, Moctezuma II reformed the empire. He reduced the privileges (and thus the costs to the empire) of the lesser nobility and narrowed the pathways of social mobility. The austerity he imposed in the imperial capital caused unrest. He also pressed the consolidation of territory by seeking to conquer the autonomous enclaves left by his predecessors. As Moctezuma targeted these enclaves, their ability to resist sapped Mexica resources and strained their morale without producing a corresponding reward for the empire in sacrifice or tribute.

By the time he reached the gates of Tenochtitlan in 1519, the Spanish conquistador Hernán Cortés had forged alliances with foes of the Aztec Empire, particularly Tlaxcala, which had so ably resisted conquest. The Tlaxcalans saw in the foreigners an opportunity that could aid their struggle against the Mexica and formed an alliance with the Spanish. Cortés's band of six hundred Spaniards arrived in Tenochtitlan accompanied by tens of thousands of Tlaxcalan soldiers.

Whatever Moctezuma made of the strangers, he received them as guests, probably because he sought to understand the nature of this encounter and its significance for his empire. Perhaps Moctezuma hesitated, losing the opportunity to act against them. Perhaps he concluded that he had no chance of defeating them, since at that moment most of the men he could count on in battle were tending to their crops and the capital had been so riddled with division and resentment of his reforms that he was powerless to act.

Either way, Cortés and his men managed the encounter skillfully and succeeded in taking Moctezuma prisoner. When the residents of Tenochtitlan rose up to expel the Spaniards, Moctezuma was killed, either at the hands of the Spaniards or by his own subjects, depending on the account. Though the Spaniards were cast out of the city, they left an unwelcome guest, smallpox. The first epidemic of the disease swept through the city in 1520, killing Moctezuma's successor, Cuitlahuac, within a matter of months. Cuauhtemoc, the last tlatoani of the Mexica, was named that same year.

The Aztec Empire and the Mexica people were not defeated by technology, cultural superiority, or a belief that the Europeans were gods. Instead the Mexica suffered a political defeat: they fell because of ruptures in their leadership due to the death of Moctezuma and his successor, as well as the willingness of allies and enemies alike to join with the Spaniards against them when they perceived an opportunity.

CHAPTER LOCATOR | How did ancient peoples of the Americas adapt to, and adapt, their environment? | What patterns shaped civilization in Mesoamerica and the Andes?

322 CHAPTER 11 THE AMERICAS

The Fall of the Incas

In 1525 Huayna Capac Inca, the grandson of Pachacuti Inca, became ill while carrying out a military campaign in present-day Ecuador, at the northern frontier of the empire. His illness was plague, introduced by Europeans waging wars of conquest in Mesoamerica, and it would kill him. But as he waged war, he also received news of the foreigners in the north and anticipated that they would come southward. From his deathbed, he urged his successor to make peace with them.

But peace did not follow Huayna Capac's death. Instead civil war erupted between two of his sons over succession to the throne. Huascar claimed it as the firstborn. His half-brother Atahualpa, Huayna Capac's favorite and an experienced military commander who had accompanied him in his Ecuadorean campaign, claimed it as well. The brothers fought for seven years, turning the empire's armies against each other. In 1532 Atahualpa vanquished and imprisoned his brother and consolidated his rule in Cuzco. That same year a group of Spaniards led by Francisco Pizarro landed on the Peruvian coast, pursuing rumors of a city of gold in the mountains.

Atahualpa agreed through emissaries to meet the Spaniards at the city of Cajamarca in northern Peru. In a demonstration of his imperial authority, he entered Cajamarca carried on a golden litter, accompanied by four military squadrons of eight thousand men each. Atahualpa met the Spanish intending not to fight a battle, but to understand them and hear them out. The meeting between Atahualpa and Pizarro reflected two deeply different worldviews.

In the scuffle that ensued at the meeting, the Spaniards took Atahualpa prisoner, and they eventually executed him. The Spaniards named a new indigenous leader, Manco Capac, whom they hoped to control. But Manco Capac turned against the Spaniards. He, and later his son Tupac Amaru, led resistance against the Spaniards until 1567. Each time the Inca forces besieged a Spanish-controlled city or town, however, their proximity to the Spaniards exposed them to European diseases. They were more successful in smaller-scale attacks, which delayed and limited Spanish colonization, but did not undo it.

QUICK REVIEW <

How did internal political divisions contribute to the fall of both the Aztec and Inca Empires?

| What were the sources of strength and prosperity, and of problems, for the Incas? | How did the Maya and Teotihuacan develop prosperous societies in the classical era? | How did the Aztecs build on earlier Mesoamerican cultures and develop new traditions? | **What did the European encounter mean for peoples of the major American empires?** | ✓ LearningCurve Check what you know. |

323

CHAPTER SUMMARY

The Inca and Aztec Empires that encountered Spanish conquerors were short-lived products of the cycle of centralization and decentralization that had characterized the Andes and Mesoamerica for thousands of years. The empires preceding those of the Incas and Aztecs had been undone when their own people turned against them, when climate changes disrupted them, or when they faced outside competition. What was new in the sixteenth century was that this outside competition came from Europeans.

The civilizations of the Andes and Mesoamerica from which the Incas and Aztecs emerged had remarkable similarities with and differences from other ancient and premodern civilizations in other regions of the world. Indigenous societies of the Americas developed extensive networks of trade. In Mesoamerica and the Andes, the domestication of crops led to the kind of bountiful production that allowed for diversification of labor among farmers, priests, nobles, merchants, and artisans. In these environments, cycles of centralization occurred in which powerful city-states emerged and embarked on campaigns of conquest, bringing vast regions under their political, religious, and cultural influence.

But civilizations of the Americas developed in unique ways as well. This was particularly true in the Andes, where peoples developed specialized patterns of farming in vertical archipelagos in their inhospitable mountain environment. Similarly, though Andean peoples did not develop writing, they instead developed the khipu into a sophisticated system of recording and communicating information.

Ultimately, the history of the peoples of the Americas was defined by their diverse experiences as they coped with varied climates, ecology, and geography. And peoples' experiences of adapting to their environments, and of transforming those environments to meet their needs, shaped the ways they understood their world. These experiences led them to produce precise calendars, highly detailed readings of the stars, and an elaborate architecture of religious beliefs through which they interpreted their relationships to their world and their place in the cosmos.

 CONNECTIONS The early sixteenth century marked the end of independent empires of the Americas and the gradual integration of American peoples into global empires seated in Europe. Spaniards were the most motivated and had their greatest success when they encountered dense, organized urban areas. Here they displaced existing overlords as the recipients of tribute in goods and labor. The Spanish were less interested in sparsely settled areas that did not have well-established systems of trade and tribute and were harder to subdue. As a result, European conquest was a surprisingly drawn-out process. Peoples of the Americas resisted conquest until well into the nineteenth century.

The incidental companion of conquest—disease—was also uneven in its effects. Over the course of the sixteenth century, epidemic diseases decimated the population of the Americas, which fell from 50 million to just 5 million. But epidemics of

CHAPTER LOCATOR | How did ancient peoples of the Americas adapt to, and adapt, their environment? | What patterns shaped civilization in Mesoamerica and the Andes?

324 CHAPTER 11
THE AMERICAS

diseases that are spread through human contact, such as measles and smallpox, are primarily urban phenomena: these diseases emerged as ancient cities grew large enough that the diseases could spread quickly among dense populations. As a result, the impact of the diseases brought by Europeans was the most severe and the most destructive in the cities of the Americas.

Since cities faced the brunt of both disease and wars of conquest, the disruptions caused by the encounter were disproportionally felt there. Whole systems of knowledge, sets of artisanal skills, political cultures, and religious thought resided in cities. Thus, as epidemics erupted, many of the most remarkable aspects of American civilizations were lost. Rural peoples and cultures were much more resilient. It was in rural areas that languages, foodways, farming practices, and approaches to healing—indeed whole worldviews—endured and evolved. This process occurred either in isolation from or in dialogue with European cultures, but local practices in rural regions were not obliterated, as they were in major cities. In the end, the European encounter destroyed the urban cultures and systems of knowledge in the Americas.

ONLINE DOCUMENT PROJECT
The Making and Remaking of Aztec History
Why did Tlacaelel believe the Aztec Empire needed a new history?
Read documents that examine Aztec history and culture, and then complete a quiz and writing assignment based on the evidence and details from this chapter. *See inside the front cover to learn more.*

What were the sources of strength and prosperity, and of problems, for the Incas?

How did the Maya and Teotihuacan develop prosperous societies in the classical era?

How did the Aztecs build on earlier Mesoamerican cultures and develop new traditions?

What did the European encounter mean for peoples of the major American empires?

✓ LearningCurve
Check what you know.

325

CHAPTER 11 STUDY GUIDE

STEP 1

GET STARTED ONLINE

LearningCurve

Now that you've read the chapter, make it stick by completing the LearningCurve activity.

STEP 2

EXPLAIN WHY IT MATTERS

Put your reading into practice. Identify each term below, and then explain why it matters in world history.

TERM	WHO OR WHAT & WHEN	WHY IT MATTERS
Mesoamerica (p. 296)		
khipu (p. 299)		
nixtamalization (p. 300)		
Olmecs (p. 302)		
Moche (p. 305)		
Inca (p. 306)		
Quechua (p. 308)		
Maya (p. 309)		
Teotihuacan (p. 309)		
Nahuatl (p. 314)		
Mexica (p. 314)		
Tenochtitlan (p. 315)		

STEP 3

MOVE BEYOND THE BASICS

To demonstrate a more advanced understanding of the three major civilizations of the Americas, fill in the chart below with descriptions of the role trade, warfare, and religion played in the society and culture of each civilization. What common characteristics did these civilizations share?

	Trade	Warfare	Religion
Maya			
Aztecs			
Inca			

STEP 4

PUT IT ALL TOGETHER

Now, take a step back and try to explain the big picture. Remember to use specific examples from the chapter in your answers.

EARLY DEVELOPMENT OF AMERICAN SOCIETIES

▶ How did geography and climate shape migration and settlement patterns in the Americas?

▶ How did the Olmec help lay the foundation for later Mesoamerican societies?

THE CLASSICAL ERA

▶ How did trade link the societies of the Americas during the classical era?

▶ Compare and contrast the classical societies of Mesoamerica and North America. How would you explain the similarities and differences you note?

AZTEC AND INCA EMPIRES

▶ Compare and contrast the imperial expansion of the Aztecs and the Incas. What factors created pressure for continued expansion in each empire?

▶ Compare and contrast imperial government in the Aztec and Inca empires. How did each empire control subject peoples and exploit their labor and resources?

LOOKING BACK, LOOKING AHEAD

▶ What important similarities are there between the histories of the Western and Eastern Hemispheres prior to 1500? How would you account for these similarities?

▶ How might European conquest and colonization of the Americas after 1500 have shaped our view of the civilizations of the Americas as they existed *prior* to 1500?

> IN YOUR OWN WORDS

Imagine that you must give an oral report to the class answering the following question: What similarities and differences were there between the societies of the Americas and other premodern societies around the world? What would be the most important points and why?

12

CULTURAL EXCHANGE IN CENTRAL AND SOUTHERN ASIA

300–1400

> **How did Mongol conquests and maritime trade facilitate cultural exchange in central and southern Asia?** Chapter 12 examines the forces that contributed to cultural exchange and transformation in Asia between 300 and 1400. From the fifth century on, groups of nomadic Turks appeared along the fringes of the settled societies of Eurasia. Much more dramatic was the rise of the Mongols in the late twelfth and early thirteenth centuries. Under the leadership of Chinggis Khan, the Mongols subdued one society after another. For a century Mongol hegemony fostered unprecedented East-West trade and contact. Over the course of several centuries, Arab and Turkish armies brought Islam to India. India continued to be the center of a very active seaborne trade, and this trade helped carry Indian ideas and practices to Southeast Asia.

Mongol Woman Women played influential roles among the Mongols. The Mongol woman portrayed in this painting is Chabi, wife of Khubilai Khan. Like other Mongols, she maintained Mongol dress even though she spent much of her time in China. (The Granger Collection, NYC — All rights reserved.)

> What aspects of nomadic life gave the nomads of Central Asia military advantages over nearby settled civilizations?

> How did Chinggis Khan and his successors conquer much of Eurasia, and how did the Mongol conquests change the regions affected?

> How did the Mongol conquests facilitate the spread of ideas, religions, inventions, and diseases?

> What was the result of India's encounters with Turks, Mongols, and Islam?

> How did states develop along the maritime trade routes of Southeast Asia and beyond?

✓ **LearningCurve**

After reading the chapter, use LearningCurve to retain what you've read.

What aspects of nomadic life gave the nomads of Central Asia military advantages over nearby settled civilizations?

Gold Belt Plaques

Like earlier nomads, the Mongols favored art with animal designs, such as these two gold belt plaques, which depict deer under trees or flowers. Belts and horses were often exchanged to seal or commemorate an alliance. (Nasser D. Khalili Collection of Islamic Art, © Nour Foundation. Courtesy of the Khalili Family Trust)

nomads
▶ Groups of people who move from place to place in search of food, water, and pasture for their animals, usually following the seasons.

steppe
▶ Grasslands that are too dry for crops but support pasturing animals; they are common across much of the center of Eurasia.

ONE EXPERIENCE ROME, PERSIA, INDIA, AND CHINA ALL SHARED was conflict with nomads who came from the very broad region referred to as Central Asia. This region was dominated by the steppe, arid grasslands that stretched from modern Hungary to Mongolia and parts of present northeast China. Initially small in number, the nomadic peoples of this region used their military superiority to conquer first other nomads, then the nearby settled societies. In the process they created settled empires of their own that drew on the cultures they absorbed.

Nomadic Society

Easily crossed by horses but too dry for crop agriculture, the grasslands could support only a thin population of nomadic herders. Following the seasons, they would break camp at least twice a year and move their animals to new pastures, going north in the spring and south in the fall.

In their search for water and good pastures, nomadic groups often came into conflict with other nomadic groups pursuing the same resources, which the two

CHAPTER LOCATOR | What aspects of nomadic life gave nomads of Central Asia advantages over settled civilizations? | How did Chinggis Khan conquer Eurasia, and how did Mongol conquests change the region?

330 CHAPTER 12 CULTURAL EXCHANGE IN CENTRAL AND SOUTHERN ASIA

ca. 320–480
Gupta Empire in India

ca. 380–450
Life of India's greatest poet, Kalidasa

ca. 450
Huns invade northern India

ca. 500
Srivijaya gains control of Strait of Malacca

ca. 500–1400
India's medieval age; caste system reaches its mature form

552
Turks rebel against Rouruan and rise to power in Central Asia

ca. 780
Borobudur temple complex begun in Srivijaya

802–1432
Khmer Empire of Cambodia

ca. 850–1250
Kingdom of the Uighurs

1030
Turks control north India

ca. 1100–1200
Buddhism declines in India

ca. 1200–1300
Easter Island society's most prosperous period

1206
Temujin proclaimed Chinggis Khan; Mongol language recorded; Delhi sultanate established

ca. 1240
The Secret History of the Mongols

1276
Mongol conquest of Song China

ca. 1300
Plague begins to spread throughout Mongol Empire

1398
Timur takes control of the Delhi sultanate

would then fight over. Groups on the losing end, especially if they were small, faced the threat of extermination or slavery, which prompted them to make alliances with other groups or move far away. Groups on the winning end of intertribal conflicts could exact tribute from those they defeated.

To get the products of nearby agricultural societies, especially grain, woven textiles, iron, tea, and wood, nomadic herders would trade their own products, such as horses and furs. When trade was difficult, they would turn to raiding to seize what they needed. Much of the time nomadic herders raided other nomads, but nearby agricultural settlements were common targets as well. The nomads' skill as horsemen and archers made it difficult for farmers and townsmen to defend against them.

Political organization among nomadic herders was generally very simple. Clans—members of an extended family—had chiefs, as did tribes (coalitions of clans). Leadership within a group was based on military prowess and was often settled by fighting. Occasionally a charismatic leader would emerge who was able to extend alliances to form confederations of tribes. Large confederations rarely lasted more than a century or so, however, and when they broke up, tribes again spent much of their time fighting with each other.

The three most wide-ranging and successful confederations were those of the Xiongnu—Huns, as they were known in the West—who emerged in the third century B.C.E. in the area near China; the Turks, who had their origins in the same area in the fourth and fifth centuries C.E.; and the Mongols, who did not become

How did the Mongol conquests facilitate the spread of religions, inventions, and diseases?

What was the result of India's encounters with Turks, Mongols, and Islam?

How did states develop along the maritime trade routes of Southeast Asia and beyond?

✓ LearningCurve
Check what you know.

important until the late twelfth century. In all three cases, the entire steppe region was eventually swept up in the movement of peoples and armies.

The Turks

In 552 a group called Turks who specialized in metalworking overthrew their overlords, the Rouruan, whose empire dominated the region from the eastern Silk Road cities of Central Asia through Mongolia. When the first Turkish khagan (ruler) died a few years later, the Turkish empire was divided between his younger brother, who took the western part (modern Central Asia), and his son, who took the eastern part (modern Mongolia). In 576 the Western Turks captured the Byzantine city of Bosporus in the Crimea.

The Eastern Turks frequently raided China and just as often fought among themselves. In the early seventh century the empire of the Eastern Turks ran up against the growing military might of the Tang Dynasty in China and soon broke apart.

In the eighth century a Turkic people called the Uighurs (Wee-gurs) formed a new empire based in Mongolia that survived about a century. It had close ties to Tang China, providing military aid but also extracting large payments in silk. During this period many Uighurs adopted religions then current along the Silk Road, notably Buddhism, Nestorian Christianity, and Manichaeism. In the ninth century this Uighur empire was destroyed by another Turkic people from north of Mongolia called the Kyrghiz. Some Uighurs fled to what is now western China. Setting up their capital city in Kucha, the Uighurs created a remarkably stable and prosperous kingdom that lasted four centuries (ca. 850–1250).

Farther west in Central Asia other groups of Turks rose to prominence. Often local Muslim forces would try to capture them, employ them as slave soldiers, and convert them. By the mid- to late tenth century many were serving in the armies of the Abbasid caliphate. Also in the tenth century Central Asian Turks began converting to Islam (which protected them from being abducted as slaves). Then they took to raiding unconverted Turks.

In the mid-eleventh century Turks had gained the upper hand in the caliphate, and the caliphs became little more than figureheads. From there Turkish power was extended into Syria, Palestine, and Asia Minor. In 1071 Seljuk Turks inflicted a devastating defeat on the Byzantine army in eastern Anatolia (see page 245). Other Turkish confederations established themselves in Afghanistan and extended their control into north India (see page 347).

In India, Persia, and Anatolia the formidable military skills of nomadic Turkish warriors made it possible for them to become overlords of settled societies. Just as the Uighurs developed a hybrid urban culture along the eastern end of the Silk Road, the Turks of Central and West Asia created an Islamic culture that drew from both Turkish and Iranian sources. Often Persian was used as the

Manichean Priests

Many religions spread through Central Asia before it became predominantly Muslim after 1300. This fragment of a tenth- to twelfth-century illustrated document, found at the Silk Road city of Turfan, is written in the Uighur language and depicts Manichean priests. (Archives Charmet/The Bridgeman Art Library)

CHAPTER LOCATOR | What aspects of nomadic life gave nomads of Central Asia advantages over settled civilizations? | How did Chinggis Khan conquer Eurasia, and how did Mongol conquests change the region?

332 CHAPTER 12 CULTURAL EXCHANGE IN CENTRAL AND SOUTHERN ASIA

administrative language of the states they formed. Nevertheless, despite the presence of Turkish overlords all along the southern fringe of the steppe, no one group of Turks was able to unite them all into a single political unit. That feat had to wait for the next major power on the steppe, the Mongols.

The Mongols

In the twelfth century ambitious Mongols did not aspire to match the Turks or other groups that had migrated west, but rather wanted to be successors to the Khitans and Jurchens, nomadic groups that had stayed in the east and mastered ways to extract resources from China. The Khitans and Jurchens had formed hybrid nomadic-urban states, with northern sections where tribesmen continued to live in the traditional way and southern sections politically controlled by the non-Chinese rulers but settled largely by taxpaying Chinese. The Khitans and Jurchens had scripts created to record their languages and adopted many Chinese governing practices. They built cities in pastoral areas that served as trading centers and places to enjoy their newly acquired wealth. In both the Khitan and Jurchen cases, their elite became culturally dual, adept in Chinese ways as well as in their own traditions.

The Mongols lived north of these hybrid nomadic-settled societies and maintained their traditional ways. They lived in tents called **yurts** rather than in houses. The yurts, about twelve to fifteen feet in diameter, were constructed of light wooden frames covered by layers of wool felt, greased to make them waterproof. The floor of a yurt was covered first with dried grass or straw, then with felt, skins, or rugs. In the center, directly under the smoke hole, was the hearth. A group of families traveling together would set up their yurts in a circle open to the south and draw up their wagons in a circle around the yurts for protection.

The Mongol diet consisted mostly of animal products. The most common meat was mutton, supplemented with wild game. When grain or vegetables could be obtained through trade, they were added to the diet. The Mongols milked sheep, goats, cows, and horses and made cheese and fermented alcoholic drinks from the milk. Wood was scarce, so dried animal dung or grasses fueled the cook fires.

Mongol women had to work very hard and had to be able to care for the animals when the men were away hunting or fighting. They normally drove the carts and set up and dismantled the yurts. They also milked the sheep, goats, and cows and made the butter and cheese. Women, like men, had to be expert riders, and many also learned to shoot. They participated actively in family decisions, especially as wives and mothers. In *The Secret History of the Mongols*, a work written in Mongolian in about 1240, the mother and wife of the Mongol leader Chinggis Khan frequently make impassioned speeches on the importance of family loyalty.

Mongol men kept as busy as the women. They made the carts and wagons and the frames for the yurts. They also made harnesses for the horses and oxen, leather saddles, and the equipment needed for hunting and war, such as bows and arrows. Men also had charge of the horses, and they milked the mares. One specialist among the nomads was the blacksmith, who made stirrups, knives, and other metal tools.

Kinship underlay most social relationships among the Mongols. Normally each family occupied a yurt, and groups of families camping together were usually

yurts
▶ Tents in which the pastoral nomads lived; they could be quickly dismantled and loaded onto animals or carts.

How did the Mongol conquests facilitate the spread of religions, inventions, and diseases? | What was the result of India's encounters with Turks, Mongols, and Islam? | How did states develop along the maritime trade routes of Southeast Asia and beyond? | ☑ LearningCurve Check what you know.

333

related along the male line. More distant patrilineal relatives were recognized as members of the same clan and could call on each other for aid. People from the same clan could not marry each other, so men had to get wives from other clans. When a woman's husband died, she would be inherited by another male in the family. Tribes were groups of clans, often distantly related. Both clans and tribes had chiefs who would make decisions on where to graze and when to retaliate against another tribe that had stolen animals or people. Women were sometimes abducted for brides. When tribes stole men from each other, they normally made them into slaves, and slaves were forced to do much of the heavy work.

Even though population was sparse in the regions where the Mongols lived, conflict over resources was endemic, and each camp had to be on the alert for attacks. Defending against attacks and retaliating against raids was as much a part of the Mongols' daily life as caring for their herds and trading with nearby settlements.

Mongol children learned to ride at a young age. The prime weapon boys had to learn to use was the compound bow, which had a pull of about 160 pounds and a range of more than 200 yards; it was well suited for using on horseback, giving Mongol soldiers an advantage in battle. Other commonly used weapons were small battle-axes and lances fitted with hooks to pull enemies off their saddles.

Hunting was a common form of military training among the Mongols. Each year tribes would organize one big hunt; mounted hunters would form a vast ring perhaps ten or more miles in circumference, then gradually shrink it down, trapping all the animals before killing them.

As with the Turks and other steppe nomads, religious practices centered around the shaman, a religious expert believed to be able to communicate with the gods. The high god of the Mongols was Heaven/Sky, but they recognized many other gods as well. Some groups of Mongols, especially those closer to settled communities, converted to Buddhism, Nestorian Christianity, or Manichaeism.

> **QUICK REVIEW**

What were the most important similarities and differences between the Mongols and the Turks?

CHAPTER LOCATOR | What aspects of nomadic life gave nomads of Central Asia advantages over settled civilizations? | How did Chinggis Khan conquer Eurasia, and how did Mongol conquests change the region?

CHAPTER 12
334 CULTURAL EXCHANGE IN CENTRAL AND SOUTHERN ASIA

The Tent of Chinggis Khan

In this fourteenth-century Persian illustration from Rashid al-Din's *History of the World*, two guards stand outside while Chinggis is in his tent. (From a book by Rashid al-din [1247–1318] [vellum], Persian School [14th century]/Bibliothèque Nationale, Paris, France/The Bridgeman Art Library)

How did Chinggis Khan and his successors conquer much of Eurasia, and how did the Mongol conquests change the regions affected?

IN THE MID-TWELFTH CENTURY the Mongols were just one of many peoples in the eastern grasslands, neither particularly numerous nor especially advanced. Why then did the Mongols suddenly emerge as an overpowering force on the historical stage? One explanation is ecological. A drop in the mean annual temperature created a subsistence crisis. As pastures shrank, the Mongols and other nomads had to look beyond the steppe to get more of their food from the agricultural world. A second reason for their sudden rise was the appearance of a single individual, the brilliant but utterly ruthless Temujin (ca. 1162–1227), later and more commonly called Chinggis Khan (sometimes spelled Genghis or Ghengis).

Chinggis Khan

In Temujin's youth, his father had built a modest tribal following. When Temujin's father was poisoned by a rival, his followers drifted away, leaving Temujin and his mother and brothers in a vulnerable position. Temujin slowly collected followers. In 1182 Temujin was captured and carried in a cage to a rival's camp. After a daring escape, he led his followers to join a stronger chieftain whom his father had

| How did the Mongol conquests facilitate the spread of religions, inventions, and diseases? | What was the result of India's encounters with Turks, Mongols, and Islam? | How did states develop along the maritime trade routes of Southeast Asia and beyond? | ✓ LearningCurve Check what you know. |

once aided. With the chieftain's help, Temujin began avenging the insults he had received.

Temujin proved to be a natural leader, and as he subdued other nomadic tribes, he built up an army of loyal followers. He mastered the art of winning allies through displays of personal courage in battle and generosity to his followers. To those who opposed him, he could be merciless. He once asserted that nothing gave more pleasure than massacring one's enemies, seizing their horses and cattle, and ravishing their women.

In 1206, at a great gathering of tribal leaders, Temujin was proclaimed **Chinggis Khan**, or Great Ruler. Chinggis decreed that Mongol, until then an unwritten language, be written down in the script used by the Uighur Turks. With this script a record was made of the Mongol laws and customs. Another measure adopted at this assembly was a postal relay system to send messages rapidly by mounted courier, suggesting that Chinggis already had ambitions to rule a vast empire.

With the tribes of Mongolia united, the energies previously devoted to infighting and vendettas were redirected to exacting tribute from the settled populations nearby, starting with the Jurchen (Jin) state that extended into north China. Because of his early experiences with intertribal feuding, Chinggis mistrusted traditional tribal loyalties, and as he fashioned a new army, he gave it a new, nontribal structure. He conscripted soldiers from all the tribes and assigned them to units that were composed of members from different tribes. He selected commanders for each unit whom he could remove at will, although he allowed commanders to pass their posts on to their sons.

After Chinggis subjugated a city, he would send envoys to cities farther out to demand submission and threaten destruction. Those who opened their city gates and submitted without fighting could join the Mongols, but those who resisted faced the prospect of mass slaughter. Not surprisingly many governors of cities and rulers of small states hastened to offer submission.

Chinggis preferred conquest to administration and did not stay in north China to set up an administrative structure. He left that to subordinates and turned his attention westward, to Central Asia and Persia, then dominated by different groups of Turks. In 1218 Chinggis proposed to the Khwarizm shah of Persia that he accept Mongol overlordship and establish trade relations. The shah ordered the envoy and the merchants who had accompanied him killed. The next year Chinggis led an army of one hundred thousand soldiers west to retaliate. Mongol forces destroyed the shah's army and sacked one Persian city after another.

After returning from Central Asia, Chinggis died in 1227 during the siege of a city in northwest China. Before he died, he instructed his sons not to fall out among themselves but instead to divide the spoils.

Chinggis's Successors

Although Mongol leaders traditionally had had to win their positions, after Chinggis died the empire was divided into four states called **khanates**, with one of the lines of his descendants taking charge of each (Map 12.1). Chinggis's third son, Ögödei, assumed the title of khan, and he directed the next round of invasions.

In 1237 representatives of all four lines led 150,000 Mongol, Turkish, and Persian troops into Europe. During the next five years, they gained control of Moscow

Chinggis Khan

▶ The title given to the Mongol ruler Temujin in 1206 and later to his successors; it means Great Ruler.

khanates

▶ The states ruled by a khan; the four units into which Chinggis divided the Mongol Empire.

CHAPTER LOCATOR | What aspects of nomadic life gave nomads of Central Asia advantages over settled civilizations? | **How did Chinggis Khan conquer Eurasia, and how did Mongol conquests change the region?**

CHAPTER 12
336 CULTURAL EXCHANGE IN CENTRAL AND SOUTHERN ASIA

Legend:
→ Mongol campaign before 1240
→ Mongol campaign after 1240
→ Route of Marco Polo, 1271–1295

MAP 12.1 ■ The Mongol Empire

The creation of the vast Mongol Empire facilitated communication across Eurasia and led to both the spread of deadly plagues and the transfer of technical and scientific knowledge. After the death of Chinggis Khan in 1227, the empire was divided into four khanates ruled by different lines of his successors. In the 1270s the Mongols conquered southern China, but most of their subsequent campaigns did not lead to further territorial gains.

> MAPPING THE PAST

ANALYZING THE MAP: Trace the campaigns of the Mongols. Which ones led to acquisition of territory, and which ones did not?

CONNECTIONS: Would the division of the Mongol Empire into separate khanates have made these areas easier for the Mongols to rule? What drawbacks might it have had from the Mongols' point of view?

and Kievan Russia and looted cities in Poland and Hungary. They were poised to attack deeper into Europe when they learned of the death of Ögödei in 1241. To participate in the election of a new khan, the army returned to the Mongols' new capital city, Karakorum.

| How did the Mongol conquests facilitate the spread of religions, inventions, and diseases? | What was the result of India's encounters with Turks, Mongols, and Islam? | How did states develop along the maritime trade routes of Southeast Asia and beyond? | ✓ LearningCurve Check what you know. |

Once Ögödei's son was certified as his successor, the Mongols turned their attention to Persia and the Middle East. In 1256 a Mongol army took northwest Iran, then pushed on to the Abbasid capital of Baghdad. When it fell in 1258, the last Abbasid caliph was murdered, and the population was put to the sword. The Mongol onslaught was successfully resisted, however, by both the Delhi sultanate (see page 347) and the Mamluk rulers in Egypt (see page 246).

Under Chinggis's grandson Khubilai Khan (r. 1260–1294), the Mongols completed their conquest of China. Proceeding deliberately, the Mongols first surrounded the Song empire in central and south China (discussed in Chapter 13) by taking its westernmost province in 1252, as well as Korea to its east in 1258; destroying the Nanzhao kingdom in modern Yunnan in 1254; and then continuing south and taking Annam (northern Vietnam) in 1257. As their invasion moved forward, the Mongols used a variety of forms of battle, employing experts in naval and siege warfare from all over their empire. During their advance toward the Chinese capital of Hangzhou, the Mongols ordered the total slaughter of the people of the major city of Changzhou, and in 1276 the Chinese empress dowager surrendered in hopes of sparing the people of the capital a similar fate.

Having overrun China and Korea, Khubilai turned his eyes toward Japan, launching invasions in 1274 and 1281. On both occasions the Mongols managed to land but were beaten back by Japanese samurai armies. Each time fierce storms destroyed the Mongol fleets. Twelve years later, in 1293, Khubilai tried sending a fleet to the islands of Southeast Asia, including Java, but it met with no more success than the fleets sent to Japan.

Why were the Mongols so successful against so many different types of enemies? Even though their population was tiny compared to the populations of the large agricultural societies they conquered, their tactics, their weapons, and their organization all gave them advantages. Like other nomads before them, they were superb horsemen and excellent archers. Their horses were extremely nimble, able

MONGOL CONQUESTS

1206	Temujin made Chinggis Khan
1215	Fall of Beijing (Jurchens)
1219–1220	Fall of Bukhara and Samarkand in Central Asia
1227	Death of Chinggis
1237–1241	Raids into eastern Europe
1257	Conquest of Annam (northern Vietnam)
1258	Conquest of Abbasid capital of Baghdad; conquest of Korea
1260	Khubilai succeeds to khanship
1274	First attempt at invading Japan
1276	Surrender of Song Dynasty (China)
1281	Second attempt at invading Japan
1293	Mongol fleet unsuccessful in invasion of Java
mid-14th century	Decline of Mongol power

CHAPTER LOCATOR | What aspects of nomadic life gave nomads of Central Asia advantages over settled civilizations? | **How did Chinggis Khan conquer Eurasia, and how did Mongol conquests change the region?**

to change direction quickly, thus allowing the Mongols to maneuver easily and ride through infantry forces armed with swords, lances, and javelins.

The Mongols were also open to trying new military technologies. To attack walled cities, they learned how to use catapults and other engines of war. At first they employed Chinese catapults, but when they learned that those used by the Turks in Afghanistan were more powerful, they adopted the better model. The Mongols also used exploding arrows and gunpowder projectiles developed by the Chinese.

The Mongols made good use of intelligence and tried to exploit internal divisions in the countries they attacked. Thus in north China they appealed to the Khitans, who had been defeated by the Jurchens a century earlier, to join them in attacking the Jurchens. In Syria they exploited the resentment of Christians against their Muslim rulers.

> **Three Generations of Mongol Conquerors:**

- Chinggis Khan: Led the first round of Mongol conquests
- Ögödei Khan: (Son of Chinggis Khan) Oversaw the westward expansion of the Mongol Empire
- Khubilai Khan: (Grandson of Chinggis Khan) Completed the Mongol conquest of China

The Mongols as Rulers

The success of the Mongols in ruling vast territories was due in large part to their willingness to incorporate other ethnic groups into their armies and governments. Whatever their original country or religion, those who served the Mongols loyally were rewarded.

Since, in Mongol eyes, the purpose of fighting was to gain riches, the Mongols would regularly loot the settlements they conquered, taking whatever they wanted, including the residents. Land would be granted to military commanders, nobles, and army units to be governed and exploited as the recipients wished. Those working the land would be given to them as serfs. The Mongols built a capital city called Karakorum in modern Mongolia, and to bring it up to the level of the cities they conquered, they transported skilled workers from those cities.

The traditional nomad disdain for farmers led some commanders to suggest turning north China into a gigantic pasture after it was conquered. In time, though, the Mongols came to realize that simply appropriating the wealth and human resources of the settled lands was not as good as extracting regular revenue from them. The Mongols gave Chinese methods of taxation a try, but soon political rivals convinced the khan that he would gain even more by letting Central Asian Muslim merchants bid against each other for licenses to collect taxes any way they could, a system called tax-farming. Ordinary Chinese found this method of tax collecting much more oppressive than traditional Chinese methods, since there was little to keep the tax collectors from seizing everything they could.

tax-farming
▶ Assigning the collection of taxes to whomever bids the most for the privilege.

By the second half of the thirteenth century there was no longer a genuine pan-Asian Mongol Empire. Much of Asia was in the hands of Mongol successor states, but these were generally hostile to each other. Khubilai was often at war

How did the Mongol conquests facilitate the spread of religions, inventions, and diseases?

What was the result of India's encounters with Turks, Mongols, and Islam?

How did states develop along the maritime trade routes of Southeast Asia and beyond?

✓ LearningCurve
Check what you know.

with the khanate of Central Asia, then held by his cousin Khaidu, and he had little contact with the khanate of the Golden Horde in south Russia. The Mongols adapted their methods of government to the existing traditions of each place they ruled, and the regions went their separate ways.

In China the Mongols resisted assimilation and purposely avoided many Chinese practices. The rulers conducted their business in the Mongol language and spent their summers in Mongolia. Khubilai discouraged Mongols from marrying Chinese and took only Mongol women into the palace. Chinese were treated as legally inferior not only to the Mongols but also to all other non-Chinese.

In Central Asia, Persia, and Russia the Mongols tended to merge with the Turkish groups already there and, like them, converted to Islam. Russia in the thirteenth century was not a strongly centralized state, and the Mongols allowed Russian princes and lords to continue to rule their territories as long as they turned over adequate tribute. The city of Moscow became the center of Mongol tribute collection and grew in importance. In the Middle East the Mongol Il-khans (as they were known in Persia) were more active as rulers, again continuing the traditions of the caliphate. In Mongolia itself, however, Mongol traditions were maintained.

In the mid-fourteenth century the Mongol dynasty in China deteriorated into civil war, and in the 1360s the Mongols withdrew back to Mongolia. There was a similar loss of Mongol power in Persia and Central Asia. Only on the south Russian steppe did the Golden Horde maintain its hold for another century.

As Mongol rule in Central Asia declined, a new conqueror emerged, Timur, also known as Tamerlane (Timur the Lame). Not a nomad but a highly civilized Turkish noble, Timur in the 1360s struck out from his base in Samarkand into Persia, north India (see page 347), southern Russia, and beyond. His armies used the terror tactics that the Mongols had perfected, massacring the citizens of cities that resisted. In the decades after his death in 1405, however, Timur's empire went into decline.

> **QUICK REVIEW**

What were the defining characteristics of Mongol government?

CHAPTER LOCATOR | What aspects of nomadic life gave nomads of Central Asia advantages over settled civilizations? | How did Chinggis Khan conquer Eurasia, and how did Mongol conquests change the region?

CHAPTER 12
340 CULTURAL EXCHANGE IN CENTRAL AND SOUTHERN ASIA

Planting Trees

The illustrations in early copies of Marco Polo's book show the elements that Europeans found most interesting. This page illustrates Khubilai's order that trees be planted along the main roads. (Illumination from *Le Livre des Merveilles du Monde* [Travels of Marco Polo], by the Paris studio of the Boucicaut Master, c. 1412/Bibliothèque Nationale, Paris/akg-images)

How did the Mongol conquests facilitate the spread of ideas, religions, inventions, and diseases?

THE MONGOL GOVERNMENTS DID MORE than any earlier political entities to encourage the movement of people and goods across Eurasia. With these vast movements came cultural accommodation as the peoples of Eurasia learned from one another. This cultural exchange involved both physical goods and the sharing of ideas, including the introduction of new religious beliefs and the adoption of new ways to organize and rule the Mongol Empire. It also facilitated the spread of the plague and the unwilling movement of enslaved captives.

The Movement of Peoples

The Mongols had never looked down on merchants the way the elites of many traditional states did, and they welcomed the arrival of merchants from distant lands. Even when different groups of Mongols were fighting among themselves, they usually allowed caravans to pass without harassing them.

The Mongol practice of transporting skilled people from the lands they conquered also brought people into contact with each other in new ways. Besides

How did the Mongol conquests facilitate the spread of religions, inventions, and diseases? | What was the result of India's encounters with Turks, Mongols, and Islam? | How did states develop along the maritime trade routes of Southeast Asia and beyond? | ✓ LearningCurve Check what you know.

those forced to move, the Mongols recruited administrators from all over. Especially prominent were the Uighur Turks of Chinese Central Asia, whose familiarity with Chinese civilization and fluency in Turkish were extremely valuable in facilitating communication.

One of those who served the Mongols was Rashid al-Din (ca. 1247–1318). A Jew from Persia and the son of an apothecary, Rashid al-Din converted to Islam at the age of thirty and entered the service of the Mongol Il-khan of Persia as a physician. He rose in government service, traveled widely, and eventually became prime minister. Aware of the great differences between cultures, he believed that the Mongols should try to rule in accord with the moral principles of the majority in each land. On that basis he convinced the Mongol khan of Persia to convert to Islam. Rashid al-Din undertook to explain the great variety of cultures by writing a world history more comprehensive than any previously written.

More Europeans made their way as far as Mongolia and China in the Mongol period than ever before. Popes and kings sent envoys to the Mongol court in the hope of enlisting the Mongols on their side in their long-standing conflict with Muslim forces over the Holy Land. European visitors were also interested in finding Christians who had been cut off from the West by the spread of Islam, and in fact there were considerable numbers of Nestorian Christians in Central Asia.

The most famous European visitor to the Mongol lands was the Venetian Marco Polo (ca. 1254–1324). In his *Travels*, Marco Polo described all the places he visited or learned about during his seventeen years away from home. He reported being warmly received by Khubilai, who impressed him enormously. He was also awed by the wealth and splendor of Chinese cities and spread the notion of Asia as a land of riches.

The Spread of Disease, Goods, and Ideas

The rapid transfer of people and goods across Central Asia spread more than ideas and inventions. It also spread diseases, the most deadly of which was the plague known in Europe as the Black Death, which scholars identify today as the bubonic plague. In the early fourteenth century, transmitted by rats and fleas, the plague began to spread from Central Asia into West Asia, the Mediterranean, and western Europe. The confusion of the mid-fourteenth century that led to the loss of Mongol power in China, Iran, and Central Asia undoubtedly owes something to the effect of the spread of the plague and other diseases. (For more on the Black Death, see Chapter 14.)

Traditionally, the historians of each of the countries conquered by the Mongols portrayed them as a scourge. Among contemporary Western historians, it is now more common to celebrate the genius of the Mongol military machine and treat the spread of ideas and inventions as an obvious good. There is no reason to assume, however, that people benefited equally from the improved communications and the new political institutions of the Mongol era. Merchants involved in long-distance trade prospered, but those enslaved and transported hundreds or thousands of miles from home would have seen themselves not as the beneficiaries of opportunities to encounter new cultures but rather as the most pitiable of victims. Moreover, the places that were ruled by Mongol governments for a cen-

CHAPTER LOCATOR | What aspects of nomadic life gave nomads of Central Asia advantages over settled civilizations? | How did Chinggis Khan conquer Eurasia, and how did Mongol conquests change the region?

CHAPTER 12
342 CULTURAL EXCHANGE IN CENTRAL AND SOUTHERN ASIA

tury or more—China, Central Asia, Persia, and Russia—do not seem to have advanced at a more rapid rate during that century than they did in earlier centuries, either economically or culturally.

In terms of the spread of technological and scientific ideas, Europe seems to have been by far the main beneficiary of increased communication, largely because in 1200 it lagged farther behind than the other areas. Chinese inventions such as printing, gunpowder, and the compass spread westward. Persian and Indian expertise in astronomy and mathematics also spread. In terms of the spread of religions, Islam probably gained the most. It came to dominate in Chinese Central Asia, which had previously been Buddhist.

QUICK REVIEW <

How did the Mongol conquests contribute to the movement of people across Eurasia?

| How did the Mongol conquests facilitate the spread of religions, inventions, and diseases? | What was the result of India's encounters with Turks, Mongols, and Islam? | How did states develop along the maritime trade routes of Southeast Asia and beyond? | ✓ LearningCurve Check what you know. |

343

What was the result of India's encounters with Turks, Mongols, and Islam?

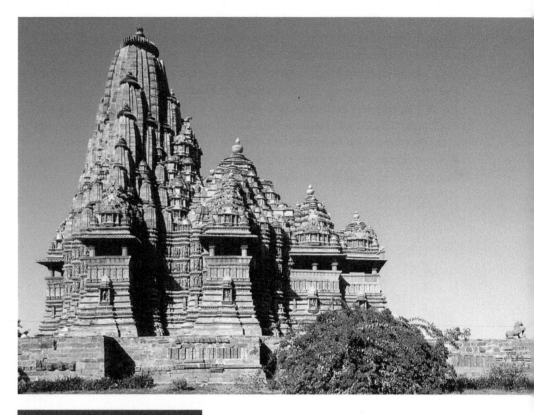

Kandariyâ Mahâdeva Hindu Temple

Built around 1050 by a local king in central India, this is one of the best-preserved Hindu temples from the medieval period. The main spire rises 100 feet, and the sides are decorated with more than six hundred stone statues. (Yvan Travert/akg-images)

AFTER THE MAURYAN EMPIRE BROKE APART in 185 B.C.E. (see page 80), India was politically divided into small kingdoms for several centuries. Only the Guptas in the fourth century would emerge to unite much of north India, though their rule was cut short by the invasion of the Huns in about 450. A few centuries later, India was profoundly shaped by Turkish nomads from Central Asia who brought their culture and, most important, Islam to India. Despite these events, the lives of most Indians remained unchanged, with the majority of the people living in villages in a society defined by caste.

The Gupta Empire, ca. 320–480

In the early fourth century a state emerged in the Ganges plain that was able to bring large parts of north India under its control. The rulers of this Indian empire, the Guptas, consciously modeled their rule after that of the Mauryan Empire, and the founder took the name of the founder of that dynasty, Chandragupta. The

CHAPTER LOCATOR | What aspects of nomadic life gave nomads of Central Asia advantages over settled civilizations? | How did Chinggis Khan conquer Eurasia, and how did Mongol conquests change the region?

Guptas united north India and received tribute from states in Nepal and the Indus Valley, thus giving large parts of India a period of peace and political unity.

The Guptas' administrative system was not as centralized as that of the Mauryans. In the central regions they drew their revenue from a tax on agriculture and maintained monopolies on key products such as metals and salt (reminiscent of Chinese practice). They also exacted labor service for the construction and upkeep of roads, wells, and irrigation systems. More distant areas were assigned to governors who were allowed considerable leeway, and governorships often became hereditary. Areas still farther away were encouraged to become vassal states.

The Gupta kings were patrons of the arts. Poets composed epics for the courts of the Gupta kings, and other writers experimented with prose romances and popular tales. India's greatest poet, Kalidasa (ca. 380–450), like Shakespeare, wrote poems as well as plays in verse.

In mathematics, too, the Gupta period could boast of impressive intellectual achievements. The so-called Arabic numerals are actually of Indian origin. Indian mathematicians developed the place-value notation system, with separate columns for ones, tens, and hundreds, as well as a zero sign to indicate the absence of units in a given column. This system greatly facilitated calculation and had spread as far as Europe by the seventh century.

The Gupta rulers were Hindus, but they tolerated all faiths. Buddhist pilgrims from other areas of Asia reported that Buddhist monasteries with hundreds or even thousands of monks and nuns flourished in the cities. The success of Buddhism did not hinder Hinduism with its many gods, which remained popular among ordinary people.

The great crisis of the Gupta Empire was the invasion of the Huns in about 450. Mustering his full might, the Gupta ruler Skandagupta (r. ca. 455–467) threw back the invaders, but they had dealt the dynasty a fatal blow.

The Gupta Empire, ca. 320–480

India's Medieval Age and the First Encounter with Islam

After the decline of the Gupta Empire, India once again broke into separate kingdoms that were frequently at war with each other. Most of the dynasties of India's medieval age (ca. 500–1400) were short-lived, but a balance of power was maintained between the major regions of India, with none gaining enough of an advantage to conquer the others (Map 12.2).

Political division fostered the development of regional cultures. Literature came to be written in India's regional languages, among them Marathi, Bengali, and Assamese. Commerce continued as before, and the coasts of India remained important in the sea trade of the Indian Ocean.

The first encounters with Islam occurred in this period. In 711 the Umayyad governor of Iraq seized the Sind area in western India (modern Pakistan). The western part of India remained part of the caliphate for centuries, but Islam did not spread much beyond this foothold. During the ninth and tenth centuries Turks from Central Asia moved into the region of today's northeastern Iran and western Afghanistan, then known as Khurasan. Converts to Islam, they first served as military forces for the caliphate in Baghdad, but as its authority weakened

How did the Mongol conquests facilitate the spread of religions, inventions, and diseases?

What was the result of India's encounters with Turks, Mongols, and Islam?

How did states develop along the maritime trade routes of Southeast Asia and beyond?

✔ LearningCurve
Check what you know.

345

MAP 12.2 ■ **South and Southeast Asia in the Thirteenth Century**

The extensive coastlines of South and Southeast Asia and the predictable monsoon winds aided seafaring in this region. Note the Strait of Malacca, through which most east-west sea trade passed.

(see pages 336–339), they made themselves rulers of an effectively independent Khurasan and frequently sent raiding parties into north India. Beginning in 997 Mahmud of Ghazni (r. 997–1030) led seventeen annual forays into India from his base in modern Afghanistan. Eventually the Arab conquerors of the Sind fell to the Turks. By 1030 the Indus Valley, the Punjab, and the rest of northwest India were in the grip of the Turks.

The new rulers encouraged the spread of Islam, but the caste system (see page 69) made it difficult to convert higher-caste Indians. After an initial period of raids and destruction of temples, the Muslim Turks came to an accommodation with the Hindus, who were classed as a protected people, like the Christians and Jews, and allowed to follow their religion. They had to pay a special tax but did not have to perform military service. Local chiefs and rajas were often allowed to remain in control of their domains as long as they paid tribute. Most Indians looked on the Muslim conquerors as a new ruling caste, capable of governing and taxing them but otherwise peripheral to their lives. The myriad castes largely governed themselves, isolating the newcomers.

Nevertheless, over the course of several centuries Islam gained a strong hold on north India, especially in the Indus Valley (modern Pakistan) and in Bengal at the mouth of the Ganges River (modern Bangladesh). Moreover, the sultanate

protected people

▶ The Muslim classification used for Hindus, Christians, and Jews; they were allowed to follow their religions but had to pay a special tax.

CHAPTER LOCATOR | What aspects of nomadic life gave nomads of Central Asia advantages over settled civilizations? | How did Chinggis Khan conquer Eurasia, and how did Mongol conquests change the region?

CHAPTER 12
346 CULTURAL EXCHANGE IN CENTRAL AND SOUTHERN ASIA

seems to have had a positive effect on the economy. Much of the wealth confiscated from temples was put to more productive use, and India's first truly large cities emerged. The Turks also were eager to employ skilled workers, giving new opportunities to low-caste manual and artisan labor.

The Muslim rulers were much more hostile to Buddhism than to Hinduism, seeing Buddhism as a competitive proselytizing religion. In 1193 a Turkish raiding party destroyed the great Buddhist university at Nalanda in Bihar. Buddhist monks were killed or forced to flee to Buddhist centers in Southeast Asia, Nepal, and Tibet. Buddhism, which had thrived for so long in peaceful and friendly competition with Hinduism, subsequently went into decline in its native land.

Hinduism, however, remained as strong as ever. South India was largely unaffected by these invasions, and traditional Hindu culture flourished there under native kings ruling small kingdoms. (See "Individuals in Society: Bhaskara the Teacher," page 348.) Devotional cults and mystical movements flourished. This was a great age of religious art and architecture in India. Extraordinary temples covered with elaborate bas-relief were built in many areas.

The Delhi Sultanate

In the twelfth century a new line of Turkish rulers arose in Afghanistan, led by Muhammad of Ghur (d. 1206). Muhammad captured Delhi and extended his control nearly throughout north India. When he fell to an assassin in 1206, one of his generals, the former slave Qutb-ud-din, seized the reins of power and established a government at Delhi, separate from the government in Afghanistan. This sultanate of Delhi lasted for three centuries, even though dynasties changed several times.

A major accomplishment of the Delhi sultanate was holding off the Mongols. Chinggis Khan and his troops entered the Indus Valley in 1221 in pursuit of the shah of Khurasan. The sultan wisely kept out of the way, and when Chinggis Khan left some troops in the area, the sultan made no attempt to challenge them. Two generations later, in 1299, a Mongol khan launched a campaign into India with two hundred thousand men, but the sultan of the time was able to defeat them. Two years later the Mongols returned and camped at Delhi for two months, but they eventually left without taking the sultan's fort. Another Mongol raid in 1306–1307 also was successfully repulsed.

During the fourteenth century, however, the Delhi sultanate was in decline and proved unable to ward off the armies of Timur (see page 339), who took Delhi in 1398. Timur's invasion left a weakened sultanate. The Delhi sultanate endured under different rulers until 1526, when it was conquered by the Mughals, a Muslim dynasty that would rule over most of northern Indian from the sixteenth into the nineteenth century.

Life in Medieval India

Local institutions played a much larger role in the lives of people in medieval India than did the state. Craft guilds oversaw conditions of work and trade, local councils handled law and order at the town or village level, and local castes gave members a sense of belonging and identity.

How did the Mongol conquests facilitate the spread of religions, inventions, and diseases?

What was the result of India's encounters with Turks, Mongols, and Islam?

How did states develop along the maritime trade routes of Southeast Asia and beyond?

✓ LearningCurve
Check what you know.

347

INDIVIDUALS IN SOCIETY
Bhaskara the Teacher

In India, as in many other societies, astronomy and mathematics were closely linked, and many of the most important mathematicians served their rulers as astronomers. Bhaskara (1114–ca. 1185) was such an astronomer-mathematician. For generations his Brahmin family had been astronomers at the Ujjain astronomical observatory in north-central India, and his father had written a popular book on astrology.

Bhaskara was a highly erudite man. A disciple wrote that he had thoroughly mastered eight books on grammar, six on medicine, six on philosophy, five on mathematics, and the four Vedas. Bhaskara eventually wrote six books on mathematics and mathematical astronomy. They deal with solutions to simple and quadratic equations and show his knowledge of trigonometry, including the sine table and relationships between different trigonometric functions, and even some of the basic elements of calculus. Earlier Indian mathematicians had explored the use of zero and negative numbers. Bhaskara developed these ideas further, in particular improving on the understanding of division by zero.

A court poet who centuries later translated Bhaskara's book titled *The Beautiful* explained its title by saying Bhaskara wrote it for his daughter named Beautiful (Lilavati) as consolation when his divination of the best time for her to marry went awry. Whether Bhaskara did or did not write this book for his daughter, many of the problems he provides in it have a certain charm:

> On an expedition to seize his enemy's elephants, a king marched two yojanas the first day. Say, intelligent calculator, with what increasing rate of daily march did he proceed, since he reached his foe's city, a distance of eighty yojanas, in a week?*
>
> Out of a heap of pure lotus flower, a third part, a fifth, and a sixth were offered respectively to the gods Siva, Vishnu, and the Sun; and a quarter was presented to Bhavani. The remaining six lotuses were given to the venerable preceptor. Tell quickly the whole number of lotus.†
>
> If eight best variegated silk scarfs, measuring three cubits in breadth and eight in length, cost a hundred nishkas, say quickly, merchant, if thou

The observatory where Bhaskara worked in Ujjain today stands in ruins. (Dinodia Photo Library)

> understand trade, what a like scarf, three and a half cubits long and half a cubit wide will cost.‡

In the conclusion to *The Beautiful*, Bhaskara wrote:

> Joy and happiness is indeed ever increasing in this world for those who have *The Beautiful* clasped to their throats, decorated as the members are with neat reduction of fractions, multiplication, and involution, pure and perfect as are the solutions, and tasteful as is the speech which is exemplified.

Bhaskara had a long career. His first book on mathematical astronomy, written in 1150 when he was thirty-six, used mathematics to calculate solar and lunar eclipses or planetary conjunctions. Thirty-three years later he was still writing on the subject, this time providing simpler ways to solve problems encountered before. Bhaskara wrote his books in Sanskrit, already a literary language rather than a vernacular language, but even in his own day some of them were translated into other Indian languages.

---

*Quotations from Haran Chandra Banerji, *Colebrooke's Translation of the Lilanvanti*, 2d ed. (Calcutta: The Book Co., 1927), pp. 80–81, 30, 51, 200. The answer is that each day he must travel 22/7 yojanas farther than the day before.

†The answer is 120.

‡The answer, from the formula $x = (1 \times 7 \times 1 \times 100) / (8 \times 3 \times 8 \times 2 \times 2)$, is given in currencies smaller than the nishka: 14 drammas, 9 panas, 1 kakini, and 6⅔ cowry shells. (20 cowry shells = 1 kakini, 4 kakini = 1 pana, 16 panas = 1 dramma, and 16 drammas = 1 nishka.)

Within a couple of decades of his death, a local ruler endowed an educational institution to study Bhaskara's works, beginning with his work on mathematical astronomy. In the text he had inscribed at the site, the ruler gave the names of Bhaskara's ancestors for six generations, as well as of his son and grandson, who had continued in his profession.

QUESTIONS FOR ANALYSIS

1. What might have been the advantages of making occupations like astronomer hereditary in India?
2. How does Bhaskara link joy and happiness to mathematical concepts?

ONLINE DOCUMENT PROJECT

What ideas and beliefs were central to Indian culture? Read a Persian account of medieval India, and then complete a quiz and writing assignment based on the evidence and details from this chapter. *See inside the front cover to learn more.*

Like peasant societies elsewhere, including in China, Japan, and Southeast Asia, agricultural life in India ordinarily meant village life. The average farmer worked a small plot of land outside the village. All the family members pooled their resources under the direction of the head of the family. These joint efforts strengthened family solidarity.

The agricultural year began with spring plowing. The traditional plow, drawn by two oxen wearing yokes and collars, had an iron-tipped share and a handle with which the farmer guided it. Rice, the most important and popular grain, was sown at the beginning of the long rainy season. Beans, lentils, and peas grew during the cold season and were harvested in the spring, when fresh food was scarce. Cereal crops such as wheat, barley, and millet provided carbohydrates and other nutrients. Some families cultivated vegetables, spices, fruit trees, and flowers in their gardens. Sugarcane was another important crop.

Farmers also raised livestock. Most highly valued were cattle, which were raised for plowing and milk, hides, and horns, but Hindus did not slaughter them for meat. Like the Islamic and Jewish prohibition on the consumption of pork, the eating of beef was forbidden among Hindus.

Local craftsmen and tradesmen were frequently organized into guilds, with guild heads and guild rules. The textile industries were particularly well developed. Textiles were produced in large quantities and traded throughout India and beyond. The cutting and polishing of precious stones was another industry associated closely with foreign trade.

In the cities shops were open to the street; families lived on the floors above. The busiest tradesmen dealt in milk and cheese, oil, spices, and perfumes. In addition to these tradesmen and merchants, a host of peddlers shuffled through towns and villages selling everything from needles to freshly cut flowers.

During the first millennium C.E., the caste system reached its mature form. Within the broad division into the four varnas (strata) of Brahmin, Kshatriya, Vaishya, and Shudra (see page 69), the population was subdivided into numerous

Men at Work

This stone frieze from the Buddhist stupa in Sanchi depicts Indian men doing a variety of everyday jobs. Although the stone was carved to convey religious ideas, we can use it as a source for such details of daily life as the sort of clothing men wore while working and how they carried loads. (Dinodia Photo Library)

jati

▶ The thousands of Indian castes.

castes, or **jati**. Each caste had a proper occupation. In addition, its members married only within the caste and ate only with other members. Members of high-status castes feared pollution from contact with lower-caste individuals and had to undertake rituals of purification to remove the taint.

Eventually Indian society comprised perhaps as many as three thousand castes. Each caste had its own governing body, which enforced the rules of the caste. Those incapable of living up to the rules were expelled, becoming outcastes. These unfortunates lived hard lives, performing tasks that others considered unclean or lowly.

For all members of Indian society regardless of caste, marriage and family were the focus of life. As in China, the family was under the authority of the eldest male, who might take several wives, and ideally sons stayed home with their parents after they married. The family affirmed its solidarity by the religious ritual of honoring its dead ancestors—a ritual that linked the living and the dead, much like ancestor worship in China (see pages 93–94). People commonly lived in extended families: grandparents, uncles and aunts, cousins, and nieces and nephews all lived together in the same house or compound.

Children in poor households worked as soon as they were able. Children in wealthier households faced the age-old irritations of learning reading, writing, and arithmetic. Less attention was paid to daughters than to sons, though in more prosperous families they were often literate. Because girls who had lost their virginity could seldom hope to find good husbands, daughters were customarily married as children, with consummation delayed until they reached puberty.

A wife was expected to have no life apart from her husband. A widow was expected to lead the hard life of the ascetic: sleeping on the ground; eating only one simple meal a day; wearing plain, undyed clothes without jewelry;

CHAPTER LOCATOR | What aspects of nomadic life gave nomads of Central Asia advantages over settled civilizations? | How did Chinggis Khan conquer Eurasia, and how did Mongol conquests change the region?

350 CHAPTER 12 CULTURAL EXCHANGE IN CENTRAL AND SOUTHERN ASIA

and shaving her head. She was viewed as inauspicious to everyone but her children, and she did not attend family festivals. Among high-caste Hindus, a widow would be praised for throwing herself on her husband's funeral pyre. Buddhist sects objected to this practice, called sati, but some Hindu religious authorities declared that by self-immolation a widow could expunge both her own and her husband's sins, so that both would enjoy eternal bliss in Heaven.

Within the home the position of a wife depended on her own intelligence and strength of character. Wives were supposed to be humble, cheerful, and diligent, even toward worthless husbands. As in other patriarchal societies, however, occasionally a woman ruled the household. For women who did not want to accept the strictures of married life, the main way out was to join a Buddhist or Jain religious community (see page 188).

sati
▶ A practice whereby a high-caste Hindu woman would throw herself on her husband's funeral pyre.

QUICK REVIEW

How would you characterize Hindu-Muslim relations during India's medieval period?

How did the Mongol conquests facilitate the spread of religions, inventions, and diseases?

What was the result of India's encounters with Turks, Mongols, and Islam?

How did states develop along the maritime trade routes of Southeast Asia. and beyond?

✓ LearningCurve
Check what you know.

How did states develop along the maritime trade routes of Southeast Asia and beyond?

Angkor Wat Temple

The Khmers built several stone temple complexes at Angkor. This aerial view catches something of the scale of the largest of these complexes, Angkor Wat.
(© Roy Garner/Alamy)

MUCH AS ROMAN CULTURE SPREAD to northern Europe and Chinese culture spread to Korea, Japan, and Vietnam, in the first millennium C.E. Indian learning, technology, and material culture spread to the mainland and islands of Southeast Asia. The spread of Indian culture was facilitated by the growth of maritime trade, but this interchange did not occur uniformly, and by 1400 there were still isolated societies in this region, most notably in the Pacific islands east of Indonesia.

Southeast Asia is a tropical region that is more like India than China. The topography of mainland Southeast Asia is marked by north-south mountain ranges separated by river valleys. It was easy for people to migrate south along these rivers but harder for them to cross the heavily forested mountains that divided the region into areas that had limited contact with each other. The indigenous population was originally mostly Malay, but migrations over the centuries brought many other peoples, including speakers of Austro-Asiatic (such as Vietnamese and Cambodian), Austronesian (such as Malay and Polynesian), and Sino-Tibetan-Burmese (such as Burmese and possibly Thai) languages, some of whom moved to the islands offshore and farther into the Pacific Ocean.

State Formation and Indian Influences

Southeast Asia was long a crossroads. Traders from China, India, Africa, and Europe either passed through the region when traveling from the Indian to the Pacific Ocean, or came for its resources, notably spices.

The northern part of modern Vietnam was under Chinese political control off and on from the second century B.C.E. to the tenth century C.E. (see page 194), but

CHAPTER LOCATOR | What aspects of nomadic life gave nomads of Central Asia advantages over settled civilizations? | How did Chinggis Khan conquer Eurasia, and how did Mongol conquests change the region?

Indian influence was of much greater significance for the rest of Southeast Asia. The first state to appear in historical records, Funan, had its capital in southern Vietnam. In the first to sixth centuries C.E. Funan extended its control over much of Indochina and the Malay Peninsula. Merchants from northwest India would offload their goods and carry them across the narrowest part of the Malay Peninsula. The ports of Funan offered food and lodging to the merchants as they waited for the winds to shift to continue their voyages. Brahmin priests and Buddhist monks from India settled along with the traders, serving the Indian population and attracting local converts. Rulers often invited Indian priests and monks to serve under them.

After the decline of Funan, maritime trade continued to grow, and petty kingdoms appeared in many places. Indian traders frequently established small settlements, generally located on the coast. Contact with the local populations led to intermarriage and the creation of hybrid cultures. Local rulers often adopted Indian customs and values, embraced Hinduism and Buddhism, and learned Sanskrit, India's classical literary language. Sanskrit gave different peoples a common mode of written expression, much as Chinese did in East Asia and Latin did in Europe.

Sanskrit
▶ India's classical literary language.

When Indian traders, migrants, and adventurers entered mainland Southeast Asia, they encountered both long-settled peoples and migrants moving southward from the frontiers of China. As in other extensive migrations, the newcomers fought one another as often as they fought the native populations. In 939 the north Vietnamese became independent of China and extended their power southward along the coast of present-day Vietnam. The Thais had long lived in what is today southwest China and north Myanmar. In the eighth century the Thai tribes united in a confederacy and expanded northward against Tang China. Like China, however, the Thai confederacy fell to the Mongols in 1253. Still farther west another tribal people, the Burmese, migrated to the area of modern Myanmar in the eighth century. They also established a state, which they ruled from their capital, Pagan, and came into contact with India and Sri Lanka.

The most important mainland state was the Khmer (kuh-MAIR) Empire of Cambodia (802–1432), which controlled the heart of the region. The Khmers were

Bayan Relief, Angkor

Among the many relief sculptures at the temples of Angkor are depictions of royal processions, armies at war, trade, cooking, cockfighting, and other scenes of everyday life. In the relief shown here, the boats and fish convey something of the significance of the sea to life in Southeast Asia. (Hervé Champollion/akg-images)

> **PICTURING THE PAST**

ANALYZING THE IMAGE: Find the boat. What do the people on it seem to be doing? What fish and animals do you see in the picture? Can you find the alligator eating a fish?
CONNECTIONS: Why would a ruler devote so many resources to decorating the walls of a temple? Why include scenes like this one?

How did the Mongol conquests facilitate the spread of religions, inventions, and diseases? | What was the result of India's encounters with Turks, Mongols, and Islam? | **How did states develop along the maritime trade routes of Southeast Asia and beyond?** | ☑ LearningCurve Check what you know.

353

indigenous to the area. Their empire eventually extended south to the sea and the northeast Malay Peninsula. Indian influence was pervasive; the impressive temple complex at Angkor Wat built in the early twelfth century was dedicated to the Hindu god Vishnu. Social organization, however, was modeled not on the Indian caste system but on indigenous traditions of social hierarchy. A large part of the population was of slave status. Generally successful in a long series of wars with the Vietnamese, the Khmers reached the peak of their power in 1219 and then gradually declined.

The Srivijayan Maritime Trade Empire

Srivijaya

▶ A maritime empire that held the Strait of Malacca and the waters around Sumatra, Borneo, and Java.

Far different from these land-based states was the maritime empire of Srivijaya, based on the island of Sumatra in modern Indonesia. From the sixth century on, it held the important Strait of Malacca, through which most of the sea traffic between China and India passed. This state, held together as much by alliances as by direct rule, was in many ways like the Gupta state of the same period in India, securing its prominence and binding its vassals and allies through its splendor and the promise of riches through trade.

Much as the Korean and Japanese rulers adapted Chinese models (see pages 195–196), the Srivijayan rulers drew on Indian traditions to justify their rule and organize their state. The Sanskrit writing system was used for government documents, and Indians were often employed as priests, scribes, and administrators. Indian mythology took hold, as did Indian architecture and sculpture. Kings and their courts, the first to embrace Indian culture, consciously spread it to their subjects.

After several centuries of prosperity, Srivijaya suffered a stunning blow in 1025. The Chola state in south India launched a large naval raid and captured the Srivijayan king and capital. Unable to hold their gains, the Indians retreated, but the Srivijayan Empire never regained its vigor.

Buddhism became progressively more dominant in Southeast Asia after 800. Mahayana Buddhism became important in Srivijaya and Vietnam, but Theravada Buddhism, closer to the original Buddhism of early India, became the dominant form in the rest of mainland Southeast Asia. Buddhist missionaries from India and Sri Lanka played a prominent role in these developments. Local converts continued the process by making pilgrimages to India and Sri Lanka to worship and to observe Indian life for themselves.

The Spread of Indian Culture in Comparative Perspective

The social, cultural, and political systems developed in India, China, and Rome all had enormous impact on neighboring peoples whose cultures were originally not as technologically advanced. Some of the mechanisms for cultural spread were similar in all three cases, but differences were important as well.

In the case of Rome and both Han and Tang China, strong states directly ruled outlying regions, bringing their civilizations with them. India's states did not have comparable bureaucratic reach. Outlying areas tended to be in the hands of local lords who had consented to recognize the overlordship of the stronger state. Moreover, most of the time India was politically divided.

The expansion of Indian culture into Southeast Asia thus came not from conquest and the extension of direct political control but from the extension of

CHAPTER LOCATOR | What aspects of nomadic life gave nomads of Central Asia advantages over settled civilizations? | How did Chinggis Khan conquer Eurasia, and how did Mongol conquests change the region?

354 CHAPTER 12
CULTURAL EXCHANGE IN CENTRAL AND SOUTHERN ASIA

trading networks, with missionaries following along. This made it closer to the way Japan adopted features of Chinese culture, often through the intermediary of Korea. In both cases, the cultural exchange was largely voluntary.

The Settlement of the Pacific Islands

Through most of Eurasia, societies became progressively less isolated over time. But in 1400 there still remained many isolated societies, especially in the islands east of modern Indonesia. As discussed in Chapter 1, *Homo sapiens* began settling the western Pacific islands very early, reaching Australia by 50,000 years ago and New Guinea by 35,000 years ago. The process did not stop there, however. The ancient Austronesians (speakers of Austronesian languages) were skilled mariners who settled numerous islands of the Pacific in subsequent centuries, generally following the coasts. Their descendants, the Polynesians, learned how to sail into the open ocean with only the stars, currents, wind patterns, paths of birds, and perhaps paths of whales and dolphins to help them navigate. They reached Tahiti and the Marquesas Islands in the central Pacific by about 200 C.E.

After reaching the central Pacific, Polynesians continued to fan out, in some cases traveling a thousand or more miles away. They reached the Hawaiian Islands in about 300 C.E., Easter Island in perhaps 1000, and New Zealand not until about 1000–1300. There even were groups who sailed west, eventually settling in Madagascar between 200 and 500.

In the more remote islands, such as Hawai'i, Easter Island, and New Zealand, the societies that developed were limited by the small range of domesticated plants and animals that the settlers brought with them and those that were indigenous to the place. Easter Island is perhaps the most extreme case. Only 15 miles wide at its widest point (only 63 square miles in total area), it is 1,300 miles from the nearest inhabited island (Pitcairn) and 2,240 miles from the coast of South America. At some point there was communication with South America, as sweet potatoes originally from there made their way to Easter Island. The

Settlement of the Pacific Islands

community that developed on the island raised chickens and cultivated sweet potatoes, taro, and sugarcane. The population is thought to have reached about fifteen thousand at Easter Island's most prosperous period, which began about 1200 C.E. It was then that its people devoted remarkable efforts to fashioning and erecting the large stone statues that still dot the island.

What led the residents of such a small island to erect more than eight hundred statues, most weighing around ten tons and standing twenty to seventy feet tall? One common theory is that they were central to the islanders' religion and that rival clans competed with each other to erect the most impressive statues. The effort they had to expend to carve them with stone tools, move them to the chosen site, and erect them would have been formidable.

After its heyday, Easter Island suffered severe environmental stress with the decline of its forests. The islanders could not make boats to fish in the ocean, and bird colonies shrank as nesting areas decreased, also reducing the food supply. Scholars still disagree on how much weight to give the many different elements

How did the Mongol conquests facilitate the spread of religions, inventions, and diseases?

What was the result of India's encounters with Turks, Mongols, and Islam?

How did states develop along the maritime trade routes of Southeast Asia and beyond?

✔ LearningCurve
Check what you know.

355

Archaeologists have excavated and restored many of Easter Island's huge statues, which display remarkable stylistic consistency, with the heads disproportionately large and the legs not visible. (Jean-Pierre De Mann/Robert Harding World Imagery)

that contributed to the decline in the prosperity of Easter Island from the age when the statues were erected.

Certainly, early settlers of an island could have a drastic impact on its ecology. When Polynesians first reached New Zealand, they found large birds up to ten feet tall. They hunted them so eagerly that within a century the birds had all but disappeared. Hunting seals and sea lions also led to their rapid depletion. But the islands of New Zealand were much larger than Easter Island, and in time the Maori (the indigenous people of New Zealand) found more sustainable ways to feed themselves, depending more and more on agriculture.

> **QUICK REVIEW**

How did Indian culture come to have such a strong influence on Southeast Asia?

CHAPTER SUMMARY

The pastoral societies that stretched across Eurasia had the great military advantage of being able to raise horses in large numbers and support themselves from their flocks of sheep, goats, and other animals. Nomadic pastoralists generally were organized on the basis of clans and tribes that selected chiefs for their military talent. Much of the time these tribes fought with each other, but several times in history leaders formed larger confederations capable of coordinated attacks on cities and towns.

From the fifth to the twelfth centuries the most successful nomadic groups on the Eurasian steppes were Turks who gained ascendancy in many of the societies from the Middle East to northern India. In the early thirteenth century, the Mongol leader Chinggis Khan conquered much of Eurasia.

After Chinggis's death, the empire was divided into four khanates ruled by four of Chinggis's descendants. For a century the Mongol Empire fostered unprecedented East-West contact. They encouraged trade and often moved craftsmen and other

CHAPTER LOCATOR | What aspects of nomadic life gave nomads of Central Asia advantages over settled civilizations? | How did Chinggis Khan conquer Eurasia, and how did Mongol conquests change the region?

CHAPTER 12
356 CULTURAL EXCHANGE IN CENTRAL AND SOUTHERN ASIA

specialists from one place to another. The Mongols were tolerant of other religions. As more Europeans made their way east, Chinese inventions such as printing and the compass made their way west. Europe especially benefited from the spread of technical and scientific ideas. Diseases also spread, including the Black Death.

India was invaded by the Mongols but not conquered. After the fall of the Gupta Empire in about 480, India was for the next millennium ruled by small kingdoms, which allowed regional cultures to flourish. For several centuries Muslim Turks formed the Delhi sultanate in north India. Over time Islam gained adherents throughout South Asia. Hinduism continued to flourish, but Buddhism declined.

Throughout the medieval period India continued to be the center of active seaborne trade, and this trade helped carry Indian ideas and practices to Southeast Asia. Local rulers used experts from India to establish strong states, such as the Khmer kingdom and the Srivijayan kingdom. Buddhism became the dominant religion throughout the region, though Hinduism also played an important role. The Pacific islands east of Indonesia remained isolated culturally for centuries.

 CONNECTIONS The societies of Eurasia became progressively more connected to each other during the centuries discussed in this chapter. One element promoting connection was the military superiority of the nomadic warriors of the steppe: first the Turks, then the Mongols, who conquered many of the settled civilizations near them. Invading Turks brought Islam to India. Connection between societies also came from maritime trade across the Indian Ocean and East Asia. Maritime trade was a key element in the spread of Indian culture to both the mainland and insular Southeast Asia. Other elements connecting these societies included Sanskrit as a language of administration and missionaries who brought both Hinduism and Buddhism far beyond their homelands.

East Asia was a key element in both the empires created by nomadic horsemen and the South Asian maritime trading networks. As discussed in Chapter 13, before East Asia had to cope with the rise of the Mongols, it experienced one of its most prosperous periods, during which China, Korea, and Japan became more distinct culturally. China's economy boomed during the Song Dynasty, and the scholar-official class, defined through the civil service examination, came more and more to dominate culture. In Korea and Japan, by contrast, aristocrats and military men gained ascendancy. Although China, Korea, and Japan all drew on both Confucian and Buddhist teachings, they ended up with elites as distinct as the Chinese scholar-official, the Korean aristocrat, and the Japanese samurai.

How did the Mongol conquests facilitate the spread of religions, inventions, and diseases? | What was the result of India's encounters with Turks, Mongols, and Islam? | How did states develop along the maritime trade routes of Southeast Asia and beyond? | ✔ **LearningCurve** Check what you know.

CHAPTER 12 STUDY GUIDE

STEP 1

GET STARTED ONLINE

 LearningCurve

Now that you've read the chapter, make it stick by completing the LearningCurve activity.

STEP 2

EXPLAIN WHY IT MATTERS

Put your reading into practice. Identify each term below, and then explain why it matters in world history.

TERM	WHO OR WHAT & WHEN	WHY IT MATTERS
nomads (p. 330)		
steppe (p. 330)		
yurts (p. 333)		
Chinggis Khan (p. 336)		
khanates (p. 336)		
tax-farming (p. 339)		
protected people (p. 346)		
jati (p. 350)		
sati (p. 351)		
Sanskrit (p. 353)		
Srivijaya (p. 354)		

STEP 3

MOVE BEYOND THE BASICS

To demonstrate a more advanced understanding of the connections Central Asian nomads helped forge among the civilizations of Eurasia, fill in the chart below with descriptions of the impact of nomadic invaders on religion, government, and commerce in China and India. What role did nomadic peoples play in stimulating cultural and commercial exchange in China and India?

	Religion	Government	Commerce
Nomadic influences in China			
Nomadic influences in India			

CENTRAL ASIAN NOMADS

► What military advantages explain the ability of Central Asian nomads to defeat the large armies of settled peoples?

► In what ways did nomadic and settled peoples cooperate in Eurasia? Under what circumstances did cooperation turn into conflict?

THE MONGOLS

► What light does the rise of Chinggis Khan to power shed on the nature of Mongol politics and society?

► How did Mongol military and political activities accelerate regional exchange? Who gained and who lost as a result of Mongol activities?

INDIA AND SOUTHEAST ASIA

► How did the arrival of Islamic conquerors alter the Indian religious landscape?

► How and why did Indian culture spread in Southeast Asia? How did the relationship between India and Southeast Asia differ from the relationship between China and its neighbors?

LOOKING BACK, LOOKING AHEAD

► How had the settled states of Eurasia responded to the threat posed by nomadic peoples prior to the rise of the Turks and the Mongols? Why did the Turks and the Mongols prove more dangerous than other nomadic confederations?

► How did the Mongols contribute to the process of global integration, a process that accelerated in the centuries after their decline?

> **IN YOUR OWN WORDS**

Imagine that you must give an oral report to the class answering the following question: **How did Mongol conquests and maritime trade facilitate cultural exchange in central and southern Asia? What would be the most important points and why?**

13

STATES AND CULTURES IN EAST ASIA

800–1400

> **Why did Chinese, Korean, and Japanese society and culture diverge after 800?** Chapter 13 examines developments in East Asia between 800 and 1400. During this period East Asia was the most advanced region of the world. The Chinese economy was strong, and China's methods of production were highly sophisticated. Philosophy and the arts all flourished. China's system of government was also advanced for its time. These strengths were not, however, matched with corresponding military might, and in 1279 China was conquered by the Mongols. During the previous millennium, basic elements of Chinese culture had spread beyond China's borders. Beginning around 800, however, the pendulum shifted toward cultural differentiation as Japan, Korea, and China developed in distinctive ways.

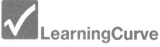**LearningCurve**

After reading the chapter, use LearningCurve to retain what you've read.

Song Chancellor Known for his stern demeanor, Sima Guang (1019–1086) was an eminent historian and a leading official.

> What made possible the expansion of the Chinese economy, and what were the outcomes of this economic growth?

> How did the civil service examinations and the scholar-official class shape Chinese society and culture, and what impact did the Mongol conquest have on them?

> How did Korean society and culture develop in an age when its northern neighbors were Khitans, Jurchens, and Mongols?

> How did the Heian form of government contribute to the cultural flowering of Japan in the period?

> What were the causes and consequences of military rule in Japan?

What made possible the expansion of the Chinese economy, and what were the outcomes of this economic growth?

Chinese Paper Money

Chinese paper currency indicated the unit of currency and the date and place of issue. The Mongols continued the use of paper money, as this note from the Mongol period attests. (National Museum of Chinese History, Beijing, China/Ancient Art and Architecture Collection Ltd./The Bridgeman Art Library)

CHINESE HISTORIANS TRADITIONALLY VIEWED dynasties as following a standard cyclical pattern. Founders were vigorous men able to recruit capable followers to serve as officials and generals. Over time, however, emperors born in the palace would get used to luxury and lack the founders' strength and wisdom. Families with wealth or political power would find ways to avoid taxes, forcing the government to impose heavier taxes on the poor. As a result, impoverished peasants would flee, the morale of those in the government and armies would decline, and the dynasty would find itself able neither to maintain internal peace nor to defend its borders.

Viewed in terms of this theory of the **dynastic cycle**, by 800 the Tang Dynasty (see pages 190–191) was in decline. It had ruled China for nearly two centuries, and its high point was in the past. A massive rebellion had wracked it in the mid-eighth century, and powerful enemies were menacing its borders. Many of the centralizing features of the government had been abandoned, with power falling more and more to regional military governors.

dynastic cycle

▶ The theory that Chinese dynasties go through a predictable cycle from early vigor and growth to subsequent decline as administrators become lax and the well-off find ways to avoid paying taxes, cutting state revenues.

CHAPTER LOCATOR | What made possible the expansion of the Chinese economy, and what were the outcomes? | How did the civil service examinations and the scholar-official class shape Chinese society?

CHAPTER 13
362 STATES AND CULTURES IN EAST ASIA

794–1185
Heian period in Japan

804
Two Japanese Buddhist monks, Saichō and Kūkai,
travel to China

935–1392
Koryŏ Dynasty in Korea

960–1279
Song Dynasty in China; emergence of scholar-official class;
invention of movable type

995–1027
Fujiwara Michinaga dominant at Heian court

ca. 1000–1010
The Tale of Genji

1119
First reported use of compass

1120s
First government-issued paper money introduced by Song

1126
Song loss of north China to the Jurchens; Song capital
relocated to Hangzhou

1130–1200
Zhu Xi, Neo-Confucian philosopher

1185–1333
Kamakura Shogunate in Japan; Zen Buddhism flourishes

1234–1368
Mongols' Yuan Dynasty in China

ca. 1275–1292
Marco Polo travels in China

Historically, Chinese political theorists always assumed that a strong, centralized government was better than a weak one or than political division, but, if
anything, the Tang toward the end of its dynastic cycle seems to have been both
intellectually and economically more vibrant than the early Tang had been. Less
control from the central government seems to have stimulated trade and economic
growth.

A government census conducted in 742 shows that China's population was
approximately 50 million. Over the next three centuries, with the expansion of
wet-field rice cultivation in central and south China, the country's food supply
steadily increased, and its population reached 100 million by 1100.

Agricultural prosperity and denser settlement patterns aided commercial-
ization of the economy. Farmers in Song China no longer merely aimed at self-
sufficiency. Instead, farmers sold their surpluses and used their profits to buy
charcoal, tea, oil, and wine. In many places farmers specialized in commercial
crops, such as sugar, oranges, cotton, silk, and tea. The need to transport the products of interregional trade stimulated the inland and coastal shipping industries.

As marketing increased, demand for money grew enormously, leading eventually to the creation of the world's first paper money. To avoid the weight and
bulk of coins for large transactions, local merchants in late Tang times started
trading receipts from deposit shops where they had left money or goods. The
early Song authorities awarded a small set of these shops a monopoly on the issuing of these certificates of deposit, and in the 1120s the government took over
the system, producing the world's first government-issued paper money.

With the intensification of trade, merchants became progressively more
specialized and organized. They set up partnerships and joint stock companies.
In the large cities merchants were organized into guilds according to the type

How did Korean society
develop when its northern
neighbors were Khitans,
Jurchens, and Mongols?

How did the Heian form
of government contribute
to the cultural flowering
of Japan in the period?

What were the causes
and consequences of
military rule in Japan?

☑ LearningCurve
Check what you know.

of product sold, and they arranged sales from wholesalers to shop owners and periodically set prices.

Foreign trade also flourished in the Song period. Chinese ships began to displace Indian and Arab merchants in the South Seas, and ship design was improved in several ways. Watertight bulkheads improved buoyancy and protected cargo. Stern-mounted rudders improved steering. Some of the ships were powered by both oars and sails and were large enough to hold several hundred men.

Also important to oceangoing travel was the perfection of the compass. The ability of a magnetic needle to point north had been known for some time, but in Song times the needle was reduced in size and attached to a fixed stem (rather than floated in water). In some instances it was put in a small protective case with a glass top, making it suitable for sea travel. The first reports of a compass used in this way date to 1119.

The Song also witnessed many advances in industrial techniques. Heavy industry, especially iron, grew astoundingly. With advances in metallurgy, iron production reached around 125,000 tons per year in 1078, a sixfold increase over the output in 800. Much of the iron was put to military purposes. Mass-production methods were used to make iron armor in small, medium, and large sizes. High-quality steel for swords was made through high-temperature metallurgy. The needs of the army also brought Chinese engineers to experiment with the use of gunpowder. In the twelfth-century wars against the Jurchens (see page 333), those defending a besieged city used gunpowder to propel projectiles at the enemy.

compass

▶ A tool developed in Song times to aid in navigation at sea; it consisted of a magnetic needle that would point north and was placed in a small protective case.

Transplanting Rice

To get the maximum yield per plot and to make it possible to grow two crops in the same field, Chinese farmers grew rice seedlings in a seedbed and then, when a field was free, transplanted the seedlings into the flooded field. Because the Song government wanted to promote up-to-date agricultural technology, in the twelfth century it commissioned a set of twelve illustrations of the steps to be followed. This painting comes from a later version of those illustrations. (*Tilling Rice*, Yuan Dynasty [ink and colour on paper], Qi, Cheng [13th century] [attr. to]/Freer Gallery of Art, Smithsonian Institution, Washington, D.C., U.S.A./The Bridgeman Art Library)

CHAPTER LOCATOR | What made possible the expansion of the Chinese economy, and what were the outcomes? | How did the civil service examinations and the scholar-official class shape Chinese society?

CHAPTER 13
364   STATES AND CULTURES IN EAST ASIA

Economic expansion fueled the growth of cities. Dozens of cities had 50,000 or more residents, and quite a few had more than 100,000, very large populations compared to other places in the world at the time. China's two successive capitals, Kaifeng (kigh-fuhng) and Hangzhou (hahng-joh), each had an estimated 1 million residents.

The medieval economic revolution shifted the economic center of China south to the Yangzi River drainage area. This area had many advantages over the north China plain. Rice, which grew in the south, provides more calories per unit of land and therefore allows denser settlement. The milder temperatures often allowed two crops to be grown on the same plot of land, first a summer crop of rice and then a winter crop of wheat or vegetables. The abundance of rivers and streams facilitated shipping, which reduced the cost of transportation and thus made regional specialization economically more feasible.

Ordinary people benefited from the Song economic revolution in many ways. There were more opportunities for the sons of farmers to leave agriculture and find work in cities. Those who stayed in agriculture had a better chance of improving their situations by taking up sideline production of wine, charcoal, paper, or textiles. Energetic farmers who grew cash crops such as sugar, tea, mulberry leaves (for silk), and cotton (recently introduced from India) could grow rich. Greater interregional trade led to the availability of more goods at rural markets.

QUICK REVIEW <

How did the Chinese economic revolution change life in the countryside?

How did Korean society develop when its northern neighbors were Khitans, Jurchens, and Mongols?

How did the Heian form of government contribute to the cultural flowering of Japan in the period?

What were the causes and consequences of military rule in Japan?

☑ LearningCurve
Check what you know.

How did the civil service examinations and the scholar-official class shape Chinese society and culture, and what impact did the Mongol conquest have on them?

IN THE TENTH CENTURY Tang China broke up into separate contending states, some of which had non-Chinese rulers. The two states that proved to be long lasting were the Song, which came to control almost all of China proper south of the Great Wall, and the Liao, whose ruling house was Khitan and which held the territory of modern Beijing and areas north (Map 13.1). Although the Song Dynasty had a much larger population, the Liao was militarily the stronger of the two. In the early twelfth century the Liao state was defeated by the Jurchens, another non-Chinese people, who founded the Jin Dynasty and went on to conquer most of north China, leaving Song to control only the south. After a century the Jin Dynasty was defeated by the Mongols, who extended their Yuan Dynasty to control all of China by 1276.

The Song Dynasty

The founder of the Song Dynasty, Taizu (r. 960–976), was a general whose troops elevated him to emperor (somewhat reminiscent of Roman practice). To make sure

CHAPTER LOCATOR | What made possible the expansion of the Chinese economy, and what were the outcomes? | **How did the civil service examinations and the scholar-official class shape Chinese society?**

366 CHAPTER 13
STATES AND CULTURES IN EAST ASIA

that such an act could not happen in the future, Taizu retired or rotated his generals and assigned civil officials to supervise them. In time these civil bureaucrats came to dominate every aspect of Song government and society. The civil service examination system established during the Sui Dynasty (see page 189) was greatly expanded to provide the dynasty with a constant flow of men trained in the Confucian classics.

Curbing the generals' power ended warlordism but did not solve the military problem of defending against the nomadic Khitans' Liao Dynasty to the north. After several attempts to push the Liao back beyond the Great Wall, the Song concluded a peace treaty with them. The Song agreed to make huge annual payments of gold and silk to the Khitans, in a sense paying them not to invade. Even so, the Song rulers had to maintain a standing army of more than a million men. By the middle of the eleventh century military expenses consumed half the government's revenues.

MAP 13.1 ■ **East Asia in 1000 and 1200**

The Song empire did not extend as far as its predecessor, the Tang, and faced powerful rivals to the north — the Liao Dynasty of the Khitans and the Xia Dynasty of the Tanguts. Koryŏ Korea maintained regular contact with Song China, but Japan, by the late Heian period, was no longer deeply involved with the mainland. By 1200 military families dominated both Korea and Japan, but the borders were little changed. On the mainland the Liao Dynasty had been overthrown by the Jurchens' Jin Dynasty, which also seized the northern third of the Song empire. Because the Song relocated its capital to Hangzhou in the south, this period is called the Southern Song period.

> MAPPING THE PAST

ANALYZING THE MAP: What were the countries of East Asia in 1000? What were the major differences in 1200?

CONNECTIONS: What connections do you see between the length of their northern borders and the histories of China, Korea, and Japan?

How did Korean society develop when its northern neighbors were Khitans, Jurchens, and Mongols?

How did the Heian form of government contribute to the cultural flowering of Japan in the period?

What were the causes and consequences of military rule in Japan?

☑ LearningCurve
Check what you know.

In the early twelfth century the military situation rapidly worsened when the Khitan state was destroyed by another tribal confederation led by the Jurchens, who quickly realized how easy it would be to defeat the Song. When they marched into the Song capital in 1126, they captured the emperor and former emperor and took them and the entire court into captivity. Song forces rallied around one of the emperor's sons who had escaped capture, and this prince re-established a Song court in the south at Hangzhou (see Map 13.1). This Southern Song Dynasty controlled only about two-thirds of the former Song territories, but the social, cultural, and intellectual life there remained vibrant until the Song fell to the Mongols in 1279.

The Scholar-Officials and Neo-Confucianism

The Song period saw the full flowering of one of the most distinctive features of Chinese civilization, the scholar-official class certified through highly competitive civil service examinations. This elite was both broader and better educated than the elites of earlier periods in Chinese history. Once the examination system was fully developed, aristocratic habits and prejudices largely disappeared.

To prepare for the examinations, men had to memorize the classics. They also had to master specific forms of composition, including poetry, and be ready to discuss policy issues, citing appropriate historical examples. Those who became officials this way had usually tried the exams several times and were on average a little over thirty years of age when they succeeded.

The invention of printing should be given some credit for the trend toward a better-educated elite. Tang craftsmen developed the art of carving words and pictures into wooden blocks, inking the blocks, and pressing paper onto them. Each block held an entire page of text. Such whole-page blocks were used for printing as early as the middle of the ninth century, and in the eleventh century movable type (one piece of type for each character) was invented, but it was rarely used because whole-block printing was cheaper. In China, as in Europe a couple of centuries later, the introduction of printing dramatically lowered the price of books, thus aiding the spread of literacy.

Among the upper class the availability of cheaper books enabled scholars to amass their own libraries. Song publishers printed the classics of Chinese literature. Works on philosophy, science, and medicine were also avidly consumed, as were Buddhist texts. Han and Tang poetry and historical works became the models for Song writers. One popular literary innovation was the encyclopedia, which first appeared in the Song period.

scholar-official class
► Chinese educated elite that included both scholars and officials. The officials had usually gained office by passing the highly competitive civil service examination. Scholars without office had often studied for the examinations but failed repeatedly.

examination system
► A system of selecting officials based on competitive written examinations.

movable type
► A system of printing in which one piece of type is used for each unique character.

> **The Accomplishments of Notable Scholar Officials:**

- Ouyang Xiu: wrote love songs, histories, and the first analytical catalogue of rubbings of ancient stone and bronze inscriptions
- Sima Guang: wrote a narrative history of China, twenty-seven hundred poems, and eight hundred letters; was also an esteemed painter, calligrapher, and theorist of the arts
- Su Song: constructed an eighty-foot-tall mechanical clock that told the time of day, the day of the month, the phase of the moon, and the position of certain stars and planets in the sky

CHAPTER LOCATOR | What made possible the expansion of the Chinese economy, and what were the outcomes? | **How did the civil service examinations and the scholar-official class shape Chinese society?**

CHAPTER 13
368 STATES AND CULTURES IN EAST ASIA

On a Mountain Path in Spring

With spare, sketchy strokes, the court painter Ma Yuan (ca. 1190–1225) depicts a scholar on an outing accompanied by his boy servant carrying a lute. The scholar gazes into the mist, his eyes attracted by a bird in flight. The poetic couplet was inscribed by Emperor Ningzong (r. 1194–1124), at whose court Ma Yuan served. It reads: "Brushed by his sleeves, wild flowers dance in the wind. / Fleeing from him, hidden birds cut short their songs." (National Palace Museum, Taipei, Taiwan/photo © AISA/ The Everett Collection)

> PICTURING THE PAST

ANALYZING THE IMAGE: Find the key elements in this picture: the scholar, the servant boy, the bird, the willow tree. Are these elements skillfully conveyed? Are there other elements in the painting that you find hard to read?

CONNECTIONS: What do you think is the reason for writing a poetic couplet on this painting? Does it enhance the experience of viewing the painting or detract from it?

The life of the educated man involved more than study for the civil service examinations and service in office. Many took to refined pursuits such as collecting antiques or old books and practicing the arts. In the Song period, the engagement of the elite with the arts led to extraordinary achievement in calligraphy and painting, especially landscape painting. A large share of the social life of upper-class men was centered on these refined pastimes, as they gathered to compose or criticize poetry, to view each other's art treasures, and to patronize young talents. (See "Individuals in Society: Shen Gua," page 370.)

Besides politics, scholars also debated issues in ethics and metaphysics. For several centuries Buddhism had been more vital than Confucianism. Beginning in the late Tang period, Confucian teachers began claiming that the teachings of the Confucian sages contained all the wisdom one needed and that a true Confucian would reject Buddhist teachings. During the eleventh century many Confucian teachers urged students to set their sights not on exam success but on the higher goals of attaining the wisdom of the sages. Metaphysical theories about the workings of the cosmos in terms of *li* (principle) and *qi* (vital energy) were developed in response to the challenge of the sophisticated metaphysics of Buddhism.

Neo-Confucianism, as this movement is generally termed, was more fully developed in the twelfth century by the immensely learned Zhu Xi (joo shee)

Neo-Confucianism
▶ The revival of Confucian thinking that began in the eleventh century, characterized by the goal of attaining the wisdom of the sages, not exam success.

How did Korean society develop when its northern neighbors were Khitans, Jurchens, and Mongols?

How did the Heian form of government contribute to the cultural flowering of Japan in the period?

What were the causes and consequences of military rule in Japan?

☑ LearningCurve
Check what you know.

In the eleventh century it was not rare for Chinese men of letters to have broad interests, but few could compare to Shen Gua (1031–1095), a man who tried his hand at everything from mathematics, geography, economics, engineering, medicine, divination, and archaeology to military strategy and diplomacy.

Shen Gua's father was an official and Shen Gua often accompanied him on his assignments, which built up his knowledge of geography. In 1063 he passed the civil service examinations, and in 1066 he received a post in the capital. He eventually held high astronomical, ritual, and financial posts and became involved in waterworks and the construction of defense walls. He was sent as an envoy to the Khitans in 1075 to try to settle a boundary dispute. When a military campaign that he advised failed in 1082, he was demoted and later retired to write.

It is from his book of miscellaneous notes that we know the breadth of his interests. In one note Shen describes how, on assignment to inspect the frontier, he made a relief map of wood and glue-soaked sawdust to show the mountains, roads, rivers, and passes. The emperor was so impressed when he saw it that he ordered all the border prefectures to make relief maps. Elsewhere Shen describes the use of petroleum and explains how to make movable type from clay. Shen Gua often applied a mathematical approach to issues that his contemporaries did not think of in those terms. He once computed the total number of possible situations on a Go board, and another time he calculated the longest possible military campaign given the limits of human carriers, who had to carry their own food as well as food for the soldiers.

Shen Gua is especially known for his scientific explanations. He explained the deflection of the compass from due south. He identified petrified bamboo and from its existence argued that the region where it was found must have been much warmer and more humid in ancient times. He argued against the theory that tides are caused by the rising and setting of the sun, demonstrating that they correlate with the cycles of the moon. He proposed switching from a lunar calendar to a solar one of 365 days, saying that even though his contemporaries would reject his idea, "surely in the future some will adopt my idea." To convince his readers that the sun and the moon

Shen Gua played Go with white and black markers on a grid-like board like this one. (Courtesy of Library of Congress, LC-USZC4-8471/8472)

were spherical, not flat, he suggested that they cover a ball with fine powder on one side and then look at it obliquely. The powder was the part of the moon illuminated by the sun, and as the viewer looked at it obliquely, the white part would be crescent shaped, like a waxing moon. Shen Gua, however, did not realize that the sun and moon had entirely different orbits, and he explained why they did not collide by positing that both were composed of *qi* (vital energy) and had form but not substance.

Shen Gua also wrote on medicine and criticized his contemporaries for paying more attention to old treatises than to clinical experience. Yet he, too, was sometimes stronger on theory than on observation. In one note he argued that longevity pills could be made from cinnabar. He reasoned that if cinnabar could be transformed in one direction, it ought to be susceptible to transformation in the opposite direction as well. Therefore, since melted cinnabar causes death, solid cinnabar should prevent death.

1. How did Shen Gua's travels add to his curiosity about the material world?
2. In what ways could Shen Gua have used his scientific interests in his work as a government official?
3. How does Shen Gua's understanding of the natural world compare to that of the early Greeks? (See pages 128–130.)

ONLINE DOCUMENT PROJECT

What cultural pursuits interested the scholar-official class? View images from the Song period, and then complete a quiz and writing assignment based on the evidence and details from this chapter. *See inside the front cover to learn more.*

(1130–1200). Besides serving in office, he wrote, compiled, or edited almost a hundred books. Although he was treated as a political threat during his lifetime, within decades of his death his writings came to be considered orthodox, and in subsequent centuries candidates for the examinations had to be familiar with his commentaries on the classics.

Women's Lives in Song Times

Families who could afford it usually tried to keep their wives and daughters within the walls of the house, rather than let them work in the fields or in shops or inns. At home there was plenty for them to do. Not only was there the work of tending children and preparing meals, but spinning, weaving, and sewing were considered women's work as well and took a great deal of time. Families that raised silkworms also needed women to do much of the work of caring for the worms. Within the home women generally had considerable say and took an active interest in issues such as the selection of marriage partners for their children.

Women tended to marry between the ages of sixteen and twenty. Their husbands were, on average, a couple of years older than they were. Marriages were arranged by their parents, who would have either called on a professional matchmaker or turned to a friend or relative for suggestions. Before a wedding took place, written agreements were exchanged, listing the prospective bride's and groom's birth dates, parents, and grandparents; the gifts that would be exchanged; and the dowry the bride would bring.

The young bride's first priority was to try to win over her mother-in-law. One way to do this was to quickly bear a son for the family. Within the patrilineal system, a woman fully secured her position in the family by becoming the mother of one of the men. Every community had older women skilled in midwifery who were called to help when a woman went into labor. If the family was well-to-do, arrangements might be made for a wet nurse to help her take care of the newborn.

Women frequently had four, five, or six children, but likely one or more would die in infancy.

Woman Attendant

The Song emperors were patrons of a still-extant temple in northern China that enshrined a statue of the "holy mother," the mother of the founder of the ancient Zhou Dynasty. The forty-two maids who attend her, one of whom is shown here, seem to have been modeled on the palace ladies who attended Song emperors. (Taiyuan Jinci/Goddess Hall/Uniphoto Press International Japan/Art and Architecture Collection Ltd.)

If a son reached adulthood and married before the woman herself was widowed, she would be considered fortunate, for she would have always had an adult man who could take care of business for her—first her husband, then her grown son.

A woman with a healthy and prosperous husband faced another challenge in middle age: her husband could bring home a **concubine**. Wives outranked concubines and could give them orders in the house, but a concubine had her own ways of getting back through her hold on the husband. The children born to a concubine were considered just as much children of the family as the wife's children, and if the wife had had only daughters and the concubine had a son, the wife would find herself dependent on the concubine's son in her old age.

Neo-Confucianism is sometimes blamed for a decline in the status of women in Song times, largely because one of the best known of the Neo-Confucian teachers, Cheng Yi, once told a follower that it would be better for a widow to die of starvation than to lose her virtue by remarrying. In later centuries this saying was often quoted to justify pressuring widows, even very young ones, to stay with their husbands' families and not remarry. In Song times, however, widows frequently remarried.

It is true that **foot binding** began during the Song Dynasty, but it was not recommended by Neo-Confucian teachers; rather it was associated with the pleasure quarters and with women's efforts to beautify themselves. Mothers bound the feet of girls aged five to eight with long strips of cloth to keep them from growing and to bend the four smaller toes under to make the foot narrow and arched. The hope was that the girl would be judged more beautiful. Foot binding spread gradually during Song times but was probably still largely an elite practice. In later centuries it became extremely common in north and central China, eventually spreading to all classes. Women with bound feet were less mobile than women with natural feet, but only those who could afford servants bound their feet so tightly that walking was difficult.

concubine

▶ A woman contracted to a man as a secondary spouse; although subordinate to the wife, her sons were considered legitimate heirs.

foot binding

▶ The practice of binding the feet of girls with long strips of cloth to keep them from growing large.

CHAPTER LOCATOR | What made possible the expansion of the Chinese economy, and what were the outcomes? | How did the civil service examinations and the scholar-official class shape Chinese society?

CHAPTER 13
372 STATES AND CULTURES IN EAST ASIA

China Under Mongol Rule

As discussed in Chapter 12, the Mongols conquered China in stages, gaining much of north China by 1215 and all of it by 1234, but not taking the south till the 1270s. The north suffered the most devastation. The non-Chinese rulers in the north, the Jin Dynasty of the Jurchen thought they had the strongest army known to history. Yet Mongol tactics frustrated them. The Mongols would take a city, plunder it, and then withdraw, letting the Jin take it back and deal with the resulting food shortages and destruction. Under these circumstances, Jurchen power rapidly collapsed.

Not until Khubilai was Great Khan was the Song Dynasty defeated and south China brought under the control of the Mongol's Yuan Dynasty. Non-Chinese rulers had gained control of north China several times in Chinese history, but none of them had been able to secure control of the region south of the Yangzi River, which required a navy. By the 1260s Khubilai had put Chinese shipbuilders to work building a fleet, crucial to his victory over Song (see page 336).

Life in China under the Mongols was much like life in China under earlier alien rulers. Once order was restored, people did their best to get on with their lives. Some were deprived of their land, business, or freedom and suffered real hardship. Yet people still spoke Chinese, followed Chinese customary practices in dividing their family property, made offerings at local temples, and celebrated the new year and other customary festivals. Teachers still taught students the classics, scholars continued to write books, and books continued to be printed.

The Mongols, like other foreign rulers before them, did not see anything particularly desirable in the social mobility of Chinese society. Preferring stability, they assigned people hereditary occupations, occupations that came with obligations to the state. The Mongols also classified the population into four grades, with the Mongols occupying the top grade. Next came various non-Chinese, such as the Uighurs and Persians. Below them were Chinese former subjects of the Jurchen, called the Han. At the bottom were the former subjects of the Song, called southerners.

The reason for codifying ethnic differences this way was to preserve the Mongols' privileges as conquerors. Chinese were not allowed to take Mongol names, and great efforts were made to keep them from passing as Mongols or marrying Mongols. To keep Chinese from rebelling, they were forbidden to own weapons or congregate in public.

As the Mongols captured Chinese territory, they recruited Chinese into their armies and government. Although some refused to serve the Mongols, others argued that the Chinese would fare better if Chinese were the administrators and could shield Chinese society from the most brutal effects of Mongol rule.

Nevertheless, government service, which had long been central to the identity and income of the educated elite in China, was not as widely available under the Mongols. The Mongols reinstituted the civil service examinations in 1315, but filled only about 2 percent of the positions in the bureaucracy through it and reserved half of those places for Mongols.

The scholar-official elite without government employment turned to alternative ways to support themselves. Those who did not have land to live off of found work as physicians, fortune-tellers, children's teachers, Daoist priests, publishers,

How did Korean society develop when its northern neighbors were Khitans, Jurchens, and Mongols? | How did the Heian form of government contribute to the cultural flowering of Japan in the period? | What were the causes and consequences of military rule in Japan? | ✓ LearningCurve Check what you know.

373

booksellers, or playwrights. Many took leadership roles at the local level, such as founding academies for Confucian learning or promoting local charitable ventures. Through such activities, scholars without government offices could assert the importance of civil over military values and see themselves as trustees of the Confucian tradition.

Since the Mongols wanted to extract wealth from China, they had every incentive to develop the economy. They encouraged trade both within China and beyond its borders and tried to keep paper money in circulation. They repaired the Grand Canal, which had been ruined during their initial conquest of north China. Chinese industries with strong foreign markets, such as porcelain, thrived. Nevertheless, the economic expansion of late Tang and Song times did not continue under the alien rule of the Jurchens and Mongols.

The Mongols' Yuan Dynasty began a rapid decline in the 1330s as disease, rebellions, and poor leadership led to disorder throughout the country. When a Chinese strongman succeeded in consolidating the south, the Mongol rulers retreated to Mongolia before he could take Beijing. By 1368 the Yuan Dynasty had given way to a new Chinese-led dynasty: the Ming.

> **QUICK REVIEW**

What values and priorities were associated with the scholar-official class?

CHAPTER LOCATOR | What made possible the expansion of the Chinese economy, and what were the outcomes? | How did the civil service examinations and the scholar-official class shape Chinese society?

CHAPTER 13
374 STATES AND CULTURES IN EAST ASIA

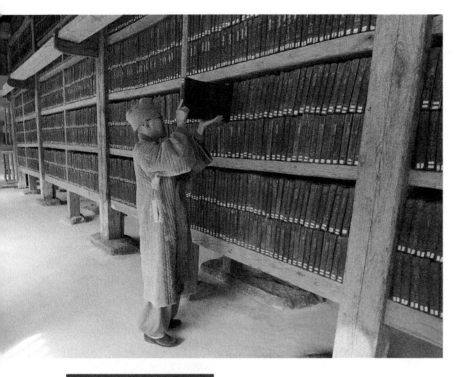

Wooden Blocks for Printing

The Heainsa Buddhist Temple in Korea has preserved the more than eighty thousand woodblocks used to print the huge Buddhist canon in the thirteenth century. The monk shown here is replacing a block. All the blocks are carved on both sides and stabilized by wooden frames that have kept them from warping. (© OUR PLACE THE WORLD HERITAGE COLLECTION, www.ourplaceworldheritage.com)

How did Korean society and culture develop in an age when its northern neighbors were Khitans, Jurchens, and Mongols?

DURING THE SILLA PERIOD, Korea was strongly tied to Tang China and avidly copied China's model (see page 195). This changed along with much else in North Asia between 800 and 1400. In this period Korea lived more in the shadows of the powerful states of the Khitans, Jurchens, and Mongols than of the Chinese.

The Silla Dynasty began to decline after the king was killed in a revolt in 780. For the next 155 years, rebellions and coups d'état followed one after the other, as different groups of nobles placed their candidates on the throne and killed as many of their opponents as they could.

The dynasty that emerged from this confusion was called Koryŏ (KAW-ree-oh) (935–1392). (The English word *Korea* derives from the name of this dynasty.) During this time Korea developed more independently of the China model than it had in Silla times. This was not because the Chinese model was rejected; the Koryŏ capital was laid out on the Chinese model, and the government was closely patterned on the Tang system. But despite Chinese influence, Korean society remained deeply aristocratic.

| How did Korean society develop when its northern neighbors were Khitans, Jurchens, and Mongols? | How did the Heian form of government contribute to the cultural flowering of Japan in the period? | What were the causes and consequences of military rule in Japan? | ✓ LearningCurve Check what you know. |

The founder of the dynasty, Wang Kon (877–943), was a man of relatively obscure background, and he needed the support of the old aristocracy to maintain control. His successors introduced civil service examinations on the Chinese model, as well as examinations for Buddhist clergy, but because the aristocrats were the best educated and the government schools admitted only the sons of aristocrats, this system served primarily to solidify their control.

At the other end of the social scale, the number of people in the serf-slave stratum seems to have increased. This lowborn stratum included not only privately held slaves but also large numbers of government slaves as well as government workers in mines, porcelain factories, and other government industries. Sometimes entire villages or groups of villages were considered lowborn. There were occasional slave revolts, and some freed slaves did rise in status, but prejudice against anyone with slave ancestors was intense. In China and Japan, by contrast, slavery was a much more minor element in the social landscape.

The commercial economy declined in Korea during this period. Except for the capital, there were no cities of commercial importance, and in the countryside the use of money declined. One industry that did flourish was ceramics.

Buddhism remained strong throughout Korea, and monasteries became major centers of art and learning. As in Song China and Kamakura Japan, Chan (Zen) and Tiantai (Tendai) were the leading Buddhist teachings (see page 191). The founder of the Koryŏ Dynasty attributed the dynasty's success to the Buddha's protection, and he and his successors were ardent patrons of the church. The entire Buddhist canon was printed in the eleventh century and again in the thirteenth. As in medieval Europe, aristocrats who entered the church occupied the major abbacies. Monasteries played the same roles as they did in China and Japan, such as engaging in money-lending and charitable works. As in Japan (but not China), some monasteries accumulated military power.

The Koryŏ Dynasty was preserved in name long after the ruling family had lost most of its power. In 1170 the palace guards massacred the civil officials at court and placed a new king on the throne. After incessant infighting among the generals and a series of coups, in 1196 the general Ch'oe Ch'ung-hon took control. The domination of Korea by the Ch'oe family was much like the contemporaneous situation in Japan, where warrior bands were seizing power. Moreover, because the Ch'oes were content to dominate the government while leaving the Koryŏ king on the throne, they had much in common with the Japanese shoguns, who followed a similar strategy.

Korea, from early times, recognized China as being in many ways senior to it, but when strong non-Chinese states emerged to its north in Manchuria, Korea was ready to accommodate them as well. Koryŏ's first neighbor to the north was the Khitan state of Liao, which in 1010 invaded and sacked the capital. To avoid destruction, Koryŏ acceded to vassal status, but Liao invaded again in 1018. This time Koryŏ was able to repel the nomadic Khitans. Afterward a defensive wall was built across the Korean peninsula south of the Yalu River. When the Jurchens and their Jin Dynasty supplanted the Khitans' Liao Dynasty, Koryŏ agreed to send them tribute as well.

As mentioned in Chapter 12, Korea was conquered by the Mongols, and the figurehead Koryŏ kings were moved to Beijing, where they married Mongol princesses, their descendants becoming more Mongol than Korean. This was a time of hardship for the Korean people. In the year 1254 alone, the Mongols enslaved

The Koryŏ Dynasty, 935–1392

CHAPTER LOCATOR | What made possible the expansion of the Chinese economy, and what were the outcomes? | How did the civil service examinations and the scholar-official class shape Chinese society?

CHAPTER 13
376   STATES AND CULTURES IN EAST ASIA

two hundred thousand Koreans and took them away. Ordinary people in Korea suffered grievously when their land was used as a launching pad for the huge Mongol invasions of Japan. In this period Korea also suffered from frequent attacks by Japanese pirates, somewhat like the depredations of the Vikings in Europe a little earlier (see page 390).

When Mongol rule in China fell apart in the mid-fourteenth century, it declined in Korea as well. Chinese rebels opposing the Mongols entered Korea and even briefly captured the capital in 1361. When the Ming Dynasty was established in China in 1368, the Koryŏ court was unsure how to respond. In 1388 a general, Yi Song-gye, was sent to oppose a Ming army at the northwest frontier. When he saw the strength of the Ming, he concluded that making an alliance was more sensible than fighting, and he led his troops back to the capital, where in 1392 he usurped the throne, founding the Chosŏn Dynasty.

QUICK REVIEW <

How did Korean society differ from Chinese society in this period?

| How did Korean society develop when its northern neighbors were Khitans, Jurchens, and Mongols? | How did the Heian form of government contribute to the cultural flowering of Japan in the period? | What were the causes and consequences of military rule in Japan? | ✓ LearningCurve Check what you know. |

> How did the Heian form of government contribute to the cultural flowering of Japan in the period?

The Shogun Minamoto Yoritomo in Court Dress

This wooden sculpture, 27.8 inches tall, was made about a half century after Yoritomo's death for use in a shrine dedicated to his memory. The bold shapes convey Yoritomo's dignity and power. (*Yoritomo [Minamotono-Yoritomo]*, wood with colored painting and quartz eyes, Kamakura Period, 1300/National Museum, Tokyo, Japan/akg-images)

AS DESCRIBED IN CHAPTER 7, during the seventh and eighth centuries the Japanese ruling house pursued a vigorous policy of adopting useful ideas, techniques, and policies from the more advanced civilization of China. The rulers built a capital along Chinese lines in Nara and fostered the growth of Buddhism. Monasteries grew so powerful in Nara, however, that in less than a century the court decided to move away from them and encourage other sects of Buddhism.

The new capital was built about twenty-five miles away at Heian (HAY-ahn; modern Kyoto). Like Nara, Heian was modeled on the Tang capital of Chang'an. For the first century at Heian the government continued to follow Chinese models, but it turned away from them with the decline of the Tang Dynasty in the late ninth century. During the Heian period (794–1185), Japan witnessed a literary and cultural flowering under the rule of the Fujiwara family.

Fujiwara Rule

Only the first two Heian emperors were much involved in governing. By 860 political management had been taken over by a series of regents from the Fujiwara family, who supplied most of the empresses in this period. The emperors contin-

CHAPTER LOCATOR | What made possible the expansion of the Chinese economy, and what were the outcomes? | How did the civil service examinations and the scholar-official class shape Chinese society?

ued to be honored, but the Fujiwaras ruled. Fujiwara dominance represented the privatization of political power and a return to clan politics. Political history thus took a very different course in Japan than in China, where, when a dynasty weakened, military strongmen would compete to depose the emperor and found their own dynasties. In Japan for the next thousand years, political contenders sought to manipulate the emperors rather than supplant them.

The Fujiwaras reached the apogee of their glory under Fujiwara Michinaga (r. 995–1027). Like many aristocrats of the period, he was learned in Buddhism, music, poetry, and Chinese literature and history. He dominated the court for more than thirty years as the father of four empresses, the uncle of two emperors, and the grandfather of three emperors. After ensuring that his sons could continue to rule, he retired to a Buddhist monastery, all the while continuing to maintain control.

By the end of the eleventh century several emperors who did not have Fujiwara mothers had found a device to counter Fujiwara control: they abdicated but continued to exercise power by controlling their young sons on the throne. This system of rule has been called **cloistered government** because the retired emperors took Buddhist orders, while maintaining control of the government from behind the scenes.

cloistered government
▶ A system in which an emperor retired to a Buddhist monastery but continued to exercise power by controlling his young son on the throne.

Aristocratic Culture

A brilliant aristocratic culture developed in the Heian period. In the capital at Heian, nobles, palace ladies, and imperial family members lived a highly refined and leisured life. In their society, niceties of birth, rank, and breeding counted for everything. The elegance of one's calligraphy and the allusions in one's poems were matters of intense concern to both men and women at court. Courtiers did not like to leave the capital, and some like the court lady Sei Shonagon shuddered at the sight of ordinary working people.

In this period a new script was developed for writing Japanese phonetically. Each symbol was based on a simplified Chinese character and represented one of the syllables used in Japanese. Although "serious" essays, histories, and government documents continued to be written in Chinese, less formal works such as poetry and memoirs were written in Japanese. Mastering the new writing system took much less time than mastering writing in Chinese and aided the spread of literacy, especially among women in court society.

In the Heian period, women played important roles at all levels of society. Women educated in the arts and letters could advance at court as attendants to the ruler's empress and other consorts. Women could inherit property from their parents, and they would compete with their brothers for shares of the family property. In political life, marrying a daughter to an emperor or shogun (see page 381) was one of the best ways to gain power, and women often became major players in power struggles.

The literary masterpiece of this period is *The Tale of Genji*, written in Japanese by Lady Murasaki over several years (ca. 1000–1010). This long narrative depicts a cast of characters enmeshed in court life, with close attention to dialogue and personality. Murasaki also wrote a diary that is similarly revealing of aristocratic culture.

Murasaki was one of many female writers in this period. The wife of a high-ranking court official wrote a poetic memoir of her unhappy twenty-year marriage

The Tale of Genji
▶ A Japanese literary masterpiece about court life written by Lady Murasaki.

How did Korean society develop when its northern neighbors were Khitans, Jurchens, and Mongols?

How did the Heian form of government contribute to the cultural flowering of Japan in the period?

What were the causes and consequences of military rule in Japan?

☑ LearningCurve
Check what you know.

to him and his rare visits. A woman wrote both an autobiography that related her father's efforts to find favor at court and a love story of a hero who travels to China. Another woman even wrote a history that concludes with a triumphal biography of Fujiwara Michinaga.

Buddhism remained very strong throughout the Heian period. A mission sent to China in 804 included two monks in search of new texts. One of the monks, Saichō, spent time at the monasteries on Mount Tiantai and brought back the Buddhist teachings associated with that mountain (called Tendai in Japanese). Tendai's basic message is that all living beings share the Buddha nature and can be brought to salvation. Once back in Japan, Saichō established a monastery on Mount Hiei outside Kyoto, which grew to be one of the most important monasteries in Japan. By the twelfth century this monastery and its many branch temples had vast lands and a powerful army of monk-soldiers to protect its interests.

Kūkai, the other monk on the 804 mission to China, came back with texts from another school of Buddhism—Shingon, "True Word," a form of Esoteric Buddhism. Esoteric Buddhism is based on the idea that teachings containing the secrets of enlightenment had been secretly transmitted from the Buddha. People can gain access to these mysteries through initiation into the mandalas (cosmic diagrams), mudras (gestures), and mantras (verbal formulas). On his return to Japan, Kūkai attracted many followers and was allowed to establish a monastery at Mount Kōya, south of Osaka. The popularity of Esoteric Buddhism was a great stimulus to Buddhist art.

Esoteric Buddhism
▶ A sect of Buddhism that maintains that the secrets of enlightenment have been secretly transmitted from the Buddha and can be accessed through initiation into the mandalas, mudras, and mantras.

> QUICK REVIEW

What were the key characteristics of Fujiwara government? How did Fujiwara government represent a departure from Chinese models of political development?

CHAPTER LOCATOR | What made possible the expansion of the Chinese economy, and what were the outcomes? | How did the civil service examinations and the scholar-official class shape Chinese society?

380 CHAPTER 13 STATES AND CULTURES IN EAST ASIA

What were the causes
and consequences of
military rule in Japan?

THE GRADUAL RISE OF A WARRIOR ELITE over the course of the Heian period
finally brought an end to the domination of the Fujiwaras and other Heian aristocratic families. In 1156 civil war broke out between the Taira and Minamoto warrior clans based in western and eastern Japan, respectively. Both clans relied on
skilled warriors, later called samurai, who were rapidly becoming a new social
class. A samurai and his lord had a double bond: in return for the samurai's loyalty and service, the lord granted him land or income. From 1159 to 1181 a Taira
named Kiyomori dominated the court, taking the position of prime minister and
marrying his daughter to the emperor. His relatives became governors of more
than thirty provinces. Still, the Minamoto clan managed to defeat the Taira, and
the Minamoto leader, Yoritomo, became **shogun**, or general-in-chief. With him
began the Kamakura Shogunate (1185–1333). This period is often referred to as
Japan's feudal period because it was dominated by a military class whose members were tied to their superiors by bonds of loyalty and supported by landed
estates rather than salaries.

shogun

▶ The Japanese general-in-chief,
whose headquarters was the
shogunate.

Military Rule

The similarities between military rule in Japan and feudalism in medieval Europe
during roughly the same period have fascinated scholars, as have the very significant differences. In Europe feudalism emerged out of the fusion of Germanic and
Roman social institutions and flowered under the impact of Muslim and Viking
invasions. In Japan military rule evolved from a combination of the native warrior
tradition and Confucian ethical principles of duty to superiors.

The emergence of the samurai was made possible by the development of
private landholding. The government land allotment system, copied from Tang
China, began breaking down in the eighth century (much as it did in China). By
the ninth century local lords had begun escaping imperial taxes and control by
commending (formally giving) their land to tax-exempt entities such as monasteries, the imperial family, and high-ranking officials. The local lord then received
his land back as a tenant and paid his protector a small rent. The monastery or
privileged individual received a steady income from the land, and the local lord
escaped imperial taxes and control. By the end of the thirteenth century most land
seems to have been taken off the tax rolls this way. Unlike peasants in medieval

How did Korean society
develop when its northern
neighbors were Khitans,
Jurchens, and Mongols?

How did the Heian form
of government contribute
to the cultural flowering
of Japan in the period?

**What were the causes
and consequences of
military rule in Japan?**

☑ LearningCurve
Check what you know.

381

Europe, where similar practices of commendation occurred, those working the land in Japan never became serfs. Moreover, Japanese lords rarely lived on the lands they had rights in, unlike English or French lords who lived on their manors.

Samurai resembled European knights in several ways. Both were armed with expensive weapons, and both fought on horseback. Just as the knight was supposed to live according to the chivalric code, so Japanese samurai were expected to live according to Bushido (or "way of the warrior"). Physical hardship was accepted as routine, and soft living was despised as weak and unworthy. Disloyalty brought social disgrace, which the samurai could avoid only through *seppuku*, ritual suicide by slashing his belly.

The Kamakura Shogunate derives its name from Kamakura, a city near modern Tokyo that was the seat of the Minamoto clan. The founder, Yoritomo, ruled the country much the way he ran his own estates, appointing his retainers to newly created offices. To cope with the emergence of hard-to-tax estates, he put military land stewards in charge of seeing to the estates' proper operation. To bring order to the lawless countryside, he appointed military governors to oversee the military and enforce the law in the provinces. They supervised the conduct of the land stewards in peacetime and commanded the provincial samurai in war.

Yoritomo's wife, Masako, protected the interests of her own family, the Hōjōs, especially after Yoritomo died. She went so far as to force her first son to abdicate when he showed signs of preferring the family of his wife to the family of his mother. She later helped her brother take power away from her father. Thus the process of reducing power holders to figureheads went one step further in 1219 when the Hōjō family reduced the shogun to a figurehead. The Hōjō family held the reins of power for more than a century until 1333.

The Mongols' two massive seaborne invasions in 1274 and 1281 (see page 336) were a huge shock to the shogunate. Although the Hōjō regents, with the help of a "divine wind" (kamikaze), repelled the Mongols, they were unable to reward their vassals in the traditional way because little booty was found among the wreckage of the Mongol fleets. Discontent grew among the samurai, and by the fourteenth century the entire political system was breaking down. Both the imperial and the shogunate families were fighting among themselves. As land grants were divided, samurai became impoverished.

The factional disputes among Japan's leading families remained explosive until 1331, when the emperor Go-Daigo tried to recapture real power. His attempt sparked an uprising by the great families, local lords, samurai, and even Buddhist monasteries. Go-Daigo destroyed the Kamakura Shogunate in 1333 but soon lost the loyalty of his followers. By 1338 one of his most important military supporters, Ashikaga Takauji, had turned on him and established the Ashikaga Shogunate, which lasted until 1573. Takauji's victory was also a victory for the samurai, who took over civil authority throughout Japan.

Cultural Trends

The cultural distance between the elites and the commoners narrowed a little during the Kamakura period. Buddhism was spread to ordinary Japanese by energetic preachers. Honen (1133–1212) propagated the Pure Land teaching, preaching that paradise could be reached through simple faith in the Buddha

Bushido
▶ Literally, the "way of the warrior"; the code of conduct by which samurai were expected to live.

Kamakura Shogunate, 1185–1333

CHAPTER LOCATOR | What made possible the expansion of the Chinese economy, and what were the outcomes? | How did the civil service examinations and the scholar-official class shape Chinese society?

382 CHAPTER 13 STATES AND CULTURES IN EAST ASIA

and repeating the name of the Buddha Amitabha. His follower Shinran (1173–1263) taught that monks should not shut themselves off in monasteries but should marry and have children. A different path was promoted by Nichiren (1222–1282), a fiery and intolerant preacher who proclaimed that to be saved people had only to invoke sincerely the Lotus Sutra, one of the most important of the Buddhist sutras. These lay versions of Buddhism found a receptive audience among ordinary people in the countryside.

It was also during the Kamakura period that **Zen** came to flourish in Japan. Zen teachings originated in Tang China, where they were known as Chan (see page 191). Rejecting the authority of the sutras, Zen teachers claimed the superiority of mind-to-mind transmission of Buddhist truth. This teaching found eager patrons among the samurai, who were attracted to its discipline and strong master-disciple bonds.

Buddhism remained central to the visual arts. Many temples in Japan still house fine sculptures done in this period. In painting, narrative hand scrolls brought to life the miracles that faith could bring and the torments of Hell awaiting unbelievers.

During the Kamakura period, war tales continued the tradition of long narrative prose works. *The Tale of the Heike* tells the story of the fall of the Taira family and the rise of the Minamoto clan. The tale reached a large and mostly illiterate audience because blind minstrels would chant sections to the accompaniment of a lute. The story is suffused with the Buddhist idea of the transience of life and the illusory nature of glory. Yet it also celebrates strength, courage, loyalty, and pride.

After stagnating in the Heian period, agricultural productivity began to improve in the Kamakura period, and the population grew, reaching perhaps 8.2 million by 1333. Much like farmers in contemporary Song China, Japanese farmers adopted new strains of rice, often double-cropped in warmer regions, made increased use of fertilizers, and improved irrigation for paddy rice. Besides farming, ordinary people made their livings as artisans, traders, fishermen, and entertainers. Although trade in human beings was banned, those who fell into debt might sell themselves or their children, and professional slave traders kidnapped women and children. A vague category of outcastes occupied the fringes of society, in a manner reminiscent of India. Buddhist strictures against killing and Shinto ideas of pollution probably account for the exclusion of butchers, leatherworkers, morticians, and lepers, but other groups, such as bamboo whisk makers, were also traditionally excluded for no obvious reason.

Zen
▶ A school of Buddhism that emphasized meditation and truths that could not be conveyed in words.

QUICK REVIEW ◁

How did competition between aristocratic clans shape the history of Japan during this period?

How did Korean society develop when its northern neighbors were Khitans, Jurchens, and Mongols?

How did the Heian form of government contribute to the cultural flowering of Japan in the period?

What were the causes and consequences of military rule in Japan?

✓ LearningCurve
Check what you know.

CHAPTER SUMMARY

The countries of East Asia—China, Japan, and Korea—all underwent major changes in the six centuries from 800 to 1400. In China the loosening of the central government's control of the economy stimulated trade and economic growth. Between 800 and 1100 China's population doubled to 100 million, reflecting in part the spread of wet-field rice cultivation, especially in the south. The economic center of China shifted from the north China plain to the south, the milder region drained by the Yangzi River.

In the Song period, the booming economy and the invention of printing allowed for expansion of the scholar-official class, which came to dominate government and society. Repeatedly, the Song government chose to pay tribute to its militarily powerful neighbors—first the Khitans, then the Jurchens, then the Mongols—to keep the peace. Eventually, however, Song fell to the Mongols.

During the Koryŏ Dynasty, Korea evolved more independently of China than it had previously, in part because it had to placate powerful non-Chinese neighbors. The commercial economy declined, and an increasing portion of the population was unfree, working as slaves for aristocrats or the government. Military strongmen dominated the government, but their armies were no match for the much larger empires to their north. The period of Mongol domination was particularly difficult.

In Heian Japan, a tiny aristocracy dominated government and society. A series of regents, most of them from the Fujiwara family and fathers-in-law of the emperors, controlled political life. The aristocratic court society put great emphasis on taste and refinement. The Heian aristocrats had little interest in life in the provinces, which gradually came under the control of military clans.

After a civil war between the two leading military clans, a military government, called the shogunate, was established. The Kamakura Shogunate was dominated by a military class of samurais. Two invasions by the Mongols caused major crises in military control. Although both times the invaders were repelled, defense costs were high. During this period culture was less centered around the capital, and Buddhism spread to ordinary people.

 CONNECTIONS East Asia faced many internal and external challenges between 800 and 1400, and the ways societies responded to them shaped their subsequent histories. In China the first four centuries of this period saw economic growth, urbanization, the spread of printing, and the expansion of the educated class. In Korea and Japan aristocratic dominance and military rule were more typical of the era. All three areas, but especially China and Korea, faced an unprecedented challenge from the Mongols. The challenges of the period did not hinder creativity in the literary and visual arts.

Europe during these six centuries, the subject of the next chapter, also faced invasions from outside; in its case, the pagan Vikings were especially dreaded. Europe had a social structure more like that of Korea and Japan than of China, with less centralization and a more dominant place in society for military men.

CHAPTER LOCATOR | What made possible the expansion of the Chinese economy, and what were the outcomes? | How did the civil service examinations and the scholar-official class shape Chinese society?

CHAPTER 13
384 STATES AND CULTURES IN EAST ASIA

The centralized church in Europe, however, was unlike anything known in East Asian history. These centuries in Europe saw a major expansion of Christendom, both through conversion and migration. Although there were scares that the Mongols would penetrate deeper into Europe, the greatest challenge in Europe was the Black Death and the huge loss of life that it caused.

ONLINE DOCUMENT PROJECT

Song Artwork

What cultural pursuits interested the scholar-official class?

View images from the Song period, and then complete a quiz and writing assignment based on the evidence and details from this chapter. *See inside the front cover to learn more.*

How did Korean society develop when its northern neighbors were Khitans, Jurchens, and Mongols?

How did the Heian form of government contribute to the cultural flowering of Japan in the period?

What were the causes and consequences of military rule in Japan?

LearningCurve
Check what you know.

CHAPTER 13 STUDY GUIDE

STEP 1

GET STARTED ONLINE

 LearningCurve

Now that you've read the chapter, make it stick by completing the LearningCurve activity.

STEP 2

EXPLAIN WHY IT MATTERS

Put your reading into practice. Identify each term below, and then explain why it matters in world history.

TERM	WHO OR WHAT & WHEN	WHY IT MATTERS
dynastic cycle (p. 362)		
compass (p. 364)		
scholar-official class (p. 368)		
examination system (p. 368)		
movable type (p. 368)		
Neo-Confucianism (p. 369)		
concubine (p. 372)		
foot binding (p. 372)		
cloistered government (p. 379)		
The Tale of Genji (p. 379)		
Esoteric Buddhism (p. 380)		
shogun (p. 381)		
Bushido (p. 382)		
Zen (p. 383)		

STEP 3

MOVE BEYOND THE BASICS

To demonstrate a more advanced understanding of the divergence of China, Korea, and Japan in the medieval period, fill in the chart below with descriptions of the major social, political, and cultural developments in the three states during the period covered in this chapter. What role did nomadic peoples play in shaping Chinese, Korean, and Japanese history during this period?

	Society	Politics	Culture
China			
Korea			
Japan			

PUT IT ALL TOGETHER

Now, take a step back and try to explain the big picture. Remember to use specific examples from the chapter in your answers.

CHINA

▶ In what ways did late Tang and Song China defy the expectations of traditional Chinese historians?

▶ Why, despite its growth and prosperity, did China become increasingly vulnerable to nomadic confederations under the Song?

KOREA

▶ In what ways was Korean society different from Chinese and Japanese society?

▶ How did Korea's leaders react to the presence of powerful nomadic confederations on their borders?

JAPAN

▶ Compare and contrast Japanese elite culture during the Heian period with Chinese elite culture under the Song. How would you explain the differences you note?

▶ How and why did the power of Japanese samurai increase during the medieval period?

LOOKING BACK, LOOKING AHEAD

▶ Compare and contrast the place of China in the East Asian world before and after the period covered in this chapter. How would you explain the differences you note?

▶ From 1500 on, East Asia would face an unprecedented maritime challenge from European states. How might developments in the period covered in this chapter have affected the ability of East Asian states to meet this challenge?

> IN YOUR OWN WORDS

Imagine that you must give an oral report to the class answering the following question: **Why did Chinese, Korean, and Japanese society and culture diverge after 800?** What would be the most important points and why?

14

EUROPE IN THE MIDDLE AGES

800–1450

> **What role did clergy, nobles, peasants, and townspeople play in medieval European society?** Chapter 14 examines the development of European civilization in the Middle Ages. Traditionally, the history of Europe has been divided into three periods — ancient, medieval, and modern. At times, the history of other parts of the world has also been fit into this three-period schema as well. Today historians often question the general applicability of such labels, and even the usefulness of the term "Middle Ages" for European history. They assert that the Middle Ages was not simply a period of stagnation between two high points but rather a time of enormous intellectual energy and creative vitality. While agrarian life continued to dominate Europe, political structures that would influence later European history began to form, and Christianity continued to spread.

Hedwig of Silesia Noblewomen in medieval Europe played a wide variety of roles. Hedwig of Silesia conducted diplomatic negotiations, ruled her husband's territory when he was away, founded monasteries, and worked to expand Christianity in eastern Europe. (The John Paul Getty Museum, Los Angeles, Ms Ludwig XI, fol. 12v [detail], Court Atelier of Duke Ludwig I of Liegnitz and Brieg [illuminator], *Vita beatae Hedwigis*, 1353. Tempera colors, colored washes and ink bound between wood boards covered with red-stained pigskin, 34.1 x 24.8 cm.)

> How did medieval rulers restore order and centralize political power?

> How did the Christian Church enhance its power and create new institutions and religious practices?

> What were the causes, course, and consequences of the Crusades?

> How did the lives of common people, nobles, and towns-people differ, and what new commercial developments increased wealth?

> What were the primary educational and cultural developments in medieval Europe?

> Why have the later Middle Ages been seen as a time of calamity and crisis?

LearningCurve
After reading the chapter, use LearningCurve to retain what you've read.

> How did medieval rulers restore order and centralize political power?

IN 800 CHARLEMAGNE, the most powerful of the Carolingians, was crowned Holy Roman emperor. After his death his empire was divided among his grandsons, and their kingdoms were weakened by nobles vying for power. In addition, beginning around 800 western Europe was invaded by several different groups. Local nobles were the strongest power, and common people turned to them for protection. By the eleventh century, however, rulers in some parts of Europe had reasserted authority and were slowly building centralized states.

Invasions and Migrations

The Vikings were pagan Germanic peoples from Norway, Sweden, and Denmark. They began to make overseas expeditions, which they themselves called *vikings*, and the word came to be used for people who went on such voyages as well. Viking assaults began around 800, and by the mid-tenth century the Vikings had brought large sections of continental Europe and Britain under their sway. In the east they sailed the rivers of Russia as far as the Black Sea. In the west they established permanent settlements in Iceland and short-lived ones in Greenland and Newfoundland in Canada (Map 14.1).

Against Viking ships navigated by experienced and fearless sailors, the Carolingian Empire, with no navy, was helpless. At first the Vikings attacked and sailed off laden with booty. Later, on returning, they settled down and colonized the areas they had conquered, often marrying local women and adopting the local languages and some of the customs.

Along with the Vikings, groups of central European steppe peoples known as Magyars (MAG-yahrz) also raided villages in the late ninth century. Moving westward, small bands of Magyars on horseback reached far into Europe. They subdued northern Italy, compelled Bavaria and Saxony to pay tribute, and penetrated into the Rhineland and Burgundy. They settled in the area that is now Hungary, became Christian, and in the eleventh century allied with the papacy.

From North Africa, the Muslims also began new encroachments in the ninth century. They already ruled most of Spain and now conquered Sicily, driving northward into central Italy and the south coast of France.

From the perspective of those living in what had been Charlemagne's empire, Viking, Magyar, and Muslim attacks contributed to increasing disorder and violence. Italian, French, and English sources often describe this period as one of terror and chaos. People in other parts of Europe might have had a different opinion. In Muslim Spain and Sicily scholars worked in thriving cities, and new crops

CHAPTER LOCATOR | **How did medieval rulers restore order and centralize political power?** | How did the Christian Church enhance its power and create new institutions?

722–1492
Reconquista, the Christian reconquest of Spain from Muslims

ca. 800–950
Viking, Magyar, and Muslim attacks on Europe

1066–1087
Reign of William the Conqueror

1086
Domesday Book

1095–1270
Crusades

1180–1270
Height of construction of cathedrals in France

1215
Magna Carta

1225–1274
Life of Saint Thomas Aquinas, author of *Summa Theologica*

1309–1376
Papacy in Avignon

1315–1322
Famine in northern Europe

ca. 1337–1453
Hundred Years' War

1347
Black Death arrives in Europe

1358
Jacquerie peasant uprising in France

1378–1417
Great Schism

1381
English Peasants' Revolt

1429
Joan of Arc leads French troops to victory at Orléans

such as cotton and sugar enhanced ordinary people's lives. In eastern Europe states such as Moravia and Hungary became strong kingdoms.

"Feudalism" and Manorialism

The large-scale division of Charlemagne's empire into three parts in the ninth century led to a decentralization of power at the local level. Civil wars weakened the power and prestige of kings, who could do little about regional violence. Likewise, the invasions of the ninth century, especially those of the Vikings, weakened royal authority. The Frankish kings were unable to halt the invaders, and the local aristocracy had to assume responsibility for defense. Thus, in the ninth and tenth centuries, aristocratic families increased their authority in their local territories, and distant and weak kings could not interfere. Common people turned for protection to the strongest power, the local nobles.

The most powerful nobles were those who gained warriors' allegiance, often symbolized in an oath-swearing ceremony of homage and fealty that grew out of earlier Germanic oaths of loyalty. In this ceremony a warrior (knight) swore his loyalty as a **vassal** to the more powerful individual, who became his lord. In return for the vassal's loyalty, aid, and military assistance, the lord promised him protection and material support. This support might be a place in the lord's household but was more likely land of the vassal's own, called a **fief** (*feudum* in Latin). The fief, which might contain forests, churches, and towns, technically still belonged to the lord, and the vassal had only the use of it. Peasants living on a fief produced the food and other goods necessary to maintain the knight. Most legal scholars and historians have identified these personal ties of loyalty cemented by grants of land as a political and social system they term **feudalism**. In the last

vassal
▶ A knight who has sworn loyalty to a particular lord.

fief
▶ A portion of land, the use of which was given by a lord to a vassal in exchange for the latter's oath of loyalty.

feudalism
▶ A medieval European political system that defines the military obligations and relations between a lord and his vassals and involves the granting of fiefs.

What were the causes, course, and consequences of the Crusades? | How did the lives of common people, nobles, and townspeople differ? | What were the primary educational and cultural developments in medieval Europe? | Why have the later Middle Ages been seen as a time of calamity and crisis? | ✓ LearningCurve Check what you know.

MAP 14.1 ■ Invasions and Migrations of the Ninth and Tenth Centuries

This map shows the Viking, Magyar, and Muslim invasions and migrations in the ninth and tenth centuries. Compare it with Map 8.2 (page 219) on the barbarian migrations of late antiquity to answer the following questions.

> MAPPING THE PAST

ANALYZING THE MAP: What similarities do you see in the patterns of migration in these two periods? What significant differences?

CONNECTIONS: How did the Vikings' expertise in shipbuilding and sailing make their migrations different from those of earlier Germanic tribes? How did this set them apart from the Magyar and Muslim invaders of the ninth century?

manorialism

▶ The economic system that governed rural life in medieval Europe, in which the landed estates of a lord were worked by the peasants under the lord's jurisdiction in exchange for his protection.

serf

▶ A peasant who lost his or her freedom and became permanently bound to the landed estate of a lord.

several decades, however, increasing numbers of medieval historians have found the idea of "feudalism" problematic, because the word was a later invention and the system was so varied and changed over time.

The economic power of the warrior class rested on landed estates, which were worked by peasants under a system of **manorialism**. Free farmers surrendered themselves and their land to the lord's jurisdiction in exchange for protection. The land was given back to them to farm, but they were tied to the land by various payments and services. Most significantly, a peasant lost his or her freedom and became a **serf**, part of the lord's permanent labor force. Unlike slaves, serfs were personally free, but they were bound to the land and unable to leave it without the lord's permission.

CHAPTER LOCATOR | How did medieval rulers restore order and centralize political power? | How did the Christian Church enhance its power and create new institutions?

By around 1000 the majority of western Europeans were serfs. In eastern Europe the transition was slower but longer lasting. Western European peasants began to escape from serfdom in the later Middle Ages, at the very point that serfs were more firmly tied to the land in eastern Europe, especially in eastern Germany, Poland, and Russia.

The Restoration of Order

The eleventh century witnessed the beginnings of political stability in western Europe. Foreign invasions gradually declined, and in some parts of Europe lords in control of large territories built up their power even further, becoming kings over growing and slowly centralizing states. In a process similar to that occurring at the same time in the West African kingdom of Ghana (see pages 280–281), rulers expanded their territories and extended their authority by developing larger bureaucracies, armies, judicial systems, and other institutions to maintain control, as well as taxation systems to pay for them. These new institutions and practices laid the foundations for modern national states. Political developments in England, France, and Germany provide good examples of the beginnings of the national state in the central Middle Ages.

The Viking Canute (r. 1016–1035) made England the center of his empire, while promoting a policy of assimilation and reconciliation between Anglo-Saxons and Vikings. At the same time, England was divided into local shires, or counties, each under the jurisdiction of a sheriff appointed by the king. When Canute's heir Edward died childless, there were three claimants to the throne. One of these, Duke William of Normandy, crossed the channel and won the English throne by defeating and killing his Anglo-Saxon rival, Harold II, at the Battle of Hastings in 1066. Later dubbed "the Conqueror," William (r. 1066–1087) limited the power of the nobles and church officials and built a unified monarchy. He retained the Anglo-Saxon institution of sheriff, but named Normans to the posts.

In 1085 William decided to conduct a systematic survey of the entire country to determine how much wealth there was and who had it. The resulting record, called the *Domesday Book* (DOOMZ-day) from the Anglo-Saxon word *doom*, meaning "judgment," provided William and his descendants with vital information for governing the country.

In 1128 William's granddaughter Matilda married a powerful French noble, Geoffrey of Anjou. Their son, who became Henry II of England, inherited provinces in northwestern France from his father. When Henry married the great heiress Eleanor of Aquitaine in 1152, he claimed lordship over Aquitaine and other provinces in southwestern France as well. The histories of England and France were thus closely intertwined in the Middle Ages.

In the early twelfth century France consisted of a number of nearly independent provinces, each governed by its local ruler. The work of unifying and enlarging France began under Philip II (r. 1180–1223), also known as Philip Augustus. By the end of his reign Philip was effectively master of northern France, and by 1300 most of the provinces of modern France had been added to the royal domain.

In central Europe the German king Otto I (r. 936–973) defeated many other lords to build up his power, based on an alliance with and control of the church. Under Otto I and his successors, a loose confederation stretching from the North Sea to the Mediterranean developed. In this confederation, later called the Holy

The Norman Conquest, 1066

What were the causes, course, and consequences of the Crusades?

How did the lives of common people, nobles, and townspeople differ?

What were the primary educational and cultural developments in medieval Europe?

Why have the later Middle Ages been seen as a time of calamity and crisis?

LearningCurve
Check what you know.

393

Roman Empire, the emperor shared power with princes, dukes, counts, city officials, archbishops, and bishops.

Frederick Barbarossa (r. 1152–1190) of the house of Hohenstaufen tried valiantly to make the Holy Roman Empire a united state. When he tried to enforce his authority over the cities of northern Italy, however, they formed a league against him in alliance with the pope and defeated him. Frederick's absence from the German part of his empire allowed the princes and other rulers of independent provinces to consolidate their power there as well, and Germany did not become a unified state.

Law and Justice

Throughout Europe in the twelfth and thirteenth centuries, the law was a hodgepodge of customs, feudal rights, and provincial practices. Rulers wanted to blend these elements into a uniform system of rules acceptable and applicable to all their peoples, though their success in doing so varied.

The French king Louis IX (r. 1226–1270) was famous for his concern for justice. Each French province, even after being made part of the kingdom of France, retained its unique laws and procedures. But Louis IX created a royal judicial system, establishing the Parlement of Paris, a kind of supreme court that heard appeals from lower courts.

Under Henry II (r. 1154–1189), England developed and extended a common law—a law common to and accepted by the entire country, unique in medieval Europe. Henry's son John (r. 1199–1216), however, met with serious disappointment after taking the throne. A combination of royal debt, increased taxation, and military failures fed popular discontent. A rebellion begun by northern barons grew, and in 1215 the barons forced him to attach his seal to the Magna Carta—the "Great Charter," which became the cornerstone of English justice and law. The Magna Carta was simply meant to assert traditional rights enjoyed by certain groups, but in time it came to signify the broader principle that everyone, including the king and the government, must obey the law.

Statements of legal principles such as the Magna Carta were not how most people experienced the law in medieval Europe. Instead they were involved in actual cases. Judges determined guilt or innocence in a number of ways. In some cases, they ordered a trial by ordeal, in which the accused might be tied hand and foot and dropped in a lake or river. People believed that water was a pure substance and would reject anything foul or unclean. Thus a person who sank was considered innocent, while a person who floated was found guilty. Trials by ordeal were relatively rare, and courts increasingly favored more rational procedures, in which judges heard testimony, sought witnesses, and read written evidence if it was available.

> **QUICK REVIEW**

How did the invasions of the ninth and tenth centuries shape European society and government?

CHAPTER LOCATOR | How did medieval rulers restore order and centralize political power?　　How did the Christian Church enhance its power and create new institutions?

CHAPTER 14
394　EUROPE IN THE MIDDLE AGES

Nearly every church had at least one image of the Virgin Mary, the most important figure of Christian devotion in medieval Europe. In this thirteenth-century wooden sculpture, she is shown holding the infant Jesus and is herself sitting on the lap of her mother, Anne. Statues such as this reinforced people's sense that the heavenly family was much like theirs, with grandparents who sometimes played important roles. (Museo Nazionale del Bargello, Florence, Italy/Scala/Art Resource, NY)

How did the Christian Church enhance its power and create new institutions and religious practices?

KINGS AND EMPERORS were not the only rulers consolidating their power in the eleventh and twelfth centuries; the papacy did as well, although the popes' efforts were sometimes challenged by medieval kings and emperors. Despite such challenges, monasteries continued to be important places for learning and devotion, and new religious orders were founded. Christianity expanded into Europe's northern and eastern regions, and Christian rulers expanded their holdings in Muslim Spain.

Papal Reforms

During the ninth and tenth centuries the church came under the control of kings and feudal lords, who chose church officials in their territories, granting them fiefs that provided an income and expecting loyalty and service in return. Church

| What were the causes, course, and consequences of the Crusades? | How did the lives of common people, nobles, and townspeople differ? | What were the primary educational and cultural developments in medieval Europe? | Why have the later Middle Ages been seen as a time of calamity and crisis? | ☑ LearningCurve Check what you know. |

offices were sometimes sold outright—a practice called *simony*. Although the Roman Church encouraged clerical celibacy, many priests were married or living with women. Wealthy Roman families chose popes from among their members; thus popes paid more attention to their families' political fortunes or their own pleasures than to the church's institutional or spiritual health. Not surprisingly, clergy at all levels who had bought their positions or had been granted them for political reasons provided little spiritual guidance and were rarely models of high moral standards.

Serious efforts to reform the church began in the eleventh century. A series of popes believed that secular or lay control over the church was largely responsible for the lack of moral leadership, so they proclaimed the church independent from secular rulers. The Lateran Council of 1059 decreed that the authority and power to elect the pope rested solely in the college of cardinals, a special group of priests from the major churches in and around Rome.

Pope Gregory VII (pontificate 1073–1085) vigorously championed reform and the expansion of papal power. He ordered all priests to give up their wives and children or face dismissal, invalidated the ordination of church officials who had purchased their offices, and placed nuns under firmer control of male authorities. He believed that the pope was the vicar of God on earth and that papal orders were the orders of God. He emphasized the political authority of the papacy, ordering that any church official selected or appointed by a layperson should be deposed, and any layperson who appointed a church official should be excommunicated—cut off from the sacraments and the Christian community.

European rulers immediately protested this restriction of their power, and the strongest reaction came from Henry IV, the ruler of Germany who later became the Holy Roman emperor. Henry continued to appoint officials, and Gregory responded by excommunicating bishops who supported Henry and threatening to depose him. In January 1077 Henry secured the pope's forgiveness, and Gregory readmitted the emperor into the Christian community. Although Henry bowed before the pope, he actually won a victory, maintaining authority over his subjects and in 1084 being crowned emperor. This victory was temporary, however, for high nobles within the empire took advantage of further conflicts with the pope to enhance their position, siding with the church to gain power.

Monastic Life

Although they were in theory cut off from the world (see page 212), monasteries and convents were deeply affected by issues of money, rank, and power. During the ninth and tenth centuries, many monasteries fell under the control and domination of local feudal lords. Powerful laymen appointed themselves or their relatives as abbots, took the lands and goods of monasteries, and spent monastic revenues.

Medieval monasteries also provided noble boys with education and opportunities for ecclesiastical careers. Although a few men who rose in the ranks of church officials were of humble origins, most were from high-status families. Social class also defined the kinds of religious life open to women. Kings and nobles usually established convents for their female relatives and other elite women, and the position of abbess, or head of a convent, became the most powerful position a woman could hold in medieval society. (See "Individuals in Society: Hildegard of Bingen," page 397.)

CHAPTER LOCATOR | How did medieval rulers restore order and centralize political power?

How did the Christian Church enhance its power and create new institutions?

CHAPTER 14
396 EUROPE IN THE MIDDLE AGES

The tenth child of a lesser noble family, Hildegard (1098–1179) was turned over to the care of an abbey in the Rhineland when she was eight years old. There she learned Latin and received a good education. She spent most of her life in various women's religious communities, two of which she founded herself. When she was a child, she began having mystical visions, often of light in the sky, but told few people about them. In middle age, however, her visions became more dramatic: "And it came to pass . . . when I was 42 years and 7 months old, that the heavens were opened and a blinding light of exceptional brilliance flowed through my entire brain. And so it kindled my whole heart and breast like a flame, not burning but warming . . . and suddenly I understood of the meaning of expositions of the books."* She wanted the church to approve of her visions and wrote first to Saint Bernard of Clairvaux, who answered her briefly and dismissively, and then to Pope Eugenius, who encouraged her to write them down. Her first work was *Scivias* (Know the Ways of the Lord), a record of her mystical visions that incorporates extensive theological learning.

Obviously possessed of leadership and administrative talents, Hildegard left her abbey in 1147 to found the convent of Rupertsberg near Bingen. There she produced *Physica* (On the Physical Elements) and *Causa et Curae* (Causes and Cures), scientific works on the curative properties of natural elements; poems; a religious play; and several more works of mysticism. She carried on a huge correspondence with scholars, prelates, and ordinary people. When she was over fifty, she left her community to preach to audiences of clergy and laity, and she was the only woman of her time whose opinions on religious matters were considered authoritative by the church.

Hildegard's visions have been explored by theologians and also by neurologists, who judge that they may have originated in migraine headaches, as she reports many of the same phenomena that migraine sufferers do: auras of light around objects, areas of blindness, feelings of intense doubt and intense euphoria. The interpretations that she develops come from her theological insight and learning, however, not from her illness. That same insight also emerges in her music, which is what she is best known for today. Eighty of her compositions survive — a huge number for a medieval composer — most of them written to

Inspired by heavenly fire, Hildegard begins to dictate her visions to her scribe. The original of this elaborately illustrated copy of *Scivias* disappeared from Hildegard's convent during World War II, but fortunately a facsimile had already been made. (Private Collection/The Bridgeman Art Library)

be sung by the nuns in her convent, so they have strong lines for female voices. Many of her songs and chants have been recorded recently by various artists and are available on compact disk, as downloads, and on several Web sites.

QUESTIONS FOR ANALYSIS

1. Why do you think Hildegard might have kept her visions secret at first? Why do you think she eventually sought church approval for them?
2. In what ways were Hildegard's accomplishments extraordinary given women's general status in the Middle Ages?

ONLINE DOCUMENT PROJECT

Why was Hildegard of Bingen considered a worthy instrument for the transmission of God's word? Read excerpts from Hildegard's correspondence, and then complete a quiz and writing assignment based on the evidence and details from this chapter. *See inside the front cover to learn more.*

*From *Scivias*, trans. Mother Columba Hart and Jane Bishop, *The Classics of Western Spirituality* (New York/Mahwah: Paulist Press, 1990).

Routines within individual monasteries varied widely from house to house and from region to region. In every monastery, however, daily life centered on the liturgy or Divine Office, psalms, and other prayers, which monks and nuns said seven times a day and once during the night. Praying was looked on as a vital service. Prayers were said for peace, rain, good harvests, the civil authorities, the monks' and nuns' families, and their benefactors. Monastic patrons in turn lavished gifts on the monasteries, which often became very wealthy, controlling large tracts of land and the peasants who farmed them. The combination of lay control and wealth created problems for monasteries as monks and nuns concentrated on worldly issues and spiritual observance and intellectual activity declined.

In the thirteenth century the growth of cities provided a new challenge for the church. Many urban people thought that the church did not meet their spiritual needs. They turned instead to heresies—that is, to versions of Christianity outside of those approved by the papacy, many of which called on the church to give up its wealth and power. Combating **heresy** became a principal task of new religious orders, most prominently the Dominicans and Franciscans, who preached and ministered to city dwellers; the Dominicans also staffed the papal Inquisition, a special court designed to root out heresy.

heresy

▶ An opinion, belief, or action counter to doctrines that church leaders defined as correct; heretics could be punished by the church.

Popular Religion

Religious practices varied widely from country to country and even from province to province. But everywhere, religion permeated everyday life.

For Christians, the village church was the center of community life, with the parish priest in charge of a host of activities. People gathered at the church for services on Sundays and holy days, breaking the painful routine of work. The feasts that accompanied celebrations were commonly held in the churchyard. In everyday life people engaged in rituals and used language heavy with religious symbolism. Everyone participated in village processions to honor the saints and ask their protection. The entire calendar was designed with reference to Christmas, Easter, and Pentecost, events in the life of Jesus and his disciples.

The Christian calendar was also filled with saints' days. Saints were individuals who had lived particularly holy lives and were honored locally or more widely for their connection with the divine. People believed that the saints possessed supernatural powers that enabled them to perform miracles, and each saint became the special property of the locality in which his or her relics—remains or possessions—rested. In return for the saint's healing powers and support, peasants would offer prayers, loyalty, and gifts. The Virgin Mary, Christ's mother, became the most important saint.

Most people in medieval Europe were Christian, but there were small Jewish communities scattered through many parts of Europe, as well as Muslims in the Iberian Peninsula, Sicily, other Mediterranean islands, and southeastern Europe. Increasing suspicion and hostility marked relations among believers in different religions throughout the Middle Ages, but there were also important similarities in the ways that each group understood and experienced their faiths. In all three traditions, every major life transition was marked by a ceremony that involved religious officials or spiritual elements. In all three faiths, death was marked by religious rituals, and the living had obligations to the dead, including prayers and special mourning periods.

CHAPTER LOCATOR | How did medieval rulers restore order and centralize political power?

How did the Christian Church enhance its power and create new institutions?

398 CHAPTER 14 EUROPE IN THE MIDDLE AGES

The Expansion of Christianity

The eleventh and twelfth centuries saw an expansion of Christianity into Scandinavia, the Baltic lands, eastern Europe, and Spain that had profound cultural consequences. The expansion was accomplished through wars, the establishment of new bishoprics, and the vast migration of Christian colonists into non-Christian territories. More and more Europeans began to think of themselves as belonging to a realm of Christianity that was political as well as religious, a realm they called Christendom.

Christian influences entered Scandinavia and the Baltic lands primarily through the creation of dioceses (church districts headed by bishops). This took place in Denmark and Norway in the tenth and eleventh centuries, and then in Sweden and Finland. In all of these areas, Christian missionaries preached, baptized, and built churches. Royal power advanced institutional Christianity, and traditional Norse religions practiced by the Vikings were outlawed. In eastern Europe the German emperor Otto I (see page 393) planted a string of dioceses along his northern and eastern frontiers, hoping to pacify the newly conquered Slavs in eastern Europe. German nobles built castles and ruthlessly crushed revolts by Slavic peoples.

The church also moved into central Europe, first into Bohemia in the tenth century and from there into Poland and Hungary in the eleventh century. In the twelfth and thirteenth centuries thousands of settlers poured into eastern Europe from the west.

The Iberian Peninsula was another area of Christian expansion. In about 950 Caliph Abd al-Rahman III (912–961) of the Umayyad Dynasty of Córdoba ruled most of the peninsula. Christian Spain consisted of a number of small kingdoms. In the eleventh century divisions and civil wars in the caliphate of Córdoba allowed Christian armies to conquer an increasingly large part of the Iberian Peninsula. By 1248 Christians held all of the peninsula save for the small state of Granada in the south.

Fourteenth-century clerical writers would call the movement to expel the Muslims the reconquista (ray-kon-KEES-tah; reconquest)—a sacred and patriotic crusade to wrest the country from "alien" Muslim hands. This religious idea became part of Spanish political culture and of the national psychology. Rulers of the Christian kingdoms of Spain increasingly passed legislation discriminating against Muslims and Jews living under Christian rule, and they attempted to exclude anyone from the nobility who could not prove "purity of blood"—that is, that they had no Muslim or Jewish ancestors.

Spain was not the only place in Europe where "blood" became a way of understanding differences among people and a basis for discriminatory laws. When Germans moved into eastern Europe and English forces took over much of Ireland, they increasingly barred local people from access to legal courts and denied them positions in monasteries or craft guilds. They banned intermarriage between ethnic groups in an attempt to maintain ethnic purity, even though everyone was Christian.

Date of Christian reconquest

☐ By 814   ☐ By 1097   ■ By 1275
■ By 910   ■ By 1150   ■ By 1492
■ By 1037   ☐ By 1190

The Reconquista, ca. 750–1492

reconquista

▶ A fourteenth-century term used to describe the long Christian crusade to wrest Spain back from the Muslims; clerics believed it was a sacred and patriotic mission.

QUICK REVIEW <

Why did efforts at church reform lead to conflict between secular and religious leaders?

| What were the causes, course, and consequences of the Crusades? | How did the lives of common people, nobles, and townspeople differ? | What were the primary educational and cultural developments in medieval Europe? | Why have the later Middle Ages been seen as a time of calamity and crisis? | ✓ LearningCurve Check what you know. |

What were the causes, course, and consequences of the Crusades?

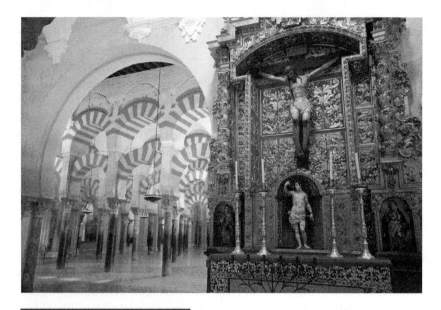

Córdoba Mosque and Cathedral

The huge arches of the Great Mosque at Córdoba dwarf the cathedral built in its center after the city was conquered by Christian armies in 1236. During the reconquista (see page 399), Christian kings often transformed mosques into churches, often by simply adding Christian elements such as crosses and altars to existing structures. (© dbimages/Alamy)

Crusades

▶ Holy wars sponsored by the papacy for the recovery of the Holy Land from the Muslims.

THE EXPANSION OF CHRISTIANITY in the Middle Ages was not limited to Europe but extended to the eastern Mediterranean in what were later termed the **Crusades**. Occurring in the late eleventh and early twelfth centuries, the Crusades were wars sponsored by the papacy to recover the holy city of Jerusalem from the Muslims.

Background and Motives

In the eleventh century the papacy had strong reasons for wanting to launch an expedition against Muslims in the East. Such an expedition would strengthen his claim to be the leader of Christian society in the West. Moreover, in 1054 a serious theological disagreement had split the Greek Church of Byzantium and the Roman Church of the West. The pope believed that a crusade would lead to strong Roman influence in Greek territories and eventually the reunion of the two churches.

Popes and other church officials gained support for war in defense of Christianity by promising spiritual benefits to those who joined a campaign or died fighting. Preachers communicated these ideas widely and told stories about warrior-saints who slew hundreds of enemies.

Religious zeal led increasing numbers of people to go on pilgrimages to holy places, including Jerusalem. The Arab Muslims who had ruled Jerusalem and the surrounding territory for centuries allowed Christian pilgrims to travel freely, but in the late eleventh century the Seljuk Turks took over Palestine, and pilgrimage became more difficult. The Byzantine emperor at Constantinople appealed to western European Christians for support. The emperor's appeal fit well with

CHAPTER LOCATOR | How did medieval rulers restore order and centralize political power? | How did the Christian Church enhance its power and create new institutions?

400 CHAPTER 14 EUROPE IN THE MIDDLE AGES

papal aims, and in 1095 Pope Urban II called for a great Christian holy war. Urban urged Christian knights who had been fighting one another to direct their energies against those he claimed were the true enemies of God, the Muslims.

The Course of the Crusades

Thousands of people of all classes responded to Urban's call, joining what became known as the First Crusade. The First Crusade was successful, mostly because of the dynamic enthusiasm of the participants, who had little more than religious zeal. They knew little of the geography or climate of the Middle East and could never agree on a leader. Adding to these disadvantages, supply lines were never set up, starvation and disease wracked the army, and the Turks slaughtered hundreds of noncombatants. Nevertheless, the army pressed on, besieging and taking several cities, including Antioch. After a monthlong siege, the Crusaders took Jerusalem in July 1099 (Map 14.2).

With Jerusalem taken, some Crusaders regarded their mission as accomplished and set off for home. Others stayed, setting up institutions to rule local territories and the Muslim population. Four small "Crusader states" — Jerusalem, Edessa, Tripoli, and Antioch — were established, and castles and fortified towns were built in these states to defend against Muslim reconquest.

Between 1096 and 1270 the crusading ideal was expressed in eight papally approved expeditions, though none after the First Crusade accomplished very much. The Muslim states in the Middle East were politically fragmented when the Crusaders first came, and it took them about a century to reorganize. They did so dramatically under Saladin (Salah al-Din), who unified Egypt and Syria. In 1187 the Muslims retook Jerusalem, but the Christians held onto port towns, and Saladin allowed pilgrims safe passage to Jerusalem. From that point on, the Crusader states were more important economically than politically or religiously, giving Italian and French merchants direct access to Eastern products.

After the Muslims retook Jerusalem, the crusading movement faced other setbacks. During the Fourth Crusade (1202–1204), Crusaders stopped in Constantinople, and when they were not welcomed, they sacked the city. The Byzantine Empire splintered into three parts and soon consisted of little more than the city of Constantinople. Moreover, the assault of one Christian people on another, made the split between the churches permanent and discredited the entire crusading movement in the eyes of many Christians.

In the late thirteenth century Turkish armies, after gradually conquering all other Muslim rulers, turned against the Crusader states. In 1291 the Christians' last stronghold, the port of Acre, fell.

Consequences of the Crusades

The Crusades testified to the religious enthusiasm of the High Middle Ages and the influence of the papacy, gave kings and the pope opportunities to expand their bureaucracies, and provided an outlet for nobles' dreams of glory. The Crusades also introduced some Europeans to Eastern luxury goods. They were also a boon to Italian merchants, who profited from outfitting military expeditions as well as from the opening of new trade routes and the establishment of trading communities in the Crusader states.

| What were the causes, course, and consequences of the Crusades? | How did the lives of common people, nobles, and townspeople differ? | What were the primary educational and cultural developments in medieval Europe? | Why have the later Middle Ages been seen as a time of calamity and crisis? | ✓ LearningCurve Check what you know. |

MAP 14.2 ■ The Crusades, 1096–1270

The Crusaders took many different sea and land routes on their way to Jerusalem, often crossing the lands of the Byzantine Empire, which led to conflict with Eastern Christians. The Crusader kingdoms in the East lasted only briefly.

Map legend:
→ First Crusade, 1096–1099
→ Second Crusade, 1147–1149
→ Third Crusade, 1189–1192
→ Fourth Crusade, 1202–1204
→ Crusade of Frederick II, 1228–1229
→ Crusades of Louis IX, 1248–1254 and 1270
■ Crusader kingdoms in the East
✦ Major battle

Despite these advantages, the Crusades had some seriously negative socio-political consequences. For one thing, they proved to be a disaster for Jewish-Christian relations. Inspired by the ideology of holy war, Christian armies on their way to Jerusalem on the First Crusade joined with local mobs to attack Jewish families and communities. Later Crusades brought similar violence, enhanced by accusations that Jews engaged in the ritual murder of Christians to use their blood in religious rites.

Legal restrictions on Jews gradually increased throughout Europe. Jews were forbidden to have Christian servants or employees, to hold public office, to appear in public on Christian holy days, or to enter Christian parts of town without a badge marking them as Jews. They were prohibited from engaging in any trade with Christians except money-lending and were banished from England and France.

The Crusades also left an inheritance of deep bitterness in Christian-Muslim relations. Each side dehumanized the other, viewing those who followed the other religion as unbelievers. The ideal of a sacred mission to conquer or convert Muslim peoples entered Europeans' consciousness and became a continuing goal. When in 1492 Christopher Columbus sailed west, he used the language of the Crusades in his diaries, and he hoped to establish a Christian base in India from which a new crusade against Islam could be launched (see page 464).

> **QUICK REVIEW**

Why did the Crusades undermine relations between Christians and non-Christians?

CHAPTER LOCATOR | How did medieval rulers restore order and centralize political power? | How did the Christian Church enhance its power and create new institutions?

402 CHAPTER 14 EUROPE IN THE MIDDLE AGES

Agricultural Work

In this scene from a German manuscript written about 1190, men and women of different ages are sowing seeds and harvesting grain. All residents of a village, including children, engaged in agricultural tasks. (Rheinisches Landesmuseum, Bonn, Germany/Giraudon/The Bridgeman Art Library)

How did the lives of common people, nobles, and townspeople differ, and what new commercial developments increased wealth?

IN THE LATE NINTH CENTURY medieval intellectuals described Christian society as composed of those who pray (the monks), those who fight (the nobles), and those who work (the peasants). This three-category model does not fully describe medieval society—there were degrees of wealth and status within each group. Also, the model does not take townspeople and the emerging commercial classes into consideration, and it completely excludes those who were not Christian, such as Jews, Muslims, and pagans. Furthermore, those who used the model, generally bishops and other church officials, ignored the fact that each of these groups was made up of both women and men. Despite—or perhaps because of—these limitations, the model of the three categories was a powerful mental construct. Therefore, we can use it to organize our investigation of life in the Middle Ages, broadening it to include groups and issues that medieval authors did not. (See page 396 for a discussion of the life of monks and nuns—"those who pray.")

The Life and Work of Peasants

The men and women who worked the land in medieval Europe made up probably more than 90 percent of the population, as they did in China, India, and other parts of the world where agriculture predominated. The evolution of localized systems of authority into more centralized states had relatively little impact on the daily lives of these peasants except when it involved warfare.

| What were the causes, course, and consequences of the Crusades? | **How did the lives of common people, nobles, and townspeople differ?** | What were the primary educational and cultural developments in medieval Europe? | Why have the later Middle Ages been seen as a time of calamity and crisis? | LearningCurve Check what you know. |

Medieval theologians lumped everyone who worked the land into the category of "those who work," but in fact there were many levels of peasants, ranging from slaves to free and sometimes very rich farmers. Most peasants were serfs, required to stay in the village and perform labor on the lord's land. Serfs were also often obliged to pay fees on common occurrences, such as marriage or inheritance of property.

Serfdom was a hereditary condition. A person born a serf was likely to die a serf, though many serfs did secure their freedom, and the economic revival that began in the eleventh century (see pages 405–406) allowed some to buy their freedom. Further opportunities for increased personal freedom came when lords organized groups of villagers to migrate to sparsely settled frontier areas or to cut down forests or fill in swamps so that there was more land available for farming. Those who took on this extra work often gained a reduction in traditional manorial obligations and an improvement of their social and legal conditions.

In the Middle Ages most European peasants, free and unfree, lived in family groups in small villages that were part of a manor, the estate of a lord (see page 391). The manor was the basic unit of medieval rural organization and the center of rural life. Within the manors of western and central Europe, villages were made up of small houses for individual families, a church, and perhaps the large house of the lord. Peasant households consisted of one married couple, their children, and perhaps one or two other relatives, such as a grandparent or unmarried aunt. In southern and eastern Europe, extended families were more likely to live in the same household or very near one another. Between one-third and one-half of children died before age five, though many people lived into their sixties.

The arable land of the manor was divided between the lord and the peasantry. A peasant family's land was not usually one particular field but a scattering of strips across many fields, some of which would be planted in grain, some in other crops, and some left unworked to allow the soil to rejuvenate. That way if one field yielded little, strips in a different field might be more bountiful.

The peasants' work was typically divided according to gender. Men and boys were responsible for clearing new land, plowing, and caring for large animals; women and girls were responsible for the care of small animals, spinning, and food preparation. Both sexes harvested and planted. Beginning in the eleventh century water mills and windmills aided in some tasks, especially grinding grain, and an increasing use of horses rather than oxen speeded up plowing.

The mainstay of the diet for peasants everywhere—and for all other classes—was bread. Peasants also ate vegetables; animals were too valuable to be used for food on a regular basis, but weaker animals were often slaughtered in the fall, and their meat was preserved with salt and eaten on great feast days such as Christmas and Easter. Ale was the universal drink of common people.

The Life and Work of Nobles

The nobility, though a small fraction of the total population, influenced all aspects of medieval culture. Nobles generally paid few taxes, and they had power over the people living on their lands. They maintained order, resolved disputes, and protected their dependents from attacks. They appointed officials who oversaw agricultural production. The liberty and privileges of the noble were inheritable, perpetuated by blood and not by wealth alone.

CHAPTER LOCATOR | How did medieval rulers restore order and centralize political power? | How did the Christian Church enhance its power and create new institutions?

404 CHAPTER 14 EUROPE IN THE MIDDLE AGES

The nobles' primary obligation was warfare, just as it was for nobles among the Mexica (see pages 314–317) and samurai in Japan (see page 381). Nobles were also obliged to attend the lord's court on important occasions.

Originally, most knights focused solely on military skills, but around 1200 a different ideal of knighthood emerged, usually termed chivalry. Chivalry was a code of conduct in which fighting to defend the Christian faith and protecting one's countrymen was declared to have a sacred purpose. Other qualities gradually became part of chivalry: bravery, generosity, honor, graciousness, mercy, and eventually gallantry toward women, which came to be called "courtly love."

Noblewomen played a large and important role in the functioning of the estate. They were responsible for managing the household's "inner economy" — cooking, brewing, spinning, weaving, and caring for yard animals. When the lord was away for long periods, his wife became the sole manager of the family properties. Often the responsibilities of the estate fell permanently to her if she became a widow.

chivalry
▶ A code of conduct that was supposed to govern the behavior of a knight.

Towns, Cities, and the Growth of Commercial Interests

Most people continued to live in villages in the Middle Ages, but the rise of towns and the growth of a new business and commercial class were central to Europe's recovery after the disorders of the tenth century. Several factors contributed to this growth: a rise in population; increased agricultural output, which provided an adequate food supply for new town dwellers; and enough peace and political stability to allow merchants to transport and sell goods.

Towns in Europe were generally enclosed by walls as were towns in China, India, and the Middle East. Most towns were first established as trading centers, with a marketplace in the middle, and they were likely to have a mint for coining money and a court for settling disputes. Residents bargained with lords to make the town politically independent, which gave them the right to hold legal courts, select leaders, and set taxes.

Townspeople also tried to acquire liberties, above all personal freedom, for themselves. It gradually developed that an individual who lived in a town for a year and a day, and was accepted by the townspeople, was free of servile obligations and status. Thus serfs who fled their manors for towns and were able to find work and avoid recapture became free of personal labor obligations. In this way the growth of towns contributed to a slow decline of serfdom in western Europe.

Merchants constituted the most powerful group in most towns, and they were often organized into merchant guilds, which prohibited nonmembers from trading, pooled members' risks, monopolized city offices, and controlled the economy of the town. Towns became centers of production as well, and artisans in particular trades formed their own craft guilds. Members of the craft guilds determined the quality, quantity, and price of the goods produced and the number of apprentices and journeymen affiliated with the guild. Formal membership in guilds was generally limited to men, but women often worked in guild shops without official membership.

Artisans generally made and sold products in their own homes, with production taking place on the ground floor. The family lived above the business on the second or third floor. As the business and the family expanded, additional stories were added.

craft guilds
▶ Associations of artisans organized to regulate the quality, quantity, and price of the goods produced as well as the number of affiliated apprentices and journeymen.

What were the causes, course, and consequences of the Crusades?

How did the lives of common people, nobles, and townspeople differ?

What were the primary educational and cultural developments in medieval Europe?

Why have the later Middle Ages been seen as a time of calamity and crisis?

☑ LearningCurve
Check what you know.

Most medieval towns and cities developed with little planning or attention to sanitation. Horses and oxen, the chief means of transportation and power, dropped tons of dung on the streets every year. It was universal practice in the early towns to dump household waste, both animal and human, into the road in front of one's house. Despite such unpleasant aspects of urban life, people wanted to get into medieval towns because they represented opportunities for economic advancement, social mobility, and improvement in legal status.

The Expansion of Trade and the Commercial Revolution

The growth of towns went hand in hand with a revival of trade as artisans and craftsmen manufactured goods for local and foreign consumption. As in the city-states of East Africa (see pages 288–290), most trade centered in towns and was controlled by merchants. They began to pool their money to finance trading expeditions, sharing the profits and also sharing the risks.

Italian cities, especially Venice, led the West in trade in general and completely dominated trade with Asia and North Africa. Merchants from Florence and Milan were also important traders, and they developed new methods of accounting and record keeping that facilitated the movement of goods and money. The towns of Bruges, Ghent, and Ypres in Flanders were leaders in long-distance trade and built up a vast industry in the manufacture of cloth, aided by ready access to wool from England. The availability of raw wool also encouraged the development of cloth manufacture within England itself.

In much of northern Europe, the Hanseatic League (known as the Hansa for short), a mercantile association of towns formed to achieve mutual security and exclusive trading rights, controlled trade. During the thirteenth century perhaps two hundred cities from Holland to Poland joined the league. At cities such as Bruges and London, Hanseatic merchants secured special concessions exempting them from all tolls and allowing them to trade at local fairs. Hanseatic merchants also established foreign trading centers.

These developments added up to what historians of Europe have called the **commercial revolution**, a direct parallel to the economic revolution going on in Song Dynasty China at the same time (see pages 366–368). In giving the transformation this name, historians point not only to an increase in the sheer volume of trade and in the complexity and sophistication of business procedures but also to the new attitude toward business and making money. Some even detect a "capitalist spirit" in which making a profit was regarded as a good thing in itself.

The commercial revolution created a great deal of new wealth, which did not escape the attention of kings and other rulers. Wealth could be taxed, and through taxation kings could create strong and centralized states. Through the activities of merchants, Europeans again saw products from Africa and Asia in city marketplaces, as they had in Roman times. The commercial revolution also provided the opportunity for thousands of serfs in western Europe to improve their social position.

- • Principal Hanseatic town
- ▲ Hanseatic trading partner

The Hanseatic League, 1300–1400

commercial revolution
▶ The transformation of the economic structure of Europe, beginning in the eleventh century, from a rural, manorial society to a more complex mercantile society.

> **QUICK REVIEW**

What are the limitations of the three-category model of medieval society? What aspects of that society does the model fail to capture?

CHAPTER LOCATOR | How did medieval rulers restore order and centralize political power? | How did the Christian Church enhance its power and create new institutions?

CHAPTER 14
406 EUROPE IN THE MIDDLE AGES

What were the primary educational and cultural developments in medieval Europe?

Notre Dame Cathedral, Paris, begun 1163

This view offers a fine example of the twin towers (left), the spire, the great rose window over the south portal (center), and the flying buttresses that support the walls and the vaults. Like hundreds of other churches in medieval Europe, it was dedicated to the Virgin Mary. With a spire rising more than 300 feet, Notre Dame was the tallest building in Europe at the time of its construction. (David R. Frazier/Photo Researchers, Inc.)

THE TOWNS THAT BECAME centers of trade and production in the High Middle Ages also developed into cultural and intellectual centers. Trade brought in new ideas as well as merchandise, and in many cities a new type of educational institution—the university—emerged. As universities appeared, so did other cultural advancements, such as new forms of architecture and literature.

Universities and Scholasticism

Since the time of the Carolingian Empire, monasteries and cathedral schools had offered the only formal instruction available. In the eleventh century in Bologna and other Italian cities, wealthy businessmen established municipal schools; in the twelfth century municipal schools in Italy and cathedral schools in France developed into much larger universities, a transformation parallel to the opening of madrasas in Muslim cities (see page 000).

The growth of the University of Bologna coincided with a revival of interest in Roman law. The study of Roman law as embodied in Justinian's *Code* (see page 206) had never completely died out in the West, but in the eleventh century

| What were the causes, course, and consequences of the Crusades? | How did the lives of common people, nobles, and townspeople differ? | **What were the primary educational and cultural developments in medieval Europe?** | Why have the later Middle Ages been seen as a time of calamity and crisis? | ✓ LearningCurve Check what you know. |

the discovery of a complete manuscript of the code in a library in northern Italy led scholars to study and teach Roman law intently.

At the Italian city of Salerno, interest in medicine had persisted for centuries. Greek and Muslim physicians there had studied the use of herbs as cures and had experimented with surgery. The twelfth century ushered in a new interest in Greek medical texts and in the work of Arab and Greek doctors. Ideas from this medical literature spread throughout Europe from Salerno and became the basis of training for physicians at other medieval universities.

Although medicine and law were important academic disciplines in the Middle Ages, theology was "the queen of sciences." Paris became the place to study theology, and in the first decades of the twelfth century students from all over Europe crowded into the cathedral school of Notre Dame in that city.

University professors were known as "schoolmen" or **Scholastics**. They developed a method of thinking, reasoning, and writing in which questions were raised and authorities cited on both sides of a question. The goal of the Scholastic method was to arrive at definitive answers and to provide a rational explanation for what was believed on faith.

One of the most famous Scholastics was Peter Abelard (1079–1142). Fascinated by logic, Abelard used a method of systematic doubting in his writing and teaching. Abelard was censured by a church council, but he was highly popular with students.

Thirteenth-century Scholastics devoted an enormous amount of time to collecting and organizing knowledge on all topics. These collections were published as summae (SOO-may), or reference books. Thomas Aquinas (1225–1274), a professor at the University of Paris, produced the most famous collection, the *Summa Theologica*, which deals with a vast number of theological questions.

Students lived in privately endowed residential colleges and were considered to be lower-level members of the clergy, so that any student accused of a crime was tried in church, rather than in city, courts. This clerical status, along with widely held ideas about women's lesser intellectual capabilities, meant that university education was restricted to men.

At all universities the standard method of teaching was the lecture. With this method the professor read a passage from the Bible, Justinian's *Code*, or one of Aristotle's treatises. He then explained and interpreted the passage. Examinations were given after three, four, or five years of study, when the student applied for a degree. If the candidate passed, he was awarded the first, or bachelor's, degree. Further study enabled the graduate to try for the master's and doctor's degrees. Degrees were technically licenses to teach. Most students, however, did not become teachers. They staffed the expanding royal and papal administrations.

Cathedrals and a New Architectural Style

In the tenth and eleventh centuries cathedrals were built in a style that resembled ancient Roman architecture, with massive walls, rounded stone arches, and small windows—features later labeled Romanesque. In the twelfth century a new style spread out from central France. It was dubbed **Gothic** by later Renaissance architects. The basic features of Gothic architecture—pointed arches, high ceilings, and exterior supports called flying buttresses that carried much of the weight of

Scholastics

▶ Medieval professors who developed a method of thinking, reasoning, and writing in which questions were raised and authorities cited on both sides of a question.

Gothic

▶ The term for the architectural and artistic style that prevailed in Europe from the mid-twelfth to the sixteenth century.

CHAPTER LOCATOR | How did medieval rulers restore order and centralize political power?   How did the Christian Church enhance its power and create new institutions?

CHAPTER 14
408   EUROPE IN THE MIDDLE AGES

the roof—allowed unprecedented interior light. Stained-glass windows were cut into the stone. Between 1180 and 1270 in France alone, eighty cathedrals, about five hundred abbey churches, and tens of thousands of parish churches were constructed in this new style. They are testimony to the deep religious faith and piety of medieval people and also to the civic pride of urban residents, for towns competed with one another to build the largest and most splendid cathedral.

Vernacular Literature and Drama

Latin was the language used in university education, scholarly writing, and works of literature. By the High Middle Ages, however, no one spoke Latin as his or her first language. The barbarian invasions, the mixture of peoples, and the usual changes in language that occurred over time resulted in a variety of local dialects that blended words and linguistic forms in various ways.

In the High Middle Ages, some authors departed from tradition and began to write in their local dialect, that is, in the everyday language of their region, which linguistic historians call the vernacular. This new **vernacular literature** gradually transformed some local dialects into literary languages, such as French, German, Italian, and English, while other local dialects, such as Breton and Bavarian, remained means of oral communication.

Stories and songs in the vernacular were composed and performed at the courts of nobles and rulers. In southern Europe, especially in Provence in southern France, poets who called themselves troubadours wrote and sang lyric verses celebrating love, desire, beauty, and gallantry. The songs of the troubadours were widely imitated in Italy, England, and Germany, so they spurred the development of vernacular literature there as well. Drama, derived from the church's liturgy, emerged as a distinct art form. Actors performed plays based on biblical themes and on the lives of the saints; these dramas were presented in the towns, first in churches and then at the marketplace. By combining comical farce based on ordinary life with serious religious scenes, plays gave ordinary people an opportunity to identify with religious figures and think about their faith.

Beginning in the fourteenth century a variety of evidence attests to the increasing literacy of laypeople. Wills and inventories reveal that many people, not just nobles, possessed books—mainly devotional texts, but also romances, manuals on manners and etiquette, histories, and sometimes legal and philosophical texts. The spread of literacy represents a response to the needs of an increasingly complex society.

vernacular literature

▶ Literature written in the everyday language of a region rather than Latin; this included French, German, Italian, and English.

QUICK REVIEW ◁

What trends and values are reflected in the emergence of vernacular literature during this period?

What were the causes, course, and consequences of the Crusades?

How did the lives of common people, nobles, and townspeople differ?

What were the primary educational and cultural developments in medieval Europe?

Why have the later Middle Ages been seen as a time of calamity and crisis?

☑ LearningCurve
Check what you know.

Why have the later Middle Ages been seen as a time of calamity and crisis?

Procession of Flagellants

In this manuscript illumination from 1349, shirtless flagellants, men and women who whipped and scourged themselves as penance for their and society's sins, walk through the Flemish city of Tournai, which had just been struck by the plague. Many people believed that the Black Death was God's punishment for humanity's wickedness. (The Flagellants at Doornik in 1349, copy of a miniature from the *Chronicle of Aegidius Li Muisis*/Private Collection/The Bridgeman Art Library)

BETWEEN 1300 AND 1450 Europeans experienced a series of shocks: climate change, economic decline, plague, war, social upheaval, and increased crime and violence. Death and preoccupation with death made the fourteenth century one of the most wrenching periods of history in Europe.

The Great Famine and the Black Death

In the first half of the fourteenth century Europe experienced a series of climate changes, especially the beginning of a period of colder and wetter weather that historical geographers label the "little ice age." Its effects were dramatic and disastrous. Population had steadily increased in the twelfth and thirteenth centuries, but with colder weather, poor harvests led to scarcity and starvation. The costs of grain, livestock, and dairy products rose sharply. Almost all of northern Europe suffered a terrible famine between 1315 and 1322, with dire social consequences: peasants were forced to sell or mortgage their lands for money to buy food, and the number of homeless people greatly increased, as did petty crime. An undernourished population was dealt a further blow in 1347 in the form of a virulent new disease, later called the **Black Death** (Map 14.3). The symptoms of

Black Death

▶ The plague that first struck Europe in 1347, killing perhaps one-third of the population.

CHAPTER LOCATOR | How did medieval rulers restore order and centralize political power? | How did the Christian Church enhance its power and create new institutions?

CHAPTER 14
410 EUROPE IN THE MIDDLE AGES

MAP 14.3 ■ The Course of the Black Death in Fourteenth-Century Europe

The plague followed trade routes as it spread into and across Europe. A few cities that took strict quarantine measures were spared.

this disease were first described in 1331 in southwestern China, then part of the Mongol Empire (see page 256). From there it spread across Central Asia by way of Mongol armies and merchant caravans, arriving in the ports of the Black Sea by the 1340s. In October 1347 Genoese ships traveling from the Crimea in southern Russia brought the plague to Messina, from which it spread across Sicily and into Italy. From Italy it traveled in all directions.

Most historians and almost all microbiologists identify the disease that spread in the fourteenth century as the bubonic plague, caused by the bacillus *Yersinia pestis*. The disease normally afflicts rats. Fleas living on the infected rats drink their blood and pass the bacteria that cause the plague on to the next rat they bite. Usually the disease is limited to rats and other rodents, but at certain points in history the fleas have jumped from their rodent hosts to humans and other animals.

Most people believed that the Black Death was caused by poisons or by "corrupted air" that carried the disease from place to place. They sought to keep poisons from entering the body by smelling or ingesting strong-smelling herbs,

What were the causes, course, and consequences of the Crusades?

How did the lives of common people, nobles, and townspeople differ?

What were the primary educational and cultural developments in medieval Europe?

Why have the later Middle Ages been seen as a time of calamity and crisis?

✓ LearningCurve
Check what you know.

Initial Stage	Appearance of boil, or *bubo* (growth the size of a nut or an apple in the armpit, the groin, or on the neck)
Secondary Stage	Appearance of black spots or blotches caused by bleeding under the skin
Final Stage	Victim begins to cough violently and spit blood; death follows in two or three days

and they tried to remove the poisons through bloodletting. They also prayed and did penance. Anxiety and fears about the plague caused people to look for scapegoats, and they found them in the Jews, who they believed had poisoned the wells of Christian communities and thereby infected the drinking water. This charge led to the murder of thousands of Jews across Europe.

Of a total English population of perhaps 4.2 million, probably 1.4 million died of the Black Death in its several visits. In Italy densely populated cities endured incredible losses. Florence lost between one-half and two-thirds of its population when the plague visited in 1348. The disease recurred intermittently in the 1360s and 1370s and reappeared many times, as late as the early 1700s in Europe.

In the short term the economic effects of the plague were severe because the death of many peasants disrupted food production. But in the long term the dramatic decline in population eased pressure on the land, and wages and per capita wealth rose for those who survived. The psychological consequences of the plague were profound. Some people sought release in wild living, while others turned to the severest forms of asceticism and frenzied religious fervor.

The Hundred Years' War

While the plague ravaged populations in Asia, North Africa, and Europe, a long international war in western Europe added further death and destruction. England and France had engaged in sporadic military hostilities from the time of the Norman Conquest in 1066 (see page 393), and in the middle of the fourteenth century these became more intense. From 1337 to 1453 the two countries intermittently fought the Hundred Years' War.

The Hundred Years' War had a number of causes. Both England and France claimed the duchy of Aquitaine in southwestern France, and the English king Edward III argued that, as the grandson of an earlier French king, he should have rightfully inherited the French throne. Nobles in provinces on the borders of France who were worried about the growing power of the French king supported Edward, as did wealthy wool merchants and clothmakers in Flanders who depended on English wool.

The war, fought almost entirely in France, consisted mainly of a series of random sieges and raids. During the war's early stages, England was successful, primarily through the use of longbows fired by well-trained foot soldiers against mounted knights and, after 1375, by early cannons. By 1419 the English had advanced to the walls of Paris. But the French cause was not lost. Though England scored the initial victories, France won the war.

CHAPTER LOCATOR | How did medieval rulers restore order and centralize political power? | How did the Christian Church enhance its power and create new institutions?

CHAPTER 14
412 EUROPE IN THE MIDDLE AGES

> PICTURING THE PAST

ANALYZING THE IMAGE: What types of weapons are the attackers and defenders using? How have the attackers on the left enhanced their position?

CONNECTIONS: This painting shows a battle that occurred in 1377, but it was painted about a hundred years later and shows the military technology available at the time it was painted, not at the time of the actual siege. Which of the weapons represent newer forms of military technology? What impact would you expect them to have on warfare?

The ultimate French success rests heavily on the actions of Joan, an obscure French peasant girl whose vision and military leadership revived French fortunes and led to victory. Born in 1412 to well-to-do peasants, Joan grew up in a pious household. During adolescence she began to hear voices, which she later said belonged to Saint Michael, Saint Catherine, and Saint Margaret. In 1428 these voices told her that the dauphin of France — Charles VII, who was uncrowned as king because of the English occupation — had to be crowned and the English expelled from France. Joan went to the French court and secured the support of the dauphin to travel, dressed as a knight, with the French army to the besieged city of Orléans.

At Orléans, Joan inspired and led French attacks, and the English retreated. As a result of her successes, Charles made Joan co-commander of the entire army,

| What were the causes, course, and consequences of the Crusades? | How did the lives of common people, nobles, and townspeople differ? | What were the primary educational and cultural developments in medieval Europe? | **Why have the later Middle Ages been seen as a time of calamity and crisis?** | LearningCurve Check what you know. |

413

and she led it to a string of military victories in the summer of 1429. Two months after the victory at Orléans, Charles VII was crowned king at Reims.

Joan and the French army continued their fight against the English. In 1430 England's allies, the Burgundians, captured Joan and sold her to the English, and the French did not intervene. In 1431 she was condemned as a heretic and burned at the stake in the marketplace at Rouen. The French army continued its victories without her, and demands for an end to the war increased among the English, who were growing tired of the mounting loss of life and the flow of money into a seemingly bottomless pit. Slowly the French reconquered Normandy and finally ejected the English from Aquitaine. At the war's end in 1453, only the town of Calais remained in English hands.

The long war had a profound impact on the two countries. In England and France the war promoted nationalism. It led to technological experimentation, especially with gunpowder weaponry, whose firepower made the protective walls of stone castles obsolete. The war also stimulated the development of the English Parliament. Edward III's constant need for money to pay for the war compelled him to summon it many times, and its representatives slowly built up their powers.

Challenges to the Church

In times of crisis or disaster people of all faiths have sought the consolation of religion, but in the fourteenth century the official Christian Church offered little solace. While local clergy eased the suffering of many, a dispute over who was the legitimate pope weakened the church as an institution. In 1309 pressure by the French monarchy led the pope to move his permanent residence to Avignon in southern France. This marked the start of seven successive papacies in Avignon. Not surprising, all these popes were French—a matter of controversy among church followers outside France. Also, the popes largely concentrated on bureaucratic and financial matters to the exclusion of spiritual objectives.

In 1376 one of the French popes returned to Rome, and when he died there several years later Roman citizens demanded an Italian pope who would remain

CHAPTER LOCATOR | How did medieval rulers restore order and centralize political power? | How did the Christian Church enhance its power and create new institutions?

414   CHAPTER 14
EUROPE IN THE MIDDLE AGES

in Rome. The cardinals elected Urban VI, but soon regretted their decision. The cardinals slipped away from Rome and declared Urban's election invalid because it had come about under threats from the Roman mob. They elected a French cardinal who took the name Clement VII (pontificate 1378–1394) and set himself up at Avignon in opposition to Urban. There were thus two popes, a situation that was later termed the Great Schism.

The powers of Europe aligned themselves with Urban or Clement along strictly political lines. France recognized the Frenchman, Clement; England, recognized Urban. The rest of Europe lined up behind one or the other. In all European countries the common people were thoroughly confused about which pope was legitimate. In the end the schism weakened the religious faith of many Christians and brought church leadership into serious disrepute.

A first attempt to heal the schism led to the installation of a third pope and a threefold split, but finally a church council meeting at Constance (1414–1418) successfully deposed the three schismatic popes and elected a new leader, who took the name Martin V (pontificate 1417–1431). In the later fifteenth century the papacy concentrated on building up its wealth and political power in Italy rather than on the concerns of the whole church. As a result, many people decided that they would need to rely on their own prayers and pious actions rather than on the institutional church for their salvation.

Allegiance to Rome
Allegiance to Avignon
Official allegiance to Rome but with shifting local allegiances

The Great Schism, 1378–1417

Peasant and Urban Revolts

The difficult conditions of the fourteenth and fifteenth centuries spurred a wave of peasant and urban revolts across Europe. In 1358, when French taxation for the Hundred Years' War fell heavily on the poor, the frustrations of the French peasantry exploded in a massive uprising called the Jacquerie (zhah-kuh-REE). Adding to the anger over taxes was the toll taken by the plague and by the famine that had struck some areas. Artisans, small merchants, and parish priests joined the peasants, and residents of both urban and rural areas committed terrible destruction. For several weeks the nobles were on the defensive, until the upper class united to repress the revolt with merciless ferocity.

Taxes and other grievances also led to the 1381 English Peasants' Revolt, involving tens of thousands of people. The Black Death had dramatically reduced the supply of labor, and peasants had demanded higher wages and fewer manorial obligations. Parliament countered with a law freezing wages and binding workers to their manors. The atmosphere of discontent was further enhanced by popular preachers who proclaimed that great disparities between rich and poor went against Christ's teachings. Moreover, decades of aristocratic violence, much of it perpetrated against the weak peasantry, had bred hostility and bitterness.

In 1380 Parliament imposed a poll tax on all citizens to fund the Hundred Years' War. This tax imposed a greater burden on the poor than on wealthier citizens, and it sparked revolt. The boy-king Richard II (r. 1377–1399) met the leaders of the revolt, agreed to charters ensuring the peasants' freedom, tricked them with false promises, and then proceeded to crush the uprising with terrible ferocity. The nobility tried to use this defeat to restore the labor obligations of serfdom, but they were not successful, and the conversion to money rents continued. In Flanders, France, and England peasant revolts often blended with conflicts

What were the causes, course, and consequences of the Crusades?

How did the lives of common people, nobles, and townspeople differ?

What were the primary educational and cultural developments in medieval Europe?

Why have the later Middle Ages been seen as a time of calamity and crisis?

LearningCurve
Check what you know.

415

involving workers in cities. Unrest also occurred in Italian, Spanish, and German cities. In Florence in 1378 the *ciompi*, or poor propertyless wool workers, revolted and briefly shared government of the city with wealthier artisans and merchants. Rebellions and uprisings everywhere revealed deep peasant and worker frustration with the socioeconomic conditions of the time.

> **QUICK REVIEW**

What were the social and economic consequences of the Black Death?

CHAPTER SUMMARY

Invasions by Vikings, Magyars, and Muslims, along with civil wars, created instability in the ninth and tenth centuries. Local nobles became the strongest powers against external threats, establishing a form of decentralized government later known as feudalism. By the twelfth century rulers in some parts of Europe had reasserted authority and were beginning to develop new institutions of government and legal codes that enabled them to assert power over lesser lords and the general population. The papacy also consolidated its power, though these moves were sometimes challenged by kings and emperors. Monasteries continued to be important places for learning and devotion, and new religious orders were founded. A papal call to retake the holy city of Jerusalem led to the Crusades.

The vast majority of medieval Europeans were peasants who lived in small villages and worked their own and their lord's land. Nobles were a tiny fraction of the total population, but they exerted great power over all aspects of life. Medieval towns and cities grew initially as trading centers and then became centers of production.

Towns also developed into cultural and intellectual centers, as trade brought in new ideas as well as merchandise. Universities offered courses of study based on classical models, and townspeople built churches and cathedrals as symbols of their Christian faith and their civic pride. New types of vernacular literature arose in which poems, songs, and stories were written down in local dialects.

In the fourteenth century a worsening climate brought poor harvests, which contributed to an international economic depression and fostered disease. The Black Death caused enormous population losses and social, psychological, and economic consequences. Additional difficulties included the Hundred Years' War, a schism among rival popes that weakened the Western Christian Church, and peasant and worker frustrations that exploded into uprisings.

CHAPTER LOCATOR | How did medieval rulers restore order and centralize political power? | How did the Christian Church enhance its power and create new institutions?

CONNECTIONS Medieval Europe continues to fascinate us today. We go to medieval fairs; visit castle-themed hotels; watch movies about knights and their conquests; play video games in which we become warriors, trolls, or sorcerers; and read stories with themes of great quests set in the Middle Ages. Characters from other parts of the world often heighten the exoticism: a Muslim soldier joins the fight against a common enemy, a Persian princess rescues the hero and his sidekick, a Buddhist monk teaches martial arts techniques. These characters from outside Europe are fictional, but they also represent aspects of reality because medieval Europe was not isolated, and political and social structures similar to those in Europe developed elsewhere.

In reality few of us would probably want to live in the real Middle Ages, when most people worked in the fields all day and even wealthy lords lived in damp and drafty castles. We do not really want to return to a time when one-third to one-half of all children died before age five and alcohol was the only real pain reliever. But the contemporary appeal of the Middle Ages is an interesting phenomenon, particularly because it stands in such sharp contrast to the attitude of educated Europeans who lived in the centuries immediately afterward. They were the ones who dubbed the period "middle." They saw their own era as the one to be celebrated, and the Middle Ages as best forgotten.

ONLINE DOCUMENT PROJECT

Hildegard of Bingen

Why was Hildegard of Bingen considered a worthy instrument for the transmission of God's word?

Read excerpts from Hildegard's correspondence, and then complete a quiz and writing assignment based on the evidence and details from this chapter. *See inside the front cover to learn more.*

| What were the causes, course, and consequences of the Crusades? | How did the lives of common people, nobles, and townspeople differ? | What were the primary educational and cultural developments in medieval Europe? | Why have the later Middle Ages been seen as a time of calamity and crisis? | ✔ LearningCurve Check what you know. |

CHAPTER 14 STUDY GUIDE

STEP 1

GET STARTED ONLINE

LearningCurve

Now that you've read the chapter, make it stick by completing the LearningCurve activity.

STEP 2

EXPLAIN WHY IT MATTERS

Put your reading into practice. Identify each term below, and then explain why it matters in world history.

TERM	WHO OR WHAT & WHEN	WHY IT MATTERS
vassal (p. 391)		
fief (p. 391)		
feudalism (p. 391)		
manorialism (p. 392)		
serf (p. 392)		
heresy (p. 398)		
reconquista (p. 399)		
Crusades (p. 400)		
chivalry (p. 405)		
craft guilds (p. 405)		
commercial revolution (p. 406)		
Scholastics (p. 408)		
Gothic (p. 408)		
vernacular literature (p. 409)		
Black Death (p. 410)		

STEP 3

MOVE BEYOND THE BASICS

To demonstrate a more advanced understanding of the social structure of medieval Europe, fill in the chart below with descriptions of the characteristics and lifestyle of the medieval peasantry, nobility, and clergy, as well as important developments and trends affecting the group's composition and status. How might you modify this model to create a better picture of the reality of medieval life?

	Characteristics and Lifestyle	Developments and Trends
Peasants		
Nobility		
Clergy		

PUT IT ALL TOGETHER Now, take a step back and try to explain the big picture. Remember to use specific examples from the chapter in your answers.

POLITICAL CONSOLIDATION AND RELIGIOUS REFORM

▶ What was the relationship between feudalism and manorialism? How did the two systems work together to shape the medieval social and political world?

▶ How and why did the agendas of secular rulers and the papacy clash in the Middle Ages?

SOCIETY, ECONOMY, AND CULTURE

▶ How did serfdom differ from slavery? How and why did Western European peasants gain increased personal liberty over the course of the Middle Ages?

▶ What made the rise of universities possible? How might larger social and economic trends have contributed to their emergence?

THE LATER MIDDLE AGES

▶ What were the social, economic, and cultural consequences of the Hundred Years' War?

▶ What factors combined to undermine European's faith in religious and political authorities? How did peasant and urban revolts reflect this lack of confidence?

LOOKING BACK, LOOKING AHEAD

▶ Argue for or against the following statement. "The Middle Ages are best understood as a period of transition, a low point of decline and disorder between the twin peaks of Classical and Renaissance civilization." What evidence can you present in support of your argument?

▶ What role might the Crusades play in contemporary Muslim-Christian relations? What connections might Muslims or Christians today make between the Crusades and the global policies of Western nations in the twenty and twenty-first centuries?

> **IN YOUR OWN WORDS**

Imagine that you must give an oral report to the class answering the following question: **What role did clergy, nobles, peasants, and townspeople play in medieval European society? What would be the most important points and why?**

15

EUROPE IN THE RENAISSANCE AND REFORMATION

1350–1600

> In what ways did the Renaissance and Reformation represent breaks from the medieval past? Chapter 15 examines cultural, intellectual, and religious change during Europe's Renaissance and Reformation. While disease, famine, and war marked the fourteenth century in much of Europe, the era also witnessed the beginnings of remarkable changes in many aspects of intellectual and cultural life. First in Italy and then elsewhere, artists and writers thought that they were living in a new golden age, later termed the Renaissance, in which Europeans recaptured the glories of the classical past. Religious reformers carried out even more dramatic changes. In the sixteenth century, long-standing calls for religious reform gained wide acceptance. In a movement termed the Protestant Reformation, Western Christianity broke into many divisions, a situation that continues today.

Portrait of Baldassare Castiglione The author and courtier Baldassare Castiglione directs his calm gaze toward the viewer in this portrait by the renowned Italian Renaissance artist Raphael. Individual portraits like this one expressed the ideals of the Renaissance: elegance, balance, proportion, and self-awareness. (© Samuel Courtauld Trust, The Courtauld Gallery, London, UK/ The Bridgeman Art Library)

> What were the major cultural developments of the Renaissance?

> What were the key social hierarchies in Renaissance Europe, and how did these hierarchies shape people's lives?

> How did the nation-states of western Europe evolve in this period?

> What were the central ideas of Protestant reformers, and why were they appealing to various groups across Europe?

> How did the Catholic Church respond to the new religious situation?

> What were the causes and consequences of religious violence, including riots, wars, and witch-hunts?

 LearningCurve

After reading the chapter, use LearningCurve to retain what you've read.

What were the major cultural developments of the Renaissance?

Italian City Scene

In this detail from a fresco, the Italian painter Lorenzo Lotto captures the mixing of social groups in a Renaissance Italian city. The crowd of men in the left foreground includes wealthy merchants in elaborate hats and colorful coats. Two mercenary soldiers (carrying a sword and a pike) wear short doublets and tight hose stylishly slit to reveal colored undergarments, while boys play with toy weapons at their feet. Clothing like that of the soldiers, which emphasized the masculine form, was frequently criticized for its expense and its "indecency." At the right, women sell vegetables and bread, which would have been a common sight at any city marketplace. (Scala/ Art Resource, NY)

Renaissance

▶ A French word meaning "rebirth," used to describe a cultural movement that began in fourteenth-century Italy and looked back to the classical past.

THE Renaissance **WAS CHARACTERIZED** by self-conscious awareness among fourteenth- and fifteenth-century Italians, particularly scholars and writers known as humanists, that they were living in a new era. Their ideas influenced education and were spread through the new technology of the printing press. Interest in the classical past and in the individual also shaped Renaissance art in terms of style and subject matter.

Wealth and Power in Renaissance Italy

Economic growth laid the material basis for the Italian Renaissance and its cultural achievements. Ambitious merchants gained political power to match their economic power and then used their money to buy luxuries and hire talent in a patronage system. Through this system, cities, groups, and individuals commissioned writers and artists to produce specific works. Thus economics, politics, and culture were interconnected.

The Renaissance began in the northern Italian city of Florence, which possessed enormous wealth as a consequence of its domination of European

patronage

▶ Financial support of writers and artists by cities, groups, and individuals, often to produce specific works or works in specific styles.

CHAPTER LOCATOR | **What were the major cultural developments of the Renaissance?** | What were the key social hierarchies in Renaissance Europe?

422 CHAPTER 15 EUROPE IN THE RENAISSANCE AND REFORMATION

1434–1737 Medici family in power in Florence	**1536** John Calvin publishes *The Institutes of the Christian Religion*
1450s Development of movable metal type in Germany	**1540** Founding of the Society of Jesus (Jesuits)
1469 Marriage of Isabella of Castile and Ferdinand of Aragon	**1545–1563** Council of Trent
1492 Spain conquers Granada; practicing Jews expelled from Spain	**1555** Peace of Augsburg
1508–1512 Michelangelo paints ceiling of the Sistine Chapel	**1558–1603** Reign of Elizabeth I in England
1513 Niccolò Machiavelli writes *The Prince*	**1560–1660** Height of European witch-hunt
1521 Diet of Worms	**1568–1578** Civil war in the Netherlands
1521–1555 Charles V's wars against Valois kings	**1572** Saint Bartholomew's Day massacre
1525 Peasant revolts in Germany	**1598** Edict of Nantes
1527 Henry VIII of England asks Pope Clement VII to annul his marriage to Catherine of Aragon	

banking. Banking profits allowed elite families to control the city's politics and culture. Although Florence was officially a republic, starting in 1434 the great Medici (MEH-duh-chee) banking family held power almost continually for centuries. They supported an academy for scholars and a host of painters, sculptors, poets, and architects. (See "Individuals in Society: Cosimo and Lorenzo de' Medici," page 430.)

In other Italian cities as well, wealthy merchants and bankers built magnificent palaces and became patrons of the arts, hiring not only architects to design and build these palaces but also artists to fill them with paintings and sculptures, and musicians and composers to fill them with music. Attractions like these appealed to the rich, social-climbing residents of Venice, Florence, Genoa, and Rome, who came to see life more as an opportunity for enjoyment than as a painful pilgrimage to Heaven.

This cultural flowering took place amid political turmoil. In the fifteenth century five powers dominated the Italian peninsula: Venice, Milan, Florence, the Papal States, and the kingdom of Naples. These powers competed furiously for territory and tried to extend their authority over smaller city-states. Whenever one Italian state appeared to gain a predominant position within the peninsula, other states combined to establish a balance of power against the threat, thereby preventing long-term political consolidation.

Italian States, 1494

How did the nation-states of western Europe evolve in this period?	What were the central ideas of Protestant reformers, and why were they appealing?	How did the Catholic Church respond to the new religious situation?	What were the causes and consequences of religious violence?	LearningCurve Check what you know.

This division facilitated outside invasions of Italy. These began in 1494 as Italy became the focus of international ambitions and the battleground of foreign armies, and Italian cities suffered severely from continual warfare for decades. Thus the failure of the city-states to form some type of federal system—or at least to establish a common foreign policy—led to centuries of subjugation by outside invaders.

The Rise of Humanism

The Renaissance was a self-conscious intellectual movement. The realization that something new and unique was happening first came to writers in the fourteenth century, especially to the Italian poet and humanist Francesco Petrarch (frahn-CHEH-skoh PEH-trahrk) (1304–1374). Along with many of his contemporaries, Petrarch sought to reconnect with the classical past, and he believed that such efforts were bringing on a new golden age of intellectual achievement.

Petrarch and other poets, writers, and artists showed a deep interest both in the physical remains of the Roman Empire and in classical Latin texts. The study of Latin classics became known as the *studia humanitates*, usually translated as "liberal studies" or the "liberal arts." People who advocated it were known as *humanists*, and their program as humanism. Like all programs of study, humanism contained an implicit philosophy: that human nature and achievements were worthy of contemplation. Humanists did not reject religion; instead they sought to synthesize Christian and classical teachings, pointing out the harmony between them.

Humanists and other Renaissance thinkers emphasized individual achievement. They were especially interested in individuals who had risen above their background to become brilliant, powerful, or unique. Such individuals had the admirable quality of *virtù* (vir-TOO), which is not virtue in the sense of moral goodness, but the ability to shape the world around them according to their will. Humanists thought that their recommended course of study in the classics would provide essential skills for all those who would take on this challenge. Just as Confucian officials did in Song China, they also taught that taking an active role in the world and working for the common good should be the aim of all educated individuals.

Humanists put their educational ideas into practice. They opened schools and academies in which pupils began with Latin grammar and rhetoric, went on to study Roman history and political philosophy, and then learned Greek in order to study Greek literature and philosophy. These classics, humanists taught, would provide models of how to write clearly, argue effectively, and speak persuasively. Gradually humanist education became the basis for intermediate and advanced education for well-to-do urban boys and men.

Humanists disagreed about education for women. Many saw the value of exposing women to classical models of moral behavior and reasoning, but they also wondered whether a program of study that emphasized eloquence and action was proper for women, whose sphere was generally understood to be private and domestic. Through tutors or programs of self-study a few women did become educated in the classics.

Humanists looked to the classical past for political as well as literary models. The best-known political theorist of this era was Niccolò Machiavelli (1469–1527),

humanism

▶ A program of study designed by Italians that emphasized the critical study of Latin and Greek literature with the goal of understanding human nature.

CHAPTER LOCATOR | What were the major cultural developments of the Renaissance? | What were the key social hierarchies in Renaissance Europe?

CHAPTER 15
424 EUROPE IN THE RENAISSANCE AND REFORMATION

author of the political treatise *The Prince* (1513). Using the examples of classical and contemporary rulers, *The Prince* argues that the function of a ruler (or a government) is to preserve order and security. To preserve the state, a ruler should use whatever means necessary—brutality, lying, manipulation—but he should not do anything that would make the populace turn against him.

Christian Humanism

In the last quarter of the fifteenth century students from the Low Countries, France, Germany, and England flocked to Italy, absorbed the "new learning" of humanism, and carried it back to their own countries. Northern humanists shared the Italians' ideas about the wisdom of ancient texts and felt even more strongly that the best elements of classical and Christian cultures should be combined. These **Christian humanists**, as they were later called, saw humanist learning as a way to bring about reform of the church and to deepen people's spiritual lives.

The Englishman Thomas More (1478–1535) began life as a lawyer, studied the classics, and entered government service. He became best known for his controversial dialogue *Utopia* (1516). *Utopia* describes a community on an island somewhere beyond Europe where all children receive a good humanist education and adults divide their days between manual labor or business pursuits and intellectual activities. The problems that plagued More's fellow citizens, such as poverty and hunger, are solved by a beneficent government. Furthermore, there is religious tolerance, and order and reason prevail.

Better known by contemporaries than Thomas More was the Dutch humanist Desiderius Erasmus (1466?–1536) of Rotterdam. His fame rested largely on his exceptional knowledge of Greek and the Bible, as well as his many publications. For Erasmus, education was the key to moral and intellectual improvement, and true Christianity was an inner attitude of the spirit, not a set of outward actions.

Christian humanists
▶ Humanists from northern Europe who thought that the best elements of classical and Christian cultures should be combined and saw humanist learning as a way to bring about reform of the church and deepen people's spiritual lives.

Printing and Its Social Impact

The impact of new ideas during this period was magnified by the invention of the printing press with movable metal type. While printing with movable type was invented in China (see page 368), movable *metal* type was actually developed in the thirteenth century in Korea, though it was tightly controlled by the monarchy and did not have the broad impact there that printing did in Europe. Printing with movable metal type developed in Germany in the middle of the fifteenth century. Several metal-smiths, most prominently Johann Gutenberg (ca. 1400–1468), transformed the metal stamps used to mark signs on jewelry into type that could be covered with ink and used to mark symbols onto a page. This type could be rearranged for every page and so used over and over. The printing revolution was also enabled by the ready availability of paper, which was made using techniques that had originated in China and spread from Muslim Spain to the rest of Europe.

The effects of the invention of movable-type printing were not felt overnight. Nevertheless, within a half century of the publication of Gutenberg's Bible of 1456, movable type had brought about radical changes. Historians estimate that somewhere between 8 million and 20 million books were printed in Europe between 1456 and 1500, many more than the total number of books that had been

How did the nation-states of western Europe evolve in this period?

What were the central ideas of Protestant reformers, and why were they appealing?

How did the Catholic Church respond to the new religious situation?

What were the causes and consequences of religious violence?

✓ LearningCurve
Check what you know.

425

produced in the West during the many millennia between the invention of writing and 1456.

Printing transformed both the private and the public lives of Europeans. In the public realm, government and church leaders both used and worried about printing. They printed laws, declarations of war, battle accounts, and propaganda, but they also attempted to censor or ban books and authors whose ideas they thought were wrong.

In the private realm, printing enabled people to read identical books so that they could more easily discuss the ideas that the books contained. Although most of the earliest books and pamphlets dealt with religious subjects, printers produced anything that would sell. Illustrations increased a book's sales, so printers published books full of woodcuts and engravings. Additionally, single-page broadsides and fly sheets allowed public events and "wonders" such as comets and two-headed calves to be experienced vicariously. Since books and other printed materials were read aloud to illiterate listeners, print bridged the gap between the written and oral cultures.

Because many laypeople could not read Latin, printers put out works in vernacular languages, fostering standardization in these languages. Works in these languages were also performed on stage. In London the works of William Shakespeare (1564–1616) were especially popular.

Art and the Artist

No feature of the Renaissance evokes greater admiration than its artistic masterpieces. In Renaissance Italy wealthy merchants, bankers, popes, and princes spent vast sums to commission art as a means of glorifying themselves and their families. Patrons varied in their level of involvement as a work progressed; some simply ordered a specific subject or scene, while others oversaw the work of the artist or architect very closely.

As a result of patronage, certain artists gained great public acclaim and adulation. In the Middle Ages, people believed that only God created, albeit through individuals, and artistic originality was not particularly valued. By contrast, Renaissance artists and humanists came to think that a work of art was the deliberate creation of a unique personality, of an individual who transcended traditions, rules, and theories.

In terms of artistic themes, religious topics remained popular among both patrons and artists. As the fifteenth century advanced and humanist ideas spread more widely, classical themes and motifs figured increasingly in painting and sculpture. Classical styles also influenced architecture, as architects designed buildings that featured arches and domes modeled on the structures of ancient Rome.

The individual portrait emerged as a distinct genre in Renaissance art. Rather than reflecting a spiritual ideal, as medieval painting and sculpture tended to do, Renaissance portraits showed human ideals, often portrayed in a more realistic style. The Florentine sculptor Donatello (1386–1466) revived the classical figure. Leonardo da Vinci (1452–1519) was particularly adept at portraying female grace and beauty. Another Florentine artist, Raphael Sanzio (1483–1520), painted hundreds of portraits, becoming the most sought-after artist in Europe (see page 421).

In the late fifteenth century the center of Renaissance art shifted from Florence to Rome, where wealthy cardinals and popes became active patrons of the

CHAPTER LOCATOR | What were the major cultural developments of the Renaissance? | What were the key social hierarchies in Renaissance Europe?

426 CHAPTER 15
EUROPE IN THE RENAISSANCE AND REFORMATION

arts. To meet this demand, Michelangelo Buonarroti (1475–1564) went to Rome from Florence in about 1500 and began the series of statues, paintings, and architectural projects from which he gained an international reputation. Most famously, between 1508 and 1512, he painted religiously themed frescoes on the ceiling and altar wall of the Sistine Chapel.

In both Italy and northern Europe most aspiring artists were educated in the workshops of older artists. By the later sixteenth century formal academies were also established to train artists. Like universities, artistic workshops and academies were male-only settings. Several women did become well known as painters during the Renaissance, but they were trained by their artist fathers and often quit painting when they married.

Women were not alone in being excluded from the institutions of Renaissance culture. Though a few talented artists such as Leonardo and Michelangelo emerged from artisanal backgrounds, most scholars and artists came from families with at least some money. The audience for artists' work was also exclusive, limited mostly to educated and prosperous citizens. In general a small, highly educated minority of literary humanists and artists created the culture of and for a social elite. In this way the Renaissance maintained, and even enhanced, a gulf between the learned minority and the uneducated multitude.

QUICK REVIEW

Who were the humanists, and what did they believe in?

| How did the nation-states of western Europe evolve in this period? | What were the central ideas of Protestant reformers, and why were they appealing? | How did the Catholic Church respond to the new religious situation? | What were the causes and consequences of religious violence? | LearningCurve Check what you know. |

427

What were the key social hierarchies in Renaissance Europe, and how did these hierarchies shape people's lives?

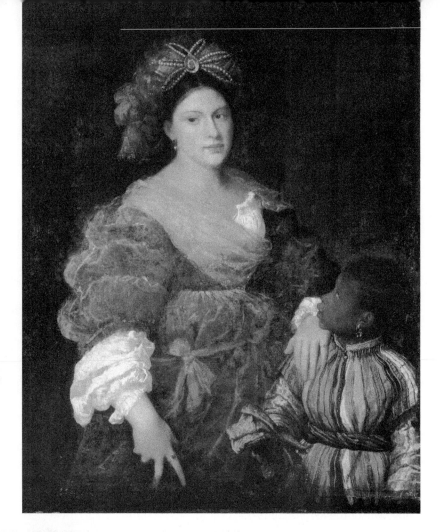

Laura de Dianti, 1523

The Venetian artist Titian portrays a young Italian woman with a gorgeous blue dress and an elaborate pearl and feather headdress accompanied by a young black page with a gold earring. Slaves from Africa and the Ottoman Empire were common in wealthy Venetian households. (Photographer: Human Bios International AG, CH-8280, Kreuzlingen, www.humanbios.com)

> PICTURING THE PAST

ANALYZING THE IMAGE: How does the artist convey the message that this woman comes from a wealthy family? How does he use the skin color of the slave to highlight the woman's fair skin, which was one of the Renaissance ideals of female beauty?

CONNECTIONS: Household slaves worked at various tasks, but they were also symbols of the exotic. What other elements does Titian include in the painting to represent foreign places and the wealth brought to Venice by overseas trade? What does this painting suggest about Venetian attitudes toward slaves, who were part of that trade?

THE DIVISION BETWEEN THE educated and uneducated was one of many social hierarchies evident in the Renaissance. Other hierarchies built on those of the Middle Ages, but also developed new features that contributed to modern social hierarchies, such as those of race, class, and gender.

CHAPTER LOCATOR | What were the major cultural developments of the Renaissance? | **What were the key social hierarchies in Renaissance Europe?**

Race and Slavery

Renaissance people did not use the word *race* the way we do, but often used *race*, *people*, and *nation* interchangeably for ethnic, national, and religious groups. They did make distinctions based on skin color that were in keeping with later conceptualizations of race, but these distinctions were interwoven with other characteristics when people thought about human differences.

Ever since the time of the Roman Republic, a few black Africans had lived in western Europe. They had come, along with white slaves, as the spoils of war. After the collapse of the Roman Empire and throughout the Middle Ages, Muslim and Christian merchants continued to import black slaves. The black population was especially concentrated in the cities of the Iberian Peninsula. By the mid-sixteenth century blacks, slave and free, constituted roughly 3 percent of the Portuguese population.

In Renaissance Portugal, Spain, and Italy, African slaves supplemented the labor force in virtually all occupations. Slaves also formed the primary workforce on the sugar plantations set up by Europeans on the Atlantic islands in the late fifteenth century (see page 475).

Until their voyages down the African coast in the late fifteenth century, Europeans had little concrete knowledge of Africans and their cultures. They perceived Africa as a remote place, the home of strange people isolated by heresy and Islam from superior European civilization. The expanding slave trade reinforced negative preconceptions about the inferiority of black Africans.

Wealth and the Nobility

By the thirteenth century, and even more so by the fifteenth, the idea of a hierarchy based on wealth was emerging. This was particularly true in cities, where wealthy merchants oversaw vast trading empires, held positions of political power, and lived in splendor rivaling that enjoyed by the richest nobles. (See "Individuals in Society: Cosimo and Lorenzo de' Medici," page 430.)

The development of a hierarchy of wealth did not mean an end to the prominence of nobles, however, and even poorer nobles still had higher status than wealthy commoners. Thus wealthy Italian merchants enthusiastically bought noble titles in the fifteenth century, and wealthy English and Spanish merchants married their daughters and sons into often-impoverished noble families. The nobility maintained its status in most parts of Europe not by maintaining rigid boundaries, but by taking in and integrating the new social elite of wealth.

Gender Roles

Renaissance people would not have understood the word *gender* to refer to categories of people, but they would have easily grasped the concept. Toward the end of the fourteenth century learned men (and a few women) began what was termed the **debate about women**, an argument about women's character and nature that would last for centuries. Misogynist critiques of women from both clerical and secular authors denounced females as devious, domineering, and demanding. In response, several authors compiled long lists of famous and

debate about women
▶ A discussion, which began in the later years of the fourteenth century, that attempted to answer fundamental questions about gender and to define the role of women in society.

| How did the nation-states of western Europe evolve in this period? | What were the central ideas of Protestant reformers, and why were they appealing? | How did the Catholic Church respond to the new religious situation? | What were the causes and consequences of religious violence? | ☑ LearningCurve Check what you know. |

INDIVIDUALS IN SOCIETY
Cosimo and Lorenzo de' Medici

The Renaissance is often described as a time of growing individualism, a development evidenced in the era's many personal portraits and individual biographies. But a person's family also remained important, even for those at the very top of society. The Medici of Florence were one of Europe's wealthiest families and used their money to influence politics and culture. The Medici got their start in banking in the late fourteenth century, with smart bets on what would happen politically in turbulent Italy and the adoption of the best new business practices. By the early fifteenth century the Medici bank had branches in Rome, Pisa, London, and other important European cities, and it served as the pope's primary banker.

Cosimo (1389–1464) and his grandson Lorenzo (1449–1492) were the most influential Medici. Not content simply with great wealth, Cosimo operated behind the scenes to gain control of the Florentine political system, although he held no office and officially the city remained a republic. Worries about his growing power led the dominant faction of the Florentine city council to exile him, but he took his money and his business with him and was soon asked to return.

Cosimo supported artists and thinkers, sponsoring what became known as the Platonic Academy, an informal group of Florence's cultural elite named in honor of Plato's famous academy in ancient Athens. Here Marsilio Ficino and other humanists translated Plato's works into Latin, making Greek learning available to a much wider European audience. Cosimo collected books and manuscripts from all over Europe, assembling an impressive library within the equally impressive Medici palace that he built in the heart of Florence.

Like his grandfather, Lorenzo was the head of the Medici bank and the de facto ruler of Florence. He, too, survived an attempt to oust him, this one led by the rival Pazzi family. The Pazzi went beyond simply trying to exile the Medici, and instead tried to murder them: Lorenzo was wounded and his brother Giuliano was killed. Medici revenge was swift and many Pazzi were executed, which led the pope — who sided with the Pazzi — to back an invasion of Florence. Lorenzo ended the conflict through personal diplomacy, and the constitution of Florence was modified to favor the Medici.

Lorenzo came to be known during his lifetime — with no irony — as "Lorenzo the Magnificent," primarily for his support for learning and the arts. As they had in Cosimo's day, a group of poets, philosophers, and

Botticelli's *Adoration of the Magi* shows many members of the Medici family and their circle, including the artist himself at the far right. (akg-images/De Agostini Picture Library)

artists spent much of their time at the Medici palace, where Lorenzo patronized writing in Italian as well as humanist scholarship in Latin and Greek. Lorenzo himself wrote love lyrics, sonnets, pastorals, odes, and carnival songs, many of them meditations on nature or on the fleetingness of human life: "Fair is youth and void of sorrow; / But it hourly flies away. / Youths and maids, enjoy today; / Nought ye know about tomorrow." The group included the humanists Ficino and Pico della Mirandola and the artists Michelangelo, Leonardo da Vinci, and Botticelli, all of them influenced by Platonic concepts of beauty and love. Botticelli's *Adoration of the Magi*, painted while he was at the Medici court, shows Cosimo (who was dead by the time the picture was painted) kneeling in front of the Virgin Mary as one of the three kings giving gifts to the infant Jesus, while a black-haired Lorenzo stands with other important Florentines on the right.

As Lorenzo reached his forties, many of the Medici bank branches began to collapse because of bad loans, and his diplomacy was not successful in maintaining a peaceful balance of power. Like many others in Florence, Lorenzo came under the spell of the charismatic preacher Savonarola, who preached that God would punish Italy for its vice and corruption. Lorenzo died before Savonarola's prediction appeared to come true when the French invaded Italy in 1494. The Medici were again ousted, but just as before, they returned, and later became the official and hereditary rulers of Florence and its environs as the Grand Dukes of Tuscany.

QUESTIONS FOR ANALYSIS

1. Renaissance people were fascinated by the quality of virtù, the ability to shape the world around one according to one's will. How did Cosimo and Lorenzo exhibit virtù?
2. The Medici created a model for very wealthy people of how to obtain political and cultural influence. Can you think of more recent examples, including contemporary ones, of those who followed this model?

ONLINE DOCUMENT PROJECT

What role did patrons play in shaping Renaissance artistic and intellectual life? Examine paintings and letters by Renaissance artists, and complete a quiz and writing assignment based on the evidence and details from this chapter. *See inside the front cover to learn more.*

praiseworthy women. Some writers, including a few women who had gained a humanist education, were interested not only in defending women but also in exploring the reasons behind women's secondary status. Beginning in the sixteenth century the debate about women also became a debate about female rulers, because in Spain, England, France, and Scotland women served as advisers to child-kings or ruled in their own right.

The dominant notion of the "true" man was that of the married head of household, so men whose class and age would have normally conferred political power but who remained unmarried were sometimes excluded from ruling positions. Actual marriage patterns in Europe left many women unmarried until late in life, but this did not lead to greater equality. Women who worked for wages, as was typical, earned about half to two-thirds of what men did even for the same work. Of all the ways in which Renaissance society was hierarchically arranged—by class, age, level of education, rank, race, occupation—gender was regarded as the most "natural" distinction and therefore the most important one to defend.

QUICK REVIEW

How did Renaissance people use the term *race*? How did ideas of race shape Renaissance society?

How did the nation-states of western Europe evolve in this period?

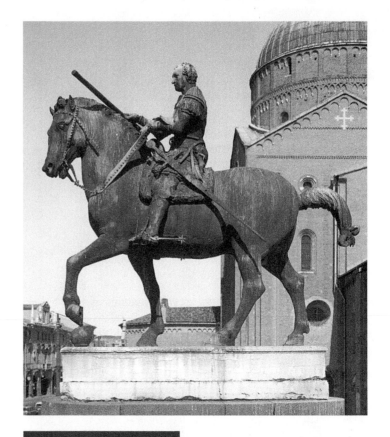

Donatello, *Gattamelata*, 1450

The Florentine sculptor Donatello's bronze statue of the powerful military captain nicknamed Gattamelata (Honey-Cat) mounted on his horse was erected in the public square of Padua. The first bronze equestrian statue made since Roman times, the larger-than-life-size work seems to capture in metal the shrewd and determined type of ruler Machiavelli described in *The Prince*. (Scala/Art Resource, NY)

BEGINNING IN THE FIFTEENTH CENTURY monarchs used aggressive methods to build up their governments. As they built and maintained power, they emphasized royal majesty and royal sovereignty and insisted on the respect and loyalty of all subjects.

France

The Black Death and the Hundred Years' War left France drastically depopulated, commercially ruined, and agriculturally weak (see page 412). Nonetheless, Charles VII (r. 1422–1461) revived the monarchy and France. He reorganized the royal council, giving increased influence to middle-class men, and strengthened royal finances through taxes on certain products and on land. Moreover, Charles created the first permanent royal army anywhere in Europe.

CHAPTER LOCATOR	What were the major cultural developments of the Renaissance?	What were the key social hierarchies in Renaissance Europe?

Two further developments strengthened the French monarchy. The marriage of Louis XII (r. 1498–1515) and Anne of Brittany added Brittany to the state. Louis XII's successor, Francis I (r. 1515–1547), and Pope Leo X reached a mutually satisfactory agreement about church and state powers in 1516 that gave French kings the power to control the appointment and thus the policies of church officials in the kingdom.

England

English society suffered severely in the fourteenth and fifteenth centuries. Between 1455 and 1471 adherents of the ducal houses of York and Lancaster waged civil wars over control of the English throne, commonly called the Wars of the Roses. The chronic disorder hurt trade, agriculture, and domestic industry, and the authority of the monarchy sank lower than it had been in centuries.

The Yorkist Edward IV (r. 1461–1483) succeeded in defeating the Lancastrian forces and after 1471 began to reconstruct the monarchy and consolidate royal power. Henry VII (r. 1485–1509) of the Welsh house of Tudor worked to restore royal prestige, to crush the power of the nobility, and to establish order and law at the local level. Under Henry VII the center of royal authority was the royal council. There Henry VII revealed his distrust of the nobility: very few great lords were among the king's closest advisers, who instead were lesser landowners and lawyers. The royal council handled any business the king put before it—executive, legislative, and judicial.

Secretive, cautious, and thrifty, Henry VII rebuilt the monarchy. He encouraged the cloth industry and built up the English merchant marine. He crushed an invasion from Ireland, secured peace with Scotland, and enhanced English prestige through the marriage of his eldest son, Arthur, to Catherine of Aragon, the daughter of Ferdinand and Isabella of Spain. When Henry VII died in 1509, he left a country at peace both domestically and internationally, a substantially augmented treasury, and the dignity and role of the Crown much enhanced.

Spain

While England and France laid the foundations of unified nation-states during the Renaissance, Spain remained a conglomerate of independent kingdoms. Even the wedding in 1469 of Isabella of Castile and Ferdinand of Aragon did not bring about administrative unity. Isabella and Ferdinand were, however, able to exert their authority in ways similar to the rulers of France and England. They curbed aristocratic power by excluding aristocrats and great territorial magnates from the royal council. They also secured from the Spanish pope Alexander VI the right to appoint bishops in Spain and in the Hispanic territories in America, enabling them to establish the equivalent of a national church. In 1492 their armies conquered Granada, the last territory held by Arabs in southern Spain.

Ferdinand and Isabella's rule also marked the start of greater persecution of the Jews. In the Middle Ages, the kings of France and England had expelled the Jews from their kingdoms, and many had sought refuge in Spain. During the long centuries of the reconquista (see page 399), Christian kings in Spain had renewed Jewish rights and privileges; in fact, Jewish industry, intelligence, and money had supported royal power.

How did the nation-states of western Europe evolve in this period?   What were the central ideas of Protestant reformers, and why were they appealing?   How did the Catholic Church respond to the new religious situation?   What were the causes and consequences of religious violence?   ✔ LearningCurve Check what you know.

433

In the fourteenth century anti-Semitism in Spain was aggravated by fiery anti-Jewish preaching, by economic dislocation, and by the search for a scapegoat during the Black Death. Anti-Semitic pogroms, violent massacres and riots directed against Jews, swept the towns of Spain, and perhaps 40 percent of the Jewish population was killed or forced to convert. Those who converted were called *conversos* (kuhn-VEHR-sohz) or New Christians. Conversos were often well educated and held prominent positions in government and business.

Such successes bred resentment. Aristocrats resented their financial dependence on conversos, the poor hated the converso tax collectors, and churchmen doubted the sincerity of their conversions. Queen Isabella shared these suspicions, and she and Ferdinand received permission from Pope Sixtus IV to establish an Inquisition to look for conversos who showed any sign of incomplete conversion.

Most conversos identified themselves as sincere Christians; many came from families that had received baptism generations before. In response, officials of the Inquisition developed a new type of anti-Semitism. A person's status as a Jew, they argued, could not be changed by religious conversion, but was in the person's blood and was heritable, so Jews could never be true Christians. Under what were known as "purity of blood" laws, having "pure Christian blood" became a requirement for noble status. Ideas about Jews developed in Spain became important components in European concepts of race.

In 1492, shortly after the conquest of Granada, Isabella and Ferdinand issued an edict expelling all practicing Jews from Spain. Of the community of perhaps 200,000 Jews, 150,000 fled. Absolute religious orthodoxy and "purity of blood" served as the theoretical foundation of the Spanish national state.

The Habsburgs

Because almost all of Europe was ruled by hereditary dynasties, claiming and holding resources involved shrewd marital strategies, for it was far cheaper to gain land by inheritance than by war. The benefits of an advantageous marriage stretched across generations, as can be seen most dramatically with the Habsburgs. The Holy Roman emperor Frederick III, a Habsburg who was the ruler of most of Austria, acquired only a small amount of territory—but a great deal of money—with his marriage to Princess Eleanore of Portugal in 1452. He arranged for his son Maximilian to marry Europe's most prominent heiress, Mary of Burgundy. Through this union with the rich and powerful duchy of Burgundy, the Austrian house of Habsburg, already the strongest ruling family in the empire, became an international power. The marriage of Maximilian and Mary angered the French, and it inaugurated centuries of conflict between the Habsburgs and the kings of France. Within the empire, German principalities that resented Austria's pre-eminence began to see that they shared interests with France.

Maximilian learned the lesson of marital politics well, marrying his son and daughter to the children of Ferdinand and Isabella, the rulers of Spain, much of southern Italy, and eventually the Spanish New World empire. His grandson Charles V (1500–1558) fell heir to a vast and incredibly diverse collection of states and peoples (Map 15.1). Charles was convinced that it was his duty to maintain the political and religious unity of Western Christendom. This conviction would be challenged far more than Charles ever anticipated.

CHAPTER LOCATOR | What were the major cultural developments of the Renaissance? | What were the key social hierarchies in Renaissance Europe?

CHAPTER 15
434 EUROPE IN THE RENAISSANCE AND REFORMATION

MAP 15.1 ■ The Global Empire of Charles V, ca. 1556

Charles V exercised theoretical jurisdiction over more European territory than anyone since Charlemagne. He also claimed authority over large parts of North and South America, although actual Spanish control was weak in much of this area.

QUICK REVIEW

How did the monarchs of England, France, and Spain seek to limit the power and autonomy of the nobility?

How did the nation-states of western Europe evolve in this period?	What were the central ideas of Protestant reformers, and why were they appealing?	How did the Catholic Church respond to the new religious situation?	What were the causes and consequences of religious violence?	✓ LearningCurve Check what you know.

What were the central ideas of Protestant reformers, and why were they appealing to various groups across Europe?

Selling Indulgences

A German single-page pamphlet shows a monk offering an indulgence, with the official seals of the pope attached, as people run to put their money in the box in exchange for his promise of heavenly bliss, symbolized by the dove above his head. Indulgences were sold widely in Germany, and they were the first Catholic practice that Luther criticized openly. This pamphlet also attacks the sale of indulgences, calling it devilish and deceitful, a point of view expressed in the woodcut by the peddler's riding on a donkey, an animal that had long been used as a symbol of ignorance. Indulgences were often printed as fill-in-the-blank forms. This one, purchased in 1521, has space for the indulgence seller's name at the top, the buyer's name in the middle, and the date at the bottom. (woodcut: akg-images; indulgence: Visual Connection Archive)

Protestant Reformation

▶ A religious reform movement that began in the early sixteenth century that split the Western Christian Church.

CALLS FOR REFORM IN THE CHURCH came from many quarters in early-sixteenth-century Europe—from educated laypeople and urban residents, from villagers and artisans, and from church officials themselves. This dissatisfaction helps explain why the ideas of Martin Luther found a ready audience. Within a decade of his first publishing his ideas, much of central Europe and Scandinavia had broken with the Catholic Church in a movement that came to be known as the **Protestant Reformation**. In addition, even more radical concepts of the Christian message were being developed and linked to calls for social change.

CHAPTER LOCATOR | What were the major cultural developments of the Renaissance? | What were the key social hierarchies in Renaissance Europe?

Criticism of the Church

Sixteenth-century Europeans were deeply pious. Many people were also highly critical of the Roman Catholic Church and its clergy. Papal conflicts with rulers and the Great Schism (see page 414) badly damaged the prestige of church leaders. Papal tax collection methods were also attacked, and some criticized the papacy itself as an institution.

In the early sixteenth century, critics of the church concentrated their attacks on clerical immorality, ignorance, and absenteeism. Charges of immorality were aimed at a number of priests who were drunkards, neglected the rule of celibacy, gambled, or indulged in fancy dress. Charges of ignorance applied to barely literate priests who delivered poor-quality sermons.

In regard to absenteeism, many clerics, especially higher ecclesiastics, held several benefices (offices) simultaneously. However, they seldom visited the communities served by the benefices. Instead, they collected revenues from all the benefices assigned to them and hired a poor priest to fulfill their spiritual duties, paying him just a fraction of the income.

There was also local resentment of clerical privileges and immunities. Priests, monks, and nuns were exempt from civic responsibilities, such as defending the city and paying taxes. Yet religious orders frequently held large amounts of urban property. City governments were increasingly determined to integrate the clergy into civic life. This brought city leaders into opposition with bishops and the papacy, which for centuries had stressed the independence of the church from lay control.

Martin Luther

By itself, widespread criticism of the church did not lead to the dramatic changes of the sixteenth century. Those resulted from the personal religious struggle of a German university professor and Augustinian friar, Martin Luther (1483–1546).

Martin Luther was a very conscientious friar, but his scrupulous observance of the religious routine, frequent confessions, and fasting gave him only temporary relief from anxieties about sin and his ability to meet God's demands. Through his study of Saint Paul's letters in the New Testament, he gradually arrived at a new understanding of Christian doctrine. His understanding is often summarized as "faith alone, grace alone, scripture alone." He believed that salvation and justification (righteousness in God's eyes) come through faith, and that faith is a free gift of God, not the result of human effort. God's word is revealed only in biblical scripture, not in the traditions of the church.

At the same time that Luther was engaged in scholarly reflections and professorial lecturing, Pope Leo X authorized a special Saint Peter's indulgence to finance his building plans in Rome. An **indulgence** was a document that substituted for penance. The archbishop who controlled the area in which Wittenberg was located, Albert of Mainz, also promoted the sale of indulgences, in his case to pay off a debt he had incurred to be named bishop of several additional territories. Albert's sales campaign promised that the purchase of indulgences would bring full forgiveness for one's own sins or buy release from purgatory for a loved one.

Luther was severely troubled that many people believed that they had no further need for repentance once they had purchased indulgences. He wrote a letter

indulgence
▶ A papal statement granting remission of a priest-imposed penalty for sin. (No one knew what penalty God would impose after death.)

How did the nation-states of western Europe evolve in this period?

What were the central ideas of Protestant reformers, and why were they appealing?

How did the Catholic Church respond to the new religious situation?

What were the causes and consequences of religious violence?

✓ LearningCurve
Check what you know.

to Archbishop Albert on the subject and enclosed in Latin his "Ninety-five Theses on the Power of Indulgences." His argument was that indulgences undermined the seriousness of the sacrament of penance and competed with the preaching of the Gospel. Luther intended his theses for academic debate, but by December 1517 they had been translated into German and were being read throughout central Europe. Luther was ordered to go to Rome, but he was able to avoid this because the ruler of the territory in which he lived protected him. The pope nonetheless ordered him to recant many of his ideas, and Luther publicly burned the letter containing the papal order. In this highly charged atmosphere, the twenty-one-year-old emperor Charles V summoned Luther to appear before the **Diet of Worms**, an assembly of representatives from the territories of the Holy Roman Empire meeting in the city of Worms in 1521. Luther, however, refused to give in to demands that he take back his ideas.

Protestant Thought and Its Appeal

As he developed his ideas, Luther gathered followers, who came to be called Protestants. At first **Protestant** meant "a follower of Luther," but with the appearance of many other reformers, it became a general term applied to all non-Catholic western European Christians.

Pulpits and printing presses spread the Protestant message all over Germany, and by the middle of the sixteenth century people of all social classes had rejected Catholic teachings and become Protestant. What was the immense appeal of Luther's religious ideas and those of other Protestants?

Educated people and humanists were attracted by Luther's ideas. He advocated a simpler personal religion based on faith, a return to the spirit of the early church, the centrality of the Scriptures in the liturgy and in Christian life, and the abolition of elaborate ceremonies—precisely the reforms the Christian humanists had been calling for. His insistence that everyone should read and reflect on the Scriptures attracted the literate middle classes. Luther's ideas also appealed to

Diet of Worms

▶ An assembly of representatives from the territories of the Holy Roman Empire convened by Charles V in the German city of Worms in 1521. It was here that Martin Luther refused to recant his writings.

Protestant

▶ Originally meaning "a follower of Luther," this term came to be generally applied to all non-Catholic western European Christians.

> Key Differences Between Catholics and Protestants:		
	Catholics	**Protestants**
How is a person saved?	By a combination of faith and good works	By faith alone
Where does religious authority lie?	In the Bible and in the traditional teachings of the church	In the Bible alone
What is the church?	The church is a clerical, hierarchical institution headed by the pope in Rome	The church is a spiritual priesthood of all believers
What is the highest form of Christian life?	The monastic and religious life	Each person should serve God in his or her individual calling

CHAPTER LOCATOR | What were the major cultural developments of the Renaissance? | What were the key social hierarchies in Renaissance Europe?

CHAPTER 15
438 EUROPE IN THE RENAISSANCE AND REFORMATION

townspeople who envied the church's wealth and resented paying for it. After cities became Protestant, the city council taxed the clergy and placed them under the jurisdiction of civil courts.

The printing press also contributed to Luther's fame and success. Many printed works included woodcuts and other illustrations, so that even those who could not read could grasp the main ideas. Hymns were also important means of conveying central points of doctrine, as was Luther's translation of the New Testament into German in 1523.

Luther worked closely with political authorities, viewing them as fully justified in reforming the church in their territories. He instructed all Christians to obey their secular rulers, whom he saw as divinely ordained to maintain order. Individuals may have been convinced of the truth of Protestant teachings on their own, but a territory became Protestant when its ruler, brought in reformers to re-educate the territory's clergy, sponsored public sermons, and confiscated church property. This happened in many of the states of the empire during the 1520s and then moved beyond the empire to Denmark-Norway and Sweden.

The Radical Reformation and the German Peasants' War

In the sixteenth century the practice of religion remained a public matter. The ruler determined the official form of religious practice in his (or occasionally her) jurisdiction. Almost everyone believed that the presence of a faith different from that of the majority represented a political threat to the security of the state.

Some individuals and groups rejected the idea that church and state needed to be united, however, and they sought to create a voluntary community of believers as they understood it to have existed in New Testament times. In terms of theology and spiritual practices, these individuals and groups varied widely, though they are generally termed "radicals" for their insistence on a more extensive break with prevailing ideas. Some adopted the custom of baptizing adult believers—for which they were given the title of "Anabaptists" by their enemies—while others saw all outward sacraments or rituals as misguided. Some groups attempted communal ownership of property. Some reacted harshly to members who deviated from the group's accepted practices, but others argued for complete religious tolerance and individualism.

Religious radicals were met with fanatical hatred and bitter persecution, including banishment and execution. Both Protestant and Catholic authorities felt threatened by the social, political, and economic implications of radicals' religious ideas and by their rejection of a state church. Their community spirit and heroism in the face of martyrdom, however, contributed to the survival of radical ideas.

Another group to challenge state authorities was the peasantry. In the early sixteenth century the economic condition of peasants varied from place to place but was generally worse than it had been in the fifteenth century and was deteriorating. Peasants demanded limitations on the new taxes and labor obligations their noble landlords were imposing. They believed that their demands conformed to the Scriptures and cited Luther as a theologian who could prove that they did.

Wanting to prevent rebellion, Luther initially sided with the peasants. But when rebellion broke out, the peasants who expected Luther's support were soon

How did the nation-states of western Europe evolve in this period? | **What were the central ideas of Protestant reformers, and why were they appealing?** | How did the Catholic Church respond to the new religious situation? | What were the causes and consequences of religious violence? | ✓ LearningCurve Check what you know.

439

disillusioned. Freedom for Luther meant independence from the authority of the Roman Church, not opposition to legally established secular powers. Firmly convinced that rebellion would hasten the end of civilized society, he wrote the tract *Against the Murderous, Thieving Hordes of the Peasants*. The nobility ferociously crushed the revolt, which became known as the German Peasants' War of 1525.

The peasants' war greatly strengthened the authority of lay rulers. Because Luther turned against the peasants who revolted, the Reformation lost much of its popular appeal after 1525, though peasants and urban rebels sometimes found a place for their social and religious ideas in radical groups. Peasants' economic conditions did moderately improve, however.

Marriage and Women's Roles

Luther and other Protestants believed that a priest's or nun's vows of celibacy went against human nature and God's commandments. Luther married a former nun, Katharina von Bora (1499–1532), who quickly had several children. Most other Protestant reformers also married, and their wives had to create a new and respectable role for themselves, pastor's wife. They were living demonstrations of their husband's convictions about the superiority of marriage to celibacy, and they were expected to be models of wifely obedience and Christian charity.

Catholics viewed marriage as a sacramental union that, if validly entered into, could not be dissolved. Protestants saw marriage as a contract in which each partner promised the other support, companionship, and the sharing of mutual goods. They believed that spouses who did not comfort or support one another endangered their own souls and the surrounding community; therefore, most Protestants came to allow divorce. Divorce remained rare, however, because marriage was such an important social and economic institution.

Protestants did not break with medieval scholastic theologians in their view that, within marriage, women were to be subject to men. Men were urged to treat their wives kindly and considerately, but also to enforce their authority, through physical coercion if necessary. A few women took the Protestant idea about the priesthood of all believers to heart and wrote religious pamphlets and hymns, but no sixteenth-century Protestants officially allowed women to hold positions of religious authority.

Because the Reformation generally brought the closing of monasteries and convents, marriage became virtually the only occupation for upper-class Protestant women. Recognizing this, women in some convents fought the Reformation or argued that they could still be pious Protestants within convent walls. Most nuns left, however, and we do not know what happened to them. The Protestant emphasis on marriage made unmarried women (and men) suspect, for they did not belong to the type of household regarded as the cornerstone of a proper, godly society.

The Reformation and German Politics

Criticism of the church was widespread in Europe in the early sixteenth century. Yet such movements could be more easily squelched by the strong central governments of Spain, France, and England. The Holy Roman Empire, in contrast,

CHAPTER LOCATOR | What were the major cultural developments of the Renaissance? | What were the key social hierarchies in Renaissance Europe?

CHAPTER 15
440   EUROPE IN THE RENAISSANCE AND REFORMATION

included hundreds of largely independent states in which the emperor had far less authority than did the monarchs of western Europe. Thus local rulers of the many states in the empire continued to exercise great power.

Luther's ideas appealed to local rulers within the empire for a variety of reasons. Though Germany was not a nation, people did have an understanding of being German because of their language and traditions. Luther frequently used the phrase "we Germans" in his attacks on the papacy, and his appeal to national feeling influenced many rulers. Also, while some German rulers were sincerely attracted to Lutheran ideas, material considerations swayed many others to embrace the new faith. The rejection of Roman Catholicism and the adoption of Protestantism would mean the legal confiscation of valuable church property. Thus many political authorities in the empire used the religious issue to extend their financial and political power and to enhance their independence from the emperor.

The Habsburg Charles V, elected as emperor in 1521, was a vigorous defender of Catholicism, so it is not surprising that the Reformation led to religious wars. Protestant territories in the empire formed military alliances, and the emperor could not oppose them effectively given other military engagements. In southeastern Europe Habsburg troops were already fighting the Ottoman Turks. Habsburg soldiers were also engaged in a series of wars with the Valois (VAL-wah) kings of France. The cornerstone of French foreign policy in the sixteenth and seventeenth centuries was the desire to keep the German states divided. Thus Europe witnessed the paradox of the Catholic king of France supporting Lutheran princes in their challenge to his fellow Catholic, Charles V.

Finally, in 1555, Charles agreed to the Peace of Augsburg, which officially recognized Lutheranism and ended religious war in Germany for many decades. Under this treaty, the political authority in each territory of the Holy Roman

How did the nation-states of western Europe evolve in this period?

What were the central ideas of Protestant reformers, and why were they appealing?

How did the Catholic Church respond to the new religious situation?

What were the causes and consequences of religious violence?

☑ LearningCurve
Check what you know.

441

Empire was permitted to decide whether the territory would be Catholic or Lutheran. His hope of uniting his empire under a single church dashed, Charles V abdicated in 1556, transferring power over his Spanish and Netherlandish holdings to his son Philip II and his imperial power to his brother Ferdinand.

England's Shift Toward Protestantism

As on the continent, the Reformation in England had economic and political as well as religious causes. The impetus for England's break with Rome was the desire of King Henry VIII (r. 1509–1547) for a new wife. When the personal matter of his need to divorce his first wife became enmeshed with political issues, a complete break with Rome resulted.

In 1527, after eighteen years of marriage, Henry's wife Catherine of Aragon had failed to produce a male child, and Henry had also fallen in love with a court lady-in-waiting, Anne Boleyn. So Henry petitioned Pope Clement VII for an annulment of his marriage to Catherine. When the pope procrastinated in granting the annulment, Henry decided to remove the English Church from papal authority.

Henry used Parliament to legalize the Reformation in England and to make himself the supreme head of the Church of England. Anne had a daughter, Elizabeth, but failed to produce a son, so Henry VIII charged her with adulterous incest and in 1536 had her beheaded. His third wife, Jane Seymour, gave Henry the desired son, Edward, but she died in childbirth. Henry went on to three more wives.

Between 1535 and 1539, Henry decided to dissolve the English monasteries primarily because he wanted their wealth. Hundreds of former church properties were sold to the middle and upper classes, strengthening the upper classes and tying them to the Tudor dynasty, to which Henry belonged. How did everyday people react to Henry's break from the Catholic Church? Recent scholarship points out that people rarely "converted" from Catholicism to Protestantism overnight. Instead they responded to the local consequences of the shift from Catholicism with a combination of resistance, acceptance, and collaboration.

Loyalty to the Catholic Church remained particularly strong in Ireland. Ireland had been claimed by English kings since the twelfth century, but in reality the English had firm control of only the area around Dublin known as the Pale. In 1536, on orders from London, the Irish Parliament, which represented only the English landlords and the people of the Pale, approved the English laws severing the church from Rome. The (English) ruling class adopted the new reformed faith, but most of the Irish people remained Roman Catholic. Irish armed opposition to the Reformation led to harsh repression by the English.

In the short reign of Henry's sickly son Edward VI (r. 1547–1553), strongly Protestant ideas exerted a significant influence on the religious life of the country. The equally brief reign of Mary Tudor (r. 1553–1558), the devoutly Catholic daughter of Catherine of Aragon, witnessed a sharp move back to Catholicism, and many Protestants fled to the continent. Mary's death raised to the throne her half sister Elizabeth (r. 1558–1603) and inaugurated the beginning of religious stability.

Elizabeth had been raised a Protestant, but at the start of her reign sharp differences existed in England. On the one hand, Catholics wanted a Roman Catholic ruler. On the other hand, a vocal number of returning exiles wanted all Catholic elements in the Church of England eliminated. Members of the latter group were

CHAPTER LOCATOR | What were the major cultural developments of the Renaissance? | What were the key social hierarchies in Renaissance Europe?

CHAPTER 15
442 EUROPE IN THE RENAISSANCE AND REFORMATION

called Puritans. Shrewdly, Elizabeth chose a middle course between Catholic and Puritan extremes. The Anglican Church, as the Church of England was called, moved in a moderately Protestant direction.

Calvinism and Its Moral Standards

John Calvin (1509–1564) was born in Noyon in northwestern France. As a young man he studied law, but in 1533 he experienced a religious crisis, as a result of which he converted from Catholicism to Protestantism. Calvin believed that God had specifically selected him to reform the church. Accordingly, he accepted an invitation to assist in the reformation of the city of Geneva. There, beginning in 1541, Calvin worked to establish a Christian society ruled by God through civil magistrates and reformed ministers.

Calvin's ideas are embodied in *The Institutes of the Christian Religion*, first published in 1536 and modified several times afterward. The cornerstone of Calvin's theology was his belief in the absolute sovereignty and omnipotence of God and the total weakness of humanity.

Calvin did not ascribe free will to human beings because that would detract from the sovereignty of God. According to his beliefs, men and women could not actively work to achieve salvation; rather, God decided at the beginning of time who would be saved and who damned. This viewpoint constitutes the theological principle called **predestination**. "This terrible decree," as even Calvin called it, did not lead to pessimism or fatalism. Instead, although Calvinists believed that one's own actions could do nothing to change one's fate, many came to believe that hard work, thrift, and moral conduct could serve as signs that one was among the "elect" chosen for salvation.

Calvin transformed Geneva into a community based on his religious principles. The most powerful organization in the city became the Consistory, a group of laymen and pastors charged with investigating and disciplining deviations from proper doctrine and conduct.

Religious refugees from France, England, Spain, Scotland, and Italy visited Calvin's Geneva, which became the model of a Christian community for many. Subsequently, the Reformed Church of Calvin served as the model for the Presbyterian Church in Scotland, the Huguenot (HYOO-guh-naht) Church in France, and the Puritan Churches in England and New England.

predestination

▶ Calvin's teaching that, by God's decree, some persons are guided to salvation and others to damnation; that God has called people not according to their works but according to his purpose and grace.

QUICK REVIEW <

What did Lutheranism and Calvinism have in common?
In what ways did they differ?

| How did the nation-states of western Europe evolve in this period? | **What were the central ideas of Protestant reformers, and why were they appealing?** | How did the Catholic Church respond to the new religious situation? | What were the causes and consequences of religious violence? | LearningCurve Check what you know. |

> How did the Catholic Church respond to the new religious situation?

BETWEEN 1517 AND 1547 Protestantism made remarkable advances. Nevertheless, the Roman Catholic Church made a significant comeback. Many historians see the developments within the Catholic Church after the Protestant Reformation as two interrelated movements, one a drive for internal reform, and the other a Counter-Reformation that actively opposed Protestantism. In both movements, papal reforms and new religious orders were important agents.

Papal Reforms and the Council of Trent

In 1542 Pope Paul III (pontificate 1534–1549) established the Supreme Sacred Congregation of the Roman and Universal Inquisition, often called the Holy Office, with jurisdiction over the Roman Inquisition, a powerful instrument of the Catholic Reformation. The Inquisition had judicial authority over all Catholics and the power to arrest, imprison, and execute.

Pope Paul III also called a general council, which met intermittently from 1545 to 1563 at Trent, an imperial city close to Italy. The decrees of the Council of Trent

Predominant religion in 1555

- Lutheran
- Calvinist (Reformed)
- Church of England
- Roman Catholic
- Eastern Orthodox
- Muslim
- → Spread of Calvinism, from 1541
- ▲ Huguenot center
- — Ottoman Empire, 1566

Penetration of Calvinism to England after 1558

Wittenberg
Martin Luther writes
Ninety-five Theses
1517

Worms
Edict of Worms
1521

Nantes
Edict of Nantes
1598

Trent
Council of Trent
1545–1563

Augsburg
Peace of Augsburg
1555

Geneva
Calvin assists in
Reformation beginning
in 1541

MAP 15.2 ■ Religious Divisions in Europe, ca. 1555

The Reformation shattered the religious unity of Western Christendom. The situation was even more complicated than a map of this scale can show. Many cities within the Holy Roman Empire, for example, accepted a different faith than did the surrounding countryside; Augsburg, Basel, and Strasbourg were all Protestant, though surrounded by territory ruled by Catholic nobles.

> MAPPING THE PAST

ANALYZING THE MAP: Which countries in Europe were the most religiously diverse? Which were the least diverse?

CONNECTIONS: Where was the first arena of religious conflict in Europe, and why did it develop there and not elsewhere? What nonreligious factors contributed to the religious divisions that developed in sixteenth-century Europe, and to what degree can they explain these divisions?

How did the nation-states of western Europe evolve in this period?

What were the central ideas of Protestant reformers, and why were they appealing?

How did the Catholic Church respond to the new religious situation?

What were the causes and consequences of religious violence?

✓ LearningCurve
Check what you know.

laid a solid basis for the spiritual renewal of the Catholic Church. It gave equal validity to the Scriptures and to tradition as sources of religious truth and authority. It reaffirmed the seven sacraments and the traditional Catholic teaching on transubstantiation (the transformation of bread and wine into the body and blood of Christ in the Eucharist). It tackled the disciplinary matters that had disillusioned the faithful. The council also required every diocese to establish a seminary for educating and training clergy. Finally, great emphasis was placed on preaching to and instructing the laity, especially the uneducated. For four centuries the doctrinal and disciplinary legislation of Trent served as the basis for Roman Catholic faith, organization, and practice.

New Religious Orders

Just as seminaries provided education, so did new religious orders, which aimed to raise the moral and intellectual level of the clergy and people. The Ursuline (UHR-suh-luhn) order of nuns, founded in 1535 by Angela Merici (1474–1540), attained enormous prestige for its education of women. The Ursulines were the first women's religious order concentrating exclusively on teaching young girls, with the goal of re-Christianizing society by training future wives and mothers. After receiving papal approval in 1565, the Ursulines rapidly spread to France and the New World.

Another important new order was the Society of Jesus, or Jesuits. Founded by Ignatius Loyola (1491–1556) in 1540, this order played a powerful international role in strengthening Catholicism in Europe and spreading the faith around the world. Under Loyola's leadership, the Society of Jesus developed into a highly centralized, tightly knit organization whose professed members vowed to go anywhere the pope said they were needed. They established schools that adopted the modern humanist curricula and methods and that educated the sons of the nobility as well as the poor. The Jesuits attracted many recruits and achieved phenomenal success for the papacy and the reformed Catholic Church, carrying Christianity around the world. Within Europe the Jesuits brought almost all of southern Germany and much of eastern Europe back to Catholicism. Also, as confessors and spiritual directors to kings, Jesuits exerted great political influence.

Jesuits

▶ Members of the Society of Jesus, founded by Ignatius Loyola and approved by the papacy in 1540, whose goal was the spread of the Roman Catholic faith through humanistic schools and missionary activity.

> **QUICK REVIEW**

What reforms were enacted by the Council of Trent?

What were the causes and consequences of religious violence, including riots, wars, and witch-hunts?

Massacre of the Huguenots, 1573

The Italian artist Giorgio Vasari depicts the Saint Bartholomew's Day massacre in Paris, one of many bloody events in the religious wars that accompanied the Reformation. Here Admiral Coligny, a leader of the French Protestants (called Huguenots), is hurled from a window while his followers are slaughtered. This fresco was commissioned by Pope Gregory XIII to decorate a hall in the Vatican Palace in Rome. Both sides used visual images to win followers and celebrate their victories. (Giorgio Vasari [1511–1574], Sala Regia, Apostolic Palace, Vatican City/De Agostini Picture Library/The Bridgeman Art Library)

IN 1559 FRANCE AND SPAIN signed the Treaty of Cateau-Cambrésis, which ended the long conflict known as the Habsburg-Valois wars. However, over the next century religious differences led to riots, civil wars, and international conflicts. Especially in France and the Netherlands, Protestants and Catholics opposed one another through preaching, teaching, and violence. This era also saw the most virulent witch persecutions in European history, as both Protestants and Catholics tried to make their cities and states more godly.

| How did the nation-states of western Europe evolve in this period? | What were the central ideas of Protestant reformers, and why were they appealing? | How did the Catholic Church respond to the new religious situation? | **What were the causes and consequences of religious violence?** | ✔ LearningCurve Check what you know. |

French Religious Wars

The costs of the Habsburg-Valois wars, waged intermittently through the first half of the sixteenth century, forced the French to increase taxes and borrow heavily. King Francis I's treaty with the pope (see page 432) gave the French crown a rich supplement of money and offices and also a vested financial interest in Catholicism. Significant numbers of French people, however, were attracted to Calvinism. Calvinism drew converts from among reform-minded members of the Catholic clergy, the industrious middle classes, and artisan groups. Additionally, some French nobles became Calvinist. By the middle of the sixteenth century perhaps one-tenth of the French population had become Huguenots, the name given to French Calvinists.

Huguenots
▶ French Calvinists.

Both Calvinists and Catholics believed that the others' books, services, and ministers polluted the community. Preachers communicated these ideas in sermons, triggering religious violence. Armed clashes between Catholic royalist nobles and Calvinist antimonarchical nobles occurred in many parts of France.

Calvinist teachings called the power of sacred images into question, and mobs in many cities destroyed statues, stained-glass windows, and paintings. Catholic mobs responded by defending the sacred images, and crowds on both sides killed their opponents, often in gruesome ways.

A particularly savage Catholic attack on Calvinists took place in Paris on August 24, 1572 , Saint Bartholomew's Day. The occasion was the marriage of the king's sister Margaret of Valois to the Protestant Henry of Navarre, which was intended to help reconcile Catholics and Huguenots. Instead Huguenot wedding guests in Paris were massacred, and other Protestants were slaughtered by mobs. Violence spread to the provinces, where thousands were killed. The Saint Bartholomew's Day massacre led to a civil war that dragged on for fifteen years.

politiques
▶ Catholic and Protestant moderates who sought to end the religious violence in France by restoring a strong monarchy and granting official recognition to the Huguenots.

What ultimately saved France was a small group of moderates of both faiths called politiques (POH-lee-teeks) who believed that only the restoration of a strong monarchy could reverse the trend toward collapse. The politiques also favored officially recognizing the Huguenots. The death of the French queen Catherine de' Medici, followed by the assassination of her son King Henry III, paved the way for the accession of Henry of Navarre, a politique who became Henry IV (r. 1589–1610).

Henry's willingness to sacrifice religious principles to political necessity saved France. He converted to Catholicism but also, in 1598, issued the Edict of Nantes (nahnt), which granted liberty of conscience (freedom of thought) and liberty of public worship to Huguenots in 150 fortified towns. By helping restore internal peace in France, the reign of Henry IV and the Edict of Nantes paved the way for French kings to claim absolute power in the seventeenth century.

Civil Wars in the Netherlands

In the Netherlands a movement for church reform developed into a struggle for Dutch independence. The Catholic emperor Charles V had inherited the seventeen provinces that compose present-day Belgium and the Netherlands (see page 434). In the Netherlands, as many other places, Lutheran ideas took root.

CHAPTER LOCATOR | What were the major cultural developments of the Renaissance? | What were the key social hierarchies in Renaissance Europe?

448 CHAPTER 15
EUROPE IN THE RENAISSANCE AND REFORMATION

Charles V had grown up in the Netherlands, however, and he was able to limit the impact of the new ideas. Charles V abdicated in 1556 and transferred power over the Netherlands to his son Philip II, who had grown up in Spain. Although Philip, like his father, opposed Protestantism, Protestant ideas spread in the Netherlands.

By the 1560s Protestants in the Netherlands were primarily Calvinists. When Spanish authorities attempted to suppress Calvinist worship and raised taxes, it sparked riots and a wave of iconoclasm. In response, Philip II sent twenty thousand Spanish troops, and from 1568 to 1578 civil war raged in the Netherlands between Catholics and Protestants and between the seventeen provinces and Spain. Eventually the ten southern provinces came under the control of the Spanish Habsburg forces. The seven northern provinces, led by Holland, formed the Union of Utrecht (the United Provinces), and in 1581 they declared their independence from Spain. The north was Protestant, and the south remained Catholic. Philip did not accept the independence of the north, and war continued. England was even drawn into the conflict, supplying money and troops to the United Provinces. Hostilities ended in 1609 when Spain agreed to a truce that recognized the independence of the United Provinces.

The Great European Witch-Hunt

Insecurity created by the religious wars contributed to persecution for witchcraft, which actually began before the Reformation in the 1480s but became especially common about 1560. Both Protestants and Catholics tried and executed those accused of being witches.

The heightened sense of God's power and divine wrath in the Reformation era was an important factor in the witch-hunts, but other factors were also significant. In the later Middle Ages, scholars and officials added a demonological component to existing ideas about witches. For them, the essence of witchcraft was making a pact with the Devil that required the witch to do the Devil's bidding. Witches were no longer simply people who used magical power to do harm and get what they wanted, but rather people used by the Devil to do what he wanted.

Trials involving this new notion of witchcraft as diabolical heresy began in Switzerland and southern Germany in the late fifteenth century; became less numerous in the early decades of the Reformation, when Protestants and Catholics were busy fighting each other; and then picked up again about 1560, spreading to much of western Europe and to European colonies in the Americas. Scholars estimate that during the sixteenth and seventeenth centuries somewhere between 100,000 and 200,000 people were officially tried for witchcraft, and between 40,000 and 60,000 were executed.

Though the gender balance of the accused varied widely in different parts of Europe, between 75 and 85 percent of those tried and executed were women, whom some demonologists viewed as weaker and so more likely to give in to the Devil. Tensions within families, households, and neighborhoods also played a role in witchcraft accusations, as grievances and jealousies led to accusations. Suspects were questioned and tortured by legal authorities, and they often implicated others.

witch-hunts
▶ Campaign against witchcraft in early modern Europe and European colonies in which hundreds of thousands of people, mostly women, were tried, and many of them executed.

How did the nation-states of western Europe evolve in this period?

What were the central ideas of Protestant reformers, and why were they appealing?

How did the Catholic Church respond to the new religious situation?

What were the causes and consequences of religious violence?

☑ LearningCurve
Check what you know.

449

Even in the sixteenth century a few individuals questioned whether witches could ever do harm, make a pact with the Devil, or engage in the wild activities attributed to them. Furthermore, doubts about trial procedures and the use of torture to extract confessions gradually spread among the same type of religious and legal authorities who had so vigorously persecuted witches. By about 1660 prosecutions for witchcraft had become less common.

> QUICK REVIEW

What sparked the French wars of religion?
How were they brought to an end?

CHAPTER SUMMARY

The Renaissance was characterized by self-conscious awareness among educated Europeans, particularly scholars and writers known as humanists, that they were living in a new era. Central to humanists were interest in the Latin classics, belief in individual potential, education for a career of public service, and, in northern Europe, the reform of church and society. Their ideas spread as a result of the development of the printing press with movable metal type, which revolutionized communication. Interest in the classical past and in the individual shaped Renaissance art in terms of style and subject matter, and patrons provided the money needed for an outpouring of painting, sculpture and architecture. Social hierarchies in the Renaissance developed new features that contributed to the modern social hierarchies of race, class, and gender. In politics, feudal monarchies gradually evolved into nation-states, as rulers used war, diplomacy, new forms of taxation, centralized institutions, and strategic marital alliances to build up their power.

Many individuals and groups had long called for reforms in the Catholic Church, providing a ready audience in the early sixteenth century for the ideas of Martin Luther. Luther and other reformers, called Protestants, developed a new understanding of Christian doctrine that emphasized faith and grace; Protestant ideas spread rapidly through preaching, hymns, and the printing press; and soon western Europe was split religiously. Local situations influenced religious patterns. In England the king's need for a church-approved divorce triggered the break with Rome, while in France and eastern Europe the ideas of John Calvin gained wide acceptance. By the middle of the sixteenth century the Roman Catholic Church had begun a process of internal reform along with opposing Protestants intellectually, politically, militarily, and institutionally. This reinvigorated Catholic Church would carry Christian ideas around the world, while in Europe religious differences led to riots, witch persecutions, civil wars, and international conflicts.

CHAPTER LOCATOR | What were the major cultural developments of the Renaissance? | What were the key social hierarchies in Renaissance Europe?

450 CHAPTER 15
EUROPE IN THE RENAISSANCE AND REFORMATION

CONNECTIONS The Renaissance and the Reformation are often seen as key to the creation of the modern world. The radical changes of these times contained many elements of continuity, however. Artists, humanists, and religious reformers looked back to the classical era and early Christianity for inspiration. Political leaders played important roles in cultural and religious developments, just as they had for centuries in Europe and other parts of the world.

The events of the Renaissance and Reformation were thus linked with earlier developments, and they were also closely connected with another important element in the modern world: European exploration and colonization (discussed in Chapter 16). Renaissance monarchs paid for maritime expeditions, expecting a large share of any profits gained and increasingly viewing overseas territory as essential to their own reputations and to a strong state. Moreover, for many, European expansion had a religious dimension and was explicitly linked to the spread of Christianity around the world. The desire for fame, wealth, and power that was central to the Renaissance, and the religious zeal central to the Reformation, were thus key to the European voyages and to colonial ventures as well.

ONLINE DOCUMENT PROJECT

Cosimo and Lorenzo de' Medici

What role did patrons play in shaping Renaissance artistic and intellectual life?

Examine paintings and letters by Renaissance artists, and complete a quiz and writing assignment based on the evidence and details from this chapter. *See inside the front cover to learn more.*

| How did the nation-states of western Europe evolve in this period? | What were the central ideas of Protestant reformers, and why were they appealing? | How did the Catholic Church respond to the new religious situation? | What were the causes and consequences of religious violence? | ✔ LearningCurve Check what you know. |

CHAPTER 15 STUDY GUIDE

 GET STARTED ONLINE

 LearningCurve

Now that you've read the chapter, make it stick by completing the LearningCurve activity.

 EXPLAIN WHY IT MATTERS

Put your reading into practice. Identify each term below, and then explain why it matters in world history.

TERM	WHO OR WHAT & WHEN	WHY IT MATTERS
Renaissance (p. 422)		
patronage (p. 422)		
humanism (p. 424)		
Christian humanists (p. 425)		
debate about women (p. 429)		
Protestant Reformation (p. 436)		
indulgence (p. 437)		
Diet of Worms (p. 438)		
Protestant (p. 438)		
predestination (p. 443)		
Jesuits (p. 446)		
Huguenots (p. 448)		
politiques (p. 448)		
witch-hunts (p. 449)		

 MOVE BEYOND THE BASICS

To demonstrate a more advanced understanding of the key differences between Catholic and Protestant beliefs and practices by filling in the chart below with descriptions of Catholic and Protestant views of salvation, the nature and role of the clergy, and the nature and role of the church. How did Protestant beliefs challenge Catholic institutions?

	View of Salvation	Nature and Role of Clergy	Nature and Role of the Church
Protestantism			
Catholicism			

STEP 4 **PUT IT ALL TOGETHER** Now, take a step back and try to explain the big picture. Remember to use specific examples from the chapter in your answers.

THE RENAISSANCE

▶ How did Renaissance ideas about individuals and their potential differ from those that prevailed in the Middle Ages?

▶ How did political and economic considerations shape the emergence, development, and spread of the Renaissance?

THE PROTESTANT REFORMATION

▶ How did Protestantism differ from earlier calls for theological and institutional reform of the Catholic Church? What explains Protestantism's remarkable success?

▶ What groups found Protestantism most appealing? Why?

THE CATHOLIC REFORMATION AND RELIGIOUS VIOLENCE

▶ Should the Catholic Reformation be considered a success? Why or why not?

▶ What connections can you make between the various forms of religious violence (riots, wars, witchcraft trials) that plagued sixteenth- and seventeenth-century Europe? What common factors and conditions contributed to each of these types of religious violence?

LOOKING BACK, LOOKING AHEAD

▶ How did medieval developments prepare the way for the Renaissance and the Reformation? What were the most important areas of continuity between medieval and early modern Europe?

▶ Many scholars and thinkers have seen the Renaissance and Reformation as marking the beginning of the "modern" Western world. Do you agree with this assessment? Why or why not?

> **IN YOUR OWN WORDS**

Imagine that you must give an oral report to the class answering the following question: In what ways did the Renaissance and Reformation represent breaks from the medieval past? What would be the most important points and why?

16

THE ACCELERATION OF GLOBAL CONTACT

1450–1600

> **What new global connections were forged in the fifteenth and sixteenth centuries?** Chapter 16 examines the causes, course, and effects of European expansion in the fifteenth and sixteenth centuries. Before 1500 Europeans were relatively marginal players in a centuries-old trading system that linked Africa, Asia, and Europe. By 1550 the European search for better access to Asian trade goods had led to a new overseas empire in the Indian Ocean and the accidental discovery of the Western Hemisphere. With this discovery South and North America were drawn into an international network of trade centers and political empires, which Europeans came to dominate. The era of globalization had begun, creating new political systems and forms of economic exchange as well as cultural assimilation, conversion, and resistance.

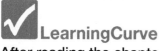 **LearningCurve**

After reading the chapter, use LearningCurve to retain what you've read.

Nezahualpilli At the time of the arrival of Europeans, Nezahualpilli was ruler of the city-state of Texcoco, the second most important city in the Aztec Empire after Tenochtitlan. (Nezahualpilli, portrait from *Codex Ixtlilxochitl*, 1582, pigment on European paper/Bibliothèque Nationale, Paris, France/De Agostini Picture Library/akg-images)

> What was the Afroeurasian trade world like prior to the era of European exploration?

> Why and how did Europeans undertake ambitious voyages of expansion?

> What was the impact of Iberian conquest and settlement on the peoples and ecologies of the Americas?

> How was the era of global contact shaped by new commodities, commercial empires, and forced migrations?

> How did new encounters shape cultural attitudes and beliefs in Europe and the New World?

What was the Afroeurasian trade world like prior to the era of European exploration?

The Port of Calicut in India

The port of Calicut, located on the west coast of India, was a center of the Indian Ocean spice trade during the Middle Ages. Vasco da Gama arrived in Calicut in 1498 and obtained permission to trade there, leading to hostilities between the Portuguese and the Arab traders who had previously dominated the port. (Private Collection/The Stapleton Collection/The Bridgeman Art Library)

THE AFROEURASIAN TRADE WORLD linked the products and people of Europe, Asia, and Africa in the fifteenth century. The West was not the dominant player in this trading system. Nevertheless, wealthy Europeans were eager consumers of luxury goods from the East, which they received through Italian middlemen.

The Trade World of the Indian Ocean

The Indian Ocean was the center of the Afroeurasian trade world, serving as a crossroads for commercial and cultural exchanges between China, India, the Middle East, Africa, and Europe (Map 16.1). From the seventh through the fourteenth centuries, the volume of this trade steadily increased, declining only during the years of the Black Death.

Merchants congregated in a series of multicultural, cosmopolitan port cities strung around the Indian Ocean. Most of these cities had some form of autonomous self-government, and mutual self-interest had largely limited violence and attempts to monopolize trade. The most developed area of this commercial web was made up of the ports surrounding the South China Sea. In the fifteenth century the port of Malacca became a great commercial entrepôt (AHN-truh-poh), a trading post to which goods were shipped for storage while awaiting redistribution to other places.

CHAPTER LOCATOR | What was the Afroeurasian trade world like prior to the era of European exploration? | Why and how did Europeans undertake ambitious voyages of expansion?

456 CHAPTER 16 THE ACCELERATION OF GLOBAL CONTACT

1271–1295
Marco Polo travels to China

1443
Portuguese establish first African trading post at Arguin

1492
Columbus lands on San Salvador

1494
Treaty of Tordesillas ratified

1518
Atlantic slave trade begins

1519–1522
Magellan's expedition circumnavigates the world

1521
Cortés conquers Aztec Empire

1533
Pizarro conquers Inca Empire

1571
Spanish establish port of Manila in the Philippines

1602
Dutch East India Company founded

The Mongol emperors opened the doors of China to the West, encouraging Europeans like the Venetian trader and explorer Marco Polo to do business there. Marco Polo's tales of his travels from 1271 to 1295 fueled Western fantasies about the Orient.

After the Mongols fell to the Ming Dynasty in 1368, China entered a period of agricultural and commercial expansion, population growth, and urbanization (see pages 612–619). Historians agree that China had the most advanced economy in the world until at least the beginning of the eighteenth century.

China also took the lead in exploration, sending Admiral Zheng He's fleet as far west as Egypt. Each of his seven expeditions from 1405 to 1433 involved hundreds of ships and tens of thousands of men (see page 633). The purpose of the voyages was primarily diplomatic, to enhance China's prestige and seek tribute-paying alliances. The high expense of the voyages in a period of renewed Mongol encroachment led to the abandonment of the maritime expeditions after the deaths of Zheng He and the emperor.

China's decision to forego large-scale exploration was a decisive turning point in world history, one that left an opening for European states to expand their role in Asian trade. Nonetheless, Zheng He's voyages left a legacy of increased Chinese trading in the South China Sea and Indian Ocean.

Another center of Indian Ocean trade was India, the crucial link between the Persian Gulf and the Southeast Asian and East Asian trade networks. The subcontinent had ancient links with its neighbors to the northwest. Trade among ports bordering the Indian Ocean was revived in the Middle Ages by Arab merchants who circumnavigated India on their way to trade in the South China Sea.

The inhabitants of India's Coromandel coast traditionally looked to Southeast Asia, where they had ancient trading and cultural ties. Hinduism and Buddhism arrived in Southeast Asia from India during the Middle Ages, and a brisk trade between Southeast Asian and Coromandel port cities persisted from that time until the arrival of the Portuguese in the sixteenth century. India itself was an important contributor of goods to the world trading system. Most of the world's pepper was grown in India, and Indian cotton and silk textiles were also highly prized.

| What was the impact of Iberian conquest and settlement on the peoples of the Americas? | How was the era of global contact shaped by new commodities and forced migrations? | How did new encounters shape cultural attitudes and beliefs in Europe and the New World? | ✓ LearningCurve Check what you know. |

MAP 16.1 ■ The Fifteenth-Century Afroeurasian Trading World

After a period of decline following the Black Death and the Mongol invasions, trade revived in the fifteenth century. Muslim merchants dominated trade, linking ports in East Africa and the Red Sea with those in India and the Malay Archipelago. The Chinese admiral Zheng He followed the most important Indian Ocean trade routes on his voyages (1405–1433), hoping to impose Ming dominance of trade and tribute.

Peoples and Cultures of the Indian Ocean

Indian Ocean trade connected peoples from the Malay Peninsula (the southern extremity of the Asian continent), India, China, and East Africa, among whom there was an enormous variety of languages, cultures, and religions. In spite of this diversity, certain sociocultural similarities linked these peoples, especially in Southeast Asia.

In comparison to India, China, or even Europe after the Black Death, Southeast Asia was sparsely populated. People were concentrated in port cities and in areas of intense rice cultivation. Another difference between Southeast Asia and

CHAPTER LOCATOR | What was the Afroeurasian trade world like prior to the era of European exploration? | Why and how did Europeans undertake ambitious voyages of expansion?

CHAPTER 16
458 THE ACCELERATION OF GLOBAL CONTACT

India, China, and Europe was the higher status of women—their primary role in planting and harvesting rice gave them authority and economic power. At marriage, which typically occurred around age twenty, the groom paid the bride (or sometimes her family) a sum of money called **bride wealth**, which remained under her control. This practice was in sharp contrast to the Chinese, Indian, and European dowry, which came under the husband's control. Property was administered jointly, in contrast to the Chinese principle and Indian practice that wives had no say in the disposal of family property. All children, regardless of gender, inherited equally.

Respect for women carried over to the commercial sphere. Women participated in business as partners and independent entrepreneurs. When Portuguese and Dutch men settled in the region and married local women, their wives continued to play important roles in trade and commerce.

In contrast to most parts of the world other than Africa, Southeast Asian peoples had an accepting attitude toward premarital sexual activity and placed no premium on virginity at marriage. Divorce carried no social stigma and was easily attainable if a pair proved incompatible. Either the woman or the man could initiate a divorce.

bride wealth

▶ In early modern Southeast Asia, a sum of money the groom paid the bride or her family at the time of marriage. This practice contrasted with the dowry in China, India, and Europe, which the husband controlled.

> **Common Features of Southeast Asian Societies:**

- Austronesian languages
- Diet based on rice, fish, palms, and palm wine
- Rice, harvested by women, as the staple of the diet
- Fishing as the chief male occupation

Trade with Africa and the Middle East

On the east coast of Africa, Swahili-speaking city-states engaged in the Indian Ocean trade, exchanging ivory, rhinoceros horn, tortoise shells, copra (dried coconut), and slaves for textiles, spices, cowrie shells, porcelain, and other goods. The most important cities were Mogadishu, Mombasa, and Kilwa, which had converted to Islam by the eleventh century.

West Africa also played an important role in world trade. In the fifteenth century most of the gold that reached Europe came from the Sudan region in West Africa. Transported across the Sahara by Arab and African traders on camels, the gold was sold in the ports of North Africa. Other trading routes led to the Egyptian cities of Alexandria and Cairo.

Inland nations that sat astride the north-south caravan routes grew wealthy from this trade. In the mid-thirteenth century the kingdom of Mali emerged as an important player on the overland trade route. In later centuries, however, the diversion of gold away from the trans-Sahara routes would weaken the inland states of Africa politically and economically.

Gold was one important object of trade; slaves were another. Long before the arrival of Europeans, Arab and

Mansa Musa

This detail from the Catalan Atlas of 1375, a world map created for the Catalan king, depicts a king of Mali, Mansa Musa, who was legendary for his wealth in gold. European desires for direct access to the trade in sub-Saharan gold helped inspire Portuguese exploration of the west coast of Africa in the fifteenth century. (Detail from the *Catalan Atlas*, 1375 [vellum], by Abraham Cresques (1325–1387)/Bibliothèque Nationale, Paris, France/The Bridgeman Art Library)

| What was the impact of Iberian conquest and settlement on the peoples of the Americas? | How was the era of global contact shaped by new commodities and forced migrations? | How did new encounters shape cultural attitudes and beliefs in Europe and the New World? | ✔ LearningCurve Check what you know. |

African merchants took West African slaves to the Mediterranean to be sold in European, Egyptian, and Middle Eastern markets and also brought eastern Europeans to West Africa as slaves. In addition, Indian and Arab merchants traded slaves in the coastal regions of East Africa.

The Middle East served as an intermediary for trade between Europe, Africa, and Asia and was also an important supplier of goods for foreign exchange. Two great rival empires, the Persian Safavids and the Turkish Ottomans, dominated the region, competing for control over western trade routes to the East. By the mid-sixteenth century the Ottomans had established control over eastern Mediterranean sea routes to trading centers in Syria, Palestine, Egypt, and the rest of North Africa.

Genoese and Venetian Middlemen

Europe constituted a minor outpost in the world trading system, for European craftsmen produced few products to rival those of Asia. However, Europeans desired luxury goods from the East, and in the late Middle Ages such trade was controlled by the Italian city-states of Venice and Genoa. Venice had opened the gateway to Asian trade in 1304, when it established formal relations with the sultan of Mamluk Egypt and started operations in Cairo. Because Eastern demand for European goods was low, Venetians funded their purchases through shipping and trade in firearms and slaves.

Venice's ancient trading rival was Genoa. By 1270, Genoa dominated the northern route to Asia through the Black Sea. From then until the fourteenth century, the Genoese expanded their trade routes as far as Persia and the Far East.

In the fifteenth century, with Venice claiming victory in the spice trade, the Genoese shifted focus from trade to finance and from the Black Sea to the western Mediterranean. When Spanish and Portuguese voyages began to explore the western Atlantic (see page 461), Genoese merchants, navigators, and financiers provided their skills and capital to the Iberian monarchs.

A major element of Italian trade was slavery. Merchants purchased slaves in the Balkans of southeastern Europe. After the loss of the Black Sea trade routes—and thus the source of slaves—to the Ottomans, the Genoese sought new supplies of slaves in the West, eventually seizing or buying and selling the Guanches (indigenous peoples from the Canary Islands), Muslim prisoners and Jewish refugees from Spain, and, by the early 1500s, both black and Berber Africans. With the growth of Spanish colonies in the New World, Genoese and Venetian merchants became important players in the Atlantic slave trade.

> **QUICK REVIEW**

What role did the peoples of Southeast Asia play in the Afroeurasian trade world? What role did Europeans play?

CHAPTER LOCATOR | What was the Afroeurasian trade world like prior to the era of European exploration? | Why and how did Europeans undertake ambitious voyages of expansion?

CHAPTER 16
460 THE ACCELERATION OF GLOBAL CONTACT

Why and how did Europeans undertake ambitious voyages of expansion?

Pepper Harvest

To break the monotony of their bland diet, Europeans had a passion for pepper, which — along with cinnamon, cloves, nutmeg, and ginger — was the main object of the Asian trade. We can appreciate the fifteenth-century expression "as dear as pepper": one kilo of pepper cost 2 grams of silver at the place of production in the East Indies and from 1 to 10 grams of silver in Alexandria, Egypt; 14 to 18 grams in Venice; and 20 to 30 grams at the markets of northern Europe. Here natives fill vats, and the dealer tastes a peppercorn for pungency. (Bibliothèque Nationale, Paris, France/Archives Charmet/The Bridgeman Art Library)

AS EUROPE RECOVERED after the Black Death, new European players entered the scene with novel technology, eager to spread Christianity and to undo Italian and Ottoman domination of trade with the East. A century after the plague, Iberian explorers began the overseas voyages that helped create the modern world, with immense consequences for their own continent and the rest of the planet.

Causes of European Expansion

European expansion had multiple causes. The first was economic. By the middle of the fifteenth century Europe was experiencing a revival of population and economic activity after the lows of the Black Death. This revival created renewed demand for luxuries, especially spices, from the East. The fall of Constantinople and the subsequent Ottoman control of trade routes created obstacles to fulfilling these demands. European merchants and rulers eager for the profits of trade thus needed to find new sources of precious metal to exchange with the Ottomans or trade routes that bypassed the Ottomans.

| What was the impact of Iberian conquest and settlement on the peoples of the Americas? | How was the era of global contact shaped by new commodities and forced migrations? | How did new encounters shape cultural attitudes and beliefs in Europe and the New World? | ✓ LearningCurve Check what you know. |

Religious fervor and the crusading spirit were another important catalyst for expansion. Just seven months separated Isabella and Ferdinand's conquest of the emirate of Granada, the last remaining Muslim state on the Iberian Peninsula, and Columbus's departure across the Atlantic. Overseas exploration thus transferred the militaristic religious fervor of the reconquista (reconquest) to new non-Christian territories. As they conquered indigenous empires, Iberians brought the attitudes and administrative practices developed during the reconquista to the Americas.

A third motivation was the dynamic spirit of the Renaissance. Like other men of the Renaissance era, explorers sought to win glory for their exploits and demonstrated a genuine interest in learning more about unknown waters. The detailed journals kept by European voyagers attest to their fascination with the new peoples and places they visited.

The people who stayed at home had a powerful impact on the voyages of discovery. Merchants provided the capital for many early voyages and had a strong say in their course. To gain authorization and financial support for their expeditions, they sought official sponsorship from the Crown. Competition among European monarchs for the prestige and profit of overseas exploration thus constituted another crucial factor in encouraging the steady stream of expeditions that began in the late fifteenth century.

The small number of Europeans who could read provided a rapt audience for tales of fantastic places and unknown peoples. Cosmography, natural history, and geography aroused enormous interest among educated people in the fifteenth and sixteenth centuries. One of the most popular books of the time was the fourteenth-century text *The Travels of Sir John Mandeville*, which purported to be a firsthand account of the author's travels in the Middle East, India, and China.

Technology and the Rise of Exploration

Technological developments in shipbuilding, navigation, and weaponry enabled European expansion. Since ancient times, most seagoing vessels had been narrow, open boats called galleys, propelled by slaves or convicts manning the oars. The need for sturdier craft, as well as population losses caused by the Black Death, forced the development of a new style of ship that would not require much manpower. Over the course of the fifteenth century the Portuguese developed the **caravel**, a small, light, three-mast sailing ship with triangular lateen sails. The caravel was much more maneuverable than the galley. When fitted with cannon, it could dominate larger vessels.

This period also saw great strides in cartography and navigational aids. Around 1410 Arab scholars reintroduced Europeans to **Ptolemy's *Geography***. Written in the second century, the work synthesized the geographical knowledge of the classical world. It represented a major improvement over medieval cartography, but it also contained significant errors. Unaware of the Americas, Ptolemy showed the world as much smaller than it is, so that Asia appeared not very far to the west of Europe.

The magnetic compass made it possible for sailors to determine their direction and position at sea. The astrolabe, an instrument invented by the ancient Greeks and perfected by Muslim navigators, was used to determine the altitude

caravel

▶ A small, maneuverable, three-mast sailing ship developed by the Portuguese in the fifteenth century that gave the Portuguese a distinct advantage in exploration and trade.

Ptolemy's *Geography*

▶ A second-century-c.e. work that synthesized the classical knowledge of geography and introduced the concepts of longitude and latitude. Reintroduced to Europeans in 1410 by Arab scholars, its ideas allowed cartographers to create more accurate maps.

CHAPTER LOCATOR | What was the Afroeurasian trade world like prior to the era of European exploration? | Why and how did Europeans undertake ambitious voyages of expansion?

CHAPTER 16

462 THE ACCELERATION OF GLOBAL CONTACT

The Portuguese Fleet Embarked for the Indies

This image shows a Portuguese trading fleet in the late fifteenth century bound for the riches of the Indies. Between 1500 and 1635 over nine hundred ships sailed from Portugal to ports on the Indian Ocean in annual fleets composed of five to ten ships. Portuguese sailors used astrolabes, such as the one pictured here, to accurately plot their position. (fleet: British Museum/HarperCollins Publishers/The Art Archive at Art Resource, NY; astrolabe: © The Trustees of the British Museum/Art Resource, NY)

of the sun and other celestial bodies. It permitted mariners to plot their latitude, that is, their precise position north or south of the equator.

Like the astrolabe, much of the new technology that Europeans used on their voyages was borrowed from the East. Gunpowder, the compass, and the stern-post rudder were Chinese inventions. Advances in cartography also drew on the rich tradition of Judeo-Arabic mathematical and astronomical learning in Iberia. In exploring new territories, European sailors thus called on techniques and knowledge developed over centuries in China, the Muslim world, and trading centers along the Indian Ocean.

The Portuguese in Africa and Asia

For centuries Portugal was a small and poor nation on the margins of European life. Yet Portugal had a long history of seafaring and navigation. Blocked from access to western Europe by Spain, the Portuguese turned to the Atlantic. Nature favored the Portuguese: winds blowing along their coast offered passage to Africa, its Atlantic islands, and, ultimately, Brazil.

In the early phases of Portuguese exploration, Prince Henry (1394–1460), a dynamic younger son of the king, played a leading role. A nineteenth-century

What was the impact of Iberian conquest and settlement on the peoples of the Americas?

How was the era of global contact shaped by new commodities and forced migrations?

How did new encounters shape cultural attitudes and beliefs in Europe and the New World?

☑ LearningCurve
Check what you know.

463

scholar dubbed Henry "the Navigator" because of his support for the study of geography and navigation and for the annual expeditions he sponsored down the western coast of Africa.

Portugal's conquest of Ceuta, an Arab city in northern Morocco, in 1415 marked the beginning of European overseas expansion. In the 1420s, under Henry's direction, the Portuguese began to settle the Atlantic islands of Madeira (ca. 1420) and the Azores (1427). In 1443 they founded their first African commercial settlement at Arguin in North Africa. By the time of Henry's death in 1460, his support for exploration had resulted in thriving sugar plantations on the Atlantic islands, the first arrival of enslaved Africans in Portugal (see page 475), and new access to African gold.

The Portuguese next established fortified trading posts, called factories, on the gold-rich Guinea coast and penetrated into the African continent all the way to Timbuktu (Map 16.2). By 1500 Portugal controlled the flow of African gold to Europe. In contrast to the Spanish conquest of the Americas (see page 468), the Portuguese did not establish large settlements in West Africa or seek to control the political or cultural lives of those with whom they traded. Instead they sought to profit by inserting themselves into pre-existing trading systems.

In 1487 Bartholomew Diaz (ca. 1451–1500) rounded the Cape of Good Hope at the southern tip of Africa (Map 16.2), but storms and a threatened mutiny forced him to turn back. A decade later Vasco da Gama (ca. 1469–1524) succeeded in rounding the Cape while commanding a fleet in search of a sea route to India. With the help of an Indian guide, da Gama reached the port of Calicut in India. He returned to Lisbon with spices and samples of Indian cloth, having proved the possibility of lucrative trade with the East via the Cape route. Thereafter, a Portuguese convoy set out for passage around the Cape every March.

Lisbon became the entrance port for Asian goods into Europe, but this was not accomplished without a fight. Muslim-controlled port city-states had long controlled the rich trade of the Indian Ocean, and they did not surrender it willingly. From 1500 to 1515 the Portuguese used a combination of bombardment and diplomatic treaties to establish trading factories at Goa, Malacca, Calicut, and Hormuz, thereby laying the foundation for a Portuguese trading empire in the sixteenth and seventeenth centuries. The acquisition of port cities and their trade routes brought riches to Portugal, but, as in Africa, the Portuguese had limited impact on the lives and religious faith of peoples beyond Portuguese coastal holdings.

Inspired by the Portuguese, Spain had also begun the quest for empire. Theirs was to be a second, entirely different mode of colonization leading to large-scale settlement and the forced assimilation of huge indigenous populations.

Spain's Voyages to the Americas

Christopher Columbus, a native of Genoa, was an experienced seaman and navigator. He had worked as a mapmaker in Lisbon and had spent time on Madeira. He was familiar with such fifteenth-century Portuguese navigational aids as *portolans*—written descriptions of the courses along which ships sailed—and the use of the compass as a nautical instrument.

Columbus was also a deeply religious man. He had witnessed the Spanish conquest of Granada and shared fully in the religious fervor surrounding that event. Like the Spanish rulers and most Europeans of his age, Columbus under-

CHAPTER LOCATOR | What was the Afroeurasian trade world like prior to the era of European exploration? | Why and how did Europeans undertake ambitious voyages of expansion?

CHAPTER 16
464   THE ACCELERATION OF GLOBAL CONTACT

Colonial
Latin America,
18th Century

MEXICO

NEW SPAIN

ATLANTIC
OCEAN

NEW
GRANADA

GUIANA

PACIFIC
OCEAN

PERU

BRAZIL

LA PLATA

CHILE

□ Spanish
viceroyalties

□ Portuguese
viceroyalties

Spanish holdings → Columbus → Cabot → Cartier → Other
Portuguese holdings → Da Gama → Magellan and crew → Frobisher

MAP 16.2 ■ Overseas Exploration and Conquest in the Fifteenth and Sixteenth Centuries

The voyages of discovery marked a dramatic new phase in the centuries-old migrations of European peoples. This map depicts the voyages of the most significant European explorers of the period.

> MAPPING THE PAST

ANALYZING THE MAP: Consider the routes and dates of the voyages shown. How might the successes of the earlier voyages have contributed to the later expeditions? Which voyage had the most impact, and why?

CONNECTIONS: Do you think the importance of these voyages was primarily economic, political, or cultural? Why?

stood Christianity as a missionary religion that should be carried to all places of the earth.

Rejected for funding by the Portuguese in 1483 and by Ferdinand and Isabella in 1486, Columbus finally won the support of the Spanish monarchy in 1492. Buoyed by the success of the reconquista and eager to earn profits from trade, the Spanish crown agreed to make him viceroy over any territory he might discover and to give him one-tenth of the material rewards of the journey.

Columbus and his small fleet left Spain on August 3, 1492. Columbus dreamed of reaching the court of the Mongol emperor, the Great Khan, not realizing that the Ming Dynasty had overthrown the Mongols in 1368. Based on Ptolemy's

| What was the impact of Iberian conquest and settlement on the peoples of the Americas? | How was the era of global contact shaped by new commodities and forced migrations? | How did new encounters shape cultural attitudes and beliefs in Europe and the New World? | ✓ LearningCurve Check what you know. |

Columbus's First Voyage to the New World, 1492–1493

Geography and other texts, he expected to pass the islands of Japan and then land on the east coast of China.

Columbus landed on an island in the Bahamas on October 12, which he christened San Salvador and claimed on behalf of the Spanish crown. In a letter he wrote to Ferdinand and Isabella on his return to Spain, Columbus described the natives as handsome, peaceful, and primitive. Believing he was somewhere off the east coast of Japan, in what he considered the Indies, he called them "Indians," a name that was later applied to all inhabitants of the Americas. Columbus concluded that they would make good slaves and could quickly be converted to Christianity.

Scholars have identified the inhabitants of the islands as the Taino (TIGH-noh) people. From San Salvador, Columbus sailed southwest, landing on Cuba on October 28. Deciding that he must be on the mainland of China near the coastal city of Quinsay (now Hangzhou), he sent a small embassy inland with letters from Ferdinand and Isabella and instructions to locate the city. Although they found no large settlement, the sight of Taino people wearing gold ornaments on Hispaniola suggested that gold was available in the region. In January, confident that its source would soon be found, he headed back to Spain to report on his discovery.

On his second voyage, Columbus took control of the island of Hispaniola and enslaved its indigenous peoples. On this and subsequent voyages, he brought with him settlers for the new Spanish territories, along with agricultural seed and livestock. Arriving in Hispaniola on his third voyage, he found revolt had broken out against his brother, whom Columbus had left behind to govern the colony. An investigatory expedition sent by the Spanish crown arrested Columbus and his brother for failing to maintain order. Columbus returned to Spain in disgrace and a royal governor assumed control of the colony.

Spain "Discovers" the Pacific

Columbus never realized the scope of his achievement: that he had found a vast continent unknown to Europeans, except for a fleeting Viking presence centuries earlier. The Florentine navigator Amerigo Vespucci (veh-SPOO-chee) (1454–1512) realized what Columbus had not. Writing about his discoveries on the coast of modern-day Venezuela, Vespucci stated: "Those new regions which we found and explored with the fleet . . . we may rightly call a New World." This letter was the first document to describe America as a continent separate from Asia. In recognition of Amerigo's bold claim, the continent was named for him.

To settle competing claims to the Atlantic discoveries, Spain and Portugal turned to Pope Alexander VI. The resulting **Treaty of Tordesillas** (tawr-duh-SEE-yuhs) in 1494 gave Spain everything to the west of an imaginary line drawn down the Atlantic and Portugal everything to the east.

The search for profits determined the direction of Spanish exploration and expansion in South America. Because its profits from Hispaniola and other Caribbean islands were insignificant compared to Portugal's enormous riches from the Asian spice trade, Spain renewed the search for a western passage to Asia. In 1519 Charles V of Spain commissioned Ferdinand Magellan (1480–1521) to find a direct sea route to Asia. Magellan sailed southwest across the Atlantic to Brazil, and after a long search along the coast he located the strait off the southern tip of South America that now bears his name (see Map 16.2). After passing through

Treaty of Tordesillas

▶ The 1494 agreement giving Spain everything west of an imaginary line drawn down the Atlantic and giving Portugal everything to the east.

CHAPTER LOCATOR | What was the Afroeurasian trade world like prior to the era of European exploration?

Why and how did Europeans undertake ambitious voyages of expansion?

CHAPTER 16
466 THE ACCELERATION OF GLOBAL CONTACT

the strait, his fleet sailed north up the west coast of South America and then headed west into the Pacific.

Terrible storms, disease, starvation, and violence haunted the expedition. Magellan himself was killed in a skirmish in the Malay Archipelago, and only one of the five ships that began the expedition made it back to Spain. This ship returned home in 1522 with only eighteen men aboard, having traveled from the east by way of the Indian Ocean, the Cape of Good Hope, and the Atlantic. The voyage—the first to circumnavigate the globe—had taken close to three years.

Despite the losses, this voyage revolutionized Europeans' understanding of the world by demonstrating the vastness of the Pacific. Magellan's expedition also forced Spain's rulers to rethink their plans for overseas commerce and territorial expansion. The westward passage to the Indies was too long and dangerous for commercial purposes. Thus Spain soon abandoned the attempt to oust Portugal from the Eastern spice trade and concentrated on exploiting its New World territories.

Early Exploration by Northern European Powers

Spain's northern European rivals also set sail across the Atlantic during the early days of exploration, searching for a northwest passage to the Indies. In 1497 John Cabot (ca. 1450–1499), a Genoese merchant living in London, landed on Newfoundland. The next year he returned and explored the New England coast. These forays proved futile, and at that time the English established no permanent colonies in the territories they explored.

News of the riches of Mexico and Peru later inspired the English to renew their efforts. Between 1576 and 1578 Martin Frobisher (ca. 1535–1594) made three voyages in and around the Canadian bay that now bears his name. Frobisher brought a quantity of ore back to England with him in hopes that it contained precious metals, but it proved to be worthless.

Early French exploration of the Atlantic was equally frustrating. Between 1534 and 1541 Frenchman Jacques Cartier (1491–1557) made several voyages and explored the St. Lawrence region of Canada, searching for a passage to the wealth of Asia. When this hope proved vain, the French turned to a new source of profit within Canada itself: trade in beavers and other furs. As had the Portuguese in Asia, French traders bartered with local peoples whom they largely treated as autonomous and equal partners. French fishermen also competed with the Spanish and English for the schools of cod they found in the Atlantic waters around Newfoundland.

QUICK REVIEW

How did the Portuguese lay the foundation for European overseas expansion?

| What was the impact of Iberian conquest and settlement on the peoples of the Americas? | How was the era of global contact shaped by new commodities and forced migrations? | How did new encounters shape cultural attitudes and beliefs in Europe and the New World? | ✓ LearningCurve Check what you know. |

What was the impact of Iberian conquest and settlement on the peoples and ecologies of the Americas?

Juan Vespucci's World Map, 1526

As chief pilot to the Spanish crown, Juan Vespucci oversaw constant revisions to royal maps necessitated by ongoing voyages of discovery and exploration. This map shows the progress of Spanish knowledge of the New World some thirty years after Columbus. (The Granger Collection, NYC — All rights reserved.)

BEFORE COLUMBUS'S ARRIVAL, the Americas were inhabited by thousands of groups of indigenous peoples with distinct languages and cultures. These groups ranged from hunter-gatherer tribes organized into tribal confederations to settled agriculturalists to large-scale empires connecting bustling cities and towns. The best estimate is that the peoples of the Americas numbered between 35 and 50 million in 1492. Their lives were radically altered by the arrival of Europeans.

Spanish Conquest of the Aztec and Inca Empires

In the first two decades after Columbus's arrival in the New World, the Spanish colonized Hispaniola, Cuba, Puerto Rico, and other Caribbean islands. Based on rumors of a wealthy mainland civilization, the Spanish governor in Cuba sponsored expeditions to the Yucatán coast of the Gulf of Mexico, including one in 1519 under the command of the **conquistador** (kahn-KEES-tuh-dawr) Hernán Cortés (1485–1547). Alarmed by Cortés's ambition, the governor decided to withdraw his support, but Cortés quickly set sail before being removed from command. Cortés and his party landed on the Mexican coast on April 21, 1519. His

conquistador

▶ Spanish for "conqueror"; a Spanish soldier-explorer, such as Hernán Cortés or Francisco Pizarro, who sought to conquer the New World for the Spanish crown.

CHAPTER LOCATOR | What was the Afroeurasian trade world like prior to the era of European exploration? | Why and how did Europeans undertake ambitious voyages of expansion?

CHAPTER 16
468   THE ACCELERATION OF GLOBAL CONTACT

camp soon received visits by delegations of Aztec leaders bearing gifts and news of their great emperor.

The Mexica Empire, also known as the Aztec Empire, comprised the Mexica people and the peoples they had conquered. At the time of the Spanish arrival, the empire was ruled by Moctezuma II (r. 1502–1520), from his capital at Tenochtitlan (tay-nawch-teet-LAHN), now Mexico City. The Aztecs were a sophisticated civilization with an advanced understanding of mathematics, astronomy, and engineering. As in European nations at the time, a hereditary nobility dominated the army, the priesthood, and the state bureaucracy and reaped the gains from the agricultural labor of the common people.

Within weeks of his arrival, Cortés acquired translators who provided vital information on the empire and its weaknesses. (See "Individuals in Society: Doña Marina / Malintzin," page 470.) Through his interpreters, Cortés learned of strong local resentment against the Aztec Empire. Realizing that he could exploit dissensions within the empire to his own advantage, Cortés forged an alliance with Tlaxcala (tlah-SKAH-lah), a subject kingdom of the Aztecs. In October a combined Spanish-Tlaxcalan force occupied the Aztec city of Cholula, second largest in the empire, and massacred thousands of inhabitants. Strengthened by this victory, Cortés formed alliances with other native kingdoms. In November 1519, with a few hundred Spanish men and some six thousand indigenous warriors, he marched on Tenochtitlan.

Moctezuma's response to the arrival of the Spanish was weak and hesitant. Unlike other native leaders, he refrained from attacking the Spaniards but instead welcomed Cortés and his men into Tenochtitlan. Moctezuma was apparently deeply impressed by Spanish victories and believed the Spanish were invincible. When Cortés took Moctezuma hostage, the emperor's influence crumbled. During the ensuing attacks and counterattacks, Moctezuma was killed. The Spaniards and their allies escaped from the city suffering heavy losses. Cortés quickly began gathering forces and making new alliances against the Aztecs. In May 1521 he led a second assault on Tenochtitlan, leading an army of approximately one thousand Spanish and seventy-five thousand native warriors.[1]

The Spanish victory in late summer 1521 was hard-won and was greatly aided by the effects of smallpox, which had devastated the besieged population of the city. After establishing a new capital in the ruins of Tenochtitlan, Cortés and other conquistadors began the systematic conquest of Mexico.

More remarkable than the defeat of the Aztec Empire was the fall of the remote Inca Empire in Peru. Living in a settlement perched more than 9,800 feet above sea level, the Incas were isolated from the Mesoamerican civilization of the Aztecs. The Incas' strength lay largely in their bureaucratic efficiency. They divided their empire into four major regions, each region into provinces, and each province into districts. Officials at each level used the extensive network of roads to transmit information and orders. The Incas used a complex system of colored and knotted cords, called khipus, for administrative bookkeeping.

By the time of the Spanish invasion, however, the Inca Empire had been weakened by a civil war over succession and an epidemic of disease, possibly smallpox, spread through trade with groups in contact with Europeans. The Spanish conquistador Francisco Pizarro (ca. 1475–1541) landed on the northern coast of Peru on May 13, 1532, the very day the Inca leader Atahualpa (ah-tuh-WAHL-puh) won control of the empire. As Pizarro advanced across the Andes toward Cuzco, the capital of the Inca Empire, Atahualpa was also heading there for his coronation.

Aztec Empire

▶ Also known as the Mexica Empire, a large and complex Native American civilization in modern Mexico and Central America that possessed advanced mathematical, astronomical, and engineering technology.

Invasion of Tenochtitlán, 1519–1521

- → Cortés's original route, 1519
- → Cortés's retreat, 1520
- → Cortés's return route, 1520–1521

→ Pizarro's route

The Conquest of Peru, 1532–1533

Inca Empire

▶ The vast and sophisticated Peruvian empire centered at the capital city of Cuzco that was at its peak in the fifteenth century.

| What was the impact of Iberian conquest and settlement on the peoples of the Americas? | How was the era of global contact shaped by new commodities and forced migrations? | How did new encounters shape cultural attitudes and beliefs in Europe and the New World? | LearningCurve Check what you know. |

In April 1519 Hernán Cortés and his followers received a number of gifts from the Tabasco people after he defeated them, including a group of twenty female captives. Among them was a young woman the Spanish baptized as Marina, which became Malin in the Nahuatl (NAH-wha-tuhl) language spoken in the Aztec Empire. Her high status and importance were recognized with the honorific title of *doña* in Spanish and the suffix *-tzin* in Nahuatl. Bernal Díaz del Castillo, who accompanied Cortés and wrote the most important contemporary history of the Aztec Empire and its conquest, claimed that Doña Marina (or Malintzin) was the daughter of a leader of a Nahuatl-speaking tribe. According to his account, the family sold Marina to Maya slave traders as a child to protect the inheritance rights of her stepbrother.

Marina possessed unique skills that immediately caught the attention of Cortés. Fluent both in Nahuatl and Yucatec Maya (spoken by a Spanish priest accompanying Cortés), she offered a way for him to communicate with the peoples he encountered. She quickly learned Spanish as well and came to play a vital role as an interpreter and diplomatic guide. Indigenous pictures and writings created after the conquest depict Malintzin as a constant presence beside Cortés as he negotiated with and fought and killed Amerindians. The earliest known images show her interpreting for Cortés as he meets with the Tlaxcalan lord Xicotencatl, forging the alliance that would prove vital to Spanish victory against the Aztecs. Malintzin also appears prominently in the images of the *Florentine Codex*, an illustrated history of the Aztec Empire and its conquest created near the end of the sixteenth century by indigenous artists working under the direction of Friar Bernardino de Sahagún. All the images depict her as a well-dressed woman standing at the center of interactions between the Spanish and Amerindians.

Malintzin bore Cortés a son, Don Martín Cortés, in 1522 and accompanied him on expeditions to Honduras between 1524 and 1526. It is impossible to know the true nature of their personal relationship. Cortés was married to a Spanish woman in Cuba at the time, and Malintzin was a slave, in no position to refuse any demands he made of her. Cortés recognized their child and provided financial support for his upbringing. Malintzin later married one of Cortés's Spanish followers, Juan Jaramillo, with whom she had a daughter. It is unknown when and how she died.

Bernal Díaz gave Malintzin high praise. In his history, written decades after the fact, he described her as beautiful and intelligent, revered by native tribesmen, and devotedly loyal to the Spanish. He stated repeatedly that it would have been impossible for them to succeed without her help. Cortés mentioned Malintzin only twice in his letters to Spanish king Charles V. He acknowledged her usefulness as his interpreter but described her only as "an Indian woman of this land," giving no hint of their personal relationship. No writings from Malintzin herself exist.

Doña Marina translating for Hernán Cortés.

Malintzin is commonly known in Mexico and Latin America as La Malinche, a Spanish rendering of her Nahuatl name. She remains a compelling and controversial figure. Popular opinion has often condemned La Malinche as a traitor to her people, whose betrayal enabled the Spanish conquest and centuries of subjugation of indigenous peoples. Other voices have defended her as an enslaved woman who had no choice but to serve her masters. As the mother of a *mestizo* (mixed-race) child, she has also been seen as a founder of the mixed-race population that dominates modern Mexico. She will always be a reminder of the complex interactions between indigenous peoples and Spanish conquistadors that led to the conquest and the new culture born from it.

QUESTIONS FOR ANALYSIS

1. Why was the role of interpreter so important in Cortés's conquest of the Aztec Empire? Why did Malintzin become such a central figure in interactions between Cortés and the Amerindians?
2. What options were open to Malintzin in following her path? If she intentionally chose to aid the Spanish, what motivations might she have had?

ONLINE DOCUMENT PROJECT

How did Spanish and Amerindian artists depict Malintzin? Examine Spanish and Amerindian representations of Malintzin's role in the conquest, and then complete a quiz and writing assignment based on the evidence and details from this chapter. *See inside the front cover to learn more.*

Like Moctezuma in Mexico, Atahualpa sent envoys to greet the Spanish. Motivated by curiosity about the Spanish, he intended to meet with them to learn more about them and their intentions. Instead the Spaniards ambushed and captured him, extorted an enormous ransom in gold, and then executed him in 1533. The Spanish then marched on to Cuzco, profiting, as with the Aztecs, from internal conflicts and forming alliances with local peoples. When Cuzco fell in 1533, the Spanish plundered immense riches in gold and silver.

A combination of factors made it possible for tiny Spanish forces to bring down the mighty empires of the Americas: the boldness and audacity of conquistadors like Cortés and Pizarro; the military superiority endowed by Spanish firepower and horses; the fervent belief in a righteous Christian God imparted by the reconquista; division within the Aztec and Inca Empires that produced native allies for the Spanish; and, of course, the devastating impact of contagious diseases among the indigenous population. Ironically, the well-organized, urban-based Aztec and Inca Empires were more vulnerable to wholesale takeover than more decentralized and fragmented groups like the Maya, whose independence was not wholly crushed until the end of the seventeenth century.

Inca Women Milking Cows

This illustration of Inca women milking cows is from a collection of illustrations by a Spanish bishop that offers a valuable view of life in Peru in the 1780s. (From *Codex Trujillo*, Bishop Baltasar Jaime Martínez Compañón, Palacio Real, Madrid, Spain/Photo: Albers Foundation/ Art Resource, NY)

Portuguese Brazil

Unlike Mesoamerica or the Andes, the territory of Brazil contained no urban empires but instead had roughly 2.5 million nomadic and settled people divided into small tribes and many different language groups. In 1500 the Portuguese crown named Pedro Álvares Cabral commander of a fleet headed for the spice trade of the Indies. En route, the fleet sailed far to the west, accidentally landing on the coast of Brazil, which Cabral claimed for Portugal under the terms of the Treaty of Tordesillas.

In the 1520s Portuguese settlers brought sugarcane production to Brazil. They initially used enslaved indigenous laborers on sugar plantations, but the rapid decline in the indigenous population soon led to the use of forcibly transported Africans. In Brazil the Portuguese thus created a new form of colonization in the Americas: large plantations worked by enslaved people. This model of slave-worked sugar plantations would spread throughout the Caribbean in the seventeenth century.

Colonial Administration

By the end of the sixteenth century the Spanish and Portuguese had successfully overcome most indigenous groups and expanded their territory throughout modern-day Mexico, the southwestern United States, and Central and South America. In Mesoamerica and the Andes, the Spanish had taken over the cities and tribute systems of the Aztecs and the Incas, basing their control on the prior existence of well-established polities with organized tribute systems.

| What was the impact of Iberian conquest and settlement on the peoples of the Americas? | How was the era of global contact shaped by new commodities and forced migrations? | How did new encounters shape cultural attitudes and beliefs in Europe and the New World? | ☑ LearningCurve Check what you know. |

While early conquest and settlement were conducted largely by private initiatives, the Spanish and Portuguese governments soon assumed more direct control. In 1503 the Spanish granted the port of Seville a monopoly over all traffic to the New World and established the House of Trade, or *Casa de Contratación*, to oversee economic matters. In 1523 Spain created the Royal and Supreme Council of the Indies, with authority over all colonial affairs subject to approval by the king. Spanish territories themselves were divided initially into two **viceroyalties**, or administrative divisions: New Spain, created in 1535; and Peru, created in 1542. In the eighteenth century, two new viceroyalties, New Granada and La Plata, were created (see Map 16.2).

Within each territory, the viceroy, or imperial governor, exercised broad military and civil authority. The viceroy presided over the *audiencia* (ow-dee-EHN-see-ah), a board of judges that served as his advisory council and the highest judicial body. As in Spain, settlement in the Americas was centered on cities and towns. In each city, the municipal council, or *cabildo*, exercised local authority.

In Portugal, the India House in Lisbon functioned much like the Spanish House of Trade, and royal representatives oversaw its possessions in West Africa and Asia, as did governors in Spanish America. To secure the vast expanse of Brazil, however, the Portuguese implemented a distinctive system of rule, called **captaincies**, in the 1530s. These were hereditary grants of land given to nobles and loyal officials who bore the costs of settling and administering their territories. Over time, the Crown secured greater power over the captaincies, appointing royal governors to act as administrators.

Throughout the Americas, the Catholic Church played an integral role in Iberian rule. The papacy allowed Portuguese and Spanish officials greater control over the church than was the case at home, allowing them to appoint clerics and collect tithes. This control helped colonial powers use the church as an instrument to indoctrinate indigenous people (see page 479).

Indigenous Population Loss and Economic Exploitation

From the time of Christopher Columbus in Hispaniola, the conquerors of the New World made use of the **encomienda system** to profit from the peoples and territories they encountered. This system was a legacy of the methods used to reward military leaders in the time of the reconquista. First in the Caribbean and then on the mainland, conquistadors granted their followers the right to employ groups of Native Americans as laborers and to demand tribute payments from them in exchange for providing food, shelter, and instruction in the Christian faith.

A 1512 Spanish law authorizing the use of the encomienda called for indigenous people to be treated fairly, but in practice the system lead to terrible abuses. Spanish missionaries publicized these abuses, leading to debates in Spain about the nature and proper treatment of indigenous people (see page 479). King Charles V responded to such complaints in 1542 with the New Laws, which set limits on the authority of encomienda holders.

The New Laws provoked a revolt among elites in Peru and were little enforced throughout Spanish territories. Nonetheless, the Crown gradually gained control over encomiendas in central areas of the empire and required indigenous people

viceroyalties
▶ The name for the four administrative units of Spanish possessions in the Americas: New Spain, Peru, New Granada, and La Plata.

captaincies
▶ A system established by the Portuguese in Brazil in the 1530s, whereby hereditary grants of land were given to nobles and loyal officials who bore the costs of settling and administering their territories

encomienda system
▶ A system whereby the Spanish crown granted the conquerors the right to forcibly employ groups of Indians; it was a disguised form of slavery.

CHAPTER LOCATOR | What was the Afroeurasian trade world like prior to the era of European exploration? | Why and how did Europeans undertake ambitious voyages of expansion?

CHAPTER 16
472 THE ACCELERATION OF GLOBAL CONTACT

to pay tributes in cash, rather than in labor. To respond to a shortage of indigenous workers, royal officials established a new government-run system of forced labor, called *repartimiento* in New Spain and *mita* in Peru. Administrators assigned a certain percentage of the inhabitants of native communities to labor for a set period each year in public works, mining, agriculture, and other tasks.

Spanish systems for exploiting the labor of indigenous peoples were both a cause of and a response to the disastrous decline in the numbers of such peoples that began soon after the arrival of Europeans. Some indigenous people died as a direct result of the violence of conquest and the disruption of agriculture and trade caused by warfare. The most important cause of death, however, was infectious disease. Having little or no resistance to diseases brought from the Old World, the inhabitants of the New World fell victim to smallpox, typhus, influenza, and other illnesses.

The pattern of devastating disease and population loss established in the Spanish colonies was repeated everywhere Europeans settled. Overall, population declined by as much as 90 percent or more but with important regional variations. In general, densely populated urban centers were worse hit than rural areas and tropical, low-lying regions suffered more than cooler, higher-altitude ones.

Colonial administrators responded to native population decline by forcibly combining dwindling indigenous communities into new settlements and imposing the rigors of the encomienda and the repartimiento. By the end of the sixteenth century the search for fresh sources of labor had given birth to the new tragedy of the Atlantic slave trade (see page 598).

Patterns of Settlement

The century after the discovery of silver in 1545 marked the high point of Iberian immigration to the Americas. Although the first migrants were men, soon whole families began to cross the Atlantic, and the European population began to increase through natural reproduction. By 1600 American-born Europeans, called *Creoles*, outnumbered immigrants.

Iberian settlement was predominantly urban in nature. Spaniards settled into the cities and towns of the former Aztec and Inca Empires as the native population dwindled through death and flight. They also established new cities in which settlers were quick to establish urban institutions familiar to them from home: city squares, churches, schools, and universities.

Despite the growing number of Europeans and the rapid decline of the native population, Europeans remained a small minority of the total inhabitants of the Americas. Iberians formed sexual relationships with native women leading to a substantial population of mixed Iberian and Indian descent known as *mestizos* (meh-STEE-zohz). The large-scale arrival of enslaved Africans, starting in Brazil in the mid-sixteenth century, added new ethnic and racial dimensions to the population (see pages 598–603).

QUICK REVIEW <

What factors help explain the conquest of the mighty Inca and Aztec Empires by the Spanish?

| What was the impact of Iberian conquest and settlement on the peoples of the Americas? | How was the era of global contact shaped by new commodities and forced migrations? | How did new encounters shape cultural attitudes and beliefs in Europe and the New World? | ✓ LearningCurve Check what you know. |

How was the era of global contact shaped by new commodities, commercial empires, and forced migrations?

A New World Sugar Refinery in Brazil

Sugar was the most important and most profitable plantation crop in the New World. This image shows the processing and refinement of sugar on a Brazilian plantation. Sugarcane was grown, harvested, and processed by African slaves who labored under brutal and ruthless conditions to generate enormous profits for plantation owners. (Bibliothèque Nationale, Paris, France/Giraudon/The Bridgeman Art Library)

THE CENTURIES-OLD AFROEURASIAN trade world was forever changed by the European voyages of discovery and their aftermath. For the first time, a truly global economy emerged in the sixteenth and seventeenth centuries, and it forged new links among far-flung peoples, cultures, and societies.

The Columbian Exchange

The travel of people and goods between the Old and New Worlds led to an exchange of animals, plants, and diseases, a complex process known as the Columbian exchange. As we have seen, the introduction of new diseases to the Americas had devastating consequences. But other results of the exchange brought benefits not only to the Europeans but also to native peoples.

Everywhere they settled, the Spanish and Portuguese brought and raised wheat. Grapes and olives brought over from Spain did well in parts of Peru and Chile. Perhaps the most significant introduction to the diet of Native Americans

Columbian exchange

▶ The exchange of animals, plants, and diseases between the Old and the New Worlds.

CHAPTER LOCATOR | What was the Afroeurasian trade world like prior to the era of European exploration? | Why and how did Europeans undertake ambitious voyages of expansion?

474 CHAPTER 16 THE ACCELERATION OF GLOBAL CONTACT

came via the meat and milk of the livestock that the early conquistadors brought with them, including cattle, sheep, and goats. The horse enabled both the Spanish conquerors and native populations to travel faster and farther and to transport heavy loads more easily.

In turn, Europeans returned home with many food crops that became central elements of their diet. Crops originating in the Americas included tomatoes, squash, pumpkins, peppers, and many varieties of beans, as well as tobacco. One of the most important of such crops was maize (corn). By the late seventeenth century, maize had become a staple in Spain, Portugal, southern France, and Italy, and in the eighteenth century it became one of the chief foods of southeastern Europe and southern China. Even more valuable was the nutritious white potato, which slowly spread from west to east, contributing everywhere to a rise in population.

While the exchange of foods was a great benefit to cultures across the world, the introduction of European pathogens to the New World had a disastrous impact on the native population. The wave of catastrophic epidemic disease that swept the Western Hemisphere after 1492 can be seen as an extension of the swath of devastation wreaked by the Black Death in the 1300s, first on Asia and then on Europe. The world after Columbus was thus unified by disease as well as by trade and colonization.

Sugar and Early Transatlantic Slavery

Two crucial and interrelated elements of the Columbian exchange were the transatlantic trade in sugar and slaves. Throughout the Middle Ages, slavery was deeply entrenched in the Mediterranean, but it was not based on race. How, then, did black African slavery enter the European picture and take root in South and then North America? In 1453 the Ottoman capture of Constantinople halted the flow of European slaves from the eastern Mediterranean. Additionally, the successes of the Christian reconquest of the Iberian Peninsula drastically diminished the supply of Muslim captives. Cut off from its traditional sources of slaves, Mediterranean Europe turned to sub-Saharan Africa, which had a long history of slave trading.

As Portuguese explorers began their voyages along the western coast of Africa, one of the first commodities they sought was slaves. While the first slaves were simply seized by small raiding parties, Portuguese merchants soon found that it was easier and more profitable to trade with African leaders, who were accustomed to dealing in enslaved people captured through warfare with neighboring powers. From 1490 to 1530 Portuguese traders brought between three hundred and two thousand enslaved Africans to Lisbon each year.

In this stage of European expansion, the history of slavery became intertwined with the history of sugar. Population increases and greater prosperity in the fifteenth century led to increasing demand for sugar. The establishment of sugar plantations on the Canary and Madeira Islands in the fifteenth century testifies to this demand.

Sugar was a particularly difficult crop to produce for profit, requiring constant, back-breaking labor. The invention of roller mills to crush the cane more efficiently meant that yields could be significantly augmented, but only if a sufficient labor force was found to supply the mills. Europeans solved the labor problem by forcing first native islanders and then transported Africans to perform the backbreaking work.

| What was the impact of Iberian conquest and settlement on the peoples of the Americas? | **How was the era of global contact shaped by new commodities and forced migrations?** | How did new encounters shape cultural attitudes and beliefs in Europe and the New World? | ✔ LearningCurve Check what you know. |

475

The Transatlantic Slave Trade

The transatlantic slave trade that would ultimately result in the forced transport of over 12 million individuals began in 1518, when Spanish king Charles V authorized traders to bring enslaved Africans to New World colonies. The Portuguese brought the first slaves to Brazil around 1550. After its founding in 1621, the Dutch West India Company transported thousands of Africans to Brazil and the Caribbean, mostly to work on sugar plantations. In the late seventeenth century, with the chartering of the Royal African Company, the English began to bring slaves to Barbados and other English colonies in the Caribbean and mainland North America.

Before 1700, when slavers decided it was better business to improve conditions, some 20 percent of slaves died on the voyage from Africa to the Americas.[2] The most common cause of death was dysentery induced by poor-quality food and water, lack of sanitation, and intense crowding. On sugar plantations, death rates among enslaved people from illness and exhaustion were extremely high. Driven by rising demands for plantation crops, the tragic transatlantic slave trade reached its height in the eighteenth century.

The Birth of the Global Economy

With Europeans' discovery of the Americas and their exploration of the Pacific, the entire world was linked for the first time in history by seaborne trade. The opening of that trade brought into being three successive commercial empires: the Portuguese, the Spanish, and the Dutch.

In the sixteenth century the Portuguese controlled the sea route to India (Map 16.3). From their bases at Goa on the Arabian Sea and at Malacca on the Malay Peninsula, ships carried goods to the Portuguese settlement at Macao. From Macao Portuguese ships loaded with Chinese silks and porcelains sailed to Japan and the Philippines, where Chinese goods were exchanged for Spanish silver from New Spain. Throughout Asia the Portuguese traded in slaves. They also exported horses from Mesopotamia and copper from Arabia to India; from India they exported hawks and peacocks for the Chinese and Japanese markets. Back to Portugal they brought Asian spices that had been purchased with textiles produced in India and with gold and ivory from East Africa. They also shipped back sugar from their colony in Brazil, produced by African slaves whom they had transported across the Atlantic.

Becoming an imperial power a few decades later than the Portuguese, the Spanish were determined to claim their place in world trade. This was greatly facilitated by the discovery of immense riches in silver in the Americas. Silver poured into Europe through the Spanish port of Seville, contributing to steep inflation across Europe. Demand for silver also created a need for slaves to work in the mines.

The Spanish Empire in the New World was basically land based, but across the Pacific the Spaniards built a seaborne empire centered at Manila in the Philippines. The city of Manila served as the transpacific bridge between Spanish America and China. In Manila Spanish traders used silver from American mines to purchase Chinese silk for European markets.

In the seventeenth century the Dutch challenged the Spanish and Portuguese Empires. The Dutch East India Company was founded in 1602 with the stated

CHAPTER LOCATOR | What was the Afroeurasian trade world like prior to the era of European exploration? | Why and how did Europeans undertake ambitious voyages of expansion?

CHAPTER 16
476 THE ACCELERATION OF GLOBAL CONTACT

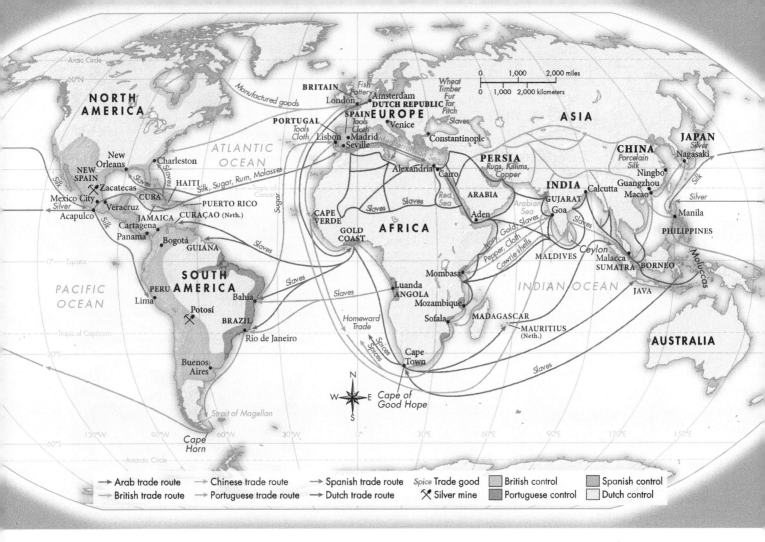

MAP 16.3 ■ **Seaborne Trading Empires in the Sixteenth and Seventeenth Centuries**

By the mid-seventeenth century trade linked all parts of the world except for Australia. Notice that trade in slaves was not confined to the Atlantic but involved almost all parts of the world.

intention of capturing the spice trade from the Portuguese. Drawing on their commercial wealth and long experience in European trade, by the end of the century the Dutch emerged as the most powerful worldwide seaborne trading power (see Chapter 19).

QUICK REVIEW ◁

How did European demand for sugar stimulate the expansion of the transatlantic slave trade?

| What was the impact of Iberian conquest and settlement on the peoples of the Americas? | **How was the era of global contact shaped by new commodities and forced migrations?** | How did new encounters shape cultural attitudes and beliefs in Europe and the New World? | ✓ LearningCurve Check what you know. |

How did new encounters shape cultural attitudes and beliefs in Europe and the New World?

Mixed Races

The unprecedented mixing of peoples in the Spanish New World colonies inspired great fascination. An elaborate terminology emerged to describe the many possible combinations of indigenous, African, and European blood, which were known collectively as *castas*. This painting belongs to a popular genre of the eighteenth century depicting couples composed of individuals of different ethnic origin and the children produced of their unions. (Schalkwijk/Art Resource, NY)

> PICTURING THE PAST

ANALYZING THE IMAGE: What do these images suggest about the racial composition of the population of Spanish America and the interaction of people with different racial and ethnic backgrounds? Who do you think the audience might have been, and why would viewers be fascinated by such images?

CONNECTIONS: What elements of this chapter might suggest that these are romanticized or idealized depictions of relations among different racial and ethnic groups?

THE AGE OF OVERSEAS EXPANSION heightened Europeans' contacts with the rest of the world. These contacts gave birth to new ideas about the inherent superiority or inferiority of different races. Religion became another means of cultural contact, as European missionaries aimed to spread Christianity in both the New World and East Asia. The East-West contacts also led to exchanges of influential cultural and scientific ideas.

CHAPTER LOCATOR | What was the Afroeurasian trade world like prior to the era of European exploration? | Why and how did Europeans undertake ambitious voyages of expansion?

Religious Conversion

Converting indigenous people to Christianity was one of the most important justifications for European expansion. The first missionaries to the New World accompanied Columbus on his second voyage, and more than 2,500 Franciscans, Dominicans, Jesuits and other friars crossed the Atlantic in the following century. Later French explorers were also accompanied by missionaries.

Catholic friars were among the first Europeans to seek an understanding of native cultures and languages as part of their effort to render Christianity comprehensible to indigenous people. They were also the most vociferous opponents of abuses committed by Spanish settlers.

Religion had been a central element of pre-Columbian societies, and many, if not all, indigenous people were receptive to the new religion that accompanied the victorious Iberians. In addition to spreading Christianity, missionaries taught indigenous peoples European methods of agriculture and instilled obedience to colonial masters. Despite the success of initial conversion efforts, authorities could not prevent the melding together of Catholic teachings with elements of pagan beliefs and practices.

European Debates About Indigenous Peoples

Iberian exploitation of the native population of the Americas began from the moment of Columbus's arrival in 1492. Denunciations of this abuse by Catholic missionaries, however, quickly followed, inspiring vociferous debates in both Europe and the colonies about the nature of indigenous peoples and how they should be treated. Bartolomé de Las Casas (1474–1566), a Dominican friar and former encomienda holder, was one of the earliest and most outspoken critics of the brutal treatment inflicted on indigenous peoples.

Mounting criticism in Spain led King Charles V to assemble a group of churchmen and lawyers to debate the issue in 1550 in the city of Valladolid. One side of the **Valladolid debate**, led by Juan Ginés de Sepúlveda, argued that conquest and forcible conversion were both necessary and justified to save indigenous people from the horrors of human sacrifice, cannibalism, and idolatry. To counter these arguments, Las Casas and his supporters depicted indigenous people as rational and innocent children, who deserved protection and tutelage from more advanced civilizations.

Elsewhere in Europe, audiences also debated these questions. Eagerly reading denunciations of Spanish abuses by critics like Las Casas, they derived the **Black Legend** of Spanish colonialism, the notion that the Spanish were uniquely brutal and cruel in their conquest and settlement of the Americas. This legend helped other European powers overlook their own record of colonial violence and exploitation.

New Ideas About Race

At the beginning of the transatlantic slave trade, most Europeans grouped Africans into the despised categories of pagan heathens or Muslim infidels. As Europeans turned to Africa for new sources of slaves, they drew on beliefs about Africans' primitiveness and barbarity to defend slavery.

Valladolid debate
▶ A debate organized by Spanish king Charles V in 1550 in the city of Valladolid that pitted defenders of Spanish conquest and forcible conversion against critics of these practices.

Black Legend
▶ The notion that the Spanish were uniquely brutal and cruel in their conquest and settlement of the Americas, an idea propagated by rival European powers.

What was the impact of Iberian conquest and settlement on the peoples of the Americas?

How was the era of global contact shaped by new commodities and forced migrations?

How did new encounters shape cultural attitudes and beliefs in Europe and the New World?

☑ LearningCurve
Check what you know.

479

Over time, the institution of slavery fostered a new level of racial inequality. Africans gradually became seen as utterly distinct from and wholly inferior to Europeans. In a transition from rather vague assumptions about Africans' non-Christian religious beliefs and general lack of civilization, Europeans developed increasingly rigid ideas of racial superiority and inferiority to safeguard the growing profits gained from plantation slavery. Black skin became equated with slavery itself as Europeans at home and in the colonies convinced themselves that blacks were destined by God to serve them as slaves in perpetuity. Support for this belief went back to the Greek philosopher Aristotle's argument that some people are naturally destined for slavery and to biblical associations between darkness and sin.

After 1700 the emergence of new methods of observing and describing nature led to the use of science to define race. Although previously the term referred to a nation or an ethnic group, henceforth "race" would be used to describe supposedly biologically distinct groups of people whose physical differences produced differences in culture, character, and intelligence. Biblical justifications for inequality thereby gave way to allegedly scientific ones (see page 736).

> **QUICK REVIEW**

How did European ideas about race change over the course of the early modern period?

CHAPTER SUMMARY

Prior to Columbus's voyages, well-developed trade routes linked the peoples and products of Africa, Asia, and Europe. Overall, Europe played a minor role in the Afroeurasian trade world. As the economy and population recovered from the Black Death, Europeans began to seek more direct and profitable access to the Afroeurasian trade world. Technological developments such as the invention of the caravel and the magnetic compass enabled explorers to undertake ever more ambitious voyages.

In the aftermath of their conquest of the Aztec and Inca Empires, the Spanish established new forms of governance to dominate native peoples and exploit their labor. The arrival of Europeans brought enormous population losses to native communities, primarily through the spread of infectious diseases. Disease was one element of the Columbian exchange, a complex transfer of germs, plants, and animals between the Old and New Worlds. These exchanges contributed to the creation of the first truly global economy. Tragically, a major component of global trade was the transatlantic slave trade, in which Europeans transported Africans to labor in the sugar plantations and silver mines of the New World. European nations vied for supremacy in global trade, with early Portuguese success in India and Asia being challenged first by the Spanish and then by the Dutch.

CHAPTER LOCATOR | What was the Afroeurasian trade world like prior to the era of European exploration? | Why and how did Europeans undertake ambitious voyages of expansion?

CHAPTER 16
480   THE ACCELERATION OF GLOBAL CONTACT

Increased contact with the outside world led Europeans to develop new ideas about cultural and racial differences. Debates occurred in Spain and its colonies over the nature of the indigenous peoples of the Americas and how they should be treated. Europeans had long held negative attitudes about Africans; as the slave trade grew, they began to express more rigid notions of racial inequality and to claim that Africans were inherently suited for slavery. Religion became another means of cultural contact, as European missionaries aimed to spread Christianity in the New World.

CONNECTIONS Just three years separated Martin Luther's attack on the Catholic Church in 1517 and Ferdinand Magellan's discovery of the Pacific Ocean in 1520. Within a few short years western Europeans' religious unity and notions of terrestrial geography were shattered. In the ensuing decades Europeans struggled to come to terms with religious differences among Protestants and Catholics at home and with the multitudes of new peoples and places they encountered abroad.

Even as the voyages of discovery contributed to the fragmentation of European culture, they also played a role in state centralization and consolidation in the longer term. Henceforth, competition to gain overseas colonies became an integral part of European politics. While Spain's enormous profits from conquest ultimately led to a weakening of its power, over time the Netherlands, England, and France used profits from colonial trade to help build modernized, centralized states.

Two crucial consequences emerged from this era of expansion. The first was the creation of enduring contacts among five of the seven continents of the globe— Europe, Asia, Africa, North America, and South America. From the sixteenth century onward, the peoples of the world were increasingly entwined in divergent forms of economic, social, and cultural exchange. The second was the growth of European power. Europeans controlled the Americas and gradually assumed control over existing trade networks in Asia and Africa. Although China remained the world's most powerful economy until at least 1800, the era of European dominance was born.

PLaunchPad

ONLINE DOCUMENT PROJECT
Interpreting Conquest

How did Spanish and Amerindian artists depict Malintzin?

Examine Spanish and Amerindian representations of Malintzin's role in the conquest, and then complete a quiz and writing assignment based on the evidence and details from this chapter. *See inside the front cover to learn more.*

What was the impact of Iberian conquest and settlement on the peoples of the Americas? | How was the era of global contact shaped by new commodities and forced migrations? | How did new encounters shape cultural attitudes and beliefs in Europe and the New World? | ✓ LearningCurve Check what you know.

481

CHAPTER 16 STUDY GUIDE

GET STARTED ONLINE

 LearningCurve

Now that you've read the chapter, make it stick by completing the LearningCurve activity.

EXPLAIN WHY IT MATTERS

Put your reading into practice. Identify each term below, and then explain why it matters in world history.

TERM	WHO OR WHAT & WHEN	WHY IT MATTERS
bride wealth (p. 459)		
caravel (p. 462)		
Ptolemy's *Geography* (p. 462)		
Treaty of Tordesillas (p. 466)		
conquistador (p. 468)		
Aztec Empire (p. 469)		
Inca Empire (p. 469)		
viceroyalties (p. 472)		
captaincies (p. 472)		
encomienda system (p. 472)		
Columbian exchange (p. 474)		
Valladolid debate (p. 479)		
Black Legend (p. 479)		

MOVE BEYOND THE BASICS

To demonstrate a more advanced understanding of the nature and impact of Spanish exploration and conquest in the Americas, fill in the chart below with descriptions of the motives behind Spanish expansion across the Atlantic. Next, identify key Spanish conquests and discoveries and the institutions of Spanish rule in the Americas. Finally, describe the impact of Spanish conquest in the New World and Europe. How do the motives you listed help explain the course of Spanish expansion in the New World?

Motives	Conquests and Discoveries	Institutions of Spanish Rule	Impact in the New World and Europe

PUT IT ALL TOGETHER

Now, take a step back and try to explain the big picture. Remember to use specific examples from the chapter in your answers.

THE AFROEURASIAN TRADE WORLD BEFORE COLUMBUS

▶ Which states were at the center of global trade prior to 1492? Why?

▶ Why were Europeans at a trading disadvantage prior to 1492? How did geography limit European participation in world trade? What role did Europe's economy and material culture play in this context?

DISCOVERY AND CONQUEST

▶ In your opinion, what was the most important motive behind European expansion? What evidence can you provide to support your position?

▶ What was the Columbian exchange? How did it transform both Europe and the Americas?

CHANGING VALUES AND BELIEFS

▶ How did European expansion give rise to new ideas about race?

▶ How did expansion complicate European's understanding of themselves and their place in the world?

LOOKING BACK, LOOKING AHEAD

▶ If Europe was at the periphery of the global trading system prior to 1492, where was it situated by the middle of the sixteenth century? What had changed? What had not?

▶ What connections can you make between our own experience of globalization in the twenty-first century and the experience of globalization in the sixteenth century? In what ways are the experiences similar? In what ways do they differ?

> IN YOUR OWN WORDS

Imagine that you must give an oral report to the class answering the following question: **What new global connections were forged in the fifteenth and sixteenth centuries?** What would be the most important points and why?

17

THE ISLAMIC WORLD POWERS

1300–1800

> **What were the strengths and weaknesses of the three great Islamic empires?** Chapter 17 examines developments in Islamic empires during the early modern period. The Ottoman Empire was one of the largest, best-organized, and most enduring political entities in world history. In Persia (now Iran) the Safavid Dynasty created a Shi'a state and presided over a brilliant culture. In India the Mughal leader Babur and his successors gained control of much of the Indian subcontinent. Although often at war with each other, these three states shared important characteristics and challenges and were strongly linked culturally. Before the end of this period, Europeans were also active in trade in these empires, especially in India.

 LearningCurve

After reading the chapter, use LearningCurve to retain what you've read.

Persian Princess The ruling houses of the Islamic empires were great patrons of art and architecture. This depiction of a princess in a garden is from an early-seventeenth-century palace built by Shah Abbas of the Safavid Dynasty in Persia. (Safavid Dynasty [fresco]. Chehel Sotun, or *The 40 Columns*, Isfahan, Iran/Giraudon/The Bridgeman Art Library)

> How were the three Islamic empires established, and what sorts of governments did they set up?

> What cultural advances occurred under the rule of the Ottoman, Safavid, and Mughal Empires?

> How did Christians, Jews, Hindus, and other non-Muslims fare under these Islamic states?

> How were the Islamic empires affected by the gradual shift toward trade routes that bypassed their lands?

> What common factors led to the decline of central power in the Islamic empires in the seventeenth and eighteenth centuries?

How were the three Islamic empires established, and what sorts of governments did they set up?

Sultan Mehmet II

Mehmet was called "the Conqueror" because at age twenty-one he captured Constantinople and ended the Byzantine Empire, but he is also known for his patronage of the arts and appreciation of beauty. (Topkapi Palace Museum, Istanbul, Turkey/Giraudon/The Bridgeman Art Library)

BEFORE THE MONGOLS ARRIVED in Central Asia and Persia, another nomadic people from the region of modern Mongolia, the Turks, had moved west, gaining control over key territories from Anatolia to Delhi in north India. As Mongol strength in Persia and Central Asia deteriorated in the late thirteenth to mid-fourteenth centuries, the Turks resumed their expansion.

In the late fourteenth century the Turkish leader Timur (1336–1405), also called Tamerlane, built a Central Asian empire from his base in Samarkand that reached into India and through Persia to the Black Sea. After his death, his sons and grandson fought each other for succession. By 1450 his empire was in rapid decline, and power devolved to the local level. Meanwhile, Sufi orders (groups of Islamic mystics) thrived, and Islam became the most important force integrating the region. It was from the many small Turkish chiefs that the founders of the three main empires emerged.

CHAPTER LOCATOR | **How were the three Islamic empires established, what governments did they set up?** | What cultural advances occurred under the rule of the Ottoman, Safavid, and Mughal Empires?

CHAPTER 17
486 THE ISLAMIC WORLD POWERS

1299–1326
Reign of Osman, founder of the Ottoman Dynasty

1299–1922
Ottoman Empire

1336–1405
Life of Timur

ca. mid-1400s
Coffeehouses become centers of Islamic male social life

1453
Ottoman conquest of Constantinople

1501–1524
Reign of Safavid Shah Isma'il

1501–1722
Safavid Empire

1520–1558
Hürrem wields influence in the Ottoman Empire as Suleiman's concubine and then wife

1520–1566
Reign of Ottoman sultan Suleiman I; period of artistic flowering in Ottoman Empire

1521
Piri Reis produces *Book of the Sea*, a navigational map book

1526–1857
Mughal Empire

1556–1605
Reign of Akbar in Mughal Empire

1570
Ottomans take control of Cyprus

1571
First major Ottoman defeat by Christians, at Lepanto

1587–1629
Reign of Shah Abbas; height of Safavid power; carpet weaving becomes major Persian industry

1631–1648
Construction of Taj Mahal under Shah Jahan in India

1658–1707
Reign of Aurangzeb; Mughal power begins to decline

1763
Treaty of Paris recognizes British control over much of India

The Ottoman Turkish Empire's Expansion

The **Ottomans** took their name from Osman (r. 1299–1326), the chief of a band of seminomadic Turks that had migrated into western **Anatolia** while the Mongols still held Persia. The Ottomans gradually expanded at the expense of other small Turkish states and the Byzantine Empire (Map 17.1). Although temporarily slowed by defeat at the hands of Timur in 1402, the Ottomans quickly reasserted themselves after Timur's death in 1405.

Osman's campaigns were intended to subdue, not to destroy. The Ottomans built their empire by absorbing the Muslims of Anatolia and by becoming the protector of the Orthodox Church and of the millions of Greek Christians in Anatolia and the Balkans. A series of victories between 1326 and 1352 made the Ottomans the masters of the Balkans. After these victories, the Ottomans made slaves of many captives and trained them as soldiers. These troops were outfitted with guns and artillery and trained to use them effectively.

In 1453, during the reign of Sultan Mehmet II (r. 1451–1481), the Ottomans conquered Constantinople, capital of the Byzantine Empire. Once Constantinople was theirs, the Ottoman

Ottomans
▶ Ruling house of the Turkish empire that lasted from 1299 to 1922.

Anatolia
▶ The region of modern Turkey.

Empire of Timur, ca. 1405

| How did Christians, Jews, Hindus, and other non-Muslims fare under these Islamic states? | How were the Islamic empires affected by trade routes that bypassed their lands? | What common factors led to the decline of central power in the Islamic empires? | ✓ LearningCurve Check what you know. |

MAP 17.1 ■ **The Ottoman Empire at Its Height, 1566**

The Ottomans, like their great rivals the Habsburgs, rose to rule a vast dynastic empire encompassing many different peoples and ethnic groups. The army and the bureaucracy served to unite the disparate territories into a single state.

> MAPPING THE PAST

ANALYZING THE MAP: Trace the coastlines of the Ottoman Empire. What were the major port cities of the empire? Which regions were encompassed within the empire at its height?

CONNECTIONS: If the Ottoman Empire is compared to Europe of the same period (see Map 18.2, page 522), which had more of its territory near the sea? How did proximity to the Mediterranean shape the politics of Ottoman-European relations in this period?

sultan

▶ An Arabic word originally used by the Seljuk Turks to mean authority or dominion; it was used by the Ottomans to connote political and military supremacy.

sultans considered themselves successors to both the Byzantine and Seljuk Turk emperors, and they quickly absorbed the rest of the Byzantine Empire. In the sixteenth century they continued to expand through the Middle East and into North Africa.

To begin the transformation of Constantinople (renamed Istanbul) into an imperial Ottoman capital, Mehmet ordered wealthy residents to participate in building mosques, markets, fountains, baths, and other public facilities. To make up for the loss of population through war, Mehmet transplanted inhabitants of other territories to the city, granting them tax remissions and possession of empty houses. He wanted them to start businesses, make Istanbul prosperous, and transform it into a microcosm of the empire.

CHAPTER LOCATOR | How were the three Islamic empires established, what governments did they set up? | What cultural advances occurred under the rule of the Ottoman, Safavid, and Mughal Empires?

Gunpowder, which was invented by the Chinese and adapted to artillery use by the Europeans, played an influential role in the expansion of the Ottoman state. In the first half of the sixteenth century, thanks to the use of this technology, the Ottomans gained control of shipping in the eastern Mediterranean and eliminated the Portuguese from the Red Sea. In 1514, under the superb military leadership of Selim (r. 1512–1520), the Ottomans turned the Safavids back from Anatolia. In addition, the Ottomans added Syria and Palestine (1516) and Egypt (1517). Before long the Ottomans had extended their rule across North Africa to Tunisia and Algeria. For the next four centuries a majority of Arabs lived under Ottoman rule.

Suleiman (r. 1520–1566) extended Ottoman dominion to its widest geographical extent (see Map 17.1). Suleiman's army crushed the Hungarians at Mohács in 1526. Three years later the Turks unsuccessfully besieged the Habsburg capital of Vienna. From the late fourteenth to the early seventeenth centuries, the Ottoman Empire was a key player in European politics. In 1525 Francis I of France and Suleiman struck an alliance; both believed that only their collaboration could prevent Habsburg domination of Europe. The Habsburg emperor Charles V retaliated by seeking an alliance with Safavid Persia. Suleiman renewed the French agreement with Francis's son, Henry II (r. 1547–1559), and this accord became the cornerstone of Ottoman policy in western Europe. Suleiman also allied with the German Protestant princes, forcing the Catholic Habsburgs to grant concessions to the Protestants. Ottoman pressure thus contributed to the official recognition of Lutheran Protestants at the Peace of Augsburg in 1555 and the consolidation of the national monarchy in France.

Though usually victorious on land, the Ottomans did not enjoy complete dominion on the seas. Competition with the Habsburgs and pirates for control of the Mediterranean led the Ottomans to conquer Cyprus in 1570 and settle thousands of Turks from Anatolia there. In response, Pope Pius V organized a Holy League against the Turks, which won a victory in 1571 at Lepanto off the west coast of Greece. Still, the Turks remained supreme on land and quickly rebuilt their entire fleet.

To the east, war with Safavid Persia occupied the sultans' attention throughout the sixteenth century. Several issues lay at the root of the long and exhausting conflict: religious antagonism between the Sunni Ottomans and the Shi'a Persians, competition to expand at each other's expense in Mesopotamia, desire to control trade routes, and European alliances. (For more on the Shi'a faith, see page 490.) Finally, in 1638 the Ottomans captured Baghdad, and the treaty of Kasr-I-Shirim established a permanent border between the two powers.

The Ottoman political system reached its classic form under Suleiman I. All authority flowed from the sultan to his public servants: provincial governors, police officers, military generals, heads of treasuries, and **viziers**. Suleiman ordered Lütfi Paşa (d. 1562), a poet and juridical scholar of slave origin, to draw up a new general code of laws that prescribed penalties for routine criminal acts. It also sought to reform bureaucratic and financial corruption. The legal code also introduced the idea of balanced government budgets. The head of the religious establishment was given the task of reconciling sultanic law with Islamic law. Suleiman's legal acts influenced many legal codes, including that of the United States.

The Ottomans ruled their more distant lands, such as those in North Africa, relatively lightly. Governors of distant provinces collected taxes and maintained trade routes, but their control did not penetrate deeply into the countryside.

viziers
▶ Chief assistants to caliphs.

How did Christians, Jews, Hindus, and other non-Muslims fare under these Islamic states? | How were the Islamic empires affected by trade routes that bypassed their lands? | What common factors led to the decline of central power in the Islamic empires? | ✓ LearningCurve Check what you know.

The Ottoman Empire's Use of Slaves

The power of the Ottoman central government was sustained through the training of slaves. Slaves were purchased from Spain, North Africa, and Venice; captured in battle; or drafted through the system known as devshirme, by which the sultan's agents compelled Christian families in the Balkans to sell their boys. The slave boys were converted to Islam and trained for the imperial civil service and the standing army. The brightest 10 percent entered the palace school, where they learned to read and write Arabic, Ottoman Turkish, and Persian in preparation for administrative jobs. Other boys were sent to Turkish farms, where they acquired physical toughness in preparation for military service. Known as janissaries (Turkish for "recruits"), they formed the elite army corps. They played a central role in Ottoman military affairs in the sixteenth century, adapting easily to the use of firearms. The devshirme system enabled the Ottomans to apply merit-based recruitment to military and administrative offices at little cost and provided a means of assimilating Christians living in Ottoman lands.

The Ottoman ruling class consisted partly of descendants of Turkish families that had formerly ruled parts of Anatolia and partly of people of varied ethnic origins who rose through the bureaucratic and military ranks, many beginning as the sultan's slaves. In return for their services to the sultan, they held landed estates for the duration of their lives. Because all property belonged to the sultan and reverted to him on the holder's death, Turkish nobles, unlike their European counterparts, did not have a local base independent of the ruler. The absence of a hereditary nobility and private ownership of agricultural land differentiates the Ottoman system from European feudalism.

Another distinctive characteristic of the Ottomans was the sultan's failure to marry. From about 1500 on, the sultans did not contract legal marriages but perpetuated the ruling house through concubinage. A slave concubine could not expect to exert power the way a local or foreign noblewoman could. (For a notable exception, see "Individuals in Society: Hürrem," page 491.) If one of the sultan's concubines delivered a boy, she raised him until the age of ten or eleven. Then the child was given a province to govern under his mother's supervision. Because succession to the throne was open to all the sultan's sons, fratricide often resulted upon his death, and the losers were blinded or executed.

Slave concubinage paralleled the Ottoman development of slave soldiers and slave viziers. All held positions entirely at the sultan's pleasure, owed loyalty solely to him, and thus were more reliable than a hereditary nobility. Great social prestige, as well as the opportunity to acquire power and wealth, was attached to being a slave of the imperial household.

The Safavid Empire in Persia

With the decline of Timur's empire after 1450, Persia was controlled by Turkish lords, with no single one dominant until 1501, when fourteen-year-old Isma'il (1487–1524) led a Turkish army to capture Tabriz and declared himself shah (king).

The strength of the early Safavid state rested on three crucial features. First, it had the loyalty and military support of nomadic Turkish Sufis known as Qizilbash (KIH-zihl-bahsh). The shah secured the loyalty of the Qizilbash by granting them

---

devshirme

▶ A process whereby the sultan's agents swept the provinces for Christian youths to be trained as soldiers or civil servants.

janissaries

▶ Turkish for "recruits"; they formed the elite army corps.

concubine

▶ A woman who is a recognized spouse but of lower status than a wife.

shah

▶ Persian word for "king."

Safavid

▶ The dynasty that encompassed all of Persia and other regions; its state religion was Shi'ism.

Qizilbash

▶ Nomadic Sufi tribesmen who were loyal to and supportive of the early Safavid state.

CHAPTER LOCATOR | How were the three Islamic empires established, what governments did they set up? | What cultural advances occurred under the rule of the Ottoman, Safavid, and Mughal Empires?

CHAPTER 17
490 THE ISLAMIC WORLD POWERS

Hürrem (1505?–1558) was born in the western Ukraine (then part of Poland), the daughter of a Ruthenian priest, and was given the Polish name Aleksandra Lisowska. When Tartars raided, they captured and enslaved her. In 1520 she was given as a gift to Suleiman on the occasion of his accession to the throne. The Venetian ambassador (probably relying on secondhand or thirdhand information) described her as "young, graceful, petite, but not beautiful." She was given the Turkish name Hürrem, meaning "joyful."

Hürrem apparently brought joy to Suleiman. Their first child was born in 1521. By 1525 they had four sons and a daughter; sources note that by that year Suleiman visited no other woman. But he waited eight or nine years before breaking Ottoman dynastic tradition by making Hürrem his legal wife, the first slave concubine so honored. For the rest of her life, Hürrem played a highly influential role in the political, diplomatic, and philanthropic life of the Ottoman state. First, great power flowed from her position as mother of the prince, the future sultan Selim II (r. 1566–1574). Then, as the intimate and most trusted adviser of the sultan, she was Suleiman's closest confidant. During his frequent trips to the far-flung corners of his multiethnic empire, Hürrem wrote him long letters filled with her love and longing for him and her prayers for his safety in battle. She also shared political information about affairs in Istanbul, the activities of the grand vizier, and the attitudes of the janissaries. At a time when some people believed that the sultan's absence from the capital endangered his hold on the throne, Hürrem acted as his eyes and ears for potential threats.

Hürrem was the sultan's contact with her native Poland, which sent more embassies to Istanbul than any other power. Through her correspondence with King Sigismund I, peace between Poland and the Ottomans was maintained. When Sigismund II succeeded his father in 1548, Hürrem sent congratulations on his accession, along with two pairs of pajamas (originally a Hindu garment but commonly worn in southwestern Asia) and six handkerchiefs. Also, she sent the shah of Persia gold-embroidered sheets and shirts that she had sewn herself, seeking to display the wealth of the sultanate and to keep peace between the Ottomans and the Safavids.

Hürrem depicted by a contemporary European artist. (© Mary Evans Picture Library/The Image Works)

The enormous stipend that Suleiman gave Hürrem permitted her to participate in his vast building program. In Jerusalem (in the Ottoman province of Palestine) she founded a hospice for fifty-five pilgrims that included a soup kitchen that fed four hundred pilgrims a day. In Istanbul Suleiman built and Hürrem endowed the Haseki (meaning "royal favorite concubine") mosque complex and a public bath for women near the Women's Market.

Perhaps Hürrem tried to fulfill two functions hitherto distinct in Ottoman political theory: those of the sultan's favorite and of mother of the prince. She also performed the conflicting roles of slave concubine and imperial wife. Many Turks resented Hürrem's interference at court. They believed she was behind the execution of Suleiman's popular son Mustafa on a charge of treason to make way for her own son to succeed as sultan.

Source: Leslie P. Peirce, *The Imperial Harem: Women and Sovereignty in the Ottoman Empire* (New York: Oxford University Press, 1993).

QUESTIONS FOR ANALYSIS

1. How does Hürrem compare to powerful women in other places, such as Empress Wu in China, Isabella of Castile, Catherine de' Medici of France, Elizabeth I of England, or any other you know about?
2. What was Hürrem's "nationality"? What role did it play in her life?

LaunchPad

ONLINE DOCUMENT PROJECT

How did Europeans view the Ottoman Empire?
Examine a Habsburg ambassador's impressions of the Ottoman Empire, and then complete a quiz and writing assignment based on the evidence and details from this chapter. *See inside front cover to learn more.*

vast grazing lands. In return, the Qizilbash supplied him with troops. Second, the Safavid state utilized the skills of urban bureaucrats and made them an essential part of the civil machinery of government.

The third source of Safavid strength was the Shi'a faith, which became the compulsory religion of the empire. The Shi'a believed that leadership among Muslims rightfully belonged to the Prophet Muhammad's descendants. Because Isma'il claimed descent from a line of twelve infallible imams (leaders) beginning with Ali (Muhammad's cousin and son-in-law), he was officially regarded as their representative on earth. Isma'il recruited Shi'a scholars to instruct and guide his people, and he persecuted and exiled Sunni **ulama**.

Safavid power reached its height under Shah Abbas (r. 1587–1629), who moved the capital from Qazvin to Isfahan. His military achievements, support for trade and commerce, and endowment of the arts earned him the epithet "the Great." In the military realm he adopted the Ottoman practice of building an army of slaves, who could serve as a counterweight to the Qizilbash, who had come to be considered a threat. He also increased the use of gunpowder weapons and made alliances with European powers against the Ottomans and Portuguese. In his campaigns against the Ottomans, Shah Abbas captured Baghdad, Mosul, and Diarbakr in Mesopotamia (Map 17.2). After Shah Abbas, Safavid power was sapped by civil war between tribal factions vying for control of the court.

ulama

▶ Religious scholars whom Sunnis trust to interpret the Qur'an and the Sunna, the deeds and sayings of Muhammad.

MAP 17.2 ■ The Safavid Empire, 1587–1629

In the late sixteenth century the power of the Safavid kingdom of Persia rested on its strong military force, its Shi'a Muslim faith, and its extraordinarily rich trade in rugs and pottery. Many of the cities on the map, such as Tabriz, Qum, and Shiraz, were great rug-weaving centers.

CHAPTER LOCATOR | How were the three Islamic empires established, what governments did they set up? | What cultural advances occurred under the rule of the Ottoman, Safavid, and Mughal Empires?

492 CHAPTER 17 THE ISLAMIC WORLD POWERS

The Mughal Empire in India

Of the three great Islamic empires of the early modern world, the Mughal Empire of India was the largest, wealthiest, and most populous. In the sixteenth century only the Ming Dynasty in China could compare.

In 1504 Babur (r. 1483–1530), a Turkish ruler forced out of a small territory in Central Asia, captured Kabul and established a kingdom in Afghanistan. Babur moved southward in search of resources to restore his fortunes. In 1526, with a force that was small but was equipped with firearms, Babur defeated the sultan of Delhi at Panipat. Babur's capture of the cities of Agra and Delhi, key fortresses of the north, paved the way for further conquests in northern India. Although many of his soldiers wished to return north with their spoils, Babur decided to stay in India.

During the reign of Babur's son Humayun (r. 1530–1540 and 1555–1556), the Mughals lost most of their territories in Afghanistan. Humayun went into temporary exile in Persia, where he developed a deep appreciation for Persian art and literature. The reign of Humayun's son Akbar (r. 1556–1605) may well have been the greatest in the history of India. Under his dynamic leadership, the Mughal state took definitive form and encompassed most of the subcontinent north of the Godavari River. No kingdom or coalition of kingdoms could long resist Akbar's armies. The once-independent states of northern India were forced into a centralized political system under the sole authority of the Mughal emperor.

To govern this vast region, Akbar developed an administrative bureaucracy centered on four co-equal ministers: finance and revenue; the army and intelligence; the judiciary and religious patronage; and the imperial household, whose jurisdiction included roads, bridges, and infrastructure throughout the empire. Under Akbar's Hindu finance minister, Raja Todar Mal, a uniform system of taxes was put in place. In the provinces imperial governors were appointed by and responsible solely to the emperor. Whereas the Ottoman sultans and Safavid shahs made extensive use of slaves for military and administrative positions, Akbar used the services of royal princes, nobles, and warrior-aristocrats. Initially these men were Muslims from Central Asia, but to reduce their influence, Akbar vigorously recruited Persians and Hindus. No single ethnic or religious faction could challenge the emperor.

Akbar's descendants extended the Mughal Empire further. His son Jahangir (r. 1605–1628) consolidated Mughal rule in Bengal. Jahangir's son Shah Jahan (r. 1628–1658) launched fresh territorial expansion. Faced with dangerous revolts by the Muslims in Ahmadnagar and the resistance of the newly arrived Portuguese in Bengal, Shah Jahan not only crushed this opposition but also strengthened his northwestern frontier. Shah Jahan's son Aurangzeb (r. 1658–1707), unwilling to wait for his father to die, deposed him and confined him for years in a small cell. A puritanically devout and strictly orthodox Muslim, as well as a skillful general and a clever diplomat, Aurangzeb ruled more of India than did any previous Mughal emperor, having extended the realm deeper into south India. His reign, however, also marked the beginning of the empire's decline. His non-Muslim subjects were not pleased with his religious zealotry, and his military campaigns were costly. In the south resistance to Mughal rule led to major uprisings. (For more on Aurangzeb's rule, see page 499.)

Mughal

▶ A term meaning "Mongol," used to refer to the Muslim empire of India, although its founders were primarily Turks, Afghans, and Persians.

Mughal territory
- ☐ In 1525
- ☐ Added, by 1539
- ☐ Added, by 1605
- ☐ Added, by 1707
- ☑ Lost, by 1707

The Mughal Empire, 1526–1857

QUICK REVIEW ◀

What role did slaves play in the government of each of the major Islamic empires?

How did Christians, Jews, Hindus, and other non-Muslims fare under these Islamic states?

How were the Islamic empires affected by trade routes that bypassed their lands?

What common factors led to the decline of central power in the Islamic empires?

☑ LearningCurve
Check what you know.

> What cultural advances occurred under the rule of the Ottoman, Safavid, and Mughal Empires?

Music in a Garden

This illustration of a courtly romance depicts several women in a garden intently listening to a musician, with cups of a beverage in their hands.

ALL THREE ISLAMIC EMPIRES presided over an extraordinary artistic and intellectual flowering. At the same time, new religious practices (and conflicts) emerged. Artistic and intellectual advances spread from culture to culture, probably because of the common Persian influence on the Turks since the tenth century. This exchange was also aided by common languages.

The Arts

One of the arts all three empires shared was carpet making. Carpet designs and weaving techniques demonstrate both cultural integration and local distinctiveness. Turkic migrants carried their weaving traditions with them as they moved but also readily adopted new motifs, especially from Persia. In Safavid Persia, Shah Abbas was determined to improve his country's export trade and built the small cottage business of carpet weaving into a national industry. Women and children were often employed as weavers, especially of the most expensive rugs, because their smaller hands could tie tinier knots.

Another art that spread from Persia to both Ottoman and Mughal lands was miniature painting, especially for book illustration. This tradition had been

CHAPTER LOCATOR | How were the three Islamic empires established, what governments did they set up? | **What cultural advances occurred under the rule of the Ottoman, Safavid, and Mughal Empires?**

494 CHAPTER 17
THE ISLAMIC WORLD POWERS

enriched by the many Chinese artists brought to Persia during the Mongol period. There was also an interplay between carpets and miniature painting, with many motifs appearing in both book illustrations and carpets.

In Mughal India, as throughout the Muslim world, books were regarded as precious objects. Time, talent, and expensive materials went into their production, and they were highly coveted because they reflected wealth, learning, and power. Akbar reportedly possessed twenty-four thousand books when he died.

City and Palace Building

In all three empires strong rulers built capital cities and imperial palaces as visible expressions of dynastic majesty. Suleiman "the Magnificent" used his fabulous wealth to adorn Istanbul with palaces, mosques, schools, and libraries, and the city reached about a million in population. The building of hospitals, roads, and bridges and the reconstruction of the water systems of the great pilgrimage sites at Mecca and Jerusalem benefited his subjects. Safavid Persia and Mughal India produced rulers with similar ambitions.

The greatest builder under the Ottomans was Mimar Sinan (1491–1588), a Greek-born devshirme recruit who rose to become imperial architect under Suleiman. His masterpieces, the Shehzade and Suleimaniye Mosques in Istanbul, which rivaled the Byzantine church of Hagia Sophia, were designed to maximize the space under the dome. His buildings expressed the discipline, power, and devotion to Islam that characterized the Ottoman Empire under Suleiman.

Shah Abbas made his capital, Isfahan, the jewel of the Safavid Empire. He had his architects place a polo ground in the center and surrounded it with palaces, mosques, and bazaars. A city of perhaps 750,000 people, Isfahan also contained 162 mosques, 48 schools, 273 public baths, and the vast imperial palace. Private houses had their own garden courts, and public gardens, pools, and parks adorned the wide streets.

Akbar in India was also a great builder. The birth of a long-awaited son, Jahangir, inspired Akbar to build a new city, Fatehpur Sikri, to symbolize the regime's Islamic foundations. He personally supervised the construction of the city, which combined the Muslim tradition of domes, arches, and spacious courts

How did Christians, Jews, Hindus, and other non-Muslims fare under these Islamic states?

How were the Islamic empires affected by trade routes that bypassed their lands?

What common factors led to the decline of central power in the Islamic empires?

✓ LearningCurve
Check what you know.

with the Hindu tradition of flat stone beams, ornate decoration, and solidity. Unfortunately, because of its bad water supply, the city was soon abandoned.

Of Akbar's successors, Shah Jahan had the most sophisticated interest in architecture. Because his capital at Agra was cramped, in 1639 he decided to found a new capital city at Delhi. In the design and layout of the buildings, Persian ideas predominated. The walled palace-fortress alone extended over 125 acres. It included private chambers for the emperor; mansions for the wives, widows, and concubines of the imperial household; huge audience rooms for the conduct of public business; baths; and vast gardens filled with flowers, trees, and thirty silver fountains spraying water. In 1650, the palace-fortress housed fifty-seven thousand people. It also boasted a covered public bazaar.

Shah Jahan's most enduring monument is the Taj Mahal. Between 1631 and 1648 twenty thousand workers toiled over the construction of this memorial in Agra to Shah Jahan's favorite wife, who died giving birth to their fifteenth child. One of the most beautiful structures in the world, the Taj Mahal is both an expression of love and a superb architectural blending of Islamic and Indian culture.

Gardens

Many of the architectural masterpieces of this age had splendid gardens attached to them. Gardens represent a distinctive and highly developed feature of Persian culture. Identified with paradise in Arab tradition, gardens served not only as centers of prayer and meditation but also as places of leisure and revelry. After the incorporation of Persia into the caliphate in the seventh century, formal gardening spread west and east through the Islamic world.

Because it evoked paradise, the garden played a large role in Muslim literature. Some scholars hold that to understand Arabic poetry, one must study Arab

CHAPTER LOCATOR | How were the three Islamic empires established, what governments did they set up? | What cultural advances occurred under the rule of the Ottoman, Safavid, and Mughal Empires?

496 CHAPTER 17 THE ISLAMIC WORLD POWERS

gardening. The secular literature of Muslim Spain, rife with references such as "a garland of verses," influenced the lyric poetry of southern France, the troubadours, and the courtly love tradition.

Intellectual Advances and Religious Trends

Between 1400 and 1800 the culture of the Islamic empires developed in many directions. Particularly notable were new movements within Islam as well as advances in mathematics, geography, astronomy, and medicine. Building on the knowledge of earlier Islamic writers and stimulated by Ottoman naval power, the geographer and cartographer Piri Reis's *Book of the Sea* (1521) contained 129 chapters, each with a map incorporating all Islamic (and Western) knowledge of the seas and navigation. In the field of astronomy, Takiyuddin Mehmet (1521–1585) built an observatory at Istanbul. He also produced *Instruments of the Observatory*, which catalogued astronomical instruments and described an astronomical clock that fixed the location of heavenly bodies with greater precision than ever before.

There were also advances in medicine. Under Suleiman the imperial palace itself became a center of medical science, and the large number of hospitals established in Istanbul and throughout the empire testifies to his support for medical research and his concern for the sick. Recurrent outbreaks of the plague posed a challenge for physicians in Muslim lands. Muhammad had once said not to go to a country where an epidemic existed but also not to leave a place because an epidemic broke out. As a consequence, when European cities began enforcing quarantines to control the spread of the plague, early Muslim rulers dismissed such efforts. By the sixteenth century, however, a better understanding of contagion led to a redefinition of the proper response to a plague epidemic.

In the realm of religion, the rulers of all three empires drew legitimacy from their support for Islam. The Sunni-Shi'a split between the Ottomans and Safavids led to efforts to define and enforce religious orthodoxy on both sides. For the Safavids this entailed suppressing Sufi movements and Sunnis, even marginalizing—sometimes massacring—the original Qizilbash warriors, who had come to be seen as politically disruptive. Sectarian conflicts within Islam were not as pronounced in Mughal lands, perhaps because Muslims were greatly outnumbered by non-Muslims, mostly Hindus.

Sufi fraternities thrived throughout the Muslim world in this era, even when the states tried to limit them. In India Sufi orders also influenced non-Muslims. The mystical Bhakti movement among Hindus involved dances, poems, and songs reminiscent of Sufi practice. The development of the new religion of the Sikhs (seeks) was also influenced by Sufis. The Sikhs traced themselves back to a teacher in the sixteenth century who argued that God did not distinguish between Muslims and Hindus but saw everyone as his children.

Despite all the signs of cultural vitality in the three Islamic empires, none of them adopted the printing press or went through the sorts of cultural expansion associated with it in China and Europe. Until 1729 the Ottoman authorities prohibited printing books in Turkish or Arabic. Printing was not banned in Mughal India, but neither did the technology spread. The copying of manuscripts was a well-established practice, and those who made their living this way sometimes organized to keep competition at bay. It also needs to be noted that by the end of this period, scientific knowledge was not keeping up with advances made in Europe (see page 550).

How did Christians, Jews, Hindus, and other non-Muslims fare under these Islamic states?

How were the Islamic empires affected by trade routes that bypassed their lands?

What common factors led to the decline of central power in the Islamic empires?

☑ LearningCurve
Check what you know.

> PICTURING THE PAST

ANALYZING THE IMAGE: What activities are people engaged in? How does the artist convey differences in the ages of those drinking coffee?

CONNECTIONS: What made coffee a popular drink for people socializing?

Coffeehouses and Their Social Impact

In the mid-fifteenth century a new social convention spread throughout the Islamic world—drinking coffee. Arab writers trace the origins of coffee drinking to Yemen Sufis, who sought a trancelike concentration on God to the exclusion of everything else and found that coffee helped them stay awake. Merchants carried the Yemenite practice to Mecca in about 1490. From Mecca, where pilgrims were introduced to it, coffee drinking spread to Egypt and Syria. In 1555 two Syrians opened a coffeehouse in Istanbul.

Coffeehouses provided a place for conversation and male sociability; there a man could entertain his friends cheaply and more informally than at home. But coffeehouses encountered religious and governmental opposition, as some authorities saw them as a threat to public morality. On the other hand, the coffee trade was a major source of profit that local notables sought to control.

Although debate over the morality of coffeehouses continued through the sixteenth century, their eventual acceptance represented a revolution in Islamic life: socializing was no longer confined to the home. In the seventeenth century coffee and coffeehouses spread to Europe.

> **Principle Arguments Against Coffeehouses:**

- Because of its composition, coffee is intoxicating, making it analogous to wine, prohibited to Muslims
- Coffee drinking was an innovation and therefore a violation of Islamic law
- Coffeehouses encouraged political discussions, facilitating sedition
- Coffeehouses attracted unemployed soldiers and other low types, encouraging immoral behavior, such as gambling, using drugs, and soliciting prostitutes
- Music at coffeehouses encouraged debauchery

> **QUICK REVIEW**

What factors facilitated cultural exchange between the Islamic empires?

CHAPTER LOCATOR | How were the three Islamic empires established, what governments did they set up? | What cultural advances occurred under the rule of the Ottoman, Safavid, and Mughal Empires?

Emperor Akbar in the City of Fatehpur Sikri

In 1569 Akbar founded the city of Fatehpur Sikri (the City of Victory) to honor the Muslim holy man Sheik Salim Chishti, who had foretold the birth of Akbar's son and heir Jahangir. Akbar is shown here seated on the cushion in the center overseeing the construction of the city. The image is contained in the Akbarnama, a book of illustrations Akbar commissioned to officially chronicle his reign. (Victoria & Albert Museum, London, UK/The Bridgeman Art Library)

How did Christians, Jews, Hindus, and other non-Muslims fare under these Islamic states?

DRAWING ON QUR'ANIC TEACHINGS, Muslims had long practiced a religious tolerance unknown in Christian Europe. Muslim rulers for the most part guaranteed the lives and property of Christians and Jews on their promise of obedience and the payment of a poll tax. In the case of the Ottomans, this tolerance was extended not only to the Christians and Jews who had been living under Muslim rule for centuries but also to the Serbs, Bosnians, Croats, and other Orthodox Christians in the newly conquered Balkans. In 1454 Rabbi Isaac Sarfati sent a letter to the Jews in the Rhineland, Swabia, Moravia, and Hungary, urging them to move to Turkey because of the good conditions for Jews there. A massive migration to Ottoman lands followed. When Ferdinand and Isabella of Spain expelled the Jews in 1492 and later, many immigrated to the Ottoman Empire.

How did Christians, Jews, Hindus, and other non-Muslims fare under these Islamic states?	How were the Islamic empires affected by trade routes that bypassed their lands?	What common factors led to the decline of central power in the Islamic empires?	✔ LearningCurve Check what you know.

The Safavid authorities made efforts to convert Armenian Christians in the Caucasus, and many seem to have embraced Islam, some more voluntarily than others. Nevertheless, the Armenian Christian Church retained its vitality, and under the Safavids Armenian Christians were prominent merchants in long-distance trade (see page 502).

Babur and his successors acquired even more non-Muslim subjects with their conquests in India, which included not only Hindus but also substantial numbers of Jains, Zoroastrians, Christians, and Sikhs. Over time, the number of Indians who converted to Islam increased, but the Mughal rulers did not force conversion.

Akbar went the furthest in promoting Muslim-Hindu accommodation. He celebrated important Hindu festivals, and he wore his uncut hair in a turban as a concession to Indian practice. Also, Akbar twice married Hindu princesses, one of whom became the mother of his heir, Jahangir, and he appointed the Spanish Jesuit Antonio Monserrate (1536–1600) as tutor to his second son, Prince Murad. Eventually, Hindus totaled 30 percent of the imperial bureaucracy. In 1579 Akbar abolished the jizya, the poll tax on non-Muslims that guaranteed their protection. These actions infuriated the ulama, and serious conflict erupted between its members and the emperor. Ultimately, Akbar issued an imperial decree declaring that the Mughal emperor had supreme authority, even above the ulama, in all religious matters, to the dismay of the Muslim religious establishment.

Some of Akbar's successors, above all Aurangzeb, sided more with the ulama. Aurangzeb appointed censors of public morals in important cities to enforce Islamic laws. He forbade sati—the self-immolation of widows on their husbands' funeral pyres—and the castration of boys to be sold as eunuchs. He also abolished all taxes not authorized by Islamic law. To compensate for the loss of revenue, in 1679 Aurangzeb reimposed the tax on non-Muslims. Aurangzeb's reversal of Akbar's religious tolerance and cultural cosmopolitanism extended further. He ordered the destruction of some Hindu temples and tried to curb Sikhism. Aurangzeb's attempts to enforce rigid Islamic norms proved highly unpopular and aroused resistance that weakened Mughal rule.

jizya

▶ A poll tax on non-Muslims.

> **QUICK REVIEW**

Which of Akbar's policies were reversed by Aurangzeb? Why?

CHAPTER LOCATOR | How were the three Islamic empires established, what governments did they set up? | What cultural advances occurred under the rule of the Ottoman, Safavid, and Mughal Empires?

CHAPTER 17
500 THE ISLAMIC WORLD POWERS

How were the Islamic empires affected by the gradual shift toward trade routes that bypassed their lands?

English Dress Made of Indian Printed Cotton Cloth

Early British traders in India were impressed with the quality of the textiles made there and began ordering designs that would be popular with the English. This dress, created around 1770–1780 in England, is made of printed cotton (chintz) from the southeastern part of India. Chintz became so popular in England that it was eventually banned because it was threatening local textile industries. (Victoria & Albert Museum, London, UK/Art Resource, NY)

IT HAS WIDELY BEEN THOUGHT that a decline in the wealth and international importance of the Muslim empires could be directly attributed to the long-term shift in trading patterns that resulted from European overseas expansion. The argument is that new sea routes enabled Europeans to acquire goods from the East without using Muslim intermediaries, so that the creation of European colonial powers beginning in the sixteenth century led directly and indirectly to the eclipse of the Ottomans, Safavids, and Mughals. Recent scholars have challenged these ideas as too simplistic. First, it was not until the eighteenth century that political decline became evident in the three Islamic empires. Second, Turkish, Persian, and Indian merchants remained very active as long-distance traders into the eighteenth century and opened up many new routes themselves. It is true that in the Islamic empires New World crops fueled population increases less rapidly than in western Europe and East Asia. But economic growth does not always correlate with population increases.

| How did Christians, Jews, Hindus, and other non-Muslims fare under these Islamic states? | **How were the Islamic empires affected by trade routes that bypassed their lands?** | What common factors led to the decline of central power in the Islamic empires? | ☑ LearningCurve Check what you know. |

Over the centuries covered in this chapter, the Islamic empires became not only more tied to European powers but also more connected to each other. Europeans gained deeper knowledge of Islamic lands, but so did residents of these lands, who more frequently traveled to other Islamic countries and wrote about their travels.

European Rivalry for Trade in the Indian Ocean

Shortly before Babur's invasion of India, the Portuguese had opened the subcontinent to Portuguese trade. In 1510 they established the port of Goa on the west coast of India as their headquarters and through an aggressive policy took control of Muslim shipping in the Indian Ocean and Arabian Sea, charging high fees to let ships through. As a result, they controlled the spice trade over the Indian Ocean for almost a century.

In 1602 the Dutch formed the Dutch East India Company with the stated goal of wresting the enormously lucrative spice trade from the Portuguese. In 1685 they supplanted the Portuguese in Ceylon (Sri Lanka). The scent of fabulous profits also attracted the English. With a charter signed by Queen Elizabeth, eighty London merchants organized the British East India Company. In 1619 Emperor Jahangir granted a British mission important commercial concessions. Soon, by offering gifts, medical services, and bribes to Indian rulers, the British East India Company was able to set up twenty-eight coastal forts/trading posts. By 1700 the company had founded the cities that became Madras and Calcutta (today called Chennai and Kolkata) and had taken over Bombay (today Mumbai), which had been a Portuguese possession (Map 17.3).

The British called their trading posts **factory-forts**. The term designated the walled compound containing company residences, offices, and warehouses. The company president exercised political authority over all residents.

Factory-forts existed to make profits from Asian-European trade, which was robust due to the popularity of Indian and Chinese wares in Europe in the late seventeenth and early eighteenth centuries. To pay for these goods, the British East India Company sold silver, copper, zinc, lead, and fabrics to the Indians. Profits grew even larger after 1700, when the company began to trade with China.

Merchant Networks in the Islamic Empires

The shifting trade patterns associated with European colonial expansion brought no direct benefit to the Ottomans and the Safavids, whose merchants could now be bypassed by Europeans seeking goods from India, Southeast Asia, or China. Yet merchants from these Islamic empires often proved adaptable, finding ways to benefit from the new trade networks.

In the case of India, the appearance of European traders led to a rapid increase in overall trade, helping Indian merchants and the Indian economy. Block-printed cotton cloth, produced by artisans working at home, was India's chief export. Through an Islamic business device involving advancing payment to artisans, banker-brokers supplied the material for production and money for

factory-forts
▶ A term first used by the British for their trading post at Surat that was later applied to all European walled settlements in India.

CHAPTER LOCATOR | How were the three Islamic empires established, what governments did they set up?   What cultural advances occurred under the rule of the Ottoman, Safavid, and Mughal Empires?

CHAPTER 17
502   THE ISLAMIC WORLD POWERS

MAP 17.3 ■ India, 1707–1805

In the eighteenth century Mughal power gradually yielded to the Hindu Marathas and to the British East India Company.

Legend:
- Northern limit of Mughal Empire in 1707
- Muslim land in 1765
- Muslim land in 1805
- Area controlled by Hindus in 1805
- Land under British East India Company rule in 1805
- Site of important battle

the artisans to live on while they worked; the cloth brokers specified the quality, quantity, and design of the finished products. This procedure resembles the later English "domestic" or "putting-out" system (see page 684), for the very good reason that the English took the idea from the Indians.

Within India the demand for cotton cloth, as well as for food crops, was so great that Akbar had to launch a wide-scale road-building campaign. From the Indian region of Gujarat, Indian merchant bankers shipped their cloth worldwide. Some scholars have compared India's international trade in the sixteenth century with that of Italian firms, such as the Medici. Indian trade actually extended over a far wider area, however. Indian merchants were often devout Hindus, Muslims, Buddhists, or Jains, evidence that undermines the argument of some Western writers, notably Karl Marx (see page 716), that religion retarded Asia's economic development.

Throughout Muslim lands both Jews and Christians were active in commerce. A particularly interesting case involves the Armenian Christians in the Safavid Empire in the sixteenth to eighteenth centuries. When the Portuguese first

How did Christians, Jews, Hindus, and other non-Muslims fare under these Islamic states?

How were the Islamic empires affected by trade routes that bypassed their lands?

What common factors led to the decline of central power in the Islamic empires?

LearningCurve
Check what you know.

appeared on the western coast of India in 1498 and began to settle in south India, they found many Armenian merchant communities already there. A few decades later Akbar invited Armenians to settle in his new capital, Agra. In 1603 Shah Abbas captured much of Armenia, taking it from the Ottomans. Because defending this newly acquired border area was difficult, he forced the Armenians to move more deeply into Persia. Among them was the merchant community of Julfa, which was moved to a new suburb of Isfahan, which was renamed New Julfa. Shah Abbas made use of the Armenian merchants as royal merchants and financiers, but their economic mainstay continued to be long-distance trade.

The trading networks of Armenian merchants stretched from Venice and Amsterdam in western Europe, Moscow in Russia, and Ottoman-controlled Aleppo and Smyrna to all the major trading cities of India and even regions farther east, including Guangzhou in southern China and Manila in the Philippines. Many Armenian communities in these cities became quite substantial. Kinship connections were regularly used to cement commercial relations, and members of the community living in these scattered cities would return to New Julfa to marry, creating new kinship connections. Business, though, was conducted through contracts. The merchant about to take a journey would borrow a sum of money to purchase goods and would contract to pay it back with interest on his return.

The Armenian merchants would sail on whatever ships were available, including Dutch and Italian ones. The merchants could often speak half a dozen languages and were comfortable in both Islamic and Christian lands. In India Armenian merchants reached an agreement with the British East India Company that recognized their rights to live in company cities and observe their own religion. By the 1660s they had settled in Manila, and a few decades later they entered what is now Malaysia and Indonesia. By the end of the seventeenth century a small group of Armenian merchants had crossed the Himalayas from India and established themselves in Lhasa, Tibet. By the mid-eighteenth century they had also settled in the Dutch colony of Batavia (Indonesia).

Armenian Brass Bowl

The inscription on this bowl dates it to 1616 and places it in New Julfa, the Armenian quarter of Isfahan. It would have been used by an Armenian Christian priest to wash his hands. (© Ana Melikian 2007)

CHAPTER LOCATOR | How were the three Islamic empires established, what governments did they set up? | What cultural advances occurred under the rule of the Ottoman, Safavid, and Mughal Empires?

CHAPTER 17
504 THE ISLAMIC WORLD POWERS

From the British East India Company to the British Empire in India

Britain's presence in India began with the British East India Company and its desire to profit from trade. Managers of the company in London discouraged all unnecessary expenses and financial risks and thus opposed missionary activities or interference in local Indian politics. Nevertheless, the company responded to political instability in India in the early eighteenth century by extending political control. The company's factories evolved into defensive installations manned by small garrisons of native troops—known as sepoys—trained in Western military weapons and tactics.

From 1740 to 1763 Britain and France were engaged in a tremendous global struggle, and India, like North America in the Seven Years' War, became a battlefield and a prize. The French won land battles, but English sea power proved decisive by preventing the landing of French reinforcements. The Treaty of Paris of 1763 recognized British control of much of India, marking the beginning of the British Empire in India.

How was Britain to govern so large a territory? Eventually, the East India Company was pushed out of its governing role because the English Parliament distrusted the company, believing it was corrupt. The Regulating Act of 1773 created the office of governor general to exercise political authority over the territory controlled by the company. The India Act of 1784 required that the governor general be chosen from outside the company, and it made company directors subject to parliamentary supervision.

Implementation of these reforms fell to three successive governors: Warren Hastings (r. 1774–1785), Lord Charles Cornwallis (r. 1786–1794), and the marquess Richard Wellesley (r. 1797–1805). Hastings sought allies among Indian princes, laid the foundations for the first Indian civil service, abolished tolls to facilitate internal trade, placed the salt and opium trades under government control, and planned a codification of Muslim and Hindu laws. Cornwallis introduced the British style of property relations in which the rents of tenant farmers supported the landlords. Wellesley was victorious over local rulers who resisted British rule, vastly extending British influence in India. Like most nineteenth-century British governors of India, Wellesley believed that British rule strongly benefited the Indians.

sepoys
▶ The native Indian troops who were trained as infantrymen.

QUICK REVIEW

How did European powers try to gain control of Indian Ocean trade?

How did Christians, Jews, Hindus, and other non-Muslims fare under these Islamic states?

How were the Islamic empires affected by trade routes that bypassed their lands?

What common factors led to the decline of central power in the Islamic empires?

✓ LearningCurve Check what you know.

What common factors led to the decline of central power in the Islamic empires in the seventeenth and eighteenth centuries?

BY THE END OF THE EIGHTEENTH CENTURY all three of the major Islamic empires were on the defensive and losing territory (Map 17.4). They faced some common problems—succession difficulties, financial strain, and loss of military superiority—but their circumstances differed in significant ways as well.

The first to fall was the Safavid Empire. Persia did not have the revenue base to maintain a large standing army. Decline in the strength of the army encouraged increased foreign aggression. In 1722 the Afghans invaded from the east, seized Isfahan, and were able to repulse an Ottoman invasion from the west. In Isfahan thousands of officials and members of the shah's family were executed. In the following century no leader emerged capable of reuniting all of Persia. In this political vacuum, Shi'a religious institutions grew stronger.

The Ottoman Empire also suffered from poor leadership. Early Ottoman practice had guaranteed that the sultans would be forceful men. The sultan's sons gained administrative experience as governors of provinces and military experience on the battlefield as part of their education. After the sultan died, any son who wanted to succeed had to contest his brothers to claim the throne, after which the new sultan would have his defeated brothers executed. Although bloody, this system led to the succession of capable, determined men. After Suleiman's reign, however, the tradition was abandoned. To prevent threats of usurpation, sons of the sultan were brought up in the harem and confined there as adults, denied roles in government. The result was a series of rulers who were minor children or incompetent adults, leaving power in the hands of high officials and the mothers of the heirs. Political factions formed around viziers, military leaders, and palace women. In the contest for political favor, the devshirme was abandoned, and political and military ranks were filled by Muslims.

The Ottoman Empire's military strength also declined. The defeat of the Turkish fleet by the Spanish off the coast of Greece at Lepanto in 1571 marked the loss of Ottoman dominance in the Mediterranean. By the terms of a peace treaty with Austria signed at Karlowitz (1699), the Ottomans lost Hungary and Transylvania,

CHAPTER LOCATOR | How were the three Islamic empires established, what governments did they set up? | What cultural advances occurred under the rule of the Ottoman, Safavid, and Mughal Empires?

506 CHAPTER 17 THE ISLAMIC WORLD POWERS

MAP 17.4 ■ The Muslim World, ca. 1700

The three great Islamic empires were adjacent to each other and of similar physical size. Many of their other neighbors were Muslim as well.

along with the tax revenues they had provided. Also, the Ottoman armies were depending more on mercenaries, and they did not keep up with the innovations in drill, command, and control that were then transforming European armies. From the late seventeenth century Ottoman armies began losing wars and territory along both northern and eastern borders. In 1774 the empire lost the lands on the northern bank of the Black Sea to Russia. In North Africa the local governors came to act more independently, sometimes starting hereditary dynasties.

Military challenges proved daunting in Mughal India as well. After defeating his father and brothers, Aurangzeb made it his goal to conquer the south. The stiffest opposition came from the Marathas, a militant Hindu group centered in the western Deccan. From 1681 until his death in 1707, Aurangzeb took many forts and won several battles, but total destruction of the Maratha guerrilla bands eluded him.

Aurangzeb's death led to thirteen years of succession struggles, shattering the empire. His eighteenth-century successors were less successful than the

How did Christians, Jews, Hindus, and other non-Muslims fare under these Islamic states?

How were the Islamic empires affected by trade routes that bypassed their lands?

What common factors led to the decline of central power in the Islamic empires?

LearningCurve
Check what you know.

Ottomans in making the dynasty the focus of loyalty. Mughal provincial governors began to rule independently, giving only minimal allegiance to the throne at Delhi. Meanwhile, the Marathas pressed steadily northward. Threats also came from the west. In 1739 the Persian adventurer Nadir Shah invaded India, defeated the Mughal army, and looted Delhi. Constant skirmishes between the Afghans and the Marathas for control of the Punjab and northern India ended in 1761 at Panipat, where the Marathas were crushed by the Afghans. At that point, India no longer had a state strong enough to impose order on the subcontinent or check the penetration of the Europeans.

In all three empires fiscal difficulties contributed to strain on the state. A long period of peace in the late sixteenth century and again in the mid-eighteenth century, as well as a decline in the frequency of visits of the plague, led to a doubling of the population. Increased population, coupled with the "little ice age" of the mid-seventeenth century, meant that the land could not sustain so many people, nor could the towns provide jobs for the thousands of agricultural workers who fled to them. The return of demobilized soldiers aggravated the problem. Inflation, famine, and widespread revolts resulted. The economic center of gravity shifted from the capital to the provinces, and politically the empire began to decentralize as well. There was a positive side to increasing provincial autonomy, however, because it drew more people into political participation, thus laying a foundation for later nationalism. At the time, however, central government officials perceived the growth in provincial power in negative terms.

> **QUICK REVIEW**

How did fiscal problems contribute to the decline of the Islamic empires?

CHAPTER SUMMARY

After the decline of the Mongols in Central Asia and Persia, many small Turkic-ruled states emerged in the region from Anatolia through Afghanistan. Three of them went on to establish large empires: the Ottomans in Anatolia, the Safavids in Persia, and the Mughals in India. The Ottoman Empire's political system reached its classic form under Suleiman I. All authority flowed from the sultan to his public servants. In Persia, the strength of the Safavid state rested in part on the skills of urban bureaucrats, who were vital to the civil machinery of government. Babur, from his base in Afghanistan, founded the Mughal Empire in India. His grandson Akbar extended Mughal rule far into India. All three empires quickly adapted to new gunpowder technologies.

Each of the three Islamic empires presided over an extraordinary artistic and intellectual flowering in everything from carpet making and book illustration to architecture and gardening, from geography and astronomy to medicine. Each of these empires drew legitimacy from their support for Islam. There were, however, key differences: the Ottomans and Mughals supported the Sunni tradition, the Safavids the Shi'a tradition.

CHAPTER LOCATOR | How were the three Islamic empires established, what governments did they set up? | What cultural advances occurred under the rule of the Ottoman, Safavid, and Mughal Empires?

CHAPTER 17
508 THE ISLAMIC WORLD POWERS

The three Islamic empires all had a substantial number of non-Muslim subjects. The Ottomans ruled over the Balkans, where most of the people were Christian, and Muslims in India were greatly outnumbered by Hindus.

European exploration opened new trade routes and enabled Europeans to trade directly with India and China, bypassing Muslim intermediaries in the Middle East. Within India British merchants increased their political control in politically unstable areas, leading before the end of the eighteenth century to a vast colonial empire in India.

By the end of the eighteenth century all three of the major Islamic empires were losing territory. The first to fall was the Safavid Empire. From the late seventeenth century Ottoman armies began losing wars along the northern and eastern borders, resulting in substantial loss of territory. Military challenges proved daunting in Mughal India as well. In all three empires, as central power declined, local notables and military strongmen seized power.

 CONNECTIONS From 1300 to 1800, Islamic civilization thrived under three dynastic houses: the Ottomans, the Safavids, and the Mughals. All three empires had a period of expansion when territory was enlarged, followed by a high point politically and culturally, and later a period of contraction, when territories broke away. At the cultural level, the borders of these three states were porous, and people, ideas, art motifs, languages, and trade flowed back and forth.

In East Asia the fifteenth through eighteenth century also saw the creation of strong, prosperous, and expanding states, though in the case of China (under the Qing Dynasty) and Japan (under the Tokugawa Shogunate) the eighteenth century was a cultural high point, not a period of decline. The Qing emperors were Manchus, from the region northeast of China proper. As in the Islamic lands, during these centuries the presence of European powers became an issue in East Asia, though the details were quite different. Although one of the commodities that the British most wanted was the tea produced in China, Britain did not extend political control in China the way it did in India. Japan managed to refuse entry to most European traders after finding their presence and their support for missionary activity disturbing. The next chapter takes up these developments in East Asia.

ONLINE DOCUMENT PROJECT

Impressions of the Ottoman Empire

How did Europeans view the Ottoman Empire?

Examine a Habsburg ambassador's impressions of the Ottoman Empire, and then complete a quiz and writing assignment based on the evidence and details from this chapter. *See inside the front cover to learn more.*

| How did Christians, Jews, Hindus, and other non-Muslims fare under these Islamic states? | How were the Islamic empires affected by trade routes that bypassed their lands? | What common factors led to the decline of central power in the Islamic empires? | ✓ LearningCurve
Check what you know. |

CHAPTER 17 STUDY GUIDE

STEP 1

GET STARTED ONLINE

 LearningCurve

Now that you've read the chapter, make it stick by completing the LearningCurve activity.

STEP 2

EXPLAIN WHY IT MATTERS

Put your reading into practice. Identify each term below, and then explain why it matters in world history.

TERM	WHO OR WHAT & WHEN	WHY IT MATTERS
Ottomans (p. 487)		
Anatolia (p. 487)		
sultan (p. 488)		
viziers (p. 489)		
devshirme (p. 490)		
janissaries (p. 490)		
concubine (p. 490)		
shah (p. 490)		
Safavid (p. 490)		
Qizilbash (p. 490)		
ulama (p. 492)		
Mughal (p. 493)		
jizya (p. 500)		
factory-forts (p. 502)		
sepoys (p. 505)		

STEP 3

MOVE BEYOND THE BASICS

To demonstrate a more advanced understanding of the empires of the Ottomans, Safavids, and Mughals, fill in the chart below with descriptions of key aspects of each empire. What role did military expansion play in all three empires?

	Government and Military	Culture and Religion	Relations with Non-Muslims	Role of Slaves
Ottomans				
Safavids				
Mughals				

STEP 4 **PUT IT ALL TOGETHER** Now, take a step back and try to explain the big picture. Remember to use specific examples from the chapter in your answers.

ORIGINS AND ORGANIZATION OF THE ISLAMIC EMPIRES

▸ How did Turkish culture and practices shape each of the empires?

▸ What common factors help explain the success of all three empires?

CULTURE AND SOCIETY OF THE ISLAMIC EMPIRES

▸ What role did religion play in the expansion and rule of each of the empires?

▸ What values and beliefs were reflected in the culture of the Islamic empires?

THE ISLAMIC EMPIRES IN THE SEVENTEENTH AND EIGHTEENTH CENTURIES

▸ What impact did European incursions have on the economies of the Islamic empires?

▸ What internal factors contributed to the decline of the Islamic empires? What about external factors?

LOOKING BACK, LOOKING AHEAD

▸ What connections can you make between the Islamic empires described in this chapter and the first Islamic empire established in the centuries following the death of Muhammad?

▸ What connections between the peoples of the Islamic empires would you expect to persist long after the onset of imperial decline? Why?

> **IN YOUR OWN WORDS**

Imagine that you must give an oral report to the class answering the following question: What were the strengths and weaknesses of the three great Islamic empires? What would be the most important points and why?

18

EUROPEAN POWER AND EXPANSION

1500–1750

> How did European central governments consolidate and expand their power in the early modern period? Chapter 17 examines the European struggle for stability in the early modern period. This struggle originated with conflicts sparked by the Protestant and Catholic Reformations in the early sixteenth century and continued with economic and social breakdown into the late seventeenth century. Between roughly 1589 and 1715 two basic patterns of government emerged from these conflicts: absolute monarchy and the constitutional state. Whether a government was constitutional or absolutist, an important foundation of state power was empire and colonialism. Jealous of Iberian overseas holdings, England, France, and the Netherlands vied for new acquisitions in Asia and the Americas, while Russia pushed its borders east to the Pacific.

Louis XIV In this painting, King Louis XIV receives foreign ambassadors to celebrate a peace treaty. The king grandly occupied the center of his court, which in turn served as the pinnacle for the French people and, at the height of his glory, for all of Europe. (Erich Lessing/Art Resource, NY)

> How did the Protestant and Catholic Reformations change power structures in Europe and shape European colonial expansion?

> How did seventeenth-century European states overcome social and economic crisis to build strong states?

> How did absolutism evolve in the seventeenth century in Spain, France, and Austria?

> Why and how did the constitutional state triumph in England and the Dutch Republic?

> How did European nations compete for global trade and empire in the Americas and Asia?

> How did Russian rulers build a distinctive absolutist monarchy and expand into a vast and powerful empire?

✓ **LearningCurve**

After reading the chapter, use LearningCurve to retain what you've read.

How did the Protestant and Catholic Reformations change power structures in Europe and shape European colonial expansion?

Jesuits in China

This European image depicts early Jesuit missionaries baptizing converts in South China. (*Archiv Gerstenberg — ullstein bild/The Granger Collection, NYC — All rights reserved.*)

Protestant Reformation

▶ A religious reform movement that began in the early sixteenth century and split the Western Christian Church.

AS A RESULT OF A MOVEMENT of religious reform known as the **Protestant Reformation**, Western Christendom broke into many divisions in the sixteenth century. This splintering happened not only for religious reasons but also because of political and social factors. Religious transformation provided a source of power for many rulers and shaped European colonial expansion.

The Protestant Reformation

In early-sixteenth-century western Europe, calls for reform in the church came from many quarters, both within and outside the church. Critics of the church concentrated their attacks on clerical immorality, ignorance, and absenteeism. Charges of immorality were aimed at a number of priests who were drunkards, neglected the rule of celibacy, gambled, or indulged in fancy dress. Charges of ignorance applied to barely literate priests who delivered poor-quality sermons.

In regard to absenteeism, many clerics, especially higher ecclesiastics, held several benefices (offices) simultaneously. However, they seldom visited the com-

CHAPTER LOCATOR | **How did the Protestant and Catholic Reformations shape colonial expansion?** | How did seventeenth-century European states overcome social and economic crisis? | How did absolutism evolve in in Spain, France, and Austria?

514
CHAPTER 18
EUROPEAN POWER AND EXPANSION

ca. 1500–1650
Consolidation of serfdom in eastern Europe

1533–1584
Reign of Ivan the Terrible in Russia

1589–1610
Reign of Henry IV in France

1598–1613
Time of Troubles in Russia

1612–1697
Caribbean islands colonized by France, England, and the Netherlands

ca. 1620–1740
Growth of absolutism in Austria and Prussia

1642–1649
English civil war, ending with the execution of Charles I

1643–1715
Reign of Louis XIV in France

1651
First of the Navigation Acts

1653–1658
Oliver Cromwell's military rule in England (the Protectorate)

1660
Restoration of English monarchy under Charles II

1665–1683
Jean-Baptiste Colbert applies mercantilism to France

1670–1671
Cossack revolt led by Stenka Razin

1682
Louis XIV moves court to Versailles

1682–1725
Reign of Peter the Great in Russia

1683–1718
Habsburgs push the Ottoman Turks from Hungary

1685
Edict of Nantes revoked

1688–1689
Glorious Revolution in England

1701–1713
War of the Spanish Succession

munities served by the benefices. Instead, they collected revenues from all the benefices assigned to them and hired a poor priest to fulfill their spiritual duties.

There was also local resentment of clerical privileges and immunities. Priests, monks, and nuns were exempt from civic responsibilities, such as defending the city and paying taxes. Yet religious orders frequently held large amounts of urban property. City governments were increasingly determined to integrate the clergy into civic life. This brought city leaders into opposition with bishops and the papacy, which for centuries had stressed the independence of the church from lay control.

This range of complaints helps explain why the ideas of Martin Luther (1483–1546), a priest and professor of theology from the German University of Wittenberg, found a ready audience. Luther and other Protestants—the word comes from a "protest" drawn up by a group of reforming princes in 1529—developed a new understanding of Christian doctrine that emphasized faith, the power of God's grace, and the centrality of the Bible. Protestant ideas were attractive to educated people and urban residents, and they spread rapidly through preaching, hymns, and the printing press.

Luther lived in the Holy Roman Empire, a loose collection of largely independent states in which the emperor had far less authority than did the monarchs of western Europe. The Habsburg emperor, Charles V, was a staunch supporter of Catholicism, but the ruler of the territory in which Luther lived protected the

| Why and how did the constitutional state triumph in England and the Dutch Republic? | How did European nations compete for trade and empire in the Americas and Asia? | How did Russian rulers build an absolutist monarchy and expand into a powerful empire? | ✓ LearningCurve Check what you know. |

reformer. Although Luther appeared before Charles V when he was summoned, he was not arrested and continued to preach and write.

Luther's ideas appealed to the local rulers of the empire for a variety of reasons. Though Germany was not a nation, people did have an understanding of being German because of their language and traditions. Luther frequently used the phrase "we Germans" in his attacks on the papacy, and his appeal to national feeling influenced many rulers. Also, while some German rulers were sincerely attracted to Lutheran ideas, material considerations swayed many others. The adoption of Protestantism would mean the legal confiscation of church properties. Thus many political authorities in the empire used the religious issue to extend their power and to enhance their independence from the emperor. Luther worked closely with political authorities, viewing them as fully justified in reforming the church in their territories. Thus, just as in the Ottoman and Safavid Empires (see Chapter 17), rulers drew their legitimacy in part from their support for religion. By 1530 many parts of the Holy Roman Empire and Scandinavia had broken with the Catholic Church.

In England the issue of the royal succession triggered that country's break with Rome, and a Protestant Church was established during the 1530s under King Henry VIII (r. 1509–1547) and reaffirmed under his daughter Elizabeth I (r. 1558–1603). Church officials were required to sign an oath of loyalty to the monarch, and people were required to attend services at the state church, which became known as the Anglican Church.

Protestant ideas also spread into France, the Netherlands, Scotland, and eastern Europe. In all these areas, a second generation of reformers built on earlier ideas to develop their own theology and plans for institutional change. The most important of the second-generation reformers was the Frenchman John Calvin (1509–1564), who reformed the city of Geneva, Switzerland. Calvin believed that God was absolutely sovereign and omnipotent and that humans had no free will. Thus men and women could not actively work to achieve salvation, because God had decided at the beginning of time who would be saved and who damned, a theological principle called predestination.

The church in Geneva served as the model for the Presbyterian Church in Scotland, the Huguenot (HYOO-guh-naht) Church in France, and the Puritan Churches in England and New England. Calvinism became the compelling force in international Protestantism, first in Europe and then in many Dutch and English colonies around the world. Calvinism was also the dominant form of Protestantism in France (Map 18.1).

The Catholic Reformation

In response to the Protestant Reformation, by the 1530s the papacy was leading a movement for reform within the Roman Catholic Church. Many historians see the developments within the Catholic Church after the Protestant Reformation as two interrelated movements, one a drive for internal reform linked to earlier reform efforts and the other a Counter-Reformation that opposed Protestantism spiritually, politically, and militarily.

Pope Paul III (pontificate 1534–1549) established the Supreme Sacred Congregation of the Roman and Universal Inquisition, often called the Holy Office, with judicial authority over all Catholics and the power to imprison and execute.

CHAPTER LOCATOR | **How did the Protestant and Catholic Reformations shape colonial expansion?** | How did seventeenth-century European states overcome social and economic crisis? | How did absolutism evolve in in Spain, France, and Austria?

CHAPTER 18
516 EUROPEAN POWER AND EXPANSION

MAP 18.1 ▪ Religious Divisions, ca. 1555

In the mid-sixteenth century, much of Europe remained Catholic. The Peace of Augsburg (1555) allowed the ruler of each territory in the Holy Roman Empire to determine the religion of its people. The northern territories of the empire became Lutheran, as did Scandinavia, while much of the southern empire remained Catholic. Sizable Calvinist populations existed in Scotland, the Netherlands and central Europe. Eastern Europe was dominated by Orthodox Christianity and the Ottoman Empire to the south and southeast was Muslim.

He also called a general council of the church, which met intermittently from 1545 to 1563 at the city of Trent. The Council of Trent laid a solid basis for the spiritual renewal of the Catholic Church. It gave equal validity to the Scriptures and to tradition as sources of religious truth and tackled problems that had disillusioned many Christians. Bishops were required to live in their dioceses and to establish a seminary for educating and training clergy. Finally, it placed great emphasis on preaching to and instructing the laity.

Just as seminaries provided education, so did new religious orders, which aimed to raise the moral and intellectual level of the clergy and people. The Ursuline (UHR-suh-luhn) order of nuns, founded by Angela Merici (1474–1540), attained enormous prestige for its education of women.

Another important new order was the Society of Jesus, or **Jesuits**. Founded by Ignatius Loyola (1491–1556) in 1540, this order played a powerful international

Jesuits

▶ Members of the Society of Jesus, founded by Ignatius Loyola and approved by the papacy in 1540, whose goal was the spread of the Roman Catholic faith through humanistic schools and missionary activity.

Why and how did the constitutional state triumph in England and the Dutch Republic? | How did European nations compete for trade and empire in the Americas and Asia? | How did Russian rulers build an absolutist monarchy and expand into a powerful empire? | ✓ LearningCurve Check what you know.

role in strengthening Catholicism in Europe and spreading the faith around the world. Recruited primarily from wealthy merchant and professional families, the Society of Jesus developed into a highly centralized organization. They established well-run schools to educate the sons of the nobility as well as the poor. The Jesuits achieved phenomenal success for the papacy and the reformed Catholic Church, carrying Christianity to the Americas, Asia, and Africa. Also, as confessors and spiritual directors to kings, Jesuits exerted great political influence.

Religious Violence

Religious differences led to riots, civil wars, and international conflicts in Europe during the sixteenth century. In the Holy Roman Empire fighting began in 1546. The initial success of Emperor Charles V led to French intervention on the side of the Protestants, lest the emperor acquire even more power. In 1555 Charles agreed to the Peace of Augsburg, which officially recognized Lutheranism and ended religious war in Germany for many decades. Under this treaty, the political authority in each territory of the Holy Roman Empire was permitted to decide whether the territory would be Catholic or Lutheran. His hope of uniting his empire under a single church dashed, Charles V abdicated in 1556, transferring power over his Spanish and Dutch holdings to his son Philip II and his imperial power to his brother Ferdinand.

In France armed clashes between Catholic royalists and Calvinist antiroyalists occurred in many parts of the country. A savage Catholic attack on Calvinists in Paris on August 24, 1572—Saint Bartholomew's Day—occurred at the marriage of the king's sister Margaret of Valois to the Protestant Henry of Navarre. The Saint Bartholomew's Day massacre initiated a civil war that dragged on for fifteen years, destroying agriculture and commercial life in many areas.

In the Netherlands the movement for church reform developed into a struggle for Dutch independence. In the 1560s Spanish authorities attempted to suppress Calvinist worship and raised taxes. Civil war broke out from 1568 to 1578 between Catholics and Protestants in the Netherlands and between the provinces of the Netherlands and Spain. Eventually the ten southern provinces came under the control of the Spanish Habsburg forces. The seven northern provinces, led by Holland, formed the Union of Utrecht (United Provinces of the Netherlands) and in 1581 declared their independence from Spain. The north was Protestant, and the south remained Catholic. Hostilities continued until 1609, when Spain agreed to a truce that recognized the independence of the northern provinces.

The era of religious wars was also the time of the most extensive witch persecutions in European history. Both Protestants and Catholics tried and executed those accused of being witches, with church officials and secular authorities acting together. The heightened sense of God's power and divine wrath in the Reformation era was an important factor in the witch-hunts, as were new demonological ideas, legal procedures involving torture, and neighborhood tensions.

> **> Witchcraft Trials: 1450–1650**
>
> - Between 100,000 and 200,000 people tried for witchcraft
> - Between 40,000 and 60,000 executed
> - Between 75 and 85 percent of those tried and executed were women

> QUICK REVIEW

How did the Reformation lead to an increase in personal and state violence in the sixteenth and seventeenth centuries?

CHAPTER LOCATOR | How did the Protestant and Catholic Reformations shape colonial expansion? | **How did seventeenth-century European states overcome social and economic crisis?** | How did absolutism evolve in in Spain, France, and Austria?

CHAPTER 18
518 EUROPEAN POWER AND EXPANSION

How did seventeenth-century European states overcome social and economic crisis to build strong states?

HISTORIANS OFTEN REFER TO THE seventeenth century as an "age of crisis" because Europe was challenged by population losses, economic decline, and social and political unrest. These difficulties were partially due to climate changes that reduced agricultural productivity. But they also resulted from military competition among European powers, the religious divides of the Reformations, increased taxation, and war.

The atmosphere of crisis encouraged governments to take emergency measures to restore order, measures that they successfully turned into long-term reforms that strengthened the power of the state. In the long run, European states proved increasingly able to impose their will on the populace.

The Social Order and Peasant Life

Peasants occupied the lower tiers of a society organized in hierarchical levels. In much of Europe, the monarch occupied the summit, celebrated as a semidivine being chosen by God to embody the state. In Catholic countries, the clergy constituted the first order of society, followed by the nobles. Christian prejudices against commerce and money meant that merchants could never lay claim to the highest honors. However, many prosperous mercantile families had bought their

Why and how did the constitutional state triumph in England and the Dutch Republic?

How did European nations compete for trade and empire in the Americas and Asia?

How did Russian rulers build an absolutist monarchy and expand into a powerful empire?

✓ LearningCurve
Check what you know.

way into the nobility through service to the monarchy in the fifteenth and sixteenth centuries, and they constituted a second tier of nobles. Those lower on the social scale, the peasants and artisans who formed the vast majority of the population, were expected to show deference to their betters.

In addition to being rigidly hierarchical, European societies were patriarchal. Religious and secular law commanded a man's wife, children, servants, and apprentices to respect and obey him. Fathers were entitled to use physical violence, imprisonment, and other forceful measures to impose their authority. These powers were balanced by expectations that a good father would care benevolently for his dependents.

In the seventeenth century the vast majority of Europeans lived in the countryside, as was the case in most parts of the world. The hub of the rural world was the small peasant village centered on a church and a manor.

In western Europe a small number of peasants owned enough land to feed themselves and possessed the livestock and plows necessary to work their land. Independent farmers were leaders of the peasant village. Below them were small landowners and tenant farmers who did not have enough land to be self-sufficient. At the bottom were villagers who worked as dependent laborers and servants. Private landowning among peasants was a distinguishing feature of western Europe. In central and eastern Europe the vast majority of peasants toiled as serfs for noble landowners, while in the Ottoman Empire all land belonged to the sultan.

Famine and Economic Crisis

In the seventeenth century a period of colder and wetter climate throughout Europe, dubbed the "little ice age" by historians, meant a shorter farming season with lower yields. A bad harvest created food shortages; a series of bad harvests could lead to famine. Recurrent famines significantly reduced the population of early modern Europe through reduced fertility, susceptibility to disease, and outright starvation.

Industry also suffered. The output of woolen textiles declined sharply in the first half of the seventeenth century. Food prices were high, wages stagnated, and unemployment soared. This economic crisis was not universal: it struck various regions at different times and to different degrees. In the middle decades of the century, for example, Spain, France, Germany, and England all experienced great economic difficulties, but these years were the golden age of the Netherlands (see page 535).

The urban poor and peasants were the hardest hit. When the price of bread rose beyond their capacity to pay, they frequently expressed their anger by rioting. Women often led these actions, since their role as mothers gave them some impunity in authorities' eyes. Historians have used the term **moral economy** for this vision of a world in which community needs predominate over competition and profit.

moral economy

▶ The early modern European view that community needs predominated over competition and profit and that necessary goods should thus be sold at a fair price.

Thirty Years' War

▶ A large-scale conflict extending from 1618 to 1648 that pitted Protestants against Catholics in central Europe, but also involved dynastic interests, notably of Spain and France.

The Thirty Years' War

Harsh economic conditions in the seventeenth century were greatly exacerbated by the decades-long conflict known as the **Thirty Years' War** (1618–1648). Shifts in the balance between the population of Protestants and Catholics in the Holy Roman Empire led to the deterioration of the Peace of Augsburg. Lutheran princes

CHAPTER LOCATOR | How did the Protestant and Catholic Reformations shape colonial expansion? | **How did seventeenth-century European states overcome social and economic crisis?** | How did absolutism evolve in in Spain, France, and Austria?

CHAPTER 18
520 EUROPEAN POWER AND EXPANSION

felt compelled to form the Protestant Union (1608), and Catholics retaliated with the Catholic League (1609). Dynastic interests were also involved; the Spanish Habsburgs strongly supported the goals of their Austrian relatives: the unity of the empire and the preservation of Catholicism within it.

The war began with a conflict in Bohemia (part of the present-day Czech Republic) between the Catholic League and the Protestant Union but soon spread through the Holy Roman Empire, drawing in combatants from across Europe. After a series of initial Catholic victories, the tide of the conflict turned due to the intervention of Sweden, under its king Gustavus Adolphus (r. 1594–1632), and then France, whose prime minister, Cardinal Richelieu, intervened on the side of the Protestants to undermine Habsburg power.

The 1648 Peace of Westphalia that ended the Thirty Years' War marked a turning point in European history. The treaties that established the peace not only ended conflicts fought over religious faith but also recognized the independent authority of more than three hundred German princes (Map 18.2, see page 522), reconfirming the emperor's severely limited authority. The Augsburg agreement of 1555 became permanent, adding Calvinism to Catholicism and Lutheranism as legally permissible creeds. The United Provinces of the Netherlands, known as the Dutch Republic, won official freedom from Spain.

The Thirty Years' War was probably the most destructive event in central Europe prior to the world wars of the twentieth century. Perhaps one-third of urban residents and two-fifths of the rural population died.

European Achievements in State-Building

In this context of warfare, economic crisis, and demographic decline, European monarchs took urgent measures to restore order and rebuild their states. In some states absolutist models of government prevailed. In others, constitutionalist forces dominated. Despite their political differences, all these states sought to protect and expand their frontiers, raise new taxes, consolidate central control, and compete for colonies and trade in the New and Old Worlds. In so doing, they followed a broad pattern of state-building and consolidation of power found across Eurasia in this period.

Rulers who wished to increase their authority encountered formidable obstacles, including poor communications, entrenched local power structures, and ethnic and linguistic diversity. Nonetheless, over the course of the seventeenth century both absolutist and constitutional governments achieved new levels of power and national unity. They did so by transforming emergency measures of wartime into permanent structures of government and by subduing privileged groups through the combined use of force and economic and social incentives. Increased state authority may be seen in four areas in particular: a tremendous growth in the size and professionalism of armies; much higher taxes; larger and more efficient bureaucracies; and territorial expansion both within Europe and overseas.

Over time, centralized power added up to something close to **sovereignty**. A state may be termed sovereign when it possesses a monopoly over the instruments of justice and the use of force within clearly defined boundaries. In a sovereign state, no nongovernmental system of courts competes with state courts in the dispensation of justice. Also, private armies present no threat to central authority. While seventeenth-century states did not acquire full sovereignty, they made important strides toward that goal.

sovereignty
▶ Authority of states that possess a monopoly over the instruments of justice and the use of force within clearly defined boundaries and in which private armies present no threat to central control; seventeenth-century European states made important advances toward sovereignty.

Why and how did the constitutional state triumph in England and the Dutch Republic?

How did European nations compete for trade and empire in the Americas and Asia?

How did Russian rulers build an absolutist monarchy and expand into a powerful empire?

☑ LearningCurve
Check what you know.

MAP 18.2 ■ Europe After the Thirty Years' War

Which country emerged from the Thirty Years' War as the strongest European power? What dynastic house was that country's major rival in the early modern period?

> **QUICK REVIEW**

How did war and famine contribute to the seventeenth-century crisis?

CHAPTER LOCATOR | How did the Protestant and Catholic Reformations shape colonial expansion? | How did seventeenth-century European states overcome social and economic crisis? | **How did absolutism evolve in in Spain, France, and Austria?**

CHAPTER 18
EUROPEAN POWER AND EXPANSION

522

Spanish Troops

The long wars that Spain fought over Dutch independence, in support of Habsburg interests in Germany, and against France left the country militarily exhausted and financially drained by the mid-1600s. In this detail from a painting by Peeter Snayers, Spanish troops — thin, emaciated, and probably unpaid — straggle away from battle. (detail, *Troops at the Siege of Aire Sur La Lys*, 1658, by Peeter Snayers [1592–1667]/Prado, Madrid, Spain/Index/The Bridgeman Art Library)

RULERS IN ABSOLUTIST STATES asserted that, because they were chosen by God, they were responsible to God alone. Under the rule of **absolutism**, monarchs claimed exclusive power to make and enforce laws, denying any other institution or group the authority to check their power. Spain, France, and Austria provide three key examples of the development of the absolutist state.

Spain

The discovery of silver at Potosí in 1541 (see page 476) had produced momentous wealth for Spain, allowing it to dominate Europe militarily. Yet Spain had inherent weaknesses that the vast wealth of empire had hidden. It was a combination of different kingdoms with their own traditions and loyalties. Spanish silver had created great wealth but also dependency. While Creoles undertook new industries in the colonies and European nations targeted Spanish colonial trade, industry and finance in Spain itself remained undeveloped.

The impact of these developments became apparent during the first half of the seventeenth century. Between 1610 and 1650 Spanish trade with the colonies

absolutism

▶ A political system common to early modern Europe in which monarchs claimed exclusive power to make and enforce laws, without checks by other institutions; this system was limited in practice by the need to maintain legitimacy and compromise with elites.

| Why and how did the constitutional state triumph in England and the Dutch Republic? | How did European nations compete for trade and empire in the Americas and Asia? | How did Russian rulers build an absolutist monarchy and expand into a powerful empire? | ☑ LearningCurve Check what you know. |

in the New World fell 60 percent due to competition from colonial industries and from Dutch and English traders. At the same time, disease decimated the enslaved workers who toiled in South American silver mines. Moreover, the mines started to run dry, and the quantity of metal produced steadily declined after 1620.

In Madrid royal expenditures constantly exceeded income. To meet state debt, the Spanish crown repeatedly devalued the coinage and declared bankruptcy, which resulted in the collapse of national credit and steep inflation. Meanwhile, commerce and manufacturing shrank. To make matters worse, in 1609 the Crown expelled some three hundred thousand Moriscos, or former Muslims, significantly reducing the pool of skilled workers and merchants.

Spanish aristocrats, attempting to maintain an extravagant lifestyle they could no longer afford, increased the rents on their estates. High rents and heavy taxes drove the peasants from the land, leading to a decline in agricultural productivity. In cities wages and production stagnated.

Spain's situation worsened with internal conflicts and fresh military defeats during the Thirty Years' War and the remainder of the seventeenth century. In the 1640s Spain faced serious revolts in Catalonia, Sicily, and the Spanish Netherlands. The Treaty of Westphalia, which ended the Thirty Years' War, compelled Spain to recognize the independence of the Dutch Republic, and another treaty in 1659 granted extensive territories to France. Finally, in 1688 the Spanish crown reluctantly recognized the independence of Portugal. With these losses, the era of Spanish dominance in Europe ended.

The Foundations of French Absolutism

At the beginning of the seventeenth century France's position appeared extremely weak. Struggling to recover from decades of religious civil war, France posed little threat to Spain's predominance in Europe. By the end of the century the countries' positions were reversed.

Henry IV (r. 1589–1610) inaugurated a remarkable recovery by defusing religious tensions and rebuilding France's economy. He issued the Edict of Nantes in 1598, allowing Huguenots (French Protestants) the right to worship in 150 traditionally Protestant towns throughout France. He invested in infrastructure and raised revenue by selling royal offices instead of charging high taxes. Despite his efforts at peace, Henry was murdered in 1610 by a Catholic zealot.

Cardinal Richelieu (1585–1642) became first minister of the French crown on behalf of Henry's young son Louis XIII (r. 1610–1643). Richelieu designed his domestic policies to strengthen royal control. He extended the use of intendants, commissioners for each of France's thirty-two districts who were appointed by and were responsible to the monarch. As the intendants' power increased under Richelieu, so did the power of the centralized French state.

Cardinal Jules Mazarin (1602–1661) succeeded Richelieu as chief minister for the next child-king, the four-year-old Louis XIV who inherited the throne from his father in 1643. Mazarin's struggle to increase royal revenues led to the uprisings of 1648–1653 known as the Fronde. In Paris magistrates of the Parlement of Paris, the nation's most important law court, were outraged by the Crown's autocratic measures. These so-called robe nobles (named for the robes they wore in court) encouraged violent protest by the common people. As rebellion spread outside

CHAPTER LOCATOR | How did the Protestant and Catholic Reformations shape colonial expansion? | How did seventeenth-century European states overcome social and economic crisis? | **How did absolutism evolve in in Spain, France, and Austria?**

524 CHAPTER 18 EUROPEAN POWER AND EXPANSION

Paris and to the sword nobles (the traditional warrior nobility), civil order broke down completely, and young Louis XIV had to flee Paris.

Much of the rebellion faded, however, when Louis XIV was declared king in his own right in 1651. The French people were desperate for peace and stability after the disorders of the Fronde and were willing to accept a strong monarch who could restore order. Louis pledged to do just that.

Louis XIV and Absolutism

During the long reign of Louis XIV (r. 1643–1715), the French monarchy reached the peak of absolutist development. Louis believed in the divine right of kings: God had established kings as his rulers on earth, and they were answerable ultimately to him alone. However, he also recognized that kings could not simply do as they pleased. They had to obey God's laws and rule for the good of the people.

Like his counterpart, the Kangxi emperor of China, who inherited his realm only two decades after the Sun King did (see page 622), Louis XIV impressed his subjects with his discipline and hard work. He ruled his realm through several councils of state and insisted on taking a personal role in many of the councils' decisions.

Although personally tolerant, Louis hated division. He insisted that religious unity was essential to the security of the state. In 1685 Louis revoked the Edict of Nantes. Around two hundred thousand Protestants, including some of the kingdom's most highly skilled artisans, fled France. Louis's insistence on "one king, one law, one religion" contrasts sharply with the religious tolerance exhibited by the Ottoman Empire (see page 499).

Despite his claims to absolute authority, there were multiple constraints on Louis's power. As a representative of divine power, he was obliged to rule in a way that seemed consistent with virtue and benevolent authority. He had to uphold the laws issued by his royal predecessors. Moreover, he also relied on the collaboration of nobles. Without their cooperation, it would have been impossible for Louis to extend his power throughout France or wage his many foreign wars.

divine right of kings
▶ The belief propagated by absolutist monarchs that they derived their power from God and were only answerable to him.

Expansion Within Europe

Louis XIV kept France at war for thirty-three of the fifty-four years of his personal rule. Under the leadership of François le Tellier, marquis de Louvois, Louis's secretary of state for war, France acquired a huge professional army. The French army almost tripled in size. Uniforms and weapons were standardized, and a system of training and promotion was devised. As in so many other matters, Louis's model was emulated across Europe.

During this long period of warfare, Louis's goal was to expand France to what he considered its natural borders. His results were mixed. During the 1660s and 1670s, French armies won a number of important victories. The wars of the 1680s and 1690s, however, brought no additional territories and placed unbearable strains on French resources.

Louis's last war, the War of the Spanish Succession (1701–1713), was endured by a French people suffering high taxes, crop failure, and widespread malnutrition and death. This war was the result of Louis's unwillingness to abide by a previous

| Why and how did the constitutional state triumph in England and the Dutch Republic? | How did European nations compete for trade and empire in the Americas and Asia? | How did Russian rulers build an absolutist monarchy and expand into a powerful empire? | ✓ LearningCurve Check what you know. |

525

Legend

- French Bourbon lands
- Spanish Bourbon lands
- Austrian Habsburg lands
- Prussian lands
- Great Britain
- Russian Empire
- — Boundary of the Holy Roman Empire

MAP 18.3 ■ Europe After the Peace of Utrecht, 1715

The series of treaties commonly called the Peace of Utrecht ended the War of the Spanish Succession and redrew the map of Europe. A French Bourbon king succeeded to the Spanish throne. France surrendered the Spanish Netherlands (later Belgium), then in French hands, to Austria and recognized the Hohenzollern rulers of Prussia. Spain ceded Gibraltar to Great Britain, for which it has been a strategic naval station ever since. Spain also granted Britain the *asiento*, the contract for supplying African slaves to America.

> **MAPPING THE PAST**

ANALYZING THE MAP: Identify the areas on the map that changed hands as a result of the Peace of Utrecht. How did these changes affect the balance of power in Europe?

CONNECTIONS: How and why did so many European countries possess scattered or discontiguous territories? What does this suggest about European politics in this period? Does this map suggest potential for future conflict?

agreement to divide Spanish possessions between France and the Holy Roman Emperor upon the death of the childless Spanish king Charles II (r. 1665–1700). In 1701 the English, Dutch, Austrians, and Prussians formed the Grand Alliance against Louis XIV. War dragged on until 1713, when it was ended by the Peace of Utrecht (Map 18.3).

The Peace of Utrecht marked the end of French expansion. Thirty-three years of war had given France the rights to all of Alsace and some commercial centers in the north. But at what price? At the time of Louis's death in 1715, an exhausted France hovered on the brink of bankruptcy.

CHAPTER LOCATOR | How did the Protestant and Catholic Reformations shape colonial expansion? | How did seventeenth-century European states overcome social and economic crisis? | **How did absolutism evolve in in Spain, France, and Austria?**

CHAPTER 18
526 EUROPEAN POWER AND EXPANSION

The Economic Policy of Mercantilism

France's ability to build armies and fight wars depended on a strong economy. Fortunately for Louis, his controller general, Jean-Baptiste Colbert (1619–1683), proved to be a financial genius. Colbert's central principle was that the wealth and the economy of France should serve the state. To this end, Colbert rigorously applied mercantilist policies to France.

Mercantilism is a collection of governmental policies for the regulation of economic activities by and for the state. It derives from the idea that a nation's international power is based on its wealth, specifically its supply of gold and silver. To accumulate wealth, a country always had to sell more goods abroad than it bought from foreign countries.

To increase exports, Colbert supported old industries and created new ones. He enacted new production regulations, created guilds to boost quality standards, and encouraged foreign craftsmen to immigrate to France. To encourage the purchase of French goods, he abolished many domestic tariffs and raised tariffs on foreign products. In 1664 Colbert founded the Company of the East Indies with hopes of competing with the Dutch for Asian trade. Colbert also sought to increase France's control over and presence in New France (Canada) (see page 835).

During Colbert's tenure as controller general, Louis was able to pursue his goals without massive tax increases and without creating a stream of new offices. The constant pressure of warfare after Colbert's death, however, undid many of his economic achievements.

mercantilism

▶ A system of economic regulations aimed at increasing the power of the state derived from the belief that a nation's international power was based on its wealth, specifically its supply of gold and silver.

The Austrian Habsburgs

Like all of central Europe, the Austrian Habsburgs emerged from the Thirty Years' War impoverished and exhausted. Their efforts to destroy Protestantism in the German lands and to turn the weak Holy Roman Empire into a real state had failed. Defeat in central Europe encouraged the Austrian Habsburgs to turn away from a quest for imperial dominance and to focus inward and eastward in an attempt to unify their diverse holdings.

Habsburg victory over Bohemia during the Thirty Years' War was an important step in this direction. Ferdinand II (r. 1619–1637) drastically reduced the power of the Bohemian Estates, the largely Protestant representative assembly. He also confiscated the landholdings of Protestant nobles and gave them to his supporters. After 1650 a large portion of the Bohemian nobility was of recent origin and owed its success to the Habsburgs.

With the support of this new nobility, the Habsburgs established direct rule over Bohemia. Under their rule, the condition of the serfs worsened substantially. The Habsburgs also successfully eliminated Protestantism in Bohemia. These changes were important steps in creating absolutist rule.

Ferdinand III (r. 1637–1657) continued to build state power. He centralized the government in the empire's German-speaking provinces, which formed the core Habsburg holdings, and established a permanent standing army. Between 1683 and 1699 the Habsburgs pushed the Ottomans from most of Hungary and Transylvania. The recovery of all the former kingdom of Hungary was completed in 1718.

Austrian Expansion, to 1699

■ Austrian Habsburg territory in 1648
□ Lands taken from Ottomans by Austrian Habsburgs, to 1699

Why and how did the constitutional state triumph in England and the Dutch Republic?

How did European nations compete for trade and empire in the Americas and Asia?

How did Russian rulers build an absolutist monarchy and expand into a powerful empire?

✔ LearningCurve
Check what you know.

Despite its reduced strength, the Hungarian nobility effectively thwarted the full development of Habsburg absolutism. Throughout the seventeenth century Hungarian nobles periodically rose in revolt against the Habsburgs. In 1703, with the Habsburgs bogged down in the War of the Spanish Succession, the Hungarians rose in one last patriotic rebellion under Prince Francis Rákóczy (RAH-coht-see). Rákóczy and his forces were eventually defeated, but the Habsburgs agreed to restore many of the traditional privileges of the Hungarian aristocracy in return for the country's acceptance of Habsburg rule.

Elsewhere, the Habsburgs made significant achievements in state-building by forging consensus with the church and the nobility. A sense of common identity and loyalty to the monarchy grew among elites in Habsburg lands. German became the language of the state, and Vienna became the political and cultural center of the empire.

The Absolutist Palace

In 1682 Louis moved his court and government to the newly renovated palace at Versailles, in the countryside southwest of Paris. The palace quickly became the center of political, social, and cultural life. The king required all great nobles to spend at least part of the year in attendance on him there.

Louis further revolutionized court life by establishing an elaborate set of etiquette rituals to mark every moment of his day, from waking up and dressing in the morning to removing his clothing and retiring at night. These rituals were far from meaningless or trivial. The king controlled immense resources and privileges; access to him meant favored treatment for government offices, military and religious posts, state pensions, honorary titles, and a host of other benefits.

A system of patronage—in which a higher-ranked individual protected a lower-ranked one in return for loyalty and services—flowed from the court to the provinces. Through this mechanism Louis gained cooperation from powerful nobles. Although they were denied public offices and posts, women played a central role in the patronage system. At court the king's wife, mistresses, and other female relatives recommended individuals for honors, advocated policy decisions, and brokered alliances between noble factions.

With Versailles as the center of European politics, French culture grew in international prestige. French became the language of polite society and international diplomacy. France inspired a cosmopolitan European culture in the late seventeenth century that looked to Versailles as its center. Moreover, Louis's rival European monarchs soon followed his example and palace building became a Europe-wide phenomenon.

> **QUICK REVIEW**

Why did Spain's situation deteriorate over the course of the seventeenth century? Why did France's improve?

CHAPTER LOCATOR | How did the Protestant and Catholic Reformations shape colonial expansion? | How did seventeenth-century European states overcome social and economic crisis? | How did absolutism evolve in in Spain, France, and Austria?

CHAPTER 18
528 EUROPEAN POWER AND EXPANSION

Puritan Occupations

These twelve engravings depict typical Puritan occupations and show that the Puritans came primarily from the artisan and lower middle classes. The governing classes and peasants made up a much smaller percentage of Puritans, and most generally adhered to the traditions of the Church of England. (Visual Connection Archive)

Why and how did the constitutional state triumph in England and the Dutch Republic?

WHILE MOST EUROPEAN NATIONS developed absolutist states in the seventeenth century, England and the Netherlands evolved toward **constitutionalism**, which is the limitation of government by law. Constitutionalism also implies a balance between the authority and power of the government, on the one hand, and the rights and liberties of the subjects, on the other.

Religious Divides and Civil War

In 1603 beloved Queen Elizabeth was succeeded by her Scottish cousin James Stuart, who ruled England as James I (r. 1603–1625). Like Louis XIV, James believed that a monarch had a divine right to his authority and was responsible only to God. James I and his son Charles I (r. 1625–1649) considered any legislative constraint on their power a threat to their divine-right prerogative. Consequently, at every meeting of Parliament between 1603 and 1640, bitter squabbles erupted between the Crown and the House of Commons.

constitutionalism

▶ A form of government in which power is limited by law and balanced between the authority and power of the government, on the one hand, and the rights and liberties of the subject or citizen, on the other; it includes constitutional monarchies and republics.

Why and how did the constitutional state triumph in England and the Dutch Republic?	How did European nations compete for trade and empire in the Americas and Asia?	How did Russian rulers build an absolutist monarchy and expand into a powerful empire?	✅ LearningCurve Check what you know.

The English Civil War, 1642–1649

☐ Parliamentarians
☐ Royalists
✳ Major battle

Religious issues also embittered relations between the king and the House of Commons. In the early seventeenth century many English people felt dissatisfied with the Church of England. Calvinist **Puritans** wanted to take the Reformation further by "purifying" the Anglican Church of Roman Catholic elements, including crown-appointed bishops. James I responded to such ideas by declaring, "No bishop, no king." His son and successor, Charles I, further antagonized subjects by marrying a French Catholic princess and supporting the high-handed policies of archbishop of Canterbury William Laud (1573–1645).

Charles avoided direct confrontation by refusing to call Parliament into session from 1629 to 1640, financing his government through extraordinary stopgap levies considered illegal by most English people. However, when Scottish Calvinists revolted against his religious policies, Charles was forced to summon Parliament to obtain funding for an army to put down the revolt. Angry with the king's behavior and sympathetic with the Scots' religious beliefs, the House of Commons passed the Triennial Act in 1641, which compelled the king to call Parliament every three years. The Commons also impeached Archbishop Laud and then threatened to abolish bishops. King Charles, fearful of a Scottish invasion, reluctantly accepted these measures. The next act in the conflict was precipitated by the outbreak of rebellion in Ireland. In 1641 the Catholic gentry of Ireland led an uprising in response to a feared invasion by British anti-Catholic forces.

Without an army, Charles I could neither come to terms with the Scots nor respond to the Irish rebellion. After a failed attempt to arrest parliamentary leaders, Charles left London and began to raise an army. In response, Parliament formed its own army, the New Model Army.

The English civil war (1642–1649) pitted the power of the king against that of Parliament. After three years of fighting, Parliament's army defeated the king's forces at the Battles of Naseby and Langport in the summer of 1645. Charles refused to concede defeat, and both sides waited for a decisive event. This arrived in the form of the army under the leadership of Oliver Cromwell, a member of the House of Commons and a devout Puritan. In 1647 Cromwell's troops captured the king and dismissed members of the Parliament who opposed Cromwell's actions. In 1649 the remaining representatives, known as the Rump Parliament, put Charles on trial for high treason. Charles was found guilty and beheaded on January 30, 1649.

The Puritan Protectorate

With the execution of Charles, the monarchy was abolished and a commonwealth, or republican government, was proclaimed. Theoretically, legislative power rested in the surviving members of Parliament, and executive power was lodged in a council of state. In fact, the army that had defeated the king controlled the government, and Oliver Cromwell controlled the army. Though called the Protectorate, the rule of Cromwell (1653–1658) was a form of military dictatorship. Reflecting Puritan ideas of morality, Cromwell's state forbade sports, kept the theaters closed, and rigorously censored the press.

On the issue of religion, Cromwell favored some degree of tolerance, and all Christians except Roman Catholics had the right to practice their faiths. Cromwell had long associated Catholicism in Ireland with sedition and heresy, and he led an army there to reconquer the country in August 1649. Following Cromwell's recon-

CHAPTER LOCATOR | How did the Protestant and Catholic Reformations shape colonial expansion? | How did seventeenth-century European states overcome social and economic crisis? | How did absolutism evolve in in Spain, France, and Austria?

530 CHAPTER 18 EUROPEAN POWER AND EXPANSION

quest, the English banned Catholicism in Ireland, executed priests, and confiscated land from Catholics for English and Scottish settlers.

The Protectorate collapsed when Cromwell died in 1658 and his ineffectual son succeeded him. Fed up with military rule, the English longed for a return to civilian government. By 1660 they were ready to restore the monarchy.

Constitutional Monarchy

The Restoration of 1660 brought to the throne Charles II (r. 1660–1685), the eldest son of Charles I. Both houses of Parliament were also restored, as was the Anglican Church. However, Charles was succeeded by his Catholic brother James II, arousing fears of a return of Catholicism. A group of eminent persons in Parliament and the Church of England offered the English throne to James's Protestant daughter Mary and her Dutch husband, Prince William of Orange. In December 1688 James II, his queen, and their infant son fled to France. Early in 1689 William and Mary were crowned king and queen of England.

In England these events, known as the Glorious Revolution, represented the final destruction of the idea of divine-right monarchy. The men who brought about the revolution framed their intentions in the **Bill of Rights of 1689**, which was formulated in direct response to Stuart absolutism. Law was to be made in Parliament; once made, it could not be suspended by the Crown. Parliament had to be called at least once every three years. The Bill of Rights also established the independence of the judiciary and mandated that there be no standing army in peacetime. Protestants could possess arms, but the Catholic minority could not. Catholics could not inherit the throne. Additional legislation granted freedom of worship to Protestant dissenters but not to Catholics.

The Glorious Revolution and the concept of representative government found its best defense in political philosopher John Locke's *Second Treatise of Civil Government* (1690). Locke (1632–1704) maintained that a government that oversteps its proper function—protecting the natural rights of life, liberty, and property— becomes a tyranny. Under a tyrannical government, he argued, the people have the natural right to rebellion.

Although the events of 1688 and 1689 brought England closer to Locke's ideal, they did not constitute a democratic revolution. The Glorious Revolution placed sovereignty in Parliament, and Parliament represented the upper classes.

Bill of Rights of 1689

▶ A bill passed by Parliament and accepted by William and Mary that limited the powers of British monarchs and affirmed those of Parliament.

The Dutch Republic

The independence of the Republic of the United Provinces of the Netherlands was recognized in 1648 in the treaty that ended the Thirty Years' War. Rejecting the rule of a monarch, the Dutch adopted a system of **republicanism**, whereby power rested in the hands of the people and was exercised through elected representatives. An oligarchy of wealthy businessmen called regents handled domestic affairs in each province's Estates, or assemblies. The provincial Estates held virtually all the power. A federal assembly, or States General, handled foreign affairs and war, but all issues had to be referred back to the local Estates for approval, and each of the seven provinces could veto any proposed legislation. Holland, the province with the largest navy and the most wealth, usually dominated the republic and the States General.

republicanism

▶ A form of government in which there is no monarch and power rests in the hands of the people as exercised through elected representatives.

| Why and how did the constitutional state triumph in England and the Dutch Republic? | How did European nations compete for trade and empire in the Americas and Asia? | How did Russian rulers build an absolutist monarchy and expand into a powerful empire? | ✓ LearningCurve Check what you know. |

531

The Young Scholar and His Wife

A new genre of painting emerged in the seventeenth century celebrating the virtues of domestic life and family. It was particularly popular in the wealthy, urban Netherlands, among prosperous families such as the couple depicted here. (*The Young Scholar and His Wife*, 1640, oil on panel by Gonzales Coques [1614–84]/Gemaeldegalerie Alte Meister, Kassel, Germany/ © Museumslandschaft Hessen Kassel/The Bridgeman Art Library)

> PICTURING THE PAST

ANALYZING THE IMAGE: What social and cultural values does this painting seem to celebrate? What insight does the painter offer into masculine and feminine roles in this society? Why do you think the husband and wife are standing separately and not together, as they probably would in a modern family portrait?

CONNECTIONS: Based on your reading in this chapter, how might the portrait of a more typical European family of 1640 differ from this one? Why would a family in the Netherlands have a different lifestyle from many families in other European countries?

In each province, the Estates appointed an executive officer, known as the stadholder. Although in theory freely chosen by the Estates, in practice the reigning prince of Orange usually held the office of stadholder in several of the seven provinces of the republic. Tensions persisted between supporters of the House of Orange and those of the staunchly republican Estates, who suspected the princes of harboring monarchical ambitions.

Global trade and commerce brought the Dutch the highest standard of living in Europe, perhaps in the world. Salaries were high, and all classes of society ate well. The moral and ethical bases of Dutch commercial wealth were thrift, frugality, and religious tolerance. Jews enjoyed a level of acceptance and assimilation in Dutch business and general culture unique in early modern Europe. (See "Individuals in Society: Glückel of Hameln," page 533.) Tolerance contributed to profits by attracting a great deal of foreign capital and investment.

> QUICK REVIEW

What limits had been put in place on the power of English kings by the end of the seventeenth century?

CHAPTER LOCATOR | How did the Protestant and Catholic Reformations shape colonial expansion? | How did seventeenth-century European states overcome social and economic crisis? | How did absolutism evolve in in Spain, France, and Austria?

CHAPTER 18
532 EUROPEAN POWER AND EXPANSION

INDIVIDUALS IN SOCIETY
Glückel of Hameln

n 1690 a Jewish widow in the small German town of Hameln in Lower Saxony sat down to write her autobiography. She wanted to distract her mind from the terrible grief she felt over the death of her husband and to provide her twelve children with a record. She told them that she was writing her memoirs "so you will know from what sort of people you have sprung, lest today or tomorrow your beloved children or grandchildren came and know naught of their family." Out of her pain and heightened consciousness, Glückel (1646–1724) produced an invaluable source for scholars.

She was born in Hamburg two years before the end of the Thirty Years' War. In 1649 the merchants of Hamburg expelled the Jews, who moved to nearby Altona, then under Danish rule. When the Swedes overran Altona in 1657–1658, the Jews returned to Hamburg "purely at the mercy of the Town Council." Glückel's narrative unfolds against a background of the constant harassment to which Jews were subjected — special papers, permits, bribes — and in Hameln she wrote, "And so it has been to this day and, I fear, will continue in like fashion."

When Glückel was "barely twelve," her father betrothed her to Chayim Hameln, and they married when she was fourteen. She describes him as "the perfect pattern of the pious Jew," a man who stopped his work every day for study and prayer, fasted, and was scrupulously honest in his business dealings. Only a few years older than Glückel, Chayim earned his living dealing in precious metals and in making small loans on pledges (pawned goods). This work required constant travel to larger cities, markets, and fairs, often in bad weather, always over dangerous roads. Chayim consulted his wife about all his business dealings. As he lay dying, a friend asked if he had any last wishes.

"None," he replied. "My wife knows everything. She shall do as she has always done." For thirty years Glückel had been his friend, full business partner, and wife. They had thirteen children, twelve of whom survived their father, eight then unmarried. As Chayim had foretold, Glückel succeeded in launching the boys in careers and in providing dowries for the girls.

Glückel's world was her family, the Jewish community of Hameln, and the Jewish communities into which her children married. Her social and business activities took her across Europe, from Amsterdam to Berlin, from Danzig to Vienna; thus her world was far from narrow or provincial. She took great pride that Prince Frederick of Cleves, later king of Prussia, danced at the wedding of her eldest daughter. The rising prosperity of Chayim's businesses allowed the couple to maintain up to six servants.

Glückel was deeply religious, and her culture was steeped in Jewish literature, legends, and mystical and secular works. Above all, she relied on the Bible. Her language, heavily sprinkled with scriptural references, testifies to a rare familiarity with the Scriptures.

Students who wish to learn about seventeenth-century business practices, the importance of the dowry in marriage, childbirth, Jewish life, birthrates, family celebrations, and even the meaning of life can gain a good deal from the memoirs of this extraordinary woman who was, in the words of one of her descendants, the poet Heinrich Heine, "the gift of a world to me."

Source: *The Memoirs of Glückel of Hameln* (New York: Schocken Books, 1977).

QUESTIONS FOR ANALYSIS

1. Consider the ways in which Glückel of Hameln was both an ordinary and an extraordinary woman of her times. Would you call her a marginal or a central person in her society? Why?
2. How might Glückel's successes be attributed to the stabilizing force of absolutism in the seventeenth century?

LaunchPad

ONLINE DOCUMENT PROJECT

What factors shaped life for European Jews in the early modern era? Read excerpts from Glückel of Hameln's memoirs and other accounts of Jewish life, and then complete a quiz and writing assignment based on the evidence and details from this chapter. *See inside the front cover to learn more.*

Although no images of Glückel exist, Rembrandt's *The Jewish Bride* suggests the mutual devotion of Glückel and her husband. (Rijksmuseum, Amsterdam, The Netherlands/The Bridgeman Art Library)

How did European nations compete for global trade and empire in the Americas and Asia?

The Fur Trade

In the early seventeenth century, European fur traders relied on Native Americans' expertise and experience, leading to the equal relations depicted in this scene from the colony of New Sweden (in modern-day Pennsylvania). The action in the background shows violence among indigenous groups, rivalries exacerbated by contact with Europeans and their trade goods. Hudson's Bay Company, the English colonial trading company, issued its own tokens as currency in the fur trade. This token, dating from the mid-nineteenth century, displays the company's crest, which says "a skin for a skin" in Latin. Two stags face each other, with a fox at the top and four beavers on the shield. Traders received tokens for the pelts they sold and could use them to purchase goods from the company's store. European demand for beaver hats, made from the felted pelts of beavers, drove the tremendous expansion of the North American fur trade in the beginning of the seventeenth century. (engraving: From *Geographia Americae with An Account of the Delaware Indians, Based on Surveys and Notes Made 1654–1656*, by Peter Lindestrom, published by The Swedish Colonial Society/Visual Connection Archive; token: © National Maritime Museum, London, UK/The Image Works)

FOR MUCH OF THE SIXTEENTH CENTURY, the Spanish and Portuguese dominated European overseas trade and colonization (see Chapter 16). In the early seventeenth century, however, England, France, and the Netherlands challenged Spain's monopoly.

CHAPTER LOCATOR | How did the Protestant and Catholic Reformations shape colonial expansion? | How did seventeenth-century European states overcome social and economic crisis? | How did absolutism evolve in in Spain, France, and Austria?

534 CHAPTER 18 EUROPEAN POWER AND EXPANSION

The Dutch Trading Empire

The so-called golden age of the Dutch Republic in the seventeenth century was built on its commercial prosperity and its highly original republican system of government. The Dutch came to dominate the European shipping business by putting profits from their original industry—herring fishing—into shipbuilding. They then took aim at Portugal's immensely lucrative Asian trade empire.

In 1599 a Dutch fleet returned to Amsterdam from a voyage to South East Asia carrying a huge cargo of spices. Those who had invested in the expedition received a 100 percent profit. The voyage led to the establishment in 1602 of the Dutch East India Company, founded with the stated intention of capturing the spice trade from the Portuguese.

In return for assisting Indonesian princes in local squabbles and disputes with the Portuguese, the Dutch won broad commercial concessions. Through agreements, seizures, and outright military aggression, they gained control of the western access to the Indonesian archipelago in the first half of the seventeenth century. Gradually, they acquired political domination over the archipelago itself. The Dutch were willing to use force more ruthlessly than the Portuguese and had superior organizational efficiency. These factors allowed them to expel the Portuguese from Ceylon and other East Indian islands in the 1660s and henceforth dominate the production and trade of spices. The company also established the colony of Cape Town on the southern tip of Africa as a provisioning point for its Asian fleets.

The Dutch also aspired to a role in the Americas (Map 18.4). Founded in 1621, the Dutch West India Company aggressively sought to open trade with North and South America and capture Spanish territories there. The company captured or destroyed hundreds of Spanish ships, seized the Spanish silver fleet in 1628, and claimed portions of Brazil and the Caribbean. The Dutch also successfully interceded in the transatlantic slave trade, establishing a large number of trading stations on the west coast of Africa. Ironically, the nation that was known as a bastion of tolerance and freedom came to be one of the principal operators of the slave trade starting in the 1640s.

Colonial Empires of England and France

England and France followed the Dutch in challenging Iberian dominance overseas. Unlike the Iberian powers, whose royal governments financed exploration and directly ruled the colonies, England, France, and the Netherlands conducted the initial phase of colonization through chartered companies with monopolies over settlement and trade in a given area.

After an unsuccessful first colony at Roanoke (in what is now North Carolina), the English colony of Virginia, founded at Jamestown in 1607, gained a steady hold by producing tobacco for a growing European market. In the 1670s English colonists from the Caribbean island of Barbados settled Carolina, where conditions were suitable for large rice plantations. During the late seventeenth century enslaved Africans replaced indentured servants as laborers on tobacco and rice plantations, and a harsh racial divide was imposed.

For the first settlers on the coast of New England, the reasons for seeking a new life in the colonies were more religious than economic. Many of these

| Why and how did the constitutional state triumph in England and the Dutch Republic? | **How did European nations compete for trade and empire in the Americas and Asia?** | How did Russian rulers build an absolutist monarchy and expand into a powerful empire? | ☑ LearningCurve Check what you know. |

535

MAP 18.4 ■ **Seventeenth-Century Dutch Commerce**
Dutch wealth rested on commerce, and commerce depended on the huge Dutch merchant marine, manned by perhaps forty-eight thousand sailors. The fleet carried goods from all parts of the globe to the port of Amsterdam.

colonists were radical Protestants escaping Anglican repression. The small and struggling outpost of Plymouth Colony (1620) was followed by Massachusetts Bay Colony (1630), which grew into a prosperous settlement. Religious disputes in Massachusetts led to the dispersion of settlers into the new communities of Providence, Connecticut, Rhode Island, and New Haven. Because New England lacked the conditions for plantation agriculture, slavery was always a minor factor there.

As the English crown grew more interested in colonial expansion, efforts were made to acquire the territory between New England in the north and Virginia in the south. The goal was to unify English holdings and minimize French and Dutch competition on the Atlantic seaboard. The results of these efforts were the mid-Atlantic colonies: the Catholic settlement of Maryland (1632); New York, captured from the Dutch in 1664; and the Quaker colony of Pennsylvania (1681).

Whereas English settlements were largely agricultural, the French established trading factories in present-day Canada, much like those in Asia and Africa. Louis XIV's capable controller general, Jean-Baptiste Colbert, established direct

CHAPTER LOCATOR | How did the Protestant and Catholic Reformations shape colonial expansion? | How did seventeenth-century European states overcome social and economic crisis? | How did absolutism evolve in in Spain, France, and Austria?

536 CHAPTER 18
EUROPEAN POWER AND EXPANSION

royal control over New France (Canada) and tried to enlarge its population by sending colonists.

French immigration to New Canada remained small compared with the stream of settlers who came to British North America; nevertheless, the French were energetic and industrious traders and explorers. Following the waterways of the St. Lawrence River, the Great Lakes, and the Mississippi River, they ventured into much of North America in the 1670s and 1680s. In 1673 the Jesuit Jacques Marquette and the merchant Louis Joliet sailed down the Mississippi as far as present-day Arkansas. In 1682 Robert de La Salle traveled the Mississippi to the Gulf of Mexico, opening the way for French occupation of Louisiana.

In the first decades of the seventeenth century, English and French captains also challenged Spain's hold over the Caribbean (see Map 19.2, page 574), seizing a number of islands. These islands acquired new importance after 1640, when the Portuguese brought sugar plantations to Brazil. Sugar and slaves quickly followed in the West Indies (see pages 475–476), making the Caribbean plantations the most lucrative of all colonial possessions.

The northern European powers also expanded in Africa and Asia. In the 1600s France and England—along with Denmark and other northern European powers—established fortified trading posts, or factories, in West Africa as bases for purchasing slaves and in India and the Indian Ocean for spices and other luxury goods. Thus, by the end of the seventeenth century, a handful of European powers possessed overseas empires that truly spanned the globe.

European Claims in North America, 1714

Mercantilism and Colonial Wars

Trade to and among European overseas possessions was governed by mercantilist economic policy (see page 527). The mercantilist notion of a "zero-sum game," in which any country's gain must come from another country's loss, led to hostile competition and outright warfare among European powers over their colonial possessions.

In England Oliver Cromwell established the first of a series of Navigation Acts in 1651, and the restored monarchy of Charles II extended them in 1660 and 1663. The acts required most goods imported into England and Scotland (Great Britain after 1707) to be carried on British-owned ships with British crews or on ships of the country producing the article. Moreover, these laws gave British merchants and shipowners a virtual monopoly on trade with British colonies. These economic regulations were intended to eliminate foreign competition and to encourage the development of a British shipping industry whose seamen could serve when necessary in the Royal Navy.

The Navigation Acts were a form of economic warfare against the Dutch, who were far ahead of the English in shipping and foreign trade in the mid-seventeenth century. In conjunction with three Anglo-Dutch wars between 1652 and 1674, the Navigation Acts seriously damaged Dutch shipping and commerce. By the late seventeenth century the Netherlands was falling behind England in shipping, trade, and settlement.

Thereafter France was England's most serious rival in the competition for overseas empire. France was continental Europe's leading military power. It was already building a powerful fleet and a worldwide system of rigidly monopolized colonial trade. But the War of the Spanish Succession, the last of Louis XIV's many

Navigation Acts
▶ Mid-seventeenth-century English mercantilist laws that greatly restricted other countries' rights to trade with England and its colonies.

Why and how did the constitutional state triumph in England and the Dutch Republic?

How did European nations compete for trade and empire in the Americas and Asia?

How did Russian rulers build an absolutist monarchy and expand into a powerful empire?

✓ LearningCurve
Check what you know.

wars (see page 525), tilted the balance in favor of England. The 1713 Peace of Utrecht forced France to cede its North American holdings in Newfoundland, Nova Scotia, and the Hudson Bay territory to Britain. Spain was compelled to give Britain control of its West African slave trade and to let Britain send one ship of merchandise into the Spanish colonies annually. These acquisitions primed Britain to take a leading role in the growing Atlantic trade of the eighteenth century, including the transatlantic slave trade (discussed in Chapter 19).

People Beyond Borders

As they seized new territories, European nations produced maps proudly outlining their possessions. The situation on the ground, however, was often much more complicated than the lines on those maps would suggest. Many groups of people lived in the contested frontiers between empires, habitually crisscrossed their borders, or carved out niches within empires where they carried out their own lives in defiance of the official rules.

Restricted from owning land and holding many occupations in Europe, Jews were eager participants in colonial trade and established closely linked mercantile communities scattered across many different empires. Similarly, a community of Christian Armenians in Isfahan in the Safavid Empire formed the center of a trade network extending from London to Manila and Acapulco. Family ties and trust within these minority groups was a tremendous advantage in generating the financial credit and cooperation necessary for international commerce. Yet Jews and Armenians were minorities where they settled and vulnerable to persecution.

The nomadic Cossacks and Tartars who inhabited the steppes of the Don River basin that bordered the Russian and Ottoman Empires are yet another example of "in-between" peoples. The Cossacks and the Tartars maintained considerable political and cultural autonomy through the seventeenth century and enjoyed a degree of peaceful interaction. By the eighteenth century, however, both Ottoman and Russian rulers had expanded state control in their frontiers and had reined in the raiding and migration of nomadic steppe peoples. As their example suggests, the assertion of state authority in the seventeenth and eighteenth centuries made it progressively harder for all of these groups to retain autonomy from the grip of empire.

> **QUICK REVIEW**

What steps did England take toward the acquisition of an overseas empire in the seventeenth century?

CHAPTER LOCATOR | How did the Protestant and Catholic Reformations shape colonial expansion? | How did seventeenth-century European states overcome social and economic crisis? | How did absolutism evolve in in Spain, France, and Austria?

538 CHAPTER 18
EUROPEAN POWER AND EXPANSION

Russian Peasants

An eighteenth-century French artist visiting Russia recorded his impressions of the daily life of the Russian people in this etching of a fish merchant pulling his wares through a snowy village on a sleigh. Two caviar vendors behind him make a sale to a young mother standing at her doorstep with her baby in her arms. (From Jean-Baptiste Le Prince's second set of Russian etchings, 1765. Private Collection/Gérard PIERSON/www.amis-paris-petersbourg.org)

How did Russian rulers build a distinctive absolutist monarchy and expand into a vast and powerful empire?

RUSSIA OCCUPIED A UNIQUE POSITION among Eurasian states. With borders straddling eastern Europe and northwestern Asia, its development into a strong imperial state drew on elements from both continents.

Mongol Rule in Russia and the Rise of Moscow

In the thirteenth century the Mongols had conquered Kievan Rus, the medieval Slavic state that included most of present-day Ukraine, Belarus, and part of northwest Russia. For two hundred years the Mongols forced the Slavic princes to submit to their rule. The princes of the Grand Duchy of Moscow, a principality within Kievan Rus, became particularly adept at serving the Mongols. Eventually the Muscovite princes were able to destroy the other princes who were their rivals for power. Ivan III (r. 1462–1505), known as Ivan the Great, greatly expanded the principality of Moscow, claiming large territories in the north and east to the Siberian frontier.

Why and how did the constitutional state triumph in England and the Dutch Republic?

How did European nations compete for trade and empire in the Americas and Asia?

How did Russian rulers build an absolutist monarchy and expand into a powerful empire?

✓ LearningCurve
Check what you know.

By 1480 Ivan III was strong enough to refuse to pay tribute to the Mongols and declare the autonomy of Moscow. To legitimize his new position, Ivan and his successors borrowed elements of Mongol rule. They forced weaker Slavic principalities to render tribute and adopted Mongol institutions such as the tax system, postal routes, and census. Loyalty from the highest-ranking nobles, or boyars, helped the Muscovite princes consolidate their power.

Another source of legitimacy lay in Moscow's claim to the political and religious inheritance of the Byzantine Empire. After the empire's capital, Constantinople, fell to the Ottomans in 1453, the princes of Moscow saw themselves as heirs of the Byzantine caesars (emperors) and guardians of the Orthodox Christian Church.

Building the Russian Empire

Developments in Russia took a chaotic turn with the reign of Ivan IV (r. 1533–1584), the famous Ivan the Terrible, who ascended to the throne at age three. His mother died when he was eight, leaving Ivan to suffer insults and neglect from the boyars at court. At age sixteen he pushed aside his hated advisers and crowned himself tsar.

After the sudden death of his wife, however, Ivan began a campaign of persecution against those he suspected of opposing him. He executed members of leading boyar families, along with their families, friends, servants, and peasants. To replace them, Ivan created a new service nobility, whose loyalty was guaranteed by their dependence on the state for land and titles.

As landlords demanded more from the serfs who survived the persecutions, growing numbers of peasants fled toward recently conquered territories to the east and south. There they joined free groups and warrior bands known as Cossacks. Ivan responded by tying serfs ever more firmly to the land. Simultaneously, he ordered that urban dwellers be bound to their towns and jobs so that he could tax them more heavily. These restrictions checked the growth of the Russian middle classes and stood in sharp contrast to economic and social developments in western Europe.

Ivan's reign was successful in defeating the remnants of Mongol power, adding vast new territories to the realm, and laying the foundations for the huge multiethnic Russian empire. In the 1550s, strengthened by an alliance with Cossack bands, he conquered the Muslim khanates of Kazan and Astrakhan and brought the fertile steppe region around the Volga River under Russian control. In the 1580s Cossacks fighting for the Russian state crossed the Ural Mountains and began the long conquest of Siberia.

Following Ivan's death, Russia entered a chaotic period known as the Time of Troubles (1598–1613). While Ivan's relatives struggled for power, the Cossacks and peasants rebelled against nobles and officials. This social explosion from below brought the nobles together. They crushed the Cossack rebellion and elected Ivan's grandnephew, Michael Romanov (r. 1613–1645), the new hereditary tsar.

Despite the turbulence of the period, the Romanov tsars, like their western European counterparts, made further achievements in territorial expansion and state-building. After a long war, Russia gained land to the west in Ukraine in 1667. By the end of the century it had completed the conquest of Siberia to the east. This vast territorial expansion brought Russian power to the Pacific Ocean

Cossacks

▶ Free groups and outlaw armies living on the borders of Russian territory from the fourteenth century onward. By the end of the sixteenth century they had formed an alliance with the Russian state.

CHAPTER LOCATOR | How did the Protestant and Catholic Reformations shape colonial expansion? | How did seventeenth-century European states overcome social and economic crisis? | How did absolutism evolve in in Spain, France, and Austria?

540 CHAPTER 18 EUROPEAN POWER AND EXPANSION

and was only checked by the powerful Qing Dynasty. The basis of Russian wealth in Siberia was furs, which the state collected by forced annual tribute payments from local peoples. Profits from furs and other natural resources, especially mining in the eighteenth century, funded expansion of the Russian bureaucracy and the army.

The growth of state power did nothing to improve the lot of the common people. In 1649 a new law code extended serfdom to all peasants in the realm, giving lords unrestricted rights over their serfs and establishing penalties for harboring runaways. The new code also removed the privileges that non-Russian elites had enjoyed within the empire and required conversion to Russian orthodoxy. Henceforth, Moscow maintained strict control of trade and administration throughout the empire.

The peace imposed by harsh Russian rule was disrupted in 1670 by a failed rebellion led by the Cossack Stenka Razin, who attracted a great army of urban poor and peasants. The ease with which Moscow crushed the rebellion testifies to the success of the Russian state in unifying and consolidating its empire.

Peter the Great and Russia's Turn to the West

Heir to his predecessors' efforts at state-building, Peter the Great (r. 1682–1725) embarked on a tremendous campaign to accelerate and complete these processes. Peter built on the service obligations of Ivan the Terrible and his successors and continued their tradition of territorial expansion. Peter's ambitions hinged on gaining access to the sea by extending Russia's borders to the Black Sea (controlled by the Ottomans) and to the Baltic Sea (dominated by Sweden).

Peter embarked on his first territorial goal by conquering the Ottoman fort of Azov in 1696 and quickly built Russia's first navy base nearby. In 1697 the tsar went on an eighteen-month tour of western European capitals. Peter was fascinated by foreign technology, and he hoped to forge an anti-Ottoman alliance to strengthen his hold on the Black Sea. Peter failed to secure a military alliance, but he did learn his lessons from the growing power of the Dutch and the English.

To realize his second goal, Peter entered the Great Northern War (1700–1721) against Sweden. After a humiliating defeat at the Battle of Narva in 1700, Peter responded with measures designed to increase state power, strengthen his military, and gain victory. He required all nobles to serve in the army or in the civil administration—for life. Peter also created schools and universities to produce skilled technicians and experts. Furthermore, he established an interlocking military-civilian bureaucracy with fourteen ranks, and he decreed that all had to start at the bottom and work toward the top. He sought talented foreigners and placed them in his service. These measures gradually combined to make the army and government more powerful and efficient.

Peter also greatly increased the service requirements of commoners. He established a regular standing army of peasant-soldiers, drafted for life. In addition, he created special regiments of Cossacks and foreign mercenaries. To fund the army, taxes on peasants increased threefold during Peter's reign. Serfs were also arbitrarily assigned to work in the growing number of factories and mines that supplied the military.

Why and how did the constitutional state triumph in England and the Dutch Republic?

How did European nations compete for trade and empire in the Americas and Asia?

How did Russian rulers build an absolutist monarchy and expand into a powerful empire?

LearningCurve
Check what you know.

541

Peter the Great

This compelling portrait by Grigory Musikiysky captures the strength and determination of the warrior-tsar in 1723, after more than three decades of personal rule. In his hand Peter holds the scepter, symbol of royal sovereignty, and across his breastplate is draped an ermine fur, a mark of honor. In the background are the battleships of Russia's new Baltic fleet and the famous St. Peter and St. Paul Fortress that Peter built in St. Petersburg. Peter the Great commissioned this magnificent new crown (left) for himself for his 1682 joint coronation with his half brother Ivan. (crown: bpk, Berlin/Kremlin Museum, Moscow, Russia/Art Resource, NY; portrait: Hermitage, St. Petersburg, Russia/The Bridgeman Art Library)

In 1709 Peter's new war machine was able to crush Sweden's army in Ukraine at Poltava (Map 18.5). Russia's victory against Sweden was conclusive in 1721, and Estonia and present-day Latvia came under Russian rule for the first time. As a result, Russia became the dominant power in the Baltic and very much a great European power.

After his victory at Poltava, Peter channeled enormous resources into building a new Western-style capital on the Baltic. The city of St. Petersburg was designed to reflect modern urban planning with wide, straight avenues; buildings set in a uniform line; and large parks. Each summer, twenty-five thousand to forty thousand peasants were sent to provide construction labor in St. Petersburg without pay.

There were other important consequences of Peter's reign. For Peter, modernization meant westernization, and both Westerners and Western ideas flowed into Russia for the first time. He required nobles to shave their heavy beards and wear Western clothing. He also required them to attend parties where young men and women would mix together and freely choose their own spouses. From these efforts a new elite class of Western-oriented Russians began to emerge.

CHAPTER LOCATOR | How did the Protestant and Catholic Reformations shape colonial expansion? | How did seventeenth-century European states overcome social and economic crisis? | How did absolutism evolve in in Spain, France, and Austria?

542   CHAPTER 18
EUROPEAN POWER AND EXPANSION

MAP 18.5 ■ The Expansion of Russia, 1462–1689

In little more than two centuries, Russia expanded from the small principality of Muscovy to an enormous multiethnic empire, stretching from the borders of western Europe through northern Asia to the Pacific.

Peter's reforms were unpopular with many Russians. For nobles, one of Peter's most detested reforms was the imposition of unigeniture—inheritance of land by one son alone. For peasants, the reign of the tsar saw a significant increase in the bonds of serfdom. Nonetheless, Peter's modernizing and westernizing of Russia paved the way for it to move somewhat closer to the European mainstream in its thought and institutions during the Enlightenment, especially under Catherine the Great (see page 568).

QUICK REVIEW

What were Peter the Great's primary goals?
How did he go about achieving them?

Why and how did the constitutional state triumph in England and the Dutch Republic?

How did European nations compete for trade and empire in the Americas and Asia?

How did Russian rulers build an absolutist monarchy and expand into a powerful empire?

✔ LearningCurve
Check what you know.

CHAPTER SUMMARY

Most parts of Europe experienced the first centuries of the early modern era as a time of crisis. Following the religious divides of the sixteenth-century Protestant and Catholic Reformations, Europeans in the seventeenth century suffered from economic stagnation, social upheaval, and renewed military conflict. Despite these obstacles, both absolutist and constitutional European states emerged from the seventeenth century with increased powers and more centralized control.

Monarchs in Spain, France, and Austria used divine right to claim they possessed absolute power and were not responsible to any representative institutions. Absolute monarchs overcame the resistance of the nobility both through military force and by affirming existing economic and social privileges. England and the Netherlands defied the general trend toward absolute monarchy, adopting distinctive forms of constitutional rule.

As Spain's power weakened in the early seventeenth century, the Netherlands, England, and France competed for access to overseas trade and territory. Mercantilist competition among these powers led to hostility and war. England emerged in the early eighteenth century with a distinct advantage over its rivals.

In Russia, Mongol conquest and rule set the stage for a harsh tsarist autocracy that was firmly in place by the time of the reign of Ivan the Terrible in the sixteenth century. The reign of Ivan and his successors saw a great expansion of Russian territory, laying the foundations for a huge multiethnic empire. Peter the Great forcibly turned Russia toward the West by adopting Western technology and culture.

 CONNECTIONS With the re-establishment of order in the second half of the century, maintaining stability was of paramount importance to European rulers. While a few nations placed their trust in constitutionally limited governments, many more were ruled by monarchs proclaiming their absolute and God-given authority. The ability to assume such power depended on cooperation from local elites, who acquiesced to state authority in exchange for privileges and payoffs. In this way, both absolutism and constitutionalism relied on political compromises forged from decades of strife.

As Spain's power weakened, other European nations bordering the Atlantic Ocean sought their own profits and glory from overseas empires. Henceforth, war among European powers would include conflicts over territories and trade in the colonies. European rulers' increased control over their own subjects thus went hand in glove with the expansion of European power in the world.

The eighteenth century was to see these power politics thrown into question by new Enlightenment aspirations for human society, which themselves derived from the inquisitive and self-confident spirit of the Scientific Revolution. These movements are explored in the next chapter. By the end of the eighteenth century demands for real popular sovereignty, colonial self-rule, and slave emancipation challenged the very bases of order so painfully achieved in the seventeenth century. Chapter 22 recounts the revolutionary movements that swept the late-eighteenth-century Atlantic world, while Chapters 25, 26, and 27 follow the story of European imperialism and the resistance of colonized peoples into the nineteenth century.

CHAPTER LOCATOR | How did the Protestant and Catholic Reformations shape colonial expansion? | How did seventeenth-century European states overcome social and economic crisis? | How did absolutism evolve in in Spain, France, and Austria?

544 CHAPTER 18 EUROPEAN POWER AND EXPANSION

Jewish Life in the Early Modern Era

What factors shaped life for European Jews in the early modern era?

Read excerpts from Glückel of Hameln's memoirs and other accounts of Jewish life, and then complete a quiz and writing assignment based on the evidence and details from this chapter. *See inside the front cover to learn more.*

| Why and how did the constitutional state triumph in England and the Dutch Republic? | How did European nations compete for trade and empire in the Americas and Asia? | How did Russian rulers build an absolutist monarchy and expand into a powerful empire? | ✔ LearningCurve Check what you know. |

545

CHAPTER 18 STUDY GUIDE

STEP 1   GET STARTED ONLINE

 LearningCurve

Now that you've read the chapter, make it stick by completing the LearningCurve activity.

STEP 2   EXPLAIN WHY IT MATTERS

Put your reading into practice. Identify each term below, and then explain why it matters in world history.

TERM	WHO OR WHAT & WHEN	WHY IT MATTERS
Protestant Reformation (p. 514)		
Jesuits (p. 517)		
moral economy (p. 520)		
Thirty Years' War (p. 520)		
sovereignty (p. 521)		
absolutism (p. 523)		
divine right of kings (p. 525)		
mercantilism (p. 527)		
constitutionalism (p. 529)		
Puritans (p. 530)		
Bill of Rights of 1689 (p. 531)		
republicanism (p. 531)		
Navigation Acts (p. 537)		
Cossacks (p. 540)		

STEP 3   MOVE BEYOND THE BASICS

To demonstrate a more advanced understanding of the growth of state power in France, Prussia, Austria, Russia, and England, fill in the chart below by describing developments in each state in four areas where seventeenth-century governments achieved new levels of control: taxation, the armed forces, bureaucracies, and the ability to compel obedience from subjects. How did the growth of the state in England differ from the growth of the state in absolutist France, Prussia, Russia, and Austria?

	Taxation	Armed Forces	Bureaucracies	Control over Subjects
France				
Prussia				
Austria				
Russia				
England				

PUT IT ALL TOGETHER Now, take a step back and try to explain the big picture. Remember to use specific examples from the chapter in your answers.

ABSOLUTIST MONARCHIES AND THE SEVENTEENTH-CENTURY CRISIS

▶ How did life for Europe's peasants change during the seventeenth century? Why was peasant life harder in eastern Europe than in western Europe?

▶ How and why did Louis XIV try to co-opt and control the French aristocracy? In practice, how "absolute" was his rule?

▶ Compare and contrast absolutism in Austria, Prussia, and Russia. What common problems and challenges did would-be absolutist rulers face in each of these three states?

CONSTITUTIONAL STATES AND THE SEVENTEENTH-CENTURY CRISIS

▶ Why did the efforts of English monarchs to build an absolutist state fail? What groups and institutions in English society were most responsible for the triumph of constitutionalism?

▶ Compare and contrast the constitutional governments of England and the Netherlands. What role did merchant elites and commercial interests play in each state?

COMPETITION FOR EMPIRE

▶ Why did northern European powers enter the competition for New World land and resources in the seventeenth century?

▶ How did England come to dominate the Atlantic economy over the course of the seventeenth century?

LOOKING BACK, LOOKING AHEAD

▶ How did the strong, centralized states of the second half of the seventeenth century differ from their fifteenth- and sixteenth-century counterparts? What new powers and responsibilities did seventeenth-century states take on?

▶ How might the state-building efforts of European powers in the seventeenth century have contributed to the acceleration of globalization that characterized the eighteenth and nineteenth centuries?

> IN YOUR OWN WORDS

Imagine that you must give an oral report to the class answering the following question: **How did European central governments consolidate and expand their power in the early modern period?** What would be the most important points and why?

19

NEW WORLDVIEWS AND WAYS OF LIFE

1540–1790

> **How and why did Europeans' understanding of the natural world and human society change in the early modern period?** Chapter 19 examines the impact of the Scientific Revolution and the Enlightenment on European life. From the mid-sixteenth century on, age-old patterns of knowledge and daily life were disrupted by a fundamental shift in the basic framework for understanding the natural world and the methods for examining it known collectively as the "Scientific Revolution." In the eighteenth century self-proclaimed members of an "Enlightenment" movement extended the use of reason from nature to human society. The expression of new ideas was encouraged by changes in the material world. During the eighteenth century ships crisscrossing the Atlantic circulated commodities, ideas, and people to all four continents bordering the ocean. As trade became more integrated and communication intensified, an Atlantic world of mixed identities and vivid debates emerged.

Free People of Color A sizable mixed-race population emerged in many European colonies in the Americas, including descendants of unions between masters and enslaved African women. The wealthiest of the free people of color, as they were called, were plantation owners with slaves of their own. (Unknown artist, *Portrait of a Young Woman*, pastel on paper, previously attributed to Jean-Etienne Liotard [1702–1789]/Saint Louis Art Museum, Missouri, USA/The Bridgeman Art Library)

> What revolutionary discoveries were made in the sixteenth and seventeenth centuries, and why did they occur in Europe?

> What intellectual and social changes occurred as a result of the Scientific Revolution?

> What new ideas about society and human relations emerged in the Enlightenment, and what new practices and institutions enabled these ideas to take hold?

> How did economic and social change and the rise of Atlantic trade interact with Enlightenment ideas?

✓ LearningCurve
After reading the chapter, use LearningCurve to retain what you've read.

What revolutionary discoveries were made in the sixteenth and seventeenth centuries, and why did they occur in Europe?

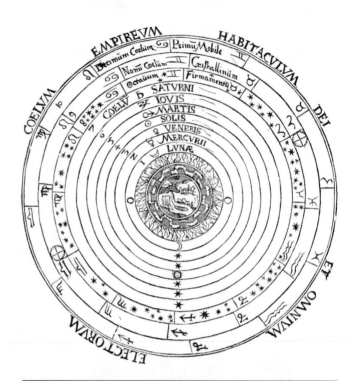

The Aristotelian Universe as Imagined in the Sixteenth Century

A round earth is at the center, surrounded by spheres of water, air, and fire. Beyond this small nucleus, the moon, the sun, and the five planets were embedded in their own rotating crystal spheres, with the stars sharing the surface of one enormous sphere. Beyond, the heavens were composed of unchanging ether. (Image Select/Art Resource, NY)

BUILDING ON DEVELOPMENTS in the Middle Ages and the Renaissance, tremendous advances in Europeans' knowledge of the natural world and techniques for establishing such knowledge took place between 1500 and 1700. Collectively known as the "Scientific Revolution," these developments were the result of many more people studying the natural world, who used new methods to answer fundamental questions about the universe and how it operated.

Why Europe?

In 1500 scientific activity flourished in many parts of the world. With the expansion of Islam into the lands of the Byzantine Empire in the seventh and eighth centuries, Muslim scholars inherited ancient Greek learning, which itself was built on centuries of borrowing from older civilizations in Egypt, Babylonia, and India. The interaction of peoples and cultures across the vast Muslim world, facilitated by religious tolerance and the common scholarly language of Arabic, was highly favorable to advances in learning.

In a great period of cultural and intellectual flourishing from 1000 to 1500, Muslim scholars thrived in cultural centers such as Baghdad and Córdoba. They established the world's first universities. In this fertile atmosphere, scholars

CHAPTER LOCATOR | **What revolutionary discoveries were made in the sixteenth and seventeenth centuries?** | What intellectual and social changes occurred as a result of the Scientific Revolution?

ca. 1500–1700 Scientific Revolution	**1762–1796** Reign of Catherine the Great of Russia
ca. 1690–1789 Enlightenment	**1765** Philosophes publish *Encyclopedia: The Rational Dictionary of the Sciences, the Arts, and the Crafts*
ca. 1700–1789 Growth of book publishing	**1780–1790** Reign of Joseph II of Austria
1720–1780 Rococo style in art and decoration	**1791** Establishment of the Pale of Settlement
1740–1786 Reign of Frederick the Great of Prussia	**1792** Establishment of mining school in Mexico City as part of reforms
ca. 1740–1789 French salons led by elite women	

surpassed the texts they had inherited in areas such as mathematics, physics, astronomy, and medicine. Arab and Persian mathematicians, for example, invented algebra, the concept of the algorithm, and decimal point notation, while Arab astronomers improved on measurements recorded in ancient works.

China was also a vital center of scientific activity, which reached a peak in the mid-fourteenth century. Among its many achievements, papermaking, gunpowder, and the use of the compass in navigation would be the most influential for the West. In Mesoamerica, civilizations such as the Maya and the Aztecs, devised complex calendar systems based on astronomical observations and developed mathematics and writing.

Given the multiple world sites of learning and scholarship, it was by no means inevitable that Europe would take the lead in scientific thought. In world history, periods of advancement produced by intense cultural interaction, such as those that occurred after the spread of Islam, are often followed by stagnation and decline during times of conflict and loss of authority. This is what happened in western Europe after the fall of the Western Roman Empire in the fifth century and in the Maya civilization after the collapse of its cultural and political centers around 900.

The re-establishment of stronger monarchies and the growth of trade in the High Middle Ages contributed to a renewal of learning in western Europe. As Europeans began to encroach on Islamic lands in Iberia, Sicily, and the eastern Mediterranean, they became aware of the rich heritage of Greek learning in these regions and the ways scholars had improved upon ancient knowledge. In the twelfth century many ancient Greek texts were translated into Latin, along with the commentaries of Arab scholars. A number of European cities created universities in which Aristotle's works dominated the curriculum.

As Europe recovered from the ravages of the Black Death in the late fourteenth and fifteenth centuries, the intellectual and cultural movement known as the Renaissance provided a crucial foundation for the Scientific Revolution. Scholars called humanists emphasized the value of acquiring knowledge for the practical purposes of life. The quest to restore the glories of the ancient past led to the rediscovery of a host of important classical texts.

What new ideas about society and human relations emerged in the Enlightenment?	How did economic and social change interact with Enlightenment ideas?	LearningCurve Check what you know.

In this period, western European universities established new professorships of mathematics, astronomy, and natural philosophy. The prestige of the new fields was low, especially mathematics, which was reserved for practical problems but not used as a tool to understand the functioning of the physical world itself. Nevertheless, these professorships eventually enabled the union of mathematics with natural philosophy that was to be a hallmark of the Scientific Revolution.

European overseas expansion in the fifteenth and sixteenth centuries provided another catalyst for new thought about the natural world. In particular, the navigational problems of long oceanic voyages in the age of expansion stimulated scientific research and invention. To help solve these problems, inventors developed many new scientific instruments. Better instruments, which permitted more accurate observations, often led to important new knowledge. Another crucial technology in this period was printing, which provided a faster and less expensive way to circulate knowledge.

Political and social conflicts were widespread in Eurasia in the sixteenth and early seventeenth centuries, but they had different results. The three large empires of the Muslim world (see Chapter 17) that arose in the wake of the Mongol Empire sought to restore order and assert legitimacy in part by imposing Islamic orthodoxy. Their failure to adopt the printing press (see page 497) can be seen as part of a wider reaction against earlier traditions of innovation. Similarly, in China after the Manchu invasion of 1644, the new Qing Dynasty legitimized its authority through stricter adherence to Confucian tradition. By contrast, western Europe remained politically fragmented into smaller competitive nations, divisions that were augmented by the religious fracturing of the Protestant Reformation. These conditions made it impossible for authorities to impose one orthodox set of ideas and thus allowed individuals to question dominant patterns of thinking.

Scientific Thought to 1550

For medieval scholars, philosophy was the path to true knowledge about the world, and its proofs consisted of the authority of ancients (as interpreted by Christian theologians) and their techniques of logical argumentation. Questions about the physical nature of the universe and how it functioned belonged to a minor branch of philosophy, called natural philosophy. Natural philosophy was based primarily on the ideas of Aristotle, the great Greek philosopher of the fourth century B.C.E. According to the Christianized version of Aristotle, a motionless earth stood at the center of the universe and was encompassed by ten separate concentric crystal spheres in which were embedded the moon, sun, planets, and stars. Beyond the spheres was Heaven with the throne of God and the souls of the saved.

Aristotle's views also dominated thinking about physics and motion on earth. Aristotle had distinguished between the world of the celestial spheres and that of the earth—the sublunar world. The sublunar realm was made up of four imperfect, changeable elements: air, fire, water, and earth. Aristotle and his followers also believed that a uniform force moved an object at a constant speed and that the object would stop as soon as that force was removed.

The work of the ancient Greek scholar Ptolemy provided the basic foundation of knowledge about the earth. Rediscovered around 1410, his *Geography* presented crucial advances on medieval cartography by representing a round earth divided into 360 degrees with the major latitude marks. However, Ptolemy's map

CHAPTER LOCATOR | What revolutionary discoveries were made in the sixteenth and seventeenth centuries? | What intellectual and social changes occurred as a result of the Scientific Revolution?

CHAPTER 19
552 NEW WORLDVIEWS AND WAYS OF LIFE

reflected the limits of ancient knowledge, showing only the continents of Europe, Africa, and Asia, with land covering three-quarters of the world.

Astronomy and Physics

The first great departure from the medieval understanding of cosmology was the work of the Polish cleric Nicolaus Copernicus (1473–1543). Without questioning the Aristotelian belief in crystal spheres, Copernicus theorized that the stars and planets, including the earth, revolved around a fixed sun. Fearing the ridicule of other astronomers, Copernicus did not publish his *On the Revolutions of the Heavenly Spheres* until 1543, the year of his death.

One astronomer who agreed with the Copernican hypothesis was the Danish astronomer Tycho Brahe (TEE-koh BRAH-hee) (1546–1601). Brahe established himself as Europe's leading astronomer with his detailed observations of a new star that appeared suddenly in 1572 and shone very brightly for almost two years. The new star, which was actually a distant exploding star, challenged the idea that the heavenly spheres were unchanging and therefore perfect. For twenty years Brahe observed the stars and planets with his naked eye in order to create new and improved tables of planetary motions.

Brahe's assistant, Johannes Kepler (1571–1630), used Brahe's data to develop three revolutionary laws of planetary motion. First, he demonstrated that the orbits of the planets around the sun are elliptical rather than circular. Second, he demonstrated that the planets do not move at a uniform speed in their orbits. When a planet is close to the sun it accelerates, and it slows as it moves farther away from the sun. Finally, Kepler's third law stated that the time a planet takes to make its complete orbit is precisely related to its distance from the sun. Kepler's contribution was monumental. Whereas Copernicus had speculated, Kepler used mathematics to prove the precise relations of a sun-centered (solar) system.

While Kepler was unraveling planetary motion, a young Florentine named Galileo Galilei (1564–1642) was challenging Aristotelian ideas about motion on earth. Galileo focused on deficiencies in Aristotle's theories of motion. He measured the movement of a rolling ball across a surface, repeating the action again and again to verify his results. In his famous acceleration experiment, he showed that a uniform force—in this case, gravity—produced a uniform acceleration. Through another experiment, he formulated the law of inertia. He found that rest was not the natural state of objects. Rather, an object continues in motion forever unless stopped by some external force. His discoveries proved Aristotelian physics wrong.

On hearing details about the invention of the telescope in Holland, Galileo made one for himself in 1609. He quickly discovered the first four moons of Jupiter, which clearly demonstrated that Jupiter could not possibly be embedded in an impenetrable crystal sphere as Aristotle and Ptolemy maintained. This discovery provided concrete evidence for the Copernican theory.

Newton's Synthesis

By about 1640 the work of Brahe, Kepler, and Galileo had been largely accepted by the scientific community despite opposition from religious leaders (see page 559). But the new findings failed to explain what forces controlled the movement of the planets and objects on earth. That challenge was taken up by English scientist Isaac Newton (1642–1727).

Copernican hypothesis
▶ The idea that the sun, not the earth, was the center of the universe.

law of inertia
▶ A law formulated by Galileo stating that motion, not rest, is the natural state of an object and that an object continues in motion forever unless stopped by some external force.

What new ideas about society and human relations emerged in the Enlightenment?

How did economic and social change interact with Enlightenment ideas?

 LearningCurve
Check what you know.

Newton arrived at some of his most basic ideas about physics in 1666 at age twenty-four but was unable to prove them mathematically. In 1684, after years of studying optics, Newton returned to physics for eighteen intensive months. The result was his towering accomplishment, a single explanatory system that integrated the astronomy of Copernicus, as corrected by Kepler's laws, with the physics of Galileo and his predecessors. Newton did this through a set of mathematical laws that explain motion and mechanics. These laws were published in 1687 in Newton's *Mathematical Principles of Natural Philosophy* (also known as the *Principia*).

The key feature of the Newtonian synthesis was the **law of universal gravitation**. According to this law, each body in the universe attracts every other body in a precise mathematical relationship, whereby the force of attraction is proportional to the quantity of matter of the objects and inversely proportional to the square of the distance between them. The whole universe was unified in one majestic system. Matter moved on earth and throughout the heavens according to the same laws, which could be understood and expressed in mathematical terms.

law of universal gravitation

▶ Newton's law that all objects are attracted to one another and that the force of attraction is proportional to the object's quantity of matter and inversely proportional to the square of the distance between them.

Natural History and Empire

At the same time that they made advances in astronomy and physics, Europeans embarked on the pursuit of knowledge about unknown geographical regions. Because they were the first to acquire a large overseas empire, the Spanish pioneered these efforts. The Spanish crown sponsored many scientific expeditions to gather information and specimens, out of which emerged new discoveries that reshaped the fields of botany, zoology, cartography, and metallurgy, among others.

Plants were a particular source of interest because they offered tremendous profits in the form of spices, medicines, dyes, and cash crops. King Philip II of Spain sent his personal physician, Francisco Hernández, to New Spain for seven years in the 1560s. Hernández filled fifteen volumes with illustrations of three

CHAPTER LOCATOR | What revolutionary discoveries were made in the sixteenth and seventeenth centuries? | What intellectual and social changes occurred as a result of the Scientific Revolution?

CHAPTER 19
554 NEW WORLDVIEWS AND WAYS OF LIFE

thousand plants previously unknown in Europe. He interviewed local healers about the plants' medicinal properties, thereby benefiting from centuries of Meso-american botanical knowledge.

Other countries followed the Spanish example as their global empires expanded, relying both on official expeditions and the private initiative of merchants, missionaries, and settlers. The stream of new information about plant and animal species overwhelmed existing intellectual frameworks. Carl Linnaeus (1707–1778) of Sweden sent his students on exploratory voyages around the world and, based on their observations and the specimens they collected, devised a system of naming and classifying living organisms still used today (with substantial revisions).

Magic and Alchemy

Recent historical research on the Scientific Revolution has focused on the contribution of ideas and practices that no longer belong to the realm of science, such as astrology and alchemy. Many of the most celebrated astronomers were also astrologers. Used as a diagnostic tool in medicine, astrology formed a regular part of the curriculum of medical schools.

Centuries-old practices of magic and alchemy also remained important traditions for natural philosophers. Early modern practitioners of magic strove to understand and control hidden connections they perceived among different elements of the natural world, such as that between a magnet and iron. The idea that objects possessed hidden or "occult" qualities that allowed them to affect other objects was a particularly important legacy of the magical tradition.

Johannes Kepler exemplifies the interaction among these different strands of interest in the natural world. His duties as court mathematician included casting horoscopes for the royal family, and he based his own life on astrological principles. He also wrote at length on cosmic harmonies and explained elliptical motion through ideas about the beautiful music created by the combined motion of the planets. Another example of the interweaving of ideas and beliefs is Sir Isaac Newton, who was both intensely religious and also fascinated by alchemy, whose practitioners believed (among other things) that base metals could be turned into gold.

QUICK REVIEW

In what ways did the work of Isaac Newton represent the culmination of the Scientific Revolution?

What new ideas about society and human relations emerged in the Enlightenment?

How did economic and social change interact with Enlightenment ideas?

LearningCurve
Check what you know.

What intellectual and social changes occurred as a result of the Scientific Revolution?

Frontispiece to *De Humani Corporis Fabrica* (*On the Structure of the Human Body*)

The frontispiece to Vesalius's pioneering work, published in 1543, shows him dissecting a corpse before a crowd of students. This was a revolutionary new hands-on approach for physicians, who usually worked from a theoretical, rather than a practical, understanding of the body. Based on direct observation, Vesalius replaced ancient ideas drawn from Greek philosophy with a much more accurate account of the structure and function of the body. (© SSPL/Science Museum/The Image Works)

THE SCIENTIFIC REVOLUTION was not accomplished by a handful of brilliant individuals working alone. Advancements occurred in many fields as scholars developed new methods to seek answers to long-standing problems with the collaboration and assistance of skilled craftsmen who invented new instruments and helped conduct experiments. These results circulated in an international intellectual community from which women were usually excluded.

The Methods of Science

The English politician and writer Francis Bacon (1561–1626) was the greatest early propagandist for the experimental method. Rejecting the Aristotelian and medieval method of using speculative reasoning to build general theories, Bacon

CHAPTER LOCATOR | What revolutionary discoveries were made in the sixteenth and seventeenth centuries? | **What intellectual and social changes occurred as a result of the Scientific Revolution?**

CHAPTER 19
556 NEW WORLDVIEWS AND WAYS OF LIFE

argued that new knowledge had to be pursued through empirical research. The researcher who wants to learn more about leaves or rocks, for example, should not speculate about the subject but should rather collect a multitude of specimens and then compare and analyze them to derive general principles. Bacon's contribution was to formalize the empirical method, which had already been used by Brahe and Galileo, into the general theory of inductive reasoning known as empiricism.

On the continent more speculative methods retained support. In 1619 the French philosopher René Descartes (day-KAHRT) (1596–1650) experienced a life-changing intellectual vision. Descartes saw that there was a perfect correspondence between geometry and algebra and that geometrical spatial figures could be expressed as algebraic equations and vice versa. A major step forward in mathematics, Descartes's discovery of analytic geometry provided scientists with an important new tool.

Descartes used mathematics to elaborate a highly influential vision of the workings of the cosmos. Drawing on ancient Greek atomist philosophies, Descartes developed the idea that matter was made up of identical "corpuscules"

MAJOR CONTRIBUTORS TO THE SCIENTIFIC REVOLUTION

Nicolaus Copernicus (1473–1543)	Published *On the Revolutions of the Heavenly Spheres* (1543); theorized that the sun, rather than the earth, was the center of the galaxy
Paracelsus (1493–1541)	Pioneered the use of chemicals and drugs to address perceived chemical imbalances
Andreas Vesalius (1514–1564)	Published *On the Structure of the Human Body* (1543)
Tycho Brahe (1546–1601)	Built observatories and compiled data for the *Rudolphine Tables*, a new table of planetary data
Francis Bacon (1561–1626)	Advocated experimental method, formalizing theory of inductive reasoning known as empiricism
Galileo Galilei (1564–1642)	Used telescopic observation to provide evidence for Copernican hypothesis; experimented to formulate laws of physics, such as inertia
Johannes Kepler (1571–1630)	Used Brahe's data to mathematically prove the Copernican hypothesis; his new laws of planetary motion united for the first time natural philosophy and mathematics; completed the *Rudolphine Tables* in 1627
William Harvey (1578–1657)	Discovered blood circulation (1628)
René Descartes (1596–1650)	Used deductive reasoning to formulate theory of Cartesian dualism
Robert Boyle (1627–1691)	Founded the modern science of chemistry; created the first vacuum; discovered Boyle's law on the properties of gases
Isaac Newton (1642–1727)	Introduced the law of universal gravitation, synthesizing the theories of Copernicus and Galileo

What new ideas about society and human relations emerged in the Enlightenment?

How did economic and social change interact with Enlightenment ideas?

☑ LearningCurve
Check what you know.

557

(tiny particles) that collided together in an endless series of motions, akin to the working of a machine. All occurrences in nature could be analyzed as matter in motion, and, according to Descartes, the total "quantity of motion" in the universe was constant. Descartes's mechanistic philosophy of the universe depended on the idea that a vacuum was impossible, which meant that every action had an equal reaction, continuing in an eternal chain reaction.

Descartes's greatest achievement was to develop his initial vision into a whole philosophy of knowledge and science. When experiments proved that sensory impressions could be wrong, Descartes decided it was necessary to doubt them and everything that could reasonably be doubted, and then, as in geometry, to use deductive reasoning from self-evident truths, which he called "first principles," to ascertain scientific laws. Descartes's reasoning ultimately reduced all substances to "matter" and "mind"—that is, to the physical and the spiritual. His view of the world as consisting of two fundamental entities is known as Cartesian dualism.

Both Bacon's inductive experimentalism and Descartes's deductive mathematical reasoning had flaws. Bacon's inability to appreciate the importance of mathematics and his obsession with practical results illustrated the limitations of antitheoretical empiricism. Likewise, some of Descartes's positions demonstrated the inadequacy of rigid, dogmatic rationalism. He believed, for example, that it was possible to deduce the whole science of medicine from first principles. Although insufficient on their own, Bacon's and Descartes's extreme approaches are combined in the modern scientific method, which began to crystallize in the late seventeenth century.

Medicine, the Body, and Chemistry

The Scientific Revolution, which began with the study of the cosmos, soon transformed understanding of the human body. For many centuries the ancient Greek physician Galen's explanation of the body carried the same authority as Aristotle's account of the universe. According to Galen, the body contained four humors: blood, phlegm, black bile, and yellow bile. Illness was believed to result from an imbalance of these humors.

Swiss physician and alchemist Paracelsus (1493–1541) was an early proponent of the experimental method in medicine and pioneered the use of chemicals and drugs to address what he saw as chemical, rather than humoral, imbalances. Another experimentalist, Flemish physician Andreas Vesalius (1514–1564), studied anatomy by dissecting human bodies. In 1543, Vesalius issued *On the Structure of the Human Body*. Its two hundred precise drawings revolutionized the understanding of human anatomy, disproving Galen. The experimental approach also led English royal physician William Harvey (1578–1657) to discover the circulation of blood through the veins and arteries in 1628.

The work of Irishman Robert Boyle (1627–1691) led to the development of modern chemistry. Following Paracelsus's lead, he undertook experiments to discover the basic elements of nature, which he believed was composed of infinitely small atoms. Boyle was the first to create a vacuum, thus disproving Descartes's belief that a vacuum could not exist in nature, and he discovered Boyle's law (1662), which states that the pressure of a gas varies inversely with volume.

CHAPTER LOCATOR | What revolutionary discoveries were made in the sixteenth and seventeenth centuries? | **What intellectual and social changes occurred as a result of the Scientific Revolution?**

CHAPTER 19
558 NEW WORLDVIEWS AND WAYS OF LIFE

Science and Religion

It is sometimes assumed that the relationship between science and religion is fundamentally hostile and that the pursuit of knowledge based on reason and proof is incompatible with faith. Yet during the Scientific Revolution most practitioners were devoutly religious and saw their work as contributing to the celebration of God's glory. However, the concept of heliocentrism, which displaced the earth from the center of the universe, threatened the understanding of the place of mankind in creation as stated in Genesis. All religions derived from the Old Testament thus faced difficulties accepting the Copernican system. The Catholic Church was initially less hostile than Protestant and Jewish religious leaders, but in the first decades of the sixteenth century its attitude changed. In 1616 the Holy Office placed the works of Copernicus and his supporters, including Kepler, on a list of books Catholics were forbidden to read.

Out of caution Galileo Galilei silenced his views on heliocentrism for several years, until 1623 saw the ascension of Pope Urban VIII, a man sympathetic to the new science. However, Galileo's 1632 *Dialogue on the Two Chief Systems of the World* went too far. Published in Italian and widely read, it openly lampooned the Aristotelian view and defended Copernicus. In 1633 Galileo was tried for heresy by the papal Inquisition. Imprisoned and threatened with torture, the aging Galileo recanted.

Science and Society

The rise of modern science had many consequences. First, it led to the rise of a new and expanding social group— the international scientific community. Members of this community were linked together by common interests and values as well as by journals and scientific societies. The personal success of scientists and scholars depended on making new discoveries, and as a result science became competitive. Second, as governments intervened to support and sometimes direct research, the new scientific community became closely tied to the state and its agendas. National academies of science were created under state sponsorship in London in 1662, Paris in 1666, Berlin in 1700, and later across Europe.

It was long believed that the Scientific Revolution was the work of exceptional geniuses. More recently, historians have emphasized the importance of skilled craftsmen in the rise of science, particularly in the

Popularizing Science

The frontispiece illustration of Fontenelle's *Conversations on the Plurality of Worlds* (1686) invites the reader to share the pleasures of astronomy with an elegant lady and an entertaining teacher. The drawing shows the planets revolving around the sun. (© Roger-Viollet/ The Image Works)

What new ideas about society and human relations emerged in the Enlightenment?	How did economic and social change interact with Enlightenment ideas?	✓ LearningCurve Check what you know.

development of the experimental method. Many artisans developed a strong interest in emerging scientific ideas, and, in turn, the practice of science in the seventeenth century relied heavily on artisans' expertise in making instruments and conducting precise experiments.

Some things did not change in the Scientific Revolution. For example, scholars willing to challenge received ideas about the natural universe did not question traditional inequalities between the sexes. Instead, the emergence of professional science may have worsened the inequality in some ways. When Renaissance courts served as centers of learning, talented noblewomen could find niches in study and research. But the rise of a scientific community raised barriers for women because the universities and academies that furnished professional credentials refused them entry.

There were, however, a number of noteworthy exceptions. In Italy universities and academies did accept women. Across Europe women worked as makers of wax anatomical models and as botanical and zoological illustrators. They were also very much involved in informal scientific communities, attending salons (see page 575), conducting experiments, and writing learned treatises.

> **QUICK REVIEW**

What contributions did Francis Bacon and René Descartes make to the development of the scientific method?

CHAPTER LOCATOR | What revolutionary discoveries were made in the sixteenth and seventeenth centuries? | What intellectual and social changes occurred as a result of the Scientific Revolution?

CHAPTER 19
560 NEW WORLDVIEWS AND WAYS OF LIFE

The French philosopher Voltaire is depicted here with his long-time companion, writer and mathematician Gabrielle-Emilie Le Tonnelier de Breteuil, marquise du Châtelet. (Château de Breteuil/Gianni Dagli Orti/ The Art Archive at Art Resource, NY)

What new ideas about society and human relations emerged in the Enlightenment, and what new practices and institutions enabled these ideas to take hold?

THE POLITICAL, INTELLECTUAL, AND religious developments of the early modern period that gave rise to the Scientific Revolution further contributed to a series of debates about key issues in eighteenth-century Europe and the wider world that came to be known as the Enlightenment. Proponents of the Enlightenment came to believe that answers to all social, political, and economic questions could be found through observation and the use of reason. Progress was possible in human society as well as science.

Enlightenment

▶ An intellectual and cultural movement in late seventeenth- and eighteenth-century Europe and its colonies that used rational and critical thinking to debate issues such as political sovereignty, religious tolerance, gender roles, and racial difference.

The Early Enlightenment

Loosely united by certain key questions and ideas, the European Enlightenment (ca. 1690–1789) was a broad intellectual and cultural movement that gained strength gradually and did not reach its maturity until about 1750. Its origins in the late seventeenth century lie in a combination of developments, including political opposition to absolutist rule, religious conflicts between Protestants

What new ideas about society and human relations emerged in the Enlightenment?	How did economic and social change interact with Enlightenment ideas?	☑ LearningCurve Check what you know.

- **The Reformation:** By shattering the unity of Western Christendom, the conflicts of the Reformation brought old religious certainties into question
- **Political Centralization:** The growing power of the state inspired questions about political sovereignty and its limits
- **Globalization:** Increased movement of peoples, goods, and ideas within and among the states of Asia, Africa, Europe, and its colonies offered examples of shockingly different ways of life and values
- **The Scientific Revolution:** The achievements of the Scientific Revolution inspired intellectuals to believe that scientific methods could be applied to human societies

and Catholics and within Protestantism, and the attempt to apply principles and practices from the Scientific Revolution to human society.

A key crucible for Enlightenment thought was the Dutch Republic, with its proud commitments to religious tolerance and republican rule. When Louis XIV demanded that all Protestants convert to Catholicism, many Huguenots fled the country and resettled in the Dutch Republic. From this haven of tolerance, French Huguenots and their supporters began to publish tracts denouncing religious intolerance and suggesting that only a despotic monarch would deny religious freedom. Their challenge to authority thus combined religious and political issues.

These dual concerns drove the career of one important early Enlightenment writer, Pierre Bayle (1647–1706), a Huguenot who took refuge from government persecution in the Dutch Republic. Bayle critically examined the religious beliefs and persecutions of the past in his *Historical and Critical Dictionary* (1697). Demonstrating that human beliefs had been extremely varied and very often mistaken, he concluded that nothing can ever be known beyond all doubt, a view known as skepticism.

The Dutch Jewish philosopher Baruch Spinoza (1632–1677) was a key figure in the transition from the Scientific Revolution to the Enlightenment. Deeply inspired by advances in the Scientific Revolution Spinoza sought to apply natural philosophy to thinking about human society. He borrowed Descartes's emphasis on rationalism and his methods of deductive reasoning but rejected the French thinker's mind-body dualism. Instead Spinoza came to espouse monism, the idea that mind and body are united in one substance and that God and nature were merely two names for the same thing. He envisioned a deterministic universe in which good and evil were merely relative values, and human actions were shaped by outside circumstances, not free will.

German philosopher and mathematician Gottfried Wilhelm von Leibniz (1646–1716), who had developed calculus independently of Isaac Newton, refuted both Cartesian dualism and Spinoza's monism. Instead he adopted the idea of an infinite number of substances, or "monads," from which all matter is composed according to a harmonious divine plan.

Out of this period of intellectual turmoil came John Locke's *Essay Concerning Human Understanding* (1690), perhaps the most important text of the early Enlightenment. In this work Locke (1632–1704) set forth a new theory about how human beings learn and form their ideas. Whereas Descartes based his deductive logic on the conviction that certain first principles, or innate ideas, are imbued

CHAPTER LOCATOR | What revolutionary discoveries were made in the sixteenth and seventeenth centuries? | What intellectual and social changes occurred as a result of the Scientific Revolution?

CHAPTER 19
562 NEW WORLDVIEWS AND WAYS OF LIFE

in humans by God, Locke insisted that all ideas are derived from experience. According to Locke, the human mind at birth is like a blank tablet, or tabula rasa, on which understanding and beliefs are inscribed by experience. Human development is therefore determined by external forces, like education and social institutions, not innate characteristics. Locke's essay contributed to the theory of sensationalism, the idea that all human ideas and thoughts are produced as a result of sensory impressions.

The Influence of the Philosophes

Divergences among the early thinkers of the Enlightenment show that, while they shared many of the same premises and questions, the answers they found differed widely. The spread of this spirit of inquiry and debate owed a great deal to the work of the philosophes, a group of influential French intellectuals.

To appeal to the public and get around the censors, the philosophes wrote novels and plays, histories and philosophies, and dictionaries and encyclopedias, all filled with satire and double meanings to spread their message. One of the greatest philosophes, the baron de Montesquieu (mahn-tuhs-KYOO) (1689–1755) pioneered this approach in *The Persian Letters* (1721). This work consists of letters supposedly written by two Persian travelers, Usbek and Rica, who as outsiders see European customs in unique ways and thereby allow Montesquieu a vantage point for criticizing existing practices and beliefs.

Disturbed by the growth in royal power under Louis XIV and inspired by the example of the physical sciences, Montesquieu set out to apply the critical method to the problem of government in *The Spirit of Laws* (1748). Arguing that forms of governments were shaped by history, geography, and customs, Montesquieu identified three main types: monarchies, republics, and despotisms. A great admirer of the English parliamentary system, Montesquieu argued for a separation of powers, with political power divided among different classes and legal estates holding unequal rights and privileges. Decades later, his theory of separation of powers had a great impact on the constitutions of the United States in 1789 and of France in 1791.

The most famous philosophe was François-Marie Arouet, known by the pen name Voltaire (1694–1778). Early in his career he was arrested twice for insulting noblemen. To avoid a prison term, Voltaire moved to England for three years, and there he came to share Montesquieu's enthusiasm for English liberties and institutions.

Returning to France, Voltaire met Gabrielle-Emilie Le Tonnelier de Breteuil, marquise du Châtelet (1706–1749), a gifted noblewoman. Madame du Châtelet invited Voltaire to live in her country house at Cirey in Lorraine. Passionate about science, she studied physics and mathematics and published the first French translation of Newton's *Principia*.

While living at Cirey, Voltaire wrote works praising England and popularizing English scientific progress. Yet, like almost all the philosophes, Voltaire was a reformer, not a revolutionary. He pessimistically concluded that the best form of government was a good monarch, since human beings "are very rarely worthy to govern themselves." Nor did Voltaire believe in social and economic equality. The only realizable equality, Voltaire thought, was that "by which the citizen

sensationalism
▶ An idea, espoused by John Locke, that all human ideas and thoughts are produced as a result of sensory impressions.

philosophes
▶ A group of French intellectuals who proclaimed that they were bringing the light of knowledge to their fellow creatures in the Age of Enlightenment.

What new ideas about society and human relations emerged in the Enlightenment?

How did economic and social change interact with Enlightenment ideas?

LearningCurve
Check what you know.

only depends on the laws which protect the freedom of the feeble against the ambitions of the strong."[1]

Voltaire's philosophical and religious positions were much more radical. Voltaire believed in God, but he rejected Catholicism in favor of **deism**, belief in a distant, noninterventionist deity. Above all, Voltaire and most of the philosophes hated religious intolerance, which they believed led to fanaticism and cruelty.

The strength of the philosophes lay in their number, dedication, and organization. Their greatest achievement was a group effort—the seventeen-volume *Encyclopedia: The Rational Dictionary of the Sciences, the Arts, and the Crafts*, edited by Denis Diderot (1713–1784) and Jean le Rond d'Alembert (1717–1783). Completed in 1765 despite opposition from the French state and the Catholic Church, the *Encyclopedia* contained hundreds of thousands of articles by leading scientists, writers, skilled workers, and progressive priests. Science and the industrial arts were exalted, religion and immortality questioned. Intolerance, legal injustice, and out-of-date social institutions were openly criticized.

After about 1770 a number of thinkers and writers began to attack the philosophes' faith in reason and progress. The most famous of these was the Swiss intellectual Jean-Jacques Rousseau (1712–1778). Like other Enlightenment think-

deism

▶ Belief in a distant, noninterventionist deity, shared by many Enlightenment thinkers.

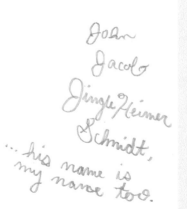

John Jacolo Jingle Heimer Schmidt, ...his name is my name too.

MAJOR FIGURES OF THE ENLIGHTENMENT

Baruch Spinoza (1632–1677)	Early Enlightenment thinker excommunicated from the Jewish community for his concept of a deterministic universe
John Locke (1632–1704)	*Essay Concerning Human Understanding* (1690)
Gottfried Wilhelm von Leibniz (1646–1716)	Early German rational philosopher and scientist
Pierre Bayle (1647–1706)	*Historical and Critical Dictionary* (1697)
Montesquieu (1689–1755)	*The Persian Letters* (1721); *The Spirit of Laws* (1748)
Voltaire (1694–1778)	Renowned French philosopher and author of more than seventy works
Gabrielle-Emilie Le Tonnelier de Breteuil, marquise du Châtelet (1706–1749)	French scholar and supporter of equal education for women
David Hume (1711–1776)	Central figure of the Scottish Enlightenment
Jean-Jacques Rousseau (1712–1778)	*The Social Contract* (1762)
Denis Diderot (1713–1784) and Jean le Rond d'Alembert (1717–1783)	Editors of *Encyclopedia: The Rational Dictionary of the Sciences, the Arts, and the Crafts* (1765)
Adam Smith (1723–1790)	Pioneering political economist and author of *An Inquiry into the Nature and Causes of the Wealth of Nations* (1776)
Immanuel Kant (1724–1804)	*What Is Enlightenment?* (1784); *On the Different Races of Man* (1775)

CHAPTER LOCATOR | What revolutionary discoveries were made in the sixteenth and seventeenth centuries? | What intellectual and social changes occurred as a result of the Scientific Revolution?

CHAPTER 19

564 NEW WORLDVIEWS AND WAYS OF LIFE

ers, Rousseau was passionately committed to individual freedom. Unlike them, however, he attacked rationalism and civilization as destroying, rather than liberating, the individual. Warm, spontaneous feeling, Rousseau believed, had to complement and correct cold intellect. Rousseau's ideals greatly influenced the early romantic movement, which rebelled against the culture of the Enlightenment in the late eighteenth century.

Rousseau also called for a rigid division of gender roles, arguing that women and men were radically different beings. According to Rousseau, because women were destined by nature to assume a passive role in sexual relations, they should also be passive in social life and devote themselves to taking care of their husbands and children. Additionally, he believed that women's love for displaying themselves in public, attending salons, and pulling the strings of power was unnatural and had a corrupting effect on both politics and society.

Rousseau's contribution to political theory in *The Social Contract* (1762) was based on two fundamental concepts: the general will and popular sovereignty. According to Rousseau, the general will is sacred and absolute, reflecting the common interests of all people, who have displaced the monarch as the holder of sovereign power. The general will is not necessarily the will of the majority, however. At times the general will may be the authentic, long-term needs of the people as correctly interpreted by a farseeing minority.

general will

▶ A concept associated with Rousseau, referring to the common interests of all the people, who have replaced the power of the monarch.

Cultural Contacts and Race

The Scientific Revolution and the political and religious conflicts of the late seventeenth century were not the only developments that influenced European thinkers. Europeans' increased interactions with non-European peoples and cultures also helped produce the Enlightenment spirit. In the wake of the great discoveries of the fifteenth and sixteenth centuries, the rapidly growing travel literature taught Europeans that the peoples of China, India, Africa, and the Americas had very different beliefs and customs. Educated Europeans began to look at truth and morality in relative, rather than absolute, terms.

The powerful and advanced nations of Asia were obvious sources of comparison with the West. During the eighteenth century Enlightenment opinion on China was divided. Voltaire and some other philosophes revered China — without ever visiting or seriously studying it — as an ancient culture replete with wisdom and learning, ruled by benevolent absolutist monarchs. They enthusiastically embraced Confucianism as a natural religion in which universal moral truths were uncovered by reason. By contrast, Montesquieu and Diderot criticized China as a despotic land ruled by fear.

Attitudes toward Islam and the Muslim world were similarly mixed. As the Ottoman military threat receded at the end of the seventeenth century, some Enlightenment thinkers assessed Islam favorably. Others, including Spinoza, saw Islamic culture as superstitious and favorable to despotism. In most cases, writing about Islam and Muslim cultures served primarily as a means to reflect on Western values and practices.

One writer with considerable personal experience in a Muslim country was Lady Mary Wortley Montagu, wife of the English ambassador to the Ottoman Empire. Her letters challenged prevailing ideas by depicting Turkish people as

What new ideas about society and human relations emerged in the Enlightenment?	How did economic and social change interact with Enlightenment ideas?	✔ LearningCurve Check what you know.

sympathetic and civilized. Montagu also disputed the notion that women were oppressed in Ottoman society.

Apart from debates about Asian and Muslim lands, the "discovery" of the New World and subsequent explorations in the Pacific Ocean also destabilized existing norms and values in Europe. One popular idea, among Rousseau and others, was that indigenous peoples of the Americas were living examples of "natural man," who embodied the essential goodness of humanity uncorrupted by decadent society.

As scientists developed taxonomies of plant and animal species in response to discoveries in the Americas, they also began to classify humans into hierarchically ordered "races" and to speculate on the origins of such races. The French naturalist Georges-Louis Leclerc, comte de Buffon (1707–1788), argued that humans originated with one species that then developed into distinct races due largely to climatic conditions.

Using the word *race* to designate biologically distinct groups of humans was new in European thought. Previously, Europeans had grouped other peoples into "nations" based on their historical, political, and cultural affiliations, rather than on supposedly innate physical differences. Unsurprisingly, when thinkers drew up a hierarchical classification of human species, their own "race" was placed at the top. Europeans had long believed they were culturally superior. The new idea that racial difference was physical and innate rather than cultural taught them they were biologically superior as well. In turn, scientific racism helped legitimate and justify the tremendous growth of slavery that occurred during the eighteenth century by depicting Africans as belonging to a biologically inferior race that was naturally fit for enslavement.

Racist ideas did not go unchallenged. The abbé Raynal's *History of the Two Indies* (1770) fiercely attacked slavery and the abuses of European colonization. *Encyclopedia* editor Denis Diderot adopted Montesquieu's technique of criticizing European attitudes through the voice of outsiders in his dialogue between Tahitian villagers and their European visitors. Former slaves, like Olaudah Equiano (see Chapter 20) and Ottobah Cugoana published eloquent memoirs testifying to the horrors of slavery and the innate equality of all humans. These challenges to racism, however, were in the minority. More often, Enlightenment thinkers, Thomas Jefferson among them, supported racial inequality.

The International Enlightenment

The Enlightenment was a movement of international dimensions, with thinkers traversing borders in a constant exchange of visits, letters, and printed materials. The Republic of Letters, as this international group of scholars and writers was called, was a truly cosmopolitan set of networks stretching from western Europe to its colonies in the Americas, to Russia and eastern Europe, and along the routes of trade and empire to Africa and Asia.

Within this broad international conversation, scholars have identified regional and national particularities. Outside of France, many strains of Enlightenment thought sought to reconcile reason with faith, rather than emphasizing the errors of religious fanaticism and intolerance. Some scholars point to a distinctive "Catholic Enlightenment" that aimed to renew and reform the church from within, looking to divine grace rather than human will as the source of social progress.

CHAPTER LOCATOR | What revolutionary discoveries were made in the sixteenth and seventeenth centuries? | What intellectual and social changes occurred as a result of the Scientific Revolution?

CHAPTER 19
566 NEW WORLDVIEWS AND WAYS OF LIFE

An actor performs the first reading of a new play by Voltaire at the salon of Madame Geoffrin in this painting from 1755. Voltaire, then in exile, is represented by a bust statue. (Painting by Gabriel Lemonnier [1743–1824], oil on canvas/De Agonstini Picture Library/Gianni Dagli Orti/The Bridgeman Art Library)

> PICTURING THE PAST

ANALYZING THE IMAGE: Which of these people do you think is the hostess, Madame Geoffrin, and why? Using details from the painting to support your answer, how would you describe the status of the people shown?
CONNECTIONS: What does this image suggest about the reach of Enlightenment ideas to common people? To women? Does the painting of the bookstore on page 572 suggest a broader reach? Why?

The Scottish Enlightenment, centered in Edinburgh, was marked by an emphasis on common sense and scientific reasoning. A central figure in Edinburgh was David Hume (1711–1776). Building on Locke's writings on learning, Hume argued that the human mind is really nothing but a bundle of impressions. These impressions originate only in sensory experiences and our habits of joining these experiences together. Since our ideas ultimately reflect only our sensory experiences, our reason cannot tell us anything about questions that cannot be verified by sensory experience (in the form of controlled experiments or mathematics), such as the origin of the universe or the existence of God. Hume further argued, in opposition to Descartes, that reason alone could not supply moral principles but that they derived instead from emotions and desires, such as feelings of approval or shame. Hume's rationalistic inquiry thus ended up undermining the Enlightenment's faith in the power of reason by emphasizing the superiority of the passions over reason in driving human behavior.

What new ideas about society and human relations emerged in the Enlightenment?	How did economic and social change interact with Enlightenment ideas?	✓ LearningCurve Check what you know.

Hume's ideas had a formative influence on another major figure of the Scottish Enlightenment, Adam Smith (1723–1790). In his *Theory of Moral Sentiments* (1759), Smith argued that social interaction produced feelings of mutual sympathy that led people to behave in ethical ways, despite inherent tendencies toward self-interest. Smith believed that the thriving commercial life of the eighteenth century was likely to produce civic virtue through the values of competition, fair play, and individual autonomy. In *An Inquiry into the Nature and Causes of the Wealth of Nations* (1776), Smith attacked the laws and regulations created by mercantilist governments that, he argued, prevented commerce from reaching its full capacity (see Chapter 18). For Smith, ordinary people were capable of forming correct judgments based on their own experience and should therefore not be hampered by government regulations. Smith's economic liberalism became the dominant form of economic thought in the early nineteenth century.

Inspired by philosophers of moral sentiments, like Hume and Smith, as well as by physiological studies of the role of the nervous system in human perception, the celebration of sensibility became an important element of eighteenth-century culture. Sensibility referred to an acute sensitivity of the nerves and brains to outside stimulus that produced strong emotional and physical reactions. Novels, plays, and other literary genres depicted moral and aesthetic sensibility as a particular characteristic of women and the upper classes. The proper relationship between reason and the emotions became a key question.

After 1760 Enlightenment ideas were hotly debated in the German-speaking states, often in dialogue with Christian theology. Immanuel Kant (1724–1804) was the greatest German philosopher of his day. Kant posed the question of the age when he published a pamphlet in 1784 titled *What Is Enlightenment?* He answered, "*Sapere Aude* (dare to know)! 'Have the courage to use your own understanding' is therefore the motto of enlightenment." He argued that if intellectuals were granted the freedom to exercise their reason publicly in print, enlightenment would surely follow. Kant was no revolutionary; he also insisted that in their private lives, individuals must obey all laws, no matter how unreasonable. Like other Enlightenment figures in central and east-central Europe, Kant thus tried to reconcile absolutism and religious faith with a critical public sphere.

Important developments in Enlightenment thought also took place in the Italian peninsula. After achieving independence from Habsburg rule (1734), the kingdom of Naples entered a period of intellectual flourishing. In northern Italy a central figure was Cesare Beccaria (1738–1794). His *On Crimes and Punishments* (1764) was a passionate plea for reform of the penal system that decried the use of torture, arbitrary imprisonment, and capital punishment and advocated the prevention of crime over its punishment.

Enlightened Absolutism and Its Limits

Some absolutist rulers tried to reform their governments in accordance with Enlightenment ideals. The result was what historians have called the enlightened absolutism of the later eighteenth century. (Similar programs of reform in France and Spain will be discussed in Chapter 22.) Influenced by the philosophes, Frederick II (r. 1740–1786) of Prussia, known as Frederick the Great, and Catherine the Great of Russia (r. 1762–1796) set out to rule in an enlightened manner. Frederick promoted religious tolerance and free speech and improved the educational system.

economic liberalism

▶ The theory, associated with Adam Smith, that the pursuit of self-interest in a competitive market suffices to improve living conditions, rendering government intervention unnecessary and undesirable.

enlightened absolutism

▶ Term coined by historians to describe the rule of eighteenth-century monarchs who, without renouncing their own absolute authority, adopted Enlightenment ideals of rationalism, progress, and tolerance.

CHAPTER LOCATOR | What revolutionary discoveries were made in the sixteenth and seventeenth centuries? | What intellectual and social changes occurred as a result of the Scientific Revolution?

CHAPTER 19
568 NEW WORLDVIEWS AND WAYS OF LIFE

Under his reign, Prussia's laws were simplified, torture of prisoners was abolished, and judges decided cases quickly and impartially. However, Frederick did not free the serfs of Prussia; instead he extended the privileges of the nobility over them.

Frederick's reputation as an enlightened prince was rivaled by that of Catherine the Great of Russia. Catherine pursued three major goals. First, she worked hard to continue Peter the Great's efforts to bring the culture of western Europe to Russia (see page 541). Catherine's second goal was domestic reform. Like Frederick, she restricted the practice of torture, allowed limited religious tolerance, and tried to improve education and local government. The philosophes applauded these measures and hoped more would follow.

These hopes were dashed by a massive uprising of serfs in 1733 under the leadership of a Cossack soldier named Emelian Pugachev. Although Pugachev was ultimately captured and executed, his rebellion shocked Russian rulers. After 1775 Catherine gave nobles absolute control of their serfs and extended serfdom into new areas. In 1785 she formally freed nobles from taxes and state service. Under Catherine the Russian nobility thus attained its most exalted position, and serfdom entered its most oppressive phase.

Catherine's third goal was territorial expansion. Her armies subjugated the last descendants of the Mongols and the Crimean Tartars and began the conquest of the Caucasus on the border between Europe and Asia. Her greatest coup was the partition of Poland, which took place in stages from 1772 to 1795 (Map 19.1).

Joseph II (r. 1780–1790), the Austrian Habsburg emperor, was perhaps the most sincere proponent of enlightened absolutism. Joseph abolished serfdom in 1781, and in 1789 he decreed that peasants could pay landlords in cash rather than through compulsory labor. When Joseph died at forty-nine, the Habsburg empire was in turmoil. His brother Leopold II (r. 1790–1792) canceled Joseph's radical edicts in order to re-establish order.

Perhaps the best examples of the limitations of enlightened absolutism are the debates surrounding the possible emancipation of the Jews. For the most part, Jews in Europe were confined to tiny, overcrowded ghettos; were excluded by law from most occupations; and could be ordered out of a kingdom at a moment's notice.

In the eighteenth century an Enlightenment movement known as the Haskalah emerged from within the European Jewish community, led by the Prussian philosopher Moses Mendelssohn (1729–1786). Christian and Jewish Enlightenment philosophers, including Mendelssohn, began to advocate for freedom and civil rights for European Jews. (See "Individuals in Society: Moses Mendelssohn and the Jewish Enlightenment," page 571.)

Arguments for tolerance won some ground, especially under Joseph II of Austria. Most monarchs, however, refused to entertain the idea of emancipation. In 1791 Catherine the Great established the Pale of Settlement, a territory encompassing modern-day Belarus, Lithuania, Latvia, Moldova, Ukraine, and parts of Poland, in which most Jews were required to live until the Russian Revolution of 1917.

The Pale of Settlement, 1791

Haskalah

▶ A Jewish Enlightenment movement led by Prussian philosopher Moses Mendelssohn.

What new ideas about society and human relations emerged in the Enlightenment?

How did economic and social change interact with Enlightenment ideas?

✓ LearningCurve
Check what you know.

569

I n 1743 a small, humpbacked Jewish boy with a stammer left his poor parents in Dessau in central Germany and walked eighty miles to Berlin, the capital of Frederick the Great's Prussia. According to one story, when the boy reached the Rosenthaler Gate, the only one through which Jews could pass, he told the inquiring watchman that his name was Moses and that he had come to Berlin "to learn." The watchman laughed and waved him through. "Go Moses, the sea has opened before you."*

In Berlin the young Mendelssohn studied Jewish law and eked out a living copying Hebrew manuscripts in a beautiful hand. But he was soon fascinated by an intellectual world that had been closed to him in the Dessau ghetto. There, like most Jews throughout central Europe, he had spoken Yiddish — a mixture of German, Polish, and Hebrew. Now, working mainly on his own, he mastered German; learned Latin, Greek, French, and English; and studied mathematics and Enlightenment philosophy. Word of his exceptional abilities spread in Berlin's Jewish community (the dwelling of 1,500 of the city's 100,000 inhabitants). He began tutoring the children of a wealthy Jewish silk merchant, and he soon became the merchant's clerk and later his partner. But his great passion remained the life of the mind and the spirit, which he avidly pursued in his off-hours.

Gentle and unassuming in his personal life, Mendelssohn was a bold thinker. Reading eagerly in works of Western philosophy dating back to antiquity, he was, as a pious Jew, soon convinced that Enlightenment teachings need not be opposed to Jewish thought and religion. He concluded that reason could complement and strengthen religion, although each would retain its integrity as a separate sphere.[†] Developing this idea in his first great work, "On the Immortality of the Soul" (1767), Mendelssohn used the neutral setting of a philosophical dialogue between Socrates and his followers in ancient Greece to argue that the human soul lived forever. In refusing to bring religion and critical thinking into conflict, he was strongly influenced by contemporary German philosophers who argued similarly on behalf of Christianity. His thoughts reflected the way the German Enlightenment generally supported established religion, in contrast to the French Enlightenment, which attacked it.

Mendelssohn's treatise on the human soul captivated the educated German public, which marveled that a Jew could have written a philosophical mas-

Lavater (right) attempts to convert Mendelssohn, in a painting of an imaginary encounter by Moritz Oppenheim. (Oil on canvas painting by Daniel Moritz Oppenheim (1800–1882)/Judah L. Magnes Memorial Museum/akg-images)

terpiece. In the excitement, a Christian zealot named Lavater challenged Mendelssohn in a pamphlet to accept Christianity or to demonstrate how the Christian faith was not "reasonable." Replying politely but passionately, the Jewish philosopher affirmed that his studies had only strengthened him in his faith, although he did not seek to convert anyone not born into Judaism. Rather, he urged tolerance in religious matters and spoke up courageously against Jewish oppression.

An Orthodox Jew and a German philosophe, Moses Mendelssohn serenely combined two very different worlds. He built a bridge from the ghetto to the dominant culture over which many Jews would pass, including his novelist daughter Dorothea and his famous grandson, the composer Felix Mendelssohn.

QUESTIONS FOR ANALYSIS

1. How did Mendelssohn seek to influence Jewish religious thought in his time?
2. How do Mendelssohn's ideas compare with those of the French Enlightenment?

ONLINE DOCUMENT PROJECT

How did Moses Mendelssohn fit into the larger Enlightenment debate about religious tolerance? Examine primary sources written by Mendelssohn and his contemporaries, and then complete a quiz and writing assignment based on the evidence and details from this chapter. *See inside the front cover to learn more.*

*H. Kupferberg, *The Mendelssohns: Three Generations of Genius* (New York: Charles Scribner's Sons, 1972), p. 3.
[†]D. Sorkin, *Moses Mendelssohn and the Religious Enlightenment* (Berkeley: University of California Press, 1996), pp. 8ff.

MAP 19.1 ■ The Partition of Poland, 1772–1795

In 1772 the threat of war between Russia and Austria arose over Russian gains from the Ottoman Empire. To satisfy desires for expansion without fighting, Prussia's Frederick the Great proposed dividing parts of Poland among Austria, Prussia, and Russia. In 1793 and 1795 the three powers partitioned the remainder, and Poland ceased to exist as an independent nation.

> **MAPPING THE PAST**

ANALYZING THE MAP: Of the three powers that divided the kingdom of Poland, which benefited the most? How did the partition affect the geographical boundaries of each state, and what was the significance? What border with the former Poland remained unchanged? Why do you think this was the case?

CONNECTIONS: Why was Poland vulnerable to partition in the later half of the eighteenth century? What does it say about European politics at the time that a country could simply cease to exist on the map? Could that happen today?

QUICK REVIEW <

How did participants in the Enlightenment build on the accomplishments of the Scientific Revolution?

What new ideas about society and human relations emerged in the Enlightenment?	How did economic and social change interact with Enlightenment ideas?	✔ LearningCurve Check what you know.

How did economic and social change and the rise of Atlantic trade interact with Enlightenment ideas?

The French Book Trade

Book consumption surged in the eighteenth century and along with it, new bookstores. This appealing bookshop in France with its intriguing ads for the latest works offers to put customers "Under the Protection of Minerva," the Roman goddess of wisdom. Large packets of books sit ready for shipment to foreign countries. (Musée des Beaux-Arts, Dijon, France/Art Resource, NY)

ENLIGHTENMENT DEBATES TOOK PLACE within a rapidly evolving material world. Agricultural reforms contributed to a rise in population that in turned fueled substantial economic growth in eighteenth-century Europe. A new public sphere emerged in the growing cities in which people exchanged opinions in cafés, bookstores, and other spaces. A consumer revolution brought fashion and imported foods into the reach of common people for the first time.

These economic and social changes were fed by an increasingly integrated Atlantic economy. Over time, the peoples, goods, and ideas that crisscrossed the ocean created distinctive Atlantic communities and identities.

Economic and Demographic Change

The seventeenth century saw important gains in agricultural productivity in north-western Europe that slowly spread throughout the continent. Using new scientific techniques of observation and experimentation, a group of scientists, government

CHAPTER LOCATOR | What revolutionary discoveries were made in the sixteenth and seventeenth centuries? | What intellectual and social changes occurred as a result of the Scientific Revolution?

572 CHAPTER 19 NEW WORLDVIEWS AND WAYS OF LIFE

officials, and a few big landowners devised agricultural practices and tools that raised crop yields dramatically, especially in England and the Netherlands. These included new forms of crop rotation, better equipment, and selective breeding of livestock. The controversial process of enclosure, fencing off common land to create privately owned fields, allowed a break with traditional methods but at the cost of reducing poor farmers' access to land.

Colonial plants also provided new sources of calories and nutrition. Introduced into Europe from the Americas—along with corn, squash, tomatoes, and many other useful plants—the potato provided an excellent new food source and offset the lack of fresh vegetables and fruits in common people's winter diet. The potato had become an important dietary supplement in much of Europe by the end of the eighteenth century.

Increases in agricultural productivity and better nutrition, combined with the disappearance of bubonic plague after 1720 and improvements in sewage and water supply, contributed to the tremendous growth of the European population in the eighteenth century. The explosion of population was a major phenomenon in all European countries, leading to a doubling of the number of Europeans between 1700 and 1835.

Population growth increased the number of rural workers with little or no land, and this in turn contributed to the development of industry in rural areas. The poor in the countryside increasingly needed to supplement their agricultural earnings with other types of work. Cottage industry, which consisted of manufacturing with hand tools in peasant cottages and work sheds, grew markedly in the eighteenth century and became a crucial feature of the European economy.

Despite the rise in rural industry, life in the countryside was insufficient to support the rapidly growing population. Many people thus left their small villages to join the tide of migration to the cities, especially after 1750.

The Atlantic Economy

European economic growth in the eighteenth century was spurred by the expansion of trade across the Atlantic Ocean. Commercial exchange in the Atlantic is often referred to as the triangle trade, designating a three-way transport of goods: European commodities to Africa; enslaved Africans to the colonies; and colonial goods back to Europe. This model highlights some of the most important flows of trade but significantly oversimplifies the picture. For example, a brisk intercolonial trade existed, with the Caribbean slave colonies importing food from other American colonies in exchange for sugar and slaves (Map 19.2).

Moreover, the Atlantic economy was inextricably linked to trade with the Indian and Pacific Oceans. The rising economic and political power of Europeans in the eighteenth century thus drew on the connections they established between the long-standing Asian and Atlantic trade worlds.

Over the course of the eighteenth century the economies of European nations bordering the Atlantic Ocean relied more and more on colonial exports. In England sales to the mainland colonies of North America and the West Indian sugar islands soared from £500,000 to £4 million (Figure 19.1). Exports to England's colonies in Ireland and India also rose substantially from 1700 to 1800.

At the core of this Atlantic world was the misery and profit of the Atlantic slave trade (see pages 598–603). The brutal practice intensified dramatically after

enclosure
▶ The controversial process of fencing off common land to create privately owned fields that increased agricultural production at the cost of reducing poor farmers' access to land.

cottage industry
▶ Manufacturing with hand tools in peasant cottages and work sheds, a form of economic activity that became important in eighteenth-century Europe.

What new ideas about society and human relations emerged in the Enlightenment? | **How did economic and social change interact with Enlightenment ideas?** | ✓ LearningCurve Check what you know.

573

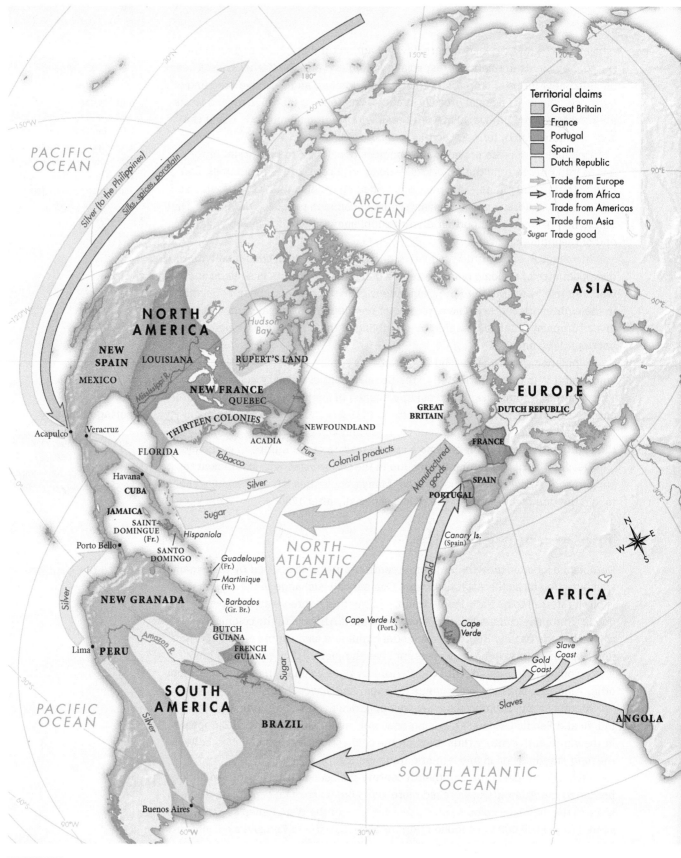

MAP 19.2 ■ The Atlantic Economy, 1701

The growth of trade encouraged both economic development and military conflict in the Atlantic basin. Four continents were linked together by the exchange of goods and slaves.

CHAPTER LOCATOR

What revolutionary discoveries were made in the sixteenth and seventeenth centuries?

What intellectual and social changes occurred as a result of the Scientific Revolution?

CHAPTER 19
574 NEW WORLDVIEWS AND WAYS OF LIFE

1700 and especially after 1750 with the growth of trade and demand for slave-produced goods. English dominance of the slave trade provided another source of large profits to the home country.

The French also profited enormously from colonial trade in the eighteenth century, even after losing their vast North American territories to England in 1763. The Caribbean colonies of Saint-Domingue (modern-day Haiti), Martinique, and Guadeloupe provided immense fortunes from slave-based plantation agriculture. The wealth generated from colonial trade fostered the confidence of the merchant classes in Nantes, Bordeaux, and other large cities, and merchants soon joined other elite groups clamoring for more political power.

The third major player in the Atlantic economy, Spain, also saw its colonial fortunes improve during the eighteenth century. Its mercantilist goals were boosted by a recovery in silver production. Spanish territory in North America expanded significantly in the second half of the eighteenth century. At the close of the Seven Years' War (1756–1763) (see page 647), Spain gained Louisiana from the French, and its influence extended westward all the way to northern California through the efforts of Spanish missionaries and ranchers.

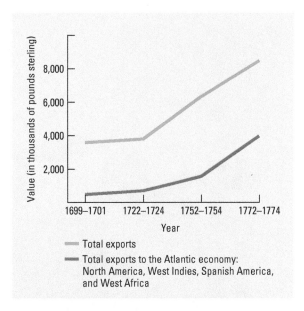

FIGURE 19.1 ■ **Exports of English Manufactured Goods, 1700–1774**

While trade between England and Europe stagnated after 1700, English exports to Africa and the Americas boomed and greatly stimulated English economic development. (Source: Data from R. Davis, "English Foreign Trade, 1700–1774," *Economic History Review*, 2nd ser., 15 [1962]: 302–303.)

Urban Life and the Public Sphere

Urban life in the Atlantic world gave rise to new institutions and practices that encouraged the spread of Enlightenment thought. From about 1700 to 1789 the production and consumption of books grew significantly. Lending libraries, book-shops, cafés, and Masonic lodges provided spaces in which urban people debated new ideas. Together these spaces and institutions helped create a new **public sphere** that celebrated open debate informed by critical reason.

Another important Enlightenment institution was the salon. In Paris from about 1740 to 1789, a number of talented, wealthy women presided over regular social gatherings named after their elegant private drawing rooms, or **salons**. There they encouraged the exchange of observations on literature, science, and philosophy with great aristocrats, wealthy middle-class financiers, high-ranking officials, and noteworthy foreigners.

Elite women also exercised great influence on artistic taste. Soft pastels, ornate interiors, sentimental portraits, and starry-eyed lovers protected by hovering cupids were all hallmarks of the rococo style they favored. Women were also closely associated with the rise of the novel as a literary genre, both as authors and readers. The novel helped popularize the cult of sensibility, which celebrated strong emotions and intimate family love.

Economic growth in the second half of the eighteenth century also enabled a significant rise in the consumption of finished goods and new foodstuffs that historians have labeled a "consumer revolution." A boom in textile production and cheap reproductions of luxury items meant that the common people could afford to follow fashion for the first time. Colonial trade made previously expensive and rare foodstuffs, such as sugar, tea, coffee, chocolate, and tobacco, widely available.

public sphere

▶ An idealized intellectual space that emerged in Europe during the Enlightenment. Here, the public came together to discuss important social, economic, and political issues.

salons

▶ Regular social gatherings held by talented and rich Parisian women in their homes, where philosophes and their followers met to discuss literature, science, and philosophy.

What new ideas about society and human relations emerged in the Enlightenment?	How did economic and social change interact with Enlightenment ideas?	LearningCurve Check what you know.

From the mid-eighteenth century on, the cities of western Europe witnessed a new proliferation of consumer goods. Items once limited to the wealthy few — such as fans (above), watches, snuffboxes, umbrellas, ornamental containers, and teapots — were now reproduced in cheaper versions for middling and ordinary people. The fashion for wide hoopskirts was so popular that the armrests of the chairs of the day, known as Louis XV chairs (left), were specially designed to accommodate them. (fan: Musée Conde, Chantilly, France/Scala/White Images/Art Resource, NY; chair: © RMN–Grand Palais/Art Resource, NY)

Culture and Community in the Atlantic World

As contacts among the Atlantic coasts of the Americas, Africa, and Europe became more frequent, and as European settlements grew into well-established colonies, new identities and communities emerged. The term *Creole* referred to people of Spanish or other European ancestry born in the Americas. Wealthy Creoles throughout the Atlantic colonies prided themselves on following European ways of life.

Over time, however, the colonial elite came to feel that their circumstances gave them different interests and characteristics from people of their home countries. Creoles adopted native foods, like chocolate, chili peppers, and squash, and sought relief from tropical disease in native remedies. Also, they began to turn against restrictions from their home countries: Creole traders and planters, along with their counterparts in English colonies, increasingly resented the regulations and taxes imposed by colonial bureaucrats, and such resentment would eventually lead to revolutions against colonial powers (discussed in Chapter 22).

CHAPTER LOCATOR | What revolutionary discoveries were made in the sixteenth and seventeenth centuries? | What intellectual and social changes occurred as a result of the Scientific Revolution?

CHAPTER 19
576 NEW WORLDVIEWS AND WAYS OF LIFE

Not all Europeans in the colonies were wealthy or well educated. Numerous poor and lower-middle-class whites worked as clerks, shopkeepers, craftsmen, and laborers. With the exception of the English colonies of North America, white Europeans made up a minority of the population, outnumbered by indigenous peoples in Spanish America and, in the Caribbean, by the growing numbers of enslaved people of African descent. Since most European migrants were men, much of the colonial population of the Atlantic world descended from unions — forced or through consent — of European men and indigenous or African women. Colonial attempts to identify and control racial categories greatly influenced developing Enlightenment thought on racial differences.

In the Spanish and French Caribbean, as in Brazil, many slave masters acknowledged and freed their mixed-race children, leading to sizable populations of free people of color. In the second half of the eighteenth century the prosperity of some free people of color brought a backlash from the white population of Saint-Domingue in the form of new race laws prohibiting nonwhites from marrying whites and forcing them to adopt distinctive attire. In the British colonies of the Caribbean and the southern mainland, by contrast, masters tended to leave their mixed-race progeny in slavery, maintaining a stark discrepancy between free whites and enslaved people of color.[2]

Restricted from owning land and holding many occupations in Europe, Jews were eager participants in the new Atlantic economy and established a network of mercantile communities along its trade routes. As in the Old World, Jews in European colonies faced discrimination. Jews were considered to be white Europeans and thus ineligible to be slaves, but they did not enjoy equal status with Christians. The status of Jews adds one more element to the complexity of Atlantic identities.

The Atlantic Enlightenment

The colonies of British North America were deeply influenced by the Scottish Enlightenment, with its emphasis on pragmatic approaches to the problems of life. Following the Scottish model, leaders in the colonies adopted a moderate, "commonsense" version of the Enlightenment that emphasized self-improvement and ethical conduct. In most cases, this version of the Enlightenment was perfectly compatible with religion and was chiefly spread through the growing colleges and universities of the colonies.

Northern Enlightenment thinkers often depicted Spain and its American colonies as the epitome of the superstition and barbarity they contested. Nonetheless, the dynasty that took power in Spain in the early eighteenth century followed its own course of enlightened absolutism, just like its counterparts in the rest of Europe. Under King Carlos III (r. 1759–1788) and his son Carlos IV (r. 1788–1808), Spanish administrators attempted to strengthen colonial rule and improve government efficiency. Enlightened administrators debated the status of indigenous peoples and whether it would be better for these peoples if they maintained their distinct legal status or were integrated into Spanish society.

Educated Creoles were well aware of the new currents of thought, and the universities, newspapers, and salons of Spanish America produced their own

What new ideas about society and human relations emerged in the Enlightenment?

How did economic and social change interact with Enlightenment ideas?

LearningCurve
Check what you know.

577

reform ideas. As in other European colonies, one effect of Enlightenment thought was to encourage Creoles to criticize the policies of the mother country and aspire toward greater autonomy.

> **QUICK REVIEW**

How did the relationship between the Americas and the rest of the world change in the seventeenth and eighteenth centuries?

CHAPTER SUMMARY

Decisive breakthroughs in astronomy and physics in the seventeenth century demolished the medieval synthesis of Aristotelian philosophy and Christian theology. The impact of these scientific breakthroughs on intellectual life was enormous, nurturing a new critical attitude in many disciplines. In addition, an international scientific community arose, and state-sponsored academies, which were typically closed to women, advanced scientific research.

Believing that all aspects of life were open to debate and skepticism, Enlightenment thinkers asked challenging questions about religious tolerance, representative government, and racial and sexual difference. Enlightenment thinkers drew inspiration from the new peoples and cultures encountered by Europeans and devised new ideas about race as a scientific and biological category. The ideas of the Enlightenment inspired absolutist rulers in central and eastern Europe, but real reforms were limited.

In the second half of the eighteenth century agricultural reforms helped produce tremendous population growth. Economic growth and urbanization favored the spread of Enlightenment thought by producing a public sphere in which ideas could be debated. The expansion of transatlantic trade made economic growth possible, as did the lowering of prices on colonial goods due to the growth of slave labor. Atlantic trade involved the exchange of commodities among Europe, Africa, and the Americas, but it was also linked with trade in the Indian and Pacific Oceans. The movement of people and ideas across the Atlantic helped shape the identities of colonial inhabitants.

 CONNECTIONS Hailed as the origin of modern thought, the Scientific Revolution must also be seen as a product of its past. Borrowing from Islamic cultural achievements, medieval universities gave rise to important new scholarship in mathematics and natural philosophy. In turn, the ambition and wealth of Renaissance patrons nurtured intellectual curiosity and encouraged scholarly research and foreign exploration. Natural philosophers

CHAPTER LOCATOR | What revolutionary discoveries were made in the sixteenth and seventeenth centuries? | What intellectual and social changes occurred as a result of the Scientific Revolution?

578 CHAPTER 19 NEW WORLDVIEWS AND WAYS OF LIFE

pioneered new methods of explaining and observing nature while drawing on centuries-old traditions of astrology, alchemy, and magic. A desire to control and profit from empire led the Spanish, followed by their European rivals, to explore and catalogue the flora and fauna of their American colonies. These efforts resulted in new frameworks in natural history.

Enlightenment ideas of the eighteenth century were a similar blend of past and present, progressive and traditional, homegrown and foreign-inspired. Enlightenment thinkers advocated universal rights and liberties but also preached the biological inferiority of non-Europeans and women. Their principles often served as much to bolster absolutist regimes as to inspire revolutionaries to fight for human rights.

New notions of progress and social improvement would drive Europeans to embark on world-changing revolutions in politics and industry (see Chapters 22 and 23) at the end of the eighteenth century. These revolutions provided the basis for modern democracy and unprecedented scientific advancement. Yet some critics have seen a darker side. For them, the mastery over nature enabled by the Scientific Revolution now threatens to overwhelm the earth's fragile equilibrium, and the Enlightenment belief in the universal application of reason can lead to intolerance of other people's spiritual, cultural, and political values.

As the era of European exploration and conquest gave way to empire building, the eighteenth century witnessed increased consolidation of global markets and bitter competition among Europeans. The eighteenth-century Atlantic world thus tied the shores of Europe, the Americas, and Africa in a web of commercial and human exchange, including the tragedy of slavery, discussed in Chapter 20. The Atlantic world maintained strong ties with trade in the Pacific and the Indian Ocean.

ONLINE DOCUMENT PROJECT
Moses Mendelssohn

How did Moses Mendelssohn fit into the larger Enlightenment debate about religious tolerance?

Examine primary sources written by Mendelssohn and his contemporaries, and then complete a quiz and writing assignment based on the evidence and details from this chapter. *See inside the front cover to learn more.*

What new ideas about society and human relations emerged in the Enlightenment?	How did economic and social change interact with Enlightenment ideas?	✔ LearningCurve Check what you know.

STEP 1 GET STARTED ONLINE

 LearningCurve

Now that you've read the chapter, make it stick by completing the LearningCurve activity.

STEP 2 EXPLAIN WHY IT MATTERS

Put your reading into practice. Identify each term below, and then explain why it matters in world history.

TERM	WHO OR WHAT & WHEN	WHY IT MATTERS
Copernican hypothesis (p. 553)		
law of inertia (p. 553)		
law of universal gravitation (p. 554)		
empiricism (p. 557)		
Enlightenment (p. 561)		
sensationalism (p. 563)		
philosophes (p. 563)		
deism (p. 564)		
general will (p. 565)		
economic liberalism (p. 568)		
enlightened absolutism (p. 568)		
Haskalah (p. 569)		
enclosure (p. 573)		
cottage industry (p. 573)		
public sphere (p. 575)		
salons (p. 575)		

STEP 3 MOVE BEYOND THE BASICS

To demonstrate a more advanced understanding of key figures of the Scientific Revolution, fill in the chart below with descriptions of the scientific discoveries of the figures listed. Be sure to include both concrete discoveries and contributions to the development of the scientific method. How did these thinkers build off of each other's discoveries and insights? What common goals did they share?

	Discoveries and Contributions
Nicolaus Copernicus	
Tycho Brahe	
Johannes Kepler	
Francis Bacon	
René Descartes	
Galileo Galilei	
Isaac Newton	

PUT IT ALL TOGETHER

Now, take a step back and try to explain the big picture. Remember to use specific examples from the chapter in your answers.

THE SCIENTIFIC REVOLUTION

► What was revolutionary about the Scientific Revolution? How did the study of nature in the sixteenth century differ from the study of nature in the Middle Ages?

► What role did religion play in the Scientific Revolution? How did religious belief both stimulate and hinder scientific inquiry?

THE ENLIGHTENMENT AND ENLIGHTENED ABSOLUTISM

► How did the Scientific Revolution contribute to the emergence of the Enlightenment? What new ideas about the power and potential of human reason were central to both developments?

► What connections can you make between the state-building ambitions of central and eastern European absolute monarchs and their embrace of Enlightenment reforms?

CONSUMERISM AND THE ATLANTIC WORLD

► How did the growth and consolidation of the Atlantic economy shape the everyday lives of eighteenth-century Europeans?

► How did Enlightenment thinkers deal with issues of gender and race? How did New World encounters shape their thinking?

LOOKING BACK, LOOKING AHEAD

► How did medieval and Renaissance developments contribute to the Scientific Revolution? Should the Scientific Revolution be seen a sharp break with the past, or the culmination of long-term, gradual change?

► A noted historian has said that the Scientific Revolution was "the real origin both of the modern world and the modern mentality." Do you agree or disagree with this characterization? Why?

> IN YOUR OWN WORDS

Imagine that you must give an oral report to the class answering the following question: How and why did Europeans' understanding of the natural world and human society change in the early modern period? What would be the most important points and why?

20

AFRICA AND THE WORLD

1400–1800

> **What were the short-term and long-term consequences of the transatlantic slave trade for African societies?** Chapter 20 examines early modern Africa. Early modern African states and societies included a wide variety of languages, cultures, political systems, and levels of economic development. African societies of this period were connected to each other and to the outside world by extensive trade networks. Modern European intrusion into Africa beginning in the fifteenth century profoundly affected these diverse societies and ancient trading networks. Most important, the intrusion led to the transatlantic slave trade, one of the greatest forced migrations in world history, through which Africa made a substantial, though involuntary, contribution to the building of the West's industrial civilization.

Waist Pendant of Benin Worn by Royalty European intrusion in Africa during the early modern period deeply affected the diverse societies of Africa. The facial features, the beard, and the ruffled collar on this Edo peoples' artifact dating from the sixteenth to the nineteenth centuries are clearly Portuguese, but the braided hair is distinctly African, probably signifying royalty. (Hip Ornament: Portuguese Face, 16th–19th century. Brass, iron. Gift of Mr. and Mrs. Klaus G. Perls, 1991 [1991.162.9]. The Metropolitan Museum of Art, New York, NY, USA/Image copyright © The Metropolitan Museum of Art/Image source: Art Resource, NY)

> What different types of economic, social, and political structures were found in the kingdoms and states along the west coast and in the Sudan?

> How did the arrival of Europeans and other foreign cultures affect the East African coast, and how did Ethiopia and the Swahili city-states respond to these incursions?

> What role did slavery play in African societies before the transatlantic slave trade began, and what was the effect of European involvement?

LearningCurve

After reading the chapter, use LearningCurve to retain what you've read.

What different types of economic, social, and political structures were found in the kingdoms and states along the west coast and in the Sudan?

The Oba of Benin

The oba's palace walls were decorated with bronze plaques that date from about the sixteenth to eighteenth centuries. This plaque vividly conveys the oba's power, majesty, and authority. The two attendants holding his arms also imply that the oba needs the support of his people. The oba's legs are mudfish, which represent fertility, peace, well-being, and prosperity, but their elongation, suggesting electric eels, relates the oba's terrifying and awesome power to the eel's jolting shock. (National Museum, Lagos, Nigeria/photo: André Held/akg-images)

IN MID-FIFTEENTH-CENTURY AFRICA, Benin and a number of other kingdoms flourished along the two-thousand-mile west coast between Senegambia and the northeastern shore of the Gulf of Guinea. Further inland, in the region of the Sudan, the kingdoms of Songhai, Kanem-Bornu, and Hausaland benefited from the trans-Saharan caravan trade. Stateless societies such as those in the region of Senegambia existed alongside these more centralized states. Despite their political differences and whether they were agricultural, pastoral, or a mixture of both, West African cultures all faced the challenges presented by famine, disease, and the slave trade.

The West Coast: Senegambia and Benin

The Senegambian states possessed a homogeneous culture and a common history. For centuries Senegambia served as an important entrepôt for desert caravan contact with North African and Middle Eastern Islamic civilizations. Through the

CHAPTER LOCATOR | What different types of economic, social, and political structures were found in the kingdoms and states along the west coast and in the Sudan? | How did the arrival of Europeans and other foreign cultures affect the East African coast, and how did Ethiopia and the Swahili city-states respond to these incursions?

CHAPTER 20
584 AFRICA AND THE WORLD

1400–1600s
Salt trade dominates West African economy

ca. 1464–1591
Songhai kingdom dominates the western Sudan

1485
Portuguese and other Europeans first appear in Benin

1493–1528
Muhammad Toure governs and expands kingdom of Songhai

1498
Portuguese explorer Vasco da Gama sails around Africa

ca. 1500–1900
Era of transatlantic slave trade

1502–1507
Portuguese erect forts at Kilwa, Zanzibar, and Sofala on Swahili coast

1529
Adal defeats Ethiopian emperor and begins systematic devastation of Ethiopia

1543
Joint Ethiopian and Portuguese force defeat Muslims in Ethiopia

1571–1603
Idris Alooma governs kingdom of Kanem-Bornu

1591
Moroccan army defeats Songhai

1658
Dutch East India Company allows importation of slaves into Cape Colony

1680s
Famine from Senegambian coast to Upper Nile

1738–1756
Major famine in West Africa

1789
Olaudah Equiano publishes autobiography

transatlantic slave trade, Senegambia came into contact with Europe and the Americas. Thus Senegambia felt the impact of Islamic culture to the north and of European influences from the maritime West.

The Senegambian peoples spoke Wolof, Serer, and Pulaar, which all belong to the West African language group. Both the Wolof-speakers and the Serer-speakers had clearly defined social classes: royalty, nobility, warriors, peasants, low-caste artisans such as blacksmiths and leatherworkers, and enslaved persons. The enslaved class consisted of individuals who were pawned for debt, house servants who could not be sold, and people who were acquired through war or purchase. Senegambian slavery varied from society to society. In some places slaves were considered chattel property and were treated as harshly as they would be later in the Western Hemisphere.

The word **chattel** originally comes from a Latin word meaning "head," as in "so many head of cattle." It reflects the notion that enslaved people are not human, but subhuman, like beasts of burden or other animals. Thus they can be treated like animals. But in Senegambia and elsewhere in Africa, many enslaved people were not considered chattel property and could not be bought and sold. Some even served as royal advisers and enjoyed great power and prestige.[1] Unlike in the Americas, where slave status passed forever from one generation to the next, in Africa the enslaved person's descendants were sometimes considered free.

Senegambia was composed of stateless societies, culturally homogeneous ethnic populations living in small groups of villages without a central capital. Among these stateless societies, **age-grade systems** evolved. Age-grades were groups of teenage males and females whom the society initiated into adulthood

chattel
▶ An item of personal property; a term used in reference to enslaved people that conveys the idea that they are subhuman, like animals, and therefore may be treated like animals.

age-grade systems
▶ Among the societies of Senegambia, groups of men and women whom the society initiated into adulthood at the same time.

What role did slavery play in African societies before the transatlantic slave trade began, and what was the effect of European involvement?

✓ LearningCurve
Check what you know.

at the same time. Age-grades cut across family ties, created community-wide loyalties, and provided a means of local law enforcement, because each age-grade was responsible for the behavior of all its members.

The typical Senegambian community was a small, self-supporting agricultural village of closely related families. The average six- to eight-acre farm supported a moderate-size family. Millet and sorghum were the staple grains in northern Senegambia; farther south, forest dwellers cultivated yams as a staple. Social life centered on the family, and government played a limited role, interceding mostly to resolve family disputes and conflicts between families.

Alongside West African stateless societies like Senegambia were kingdoms and states ruled by kings who governed defined areas through bureaucratic hierarchies. The great forest kingdom of Benin emerged in the fifteenth and sixteenth centuries in what is now southern Nigeria (see Map 20.1). Over time, the position

MAP 20.1 ▪ West African Societies, ca. 1500–1800

The coastal region of West Africa witnessed the rise of a number of kingdoms in the sixteenth century.

> MAPPING THE PAST

ANALYZING THE MAP: What geographical features defined each of the kingdoms shown here? Consider rivers, lakes, oceans, deserts, and forests. How might they have affected the size and shape of these kingdoms?
CONNECTIONS: Compare this map to the spot map of the slave coast of West Africa on page 590. Consider the role that rivers and other geographical factors played in the development of the West African slave trade. Why were Luanda and Benguela the logical Portuguese sources for slaves?

- Songhai, ca. 1500
- Kanem-Bornu, ca. 1500
- Benin, ca. 1625
- Kongo, ca. 1625
- Area occupied by Fulani people

CHAPTER LOCATOR | What different types of economic, social, and political structures were found in the kingdoms and states along the west coast and in the Sudan? | How did the arrival of Europeans and other foreign cultures affect the East African coast, and how did Ethiopia and the Swahili city-states respond to these incursions?

586 CHAPTER 20
AFRICA AND THE WORLD

of its **oba**, or king, was exalted, bringing stability to the state. In the later fifteenth century the oba Ewuare strengthened his army and pushed Benin's borders as far as the Niger River in the east, westward into Yoruba country, and south to the Gulf of Guinea. During the late sixteenth and seventeenth centuries the office of the oba evolved from a warrior-kingship to a position of spiritual leadership.

At its height in the late sixteenth century, Benin controlled a vast territory, and European visitors described a sophisticated society. A Dutch visitor in the early 1600s, possibly Dierick Ruiters, described the capital, Benin City, as possessing a great, wide, and straight main avenue down the middle, with many side streets crisscrossing it. Visitors noted that Benin City was kept scrupulously clean and had no beggars and that public security was so effective that theft was unknown. The period also witnessed remarkable artistic creativity in ironwork, carved ivory, and especially bronze portrait busts. Over nine hundred brass plaques survive, providing important information about Benin court life, military triumphs, and cosmological ideas.

In 1485 Portuguese and other Europeans began to appear in Benin in pursuit of trade, and over the next couple of centuries Benin grew rich from the profits made through the slave trade and the export of tropical products. Its main European trading partners along this stretch of the so-called slave coast were the Dutch and Portuguese.

The Sudan: Songhai, Kanem-Bornu, and Hausaland

The Songhai kingdom, a successor state of the kingdoms of Ghana (ca. 900–1100) and Mali (ca. 1200–1450), dominated the whole Niger region of the western and central Sudan (see Map 20.1). The imperial expansion of Songhai (song-GUY) began during the reign of the Songhai king Sonni Ali (r. ca. 1464–1492) and continued under his eventual successor, Muhammad Toure (r. 1493–1528). From his capital at Gao, Toure extended his rule as far north as the salt-mining center at **Taghaza** in the western Sahara and as far east as Agades and Kano. A convert to Islam, Toure tried to bring about greater centralization in his own territories by building a strong army, improving taxation procedures, and replacing local Songhai officials with more efficient Arabs in an effort to substitute royal institutions for ancient kinship ties.

When the scholar Leo Africanus (ca. 1465–1550) visited Timbuktu, the second-largest city of the empire, in 1513 he was impressed by its intellectual climate. "Here [is] a great store of doctors, judges, priests, and other learned men, that are bountifully maintained at the King's court," he reported.[2] Many of these Islamic scholars had studied in Cairo and other Muslim learning centers. They gave Timbuktu a reputation for intellectual sophistication, religious piety, and moral justice.

Songhai under Muhammad Toure seems to have enjoyed economic prosperity. The elite had immense wealth, and expensive North African and European luxuries were much in demand. The existence of many shops and markets implies the development of an urban culture. In Timbuktu merchants, scholars, judges, and artisans constituted a distinctive bourgeoisie, or middle class. The presence of

oba
▶ The title of the king of Benin.

Taghaza
▶ A settlement in the western Sahara, the site of the main salt-mining center.

What role did slavery play in African societies before the transatlantic slave trade began, and what was the effect of European involvement?

☑ LearningCurve
Check what you know.

587

many foreign merchants, including Jews and Italians, gave the city a cosmopolitan atmosphere.

Slavery played an important role in Songhai's economy. On the royal farms scattered throughout the kingdom, enslaved people produced rice for the royal granaries. Slaves could possess their own slaves, land, and cattle, but they could not bequeath any of this property. Muhammad Toure greatly increased the number of royal slaves. He bestowed slaves on favorite Muslim scholars, who thus gained a steady source of income. Slaves were also sold at the large market at Gao, where traders from North Africa bought them to resell later in Cairo, Constantinople, Lisbon, Naples, Genoa, and Venice.

Despite its considerable economic and cultural strengths, Songhai had serious internal problems. Islam never took root in the countryside, and Muslim officials alienated the king from his people. Muhammad Toure's reforms were a failure. He governed diverse peoples who were often hostile to one another, and no cohesive element united them. Moreover, revolts, conspiracies, and palace intrigues followed the death of every king, and only three of the nine rulers in the dynasty begun by Muhammad Toure died natural deaths. Muhammad Toure himself was murdered by one of his sons. His death began a period of political instability that led to the kingdom's slow disintegration. The empire came to an end in 1591 when a Moroccan army of three thousand soldiers—many of whom were slaves of European origin equipped with European muskets—crossed the Sahara and inflicted a crushing defeat on the Songhai at Tondibi.

East of Songhai lay the kingdoms of Kanem-Bornu and Hausaland (see Map 20.1). Under the dynamic military leader Idris Alooma (r. 1571–1603), Kanem-Bornu gained jurisdiction over an extensive area. Well drilled and equipped with firearms, his standing army and camel-mounted cavalry decimated warriors fighting with spears and arrows. Idris Alooma perpetuated a form of feudalism by granting land to able fighters in return for loyalty and the promise of future military assistance. Kanem-Bornu shared in the trans-Saharan trade, shipping eunuchs and young girls to North Africa in return for horses and firearms.

A devote Muslim, Idris Alooma built mosques at his capital city of N'gazargamu and substituted Muslim courts and Islamic law for African tribunals and ancient customary law. His eighteenth-century successors lacked his vitality and military skills, however, and the empire declined.

Between Songhai and Kanem-Bornu were the lands of the Hausa, an agricultural people who lived in small villages. Hausa merchants carried on a sizable trade in slaves and kola nuts with North African communities across the Sahara. Trading posts evolved into important Hausa city-states like Kano and Katsina, through which Islamic influences entered the region. Kano and Katsina became Muslim intellectual centers and in the fifteenth century attracted scholars from Timbuktu. As in Songhai and Kanem-Bornu, however, Islam made no strong imprint on the Hausa masses until the nineteenth century.

The Lives of the People of West Africa

Wives and children were highly desired in African societies because they could clear and cultivate the land and because they brought prestige, social support, and security in old age. The results were intense competition for women, inequal-

CHAPTER LOCATOR | What different types of economic, social, and political structures were found in the kingdoms and states along the west coast and in the Sudan? | How did the arrival of Europeans and other foreign cultures affect the East African coast, and how did Ethiopia and the Swahili city-states respond to these incursions?

CHAPTER 20
588   AFRICA AND THE WORLD

ity of access to them, an emphasis on male virility and female fertility, and serious tension between male generations. Polygyny was almost universal.

Men acquired wives in two ways. In some cases, couples simply eloped and began their union. More commonly, a man's family gave bride wealth to the bride's family. Because it took time for a young man to acquire the bride wealth, all but the richest men delayed marriage until about age thirty. Women married at about the onset of puberty.

The easy availability of land in Africa reduced the kinds of generational conflict that occurred in western Europe, where land was scarce. Competition for wives between male generations, however, was fierce. On the one hand, myth and folklore stressed respect for the elderly, and the older men in a community imposed their authority over the younger ones. On the other hand, young men possessed the powerful asset of their labor, which could easily be turned into independence where so much land was available.

Children were the primary goal of marriage. A woman might have six widely spaced pregnancies in her fertile years; the universal practice of breast-feeding infants for two, three, or even four years may have inhibited conception. Long intervals between births due to food shortages also may have limited pregnancies and checked population growth.

Both nuclear and extended families were common in West Africa. Nuclear families averaged only five or six members, but the household of a Big Man (a local man of power) included his wives, married and unmarried sons, unmarried daughters, poor relations, dependents, and scores of children. Extended families were common among the Hausa and Mandinka peoples. On the Gold Coast in the seventeenth century, a well-to-do man's household might number 150 people, in the Kongo region in west-central Africa, several hundred.

In agriculture men did the heavy work of felling trees and clearing the land; women then planted, weeded, and harvested. Between 1000 and 1400, cassava (manioc), bananas, and plantains came to West Africa from Asia. In the sixteenth century the Portuguese introduced maize (corn), sweet potatoes, and new varieties of yams from the Americas. Fish supplemented the diets of people living near bodies of water.

Disease posed perhaps the biggest obstacle to population growth. Malaria, spread by mosquitoes and rampant in West Africa, was the greatest killer, especially of infants. West Africans developed a relatively high degree of immunity to malaria and other parasitic diseases. Acute strains of smallpox introduced by Europeans certainly did not help population growth, nor did venereal syphilis, which possibly originated in Latin America. As in Chinese and European communities in the early modern period, the sick depended on folk medicine. African medical specialists administered a variety of treatments. Still, disease was common where the diet was poor and lacked adequate vitamins.

The devastating effects of famine represented another major check on population growth. Drought, excessive rain, swarms of locusts, and rural wars that

Queen Mother and Attendants

As in Ottoman, Chinese, and European societies, the mothers of African rulers sometimes exercised considerable political power because of their influence on their sons. African kings granted the title Queen Mother as a badge of honor. In this figure, the long beaded cap, called "chicken's beak," symbolizes the mother's rank, as do her elaborate neck jewelry and attendants. (Culture: Edo peoples. Culture: Court of Benin. Altar Tableau: Queen Mother and Attendants, 18th century. Brass. Front, view #1. Gift of Mr. and Mrs. Klaus G. Perls, 1991 [1991.17.111]. The Metropolitan Museum of Art, New York, NY, USA/Image copyright © The Metropolitan Museum of Art/Image source: Art Resource, NY)

What role did slavery play in African societies before the transatlantic slave trade began, and what was the effect of European involvement?

LearningCurve
Check what you know.

prevented land cultivation all meant later food shortages. In the 1680s famine extended from the Senegambian coast to the Upper Nile, and many people sold themselves into slavery for food. In the eighteenth century "slave exports" reached their peak in times of famine.

Because the Americas had been isolated from the Eurasian-African landmass for thousands of years, parasitic diseases common in Europe, Africa, and Asia were unknown in the Americas before the Europeans' arrival. Enslaved Africans taken to the Americas brought with them the diseases common to tropical West Africa. Thus the hot, humid disease environment in the American tropics, where the majority of enslaved Africans lived and worked, became more "African." On the other hand, cold-weather European diseases, such as chicken pox, mumps, measles, and influenza, prevailed in the northern temperate zone in North America and the southern temperate zone in South America. This difference in disease environment partially explains why Africans made up the majority of the unskilled labor force in the tropical areas of the Americas, and Europeans made up the majority of the unskilled labor force in the Western Hemisphere temperate zones, such as the northern United States and Canada.

Trade and Industry

As in all premodern societies, West African economies rested on agriculture. There was some trade and industry, but population shortages encouraged local self-sufficiency, slowed transportation, and hindered exchange. There were very few large markets, and their relative isolation from the outside world and failure to attract large numbers of foreign merchants limited technological innovation.

For centuries black Africans had exchanged goods with North African merchants in centers such as Gao and Timbuktu. This long-distance trans-Saharan trade was conducted and controlled by Muslim-Berber merchants using camels. The two primary goods exchanged were salt, which came from salt mines in North Africa, and gold, which came mainly from gold mines in modern-day Mali, and later, modern Ghana.

As elsewhere around the world, water was the cheapest method of transportation, and many small dugout canoes and larger trading canoes plied the Niger and its delta region (see Map 20.1). On land West African peoples used pack animals rather than wheeled vehicles; only a narrow belt of land in the Sudan was suitable for animal-drawn carts. When traders reached an area infested with tsetse flies, they transferred each animal's load to human porters. Such difficulties in transport severely restricted long-distance trade, so most people relied on the regional exchange of local specialties.

West African communities had a well-organized market system. At informal markets on riverbanks, fishermen bartered fish for local specialties. More formal markets existed within towns and villages or on neutral ground between them. Markets also rotated among neighboring villages on certain days. Local sellers were usually women; traders from afar were men.

The salt trade dominated the West African economies in the fifteenth, sixteenth, and seventeenth centuries. The main salt-mining center was at Taghaza (see Map 20.1) in the western Sahara. In the most wretched conditions, slaves dug the salt from desiccated lakes and loaded heavy blocks onto camels' backs. **Tuareg** warriors and later Moors (peoples of Berber and Arab descent) traded

West African Trade Routes

Tuareg

▶ Along with the Moors, warriors who controlled the north-south trans-Saharan trade in salt.

CHAPTER LOCATOR | What different types of economic, social, and political structures were found in the kingdoms and states along the west coast and in the Sudan? | How did the arrival of Europeans and other foreign cultures affect the East African coast, and how did Ethiopia and the Swahili city-states respond to these incursions?

CHAPTER 20
590 AFRICA AND THE WORLD

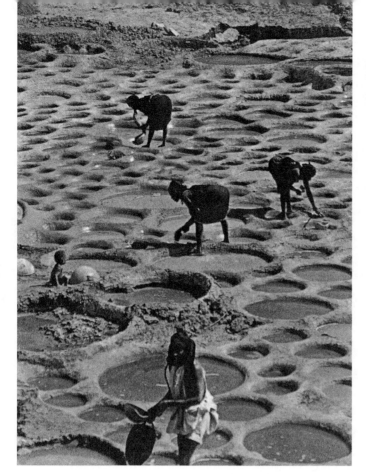

their salt south for gold, grain, slaves, and kola nuts. **Cowrie shells**, imported from the Maldives in the Indian Ocean by way of Gujarat (see page 502) and North Africa, served as the medium of exchange. Gold continued to be mined and shipped from Mali until South American bullion flooded Europe in the sixteenth century. Thereafter, its production in Africa steadily declined.

West African peoples engaged in many crafts, such as basket weaving and potterymaking. Ironworking became hereditary in individual families; such expertise was regarded as family property. The textile industry had the greatest level of specialization. The earliest fabric in West Africa was made of vegetable fiber. Muslim traders introduced cotton and its weaving in the ninth century.

cowrie shells
► Imported from the Maldives, they served as the medium of exchange in West Africa.

QUICK REVIEW <

What role did trade play in West African society?

What role did slavery play in African societies before the transatlantic slave trade began, and what was the effect of European involvement?

✓ LearningCurve
Check what you know.

How did the arrival of Europeans and other foreign cultures affect the East African coast, and how did Ethiopia and the Swahili city-states respond to these incursions?

Chinese Porcelain Plates

Embedded in an eighteenth-century Kunduchi pillar tomb, these Chinese plates testify to the enormous Asian-African trade that flourished in the four-teenth to sixteenth centuries. Kunduchi, whose ruins lie north of Dar es Salaam in present-day Tanzania, was one of the Swahili city-states. (Werner Forman Archive/ The Bridgeman Art Library)

> PICTURING THE PAST

ANALYZING THE IMAGE: How many Chinese plates can you identify? What features identify this as a tomb?

CONNECTIONS: Why would a Muslim African want a Chinese plate embedded in his tomb? What does this suggest about his status, occupation, and wealth?

EAST AFRICA IN THE EARLY modern period faced repeated incursions from foreign powers. At the beginning of the sixteenth century Ethiopia faced challenges from the Muslim state of Adal, and then from Europeans. Jesuit attempts to impose Roman Catholic practices met with fierce resistance and ushered in a centuries-long period of hostility to foreigners. The wealthy Swahili city-states along the southeastern African coast also resisted European intrusions in the sixteenth century, with even more disastrous results.

CHAPTER LOCATOR | What different types of economic, social, and political structures were found in the kingdoms and states along the west coast and in the Sudan?

How did the arrival of Europeans and other foreign cultures affect the East African coast, and how did Ethiopia and the Swahili city-states respond to these incursions?

Muslim and European Incursions in Ethiopia, ca. 1500–1630

At the beginning of the sixteenth century the powerful East African kingdom of Ethiopia extended from Massawa in the north to several tributary states in the south (Map 20.2), but the ruling Solomonic dynasty in Ethiopia, in power since the thirteenth century, faced serious external threats. Alone among the states in northeast and eastern Africa, Ethiopia was a Christian kingdom that practiced **Coptic Christianity**, an orthodox form of the Christian faith that originated in Egypt in 451. By the early 1500s Ethiopia was an island of Christianity surrounded by a sea of Muslim states.

Adal, a Muslim state along the southern base of the Red Sea, began incursions into Ethiopia, and in 1529 the Adal general Ahmad ibn-Ghazi inflicted a disastrous defeat on the Ethiopian emperor Lebna Dengel (r. 1508–1540). Ibn-Ghazi followed up his victory with systematic devastation of the land; destruction of many Ethiopian artistic and literary works, churches, and monasteries; and the forced conversion of thousands to Islam. Lebna Dengel fled to the mountains and appealed to Portugal for assistance. The Portuguese came to his aid, but Dengel was killed in battle before the Portuguese arrived. The Muslim occupation of Christian Ethiopia, which began around 1531, ended in 1543, after a joint Ethiopian and Portuguese force defeated a larger Muslim army at the Battle of Wayna Daga.

In the late twelfth century tales of Prester John, rumored to be a powerful Christian monarch ruling a vast and wealthy African empire, reached western Europe. The search for Prester John, as well as for gold and spices, spurred the Portuguese to undertake a series of trans-African expeditions that reached Timbuktu and Mali in the 1480s and the Ethiopian court by 1508. It was their desire to convert Ethiopians from Coptic Christianity to Roman Catholicism that motivated the Portuguese to aid the Ethiopians in defeating Adal's Muslim forces.

No sooner had the Muslim threat ended than Ethiopia encountered three more dangers. The Galla moved northward in great numbers in the 1530s, occupying portions of Harar, Shoa, and Amhara. The Ethiopians could not defeat

Coptic Christianity

▶ Orthodox form of Christianity from Egypt practiced in Ethiopia.

MAP 20.2 ■ **East Africa in the Sixteenth Century**

In early modern times, the Christian kingdom of Ethiopia, first isolated and then subjected to Muslim and European pressures, played an insignificant role in world affairs. But the East African city-states, which stretched from Sofala in the south to Mogadishu in the north, had powerfully important commercial relations with Mughal India, China, the Ottoman world, and southern Europe.

What role did slavery play in African societies before the transatlantic slave trade began, and what was the effect of European involvement?

✓ LearningCurve
Check what you know.

This wall painting of Saint George slaying a dragon resides in the stone-carved Church of Saint George in Lalibela, Ethiopia, and attests to the powerful and pervasive Christian influence on Ethiopian culture. (Galen R. Frysinger)

them militarily, and the Galla were not interested in assimilation. For the next two centuries the two peoples lived together in an uneasy truce. Simultaneously, the Ottoman Turks seized Massawa and other coastal cities. Then the Jesuits arrived and attempted to force Roman Catholicism on the Ethiopian people. Since Ethiopian national sentiment was closely tied to Coptic Christianity, violent rebellion and anarchy ensued.

In 1633 the Jesuit missionaries were expelled. For the next two centuries hostility to foreigners, weak political leadership, and regionalism characterized Ethiopia. Civil conflicts between Galla and Ethiopians erupted continually. The Coptic Church, though lacking strong authority, survived as the cornerstone of Ethiopian national identity.

The Swahili City-States and the Arrival of the Portuguese, ca. 1500–1600

Swahili

▶ Meaning "People of the Coast," the term used for the people living along the East African coast and on nearby islands.

The word Swahili means "People of the Coast" and refers to the people living along the East African coast and on the nearby islands. Although predominantly a Bantu-speaking people, the Swahili have incorporated significant aspects of Arab culture. The Arabic alphabet was used for the first written works in Swahili and

CHAPTER LOCATOR | What different types of economic, social, and political structures were found in the kingdoms and states along the west coast and in the Sudan? | How did the arrival of Europeans and other foreign cultures affect the East African coast, and how did Ethiopia and the Swahili city-states respond to these incursions?

CHAPTER 20
594 AFRICA AND THE WORLD

roughly 35 percent of Swahili words come from Arabic. By the eleventh century the Swahili had accepted Islam, which provided a common identity and unifying factor for all the peoples along coastal East Africa. Living on the Indian Ocean coast, the Swahili also felt the influences of Indians, Indonesians, Persians, and even the Chinese.

Swahili civilization was overwhelmingly maritime. A fertile, well-watered, and intensely cultivated stretch of land extending down the coast yielded valuable crops. The region's considerable prosperity, however, rested on trade and commerce. The Swahili acted as middlemen in an Indian Ocean–East African economy that might be described as early capitalism. In the fifteenth century the cosmopolitan city-states of Mogadishu, Pate, Lamu, Mombasa, and especially Kilwa enjoyed a worldwide reputation for commercial prosperity and high living standards.[3]

The arrival of the Portuguese explorer Vasco da Gama (see Map 16.2, page 465) in 1498 spelled the end of the Swahili cities' independence. Lured by the spice trade, da Gama wanted to build a Portuguese maritime empire in the Indian Ocean. Some Swahili rulers quickly agreed to a trading alliance with the Portuguese. Others were tricked into commercial agreements. Swahili rulers who rejected Portuguese overtures saw their cities bombarded and attacked. To secure alliances made between 1502 and 1507, the Portuguese erected forts at the southern port cities of Kilwa, Zanzibar, and Sofala. These fortified markets and trading posts served as the foundation of Portuguese commercial power on the Swahili coast. The better-fortified northern cities, such as Mogadishu, survived as important entrepôts for goods to India.

The Portuguese presence in the south did not yield the expected commercial fortunes. Rather than accept Portuguese commercial restrictions, the residents deserted the towns, and the town economies crumbled. Large numbers of Kilwa's people, for example, immigrated to northern cities. The gold flow from inland mines to Sofala slowed to a trickle. Swahili noncooperation successfully prevented the Portuguese from gaining control of the local coastal trade.

In the late seventeenth century pressures from the northern European maritime powers—the Dutch, French, and English, aided greatly by Omani Arabs—combined with local African rebellions to bring about the collapse of Portuguese influence in Africa. A Portuguese presence remained only at Mozambique in the far south and Angola on the west coast.

QUICK REVIEW

What distinctive features characterized East African coastal societies?

What role did slavery play in African societies before the transatlantic slave trade began, and what was the effect of European involvement?

LearningCurve
Check what you know.

What role did slavery play in African societies before the transatlantic slave trade began, and what was the effect of European involvement?

THE ENSLAVEMENT OF HUMAN BEINGS was practiced in some form or another all over Africa—indeed, all over the world. Sanctioned by law and custom, enslaved people served critical and well-defined roles in the social, political, and economic organization of many African societies.

Over time, the trans-Saharan slave trade became less important than the transatlantic trade, which witnessed an explosive growth during the seventeenth and eighteenth centuries. The millions of enslaved Africans forcibly exported to the Americas had a lasting impact on African society and led ultimately to a wider use of slaves within Africa itself.

The Institution of Slavery in Africa

Islamic practices strongly influenced African slavery. African rulers justified enslavement with the Muslim argument that prisoners of war could be sold and that captured people were considered chattel. Between 650 and 1600 Muslims transported perhaps as many as 4.82 million black slaves across the trans-Saharan

CHAPTER LOCATOR | What different types of economic, social, and political structures were found in the kingdoms and states along the west coast and in the Sudan? | How did the arrival of Europeans and other foreign cultures affect the East African coast, and how did Ethiopia and the Swahili city-states respond to these incursions?

CHAPTER 20
596 AFRICA AND THE WORLD

trade route.[4] In the fourteenth and fifteenth centuries the rulers and elites of Mali and Benin imported thousands of white Slavic slave women, symbols of wealth and status, who had been seized in slave raids from the Balkans and Caucasus regions of the eastern Mediterranean by Turks, Mongols, and others.[5]

Meanwhile, the flow of black people to Europe, begun during the Renaissance, continued. In the seventeenth and eighteenth centuries as many as two hundred thousand Africans entered European societies. Some arrived as slaves, others as servants; the legal distinction was not always clear. Eighteenth-century London, for example, had more than ten thousand blacks, most of whom arrived as sailors on Atlantic crossings or as personal servants brought from the West Indies. London's black population constituted a well-organized, self-conscious subculture, with black pubs, black churches, and black social groups assisting the black poor and unemployed. Some black people attained wealth and position.

In 1658 the Dutch East India Company (see page 476) began to allow the importation of slaves into the Cape Colony, which the company had founded on the southern tip of Africa in 1652. Over the next century and a half about 75 percent of the slaves brought into the colony came from Dutch East India Company colonies in India and Southeast Asia or from Madagascar; the remaining 25 percent came from Africa. Most worked long and hard as field hands and at any other menial or manual forms of labor needed by their European masters. The Dutch East India Company was the single largest slave owner in the Cape Colony, employing its slaves on public works and company farms.

Although in the seventeenth and eighteenth centuries Holland enjoyed a Europe-wide reputation for religious tolerance and intellectual freedom (see page 535), in the Cape Colony the Dutch used a strict racial hierarchy and heavy-handed paternalism to maintain control over enslaved native and foreign-born peoples. In Muslim society the offspring of a free man and an enslaved woman were free, but in southern Africa such children remained enslaved. Because enslaved males greatly outnumbered enslaved females in the Cape Colony, marriage and family life were almost nonexistent. Because there were few occupations requiring special skills, those enslaved in the colony lacked opportunities to earn manumission, or freedom. And in contrast with North and South America and with Muslim societies, in the Cape Colony only a very small number of those enslaved won manumission.[6]

The slave trade expanded greatly in East Africa's savanna and Horn regions in the late eighteenth century and the first half of the nineteenth century. Why this increased demand? Merchants and planters wanted slaves to work the sugar plantations on the Mascarene Islands, located east of Madagascar; the clove plantations on Zanzibar and Pemba; and the food plantations along the Kenyan coast. The eastern coast also exported enslaved people to the Americas, particularly to

KITCHIN STUFF.

Below Stairs

The prints and cartoons of Thomas Rowlandson (1756–1827) testify to the sizable numbers of blacks in eighteenth-century London, where they worked in naval and military service as well as domestic service. Here the household cook, maid, and footman relax before the kitchen fire. Interracial marriages were not uncommon. (© The Trustees of The British Museum/Art Resource, NY)

Cape Colony, ca. 1750

What role did slavery play in African societies before the transatlantic slave trade began, and what was the effect of European involvement?

LearningCurve
Check what you know.

597

Brazil. In the late eighteenth and early nineteenth centuries, precisely when the slave trade to North America and the Caribbean declined, the Arabian and Asian markets expanded.

The Transatlantic Slave Trade

Although the trade in African people was a worldwide phenomenon, the transatlantic slave trade involved the largest number of enslaved Africans. This forced migration of millions of human beings, extending from the early sixteenth to the late nineteenth centuries, represents one of the most inhumane, unjust, and shameful tragedies in human history. It also immediately provokes a troubling question: why, in the seventeenth and eighteenth centuries, did enslavement in the Americas become exclusively African?

European settlers first enslaved indigenous peoples, the Amerindians, to mine the silver and gold discovered in the New World (see page 476). When they proved ill suited to the harsh rigors of mining, the Spaniards brought in Africans.

Why did the Spaniards turn to Africa to solve their labor problem? One theory holds that in the Muslim and Arab worlds by the tenth century, an association had developed between blackness and menial slavery. Although the great majority of enslaved persons in the Islamic world were white, a racial element existed in Muslim perceptions: not all slaves were black, but blacks were identified with slavery. In Europe, after the arrival of tens of thousands of sub-Saharan Africans in the Iberian Peninsula during the fifteenth century, Christian Europeans also began to make a strong association between slavery and black Africans. Therefore, Africans seemed the "logical" solution to the labor shortage in the Americas.[7]

Another important question relating to the African slave trade is this: why were African peoples enslaved in a period when serfdom was declining in western Europe, and when land was so widely available and much of the African continent had a labor shortage? The answer seems to lie in a technical problem related to African agriculture. African conditions were unsuitable for plowing with draft animals, and most work had to be done by hand with the hoe. Productivity, therefore, was low. Thus, in precolonial Africa the individual's agricultural productivity was low, so his or her economic value to society was less than the economic value of a European peasant in Europe. Enslaved persons in the Americas were more productive than free producers in Africa. And European slave dealers were very willing to pay a price higher than the value of an African's productivity in Africa.

The incidence of disease in the Americas also helps explain African enslavement. Smallpox took a terrible toll on Native Americans, and between 30 and 50 percent of Europeans exposed to malaria succumbed to that sickness. Africans had developed some immunity to both diseases, and in the Americas they experienced the lowest mortality rate of any people, making them, ironically, the most suitable workers for the environment.

Portuguese colonization of Brazil began in the early 1530s, and in 1551 the Portuguese founded a sugar colony at Bahia. Between 1551 and 1575, before the North American slave traffic began, the Portuguese delivered more African slaves to Brazil than ever reached British North America (Figure 20.1). Portugal essentially monopolized the slave trade until 1600 and continued to play a significant

The Slave Coast
of West Africa

CHAPTER LOCATOR | What different types of economic, social, and political structures were found in the kingdoms and states along the west coast and in the Sudan? | How did the arrival of Europeans and other foreign cultures affect the East African coast, and how did Ethiopia and the Swahili city-states respond to these incursions?

CHAPTER 20
598 AFRICA AND THE WORLD

role in the seventeenth century, though the trade was increasingly taken over by the Dutch, French, and English. From 1690 until the British House of Commons abolished the slave trade in 1807, England was the leading carrier of African slaves.

Population density and supply conditions along the West African coast and the sailing time to New World markets determined the sources of slaves. As the demand for slaves rose, slavers moved down the West African coast from Senegambia to the more densely populated hinterlands of the Bight of Benin and the Bight of Biafra. The abundant supply of Africans to enslave in Angola, the region south of the Congo River, and the quick passage from Angola to Brazil and the Caribbean established that region as the major coast for Portuguese slavers.

Transatlantic wind patterns partly determined exchange routes. Shippers naturally preferred the swiftest crossing—that is, from the African port nearest the latitude of the intended American destination. Thus Portuguese shippers carried their cargoes from Angola to Brazil, and British merchants sailed from the Bight of Benin to the Caribbean. The great majority of enslaved Africans were intended for the sugar and coffee plantations extending from the Caribbean islands to Brazil. Angola produced 26 percent of all African slaves and 70 percent of all Portuguese slaves. Trading networks extending deep into the interior culminated at two major ports on the Angolan coast, Luanda and Benguela. The Portuguese acquired a few slaves through warfare but secured the vast majority through trade with African dealers. Whites did not participate in the inland markets, which were run solely by Africans.

Almost all Portuguese shipments went to satisfy the virtually insatiable Brazilian demand for slaves. The so-called Middle Passage was the horrific journey experienced by Africans from freedom to enslavement in the Americas. Packed tightly into nearly airless holds, enslaved Africans were treated as animals, with large numbers succumbing to disease, malnutrion, and despair before they reached their destination.

Olaudah Equiano (see "Individuals in Society: Olaudah Equiano," page 600) describes the experience of his voyage as a captured slave from Benin to Barbados in the Caribbean:

> The stench of the hold while we were on the coast was so intolerably loathsome that it was dangerous to remain there for any time, and some of us had been permitted to stay on the deck for the fresh air; but now that the whole

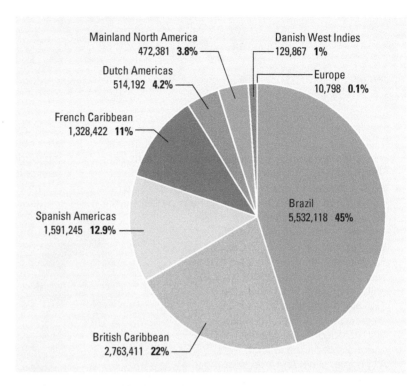

FIGURE 20.1 ■ **Estimated Slave Imports by Destination, 1501–1866**

Brazil was the single largest importer of African slaves from 1501 to 1866. But when taken cumulatively, the British, French, Dutch, and Danish colonies of the Caribbean rivaled the much larger colony of Brazil for numbers of slaves imported from Africa.

(Source: Data from Emory University. "Assessing the Slave Trade: Estimates," in *Voyages: The Trans-Atlantic Slave Trade Database*. 2009. http://www.slavevoyages.org.)

Middle Passage

▶ African slaves' voyage across the Atlantic to the Americas, a long and treacherous journey during which slaves endured appalling and often deadly conditions.

What role did slavery play in African societies before the transatlantic slave trade began, and what was the effect of European involvement?

 LearningCurve
Check what you know.

The transatlantic slave trade was a mass movement involving millions of human beings. It was also the sum of individual lives spent partly or entirely in slavery. Most of those lives remain hidden to us. Olaudah Equiano (1745–1797) represents a rare window into the slaves' obscurity; he is probably the best-known African slave.

In his autobiography, *The Interesting Narrative of the Life of Olaudah Equiano* (1789), Equiano says that he was born in Benin (modern Nigeria) of Ibo ethnicity.* His father, one of the village elders (or chieftains), presided over a large household that included "many slaves," prisoners captured in local wars. All people, slave and free, shared in the cultivation of family lands. One day, when all the adults were in the fields, two strange men and a woman broke into the family compound, kidnapped the eleven-year-old Olaudah and his sister, tied them up, and dragged them into the woods. Brother and sister were separated, and Olaudah was sold several times to various dealers before reaching the coast. As it took six months to walk there, his home must have been far inland. The sea, the slave ship, and the strange appearance of the white crew terrified the boy (see page 599). Equiano's master took him to Jamaica, to Virginia, and then to England, where he placed him in the custody of a kind family. They gave him the rudiments of an education, and he was baptized a Christian.

Equiano soon went to sea as a captain's boy (servant), serving in the Royal Navy during the Seven Years' War (see page 647). On shore at Portsmouth, England, after one battle, Equiano was urged by his master to read, study, and learn basic mathematics. This education served him well, for after a voyage to the West Indies, his master sold him to a Philadelphia Quaker, Robert King, who was a rum and

In this 1789 portrait, Olaudah Equiano holds his Bible, open to the book of Acts. (1789 mezzotint, British Library, London, UK/© British Library Board. All Rights Reserved./The Bridgeman Art Library)

sugar merchant. Equiano worked as a clerk in King's warehouse, as a longshoreman loading and unloading cargo ships, and at sea where he developed good navigational skills; King paid him for his work. Equiano became an entrepreneur himself, buying and selling small goods in the islands and mainland ports.

Determined to buy his freedom, Equiano had amassed enough money by 1766, and King signed the deed of manumission. Equiano was twenty-one years old; he had been a slave for ten years.

Equiano returned to London and used his remaining money to hire tutors to teach him hairdressing, mathematics, and how to play the French horn. When money was scarce, he found work as a merchant seaman, traveling to Portugal, Nice, Genoa, Naples, and Turkey. He even participated in an Arctic expedition.

Equiano's *Narrative* reveals a complex and sophisticated man. He had a strong constitution and an equally strong character. His Christian faith undoubtedly sustained him. On the title page of his book, he cited a verse from Isaiah (12:2): "The Lord Jehovah is my strength and my song." The very first thought that came to his mind the day he was freed was a passage from Psalm 126: "I glorified God in my heart, in whom I trusted."

Equiano loathed the brutal slavery he saw in the West Indies and the vicious racism he experienced in the North American colonies. He respected the fairness of Robert King, admired British navigational and industrial technologies, and had many close white friends. He once described himself as "almost an Englishman." He was also involved in the black communities in the West Indies and in London. Equiano's *Narrative* is a well-documented argument for the abolition of slavery and a literary classic that went through nine editions before his death.

Olaudah Equiano's *Narrative*, with its horrific descriptions of slavery, proved influential, and after its publication Equiano became active in the abolition movement. He spoke to large crowds in the industrial cities of Manchester and Birmingham in England, arguing that it was in the business interests of manufacturers to support abolition, as Africa was a huge,

*Recent scholarship has re-examined Equiano's life and raised some questions about his African origins and his experience of the Middle Passage. To explore the debate over Equiano's authorship of the African and Middle Passage portions of his autobiography, see Vincent Carretta, *Equiano, the African: Biography of a Self-Made Man* (New York: Penguin, 2007).

virtually untapped market for English cloth. Though he died in 1797, ten years before its passage, Equiano significantly advanced the abolitionist cause that led to the Slave Trade Act of 1807.

Source: *Equiano's Travels: The Interesting Narrative of the Life of Olaudah Equiano*, ed. Paul Edwards (Portsmouth, N.H.: Heinemann, 1996).

QUESTIONS FOR ANALYSIS

1. How typical was Olaudah Equiano's life as a slave? How atypical?
2. Describe Equiano's culture and his sense of himself.

ONLINE DOCUMENT PROJECT

What role did slave accounts play in antislavery activism? Read several first-person accounts of slavery, and then complete a quiz and writing assignment based on the evidence and details from this chapter. *See inside the front cover to learn more.*

ship's cargo were confined together it became absolutely pestilential. The closeness of the place and the heat of the climate, added to the number in the ship, which was so crowded that each had scarcely room to turn himself, almost suffocated us. This produced copious perspirations, so that the air soon became unfit for respiration from a variety of loathsome smells, and brought on a sickness among the slaves, of which many died. . . . This wretched situation was again aggravated by the galling of the chains, now become insupportable, and the filth of the necessary tubs [of human waste], into which the children often fell and were almost suffocated. The shrieks of the women and the groans of the dying rendered the whole a scene of horror almost inconceivable.[8]

Although the demand was great, Portuguese merchants in Angola and Brazil sought to maintain only a steady trickle of slaves from the African interior to Luanda and across the ocean to Bahia and Rio de Janeiro: a flood of slaves would have depressed the American market. Planters and mine operators from the provinces traveled to Rio to buy slaves. Between 1795 and 1808 approximately 10,000 Angolans per year stood in the Rio slave market. In 1810 the figure rose to 18,000; in 1828 it reached 32,000.[9]

The English ports of London, Bristol, and particularly Liverpool dominated the British slave trade. In the eighteenth century Liverpool was the world's greatest slave-trading port. In all three cities, small and cohesive merchant classes exercised great public influence. The cities also had huge stores of industrial products for export, growing shipping industries, and large amounts of ready cash for investment abroad.

Slaving ships from Bristol plied back and forth along the Gold Coast, the Bight of Benin, Bonny, and Calabar looking for African traders who were willing to supply them with slaves. Liverpool's ships drew enslaved people from Gambia, the Windward Coast, and the Gold Coast. British ships carried textiles, gunpowder and flint, beer and spirits, British and Irish linens, and woolen cloth to Africa. A collection of goods was grouped together

Peddlers in Rio de Janeiro

A British army officer sketched this early-nineteenth-century scene of everyday life in Rio de Janeiro, Brazil. The ability to balance large burdens on the head meant that the person's hands were free for other use. Note the player (on the left) of a musical instrument originating in the Congo. On the right a woman gives alms to the man with the holy image in return for being allowed to kiss the image as an act of devotion. We do not know whether the peddlers were free and self-employed or were selling for their owners. (From "Views and Costumes of the City and Neighborhood of Rio de Janeiro, Brazil," in *Drawings Taken by Lieutenant Henry Chamberlain, During the Years 1819 and 1820* [London: Columbian Press, 1822]/ Visual Connection Archive)

sorting

▶ A collection or batch of British goods that would be traded for a slave or for a quantity of gold, ivory, or dyewood.

shore trading

▶ A process for trading goods in which European ships sent boats ashore or invited African dealers to bring traders and slaves out to the ships.

into what was called the sorting. An English sorting might include bolts of cloth, firearms, alcohol, tobacco, and hardware; this batch of goods was traded for an enslaved individual or a quantity of gold, ivory, or dyewood.[10]

European traders had two systems for exchange. First, especially on the Gold Coast, they established factory-forts. (For more on factory-forts, see page 502.) These fortified trading posts were expensive to maintain but proved useful for fending off European rivals. Second, they used shore trading, in which European ships sent boats ashore or invited African dealers to bring traders and enslaved Africans out to the ships.

The shore method of buying slaves allowed the ship to move easily from market to market. The final prices of those enslaved depended on their ethnic origin, their availability when the shipper arrived, and their physical health when offered for sale in the West Indies or the North or South American colonies.

The supply of slaves for the foreign market was controlled by a small, wealthy African merchant class or by a state monopoly. By contemporary standards, slave raiding was a costly operation, and only black African entrepreneurs with sizable capital and labor could afford to finance and direct raiding drives.

The transatlantic slave trade that the British, as well as the Dutch, Portuguese, French, Americans, and others, participated in was part of a much larger trading network that is known as the triangle trade. European merchants sailed to Africa on the first leg of the voyage to trade European manufactured goods for enslaved Africans. When they had filled their ships' holds with enslaved peoples,

CHAPTER LOCATOR | What different types of economic, social, and political structures were found in the kingdoms and states along the west coast and in the Sudan? | How did the arrival of Europeans and other foreign cultures affect the East African coast, and how did Ethiopia and the Swahili city-states respond to these incursions?

602 CHAPTER 20 AFRICA AND THE WORLD

they headed across the Atlantic on the second leg of the voyage, the Middle Passage. When they reached the Americas, the merchants unloaded and sold their human cargoes and used the profits to purchase raw materials—such as cotton, sugar, and indigo—that they then transported back to Europe, completing the third leg of the commercial triangle.

> **The Triangle Trade:**

- Africa: Europeans trade manufactured goods for enslaved Africans
- The Americas: Enslaved Africans are sold and raw materials are purchased
- Europe: Raw materials are sold and manufactured goods are purchased

Enslaved African people had an enormous impact on the economies and cultures of the Portuguese and Spanish colonies of South America and the Dutch, French, and British colonies of the Caribbean and North America. For example, on the sugar plantations of Mexico and the Caribbean; on the North American cotton, rice, and tobacco plantations; and in Peruvian and Mexican silver and gold mines, enslaved Africans not only worked in the mines and fields but also filled skilled, supervisory, and administrative positions and performed domestic service. In the United States enslaved Africans and their descendants influenced many facets of American culture, such as language, music (ragtime and jazz), dance, and diet. But the importance of the slave trade extended beyond the Atlantic world. Both the expansion of capitalism and the industrialization of Western societies; Egypt; and the nations of West, Central, and South Africa were related in one way or another to the traffic in African people.

Impact on African Societies

What economic impact did European trade have on African societies? Africans possessed technology well suited to their environment. Over the centuries they had cultivated a wide variety of plant foods; developed plant and animal husbandry techniques; and mined, smelted, and otherwise worked a great variety of metals. Apart from a handful of items, most notably firearms, European goods presented no novelty to Africans. Africans exchanged slaves, ivory, gold, pepper, and animal skins for those goods. African states eager to expand or to control commerce bought European firearms, although the difficulty of maintaining guns often gave gun owners only marginal superiority over skilled bowmen.[11]

The African merchants who controlled the production of exports gained the most from foreign trade. Slave-trading entrepôts, which provided opportunities for traders and for farmers who supplied foodstuffs to towns, caravans, and slave ships, prospered. But such economic returns did not spread very far.[12] International trade did not lead to Africa's economic development. Africa experienced neither technological growth nor the gradual spread of economic benefits in early modern times.

As in the Islamic world, women in sub-Saharan Africa also engaged in the slave trade. In Guinea these women slave merchants and traders were known as *nhara*. They acquired considerable riches, often by marrying the Portuguese merchants and serving as go-betweens for these outsiders who were not familiar with the customs and languages of the African coast.

What role did slavery play in African societies before the transatlantic slave trade began, and what was the effect of European involvement?

 LearningCurve
Check what you know.

Sapi-Portuguese Saltcellar

Contact with the Sapi people of present-day Sierra Leone in West Africa led sixteenth-century Portuguese traders to commission this ivory saltcellar, for which they brought Portuguese designs. But the object's basic features — a spherical container and separate lid on a flat base, with men and/or women supporting, or serving as, beams below — are distinctly African. Here a Portuguese caravel sits on top with a man in the crow's nest. Four men stand below: two finely carved, regally dressed, and fully armed noblemen facing forward and two attendants in profile. (© akg-images/The Image Works)

The intermarriage of French traders and Wolof women in Senegambia created a métis, or mulatto, class. In the emerging urban centers at Saint-Louis, members of this small class adopted the French language, the Roman Catholic faith, and a French manner of life, and they exercised considerable political and economic power. However, European cultural influences did not penetrate West African society beyond the seacoast.

The political consequences of the slave trade varied from place to place. The trade enhanced the power and wealth of some kings and warlords in the short run but promoted conditions of instability and collapse over the long run. In the Kongo kingdom the perpetual Portuguese search for Africans to enslave undermined the monarchy, destroyed political unity, and led to constant disorder and warfare; power passed to the village chiefs. Likewise in Angola, the slave trade decimated and scattered the population and destroyed the local economy. By contrast, the military kingdom of Dahomey, which entered into the slave trade in the eighteenth century and made it a royal monopoly, prospered enormously. Dahomey's economic strength rested on the slave trade. The royal army raided deep into the interior, and in the late eighteenth century Dahomey became one of the major West African sources of slaves. When slaving expeditions failed to yield sizable catches and when European demand declined, the resulting depression in the Dahomean economy caused serious political unrest. Iboland, inland from the Niger Delta, from whose great port cities of Bonny and Brass the British drained tens of thousands of enslaved Africans, experienced minimal political effects. A high birthrate kept pace with the incursions of the slave trade, and Ibo societies remained demographically and economically strong.

What demographic impact did the slave trade have on Africa? Between approximately 1501 and 1866 more than 12 million Africans were forcibly exported to the Americas, 6 million were traded to Asia, and 8 million were retained as slaves within Africa. Figure 20.2 shows the estimated number of slaves shipped to the Americas in the transatlantic slave trade. Export figures do not include the approximately 10 to 15 percent who died during procurement or in transit.

The early modern slave trade involved a worldwide network of relationships among markets in the Middle East, Africa, Asia, Europe, and the Americas. But Africa was the crucible of the trade. There is no small irony in the fact that Africa, which of all the continents was most desperately in need of population because of its near total dependence on labor-intensive agriculture and pastoralism, lost so many millions to the trade. Although the British Parliament abolished the slave trade in 1807 and traffic in Africans to Brazil and Cuba gradually declined, within Africa the trade continued at the levels of the peak years of the transatlantic trade, 1780–1820. In the later nineteenth century developing African industries, using slave labor, produced a variety of products for domestic consumption and export. Again, there is irony in the fact that in the eighteenth century European demand for slaves expanded the trade (and wars) within Africa, yet in the nineteenth century European imperialists defended territorial aggrandizement by arguing that they were "civilizing" Africans by abolishing slavery. But after 1880 European businessmen (and African governments) did not push abolition; they wanted cheap labor.

Markets in the Americas generally wanted young male slaves. Asian and African markets preferred young females. Women were sought for their reproductive value, as sex objects, and because their economic productivity was not threatened by the possibility of physical rebellion, as might be the case with young men. Consequently, two-thirds of those exported to the Americas were male, one-third female. As a result, the population on Africa's western coast became predominantly female; the population in the East African savanna and Horn regions was predominantly male. The slave trade therefore had significant consequences for the institutions of marriage, the local trade in enslaved people (as these local populations became skewed with too many males or too many females), and the sexual division of labor. Although Africa's overall population may have shown modest growth from roughly 1650 to 1900, that growth was offset by declines in the Horn and on the eastern and western coasts. While Europe and Asia experienced considerable demographic and economic expansion in the eighteenth century, Africa suffered a decline.[13]

FIGURE 20.2 ■ The Transatlantic Slave Trade, 1501–1866

The volume of slaves involved in the transatlantic slave trade peaked during the eighteenth century. These numbers show the slaves who embarked from Africa and do not reflect the 10 to 15 percent of enslaved Africans who died in transit. (Source: Data from Emory University. "Assessing the Slave Trade: Estimates," in *Voyages: The Trans-Atlantic Slave Trade Database.* 2009. http://www.slavevoyages.org.)

QUICK REVIEW

How did the transatlantic slave trade shape African demographic trends?

What role did slavery play in African societies before the transatlantic slave trade began, and what was the effect of European involvement?

LearningCurve
Check what you know.

CHAPTER SUMMARY

In the early modern world, West African kingdoms and stateless societies existed side by side. Both had predominantly agricultural economies. Stateless societies revolved around a single village or group of villages without a central capital or ruler. Kings ruled over defined areas through bureaucratic hierarchies. The Sudanic empires controlled the north-south trans-Saharan trade in gold, salt, and other items. Led by predominantly Muslim rulers, these kingdoms belonged to a wider Islamic world, allowing them access to vast trade networks and some of the most advanced scholarship in the world. Still, Muslim culture affected primarily the royal and elite classes, seldom reaching the masses.

Europeans believed a wealthy (mythical) Christian monarch named Prester John ruled the Christian kingdom of Ethiopia. This fable attracted Europeans to Ethiopia, and partly explains why the Portuguese helped the Ethiopians fight off Muslim incursions. Jesuit missionaries tried to convert Ethiopians to Roman Catholicism but were fiercely resisted and expelled in 1633.

Swahili city-states on Africa's southeastern coast possessed a Muslim and mercantile culture. The Swahili acted as middlemen in the East African–Indian Ocean trade network, which, in the late fifteenth and early sixteenth centuries, Portugal sought to conquer and control. Swahili rulers who refused to form trading alliances with the Portuguese were attacked. The Portuguese presence caused the economic decline and death of many Swahili cities.

Slavery existed across Africa before Europeans arrived. Enslaved people were treated relatively benignly in some societies but elsewhere as chattel possessions, suffering harsh and brutal treatment. European involvement in the slave trade began around 1550, when the Portuguese purchased Africans to work in Brazil. The Dutch East India Company used enslaved Africans and southeast Asians in their Cape Colony. African entrepreneurs and merchants partnered in the trade, capturing people in the interior and exchanging them for firearms, liquor, and other goods with European slave ships. Though some kingdoms experienced a temporary rise of wealth and power, over time the slave trade was largely destabilizing. The individual suffering and social disruption in Africa caused by the enslavement of millions of Africans is impossible to estimate.

 CONNECTIONS During the period from 1400 to 1800 many parts of Africa experienced a profound transition with the arrival of Europeans all along Africa's coasts. Ancient trade routes, such as those across the Sahara Desert or up and down the East African coast, were disrupted. In West Africa trade routes that had been purely internal now connected with global trade networks at European coastal trading posts. Along Africa's east coast the Portuguese attacked Swahili city-states in their effort to take control of the Indian Ocean trade nexus.

The most momentous consequence of the European presence along Africa's coast, however, was the introduction of the transatlantic slave trade. For more than three centuries Europeans, with the aid of African slave traders, enslaved millions of African men and women. Although many parts of Africa were untouched by the

CHAPTER LOCATOR | What different types of economic, social, and political structures were found in the kingdoms and states along the west coast and in the Sudan? | How did the arrival of Europeans and other foreign cultures affect the East African coast, and how did Ethiopia and the Swahili city-states respond to these incursions?

606 CHAPTER 20 AFRICA AND THE WORLD

transatlantic slave trade, at least directly, areas where Africans were enslaved experienced serious declines in agricultural production, little progress in technological development, and significant increases in violence.

As we saw in Chapter 17 and will see in Chapter 21, early European commercial contacts with the empires of the Middle East and of South and East Asia were similar in many ways to those with Africa. Initially, the Portuguese, and then the English, Dutch, and French, did little more than establish trading posts at port cities and had to depend on the local people to bring them trade goods from the interior. Tropical diseases, particularly in India and Southeast Asia, took heavy death tolls on the Europeans, as they did in tropical Africa. What is more, while it was possible for the Portuguese to attack and conquer the individual Swahili city-states, Middle Eastern and Asian empires were, like the West African kingdoms, economically and militarily powerful enough to dictate terms of trade with the Europeans.

Resistance to enslavement took many forms on both sides of the Atlantic. In Haiti, as discussed in Chapter 22, resistance led to revolution and independence, marking the first successful uprising of non-Europeans against a colonial power. At the end of the nineteenth century, as described in Chapter 25, Europeans used the ongoing Arab-Swahili slave raids from Africa's eastern coast far into the interior as an excuse to invade and eventually colonize much of central and eastern Africa. The racial discrimination that accompanied colonial rule in Africa set the stage for a struggle for equality that led to eventual independence after World War II.

ONLINE DOCUMENT PROJECT

African Voices in the Antislavery Movement

What role did slave accounts play in antislavery activism?

Read several first-person accounts of slavery, and then complete a quiz and writing assignment based on the evidence and details from this chapter. *See inside the front cover to learn more.*

What role did slavery play in African societies before the transatlantic slave trade began, and what was the effect of European involvement?

✓ LearningCurve
Check what you know.

CHAPTER 20 STUDY GUIDE

STEP 1

GET STARTED ONLINE

 LearningCurve

Now that you've read the chapter, make it stick by completing the LearningCurve activity.

STEP 2

EXPLAIN WHY IT MATTERS

Put your reading into practice. Identify each term below, and then explain why it matters in world history.

TERM	WHO OR WHAT & WHEN	WHY IT MATTERS
chattel (p. 585)		
age-grade systems (p. 585)		
oba (p. 587)		
Taghaza (p. 587)		
Tuareg (p. 590)		
cowrie shells (p. 591)		
Coptic Christianity (p. 593)		
Swahili (p. 594)		
Middle Passage (p. 599)		
sorting (p. 602)		
shore trading (p. 602)		

STEP 3

MOVE BEYOND THE BASICS

To demonstrate a more advanced understanding of early modern West and East Africa, fill in the chart below with descriptions of key aspects of each region. What were the most important differences between West African and East African states?

	Political Organization	Economy and Commerce	Relationship to Europe and the Muslim World	Slavery and the Slave Trade
West Africa				
East Africa				

PUT IT ALL TOGETHER   Now, take a step back and try to explain the big picture. Remember to use specific examples from the chapter in your answers.

WEST AFRICA

▶ What was the relationship between stateless societies and the dominant states of West Africa?

▶ How did the slave trade shape marriage patterns and family structure in West Africa?

EAST AFRICA

▶ What was the legacy for Ethiopia of early modern conflicts among Muslims, Coptic Christians, and Roman Catholics?

▶ Why was the arrival of the Portuguese an economic disaster for East Africa?

THE AFRICAN SLAVE TRADE

▶ What economic forces, both inside Africa and in the larger Atlantic world, contributed to the growth of the transatlantic slave trade?

▶ How and why did enslavement in the Americas become exclusively African?

LOOKING BACK, LOOKING AHEAD

▶ How did the transatlantic slave trade build on earlier African labor practices and commercial connections? How were older patterns of trade and exchange disrupted by the demand for African slaves in the Americas?

▶ What connections can you make between the colonization and exploitation of Africa by industrialized nations in the nineteenth and twentieth centuries and the transatlantic slave trade?

> **IN YOUR OWN WORDS**

Imagine that you must give an oral report to the class answering the following question: What were the short-term and long-term consequences of the transatlantic slave trade for African societies? What would be the most important points and why?

21
CONTINUITY AND CHANGE IN EAST ASIA
1400–1800

> **What fueled population and economic growth in East Asia between 1400 and 1800?** Chapter 21 examines major developments in China and Japan from 1400 to 1800. Under the Ming (1368–1644), China saw agricultural reconstruction, commercial expansion, and the rise of a vibrant urban culture. In the early seventeenth century, after the Ming Dynasty fell into disorder, the non-Chinese Manchus founded the Qing Dynasty (1644–1911) and added Taiwan, Mongolia, Tibet, and Xinjiang to their realm. In Japan the fifteenth century saw the start of a long period of civil war. At the end of the sixteenth century, Hideyoshi (HEE-deh-YOH-shee) became the supreme ruler. After his death, power was seized by Tokugawa Ieyasu (toh-koo-GAH-wuh ee-eh-YAH-soo). Under the Tokugawa Shogunate (1603–1867), Japan restricted contact with the outside world and social mobility among its own people. Yet Japan thrived, as agricultural productivity increased and a lively urban culture developed.

Kabuki Actor Urban entertainment flourished in Japan under the rule of the Tokugawa shoguns. This late-eighteenth-century woodblock print was made for the many fans of the Kabuki actor Matsumoto Yonesaburo, who specialized in performing female roles. (Private Collection/Photo © Boltin Picture Library/The Bridgeman Art Library)

> What sort of state and society developed in China after the Mongols were ousted?

> Did the return of alien rule with the Manchus have any positive consequences for China?

> How did Japan change during this period of political instability?

> What was life like in Japan during the Tokugawa peace?

> How did the sea link the countries of East Asia, and what happened when Europeans entered this maritime sphere?

LearningCurve
After reading the chapter, use LearningCurve to retain what you've read.

What sort of state and society developed in China after the Mongols were ousted?

Portrait of a Scholar-Official

The official Jiang Shunfu arranged to have his portrait painted wearing an official robe and hat and followed by two boy attendants, one holding a lute wrapped in cloth. During Ming and Qing times, the rank of an official was made visible by the badges he wore on his robes. The pair of cranes on Jiang's badge shows he held a first-rank post in the civil service hierarchy. (From *Mingqing renwuxiaoxiang huaxuan* [Nanjing: Nanjing Bowuguan], pl 16/Visual Connection Archive)

THE OVERTHROW OF THE MONGOLS and the establishment of the Ming Dynasty ushered in an era of peace, prosperity, and lively urban culture. By the beginning of the seventeenth century, however, the Ming government was beset by fiscal, military, and political problems.

Ming Dynasty

▶ The Chinese dynasty in power from 1368 to 1644; it marked a period of agricultural reconstruction, foreign expeditions, commercial expansion, and vibrant urban culture.

The Rise of Zhu Yuanzhang and the Founding of the Ming Dynasty

The founder of the **Ming Dynasty**, Zhu Yuanzhang (1328–1398) (JOO yoowan-JAHNG), began life in poverty during the last decades of the Mongol Yuan Dynasty. His home region was hit by drought and then plague in the 1340s, and when he

1368–1644 Ming Dynasty in China	**1603–1867** Tokugawa Shogunate in Japan
1405–1433 Zheng He's naval expeditions	**1615** Battle of Osaka leads to persecution of Christians in Japan
1407–1420 Construction of Beijing as Chinese capital	**1629** Tokugawa government bans actresses from the stage
1467–1600 Period of civil war in Japan	**1639** Japan closes its borders
ca. 1500–1600 Increased availability of books for general audiences in China	**1644–1911** Qing Dynasty in China
1549 First Jesuit missionaries land in Japan	**1793** Lord Macartney's diplomatic visit to China
1557 Portuguese set up trading base at Macao	

was only sixteen years old, his father, oldest brother, and that brother's wife all died. With no relatives to turn to, Zhu Yuanzhang asked a monastery to accept him as a novice. The monks soon sent Zhu out to beg for food, and for three or four years he wandered through central China. Only after he returned to the monastery did he learn to read.

In 1351 members of a religious sect known as the Red Turbans rose in rebellion against the government. Red Turban teachings drew on Manichaean ideas about the incompatibility of the forces of good and evil as well as on the cult of the Maitreya Buddha, who according to believers would in the future bring his paradise to earth to relieve human suffering. When the temple where Zhu Yuanzhang was living was burned down in the fighting, Zhu joined the rebels and rose rapidly.

Zhu and his followers developed into brilliant generals, and gradually they defeated one rival after another. In 1356 Zhu took the city of Nanjing and made it his base. In 1368 his armies took Beijing, and Zhu Yuanzhang declared himself emperor of the Ming (Bright) Dynasty. As emperor, he is known as Taizu (TIGH-dzoo) or the Hongwu emperor.

Taizu started his reign wanting to help the poor. To lighten the weight of government taxes and compulsory labor, he ordered a full-scale registration of cultivated land and population so that these burdens could be assessed more fairly.

Although in many ways anti-Mongol, Taizu retained some Yuan practices. One was setting up provinces as the administrative layer between the central government and the prefectures (local governments a step above counties). Another was the hereditary service obligation for both artisan and military households.

Garrisons were concentrated along the northern border and near the capital at Nanjing. Each garrison was allocated a tract of land that the soldiers took turns cultivating to supply their own food. Although in theory this system should have provided the Ming with a large but inexpensive army, the reality was less satisfactory. Garrisons were rarely self-sufficient. Furthermore, men compelled to

Ming China, ca. 1600

How did Japan change during this period of political instability?	What was life like in Japan during the Tokugawa peace?	How did the sea link the countries of East Asia, and what happened when Europeans entered this maritime sphere?	✓ LearningCurve Check what you know.

613

become soldiers did not necessarily make good fighting men, and desertion was difficult to prevent. Consequently, like earlier dynasties, the Ming turned to non-Chinese northerners for much of its armed forces.

Taizu had deeply ambivalent feelings about men of education and sometimes brutally humiliated them in open court. His behavior was so erratic that it is most likely that he suffered from some form of mental illness. When literary men began to avoid official life, Taizu made it illegal to turn down appointments or to resign from office. In 1376 Taizu had thousands of officials killed because they were found to have taken shortcuts in their handling of paperwork for the grain tax. In 1380 Taizu concluded that his chancellor was plotting to assassinate him, and thousands only remotely connected to the chancellor were executed. From then on, Taizu acted as his own chancellor, dealing directly with the heads of departments and ministries.

The next important emperor, called Chengzu or the Yongle emperor (r. 1403–1425), was also a military man. One of Taizu's younger sons, he took the throne by force from his nephew and often led troops into battle against the Mongols. Like his father, Chengzu was willing to use terror to keep government officials in line.

Early in his reign, Chengzu decided to move the capital from Nanjing to Beijing, which had been his own base as a prince and the capital during Mongol times. Constructed between 1407 and 1420, Beijing was a planned city. Like Chang'an in Sui-Tang times (581–907), it was arranged like a set of boxes within boxes and built on a north-south axis. The main outer walls were forty feet high and nearly fifteen miles around. Inside was the Imperial City, with government offices, and within that the palace itself, called the Forbidden City.

The areas surrounding Beijing were not nearly as agriculturally productive as those around Nanjing. To supply Beijing with grain, the Yuan Grand Canal connecting the city to the rice basket of the Yangzi River regions was broadened, deepened, and supplied with more locks and dams.

Forbidden City

The palace complex in Beijing, commonly called the Forbidden City, was built in the early fifteenth century when the capital was moved from Nanjing to Beijing. Audience halls and other important state buildings are arranged on a north-south axis with huge courtyards between them, where officials would stand during ceremonies. (sinopictures/Wenxiao–ullstein bild/The Granger Collection, NYC — All rights reserved)

CHAPTER LOCATOR | What sort of state and society developed in China after the Mongols were ousted? | Did the return of alien rule with the Manchus have any positive consequences for China?

614 CHAPTER 21 CONTINUITY AND CHANGE IN EAST ASIA

Problems with the Imperial Institution

Taizu had decreed that succession should go to the eldest son of the empress or to the son's eldest son if the son predeceased his father, the system generally followed by earlier dynasties. In Ming times, the flaws in this system became apparent as one mediocre, obtuse, or erratic emperor followed another.

Because Taizu had abolished the position of chancellor, emperors turned to secretaries and eunuchs to manage the paperwork. Eunuchs were essentially slaves. Society considered eunuchs the basest of servants, and Confucian scholars heaped scorn on them. Yet Ming emperors, like rulers in earlier dynasties, often preferred the always-compliant eunuchs to high-minded, moralizing civil service officials.

In Ming times, the eunuch establishment became huge. By the late fifteenth century the eunuch bureaucracy had grown as large as the civil service. After 1500 the eunuch bureaucracy grew even more rapidly, and by the mid-sixteenth century seventy thousand eunuchs were in service throughout the country, with ten thousand in the capital. Tension between the two bureaucracies was high. In 1420 Chengzu set up a eunuch-run secret service to investigate cases of suspected corruption and sedition in the regular bureaucracy. Eunuch control over vital government processes became a severe problem.

In hope of persuading emperors to make reforms, many Ming officials risked their careers and lives by speaking out and engaging in public protests. The Confucian tradition celebrated these acts of political protest as heroic. Rarely, however, did they succeed in moving an emperor to change his mind.

Although the educated public complained about the performance of emperors, no one proposed or even imagined alternatives to imperial rule. High officials were forced to find ways to work around uncooperative emperors, but they were not able to put in place institutions that would limit the damage an emperor could do. Knowing that strong emperors often acted erratically, many high officials came to prefer weak emperors who let them take care of the government.

The Mongols and the Great Wall

The early Ming emperors feared the formation of another great Mongol military machine of the sort Chinggis Khan (ca. 1162–1227) had put together two centuries earlier. Although in Ming times the Mongols were never united in a pan-Mongol federation, groups of Mongols could and did raid. Twice they threatened the dynasty: in 1449 the khan of the western Mongols captured the Chinese emperor, and in 1550 Beijing was surrounded by the forces of the khan of the Mongols in Inner Mongolia. Fearful of anything that might strengthen the Mongols, Ming officials were reluctant to grant any privileges to Mongol leaders, such as trading posts along the borders. Instead they wanted the different groups of Mongols to trade only through the formal tribute system. When trade was finally liberalized in 1570, friction was reduced.

Two important developments shaped Ming-Mongol relations: the construction of the Great Wall, and closer relations between Mongolia and Tibet. The Great Wall extends about 1,500 miles from northeast of Beijing into Gansu province. In the eastern 500 miles, the wall averages about 35 feet high and 20 feet across, with lookout towers every half mile.

Whether the wall did much to protect Ming China from the Mongols is still debated. Perhaps of more significance was the spread of Tibetan Buddhism

How did Japan change during this period of political instability?

What was life like in Japan during the Tokugawa peace?

How did the sea link the countries of East Asia, and what happened when Europeans entered this maritime sphere?

✔ LearningCurve
Check what you know.

615

among the Mongols. The Tibetan Buddhist Tsong-kha-pa (1357–1419) founded the Yellow Hat, or Gelug-pa, sect, whose heads later became known as the Dalai Lamas. In 1577 the third Dalai Lama accepted the invitation of Altan Khan to visit Mongolia, and the khan declared Tibetan Buddhism to be the official religion of all the Mongols. The Dalai Lama gave the khan the title "King of Religion," and the khan swore that the Mongols would renounce blood sacrifice. When the third Dalai Lama's reincarnation was found to be the great-grandson of Altan Khan, the ties between Tibet and Mongolia, not surprisingly, became even stronger. From the perspective of Ming China, the growing influence of Buddhism among the Mongols seemed a positive development, as Buddhist emphasis on nonviolence was expected to counter the Mongols' love of war.

The Examination Life

In sharp contrast to Europe in this era, Ming China had few social barriers. It had no hereditary aristocracy that could have limited the emperor's absolute power. Although China had no titled aristocracy, it did have an elite whose status was based above all on government office acquired through education. Unlike in many European countries of the era, China's merchants did not become a politically articulate bourgeoisie. Instead the politically active class was that of the scholars who Confucianism taught should aid the ruler in running the state. Merchants tried to marry into the scholar class in order to rise in the world.

Thus, despite the harsh and arbitrary ways in which the Ming emperors treated their civil servants, educated men were eager to enter the government. Reversing the policies of the Mongol Yuan Dynasty, the Ming government recruited almost all its officials through civil service examinations. To become officials, candidates had to pass examinations at the prefectural, the provincial, and the capital levels. To keep the wealthiest areas from dominating the exams, quotas were established for the number of candidates that each province could send on to the capital.

Of course, boys from well-to-do families had a significant advantage because their families could start their education with tutors at age four or five, though less costly schools were becoming increasingly available as well. Families that for generations had pursued other careers—for example, as merchants or physicians— had more opportunities than ever for their sons to become officials through the exams. (See "Individuals in Society: Tan Yunxian, Woman Doctor," page 617.) Clans sometimes operated schools for their members. Most of those who attended school stayed only a few years, but students who seemed most promising moved on to advanced schools where they practiced essay writing and studied the essays of men who had succeeded in the exams.

The examinations at the prefecture level lasted a day and drew hundreds if not thousands of candidates. The provincial and capital examinations were given in three sessions spread out over a week. In the first session, candidates wrote essays on passages from the classics. In the second and third sessions, candidates had to write essays on practical policy issues and on a passage from the *Classic of Filial Piety* (a brief text celebrating devotion to parents and other superiors). In addition, they had to show that they could draft state papers such as edicts, decrees, and judicial rulings. Reading the dynastic histories was a good way to prepare for policy questions and state paper exercises.

civil service examinations
▶ A highly competitive series of written tests held at the prefecture, province, and capital levels to select men to become officials.

INDIVIDUALS IN SOCIETY
Tan Yunxian, Woman Doctor

The grandmother of Tan Yunxian (1461–1554) was the daughter of a physician, and her husband had married into her home to learn medicine himself. At least two of their sons — including Yunxian's father — passed the civil service examination and became officials, raising the social standing of the family considerably. The grandparents wanted to pass their medical knowledge down to someone, and because they found Yunxian very bright, they decided to teach it to her.

Tan Yunxian married and raised four children but also practiced medicine, confining her practice to women. At age fifty she wrote an autobiographical account, *Sayings of a Female Doctor*. In the preface she described how, under her grandmother's tutelage, she had first memorized the *Canon of Problems* and the *Canon of the Pulse*. Then when her grandmother had time, she asked her granddaughter to explain particular passages in these classic medical treatises.

Tan Yunxian began the practice of medicine by treating her own children, asking her grandmother to check her diagnoses. When her grandmother was old and ill, she gave Yunxian her notebook of prescriptions and her equipment for making medicines, telling her to study them carefully. Later, Yunxian herself became seriously ill and dreamed of her grandmother telling her on what page of which book to find the prescription that would cure her. When she recovered, she began her medical career in earnest.

Tan Yunxian's book records the cases of thirty-one patients she treated, most of them women with chronic complaints rather than critical illnesses. Many of the women had what the Chinese classed as women's complaints, such as menstrual irregularities, repeated miscarriages, barrenness, and postpartum fatigue. Some had ailments that men too could suffer, such as coughs, nausea, insomnia, diarrhea, rashes, and swellings. Like other literati physicians, Yunxian regularly prescribed herbal medications. She also practiced moxibustion, the technique of burning moxa (dried artemisia) at specified points on the body with the goal of stimulating the circulation of qi (life energy). Because the physician applying the moxa had to touch the patient, male physicians could not perform moxibustion on women.

Yunxian's patients included working women, and Yunxian seems to have thought that their problems often sprang from overwork. One woman came to her because she had had vaginal bleeding for three years. When questioned, the woman told Yunxian that she worked all day with her husband at their kiln making bricks and tiles. Yunxian's diagnosis was overwork, and she gave the woman pills to replenish her yin energies. A boatman's wife came to her complaining of numbness in her hands. When the woman told Yunxian that she worked in the wind and rain handling the boat,

Tan Yunxian would have consulted traditional herbals, like this one, with sketches of plants of medicinal value and descriptions of their uses. (Wellcome Trust, London)

the doctor advised some time off. In another case Yunxian explained to a servant girl that she had gone back to work too soon after suffering a wind damage fever.

By contrast, when patients came from upper-class families, Tan Yunxian believed negative emotions were the source of their problems, particularly if a woman reported that her mother-in-law had scolded her or that her husband had recently brought a concubine home. Yunxian told two upper-class women who had miscarried that they lost their babies because they had hidden their anger, causing fire to turn inward and destabilize the fetus.

Tan Yunxian herself lived a long life, dying at age ninety-three.

Source: Based on Charlotte Furth, *A Flourishing Yin: Gender in China's Medical History, 960–1665* (Berkeley: University of California Press, 1999), pp. 285–295.

QUESTIONS FOR ANALYSIS

1. Why do you think Tan Yunxian treated only women? Why might she have been more effective with women patients than a male physician would have been?
2. What do you think of Yunxian's diagnoses? Do you think she was able to help many of her patients?

ONLINE DOCUMENT PROJECT

What kinds of treatments did Chinese doctors employ? Examine artwork depicting Chinese medical practices, and then complete a quiz and writing assignment based on the evidence and details from this chapter. *See inside the front cover to learn more.*

617

Everyday Life in Ming China

For civil servants and almost everyone else, everyday life in Ming China followed patterns established in earlier periods. The family remained central to most people's lives, and almost everyone married. Beyond the family, people's lives were shaped by the type of work they did and where they lived.

Large towns and cities proliferated in Ming times. In these urban areas small businesses manufactured textiles, paper, and luxury goods such as silks and porcelains. The southeast became a center for the production of cotton and silks; other areas specialized in the grain and salt trades and in silver.

Printing was invented in Tang times (618–907) and had a great impact on the life of the educated elite in Song times (960–1279), but not until Ming times did it transform the culture of the urban middle classes. By the late Ming period, publishing houses were putting out large numbers of books aimed at general audiences. To make their books attractive in the marketplace, entrepreneurial book publishers commissioned artists to illustrate them. By the sixteenth century more and more books were being published in the vernacular language (the language people spoke), especially short stories, novels, and plays. Ming vernacular short stories depicted a world much like that of their readers, full of shop clerks and merchants, monks and prostitutes, students and matchmakers.

The full-length novel made its first appearance during the Ming period. The plots of the early novels were heavily indebted to story cycles developed by oral storytellers over the course of several centuries. Competing publishers brought out their own editions of popular novels, sometimes adding new illustrations or commentaries.

> ### > Popular Ming Novels:

- *Water Margin*: an episodic tale of a band of bandits
- *The Romance of the Three Kingdoms*: a work of historical fiction based on the exploits of the generals and statesmen contending for power at the end of the Han Dynasty
- *The Journey to the West*: a fantastic account of the Tang monk Xuanzang's travels to India
- *Plum in the Golden Vase*: novel of manners about a lustful merchant with a wife and five concubines

The Chinese found recreation and relaxation in many ways besides reading. The affluent indulged in an alcoholic drink made from fermented and distilled rice, and once tobacco was introduced from the Americas, both men and women took up pipes. Plays were also very popular, and people not only enjoyed play performances but also avidly read the play scripts.

Rice supplied most of the calories of the population in central and south China. (In north China, wheat, made into steamed or baked bread or into noodles, served as the dietary staple.) In the south, terracing and irrigation of mountain slopes, introduced in the eleventh century, had increased rice harvests. Other innovations also brought good results. Farmers began to stock the rice paddies with fish, which continuously fertilized the rice fields, destroyed malaria-bearing mosquitoes, and enriched the diet. Farmers also grew cotton, sugarcane, and indigo as commercial crops. New methods of crop rotation allowed for continuous cultivation and for more than one harvest per year from a single field.

CHAPTER LOCATOR | What sort of state and society developed in China after the Mongols were ousted? | Did the return of alien rule with the Manchus have any positive consequences for China?

CHAPTER 21
618 CONTINUITY AND CHANGE IN EAST ASIA

The Ming rulers promoted the repopulation and colonization of war-devastated regions through reclamation of land and massive transfers of people. Immigrants to these areas received large plots and exemption from taxation for many years. Reforestation played a dramatic role in the agricultural revolution. In 1391 the Ming government ordered 50 million trees planted in the Nanjing area to produce lumber for the construction of a maritime fleet. In 1392 each family holding a land grant in Anhui province had to plant two hundred mulberry, jujube, and persimmon trees. In 1396 peasants in the present-day provinces of Hunan and Hubei in central China planted 84 million fruit trees. Historians have estimated that 1 billion trees were planted during Taizu's reign.

Increased food production led to steady population growth and the multiplication of markets, towns, and small cities. Larger towns had permanent shops; smaller towns had periodic markets. Tradesmen carrying their wares on their backs and craftsmen—carpenters, barbers, joiners, locksmiths—moved constantly from market to market.

Ming Decline

Beginning in the 1590s the Ming government was beset by fiscal, military, and political problems. The government went nearly bankrupt helping defend Korea against a Japanese invasion (see pages 634–635). Then came a series of natural disasters: floods, droughts, locusts, and epidemics ravaged one region after another. At the same time, a "little ice age" brought a drop in average temperatures that shortened the growing season and reduced harvests. In areas of serious food shortages, gangs of army deserters and laid-off soldiers began scouring the countryside in search of food. Once the gangs had stolen all their grain, hard-pressed farmers joined them just to survive. The Ming government had little choice but to try to increase taxes to deal with these threats, but the last thing people needed was heavier taxes.

Adding to the hardship was a sudden drop in the supply of silver. In place of the paper money that had circulated in Song and Yuan times, silver ingots came into general use as money in Ming times. Much of this silver originated in either Japan or the New World and entered China as payment for the silk and porcelains exported from China. When events in Japan and the Philippines led to disruption of trade, silver imports dropped. This led to deflation in China, which caused real rents to rise. Soon there were riots among urban workers and tenant farmers. In 1642 a group of rebels cut the dikes on the Yellow River, causing massive flooding. A smallpox epidemic soon added to the death toll. In 1644 the last Ming emperor, in despair, took his own life when rebels entered Beijing, opening the way for the start of a new dynasty.

QUICK REVIEW <

What were the defining characteristics of Ming government?

How did Japan change during this period of political instability?

What was life like in Japan during the Tokugawa peace?

How did the sea link the countries of East Asia, and what happened when Europeans entered this maritime sphere?

 LearningCurve
Check what you know.

Did the return of alien rule with the Manchus have any positive consequences for China?

Presenting a Horse to the Emperor

This detail from a 1757 hand scroll shows the Qianlong emperor, seated, receiving envoys from the Kazakhs. Note how the envoy, presenting a pure white horse, is kneeling to the ground performing the kowtow, which involved lowering his head to the ground as an act of reverence. The artist was Guiseppe Castiglione, an Italian who worked as a painter in Qianlong's court. (by Father Guiseppe Castiglione [1688–1766]; Musée des Arts Asiatiques-Guimet/© RMN–Grand Palais/Art Resource, NY)

Qing Dynasty

▶ The dynasty founded by the Manchus that ruled China from 1644 to 1911.

THE NEXT DYNASTY, THE Qing Dynasty (1644–1911), was founded by the Manchus, a non-Chinese people who were descended from the Jurchens. In the late sixteenth century the Manchus began expanding their territories, and in 1644 they founded the Qing Dynasty, which brought peace and in time prosperity. Successful Qing military campaigns extended the borders into Mongol, Tibetan, and Uighur regions, creating a multiethnic empire that was larger than any earlier Chinese dynasty.

The Rise of the Manchus

In the Ming period, the Manchus lived in dispersed communities in what is loosely called Manchuria (the northeast of modern-day China). In the more densely populated southern part of Manchuria, the Manchus lived in close contact with Mon-

CHAPTER LOCATOR | What sort of state and society developed in China after the Mongols were ousted? | Did the return of alien rule with the Manchus have any positive consequences for China?

Cultural groups, by predominant economic activity

Agricultural
- Han

Nomadic/Agricultural
- Tibetan
- Mongol
- Turkic

Hunting/Fishing/Agricultural
- Tungusic, Manchu

Fishing/Gathering/Agricultural
- Thai, Miao-Yao, Mon-Khmer
- Malayo-Polynesian

- Other

MAP 21.1 ■ The Qing Empire, ca. 1800

The sheer size of the Qing Empire in China almost inevitably led to its profound cultural influence on the rest of Asia.

> MAPPING THE PAST

ANALYZING THE MAP: How many different cultural groups are depicted? Which occupied the largest territories? Where was crop agriculture most prevalent?

CONNECTIONS: What geographical and political factors limited the expansion of the Qing Empire?

---

gols, Koreans, and Chinese (Map 21.1). They were not nomads but rather hunters, fishers, and farmers. Like the Mongols, they also were excellent horsemen and archers and had a strongly hierarchical social structure, with elites and slaves. Slaves, often Korean or Chinese, were generally acquired through capture. Manchu villages were generally small and often at odds with each other over resources. Interspersed among these Manchu settlements were groups of nomadic Mongols who lived in tents.

The Manchus credited their own rise to Nurhaci (1559–1626). Over several decades, he united the Manchus and expanded their territories. Like Chinggis Khan, who had reorganized the Mongol armies to reduce the importance of tribal affiliations, Nurhaci created a new social basis for his armies in units called **banners**. Each banner was made up of a set of military companies and included the families and slaves of the soldiers. Each company had a hereditary captain, often from Nurhaci's own lineage. When new groups were defeated, their members were distributed among several banners to lessen their potential for subversion.

banners

▶ Units of the Qing army, composed of soldiers, their families, and slaves.

How did Japan change during this period of political instability?

What was life like in Japan during the Tokugawa peace?

How did the sea link the countries of East Asia, and what happened when Europeans entered this maritime sphere?

☑ LearningCurve
Check what you know.

The Manchus entered China by invitation of the distinguished Ming general Wu Sangui, who was near the eastern end of the Great Wall when he heard that the rebels had captured Beijing. The Manchus proposed to Wu that they join forces and liberate Beijing. Wu opened the gates of the Great Wall to let the Manchus in, and within a couple of weeks they occupied Beijing. When the Manchus made clear that they intended to conquer the rest of the country and take the throne themselves, Wu and many other Chinese generals joined forces with them. Before long, China was again under alien rule.

Once securely in power, the Qing put in place policies and institutions that gave China a respite from war and disorder. Most of the political institutions of the Ming Dynasty were taken over relatively unchanged, including the examination system.

After peace was achieved, population growth took off. Between 1700 and 1800 the Chinese population seems to have nearly doubled, from about 150 million to over 300 million. Population growth during the eighteenth century has been attributed to many factors: global warming that extended the growing season, expanded use of New World crops, slowing of the spread of new diseases that had accompanied the sixteenth-century expansion of global traffic, and the efficiency of the Qing government in providing relief in times of famine.

Competent and Long-Lived Emperors

For more than a century, China was ruled by only three rulers, each of them hardworking, talented, and committed to making the Qing Dynasty a success. Two, the Kangxi and Qianlong emperors, had exceptionally long reigns.

Kangxi (r. 1661–1722) proved adept at meeting the expectations of both the Chinese and the Manchu elites. Kangxi (KAHNG-shee) could speak, read, and write Chinese and made efforts to persuade educated Chinese that the Manchus had a legitimate claim to rule, even trying to attract Ming loyalists who had been unwilling to serve the Qing. He undertook a series of tours of the south, where Ming loyalty had been strongest, and he held a special exam to select men to compile the official history of the Ming Dynasty.

Qianlong (chyan-loong) (r. 1722–1735) understood that the Qing's capacity to hold the multiethnic empire together rested on their ability to appeal to all those they ruled. Besides speaking Manchu and Chinese, Qianlong learned to converse in Mongolian, Uighur, Tibetan, and Tangut, and he addressed envoys in their own languages. He became as much a patron of Tibetan Buddhism as of Chinese Confucianism. He initiated a massive project to translate the Tibetan Buddhist canon into Mongolian and Manchu and had huge multilingual dictionaries compiled.

To demonstrate to the Chinese scholar-official elite that he was a sage emperor, Qianlong worked on affairs of state from dawn until early afternoon and then turned to reading, painting, and calligraphy. He was ostentatious in his devotion to his mother, visiting her daily and tending to her comfort with all the devotion of the most filial Chinese son.

Through Qianlong's reign, China remained an enormous producer of manufactured goods and led the way in assembly-line production. The government operated huge textile factories, but some private firms were even larger. Hangzhou had a textile firm that gave work to 4,000 weavers, 20,000 spinners, and 10,000 dyers and finishers. The porcelain kilns at Jingdezhen employed the division of labor on a large scale and were able to supply porcelain to much of the world. The growth of the economy benefited the Qing state, and the treasury became so full that the Qianlong emperor was able to cancel taxes on several occasions.

Imperial Expansion

The Qing Dynasty put together a multiethnic empire that was larger than any earlier Chinese dynasty. Taiwan was acquired in 1683. In 1696 Kangxi led an army of eighty thousand men into Mongolia, and within a few years Manchu supremacy was accepted there. Cannon and muskets gave Qing forces military superiority over the Mongols, who were armed only with bows and arrows. Thus the Qing could dominate the steppe cheaply, effectively ending two thousand years of Inner Asian military advantage.

In the 1720s the Qing established a permanent garrison of banner soldiers in Tibet. By this time, the expanding Qing and Russian Empires were nearing each other. In 1689 the Manchu and the Russian rulers approved a treaty defining their borders in Manchuria and regulating trade. Another treaty in 1727 allowed a Russian ecclesiastical mission to reside in Beijing and a trade caravan to make a trip from Russia to Beijing once every three years.

The last region to be annexed was Chinese Turkestan (the modern province of Xinjiang). Both the Han and the Tang Dynasties had stationed troops in the region, exercising loose overlordship, but neither the Song nor the Ming had tried to control the area. The Qing won the region in the 1750s through a series of campaigns against Uighur and Dzungar Mongol forces.

QUICK REVIEW

What factors and developments help explain Qing success?

| How did Japan change during this period of political instability? | What was life like in Japan during the Tokugawa peace? | How did the sea link the countries of East Asia, and what happened when Europeans entered this maritime sphere? | ✓ LearningCurve Check what you know. |

623

How did Japan change during this period of political instability?

Matsumoto Castle

Hideyoshi built Matsumoto Castle between 1594 and 1597. Designed to be impregnable, it was surrounded by a moat and had a base constructed of huge stones. In the sixteenth and early seventeenth centuries Spanish and Portuguese missionaries compared Japanese castles favorably to European castles of the period. (Adina Tovy/Robert Harding World Imagery)

IN THE TWELFTH CENTURY Japan entered an age that can be compared to Europe's feudal age. The Kamakura Shogunate (1185–1333) had its capital in the east, at Kamakura. It was succeeded by the Ashikaga Shogunate (1338–1573), which returned the government to Kyoto (KYOH-toh) and helped launch, during the fifteenth century, the great age of Zen-influenced Muromachi culture. The sixteenth century brought civil war over succession to the shogunate, leading to the building of massive castles and the emergence of rulers of obscure origins who eventually unified the realm.

Muromachi Culture

The headquarters of the Ashikaga shoguns were on Muromachi Street in Kyoto, and the refined and elegant style that they promoted is often called Muromachi culture. The shoguns patronized Zen Buddhism, the school of Buddhism associated with meditation and mind-to-mind transmission of truth.

CHAPTER LOCATOR | What sort of state and society developed in China after the Mongols were ousted? | Did the return of alien rule with the Manchus have any positive consequences for China?

CHAPTER 21
624 CONTINUITY AND CHANGE IN EAST ASIA

Zen ideas of simplicity permeated the arts. The Silver Pavilion built by the shogun Yoshimasa (r. 1449–1473) epitomizes Zen austerity. A white sand cone constructed in the temple garden was designed to reflect moonlight. Yoshimasa was also influential in the development of the tea ceremony. Aesthetes celebrated the beauty of imperfect objects, such as plain or misshapen cups or pots. Spare monochrome paintings fit into this aesthetic, as did simple asymmetrical flower arrangements.

The shoguns were also patrons of the No theater. No drama originated in popular forms of entertainment, including comical skits and dances directed to the gods. It was transformed into high art by Zeami (1363–1443), an actor and playwright. No was performed on a bare stage with a pine tree painted across the backdrop. One or two actors wearing brilliant brocade robes performed, using stylized gestures and stances. The actors were accompanied by a chorus and a couple of musicians playing drums and flute. Many of the stories concerned ghosts consumed by jealous passions or the desire for revenge. Zeami argued that the most meaningful moments came during silence, when the actor's spiritual presence allowed the audience to catch a glimpse of the mysterious and inexpressible.

Nō theater
▶ A type of Japanese theater in which performers convey emotions and ideas as much through gestures, stances, and dress as through words.

Civil War

Civil war began in Kyoto in 1467 as a struggle over succession to the shogunate. Rival claimants and their followers burned down temples and mansions, destroying much of the city and its treasures. Once Kyoto was laid waste, war spread to outlying areas. When the shogun could no longer protect cities, merchants banded together to hire mercenaries. In the political vacuum, the Lotus League, a commoner-led religious sect united by faith in the saving power of the Lotus Sutra, set up a commoner-run government that collected taxes and settled disputes. In 1536, during eight days of fighting, the powerful Buddhist monastery Enryakuji attacked the League and its temples; burned much of the city; and killed men, women, and children thought to be believers.

In these confused and violent circumstances, power devolved to the local level, where warlords, called daimyo (DIGH-myoh), built their power bases. To raise revenues, they surveyed the land and promoted irrigation and trade. Many of the most successful daimyo were self-made men who rose from obscurity.

daimyo
▶ Regional lords in Japan, many of whom were self-made men.

The violence of the period encouraged castle building. The castles were built not on mountaintops but on level plains, and they were surrounded by moats and walls made from huge stones. Inside a castle was a many-storied keep. Though relatively safe from incendiary missiles, the keeps were vulnerable to Western-style cannon, introduced in the 1570s.

The Victors: Nobunaga and Hideyoshi

The first daimyo to gain a predominance of power was Oda Nobunaga (1534–1582). A samurai of the lesser daimyo class, he recruited followers from masterless samurai. After he won control of his native province in 1559, he immediately set out to extend his power through central Japan. A key step was destroying the military power of the great monasteries. To increase revenues, he minted coins

| How did Japan change during this period of political instability? | What was life like in Japan during the Tokugawa peace? | How did the sea link the countries of East Asia, and what happened when Europeans entered this maritime sphere? | ✓ LearningCurve Check what you know. |

625

MING CHINA

KOREA

Sea of Japan

JAPAN

• Edo

• Kyoto

Takamatsu

Kagoshima

→ Reunification campaign
→ Campaign against Korea

Hideyoshi's Campaigns in Japan and Korea, 1592–1598

and promoted trade by eliminating customs barriers and opening the little fishing village of Nagasaki to foreign commerce; it soon became Japan's largest port.

In 1582, in an attempted coup, Nobunaga was forced by one of his vassals to commit suicide. His general and staunchest adherent, Toyotomi Hideyoshi (1537–1598), avenged him and continued the drive toward unification of the daimyo-held lands.

Like the Ming founder, Hideyoshi was a peasant's son who rose to power through military talent. A series of campaigns brought all of Japan under Hideyoshi's control. Hideyoshi soothed the vanquished daimyo as Nobunaga had done—with lands and military positions—but he also required them to swear allegiance and to obey him down to the smallest particular. For the first time in over two centuries, Japan had a single ruler.

Hideyoshi did his best to ensure that future peasants' sons would not be able to rise as he had. His great sword hunt of 1588 collected weapons from farmers, who were no longer allowed to wear swords. Restrictions were also placed on samurai; they were prohibited from leaving their lord's service or switching occupations. To improve tax collection, Hideyoshi ordered a survey of the entire country. His surveys not only tightened tax collection, but also registered each peasant household and tied the peasants to the land. With the country pacified, Hideyoshi embarked on an ill-fated attempt to conquer Korea and China that ended only with his death, discussed later in the chapter (see page 634).

> ## QUICK REVIEW

Who held power during Japan's Middle Ages? How did they wield it?

CHAPTER LOCATOR | What sort of state and society developed in China after the Mongols were ousted? | Did the return of alien rule with the Manchus have any positive consequences for China?

CHAPTER 21

626 CONTINUITY AND CHANGE IN EAST ASIA

What was life like in Japan during the Tokugawa peace?

Daimyo Procession

The system of alternate residence meant that some daimyo were always on the road. The constant travel of daimyo with their attendants between their domains and Edo, the shogun's residence, stimulated construction of roads, inns, and castle-towns. (*Daimyo's Processions Passing Along the Tokaido*, by Utagawa Sadahide [1807–1873]/triptych of polychrome woodblock prints; ink and color on paper, Edo period [1615–1868]. Bequest of William S. Lieberman, 2005, accession 2007.49.290a–c/Metropolitan Museum of Art, New York, NY, USA/Image copyright © The Metropolitan Museum of Art/Image source: Art Resource, NY)

ON HIS DEATHBED, Hideyoshi set up a council of regents to govern during the minority of his infant son. The strongest regent was Hideyoshi's long-time supporter Tokugawa Ieyasu (1543–1616). In 1600 at Sekigahara, Ieyasu smashed a coalition of daimyo defenders of the heir and began building his own government. In 1603 he took the title "shogun." The Tokugawa Shogunate that Ieyasu fashioned lasted until 1867. This era is also called the Edo period after the location of the shogunate, starting Tokyo's history as Japan's most important city (Map 21.2).

Tokugawa Government

Over the course of the seventeenth century the Tokugawa shoguns worked to consolidate relations with the daimyo. In a scheme resembling the later residency requirements imposed by Louis XIV in France (see page 528) and Peter the Great in Russia (see page 541), Ieyasu set up the **alternate residence system**, which compelled the lords to live in Edo every other year and to leave their wives and sons there—essentially as hostages.

The peace imposed by the Tokugawa Shogunate brought a steady rise in population to about 30 million people by 1800. To maintain stability, the early

Tokugawa Shogunate

▶ The Japanese government in Edo founded by Tokugawa Ieyasu. It lasted from 1603 to 1867.

alternate residence system

▶ Arrangement in which lords lived in Edo every other year and left their wives and sons there as hostages.

How did Japan change during this period of political instability?

What was life like in Japan during the Tokugawa peace?

How did the sea link the countries of East Asia, and what happened when Europeans entered this maritime sphere?

 LearningCurve
Check what you know.

627

Tokugawa shoguns froze social status. Laws rigidly prescribed what each class could and could not do. Daimyo, for example, were prohibited from moving troops outside their frontiers, making alliances, and coining money. As intended, these rules protected the Tokugawa shoguns from daimyo attack and helped ensure a long era of peace.

The early Tokugawa shoguns also restricted the construction and repair of castles — symbols, in Japan as in medieval Europe, of feudal independence. Continuing Hideyoshi's policy, the Tokugawa regime enforced a policy of complete separation of samurai and peasants. Samurai were defined as those permitted to carry swords. They had to live in castles, and they depended on stipends from their lords, the daimyo. Samurai were effectively prevented from establishing ties to the land, so they could not become landholders. Likewise, merchants and artisans had to live in towns and could not own land.

After 1639 Japan limited its contacts with the outside world because of concerns about both the loyalty of subjects converted to Christianity by European missionaries and about the imperialist ambitions of European powers (discussed below). However, China remained an important trading partner and source of ideas. The Edo period also saw the development of a school of native learning that rejected Buddhism and Confucianism as alien and tried to identify a distinctly Japanese sensibility.

MAP 21.2 ■ Tokugawa Japan, 1603–1867

The lands that the shogunate directly controlled were concentrated near its capital at Edo. The daimyo of distant places, such as the island of Kyushu, were required to make long journeys to and from Edo every year.

CHAPTER LOCATOR

What sort of state and society developed in China after the Mongols were ousted?

Did the return of alien rule with the Manchus have any positive consequences for China?

CHAPTER 21
628 CONTINUITY AND CHANGE IN EAST ASIA

Commercialization and the Growth of Towns

During the civil war period, warfare seems to have promoted social and economic change, much as it had in China during the Warring States Period (403–221 B.C.E.). Trade grew, and greater use was made of coins imported from Ming China. Markets began appearing at river crossings, at the entrances to temples and shrines, and at other places where people congregated. Towns and cities sprang up all around the country, some of them around the new castles. Traders and artisans dealing in a specific product began forming guilds. Foreign trade also flourished, despite chronic problems with pirates who raided the Japanese, Korean, and Chinese coasts (see pages 634–635).

In most cities, merchant families with special privileges from the government controlled the urban economy. Frequently, a particular family dominated the trade in a particular product and then branched out into other businesses. Japanese merchant families also devised distinct patterns and procedures for their business operations. What today is called "family-style management principles" determined the age of apprenticeship (between eleven and thirteen); the employee's detachment from past social relations and adherence to the norms of a particular family business; salaries; seniority as the basis of promotion, although job performance at the middle rungs determined who reached the higher ranks; and the time for retirement. All employees in a family business were expected to practice frugality, resourcefulness, self-denial, and careful accounting. These values formed the basis of what has been called the Japanese "industrious revolution." They help to explain how, after the Meiji (MAY-jee) Restoration of 1867 (see page 796), Japan was able to industrialize rapidly and compete successfully with the West.

In the seventeenth century underemployed farmers and samurai thronged to the cities. As a result, Japan's cities grew tremendously. Kyoto became the center for the manufacture of luxury goods like lacquer, brocade, and fine porcelain. Osaka was the chief market, especially for rice. Edo was a center of consumption by the daimyo, their vassals, and government bureaucrats. Both Osaka and Edo reached about a million residents.

Two hundred fifty towns came into being in this period. Most ranged in size from 3,000 to 20,000 people, but a few, such as Hiroshima, Kagoshima, and Nagoya, had populations of between 65,000 and 100,000. In addition, perhaps two hundred towns along the main road to Edo emerged to meet the needs of men traveling on the alternate residence system. In the eighteenth century perhaps 4 million people, 15 percent of the Japanese population, resided in cities or towns.

The Life of the People in the Edo Period

The Tokugawa shoguns brought an end to civil war by controlling the military. Stripped of power and required to spend alternate years at Edo, many of the daimyo and samurai passed their lives in idle pursuit of pleasure. They spent extravagantly on fine silks, paintings, concubines, boys, the theater, and the redecoration of their castles. These temptations, as well as more sophisticated pleasures and the heavy costs of maintaining alternate residences at Edo, gradually bankrupted the warrior class.

All major cities contained places of amusement for men—teahouses, theaters, restaurants, and houses of prostitution. Desperately poor parents sometimes sold

How did Japan change during this period of political instability?

What was life like in Japan during the Tokugawa peace?

How did the sea link the countries of East Asia, and what happened when Europeans entered this maritime sphere?

☑ LearningCurve
Check what you know.

629

Interior View of a Theater

Complex kabuki plays, which dealt with heroes, loyalty, and tragedy and included music and dance, became the most popular form of entertainment in Tokugawa Japan for all classes. Movable scenery and lighting effects made possible the staging of storms, fires, and hurricanes. (woodblock print by Okumura Masanobu, 18th century/Private Collection/J.T. Vintage/The Bridgeman Art Library)

> PICTURING THE PAST

ANALYZING THE IMAGE: How many people are performing in this scene? Are there more men or women in the audience? How do you distinguish them? Are any of the men samurai?
CONNECTIONS: What connections do you see between the popularity of kabuki plays and other aspects of Japanese life in this period?

their daughters to entertainment houses (as they did in China and medieval Europe), and the most attractive or talented girls, trained in singing, dancing, and conversational arts, became courtesans, later called geishas (GAY-shahz), "accomplished persons."

Another form of entertainment in the cities was **kabuki theater**, patronized by both merchants and samurai. An art form created by townspeople, kabuki originated in crude, bawdy skits dealing with love and romance. Because actresses were thought to corrupt public morals, the Tokugawa government banned them from the stage in 1629. From that time on, men played all the parts. Homosexuality, long accepted in Japan, was widely practiced among the samurai, who pursued the actors and spent profligately on them. Some moralists and bureaucrats complained from time to time, but the Tokugawa government decided to accept kabuki and prostitution as necessary evils.

Cities were also the center for commercial publishing. As in contemporary China, the reading public eagerly purchased fiction and the scripts for plays. The art of color woodblock printing also was perfected during this period. Many of the surviving prints, made for a popular audience, depict the theater and women of the entertainment quarters.

kabuki theater
▶ A popular form of Japanese drama that brings together dialogue, dance, and music to tell stories. The actors wear colorful costumes and dramatic makeup.

CHAPTER LOCATOR | What sort of state and society developed in China after the Mongols were ousted? | Did the return of alien rule with the Manchus have any positive consequences for China?

Almost as entertaining as attending the theater was watching the long processions of daimyo, their retainers, and their luggage as they passed back and forth to and from Edo twice a year. The shogunate prohibited travel by commoners, but they could get passports to take pilgrimages, visit relatives, or seek the soothing waters of medicinal hot springs. Setting out on foot, groups of villagers would travel to such shrines as Ise, often taking large detours to visit Osaka or Edo to sightsee or attend the theater.

According to Japanese tradition, farmers deserved respect. In practice, however, peasants were often treated callously. Government regulations described them as "people without sense or forethought," a characterization used to justify strict control over almost every aspect of their lives.

During the seventeenth and eighteenth centuries daimyo and upper-level samurai paid for their extravagant lifestyles by raising taxes on their subordinate peasants from 30 or 40 percent of the rice crop to 50 percent. Not surprisingly, this angered peasants, and peasant protests became chronic during the eighteenth century. Natural disasters also added to the peasants' misery. In 1783 Mount Asama erupted, spewing volcanic ash that darkened the skies all summer; the resulting crop failures led to famine. When famine recurred again in 1787, commoners rioted for five days in Edo. The shogunate responded by trying to control the floating population of day laborers without families in the city. At one point they were rounded up and transported to work the gold mines in an island off the north coast, where most of them died within two or three years.

This picture of peasant hardship tells only part of the story. Agricultural productivity increased substantially during the Tokugawa period. Peasants who improved their lands and increased their yields continued to pay the same assessed tax and could pocket the surplus as profit. As those without land drifted to the cities, peasants left in the countryside found ways to improve their livelihoods. At Hirano near Osaka, for example, 61.7 percent of all arable land was sown in cotton. In many rural places, as many peasants worked in the manufacture of silk, cotton, or vegetable oil as in the production of rice.

In comparison to farmers, merchants had a much easier life, even if they had no political power. By contemporary standards anywhere in the world, the Japanese mercantile class lived well. In 1705 the shogunate confiscated the property of a merchant in Osaka at the urging of influential daimyo and samurai who owed the merchant gigantic debts. The government seized 50 pairs of gold screens, 360 carpets, several mansions, 48 granaries and warehouses scattered around the country, and hundreds of thousands of gold pieces. Few merchants possessed such fabulous wealth, but many lived very comfortably.

Within a village, some families would be relatively well-off, others barely able to get by. The village headman generally came from the richest family, but he consulted a council of elders on important matters. Women in better-off families were much more likely to learn to read than women in poor families. Daughters of wealthy peasants studied penmanship, the Chinese classics, poetry, and the proper forms of correspondence, and they rounded out their education with

Edo Craftsman at Work

Less than 3 inches tall, this ivory figure shows a parasol maker seated on the floor (the typical Japanese practice) eating his lunch, his tools by his side. (Photo © Boltin Picture Library/The Bridgeman Art Library)

How did Japan change during this period of political instability?

What was life like in Japan during the Tokugawa peace?

How did the sea link the countries of East Asia, and what happened when Europeans entered this maritime sphere?

✓ LearningCurve
Check what you know.

631

travel. By contrast, girls from middle-level peasant families might have had from two to five years of formal schooling focused on moral instruction intended to instill virtue.

By the fifteenth and sixteenth centuries Japan's family and marriage systems had evolved in the direction of a patrilocal, patriarchal system more like China's, and Japanese women had lost the prominent role in high society that they had occupied during the Heian period. It became standard for women to move into their husbands' homes, where they occupied positions subordinate to both their husbands and their mothers-in-law. In addition, elite families stopped dividing their property among all their children; instead they retained it for the sons alone or increasingly for a single son who would continue the family line. Wedding rituals involved both the exchange of betrothal gifts and the movement of the bride from her parents' home to her husband's home. She brought with her a trousseau that provided her with clothes and other items she would need for daily life, but not with land, which would have given her economic autonomy. On the other hand, her position within her new family was more secure, for it became more difficult for a husband to divorce his wife. She also gained authority within the family. If her husband was away, she managed family affairs. If her husband fathered children with concubines, she was their legal mother.

A peasant wife shared responsibility for the family's economic well-being with her husband. If of poor or middling status, she worked alongside her husband in the fields. If they were farm hands and worked for wages, the wife invariably earned a third or a half less than her husband. Wives of prosperous farmers never worked in the fields, but they reeled silk, wove cloth, helped in any family business, and supervised the maids. When cotton growing spread to Japan in the sixteenth century, women took on the jobs of spinning and weaving it. Whatever their economic status, Japanese women, like women everywhere in the world, tended the children. Families were growing smaller in this period in response to the spread of single-heir inheritance.

How was divorce initiated, and how frequent was it? Among the elite, the husband alone could initiate divorce; all he had to do was order his wife to leave or send her possessions to her parents' home. For the wife, divorce carried a stigma, but she could not prevent it or insist on keeping her children. Widows and divorcées of the samurai elite were not expected to remarry. Among the peasant classes, by contrast, divorce seems to have been fairly common. A poor woman wanting a divorce could simply leave her husband's home. It was also possible to secure divorce through a temple. If a married woman entered the temple and performed rites there for three years, her marriage bond was dissolved.

> **QUICK REVIEW**

How did government policy shape social and economic development under the Tokugawa Shogunate?

How did the sea link the countries of East Asia, and what happened when Europeans entered this maritime sphere?

Dutch in Japan

The Japanese were curious about the appearance, dress, and habits of the Dutch who came to the enclave of Deshima to trade. In this detail from a long hand scroll, Dutch traders are shown interacting with a Japanese samurai in a room with Japanese tatami mats on the floor. Note also the Western musical instrument. (Private Collection/The Bridgeman Art Library)

IN THE PERIOD 1400–1800 maritime trade and piracy connected China and Japan to each other and also to Korea, Southeast Asia, and Europe. Both Korea and Japan relied on Chinese coinage, and China relied on silver from Japan. During the fifteenth century China launched overseas expeditions. Japan was a major base for pirates. In the sixteenth century European traders appeared, eager for Chinese porcelains and silks. Christian missionaries followed. Political changes in Europe changed the international makeup of the European traders in East Asia, with the dominant groups first the Portuguese, next the Dutch, and then the British.

Zheng He's Voyages

Early in the Ming period, the Chinese government tried to revive the tribute system of the Han (206–220 C.E.) and Tang (618–907) Dynasties, when China had dominated East Asia and envoys had arrived from dozens of distant lands. To invite more countries to send missions, the third Ming emperor (Chengzu, or

| How did Japan change during this period of political instability? | What was life like in Japan during the Tokugawa peace? | **How did the sea link the countries of East Asia, and what happened when Europeans entered this maritime sphere?** | ☑ LearningCurve Check what you know. |

Yongle) authorized a series of voyages to the Indian Ocean under the command of the Muslim eunuch Zheng He (1371–1433).

Zheng He's father had made the trip to Mecca, and the seven voyages that Zheng led between 1405 and 1433 followed old Arab trade routes. The first of the seven was made by a fleet of 317 ships. Each expedition involved from twenty thousand to thirty-two thousand men. Their itineraries included stops in Vietnam, Malaysia, Indonesia, Sri Lanka, India, and, in the later voyages, Hormuz (on the coast of Persia) and East Africa. At each stop Zheng He went ashore to visit rulers, transmit messages of China's peaceful intentions, and bestow lavish gifts. Rulers were invited to come to China or send envoys and were offered accommodation on the return voyages. Near the Straits of Malacca, Zheng He's fleet battled Chinese pirates, bringing them under control. Zheng He made other shows of force as well, deposing rulers deemed unacceptable in Java, Sumatra, and Sri Lanka.

Why were these voyages abandoned? Officials complained about their cost and modest returns. As a consequence, after 1474 all the remaining ships with three or more masts were broken up and used for lumber. China did not pull back from trade in the South China Sea and Indian Ocean, but the government no longer promoted trade, leaving the initiative to private merchants and migrants.

Piracy and Japan's Overseas Adventures

One goal of Zheng He's expeditions was to suppress piracy, which had become a problem all along the China coast. Already in the thirteenth century social disorder and banditry in Japan had expanded into seaborne banditry, some of it within the Japanese islands around the Inland Sea (Map 21.3), but also in the straits between Korea and Japan. Although the pirates were called the "Japanese pirates" by both the Koreans and the Chinese, pirate gangs in fact recruited from all countries. The Ryūkyū (ryoo-kyoo) Islands and Taiwan became major bases.

Possibly encouraged by the exploits of these bandits, Hideyoshi, after his victories in unifying Japan, decided to extend his territory across the seas. In 1590, after receiving congratulations from Korea on his victories, Hideyoshi sent a letter asking the Koreans to allow his armies to pass through their country, declaring that his real target was China. He also sent demands for submission to countries of Southeast Asia and to the Spanish governor of the Philippines.

In 1592 Hideyoshi mobilized 158,000 soldiers and 9,200 sailors for his invasion and equipped them with muskets and cannon, which had recently been introduced into Japan. His forces overwhelmed Korean defenders and reached Seoul within three weeks and Pyongyang in two months. A few months later, in the middle of winter, Chinese armies arrived to help defend Korea, and Japanese forces were pushed back from Pyongyang. A stalemate lasted till 1597, when Hideyoshi sent new troops. This time the Ming army and the Korean navy were more successful in resisting the Japanese. In 1598, after Hideyoshi's death, the Japanese army withdrew, but Korea was left devastated.

After recovering from the setbacks of these invasions, Korea began to advance socially and economically. During the Chosŏn Dynasty (1392–1910), the Korean elite (the yangban) turned away from Buddhism and toward strict Neo-Confucian orthodoxy. As agricultural productivity improved, the population began to grow. With economic advances, slavery declined. When slaves ran away, land-

CHAPTER LOCATOR | What sort of state and society developed in China after the Mongols were ousted? | Did the return of alien rule with the Manchus have any positive consequences for China?

CHAPTER 21
634 CONTINUITY AND CHANGE IN EAST ASIA

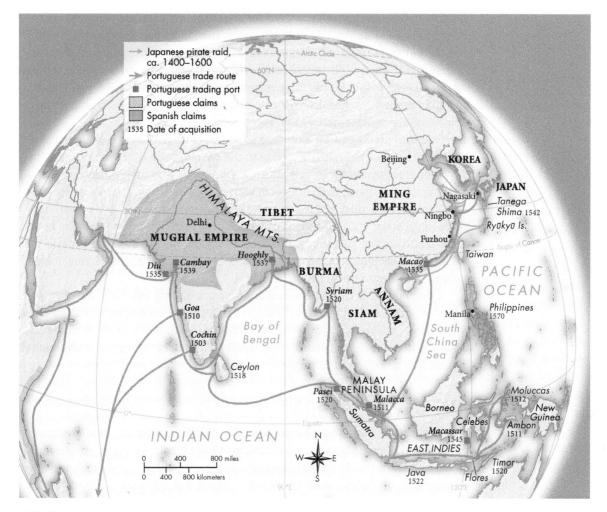

MAP 21.3 ■ East Asia, ca. 1600

Pirates and traders often plied the same waters as seaborne trade grew in the sixteenth century. The Portuguese were especially active in setting up trading ports.

owners found that it was less expensive to replace them with sharecroppers than to recapture them. Between 1750 and 1790 the slave population dropped from 30 percent to 5 percent of the population. The hold of the yangban elite, however, remained strong.

Europeans Enter the Scene

In the sixteenth century Portuguese, Spanish, and Dutch merchants and adventurers began to participate in the East Asian maritime world (see Chapter 16). The trade between Japan, China, and Southeast Asia was very profitable, and the European traders wanted a share of it. They also wanted to develop trade between Asia and Europe.

The Portuguese and Dutch were not reluctant to use force to gain control of trade, and they seized many outposts along the trade routes. Moreover, they made little distinction between trade, smuggling, and piracy. In 1521 the Ming tried to

How did Japan change during this period of political instability?

What was life like in Japan during the Tokugawa peace?

How did the sea link the countries of East Asia, and what happened when Europeans entered this maritime sphere?

✓ LearningCurve
Check what you know.

635

ban the Portuguese from China. Two years later an expeditionary force commissioned by the Portuguese king to negotiate a friendship treaty defeated its mission by firing on Chinese warships near Guangzhou. In 1557, without informing Beijing, local Chinese officials decided that the way to regulate trade was to allow the Portuguese to build a trading post near the mouth of the Pearl River. The city they built there—Macao—became the first destination for Europeans going to China until the nineteenth century.

European products were not in demand in China, but silver was. Japan had supplied much of China's silver, but with the development of silver mines in the New World, European traders began supplying large quantities of silver to China, allowing the expansion of China's economy.

Chinese were quick to take advantage of the new trading ports set up by European powers. Manila, under Spanish control, and Taiwan and Batavia, both under Dutch control, all attracted thousands of Chinese colonists. Local people felt the intrusion of Chinese more than of Europeans, and riots against Chinese led to massacres on several occasions.

A side benefit of the appearance of European traders was New World crops. Sweet potatoes, maize, peanuts, tomatoes, chili peppers, tobacco, and other crops were quickly adopted in East Asia. Sweet potatoes and maize in particular facilitated population growth because they could be grown on land previously thought too sandy or too steep to cultivate.

Christian Missionaries

The Spanish and Portuguese kings supported missionary activity, and merchant vessels soon brought Catholic missionaries to East Asia. The Jesuit priest Francis Xavier had worked in India and the Indies before China and Japan attracted his attention. In 1549 he landed on Kyushu, Japan's southernmost island (see Map 21.2). After he was expelled by the local lord, he traveled throughout western Japan as far as Kyoto, proselytizing wherever warlords allowed. He soon made many converts among the poor and even some among the daimyo. Xavier then set his sights on China but died on an uninhabited island off the China coast in 1552.

Other missionaries carried on his work, and by 1600 there were three hundred thousand baptized Christians in Japan. Most of them lived on Kyushu, where the shogun's power was weakest and the loyalty of the daimyo most doubtful. In 1615 bands of Christian samurai supported Tokugawa Ieyasu's enemies at the Battle of Osaka. A couple of decades later, thirty thousand peasants in the heavily Catholic area of northern Kyushu revolted. The Tokugawa shoguns thus came to associate Christianity with domestic disorder and insurrection. Accordingly, what had been mild persecution of Christians became ruthless repression after 1639.

Meanwhile, in China the Jesuits concentrated on gaining the linguistic and scholarly knowledge they would need to convert the educated class. The Jesuit Matteo Ricci studied for years in Macao before setting himself up in Nanjing and trying to win over members of the educated class. In 1601 he was given permission to reside in Beijing, where he made several high-placed conversions. He also interested educated Chinese men in Western geography, astronomy, and Euclidean mathematics.

Ricci and his Jesuit successors believed that Confucianism was compatible with Christianity. The Jesuits thought that both faiths shared similar concerns

CHAPTER LOCATOR | What sort of state and society developed in China after the Mongols were ousted?   Did the return of alien rule with the Manchus have any positive consequences for China?

CHAPTER 21
636   CONTINUITY AND CHANGE IN EAST ASIA

Among the objects produced in China that were in high demand in Europe in the seventeenth and eighteenth centuries were colorful porcelains. In this period Chinese potters perfected the use of overglaze enamels, which allowed the application of many colors to a single object. Blue, green, yellow, orange, and red all appear on this 18-inch-tall vase. (Vase, Qing dynasty, Kangxi period [1662–1722], late 17th–early 18th century. Porcelain painted in overglaze famille verte enamels and gold. Bequest of John D. Rockefeller Jr., 1960 [61.200.66], The Metropolitan Museum of Art, New York, NY, USA/Image copyright © The Metropolitan Museum of Art/Image Source: Art Resource, NY)

for morality and virtue. The Franciscan and Dominican friars disagreed with the Jesuit position. In 1715 religious and political quarrels in Europe led the pope to decide that the Jesuits' accommodating approach was heretical. Angry at this insult, the Kangxi emperor forbade all Christian missionary work in China.

Learning from the West

Although both China and Japan ended up prohibiting Christian missionary work, other aspects of Western culture were seen as impressive and worth learning. The closed-country policy that Japan instituted in 1639 restricted Japanese from leaving the country and kept European merchants in small enclaves. Still, Japanese interest in Europe did not disappear. Through the Dutch enclave of Deshima on a tiny island in Nagasaki harbor, a stream of Western ideas and inventions trickled into Japan in the eighteenth century.

In China, too, both scholars and rulers showed an interest in Western learning. The Kangxi emperor frequently discussed scientific and philosophical questions with the Jesuits at court. In addition, he had translations made of a collection of Western works on mathematics and the calendar. The court was impressed with the Jesuits' skill in astronomy and quickly appointed them to the Board of Astronomy. In 1674 the emperor asked them to re-equip the observatory with European instruments. Firearms and mechanical clocks were also widely admired. The court established its own clock and watch factory, and in 1673 the emperor insisted that the Jesuits manufacture cannon for him and supervise gunnery practice.

Admiration was not one-sided. In the early eighteenth century China enjoyed a positive reputation in Europe. Voltaire wrote of the rationalism of Confucianism and saw advantages to the Chinese political system. Chinese medical practice also drew European interest. One Chinese practice that Europeans adopted was "variolation," an early form of smallpox inoculation.

The Shifting International Environment in the Eighteenth Century

The East Asian maritime world underwent many changes from the sixteenth to the eighteenth centuries. As already noted, the Japanese pulled back their own traders and limited opportunities for Europeans to trade in Japan. In China the Qing government limited trading contacts with Europe to Guangzhou in the far

How did Japan change during this period of political instability?

What was life like in Japan during the Tokugawa peace?

How did the sea link the countries of East Asia, and what happened when Europeans entered this maritime sphere?

LearningCurve
Check what you know.

637

south in an attempt to curb piracy. Portugal lost many of its bases to the Dutch, and by the eighteenth century the British had become as active as the Dutch.

By the late eighteenth century Britain had become a great power and did not see why China should be able to dictate the terms of trade. Wanting to renegotiate relations, King George III sent Lord George Macartney to China with six hundred cases of British goods. The Qianlong emperor was, however, not impressed. The Qing court was as intent on maintaining the existing system of regulated trade as Britain was intent on doing away with it.

> **QUICK REVIEW**

How did the governments of China and Japan respond to the arrival of Europeans in East Asia in the sixteenth and seventeenth centuries?

CHAPTER SUMMARY

After the fall of the Mongols, China was ruled by the native Ming Dynasty for nearly three centuries. Despite the poor quality of most Ming emperors, China thrived in many ways. Population grew as food production increased. Educational levels were high as more and more men prepared for the civil service examinations. Urban culture was lively, and publishing houses put out novels, short stories, and plays in the vernacular language for large audiences.

In 1644 the Ming Dynasty fell to the non-Chinese Manchus. The Manchu rulers proved more competent than the Ming emperors and were able to both maintain peace and expand the empire. Population grew steadily under Manchu rule.

During the fifteenth and sixteenth centuries Japan was fragmented by civil war. As daimyo attacked and defeated each other, power was gradually consolidated, until Hideyoshi gained control of most of the country. Japan also saw many cultural developments during this period, including the increasing influence of Zen ideas on the arts and the rise of Nō theater.

After Hideyoshi's death, power was seized by Tokugawa Ieyasu, the founder of the Tokugawa Shogunate. The early rulers tried to create stability by freezing the social structure and limiting foreign contact to the city of Nagasaki. As the wealth of the business classes grew, the samurai, now dependent on fixed stipends, became progressively poorer. Samurai and others in search of work and pleasure streamed into the cities.

Between 1400 and 1800 maritime trade connected the countries of Asia, but piracy was a perpetual problem. Early in this period China sent out naval expeditions looking to promote diplomatic contacts, reaching as far as Africa. In the sixteenth century European traders arrived in China and Japan and soon developed profitable trading relationships. The Chinese economy became so dependent on huge imports of silver acquired through this trade that a cutoff in supplies caused severe hardship. Trade with Europe also brought New World crops and new ideas. The Catholic missionaries who began to arrive in Asia introduced

CHAPTER LOCATOR | What sort of state and society developed in China after the Mongols were ousted? | Did the return of alien rule with the Manchus have any positive consequences for China?

CHAPTER 21
638   CONTINUITY AND CHANGE IN EAST ASIA

Western science and learning as well as Christianity, until they were banned in both Japan and China. Although the shogunate severely restricted trade, some Western scientific ideas and technology entered Japan through the port of Nagasaki. Chinese, too, took an interest in Western painting, astronomy, and firearms. Because Europeans saw much to admire in East Asia in this period, ideas also flowed from East to West.

CONNECTIONS

During the four centuries from 1400 to 1800, the countries of East Asia became increasingly connected. At the same time, their cultures and social structures were in no sense converging. The elites of the three countries were very different: in both Korea and Japan elite status was hereditary, while in China the key route to status and power involved doing well on a written examination. In Japan the samurai elite were expected to be skilled warriors, but in China and Korea the highest prestige went to men of letters.

By the end of this period, East Asian countries found themselves in a rapidly changing international environment, mostly because of revolutions occurring far from their shores. The next two chapters take up the story of these revolutions, first the political ones in America, France, and Haiti, and then the Industrial Revolution that began in Britain. In time, these revolutions would profoundly alter East Asia as well.

ONLINE DOCUMENT PROJECT
Chinese Medicine
What kinds of treatments did Chinese doctors employ?

Examine artwork depicting Chinese medical practices, and then complete a quiz and writing assignment based on the evidence and details from this chapter. *See inside the front cover to learn more.*

How did Japan change during this period of political instability?

What was life like in Japan during the Tokugawa peace?

How did the sea link the countries of East Asia, and what happened when Europeans entered this maritime sphere?

☑ LearningCurve
Check what you know.

CHAPTER 21 STUDY GUIDE

STEP 1

GET STARTED ONLINE

 LearningCurve

Now that you've read the chapter, make it stick by completing the LearningCurve activity.

STEP 2

EXPLAIN WHY IT MATTERS

Put your reading into practice. Identify each term below, and then explain why it matters in world history.

TERM	WHO OR WHAT & WHEN	WHY IT MATTERS
Ming Dynasty (p. 612)		
civil service examinations (p. 616)		
Qing Dynasty (p. 620)		
banners (p. 621)		
Nō theater (p. 625)		
daimyo (p. 625)		
Tokugawa Shogunate (p. 627)		
alternate residence system (p. 627)		
kabuki theater (p. 630)		

STEP 3

MOVE BEYOND THE BASICS

To demonstrate a more advanced understanding of Qing China and Tokugawa Japan, fill in the chart below with descriptions of key aspects of each empire: social and economic developments, nature and role of elites, and relations with Europeans. How and why did Japanese and Chinese society and culture diverge in this period?

	Social and Economic Developments	Nature and Role of Elites	Relations with Europeans
Qing China			
Tokugawa Japan			

PUT IT ALL TOGETHER

Now, take a step back and try to explain the big picture. Remember to use specific examples from the chapter in your answers.

CHINA UNDER THE MING AND THE QING

► How did Ming officials manage the government when emperors were incompetent? How did this ultimately contribute to the Ming's decline?

► How did the Qing respond to the challenge of ruling a multiethnic empire?

WAR AND PEACE IN JAPAN

► How did the role of the samurai in Japanese society and government change between 1400 and 1800?

► What explains the emergence of a vibrant urban culture during the Tokugawa Shogunate?

THE ASIAN MARITIME SPHERE

► What do Zheng He's voyages tell us about Chinese attitudes toward overseas trade, expansion, and international relations?

► Why did both the Japanese and Chinese have mixed feelings about European culture? What did they admire? What did they dislike and fear?

LOOKING BACK, LOOKING AHEAD

► What explains the cultural divergence between China and Japan in this period?

► What trends in the relationship between Asia and Europe were emerging by the end of this period? How did Asian governments respond to the changes that were beginning to take place?

> **IN YOUR OWN WORDS**

Imagine that you must give an oral report to the class answering the following question: What fueled population and economic growth in East Asia between 1400 and 1800? What would be the most important points and why?

22
REVOLUTIONS IN THE ATLANTIC WORLD

1775–1825

> How did revolution change the Atlantic world? What aspects of Atlantic society and politics were left unchanged? Chapter 22 examines the wave of revolutions that rocked the Atlantic world from 1775 to 1825. The revolutionary era began in North America in 1775, where the United States of America won freedom from Britain in 1783. Then in 1789 France became the leading revolutionary nation. It established first a constitutional monarchy, then a radical republic, and finally a new empire under Napoleon that would last until 1815. Inspired both by the ideals of the revolution on the continent and by internal colonial conditions, the slaves in the French colony of Saint Domingue rose up in 1791, followed by colonial settlers, indigenous people, and slaves in Spanish America. In Europe and its colonies abroad, the world of modern politics was born.

Jean-Baptiste Belley Born in Senegal and enslaved in the colony of Saint-Domingue, Jean-Baptiste Belley fought in the American War of Independence and was elected as a deputy to the French National Convention. His career epitomizes the transnational connections of the era of Atlantic revolutions. (*Jean-Baptiste Belley* [1747–1805], Deputy of Santo Domingo at the French Convention, by Anne-Louis Girodet de Roussy-Trioson [1767–1824], 1797, oil on canvas. Inv. MV4616. Photo: Gérard Blot/Châteaux de Versailles et de Trianon, Versailles, France/© RMN–Grand Palais/Art Resource, NY)

LearningCurve
After reading the chapter, use LearningCurve to retain what you've read.

> What were the factors behind the age of revolution in the Atlantic world?

> Why and how did American colonists forge a new, independent nation?

> How did the events of 1789 result in a constitutional monarchy in France, and what were the consequences?

> How did Napoleon Bonaparte assume control of France and much of Europe, and what factors led to his downfall?

> How did slave revolt on colonial Saint-Domingue lead to the creation of the independent nation of Haiti in 1804?

> Why and how did the Spanish and Portuguese colonies of North and South America shake off European domination and develop into national states?

What were the factors behind the age of revolution in the Atlantic world?

The Three Estates

French inhabitants were legally divided into three orders, or estates: the clergy, the nobility, and everyone else. In this political cartoon from 1789 a peasant of the third estate struggles under the weight of a happy clergyman and a plumed nobleman. The caption — "Let's hope this game ends soon" — sets forth a program of reform that any peasant could understand. (Musée de la Ville de Paris, Musée Carnavalet, Paris, France/The Bridgeman Art Library)

THE ORIGINS OF REVOLUTIONS in the Atlantic world were complex, and no one cause lay behind them. However, a series of shared factors helped set the stage for reform. They included: fundamental social and economic changes and political crises that eroded state authority; the impact of political ideas derived from the Enlightenment; and, perhaps most important, imperial competition and financial crises generated by the expenses of imperial warfare.

Social Change

Eighteenth-century European society was legally divided into groups with special privileges, such as the nobility and the clergy, and groups with special burdens, such as the peasantry. Nobles were the largest landowners. They enjoyed exemption from many taxes and exclusive rights such as hunting and bearing swords.

CHAPTER LOCATOR | What were the factors behind the age of revolution in the Atlantic world? | Why and how did American colonists forge a new, independent nation?

CHAPTER 22
644 REVOLUTIONS IN THE ATLANTIC WORLD

1715–1774
Reign of Louis XV in France

1743–1803
Life of Toussaint L'Ouverture

1756–1763
Seven Years' War

1763
Treaty of Paris

1774–1792
Reign of Louis XVI in France

1775
Thomas Paine publishes *Common Sense*

1775–1783
American Revolution

1789–1799
French Revolution

1790
Edmund Burke publishes *Reflections on the Revolution in France*

1791–1804
Haitian Revolution

1799–1814
Reign of Napoleon Bonaparte in France

In most countries, various middle-class groups—professionals, merchants, and guild masters—enjoyed privileges that allowed them to monopolize all sorts of economic activity.

Traditional prerogatives persisted in societies undergoing dramatic change. Due to increased agricultural production, Europe's population rose rapidly after 1750, and its cities and towns swelled in size. Inflation kept pace with demography, making it increasingly difficult for urban people to find affordable food and living space. One way they kept up, and even managed to participate in the new consumer revolution (see page 575), was by working harder and for longer hours. More positive developments were increased schooling and a rise in literacy rates, particularly among urban men.

Economic growth created new inequalities between rich and poor. While the poor struggled with rising prices, investors grew rich from the spread of rural manufacture and overseas trade. Old distinctions between landed aristocracy and city merchant began to fade as enterprising nobles put money into trade and rising middle-class bureaucrats and merchants bought landed estates and noble titles. Marriages between nobles and wealthy, educated commoners (called the *bourgeoisie* [boorzh-wah-ZEE] in France) served both groups' interests, and a mixed-caste elite began to take shape.

Another social change involved the racial regimes established in European colonies. By the late eighteenth century European law accepted that only Africans and people of African descent were subject to slavery. Even free people of color—a term for nonslaves of African or mixed African-European descent—were subject to significant restrictions on their legal rights. Racial privilege conferred a new dimension of entitlement on European settlers in the colonies, and they used extremely brutal methods to enforce it.

In Spanish America and Brazil, people of European and African descent intermingled with the very large indigenous population. Until the reforms of Charles III, indigenous people and Spaniards were required by law to live in separate communities, although many of the former secretly fled to Spanish cities and

How did the events of 1789 result in a constitutional monarchy in France?

How did Napoleon Bonaparte assume control of France and much of Europe?

How did slave revolt on colonial Saint-Domingue lead to the creation of Haiti in 1804?

How did the Spanish and Portuguese colonies of the Americas shake off European domination?

☑ LearningCurve
Check what you know.

haciendas to escape forced labor obligations. Mestizos (meh-STEE-zohz), people of mixed European and indigenous descent, held a higher social status than other nonwhites, but a lower status than Europeans.

Demands for Liberty and Equality

In addition to destabilizing social changes, the ideals of liberty and equality helped fuel revolutions in the Atlantic world. The call for liberty was first of all a call for individual human rights. Supporters of the cause of individual liberty (who became known as "liberals" in the early nineteenth century) demanded freedom to worship according to the dictates of their consciences, an end to censorship, and freedom from arbitrary laws and from judges who simply obeyed orders from the government.

The call for liberty was also a call for a new kind of government. Reformers believed that the people had sovereignty—that is, that the people alone had the authority to make laws limiting an individual's freedom of action. In practice, this system of government meant choosing legislators who represented the people and were accountable to them. Monarchs might retain their thrones, but their rule should be constrained by the will of the people.

Equality was a more ambiguous idea. Eighteenth-century liberals argued that, in theory, all citizens should have identical rights and liberties. However, they accepted a number of distinctions. First, most male eighteenth-century liberals believed that equality between men and women was neither practical nor desirable. Second, few questioned the superiority of people of European descent over those of indigenous or African origin.

Finally, liberals never believed that everyone should be equal economically. Great differences in wealth and income between rich and poor were perfectly acceptable, so long as every free white male had a legally equal chance at economic gain. However limited they appear to modern eyes, these demands for liberty and equality were revolutionary, given that a privileged elite had long existed with little opposition.

The two most important Enlightenment references for late-eighteenth-century liberals were John Locke and the baron de Montesquieu. Locke maintained that England's long political tradition rested on "the rights of Englishmen" and on representative government through Parliament. He argued that if a government oversteps its proper function of protecting the natural rights of life, liberty, and private property, it becomes a tyranny. Montesquieu was also an admirer of England's Parliament. He believed that powerful "intermediary groups"—such as the judicial nobility of which he was a proud member—offered the best defense of liberty against despotism.

The Atlantic revolutions began with aspirations for equality and liberty among the social elite. Soon, however, dissenting voices emerged as some revolutionaries became frustrated with the limitations of liberal notions of equality and liberty and clamored for a fuller realization of these concepts. Depending on location, their demands included political rights for women and free people of color, the emancipation of slaves, better treatment of indigenous people, and government regulations to reduce economic inequality. The age of revolution was thus characterized by bitter conflicts over how far reform should go and to whom it should apply.

CHAPTER LOCATOR | What were the factors behind the age of revolution in the Atlantic world? | Why and how did American colonists forge a new, independent nation?

CHAPTER 22
646 REVOLUTIONS IN THE ATLANTIC WORLD

The Seven Years' War

The roots of revolutionary ideology could be found in Enlightenment texts, but it was by no means inevitable that such ideas would result in revolution. Instead events — political, economic, and military — created crises that opened the door for radical action. One of the most important was the global conflict known as the Seven Years' War (1756–1763).

The war's battlefields stretched from central Europe to India to North America, pitting a new alliance of England and Prussia against the French, Austrians, and, later, Spanish. Its origins were in conflicts left unresolved at the end of the War of the Austrian Succession in 1748, during which Prussia had seized the Austrian territory of Silesia. In central Europe, Austria's monarch Maria Theresa vowed to win back Silesia, and to crush Prussia. By the end of the Seven Years' War, Maria Theresa had almost succeeded, but Prussia survived with its boundaries intact.

In North America the encroachment of English settlers into territory claimed by the French in the Ohio Valley resulted in skirmishes that soon became war. French forces achieved major victories until 1758, but the tide of the conflict turned when the British diverted resources from the war in Europe, using superior sea power to destroy the French fleet and choke French commerce around the world.

British victory on all colonial fronts was ratified in the 1763 **Treaty of Paris**. Canada and all French territory east of the Mississippi River passed to Britain, and France ceded Louisiana to Spain as compensation for Spain's loss of Florida to Britain. France also gave up most of its holdings in India, opening the way to British dominance on the subcontinent (Map 22.1).

The war was costly for all participants and, in its aftermath, British, French, and Spanish governments had to increase taxes to repay loans, raising a storm of protest and demands for political reform. Since the Caribbean colony of Saint-Domingue remained French, revolutionary turmoil in the mother country would directly affect its population. The seeds of revolutionary conflict in the Atlantic world were thus sown.

Treaty of Paris

▶ The 1763 peace treaty that ended the Seven Years' War, according vast French territories in North America and India to Britain and Louisiana to Spain.

How did the events of 1789 result in a constitutional monarchy in France? | How did Napoleon Bonaparte assume control of France and much of Europe? | How did slave revolt on colonial Saint-Domingue lead to the creation of Haiti in 1804? | How did the Spanish and Portuguese colonies of the Americas shake off European domination? | ✔ LearningCurve Check what you know.

647

MAP 22.1 ■ European Claims in North America and India Before and After the Seven Years' War, 1755–1763

As a result of the war, France lost its vast territories in North America and India. In an effort to avoid costly conflicts with Native Americans living in the newly conquered territory, the British government in 1763 prohibited colonists from settling west of the Appalachian Mountains. One of the few remaining French colonies in the Americas, Saint-Domingue (on the island of Hispaniola) was the most profitable plantation in the New World.

> ## QUICK REVIEW

How did imperial rivalries contribute to the outbreak of revolutions across the Atlantic world?

CHAPTER LOCATOR │ What were the factors behind the age of revolution in the Atlantic world?   Why and how did American colonists forge a new, independent nation?

CHAPTER 22
648 REVOLUTIONS IN THE ATLANTIC WORLD

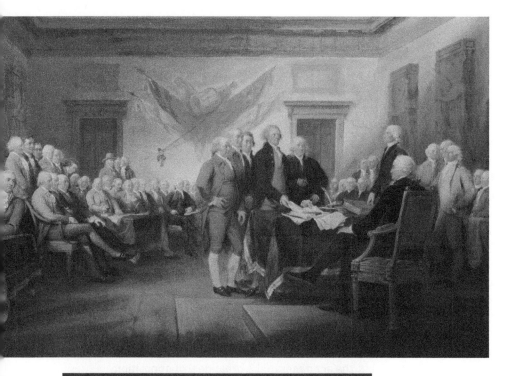

The Signing of the Declaration of Independence, July 4, 1776

John Trumbull's famous painting shows the dignity and determination of America's revolutionary leaders. An extraordinarily talented group, they succeeded in rallying popular support without losing power to more radical forces in the process. (Photo © Boltin Picture Library/The Bridgeman Art Library)

INCREASED TAXES AND GOVERNMENT control sparked colonial protests in the New World, where the era of liberal political revolution began. Participants in the revolution believed they were demanding only the traditional rights of English men and women. But those traditional rights were liberal rights, and in the American context they had strong democratic and popular overtones.

The Origins of the Revolution

The high cost of the Seven Years' War doubled the British national debt. Anticipating further expenses to defend newly conquered territories, the British government broke with tradition and announced that it would maintain a large army in North America and tax the colonies directly. In 1765 Parliament passed the Stamp Act, which levied taxes on a long list of commercial and legal documents, diplomas, newspapers, almanacs, and playing cards. These measures seemed perfectly reasonable to the British, for a much heavier stamp tax already existed in Britain, and proceeds from the tax were to fund the defense of the colonies. Nonetheless, the colonists vigorously protested the Stamp Act by rioting and by boycotting British goods. Thus Parliament reluctantly repealed it.

This dispute raised an important political issue. The British government believed that Americans were represented in Parliament, albeit indirectly (like most British people), and that Parliament ruled throughout the empire. Many Americans felt otherwise, and came to see British colonial administration and parliamentary supremacy as grave threats to existing American liberties.

Americans' resistance to these threats was fed by the great degree of independence they had long enjoyed. In British North America, unlike in England and Europe, religious freedom was taken for granted. Colonial assemblies made the important laws, which were seldom overturned by the British government. Also, the right to vote was much more widespread than in England.

Moreover, greater political equality was matched by greater social and economic equality, at least for the free population. There was no hereditary nobility, and independent farmers dominated colonial society. This was particularly true in the northern colonies, where the revolution originated.

In 1773 disputes over taxes and representation flared up again. Under the Tea Act of that year, the East India Company secured a profitable monopoly on the tea trade, and colonial merchants were excluded. The price on tea was actually lowered for colonists, but the act generated a great deal of opposition because of its impact on local merchants.

In protest, Boston men disguised as Native Americans held a rowdy Tea Party in which they boarded East India Company ships and threw tea from them into the harbor. In response, the so-called Coercive Acts of 1774 instated a series of harsh measures. County conventions in Massachusetts urged that the acts be "rejected as the attempts of a wicked administration to enslave America." Other colonial assemblies joined in the denunciations. In September 1774 the First Continental Congress met in Philadelphia. The more radical members of this assembly argued successfully against concessions to the English crown. The British Parliament also rejected compromise, and in April 1775 fighting between colonial and British troops began at Lexington and Concord.

Independence from Britain

As fighting spread, the colonists moved slowly toward open calls for independence. The uncompromising attitude of the British government and its use of German mercenaries did much to dissolve loyalties to the home country and to unite the separate colonies. *Common Sense* (1775), a brilliant attack by the recently arrived English radical Thomas Paine (1737–1809), also mobilized public opinion in favor of independence.

On July 4, 1776, the Second Continental Congress adopted the **Declaration of Independence**. Written by Thomas Jefferson and others, this document listed the tyrannical acts committed by George III (r. 1760–1820) and proclaimed the natural rights of mankind and the sovereignty of the American states. The Declaration of Independence in effect universalized the traditional rights of English people and made them the rights of all mankind.

After the Declaration of Independence, the conflict often took the form of a civil war pitting patriots against Loyalists, those who maintained an allegiance

Declaration of Independence

▶ The 1776 document in which the American colonies declared independence from Great Britain and recast traditional English rights as universal human rights.

CHAPTER LOCATOR | What were the factors behind the age of revolution in the Atlantic world? | Why and how did American colonists forge a new, independent nation?

CHAPTER 22
650   REVOLUTIONS IN THE ATLANTIC WORLD

to the Crown. The Loyalists were few in number in New England and Virginia, but more common in the Deep South and on the western frontier. British commanders also recruited Loyalists from enslaved people by promising freedom to any slave who left his master to fight for the mother country.

On the international scene, the French wanted revenge against the British for the humiliating defeats of the Seven Years' War. Thus they sympathized with the rebels and supplied guns and gunpowder from the beginning of the conflict. In 1778 the French government offered the Americans a formal alliance, and in 1779 and 1780 the Spanish and Dutch declared war on Britain. Catherine the Great of Russia helped organize the League of Armed Neutrality to protect neutral shipping rights and succeeded in hampering Britain's naval power.

Thus by 1780 Britain was engaged in an imperial war against most of Europe as well as the thirteen colonies. In these circumstances, and in the face of severe reverses in India, in the West Indies, and at Yorktown in Virginia, a new British government decided to cut its losses and end the war. Under the Treaty of Paris of 1783, Britain recognized the independence of the thirteen colonies and ceded all its territory between the Allegheny Mountains and the Mississippi River to the Americans.

Loyalist Strength in the Colonies, ca. 1774–1776

KEY EVENTS OF THE AMERICAN REVOLUTION

1765	Britain passes the Stamp Act
1773	Britain passes the Tea Act
1774	Britain passes the Coercive Acts in response to the Tea Party in the colonies; the First Continental Congress refuses concessions to the English crown
April 1775	Fighting begins between colonial and British troops
July 4, 1776	The Second Continental Congress adopts the Declaration of Independence
1777–1780	The French, Spanish, and Dutch side with the colonists against Britain
1783	The Treaty of Paris recognizes the independence of the American colonies
1787	The U.S. Constitution is signed
1791	The first ten amendments to the Constitution are ratified (the Bill of Rights)

Framing the Constitution

The liberal program of the American Revolution was consolidated by the federal Constitution, the Bill of Rights, and the creation of a national republic. Assembling in Philadelphia in the summer of 1787, the delegates to the Constitutional Convention were determined to end the period of economic depression, social uncertainty, and leadership under a weak central government that had followed independence. The delegates thus decided to grant the federal, or central, government important powers: regulation of domestic and foreign trade, the right to tax, and the means to enforce its laws.

When the results of the Constitutional Convention were presented to the states for ratification, a great public debate began. The opponents of the proposed

How did the events of 1789 result in a constitutional monarchy in France?

How did Napoleon Bonaparte assume control of France and much of Europe?

How did slave revolt on colonial Saint-Domingue lead to the creation of Haiti in 1804?

How did the Spanish and Portuguese colonies of the Americas shake off European domination?

LearningCurve
Check what you know.

651

Antifederalists

▶ Opponents of the American Constitution who felt it diminished individual rights and accorded too much power to the federal government at the expense of the states.

Constitution—the Antifederalists—charged that the framers of the new document had taken too much power from the individual states and made the federal government too strong. Moreover, many Antifederalists feared for the individual freedoms for which they had fought. To overcome these objections, the Federalists promised to spell out these basic freedoms as soon as the new Constitution was adopted. The result was the first ten amendments to the Constitution, which the first Congress passed shortly after it met in New York in March 1789. These amendments, ratified in 1791, formed an effective Bill of Rights to safeguard the individual.

Limitations of Liberty and Equality

The American Constitution and the Bill of Rights exemplified the strengths and the limits of what came to be called classical liberalism. Liberty meant individual freedoms and political safeguards. Liberty also meant representative government, but it did not mean democracy, with its principle of one person, one vote. Equality meant equality before the law, not equality of political participation or wealth. It did not mean equal rights for slaves, Native Americans, or women.

A vigorous abolitionist movement during the 1780s led to the passage of emancipation laws in all northern states, but slavery remained prevalent in the South, and discord between pro- and antislavery delegates roiled the Constitutional Convention of 1787. The result was a set of compromises that ensured that slavery would endure in the United States for the foreseeable future.

The new republic also failed to protect the Native American tribes whose lands fell within or alongside the territory ceded by Britain at the Treaty of Paris. The 1787 Constitution promised protection to Native Americans and guaranteed that their land would not be taken without consent. Nonetheless, the rights and interests of Native Americans were generally ignored as a growing colonial population pushed westward.

Women played a vital role in the American Revolution. Women were essential participants in boycotts of British goods, which squeezed profits from British merchants and fostered the revolutionary spirit. After the outbreak of war, women raised funds for the Continental Army and took care of homesteads, workshops, and other businesses when their men went off to fight. Women did not, however, receive the right to vote in the new Constitution, an omission confirmed by a clause added in 1844.

> **QUICK REVIEW**

What did proponents of the American Revolution mean by the terms "liberty" and "equality"?

CHAPTER LOCATOR | What were the factors behind the age of revolution in the Atlantic world? | Why and how did American colonists forge a new, independent nation?

CHAPTER 22
652 REVOLUTIONS IN THE ATLANTIC WORLD

The Tennis Court Oath, June 20, 1789

Painted two years after the event shown, this dramatic painting by Jacques-Louis David depicts a crucial turning point in the early days of the Revolution. On June 20 delegates of the third estate arrived at their meeting hall in the Versailles palace to find the doors closed and guarded. Fearing the king was about to dissolve their meeting by force, the deputies reassembled at a nearby indoor tennis court and swore a solemn oath not to disperse until they had been recognized as the National Assembly. (Musée de la Ville de Paris, Musée Carnavalet, Paris, France/Giraudon/The Bridgeman Art Library)

How did the events of 1789 result in a constitutional monarchy in France, and what were the consequences?

ALTHOUGH INSPIRED IN PART by events in North America, the French Revolution did not mirror the American example. It was more radical and more complex, more influential and more controversial. For Europeans and most of the rest of the world, it was the great revolution of the eighteenth century, the revolution that opened the modern era in politics.

Breakdown of the Old Order

As did the American Revolution, the French Revolution had its immediate origins in the financial difficulties of the government. The efforts of the ministers of King Louis XV (r. 1715–1774) to raise taxes to meet the expenses of the War of the Austrian Succession and the Seven Years' War were thwarted by the high courts, known as the parlements. The noble judges of the parlements resented this threat to their exemption from taxation and decried the government's actions as a form of royal despotism.

How did the events of 1789 result in a constitutional monarchy in France?	How did Napoleon Bonaparte assume control of France and much of Europe?	How did slave revolt on colonial Saint-Domingue lead to the creation of Haiti in 1804?	How did the Spanish and Portuguese colonies of the Americas shake off European domination?	✓ LearningCurve Check what you know.

When renewed efforts to reform the tax system similarly failed in 1776, the government was forced to finance its enormous expenditures during the American war with borrowed money. As a result, the national debt soared. In 1786 the finance minister informed King Louis XVI (r. 1774–1792) that the nation was on the verge of bankruptcy.

> **> France's Annual Budget (1786):**

- 50 percent: Interest payments on the national debt
- 25 percent: Maintenance of the military
- 6 percent: Expenses of the royal family and the court
- Less than 20 percent: Productive functions of the state, such as transportation and general administration

Louis XVI's minister of finance convinced the king to call an assembly of notables in 1787 to gain support for major fiscal reforms. The assembled notables declared that sweeping tax changes required the approval of the Estates General, the representative body of all three estates. Louis XVI's efforts to reject their demands failed, and in July 1788 he reluctantly called the Estates General into session.

Estates General

▶ Traditional representative body of the three estates of France that met in 1789 in response to imminent state bankruptcy.

The National Assembly

The Estates General was a legislative body with representatives from the three orders of society: the clergy, nobility, and commoners. On May 5, 1789, the twelve hundred newly elected delegates of the three estates gathered in Versailles for the opening session of the Estates General. They met in an atmosphere of deepening economic crisis, triggered by a poor grain harvest in 1788.

The Estates General was almost immediately deadlocked by arguments about voting procedures. The government insisted that each estate should meet and vote separately. Critics had demanded instead a single assembly dominated by the third estate. In his famous pamphlet "What Is the Third Estate?" the abbé Emmanuel Joseph Sieyès argued that the nobility was a tiny, overprivileged minority and that commoners constituted the true strength of the French nation. The issue came to a crisis in June 1789 when delegates of the third estate refused to meet until the king ordered the clergy and nobility to sit with them in a single body. On June 20 the delegates of the third estate moved to a large indoor tennis court where they swore the famous Oath of the Tennis Court, pledging not to disband until they had been recognized as a National Assembly and had written a new constitution.

National Assembly

▶ French representative assembly formed in 1789 by the delegates of the third estate and some members of the clergy, the second estate.

The king's response was disastrously ambivalent. Although he made a conciliatory speech accepting the deputies' demands, he called a large army toward the capital to bring the Assembly under control, and on July 11 he dismissed his finance minister and other liberal ministers. On July 14, 1789, several hundred common people, angered by the king's actions, stormed the Bastille (ba-STEEL), a royal prison. Ill-judged severity on the part of the Crown thus led to the first episodes of popular violence.

Uprisings also rocked the countryside. In the summer of 1789 throughout France peasants began to rise in insurrection against their lords. Fear of maraud-

CHAPTER LOCATOR | What were the factors behind the age of revolution in the Atlantic world? | Why and how did American colonists forge a new, independent nation?

CHAPTER 22
654 REVOLUTIONS IN THE ATLANTIC WORLD

ers and vagabonds hired by vengeful landlords—called the Great Fear by contemporaries—seized the rural poor and fanned the flames of rebellion.

The National Assembly responded to the swell of popular anger with a surprise maneuver on the night of August 4, 1789. By a decree of the Assembly, all the old noble privileges were abolished along with tithes paid to the church. On August 27, 1789, the Assembly further issued the Declaration of the Rights of Man and of the Citizen, guaranteeing equality before the law, representative government for a sovereign people, and individual freedom.

The National Assembly's declaration had little practical effect for the poor and hungry people of Paris. The economic crisis worsened after the fall of the Bastille, as aristocrats fled the country and the luxury market collapsed. Foreign markets also shrank, and unemployment among the urban working class grew.

Constitutional Monarchy

The next two years, until September 1791, saw the consolidation of the liberal revolution. In June 1790 the National Assembly abolished the nobility, and in July the king swore to uphold the as-yet-unwritten constitution. The king remained the head of state, but all lawmaking power now resided in the National Assembly, elected by the wealthiest half of French males. The constitution finally passed in September 1791 was the first in French history. It legalized divorce and broadened women's rights to inherit property and to obtain financial support for illegitimate children from fathers, but excluded women from political office and voting.

In addition to ruling on women's rights, the National Assembly replaced the patchwork of historic provinces with eighty-three departments of approximately equal size. The deputies prohibited monopolies, guilds, and workers' associations and abolished barriers to trade within France. Thus the National Assembly applied the spirit of the Enlightenment in a thorough reform of France's laws and institutions.

The National Assembly also imposed a radical reorganization on religious life. It granted religious freedom to the small minority of French Jews and Protestants. Furthermore, in November 1789 it nationalized the property of the Catholic Church and abolished monasteries.

In July 1790 the Civil Constitution of the Clergy established a national church with priests chosen by voters. The National Assembly then forced the Catholic clergy to take an oath of loyalty to the new government. The pope formally condemned this measure, and only half the priests of France swore the oath. Many sincere Christians, especially those in the countryside, were also upset by these changes in the religious order. The attempt to remake the Catholic Church, like the abolition of guilds and workers' associations, sharpened the conflict between the educated classes and the common people that had been emerging in the eighteenth century.

The National Convention

The outbreak and progress of revolution in France produced great excitement and a sharp division of opinion in Europe and the United States. Liberals and radicals saw a triumph of liberty over despotism, while conservative leaders were deeply troubled by the aroused spirit of reform.

| How did the events of 1789 result in a constitutional monarchy in France? | How did Napoleon Bonaparte assume control of France and much of Europe? | How did slave revolt on colonial Saint-Domingue lead to the creation of Haiti in 1804? | How did the Spanish and Portuguese colonies of the Americas shake off European domination? | ✔ LearningCurve Check what you know. |

655

Jacobin club

▶ A political club during the French Revolution to which many of the deputies of the Legislative Assembly belonged.

Mountain

▶ Led by Robespierre, the French National Convention's radical faction, which led the Convention in 1793.

Girondists

▶ A moderate group that fought for control of the French National Convention in 1793.

sans-culottes

▶ The laboring poor of Paris, so called because the men wore trousers instead of the knee breeches of the aristocracy and middle class; the term came to refer to the militant radicals of the city.

Areas of French Insurrection, 1793

The kings and nobles of continental Europe, who had at first welcomed the revolution in France as weakening a competing power, now feared its impact. In June 1791 the royal family was arrested and returned to Paris after a failed attempt to escape France. To the monarchs of Austria and Prussia, the arrest of a crowned monarch was unacceptable. Two months later they issued the Declaration of Pillnitz, proclaiming their willingness to intervene in France to restore Louis XVI's rule, if necessary.

The new French representative body, called the Legislative Assembly, was dominated by members of the Jacobin club. The Jacobins and other deputies reacted with patriotic fury to the Declaration of Pillnitz, and in April 1792 France declared war on Francis II of Austria, the Habsburg monarch.

France's crusade against tyranny went poorly at first. Prussian forces joined Austria against the French, who broke and fled at their first military encounter with this First Coalition of antirevolutionary foreign powers. The Legislative Assembly declared the country in danger, and volunteers rallied to the capital. In August the Assembly suspended the king from all his functions and imprisoned him.

The fall of the monarchy marked a rapid radicalization of the Revolution. In late September 1792 a new assembly, called the National Convention, was elected by universal manhood suffrage. The Convention proclaimed France a republic, a nation in which the people, instead of a monarch, held sovereign power. Under the leadership of the Mountain, the radical faction of the Jacobin club led by Maximilien Robespierre and Georges Jacques Danton, the Convention tried and convicted the king for treason. On January 21, 1793, Louis was executed. His wife, Marie Antoinette, suffered the same fate later that year.

In February 1793 the National Convention declared war on Britain, the Dutch Republic, and Spain. Republican France was now at war with almost all of Europe, and it faced mounting internal opposition. Peasants in western France revolted against being drafted into the army, with the Vendée region of Brittany emerging as the epicenter of revolt. Devout Catholics, royalists, and foreign agents encouraged their rebellion.

By March 1793 the National Convention was locked in struggle between two factions of the Jacobin club, the radical Mountain and the more moderate Girondists. With the middle-class delegates so bitterly divided, the laboring poor of Paris once again emerged as the decisive political factor. The laboring poor and the petty traders were often known as the sans-culottes (san-koo-LAHT; "without breeches") because their men wore trousers instead of the knee breeches of the wealthy. They demanded radical political action to guarantee them their daily bread. The Mountain, sensing an opportunity to outmaneuver the Girondists, joined with sans-culotte activists to engineer a popular uprising. On June 2, 1793, armed sans-culottes invaded the Convention and forced its deputies to arrest twenty-nine Girondist deputies for treason. All power passed to the Mountain.

This military and political crisis led to the most radical period of the Revolution, which lasted from spring 1793 until summer 1794. To deal with threats from within and outside France, the Convention formed the Committee of Public Safety in April 1793. Led by Robespierre, the Committee advanced on several fronts in 1793 and 1794. First, in September 1793 Robespierre and his coworkers established a planned economy. Rather than let supply and demand determine prices, the government set maximum allowable prices for key products. Though the state was too weak to enforce all its price regulations, it did fix the price of bread in Paris at levels the poor could afford.

CHAPTER LOCATOR | What were the factors behind the age of revolution in the Atlantic world? | Why and how did American colonists forge a new, independent nation?

Contrasting Visions of the Sans-Culottes

These two images offer profoundly different representations of a sans-culotte woman. The image on the left was created by a French artist, while the image on the right is English. The French words above the image on the right read in part, "Heads! Blood! Death! . . . I am the Goddess of Liberty! . . . Long Live the Guillotine!" (left: Musée de la Ville de Paris, Musée Carnavalet, Paris, France/ Archives Charmet/The Bridgeman Art Library; right: by James Gillray [1757–1815]. © Courtesy of the Warden and Scholars of New College, Oxford, UK/The Bridgeman Art Library)

> **> PICTURING THE PAST**

ANALYZING THE IMAGE: How would you describe the woman on the left? What qualities does the artist seem to ascribe to her, and how do you think these qualities relate to the sans-culottes and the French Revolution? How would you characterize the facial expression and attire of the woman on the right? How does the inclusion of the text contribute to your impressions of her?
CONNECTIONS: What does the contrast between these two images suggest about differences between French and English perceptions of the sans-culottes and of the French Revolution? Why do you think the artists have chosen to depict women?

The government also put the people to work producing arms, munitions, and uniforms for the war effort. The government told craftsmen what to produce, nationalized many small workshops, and requisitioned raw materials and grain. These economic reforms amounted to an emergency form of socialism, which thoroughly frightened Europe's propertied classes and greatly influenced the subsequent development of socialist ideology.

Second, the **Reign of Terror** (1793–1794) enforced compliance with republican beliefs and practices. Special revolutionary courts tried "enemies of the nation" for political crimes. As a result, some forty thousand French men and women were executed or died in prison. Presented as a necessary measure to save the republic, the Terror was a weapon directed against all suspected of opposing the revolutionary government.

In their efforts to impose unity, the Jacobins also took actions to suppress women's participation in political debate, which they perceived as disorderly and a distraction from women's proper place in the home. On October 30, 1793, the National Convention declared, "The clubs and popular societies of women, under whatever denomination are prohibited."

The third element of the Committee's program was to bring about a cultural revolution that would transform former royal subjects into republican citizens.

Reign of Terror

▶ The period from 1793 to 1794, during which Robespierre's Committee of Public Safety tried and executed thousands suspected of treason and a new revolutionary culture was imposed.

How did the events of 1789 result in a constitutional monarchy in France?

How did Napoleon Bonaparte assume control of France and much of Europe?

How did slave revolt on colonial Saint-Domingue lead to the creation of Haiti in 1804?

How did the Spanish and Portuguese colonies of the Americas shake off European domination?

LearningCurve Check what you know.

KEY EVENTS OF THE FRENCH REVOLUTION

May 5, 1789	Estates General meets at Versailles
June 20, 1789	Oath of the Tennis Court
July 14, 1789	Storming of the Bastille
July–August 1789	Great Fear
August 4, 1789	National Assembly abolishes feudal privileges
August 27, 1789	National Assembly issues Declaration of the Rights of Man and of the Citizen
July 1790	Civil Constitution of the Clergy establishes a national church; Louis XVI agrees to a constitutional monarchy
June 1791	Royal family is arrested while attempting to flee France
August 1791	Austria and Prussia issue the Declaration of Pillnitz
April 1792	France declares war on Austria
August 1792	Legislative Assembly takes Louis XVI prisoner and suspends him from functions
September 1792	National Convention declares France a republic and abolishes monarchy
January 21, 1793	Louis XVI is executed
February 1793	France declares war on Britain, the Dutch Republic, and Spain; revolts take place in some provinces
March 1793	Struggle between Girondists and the Mountain
June 1793	Sans-culottes invade the National Convention; Girondist leaders are arrested
September 1793	Price controls are instituted to aid the poor
1793–1794	Reign of Terror
Spring 1794	French armies are victorious on all fronts
July 1794	Robespierre is executed; Thermidorian reaction begins
1795	Economic controls are abolished, and suppression of the sans-culottes begins
1795–1799	Directory rules
1798–1799	Austria, Britain, and Russia form the Second Coalition against France
1799	Napoleon Bonaparte overthrows the Directory and seizes power

The government sponsored revolutionary art and songs as well as secular holidays and open-air festivals to celebrate republican virtues. It also attempted to rationalize daily life by adopting the decimal system for weights and measures and a new calendar based on ten-day weeks. A campaign of de-Christianization aimed to eliminate Catholic symbols and beliefs. Fearful of the hostility aroused in rural France, however, Robespierre called for a halt to de-Christianization measures in mid-1794.

The final element in the program of the Committee of Public Safety was its appeal to a new sense of national identity and patriotism. With a common language and a common tradition reinforced by the revolutionary ideals of popular sovereignty and democracy, many French people developed an intense emotional attachment to the nation. This was the birth of modern nationalism, the strong identification with one's nation, which would have a profound effect on subsequent European history.

CHAPTER LOCATOR | What were the factors behind the age of revolution in the Atlantic world? | Why and how did American colonists forge a new, independent nation?

To defend the nation, a decree of August 1793 imposed a draft on all unmarried young men. By January 1794 French armed forces outnumbered those of their enemies almost four to one. By spring 1794 French armies were victorious on all fronts and domestic revolt was largely suppressed. The republic was saved.

The Directory

The success of French armies led the Committee of Public Safety to relax emergency economic controls, but they extended the political Reign of Terror. The revolutionary tribunals sent many critics to the guillotine, including long-standing collaborators whom Robespierre believed had turned against him. A group of radicals and moderates in the Convention, knowing that they might be next, organized a conspiracy. They howled down Robespierre when he tried to speak to the National Convention on July 27, 1794—a date known as 9 Thermidor according to France's newly adopted republican calendar. The next day it was Robespierre's turn to be guillotined.

The respectable middle-class lawyers and professionals who had led the liberal Revolution of 1789 then reasserted their authority. This period of **Thermidorian reaction**, as it was called, harkened back to the moderate beginnings of the Revolution. In 1795 the National Convention abolished many economic controls and severely restricted local political organizations. In addition, the middle-class members of the National Convention wrote a new constitution restricting eligibility to serve as a deputy to men of substantial means. Real power lay with a new five-man executive body, called the Directory. France's new rulers continued to support military expansion abroad, but war was no longer so much a crusade as a response to economic problems. Large, victorious armies reduced unemployment at home. However, the French people quickly grew weary of the corruption and ineffectiveness that characterized the Directory. This general dissatisfaction revealed itself clearly in the national elections of 1797, which returned a large number of conservative and even monarchist deputies. Fearing for their survival, the Directory used the army to nullify the elections and began to govern dictatorially. Two years later Napoleon Bonaparte ended the Directory in a coup d'état (koo day-TAH) and substituted a strong dictatorship for a weak one. While claiming to uphold revolutionary values, Napoleon would install authoritarian rule.

Thermidorian reaction

▶ A reaction in 1794 to the violence of the Reign of Terror, resulting in the execution of Robespierre and the loosening of economic controls.

The Execution of Robespierre

Completely wooden except for the heavy iron blade, the guillotine was devised by a French revolutionary doctor named Guillotin as a humane method of execution. The guillotine was painted red for Robespierre's execution. Large crowds witnessed the execution in a majestic public square in central Paris, then known as the Place de la Revolution and now called the Place de la Concorde (Harmony Square). (Musée de la Ville de Paris, Musée Carnavalet, Paris, France/Giraudon/The Bridgeman Art Library)

QUICK REVIEW <

How and why did the French Revolution change between 1789 and 1799?

How did the events of 1789 result in a constitutional monarchy in France?

How did Napoleon Bonaparte assume control of France and much of Europe?

How did slave revolt on colonial Saint-Domingue lead to the creation of Haiti in 1804?

How did the Spanish and Portuguese colonies of the Americas shake off European domination?

✔ LearningCurve
Check what you know.

How did Napoleon Bonaparte assume control of France and much of Europe, and what factors led to his downfall?

The Coronation of Napoleon, 1804

In this detail from a grandiose painting by Jacques-Louis David, Napoleon, instead of the pope, prepares to crown his wife, Josephine, in an elaborate ceremony in Notre Dame Cathedral. Napoleon, the ultimate upstart, also crowned himself. Pope Pius VII, seated glumly behind the emperor, is reduced to being a spectator. (Photo by Jacques-Louis David [1748–1825]/Louvre, Paris, France/ The Bridgeman Art Library)

NAPOLEON BONAPARTE (1769–1821) sought to put an end to civil strife in France in order to create unity and consolidate his rule. And he did. But Napoleon saw himself as a man of destiny, and the glory of war and the dream of universal empire proved irresistible.

Napoleon's Rule of France

Born on the Mediterranean island of Corsica, Napoleon left home and became a lieutenant in the French artillery in 1785. Rising rapidly in the new army, Napoleon was placed in command of French forces in Italy and won brilliant victories there in 1796 and 1797. His next campaign, in Egypt, was a failure, but Napoleon returned to France before the fiasco was generally known. French aggression in Egypt and elsewhere provoked the British to organize a new alliance in 1798, the Second Coalition, which included Austria and Russia.

Napoleon soon learned that some prominent members of the legislature were plotting against the Directory. The dissatisfaction of these plotters stemmed not

CHAPTER LOCATOR | What were the factors behind the age of revolution in the Atlantic world? | Why and how did American colonists forge a new, independent nation?

660 CHAPTER 22
REVOLUTIONS IN THE ATLANTIC WORLD

so much from the fact that the Directory was a dictatorship as from the fact that it was a weak dictatorship.

The young Napoleon, nationally revered for his heroism, was an ideal figure of authority. On November 9, 1799, Napoleon and his conspirators ousted the Directors, and the following day soldiers disbanded the legislature. Napoleon was named first consul of the republic, and a new constitution consolidating his position was overwhelmingly approved in a plebiscite in December 1799. Republican appearances were maintained, but Napoleon became the real ruler of France.

Napoleon worked to maintain order and end civil strife by appeasing powerful groups in France, offering them favors in return for loyal service. Napoleon's bargain with the middle class was codified in the Civil Code of March 1804, also known as the Napoleonic Code, which reasserted two of the fundamental principles of the Revolution of 1789: equality of all male citizens before the law and absolute security of wealth and private property. Napoleon and the leading bankers of Paris established the privately owned Bank of France in 1800, which served the interests of both the state and the financial oligarchy. Napoleon won over peasants by defending the gains in land and status they had won during the Revolution.

At the same time, Napoleon consolidated his rule by recruiting disillusioned revolutionaries for the network of government officials. Nor were members of the old nobility slighted. In 1800 and again in 1802 Napoleon granted amnesty to noble émigrés on the condition that they return to France and take a loyalty oath. Members of this returning elite soon occupied high posts in the expanding centralized state. Napoleon also created a new imperial nobility to reward his most talented generals and officials.

Furthermore, Napoleon sought to restore the Catholic Church in France so that it could serve as a bulwark of social stability. Napoleon and Pope Pius VII (pontificate 1800–1823) signed the Concordat of 1801. Under this agreement the pope gained the right for French Catholics to practice their religion freely, but Napoleon's government now nominated bishops, paid the clergy, and exerted great influence over the church in France.

Order and unity had a price: authoritarian rule. Women lost many of the gains they had made in the 1790s. Under the Napoleonic Code, women were dependents of either their fathers or their husbands, and they could not make contracts or have bank accounts in their own names. Napoleon also curtailed free speech and freedom of the press and manipulated voting in the occasional elections. After 1810 political suspects were held in state prisons, as they had been during the Terror.

Napoleon's Expansion in Europe

After coming to power in 1799, Napoleon sent peace feelers to Austria and Britain, the dominant powers of the Second Coalition. When these overtures were rejected, French armies led by Napoleon decisively defeated the Austrians. Subsequent treaties with Austria in 1801 and Britain in 1802 consolidated France's hold on the territories its armies had won up to that point.

In 1802 Napoleon was secure but still driven to expand his power. Aggressively redrawing the map of German-speaking lands so as to weaken Austria and encourage the secondary states of southwestern Germany to side with France,

Napoleonic Code

▶ French civil code promulgated in 1804 that reasserted the 1789 principles of the equality of all male citizens before the law and the absolute security of wealth and private property.

| How did the events of 1789 result in a constitutional monarchy in France? | **How did Napoleon Bonaparte assume control of France and much of Europe?** | How did slave revolt on colonial Saint-Domingue lead to the creation of Haiti in 1804? | How did the Spanish and Portuguese colonies of the Americas shake off European domination? | ☑ LearningCurve Check what you know. |

661

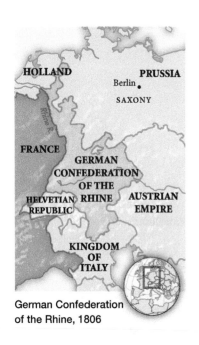

German Confederation
of the Rhine, 1806

Napoleon tried to restrict British trade with all of Europe. He then plotted to attack Britain, but his Mediterranean fleet was destroyed by Lord Nelson at the Battle of Trafalgar on October 21, 1805.

Austria, Russia, and Sweden joined with Britain to form the Third Coalition against France shortly before the Battle of Trafalgar. Yet the Austrians and the Russians were no match for Napoleon, who scored a brilliant victory over them at the Battle of Austerlitz in December 1805. Russia decided to pull back, and Austria accepted large territorial losses in return for peace as the Third Coalition collapsed.

Napoleon then reorganized the German states to his liking. In 1806 he abolished many tiny German states as well as the Holy Roman Empire and established by decree the German Confederation of the Rhine, a union of fifteen German states minus Austria, Prussia, and Saxony.

Napoleon's intervention in German affairs alarmed the Prussians, who mobilized their armies. In October 1806 Napoleon attacked them and won two more victories at Jena and Auerstädt. The war with Prussia, now joined by Russia, continued into the following spring. After Napoleon won another victory, Alexander I of Russia was ready to negotiate for peace. In the treaties of Tilsit in 1807, Prussia lost half its population through land concessions, while Russia accepted Napoleon's reorganization of western and central Europe and promised to enforce Napoleon's economic blockade against British goods.

The Grand Empire and Its End

Grand Empire

▶ The empire over which Napoleon and his allies ruled, encompassing virtually all of Europe except Great Britain.

Continental System

▶ A blockade imposed by Napoleon to halt all trade between continental Europe and Britain, thereby weakening the British economy and military.

Napoleon's so-called Grand Empire had three parts. The core, or first part, was an ever-expanding France (Map 22.2). The second part consisted of a number of dependent satellite kingdoms. The third part comprised the independent but allied states of Austria, Prussia, and Russia. After 1806 both satellites and allies were expected to support Napoleon's Continental System, a blockade in which no ship coming from Britain or her colonies was permitted to dock at any port that was controlled by the French. The blockade was intended to destroy the British economy and, thereby, its ability to wage war.

In the areas incorporated into France and in the satellites, French rule sparked patriotic upheavals and encouraged the growth of reactive nationalism. The first great revolt occurred in Spain. In 1808 Napoleon deposed Spanish king Ferdinand VII and placed his own brother Joseph on the throne. A coalition of Catholics, monarchists, and patriots rebelled against this attempt to turn Spain into a satellite of France. French armies occupied Madrid, but the foes of Napoleon fled to the hills and waged guerrilla warfare. Events in Spain sent a clear warning: resistance to French imperialism was growing.

Yet Napoleon pushed on. In 1810, when the Grand Empire was at its height, Britain still remained at war with France, helping the guerrillas in Spain and Portugal. The Continental System was a failure. Instead of harming Britain, the system provoked the British to set up a counter-blockade, which created hard times for French consumers. Perhaps looking for a scapegoat, Napoleon turned on Alexander I of Russia, who in 1811 openly repudiated Napoleon's prohibitions against British goods.

Napoleon's invasion of Russia began in June 1812 with a force that eventually numbered 600,000. Originally planning to winter in the Russian city of Smolensk,

CHAPTER LOCATOR | What were the factors behind the age of revolution in the Atlantic world? | Why and how did American colonists forge a new, independent nation?

CHAPTER 22
662 REVOLUTIONS IN THE ATLANTIC WORLD

MAP 22.2 ■ Napoleonic Europe in 1812

At the height of the Grand Empire in 1810, Napoleon had conquered or allied with every major European power except Britain. But in 1812, angered by Russian repudiation of his ban on trade with Britain, Napoleon invaded Russia with disastrous results. Compare this map with Map 18.3 (page 526), which shows the division of Europe in 1715.

> **MAPPING THE PAST**

ANALYZING THE MAP: How had the balance of power shifted in Europe from 1715 to 1812? What changed, and what remained the same? What was the impact of Napoleon's wars on Germany, the Italian peninsula, and Russia?

CONNECTIONS: Why did Napoleon achieve vast territorial gains where Louis XIV did not?

Napoleon recklessly pressed on toward Moscow (see Map 22.2). The Battle of Borodino that followed was a draw. Alexander ordered the evacuation of Moscow, which the Russians then burned in part, and he refused to negotiate. Finally, after five weeks in the scorched city, Napoleon ordered a disastrous retreat. When the

| How did the events of 1789 result in a constitutional monarchy in France? | **How did Napoleon Bonaparte assume control of France and much of Europe?** | How did slave revolt on colonial Saint-Domingue lead to the creation of Haiti in 1804? | How did the Spanish and Portuguese colonies of the Americas shake off European domination? | ✓ LearningCurve Check what you know. |

frozen remnants of Napoleon's army staggered into Poland and Prussia in December, 370,000 men had died and another 200,000 had been taken prisoner.

Leaving his troops to their fate, Napoleon raced to Paris to raise another army. Meanwhile, Austria and Prussia deserted Napoleon and joined Russia and Britain in the Treaty of Chaumont in March 1814, by which the four powers formed the Quadruple Alliance to defeat the French emperor. Less than a month later, on April 4, 1814, a defeated Napoleon abdicated his throne. The victorious allies then exiled Napoleon to the island of Elba off the coast of Italy.

In February 1815 Napoleon staged a daring escape from Elba. Landing in France, he issued appeals for support and marched on Paris. But Napoleon's gamble was a desperate long shot, for the allies were united against him. At the end of a frantic period known as the Hundred Days, they crushed his forces at Waterloo on June 18, 1815, and imprisoned him on the island of St. Helena, off the western coast of Africa. The restored Bourbon dynasty took power under Louis XVIII, a younger brother of Louis XVI.

> **QUICK REVIEW**

What kind of state did Napoleon create?
From which social groups did he draw his support?

CHAPTER LOCATOR | What were the factors behind the age of revolution in the Atlantic world? | Why and how did American colonists forge a new, independent nation?

CHAPTER 22
664 REVOLUTIONS IN THE ATLANTIC WORLD

How did slave revolt on colonial Saint-Domingue lead to the creation of the independent nation of Haiti in 1804?

Saint-Domingue Slave Life

Although the brutal conditions of plantation slavery left little time or energy for leisure, slaves on Saint-Domingue took advantage of their day of rest on Sunday to engage in social and religious activities. The law officially prohibited slaves of different masters from mingling together, but such gatherings were often tolerated if they remained peaceful. This image depicts a fight between two slaves, precisely the type of unrest and violence feared by authorities. (Musée du Nouveau Monde, La Rochelle, France/Scala/White Images/Art Resource, NY)

PRIOR TO 1789 SAINT-DOMINGUE, the French colony that was to become Haiti, reaped huge profits through a ruthless system of slave-based plantation agriculture. News of revolution in France lit a powder keg of contradictory aspirations among white planters, free people of color, and slaves. Free people of color and, later, the enslaved rose up to claim their freedom. They succeeded, despite invasion by the British and Spanish and Napoleon Bonaparte's bid to reimpose French control. In 1804 Haiti became the only nation in history to claim its freedom through slave revolt.

Revolutionary Aspirations in Saint-Domingue

On the eve of the French Revolution, Saint-Domingue was inhabited by a variety of social groups who resented and mistrusted one another. The European population included French colonial officials, wealthy plantation owners and merchants,

How did the events of 1789 result in a constitutional monarchy in France? | How did Napoleon Bonaparte assume control of France and much of Europe? | **How did slave revolt on colonial Saint-Domingue lead to the creation of Haiti in 1804?** | How did the Spanish and Portuguese colonies of the Americas shake off European domination? | ✓ LearningCurve Check what you know.

665

and poor artisans and clerks. Vastly outnumbering the white population were the colony's five hundred thousand enslaved people, along with a sizable population of some forty thousand free people of African and mixed African and European descent. Members of this last group referred to themselves as "free people of color."

Most of the island's enslaved population performed grueling toil in the island's sugar plantations. The highly outnumbered planters used extremely harsh methods, such as beating, maiming, and executing slaves, to maintain their control. The 1685 Code Noir (Black Code) that legally regulated slavery was intended to provide minimal standards of humane treatment, but its tenets were rarely enforced. Masters calculated that they could earn more by working slaves ruthlessly and purchasing new ones when they died than by providing the food, rest, and medical care needed to allow the enslaved population to reproduce naturally. This meant that a constant inflow of newly enslaved people from Africa was necessary to work the plantations.

Despite their brutality, slaveholders on Saint-Domingue freed a certain number of their slaves, mostly their own mixed-race children, thereby producing one of the largest populations of free people of color in any slaveholding colony. The Code Noir had originally granted free people of color the same legal status as whites. From the 1760s on, however, colonial administrators began rescinding these rights, and by the time of the French Revolution free people of color were subject to many discriminatory laws.

The political and intellectual turmoil of the 1780s, with its growing rhetoric of liberty, equality, and fraternity, raised new challenges and possibilities for each of Saint-Domingue's social groups. For enslaved people, news of abolitionist movements in France led to hopes that the mother country might grant them freedom. Free people of color looked to reforms in Paris as a means of gaining political enfranchisement and reasserting equal status with whites. The white elite, however, was determined to protect its way of life, including slaveholding. They hoped to gain control of their own affairs, as had the American colonists before them.

The National Assembly frustrated the hopes of all these groups. Cowed by colonial representatives who claimed that support for free people of color would result in slave insurrection, the Assembly refused to extend French constitutional safeguards to the colonies. At the same time, however, the Assembly also reaffirmed French monopolies over colonial trade, thereby angering planters as well.

In July 1790 Vincent Ogé (aw-ZHAY) (ca. 1750–1791), a free man of color, returned to Saint-Domingue from Paris determined to win rights for his people. He raised an army and sent letters to the new Provincial Assembly of Saint-Domingue demanding political rights for all free citizens. When Ogé's demands were refused, he and his followers turned to armed insurrection. After initial victories, his army was defeated, and Ogé was executed by colonial officials. Revolutionary leaders in Paris were more sympathetic to Ogé's cause. In May 1791 the National Assembly granted political rights to free people of color born to two free parents who possessed sufficient property. When news of this legislation arrived in Saint-Domingue, the colonial governor refused to enact it. Violence then erupted between groups of whites and free people of color in parts of the colony.

CHAPTER LOCATOR | What were the factors behind the age of revolution in the Atlantic world? | Why and how did American colonists forge a new, independent nation?

CHAPTER 22
666   REVOLUTIONS IN THE ATLANTIC WORLD

The Outbreak of Revolt

Just as the sans-culottes helped push forward more radical reforms in France, the second stage of revolution in Saint-Domingue also resulted from decisive action from below. In August 1791 slaves took events into their own hands. Revolts began on a few plantations on the night of August 22. As the uprising spread, rebels joined together in an ever-growing slave army. During the next month enslaved combatants attacked and destroyed hundreds of sugar and coffee plantations.

On April 4, 1792, as war loomed with the European states, the National Assembly issued a decree extending full citizenship rights to free men of color. The Assembly hoped this measure would win the loyalty of free men of color and their aid in defeating the slave rebellion.

Warfare in Europe soon spread to Saint-Domingue (Map 22.3). Since the beginning of the slave insurrection, the Spanish colony of Santo Domingo, on the eastern side of the island of Hispaniola, had supported rebel slaves. In early 1793

MAP 22.3 ■ The War of Haitian Independence, 1791–1804

Neighbored by the Spanish colony of Santo Domingo, Saint-Domingue was the most profitable European colony in the Caribbean. In 1791 slave revolts erupted in the north near Le Cap, which had once been the capital. In 1770 the French had transferred the capital to Port-au-Prince, which in 1804 became capital of the newly independent Haiti.

How did the events of 1789 result in a constitutional monarchy in France?

How did Napoleon Bonaparte assume control of France and much of Europe?

How did slave revolt on colonial Saint-Domingue lead to the creation of Haiti in 1804?

How did the Spanish and Portuguese colonies of the Americas shake off European domination?

✓ LearningCurve
Check what you know.

667

the Spanish began to bring slave leaders and their soldiers into the Spanish army. Toussaint L'Ouverture (TOO-sahn LOO-vair-toor) (1743–1803), a freed slave who had joined the revolt, was named a Spanish officer. In September the British navy blockaded the colony, and invading British troops captured French territory on the island. For the Spanish and British, revolutionary chaos provided a tempting opportunity to capture a profitable colony.

Desperate for forces to oppose France's enemies, commissioners sent by the newly elected National Convention promised freedom to slaves who fought for France. By October 1793 the commissioners had abolished slavery throughout the colony. On February 4, 1794, the Convention ratified the abolition of slavery and extended it to all French territories.

The tide of battle began to turn when Toussaint L'Ouverture switched sides. By 1796 the French had regained control of the colony, and L'Ouverture had emerged as a key military leader. (See "Individuals in Society: Toussaint L'Ouverture," page 669.) In May 1796 he was named commander of the western province of Saint-Domingue (see Map 22.3).

The War of Haitian Independence

With Toussaint L'Ouverture acting increasingly as an independent ruler of the western province of Saint-Domingue, another general, André Rigaud (1761–1811), set up his own government in the southern peninsula. Tensions mounted between L'Ouverture and Rigaud. While L'Ouverture was a freed slave of African

KEY EVENTS OF THE HAITIAN REVOLUTION

1760s	Colonial administrators begin rescinding the rights of free people of color
July 1790	Vincent Ogé leads a failed rebellion to gain rights for free people of color
August 1791	Slave revolts begin
April 4, 1792	National Assembly enfranchises all free blacks and free people of color
September 1793	British troops invade Saint-Domingue
February 4, 1794	National Convention ratifies the abolition of slavery and extends it to all French territories
May 1796	Toussaint L'Ouverture is named commander of Saint-Domingue
1800	After invading the south of Saint-Domingue, L'Ouverture gains control of the entire colony
1802	French general Charles-Victor-Emmanuel Leclerc arrests L'Ouverture and deports him to France
1803	L'Ouverture dies
1804	After defeating French forces, Jean Jacques Dessalines declares the independence of Saint-Domingue and the creation of the sovereign nation of Haiti

CHAPTER LOCATOR | What were the factors behind the age of revolution in the Atlantic world? | Why and how did American colonists forge a new, independent nation?

CHAPTER 22
668 REVOLUTIONS IN THE ATLANTIC WORLD

INDIVIDUALS IN SOCIETY
Toussaint L'Ouverture

Little is known of the early life of Saint-Domingue's brilliant military and political leader Toussaint L'Ouverture. He was born in 1743 on a plantation outside Le Cap owned by the Count de Bréda. According to tradition, L'Ouverture was the eldest son of a captured African prince from modern-day Benin. Toussaint Bréda, as he was then called, occupied a privileged position among slaves. Instead of performing backbreaking labor in the fields, he served his master as a coachman and livestock keeper. He also learned to read and write French and some Latin, but he was always more comfortable with the Creole dialect.

During the 1770s the plantation manager emancipated L'Ouverture, who subsequently leased his own small coffee plantation, worked by slaves. He married Suzanne Simone, who already had one son, and the couple had another son during their marriage. In 1791 he joined the slave uprisings that swept Saint-Domingue, and he took on the *nom de guerre* (war name) L'Ouverture, meaning "the opening." L'Ouverture rose to prominence among rebel slaves allied with Spain and by early 1794 controlled his own army. A devout Catholic who led a frugal and ascetic life, L'Ouverture impressed others with his enormous physical energy, intellectual acumen, and air of mystery. In 1794 he defected to the French side and led his troops to a series of victories against the Spanish. In 1795 the National Convention promoted L'Ouverture to brigadier general.

Over the next three years L'Ouverture successively eliminated rivals for authority on the island. First he freed himself of the French commissioners sent to govern the colony. With a firm grip on power in the northern province, L'Ouverture defeated General André Rigaud in 1800 to gain control in the south. His army then marched on the capital of Spanish Santo Domingo on the eastern half of the island, meeting little resistance. The entire island of Hispaniola was now under his command.

With control in his hands, L'Ouverture was confronted with the challenge of building a post-

Equestrian portrait of Toussaint L'Ouverture. (Bibliothèque Nationale, Paris, France/Archives Charmet/ The Bridgeman Art Library)

emancipation society, the first of its kind. The task was made even more difficult by the chaos wreaked by war, the destruction of plantations, and bitter social and racial tensions. For L'Ouverture the most pressing concern was to re-establish the plantation economy. Without revenue to pay his army, the gains of the rebellion could be lost. He therefore encouraged white planters to return and reclaim their property. He also adopted harsh policies toward former slaves, forcing them back to their plantations and restricting their ability to acquire land. When they resisted, he sent troops across the island to enforce submission. L'Ouverture's 1801 constitution reaffirmed his draconian labor policies and named L'Ouverture governor for life, leaving Saint-Domingue as a colony in name alone. In June 1802 French forces arrested L'Ouverture and jailed him at Fort de Joux in France's Jura Mountains near the Swiss border. He died of pneumonia on April 7, 1803, leaving his lieutenant, Jean Jacques Dessalines, to win independence for the new Haitian nation.

QUESTIONS FOR ANALYSIS

1. Toussaint L'Ouverture was both slave and slave owner. How did each experience shape his life and actions?
2. What did L'Ouverture and Napoleon Bonaparte have in common? How did they differ?

LaunchPad

ONLINE DOCUMENT PROJECT

How did the French Revolution affect France's Caribbean colonies? Examine reactions of slaves and free men of color to the French Revolution, and then complete a quiz and writing assignment based on the evidence and details from this chapter. *See inside the front cover to learn more.*

descent, Rigaud belonged to the elite group of free people of color. This elite resented the growing power of former slaves like L'Ouverture, who in turn accused the elite of adopting the prejudices of white settlers. Civil war broke out between the two sides in 1799, when L'Ouverture's forces, led by his lieutenant, Jean Jacques Dessalines (1758–1806), invaded the south. Victory over Rigaud in 1800 gave L'Ouverture control of the entire colony.

This victory was soon challenged by Napoleon, who had his own plans for using the profits from a re-established system of plantation slavery as a basis for expanding the French empire. In 1802 Toussaint L'Ouverture was arrested and deported to France, along with his family, where he died in 1803.

It was left to L'Ouverture's lieutenant, Jean Jacques Dessalines, to unite the resistance, and he led it to a crushing victory over French forces. On January 1, 1804, Dessalines formally declared the independence of Saint-Domingue and the creation of the new sovereign nation of Haiti, the name used by the pre-Columbian inhabitants of the island.

> **QUICK REVIEW**

How did tensions between slaves and free people of color shape the Haitian Revolution?

CHAPTER LOCATOR | What were the factors behind the age of revolution in the Atlantic world? | Why and how did American colonists forge a new, independent nation?

CHAPTER 22
670   REVOLUTIONS IN THE ATLANTIC WORLD

Triumph of Bolívar

Bolívar was treated as a hero everywhere he went in
South America. (akg-images)

Why and how did the Spanish and Portuguese colonies of North and South America shake off European domination and develop into national states?

THE LATIN AMERICAN MOVEMENTS for independence drew strength from
unfair taxation and trade policies, Spain's declining control over its Latin American
colonies, racial and class discrimination, and the spread of revolutionary
ideas. Between 1806 and 1825 the Spanish colonies in Latin America were con-
vulsed by upheavals that ultimately resulted in their separation from Spain.

The Origins of the Revolutions Against Colonial Powers

Spain's humiliating defeat in the War of the Spanish Succession (1701–1713; see
page 537) prompted demands for sweeping reform of all of Spain's institutions,
including its colonial policies and practices. The new Bourbon dynasty initiated

How did the events
of 1789 result in a
constitutional monarchy
in France?

How did Napoleon
Bonaparte assume
control of France and
much of Europe?

How did slave revolt on
colonial Saint-Domingue
lead to the creation of
Haiti in 1804?

**How did the Spanish and
Portuguese colonies of
the Americas shake off
European domination?**

✓ LearningCurve
Check what you know.

a decades-long effort known as the Bourbon reforms, which aimed to improve administrative efficiency and increase central control. Under Charles III (r. 1759–1788), Spanish administrators drew on Enlightenment ideals of rationalism and progress to strengthen colonial rule and thereby increase the fortunes and power of the Spanish state. They created a permanent standing army and enlarged colonial militias, sought to bring the church under tighter control, and dispatched intendants (government commissioners) with extensive new powers to oversee the colonies.

Additionally, Spain ended its policy of insisting on monopoly over trade with its colonies. Instead it adopted a policy of free trade in order to compete with Great Britain and Holland in the struggle for empire. In Latin America these actions stimulated the production and export of agricultural commodities that were in demand in Europe. Colonial manufacturing, however, which had been growing steadily, suffered a heavy blow under free trade. Colonial textiles and china, for example, could not compete with cheap Spanish products.

Madrid's tax reforms also aggravated discontent. Like Great Britain, Spain believed its colonies should bear some of the costs of their own defense. Accordingly, Madrid raised the prices of its monopoly products—tobacco and liquor—and increased sales taxes on many items. War with revolutionary France in the 1790s led to additional taxes and forced loans, all of which were widely resented. Moreover, new taxes took a heavy toll on indigenous communities, which bore the brunt of all forms of taxation and suffered from the corruption and brutality of tax collectors. Riots and protest movements met with harsh repression.

Political conflicts beyond the colonies also helped drive aspirations for independence. The French Revolution and the Napoleonic Wars, which involved France's occupation of Spain and Britain's domination of the seas, isolated Spain from Latin America. As a result, Spain's control over its Latin American colonies diminished.

Racial, ethnic, and class privileges also fueled discontent. The Creoles—people of Spanish or other European descent born in the Americas (see page 576)—resented the economic and political dominance of the peninsulares (puh-nihn-suh-LUHR-ayz), as the colonial officials and other natives of Spain or Portugal were called. The Creoles wanted to free themselves from Spain and Portugal and to rule the colonies themselves. They had little interest in improving the lot of the Indians, the mestizos of mixed Spanish and Indian background, or the mulattos of mixed Spanish and African heritage.

As in Saint-Domingue, a racial backlash against the growing numbers and social prominence of people of mixed racial origin occurred in the last quarter of the eighteenth century. In 1776 King Charles III outlawed marriages between whites and any person with Indian or African blood. A number of cities issued ordinances prohibiting nonwhites from joining guilds, serving in the militia, and mixing with whites in public.

A final factor contributing to rebellion was cultural and intellectual ideas. One set of such ideas was Enlightenment thought, which had been trickling into Latin America for decades (see Chapter 19). By 1800 the Creole elite throughout Latin America was familiar with liberal Enlightenment political thought and its role in inspiring colonial revolt.

Another important set of ideas consisted of indigenous traditions of justice and political rule, which often looked back to an idealized precolonial past. During

Creoles

▶ People of Spanish or other European descent born in the Americas.

peninsulares

▶ A term for natives of Spain and Portugal.

the eighteenth century these ideas served as a rallying point for Indians and non-Indians alike. Creoles took advantage of indigenous symbols, but this did not mean they were prepared to view Indians and mestizos as equals.

Resistance, Rebellion, and Independence

The mid-eighteenth century witnessed frequent Andean Indian rebellions. In 1780, under the leadership of a descendant of the Inca rulers who took the name Túpac Amaru II, a massive insurrection exploded. Creoles joined forces with Spaniards and Indian nobles to crush the rebellion, shocked by the radical social and economic reforms promised by its leaders.

As news of the rebellion of Túpac Amaru II trickled northward, it helped stimulate the 1781 Comuneros Revolt in the New Granada viceroyalty (see Map 22.4). In this uprising, an Indian and mestizo peasant army commanded by Creole captains marched on Bogotá. Dispersed by the ruling Spanish, who made promises they did not intend to keep, the revolt in the end did little to improve the Indians' lives.

While these revolts shook authorities, two events outside of Spanish America did more to shape the ensuing struggle for independence. First, the revolution on Saint-Domingue and the subsequent independence of the nation of Haiti in 1804 convinced Creole elites, many of whom were slaveholders, of the dangers of slave revolt and racial warfare (see Map 22.3). Their plans and strategies would henceforth be shaped by their determination to avoid a similar outcome in Spanish America.

Second, in 1808 Napoleon Bonaparte deposed Spanish king Ferdinand VII and placed his own brother on the Spanish throne (see page 662). The Creoles in Latin America claimed that the removal of the legitimate king shifted sovereignty to the people—that is, to themselves.

The great hero of the movement for independence was Simón Bolívar (1783–1830). Under his leadership, a regional congress in Caracas declared the independence of the United States of Venezuela in July 1811 and quickly drafted a constitution guaranteeing freedom of the press and racial equality. The republic failed after only one year, but Bolívar continued to fight royalist forces for the next eight years, with assistance from the newly formed Haitian republic. His victories over Spanish armies won him the presidency of the new republic of Gran Colombia (formerly the New Granada viceroyalty) in 1819. The territories of Gran Colombia, however, soon splintered (see Map 22.4), and a sadly disillusioned Bolívar went into exile.

In 1808, after Napoleon's coup, the Spanish viceroy assumed control of the government of New Spain from its capital in Mexico City. Meanwhile, groups of rebels plotted to overthrow royalist power. Under the leadership of two charismatic priests, poor Creoles and indigenous peasants rose up against the Spanish. This movement from below fell to royalist forces, but in 1821 a new movement commanded by Creole elites succeeded in winning independence from Spain.

Although Creole officers dominated rebel armies, their success depended on a rank and file largely composed of nonwhites. These included many blacks and free people of color. In Mexico many indigenous people also fought for the patriots, but elsewhere Indians were often indifferent to independence or felt their status was more secure with the royal government than with the Creoles.

How did the events of 1789 result in a constitutional monarchy in France?

How did Napoleon Bonaparte assume control of France and much of Europe?

How did slave revolt on colonial Saint-Domingue lead to the creation of Haiti in 1804?

How did the Spanish and Portuguese colonies of the Americas shake off European domination?

LearningCurve
Check what you know.

673

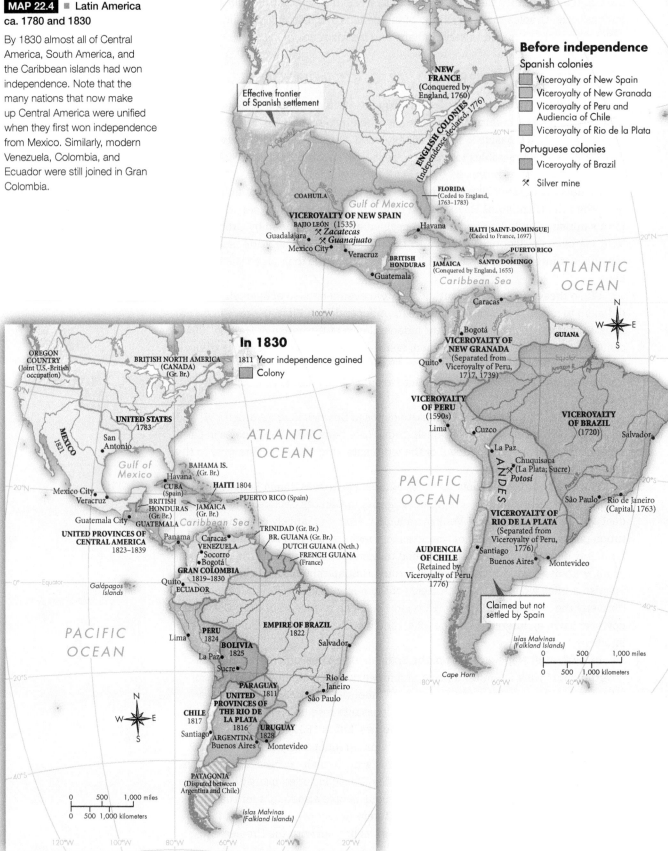

MAP 22.4 ■ Latin America ca. 1780 and 1830

By 1830 almost all of Central America, South America, and the Caribbean islands had won independence. Note that the many nations that now make up Central America were unified when they first won independence from Mexico. Similarly, modern Venezuela, Colombia, and Ecuador were still joined in Gran Colombia.

Before independence

Spanish colonies
- Viceroyalty of New Spain
- Viceroyalty of New Granada
- Viceroyalty of Peru and Audiencia of Chile
- Viceroyalty of Rio de la Plata

Portuguese colonies
- Viceroyalty of Brazil

⚒ Silver mine

In 1830

1811 Year independence gained
☐ Colony

CHAPTER LOCATOR | What were the factors behind the age of revolution in the Atlantic world? | Why and how did American colonists forge a new, independent nation?

In the 1830s regional separatism resulted in New Spain's breakup into five separate countries. The failure of political union in New Spain and Gran Colombia isolated individual countries, prevented collective action, and later paved the way for the political and economic intrusion of the United States and other powers.

Brazil followed a different path to independence. When Napoleon's troops entered Portugal, the royal family fled to Brazil and made Rio de Janeiro the capital of the Portuguese Empire. The king returned to Portugal in 1821, leaving his son Pedro in Brazil as regent. Under popular pressure, Pedro proclaimed Brazil's independence in 1822, issued a constitution, and even led resistance against Portuguese troops. He accepted the title Emperor Pedro I (r. 1822–1831). Even though Brazil was a monarchy, Creole elites dominated society as they did elsewhere in Latin America.

KEY EVENTS IN EARLY LATIN AMERICAN REVOLUTIONS

1759–1788	Reign of Charles III, who instituted administrative and economic reforms
1794	Colombian Antonio Nariño publishes the French Declaration of the Rights of Man and of the Citizen
July 1811	Regional congress in Caracas declares independence of the United States of Venezuela
1822	Proclamation of Brazil's independence from Portugal
1826	Call by Simón Bolívar for Panama conference on Latin American union
1830s	New Spain breaks up into five separate countries
1888	Emancipation of slaves in Brazil

The Aftermath of Revolution in the Atlantic World

The aftermath of the Atlantic revolutions brought extremely different fortunes to the new nations that emerged from them. France returned to royal rule with the restoration of the Bourbon monarchy in 1815. A series of revolutionary crises ensued in the nineteenth century as succeeding generations struggled over the legacies of monarchicalism, republicanism, and Bonapartism. It was not until 1871 that republicanism finally prevailed (see Chapter 24). The transition to an independent republic was permanent and relatively smooth in the United States. Nevertheless, the unresolved conflict over slavery would lead to catastrophic civil war in 1860. The independent nation of Haiti was built on the only successful slave revolt in history, but the need for revenue from plantation agriculture soon led to the return of coercive labor requirements, if not outright slavery.

The newly independent nations of Latin America had difficulty achieving political stability when the wars of independence ended. The economic lives of most Latin American countries were disrupted during the years of war. Mexico and Venezuela in particular suffered great destruction of farmland and animals.

How did the events of 1789 result in a constitutional monarchy in France?

How did Napoleon Bonaparte assume control of France and much of Europe?

How did slave revolt on colonial Saint-Domingue lead to the creation of Haiti in 1804?

How did the Spanish and Portuguese colonies of the Americas shake off European domination?

LearningCurve
Check what you know.

Between 1836 and 1848 Mexico lost half its territory to the United States, and other countries, too, had difficulty defending themselves from their neighbors. The Creole leaders of the revolutions had little experience in government, and the wars left a legacy of military, not civilian, leadership.

> QUICK REVIEW

How did events and developments in Europe influence revolutionary struggles in Latin America?

CHAPTER SUMMARY

From 1775 to 1825 a wave of revolution sweep through the Atlantic world. Its origins included long-term social and economic changes, Enlightenment ideals of liberty and equality, and the costs of colonial warfare. British efforts to raise taxes after the Seven Years' War aroused violent protest in the American colonies. In 1776 the Second Continental Congress issued the Declaration of Independence, and by 1783 Britain had recognized the independence of the thirteen colonies.

In 1789 delegates to the Estates General defied royal authority to declare themselves a National Assembly, which promulgated France's first constitution in 1791. Led by the Jacobin club, the Assembly waged war on Austria and Prussia and proclaimed France a republic. From the end of 1793, under the Reign of Terror, the Revolution pursued internal and external enemies ruthlessly and instituted economic controls to aid the poor. The weakness of the Directory government after the fall of Robespierre enabled Napoleon Bonaparte to claim control of France. Napoleon's relentless military ambitions allowed him to spread French power through much of Europe but ultimately led to his downfall.

After a failed uprising by free men of color, slaves rose in revolt in the French colony of Saint-Domingue in August 1791. Their revolt, combined with the outbreak of war and the radicalization of the French Revolution, led to a sequence of conflicts and rebellions that culminated in independence for the new Haitian nation in 1804.

Latin American independence movements drew strength from Spain's unpopular policies. Under the leadership of Simón Bolívar, the United States of Venezuela claimed independence in 1811. Led by Creole officers but reliant on nonwhite soldiers, rebel armies successfully fought Spanish forces over the next decade. Despite Bolivar's efforts to build a unified state, in the1830s New Spain split into five separate countries. In Brazil the royal regent proclaimed independence in 1822 and reigned as emperor of the new state.

CHAPTER LOCATOR | What were the factors behind the age of revolution in the Atlantic world? | Why and how did American colonists forge a new, independent nation?

CHAPTER 22
676 REVOLUTIONS IN THE ATLANTIC WORLD

CONNECTIONS The Atlantic world formed an essential context for a great revolutionary wave in the late eighteenth and early nineteenth centuries. The movement of peoples, commodities, and ideas across the Atlantic Ocean in the eighteenth century created a world of common debates, conflicts, and aspirations. Moreover, the high stakes of colonial empire heightened competition among European states, leading to a series of wars that generated crushing costs for overburdened treasuries. For both the British in their North American colonies and the French at home, the desperate need for new taxes weakened government authority and opened the door to revolution. In turn, the ideals of the French Revolution inspired slaves and free people of color in Saint-Domingue to rise up and claim the promise of liberty, equality, and fraternity for people of all races.

The chain reaction did not end with the liberation movements in Spanish America that followed the Haitian Revolution. Throughout the nineteenth and early twentieth centuries periodic convulsions occurred in Europe, the Americas, and elsewhere as successive generations struggled over political rights first proclaimed by late-eighteenth-century revolutionaries. Meanwhile, as dramatic political events unfolded, a parallel economic revolution was gathering steam. This was the Industrial Revolution, originating around 1780 and accelerating through the end of the eighteenth century (see Chapter 23). After 1815 the twin forces of industrialization and democratization would combine to transform Europe and the world.

ONLINE DOCUMENT PROJECT

The Rights of Which Men?

How did the French Revolution affect France's Caribbean colonies?

Examine reactions of slaves and free men of color to the French Revolution, and then complete a quiz and writing assignment based on the evidence and details from this chapter. *See inside the front cover to learn more.*

How did the events of 1789 result in a constitutional monarchy in France?

How did Napoleon Bonaparte assume control of France and much of Europe?

How did slave revolt on colonial Saint-Domingue lead to the creation of Haiti in 1804?

How did the Spanish and Portuguese colonies of the Americas shake off European domination?

☑ LearningCurve
Check what you know.

677

CHAPTER 22 STUDY GUIDE

STEP 1

GET STARTED ONLINE

 LearningCurve

Now that you've read the chapter, make it stick by completing the LearningCurve activity.

STEP 2

EXPLAIN WHY IT MATTERS

Put your reading into practice. Identify each term below, and then explain why it matters in world history.

TERM	WHO OR WHAT & WHEN	WHY IT MATTERS
Treaty of Paris (p. 647)		
Declaration of Independence (p. 650)		
Antifederalists (p. 652)		
Estates General (p. 654)		
National Assembly (p. 656)		
Jacobin club (p. 656)		
Mountain (p. 656)		
Girondists (p. 656)		
sans-culottes (p. 656)		
Reign of Terror (p. 657)		
Thermidorian reaction (p. 659)		
Napoleonic Code (p. 661)		
Grand Empire (p. 662)		
Continental System (p. 662)		
Creoles (p. 672)		
peninsulares (p. 672)		

STEP 3

MOVE BEYOND THE BASICS

To demonstrate a more advanced understanding of the four main phases of the French Revolution, fill in the chart below with descriptions of the leaders and key groups that shaped important developments, the policies and reforms initiated during each phase, and the groups that gained and lost the most as a result of those policies. What role did violence play in the transition between each phase of the Revolution?

	Leaders and Key Groups	Policies and Reforms	Winners and Losers
The First Revolution: 1789–1791			
The Second Revolution: 1791–1794			
The Directory: 1795–1799			
Napoleonic France: 1799–1815			

STEP 4 **PUT IT ALL TOGETHER** Now, take a step back and try to explain the big picture. Remember to use specific examples from the chapter in your answers.

THE AGE OF REVOLUTIONS BEGINS

▶ How did social, economic, ideological, and fiscal problems combine to spark the age of revolutions?

▶ How did the relative social and political equality enjoyed by white inhabitants of the British North American colonies shape the American Revolution?

THE FRENCH REVOLUTION

▶ What role did the poor people of France play in shaping the French Revolution? At what points did they take control of events from elite and middle-class leaders?

▶ How was violence used as a political tool during the period of the Second Revolution? What justifications were offered for its use? In your opinion, how valid were these justifications?

THE NAPOLEONIC ERA AND THE HAITIAN REVOLUTION

▶ Should Napoleon be considered a "revolutionary"? Why or why not?

▶ How did the people of Saint-Domingue react to the news of revolution in France? How would you explain their reaction? How did the French Revolution contribute to increasing social and political tensions in Saint-Domingue?

LOOKING BACK, LOOKING AHEAD

▶ What was revolutionary about the age of revolution? How did the states that emerged out of the eighteenth-century revolutions differ from the states that predominated in previous centuries?

▶ In what sense did the age of revolution mark the beginning of modern politics in Europe and the Americas?

> **IN YOUR OWN WORDS**

Imagine that you must give an oral report to the class answering the following question: **How did revolution change the Atlantic world? What aspects of Atlantic society and politics were left unchanged? What would be the most important points and why?**

23
THE REVOLUTION IN ENERGY AND INDUSTRY

1760–1850

> **What were the social, cultural, and economic consequences of the Industrial Revolution?**

Chapter 23 examines the Industrial Revolution. The Industrial Revolution began in Great Britain around 1780 and soon began to influence continental Europe and the United States. Industrialization profoundly modified human experience. It changed patterns of work, transformed the social structure, and eventually altered the international balance of political power in favor of the most rapidly industrialized nations, especially Great Britain. What was most remarkable about the Industrial Revolution was that it inaugurated a period of sustained economic and demographic growth that has continued to the present.

 LearningCurve
After reading the chapter, use LearningCurve to retain what you've read.

Young Factory Worker Children composed a substantial element of the workforce in early factories, where they toiled long hours in dangerous and unsanitary conditions. Until a mechanized process was invented at the end of the nineteenth century, boys working in glass-bottle factories, like the youth pictured here, stoked blazing furnaces with coal and learned to blow glass. (Detail, *Interior of a Furnace*, 1865, oil on canvas by Charles Housez [1822–1888]/© Boume Gallery, Reigate, Surrey, UK/The Bridgeman Art Library)

> Why did the Industrial Revolution begin in Britain, and how did it develop between 1780 and 1850?

> How did countries in Europe and around the world respond to the challenge of industrialization after 1815?

> How did work evolve during the Industrial Revolution, and how did daily life change for working people?

> How did the changes brought about by the Industrial Revolution lead to new social classes, and how did people respond to the new structure?

Why did the Industrial Revolution begin in Britain, and how did it develop between 1780 and 1850?

Woman Working a Spinning Jenny

The loose cotton strands on the slanted bobbins shown in this illustration of Hargreaves's spinning jenny passed up to the sliding carriage and then on to the spindles (inset) in back for fine spinning. The worker, almost always a woman, regulated the sliding carriage with one hand, and with the other she turned the crank on the wheel to supply power. By 1783 one woman could spin a hundred threads at a time. (spinning jenny: © Mary Evans Picture Library/The Image Works; spindle: Picture Research Consultants & Archives)

THE INDUSTRIAL REVOLUTION ORIGINATED from a unique combination of possibilities and constraints in late-eighteenth-century Britain. With no models to copy and no idea of what to expect, Britain pioneered not only in industrial technology but also in social relations and urban living.

Why Britain?

Why did the Industrial Revolution originate in western Europe, and Britain in particular, rather than in other parts of the world, such as Asia? The best answer seems to be that Britain possessed a unique set of possibilities and constraints — abundant coal, high wages, a relatively peaceful and centralized government, well-developed financial systems, innovative culture, highly skilled craftsmen, and a strong position in empire and global trade — that spurred its people to adopt a capital-intensive, machine-powered system of production.

CHAPTER LOCATOR | **Why did the Industrial Revolution begin in Britain, and how did it develop?** | How did countries respond to the challenge of industrialization?

ca. 1765
Hargreaves invents spinning jenny; Arkwright creates water frame

1769
Watt patents modern steam engine

ca. 1780–1850
Industrial Revolution and accompanying population boom in Great Britain

1799
Combination Acts passed in England

1805
Egypt begins process of modernization

1810
Strike of Manchester, England, cotton spinners

1824
British Combination Acts repealed

1829
Stephenson's *Rocket*; first important railroad

1830s
Industrial banks promote rapid industrialization of Belgium

1833
Factory Act passed in England

1834
Creation of a *Zollverein* (customs union) among many German states

1842
Mines Act passed in England

1844
Engels, *The Condition of the Working Class in England*

1850s
Japan begins to adopt Western technologies; industrial gap widens between the West and the rest of the world

1851
Great Exhibition held at Crystal Palace in London

1860s
Germany and the United States begin to industrialize rapidly

Thus a number of factors came together over the long term to give rise to the Industrial Revolution in Britain. The Scientific Revolution and the Enlightenment fostered a new worldview that embraced progress and the role of research and experimentation in understanding and mastering the natural world. Moreover, Britain's intellectual culture emphasized the public sharing of knowledge, including that of scientists and technicians from other countries.

In the economic realm, the seventeenth-century expansion of rural industry produced a surplus of English woolen cloth. Exported throughout Europe, English cloth brought commercial profits and high wages. By the eighteenth century the expanding Atlantic economy and trade with India and China were also serving Britain well. The mercantilist colonial empire Britain aggressively built, augmented by a strong position in Latin America and in the transatlantic slave trade, provided raw materials like cotton and a growing market for British manufactured goods (see Chapter 19). Strong demand for British manufacturing meant that British workers earned high wages compared to the rest of the world's laborers.

Agriculture also played an important role in bringing about the Industrial Revolution. English farmers were second only to the Dutch in productivity in 1700, and they were continually adopting new methods of farming (see page 572). Because of increasing efficiency, landowners were able to produce more food with a smaller workforce. The enclosure movement had deprived many small landowners of their land, leaving the landless poor to work as hired agricultural laborers or in rural industry. These groups created a pool of potential laborers for the new factories.

How did work evolve during the Industrial Revolution, and how did daily life change for working people?

How did the changes brought about by the Industrial Revolution lead to new social classes, and how did people respond to the new structure?

☑ LearningCurve
Check what you know.

683

Industrial areas
- ▢ Coal deposit
- ○ Metal goods
- ▢ Woolen cloth
- — Canals, 1800
- — Navigable rivers

Cottage Industry and
Transportation in Great
Britain in the 1700s

Industrial Revolution

▶ A term first coined in the
1830s to describe the burst of
major inventions and economic
expansion that took place in
certain industries, such as cotton
textiles and iron, between 1780
and 1850.

Abundant food and high wages in turn meant that the ordinary English family no longer had to spend almost everything it earned just to buy bread. Thus the family could spend more on manufactured goods. They could also pay to send their children to school. Britain's populace enjoyed high levels of education compared to the rest of Europe. Moreover, in the eighteenth century the members of the average British family—including women and girls—were redirecting their labor away from unpaid work for household consumption and toward work for wages that they could spend on goods.

Britain also benefited from rich natural resources and a well-developed infrastructure. In an age when it was much cheaper to ship goods by water than by land, no part of England was more than fifty miles from navigable water. Beginning in the 1770s a canal-building boom enhanced this advantage. Rivers and canals provided easy movement of England and Wales's enormous deposits of iron and coal. The abundance of coal combined with high wages in manufacturing placed Britain in a unique position among the nations of the world: its manufacturers had extremely strong incentives to develop technologies to draw on the power of coal to increase workmen's productivity. In regions with lower wages, such as India and China, the costs of mechanization outweighed potential gains in productivity.

A final factor favoring British industrialization was the British state and its policies. Britain's parliamentary system taxed its population aggressively and spent the money on a navy to protect imperial commerce and on an army that could be used to quell uprisings by disgruntled workers. Starting with the Navigation Acts under Oliver Cromwell (see Chapter 18), the British state also adopted aggressive tariffs, or duties, on imported goods to protect its industries.

All these factors combined to initiate the Industrial Revolution, a term first coined to describe the burst of major inventions and technical changes that took place in certain industries. This technical revolution went hand in hand with an impressive quickening in the annual rate of industrial growth in Britain. Whereas industry had grown at only 0.7 percent between 1700 and 1760 (before the Industrial Revolution), it grew at the much higher rate of 3 percent between 1801 and 1831, when industrial transformation was in full swing.[1]

Technological Innovations and Early Factories

The pressure to produce more goods for a growing market and to reduce the labor costs of manufacturing was directly related to the first decisive breakthrough of the Industrial Revolution: the creation of the world's first machine-powered factories in the British cotton textile industry. Technological innovations in the manufacture of cotton cloth led to a new system of production and social relationships.

The putting-out system that developed in the seventeenth-century textile industry involved a merchant who loaned, or "put out," raw materials to cottage workers who processed the raw materials in their own homes and returned the finished products to the merchant. There was always a serious imbalance in textile production based on cottage industry: the work of four or five spinners was needed to keep one weaver steadily employed. During the eighteenth century the putting-out system grew across Europe, but most extensively in Britain. The growth of demand only increased pressures on the supply of thread.

CHAPTER LOCATOR | Why did the Industrial Revolution begin in Britain, and how did it develop? | How did countries respond to the challenge of industrialization?

CHAPTER 23
684 THE REVOLUTION IN ENERGY AND INDUSTRY

Many a tinkering worker knew that devising a better spinning wheel promised rich rewards. It proved hard to spin the traditional raw materials—wool and flax—with improved machines, but cotton was different. Cotton textiles had first been imported into Britain from India by the East India Company. By 1760 a tiny domestic cotton industry had emerged in northern England based on imported raw materials, but it could not compete with cloth produced by workers in India and other parts of Asia. International competition thus drove English entrepreneurs to invent new technologies to bring down labor costs.

After many experiments over a generation, a carpenter and jack-of-all-trades, James Hargreaves, invented his cotton-spinning jenny about 1765. At almost the same moment, a barber-turned-manufacturer named Richard Arkwright invented (or possibly pirated) another kind of spinning machine, the water frame. These breakthroughs produced an explosion in the infant cotton textile industry in the 1780s. By 1790 the new machines were producing ten times as much cotton yarn as had been made in 1770.

Hargreaves's **spinning jenny** was simple, inexpensive, and powered by hand. In early models from six to twenty-four spindles were mounted on a sliding carriage, and each spindle spun a fine, slender thread. Arkwright's **water frame** employed a different principle. It quickly acquired a capacity of several hundred spindles driven by waterpower. The water frame required large specialized mills located beside rivers and factories that employed as many as one thousand workers from the very beginning. The major drawback of the water frame was that it could spin only a coarse, strong thread. Around 1790 a hybrid machine invented by Samuel Crompton proved capable of spinning very fine and strong thread in large quantities. Gradually, all cotton spinning was concentrated in large-scale factories.

These revolutionary developments in the textile industry allowed British manufacturers to produce vast quantities of both fine and coarse cotton thread. Families using cotton in cottage industry were freed from their constant search for adequate yarn from scattered part-time spinners, because all the thread needed could be spun in the cottage on the jenny or obtained from a nearby factory. The income of weavers, now hard-pressed to keep up with the spinners, rose markedly until about 1792. In response, mechanics and capitalists sought to invent a power loom to save on labor costs. This Edmund Cartwright achieved in 1785. But the power looms of the factories worked poorly at first and did not fully replace handlooms until the 1820s.

Working conditions in the early cotton factories were so poor that adult workers were reluctant to work in them. Factory owners often turned to orphans and abandoned children instead. By placing them in "apprenticeship" with factory owners, parish officers charged with caring for such children saved money. The owners gained workers over whom they exercised almost the authority of slave owners. Housed, fed, and locked up nightly in factory dormitories, the young workers labored thirteen or fourteen hours a day, six days a week, for little or no pay.

The Steam Engine Breakthrough

Well into the eighteenth century, Europe, like other areas of the world, relied mainly on wood for energy, and human beings and animals performed most work. This dependence meant that Europe and the rest of the world remained poor in energy and power.

spinning jenny

▶ A simple, inexpensive, hand-powered spinning machine created by James Hargreaves in 1765.

water frame

▶ A spinning machine created by Richard Arkwright that had a capacity of several hundred spindles and used waterpower; it therefore required a larger and more specialized mill—a factory.

How did work evolve during the Industrial Revolution, and how did daily life change for working people?

How did the changes brought about by the Industrial Revolution lead to new social classes, and how did people respond to the new structure?

LearningCurve
Check what you know.

685

By the eighteenth century wood was in ever-shorter supply in Britain. Processed wood (charcoal) was mixed with iron ore in blast furnaces to produce pig iron that could be processed into steel, cast iron, or wrought iron. The iron industry's appetite for wood was enormous, and by 1740 the British iron industry was stagnating. As wood became ever more scarce, the British looked to coal as an alternative. The real breakthrough came when industrialists began to use coal to produce mechanical energy and to power machinery.

To produce more coal, mines had to be dug deeper and deeper and were constantly filling with water. Mechanical pumps, usually powered by animals walking in circles at the surface, had to be installed. Animal power was expensive and bothersome. In an attempt to overcome these disadvantages, Thomas Savery in 1698 and Thomas Newcomen in 1705 invented the first primitive steam engines. Both engines burned coal to produce steam that drove the water pumps.

In 1763 a gifted young Scot named James Watt (1736–1819) was drawn to a critical study of the steam engine. Watt worked at the University of Glasgow as a skilled craftsman making scientific instruments. In 1763 Watt was called on to repair a Newcomen engine being used in a physics course. Watt discovered that the Newcomen engine could be significantly improved by adding a separate condenser. This invention, patented in 1769, greatly increased the efficiency of the steam engine.

To make his invention a practical success, Watt needed skilled workers, precision parts, and capital, and the relatively advanced nature of the British economy proved essential. A partnership in 1775 with Matthew Boulton, a wealthy English industrialist, provided Watt with adequate capital and exceptional skills in salesmanship that equaled those of the renowned pottery king, Josiah Wedgwood. (See "Individuals in Society: Josiah Wedgwood.) Among Britain's highly skilled locksmiths, tinsmiths, and millwrights, Watt found mechanics who could install, regulate, and repair his sophisticated engines. From ingenious manufacturers, Watt was gradually able to purchase precision parts. By the late 1780s the firm of Boulton and Watt had made the steam engine a practical and commercial success in Britain.

The coal-burning steam engine of Watt and his followers was the Industrial Revolution's most fundamental advance in technology. For the first time in history, humanity had, at least for a few generations, almost unlimited power at its disposal. Steam power began to replace waterpower in cotton-spinning mills during the 1780s, contributing greatly to that industry's phenomenal rise. Steam also took the place of waterpower in flour mills, in the malt mills used in breweries, in the flint mills supplying the pottery industry, and in the mills exported by Britain to the West Indies to crush sugarcane.

The British iron industry was also radically transformed. After 1770 the adoption of steam-driven bellows in blast furnaces allowed for great increases in the quantity of pig iron produced by British ironmakers. In the 1780s Henry Cort developed the puddling furnace, which allowed pig iron to be refined with coke, a smokeless and hot-burning fuel produced by heating coal to rid it of impurities.

Cort also developed steam-powered rolling mills, which were capable of spewing out finished iron in every shape and form. The economic consequence of these technical innovations was a great boom in the British iron industry. Once scarce and expensive, iron became the cheap, basic, indispensable building block of the British economy.

steam engines

▶ A breakthrough invention by Thomas Savery in 1698 and Thomas Newcomen in 1705 that burned coal to produce steam, which was then used to operate a pump; the early models were superseded by James Watt's more efficient steam engine, patented in 1769.

CHAPTER LOCATOR | Why did the Industrial Revolution begin in Britain, and how did it develop? | How did countries respond to the challenge of industrialization?

CHAPTER 23
686   THE REVOLUTION IN ENERGY AND INDUSTRY

As the making of cloth and iron was revolutionized by technical change and factory organization, so, too, were the production and consumption of pottery. Acquiring beautiful tableware became a craze for eighteenth-century consumers, and continental monarchs often sought prestige in building royal china works. But the grand prize went to Josiah Wedgwood, who wanted to "astonish the world."

The twelfth child of a poor potter, Josiah Wedgwood (1730–1795) grew up in the pottery district of Staffordshire in the English Midlands, where many tiny potteries made simple earthenware utensils for sale in local markets. Having grown up as an apprentice in the family business inherited by his oldest brother, Wedgwood struck off on his own in 1752. Soon manager of a small pottery, Wedgwood learned that new products recharged lagging sales. Studying chemistry and determined to succeed, Wedgwood spent his evenings experimenting with different chemicals and firing conditions.

In 1759, after five years of tireless efforts, Wedgwood perfected a beautiful new green glaze. Now established as a master potter, he opened his own factory and began manufacturing teapots and tableware finished in his green and other unique glazes, or adorned with printed scenes far superior to those being produced by competitors. Wedgwood's products caused a sensation among consumers, and his business quickly earned substantial profits. Subsequent breakthroughs, including ornamental vases imitating classical Greek models and jasperware for jewelry, contributed greatly to Wedgwood's success.

Competitors were quick to copy Wedgwood's new products and sell them at lower prices. Thus Wedgwood and his partner, Thomas Bentley, sought to cultivate an image of superior fashion, taste, and quality in order to develop and maintain a dominant market position. They did this by first capturing the business of the trendsetting elite. In one brilliant coup the partners first sold a very large cream-colored dinner set to Britain's queen, which they quickly christened "Queen's ware" and sold as a very expensive, must-have luxury to English aristocrats. Equally brilliant was Bentley's suave expertise in the elegant London showroom selling Wedgwood's imitation Greek vases, which became the rage after the rediscovery of the cities of Pompeii and Herculaneum in the mid-eighteenth century.

Josiah Wedgwood perfected jasperware, a fine-grained pottery usually made in "Wedgwood blue" with white decoration. This elegant cylindrical vase, decorated in the form of a miniature Roman household altar, was destined for the luxury market. (Josiah Wedgwood [1730–1795]. Vase, 18th century. Jasperware. Vase [09.194.7]: English [Staffordshire, Etruria]. Rogers Fund, 1909 [09.194.7-9], designed by John Flaxman [1755–1826]. Metropolitan Museum of Art, New York, NY, USA/ Image copyright © The Metropolitan Museum of Art/Image source: Art Resource, NY)

Above all, once Wedgwood had secured his position as the luxury market leader, he was able to successfully extend his famous brand to the growing middle class, capturing an enormous mass market for his "useful ware." Thus, when sales of a luxury good grew "stale," Wedgwood made tasteful modifications and sold it to the middling classes for twice the price his competitors could charge. This unbeatable combination of mass appeal and high prices brought Wedgwood great fame all across Europe and enormous wealth.

A workaholic with an authoritarian streak, Wedgwood contributed substantially to the development of the factory system. In 1769 he opened a model factory on a new canal he had promoted. With two hundred workers in several departments, Wedgwood exercised tremendous control over his workforce, imposing fines for many infractions, such as being late, drinking on the job, or wasting material. He wanted, he said, to create men who would be like "machines" that "cannot err." Yet Wedgwood also recognized the value in treating workers well. He championed a division of labor that made most workers specialists who received ongoing training. He also encouraged employment of family groups, who were housed in company row houses with long, narrow backyards suitable for raising vegetables and chickens. Paying relatively high wages and providing pensions and some benefits, Wedgwood developed a high-quality labor force that learned to accept his rigorous discipline and carried out his ambitious plans.

QUESTIONS FOR ANALYSIS

1. How and why did Wedgwood succeed?
2. Was Wedgwood a good boss or a bad one? Why?
3. How did Wedgwood exemplify the new class of factory owners?

ONLINE DOCUMENT PROJECT

How were social and economic change connected in nineteenth-century England? Read sources on early industrial manufacturing, and then complete a quiz and writing assignment based on the evidence and details from this chapter. *See inside the front cover to learn more.*

Steam-Powered Transportation

Rocket

▶ The name given to George Stephenson's effective locomotive that was first tested in 1829 on the Liverpool and Manchester Railway and reached a maximum speed of 35 miles per hour.

The first steam locomotive was built by Richard Trevithick after much experimentation. George Stephenson's locomotive named *Rocket* sped down the track of the just-completed Liverpool and Manchester Railway at a maximum speed of 35 miles per hour in 1829. The line from Liverpool to Manchester was a financial as well as a technical success, and many private companies were organized to build more rail lines. Within twenty years they had completed the main trunk lines of Great Britain (Map 23.1). Other countries were quick to follow, with the first steam-powered trains operating in the United States in the 1830s and in Brazil, Chile, Argentina, and the British colonies of Canada, Australia, and India in the 1850s (Figure 23.1).

The arrival of the railroad had many significant consequences. It dramatically reduced the cost and uncertainty of shipping freight over land. Previously, markets had tended to be small and local; as the barrier of high transportation costs was lowered, markets became larger and even nationwide. Larger markets encouraged larger factories with more sophisticated machinery in a growing number of industries. Such factories could make goods more cheaply and gradually subjected most cottage workers and many urban artisans to severe competitive pressures. In all countries, the construction of railroads created a strong demand for unskilled labor and contributed to the growth of a class of urban workers.

The railroad also had a tremendous impact on cultural values and attitudes. The last and culminating invention of the Industrial Revolution, the railroad dramatically revealed the power and increased the speed of the new age. Some great painters, notably Joseph M. W. Turner (1775–1851) and Claude Monet (1840–1926), succeeded in expressing the sense of power and awe railroads inspired. So did the massive new train stations, the cathedrals of the industrial age.

The steam engine also transformed water travel. French engineers completed the first steamships in the 1770s, and the first commercial steamships came into use in North America several decades later. The steamship brought the advantages of the railroad—speed, reliability, efficiency—to water travel.

Towns with over 20,000 people are shown

50   400   2.4
Thousand   Million

Cities with over 100,000 people are labeled

▮ Exposed coal deposit
▢ Industrial area
┼┼┼ Principal railroad

0   50   100 miles
0   50   100 kilometers

MAP 23.1 ■ The Industrial Revolution in Great Britain, ca. 1850

Industry concentrated in the rapidly growing cities of the north and the center of England, where rich coal and iron deposits were close to one another.

CHAPTER LOCATOR | Why did the Industrial Revolution begin in Britain, and how did it develop? | How did countries respond to the challenge of industrialization?

CHAPTER 23
688   THE REVOLUTION IN ENERGY AND INDUSTRY

The International Sleeping-Car Company was founded in 1872, inspired by the model of the American Pullman night trains. It quickly became the most important operator of sleeping and dining cars in Europe. The company's posters, like the one pictured here, appealed to wealthy and middle-class customers by emphasizing the luxury and spaciousness of its accommodations. The company's most famous line was the Orient Express (1883–2009), which ran from Paris to Istanbul. (Kharbine-Tapabor/The Art Archive at Art Resource, NY)

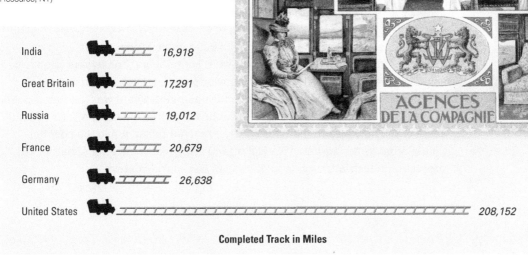

COMP^{IE} INTERNATIONALE DES WAGONS-LITS & DES GRANDS EXPRESS EUROPEENS

AGENCES DE LA COMPAGNIE

India	16,918
Great Britain	17,291
Russia	19,012
France	20,679
Germany	26,638
United States	208,152

Completed Track in Miles

FIGURE 23.1 ■ Railroad Track Mileage, 1890

Steam railroads were first used by the general public for shipping in England in the 1820s, and they quickly spread to other countries. The United States was an early adopter of railroads and by 1890 had surpassed all other countries in miles of track, as shown in this figure.

Industry and Population

In 1851 London hosted an industrial fair called the Great Exhibition in the newly built **Crystal Palace**. The building was made entirely of glass and iron, both of which were now cheap and abundant. Sponsored by the British royal family, the exhibition celebrated the new era of industrial technology and the kingdom's role as world economic leader.

As the British economy significantly increased its production of manufactured goods, the gross national product (GNP) rose roughly fourfold at constant prices between 1780 and 1851. At the same time, the population of Britain boomed, growing from about 9 million in 1780 to almost 21 million in 1851. Thus growing numbers consumed much of the increase in total production.

Rapid population growth in Great Britain was key to industrial development. More people meant a more mobile labor force, with a wealth of young workers in need of employment and ready to go where the jobs were. Sustaining the dramatic increase in population, in turn, was only possible through advances in agriculture

Crystal Palace

▶ The location of the Great Exhibition in 1851 in London, an architectural masterpiece made entirely of glass and iron.

How did work evolve during the Industrial Revolution, and how did daily life change for working people?

How did the changes brought about by the Industrial Revolution lead to new social classes, and how did people respond to the new structure?

 LearningCurve
Check what you know.

and industry. Many contemporaries feared that the rapid growth in population would inevitably lead to disaster. In his *Essay on the Principle of Population* (1798), Thomas Malthus (1766–1834) argued that population would always tend to grow faster than the food supply. Malthus concluded that the only hope of warding off such "positive checks" to population growth as war, famine, and disease was "prudential restraint." That is, young men and women had to limit the growth of population by marrying late in life. But Malthus was not optimistic about this possibility. The powerful attraction of the sexes would cause most people to marry early and have many children.

Economist David Ricardo (1772–1823) spelled out the pessimistic implications of Malthus's thought. Ricardo's depressing iron law of wages posited that, because of the pressure of population growth, wages would always sink to subsistence level. That is, wages would be just high enough to keep workers from starving.

Malthus, Ricardo, and their followers were proved wrong in the long run. However, until the 1820s, or even the 1840s, contemporary observers might reasonably have concluded that the economy and the total population were racing neck and neck, with the outcome very much in doubt. There was another problem as well. Perhaps workers, farmers, and ordinary people did not get their rightful share of the new wealth. Perhaps only the rich got richer, while the poor got poorer or made no progress. We will turn to this great issue after situating the process of industrialization in its European and global context.

iron law of wages
▶ Theory proposed by English economist David Ricardo suggesting that the pressure of population growth prevents wages from rising above the subsistence level.

> **QUICK REVIEW**

What role did technology play in the early phases of the Industrial Revolution?

CHAPTER LOCATOR | Why did the Industrial Revolution begin in Britain, and how did it develop? | How did countries respond to the challenge of industrialization?

CHAPTER 23
690 THE REVOLUTION IN ENERGY AND INDUSTRY

The Borsig ironworks in Berlin mastered the new British method of smelting iron ore with coke. Germany, especially the state of Prussia, was well endowed with both iron and coal, and the rapid exploitation of these resources after 1840 transformed a poor agricultural country into an industrial powerhouse. (Stiftung Stadtmuseum/akg-images)

How did countries in Europe and around the world respond to the challenge of industrialization after 1815?

AS NEW TECHNOLOGIES and a new organization of labor began to revolutionize production in Britain, other countries took notice and began to emulate its example. With the end of the Napoleonic Wars, the nations of the European continent quickly adopted British inventions and achieved their own pattern of technological innovation and economic growth. By the last decades of the nineteenth century, western European countries as well as the United States and Japan had industrialized their economies to a considerable, albeit varying, degree.

National and International Variations

Comparative data on industrial production in different countries over time help give us an overview of what happened. One set of data, the work of a Swiss scholar, compares the level of industrialization on a per capita basis in several countries from 1750 to 1913. These data are far from perfect, but they reflect basic trends and are presented in Table 23.1 for closer study.

Table 23.1 presents a comparison of how much industrial product was produced, on average, for each person in a given country in a given year. All the numbers are expressed in terms of a single index number of 100, which equals the per capita level of industrial goods in Great Britain and Ireland in 1900. Every number in the table is thus a percentage of the 1900 level in Britain and is directly

How did work evolve during the Industrial Revolution, and how did daily life change for working people?

How did the changes brought about by the Industrial Revolution lead to new social classes, and how did people respond to the new structure?

 LearningCurve
Check what you know.

691

TABLE 23.1 ■ Per Capita Levels of Industrialization, 1750–1913

	1750	1800	1830	1860	1880	1900	1913
Great Britain	10	16	25	64	87	100	115
Belgium	9	10	14	28	43	56	88
United States	4	9	14	21	38	69	126
France	9	9	12	20	28	39	59
Germany	8	8	9	15	25	52	85
Austria-Hungary	7	7	8	11	15	23	32
Italy	8	8	8	10	12	17	26
Russia	6	6	7	8	10	15	20
China	8	6	6	4	4	3	3
India	7	6	6	3	2	1	2

Note: All entries are based on an index value of 100, equal to the per capita level of industrialization in Great Britain in 1900. Data for Great Britain include Ireland, England, Wales, and Scotland.

Source: P. Bairoch, "International Industrialization Levels from 1750 to 1980," *Journal of European Economic History* 11 (Spring 1982): 294, U.S. Journals at Cambridge University Press. Reprinted by permission.

comparable with other numbers. The countries are listed in roughly the order that they began to use large-scale, power-driven technology.

What does this overview tell us? First, one sees in the first column that in 1750 all countries were fairly close together, including non-Western areas such as China and India. However, the column headed 1800 shows that Britain had opened up a noticeable lead over all countries by 1800, and that gap progressively widened as the British Industrial Revolution accelerated through 1830 and reached full maturity by 1860.

Second, the table shows that Western countries began to emulate the British model successfully over the nineteenth century, with significant variations in the timing and in the extent of industrialization. Belgium led in adopting Britain's new technology, and it experienced a truly revolutionary surge between 1830 and 1860. France developed factory production more gradually and did not experience "revolutionary" acceleration in the growth of overall industrial output. Slow but steady economic growth in France was overshadowed by the spectacular rise of Germany and the United States after 1860 in what has been termed the "Second Industrial Revolution." In general, eastern and southern Europe began the process of industrialization later than northwestern and central Europe. Nevertheless, these regions made real progress in the late nineteenth century, as growth after 1880 in Austria-Hungary, Italy, and Russia suggests. This meant that all European states as well as the United States managed to raise per capita industrial levels in the nineteenth century.

These increases stood in stark contrast to the decreases that occurred at the same time in many non-Western countries, most notably in China and India as Table 23.1 shows. European countries industrialized to a greater or lesser extent even as most of the non-Western world stagnated. Japan, which is not included in this table, stands out as an exceptional area of non-Western industrial growth in

CHAPTER LOCATOR | Why did the Industrial Revolution begin in Britain, and how did it develop? | How did countries respond to the challenge of industrialization?

CHAPTER 23
692 THE REVOLUTION IN ENERGY AND INDUSTRY

the second half of the nineteenth century. After the forced opening of the country to the West in the 1850s, Japanese entrepreneurs began to adopt Western technology and manufacturing methods, resulting in a production boom by the late nineteenth century (see Chapter 26). Differential rates of wealth- and power-creating industrial development, which heightened disparities within Europe, also greatly magnified existing inequalities between Europe and the rest of the world (see Chapter 25).

Industrialization in Continental Europe

Throughout Europe the eighteenth century was an era of agricultural improvement, population increase, expanding foreign trade, and growing cottage industry. Thus, when the pace of British industry began to accelerate in the 1780s, continental businesses began to adopt the new methods as they proved their profitability. During the period of the revolutionary and Napoleonic Wars, from 1793 to 1815, however, western Europe experienced tremendous political and social upheaval that temporarily halted economic development. With the return of peace in 1815, however, western European countries again began to play catch-up.

They faced significant challenges. In the newly mechanized industries, British goods were being produced very economically, and these goods had come to dominate world markets. In addition, British technology had become so advanced that very few engineers or skilled technicians outside England understood it. Moreover, the technology of steam power involved large investments in the iron and coal industries and, after 1830, required the existence of railroads. Continental business people had great difficulty amassing the large sums of money the new methods demanded, and laborers bitterly resisted the move to working in factories. All these factors slowed the spread of mechanization (Map 23.2).

Nevertheless, western European nations possessed a number of advantages that helped them respond to these challenges. First, most had rich traditions of putting-out enterprise, merchant capitalism, and skilled urban trades. These assets gave their firms the ability to adapt and survive in the face of new market conditions. Second, continental capitalists did not need to develop their own advanced technology. Instead, they could "borrow" the new methods developed in Great Britain, as well as the engineers and some of the financial resources they lacked. Finally, European countries had strong, independent governments that were willing to use the power of the state to promote industry and catch up with Britain.

Agents of Industrialization

Western European success in adopting British methods took place despite the best efforts of the British to prevent it. The British realized the great value of their technical discoveries and tried to keep their secrets to themselves. Until 1825 it was illegal for artisans and skilled mechanics to leave Britain; until 1843 the export of textile machinery and other equipment was forbidden. Many talented, ambitious workers, however, slipped out of the country illegally and introduced the new methods abroad.

Thus British technicians and skilled workers were a powerful force in the spread of early industrialization. A second agent of industrialization consisted of talented European entrepreneurs such as Fritz Harkort (1793–1880). Serving in England as a Prussian army officer during the Napoleonic Wars, Harkort was impressed with what he saw. Harkort set up shop building steam engines in the

How did work evolve during the Industrial Revolution, and how did daily life change for working people?

How did the changes brought about by the Industrial Revolution lead to new social classes, and how did people respond to the new structure?

LearningCurve
Check what you know.

693

MAP 23.2 ■ Continental Industrialization, ca. 1850

Although continental countries were beginning to make progress by 1850, they still lagged far behind Britain. For example, continental railroad building was still in an early stage, whereas the British rail system was essentially complete (see Map 23.1). Coal played a critical role in nineteenth-century industrialization, both as a power source for steam engines and as a raw material for making iron and steel.

> **MAPPING THE PAST**

ANALYZING THE MAP: Locate the major exposed (that is, known) coal deposits in 1850. Which countries and areas appear rich in coal resources, and which appear poor? Is there a difference between northern and southern Europe?
CONNECTIONS: What is the relationship between known coal deposits and emerging industrial areas in continental Europe? In England (see Map 23.1)?

Ruhr Valley, on the western border with France. In spite of problems obtaining skilled workers and machinery, Harkort succeeded in building and selling engines. However, his ambitious efforts failed to turn a profit. His career illustrates both the great efforts of a few important business leaders to duplicate the British achievement and the difficulty of the task.

National governments played an even more important role in supporting industrialization in continental Europe than in Britain. **Tariff protection** was one such support. The French, for example, responded to a flood of cheap British goods in 1815, after the Napoleonic Wars, by laying high taxes on imported goods. Customs agreements emerged among some German states starting in 1818, and in 1834 a number of states signed a treaty creating a customs union, or *Zollverein*. The treaty allowed goods to move between member states without tariffs, while erecting a single uniform tariff against other nations.

After 1815 continental governments also bore the cost of building roads, canals, and railroads to improve transportation. Belgium led the way in the 1830s and 1840s, building a state-owned railroad network that stimulated the development of heavy industry and made the country an early industrial leader. In France

tariff protection

▶ A government's way of supporting and aiding its own economy by laying high taxes on imported goods from other countries, as when the French responded to the flood of cheaper British goods in their country by imposing high tariffs on some imported products.

CHAPTER LOCATOR | Why did the Industrial Revolution begin in Britain, and how did it develop? | How did countries respond to the challenge of industrialization?

CHAPTER 23
694 THE REVOLUTION IN ENERGY AND INDUSTRY

the state shouldered all the expense of acquiring and laying roadbed, including bridges and tunnels.

Finally, banks, like governments, also played a larger and more creative role on the continent than in Britain. Previously, almost all banks in Europe had been private. Because of the possibility of unlimited financial loss, the partners of private banks generally avoided industrial investment as being too risky.

In the 1830s two important Belgian banks pioneered in a new direction. They received permission from the growth-oriented government to establish themselves as corporations enjoying limited liability. That is, if the bank went bankrupt, stockholders would lose only their original investments in the bank's common stock, and they could not be forced to pay for additional losses out of other property they owned. Limited liability helped these banks attract investors. They mobilized impressive resources for investment in big companies, became industrial banks, and successfully promoted industrial development. Similar corporate banks became important in France and Germany in the 1850s and 1860s.

The combined efforts of skilled workers, entrepreneurs, governments, and industrial banks meshed successfully between 1850 and the financial crash of 1873. In Belgium, France, and the German states key indicators of modern industrial development increased at average annual rates of 5 to 10 percent. As a result, rail networks were completed in western Europe and much of central Europe, and the leading continental countries mastered the industrial technologies that had first been developed in Great Britain. In the early 1870s Britain was still Europe's most industrial nation, but a select handful of countries were closing the gap.

The Global Picture

The Industrial Revolution did not extend outside of Europe prior to the 1860s, with the exception of the United States and Japan. In many countries, national governments and pioneering entrepreneurs promoted industrialization, but fell short of transitioning to an industrial economy. For example, in Russia the

Press for Packing Indian Cotton, 1864

British industrialization destroyed a thriving Indian cotton textile industry, whose weavers could not compete with cheap British imports. India continued to supply raw cotton to British manufacturers. (English wood engraving, 1864/The Granger Collection, NYC — All rights reserved.)

How did work evolve during the Industrial Revolution, and how did daily life change for working people?

How did the changes brought about by the Industrial Revolution lead to new social classes, and how did people respond to the new structure?

LearningCurve
Check what you know.

imperial government brought steamships to the Volga River and a railroad to the capital, St. Petersburg, in the first decades of the nineteenth century. By mid-century ambitious entrepreneurs had established steam-powered cotton factories using imported British machines. However, these advances did not lead to overall industrialization of the country. Instead Russia confirmed its role as provider of raw materials, especially timber and grain, to the hungry West.

Egypt, a territory of the Ottoman empire, similarly began an ambitious program of modernization after a reform-minded viceroy took power in 1805. This program included the use of imported British technology and experts in textile manufacture and other industries (see page 731). These industries, however, could not compete with lower-priced European imports. Like Russia, Egypt fell back on agricultural exports, such as sugar and cotton, to European markets.

Such examples of faltering efforts at industrialization could be found in many other places in the Middle East, Asia, and Latin America. Where European governments maintained direct or indirect control, they acted to maintain colonial markets as both sources of raw materials and consumers for their own products, rather than encouraging the spread of industrialization. In India millions of poor textile workers lost their livelihood because they could not compete with industrially produced British cotton. The British charged stiff import duties on Indian cottons entering the kingdom, but prohibited the Indians from doing the same to British imports. The arrival of railroads in India in the mid-nineteenth century served the purpose of agricultural rather than industrial development.

Latin American economies were disrupted by the early-nineteenth-century wars of independence (see Chapter 22). As these countries' economies recovered in the mid-nineteenth century, they increasingly adopted steam power for sugar and coffee processing and for transportation. Like elsewhere, this technology first supported increased agricultural production for export and only later drove domestic industrial production.

The rise of industrialization in Britain, western Europe, and the United States thus caused other regions of the world to become increasingly economically dependent. Instead of industrializing, many territories underwent a process of deindustrialization or delayed industrialization. In turn, relative economic weakness made them vulnerable to the new wave of imperialism undertaken by industrialized nations in the second half of the nineteenth century (see Chapters 25 and 26).

As for China, it did not adopt mechanized production until the end of the nineteenth century, but continued as a market-based, commercial society with a massive rural sector and industrial production based on traditional methods. In the 1860s and 1870s, when Japan was successfully adopting industrial methods, the Chinese government showed similar interest in Western technology and science. However, China faced widespread uprisings in the mid-nineteenth century, which drained attention and resources to the military; moreover, after the Boxer Rebellion of 1898–1900 (see page 794), Western powers forced China to pay massive indemnities, further reducing its capacity to promote industrialization.

> **QUICK REVIEW**

Why did British practices spread to continental Europe, but not to most of the rest of the world?

CHAPTER LOCATOR | Why did the Industrial Revolution begin in Britain, and how did it develop? | How did countries respond to the challenge of industrialization?

CHAPTER 23
696   THE REVOLUTION IN ENERGY AND INDUSTRY

How did work evolve during the Industrial Revolution, and how did daily life change for working people?

Workers at a U.S. Mill

Female workers at a U.S. cotton mill in 1890 take a break from operating belt-driven weaving machines to pose for this photograph, accompanied by their male supervisor. The first textile mills, established in the 1820s in Massachusetts, employed local farm girls. As competition intensified, conditions deteriorated and the mills increasingly relied on immigrant women who had few alternatives to the long hours, noise, and dangers of factory work. By 1900 more than 1 million women worked in factories in the United States. (Courtesy of George Eastman House, International Museum of Photography and Film, accession number 1966:0039:0013)

HAVING FIRST EMERGED in the British countryside in the late eighteenth century, factories and industrial labor began migrating to cities by the early nineteenth century. For some people, the Industrial Revolution brought improvements, but living and working conditions for the poor stagnated or even deteriorated until around 1850, especially in overcrowded industrial cities.

Work in Early Factories

The first factories of the Industrial Revolution were cotton mills, which began functioning in the 1770s along fast-running rivers and streams and were often located in sparsely populated areas. Cottage workers, accustomed to the putting-out system, were reluctant to work in the new factories even when they received relatively good wages. In a factory, workers had to keep up with the machine and follow its relentless tempo. Moreover, they had to show up every day, on time, and work long, monotonous hours under the constant supervision of demanding overseers.

| How did work evolve during the Industrial Revolution, and how did daily life change for working people? | How did the changes brought about by the Industrial Revolution lead to new social classes, and how did people respond to the new structure? | LearningCurve Check what you know. |

697

Cottage workers were not used to that way of life. All members of the family worked hard and long, but in spurts, setting their own pace. Women and children could break up their long hours of spinning with other tasks. On Saturday afternoon the head of the family delivered the week's work to the merchant manufacturer and got paid. Saturday night was a time of relaxation and drinking, especially for men.

Also, early factories resembled English poorhouses, where totally destitute people went to live at public expense. The similarity between large brick factories and large stone poorhouses increased the cottage workers' fear of factories and their hatred of factory discipline. It was cottage workers' reluctance to work in factories that prompted early cotton mill owners to turn to pauper children.

Working Families and Children

By the 1790s the early labor pattern was rapidly changing. The use of pauper apprentices was in decline, and in 1802 it was forbidden by Parliament. Many more textile factories were being built, mainly in urban areas, where they could use steam power rather than waterpower and attract a workforce more easily than in the countryside. People came from near and far to work in the cities. Collectively, these wage laborers came to be known as the "working class," a term first used in the late 1830s.

In some cases, workers accommodated to the system by carrying over familiar working traditions. Some came to the mills and the mines as family units, as they had worked on farms and in the putting-out system. The mill or mine owner bargained with the head of the family and paid him or her for the work of the whole family.

Ties of kinship were particularly important for newcomers, who often traveled great distances to find work. Many urban workers in Great Britain were from Ireland. They were forced out of rural Ireland by population growth and deteriorating economic conditions from 1817. Their numbers increased dramatically during the desperate years of the potato famine, from 1845 to 1851. Like many other immigrant groups held together by ethnic and religious ties, the Irish worked together, formed their own neighborhoods, and maintained their cultural traditions.

In the early decades of the nineteenth century, however, technical changes made it less and less likely that workers could continue to labor in family groups. As control and discipline passed into the hands of impersonal managers and overseers, adult workers began to protest against inhuman conditions on behalf of their children. Some enlightened employers and social reformers in Parliament agreed that more humane standards were necessary, and they used widely circulated parliamentary reports to influence public opinion.

Factory Act of 1833

▶ English law that led to a sharp decline in the employment of children by limiting the hours that children over age nine could work and banning employment of children younger than nine.

These efforts resulted in a series of British Factory Acts from 1802 to 1833 that progressively limited the workday of child laborers and set minimum hygiene and safety requirements. The Factory Act of 1833 installed a system of full-time professional inspectors to enforce the provisions of previous acts. The Factory Acts constituted significant progress in preventing the exploitation of children. One unintended drawback of restrictions on child labor, however, was that they broke the pattern of whole families working together in the factory, because efficiency required standardized shifts for all workers. After 1833 the number of children employed in industry declined rapidly.

CHAPTER LOCATOR | Why did the Industrial Revolution begin in Britain, and how did it develop? | How did countries respond to the challenge of industrialization?

CHAPTER 23
698 THE REVOLUTION IN ENERGY AND INDUSTRY

The Sexual Division of Labor

With the restriction of child labor and the collapse of the family work pattern in the 1830s came a new sexual division of labor. By 1850 the man was emerging as the family's primary wage earner, while the married woman found only limited job opportunities. Generally denied good jobs at high wages in the growing urban economy, wives were expected to concentrate on their duties at home. Evolving gradually, but largely in place by 1850, this new pattern of separate spheres in Britain constituted a major development in the history of women and of the family.

> ### The Sexual Division of Labor:

- Married women from the working classes were much less likely to work full-time for wages outside the house after the first child arrived
- Married women who did work for wages outside the house usually came from the poorest families
- Poor married or widowed women had to compete with young unmarried women for the limited employment opportunities available to women
- All women were generally confined to low-paying, dead-end jobs

Several factors combined to create this new sexual division of labor. First, the new and unfamiliar discipline of the clock and the machine was especially hard on married women of the laboring classes. Factory discipline conflicted with child care in a way that labor on the farm or in the cottage had not.

Second, running a household in conditions of urban poverty was an extremely demanding job in its own right. There were no supermarkets or public transportation. Shopping and feeding the family constituted a never-ending challenge. Taking on a brutal job outside the house had limited appeal for the average married woman from the working class. Thus many women might well have accepted the emerging division of labor as the best available strategy for family survival in the industrializing society.[2]

Third, to a large degree the young, generally unmarried women who did work for wages outside the home were segregated from men and confined to certain "women's jobs" because the new sexual division of labor replicated long-standing patterns of gender segregation and inequality. In the preindustrial economy, a small sector of the labor market had always been defined as "women's work," especially tasks involving needlework, spinning, food preparation, child care, and nursing. This traditional sexual division of labor took on new overtones, however, in response to the factory system. The growth of factories and mines brought unheard-of opportunities for girls and boys to mix on the job, free of familial supervision. Such opportunities led to more unplanned pregnancies and fueled the illegitimacy explosion that had begun in the late eighteenth century and that gathered force until at least 1850. Thus segregation of jobs by gender was partly an effort by older people to help control the sexuality of working-class youths.

Investigations into the British coal industry before 1842 provide a graphic example of this concern. The middle-class men leading the inquiry professed horror at the sight of girls and women working without shirts, which was a common

How did work evolve during the Industrial Revolution, and how did daily life change for working people? | How did the changes brought about by the Industrial Revolution lead to new social classes, and how did people respond to the new structure? | ✔ LearningCurve Check what you know.

699

practice because of the heat, and they quickly assumed the prevalence of licentious sex with the male miners. In fact, most girls and married women worked for related males in a family unit that provided considerable protection and restraint. Yet many witnesses from the working class also believed that the mines were inappropriate and dangerous places for women and girls. Some miners stressed particularly the danger of sexual aggression for girls working past puberty. The **Mines Act of 1842** prohibited underground work for all women and girls as well as for boys under ten.

A final factor encouraging working-class women to withdraw from paid labor was the domestic ideals emanating from middle-class women, who had largely embraced the "separate spheres" ideology. Middle-class reformers published tracts and formed societies to urge poor women to devote more care and attention to their homes and families.

Living Standards for the Working Class

Although the evidence is complex and sometimes contradictory, most historians now agree that overall living standards for the working class did not rise substantially until the 1840s at least. Factory wages began to rise after 1815, but these gains were modest and were offset by a decline in married women's and children's participation in the labor force, meaning that many households had less total income than before. Moreover, many people still worked outside the factories as cottage workers or rural laborers, and in those sectors wages declined. Thus the increase in the productivity of industry did not lead to an increase in the purchasing power of the British working classes. Only after 1830, and especially after 1840, did real wages rise substantially, so that the average worker earned roughly 30 percent more in real terms in 1850 than in 1770.[3] Up to that point, the harshness of labor in the new industries probably outweighed their benefits as far as working people were concerned.

As the factories moved to urban areas, workers followed them in large numbers, leading to an explosion in the size of cities, especially in the north of England. Life in the new industrial cities, such as Manchester and Glasgow, was grim. Given extremely high rates of infant mortality, average life expectancy was around only twenty-five to twenty-seven years, some fifteen years less than the national average.[4] Migrants to the booming cities found expensive, hastily constructed, overcrowded apartments and inadequate sanitary systems.

Another way to consider the workers' standard of living is to look at the goods they purchased, which also suggest stagnant or declining living standards until the middle of the nineteenth century. One important area of improvement was in the consumption of cotton goods, which became much cheaper and could be enjoyed by all classes. However, in other areas, food in particular, the modest growth in factory wages was not enough to compensate for rising prices.

From the 1840s onward, matters improved considerably as wages made substantial gains and the prices of many goods dropped. A greater variety of foods became available, including the first canned goods. Some of the most important advances were in medicine. Smallpox vaccination became routine, and surgeons began to use anesthesia in the late 1840s. By 1850 trains and steamships had revolutionized transportation for the masses, while the telegraph made instant

Mines Act of 1842

▶ English law prohibiting underground work for all women and girls as well as for boys under ten.

CHAPTER LOCATOR | Why did the Industrial Revolution begin in Britain, and how did it develop? | How did countries respond to the challenge of industrialization?

700 CHAPTER 23
THE REVOLUTION IN ENERGY AND INDUSTRY

communication possible for the first time in human history. Gaslights greatly expanded the possibilities of nighttime activity.

In addition to the technical innovations that resulted from industrialization, other, less tangible changes were also taking place. As young men and women migrated away from their villages to seek employment in urban factories, many close-knit rural communities were destroyed. The loss of skills and work autonomy, along with the loss of community, must be included in the assessment of the Industrial Revolution's impact on the living conditions of the poor.

QUICK REVIEW <

How did industrialization change European family life?

| How did work evolve during the Industrial Revolution, and how did daily life change for working people? | How did the changes brought about by the Industrial Revolution lead to new social classes, and how did people respond to the new structure? | LearningCurve Check what you know. |

701

How did the changes brought about by the Industrial Revolution lead to new social classes, and how did people respond to the new structure?

IN GREAT BRITAIN industrial development led to the creation of new social groups and intensified long-standing problems between capital and labor. A new class of factory owners and industrial capitalists arose. The demands of modern industry regularly brought the interests of the middle-class industrialists into conflict with those of the people who worked for them—the working class. As observers took note of these changes, they raised new questions about how industrialization affected social relationships. Meanwhile, enslaved labor in European colonies contributed to the industrialization process in multiple ways.

CHAPTER LOCATOR | Why did the Industrial Revolution begin in Britain, and how did it develop? | How did countries respond to the challenge of industrialization?

The New Class of Factory Owners

Early industrialists operated in a highly competitive economic system. There were countless production problems, and success and large profits were by no means certain. Manufacturers therefore waged a constant battle to cut their production costs and stay afloat. Much of the profit had to go back into the business for new and better machinery.

Most early industrialists drew upon their families and friends for labor and capital, but they came from a variety of backgrounds. Many were from well-established merchant families with rich networks of contacts and support. Others were of modest means, especially in the early days. Artisans and skilled workers of exceptional ability had unparalleled opportunities. Members of ethnic and religious groups who had been discriminated against in the traditional occupations controlled by the landed aristocracy jumped at the new chances and often helped each other.

As factories and firms grew larger, and opportunities declined, it became harder for a gifted but poor young mechanic to start a small enterprise and end up as a wealthy manufacturer. Expensive, formal education became more important for young men as a means of success and advancement. In Britain by 1830 and in France and Germany by 1860, leading industrialists were more likely to have inherited their well-established enterprises, and they were financially much more secure than their struggling parents had been.

Just like working-class women, the wives and daughters of successful businessmen also found fewer opportunities for active participation in Europe's business world. Rather than contributing as vital partners in a family-owned enterprise, as so many middle-class women had done before, these women were increasingly valued for their ladylike gentility.

Responses to Industrialization

From the beginning, the British Industrial Revolution had its critics. Among the first were the romantic poets, including William Blake (1757–1827) and William Wordsworth (1770–1850). Some handicraft workers—notably the Luddites, who attacked factories in northern England in 1811 and later—smashed the new machines, which they believed were putting them out of work. Doctors and reformers wrote of problems in the factories and new towns, while Malthus and Ricardo concluded that workers would earn only enough to stay alive.

This pessimistic view was accepted and reinforced by Friedrich Engels (1820–1895), the future revolutionary and colleague of Karl Marx (see Chapter 24). After studying conditions in northern England, this young son of a wealthy Prussian cotton manufacturer published in 1844 *The Condition of the Working Class in England*, a blistering indictment of the capitalist classes. Engels's extremely influential account of capitalist exploitation and increasing worker poverty was embellished by Marx and later socialists (see Chapter 24).

Analysis of industrial capitalism, often combined with reflections on the French Revolution, led to the development of a new overarching interpretation—a new paradigm—regarding social relationships. Briefly, this paradigm argued that individuals were members of separate classes based on their relationship to

Luddites

▶ Group of handicraft workers who attacked factories in northern England in 1811 and after, smashing the new machines that they believed were putting them out of work.

How did work evolve during the Industrial Revolution, and how did daily life change for working people? | How did the changes brought about by the Industrial Revolution lead to new social classes, and how did people respond to the new structure? | ✓ LearningCurve Check what you know.

703

Ford Maddox Brown, *Work*

This midcentury painting provides a rich and realistic visual representation of the new concepts of social class that had become common by 1850. (Birmingham Museums and Art Gallery, Birmingham, UK/ The Bridgeman Art Library)

> PICTURING THE PAST

ANALYZING THE IMAGE: Describe the different types of work shown. What different social classes are depicted, and what kinds of work and leisure are the members of the different social classes engaged in?
CONNECTIONS: What does this painting and its title suggest about the artist's opinion of the work of common laborers?

the means of production, that is, the machines and factories that dominated the new economy. As owners of expensive industrial machinery and as dependent laborers in their factories, the two main groups of society had separate and conflicting interests. Accordingly, the comfortable, well-educated "public" of the eighteenth century came increasingly to be defined as the middle class and the "people" gradually began to perceive themselves as composing a modern working class. And while the new class interpretation was open to criticism, it appealed to many because it seemed to explain what was happening. Therefore, conflicting classes existed, in part, because many individuals came to believe they existed and developed an awareness that they belonged to a particular social class—what Karl Marx called **class-consciousness**.

class-consciousness

▶ An individual's sense of class differentiation, a term introduced by Karl Marx.

The Early Labor Movement in Britain

Not everyone worked in large factories and coal mines during the Industrial Revolution. In 1850 more British people still worked on farms than in any other single occupation. The second-largest occupation was domestic service, with more than 1 million household servants, 90 percent of whom were women.

CHAPTER LOCATOR | Why did the Industrial Revolution begin in Britain, and how did it develop? | How did countries respond to the challenge of industrialization?

CHAPTER 23
704 THE REVOLUTION IN ENERGY AND INDUSTRY

Within industry itself, the pattern of artisans working with hand tools in small shops remained unchanged in many trades, even as others were revolutionized by technological change. For example, the British iron industry was completely dominated by large-scale capitalist firms by 1850. Yet the firms that fashioned iron into small metal goods employed on average fewer than ten wage workers who used handicraft skills.

Working-class solidarity and class-consciousness developed in small workshops as well as in large factories. In the northern factory districts, anticapitalist sentiments were frequent by the 1820s. Commenting in 1825 on a strike in the woolen center of Bradford and the support it had gathered from other regions, one newspaper claimed with pride that "it is all the workers of England against a few masters of Bradford."[5]

Such sentiments ran contrary to the liberal tenets of economic freedom. Liberal economic principles were embraced by statesmen and middle-class business owners in the late eighteenth century and continued to gather strength in the early nineteenth century. In 1799 Parliament passed the Combination Acts, which outlawed unions and strikes. In 1813 and 1814 Parliament repealed an old law regulating the wages of artisans and the conditions of apprenticeship. As a result of these and other measures, certain skilled artisan workers found aggressive capitalists ignoring traditional work rules and trying to flood their trades with unorganized women workers and children to beat down wages.

The capitalist attack on artisan guilds and work rules was bitterly resented by many craftworkers, who subsequently played an important part in Great Britain and in other countries in gradually building a modern labor movement. The Combination Acts were widely disregarded by workers. Craftsmen continued to take collective action, and societies of skilled factory workers also organized unions. Unions sought to control the number of skilled workers, to limit apprenticeship to members' own children, and to bargain with owners over wages. In the face of widespread union activity, Parliament repealed the Combination Acts in 1824, and unions were tolerated, though not fully accepted, after 1825.

The next stage in the development of the British trade-union movement was the attempt to create a single large national union. This effort was led not so much by working people as by social reformers such as Robert Owen. Owen, a self-made cotton manufacturer, had pioneered in industrial relations by combining firm discipline with concern for the health, safety, and hours of his workers. After 1815 he experimented with cooperative and socialist communities. Then in 1834 Owen organized one of the largest and most visionary of the early national unions, the Grand National Consolidated Trades Union.

When Owen's and other grandiose schemes collapsed, the British labor movement moved once again after 1851 in the direction of craft unions. These unions won real benefits for members by fairly conservative means and thus became an accepted part of the industrial scene.

British workers also engaged in direct political activity in defense of their interests. After the collapse of Owen's national trade union, many working people went into the Chartist movement, which fought for universal manhood suffrage. Workers were also active in campaigns to limit the workday in factories to ten hours and to permit duty-free importation of wheat into Great Britain to secure cheap bread. Thus working people developed a sense of their own identity and

Combination Acts

▶ English laws passed in 1799 that outlawed unions and strikes, favoring capitalist business owners over skilled artisans. Bitterly resented and widely disregarded by many craft guilds, the acts were repealed by Parliament in 1824.

How did work evolve during the Industrial Revolution, and how did daily life change for working people? | **How did the changes brought about by the Industrial Revolution lead to new social classes, and how did people respond to the new structure?** | ✓ LearningCurve Check what you know.

705

played an active role in shaping the new industrial system. They were neither helpless victims nor passive beneficiaries.

The Impact of Slavery

Another mass labor force of the Industrial Revolution was composed of the millions of enslaved men, women, and children who toiled in European colonies in the Caribbean and in North and South America. Historians have long debated the extent to which revenue from slavery contributed to Britain's achievements in the Industrial Revolution.

Most now agree that profits from colonial plantations and slave trading were a small portion of British national income in the eighteenth century. Nevertheless, the impact of slavery on Britain's economy was much broader than direct profits alone. In the mid-eighteenth century the need for items to exchange for colonial cotton, sugar, tobacco, and slaves stimulated demand for British manufactured goods in the Caribbean, North America, and West Africa. Britain's dominance in the slave trade also led to the development of finance and credit institutions that would help early industrialists obtain capital for their businesses.

The British Parliament abolished the slave trade in 1807 and freed all slaves in British territories in 1833, but by 1850 most of the cotton processed by British mills was supplied by the coerced labor of slaves in the southern United States. Thus the Industrial Revolution cannot be detached from the Atlantic world and the misery of slavery it included.

> **QUICK REVIEW**

What steps did working-class people take to shape the conditions under which they labored?

CHAPTER SUMMARY

As markets for manufactured goods increased both domestically and overseas, Britain was able to respond with increased production, largely because of its stable government, abundant natural resources, and flexible labor force. The first factories arose as a result of innovations in the textile industry. The demand for improvements in energy led to innovations and improvements in the steam engine, which transformed the iron industry, among others. In the early nineteenth century transportation of goods was greatly enhanced with the adoption of steam-powered trains and ships.

After 1815 continental European countries gradually built on England's technical breakthroughs. Newly established corporate banks worked in conjunction with government interventions in finance and tariff controls to promote railroads and other industries. Beginning around 1850 Japan and the United States also

CHAPTER LOCATOR | Why did the Industrial Revolution begin in Britain, and how did it develop? | How did countries respond to the challenge of industrialization?

CHAPTER 23
706 THE REVOLUTION IN ENERGY AND INDUSTRY

began to rapidly industrialize, but generally the Industrial Revolution spread more slowly outside of Europe, as many countries were confined to producing agricultural goods and other raw materials to serve European markets.

The rise of modern industry had a profound impact on society, beginning in Britain in the late eighteenth century. Industrialization led to the growing size and wealth of the middle class and the rise of a modern industrial working class. Improvements in the standard of living came slowly, but they were substantial by 1850. Married women withdrew increasingly from wage work and concentrated on child care and household responsibilities. The era of industrialization also fostered new attitudes toward child labor, encouraged protective factory legislation, and called forth a new sense of class feeling and an assertive labor movement. Slave labor in European colonies contributed to the rise of the Industrial Revolution.

CONNECTIONS For much of its history, Europe lagged behind older and more sophisticated civilizations in China and the Middle East. And yet by 1800 Europe had broken ahead of the other regions of the world in terms of wealth and power.

One important prerequisite for the rise of Europe was its growing control over world trade, first in the Indian Ocean in the sixteenth and seventeenth centuries and then in the eighteenth-century Atlantic world. A second crucial factor in the rise of Europe was the Industrial Revolution, which dramatically increased the pace of production and distribution while reducing their cost, thereby allowing Europeans to control other countries first economically and then politically. By the middle of the nineteenth century the gap between Western industrial production and standards of living and those of the non-West had grown dramatically, bringing with it the economic dependence of non-Western nations, meager wages for their largely impoverished populations, and increasingly aggressive Western imperial ambitions (see Chapter 25).

ONLINE DOCUMENT PROJECT
Inventing a New Workforce

How were social and economic change connected in nineteenth-century England?

Read sources on early industrial manufacturing, and then complete a quiz and writing assignment based on the evidence and details from this chapter. *See inside the front cover to learn more.*

| How did work evolve during the Industrial Revolution, and how did daily life change for working people? | How did the changes brought about by the Industrial Revolution lead to new social classes, and how did people respond to the new structure? | ✔ LearningCurve Check what you know. |

CHAPTER 23 STUDY GUIDE

STEP 1 GET STARTED ONLINE

✓ **LearningCurve**

Now that you've read the chapter, make it stick by completing the LearningCurve activity.

STEP 2 EXPLAIN WHY IT MATTERS

Put your reading into practice. Identify each term below, and then explain why it matters in world history.

TERM	WHO OR WHAT & WHEN	WHY IT MATTERS
Industrial Revolution (p. 684)		
spinning jenny (p. 685)		
water frame (p. 685)		
steam engines (p. 686)		
Rocket (p. 688)		
Crystal Palace (p. 689)		
iron law of wages (p. 690)		
tariff protection (p. 694)		
Factory Act of 1833 (p. 698)		
separate spheres (p. 699)		
Mines Act of 1842 (p. 700)		
Luddites (p. 703)		
class-consciousness (p. 704)		
Combination Acts (p. 705)		

STEP 3 MOVE BEYOND THE BASICS

To demonstrate a more advanced understanding of the changes brought on by the process of industrialization, fill in the chart below with descriptions of key aspects of work and home life for cottage and factory workers. How did industrialization change the way that workers thought about themselves and their communities?

	Cottage Industry	Factory Work
Nature of Work		
Work and Gender		
Work and Children		
Relationship to Home Life		
Identity/Class-Consciousness		

STEP 4 PUT IT ALL TOGETHER

Now, take a step back and try to explain the big picture. Remember to use specific examples from the chapter in your answers.

THE INDUSTRIAL REVOLUTION IN BRITAIN

▶ What advantages help explain Britain's early industrialization? How did those advantages combine to spark the Industrial Revolution?

▶ How did British innovators solve the eighteenth-century energy crisis? How did their solution help transform the British economy?

INDUSTRIALIZATION IN CONTINENTAL EUROPE

▶ Compare and contrast conditions in Continental Europe before and after 1815. What made conditions after 1815 more favorable to industrialization than conditions before 1815?

▶ What role did government play in continental industrialization? How did continental governments work with private individuals and companies to promote economic development?

RELATIONS BETWEEN CAPITAL AND LABOR

▶ How did ideas about "women's work" change as a result of industrialization?

▶ What is class-consciousness? How did industrialization help produce a new sense among workers of their own social identity?

LOOKING BACK, LOOKING AHEAD

▶ How did developments between 1600 and 1800 contribute to the rise of Europe to world dominance in the nineteenth century?

▶ Argue for or against the following proposition: "Given contemporary trends, the dominance of the West in the nineteenth and twentieth centuries should be seen as a temporary aberration, rather than as a fundamental and permanent shift in the global balance of power."

> ### IN YOUR OWN WORDS

Imagine that you must give an oral report to the class answering the following question: What were the social, cultural, and economic consequences of the Industrial Revolution? What would be the most important points and why?

24

IDEOLOGIES OF CHANGE IN EUROPE

1815–1914

> What role did social conflict play in nineteenth-century European politics? Chapter 25 examines political and ideological conflict in nineteenth-century Europe. After 1815 the powers that defeated Napoleon united under a revived conservatism to stamp out the spread of liberal and democratic reforms. In response, powerful ideologies — liberalism, nationalism, and socialism — emerged to oppose conservatism. All played critical roles in the great popular upheaval that eventually swept across Europe in the revolutions of 1848. These revolutions failed, however, and gave way to more sober — and more successful — nation building in the 1860s. European political leaders and middle-class nationalists also began to deal effectively with the challenges of the emerging urban society. One way they did so was through nationalism — mass identification with a nation-state that was increasingly responsive to the needs of its people.

Christabel Pankhurst, Militant Suffragette Christabel Pankhurst led the British Women's Social and Political Union, whose motto was "deeds, not words." This photo was taken in 1912 in Paris, where Pankhurst was living to avoid arrest for her increasingly violent actions to obtain the vote for women, including bombing the home of the future prime minister. Women in Britain and many other countries gained the right to vote in the years immediately after World War I. (© Hulton-Deutsch Collection/Corbis)

> How did the allies fashion a peace settlement in 1815, and what radical ideas emerged between 1815 and 1848?

> Why did revolutions triumph briefly throughout most of Europe in 1848, and why did they fail?

> How did strong leaders and nation building transform Italy, Germany, and Russia?

> What was the impact of urban growth on cities, social classes, families, and ideas?

> How did nationalism and socialism shape European politics in the decades before the Great War?

✓ **LearningCurve**

After reading the chapter, use LearningCurve to retain what you've read.

How did the allies fashion a peace settlement in 1815, and what radical ideas emerged between 1815 and 1848?

LA BALANCE POLITIQUE.

Adjusting the Balance

The Englishman on the left uses his money to counterbalance the people that the Prussian and the fat Metternich are gaining in Saxony and Italy. Alexander I sits happily on his prize, Poland. This cartoon captures the essence of how the educated public thought about the balance-of-power diplomacy resulting in the Treaty of Vienna. ("*La Balance Politique*," 1815, colored etching/Deutsches Historisches Museum, Berlin, Germany/© DHM/The Bridgeman Art Library)

Congress of Vienna
▶ A meeting of the Quadruple Alliance (Russia, Prussia, Austria, Great Britain) and France held in 1814–1815 to fashion a general peace settlement that attempted to redraw Europe's political map after the defeat of Napoleonic France.

conservatism
▶ A political philosophy that stressed retaining traditional values and institutions, including hereditary monarchy and a strong landowning aristocracy.

AFTER FINALLY DEFEATING NAPOLEON, the conservative aristocratic monarchies of Russia, Prussia, Austria, and Great Britain—known as the Quadruple Alliance (see Chapter 22)—agreed to meet at the Congress of Vienna to fashion a lasting peace settlement. By carefully managing the European balance of power and embracing conservative restoration, they brokered an agreement that contributed to fifty years without major warfare in Europe (see Map 24.1, page 714).

In the years following the peace settlement, intellectuals and social observers sought to harness the radical ideas of the revolutionary age to new political movements. Many rejected conservatism, a political philosophy that stressed retaining traditional values and institutions. Radical thinkers developed alternative ideologies and tried to convince society to act on them.

The Political and Social Situation after 1815

When the Quadruple Alliance, along with representatives of minor powers, met together at the Congress of Vienna they combined leniency toward France with strong defensive measures. The Low Countries—Belgium and Holland—were

CHAPTER LOCATOR | **How did the allies fashion a peace settlement in 1815?** | Why did revolutions throughout Europe in 1848 triumph and why did they fail?

ca. 1790s–1840s
Romantic movement in literature and the arts

1814–1815
Congress of Vienna

1832
Reform Bill in Britain

ca. 1840s–1890s
Realism is dominant in Western literature

1845–1851
Great Famine in Ireland

1848
Revolutions in France, Austria, and Prussia; Marx and Engels, *The Communist Manifesto*; first public health law in Britain

1854
Pasteur studies fermentation and develops pasteurization

1854–1870
Development of germ theory

1859
Darwin, *On the Origin of Species by the Means of Natural Selection*

1859–1870
Unification of Italy

1861
Freeing of Russian serfs

1866–1871
Unification of Germany

1873
Stock market crash spurs renewed anti-Semitism in central and eastern Europe

1883
First social security laws to help workers in Germany

1889–1914
Second Socialist International

1890–1900
Massive industrialization surge in Russia

1904–1905
Russo-Japanese War

1905
Revolution in Russia

1906–1914
Social reform in Britain

united under an enlarged Dutch monarchy capable of opposing France more effectively. Prussia received considerably more territory along France's eastern border to stand as a "sentinel on the Rhine" against renewed French aggression. At the same time, France did not have to pay any war reparations and it did not lose large amounts of territory.

In their moderation toward France, the allies were motivated by self-interest and traditional ideas about the balance of power. To the peacemakers, especially to Klemens von Metternich (1773–1859), Austria's foreign minister, the balance of power meant an international equilibrium of political and military forces that would discourage aggression by any state or combination of states. The Quadruple Alliance members, therefore, agreed to meet periodically to discuss their common interests and to consider appropriate measures to maintain peace in Europe. This agreement marked the beginning of the European "congress system," which lasted long into the nineteenth century.

Conservatism After 1815

The peace settlement's domestic side was much less moderate. In 1815, under Metternich's leadership, Austria, Prussia, and Russia formed the Holy Alliance, dedicated to crushing the ideas and politics of the revolutionary era. Metternich's

| How did strong leaders and nation building transform Italy, Germany, and Russia? | What was the impact of urban growth on cities, social classes, families, and ideas? | How did nationalism and socialism shape politics in the decades before the Great War? | ✓ LearningCurve Check what you know. |

MAP 24.1 ■ Europe in 1815

In 1815 Europe contained many different states, but after the defeat of Napoleon international politics was dominated by the five Great Powers: Russia, Prussia, Austria, Great Britain, and France. (The number rises to six if one includes the Ottoman Empire.)

> MAPPING THE PAST

ANALYZING THE MAP: Trace the political boundaries of each Great Power, and compare their geographical strengths and weaknesses. What territories did Prussia and Austria gain as a result of the war with Napoleon?

CONNECTIONS: How did Prussia's and Austria's territorial gains contribute to the balance of power established at the Congress of Vienna? What other factors enabled the Great Powers to achieve such a long-lasting peace?

policies dominated the entire German Confederation of thirty-eight independent German states (Map 24.1). It was through the German Confederation that Metternich had the repressive Karlsbad Decrees issued in 1819. These decrees required the member states to root out radical ideas in their universities and newspapers, and a permanent committee was established to investigate and punish any liberal or radical organizations.

CHAPTER LOCATOR | **How did the allies fashion a peace settlement in 1815?** | Why did revolutions throughout Europe in 1848 triumph and why did they fail?

Adhering to a conservative political philosophy, Metternich believed that strong governments were needed to protect society from its worst instincts. Like many European conservatives of his time, Metternich believed that liberalism (see below), as embodied in revolutionary America and France, had been responsible for a generation of war with untold bloodshed and suffering.

Another belief that Metternich opposed, which was often allied with liberalism, was nationalism, the idea that each national group had a right to establish its own independent government. The Habsburg's Austrian Empire was a dynastic state dominated by Germans but containing many other national groups. This multinational state was both strong and weak. It was strong because of its large population and vast territories, but weak because of its many and potentially dissatisfied nationalities. In these circumstances, Metternich opposed both liberalism and nationalism, for Austria could not accommodate those ideologies and remain a powerful empire.

Liberalism and the Middle Class

The principal ideas of liberalism—liberty and equality—were by no means defeated in 1815. Liberalism demanded representative government and equality before the law. The idea of liberty also meant specific individual freedoms: freedom of the press, freedom of speech, freedom of assembly, and freedom from arbitrary arrest.

Liberalism faced more radical ideological competitors in the early nineteenth century. Opponents of liberalism especially criticized its economic principles, which called for unrestricted private enterprise and no government interference in the economy. This philosophy was popularly known as the doctrine of laissez faire (lay-say FEHR). In early-nineteenth-century Britain economic liberalism was embraced most enthusiastically by business groups and thus became a doctrine associated with business interests.

In the early nineteenth century liberal political ideals also became more closely associated with narrow class interests. Early-nineteenth-century liberals favored representative government, but they generally wanted property qualifications attached to the right to vote and to serve in Parliament.

As liberalism became increasingly identified with the middle class after 1815, some intellectuals and foes of conservatism felt that liberalism did not go nearly far enough. They called for replacing monarchical rule with republics, for democracy through universal male suffrage, and for greater economic and social equality. These democrats and republicans were more radical than the liberals, and they were more willing to endorse violence to achieve goals. As a result, liberals and radical republicans could join forces against conservatives only up to a point.

The Growing Appeal of Nationalism

Nationalism was a second radical ideology that emerged in the years after 1815. Early advocates of the "national idea" argued that the members of what we would call today an ethnic group had its own genius and its own cultural unity, which were manifested especially in a common language, history, and territory.

liberalism
▶ A philosophy whose principal ideas were equality and liberty; liberals demanded representative government and equality before the law as well as such individual freedoms as freedom of the press, freedom of speech, freedom of assembly, and freedom from arbitrary arrest.

laissez faire
▶ A doctrine of economic liberalism advocating unrestricted private enterprise and no government interference in the economy.

nationalism
▶ The idea that each people had its own genius and its own cultural unity, which manifested itself especially in a common language and history and could serve as the basis for an independent political state.

How did strong leaders and nation building transform Italy, Germany, and Russia?

What was the impact of urban growth on cities, social classes, families, and ideas?

How did nationalism and socialism shape politics in the decades before the Great War?

✔ LearningCurve
Check what you know.

715

In fact, such cultural unity was more a dream than a reality as local dialects abounded, historical memory divided the inhabitants of the different states as much as it unified them, and a variety of ethnic groups shared the territory of most states.

Nevertheless, many European nationalists sought to make the territory of each people coincide with well-defined boundaries in an independent nation-state. It was this political goal that made nationalism so explosive in central and eastern Europe after 1815, when there were either too few states (Austria, Russia, and the Ottoman Empire) or too many (the Italian peninsula and the German Confederation), and when different peoples overlapped and intermingled.

Between 1815 and 1850 most people who believed in nationalism also believed in either liberalism or radical democratic republicanism. A common faith in the creativity and nobility of the people was perhaps the single most important reason for the linking of these two concepts. Liberals and especially democrats saw the people as the ultimate source of all good government. They agreed that the benefits of self-government would only be possible if the people were united by common traditions that transcended class and local interests. Thus individual liberty and love of a free nation overlapped greatly.

Yet early nationalists also stressed the differences among peoples, and they developed a strong sense of "we" and "they." Thus, while European nationalism's main thrust was liberal and democratic, below the surface lurked ideas of national superiority and national mission.

The Birth of Socialism

socialism

▶ A radical political doctrine that opposed individualism and the fragmentation of society and that advocated international cooperation and a sense of community; key ideas were economic planning, greater economic equality, and state regulation of property.

Socialism, the new radical doctrine after 1815, began in France. Early French socialists shared a sense of disappointment in the outcome of the French Revolution. They were also alarmed by the rise of laissez faire and the emergence of modern industry, which they saw as fostering inequality and selfish individualism. There was, they believed, an urgent need for a further reorganization of society to establish cooperation and a new sense of community.

Early French socialists felt an intense desire to help the poor, and they preached greater economic equality between the rich and the poor. Inspired by the economic planning implemented in revolutionary France (see Chapter 22), they argued that the government should rationally organize the economy to control prices and prevent unemployment. Socialists also believed that government should regulate private property or that private property should be abolished and replaced by state or community ownership.

> **Early French Socialists:**

- Henri de Saint-Simon (1760–1825): Believed that the key to progress was technocratic government and economic planning
- Charles Fourier (1772–1837): Envisaged a socialist utopia of self-sufficient communities; called for the abolition of marriage, free unions based only on love, and sexual freedom
- Pierre-Joseph Proudhon (1809–1865): Argued that property was profit stolen from the workers who actually produced all wealth

CHAPTER LOCATOR | How did the allies fashion a peace settlement in 1815?

Why did revolutions throughout Europe in 1848 triumph and why did they fail?

716   CHAPTER 24   IDEOLOGIES OF CHANGE IN EUROPE

Up to the 1840s France was the center of socialism, as it had been the center of revolution in Europe, but in the following decades the German intellectual Karl Marx (1818–1883) would weave the diffuse strands of social thought into a distinctly modern ideology. In 1848 the thirty-year-old Karl Marx and the twenty-eight-year-old Friedrich Engels (see page 703) published *The Communist Manifesto*, which became the guiding text of socialism.

Marx argued that middle-class interests and those of the industrial working class were inevitably opposed to each other. According to the *Manifesto*, the "history of all previously existing society is the history of class struggles." In Marx's view, one class had always exploited the other, and, with the advent of modern industry, society was split more clearly than ever before: between the middle class—the bourgeoisie—and the modern working class—the proletariat.

Just as the bourgeoisie had triumphed over the feudal aristocracy in the French Revolution, Marx predicted that the proletariat would conquer the bourgeoisie in a new revolution. While a tiny majority owned the means of production and grew richer, the ever-poorer proletariat was constantly growing in size and in class-consciousness. Marx believed that the critical moment when class conflict would result in revolution was very near.

bourgeoisie
▶ The well-educated, prosperous, middle-class groups.

proletariat
▶ The Marxist term for the modern working class.

QUICK REVIEW <

What connections were there between liberalism and nationalism in the first half of the nineteenth century?

How did strong leaders and nation building transform Italy, Germany, and Russia?

What was the impact of urban growth on cities, social classes, families, and ideas?

How did nationalism and socialism shape politics in the decades before the Great War?

LearningCurve
Check what you know.

Why did revolutions triumph briefly throughout most of Europe in 1848, and why did they fail?

Das merkwürdige Jahr 1848. ____ Eine neue Bilderzeitung.

Street Fighting in Berlin, 1848

This contemporary lithograph portrays a street battle on March 18, 1848, between Prussian troops loyal to King Frederick William IV and civilian men and women demonstrators. The king withdrew his troops the following day rather than kill anymore of his "beloved Berliners." Revolutionaries across Europe often dug up paving stones and used them as weapons. The tricolor flag achieved prominence during the revolution as the symbol of a united and democratic Germany. (akg-images)

AS LIBERAL, NATIONALIST, AND SOCIALIST FORCES battered the conservatism of 1815, social and economic conditions continued to deteriorate for many Europeans, adding to the mounting pressures. In some countries, such as Great Britain, change occurred gradually and largely peacefully, but in 1848 radical political and social ideologies combined with economic crisis to produce revolutionary movements that demanded an end to repressive government.

Social and Economic Conflict

The slow and uneven spread of industrialization in Europe after 1815 (see Chapter 23) meant that the benefits of higher productivity were not felt by many. In Great Britain, the earliest adopter of industrial methods, living standards did not rise until the 1840s, and this trend took longer to spread to the continent. Most of

CHAPTER LOCATOR | How did the allies fashion a peace settlement in 1815? | **Why did revolutions throughout Europe in 1848 triumph and why did they fail?**

718 CHAPTER 24 IDEOLOGIES OF CHANGE IN EUROPE

the continent remained agricultural, and the traditional social hierarchy, dominated by a landowning aristocracy, persisted. In the early nineteenth century the pressures of a rapidly growing population, the adoption of new forms of agriculture, and the spread of exploitative rural industry destabilized these existing patterns.

Many of the social conflicts that ensued resembled those of the eighteenth century. Peasants resented the demands of their noble landlords and state tax collectors. Many lost access to collective land due to enclosure and the adoption of more efficient farming techniques. The growing number of cottage workers resisted exploitation by merchant capitalists, and journeymen battled masters in urban industries. Serfdom still existed in the Hungarian provinces of the Austrian Empire, Prussian Silesia, and Russia.[1]

What transformed these conflicts was the political ideologies born from the struggles and unfulfilled hopes of the French Revolution—liberalism, nationalism, and socialism—as well as the newly invigorated conservatism that stood against them. These ideologies helped turn economic and social conflicts into the revolutions of 1848.

Liberal Reform in Great Britain

The English parliamentary system guaranteed basic civil rights, but only about 8 percent of the population could vote for representatives to Parliament. By the 1780s there was growing interest in reform, but the French Revolution threw the British aristocracy into a panic. After 1815 the British government put down popular protests over unemployment and the high cost of grain caused by the Napoleonic Wars with repressive legislation and military force.

By the early 1830s the social and economic changes created by industrialization began to be felt in politics. In 1832 continuous pressure from the liberal middle classes and popular unrest convinced the king and the House of Lords that they needed to act. The Reform Bill of 1832 moved British politics in a more democratic direction by giving new industrial areas increased representation in the House of Commons and by increasing the number of voters by about 50 percent. Two years later, the New Poor Law called for unemployed and indigent families to be placed in harsh workhouses rather than receiving aid from local parishes to remain in their own homes. With this act, Britain's rulers sought to relieve middle-class taxpayers of the burden of poor relief and to encourage unemployed rural workers to migrate to cities and take up industrial work.

Thus limited democratic reform was counterbalanced by harsh measures against the poor, both linked to the new social and economic circumstances of the Industrial Revolution. Many working people protested their exclusion from voting and the terms of the New Poor Law. Between 1838 and 1848 they joined the Chartist movement (see page 704), which demanded universal male suffrage. In 1847 the ruling conservative party, known as the Tories, sought to appease working people with the Ten Hours Act, which limited the workday for women and young people in factories to ten hours. Tory aristocrats championed such legislation in order to compete with the middle class for working-class support.

This competition meant that the Parliamentary state functioned well in eliciting support from its people and thereby managed unrest without the outbreak of revolution. Another factor favoring Great Britain's largely peaceful evolution in

How did strong leaders and nation building transform Italy, Germany, and Russia?　|　What was the impact of urban growth on cities, social classes, families, and ideas?　|　How did nationalism and socialism shape politics in the decades before the Great War?　|　✓ LearningCurve Check what you know.

719

the nineteenth century was the fact that living standards had begun to rise significantly by the 1840s, as the benefits of industrialization finally began to be felt. Thus England avoided the violence and turmoil of the revolutions of 1848 that shook continental Europe.

The people of Ireland did not benefit from these circumstances. Long ruled as a conquered people, the population was mostly composed of Irish Catholic peasants who rented their land from a tiny minority of Protestant landowners, many of whom resided in England. Ruthlessly exploited and growing rapidly in numbers, the rural population around 1800 lived under abominable conditions.

In spite of terrible conditions, Ireland's population doubled from 4 million to 8 million between 1780 and 1840, fueled in large part by the calories and nutritive qualities of the potato. However, the potato crop failed in 1845, 1846, 1848, and 1851 in Ireland and throughout much of Europe. Many suffered in Europe, but in Ireland, where dependency on the potato was much more widespread, the result was starvation and death. The British government, committed to laissez-faire economic policies, reacted slowly and utterly inadequately. One and a half million died, while another million fled between 1845 and 1851, primarily to the United States and Great Britain. The Great Famine, as this tragedy came to be known, intensified anti-British feeling and promoted Irish nationalism.

Revolutions in France

Louis XVIII's Constitutional Charter of 1814 was essentially a liberal constitution. It protected economic and social gains made by the middle class and the peasantry in the French Revolution, recognized intellectual and artistic freedom, and created a parliament with upper and lower houses. The charter was anything but democratic, however. Only a tiny minority of males had the right to vote for the legislative deputies who, with the king and his ministers, made the nation's laws.

Louis's conservative successor, Charles X (r. 1824–1830), wanted to re-establish the old order in France. To rally French nationalism and gain popular support, he exploited a long-standing dispute with Muslim Algeria. In June 1830 a French force crossed the Mediterranean and took the capital of Algiers. Buoyed by this success, Charles overplayed his hand and repudiated the Constitutional Charter. After three days of uprisings in Paris, which sparked a series of revolts by frustrated liberals and democrats across Europe, Charles fled. His cousin Louis Philippe (r. 1830–1848) accepted the Constitutional Charter of 1814 and assumed the title of the "king of the French people." Still, the situation in France remained fundamentally unchanged. Political and social reformers and the poor of Paris were bitterly disappointed.

During the 1840s this sense of disappointment was worsened by bad harvests and the slow development of industrialization. Similar conditions prevailed across continental Europe, which was soon rocked by insurrections. In February full-scale revolution broke out in France, and its shock waves ripped across the continent.

Louis Philippe had refused to approve social legislation or consider electoral reform. Frustrated desires for change, high-level financial scandals, and crop failures in 1845 and 1846 united diverse groups of the king's opponents, including merchants, intellectuals, shopkeepers, and workers. In February 1848, as popular revolt broke out, barricades went up, and Louis Philippe abdicated.

CHAPTER LOCATOR | How did the allies fashion a peace settlement in 1815? | Why did revolutions throughout Europe in 1848 triumph and why did they fail?

CHAPTER 24
720 IDEOLOGIES OF CHANGE IN EUROPE

The Triumph of Democratic Republics

This French illustration offers an opinion of the initial revolutionary breakthrough in 1848. The peoples of Europe, joined together around their respective national banners, are achieving republican freedom, which is symbolized by the Statue of Liberty and the discarded crowns. The woman wearing pants at the base of the statue — very radical attire — represents feminist hopes for liberation. (Lithograph by Frederic Sorrieu [1807–ca. 1861]. Musée de la Ville de Paris, Musée Carnavalet, Paris, France/Giraudon/The Bridgeman Art Library)

> PICTURING THE PAST

ANALYZING THE IMAGE: How many different flags can you count and/or identify? How would you characterize the types of people marching and the mood of the crowd?

CONNECTIONS: What do the angels, Statue of Liberty, and discarded crowns suggest about the artist's view of the events of 1848? Do you think this illustration was created before or after the collapse of the revolution in France? Why?

The revolutionaries quickly drafted a democratic, republican constitution for France's Second Republic, granting the right to vote to every adult male. Slaves in the French colonies were freed, the death penalty was abolished, and national workshops were established for unemployed Parisian workers.

Yet there were profound differences within the revolutionary coalition in Paris. The socialism promoted by radical republicans frightened not only the liberal middle and upper classes but also the peasants, many of whom owned land. When the French masses voted for delegates to the new Constituent Assembly in late April 1848, the monarchists won a clear majority. When the new government dissolved the national workshops in Paris, workers rose in a spontaneous insurrection. After three terrible "June Days" and the death or injury of more than ten thousand people, the republican army stood triumphant in a sea of working-class blood and hatred.

The revolution in France thus ended in failure. The middle and working classes had turned against each other. In place of a generous democratic republic,

How did strong leaders and nation building transform Italy, Germany, and Russia?

What was the impact of urban growth on cities, social classes, families, and ideas?

How did nationalism and socialism shape politics in the decades before the Great War?

LearningCurve
Check what you know.

721

the Constituent Assembly completed a constitution featuring a strong executive. This allowed Louis Napoleon, nephew of Napoleon Bonaparte, to win a landslide victory in the December 1848 election based on promises to lead a strong government in favor of popular interests.

President Louis Napoleon at first shared power with a conservative National Assembly. But in 1851 Louis Napoleon dismissed the Assembly and seized power in a coup d'état. A year later he called on the French to make him hereditary emperor, and 97 percent voted to do so in a national plebiscite. Louis Napoleon then ruled France's Second Empire as Napoleon III, initiating policies favoring economic growth and urban development to appease the populace.

The Revolutions of 1848 in Central Europe

Throughout central Europe, social conflicts were exacerbated by the economic crises of 1845 to 1846. News of the upheaval in France in 1848 provoked the outbreak of revolution. Liberals demanded written constitutions, representative government, and greater civil liberties from authoritarian regimes. When governments hesitated, popular revolts followed. Urban workers and students allied with middle-class liberals and peasants. In the face of these coalitions, monarchs made hasty concessions. Soon, however, popular revolutionary fronts broke down as they had in France.

Compared with the situation in France, where political participation by working people reached its peak, revolts in central Europe tended to be dominated by social elites. They were also more sharply divided between moderate constitutionalists and radical republicans. The revolution in the Austrian Empire began in 1848 in Hungary, when nationalistic Hungarians demanded national autonomy, full civil liberties, and universal suffrage. When Viennese students and workers also took to the streets and peasant disorders broke out, the Habsburg emperor Ferdinand I (r. 1835–1848) capitulated and promised reforms and a liberal constitution. The coalition of revolutionaries was not stable, however. When the monarchy abolished serfdom, the newly free peasants lost interest in the political and social questions agitating the cities.

The revolutionary coalition was also weakened and ultimately destroyed by conflicting national aspirations. In March the Hungarian revolutionary leaders pushed through an extremely liberal constitution, but they also sought to create a unified Hungarian nation. The minority groups that formed half the population objected that such unification would hinder their own political autonomy and cultural independence. Likewise, Czech nationalists based in Bohemia and the city of Prague came into conflict with German nationalists. Thus nationalism within the Austrian Empire enabled the monarchy to play off one ethnic group against the other.

The monarchy's first breakthrough came in June when the army crushed a working-class revolt in Prague. In October the predominantly peasant troops of the regular Austrian army attacked the student and working-class radicals in Vienna and retook the city. When Ferdinand I abdicated in favor of his young nephew, Franz Joseph (see page 741), only Hungary had yet to be brought under control. Nicholas I of Russia (r. 1825–1855) obligingly lent his support. In June 1849, 130,000 Russian troops poured into Hungary and subdued the country. For a number of years the Habsburgs ruled Hungary as a conquered territory.

CHAPTER LOCATOR | How did the allies fashion a peace settlement in 1815? | **Why did revolutions throughout Europe in 1848 triumph and why did they fail?**

After Austria, Prussia was the largest and most influential kingdom in the German Confederation. Prior to 1848, middle-class Prussian liberals had sought to reshape Prussia into a liberal constitutional monarchy, which would lead the confederation's thirty-eight states into a unified nation. When artisans and factory workers in Berlin exploded in revolt in March 1848 and joined with middle-class liberals against the monarchy, Prussian king Frederick William IV (r. 1840–1861) caved in. On March 21 he promised to grant Prussia a liberal constitution and to merge Prussia into a new national German state.

Elections were held across the German Confederation for a national parliament, which convened to write a federal constitution for a unified German state. Members of the new parliament completed drafting a liberal constitution in March 1849 and elected King Frederick William of Prussia emperor of the new German national state. By early 1849, however, Frederick William had reasserted his royal authority, contemptuously refusing to accept the "crown from the gutter." When Frederick William tried to get the small monarchs of Germany to elect him emperor on his own terms, with authoritarian power, Austria balked. Supported by Russia, Austria forced Prussia to renounce all its unification schemes in late 1850.

Thus, across Europe, the uprisings of 1848, which had been inspired by the legacy of the late-eighteenth-century revolutionary era, were unsuccessful. Reform movements splintered into competing factions, while the forces of order proved better organized and more united, on both a domestic and international level.

QUICK REVIEW

How did Britain avoid the waves of revolutionary upheaval that struck the continent?

| How did strong leaders and nation building transform Italy, Germany, and Russia? | What was the impact of urban growth on cities, social classes, families, and ideas? | How did nationalism and socialism shape politics in the decades before the Great War? | ✓ LearningCurve Check what you know. |

How did strong leaders and nation building transform Italy, Germany, and Russia?

The Fruits of Terrorism

In the late 1870s a small group of revolutionaries believed that killing the tsar could destroy the Russian state. Succeeding in blowing up the reforming Alexander II after several near misses, the five assassins, including one woman, were quickly caught and hanged. Russia entered an era of reaction and harsh authoritarian rule. (Visual Connection Archive)

LOUIS NAPOLEON'S TRIUMPH IN 1848 and his authoritarian rule in the 1850s provided Europe's victorious forces of order with a new political model. To what extent might the expanding urban middle classes and even portions of the working classes rally to a strong and essentially conservative national state that also promised change? In central Europe a resounding answer came with the national unification of Italy and Germany.

The Russian empire also experienced profound political crises in this period, but they were unlike those in Italy or Germany because Russia was already a vast multinational state. It became clear to Russian leaders that they had to embrace the process of **modernization**, defined narrowly as the changes that enable a country to compete effectively with the leading countries at a given time.

modernization

▶ The changes that enable a country to compete effectively with the leading countries at a given time.

Cavour, Garibaldi, and the Unification of Italy

Italy had never been a united nation prior to 1850. A battleground for the Great Powers after 1494, Italy was reorganized in 1815 at the Congress of Vienna. Austria received the northern provinces of Lombardy and Venetia. Sardinia and

CHAPTER LOCATOR | How did the allies fashion a peace settlement in 1815? | Why did revolutions throughout Europe in 1848 triumph and why did they fail?

CHAPTER 24
724 IDEOLOGIES OF CHANGE IN EUROPE

Piedmont fell under the rule of an Italian monarch, and Tuscany shared north-central Italy with several smaller states. The papacy ruled over central Italy and Rome, while a branch of the Bourbons ruled Naples and Sicily (Map 24.2).

After 1815 the goal of a unified Italian nation captivated many Italians, but there was no agreement on how it could be achieved. In 1848 the idealistic nationalist Giuseppe Mazzini's efforts to form a democratic Italian republic were crushed by Austrian forces. Temporarily driven from Rome during the upheavals of 1848, a frightened Pope Pius IX (pontificate 1846–1878) turned against most modern trends, including national unification. At the same time, Victor Emmanuel, king of independent Sardinia, retained the moderate liberal constitution granted under duress in March 1848. To the Italian middle classes, Sardinia (see Map 24.2) appeared to be a liberal, progressive state ideally suited to drive Austria out of northern Italy and achieve the goal of national unification.

Sardinia had the good fortune of being led by Count Camillo Benso di Cavour. Gavour's national goals were limited and realistic. Until 1859 he sought unity only for the states of northern and perhaps central Italy in a greatly expanded kingdom of Sardinia.

MAP 24.2 ■ The Unification of Italy, 1859–1870

The leadership of Sardinia-Piedmont, nationalist fervor, and Garibaldi's attack on the Kingdom of the Two Sicilies were decisive factors in the unification of Italy.

Legend:
- Kingdom of Sardinia-Piedmont before 1859
- To Kingdom of Sardinia-Piedmont, 1859
- To Kingdom of Sardinia-Piedmont, 1860
- To Kingdom of Italy, 1866, 1870
- Major battle
- Northern boundary of Kingdom of Italy after unification

How did strong leaders and nation building transform Italy, Germany, and Russia?

What was the impact of urban growth on cities, social classes, families, and ideas?

How did nationalism and socialism shape politics in the decades before the Great War?

LearningCurve
Check what you know.

In the 1850s Cavour worked to consolidate Sardinia as a liberal constitutional state capable of leading northern Italy. He worked out a secret alliance with Napoleon III, and in July 1858 he goaded Austria into attacking Sardinia. The combined Franco-Sardinian forces were victorious, but Napoleon III decided on a compromise peace with the Austrians in July 1859 to avoid offending French Catholics by supporting an enemy of the pope. Sardinia would receive only Lombardy, the area around Milan. Cavour resigned in protest.

Popular revolts and Italian nationalism salvaged Cavour's plans. While the war against Austria raged in the north, dedicated nationalists in central Italy had risen and driven out their rulers. Cavour returned to power in early 1860, and the people of central Italy voted overwhelmingly to join a greatly enlarged kingdom of Sardinia. Cavour had achieved his original goal of a north Italian state (see Map 24.2).

For superpatriots such as Giuseppe Garibaldi (1807–1882), the job of unification was still only half done. Having led a unit of volunteers to several victories over Austrian troops in 1859, Garibaldi emerged in 1860 as an independent force in Italian politics. (See "Individuals in Society: Giuseppe Garibaldi," page 727.)

Secretly supported by Cavour, Garibaldi landed on the shores of Sicily in May 1860. His guerrilla band captured the imagination of the Sicilian peasantry, which rose in rebellion. Garibaldi captured Palermo and crossed to the mainland. When Garibaldi and Victor Emmanuel rode through Naples to cheering crowds, they symbolically sealed the union of north and south, of monarch and people.

The new kingdom of Italy, which did not include Venice until 1866 or Rome until 1870, was a parliamentary monarchy under Victor Emmanuel, neither radical nor democratic. Only a small minority of Italian males could vote. Despite political unity, the propertied classes and the common people were divided. A great social and cultural gap separated the industrializing north from the agrarian south.

Bismarck and German Unification

In the aftermath of 1848 the German states, particularly Austria and Prussia, were locked in a political stalemate, each seeking to block the power of the other within the German Confederation. At the same time, powerful economic forces were undermining the political status quo. Modern industry was growing rapidly within the German customs union, or *Zollverein*. By 1853 all the German states except Austria had joined the customs union, and a new Germany excluding Austria was becoming an economic reality. Rising prosperity from the rapid growth of industrialization after 1850 gave new impetus to middle-class liberals.

By 1859 liberals had assumed control of the parliament that emerged from the upheavals of 1848 in Prussia. The national uprising in Italy in 1859, however, convinced Prussia's tough-minded William I (r. 1861–1888) that political change and even war with Austria or France was possible. William I pushed to raise taxes and increase the defense budget to double the army's size. The Prussian parliament, reflecting the middle class's desire for a less militaristic society, rejected the military budget in 1862, and the liberals triumphed in new elections. King William then called on Count Otto von Bismarck to head a new ministry and defy the parliament.

When Otto von Bismarck (1815–1898) took office as chief minister in 1862, he declared that government would rule without parliamentary consent. Bismarck

CHAPTER LOCATOR | How did the allies fashion a peace settlement in 1815? | Why did revolutions throughout Europe in 1848 triumph and why did they fail?

726   CHAPTER 24   IDEOLOGIES OF CHANGE IN EUROPE

INDIVIDUALS IN SOCIETY
Giuseppe Garibaldi

When Giuseppe Garibaldi visited England in 1864, he received the most triumphant welcome ever given to any foreigner. Honored and feted by politicians and high society, he also captivated the masses. An unprecedented crowd of a half-million people cheered his carriage through the streets of London. These ovations were no fluke. In his time, Garibaldi was probably the most famous and most beloved figure in the world.* How could this be?

A rare combination of wild adventure and extraordinary achievement partly accounted for his demigod status. Born in Nice, Garibaldi went to sea at fifteen and sailed the Mediterranean for twelve years. At seventeen his travels took him to Rome, and he was converted in an almost religious experience to the "New Italy, the Italy of all the Italians." As he later wrote in his best-selling *Autobiography*, "The Rome that I beheld with the eyes of youthful imagination was the Rome of the future — the dominant thought of my whole life."

Sentenced to death in 1834 for his part in a revolutionary uprising in Genoa, Garibaldi barely escaped to South America. For twelve years he led a guerrilla band in Uruguay's struggle for independence from Argentina. "Shipwrecked, ambushed, shot through the neck," he found in a tough young woman, Anna da Silva, a mate and companion in arms. Their first children nearly starved in the jungle while Garibaldi, clad in his long red shirt, fashioned a legend as a fearless freedom fighter.

After he returned to Italy in 1848, the campaigns of his patriotic volunteers against the Austrians in 1848 and 1859 mobilized democratic nationalists. The stage was set for his volunteer army to liberate Sicily against enormous odds, astonishing the world and creating a large Italian state. Garibaldi's achievement matched his legend.

A brilliant fighter, the handsome and inspiring leader was an uncompromising idealist of absolute integrity. He never drew personal profit from his exploits, continuing to milk his goats and rarely possessing more than one change of clothing. When Victor Emmanuel offered him lands and titles after his great victory in 1860, even as the left-leaning volunteers were disbanded and humiliated, Garibaldi declined, saying he could not be bought off. Returning to his farm on a tiny rocky island, he denounced the government without hesitation when he concluded that it was betraying the dream of unification with its ruthless rule in the south. Yet even after a duplicitous Italian government caused two later attacks on Rome

Giuseppe Garibaldi, the charismatic leader, shown in a portrait painted in 1850. (1850 oil on canvas painting by Auguste Etienne [1794–1865]. Musée de l'Armee/akg-images)

to fail, his faith in the generative power of national unity never wavered. Garibaldi showed that ideas and ideals count in history.

Above all, millions of ordinary men and women identified with Garibaldi because they believed that he was fighting for them. They recognized him as one of their own and saw that he remained true to them in spite of his triumphs, thereby ennobling their own lives and aspirations. Welcoming runaway slaves as equals in Latin America, advocating the emancipation of women, introducing social reforms in the south, and pressing for free education and a broader suffrage in the new Italy, Garibaldi the national hero fought for freedom and human dignity. The common people understood and loved him for it.

QUESTIONS FOR ANALYSIS

1. Why was Garibaldi so famous and popular?
2. Nationalism evolved and developed in the nineteenth century. How did Garibaldi fit into this evolution? What kind of a nationalist was he?

ONLINE DOCUMENT PROJECT

How did Italian nationalists respond to unification? Examine evidence from the period following Italian unification, and then complete a quiz and writing assignment based on the evidence and details from this chapter. *See inside the front cover to learn more.*

*Denis Mack Smith, *Garibaldi: A Great Life in Brief* (New York: Alfred A. Knopf, 1956), pp. 136–147; Denis Mack Smith, "Giuseppe Garibaldi," *History Today*, August 1991, pp. 20–26.

727

MAP 24.3 ■ The Unification of Germany, 1866–1871

This map shows how Prussia expanded and a new German Empire was created through two wars, the Austro-Prussian War of 1866 and the Franco-Prussian War of 1870–1871.

had the Prussian bureaucracy continue to collect taxes even though the parliament refused to approve the budget, and he reorganized the army. For their part, the voters of Prussia continued to express their opposition by sending large liberal majorities to the parliament from 1862 to 1866.

In 1866 Bismarck launched the Austro-Prussian War with the intent of expelling Austria from German politics. The war lasted only seven weeks, as the reorganized Prussian army defeated Austria decisively. Bismarck forced Austria to withdraw from German affairs and dissolved the existing German Confederation. The mainly Protestant states north of the Main River were grouped in the new North German Confederation, led by an expanded Prussia (Map 24.3). Each state retained its own local government, but the federal government—William I and Bismarck—controlled the army and foreign affairs.

To make peace with the liberal middle class and the nationalist movement, Bismarck asked the Prussian parliament to approve after the fact all the government's "illegal" spending between 1862 and 1866. Overawed by Bismarck's achievements, middle-class liberals now jumped at the chance to cooperate, opting for national unity and military glory over the battle for truly liberal institutions. Bismarck also followed Napoleon III's example by creating a legislature with members of the lower house elected by universal male suffrage, allowing him to bypass the middle class and appeal directly to the people if necessary.

The final act in the drama of German unification followed quickly with a patriotic war against France. The apparent issue — whether a distant relative of Prussia's William I might become king of Spain — was only a diplomatic pretext. By 1870, alarmed by Prussia's growing power, French leaders had decided on a war to teach Prussia a lesson.

As soon as war against France began in 1870, Bismarck had the whole-hearted support of the south German states. The Germans quickly defeated Louis Napoleon's armies at Sedan on September 1, 1870. Three days later French patriots in Paris proclaimed yet another French republic and vowed to continue fighting. But after five months, in January 1871, a starving Paris surrendered, and France accepted Bismarck's harsh peace terms. By this time the south German states had agreed to join a new German Empire.

The Franco-Prussian War released an enormous surge of patriotic feeling in Germany. The new German Empire had become Europe's most powerful state, and most Germans were enormously proud. Semi-authoritarian nationalism and a "new conservatism," which was based on an alliance of the propertied classes and sought the active support of the working classes, had triumphed in Germany.

The Modernization of Russia

In the 1850s Russia was a poor agrarian society with a rapidly growing population. Almost 90 percent of the population lived off the land, and serfdom was still the basic social institution. Then the Crimean War of 1853 to 1856 arose from the breakdown of the balance of power established at the Congress of Vienna, European competition over influence in the Middle East, and Russian desires to expand into European territories held by the Ottoman Empire. France and Great Britain, aided by Sardinia and the Ottoman Empire, inflicted a humiliating defeat on Russia.

Russia's military defeat showed that it had fallen behind the industrializing nations of western Europe. Moreover, the war had caused hardship and raised the specter of massive peasant rebellion. Military disaster thus forced the new tsar, Alexander II (r. 1855–1881), and his ministers along the path of rapid social change and general modernization.

The first and greatest of the reforms was the freeing of the serfs in 1861. The emancipated peasants received, on average, about half of the land, which was to be collectively owned by peasant villages. The prices for the land were high, and collective ownership limited the possibilities of agricultural improvement and migration to urban areas. Thus the effects of the reform were limited. More successful was reform of the legal system, which established independent courts and equality before the law. The government also relaxed censorship and partially liberalized policies toward Russian Jews.

The Crimean War, 1853–1856

| How did strong leaders and nation building transform Italy, Germany, and Russia? | What was the impact of urban growth on cities, social classes, families, and ideas? | How did nationalism and socialism shape politics in the decades before the Great War? | ✔ LearningCurve Check what you know. |

Russia's greatest strides toward modernization were economic rather than political. Rapid, government-subsidized railroad construction to 1880 enabled agricultural Russia to export grain and thus earn money for further industrialization. Russia began seizing territory in far eastern Siberia, on the border with China; in Central Asia, north of Afghanistan; and in the Islamic lands of the Caucasus.

In 1881 an anarchist assassinated Alexander II, and the reform era came to an abrupt end. Political modernization remained frozen until 1905, but economic modernization sped forward in the massive industrial surge of the 1890s. The key leader was Sergei Witte (suhr-GAY VIH-tuh), the energetic minister of finance. Under Witte's leadership, the government doubled Russia's railroad network by the end of the century and promoted Russian industry with high protective tariffs.

By 1900 Russia was catching up with western Europe and expanding its empire in Asia. By 1903 Russia had established a sphere of influence in Chinese Manchuria and was eyeing northern Korea. When the protests of equally imperialistic Japan were ignored, the Japanese launched a surprise attack on Russian forces in Manchuria in February 1904. After Japan scored repeated victories Russia was forced in September 1905 to accept a humiliating defeat.

Military disaster in East Asia brought political upheaval at home. On January 22, 1905, workers peacefully protesting for improved working conditions and higher wages were attacked by the tsar's troops outside the Winter Palace. This event, known as Bloody Sunday, set off a wave of strikes, peasant uprisings, and troop mutinies across Russia. The revolutionary surge culminated in October 1905 in a paralyzing general strike, which forced the government to capitulate. The tsar, Nicholas II (r. 1894–1917), issued the October Manifesto, which granted full civil rights and promised a popularly elected Duma (DOO-muh; parliament) with real legislative power.

Under the new constitution, Nicholas II retained great powers and the Duma had only limited authority. The middle-class liberals, the largest group in the newly elected Duma, were badly disappointed, and efforts to cooperate with the tsar's ministers soon broke down. In 1907 Nicholas II and his reactionary advisers rewrote the electoral law so as to increase greatly the weight of the propertied classes. On the eve of World War I, Russia was partially modernized, a conservative constitutional monarchy with an agrarian but industrializing economy.

The Russian Revolution of 1905

- ☐ Area of peasant unrest
- ● Major strikes and mutinies

St. Petersburg
Moscow
RUSSIA
Warsaw
Black Sea

October Manifesto

▶ The result of a great general strike in Russia in October 1905, it granted full civil rights and promised a popularly elected Duma (parliament) with real legislative power.

> **QUICK REVIEW**

What role did war play in Italian and German unification?

CHAPTER LOCATOR | How did the allies fashion a peace settlement in 1815? | Why did revolutions throughout Europe in 1848 triumph and why did they fail?

What was
the impact of
urban growth
on cities,
social classes,
families, and
ideas?

This wistful painting of a Spanish square on a rainy day, by Enrique Martínez Cubells y Ruiz (1874–1917), includes a revealing commentary on how scientific discoveries transformed urban life. Coachmen wait atop their expensive hackney cabs for a wealthy clientele, while modern electric streetcars that carry the masses converge on the square from all directions. In this way the development of electricity brought improved urban transportation and enabled the city to expand to the suburbs.
(Museo Muncipal, Madrid, Spain/Giraudon/The Bridgeman Art Library)

BY 1900 WESTERN EUROPE WAS urban and industrial as surely as it had been rural and agrarian in 1800. Rapid urban growth in the nineteenth century worsened long-standing overcrowding and unhealthy living conditions, lending support to voices calling for revolutionary change. In response, government leaders, city planners, reformers, and scientists urgently sought solutions to these challenges.

Urban Development

Since the Middle Ages, European cities had been congested, dirty, and unhealthy. Industrialization greatly worsened these conditions. The steam engine freed industrialists from dependence on the energy of streams and rivers so that by 1800 there was every incentive to build new factories in cities, which had better shipping facilities and a large and ready workforce. Therefore, as industry grew, overcrowded and unhealthy cities expanded rapidly.

| How did strong leaders and nation building transform Italy, Germany, and Russia? | **What was the impact of urban growth on cities, social classes, families, and ideas?** | How did nationalism and socialism shape politics in the decades before the Great War? | ✔️ LearningCurve Check what you know. |

In the 1820s and 1830s people in Britain and France began to worry about the condition of their cities. Parks and open areas were almost nonexistent, and narrow houses were built wall to wall in long rows. Highly concentrated urban populations lived in extremely unsanitary conditions, with open drains and sewers flowing alongside or down the middle of unpaved streets.

The urban challenge—and the growth of socialist movements calling for radical change—eventually brought an energetic response from a generation of reformers. The most famous early reformer was Edwin Chadwick, a British official. Collecting detailed reports from local officials and publishing his findings in 1842, Chadwick concluded that the stinking excrement of communal outhouses could be carried off by water through sewers at less than one-twentieth the cost of removing it by hand. In 1848 Chadwick's report became the basis of Great Britain's first public health law, which created a national health board and gave cities broad authority to build modern sanitary systems. Such sanitary movements won dedicated supporters in the United States, France, and Germany from the 1840s on.

Early sanitary reformers were handicapped by the prevailing miasmatic theory of disease—the belief that people contract disease when they breathe foul odors. In the 1840s and 1850s keen observation by doctors and public health officials suggested that contagion spread through physical contact with filth and not by its odors, thus weakening the miasmatic idea. An understanding of how this occurred came out of the work of Louis Pasteur (1822–1895), who developed the **germ theory** of disease. By 1870 the work of Pasteur and others had demonstrated that specific living organisms caused specific diseases and that those organisms could be controlled. These discoveries led to the development of a number of effective vaccines. Surgeons also applied the germ theory in hospitals, sterilizing not only the wound but everything else that entered the operating room.

The achievements of the bacterial revolution coupled with the public health movement saved millions of lives, particularly after about 1890. In England, France, and Germany death rates declined dramatically, and diphtheria, typhoid, typhus, cholera, and yellow fever became vanishing diseases in the industrializing nations.

More effective urban planning after 1850 also improved the quality of urban life. France took the lead during the rule of Napoleon III (r. 1848–1870), who believed that rebuilding Paris would provide employment, improve living conditions, and glorify and strengthen his empire. Baron Georges Haussmann (1809–1884), whom Napoleon III placed in charge of Paris, destroyed the old medieval core of Paris to create broad tree-lined boulevards, long open vistas, monumental buildings, middle-class housing, parks, and improved sewers and aqueducts. The rebuilding of Paris stimulated urban development throughout Europe, particularly after 1870.

Mass public transportation was also of great importance in the improvement of urban living conditions. In the 1890s countries in North America and Europe adopted an American transit innovation, the electric streetcar. Millions of riders hopped on board during the workweek. On weekends and holidays streetcars carried city people on outings to parks and the countryside, racetracks, and music halls.[2] Electric streetcars also gave people of modest means access to improved housing, as the still-crowded city was able to expand and become less congested.

Industrialization and the growth of global trade also led to urbanization outside of Europe. The tremendous appetite of industrializing nations for raw materials, food, and other goods caused the rapid growth of port cities and mining

germ theory

▶ The idea that disease is caused by the spread of living organisms that can be controlled.

CHAPTER LOCATOR | How did the allies fashion a peace settlement in 1815? | Why did revolutions throughout Europe in 1848 triumph and why did they fail?

732 CHAPTER 24 IDEOLOGIES OF CHANGE IN EUROPE

centers across the world. Many of these new cities consciously emulated European urban planning. For example, from 1880 to 1910 the Argentine capital of Buenos Aires modernized rapidly. The development of Buenos Aires was greatly stimulated by the arrival of many Italian and Spanish immigrants, part of a much larger wave of European migration in this period (see Chapter 27).

Social Inequality and Class

By 1850 at the latest, the wages and living conditions of the working classes were finally improving. Greater economic rewards, however, did not significantly narrow the gap between rich and poor. In fact, economic inequality worsened in Europe over the course of the nineteenth century and reached its height on the eve of World War I.

Despite extreme social inequality, society had not split into two sharply defined opposing classes, as Marx had predicted. Instead economic specialization created an almost unlimited range of jobs, skills, and earnings; one group or subclass blended into another in a complex, confusing hierarchy.

Between the tiny elite of the very rich and the sizable mass of the dreadfully poor existed a range of subclasses, each filled with individuals struggling to rise or at least to hold their own in the social order. A confederation of middle classes was loosely linked by occupations requiring mental, rather than physical, skill. As the upper middle class, composed mainly of successful business families, gained in income and progressively lost all traces of radicalism after the trauma of 1848, they were drawn toward the aristocratic lifestyle.

One step below was a much larger group of moderately successful industrialists and merchants, professionals in law and medicine, and midlevel managers of large public and private institutions. The expansion of industry and technology called for experts with specialized knowledge, and the most valuable of the specialties became solid middle-class professions. Next came independent shopkeepers, small traders, and tiny manufacturers—the lower middle class. Industrialization and urbanization also diversified the lower middle class and expanded the number of white-collar employees. White-collar employees were propertyless, but generally they were fiercely committed to the middle class and to the ideal of moving up in society.

Food, housing, clothes, and behavior all expressed middle-class values. Employment of at least one full-time maid was the clearest sign that a family had crossed the divide from the working classes into the middle classes. Freed from domestic labor, the middle-class wife directed her servants, supervised her children's education, and used her own appearance and that of her home to display the family's status. The middle classes shared a code of expected behavior and morality, which stressed hard work, self-discipline, and personal achievement.

At the beginning of the twentieth century about four out of five Europeans belonged to the working classes, that is people whose livelihoods depended primarily on physical labor. Many of them were small landowning peasants and hired farm hands, especially in eastern Europe. The urban working classes were even less unified than the middle classes. Economic development and increased specialization during the nineteenth century expanded the traditional range of working-class skills, earnings, and experiences. Skilled, semiskilled, and unskilled workers accordingly developed widely divergent lifestyles and cultural values,

| How did strong leaders and nation building transform Italy, Germany, and Russia? | **What was the impact of urban growth on cities, social classes, families, and ideas?** | How did nationalism and socialism shape politics in the decades before the Great War? | ☑ LearningCurve Check what you know. |

733

Hudson's Soap Advertising Postcard, ca. 1903

Early-twentieth-century advertisements, such as this one for Hudson's Soap, reflected the strict class divisions of society.
(Amoret Tanner Collection/The Art Archive at Art Resource, NY)

The Happiness of the Drawing Room *depends upon* the Comfort of the Kitchen.

For the People
HUDSON'S SOAP

and their differences contributed to a keen sense of social status and hierarchy within the working classes.

Highly skilled workers, who made up about 15 percent of the working classes, became known as the labor aristocracy. They were led by construction bosses and factory foremen. The labor aristocracy also included members of the traditional highly skilled handicraft trades that had not transitioned to mechanized production, as well as new kinds of skilled workers such as shipbuilders and railway locomotive engineers.

Below the labor aristocracy stood the complex world of semiskilled and unskilled urban workers. A large number of the semiskilled were factory workers who earned good wages and whose relative importance in the labor force was increasing. Below the semiskilled workers was a larger group of unskilled workers that included day laborers and domestic servants.

To make ends meet, many working-class wives had to join the ranks of working women in the "sweated industries." These industries resembled the old putting-out and cottage industries of earlier times, and they were similar to what we call sweatshops today. The women normally worked at home and were paid by the piece, often making clothing after the advent of the sewing machine in the 1850s.

Despite their harsh lives, the urban working classes found outlets for fun and recreation. Across Europe drinking remained a favorite working-class leisure-time activity along with sports and music halls. Religion continued to provide working people with solace and meaning, although church attendance among the urban working classes declined in the late nineteenth century, especially among men.

The Changing Family

Industrialization and the growth of modern cities also brought great changes to the lives of women and families. As economic conditions improved, only women in poor families tended to work outside the home. The ideal became separate

CHAPTER LOCATOR | How did the allies fashion a peace settlement in 1815? | Why did revolutions throughout Europe in 1848 triumph and why did they fail?

spheres (see page 699), the strict division of labor by sex. This rigid division meant that married women faced great obstacles if they needed or wanted to move into the world of paid employment outside the home. Well-paying jobs were off-limits to women, and a woman's wage was almost always less than a man's, even for the same work.

Because they needed to be able to support their wives, middle-class men did not marry until they were well established in their careers. The system encouraged marriages between much older men and younger women, who had little experience with adult life. Men were encouraged to see themselves as the protectors of their fragile and vulnerable wives.

As the ideology and practice of rigidly separate spheres narrowed women's horizons, their control and influence in the home became increasingly strong throughout Europe in the late nineteenth century. The comfortable home run by the middle-class wife was idealized as a warm shelter in a hard and impersonal urban world. By 1900 working-class families had adopted many middle-class values, but they did not have the means to fully realize the ideals of domestic comfort or separate spheres. Nevertheless, the working-class wife generally determined how the family's money was spent and took charge of all major domestic decisions. The woman's guidance of the household went hand in hand with the increased emotional importance of home and family for all social groups.

Ideas about sexuality within marriage varied. Many French marriage manuals of the late 1800s stressed that women had legitimate sexual needs. In the more puritanical United States, however, sex manuals recommended sexual abstinence for unmarried men and limited sexual activity for married men. Respectable women were thought to experience no sexual pleasure at all from sexual activity.

Medical doctors in both Europe and the United States began to study sexual desires and behavior more closely, and to determine what was considered "normal" and "abnormal." Same-sex attraction, labeled "homosexuality" for the first time, was identified as a "perversion." Governments increasingly regulated prostitution, the treatment of venereal disease, and access to birth control in ways that were shaped by class and gender hierarchies. Medical science also turned its attention to motherhood, and a wave of books instructed middle-class women on how to be better mothers.

Ideas about sexuality and motherhood were inextricably tied up with ideas about race. As European nations embarked on imperialist expansion in the second half of the nineteenth century, the need to maintain the racial superiority that justified empire led to increased concerns about the possible dilution or weakening of the European races. Maintaining healthy bodies, restricting sexuality, preventing interracial marriages, and ensuring that women properly raised their children were all components of racial strength, in the eyes of many European thinkers.

Women in industrializing countries also began to limit the number of children they bore. This revolutionary reduction in family size, in which the comfortable and well-educated classes took the lead, was founded on parents' desire to improve their economic and social position and that of their children. By having fewer youngsters, parents could give those they had advantages, from music lessons to expensive university educations.

The ideal of separate spheres and the rigid gender division of labor meant that middle-class women lacked legal rights and faced discrimination in education and employment. Organizations founded by middle-class feminists campaigned

How did strong leaders and nation building transform Italy, Germany, and Russia?

What was the impact of urban growth on cities, social classes, families, and ideas?

How did nationalism and socialism shape politics in the decades before the Great War?

☑ LearningCurve
Check what you know.

735

for legal equality as well as for access to higher education and professional employment. In the late nineteenth century middle-class women scored some significant victories, such as the 1882 law giving British married women full property rights. Rather than contesting existing notions of women as morally superior guardians of the home, feminists drew on these ideas for legitimacy in speaking out about social issues.

Socialist women leaders usually took a different path. They argued that the liberation of working-class women would come only with the liberation of the entire working class. In the meantime, they championed the cause of working women and won some practical improvements. In a general way, these different approaches to women's issues reflected the diversity of classes and political views in urban society.

Science for the Masses

Breakthroughs in industrial technology stimulated basic scientific inquiry as researchers sought to explain how such things as steam engines and blast furnaces actually worked. The result from the 1830s onward was an explosive growth of fundamental scientific discoveries that were increasingly transformed into material improvements for the general population.

A perfect example of the translation of better scientific knowledge into practical human benefits was the development of the branch of physics known as thermodynamics, the study of the relationship between heat and mechanical energy. By midcentury physicists had formulated the fundamental laws of thermodynamics, which were then applied to mechanical engineering, chemical processes, and many other fields. Electricity was transformed from a curiosity in 1800 to a commercial form of energy. By 1890 the internal combustion engine fueled by petroleum was an emerging competitor to steam and electricity.

Everyday experience and innumerable articles in newspapers and magazines impressed the importance of science on the popular mind. The methods of science acquired unrivaled prestige after 1850. Many educated people came to believe that the union of careful experiment and abstract theory was the only reliable route to truth and objective reality. The Enlightenment idea that natural processes were determined by rigid laws, leaving little room for either divine intervention or human will, won broad acceptance.

Living in an era of rapid change, nineteenth-century thinkers in Europe were fascinated with the idea of evolution and dynamic development. The most influential of all nineteenth-century evolutionary thinkers was Charles Darwin (1809–1882). Darwin believed that all life had gradually evolved from a common ancestral origin in an unending "struggle for survival." Darwin's theory of **evolution** is summarized in the title of his work *On the Origin of Species by the Means of Natural Selection* (1859). He argued that small variations within individuals in one species enabled them to acquire more food and better living conditions and made them more successful in reproducing, thus allowing them to pass their genetic material to the next generation. When a number of individuals within a species became distinct enough that they could no longer interbreed successfully with others, they became a new species.

Darwin's theory of natural selection provoked resistance, particularly because he extended the theory to humans. His findings reinforced the teachings of secu-

evolution

▶ The idea, developed by Charles Darwin, that all life had gradually evolved from a common origin through a process of natural selection; as applied by thinkers in many fields, the idea stressed gradual change and continuous adjustment.

larists such as Marx, who scornfully dismissed religious belief in favor of agnostic or atheistic materialism. Many writers also applied the theory of biological evolution to human affairs. Herbert Spencer (1820–1903), an English philosopher, saw the human race as driven forward to ever-greater specialization and progress by a brutal economic struggle that determines the "survival of the fittest." The idea that human society also evolves, and that the stronger will become powerful and prosperous while the weaker will be conquered or remain poor, became known as Social Darwinism. Powerful nations used this ideology to justify nationalism and expansion, and colonizers to justify imperialism.

Not only did science shape society, but society also shaped science. As nations asserted their differences from one another, they sought "scientific" proof for those differences, which generally meant proof of their own superiority. European and American scientists, anthropologists, and physicians sought to prove that whites were more intelligent than other races, and that northern Europeans were more advanced than southern Europeans. Africans were described and depicted as "missing links" between chimpanzees and Europeans. This scientific racism extended to Jews, who were increasingly described as a separate and inferior race, not a religious group.

Social Darwinism
▶ The application of the theory of biological evolution to human affairs, it sees the human race as driven to ever-greater specialization and progress by an unending economic struggle that determines the survival of the fittest.

Cultural Shifts

In part a revolt against what was perceived as the cold rationality of the Enlightenment, romanticism was characterized by a belief in emotional exuberance, unrestrained imagination, and spontaneity in both art and personal life. Preoccupied with emotional excess, romantic works explored the awesome power of love and desire and of hatred, guilt, and despair. Where Enlightenment thinkers embraced secularization and civic life, romantics delved into religious ecstasy and the hidden recesses of the self. The romantics were passionately moved by nature and decried the growth of modern industry and industrial cities.

romanticism
▶ A movement in art, literature, and music characterized by a belief in emotional exuberance, unrestrained imagination, and spontaneity in both art and personal life.

The French romantic painter Eugène Delacroix (oo-ZHEHN deh-luh-KWAH) (1798–1863) depicted dramatic, colorful scenes that stirred the emotions. He frequently painted non-European places and people, whether lion hunts in Morocco or women in a sultan's harem. Like other romantic works, Delacroix's art reveals the undercurrents of desire and fascination within Europe's imperial ambitions in "exotic" and "savage" places in the nineteenth century.

It was in music that romanticism realized most fully and permanently its goals of free expression and emotional intensity. Abandoning well-defined structures, the great romantic composers used a wide range of forms to create musical landscapes and evoke powerful emotion. The first great romantic composer is among the most famous today, Ludwig van Beethoven (1770–1827).

Romanticism also found a distinctive voice in poetry. In 1798 William Wordsworth (1770–1850) and his fellow romantic poet Samuel Taylor Coleridge (1772–1834) published their *Lyrical Ballads*, which abandoned flowery classical conventions for the language of ordinary speech. Wordsworth described his conception of poetry as the "spontaneous overflow of powerful feeling recollected in tranquility."

Victor Hugo's (1802–1885) powerful novels exemplified the romantic fascination with fantastic characters, strange settings, and human emotions. The hero of Hugo's famous *Hunchback of Notre Dame* (1831) is the great cathedral's deformed

How did strong leaders and nation building transform Italy, Germany, and Russia?

What was the impact of urban growth on cities, social classes, families, and ideas?

How did nationalism and socialism shape politics in the decades before the Great War?

☑ LearningCurve
Check what you know.

737

bell-ringer, a "human gargoyle" overlooking the teeming life of fifteenth-century Paris.

The study of history became a romantic passion. History was the key to a universe that was now perceived to be organic and dynamic, not mechanical and static as the Enlightenment thinkers had believed. Historical studies supported the development of national aspirations and encouraged entire peoples to seek in the past their special destinies.

In central and eastern Europe, in particular, literary romanticism and early nationalism reinforced each other. Romantics turned their attention to peasant life and transcribed the folk songs, tales, and proverbs that the cosmopolitan Enlightenment had disdained. The brothers Jacob and Wilhelm Grimm were particularly successful at rescuing German fairy tales from oblivion. In the Slavic lands romantics played a decisive role in converting spoken peasant languages into modern written languages.

Beginning in the 1840s romanticism gave way to a new artistic genre, realism. Influenced by the growing prestige of science in this period, realist writers believed that literature should depict life exactly as it is. Forsaking poetry for prose and the personal, emotional viewpoint of the romantics for strict scientific objectivity, the realists simply observed and recorded.

Realist writers focused on creating fiction based on contemporary everyday life. Beginning with a dissection of the middle classes, from which most of them sprang, many realists eventually focused on the working classes, especially the urban working classes, which had been neglected in literature before this time. The realists put a microscope to unexplored and taboo topics — sex, strikes, violence, alcoholism — shocking middle-class critics.

The realists' claims of objectivity did not prevent the elaboration of a definite worldview. Realists such as the famous French novelist Émile Zola (1840–1902) and English novelist Thomas Hardy (1840–1928) were determinists. They believed that human beings, like atoms, are components of the physical world and that all human actions are caused by unalterable natural laws: heredity and environment determine human behavior; good and evil are merely social conventions. They were also critical of the failures of industrial society; by depicting the plight of poor workers, they hoped to bring about positive social change.

> **QUICK REVIEW**

Why did growing economic inequality not lead to increasing class conflict in the second half of the nineteenth century?

CHAPTER LOCATOR | How did the allies fashion a peace settlement in 1815? | Why did revolutions throughout Europe in 1848 triumph and why did they fail?

CHAPTER 24
738 IDEOLOGIES OF CHANGE IN EUROPE

Le Petit Journal

SUPPLÉMENT ILLUSTRÉ

DIMANCHE 13 JANVIER 1895

LE TRAITRE

How did nationalism and socialism shape European politics in the decades before the Great War?

The Traitor: Degradation of Alfred Dreyfus

After being arrested and convicted in a secret court martial for treason, Captain Dreyfus bravely stood at attention during a public degradation ceremony. While the officer on duty tore off his stripes, ripped off his honors, and broke his sword in two, Dreyfus shouted out, "You are degrading an innocent man! Long live France! Long live the army!" (Le Petit Journal, 13 January 1895/engraving by Henri Meyer [1844–99]/Private Collection/The Bridgeman Art Library)

AFTER 1871 NATIONALISM SERVED, for better or worse, as a new unifying political principle. At the same time, socialist parties grew rapidly. Governing elites manipulated national feeling to create a sense of unity to divert attention from underlying class conflicts, and increasingly channeled national sentiment in an antiliberal and militaristic direction, tolerating anti-Semitism and waging wars in non-Western lands. This policy helped manage domestic conflicts, but only at the expense of increasing the international tensions that erupted in World War I.

Trends in Suffrage

There were good reasons why ordinary people felt increasing loyalty to their governments in central and western Europe. More people could vote. By 1914 universal male suffrage had become the rule rather than the exception. Ordinary men felt they were becoming "part of the system."

| How did strong leaders and nation building transform Italy, Germany, and Russia? | What was the impact of urban growth on cities, social classes, families, and ideas? | **How did nationalism and socialism shape politics in the decades before the Great War?** | LearningCurve Check what you know. |

Women also began to demand the right to vote. The first important successes occurred in Scandinavia and Australia. In Sweden taxpaying single women and widows could vote in municipal elections after 1862. Australia and Finland gave women the right to vote in national elections and stand for parliament in 1902 and 1906, respectively. In the western United States, women could vote in twelve states by 1913.

As the right to vote spread, politicians and parties in national parliaments usually represented the people more responsively. The multiparty system prevailing in most countries meant that parliamentary majorities were built on shifting coalitions, which gave political parties leverage to obtain benefits for their supporters. Governments also passed laws to alleviate general problems, thereby acquiring greater legitimacy and appearing more worthy of support.

The German Empire

The new German Empire was a federal union of Prussia and twenty-four smaller states. Unifying the whole was a strong national government with a chancellor — Bismarck until 1890 — and a popularly elected parliament called the Reichstag. Although Bismarck repeatedly ignored the wishes of the parliamentary majority, he nonetheless preferred to win the support of the Reichstag to lend legitimacy to his policy goals.

Bismarck was a fierce opponent of socialism. In 1878 he pushed through a law outlawing the German Social Democratic Party, but he was unable to force socialism out of existence. Bismarck then urged the Reichstag to enact new social welfare measures to gain the allegiance of the working classes. In 1883 the Reichstag created national health insurance, followed in 1884 by accident insurance and in 1889 by old-age pensions and retirement benefits. Together, these laws created a national social security system that was the first of its kind anywhere, funded by contributions from wage earners, employers, and the state.

Under Kaiser William I (r. 1861–1888), Bismarck had managed the domestic and foreign policies of the state. In 1890 the new emperor, William II (r. 1888–1918), eager to rule in his own right and to earn the workers' support, forced Bismarck to resign. Following Bismarck's departure, the Reichstag passed new laws to aid workers and to legalize socialist political activity.

Although William II was no more successful than Bismarck in getting workers to renounce socialism, in the years before World War I the Social Democratic Party broadened its base and adopted a more patriotic tone. German socialists identified increasingly with the German state and concentrated on gradual social and political reform.

Republican France

Although Napoleon III's reign made some progress in reducing antagonisms between classes, the Franco-Prussian war undid these efforts, and in 1871 France seemed hopelessly divided once again. The republicans who proclaimed the Third Republic in Paris refused to admit defeat. They defended Paris with great heroism for weeks, until they were starved into submission by German armies in January 1871. When national elections then sent a large majority of conservatives and mon-

CHAPTER LOCATOR | How did the allies fashion a peace settlement in 1815? | Why did revolutions throughout Europe in 1848 triumph and why did they fail?

CHAPTER 24
740   IDEOLOGIES OF CHANGE IN EUROPE

archists to the National Assembly, France's leaders decided they had no choice but to surrender Alsace and Lorraine to Germany. The traumatized Parisians exploded in patriotic frustration and proclaimed the Paris Commune in March 1871.

Commune leaders wanted to govern Paris without interference from the conservative French countryside. The National Assembly, led by conservative politician Adolphe Thiers, ordered the French army into Paris and brutally crushed the Commune. Twenty thousand people died in the fighting. Out of this tragedy France slowly formed a new national unity, achieving considerable stability before 1914.

The moderate republicans who governed France sought to preserve their creation by winning the loyalty of the next generation. Trade unions were fully legalized, and France acquired a colonial empire (see Chapter 25). A series of laws between 1879 and 1886 established free compulsory elementary education for both girls and boys, thereby greatly reducing the role of parochial Catholic schools, which had long been hostile to republicanism. In France and throughout the world, the general expansion of public education served as a critical nation- and nationalism-building tool in the late nineteenth century.

Although the educational reforms of the 1880s disturbed French Catholics, many of them rallied to the republic in the 1890s, and tensions between church and state eased. Unfortunately, the Dreyfus affair changed all that. In 1894 Alfred Dreyfus, a Jewish captain in the French army, was falsely accused and convicted of treason. In 1898 and 1899 the case split France apart. On one side was the army, which had manufactured evidence against Dreyfus, joined by anti-Semites and most of the Catholic establishment. On the other side stood the civil libertarians and most of the more radical republicans.

This battle, which eventually led to Dreyfus's being declared innocent, revived militant republican feeling against the church. Between 1901 and 1905 the government severed all ties between the state and the Catholic Church after centuries of close relations.

Dreyfus affair

▶ A divisive case in which Alfred Dreyfus, a Jewish captain in the French army, was falsely accused and convicted of treason. The Catholic Church sided with the anti-Semites against Dreyfus; after Dreyfus was declared innocent, the French government severed all ties between the state and the church.

Great Britain and the Austro-Hungarian Empire

The development of Great Britain and Austria-Hungary, two leading but quite different powers, throws a powerful light on the dynamics of nationalism in Europe before 1914. At home Britain made more of its citizens feel a part of the nation by passing consecutive voting rights bills that culminated with the establishment of universal male suffrage in 1884. Moreover, extensive social welfare measures were passed in a spectacular rush between 1906 and 1914. The state was integrating the urban masses socially as well as politically.

On the eve of World War I, however, the unanswered question of Ireland brought Great Britain to the brink of civil war. The terrible Irish famine of the 1840s and early 1850s had fueled an Irish revolutionary movement. The English slowly granted concessions, and in 1913 the British Parliament passed a bill granting Ireland self-government, or home rule.

Irish Protestants in the northern counties of Ulster, however, vowed to resist home rule, fearing they would fall under the control of the majority Catholics. Unable to resolve the conflict as World War I started in August 1914, the British government postponed indefinitely the whole question of Irish home rule.

How did strong leaders and nation building transform Italy, Germany, and Russia?

What was the impact of urban growth on cities, social classes, families, and ideas?

How did nationalism and socialism shape politics in the decades before the Great War?

LearningCurve
Check what you know.

741

The Irish dilemma helps one appreciate how desperate the situation in the Austro-Hungarian Empire had become by the early twentieth century. Following its defeat by Prussia in 1866, a weakened Austria was forced to establish the so-called dual monarchy. The empire was divided in two, and the nationalistic Magyars gained virtual independence for Hungary. The two states were joined only by a shared monarch and common ministries for finance, defense, and foreign affairs. Still, the disintegrating force of competing nationalisms continued unabated, and the Austro-Hungarian Empire was progressively weakened and eventually destroyed by the conflicting national aspirations of its different ethnic groups. It was these ethnic conflicts in the Balkans that touched off the Great War in 1914 (see Chapter 28).

Jewish Emancipation and Modern Anti-Semitism

Revolutionary changes in political principles and the triumph of the nation-state brought equally revolutionary changes in Jewish life in western and central Europe. Beginning in France in 1791, Jews gradually gained their civil rights. In the 1850s and 1860s liberals in Austria, Italy, and Prussia pressed successfully for legal equality. In 1871 the constitution of the new German Empire abolished all restrictions on Jewish marriage, choice of occupation, place of residence, and property ownership. Exclusion from government employment and discrimination in social relations remained, however, in central Europe.

By 1871 a majority of Jews in western and central Europe had improved their economic situations and entered the middle classes. Most Jews identified strongly with their respective nation-states and considered themselves patriotic citizens.

Vicious anti-Semitism reappeared after the stock market crash of 1873, beginning in central Europe. Drawing on long traditions of religious intolerance, this

"The Expulsion of the Jews from Russia"

So reads this postcard, correctly suggesting that Russian government officials often encouraged popular anti-Semitism and helped drive many Jews out of Russia in the late nineteenth century. The road signs indicate that these poor Jews are crossing into Germany, where they will find a grudging welcome and a meager meal at the Jolly Onion Inn. Other Jews from eastern Europe settled in France and Britain, thereby creating small but significant Jewish populations in both countries for the first time since they had expelled most of their Jews in the Middle Ages. (Alliance Israelite Universele, Paris, France/Archives Charmet/The Bridgeman Art Library)

CHAPTER LOCATOR | How did the allies fashion a peace settlement in 1815? | Why did revolutions throughout Europe in 1848 triumph and why did they fail?

CHAPTER 24
742 IDEOLOGIES OF CHANGE IN EUROPE

hostility also drew on modern, supposedly scientific ideas about Jews as a separate race (see page 736). Anti-Semitic beliefs were particularly popular among conservatives, extremist nationalists, and people who felt threatened by Jewish competition.

Anti-Semites also created modern political parties. In Austrian Vienna in the early 1890s, Karl Lueger (LOO-guhr), the popular mayor of Vienna from 1897 to 1910, combined fierce anti-Semitic rhetoric with his support of municipal ownership of basic services. In response to spreading anti-Semitism, a Jewish journalist named Theodor Herzl (1860–1904) turned from German nationalism to advocate Jewish political nationalism, or Zionism, and the creation of a Jewish state.

Before 1914 anti-Semitism was most oppressive in eastern Europe, where Jews also suffered from terrible poverty. In the Russian empire officials used anti-Semitism to channel popular discontent away from the government. In 1881–1882 a wave of violent pogroms commenced in southern Russia. The police and the army stood aside for days while peasants assaulted Jews and looted and destroyed their property. Official harassment continued in the following decades, and many Russian Jews emigrated to western Europe and the United States.

Zionism

► The movement toward Jewish political nationhood started by Theodor Herzl.

The Socialist Movement

Socialism appealed to large numbers of working men and women in the late nineteenth century, and the growth of socialist parties after 1871 was phenomenal. By 1912 the German Social Democratic Party, which espoused Marxist principles, had millions of followers and was the Reichstag's largest party. Socialist parties also grew in other countries, and Marxist socialist parties were linked together in an international organization.

As socialist parties grew and attracted large numbers of members, they looked more and more toward gradual change and steady improvement for the working class and less and less toward revolution. Workers themselves were progressively less inclined to follow radical programs for several reasons. As workers gained the right to vote and won real benefits, their attention focused more on elections than on revolutions. Workers were also not immune to nationalistic patriotism. Nor were workers a unified social group. Perhaps most important of all, workers' standard of living rose steadily after 1850, and the quality of life improved substantially in urban areas.

The growth of labor unions reinforced this trend toward moderation. In Great Britain new unions that formed for skilled workers after 1850 avoided radical politics and concentrated on winning better wages and hours for their members through collective bargaining and compromise. After 1890 unions for unskilled workers developed in Britain.

German unions were not granted important rights until 1869, and until the Anti-Socialist Laws were repealed in 1890 the government frequently harassed them as socialist fronts. But after most legal harassment was eliminated, union membership skyrocketed.

The German trade unions and their leaders were thoroughgoing revisionists. Revisionism was an effort by various socialists to update Marxist doctrines to reflect the realities of the time. The socialist Eduard Bernstein (1850–1932) argued in his *Evolutionary Socialism* in 1899 that Marx's predictions of ever-greater poverty for workers had been proved false. Therefore, Bernstein suggested, socialists

revisionism

► An effort by various socialists to update Marxist doctrines to reflect the realities of the time.

How did strong leaders and nation building transform Italy, Germany, and Russia?

What was the impact of urban growth on cities, social classes, families, and ideas?

How did nationalism and socialism shape politics in the decades before the Great War?

✓ LearningCurve
Check what you know.

743

should reform their doctrines and win gradual evolutionary gains for workers through legislation, unions, and further economic development.

Socialist parties in other countries had clear-cut national characteristics. Russians and socialists in the Austro-Hungarian Empire tended to be the most radical. In Great Britain the socialist but non-Marxist Labour Party formally committed to gradual reform. In Spain and Italy anarchism, seeking to smash the state rather than the bourgeoisie, dominated radical thought and action.

In short, socialist policies and doctrines varied from country to country. Socialism itself was to a large extent "nationalized." This helps explain why almost all socialist leaders supported their governments when war came in 1914.

> **QUICK REVIEW**

How did political elites gain the loyalty of elements of the working classes in the late nineteenth century?

CHAPTER SUMMARY

In 1814 the victorious allied powers sought to restore peace and stability in Europe. The conservative powers used intervention and repression as they sought to prevent the spread of subversive ideas and radical changes in politics. After 1815 ideologies of liberalism, nationalism, and socialism all developed to challenge the new order. The growth of these forces culminated in the liberal and nationalistic revolutions of 1848, revolutions that were crushed by resurgent conservative forces. In the second half of the nineteenth century Italy and Germany became unified nation-states, while Russia undertook a modernization program and struggled with popular discontent.

Living conditions in rapidly growing industrial cities declined until the mid-nineteenth century, when governments undertook major urban development. Major changes in the class structure and family life occurred, as the separate spheres ideology strengthened, and the class structure became more complex and diversified. The prestige of science grew tremendously, and scientific discoveries challenged the traditional religious understanding of the world. In the realm of literature and the arts, the romantic movement reinforced the spirit of change. Romanticism gave way to realism in the 1840s.

Western society became increasingly nationalistic as well as urban and industrial in the late nineteenth century. Nation-states became more responsive to the needs of their people, and they enlisted widespread support as political participation expanded, educational opportunities increased, and social security systems took shape. Even socialism became increasingly national in orientation, gathering strength as a champion of working-class interests in domestic politics. Yet even though nationalism served to unite peoples, it also drove them apart and contributed to the tragic conflicts of the twentieth century.

CHAPTER LOCATOR | How did the allies fashion a peace settlement in 1815? | Why did revolutions throughout Europe in 1848 triumph and why did they fail?

CHAPTER 24
744   IDEOLOGIES OF CHANGE IN EUROPE

CONNECTIONS Much of world history in the past two centuries can be seen as a struggle over the unfinished legacies of the late-eighteenth-century revolutions in politics and economics. Although defeated in 1848, the new political ideologies associated with the French Revolution re-emerged decisively after 1850. Nationalism, with its commitment to the nation-state, became the most dominant of the new ideologies.

After 1870 nationalism and militarism, its frequent companion, touched off increased competition between the major European powers for raw materials and markets for manufactured goods. As discussed in the next two chapters, during the last decades of the nineteenth century Europe colonized nearly all of Africa and large areas in Asia. In Europe itself nationalism promoted bitter competition between states, threatening the very progress and unity it had helped to build. In 1914 the power of unified nation-states turned on itself, unleashing an unprecedented conflict among Europe's Great Powers. Chapter 28 tells the story of this First World War.

Nationalism also sparked worldwide challenges to European dominance by African and Asian leaders who fought to liberate themselves from colonialism, and it became a rallying cry in nominally independent countries like China and Japan, whose leaders sought freedom from European and American influence and a rightful place among the world's leading nations. Chapters 25, 26, and 33 explore these developments. Likewise, Chapter 33 discusses how the problems of rapid urbanization and the huge gaps between rich and poor caused by economic transformations in America and Europe in the 1800s are now the concern of policymakers in Africa, Asia, and Latin America.

Another important ideology of change, socialism, remains popular in Europe, which has seen socialist parties democratically elected to office in many countries. Marxist revolutions that took absolute control of entire countries, as in Russia, China, and Cuba, occurred in the twentieth century.

ONLINE DOCUMENT PROJECT

Competing Visions of a United Italy

How did Italian nationalists respond to unification?

Examine evidence from the period following Italian unification, and then complete a quiz and writing assignment based on the evidence and details from this chapter. *See inside the front cover to learn more.*

How did strong leaders and nation building transform Italy, Germany, and Russia?

What was the impact of urban growth on cities, social classes, families, and ideas?

How did nationalism and socialism shape politics in the decades before the Great War?

☑ LearningCurve
Check what you know.

CHAPTER 24 STUDY GUIDE

STEP 1 GET STARTED ONLINE

LearningCurve

Now that you've read the chapter, make it stick by completing the LearningCurve activity.

STEP 2 EXPLAIN WHY IT MATTERS

Put your reading into practice. Identify each term below, and then explain why it matters in world history.

TERM	WHO OR WHAT & WHEN	WHY IT MATTERS
Congress of Vienna (p. 712)		
conservatism (p. 712)		
liberalism (p. 715)		
laissez faire (p. 715)		
nationalism (p. 715)		
socialism (p. 716)		
bourgeoisie (p. 717)		
proletariat (p. 717)		
modernization (p. 724)		
October Manifesto (p. 730)		
germ theory (p. 732)		
evolution (p. 736)		
Social Darwinism (p. 737)		
romanticism (p.737)		
Dreyfus affair (p. 741)		
Zionism (p. 743)		
revisionism (p. 743)		

STEP 3 MOVE BEYOND THE BASICS

To demonstrate a more advanced understanding of the new ideologies that shaped European history in the nineteenth century, fill in the chart below with the key characteristics and beliefs associated with liberalism, conservatism, nationalism, and socialism. How were each of these four ideologies shaped by memories of the French Revolution?

	Key Characteristics and Beliefs
Liberalism	
Conservatism	
Nationalism	
Socialism	

STEP 4

PUT IT ALL TOGETHER

Now, take a step back and try to explain the big picture. Remember to use specific examples from the chapter in your answers.

REACTION AND REVOLUTION

▸ What were the goals of the participants in the Congress of Vienna? How did their experience of the French Revolution and the Napoleonic Wars shape their vision of postwar Europe?

▸ What explains the near simultaneous eruption of revolution across Europe in 1848? How did revolution in one country help trigger revolution in another? Why did all of the revolutions of 1848 fail?

NATION BUILDING IN ITALY, GERMANY, AND RUSSIA

▸ How did Bismarck use war to promote German unification under Prussian leadership? How did he use war to tame his domestic opponents?

▸ What did Russian leaders mean by "modernization"? How successful were their modernization efforts?

LATE NINETEENTH-CENTURY SOCIETY, CULTURE, AND POLITICS

▸ What explains the increasing social diversity of nineteenth-century Europe? What were the economic and political implications of this diversity?

▸ How did governments across Europe work to cement the loyalty of their citizens in the late nineteenth century? How effective were their efforts?

LOOKING BACK, LOOKING AHEAD

▸ How did nineteenth-century nation-states differ from their eighteenth-century counterparts? What role did industrialization and new political ideologies play in producing the differences you note?

▸ In what sense were the societies and states that developed in nineteenth-century Europe "modern"? What fundamental features of contemporary nation-states emerged in the period covered in this chapter?

> ## IN YOUR OWN WORDS

Imagine that you must give an oral report to the class answering the following question: What role did social conflict play in nineteenth-century European politics? What would be the most important points and why?

25

AFRICA, THE OTTOMAN EMPIRE, AND THE NEW IMPERIALISM

1800–1914

> How and why did Western nations strive for global dominance over the course of the nineteenth century? Chapter 25 examines nineteenth-century Western imperialism in Africa and the Middle East. As the process of industrialization advanced, European commercial interests went in search of new sources of raw materials and markets for their manufactured goods. At the same time, millions of Europeans and Asians picked up stakes and emigrated abroad. What began as a relatively peaceful exchange of products with Africa and Asia in the early nineteenth century had transformed by century's end into a frenzy of imperialist occupation and domination that had a profound impact on both colonizer and colonized. The political annexation of territory in the 1880s — the "new imperialism," as it is often called by historians — was the capstone of Western society's underlying economic and technological transformation.

Sengbe Pieh Enslaved in 1839, Pieh (later known as Joseph Cinqué) led a famous revolt on the slave ship *Amistad*. He and his fellow slaves were charged with mutiny and murder, but in March 1840 the U.S. Supreme Court found them innocent because they had been illegally captured and sold. They returned to their native Sierra Leone as free men. (Oil on canvas by Nathaniel Jocelyn, 1839/The Granger Collection, New York — All rights reserved.)

> What were the most significant changes in Africa during the nineteenth century, and why did they occur?

> What were the causes and consequences of European empire building after 1880?

> How did the Ottoman Empire and Egypt try to modernize themselves, and what were the most important results?

> What were the global consequences of European industrialization between 1800 and 1914?

> What fueled migration, and what was the general pattern of this unprecedented movement of people?

✓ **LearningCurve**

After reading the chapter, use LearningCurve to retain what you've read.

What were the most significant changes in Africa during the nineteenth century, and why did they occur?

Brutality in the Congo

No Africans suffered more violent and brutal treatment under colonial rule than those living in Belgian king Leopold the II's Congo Free State. When not having their hands, feet, or heads cut off as punishment, Africans were whipped with *chicottes*, whips made of dried hippopotamus hide. Some Congolese were literally whipped to death. (© TopFoto/The Image Works)

FROM THE BEGINNING OF THE NINETEENTH CENTURY to the global depression of the 1930s, the different regions of Africa experienced gradual but monumental change. The transatlantic slave trade declined and practically disappeared by the late 1860s. In the early nineteenth century Islam expanded its influence south of the Sahara, but Africa generally remained free of European political control. After about 1880 Africa was divided and largely conquered by Europeans, and by 1900 the foreigners were consolidating their authoritarian empires.

Trade and Social Change

The most important development in West Africa before the European conquest was the decline of the Atlantic slave trade and the simultaneous rise in exports of **palm oil** and other commodities. This shift in African foreign trade marked the beginning of modern economic development in sub-Saharan Africa.

Although the trade in enslaved Africans was a global phenomenon, the transatlantic slave trade between Africa and the Americas became the most extensive

palm oil

▶ A West African tropical product often used to make soap; the British encouraged its cultivation as an alternative to the slave trade.

CHAPTER LOCATOR | **What were the most significant changes in Africa during the nineteenth century?** | What were the causes and consequences of European empire building after 1880?

CHAPTER 25
750 AFRICA, THE OTTOMAN EMPIRE, AND THE NEW IMPERIALISM

1805–1849
Muhammad Ali modernizes Egypt

1808–1839
Mahmud II rules Ottoman state and enacts reforms

1809
Uthman dan Fodio founds Sokoto caliphate

1830
France begins conquest of Algeria

1839–1876
Western-style reforms (Tanzimat) in Ottoman Empire

1860s
Transatlantic slave trade declines rapidly

1869
Completion of Suez Canal

1875
Ottoman state declares partial bankruptcy; European creditors take over

1876
Europeans take financial control in Egypt

1880
Western and central Sudan unite under Islam

1880–1900
Most of Africa falls under European rule

1880–1914
Height of new imperialism in Asia and Africa

1879–1882
Ahmed Arabi leads revolt against foreign control of Egypt

1884–1885
Berlin Conference

1899
Kipling, "The White Man's Burden"; Amin, *The Liberation of Women*

1899–1902
South African War

1902
Conrad, *Heart of Darkness*; Hobson, *Imperialism*

1908
Young Turks seize power in Ottoman Empire

and significant portion of it (see pages 598–603). After 1775 a broad campaign to abolish slavery, in which British women played a critical role, developed in Britain and grew into one of the first peaceful mass political movements based on the mobilization of public opinion in British history. Abolitionists also argued for a transition to legitimate (nonslave) trade, to end both the transatlantic slave trade and the internal African slave systems. In 1807 Parliament declared the slave trade illegal. Britain then established the antislavery West Africa Squadron, using its navy to seize slave runners' ships, liberate the captives, and settle them in the British port of Freetown, in Sierra Leone, as well as in Liberia (see Map 25.1, page 755). Freed American slaves had established the colony of Liberia in 1821–1822.

British action had a limited impact at first. Britain's West Africa Squadron intercepted fewer than 10 percent of all slave ships, and the demand for slaves remained high on the expanding and labor-intensive sugar and coffee plantations of Cuba and Brazil until the 1850s and 1860s. In the United States, President Thomas Jefferson signed into law an act that banned slave importation from January 1, 1808. From that time on, natural increase (slaves having children) mainly accounted for the subsequent growth of the African American slave population before the Civil War. Strong financial incentives remained, however, for Portuguese and other European slave traders and for those African rulers who relied on profits from the trade for power and influence.

As more nations joined Britain in outlawing the slave trade, shipments of human cargo slackened along the West African coast (see Map 25.1, page 755).

How did the Ottoman Empire and Egypt try to modernize themselves? | What were the global consequences of European industrialization? | What fueled migration, and what was the pattern of this movement of people? | ✓ LearningCurve Check what you know.

751

The first step towards lightening

The White Man's Burden

is through teaching the virtues of cleanliness.

Pears' Soap

is a potent factor in brightening the dark corners of the earth as civilization advances, while amongst the cultured of all nations it holds the highest place—it is the ideal toilet soap.

> PICTURING THE PAST

ANALYZING THE IMAGE: Which elements or words in this advertisement suggest the Western ideal of "civilization"? Which elements or words are used to describe non-Europeans?
CONNECTIONS: How might the English maxim "Cleanliness is next to godliness" relate to this advertisement? How can Pears' Soap lighten "the white man's burden" and brighten "the dark corners of the earth"?

At the same time the ancient but limited shipment of slaves across the Sahara and from the East African coast into the Indian Ocean and through the Red Sea expanded dramatically. Only in the 1860s did this trade begin to decline rapidly. As a result of these shifting currents, total slave exports from all regions of sub-Saharan Africa declined only marginally. Abolitionists failed to achieve their vision of "legitimate" commerce in tropical products quickly replacing illegal slave exports.

Nevertheless, beginning in West Africa, trade in tropical products did make steady progress for several reasons. First, with Britain encouraging palm tree cultivation as an alternative to the slave trade, palm oil sales from West Africa to Britain surged. Second, the sale of palm oil admirably served the self-interest of industrializing Europe. Manufacturers used palm oil to lubricate their giant machines and to make cheap soap and other cosmetics. Third, peanut production for export also grew rapidly, in part because both small, independent African family farmers and large-scale enterprises could produce peanuts for the substantial American and European markets.

Finally, powerful West African rulers and warlords who had benefited from the Atlantic slave trade redirected some of their slaves' labor into the production of legitimate goods for world markets. This was possible because local warfare and slave raiding continued to enslave large numbers of people in sub-Saharan Africa, so slavery and slave markets remained strong. Although some enslaved captives might still be sold abroad, now women were often kept as wives, concubines, or servants, while men were used to transport goods, mine gold, grow crops, and serve in slave armies. Thus, the transatlantic slave trade's slow decline coincided with the most intensive use of slaves within Africa.

All the while, a new group of African merchants was emerging to handle legitimate trade, and some grew rich. Women were among the most successful

CHAPTER LOCATOR | What were the most significant changes in Africa during the nineteenth century? | What were the causes and consequences of European empire building after 1880?

752 CHAPTER 25 AFRICA, THE OTTOMAN EMPIRE, AND THE NEW IMPERIALISM of these merchants. There is a long tradition of West African women being actively involved in trade (see pages 603–605), but the arrival of Europeans provided new opportunities. The African wife of a European trader served as her husband's interpreter and learned all aspects of his business. If the husband died, the African wife inherited his commercial interests, including his inventory and his European connections. Many such widows used their considerable business acumen to make small fortunes.

By the 1850s and 1860s legitimate African traders, flanked by Western-educated African lawyers, teachers, and journalists, had formed an emerging middle class in the West African coastal towns. Unfortunately for West Africans, in the 1880s and 1890s African business leadership gave way to imperial subordination.

Islamic Revival and Expansion in Africa

The Sudanic savanna is that vast belt of flat grasslands across Africa below the Sahara's southern fringe (the Sahel). By the early eighteenth century Islam had been practiced throughout this region for five hundred to one thousand years, depending on the area. City dwellers, political rulers, and merchants in many small states were Muslim. Yet the rural peasant farmers and migratory cattle raisers—the vast majority of the population—generally held onto traditional animist practices. Muslim rulers did not try to convert their subjects in the countryside or enforce Islamic law.

A powerful Islamic revival began in the eighteenth century and gathered strength in the early nineteenth century. In essence, Muslim scholars and fervent religious leaders arose to wage successful jihads, or religious wars, against both animist rulers and Islamic states they deemed corrupt. The new reformist rulers believed African cults and religious practice could no longer be tolerated, and they often effected mass conversions of animists to Islam.

The most important of these revivalist states, the Sokoto caliphate, illustrates the pattern of Islamic revival in Africa. It was founded by Uthman dan Fodio (1754–1817), a Muslim teacher who first won followers in the Muslim state of Gobir in the northern Sudan. After his religious community was attacked by Gobir's rulers, Uthman launched the jihad of 1804, one of the most important events in nineteenth-century West Africa. Uthman claimed the Hausa rulers of Muslim Gobir were idolaters who killed and plundered their subjects without any regard for Islamic law.[1] He recruited young religious students and discontented Fulani cattle raisers to form the backbone of his jihadi fighters and succeeded in overthrowing the Hausa rulers and expanding Islam into the Sudan. In 1809 Uthman established the new Sokoto caliphate (see Map 25.1, page 755).

The triumph of the Sokoto caliphate had profound consequences for Africa and the Sudan. First, the caliphate was governed by a sophisticated written constitution based on Islamic history and law. This government of laws, rather than men, provided stability and made Sokoto one of the most prosperous regions in tropical Africa. Second, because of Sokoto and other revivalist states, Islam became much more widely and deeply rooted in sub-Saharan Africa than ever before. Finally, as one historian explained, Islam had always approved of slavery for non-Muslims and Muslim heretics, and "the jihads created a new slaving frontier on the basis of rejuvenated Islam."[2] In 1900 the Sokoto caliphate had at least 1 million and perhaps as many as 2.5 million slaves.

jihad
▶ Religious war waged by Muslim scholars and religious leaders against both animist rulers and Islamic states that they deemed corrupt.

Sokoto caliphate
▶ Founded in 1809 by Uthman dan Fodio, this African state was based on Islamic history and law.

How did the Ottoman Empire and Egypt try to modernize themselves? | What were the global consequences of European industrialization? | What fueled migration, and what was the pattern of this movement of people? | ✓ LearningCurve Check what you know.

753

Islam also expanded in East Africa. From the 1820s on, Arab merchants and adventurers pressed far into the interior in search of slaves and ivory, converting and intermarrying with local Nyamwezi (nyahm-WAY-zee) elites and establishing small Muslim states. The Arab immigrants brought literacy, administrative skills, and increased trade and international contact, as well as the intensification of slavery, to East Africa. In 1870, before Christian missionaries and Western armies began to arrive in force and halt Islam's spread, it appeared that most of the East and Central African populations would accept Islam within a generation.[3]

The Scramble for Africa, 1880–1914

Between 1880 and 1914 Britain, France, Germany, Belgium, Spain, and Italy scrambled for African possessions as if their national livelihoods were at stake. In 1880 Europeans controlled barely 20 percent of the African continent, mainly along the coast; by 1914 they controlled over 90 percent. Only Ethiopia in northeast Africa and Liberia on the West African coast remained independent (Map 25.1).

In addition to the general causes underlying Europe's imperialist burst after 1880, certain events and individuals stand out. First, as the antislavery movement succeeded in shutting down the Atlantic slave trade by the late 1860s, slavery's persistence elsewhere attracted growing attention in western Europe and the Americas. Missionaries played a key role in publicizing the horrors of slave raids and the suffering of thousands of enslaved Africans. The public was led to believe that European conquest and colonization would end this human tragedy by bringing, in Scottish missionary David Livingstone's famous phrase, "Commerce, Christianity, and Civilization" to Africa.

King Leopold II (r. 1865–1909) of Belgium also played a crucial role. His agents signed treaties with African chiefs and planted Leopold's flag along the Congo River. By 1883 Europe had caught "African fever," and the race for territory was on. To lay down some rules for this imperialist competition, French premier Jules Ferry and German chancellor Otto von Bismarck arranged a European conference on Africa in Berlin in 1884–1885. The **Berlin Conference** established the principle that a nation could establish a colony only if it had effectively taken possession of the territory through signed treaties with local leaders and had begun to develop it economically.

In addition to developing rules for imperialist competition, participants at the Berlin Conference also promised to stop black and Islamic slave dealers and to bring Christianity and civilization to Africa. In truth, however, these ideals ran a distant second to, and were not allowed to interfere with, the nations' primary goal of commerce—holding on to their old markets and exploiting new ones.

The Berlin Conference coincided with Germany's emergence as an imperial power. In 1884 and 1885 Bismarck's Germany established **protectorates** over a number of small African kingdoms and societies (see Map 25.1). In acquiring colonies, Bismarck cooperated with France's Jules Ferry against the British. The French expanded into West Africa and also formed a protectorate on the Congo River. Meanwhile, the British began enlarging their West African enclaves and pushed northward from the Cape Colony and westward from the East African coast.

The British also moved southward from Egypt, which they had seized in 1882 (see page 767), but were blocked in the eastern Sudan by fiercely independent

Berlin Conference

▶ A meeting of European leaders held in 1884–1885 to lay down basic rules for imperialist competition in sub-Saharan Africa.

protectorate

▶ An autonomous state or territory partly controlled and protected by a stronger outside power.

CHAPTER LOCATOR | What were the most significant changes in Africa during the nineteenth century? | What were the causes and consequences of European empire building after 1880?

CHAPTER 25
754 AFRICA, THE OTTOMAN EMPIRE, AND THE NEW IMPERIALISM

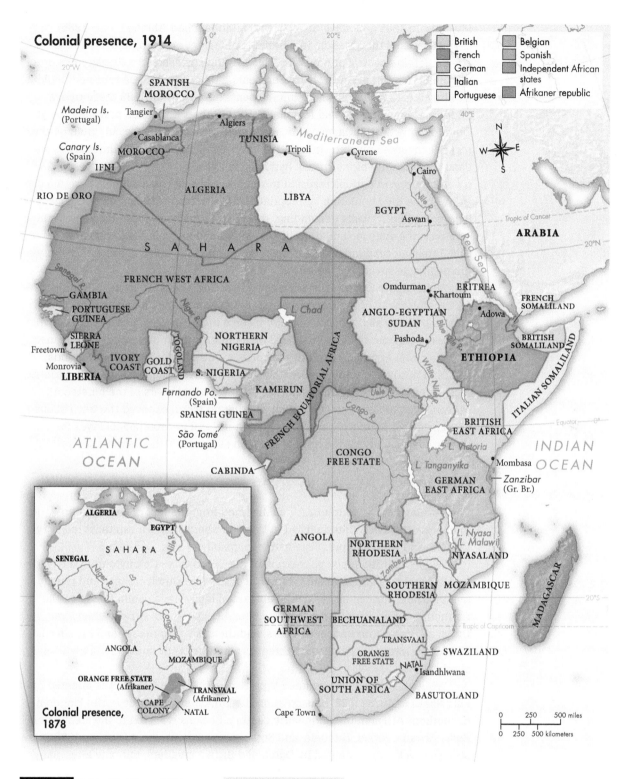

Colonial presence, 1914

British	Belgian
French	Spanish
German	Independent African states
Italian	
Portuguese	Afrikaner republic

Madeira Is.
(Portugal)

Canary Is.
(Spain)

SPANISH
MOROCCO

Tangier

Algiers

Casablanca

TUNISIA

Tripoli

Cyrene

Mediterranean Sea

Cairo

40°E

IFNI

MOROCCO

RIO DE ORO

ALGERIA

LIBYA

EGYPT

Aswan

Tropic of Cancer

ARABIA

20°N

S A H A R A

Red Sea

FRENCH WEST AFRICA

Omdurman

Khartoum

ERITREA

FRENCH
SOMALILAND

GAMBIA

Senegal R.

Niger R.

L. Chad

ANGLO-EGYPTIAN
SUDAN

Adowa

Blue Nile

PORTUGUESE
GUINEA

SIERRA
LEONE

Freetown

NORTHERN
NIGERIA

Fashoda

ETHIOPIA

BRITISH
SOMALILAND

ITALIAN SOMALILAND

Monrovia

IVORY
COAST

GOLD
COAST

TOGOLAND

S. NIGERIA

White Nile

LIBERIA

KAMERUN

Fernando Po.
(Spain)

SPANISH GUINEA

Uele R.

São Tomé
(Portugal)

FRENCH EQUATORIAL AFRICA

Congo R.

BRITISH
EAST AFRICA

Equator

0°

INDIAN
OCEAN

ATLANTIC
OCEAN

CABINDA

CONGO
FREE STATE

L. Victoria

L. Tanganyika

Mombasa

GERMAN
EAST AFRICA

Zanzibar
(Gr. Br.)

ANGOLA

NORTHERN
RHODESIA

L. Nyasa
(L. Malawi)

NYASALAND

Zambezi R.

SOUTHERN
RHODESIA

MOZAMBIQUE

MADAGASCAR

20°S

GERMAN
SOUTHWEST
AFRICA

BECHUANALAND

Tropic of Capricorn

TRANSVAAL

ORANGE
FREE STATE

SWAZILAND

NATAL

Isandhlwana

UNION OF
SOUTH AFRICA

BASUTOLAND

Cape Town

| 0 | 250 | 500 miles |
| 0 | 250 | 500 kilometers |

Colonial presence, 1878

ALGERIA

EGYPT

SAHARA

SENEGAL

Nile R.

Niger R.

Congo R.

ANGOLA

MOZAMBIQUE

ORANGE FREE STATE
(Afrikaner)

TRANSVAAL
(Afrikaner)

CAPE
COLONY

NATAL

MAP 25.1 ■ The Partition of Africa

The European powers carved up Africa after 1880 and built vast political empires.

> MAPPING THE PAST

ANALYZING THE MAP: What European countries were leading imperialist states in Africa, and what lands did they hold? What countries maintained political independence?

CONNECTIONS: The late nineteenth century was the high point of European imperialism. What were the motives behind the rush for land and empire in Africa?

How did the Ottoman Empire and Egypt try to modernize themselves?

What were the global consequences of European industrialization?

What fueled migration, and what was the pattern of this movement of people?

✓ LearningCurve
Check what you know.

Muslims. In 1881 a pious Sudanese leader, Muhammad Ahmad (1844–1885), proclaimed himself the "Mahdi" (a messianic redeemer of Islam) and led a revolt against foreign control of Egypt. In 1885 his army massacred a British force, forcing the British to retreat to Cairo. Ten years later a British force returned, building a railroad to supply arms and reinforcements as it went. In 1898 these troops, under the command of Field Marshal Horatio Hubert Kitchener, met their foe at Omdurman, where Sudanese Muslims armed with spears were cut down by the recently invented machine gun. In the end eleven thousand Muslim fighters lay dead. Only twenty-eight Britons had been killed.

All European nations resorted to some violence in their colonies to retain control, subdue the population, appropriate land, and force African laborers to work long hours at physically demanding, and often dangerous, jobs. In no colony, however, was the violence and brutality worse than in Leopold II's Congo Free State. The European companies operating in the Congo Free State introduced slavery, unimaginable savagery, and terror.

Profits in the Congo Free State came first from the ivory trade, but in the 1890s, after many of the Congo's elephant herds had been decimated, rubber surpassed ivory as the colony's major income producer. Violence and brutality increased exponentially as industrial demand for rubber increased. Europeans and their well-armed mercenaries terrorized entire regions, cutting off hands, feet, and heads and wiping out whole villages to send the message that Africans must either work for the Europeans or die. In the first years of the nineteenth century, human rights activists such as Edmund Morel exposed the truth about the horrific conditions in the Congo Free State, and in 1908 Leopold was forced to turn over his private territory to Belgium as a colony, the Belgian Congo.

Southern Africa in the Nineteenth Century

The development of southern Africa diverged from the rest of sub-Saharan Africa in important ways. Whites settled in large numbers, modern capitalist industry took off, and British imperialists had to wage all-out war.

When the British took possession of the Dutch Cape Colony during the Napoleonic Wars, there were about twenty thousand free Dutch citizens and twenty-five thousand African slaves, with substantial mixed-race communities on the northern frontier of white settlement. After 1815 powerful African chiefdoms, Dutch settlers—first known as Boers, and then as Afrikaners—and British colonial forces waged a complicated three-cornered battle to build strong states in southern Africa.

Afrikaners
▶ Descendants of the Dutch settlers in the Cape Colony in southern Africa.

While the British consolidated their rule in the Cape Colony, the talented Zulu king Shaka (r. 1818–1828) was creating the largest and most powerful kingdom in southern Africa in the nineteenth century. Shaka's wars led to the creation of Zulu, Tswana, Swazi, Ndebele, and Sotho states in southern Africa. By 1890 these states were largely subdued by Dutch and British invaders, but only after many hard-fought frontier wars.

Between 1834 and 1838 the British abolished slavery in the Cape Colony and introduced racial equality before the law to protect African labor. In 1836 about ten thousand Afrikaner cattle ranchers and farmers, resentful of equal treatment of blacks by British colonial officials and missionaries after the abolition of slavery, began to make their so-called Great Trek northward into the interior. In 1845

CHAPTER LOCATOR | What were the most significant changes in Africa during the nineteenth century? | What were the causes and consequences of European empire building after 1880?

CHAPTER 25
756 AFRICA, THE OTTOMAN EMPIRE, AND THE NEW IMPERIALISM

Diamond Mining in South Africa

At first, both black and white miners could own and work claims at the diamond diggings, as this early photo suggests. However, as the industry expanded and was monopolized by European financial interests, white workers claimed the supervisory jobs, and blacks were limited to dangerous low-wage labor. (Robert Harvey/© Hulton-Deutsch Collection/Corbis)

another group of Afrikaners joined them north of the Orange River. Over the next thirty years Afrikaner and British settlers reached a mutually advantageous division of southern Africa. The British ruled the strategically valuable colonies of Cape Colony and Natal (nuh-TAL) on the coast, and the Afrikaners controlled the ranch-land republics of Orange Free State and the Transvaal in the interior.

The discovery of incredibly rich deposits of diamonds in 1867 near Kimberley, and of gold in 1886 in the Afrikaners' Transvaal Republic around modern Johannesburg, revolutionized the southern African economy, making possible large-scale industrial capitalism and transforming the lives of all its peoples. The extraction of these minerals, particularly the deep-level gold deposits, required big foreign investment, European engineering expertise, and an enormous labor force. Thus small-scale miners soon gave way to powerful financiers, particularly Cecil Rhodes (1853–1902). Rhodes came from a large middle-class British family and at seventeen went to southern Africa to seek his fortune. By 1888 Rhodes's firm, the De Beers mining company, monopolized the world's diamond industry and earned him fabulous profits.

How did the Ottoman Empire and Egypt try to modernize themselves?

What were the global consequences of European industrialization?

What fueled migration, and what was the pattern of this movement of people?

☑ LearningCurve
Check what you know.

757

The mining bonanza whetted the appetite of British imperialists led by the powerful Rhodes. Between 1888 and 1893 Rhodes used missionaries and his British South Africa Company, chartered by the British government, to force African chiefs to accept British protectorates, and he managed to add Southern and Northern Rhodesia (modern-day Zimbabwe and Zambia) to the British Empire.

Southern Rhodesia is one of the most egregious examples of Europeans misleading African rulers to take their land. In 1888 the Ndebele (or Matabele) king, Lobengula (1845–1894), ruler over much of modern southwestern Zimbabwe, met with three of Rhodes's men, led by Charles Rudd, and signed the Rudd Concession. Lobengula believed he was simply allowing a handful of British fortune hunters a few years of gold prospecting in Matabeleland. Lobengula had been misled, however, by the resident London Missionary Society missionary (and Lobengula's supposed friend), the Reverend Charles Helm, as to the document's true meaning and Rhodes's hand behind it. Even though Lobengula soon repudiated the agreement, he opened the way for Rhodes's seizure of the territory.

The Transvaal gold fields still remained in Afrikaner hands, however, so Rhodes and the imperialist clique initiated a series of events that sparked the South African War of 1899–1902 (also known as the Anglo-Boer War). Often considered the first "total war," this conflict witnessed the British use of a scorched-earth strategy to destroy Afrikaner property, and concentration camps to detain Afrikaner families and their servants, thousands of whom died of illness.

The long and bitter war divided whites in South Africa, but South Africa's blacks were the biggest losers. The British had promised the Afrikaners representative government in return for surrender in 1902, and they made good on their pledge. In 1910 the Cape Colony, Natal, the Orange Free State, and the Transvaal formed a new self-governing Union of South Africa. After the peace settlement, because the white minority held almost all political power in the new union, and because Afrikaners outnumbered English-speakers, the Afrikaners began to regain what they had lost on the battlefield. South Africa, under a joint British-Afrikaner government within the British Empire, began the creation of a modern segregated society that culminated in an even harsher system of racial separation, or apartheid, after World War II.

The Struggle for South Africa, 1878

- Boer republics
- British territory
- Battle

KALAHARI DESERT
TRANSVAAL
ZULULAND
ORANGE FREE STATE
NATAL
CAPE COLONY
Cape Town
ATLANTIC OCEAN
INDIAN OCEAN

Colonialism's Impact After 1900

By 1900 much of Africa had been conquered and a system of colonial administration was taking shape. In general, this system weakened or shattered the traditional social order and challenged accepted values.

The self-proclaimed political goal of the French and the British — the principal colonial powers — was to provide good government for their African subjects, especially after World War I. "Good government" meant, above all, law and order. It meant strong, authoritarian government, which maintained a small army, built up an African police force, and included a modern bureaucracy capable of taxing and governing the population. Many African leaders and their peoples had chosen not to resist the invaders' superior force, and others stopped fighting and turned to other, less violent means of resisting colonial rule. Thus the goal of law and order was widely achieved.

Colonial governments demonstrated much less interest in providing basic social services. Education, public health, hospital, and other social service

CHAPTER LOCATOR | What were the most significant changes in Africa during the nineteenth century? | What were the causes and consequences of European empire building after 1880?

758 CHAPTER 25 AFRICA, THE OTTOMAN EMPIRE, AND THE NEW IMPERIALISM expenditures increased after the Great War but still remained small. Europeans feared the political implications of mass education and typically relied instead on the modest efforts of state-subsidized mission schools. Moreover, they tried to make even their poorest colonies pay for themselves. Thus government workers' salaries normally absorbed nearly all tax revenues.

Economically, the colonial goal was to draw the African interior into the world economy on terms favorable to the dominant Europeans. The key was railroads linking coastal trading centers to interior outposts. Cheap, dependable transportation facilitated easy shipment of raw materials out and manufactured goods in. Railroads had two other important outcomes: they allowed quick troop movements to put down local unrest, and they allowed many African peasants to earn wages for the first time.

The focus on economic development and low-cost rule explains why colonial governments were reluctant to move decisively against slavery within Africa. Officials feared that an abrupt abolition of slavery where it existed would disrupt production and lead to costly revolts by powerful slaveholding elites, especially in Muslim areas. Thus colonial regimes settled for halfway measures designed to satisfy humanitarian groups in Europe and also make all Africans, free or enslaved, participate in a market economy and work for wages. Even this cautious policy emboldened many slaves to run away, thereby facilitating a rapid decline of slavery within Africa.

Colonial governments also often imposed head or hut taxes. Payable only in labor or European currency, these taxes compelled Africans to work for their white overlords. In some regions, particularly in West Africa, African peasants continued to respond freely to the new economic opportunities by voluntarily shifting to export crops on their own farms. Overall, the result of these developments was an increase in wage work and production geared to the world market and a decline in nomadic herding and traditional self-sufficient farming of sustainable crops. In sum, the imposition of bureaucratic Western rule and the gradual growth of a world-oriented cash economy after 1900 had a revolutionary impact on large parts of Africa.

QUICK REVIEW

How and why did European nations engage
in the "scramble for Africa"?

How did the Ottoman Empire and Egypt try to modernize themselves?

What were the global consequences of European industrialization?

What fueled migration, and what was the pattern of this movement of people?

☑ LearningCurve
Check what you know.

> What were the causes and consequences of European empire building after 1880?

Tools for Empire Building

Western technological advances aided imperialist ambitions in Africa. The Maxim gun was highly mobile and could lay down a continuous barrage that decimated charging enemies, as in the slaughter of Muslim tribesman at the Battle of Omdurman in Sudan. Quinine, first taken around 1850 to prevent the contraction of malaria, enabled Europeans to move safely into the African interior and overwhelm native peoples. And the development of the electromagnetic telegraph in the 1840s permitted rapid long-distance communications for the first time in history. (gun: Private Collection/Peter Newark Military Pictures/The Bridgeman Art Library; quinine: Wellcome Library, London; telegraph: John D. Jenkins, www.sparksmuseum.com)

WESTERN EXPANSION INTO AFRICA AND ASIA reached its apex between about 1880 and 1914. In those years the leading European nations sent streams of money and manufactured goods to both continents and also rushed to create or enlarge vast overseas political empires. This frantic activity differed sharply with the limited economic penetration of non-Western territories between 1816 and 1880, which, albeit by naked military force, had left a China or a Japan "opened" but politically independent (see Chapter 26). By contrast,

CHAPTER LOCATOR | What were the most significant changes in Africa during the nineteenth century? | **What were the causes and consequences of European empire building after 1880?**

late-nineteenth-century empires recalled the old European colonial empires of the seventeenth and eighteenth centuries and led contemporaries to speak of the **new imperialism**.

Causes of the New Imperialism

Economic motives played an important role in the extension of political empires, especially of the British Empire. By the 1870s France, Germany, and the United States were rapidly industrializing. For a century Great Britain had been the "workshop of the world," the dominant modern industrial power. Now it was losing its industrial leadership, as its share of global manufacturing output dropped from 33 percent to just 14 percent between 1870 and 1914, and facing increasingly tough competition in foreign markets. In this changing environment of widening economic internationalism, the world experienced one of the worse economic depressions in history, the Long Depression, which lasted from 1873 to 1879. To protect home industries, America and Europe (except for Britain and the Netherlands) raised tariff barriers, abandoning the century-long practice of free trade and laissez-faire capitalism (see page 715). Unable to export their goods and faced with excess production, market saturation, and high unemployment, Britain, the other European powers, and the United States turned to imperial expansion, seeking African and Asian colonies to sell their products and acquire cheap raw materials. The Long Depression was arguably the single most important spark touching off the age of new imperialism.

Economic gains from the new imperialism proved limited, however, before 1914. The new colonies were too poor to buy much, and they offered few immediately profitable investments. Nonetheless, colonies became important for political and diplomatic reasons. Each leading European country considered them crucial to national security, military power, and international prestige.

Colonial rivalries reflected the increasing aggressiveness of Social Darwinian theories of brutal competition among races (see page 736). From a Social Darwinist perspective, European nations, considered as racially distinct parts of the dominant white race, had to seize colonies to prove their strength and virility. Moreover, since racial struggle was nature's inescapable law, the conquest of "inferior" peoples was just. Social Darwinism and harsh racial doctrines fostered imperialist expansion.

So, too, did the industrial world's unprecedented technological and military superiority. Three developments were crucial. First, the rapidly firing machine gun was an ultimate weapon in many unequal battles. Second, newly discovered **quinine** effectively controlled malaria attacks, which had previously decimated Europeans in the tropics. Third, the introduction of steam power (see page 688) strengthened the Western powers in two ways. Militarily, they could swiftly transport their armies by sea or rail where they were most needed. Economically, steamships with ever-larger cargoes now made round-trip journeys to far-flung colonies much more quickly and economically. Small steamboats could travel back and forth along the coast and also carry goods up and down Africa's great rivers. Likewise, freight cars pulled by powerful steam engines replaced the thousands of African porters hitherto responsible for carrying raw materials from the interior to the coast. Never before—and never again after 1914—would the

new imperialism

▶ The late-nineteenth-century drive by European countries to create vast political empires abroad.

quinine

▶ An agent that proved effective in controlling attacks of malaria, which had previously decimated Europeans in the tropics.

How did the Ottoman Empire and Egypt try to modernize themselves?

What were the global consequences of European industrialization?

What fueled migration, and what was the pattern of this movement of people?

✓ LearningCurve
Check what you know.

technological gap between the West and the non-Western regions of the world be so great.

Domestic political and class conflicts also contributed to overseas expansion. Conservative political leaders often manipulated colonial issues in order to divert popular attention from domestic problems and to create a false sense of national unity. Imperial propagandists relentlessly stressed that colonies benefited workers as well as capitalists, and they encouraged the masses to savor foreign triumphs and imperial glory.

Finally, special-interest groups in each country were powerful agents of expansion. Shipping companies wanted lucrative subsidies. White settlers wanted more land. Missionaries and humanitarians wanted to spread religion and stop the slave trade. Military men and colonial officials foresaw rapid advancement and high-paid positions in growing empires. The actions of such groups pushed the course of empire forward.

A "Civilizing Mission"

To rationalize imperialist expansion, Europeans and Americans argued they could and should "civilize" supposedly primitive non-Western peoples. According to this view, Africans and Asians would benefit from Western educations, modern economies, cities, advanced medicine, and higher living standards and eventually might be ready for self-government and Western democracy.

Another argument was that imperial government protected colonized peoples from ethnic warfare, the slave trade within Africa, and other forms of exploitation by white settlers and business people. Thus the French spoke of their sacred "civilizing mission." In 1899 Rudyard Kipling (1865–1936), perhaps the most influential British writer of the 1890s, exhorted Westerners to unselfish service in distant lands (while warning of the high costs involved) in his poem "The White Man's Burden." Kipling's poem, written in response to America's seizure of the Philippines after the Spanish-American War, and his concept of a **white man's burden** won wide acceptance among American imperialists. This principle was an important factor in the decision to rule, rather than liberate, the Philippines after the Spanish-American War (see page 838). Like their European counterparts, these Americans believed their civilization had reached unprecedented heights, enabling them to bestow unique benefits on all "less advanced" peoples.

Imperialists also claimed that peace and stability under European or American dominion permitted the spread of Christianity. In Africa Catholic and Protestant missionaries competed with Islam south of the Sahara, seeking converts and building schools. Many Africans' first real contact with Europeans and Americans was in mission schools. Some peoples, such as the Ibo in Nigeria, became highly Christianized. Such successes in black Africa contrasted with the general failure of missionary efforts in the Islamic world and in much of Asia.

Critics of Imperialism

Imperial expansion aroused sharp, even bitter, critics. One forceful attack was delivered in 1902, after the unpopular South African War, by radical English economist J. A. Hobson (1858–1940) in his *Imperialism*. Hobson contended that the

white man's burden

▶ The idea that Europeans could and should civilize more primitive nonwhite peoples and that imperialism would eventually provide nonwhites with modern achievements and higher standards of living.

CHAPTER LOCATOR | What were the most significant changes in Africa during the nineteenth century?

What were the causes and consequences of European empire building after 1880?

CHAPTER 25
762 AFRICA, THE OTTOMAN EMPIRE, AND THE NEW IMPERIALISM

rush to acquire colonies resulted from the economic needs of unregulated (by governments) capitalism. Moreover, Hobson argued, the quest for empire diverted popular attention away from domestic reform and the need to reduce the great gap between rich and poor at home. These and similar arguments had limited appeal because most people fervently believed imperialism was economically profitable for the homeland. Both Hobson and public opinion were wrong, however. Most British and European investors put the bulk of their money in the United States, Canada, Russia and other industrializing countries. Sub-Saharan Africa accounted for less than 5 percent of British exports in 1890, and British investments in Africa flowed predominantly to the mines in southern African. Thus, while some sectors of the British economy did profit from imperial conquests, and trade with these conquests was greater just before the Great War than in 1870, overall profits from imperialism were marginal at best.

Hobson and many Western critics struck home, however, with their moral condemnation of whites imperiously ruling nonwhites. Kipling and his kind were lampooned as racist bullies whose rule rested on brutality, racial contempt, and the Maxim machine gun. Polish-born novelist Joseph Conrad (1857–1924), in *Heart of Darkness* (1902), castigated the "pure selfishness" of Europeans in "civilizing" Africa.

Critics charged Europeans with applying a degrading double standard and failing to live up to their own noble ideals. At home Europeans had won or were winning representative government, individual liberties, and a certain equality of opportunity. In their empires Europeans imposed military dictatorships on Africans and Asians, forced them to work involuntarily, and discriminated against them shamelessly.

African and Asian Resistance

Initially African and Asian rulers often responded to imperialist incursions by trying to drive the unwelcome foreigners away, as in China and Japan (see Chapter 26). Violent antiforeign reactions exploded elsewhere again and again, but the industrialized West's superior military technology almost invariably prevailed. In addition, Europeans sought to divide and conquer by giving special powers and privileges to some individuals and groups from among the local population, including traditional leaders such as chiefs, landowners, and religious figures, and Western-educated professionals and civil servants, including police officers and military officers. These local elites recognized the imperial power realities in which they were enmeshed, and manipulated them to maintain or gain authority over the masses. Some concluded that the West was superior in certain ways and that they needed to reform and modernize their societies by copying some European achievements. By ruling indirectly through a local elite, a relatively small number of Europeans could maintain control over much larger populations without constant rebellion and protest. European empires were won by force, but they were maintained by cultural as well as military and political means.

Nevertheless, imperial rule was in many ways an imposing edifice built on sand. Acceptance of European rule was shallow and weak among the colonized masses. They were often quick to follow determined charismatic personalities who came to oppose the Europeans. Such leaders always arose, both when

| How did the Ottoman Empire and Egypt try to modernize themselves? | What were the global consequences of European industrialization? | What fueled migration, and what was the pattern of this movement of people? | ✓ LearningCurve Check what you know. |

763

Europeans ruled directly, or indirectly through native governments, for at least two basic reasons.

First, the nonconformists—the eventual anti-imperialist leaders—developed a burning desire for human dignity. They felt such dignity was incompatible with, and impossible under, foreign rule. Second, potential leaders found in the Western world the necessary ideologies and justification for their protest. Above all, they found themselves attracted to the nineteenth-century Western ideology of nationalism, which asserted that every people had the right to control their own destiny (see Chapter 24). After 1917 anti-imperialist revolt found another weapon in Lenin's version of Marxist socialism.

> ## QUICK REVIEW

What were the defining characteristics of the "new imperialism"?

CHAPTER LOCATOR | What were the most significant changes in Africa during the nineteenth century? | What were the causes and consequences of European empire building after 1880?

CHAPTER 25

764 AFRICA, THE OTTOMAN EMPIRE, AND THE NEW IMPERIALISM

How did the Ottoman Empire and Egypt try to modernize themselves, and what were the most important results?

Egyptian Travel Guide

Ismail's efforts to transform Cairo were fairly successful. As a result, European tourists could more easily visit the country that their governments dominated. Ordinary Europeans were lured to exotic lands by travel books like this colorful "Official Guide" to an exhibition on Cairo held in Berlin. (Private Collection/Archives Charmet/The Bridgeman Art Library)

STRETCHING FROM WEST AFRICA into southeastern Europe and across Southwest Asia to the East Indies, Islamic civilization competed successfully with western Europe for centuries. Beginning in the late seventeenth century, however, the rising absolutist states of Austria and Russia began to challenge the Ottoman Empire and gradually to reverse Ottoman rule in southeastern Europe. In the nineteenth century European industrialization and nation building further altered the long-standing balance of power, and Western expansion eventually posed a serious challenge to Muslims everywhere.

Decline and Reform in the Ottoman Empire

Although the Ottoman Empire began a slow decline after Suleiman the Magnificent in the sixteenth century, the relationship between the Ottomans and the Europeans in about 1750 was still one of roughly equal strength. This parity

How did the Ottoman Empire and Egypt try to modernize themselves?	What were the global consequences of European industrialization?	What fueled migration, and what was the pattern of this movement of people?	✓ LearningCurve Check what you know.

began to change quickly and radically, however, in the later eighteenth century, as the Ottomans fell behind western Europe in science, industrial skill, and military technology.

A transformation of the army was absolutely necessary to battle the Europeans more effectively and enhance the sultanate's authority within the empire. There were two primary obstacles to change, however. First, Ottoman military weakness reflected the decline of the sultan's "slave army," the so-called janissary corps (see page 490). With time, the janissaries—boys and other slaves raised in Turkey as Muslims, then trained to serve in the Ottoman infantry's elite corps—became a corrupt and privileged hereditary caste, absolutely opposed to any military innovations that might undermine their high status. Second, the empire was no longer a centralized military state. Instead local governors were becoming increasingly independent, pursuing their own interests and even seeking to establish their own governments and hereditary dynasties.

Sultan Selim III (r. 1789–1807) understood these realities, but when he tried to reorganize the army, the janissaries refused to use any "Christian" equipment. In 1807 they revolted and executed Selim in a palace revolution, one of many that plagued the Ottoman state. Selim's successor, the reform-minded Mahmud II (r. 1808–1839), proceeded cautiously, picking loyal officers and building his dependable artillery corps. In 1826 his council ordered the janissaries to drill in the European manner. As expected, the janissaries revolted and charged the palace, where they were mowed down by the waiting artillery.

The destruction and abolition of the janissaries cleared the way for building a new army, but it came too late to stop the rise of Muhammad Ali, the Ottoman governor in Egypt. In 1831 his French-trained forces occupied the Ottoman province of Syria and appeared ready to depose Mahmud II. The Ottoman sultan survived, but only with help from Britain, Russia, and Austria. The Ottomans were saved again in 1839, after their forces were routed trying to drive Muhammad Ali from Syria. In the last months of 1840 Russian diplomatic efforts, British and Austrian naval blockades, and threatened military action convinced Muhammad Ali to return Syria to the Ottomans. European powers preferred a weak and dependent Ottoman state to a strong and revitalized Muslim entity under a leader such as Muhammad Ali.

In 1839, realizing their precarious position, liberal Ottoman statesmen launched an era of radical reforms, which lasted until 1876 and culminated in a constitution and a short-lived parliament. Known as the Tanzimat, these reforms were designed to remake the empire on a western European model. The new decrees called for Muslim, Christian, and Jewish equality before the law and in business, security of life and property, and a modernized administration and military. New commercial laws allowed free importation of foreign goods, as British advisers demanded, and permitted foreign merchants to operate freely throughout an economically dependent empire. Under British pressure, slavery in the empire was drastically curtailed, though not abolished completely. Of great significance, growing numbers among the elite and the upwardly mobile embraced Western education, adopted Western manners and artistic styles, and accepted secular values to some extent.

The Tanzimat achieved only partial success. The Ottoman state and society failed to regain its earlier power and authority for several reasons. First, implementation of the reforms required a new generation of well-trained and trust-

Tanzimat

▶ A set of radical reforms designed to remake the Ottoman Empire on a western European model.

CHAPTER LOCATOR | What were the most significant changes in Africa during the nineteenth century? | What were the causes and consequences of European empire building after 1880?

CHAPTER 25
766 AFRICA, THE OTTOMAN EMPIRE, AND THE NEW IMPERIALISM

worthy officials, and that generation did not exist. Second, the liberal reforms failed to halt the growth of nationalism among Christian subjects in the Balkans (see below and Chapter 28), which resulted in crises and defeats that undermined all reform efforts. Third, the Ottoman initiatives did not curtail the appetite of Western imperialism, and European bankers gained a stranglehold on Ottoman finances. In 1875 the Ottoman state had to declare partial bankruptcy and place its finances in the hands of European creditors.

Finally, the elaboration of equal rights for citizens and religious communities failed to create greater unity within the state. Religious disputes increased, worsened by the Great Powers' relentless interference. This development embittered relations between religious communities, distracted the government from its reform mission, and split Muslims into secularists and religious conservatives. Islamic conservatives became the most dependable supporters of Sultan Abdül-hamid II (r. 1876–1909), who abandoned the model of European liberalism in his long and repressive reign.

Meanwhile, the Ottoman Empire gradually lost control of its vast territories. Serbian nationalists rebelled and forced the Ottomans to grant Serbia local autonomy in 1816. The Greeks revolted against Ottoman rule in 1821 and won their national independence in 1830. As the Ottomans dealt with these uprisings by their Christian subjects in Europe, they failed to defend their Islamic provinces in North Africa. In 1830 French armies began their conquest of the Arabic-speaking province of Algeria.

Finally, during the Russo-Turkish War (1877–1878), absolutist Russia and a coalition of Balkan countries pushed southward into Ottoman lands and won a decisive victory. At the Congress of Berlin in 1878, the European Great Powers and the Ottoman Empire met to formally recognize Bulgarian, Romanian, Serbian, and Montenegrin independence. The Ottomans also lost territory to the Russians in the Caucasus, Austria-Hungary occupied the Ottoman provinces of Bosnia-Herzegovina and Novi Pazar, and Great Britain took over Cyprus.

The combination of declining international power and conservative tyranny eventually led to a powerful resurgence of the modernizing impulse among idealistic Turkish exiles in Europe and young army officers in Istanbul. These fervent patriots, the so-called **Young Turks**, seized power in the 1908 revolution, overthrowing Sultan Abdülhamid II. They made his brother Mehmed V (r. 1909–1918) the figurehead sultan and forced him to implement reforms. Though they failed to stop the rising tide of anti-Ottoman nationalism in the Balkans, the Young Turks did help prepare the way for the birth of modern secular Turkey after the defeat and collapse of the Ottoman Empire in World War I (see pages 864–866).

Egypt: From Reform to British Occupation

Egypt had been ruled by a succession of foreigners from 525 B.C.E. to the Ottoman conquest in the early sixteenth century. In 1798, as France and Britain prepared for war in Europe, Napoleon Bonaparte invaded Egypt, thereby threatening British access to India, and occupied the territory for three years. Into the power vacuum left by the French withdrawal stepped an extraordinary Albanian-born Turkish general, Muhammad Ali (1769–1849).

Appointed Egypt's governor in 1805, Muhammad Ali set out to build his own state on the strength of a large, powerful army organized along European lines.

Ottoman Decline in the Balkans, 1818–1830

Young Turks
▸ Fervent patriots who seized power in the revolution of 1908, forcing the conservative sultan to implement reforms; they helped pave the way for the birth of modern secular Turkey.

How did the Ottoman Empire and Egypt try to modernize themselves?

What were the global consequences of European industrialization?

What fueled migration, and what was the pattern of this movement of people?

✓ LearningCurve
Check what you know.

767

He also reformed the government and promoted modern industry. (See "Individuals in Society: Muhammad Ali," page 769.) For a time Muhammad Ali's ambitious strategy seemed to work, but it eventually foundered when his armies occupied Syria and he threatened the Ottoman sultan, Mahmud II. In the face of European military might and diplomatic entreaties, Muhammad Ali agreed to peace with his Ottoman overlords and withdrew. In return he was given unprecedented hereditary rule over Egypt and Sudan. By his death in 1849, Muhammad Ali had established a strong and virtually independent Egyptian state within the Ottoman Empire.

To pay for a modern army and industrialization, Muhammad Ali encouraged the development of commercial agriculture geared to the European market, which had profound social implications. Egyptian peasants had been largely self-sufficient, growing food on state-owned land allotted to them by tradition. High-ranking officials and members of Muhammad Ali's family began carving private landholdings out of the state domain, and they forced the peasants to grow cash crops for European markets.

Muhammad Ali's modernization policies attracted growing numbers of Europeans to the banks of the Nile. Europeans served as army officers, engineers, doctors, government officials, and police officers. Others worked in trade, finance, and shipping. Above all, Europeans living in Egypt combined with landlords and officials to continue steering commercial agriculture toward exports. As throughout the Ottoman Empire, Europeans enjoyed important commercial and legal privileges and formed an economic elite.

The Suez Canal, 1869

Following in his grandfather's footsteps, Ismail (r. 1863–1879) was a westernizing autocrat. He promoted cotton production, and exports to Europe soared. Ismail also borrowed large sums, and with his support the Suez Canal was completed by a French company in 1869, shortening the voyage from Europe to Asia by thousands of miles. Cairo acquired modern boulevards and Western hotels.

Major cultural and intellectual changes accompanied the political and economic ones. The Arabic of the masses, rather than the conqueror's Turkish, became the official language, and young, European-educated Egyptians helped spread new skills and ideas in the bureaucracy. A host of writers, intellectuals, and religious thinkers responded to the novel conditions with innovative ideas that had a powerful impact in Egypt and other Muslim societies.

Three influential figures who represented broad families of thought were especially significant. The teacher and writer Jamal al-Din al-Afghani (1838/39–1897) argued for the purification of Islamic religious belief, Muslim unity, and a revolutionary overthrow of corrupt Muslim rulers and foreign exploiters. The more moderate Muhammad Abduh (1849–1905) launched the modern Islamic reform movement. Abduh concluded that Muslims should adopt a flexible, reasoned approach to change, modernity, science, social questions, and foreign ideas and not reject these out of hand.

Finally, the writer Qasim Amin (1863–1908) represented those who found inspiration in the West in the late nineteenth century. In his influential book *The Liberation of Women* (1899), Amin argued forcefully that superior education for European women had contributed greatly to the Islamic world's falling far behind the West. In his view, the rejuvenation of Muslim societies required greater equality for women.

CHAPTER LOCATOR | What were the most significant changes in Africa during the nineteenth century? | What were the causes and consequences of European empire building after 1880?

CHAPTER 25
768 AFRICA, THE OTTOMAN EMPIRE, AND THE NEW IMPERIALISM

INDIVIDUALS IN SOCIETY
Muhammad Ali

The dynamic leader Muhammad Ali stands across the history of modern Egypt like a colossus. Yet the essence of the man remains a mystery, and historians vary greatly in their interpretations of him. Sent by the Ottomans, with Albanian troops, to oppose the French occupation of Egypt in 1799, Muhammad Ali maneuvered skillfully after the French withdrawal in 1802. In 1805 he was named pasha, or Ottoman governor, of Egypt. Only the Mamluks remained as rivals. Originally an elite corps of Turkish slave soldiers, the Mamluks had become a semifeudal military ruling class living off the Egyptian peasantry. In 1811 Muhammad Ali offered to make peace, and he invited the Mamluk chiefs and their retainers to a banquet in Cairo's Citadel. As the unsuspecting guests processed through a narrow passage, his troops opened fire, slaughtering all the Mamluk leaders.

After eliminating his foes, Muhammad Ali embarked on a program of radical reforms. He reorganized agriculture and commerce, reclaiming most of the cultivated land for the state domain, which he controlled. He also established state agencies to monopolize, for his own profit, the sale of agricultural goods. Commercial agriculture geared to exports to Europe developed rapidly, especially after the successful introduction of high-quality cotton in 1821. Canals and irrigation systems along the Nile were rebuilt and expanded.

Muhammad Ali used his growing revenues to recast his army along European lines. He recruited French officers to train the soldiers. As the military grew, so did the need for hospitals, schools of medicine and languages, and secular education. Young Turks and some Egyptians were sent to Europe for advanced study. The ruler boldly financed factories to produce uniforms and weapons, and he prohibited the importation of European goods so as to protect Egypt's infant industries. In the 1830s state factories were making one-fourth of Egypt's cotton into cloth. Above all, Muhammad Ali drafted Egyptian peasants into the military for the first time, thereby expanding his army to one hundred thousand men. It was this force that conquered the Ottoman province of Syria, threatened the sultan in Istanbul, and triggered European intervention. Grudgingly recognized by his Ottoman overlord as Egypt's hereditary ruler in 1841, Muhammad Ali nevertheless had to accept European and Ottoman demands to give up Syria and

Muhammad Ali, the Albanian-born ruler of Egypt, in 1839. (© Mary Evans Picture Library/The Image Works)

abolish his monopolies and protective tariffs. The old ruler then lost heart; his reforms languished, and his factories disappeared.

In the attempt to understand Muhammad Ali and his significance, many historians have concluded that he was a national hero, the "founder of modern Egypt." His ambitious state-building projects — hospitals, schools, factories, and the army — were the basis for an Egyptian reawakening and eventual independence from the Ottomans' oppressive foreign rule. Similarly, state-sponsored industrialization promised an escape from poverty and Western domination, which was foiled only by European intervention and British insistence on free trade.

A growing minority of historians question these views. They see Muhammad Ali primarily as an Ottoman adventurer. In their view, he did not aim for national independence for Egypt, but rather "intended to carve out a small empire for himself and for his children after him."* Paradoxically, his success, which depended on heavy taxes and brutal army service, led to Egyptian nationalism among the Arabic-speaking masses, but that new nationalism was directed against Muhammad Ali and his Turkish-speaking entourage. Continuing research into this leader's life will help resolve these conflicting interpretations.

*K. Fahmy, *All the Pasha's Men: Mehmed Ali, His Army, and the Making of Modern Egypt* (Cambridge: Cambridge University Press, 1997), p. 310.

QUESTIONS FOR ANALYSIS

1. Which of Muhammad Ali's actions support the interpretation that he was the founder of modern Egypt? Which actions support the opposing view?
2. After you have studied Chapter 26, compare Muhammad Ali and the Meiji reformers in Japan. What accounts for the similarities and differences?

ONLINE DOCUMENT PROJECT

How did reformers address the challenges facing the Ottoman Empire in the nineteenth century? Read excerpts from Ottoman reformers, and then complete a quiz and writing assignment based on the evidence and details from this chapter. *See inside the front cover to learn more.*

Egypt changed rapidly during Ismail's rule, but his projects were reckless and enormously expensive. By 1876 the Egyptian government could not pay the interest on its debt. Rather than let Egypt go bankrupt and repudiate its loans, France and Great Britain intervened, forcing Ismail to appoint French and British commissioners to oversee Egyptian finances. This meant that Europeans would determine the state budget and in effect rule Egypt.

Foreign financial control evoked a violent nationalistic reaction. Continuing diplomatic pressure, which forced Ismail to abdicate in favor of his weak son, Tewfiq (r. 1879–1892), resulted in bloody anti-European riots in Alexandria in 1882. In response, the British fleet bombarded Alexandria, and a British expeditionary force occupied all of Egypt. British armies remained in Egypt until 1956.

Initially the British maintained the fiction that Egypt was an autonomous province of the Ottoman Empire. In reality, British consul, General Evelyn Baring, later Lord Cromer, ruled the country after 1883. Baring was a paternalistic reformer. He initiated tax reforms and made some improvements to conditions for peasants. Foreign bondholders received their interest payments, while Egyptian nationalists chafed under foreign rule.

> **QUICK REVIEW**

How did European nations undermine reform efforts in the Ottoman Empire and in Egypt?

CHAPTER LOCATOR | What were the most significant changes in Africa during the nineteenth century? | What were the causes and consequences of European empire building after 1880?

CHAPTER 25
770   AFRICA, THE OTTOMAN EMPIRE, AND THE NEW IMPERIALISM

What were the global consequences of European industrialization between 1800 and 1914?

British East African Railway Poster

Europeans constructed railroads in most of their African colonies to haul raw materials from the interior to coastal ports and to transport colonial officials, white settlers, and foreign tourists. Britain's East African railroad line from Kampala, Uganda, to the Kenyan port city of Mombasa was one of the most famous and most romanticized. Indians from British India did much of the construction and then remained in Kenya to form substantial Indian communities. President Theodore Roosevelt rode this train while on his 1909 African safari.
(Advertising Archive/Courtesy The Everett Collection)

OVER THE COURSE OF THE NINETEENTH CENTURY the Industrial Revolution expanded and transformed economic relations across the face of the earth. As a result, the world's total income grew as never before, and international trade boomed. Western nations used their superior military power to force non-Western nations to open their doors to Western economic interests. Consequently, the largest share of the ever-increasing gains from trade flowed to the West, resulting in a stark division between rich and poor countries.

The Rise of Global Inequality

A gap between the industrializing regions (Europe, North America, Japan) and the nonindustrializing regions (mainly Africa, Asia, and Latin America) opened and grew steadily throughout the nineteenth century (Figure 25.1). Moreover, this pattern of uneven global development became institutionalized, built into the structure of the world economy.

| How did the Ottoman Empire and Egypt try to modernize themselves? | **What were the global consequences of European industrialization?** | What fueled migration, and what was the pattern of this movement of people? | LearningCurve Check what you know. |

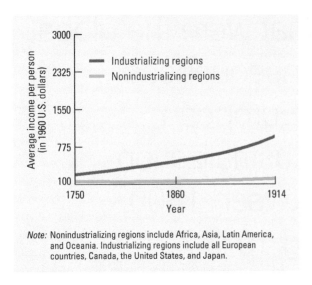

FIGURE 25.1 ■ The Growth of Average Income per Person Worldwide, 1750–1914

(Source of data: P. Bairoch and M. Lévy-Leboyer, eds., *Disparities in Economic Development Since the Industrial Revolution*, published 1981, Macmillan Publishers.)

Note: Nonindustrializing regions include Africa, Asia, Latin America, and Oceania. Industrializing regions include all European countries, Canada, the United States, and Japan.

In 1750 the average living standard was no higher in Europe as a whole than in the rest of the world. By 1914 the average person in the wealthiest countries had an income four or five times as great (and in Great Britain nine or ten times as great) as an average person's income in the poorest countries of Africa and Asia. The rise in average income and well-being reflected the rising level of industrialization in Great Britain and then in the other developed countries before World War I.

The reasons for these enormous income disparities have generated a great deal of debate. One school of interpretation stresses that the West used science, technology, capitalist organization, and even its critical worldview to create its wealth and greater physical well-being. An opposing school argues that the West used its political, economic, and military power to steal much of its riches through its rapacious colonialism in the nineteenth and twentieth centuries.

These issues are complex, and there are few simple answers. As noted in Chapter 23, the wealth-creating potential of technological improvement and more intensive capitalist organization was great. At the same time, the initial breakthroughs in the late eighteenth century rested in part on Great Britain's having already used political force to dominate a substantial part of the world economy. In the nineteenth century other industrializing countries joined with Britain to extend Western dominion over the entire world economy. Unprecedented wealth was created, but the lion's share of that new wealth flowed to the West and its propertied classes and to a tiny indigenous elite of cooperative rulers, landowners, and merchants.

The World Market

World trade was a powerful stimulus to economic development in the nineteenth century. In 1913 the value of world trade was about twenty-five times what it had been in 1800, even though prices of manufactured goods and raw materials were lower in 1913 than in 1800. In a general way, this enormous increase in international commerce summed up the growth of an interlocking world economy centered in Europe.

Great Britain played a key role in using trade to tie the world together economically. In 1815 Britain already possessed a colonial empire. The technological breakthroughs of the Industrial Revolution encouraged British manufacturers to seek export markets around the world. After Parliament repealed laws restricting grain importation in 1846, Britain also became the world's leading importer of foreign goods. Free access to Britain's market stimulated the development of mines and plantations in Africa and Asia.

The conquest of distance facilitated the growth of trade. Wherever railroads were built, they drastically reduced transportation costs, opened new economic opportunities, and called forth new skills and attitudes. Much of the railroad construction undertaken in Africa, Asia, and Latin America connected seaports with inland cities and regions, as opposed to linking and developing cities and regions

CHAPTER LOCATOR | What were the most significant changes in Africa during the nineteenth century?

What were the causes and consequences of European empire building after 1880?

within a country. Thus railroads dovetailed with Western economic interests, facilitating the inflow and sale of Western manufactured goods and the export and development of local raw materials.

Steam power also revolutionized transportation by sea. Steam power was first used to supplant sails on the world's oceans in the late 1860s. Passenger and freight rates tumbled, and the shipment of low-priced raw materials from one continent to another became feasible.

The revolution in land and sea transportation helped European settlers seize vast, thinly populated territories and produce agricultural products and raw materials for sale in Europe. Improved transportation enabled Asia, Africa, and Latin America to export agricultural commodities and industrial raw materials.

Intercontinental trade was enormously facilitated by the Suez Canal and the Panama Canal (see page 839). Of great importance, too, was large and continual investment in modern port facilities. Finally, transoceanic telegraph cables inaugurated rapid communications among the world's financial centers and linked world commodity prices in a global network.

The growth of trade and the conquest of distance encouraged Europeans to make massive foreign investments beginning about 1840, but not to European colonies or protectorates in Asia and Africa. About three-quarters of total European investment went to other European countries, the United States and Canada, Australia and New Zealand, and Latin America. Much of this investment was peaceful and mutually beneficial for lenders and borrowers. The victims were Native Americans, Australian Aborigines, New Zealand Maoris, and other native peoples who were displaced and decimated by an aggressively expanding Western society (see Chapter 27).

QUICK REVIEW

What role did technology play in late nineteenth-century globalization?

How did the Ottoman Empire and Egypt try to modernize themselves?

What were the global consequences of European industrialization?

What fueled migration, and what was the pattern of this movement of people?

☑ LearningCurve
Check what you know.

What fueled migration, and what was the general pattern of this unprecedented movement of people?

Steerage Passengers, 1902

Conditions for steerage passengers traveling from Europe to the Americas were cramped, as evidenced by this photo from 1902. (Private Collection/Peter Newark American Pictures/The Bridgeman Art Library)

great migration

▶ The mass movement of people from Europe in the nineteenth century, one reason that the West's impact on the world was so powerful and complex.

A POIGNANT HUMAN DRAMA WAS INTERWOVEN with this worldwide economic expansion: millions of people left their ancestral lands in one of history's greatest migrations, the so-called **great migration**. In the early eighteenth century the world's population entered a period of rapid growth that continued unabated through the nineteenth and twentieth centuries. Europe's population (including Asiatic Russia) more than doubled during the nineteenth century. Since African and Asian populations increased more slowly than those in Europe, Europeans and peoples of predominantly European origin jumped from about 22 percent of the world's total in 1850 to a high of about 38 percent in 1930.

CHAPTER LOCATOR | What were the most significant changes in Africa during the nineteenth century? | What were the causes and consequences of European empire building after 1880?

Rapid population growth led to relative overpopulation in area after area in Europe and was a driving force behind emigration and Western expansion. Millions of country folk moved to nearby cities, and the more adventuresome went abroad, in search of work and economic opportunity. Wars, famine, poverty, and, particularly in the case of Russian and eastern European Jews, bigotry and discrimination were also leading causes for emigrants to leave their ancestral homelands. More than 60 million people left Europe over the course of the nineteenth century, primarily for the rapidly growing "areas of European settlement" — North and South America, Australia, New Zealand, and Siberia (see Chapter 27).

The European migrant was most often a small peasant landowner or a village craftsman whose traditional way of life was threatened by too little land, estate agriculture, and cheap factory-made goods. Determined to maintain or improve their precarious status, the vast majority of migrants were young and often unmarried. Many European migrants returned home after some time abroad.

Ties of family and friendship played a crucial role in the movement of peoples. Over several years a given province or village might lose significant numbers of its inhabitants to migration. These then settled together in rural enclaves or tightly knit urban neighborhoods in foreign lands thousands of miles away. Very often a strong individual—a businessman, a religious leader—blazed the way, and others followed, forming a **migration chain**.

migration chain

▶ The movement of peoples in which one strong individual blazes the way and others follow.

A substantial number of Asians—especially Chinese, Japanese, Indians, and Filipinos—also responded to population pressure and rural hardship with temporary or permanent migration. At least 3 million Asians moved abroad before 1920. Most went as indentured laborers to work on the plantations or in the gold mines of Latin America, southern Asia, Africa, California, Hawaii, and Australia (see Chapter 26). White estate owners often used Asians to replace or supplement black Africans after the suppression of the Atlantic slave trade.

Asian migration would undoubtedly have been much greater if planters and mine owners desiring cheap labor had had their way. But usually they did not. Asians fled the plantations and gold mines as soon as possible, seeking greater opportunities in trade and towns. Here, however, they came into conflict with white settlers, who demanded a halt to Asian immigration. By the 1880s Americans and Australians were building **great white walls**—discriminatory laws designed to keep Asians out.

great white walls

▶ Discriminatory laws built by Americans and Australians to keep Asians from settling in their countries in the 1880s.

The general policy of "whites only" in the lands of large-scale European settlement meant that Europeans and people of European ancestry reaped the main benefits of the great migration. By 1913 people in Australia, Canada, and the United States all had higher average incomes than did people in Great Britain, still Europe's wealthiest nation. This, too, contributed to Western dominance in the increasingly lopsided world.

Within Asia and Africa the situation was different. Migrants from south China frequently settled in Dutch, British, and French colonies of Southeast Asia, where they established themselves as peddlers and small shopkeepers (see Chapter 26). These "overseas Chinese" gradually emerged as a new class of entrepreneurs and office workers. Traders from India and modern-day Lebanon performed the same function in much of sub-Saharan Africa after European colonization in the

How did the Ottoman Empire and Egypt try to modernize themselves?

What were the global consequences of European industrialization?

What fueled migration, and what was the pattern of this movement of people?

☑ LearningCurve
Check what you know.

775

late nineteenth century. Thus in some parts of Asia and Africa the business class was both Asian and foreign, protected and tolerated by Western imperialists who found these business people useful.

> ## > QUICK REVIEW

Why did so many Europeans leave their homelands and settle overseas in the late nineteenth and early twentieth centuries?

CHAPTER SUMMARY

Following Europe's Industrial Revolution in the late eighteenth and early nineteenth centuries, European demands for raw materials and new markets reoriented Africa's economy. The transatlantic slave trade declined dramatically as Africans began producing commodities for export. This legitimate trade in African goods proved profitable and led to the emergence of a small black middle class. Islam revived and expanded until about 1870.

After 1880 a handful of Western nations seized most of Africa and parts of Asia and rushed to build authoritarian empires. The reasons for this empire building included trade rivalries, competitive nationalism in Europe, and self-justifying claims of a civilizing mission.

The Ottoman Empire and Egypt prepared to become modern nation-states in the twentieth century by introducing reforms to improve the military, provide technical and secular education, and expand personal liberties. They failed, however, to defend themselves from Western imperialism. The Ottoman Empire lost territory but survived in a weakened condition. Egypt's Muhammad Ali reformed the government and promoted modern industry, but Egypt went bankrupt and was conquered and ruled by Britain.

Population pressures at home and economic opportunities abroad caused millions of European emigrants to resettle in the sparsely populated areas of European settlement in North and South America, Australia, and Asiatic Russia. Migration from Asia was much more limited, mainly because European settlers raised high barriers to prevent the settlement of Asian immigrants.

CHAPTER LOCATOR | What were the most significant changes in Africa during the nineteenth century? | What were the causes and consequences of European empire building after 1880?

CHAPTER 25
776 AFRICA, THE OTTOMAN EMPIRE, AND THE NEW IMPERIALISM

CONNECTIONS By the end of the nineteenth century broader industrialization across Europe increased the need for raw materials and markets, and with it came a rush to create or enlarge vast political empires abroad. The new imperialism was aimed primarily at Africa and Asia, and in the years before 1914 the leading European nations not only created empires abroad, but also continued to send massive streams of migrants, money, and manufactured goods around the world. (The impact of this unprecedented migration is taken up in the next two chapters.)

European influence also grew in the Middle East. Threatened by European military might, modernization, and Christianity, Turks and Arabs tried to implement reforms that would assure their survival and independence but also endeavored to retain key aspects of their cultures, particularly Islam. Although they made important advances in the modernization of their economies and societies, their efforts were not enough to overcome Western imperialism. With the end of World War I and the collapse of the Ottoman Empire, England and France divided much of the Middle East into colonies and established loyal surrogates as rulers in other, nominally independent, countries. Chapter 29 will take up the story of these developments.

As European imperialism was dividing the world after the 1880s, the leading European states were also dividing themselves into two opposing military alliances. As Chapter 28 will show, when the two armed camps stumbled into war in 1914, the results were disastrous. World War I set the stage for a new anti-imperialist struggle in Africa and Asia for equality and genuine independence (see Chapters 32 and 33).

ONLINE DOCUMENT PROJECT
Reform Movements in the Late Ottoman Empire
How did reformers address the challenges facing the Ottoman Empire in the nineteenth century?

Read excerpts from Ottoman reformers, and then complete a quiz and writing assignment based on the evidence and details from this chapter. *See inside the front cover to learn more.*

How did the Ottoman Empire and Egypt try to modernize themselves?	What were the global consequences of European industrialization?	What fueled migration, and what was the pattern of this movement of people?	☑ LearningCurve Check what you know.

CHAPTER 25 STUDY GUIDE

STEP 1 GET STARTED ONLINE

 LearningCurve

Now that you've read the chapter, make it stick by completing the LearningCurve activity.

STEP 2 EXPLAIN WHY IT MATTERS

Put your reading into practice. Identify each term below, and then explain why it matters in world history.

TERM	WHO OR WHAT & WHEN	WHY IT MATTERS
palm oil (p. 750)		
jihad (p. 753)		
Sokoto caliphate (p. 753)		
Berlin Conference (p. 754)		
protectorate (p. 754)		
Afrikaners (p. 756)		
new imperialism (p. 761)		
quinine (p. 761)		
white man's burden (p. 762)		
Tanzimat (p. 766)		
Young Turks (p. 767)		
great migration (p. 774)		
migration chain (p. 775)		
great white walls (p. 775)		

STEP 3 MOVE BEYOND THE BASICS

To demonstrate a more advanced understanding of the "New Imperialism" of the late nineteenth century, fill in the chart below with descriptions of the causes, motives, and characteristics of Western expansion before and after 1880. How did the nature of Western domination change after 1880? How would you explain the changes you note?

	Causes and Motives	Key Characteristics
Western Expansion Before 1880		
Western Expansion After 1880		

PUT IT ALL TOGETHER Now, take a step back and try to explain the big picture. Remember to use specific examples from the chapter in your answers.

THE NEW IMPERIALISM

▶ How did Western pressure shape African development before 1880? How about after 1880?

▶ How did Westerners justify imperialism? How did Western critics of imperialism challenge such justifications?

MODERNIZATION AND REFORM IN THE ISLAMIC HEARTLAND

▶ How did Ottoman and Egyptian leaders use Western ideas and culture to resist Western domination?

▶ Should the modernization efforts of the Ottomans and Egyptian be deemed "failures"? Why or why not?

GLOBALIZATION, INDUSTRIALIZATION, AND MIGRATION

▶ Who benefitted the most from the economic growth and globalization of the nineteenth century? Why?

▶ Compare and contrast European and Asian migration during the nineteenth century. What important differences do you note? What common factors help explain the movements of both groups of migrants?

LOOKING BACK, LOOKING AHEAD

▶ What place did Europe have in the world economy in 1750? What about 1900? How would you explain the differences you note?

▶ What connections might one make between nineteenth-century European imperialism and the disastrous wars that befell Europe if the first half of the twentieth century?

> **IN YOUR OWN WORDS**

Imagine that you must give an oral report to the class answering the following question: **How and why did Western nations strive for global dominance over the course of the nineteenth century?** What would be the most important points and why?

26

ASIA AND THE PACIFIC IN THE ERA OF IMPERIALISM

1800–1914

> **> How did Asian leaders respond to the challenges posed by Western imperialism?**

Chapter 26 examines the impact of nineteenth-century Western imperialism on Asia. At the beginning of the century Spain, the Netherlands, and Britain had colonies in the Philippines, modern Indonesia, and India, respectively. By the end of the century most of the southern tier of Asia, from India to the Philippines, had been colonized. Not all the countries in Asia were reduced to colonies. Although Western powers put enormous pressures on China, it remained politically independent. Much more impressively, Japan became the first non-Western nation to meet successfully the many-sided challenge of Western expansion. By the end of this period Japan had become an industrialized, imperialist power itself.

Rammohun Roy The expansion of British power in India posed intellectual and cultural challenges to the native elite. Among those who rose to this challenge was writer and reformer Rammohun Roy, depicted here. (V&A Images, London, UK/Art Resource, NY)

> In what ways did India change as a consequence of British rule?

> Why were most but not all Southeast Asian societies reduced to colonies?

> Was China's decline in the nineteenth century due more to internal problems or to Western imperialism?

> How was Japan able to quickly master the challenges posed by the West?

> What were the causes and consequences of the vast movement of people in the Pacific region?

> What explains the similarities and differences in the experiences of Asian countries in this era?

LearningCurve
After reading the chapter, use LearningCurve to retain what you've read.

In what ways did India change as a consequence of British rule?

British and Sikh Leaders at Lahore

The Sikh kingdom in the Punjab fell to the British in a brief war in 1845–1846. This painting depicts the British and Sikh representatives who negotiated the resulting treaty, which gave Britain control of the region. (© The Trustees of the British Museum/Art Resource, NY)

ARRIVING IN INDIA IN THE SEVENTEENTH CENTURY, the British East India Company outmaneuvered French and Dutch rivals and was there to pick up the pieces as the Mughal Empire decayed during the eighteenth century (see pages 506–508). By 1757 the company had gained control over much of India. During the nineteenth century the British government replaced the company, progressively unified the subcontinent, and harnessed its economy to British interests.

The Evolution of British Rule

In India the British ruled with the cooperation of local princely allies, whom they could not afford to offend. To assert their authority, the British disbanded and disarmed local armies, introduced simpler private property laws, and enhanced the powers of local princes and religious leaders, both Hindu and Muslim. The British administrators were on the whole competent and concerned about the welfare of the Indian peasants. Slavery was outlawed and banditry suppressed, and new laws designed to improve women's position in society were introduced.

CHAPTER LOCATOR | **In what ways did India change as a consequence of British rule?** | Why were most but not all Southeast Asian societies reduced to colonies?

1825 King Minh Mang outlaws teaching of Christianity in Vietnam	**1869** Suez Canal opens
1830 Dutch institute Culture System in Indonesia	**1872** Universal public schools established in Japan
1839–1842 Opium War	**1885** Foundation of Indian National Congress
1851–1864 Taiping Rebellion in China	**1894–1895** Japan defeats China in Sino-Japanese War and gains control of Taiwan
1853 Commodore Perry opens Japanese ports to foreign trade	**1898** United States takes control of Philippines from Spain
1857 Great Mutiny / Great Revolt by Indian sepoys against British rule	**1900** Boxer Rebellion in China
1858 British Parliament begins to rule India	**1904** Japan attacks Russia and starts Russo-Japanese War
1859–1885 Vietnam becomes a colony of France	**1910** Korea becomes a province of Japan
1867 Meiji Restoration in Japan	**1912** China's monarchy is replaced by a republic

The last armed resistance to British rule occurred in 1857. By that date the British military presence in India had grown to include two hundred thousand Indian sepoy troops and thirty-eight thousand British officers. In 1857 groups of sepoys, especially around Delhi, revolted in what the British called the **Great Mutiny** and the Indians called the **Great Revolt**. The sepoys' grievances were many, ranging from the use of fat from cows (sacred to Hindus) and pigs (regarded as filthy by Muslims) to grease rifle cartridges to high tax rates and the incorporation of low-caste soldiers into the army. The insurrection spread rapidly throughout northern and central India before it was finally crushed. Thereafter, although princely states were allowed to continue, Britain ruled India much more tightly. Moreover, the British in India acted more like an occupying power and mixed less with the Indian elite.

After 1858 India was ruled by the British Parliament in London and administered by a civil service in India, the upper echelons of which were all white. In 1900 this elite consisted of fewer than 3,500 top officials for a population of 300 million.

The Socioeconomic Effects of British Rule

The impact of British rule on the Indian economy was multifaceted. In the early stages, the British East India Company expanded agricultural production, creating large plantations. Early crops were opium to export to China (see page 791) and

Great Mutiny / Great Revolt

▶ The terms used by the British and the Indians, respectively, to describe the last armed resistance to British rule in India, which occurred in 1857.

The Great Revolt / Great Mutiny, 1857

Was China's decline due more to internal problems or to Western imperialism?	How was Japan able to quickly master the challenges posed by the West?	What were the causes and consequences of the vast movement of people in the Pacific region?	What explains the similarities and differences between Asian countries in this era?	✓ LearningCurve Check what you know.

tea to substitute for imports from China. India gradually replaced China as the leading exporter of tea to Europe. Clearing land for tea and coffee plantations, along with massive commercial logging operations, led to extensive deforestation.

To aid the transport of goods, people, and information, the colonial administration invested heavily in India's infrastructure. By 1855 India's major cities had all been linked by telegraph and railroads, and postal service was being extended to local villages. Irrigation also received attention, and by 1900 India had the world's most extensive irrigation system.

At the same time, Indian production of textiles suffered a huge blow. Britain imported India's raw cotton but exported machine-spun yarn and machine-woven cloth, displacing millions of Indian hand-spinners and hand-weavers. By 1900 India was buying 40 percent of Britain's cotton exports. Not until 1900 were small steps taken toward industrializing India.

Although the economy expanded, the poor did not see much improvement in their standard of living. Tenant farming and landlessness increased with the growth in plantation agriculture. Increases in production were eaten up by increases in population. There was also a negative side to improved transportation. As Indians traveled more widely on the convenient trains, disease spread, especially cholera, which is transmitted by exposure to contaminated water.

The British and the Indian Educated Elite

The Indian middle class probably gained more than the poor from British rule, because they were the ones to benefit from the English-language educational system Britain established in India. Missionaries also established schools with Western curricula High-caste Hindus came to form a new elite profoundly influenced by Western thought and culture.

By creating a well-educated, English-speaking Indian elite and a bureaucracy aided by a modern communication system, the British laid the groundwork for a unified, powerful state. Britain placed under the same general system of law and administration the various Hindu and Muslim peoples of the subcontinent who had resisted one another for centuries. University graduates tended to look on themselves as Indians more than as residents of separate states and kingdoms, a necessary step for the development of Indian nationalism.

CHAPTER LOCATOR | In what ways did India change as a consequence of British rule? | Why were most but not all Southeast Asian societies reduced to colonies?

CHAPTER 26
784 ASIA AND THE PACIFIC IN THE ERA OF IMPERIALISM

Some Indian intellectuals sought to reconcile the values of the modern West and their own traditions. Rammohun Roy (1772–1833) founded a college that offered instruction in Western languages and subjects. He also founded a society to reform traditional customs, especially child marriage, the caste system, and restrictions on widows. He espoused a modern Hinduism founded on the *Upani-shads* (oo-PAH-nih-shadz), the ancient sacred texts of Hinduism.

The more that Western-style education was developed in India, the more the inequalities of the system became apparent to educated Indians. Indians were eligible to take the examinations for entry into the elite Indian Civil Service, the bureaucracy that administered the Indian government, but the exams were given in England. Since few Indians could travel such a long distance to take the test, in 1870 only 1 of the 916 members of the service was Indian. In other words, no matter how Anglicized educated Indians became, they could never become the white rulers' equals. The top jobs, the best clubs, the modern hotels, and even certain railroad compartments were sealed off to brown-skinned men and women. Most of the British elite considered all Indians to be racially inferior.

The peasant masses might accept such inequality as the latest version of age-old class and caste hierarchies, but the well-educated, English-speaking elite eventually could not. They had studied not only Milton and Shakespeare but also English traditions of democracy, liberty, and national pride.

In the late nineteenth century the colonial ports of Calcutta, Bombay, and Madras, now all linked by railroads, became centers of intellectual ferment. In these and other cities, newspapers in English and in regional languages gained influence. Lawyers trained in English law began agitating for Indian independence. By 1885, when a group of educated Indians came together to found the Indian National Congress, demands were increasing for equality and self-government. The Congress Party called for more opportunities for Indians in the Indian Civil Service and reallocation of the government budget from military expenditures to the alleviation of poverty. The party advocated unity across religious and caste lines, but most members were upper-caste, Western-educated Hindus.

Defending British possessions in India became a key element of Britain's foreign policy during the nineteenth century and led to steady expansion of the territory Britain controlled in Asia. By 1852, the British had annexed all of the kingdom of Burma, administering it as a province of India. The establishment of a British base in Singapore was followed by expansion into Malaya (now Malaysia) in the 1870s and 1880s. In both Burma and Malaya, Britain tried to foster economic development, building railroads and promoting trade. Burma became a major exporter of timber and rice, Malaya of tin and rubber. So many laborers were brought into Malaya for the expanding mines and plantations that its population came to be approximately one-third Malay, one-third Chinese, and one-third Indian.

Indian Civil Service

▶ The bureaucracy that administered the government of India. Entry into its elite ranks was through examinations that Indians were eligible to take, but these tests were offered only in England.

Indian National Congress

▶ A political association formed in 1885 that worked for Indian self-government.

QUICK REVIEW ◂

Why did opposition to British rule among Indian elites increase in the late nineteenth century?

Was China's decline due more to internal problems or to Western imperialism?

How was Japan able to quickly master the challenges posed by the West?

What were the causes and consequences of the vast movement of people in the Pacific region?

What explains the similarities and differences between Asian countries in this era?

 LearningCurve
Check what you know.

MAP 26.1 ■ Asia in 1914

India remained under British rule, while China precariously preserved its political independence. The Dutch Empire in modern-day Indonesia was old, but French control of Indochina was a product of the new imperialism.

> MAPPING THE PAST

ANALYZING THE MAP: Consider the colonies of the different powers on this map. What European countries were leading imperialist states, and what lands did they hold? Can you see places where colonial powers were likely to come into conflict with each other?

CONNECTIONS: Do the sizes of the various colonial territories as seen on this map adequately reflect their importance to the countries that possessed them? If not, what else should be taken into account in thinking about the value of these sorts of colonial possessions?

CHAPTER LOCATOR | In what ways did India change as a consequence of British rule? | Why were most but not all Southeast Asian societies reduced to colonies?

The French Governor General and the Vietnamese Emperor

The twelfth emperor of the Nguyen Dynasty, Khai Dinh (1885–1925), had to find ways to get along with the French governor general (in this picture, Albert Sarraut) if he wished to preserve his dynasty. Seen here in 1917 or 1918, he had adopted Western leather shoes but otherwise tried to keep a distinct Vietnamese identity in his dress. (© Maurice-Louis Branger/Roger-Viollet/Getty Images)

Why were most but not all Southeast Asian societies reduced to colonies?

AT THE BEGINNING OF THE NINETEENTH CENTURY only a small part of Southeast Asia was under direct European control. By the end of the century most of the region would be in foreign hands.

The Dutch East Indies

Although Dutch forts and trading posts in the East Indies dated back to the seventeenth century, in 1816 the Dutch ruled little more than the island of Java. Thereafter they gradually brought almost all of the 3,000-mile-long archipelago under their political authority. In extending their rule, the Dutch, like the British in India, brought diverse peoples with different languages and distinct cultural traditions into a single political entity (see Map 26.1).

Taking over the Dutch East India Company in 1799, the Dutch government modified the company's loose control of Java and gradually built a modern

| Was China's decline due more to internal problems or to Western imperialism? | How was Japan able to quickly master the challenges posed by the West? | What were the causes and consequences of the vast movement of people in the Pacific region? | What explains the similarities and differences between Asian countries in this era? | ✔️ **LearningCurve** Check what you know. |

bureaucratic state. Javanese resistance to Dutch rule led to the bloody Java War (1825–1830). In 1830, after the war, the Dutch established a particularly exploitive policy called the Culture System. Under this system, Indonesian peasants were forced to plant a fifth of their land in export crops, especially coffee and sugar, to turn over to the Dutch as tax.

At the end of the nineteenth century the Dutch began to encourage Western education in the East Indies. The children of local rulers and privileged elites, much like their counterparts in India, encountered new ideas in Dutch-language schools. They began to question the long-standing cooperation of local elites with Dutch colonialism, and they searched for a new national identity. Thus anticolonial nationalism began to take shape in the East Indies in the early twentieth century, and it would blossom after World War I.

Mainland Southeast Asia

Unlike India and Java, mainland Southeast Asia had escaped European rule during the eighteenth century. In 1802 the Nguyen Dynasty came to power in Vietnam, putting an end to thirty years of peasant rebellion and civil war. Working through a centralizing scholar bureaucracy fashioned on the Chinese model, the Nguyen (gwihn) Dynasty energetically built irrigation canals, roads and bridges, and impressive palaces in Hue (hway), the new capital city. Construction placed a heavy burden on the peasants drafted to do the work, and this hardship contributed to a resurgence of peasant unrest.

Roman Catholic missionaries from France posed a second, more dangerous threat to Vietnam's Confucian ruling elite. The king and his advisers believed that Christianity would undermine Confucian moral values and the unity of the Vietnamese state. In 1825 King Minh Mang (r. 1820–1841) outlawed the teaching of Christianity, and soon his government began executing Catholic missionaries and Vietnamese converts. In response, in 1859–1860 a French naval force seized Saigon and three surrounding provinces in southern Vietnam, making that part of Vietnam a French colony. In 1884–1885 France launched a second war against Vietnam and conquered the rest of the country. Laos and Cambodia were added to form French Indochina in 1887. In all three countries the local rulers were left on their thrones, but France dominated and tried to promote French culture.

After the French conquest, Vietnamese patriots continued to resist the colonial occupiers. After Japan's victory over Russia in 1905 (see page 799), a new generation of nationalists saw Japan as a model for Vietnamese revitalization and freedom. They went to Japan to study and planned for anticolonial revolution in Vietnam.

In all of Southeast Asia, only Siam succeeded in preserving its independence. Siam was sandwiched between the British in Burma and the French in Indochina. Siam's very able King Chulalongkorn (r. 1868–1910) took advantage of this situation to play the two competitors against each. Chulalongkorn outlawed slavery and implemented modernizing reforms that centralized the government so that it could more effectively control outlying provinces coveted by the imperialists. Independent Siam gradually developed a modern centralizing state similar to those constructed by Western imperialists in their Asian possessions.

CHAPTER LOCATOR | In what ways did India change as a consequence of British rule? | Why were most but not all Southeast Asian societies reduced to colonies?

CHAPTER 26

788 ASIA AND THE PACIFIC IN THE ERA OF IMPERIALISM

The Philippines

The United States became one of the imperialist powers in Asia when it took the Philippines from Spain in 1898. The government of Spain encouraged Spaniards to colonize the Philippines through the encomienda system (see page 472): Spaniards who had served the Crown were rewarded with grants giving them the exclusive right to control public affairs and collect taxes in a specific locality of the Philippines. A local Filipino elite also developed, aided by the Spanish introduction of private ownership of land. Manila developed into an important entrepôt in the galleon trade between Mexico and China, and this trade also attracted a large Chinese community, which handled much of the trade within the Philippines.

In the late nineteenth century wealthy Filipinos began to send their sons to study abroad, and a movement to press Spain for reforms emerged among those who had been abroad. When the Spanish cracked down on critics, a rebellion erupted in 1896. (See "Individuals in Society: José Rizal," page 790.)

In 1898 war between Spain and the United States broke out in Cuba (see page 838), and in May the American naval officer Commodore George Dewey sailed into Manila Bay and sank the Spanish fleet anchored there. Dewey called on the Filipino rebels to help defeat the Spanish forces, but when the rebels declared independence, the U.S. government refused to recognize them. U.S. forces fought the Filipino rebels, and by the end of the insurrection in 1902 the war had cost the lives of five thousand Americans and about two hundred thousand Filipinos. In the following years the United States introduced a form of colonial rule that included public works and economic development projects, improved education and medicine, and, in 1907, an elected legislative assembly.

QUICK REVIEW <

How did Siam avoid the fate of the rest of Southeast Asia?

| Was China's decline due more to internal problems or to Western imperialism? | How was Japan able to quickly master the challenges posed by the West? | What were the causes and consequences of the vast movement of people in the Pacific region? | What explains the similarities and differences between Asian countries in this era? | ✓ LearningCurve Check what you know. |

INDIVIDUALS IN SOCIETY
José Rizal

In the mid-seventeenth century a Chinese merchant immigrated to the Philippines and married a woman who was half Chinese, half Filipino. Because of anti-Chinese animosity, he changed his name to Mercado, Spanish for "merchant."

Mercado's direct patrilineal descendant, José Rizal (1861–1896), was born into a well-to-do family that leased a plantation from Dominican friars. Both of his parents were educated, and he was a brilliant student himself. In 1882, after completing his studies at the Jesuit-run college in Manila, he went to Madrid to study medicine. During his ten years in Europe he not only earned a medical degree in Spain and a Ph.D. in Germany but he also found time to learn several European languages and make friends with scientists, writers, and political radicals.

While in Europe, Rizal became involved with Filipino revolutionaries and contributed numerous articles to their newspaper, *La Solidaridad*, published in Barcelona. Rizal advocated making the Philippines a province of Spain, giving it representation in the Spanish parliament, replacing Spanish friars with Filipino priests, and making Filipinos and Spaniards equal before the law. He spent a year at the British Museum doing research on the early phase of the Spanish colonization of the Philippines. He also wrote two novels.

The first novel, written in Spanish, was fired by the passions of nationalism. In satirical fashion, it depicts a young Filipino of mixed blood who studies for several years in Europe before returning to the Philippines to start a modern secular school in his hometown and to marry his childhood sweetheart. The church stands in the way of his efforts, and the colonial administration proves incompetent. The novel ends with the hero being gunned down after the friars falsely implicate him in a revolutionary conspiracy. Rizal's own life ended up following this narrative surprisingly closely.

In 1892 Rizal left Europe, stopped briefly in Hong Kong, and then returned to Manila to help his family with a lawsuit. Though he secured his relatives' release from jail, he ran into trouble himself.

Because his writings were critical of the power of the church, he made many enemies, some of whom had him arrested. He was sent into exile to a Jesuit mission town on the relatively primitive island of Mindanao. There he founded a school and a hospital, and the Jesuits tried to win him back to the church. He kept busy during his four years in exile, not only teaching English, science, and self-defense, but also maintaining his correspondence with scientists in Europe. When a nationalist secret society rose in revolt in 1896, Rizal, in an effort to distance himself, volunteered to go to Cuba to help in an outbreak of yellow fever. Although he had no connections with the secret society and was on his way across the ocean, Rizal was arrested and shipped back to Manila.

Tried for sedition by the military, Rizal was found guilty. When handed his death certificate, Rizal struck out the words "Chinese half-breed" and wrote "pure native." He was publicly executed by a firing squad in Manila at age thirty-five, making him a martyr of the nationalist cause.

José Rizal. (Courtesy of the Library of Congress, LC-USZ62-43453)

QUESTIONS FOR ANALYSIS

1. How did Rizal's comfortable family background contribute to his becoming a revolutionary?
2. How would Rizal's European contemporaries have reacted to his opposition to the Catholic Church?

LaunchPad

ONLINE DOCUMENT PROJECT

How did Filipinos and Americans respond to Spanish and American imperialism? Examine documents about the Philippines during the Spanish-American war, and then complete a quiz and writing assignment based on the evidence and details from this chapter. *See inside the front cover to learn more.*

Treaty of Nanjing

The settlement reached by Britain and China in 1842 was written in both English and Chinese. The chief negotiators of both sides signed the document, and the seals of both countries were placed on it. The Chinese seal was impressed with red ink in the traditional way, while the British used wax. (© Mary Evans Picture Library/National Archives, UK/The Image Works)

Was China's decline in the nineteenth century due more to internal problems or to Western imperialism?

IN 1800 MOST CHINESE HAD NO REASON to question the concept of China as the central kingdom. A century later China's world standing had sunk precipitously. In 1900 foreign troops marched into China's capital to protect foreign nationals, and more and more Chinese had come to think that their government, society, and cultural values needed to be radically changed.

The Opium War

Seeing little to gain from trade with European countries, the Qing (Manchu) emperors, who had been ruling China since 1644 (see pages 620–622), permitted Europeans to trade only at the port of Guangzhou (Canton) and only through licensed Chinese merchants. Initially, the balance of trade was in China's favor. Great Britain and the other Western nations used silver to pay for tea, because they had not been able to find anything the Chinese wanted to buy. By the 1820s, however, the British had found something the Chinese would buy: opium. Grown

| **Was China's decline due more to internal problems or to Western imperialism?** | How was Japan able to quickly master the challenges posed by the West? | What were the causes and consequences of the vast movement of people in the Pacific region? | What explains the similarities and differences between Asian countries in this era? | ✓ LearningCurve Check what you know. |

791

legally in British-occupied India, opium was smuggled into China, where its use and sale were illegal. Huge profits and the cravings of addicts led to rapid increases in sales. At this point it was China that suffered a drain of silver because it was importing more than it was exporting.

To deal with this crisis, the Chinese government dispatched Lin Zexu to Guangzhou in 1839. He dealt harshly with Chinese who purchased opium and seized the opium stores of British merchants. Lin even wrote to Queen Victoria, calling on her to intervene.

Although for years foreign merchants had accepted Chinese rules, by 1839 the British, the dominant group, were ready to flex their muscles. British merchants wanted to create a market for their goods in China and get tea more cheaply by trading closer to its source in central China. They also wanted a European-style diplomatic relationship with China. With the encouragement of their merchants in China, the British sent an expeditionary force from India with forty-two warships.

With its control of the seas, the British easily shut down key Chinese ports and forced the Chinese to negotiate. Dissatisfied with the resulting agreement, the British sent a second, larger force, which took even more coastal cities. This Opium War was settled at gunpoint in 1842. The resulting treaties opened five ports to international trade, fixed the tariff on imported goods at 5 percent, imposed an indemnity of 21 million ounces of silver on China to cover Britain's war expenses, and ceded the island of Hong Kong to Britain. Through the clause on extraterritoriality, British subjects in China became answerable only to British law, even in disputes with Chinese. The treaties also had a "most-favored nation" clause, which meant that whenever one nation extracted a new privilege from China, it was extended automatically to Britain.

The treaties satisfied neither side. China continued to refuse to accept foreign diplomats at its capital in Beijing, and the expansion of trade fell far short of Western expectations. Between 1856 and 1860 Britain and France renewed hostilities with China. British and French troops occupied Beijing and set the emperor's summer palace on fire. Another round of harsh treaties gave European merchants and missionaries greater privileges and forced the Chinese to open several more cities to foreign trade.

Internal Problems

China's problems in the nineteenth century were not all of foreign origin. By 1850 China had a population of more than 400 million. As the population grew, farm size shrank, surplus labor suppressed wages, and conflicts over rights to water and tenancy increased. Hard times also led to increased female infanticide, as families felt that they could not afford to raise more than two or three children and saw sons as necessities.

These economic and demographic circumstances led to some of the most destructive rebellions in China's history. The worst was the Taiping Rebellion (1851–1864), in which some 20 million people lost their lives.

The Taiping (TIGH-ping) Rebellion was initiated by Hong Xiuquan (hong show-chwan) (1814–1864). Hong believed he was Jesus's younger brother and that he had a mission to wipe out evil in China. He soon gathered followers, whom he instructed to destroy idols and ancestral temples, give up opium and alcohol,

Opium War

▶ The 1839–1842 war between the British and the Chinese over limitations on trade and the importation of opium into China.

extraterritoriality

▶ The legal principle that exempts individuals from local law, applicable in China because of the agreements reached after China's loss in the Opium War.

Taiping Rebellion

▶ A massive rebellion by believers in the religious teachings of Hong Xiuquan, begun in 1851 and not suppressed until 1864.

CHAPTER LOCATOR | In what ways did India change as a consequence of British rule? | Why were most but not all Southeast Asian societies reduced to colonies?

792 CHAPTER 26 ASIA AND THE PACIFIC IN THE ERA OF IMPERIALISM and renounce foot binding and prostitution. In 1851 he declared himself king of the Heavenly Kingdom of Great Peace (Taiping), an act of open insurrection.

By 1853 the Taiping rebels, as Hong's followers were known, had moved north and established their capital at the major city of Nanjing, which they held onto for a decade. There, they set about creating a utopian society based on the equalization of landholdings and the equality of men and women. To suppress the Taipings, the Manchus had to turn to Chinese scholar-officials, who raised armies on their own, revealing the Manchus' military weakness.

The Self-Strengthening Movement

After the various rebellions were suppressed, forward-looking reformers began addressing the Western threat. Under the slogan "self-strengthening," they set about modernizing the military along Western lines. Some of the most progressive reformers also initiated new industries, which in the 1870s and 1880s included railway lines, steam navigation companies, coal mines, telegraph lines, and cotton spinning and weaving factories.

Despite the enormous effort put into trying to catch up, China was humiliated yet again at the end of the nineteenth century. First came the discovery that Japan had so successfully modernized that it posed a threat to China. Then in 1894 Japanese efforts to separate Korea from Chinese influence led to the brief Sino-Japanese War in which China was decisively defeated. China's helplessness in the face of aggression led to a scramble among the European powers for

Chinese Rebellions, 1851–1911

China's First Railroad

Soon after this 15-mile-long railroad was constructed near Shanghai in 1876 by the British firm of Jardine, Matheson, and Company, the provincial governor bought it in order to tear it out. Many Chinese of the period saw the introduction of railroads as harmful not only to the balance of nature but also to people's livelihoods, because the railroads eliminated jobs in transport like dragging boats along canals or driving pack horses. (Private Collection/Visual Connection Archive)

| Was China's decline due more to internal problems or to Western imperialism? | How was Japan able to quickly master the challenges posed by the West? | What were the causes and consequences of the vast movement of people in the Pacific region? | What explains the similarities and differences between Asian countries in this era? | ✓ LearningCurve Check what you know. |

concessions and protectorates in China. At the high point of this rush in 1898, it appeared that the European powers might actually divide China among themselves, the way they had recently divided Africa.

Republican Revolution

China's humiliating defeat in the Sino-Japanese War in 1895 led to a renewed drive for reform. In 1898 a group of educated young reformers gained the support of the twenty-seven-year-old Qing emperor. They proposed redesigning China as a constitutional monarchy with modern financial and educational systems. For three months the emperor issued a series of reform decrees. But the Manchu establishment and the empress dowager felt threatened and not only suppressed the reform movement but imprisoned the emperor as well. Hope for reform from the top was dashed.

A period of violent reaction swept the country, reaching its peak in 1900 with the uprising of a secret society that foreigners dubbed the Boxers. The Boxers blamed China's ills on foreigners, especially Christian missionaries. After the Boxers laid siege to the foreign legation quarter in Beijing, a dozen nations including Japan sent twenty thousand troops to lift the siege. In the negotiations that followed, China had to accept a long list of harsh penalties.

After this defeat, gradual reform lost its appeal. More and more Chinese were studying abroad and learning about Western political ideas, including democracy and revolution. The most famous was Sun Yatsen (1866–1925). Sent by his peasant family to Hawaii, he learned English and then continued his education in Hong Kong. From 1894 on, he spent his time abroad organizing revolutionary societies. He joined forces with Chinese student revolutionaries studying in Japan, and together they sparked the 1911 Revolution, which brought China's monarchy to an end in 1912, to be replaced by a Western-style republic. China had escaped direct foreign rule but would never be the same.

Boxers

▶ A Chinese secret society that blamed the country's ills on foreigners, especially missionaries, and rose in rebellion in 1900.

1911 Revolution

▶ The uprising that brought China's monarchy to an end.

> QUICK REVIEW

Why were Chinese efforts at modernization and reform largely ineffective?

CHAPTER LOCATOR | In what ways did India change as a consequence of British rule? | Why were most but not all Southeast Asian societies reduced to colonies?

CHAPTER 26
794 ASIA AND THE PACIFIC IN THE ERA OF IMPERIALISM

How was Japan able to quickly master the challenges posed by the West?

Japan's Modernized Army

A set of woodblock prints depicting the new sights of Tokyo included this illustration of a military parade ground. The soldiers' brightly colored Western-style uniforms undoubtedly helped make this a sight worth seeing.

DURING THE NINETEENTH CENTURY, while China's standing in the world plummeted, Japan's was rising. During the eighteenth century Japan (much more effectively than China) kept foreign merchants and missionaries at bay. It limited trade to a single port (Nagasaki), where only the Dutch were allowed, and forbade Japanese to travel abroad. Because Japan's land and population were so much smaller than China's, the Western powers never expected much from Japan as a trading partner and did not press it as urgently. Still, the European threat was part of what propelled Japan to modernize.

The "Opening" of Japan

Wanting to play a greater role in the Pacific, the United States decided to force the Japanese to open their ports to trade. In 1853 Commodore Matthew Perry steamed into Edo (now Tokyo) Bay and demanded diplomatic negotiations with

| Was China's decline due more to internal problems or to Western imperialism? | **How was Japan able to quickly master the challenges posed by the West?** | What were the causes and consequences of the vast movement of people in the Pacific region? | What explains the similarities and differences between Asian countries in this era? | ✓ LearningCurve Check what you know. |

795

gunboat diplomacy

▶ The imposition of treaties and agreements under threat of military violence, such as the opening of Japan to trade after Commodore Perry's demands.

the emperor. Under threat of gunboat diplomacy, and after consulting with the daimyo (major lords), Japanese officials signed a treaty with the United States that opened two ports and permitted trade.

Japan at this time was a complex society. The emperor in Kyoto had no effective powers. For more than two hundred years real power had been in the hands of the Tokugawa shogun in Edo (see pages 627–628). The country was divided into numerous domains, each under a daimyo. Each daimyo had under him samurai, who had hereditary stipends and privileges, such as the right to wear a sword. Peasants and merchants were also legally distinct classes, and in theory social mobility from peasant to merchant or merchant to samurai was impossible. After two centuries of peace, there were many more samurai than were needed to administer or defend the country, and many lived very modestly. They were proud, however, and felt humiliated by the sudden American intrusion and the unequal treaties that the Western countries imposed. Some began agitating against the shogunate under the slogan "Revere the emperor and expel the barbarians."

When foreign diplomats and merchants began to settle in Yokohama after 1858, radical samurai reacted with a wave of antiforeign terrorism and antigovernment assassinations. The Western response was swift and unambiguous. They sent an allied fleet of American, British, Dutch, and French warships to demolish key Japanese forts, further weakening the power and prestige of the shogun's government.

The Meiji Restoration

In 1867 a coalition of reform-minded daimyo led a coup that ousted the Tokugawa Shogunate. The samurai who led this coup declared a return to direct rule by the emperor. This emperor was called the Meiji (MAY-jee) emperor and this event the Meiji Restoration, a great turning point in Japanese history.

The domain leaders who organized the coup, called the Meiji Oligarchs, moved the boy emperor to Tokyo castle. They used the young sovereign to win over both the lords and the commoners. Real power, however, remained in the hands of the oligarchs.

Meiji Restoration

▶ The 1867 ousting of the Tokugawa Shogunate that "restored" the power of the Japanese emperors.

The battle cry of the Meiji reformers had been "strong army, rich nation." How were these goals to be accomplished? Convinced that they could not beat the West until they had mastered the secrets of its military and industrial might, they dropped their antiforeign attacks and initiated a series of measures to reform Japan along modern Western lines. Within four years a delegation was traveling the world to learn what made the Western powers strong. Its members examined everything from the U.S. Constitution to the factories, shipyards, and railroads that made the European landscape so different from Japan's.

Japan under the shoguns had been decentralized, with most of the power over the population in the hands of the many daimyo. By elevating the emperor, the oligarchs were able to centralize the government. In 1871 they abolished the domains and merged the domain armies. Following the example of the French Revolution, they dismantled the four-class legal system and declared everyone equal. This amounted to stripping the samurai (7 to 8 percent of the population) of their privileges. Not surprisingly, some samurai rose up against their loss of privileges. None of these uncoordinated uprisings made any difference.

CHAPTER LOCATOR | In what ways did India change as a consequence of British rule? | Why were most but not all Southeast Asian societies reduced to colonies?

CHAPTER 26
796 ASIA AND THE PACIFIC IN THE ERA OF IMPERIALISM

Several leaders of the Meiji Restoration, in France on a fact-finding mission during the Franco-Prussian War of 1870–1871, were impressed by the active participation of French citizens in the defense of Paris. For Japan to survive in the hostile international environment, they concluded, ordinary people had to be trained to fight. Consequently, a conscription law, modeled on the French law, was issued in 1872. To improve the training of soldiers, the new War College was organized along German lines, and German instructors were recruited to teach there. Young samurai were trained to form the new professional officer corps.

Many of the new institutions established in the Meiji period reached down to the local level. Schools open to all were rapidly introduced beginning in 1872. Teachers were trained in newly established teachers' colleges. Another modern institution that reached the local level was a national police force. In 1884 police training schools were established in every prefecture, and within a few years police stations were set up throughout the country. Policemen came to act as local agents of the central government. They not only dealt with crime but also enforced public health rules, conscription laws, and codes of behavior.

In 1889 Japan became the first non-Western country to adopt the constitutional form of government. A commission sent abroad to study European constitutional governments had come to the conclusion that the German constitutional monarchy would provide the best model for Japan, rather than the more democratic governments of the British, French, and Americans. Japan's new government had a two-house parliament, called the Diet. The upper house of lords was drawn largely from former daimyo and nobles, and the lower house was elected by a limited electorate (about 5 percent of the adult male population in 1890). Although Japan now had a government based on laws, it was authoritarian rather than democratic. The emperor had the right to appoint the prime minister and cabinet. He did not have to ask the Diet for funds because wealth assigned to the imperial house was entrusted to the Imperial Household Ministry, which was outside the government's control.

> ### > Japan's 1889 Constitution:

- Based on the German constitutional monarchy
- Two-house parliament (Diet)
- Upper house drawn largely from former daimyo and nobles
- Lower house elected by limited electorate
- Emperor remained outside of Diet's control

Cultural change during the Meiji period was as profound as political change. For more than a thousand years China had been the major source of ideas and technologies introduced into Japan. But in the late nineteenth century China, beset by Western pressure, had become an object lesson on the dangers of stagnation. The influential author Fukuzawa Yukichi began urging Japan to pursue "civilization and enlightenment," by which he meant Western civilization. Soon Japanese were being told to conform to Western taste, eat meat, wear Western-style clothes, and drop customs that Westerners found odd.

Was China's decline due more to internal problems or to Western imperialism?

How was Japan able to quickly master the challenges posed by the West?

What were the causes and consequences of the vast movement of people in the Pacific region?

What explains the similarities and differences between Asian countries in this era?

☑ LearningCurve
Check what you know.

797

Industrialization

The leaders of the Meiji Restoration, wanting to strengthen Japan's military capacity, promoted industrialization. The government paid foreign experts to help with industrialization, and Japanese were encouraged to go abroad to study science and engineering.

The government played an active role in getting railroads, mines, and factories started. Early on, the Japanese government decided to compete with China in the export of tea and silk to the West. Introducing the mechanical reeling of silk gave Japan a strong price advantage in the sale of silk, and Japan's total foreign trade increased tenfold from 1877 to 1900. The next stage was to develop heavy industry. The huge indemnity exacted from China in 1895 was used to establish the Yawata Iron and Steel Works. The third stage of Japan's industrialization would today be called import substitution. Factories such as cotton mills were set up to help cut the importation of Western consumer goods.

Most of the great Japanese industrial conglomerates known as *zaibatsu* (zigh-BAHT-dzoo), such as Mitsubishi, got their start in this period, often founded by men with government connections. Sometimes the government set up plants that it then sold to private investors at bargain prices. Successful entrepreneurs were treated as patriotic heroes.

As in Europe, the early stages of industrialization brought hardship to the countryside. Farmers often rioted as their incomes failed to keep up with prices or as their tax burdens grew. Workers in modern industries were no happier, and in 1898 railroad workers went on strike for better working conditions and overtime pay. Still, rice production increased, death rates dropped as public health was improved, and the population grew from about 33 million in 1868 to about 45 million in 1900.

Japan's First Skyscraper

Meiji Japan's fascination with things Western led to the construction of Western-style buildings. Japan's first elevator made possible this twelve-story tower built in Tokyo in 1890. Situated in the entertainment district, it was filled with shops, theaters, bars, and restaurants. ("Pavilion Above the Clouds," Sugoroku 1890, Utagawa Kunimasa IV [1848–1920]/Mead Art Museum, Amherst College, MA, USA/ The Bridgeman Art Library)

> PICTURING THE PAST

ANALYZING THE IMAGE: Locate all the people in this picture. How are they dressed? What are they doing?

CONNECTIONS: Keeping in mind that the building in this picture was built in 1890, what connections can you draw between the politics of the period and this visual celebration of a new style of architecture?

CHAPTER LOCATOR | In what ways did India change as a consequence of British rule? | Why were most but not all Southeast Asian societies reduced to colonies?

CHAPTER 26
798 ASIA AND THE PACIFIC IN THE ERA OF IMPERIALISM

Japan as an Imperial Power

During the course of the Meiji period, Japan became an imperial power, making Taiwan and Korea into its colonies. The conflicts that led to Japanese acquisition of both of them revolved around Korea.

In the second half of the nineteenth century Korea found itself caught between China, Japan, and Russia, each trying to protect or extend its sphere of influence. Westerners also began demanding that Korea be "opened." Matters were complicated by the rise in the 1860s of a religious cult, the Tonghak movement, that had strong xenophobic elements. Although the government executed the cult founder in 1864, this cult continued to gain support, especially among impoverished peasants. Thus, like China in the same period, the Korean government faced simultaneous internal and external threats.

In 1871 the U.S. minister to China took five warships to try to open Korea, but left after exchanges of fire resulted in 250 Koreans dead without any progress in getting the Korean government to make concessions. Japan tried next and in 1876 forced the Korean government to sign an unequal treaty and open three ports to Japanese trade. On China's urging, Korea also signed treaties with the European powers in an effort to counterbalance Japan.

Japanese Expansion, 1875–1914

Over the next couple of decades reformers in China and Japan tried to encourage Korea to adopt its own self-strengthening movement, but Korean conservatives did their best to undo reform efforts. In 1894, when the religious cult rose in a massive revolt, both China and Japan sent military forces, claiming to come to the Korean government's aid. They ended up fighting each other instead in what is known as the Sino-Japanese War (see page 793). With Japan's decisive victory, it gained Taiwan from China and was able to make Korea a protectorate. In 1910 Korea was formally annexed as a province of Japan.

Japan also competed aggressively with the leading European powers for influence and territory in China, particularly in the northeast (Manchuria). There Japanese and Russian imperialism met and collided. In 1904 Japan attacked Russian forces and, after its 1905 victory in the bloody **Russo-Japanese War**, emerged with a foothold in China—Russia's former protectorate over Port Arthur (see Map 26.1).

Russo-Japanese War

▶ The 1904–1905 war between Russia and Japan fought over imperial influence and territory in northeast China (Manchuria).

Japan's victories over China and Russia changed the way European nations looked at Japan. Through negotiations Japan was able to eliminate extraterritoriality in 1899 and gain control of its own tariffs in 1911. Within Japan, the success of the military in raising Japan's international reputation added greatly to its political influence.

QUICK REVIEW <

What kind of government and society did Japanese leaders seek to create during the Meiji period?

| Was China's decline due more to internal problems or to Western imperialism? | **How was Japan able to quickly master the challenges posed by the West?** | What were the causes and consequences of the vast movement of people in the Pacific region? | What explains the similarities and differences between Asian countries in this era? | LearningCurve Check what you know. |

> What were the causes and consequences of the vast movement of people in the Pacific region?

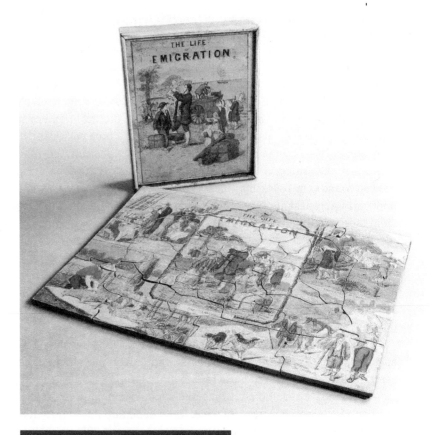

The "Life of Emigration" Puzzle, ca. 1840

Some of the advertising designed to attract people to move to Australia was aimed at children, such as this wooden puzzle depicting the life of a family moving from Britain to Australia. (Photograph courtesy of the State Library of South Australia, S.A. Memory website)

THE NINETEENTH CENTURY WAS MARKED by extensive movement of people into, across, and out of Asia and the broad Pacific region. Many of these migrants moved from one Asian country to another, but there was also a growing presence of Europeans in Asia, a consequence of the increasing integration of the world economy (see pages 771–772).

Settler Colonies in the Pacific: Australia and New Zealand

The largest share of the Europeans who moved to the Pacific region in the nineteenth century went to the settler colonies in Australia and New Zealand (Map 26.2). In the 1770s the English explorer James Cook visited New Zealand, Australia, and Hawaii. All three of these places in time became destinations for migrants.

CHAPTER LOCATOR | In what ways did India change as a consequence of British rule? | Why were most but not all Southeast Asian societies reduced to colonies?

As discussed in Chapter 12, between 200 and 1300 C.E. Polynesians settled numerous islands of the Pacific, from New Zealand in the south to Hawaii in the north and Easter Island in the east. Thus most of the lands that explorers like Cook encountered were occupied by societies with chiefs, crop agriculture, domestic animals, excellent sailing technology, and often considerable experience in warfare. Australia had been settled millennia earlier by a different population. When Cook arrived in Australia, it was occupied by about three hundred thousand Aborigines who lived entirely by food gathering, fishing, and hunting. Like the Indians of Central and South America, the people in all these lands fell victim to Eurasian diseases and died in large numbers.

Australia was first developed by Britain as a penal colony. Between 1787 and 1869, when the penal colony system was abolished, a total of 161,000 convicts were transported to Australia. After the end of the Napoleonic Wars in 1815, a

MAP 26.2 ■ Australia

Because of the vast deserts in western Australia, cities and industries developed mainly in the east. Australia's early geographical and cultural isolation bred a sense of inferiority. Air travel, the communications revolution, and the massive importation of Japanese products and American popular culture have changed that.

Was China's decline due more to internal problems or to Western imperialism?

How was Japan able to quickly master the challenges posed by the West?

What were the causes and consequences of the vast movement of people in the Pacific region?

What explains the similarities and differences between Asian countries in this era?

✔ LearningCurve
Check what you know.

steady stream of non-convicts voluntarily immigrated to Australia. Raising sheep proved suitable to Australia's climate, and wool exports steadily increased. To encourage migration, the government offered free passage and free land to immigrants. By 1850 Australia had five hundred thousand inhabitants. The discovery of gold in Victoria in 1851 quadrupled that number in a few years. The gold rush also provided the financial means for cultural development. Public libraries, museums, art galleries, and universities opened in the thirty years after 1851. These institutions dispensed a distinctly British culture.

Not everyone in Australia was of British origin, however. Chinese and Japanese built the railroads and ran the shops in the towns and the market gardens nearby. Filipinos and Pacific Islanders did the hard work in the sugarcane fields. Afghans and their camels controlled the carrying trade in some areas. But fear that Asian labor would lower living standards and undermine Australia's distinctly British culture led to efforts to keep Australia white.

Australia gained independence in stages. In 1850 the British Parliament passed the Australian Colonies Government Act, which allowed the four most populous colonies—New South Wales, Tasmania, Victoria, and South Australia—to establish colonial legislatures, determine the franchise, and frame their own constitutions. In 1902 Australia became one of the first countries in the world to give women the vote.

By 1900 New Zealand's population had reached 750,000, only a fifth of Australia's. One major reason more people had not settled these fertile islands was the resistance of the native Maori people. They quickly mastered the use of muskets and tried for decades to keep the British from taking their lands.

Foreign settlement in Hawaii began gradually. Initially, whalers stopped there for supplies, as they did at other Pacific Islands. Missionaries and businessmen came next, and soon other settlers followed, both whites and Asians. A plantation economy developed centered on sugarcane. In the 1890s leading settler families overthrew the native monarchy, set up a republic, and urged the United States to annex Hawaii, which it did in 1898.

Asian Emigration

Like Europeans, Asians left their native countries in unprecedented numbers in the nineteenth century (Map 26.3). As in Europe, both push and pull factors prompted people to leave home. China and India were extremely densely populated countries—China with more than 400 million people in the mid-nineteenth century, India with more than 200 million. Not surprisingly, these two giants were the leading exporters of people in search of work or land. On the pull side were the new opportunities created by the flow of development capital into previously underdeveloped areas. In many of the European colonies in Asia the business class came to consist of both Asian and European migrants. Asian diasporas formed in many parts of the world, with the majority in Asia itself, especially Southeast Asia.

By the nineteenth century the Chinese formed key components of mercantile communities throughout Southeast Asia. Chinese often assimilated in Siam and Vietnam, but they rarely did so in Muslim areas such as Java, Catholic areas such as the Philippines, and primitive tribal areas such as northern Borneo. In these places distinct Chinese communities emerged.

CHAPTER LOCATOR | In what ways did India change as a consequence of British rule? | Why were most but not all Southeast Asian societies reduced to colonies?

802 CHAPTER 26 ASIA AND THE PACIFIC IN THE ERA OF IMPERIALISM

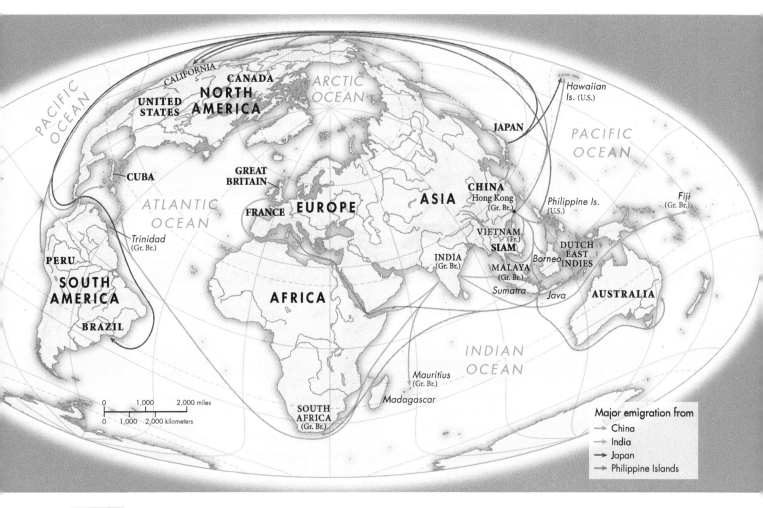

MAP 26.3 ■ Emigration out of Asia, 1820–1914

As steamships made crossing oceans quicker and more reliable, many people in Asia left their home countries to find new opportunities elsewhere. European imperialism contributed to this flow, especially by recruiting workers for newly established plantations or mines. Many emigrants simply wanted to work a few years to build their savings and planned to return home. Often, however, they ended up staying in their new countries and forming families there.

With the growth in trade that accompanied the European imperial expansion, Chinese began to settle in the islands of Southeast Asia in larger numbers. After Singapore was founded by the British in 1819, Chinese rapidly poured in, soon becoming the dominant ethnic group. In British-controlled Malaya, some Chinese built great fortunes in the tin business, while others worked in the mines. Chinese also settled in the Spanish-controlled Philippines and in Dutch-controlled Indonesia.

Discovery of gold in California in 1848, Australia in 1851, and Canada in 1858 encouraged Chinese to book passage to those places. In California few arrived soon enough to strike gold, but thousands found work building railroads, and others took up mining in Wyoming and Idaho.

Indian entrepreneurs were similarly attracted by the burgeoning commerce of the growing British Empire. The bulk of Indian emigrants were indentured laborers,

indentured laborers
▶ Laborers who, in exchange for passage, agreed to work for a number of years, specified in a contract.

Was China's decline due more to internal problems or to Western imperialism?

How was Japan able to quickly master the challenges posed by the West?

What were the causes and consequences of the vast movement of people in the Pacific region?

What explains the similarities and differences between Asian countries in this era?

✓ LearningCurve
Check what you know.

803

recruited under contract. The rise of indentured labor from Asia was a direct result of the outlawing of the African slave trade in the early nineteenth century by Britain and the United States. Sugar plantations in the Caribbean and elsewhere needed new sources of workers, and planters in the British colonies discovered that they could recruit Indian laborers to replace blacks. After the French abolished slavery in 1848, they recruited workers from India as well. Later in the century many Indians emigrated to British colonies in Africa, the largest numbers to South Africa.

Indentured laborers secured as substitutes for slaves were often treated little better than slaves. In response to such abuse, the Indian colonial government established regulations stipulating a maximum indenture period of five years, after which the migrant would be entitled to passage home. Even though government "protectors" were appointed at the ports of embarkation, exploitation of indentured workers continued largely unchecked.

In areas outside the British Empire, China offered the largest supply of ready labor. Starting in the 1840s contractors arrived at Chinese ports to recruit labor for plantations and mines in Cuba, Peru, Hawaii, Sumatra, South Africa, and elsewhere. Chinese laborers did not have the British government to protect them and seem to have suffered even more than Indian workers.

Canadian Immigration Certificate

This certificate proved that the eleven-year-old boy in the photograph had a legal right to be in Canada, as the $500 head tax required for immigration of Chinese had been paid. The head tax on Chinese immigrants introduced in 1885 started at $50, but it was raised to $100 in 1900 and to $500 in 1903. Equal to about what a laborer could earn in two years, the tax succeeded in its goal of slowing the rate of Asian immigration to Canada. (Head tax certificate for Jung Bak Hun, issued January 3, 1919/© Government of Canada. Reproduced with the permission of the Minister of Public Works and Government Services Canada [2013]/Library and Archives Canada/Canada. Department of Employment and Immigration fonds/RG76-D-2-g, Vol. 712, C.I.5 certificate #88103)

CHAPTER LOCATOR | In what ways did India change as a consequence of British rule? | Why were most but not all Southeast Asian societies reduced to colonies?

CHAPTER 26
804 ASIA AND THE PACIFIC IN THE ERA OF IMPERIALISM

India and China sent more people abroad than any other Asian countries during this period, but they were not alone. As Japan started to industrialize, its cities could not absorb all those forced off the farms, and people began emigrating in significant numbers, many to Hawaii and later to South America. Emigration from the Philippines also was substantial, especially after it became a U.S. territory in 1898.

Asian migration to the United States, Canada, and Australia would undoubtedly have been greater if it had not been so vigorously resisted by the white settlers in those regions. In 1882 Chinese were barred from becoming American citizens, and the immigration of Chinese laborers was suspended. Australia also put a stop to Asian immigration with the Commonwealth Immigration Restriction Act of 1901, which established the "white Australia policy" that remained on the books until the 1970s.

Most of the Asian migrants discussed so far were illiterate peasants or business people, not members of traditional educated elites. By the beginning of the twentieth century, however, another group of Asians was going abroad in significant numbers: students. Most of these students traveled abroad to learn about Western science, law, and government in the hope of strengthening their own countries. On their return they contributed enormously to the intellectual life of their societies, increasing understanding of the modern Western world and also becoming the most vocal advocates of overthrowing the old order and driving out the colonial masters.

Among the most notable of these foreign-educated radicals were Mohandas Gandhi (1869–1948) and Sun Yatsen (see page 794). Sun developed his ideas about the republican form of government while studying in Hawaii and Hong Kong. Gandhi, after studying law in Britain, took a job in South Africa, where he became involved in trying to defend the interests of the Indians who lived and worked there. It was there that he gradually elaborated his idea of passive resistance.

QUICK REVIEW

Why did so many Asians migrate during this period?
Where did they most often go?

| Was China's decline due more to internal problems or to Western imperialism? | How was Japan able to quickly master the challenges posed by the West? | **What were the causes and consequences of the vast movement of people in the Pacific region?** | What explains the similarities and differences between Asian countries in this era? | LearningCurve Check what you know. |

What explains the
similarities and
differences in the
experiences of Asian
countries in this era?

AT THE START OF THE NINETEENTH CENTURY the societies of Asia varied much more than those of any other part of the world. In the temperate zones of East Asia, the old established monarchies of China, Japan, and Korea were all densely populated and boasted long literary traditions and traditions of unified governments. They had ties to each other that dated back many centuries and shared many elements of their cultures. South of them, in the tropical and sub-tropical regions, cultures were more diverse. India was just as densely populated as China, Japan, and Korea, but politically and culturally less unified. In both India and Southeast Asia, Islam was much more important than it was in East Asia. All the countries with long written histories and literate elites were at a great remove from the thinly populated and relatively primitive areas without literate cultures and sometimes even without agriculture, such as Australia and some of the islands of the Philippines and Indonesia.

The nineteenth century gave the societies of Asia more in common in that all of them in one way or another had come into contact with the expanding West. Still, the Western powers did not treat all the countries the same way. Western powers initially wanted manufactured goods from the more developed Asian societies, especially Indian cotton textiles and Chinese porcelains. At the beginning of the nineteenth century Britain had already gained political control over large parts of India and was intent on forcing China to trade on terms more to its benefit. It paid virtually no attention to Korea and Japan, not seeing in them the same potential for profit. The less developed parts of Asia also attracted increasing Western interest, not because they could provide manufactured goods, but because they offered opportunities for Western development, much as the Americas had earlier.

The West that the societies of Asia faced during the nineteenth century was itself rapidly changing, and the steps taken by Western nations to gain power in

CHAPTER LOCATOR | In what ways did India change as a consequence of British rule? | Why were most but not all Southeast Asian societies reduced to colonies?

Asia naturally also changed over time. Western science and technology were making rapid advances, which gave European armies progressively greater advantages in weaponry. The Industrial Revolution made it possible for countries that industrialized early, such as Britain, to produce huge surpluses of goods for which they had to find markets; this development shifted their interest in Asia from a place to buy goods to a place to sell goods. Britain had been able to profit from its colonization of India, and this profit both encouraged it to consolidate its rule and invited its European rivals to look for their own colonies.

There were some commonalities in the ways Asian countries responded to pressure from outside. In the countries with long literary traditions, often the initial response of the established elite was to try to drive the unwelcome foreigners away. This was the case in China, Japan, and Korea in particular. Violent antiforeign reactions exploded again and again, but the superior military technology of the industrialized West almost invariably prevailed. Some Asian leaders insisted on the need to preserve their cultural traditions at all costs. Others came to the opposite conclusion that the West was indeed superior in some ways and that they would have to adopt European ideas or techniques for their own purposes. The struggles between the traditionalists and the westernizers were often intense. As nationalism took hold in the West, it found a receptive audience among the educated elites in Asia. How could the assertion that every people had the right to control its own destiny not appeal to the colonized?

Whether they were colonized or not, most countries in Asia witnessed the spread of new technologies between 1800 and 1914. Railroads, telegraphs, modern sanitation, and a wider supply of inexpensive manufactured goods brought fundamental changes in everyday life not only to lands under colonial rule, such as India and Vietnam, but also, if less rapidly, to places that managed to remain independent, such as China and Japan. In fact, the transformation of Japan between 1860 and 1900 was extraordinary. By 1914 Japan had urban conveniences and educational levels comparable to those in Europe.

QUICK REVIEW <

What common factor shaped the development of all
Asian societies in the nineteenth century?

| Was China's decline due more to internal problems or to Western imperialism? | How was Japan able to quickly master the challenges posed by the West? | What were the causes and consequences of the vast movement of people in the Pacific region? | **What explains the similarities and differences between Asian countries in this era?** | LearningCurve Check what you know. |

CHAPTER SUMMARY

In the nineteenth century the countries of Asia faced new challenges. In India Britain extended its rule to the whole subcontinent, though often the British ruled indirectly through local princes. Britain brought many modern advances to India, such as railroads and schools. Slavery was outlawed, as was widow suicide and infanticide. Resistance to British rule took several forms. In 1857 Indian soldiers in the employ of the British rose in a huge revolt, and after Britain put down this rebellion it ruled India much more tightly. Indians who received English education turned English ideas of liberty and representative rule against the British and founded the Indian National Congress, which called for Indian independence.

In Southeast Asia by the end of the nineteenth century most countries had been made colonies of Western powers, which developed them as exporters of agricultural products or raw materials. The principal exception was Siam (Thailand), whose king was able to play the English and French off against each other and institute centralizing reforms. In the Philippines more than three centuries of Spanish rule ended in 1898, but Spain was replaced by another colonial power: the United States.

In the nineteenth century China's world standing declined as a result of both foreign intervention and internal unrest. The government's efforts to suppress opium imports from Britain led to military confrontation with the British and to numerous concessions that opened China to trade on Britain's terms. Within its borders, China faced unprecedented population pressure and worsening economic conditions that resulted in uprisings in several parts of the country. Further humiliations by the Western powers led to concerted efforts to modernize, but China never quite caught up. Inspired by Western ideas of republican government, revolutionaries tried to topple the dynasty, finally succeeding in 1911–1912.

Japan was the one Asian country to quickly transform itself when confronted by the military strength of the West. It did this by overhauling its power structure. The Meiji centralized and strengthened Japan's power by depriving the samurai of their privileges, writing a constitution, instituting universal education, and creating a modern army. At the same time they guided Japan toward rapid industrialization. By the early twentieth century Japan had become an imperialist power with colonies in Korea and Taiwan.

The nineteenth century was also a great age of migration. Citizens of Great Britain came east in large numbers. Subjects of Asian countries also went abroad, often leaving one Asian country for another. Asian students traveled to Europe, Japan, or the United States to continue their educations. Millions more left in search of work. With the end of the African slave trade, recruiters from the Americas and elsewhere went to India and China to secure indentured laborers. Asian diasporas formed in many parts of the world.

By the turn of the twentieth century the countries in the Asia and Pacific region varied greatly in wealth and power. There are several reasons for this. The countries did not start with equivalent circumstances. Some had long traditions of unified rule; others did not. Some had manufactured goods that Western powers wanted; others offered raw materials or cheap labor. The timing of the arrival of Western powers also made a difference, especially because Western military superiority increased over time. European Great Power rivalry had a

In what ways did India change as a consequence of British rule?

Why were most but not all Southeast Asian societies reduced to colonies?

major impact, especially after 1860. Similarities in the experiences of Asian countries are also notable and include many of the benefits (and costs) of industrialization seen elsewhere in the world, such as modernizations in communication and transportation, extension of schooling, and the emergence of radical ideologies.

 CONNECTIONS The nineteenth century brought Asia change on a much greater scale than did any earlier century. Much of the change was political—old political orders were ousted or reduced to tokens by new masters, often European colonial powers. Old elites found themselves at a loss when confronted by the European powers with their modern weaponry and modern armies. Cultural change was no less dramatic as the old elites pondered the differences between their traditional values and the ideas that seemed to underlie the power of the European states. In several places ordinary people rose in rebellion, probably in part because they felt threatened by the speed of cultural change. Material culture underwent major changes as elites experimented with Western dress and architecture and ordinary people had opportunities to travel on newly built railroads.

In the Americas, too, the nineteenth century was an era of unprecedented change and movement of people. Colonial empires were being overturned there, not imposed as they were in Asia in the same period. The Americas were on the receiving end of the huge migrations taking place, while Asia, like Europe, was much more an exporter of people. The Industrial Revolution brought change to all these areas, both by making available inexpensive machine-made products and by destroying some old ways of making a living. Intellectually, in both Asia and the Americas the ideas of nationalism and nation building shaped how people, especially the more educated, thought about the changes they were experiencing.

ONLINE DOCUMENT PROJECT
Imperialism in the Philippines

How did Filipinos and Americans respond to Spanish and American imperialism?

Examine documents about the Philippines during the Spanish-American war, and then complete a quiz and writing assignment based on the evidence and details from this chapter. *See inside the front cover to learn more.*

Was China's decline due more to internal problems or to Western imperialism?

How was Japan able to quickly master the challenges posed by the West?

What were the causes and consequences of the vast movement of people in the Pacific region?

What explains the similarities and differences between Asian countries in this era?

LearningCurve
Check what you know.

CHAPTER 26 STUDY GUIDE

 GET STARTED ONLINE

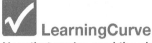 **LearningCurve**

Now that you've read the chapter, make it stick by completing the LearningCurve activity.

 EXPLAIN WHY IT MATTERS

Put your reading into practice. Identify each term below, and then explain why it matters in world history.

TERM	WHO OR WHAT & WHEN	WHY IT MATTERS
Great Mutiny / Great Revolt (p. 783)		
Indian Civil Service (p. 785)		
Indian National Congress (p. 785)		
Java War (p. 788)		
Nguyen Dynasty (p. 788)		
Opium War (p. 792)		
extraterritoriality (p. 792)		
Taiping Rebellion (p. 792)		
Boxers (p. 794)		
1911 Revolution (p. 794)		
gunboat diplomacy (p. 796)		
Meiji Restoration (p. 796)		
Russo-Japanese War (p. 799)		
indentured laborers (p. 803)		

 MOVE BEYOND THE BASICS

To demonstrate a more advanced understanding of the experiences of India, China, and Japan in the era of imperialism, fill in the chart below with descriptions of the nature and extent of Western intervention, the economic impact of the Western presence, and the efforts of the peoples of each society to respond to and resist Western expansion. What connections can you make between the nature of Western intervention and its economic impact in each society?

	Nature of Western Intervention	Economic Impact	Response and Resistance
India			
China			
Japan			

STEP 4

PUT IT ALL TOGETHER

Now, take a step back and try to explain the big picture. Remember to use specific examples from the chapter in your answers.

INDIA AND SOUTHEAST ASIA

▶ What motives underlay British efforts to shape India's society and economy? What role did Indians play in implementing British policy?

▶ Why was Siam able to resist colonization while much of the rest of Southeast Asia was not?

CHINA AND JAPAN

▶ Why was Japan so much more successful than China at resisting Western domination?

▶ Argue for or against the following statement. "By the end of the nineteenth century, Japan had become, for all intents and purposes, a Western imperial power."

REGIONAL TRENDS

▶ How did global economic and political developments influence Asian migration patterns in the nineteenth century?

▶ How did conflicts between "modernizers" and "traditionalists" shape the development of Asian societies in the nineteenth century?

LOOKING BACK, LOOKING AHEAD

▶ How did Europeans' desire to gain access to the wealth of Asia shape world history from 1500 to 1900?

▶ What connections might one make between the events of the second half of the nineteenth century and role of Japan in regional and world affairs in the first half of the twentieth century?

> IN YOUR OWN WORDS

Imagine that you must give an oral report to the class answering the following question: How did Asian leaders respond to the challenges posed by Western imperialism? What would be the most important points and why?

27

THE AMERICAS IN THE AGE OF LIBERALISM

1810–1910

> How did liberal political and economic ideas shape the development of the Americas in the nineteenth century? Chapter 27 examines major trends in the nineteenth-century Americas. In the United States, Cuba, and Brazil slavery endured until the second half of the nineteenth century. In Spanish America land remained concentrated in the hands of colonial elites. By 1900 millions of immigrants from Europe, the Middle East, and Asia had settled in the Americas. New political systems and governing institutions emerged quickly in the United States, Canada, and Brazil, while in much of the rest of the continent political rivals struggled to share power. The United States managed to nurture internal markets and assume an influential place in both Atlantic and Pacific trade. Across Latin America, new nations with weak internal markets and often poorly consolidated political systems struggled to accumulate capital or industrialize.

Yaqui Woman Indians across the Americas found their world under assault during the nineteenth century as new nation-states completed the process of territorial consolidation begun in the colonial era. Yaqui people like the woman depicted here faced the dual pressures of the United States' westward expansion and Mexico's integration of northern borderlands. (Library of Congress LC-USZ62-104492)

LearningCurve
After reading the chapter, use LearningCurve to retain what you've read.

> How and why did the process of nation-state consolidation vary across the Americas?

> Why did slavery last longer in the United States, Brazil, and Cuba than in the other republics of the Americas? How did patterns of resistance shape slavery and abolition?

> As Latin America became more integrated into the world economy, how did patterns of economic growth shape social relations and political culture?

> What factors shaped immigration patterns to the Americas? How did immigrants shape — and how were they shaped by — their new settings?

> In what ways did U.S. policies in the Caribbean and Central America resemble European imperialism? How did U.S. foreign policy depart from European imperialism?

How and why did the process of nation-state consolidation vary across the Americas?

Market Vendors in Mexico

Women sell fruits and vegetables at a market in San Luis Potosí, Mexico, around 1910 (© ullstein — Haeckel-Archiv/The Image Works)

AT THE MOMENT OF THEIR INDEPENDENCE, none of the nations of the Americas had consolidated what would become their national territory, and that process often took place violently. In countries such as Mexico and Argentina new governments failed to establish the trust needed for political stability. In the United States long-standing tensions and disagreements culminated in the Civil War, while in Cuba nationalists fought a long struggle for independence from Spain.

Liberalism and Caudillos in Spanish America

liberalism
▶ A philosophy whose principal ideas were equality and liberty; liberals demanded representative government and equality before the law as well as such individual freedoms as freedom of the press, freedom of speech, freedom of assembly, and freedom from arbitrary arrest.

The nations that gained independence from the Spanish Empire in the Americas drew upon ideological currents that circulated in the Atlantic in the age of revolution in order to establish new frameworks of government and social organization (see Chapter 22). The dominant ideology of the era was liberalism. Liberals sought to create representative republics with strong central governments framed by constitutions that defined and protected individual rights, in particular the right to freely own and buy and sell private property. Beginning with the United States, colonies that became independent nations in the Americas all adopted liberal constitutions.

CHAPTER LOCATOR | **How and why did the process of nation-state consolidation vary across the Americas?** | Why did slavery last longer in the U.S., Brazil, and Cuba than in other republics of the Americas?

814 CHAPTER 27 THE AMERICAS IN THE AGE OF LIBERALISM

1810–1825
Wars of independence in Latin America

1845
First use of term *manifest destiny* in United States; Texas and Florida admitted into United States

1845–1847
Mexican-American War

1857–1861
Mexican Wars of Reform

1861–1865
U.S. Civil War

1865–1870
Paraguay War (War of Triple Alliance)

1867
Dominion of Canada formed

1868–1878
Cuban Ten Years' War

1879–1883
War of the Pacific

1886
Abolition of slavery in Cuba

1888
Abolition of slavery in Brazil

1889
Brazilian monarchy overthrown and republic established

1898
Spanish-American War

1904
United States secures the rights to build and control the Panama Canal

1910
Mexican Revolution

1914
Panama Canal completed

The U.S. Constitution, in its earliest form, is an example of classic liberalism: it defined individual rights, but those individual rights were subordinated to property rights. Slaves were considered property rather than individuals with constitutional rights. Only property owners could vote, only men could own property, and the new government did not recognize the property of Indians. Thus, liberalism mainly served and protected oligarchs—the small number of individuals and families who had monopolized political power and economic resources since the colonial era. Liberalism preserved slavery, created tools that allowed the wealthy and powerful to continue to concentrate land ownership in the countryside, gave industrialists a free hand over their workers, and concentrated political power in the hands of those who held economic power.

By the end of the nineteenth century liberalism commingled with other ideologies such as Social Darwinism and scientific racism (see pages 736–737). This combination inspired the imperial ambitions of the United States toward Mexico and the Circum-Caribbean, the region that includes the Antilles as well as the lands that bound the Caribbean in Central America, southern North America, and northern South America.

Though liberalism provided the political and economic framework that replaced colonialism, nations of the Americas took different approaches. The United States deferred questions about centralized federal power over local state authority, as well as the legality of slavery, until its Civil War (1861–1865). After the North prevailed, economic growth under its liberal economic model accelerated. In Spanish America wars of independence left behind a weak consensus about government, which led to long cycles of civil war across many countries.

oligarchs
▶ The small number of individuals and families that monopolized political power and economic resources.

Circum-Caribbean
▶ The region encompassing the Antilles islands as well as the lands that bound the Caribbean Sea in Central America, southern North America, and northern South America.

How did patterns of economic growth shape social and political culture in Latin America?

What factors shaped immigration patterns to the Americas?

How did U.S. policies in the Caribbean and Central America resemble European imperialism?

✓ LearningCurve
Check what you know.

caudillismo

▶ Government by charismatic figures who rule through personal power rather than the functioning of public institutions.

The lack of a shared political culture among powerful groups in Spanish America created a crisis of confidence. Large landowners held great local power that they refused to yield to politicians in a distant capital. Political factions feared that if a rival faction won power, it would not abide by the rules and limits framed by the constitution, or that a rival would use its governing authority to crush its opponents. The power vacuum that resulted was often filled by caudillos, strong leaders who came to power and governed through their personal charisma and leadership abilities. This form of leadership is known as caudillismo. The rule of a caudillo, anchored in his charisma and the loyalty of his followers, often provided temporary stability amid the struggles between liberals and conservatives, but caudillos cultivated their own prestige at the expense of building stable political institutions.

Mexico and the United States

The rumblings of independence first stirred Mexico in 1810. A century later, in 1910, the country was engulfed in the Mexican Revolution. In the century between these events, Mexico declined politically and economically from its status as the most prosperous and important colony of the Spanish Empire. It lost most of its national territory as Central American provinces broke away and as the United States expanded westward and captured, purchased, or otherwise wrangled away Mexico's northern lands.

Mexicans experienced political stabilization and economic growth again in the second half of the nineteenth century when liberal leaders, especially the dictator Porfirio Díaz (r. 1876–1910), imposed order and attracted foreign investment. But as Díaz himself is said to have remarked, "Poor Mexico, so far from God, so close to the United States."[1] The United States pursued territorial expansion under the doctrine of manifest destiny, by which the United States would absorb all the territory spanning from its original Atlantic states to the Pacific Ocean. In the process, the United States took over lands belonging to Indian nations and to Mexico (Map 27.1). And as the United States grew economically, investors from the United States drove railroad construction and land speculation in Mexico that stripped lands away from peasants, who rose up in the 1910 revolution.

manifest destiny

▶ The belief that God had foreordained the United States to cover the entire continent.

Mexico's woes after independence resulted mainly from the inability of its political leaders to establish a consensus about how to govern the new nation. The general who led the war against Spain, Agustín de Iturbide, proclaimed himself emperor in 1822. When he was deposed a year later, the country's southern provinces broke away, forming the new nations of Guatemala, Honduras, Nicaragua, El Salvador, and Costa Rica. For the next three decades, power in Mexico rested in the hands of regional caudillos and local bosses. The presidency changed hands frequently as rival factions competed against each other.

By contrast, the United States established a clearer vision of government, a vision embodied in the 1789 Constitution. Deep differences of opinion remained over questions such as the power of the federal government relative to state governments, which played out in debates about the future of slavery and of westward expansion. These differences created regional tensions that lasted throughout the early nineteenth century and culminated in the Civil War (1861–1865).

Economically, the United States remained integrated into the expanding and industrializing British Empire. But the United States faced deepening regional

CHAPTER LOCATOR | How and why did the process of nation-state consolidation vary across the Americas? | Why did slavery last longer in the U.S., Brazil, and Cuba than in other republics of the Americas?

816   CHAPTER 27   THE AMERICAS IN THE AGE OF LIBERALISM

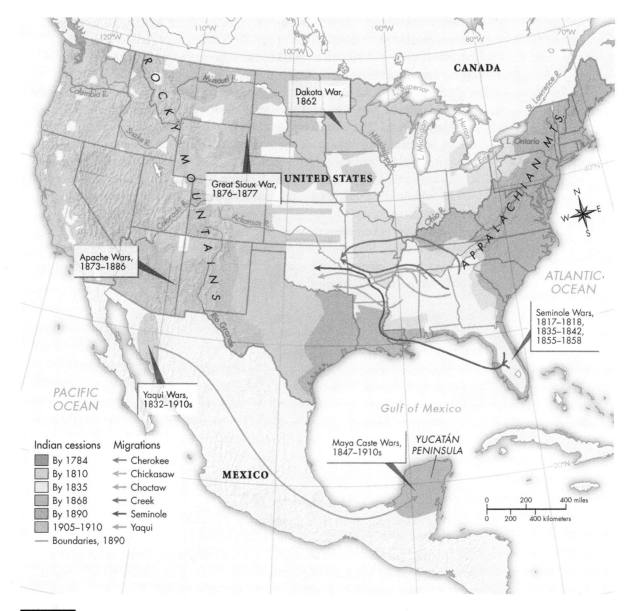

MAP 27.1 ■ Displacement of Indigenous Peoples, 1780s–1910s

The United States and Mexico waged repeated wars to claim the lands of Native American nations. This was the last stage of the process of conquest and dispossession that began with the arrival of Europeans in the Americas three centuries earlier. As national armies seized native lands, thousands of displaced native peoples were forcibly removed, leading to the deaths of thousands and the destruction of cultures.

differences: in the first half of the nineteenth century the North's economy and population grew faster than the South's, and the North became the center of immigration, banking, and industrialization. In the South slavery and tenant farming kept much of the population at the economic margins and weakened internal markets. Slavery also inhibited immigration, because immigrants avoided settling in areas where they had to compete for work with unfree labor.

The dichotomy between the economies of the U.S. North and South repeated itself in the difference between the economies of the United States and Latin

How did patterns of economic growth shape social and political culture in Latin America?

What factors shaped immigration patterns to the Americas?

How did U.S. policies in the Caribbean and Central America resemble European imperialism?

✓ LearningCurve
Check what you know.

America. The Spanish imperial economy imploded. Latin American economies were organized around the export of agricultural and mineral commodities like sugar and silver, not around internal markets as in the United States, and these export economies were disrupted by the independence process.

The fate of the major silver mine in Mexico illustrates the challenges presented by independence. La Valenciana in central Mexico was the most productive silver mine in the world. The machinery required to keep the mine functioning was destroyed during the wars of independence (1810–1821) and the mine ceased operation. Neither private investors nor the new government had the capital necessary to reactivate the mine after independence. Without the private profits, wages, and taxation that mining produced, Mexico's economy withered and its credit networks collapsed.

Thus, after independence, Mexico entered a vicious cycle: without capital and economic activity, tax revenues evaporated, public administration disintegrated, and the national government became unmanageable. In turn, the lack of political stability drove investors away.

> ## > Mexico Falls Behind the United States:

- 1800: Mexico produced half the goods and services that the United States did
- 1845: Mexico produced only 8 percent as much as the United States
- 1821: Mexico had a population of 6.2 million, while the United States had 3.9 million
- 1900: Mexico's population had risen to 13.6 million, while the U.S. population had increased to 76 million

Politically and economically weakened after independence, Mexico was vulnerable to expansionist pressure from the United States. At independence, Mexico's northern territories included much of what is today the U.S. Southwest and West. These northern territories attracted the interest of U.S. politicians, settlers, and land speculators. In the 1820s settlers from the U.S. South petitioned the Mexican government for land grants in the province of Texas, in return for which they would adopt Mexican citizenship. The U.S. government encouraged these settlers to declare the independence of Texas in 1836.

After Texas and Florida became U.S. states in 1845, President James Polk expanded its westward border, precipitating the Mexican-American War (1845–1847). In the Treaty of Guadalupe Hidalgo (1848), that followed Mexican defeat, Mexico ceded half its territory, including California, Nevada, Arizona, New Mexico, and parts of Colorado and Utah, to the United States.

Treaty of Guadalupe Hidalgo

▶ The 1848 treaty between the United States and Mexico in which Mexico ceded large tracts of land to the United States.

Liberal Reform in Mexico

In 1853 Mexican president Santa Anna unintentionally ushered in a new era of liberal political consolidation and economic reform by triggering a backlash against his sale of territory along the northern border to the United States. Many Mexicans saw his act as a betrayal of the nation and threw their support behind a new generation of liberal leaders. Beginning with the presidency of Ignacio Comonfort (pres. 1855–1858), these liberals carried out sweeping legal and economic changes called *La Reforma*, or "the reform."

CHAPTER LOCATOR | How and why did the process of nation-state consolidation vary across the Americas? | Why did slavery last longer in the U.S., Brazil, and Cuba than in other republics of the Americas?

CHAPTER 27
818 THE AMERICAS IN THE AGE OF LIBERALISM

Liberal reformers sought to make all individuals equal under the law and established property ownership as a basic right and national goal. The first major step in La Reforma was the Juarez Law (1855), which abolished legal privileges for military officers and members of the clergy. An even more consequential measure, the **Lerdo Law** (1856), banished another legacy of colonialism: "corporate lands," meaning lands owned by groups or institutions, such as the Catholic Church, rather than by individual property owners. Liberals wanted to redistribute church-owned lands among farmers who would own them as private parcels and who would profit from working them efficiently.

These liberal reforms triggered a backlash from conservative landowners and the church. When liberals enshrined these laws and other reforms in a new constitution ratified in 1857, the Catholic Church threatened to excommunicate anyone who swore allegiance to it. Conservatives revolted, triggering a civil war called the Wars of Reform (1857–1861). Liberal forces led by Benito Juárez defeated the conservatives, who then conspired with French emperor Napoleon III to invite a French invasion of Mexico in 1862. French victory led to the installation of Napoleon III's Austrian cousin Maximilian of Habsburg as emperor of Mexico.

The deposed Juárez led a guerrilla war against the French troops backing Maximilian. Juárez's nationalists prevailed, restored Mexico's republic, and executed Maximilian. Conservatives had been completely discredited: they had conspired with another country to install a foreign leader through a military invasion.

Lerdo Law
▶ An 1856 Mexican law that barred corporate landholdings.

Brazil: A New World Monarchy

Brazil gained independence in 1822 as a monarchy ruled by Emperor Pedro I, the son and heir of Portuguese emperor João IV. The creation of a Brazilian monarchy marked the culmination of a process that began in 1808, when Napoleon's armies crossed the Pyrenees from France to invade the Iberian Peninsula. Napoleon toppled the Spanish crown, but the Portuguese royal family, many of the government's bureaucrats, and most of the aristocracy fled aboard British warships to Portugal's colony, Brazil.

Before the seat of Portuguese power relocated to Brazil, colonial policies had restricted many activities in Brazil in order to keep the colony dependent and subordinate to Portugal. It was only with the arrival of the imperial court that Brazil gained its first printing press, library, and military and naval academies, as well as schools for engineering, medicine, law, and the arts.

With the flight of the emperor to Brazil in 1808 and the declaration of independence by his son in 1822, Brazil achieved something that had eluded Spanish-American nations: it retained the unifying symbol of the monarchy and continued to build upon the infrastructure of colonial administration. A liberal constitution adopted in 1824 lasted until a republican military coup in 1889. It established a two-chamber parliamentary system and a role for the emperor as a guide and intermediary in political affairs. Pedro I was not adept in this role and abdicated in 1831, leaving behind a regency governing in the name of his five-year-old son, Pedro II. In 1840 Pedro II declared himself an adult and assumed the throne. His rule, which lasted forty-nine years, provided the country with unusual political stability that helped keep Brazil from dividing into separate nations, as occurred in Spanish America, and avoided the internal strife that characterized the United States during that period.

How did patterns of economic growth shape social and political culture in Latin America?

What factors shaped immigration patterns to the Americas?

How did U.S. policies in the Caribbean and Central America resemble European imperialism?

☑ LearningCurve
Check what you know.

neocolonialism

▶ The re-establishment of political and economic influence over regions after they have ceased to be formal colonies.

The nature of Brazil's independence nonetheless constrained its growth in the nineteenth century. Portugal had been economically and militarily dependent on Britain, and Britain transferred this dependency onto Brazil. Britain negotiated with Brazil a "Friendship Treaty" that allowed British industrial goods to enter the country with very low tariffs and granted British citizens in Brazil the right to be tried by British rather than Brazilian judges. The flood of cheap British imports inhibited Brazilian industrialization. British economic and political influence, as well as the special privileges enjoyed by British citizens in Brazil, were examples of neocolonialism, the influence that European powers and the United States exerted over politically and economically weaker countries after they gained their independence.

> **QUICK REVIEW**

Why did Mexico struggle economically in the first half of the nineteenth century?

CHAPTER LOCATOR | How and why did the process of nation-state consolidation vary across the Americas? | Why did slavery last longer in the U.S., Brazil, and Cuba than in other republics of the Americas?

CHAPTER 27
820 THE AMERICAS IN THE AGE OF LIBERALISM

Why did slavery last longer in the United States, Brazil, and Cuba than in other republics of the Americas? How did patterns of resistance shape slavery and abolition?

Slave Labor in Rio de Janeiro, Brazil

This lithograph by French traveler Jean-Baptiste Debret shows different facets of urban slavery in Rio de Janeiro. In the foreground slaves lay paving stones in a plaza, while behind them other slaves peddle food. A funeral procession passes in the background. (from *Voyage Pittoresque et Historique au Bresil*, 1824 color lithograph by Jean-Baptiste Debret [1768–1848] published in 1839/Bibliotheque Nationale, Paris, France/Archives Charmet/The Bridgeman Art Library)

ACROSS THE FORMER COLONIES OF SPANISH AMERICA, the abolition of slavery quickly followed independence. Abolitionist pressure from Britain ended slavery in its Caribbean colonies in 1834, and the British navy suppressed the Atlantic slave trade. But slavery endured well into the nineteenth century in the United States, Cuba, and Brazil. In each of these countries the question of abolition became entwined with the disputes over the nature of government and authority.

Slave Societies in the Americas

Africans and their descendants were enslaved in every country of the Americas, from Canada to Chile. The experiences in slavery and freedom for Africans and African Americans, broadly defined here as the descendants of slaves brought from Africa to anywhere in the New World, varied considerably. Several factors

| How did patterns of economic growth shape social and political culture in Latin America? | What factors shaped immigration patterns to the Americas? | How did U.S. policies in the Caribbean and Central America resemble European imperialism? | LearningCurve Check what you know. |

Slaves Sold South from Richmond, 1853

This scene was painted by a British artist, based on scenes he witnessed in the U.S. South twenty years after slavery was abolished in the British Empire. Being "sold south," as this image depicts, was a terrifying fate. In addition to having their families ripped apart, those who were sold were sent to plantations where the labor regimes were famously harsh. Note the ways in which the artist depicts not only the slave families but also the white, mixed, and free black traders. (*After the Sale: Slaves Going South from Richmond*, 1853 [oil on canvas], by Eyre Crowe [1824–1910]/© Chicago History Museum, U.S.A./The Bridgeman Art Library)

> PICTURING THE PAST

ANALYZING THE IMAGE: How are images of families used in this depiction of slavery? How are whites and free blacks represented?

CONNECTIONS: Can you think of other examples of art with social or political messages? How would this painting compare in its effectiveness?

shaped their experiences: the nature of slave regimes in different economic regions, patterns of manumission (individual slaves gaining their freedom), the nature of abolition (the ending of the institution of slavery), and the proportion of the local population they represented.

The settlement of Africans as slaves was the most intense in areas that relied on plantation agriculture. Plantations were an unusual kind of farming: they were typically enormous tracts of land dedicated to cultivating a single crop on a scale so great that plantation regions usually supplied distant global markets. The massive scale of this kind of agriculture, along with the practice of importing African labor to sustain it, originated in the sugar region of northeastern Brazil under the Portuguese. African slaves played many other roles as well. From Buenos Aires to Boston, slavery was also widespread in port cities, fed by easy access to the slave trade and the demand for street laborers such as porters. And across the Americas, slaves—especially slave women—were forced into domestic service, a role that added sexual abuse to the miseries that slaves endured.

CHAPTER LOCATOR | How and why did the process of nation-state consolidation vary across the Americas? | Why did slavery last longer in the U.S., Brazil, and Cuba than in other republics of the Americas?

CHAPTER 27
822 THE AMERICAS IN THE AGE OF LIBERALISM

Independence and Abolition

Slavery and abolition became intertwined with the process of political independence. The different relationships between independence and abolition in the United States and Haiti shaped perceptions across the rest of the continent. In Haiti national independence was achieved amid a social revolution in which slaves turned against their oppressors. By contrast, the United States gained its independence in a war that created a liberal political regime that preserved the institution of slavery. When colonial elites elsewhere on the continent contemplated independence, they weighed whether the U.S. or the Haitian experience awaited them. As a result, in colonies where the unfree population was the largest, independence movements proceeded more gradually.

British efforts to keep their North American colonies, as well as a combination of moral and economic appeals for the abolition of slavery in British territories, hastened the end of the slave trade to the Americas. When British forces fought to prevent the independence of the United States, they offered freedom to slaves who joined them. Many slaves did so, and after the British defeat and withdrawal, they dispersed to Spanish Florida, the Caribbean, and West Africa.

In 1808 British abolitionists pressured their government to end the Atlantic slave trade to British colonies, and in 1834 Britain abolished slavery in Canada and its Caribbean colonies. In order to reduce economic competition with other countries still importing slaves and still using slave labor, the British government pressured other nations to follow suit. A British naval squadron patrolled the Atlantic to suppress the slave trade. The squadron captured slave ships, freed the slaves they carried, and resettled them in a colony the British government established in Sierra Leone in 1787 to settle former slaves who had sided with Britain in the American Revolution.

Unlike in the United States, in Spanish America independence forces enlisted the participation of slaves and offered freedom in return. As rebels triumphed, new national governments enacted gradual abolition. The first step toward abolition was typically taken through **free womb laws** that granted freedom to children born to slaves. These laws, passed across independent Spanish America between 1811 and 1825, created gradual abolition but did not impose an immediate financial loss on slaveholders. Similar laws hastened the abolition of slavery in the Northern states of the United States.

free womb laws
▶ A gradual form of abolition through which children born to slaves gain their freedom.

In Spanish America the conflicts that continued after independence accelerated the abolition process: within the cycle of violence and civil wars, rival factions competed to enlist the support of slaves and free blacks. In 1854 Peru became the last country in Spanish America to fully abolish slavery. The combination of free womb laws and manumission as a reward for military service meant that, unlike in the United States, by the time slavery was abolished in Latin American countries, most blacks had already gained their freedom (Map 27.2).

In the United States, even if independence occurred without abolition, the questions of nation building and slavery remained connected. The determination of Southern states to protect the slave regime was enshrined in the U.S. Constitution, which granted individual states considerable autonomy in such questions as slavery and freedom. As slavery was abolished in Northern states, westward expansion tested the political compromise between the North and South, culminating in the Civil War.

How did patterns of economic growth shape social and political culture in Latin America?

What factors shaped immigration patterns to the Americas?

How did U.S. policies in the Caribbean and Central America resemble European imperialism?

☑ LearningCurve
Check what you know.

MAP 27.2 ■ Abolition in the Americas

The process of abolition in the Americas was gradual and varied across regions. In some areas, such as Mexico and parts of New England, slavery was abolished soon after independence, while in the U.S. South it lasted until the end of the Civil War. In Texas, slavery was abolished by the Mexican government, but when Texas became part of the United States, slavery was legally reinstated. In British territories, slavery was abolished in 1834. Across Latin America the abolition of slavery was hastened by civil wars that mobilized slaves as combatants. The last country to abolish slavery, Brazil, did so only in 1888.

> MAPPING THE PAST

ANALYZING THE MAP: How did the United States resemble Latin America in its patterns of abolition?
CONNECTIONS: Why did some countries abolish slavery earlier, and why did others do so much later?

Tensions between the North and the South reached a breaking point when Abraham Lincoln, committed to checking the spread of slavery, was elected president in 1860. Southern political leaders, fearing that Lincoln might abolish slavery, seceded and formed a new nation, the Confederate States of America. Lincoln declared the secession illegal and declared war on the seceding states to preserve the territorial integrity of the United States. The ensuing civil war resulted in the deaths of over 750,000 combatants and civilians.

The Emancipation Proclamation, which became effective January 1, 1863, abolished slavery in all states that remained opposed to the Union. It was intended as leverage to bring the rebel states back into the Union, not to abolish slavery altogether, because it freed slaves only in states that had seceded. Nevertheless, the proclamation hastened the demise of slavery. In 1865 Southern rebel states surrendered after Northern armies decimated their industrial, agricultural, and military capacity. Months later, the Thirteenth Amendment to the Constitution fully abolished slavery.

Two aspects made slavery in the United States different from slavery in Latin America: gradual abolition in the North made it a regional rather than a national institution, and the U.S. Civil War, followed by military occupation of the South (1865–1877), created a lasting regional backlash that codified racial segregation. This did not make the South entirely racist and the North entirely antiracist: segregation is a form of racism but hardly the only one. Instead race relations in the northern and western states of the United States resembled those of Latin America, where racial prejudice and the marginalization of African Americans were perpetuated through largely informal practices and values. Meanwhile,

CHAPTER LOCATOR | How and why did the process of nation-state consolidation vary across the Americas? | Why did slavery last longer in the U.S., Brazil, and Cuba than in other republics of the Americas?

CHAPTER 27
824 THE AMERICAS IN THE AGE OF LIBERALISM

the U.S. South erected a distinct legal edifice preserving white privilege that best resembled the oppressive white-minority regimes of South Africa and Rhodesia (see page 1007).

Abolition in Cuba and Brazil

Cuba and Brazil followed long and indirect paths to abolition. In Cuba nationalist rebels fought for independence from Spain in the Ten Years' War (1868–1878). Many slaves and free blacks joined the failed anticolonial struggle. Spanish authorities sought to defuse the tensions feeding that struggle by enacting the Moret Law in 1870, which granted freedom to slaves who fought on the Spanish side in the war, to the children of slaves born since 1868, and to slaves over age sixty. By 1878 Spanish forces had defeated the nationalists, but the conflict set in motion an irreversible process of abolition. In Brazil the 1871 Law of the Free Womb also granted freedom to children born to slaves, and an 1885 law granted freedom to slaves over age sixty. Slavery was finally abolished completely in Cuba in 1886 and in Brazil in 1888, making them the last regions of the Americas to end slavery.

Abolition did not come about solely through laws from the top down. Social pressure, often exerted by slaves themselves, contributed to abolition. For example, in Cuba many officers in the nationalist army, including its second-in-command, General Antonio Maceo, were free black abolitionists. In Brazil free blacks like engineer André Rebouças, journalist José do Patrocínio, and novelist Joaquim Machado de Assis were fervent abolitionists who shaped public opinion against slavery and found common cause with a republican movement that saw both slavery and monarchy as outdated.

Slave resistance, in its many forms, also intensified in the last years of the nineteenth century. Slaves ran off from plantations in growing numbers. In many cases, they settled in communities of runaway slaves, particularly in Brazil, where the vast interior offered opportunities to resettle out of the reach of former masters. In the years preceding abolition, in some regions of Brazil slave flight became so widespread that slaves might simply leave their plantation and hire themselves out to a nearby planter whose own slaves had also run away. In the end, the costs of slavery had become unsustainable.

QUICK REVIEW

What connection was there between independence struggles in Spanish America and the abolition of slavery in former Spanish colonies?

How did patterns of economic growth shape social and political culture in Latin America?

What factors shaped immigration patterns to the Americas?

How did U.S. policies in the Caribbean and Central America resemble European imperialism?

☑ LearningCurve
Check what you know.

> As Latin America became more integrated into the world economy, how did patterns of economic growth shape social relations and political culture?

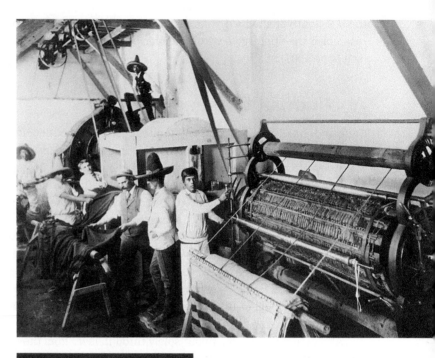

The Growth of Industry in Mexico

Workers at a textile mill in Mexico around 1900.
(© akg-images/The Image Works)

THE CONSOLIDATION OF A LIBERAL ORDER in the Americas through reforms that began in the 1850s and accelerated through conflicts like Mexico's Wars of Reform, the U.S. Civil War, and the Paraguay War in South America created stable conditions for a return of foreign investment that brought economic growth. But reforms intended to create a dynamic class of rural farmers served the opposite ends. In particular, liberalism created new economic pressures against rural workers and indigenous communities.

The Porfiriato and Liberal Stability in Mexico

When Porfirio Díaz became president of Mexico in 1876, he inherited a country in which much had been achieved: President Juárez had established national unity against the French invasion. He and his generation of liberal leaders and policy-makers had also created a national legal and political framework based on the 1857 constitution. Conservatives had been defeated and discredited. But it was a country that faced enormous challenges: per capita income was less than it had been at independence in 1821. The country had barely four hundred miles

CHAPTER LOCATOR | How and why did the process of nation-state consolidation vary across the Americas? | Why did slavery last longer in the U.S., Brazil, and Cuba than in other republics of the Americas?

826 CHAPTER 27
THE AMERICAS IN THE AGE OF LIBERALISM

of railroad tracks. The Mexican government was bankrupt and in debt. Díaz's first challenge was to attract foreign investment.

Porfirio Díaz built a regime—the Porfiriato—with unprecedented stability and ruled, with a single term out of power, from 1876 to 1911. He ruled by the mantra *pan o palo*, "bread or the stick," rewarding supporters and ruthlessly punishing opponents. The political stability he created made Mexico a haven for foreign investment, particularly from the United States. Investment in industry increased from 25,000 to 30 million pesos, and the value of manufacturing doubled. Foreign trade increased tenfold, and the country became the third largest oil producer. Railroads rapidly expanded, facilitating the shipment of goods to the United States and connecting regions long isolated from each other and from national markets.

The Porfiriato was a modernizing regime, staffed with technocrats called *científicos*: engineers, agronomists, and other experts to whom Díaz granted great autonomy and lavish rewards. By contrast, the Porfiriato considered indigenous peoples racially inferior and suppressed them, often violently, using the mission of modernization and economic development to justify a range of abuses.

Economic progress enriched Díaz and his allies but proved perilous to rural communities. The rise in foreign investment and economic activity made land more valuable, which made small landholders vulnerable. The Lerdo Law, intended to encourage the growth of small farmers, now served the opposite goal as large landowners and speculative investors used it to challenge the legal rights to lands across the Mexican countryside. In addition, the 1883 Law of Barren Lands allowed real estate companies to identify land that was not being cultivated so it could be surveyed and auctioned off. The abuse of these laws by land speculators with ties to the regime, along with intimidation and violence, had devastating consequences: by 1910, 80 percent of rural peasants had no land. The increase in land values paradoxically reduced production: speculators from the United States bought large tracts of land not to farm but to hold as investments.

The Porfiriato and its liberal ideology favored the needs of foreign investors over its own citizens. Most of Mexico's 1910 population of 12 million remained tied to the land. The expansion of railroads into that land made it valuable, and liberal reforms provided the tools to transfer that value from peasants to capitalists. Given Mexico's proximity to the United States, that process was swifter and more intense than elsewhere in Latin America, and it led to the first great social upheaval of the twentieth century, the Mexican Revolution that erupted in 1910.

Porfiriato

▶ The regime of Porfirio Díaz, who presided in Mexico from 1876 to 1880 and again from 1884 to 1910.

Liberal Consolidation in South America

As in the United States and Mexico, the process of liberal nation-state consolidation in South America took place through military conflict. The War of the Triple Alliance, or Paraguay War (1865–1870), in which Paraguay fought Brazil, Argentina, and Uruguay, played a similar role to Mexico's Wars of Reform and the U.S. Civil War in consolidating liberalism in South America. In 1865 Paraguayan leader Francisco Solano López declared war against the three neighboring countries after political competition between Argentina and Brazil threatened Paraguay's use of Uruguay's Atlantic port in Montevideo. Landlocked Paraguay depended on Montevideo as a shipping point for its imports and exports. Paraguay fought a five-year war against much larger neighbors until it was defeated in 1870.

| How did patterns of economic growth shape social and political culture in Latin America? | What factors shaped immigration patterns to the Americas? | How did U.S. policies in the Caribbean and Central America resemble European imperialism? | LearningCurve Check what you know. |

827

The war was devastating for Paraguay, which lost more than half its national population, including most adult men. But victory, too, was traumatic for Argentina and Brazil. Argentines and Brazilians asked themselves why it had taken five years to defeat a much smaller neighbor. The war prompted debates about the need for economic modernization and the reform of national governments.

In Brazil, where Emperor Pedro II's calls for volunteers to enlist in the army fell on deaf ears, the army enlisted slaves who, if they served honorably and survived, would be granted freedom. What did it mean when the free citizens of a nation would not mobilize to defend it, and when a nation prevailed only through the sacrifices borne by its slaves? For many, especially military officers who were veterans of the conflict, the lesson was that being a monarchy that relied on slavery made Brazil a backward nation. Veteran officers and liberal opponents of the war formed a movement to create a liberal republic and abolish slavery. These republicans overthrew monarchy in 1889 and installed a liberal regime that lasted until 1930.

In Argentina, after the war with Paraguay, a succession of liberal leaders beginning with Domingo Sarmiento (pres. 1868–1874) also pressed modernizing reforms. Economic measures in Argentina were the most far-reaching and drew on the experience of the United States in settling its western frontier as a model. In a military campaign called the Conquest of the Desert (1878–1885), Argentine troops took control of the lands of Mapuche Indians in the southern region of Patagonia and opened new lands for sale to ranchers. The wars were accompanied by ambitious railroad construction that linked inland areas to the coast, the introduction of barbed wire fencing that intensified ranching capabilities, and the development of new strains of cattle and wheat that increased production. The Conquest of the Desert and the government's land distribution policies transformed Argentina's countryside into highly productive ranch lands and farmlands whose exports competed directly with the ranches of the North American West.

Latin America Re-enters the World Economy

The wars of independence in Spanish America interrupted the Atlantic and Pacific trade networks that had sustained the region's colonial economies. Amid the political instability that followed independence, investment dried up and trade networks collapsed. For rural peasants and indigenous communities, this was a benefit in disguise: the decline of trade made lands less valuable. The rents landowners could charge tenant farmers decreased, making it easier for peasants to gain access to land.

By the second half of the nineteenth century Latin American elites reached a compromise that combined liberal political ideas about the way national government should be structured with liberal economic policies that favored large landowners. Political stability and economic growth returned. Foreign investment intensified. By the turn of the twentieth century Latin American countries were firmly tied to the world economy. Indigenous and rural communities paid a high price for this return to economic growth: as the value of agricultural exports increased, so did the value of land. Governments, foreign investors, and large landowners seized lands through war, legal action, or coercion at a dizzying rate.

As Latin American governments stabilized, they consolidated control of national territory in part by eliminating, subjugating, or displacing indigenous

CHAPTER LOCATOR | How and why did the process of nation-state consolidation vary across the Americas? | Why did slavery last longer in the U.S., Brazil, and Cuba than in other republics of the Americas?

CHAPTER 27
828 THE AMERICAS IN THE AGE OF LIBERALISM

communities. Through this process, Latin American governments opened new lands for private ownership.

After the Conquest of the Desert in the 1870s and 1880s, the Argentine government sold off lands it took from indigenous communities. The land was inexpensive, but because it was sold in such large parcels, the few who could purchase it did so by mortgaging existing landholdings. Consequently, more than 20 million acres were sold to just 381 landowners, who created vast estates known as latifundios. In contrast, the Brazilian Land Law of 1850 restricted land ownership by prohibiting anyone from gaining title to land by settling it. The law was a response to pressure from Britain to end the slave trade: planters used the law to keep slaves or free workers on their plantations by preventing them from setting out to farm on their own.[2]

latifundios
▶ Large landed estates.

Liberal economic policies and the intensification of foreign trade concentrated land in the hands of wealthy exporters. Governments represented the interests of large landowners by promoting commodity exports and industrial imports. Brazil became the world's largest exporter of coffee and experienced a brief but intense boom in rubber production. Argentina's conquests on the frontier and economic modernization made it one of the most efficient and profitable exporters of grains and beef. Chile and Peru served the international market for fertilizers by exporting nitrates and bat guano.

These export booms depended on imported capital and technology. In the Circum-Caribbean this came mostly from investors in the United States, while in South America it came from Britain. (See "Individuals in Society: Henry Meiggs, Promoter and Speculator," page 830.) British capital and technology built Argentina's network of railroads and refrigerated meatpacking plants. By 1890 British companies controlled 90 percent of Chile's nitrate-mining industry.

The rise in the quantity and value of primary commodity exports concentrated wealth in the hands of oligarchs. Large landowners, such as Brazilian coffee planters, relied on cheap labor provided by slaves until 1888 and, increasingly, by tenant farmers and free laborers who worked for little pay. The exported coffee produced by these workers reaped profits so great that, although coffee planters were the main slaveholders, they could afford to give up slavery and pursue immigrant labor from Europe. In the late nineteenth century planters united to create colonization companies in southern European cities that promoted and subsidized immigration to Brazil. The planters combined economic liberalism with Social Darwinism: they believed that free workers were more efficient than slave laborers and that white workers were more productive than black ones.

QUICK REVIEW <

What groups benefitted most from economic growth in Latin America in the second half of the nineteenth century?

How did patterns of economic growth shape social and political culture in Latin America?

What factors shaped immigration patterns to the Americas?

How did U.S. policies in the Caribbean and Central America resemble European imperialism?

 LearningCurve
Check what you know.

INDIVIDUALS IN SOCIETY
Henry Meiggs, Promoter and Speculator

The challenges in building the Callo-Lima-Oroya railroad across the Andes can be imagined from this picture of one of its many bridges. (From Elio Galessio, *Ferrocarriles del Perú: Un viaje a través de su Historia*. Reproduced with permission of the author.)

All throughout the Americas in the nineteenth century, opportunities beckoned. Henry Meiggs, born in upstate New York in 1811, responded to several of them, building and losing fortunes in Brooklyn, San Francisco, Chile, and Peru.

Meiggs, with only an elementary school education, began work at his father's shipyard. He soon started his own lumber business and did well until he lost everything in the financial panic of 1837. He rebuilt his business, and when gold was discovered in California in 1848, he filled a ship with lumber and sailed around Cape Horn to San Francisco, where he sold his cargo for $50,000, twenty times what he had paid for it. He then entered the lumber business, organizing crews of five hundred men to fell huge California redwoods and bring them to his steam sawmills. As his business flourished, he began speculating in real estate, which led to huge debts when the financial crisis of 1854 hit. In an attempt to save himself and his friends, Meiggs forged warrants for more than $900,000; when discovery of the fraud seemed imminent, he sailed with his wife and children for South America.

Although at one point Meiggs was so strapped for cash that he sold his watch, within three years of arriving in Chile, he had secured his first railway contract, and by 1867 he had built about 200 miles of rail lines in that country. In 1868 he went to Peru, which had less than 60 miles of track at the time. In the next nine years he would add 700 more.

Meiggs was not an engineer, but he was a good manager. He recruited experienced engineers from abroad and arranged purchase of foreign rolling stock, rails, and ties, acting as a promoter and developer. Much of the funding came from international investors in Peruvian bonds.

The most spectacular of the rail lines Meiggs built was Peru's Callao-Lima-Oroya line, which crosses the Andes at about seventeen thousand feet above sea level, making it the highest standard-gauge railway in the world. Because water was scarce in many areas along the construction site, it had to be transported up to workers, who were mostly local people. Dozens of bridges and tunnels had to be built, and casualties were high. Eight hundred people were invited to the banquet that marked the beginning of work on the Oroya Railway. Meiggs drummed up enthusiasm at the event by calling the locomotive the "irresistible battering ram of modern civilization."

In Peru Meiggs became known for his extravagance and generosity, and some charged that he bribed Peruvian officials on a large scale to get his projects approved. He was a good speaker and loved to entertain lavishly. In one example of his generosity, he distributed thousands of pesos and soles to the victims of the earthquake of 1868. He also contributed to the beautification of Lima by tearing down an old wall and putting a seven-mile-long park in its place.

Always the speculator, in 1877 Meiggs died poor, his debts exceeding his assets. He was beloved, however, and more than twenty thousand Peruvians, many of whom had labored on his projects, attended his funeral at a Catholic church in Lima.

QUESTIONS FOR ANALYSIS

1. What accounts for the changes in fortune that Meiggs experienced?
2. Were the Latin American governments that awarded contracts to Meiggs making reasonable decisions?
3. Should it matter whether Meiggs had to bribe officials to get the railroads built? Why or why not?

ONLINE DOCUMENT PROJECT

How did investors like Henry Meiggs fit into the larger context of Latin American nation building? Read descriptions of Latin America's past and visions of its future, and then complete a quiz and writing assignment based on the evidence and details from this chapter. *See inside the front cover to learn more.*

What factors shaped immigration patterns to the Americas? How did immigrants shape — and how were they shaped by — their new settings?

Immigrants in the Americas

Indian immigrants at a Jamaican banana plantation (top) and German immigrants in Brazil (bottom) at the turn of the twentieth century. Immigrants brought new cultures and worldviews to the Americas. (Jamaica: *Picturesque Jamaica*, by Adolphe Duperly & Son, England, circa 1905/Brazil: © The Print Collector/Heritage/The Image Works; © SZ Photo/Scherl/The Image Works)

DURING THE LATE NINETEENTH and early twentieth centuries unprecedented numbers of people from Europe, Asia, and the Middle East settled across North and South America. The largest wave of immigrants — some 28 million between 1860 and 1914 — settled in the United States. Another 8 million had settled in Argentina and Brazil by 1930. This cycle of immigration was a product of liberal political and economic reforms that abolished slavery, established stable political systems, and created a framework for integrating immigrants as factory and farm laborers.

| How did patterns of economic growth shape social and political culture in Latin America? | **What factors shaped immigration patterns to the Americas?** | How did U.S. policies in the Caribbean and Central America resemble European imperialism? | ✔️ LearningCurve Check what you know. |

Immigration to Latin America

In 1852 the Argentine political philosopher Juan Bautista Alberdi published *Bases and Points of Departure for Argentine Political Organization*, in which he argued that the development of his country depended on immigration. Indians and blacks, Alberdi maintained, lacked basic skills, and it would take too long to train them. Thus he pressed for massive immigration from northern Europe and the United States. Alberdi's ideas, guided by the aphorism "to govern is to populate," won immediate acceptance and were even incorporated into the Argentine constitution, which declared, "The Federal government will encourage European immigration." Other Latin American countries adopted similar policies promoting immigration to achieve similar goals.

Coffee barons in Brazil, *latifundiarios* (owners of vast estates) in Argentina, or investors in nitrate and copper mining in Chile made enormous profits that they reinvested in new factories. Latin America had been tied to the Industrial Revolution in Britain and northern Europe from the outset as a provider of raw materials and as a consumer of industrial goods. In the major exporting countries of Argentina, Brazil, and Mexico, domestic industrialization now began to take hold in the form of textile mills, food-processing plants, and mechanized transportation such as modern ports and railroads.

By the turn of the twentieth century, an industrial working-class had begun to emerge. In Brazil and Argentina these workers, who were mainly European immigrants, proved unexpectedly contentious: they brought with them radical ideologies that challenged liberalism, particularly anarchism and anarcho-syndicalism, a version of anarchism that advocated placing power in the hands of workers' unions. These workers clashed with bosses and political leaders who rejected the idea that workers had rights. The authorities suppressed worker organizations such as unions, and they resisted implementing labor laws such as a minimum wage, restrictions on child labor, the right to strike, or factory safety regulations.

Although Europe was a significant source of immigrants to Latin America, so were Asia and the Middle East. For example, in the late nineteenth and early twentieth centuries large numbers of Japanese arrived in Brazil, and by 1920 Brazil had the largest Japanese community in the world outside of Japan. From the Middle East, Lebanese, Turks, and Syrians also entered Brazil. Between 1850 and 1880, South Asian laborers went to Trinidad, Jamaica, St. Lucia, Grenada, and St. Vincent, mostly as indentured servants. When slavery was abolished in Cuba in 1886, some of the work in the sugarcane fields was done by Chinese indentured servants. Likewise, the abolition of slavery in Mexico led to the arrival of thousands of Chinese bonded servants.

Thanks to the influx of new arrivals, Buenos Aires, São Paulo, Mexico City, Montevideo, Santiago, and Havana experienced spectacular growth. By 1914 Buenos Aires in particular had emerged as one of the most cosmopolitan cities in the world, with a population of 3.6 million.

Immigrants brought wide-ranging skills that helped develop industry and commerce. In Argentina, Italian and Spanish settlers stimulated the expansion of the cattle industry and the development of the wheat and shoe industries. In Brazil, Swiss immigrants built the cheese business, Italians gained a leading role in the coffee industry, and Japanese farmers made the country self-sufficient in rice production. In Peru, Italians became influential in banking and the restaurant

anarcho-syndicalism
▶ A radical ideology that proposed the revolutionary reorganization of society into an egalitarian community ruled by workers' unions.

CHAPTER LOCATOR | How and why did the process of nation-state consolidation vary across the Americas? | Why did slavery last longer in the U.S., Brazil, and Cuba than in other republics of the Americas?

CHAPTER 27
832 THE AMERICAS IN THE AGE OF LIBERALISM

business, while the French dominated dressmaking as well as the jewelry and pharmaceutical businesses. Chinese laborers built Peruvian railroads, and in sections of large cities such as Lima, the Chinese dominated the ownership of shops and restaurants.

Immigration to the United States

After the Civil War ended in 1865, the United States underwent an industrial boom powered by exploitation of the country's natural resources. The federal government turned over vast amounts of land and mineral resources to private industrialists for development. In particular, railroad companies—the foundation of industrial expansion—received 130 million acres. By 1900 the U.S. railroad system, was 193,000 miles long, connected every part of the nation, and represented 40 percent of the railroad mileage in the world, and it was all built by immigrant labor.

Between 1860 and 1914, 28 million immigrants came to the United States. Though many became rural homesteaders, industrial America developed on the sweat and brawn of immigrants. As in South America, immigration fed the growth of cities.

Working conditions for new immigrants were often deplorable. Industrialization had created a vast class of workers who depended entirely on wage labor. Employers paid women and children much less than men. Because business owners resisted government efforts to install costly safety devices, working conditions in mines and mills were frightful. In 1913 alone, even after some safety measures had been instituted, twenty-five thousand people died in industrial accidents.

Immigrants in Hawaii

Fruit store owned and run by Chinese immigrants in Honolulu, Hawaii, around 1905.
(The Art Archive at Art Resource, NY)

How did patterns of economic growth shape social and political culture in Latin America?

What factors shaped immigration patterns to the Americas?

How did U.S. policies in the Caribbean and Central America resemble European imperialism?

LearningCurve
Check what you know.

833

"The Chinese Must Go!"

Anti-immigrant sentiment intensified as immigration to the United States accelerated in the late nineteenth and early twentieth centuries. This 1880 campaign advertisement presented Chinese immigrants as a threat to native-born workers.

Workers responded to these conditions with strikes, violence, and, gradually, unionization.

Immigrants faced more than economic exploitation: they were also subjected to harsh ethnic stereotypes and faced pressure to assimilate culturally. An economic depression in the 1890s increased resentment toward immigrants. Powerful owners of mines, mills, and factories fought the organization of labor unions, fired thousands of workers, slashed wages, and ruthlessly exploited their workers. Workers in turn feared that immigrant labor would drive salaries lower. Some of this antagonism sprang from racism, some from old Protestant suspicions of Roman Catholicism, the faith of many of the new arrivals. Long-standing anti-Semitism against Jewish immigrants from eastern Europe intensified, while increasingly violent agitation against Asians led to race riots in California and finally culminated in the Chinese Exclusion Act of 1882, which denied Chinese laborers entrance to the country. Japanese immigration to the United States was restricted in 1907, so later Japanese immigrants settled in South America, especially Brazil.

Immigrants were received very differently in Latin America, where oligarchs encouraged immigration from Europe, the Middle East, and Japan because they believed these "whiter" workers were superior to native-born, often racially mixed workers. By contrast, in the United States the descendants of northern European Protestants developed prejudices and built social barriers out of their belief that Catholic Irish, southern and eastern European, or Jewish immigrants were not white enough.

CHAPTER LOCATOR | How and why did the process of nation-state consolidation vary across the Americas? | Why did slavery last longer in the U.S., Brazil, and Cuba than in other republics of the Americas?

834 CHAPTER 27
THE AMERICAS IN THE AGE OF LIBERALISM

Immigration to Canada

Canada was sparsely populated in the nineteenth century relative to other areas of the Americas. Provinces of the British colony gained governing autonomy after 1840 and organized a national government, the Dominion of Canada, in 1867 (Map 27.3). As in the United States and Latin America, the native peoples were pushed aside by Canada's development plans, and their population dropped by half or more during the century, many succumbing to the newcomers' diseases. French Canadians were the largest minority in the population, and they remained different in language, law, and religion.

Immigration to Canada increased in the 1890s. Between 1897 and 1912, 961,000 people entered Canada from the British Isles, 594,000 from Europe, and 784,000 from the United States. Some immigrants went to work in the urban factories of Hamilton, Toronto, and Montreal. However, most immigrants from continental Europe—Poles, Germans, Scandinavians, and Russians—flooded the midwestern plains and soon transformed the prairies into one of the world's greatest

MAP 27.3 ■ The Dominion of Canada, 1871

Shortly after the Dominion of Canada came into being as a self-governing nation within the British Empire in 1867, new provinces were added. Vast areas of Canada were too sparsely populated to achieve provincial status. Alberta and Saskatchewan did not become part of the Dominion until 1905; Newfoundland was added only in 1949.

How did patterns of economic growth shape social and political culture in Latin America?

What factors shaped immigration patterns to the Americas?

How did U.S. policies in the Caribbean and Central America resemble European imperialism?

LearningCurve
Check what you know.

Russian Immigrant Women in Saskatchewan

These women were Doukhobors, members of a Christian religious sect who came to Canada from Russia seeking religious freedom from tsarist persecution. While most of the men took railroad jobs, the women planted the vast plains with rye, wheat, oats, and flax. Their farms and orchards flourished, and the Doukhobors played an important role in the development of western Canada. (Saskatchewan Archives Board, photo no. R-B 1964)

grain-growing regions. Mining also expanded, and British Columbia, Ontario, and Quebec produced large quantities of wood pulp, much of it sold to the United States. Canada's great rivers were harnessed to supply hydroelectric power for industrial and domestic use. But Canada remained a predominantly agricultural country, with less than 10 percent of its population engaged in manufacturing.

> **QUICK REVIEW**

How did racial attitudes shape immigration to the Americas in the second half of the nineteenth century?

CHAPTER LOCATOR | How and why did the process of nation-state consolidation vary across the Americas? | Why did slavery last longer in the U.S., Brazil, and Cuba than in other republics of the Americas?

836 CHAPTER 27
THE AMERICAS IN THE AGE OF LIBERALISM

In what ways did U.S. policies in the Caribbean and Central America resemble European imperialism? How did U.S. foreign policy depart from European imperialism?

BY 1890 THE UNITED STATES HAD CLAIMED the contiguous territories it acquired through purchase, war, and displacement. Its frontier was closed. The United States redirected its expansionist pressures outward, beginning with the remnants of the Spanish Empire: Cuba and Puerto Rico in the Caribbean, and the Philippine Islands and Guam in the Pacific.

U.S. Intervention in Latin America

Between 1898 and 1932 the U.S. government intervened militarily thirty-four times in ten nations in the Caribbean and Central America to extend and protect its economic interests. U.S. influence in the Circum-Caribbean was not new, however, and stretched back to the early nineteenth century. In 1823 President James Monroe proclaimed in the Monroe Doctrine that the United States would keep European influence out of Latin America. This bold assertion established Latin America as part of the U.S. sphere of influence. U.S. interventions in Latin America were also a byproduct of the manifest destiny ideal of consolidating national territory from the Atlantic to the Pacific. Often the easiest way to connect the two sides of the continent was through Latin America.

The California gold rush of the 1840s created pressure to move people and goods quickly and inexpensively between the eastern and western parts of the United States decades before its transcontinental railroad was completed in 1869. It was cheaper, faster, and safer to travel to the east or west coast of Mexico and Central America, traverse the continent where it was narrower, and continue the voyage by sea. The Panama Railway, the first railroad constructed in Central America, served exactly this purpose and was built with U.S. investment in 1855.

Monroe Doctrine
▶ Established a U.S. sphere of influence over the Americas by opposing European imperialism on the continent.

How did patterns of economic growth shape social and political culture in Latin America?

What factors shaped immigration patterns to the Americas?

How did U.S. policies in the Caribbean and Central America resemble European imperialism?

✓ LearningCurve
Check what you know.

837

Planters and politicians in the U.S. South, who faced pressure from northern abolitionists against the westward territorial expansion of the slave regime, responded by seeking opportunities to annex new lands in Latin America and the Caribbean. They eyed Cuba, the Dominican Republic, El Salvador, and Nicaragua. In Nicaragua, Tennessean William Walker employed a mercenary army to depose the government and install himself as president (1856–1857). One of his first acts was to reinstate slavery. He was overthrown by armies sent from Costa Rica, El Salvador, and Honduras.

By the end of the nineteenth century U.S. involvement in Latin America had intensified, first through private investment and then through military force. In 1893 a group of New York investors bought the foreign debt of the Dominican Republic and took control of its customs houses in order to repay investors and creditors. After the government propped up by the U.S. company fell, President Theodore Roosevelt intervened, introducing what would be known as the Roosevelt Corollary to the Monroe Doctrine, which stated that the United States, as a civilized nation, would correct the "chronic wrongdoing" of its neighbors, such as failure to protect U.S. investments.

To this end, in 1903 and 1904 Roosevelt deployed Marines to the Dominican Republic to protect the investments of U.S. firms. Marines occupied and governed the Dominican Republic again from 1916 to 1924. The violent and corrupt dictator Rafael Trujillo ruled from 1930 to 1961 with the support of the United States. When he eventually defied the United States, he was assassinated by rivals acting with the encouragement of the Central Intelligence Agency.

Versions of the Dominican Republic's experience played out across the Circum-Caribbean. These military occupations followed a similar pattern of using military force to protect private U.S. companies' investments. During repeated occupations, the U.S. military ruled like dictators and violently suppressed protest and resistance. And as U.S. forces departed, they left power in the hands of dictators who served U.S. interests. These dictators governed not through popular consent but through force, corruption, and the support of the United States.

Roosevelt Corollary

▶ A corollary to the Monroe Doctrine stating that the United States would "correct" what it saw as wrongdoing in neighboring countries.

The Spanish-American War

In Cuba a second war of independence erupted in 1895 after it had failed to gain freedom from Spain in the Ten Years' War (1868–1878). A brutal war of attrition ensued, and by 1898 the countryside was in ruins and Spanish colonial control was restricted to a handful of cities. Cuban nationalists were on the verge of defeating the Spanish forces and gaining independence. But before they could realize this goal, the United States intervened.

The U.S. intervention began with a provocative act: sailing the battleship *Maine* into Havana harbor. This was an aggressive act because the battleship was capable of bombarding the entire city. But soon after it laid anchor, the *Maine* exploded and sank, killing hundreds of sailors. The U.S. government accused Spain of sinking the warship, a charge Spain denied, and demanded that the Spanish government provide restitution. Regardless of the cause, the sinking of the *Maine* led to war between Spain and the United States over control of Cuba and the Philippines. From April to August 1898 the U.S. Navy and Marines fought and defeated Spanish forces in the Pacific and the Caribbean. With its victory, the

CHAPTER LOCATOR | How and why did the process of nation-state consolidation vary across the Americas?　Why did slavery last longer in the U.S., Brazil, and Cuba than in other republics of the Americas?

838 CHAPTER 27
THE AMERICAS IN THE AGE OF LIBERALISM

United States acquired Guam and Puerto Rico and launched a military occupation of Cuba and the Philippines.

Puerto Rico and Guam became colonies directly ruled by U.S. administrators, and residents of both island territories did not gain the right to elect their own leaders until after the Second World War. They remained commonwealths (territories that are not states) of the United States. The U.S. government also established direct rule in the Philippines, brushing aside the government established by Filipino nationalists who had fought for freedom from Spain. Nationalists then fought against the Unites States in an unsuccessful effort to establish an independent government in the Philippine-American War (1899–1902).

Cuba alone gained formal independence, but U.S. pressure limited that independence. The Platt Amendment, which the United States imposed as a condition of Cuban independence, gave the United States the power to cancel laws passed by the Cuban congress, withheld the Cuban government's right to establish foreign treaties, and granted the United States control over Guantanamo Bay, where it established a permanent naval base. Moreover, the United States militarily occupied Cuba in 1899–1902, 1906–1908, and 1912. Between 1917 and 1922 U.S. administrator Enoch Crowder governed the island.

The constraints that the U.S. government imposed on Cuban politics, along with its willingness to deploy troops and periodically establish military rule, created a safe and fertile environment for U.S. investment. By 1919 half of the island's sugar mills were owned by U.S. businesses. Small farms were consolidated into massive estates as twenty-two companies took hold of 20 percent of Cuba's national territory. U.S. companies like Coca-Cola and Hershey were among the new landowners that took control of their most important ingredient: sugar.

The United States imported its prevailing racial policies to its new Caribbean territories. In Cuba, U.S. authorities encouraged political parties to exclude black Cubans. Black war veterans established the Independent Party of Color in 1908 in order to press for political inclusion. The party was banned in 1910, and in 1912 its leaders organized a revolt that led to a violent backlash by the army and police, supported by U.S. Marines. The campaign against members of the party was followed by a wave of lynchings of black Cubans across the island.

In Puerto Rico the influence of U.S. racism was more direct. The United States carried out the involuntary sterilization of thousands of Puerto Rican women as part of a policy aimed at addressing what the government saw as overpopulation on the island. In addition, Puerto Rican men drafted into U.S. military service were organized into segregated units, as African Americans were.

The Panama Canal

U.S. imperialism in the Caribbean extended beyond Cuba and Puerto Rico to the prize the United States had pursued for decades: a canal to connect the Atlantic and Pacific Oceans. The canal would transport cargo between the east and west of the United States much less expensively than rail. In the mid-nineteenth century the U.S. railroad tycoon Cornelius Vanderbilt tried but failed to build a canal through Nicaragua. Later in the century, a consortium of French investors pursued the construction of a canal in the Columbian province of Panama. Engineers and laborers completed some excavation before the French company went bankrupt.

How did patterns of economic growth shape social and political culture in Latin America?

What factors shaped immigration patterns to the Americas?

How did U.S. policies in the Caribbean and Central America resemble European imperialism?

LearningCurve
Check what you know.

839

After the Spanish-American War, U.S. authorities negotiated with the Colombian government for the right to continue the project started by the French company, but the Colombian congress balked at the U.S. government's demand that it should have territorial control of the canal. The U.S. government responded by encouraging an insurrection in Panama City and recognized the rebels as leaders of the new country of Panama. With the 1904 Isthmian Canal Convention, the new Panamanian government gave the United States permanent control over the canal and the land upon which it was built, which became known as the Canal Zone. The Canal Zone became an unincorporated U.S. territory.

Tens of thousands of migrant workers from around the Caribbean provided labor for construction of the canal, which opened in 1914. U.S. authorities instituted the same segregationist policies applied in their other Caribbean territories. Workers were divided into a "gold roll" of highly paid white U.S. workers and a "silver role" of mostly black workers, who came from Barbados, Panama, Nicaragua, Colombia and other parts of the Caribbean. They were paid lower wages, faced much higher rates of death and injury, and lived in less healthy conditions. The Canal Zone itself functioned as a segregated enclave: U.S. residents could move freely between it and Panamanian territory, but it was closed to Panamanians except those who entered through labor contracts.

> **QUICK REVIEW**

What motives were behind the United States' repeated military interventions in Latin America? How did the United States justify its actions?

CHAPTER SUMMARY

In the century after independence, political consolidation and economic integration varied across the Americas. The North of the United States became the continent's main engine of capital accumulation, immigration, and industrialization. In other regions political and economic conditions produced different results. In the U.S. South and Brazil reliance on slavery weakened internal markets, inhibited immigration, and slowed industrialization. In Spanish America the lack of a governing consensus until the second half of the nineteenth century led new countries to fall behind not only relative to other regions of the world but even relative to their past colonial experiences.

The cycle of war that began in the 1850s and continued for the next two decades reshaped the Americas politically and economically, consolidating a liberal order that placed great wealth in few hands while dealing misery and dislocation to many others. Liberalism had a modernizing influence on trade and industry, but it further concentrated wealth. Just as the United States waged wars against the Indians and pushed its frontier westward, so too did the countries of Latin America. Racial prejudice kept most African Americans at the social and economic margins.

CHAPTER LOCATOR | How and why did the process of nation-state consolidation vary across the Americas? | Why did slavery last longer in the U.S., Brazil, and Cuba than in other republics of the Americas?

840 CHAPTER 27 THE AMERICAS IN THE AGE OF LIBERALISM

By the beginning of the twentieth century, the economies of American nations were tightly integrated into the world economy, and powerful currents of immigration further deepened ties between countries. Industrialization that began in the northeast of the United States developed elsewhere in the continent, but the lead in industrialization held by the United States allowed it to increasingly impose its will over other nations. The economic and social dislocations produced by the liberal model of export-oriented economic growth also awoke growing social demands by the rural and urban poor. These boiled over the most dramatically in Mexico's 1910 revolution, but in cities to the south such as Buenos Aires, Argentina, and Santiago, Chile, workers' demands for the right to organize for better wages and for political representation were becoming too insistent to ignore.

 CONNECTIONS In the Americas the century or so between independence and World War I was a time of nation building. Colonial governments were overthrown, new constitutions were written, settlement was extended, slavery was ended, and immigrants from around the world settled across the continents. On the eve of World War I, there was reason to be optimistic about the future of all these countries.

World War I, the topic of the next chapter, affected these countries in a variety of ways. Canada followed Britain into the war in 1914 and sent six hundred thousand men to fight. The United States did not join the war until 1917, but quickly mobilized several million men and in 1918 began sending soldiers and materials in huge numbers. Even countries that maintained neutrality, as all the Latin American countries other than Brazil did, felt the economic impact of the war deeply, especially the increased demand for food and manufactured goods. For the working class the global demand for exported foods drove up the cost of living, but the profits that oligarchs accummulated fueled the process of industrialization.

 LaunchPad

ONLINE DOCUMENT PROJECT

Nation Building in Postcolonial Latin America

How did investors like Henry Meiggs fit into the larger context of Latin American nation building?

Read descriptions of Latin America's past and visions of its future, and then complete a quiz and writing assignment based on the evidence and details from this chapter. *See inside the front cover to learn more.*

How did patterns of economic growth shape social and political culture in Latin America?

What factors shaped immigration patterns to the Americas?

How did U.S. policies in the Caribbean and Central America resemble European imperialism?

✓ LearningCurve
Check what you know.

CHAPTER 27 STUDY GUIDE

STEP 1

GET STARTED ONLINE

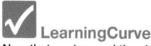

LearningCurve
Now that you've read the chapter, make it stick by completing the LearningCurve activity.

STEP 2

EXPLAIN WHY IT MATTERS

Put your reading into practice. Identify each term below, and then explain why it matters in world history.

TERM	WHO OR WHAT & WHEN	WHY IT MATTERS
liberalism (p. 814)		
oligarchs (p. 815)		
Circum-Caribbean (p. 815)		
caudillismo (p. 816)		
manifest destiny (p. 816)		
Treaty of Guadalupe Hidalgo (p. 818)		
Lerdo Law (p. 819)		
neocolonialism (p. 820)		
free womb laws (p. 823)		
Porfiriato (p. 827)		
latifundios (p. 829)		
anarcho-syndicalism (p. 832)		
Monroe Doctrine (p. 837)		
Roosevelt Corollary (p. 838)		

STEP 3

MOVE BEYOND THE BASICS

To demonstrate a more advanced understanding of the development of the United States and the independent nations of Latin America in the nineteenth century, fill in the chart below with descriptions of the nature of government and degree of democratization, economic development, and the impact of race on society. How did race shape American societies in both South and North America?

	Government and Democracy	Economic Development	Race and Society
United States			
Latin America			

STEP 4 **PUT IT ALL TOGETHER** Now, take a step back and try to explain the big picture. Remember to use specific examples from the chapter in your answers.

NEW NATIONS AND THE ABOLITION OF SLAVERY

▶ What role did political liberalism play in Latin American independence movements?

▶ How did the various new nations of the Americas deal with the issue of slavery? How would you explain the differences you note?

ECONOMIC AND DEMOGRAPHIC TRENDS

▶ Why did so many Latin American nations develop economies focused on the export of commodities? What were the advantages and disadvantages of such an approach to economic growth?

▶ What forces drew new immigrants to the Americas in the second half of the nineteenth century?

A NEW AMERICAN EMPIRE

▶ Why did so many Americans look to Latin America for new opportunities at the end of the nineteenth century?

▶ What policies and practices did the United States use to control the governments and economies of its Latin American neighbors?

LOOKING BACK, LOOKING AHEAD

▶ How did the process of nation building in the Americas differ from the nation building in Italy and Germany (see Chapter 24) that occurred in roughly the same time period?

▶ What new opportunities and challenges might the devastation of old nations of Europe in World War I have created for the new nations covered in this chapter?

> **IN YOUR OWN WORDS**

Imagine that you must give an oral report to the class answering the following question: How did liberal political and economic ideas shape the development of the Americas in the nineteenth century? What would be the most important points and why?

28

WORLD WAR AND REVOLUTION

1914–1929

> In what ways did the First World War represent a fundamental turning point in world history?

Chapter 28 examines the First World War, the Russian Revolution, and the decade that followed these cataclysmic events. The First World War was long, global, indecisive, and tremendously destructive. All of the major combatant nations were traumatized and transformed by the war. In Russia, military defeat once again led to social and political unrest. This time, however, the tsarist regime did not survive and was replaced by history's first Communist state. When the war was finally over, the victorious Allies, led by Britain, France, and the United States, met in Paris to plan the peace to come. In the end, few left Paris satisfied with the results. The peace and prosperity the delegates sought lasted barely a decade.

LearningCurve

After reading the chapter, use LearningCurve to retain what you've read.

Senegalese Soldier A *tirailleur* (literally, "skirmisher") from French West Africa who fought in Europe during the Great War. Across the bottom of this postcard image from the era, the soldier proclaimed his loyalty with the phrase "Glory to the Greater France," meaning France and its colonies. Note the two German *pickelhaube* (spike helmets) he wears on his head. (Private Collection/Archives Charmet/The Bridgeman Art Library)

> What were the long-term and immediate causes of World War I, and how did the conflict become a global war?

> How did total war affect the home fronts of the major combatants?

> What factors led to the Russian Revolution, and what was its outcome?

> What were the global consequences of the First World War?

> How did leaders deal with the political dimensions of uncertainty and try to re-establish peace and prosperity in the interwar years?

> In what ways were the anxieties of the postwar world expressed or heightened by revolutionary ideas in modern thought, art, and science and in new forms of communication?

What were the long-term and immediate causes of World War I, and how did the conflict become a global war?

Henri de Groux, *The Assault, Verdun*

An eerie portrayal by Belgian artist Henri de Groux (1867–1930) of French troops moving forward in a thick haze of smoke and perhaps clouds of diphosgene, a poisonous gas first used by the Germans at Verdun on June 22, 1916. (Musées des Deux Guerres Mondiales, Paris, France/The Bridgeman Art Library)

THE FIRST WORLD WAR CLEARLY MARKED a major break in the course of world history. The maps of Europe and southwest Asia were redrawn, nationalist movements took root and spread across Asia (see Chapter 29), America consolidated its position as a global power, and the world experienced, for the first time, industrialized, total war. Europe's Great Powers started the war and suffered the most. Imperialism also brought the conflict to the Middle East, Africa, and Asia, making this a global war of unprecedented scope.

Origins and Causes of the Great War

Any study of the Great War's origins must begin with nationalism (see Chapter 24), one of the major ideologies of the nineteenth century, and its armed companion, militarism, the glorification of the military as the supreme ideal of the state with all other interests subordinate to it. European concerns over national security, economies, welfare, identities, and overseas empires set nation against nation, alliance against alliance, and army against army until they all went to war at once.

militarism

▶ The glorification of the military as the supreme ideal of the state with all other interests subordinate to it.

CHAPTER LOCATOR | **What were the long-term and immediate causes of World War I, how did it become a global war?** | How did total war affect the home fronts of the major combatants?

1914
Assassination of Archduke Franz Ferdinand; Ottoman Empire joins Central Powers; German victories on the eastern front

1914–1918
World War I

1914
Japan joins the Triple Entente and seizes German holdings in China

1915
Italy joins the Triple Entente; German submarine sinks the *Lusitania*; Japan expands into southern Manchuria

1916
Battles of Verdun and the Somme; Irish Easter Rebellion; German Auxiliary Service Law requires seventeen- to sixty-year-old males to work for war effort; Rasputin murdered

1916–1918
Growth of antiwar sentiment throughout Europe

1917
United States declares war on Germany; Bolshevik Revolution in Russia

1917–1922
Civil war in Russia

1918
Treaty of Brest-Litovsk; revolution in Germany

1919
Treaty of Versailles; Freudian psychology gains popularity; Rutherford splits the atom; Bauhaus school founded

1920s
Existentialism, Dadaism, and surrealism gain prominence

1923
French and Belgian armies occupy the Ruhr

1924
Dawes Plan

1926
Germany joins League of Nations

1928
Kellogg-Briand Pact

Competition between nations intensified greatly when Germany became a unified nation-state and the most powerful country in Europe in 1871 (see page 726). A new era in international relations began, as Chancellor Bismarck declared Germany a "satisfied" power, having no territorial ambitions within Europe and desiring only peace.

But how to preserve the peace? Bismarck's first concern was to keep rival France diplomatically isolated and without military allies. His second concern was to prevent Germany from being dragged into a war between the two rival empires, Austria-Hungary and Russia, as they sought to fill the power vacuum created in the Balkans by the Ottoman Empire's decline (see pages 765–767). To these ends, Bismarck brokered a series of treaties and alliances, all meant to ensure the balance of power in Europe and to prevent the outbreak of war.

In 1890 Germany's new emperor, William II, forced Bismarck to resign and then abandoned many of Bismarck's efforts to ensure German security through promoting European peace and stability. William refused to renew a nonaggression pact Bismarck had signed with Russia, for example, which prompted France to court the tsar, offering loans and arms, and sign a Franco-Russian Alliance in 1892. With France and Russia now allied against Germany, Austria, and Italy, Great Britain's foreign policy became increasingly crucial. Many Germans and some Britons felt that the racially related Germanic and Anglo-Saxon peoples were natural allies. However, the good relations that had prevailed between Prussia and Great Britain since the mid-eighteenth century gave way after 1890 to a bitter Anglo-German rivalry.

There were several reasons for this development. Germany and Great Britain's commercial rivalry in world markets and Kaiser William's publicly expressed

| What factors led to the Russian Revolution, and what was its outcome? | What were the global consequences of the First World War? | How did leaders deal with the political dimensions of uncertainty in the interwar years? | In what ways were the anxieties of the postwar world expressed in new forms of communication? | ✓ LearningCurve Check what you know. |

intention to create a global German empire unsettled the British. Germany's decision in 1900 to add a fleet of big-gun battleships to its already-expanding navy also heightened tensions. British leaders considered the new battleships to be a military challenge to their long-standing naval supremacy. This decision coincided with the South African War (see page 756) between the British and the Afrikaners, which revealed widespread anti-British feeling around the world.

Thus British leaders set about shoring up their exposed position with their own alliances and agreements. Britain improved its relations with the United States, concluded an alliance with Japan in 1902, and in the Anglo-French Entente of 1904 settled all outstanding colonial disputes with France. Frustrated by Britain's closer relationship with France, Germany's leaders decided to test the entente's strength by demanding an international conference to challenge French control over Morocco. At the Algeciras (Spain) Conference in 1906, Germany's crude bullying only forced France and Britain closer together.

The Moroccan crisis was something of a diplomatic revolution. Britain, France, Russia, and even the United States began to view Germany as a potential threat. At the same time, German leaders began to suspect sinister plots to encircle Germany and block its development as a world power. In 1907 Russia and Britain settled their outstanding differences and signed the Anglo-Russian Agreement. This treaty, together with the earlier Franco-Russian Alliance of 1892 and Anglo-French Entente of 1904, served as a catalyst for the Triple Entente, the alliance of Great Britain, France, and Russia in the First World War (Map 28.1).

Triple Entente

▶ The alliance of Great Britain, France, and Russia in the First World War.

MAP 28.1 ■ European Alliances at the Outbreak of World War I, 1914

By the time war broke out, Europe was divided into two opposing alliances: the Triple Entente of Britain, France, and Russia and the Triple Alliance of Germany, Austria-Hungary, and Italy. Italy switched sides and joined the Entente in 1915.

Triple Alliance, 1882–1915

Triple Entente, 1907–1917

Neutral

Sarajevo
June 28, 1914
Assassination of Archduke
Franz Ferdinand triggers WWI

CHAPTER LOCATOR | What were the long-term and immediate causes of World War I, how did it become a global war? | How did total war affect the home fronts of the major combatants?

By 1909 Britain was psychologically, if not officially, in the Franco-Russian camp. Europe's leading nations were divided into two hostile blocs, both ill-prepared to deal with upheaval in the Balkans.

The Outbreak of War

By 1903 Balkan nationalism was asserting itself again. Serbia led the way, becoming openly hostile to both Austria-Hungary and the Ottoman Empire. The Slavic Serbs looked to Slavic Russia for support of their national aspirations. In 1908, to block Serbian expansion, Austria formally annexed Bosnia and Herzegovina. Serbia erupted in rage but could do nothing without Russia's support.

Then two nationalist wars, the first and second Balkan wars in 1912 and 1913, finally destroyed the centuries-long Ottoman presence in Europe (Map 28.2). This sudden but long-expected event elated Balkan nationalists but dismayed Austria-Hungary's leaders who feared that Austria-Hungary might next be broken apart.

Within this tense context, Serbian nationalist Gavrilo Princip assassinated Archduke Franz Ferdinand, heir to the Austro-Hungarian throne, and his wife, Sophie, on June 28, 1914, during a state visit to the Bosnian capital of Sarajevo.

MAP 28.2 ■ The Balkans, 1878–1914

The Ottoman Empire suffered large territorial losses after the Congress of Berlin in 1878 but remained a power in the Balkans. By 1914 ethnic boundaries that did not follow political boundaries had formed, and Serbian national aspirations threatened Austria-Hungary.

| What factors led to the Russian Revolution, and what was its outcome? | What were the global consequences of the First World War? | How did leaders deal with the political dimensions of uncertainty in the interwar years? | In what ways were the anxieties of the postwar world expressed in new forms of communication? | ☑ LearningCurve Check what you know. |

Austria-Hungary's leaders held Serbia responsible and on July 23 presented Serbia with an unconditional ultimatum that included demands amounting to Austrian control of the Serbian state. When Serbia replied moderately but evasively, Austria declared war.

Of prime importance in Austria-Hungary's fateful decision was Germany's unconditional support. Kaiser William II and his chancellor, Theobald von Bethmann-Hollweg, realized that war between Austria and Russia was likely, for Russia could not stand by and watch the Serbs be crushed. Yet Bethmann-Hollweg hoped that while Russia (and its ally France) might go to war, Great Britain would remain neutral.

Anticipating a possible conflict, Europe's military leaders had been drawing up war plans and timetables for years, and now these, rather than diplomacy, began to dictate policy. Tsar Nicholas II ordered a partial mobilization against Austria-Hungary but almost immediately found this was impossible. Russia had assumed a war with both Austria and Germany, and it could not mobilize against one without mobilizing against the other. Therefore, Russia ordered full mobilization and in effect declared general war. The German general staff had also prepared for a two-front war. Its Schlieffen plan called for first knocking out France with a lightning attack through neutral Belgium to capture Paris before turning on a slower-to-mobilize Russia. On August 3 German armies invaded Belgium. Great Britain declared war on Germany the following day. In each country the great majority of the population rallied to defend its nation and enthusiastically embraced war in August 1914.

The Schlieffen Plan

◄- - Planned German offensive
◄— Actual German offensive
▢ Neutral nations

GREAT BRITAIN
NETHERLANDS
BELGIUM
GERMANY
Brussels
Rhine R.
LUX.
Reims
Paris
•Metz
Seine R.
Marne R.
FRANCE
0   100   200 mi.
0   100   200 km
SWITZ.

Stalemate and Slaughter

When the Germans invaded Belgium in August 1914, the Belgian army defended its homeland and then fell back to join a rapidly landed British army corps near the Franco-Belgian border. Instead of quickly capturing Paris in a vast encircling movement, German soldiers were advancing slowly along an enormous front. On September 6 the French attacked the German line at the Battle of the Marne. For three days France threw everything into the attack, forcing the Germans to fall back (Map 28.3).

The two stalled armies now dug in behind rows of trenches, mines, and barbed wire. A "no-man's land" of one hundred to three hundred yards lay between the two combatants. Eventually an unbroken line of trenches stretched over four hundred miles from the Belgian coast to the Swiss frontier. By November 1914 the slaughter on the western front had begun in earnest. For four years battles followed the same plan: after ceaseless heavy artillery shelling to "soften up" the enemy, young soldiers went "over the top" of the trenches in frontal attacks on the enemy's line.

The human cost of **trench warfare** was staggering, while territorial gains were minuscule. In the Battle of the Somme in summer 1916, the British and French gained an insignificant 125 square miles at a cost of 600,000 dead or wounded. The Germans lost 500,000 men. That same year the unsuccessful German campaign against Verdun cost 700,000 lives on both sides. The slaughter was made even greater by new weapons of war—including chemical gases, tanks, airplanes, flamethrowers, and the machine gun.

trench warfare

▶ Fighting behind rows of trenches, mines, and barbed wire; used in World War I with a staggering cost in lives and minimal gains in territory.

CHAPTER LOCATOR | What were the long-term and immediate causes of World War I, how did it become a global war? | How did total war affect the home fronts of the major combatants?

CHAPTER 28
850 WORLD WAR AND REVOLUTION

The Western Front

Germany, 1914

Greatest extent of territory gained by Germany, Sept. 1914

Front at beginning of 1915

German offensive, Summer 1918

Major battle

MAP 28.3 ■ **The First World War in Europe**

The trench war on the western front was concentrated in Belgium and northern France (inset), while the war in the east encompassed an enormous territory.

On the eastern front, the Russians moved into eastern Germany but suffered appalling losses against the Germans at the Battles of Tannenberg and the Masurian Lakes in August and September 1914 (see Map 28.3). German and Austrian forces then reversed the Russian advances of 1914 and forced the Russians to retreat deep into their own territory in the 1915 eastern campaign. A staggering 2.5 million Russians were killed, wounded, or taken prisoner.

These changing tides of victory and hopes of territorial gains brought neutral countries into the war. In May 1915 Italy joined the Triple Entente of Great Britain, France, and Russia in return for promises of Austrian territory. In September Bulgaria joined the Triple Alliance in order to settle old scores with Serbia.

The War Becomes Global

In October 1914 the Ottoman Empire joined with Austria and Germany, by then known as the Central Powers. A German alliance permitted the Turks to renounce the limitations on Ottoman sovereignty imposed by Europeans in the nineteenth century and also to settle old grievances with Russia, the Turks' historic enemy.

The entry of the Ottoman Turks pulled the entire Middle East into the war and made it truly a global conflict. While Russia attacked the Ottomans in the Caucasus, the British protected their rule in Egypt. In 1915, at the Battle of Gallipoli, British forces tried to take the Dardanelles and Constantinople from the Ottoman Turks but were badly defeated. Casualties were high on both sides and included thousands of Australians and New Zealanders.

The British had more success inciting Arabs to revolt against their Turkish overlords. The foremost Arab leader was Hussein ibn-Ali (1856–1931), who governed much of the Ottoman Empire's territory along the Red Sea (see Map 29.1, page 889). In 1915 Hussein won vague British commitments for an independent Arab kingdom. In return, he joined forces with the British under T. E. Lawrence, who in 1917 led Arab tribesmen and Indian soldiers in a successful guerrilla war against the Turks on the Arabian peninsula. In the Ottoman province of Iraq, Britain occupied Basra in 1914 and captured Baghdad in 1917. In 1918 British armies, aided by imperial forces from Egypt, India, Australia, and New Zealand, smashed the old Ottoman state. Thus war brought revolutionary change to the Middle East (see pages 888–895).

Japan, allied with the British since 1902, joined the Triple Entente on August 23, 1914, and began attacking German-controlled colonies and territories in the Pacific. Later that year Japan seized Germany's holdings on the Shandong (Shantung) Peninsula in China.

War also spread to colonies in Africa and East Asia. Colonized peoples provided critical supplies and fought in Europe, Africa, and the Ottoman Empire. More than a million Africans and Asians served in the various armies of the warring powers, with more than double that number serving as porters to carry equipment.

Many of these men joined up to get clothes (uniforms), food, and money for enlisting. Others did so because colonial recruiters promised them better lives when they returned home. Most were illiterate and had no idea of why they were going or what they would experience.

The war had a profound impact on these colonial troops. Fighting against and killing Europeans destroyed the impression that the Europeans were superhuman.

CHAPTER LOCATOR | What were the long-term and immediate causes of World War I, how did it become a global war? | How did total war affect the home fronts of the major combatants?

852   CHAPTER 28
WORLD WAR AND REVOLUTION

New concepts like nationalism and individual freedoms—ideals for which the Europeans were supposedly fighting—were carried home to become rallying cries for future liberation struggles.

A crucial turning point in the expanding conflict came in April 1917 when the United States declared war on Germany. American intervention grew out of the war at sea and sympathy for the Triple Entente. At the beginning of the war Britain and France established a naval blockade to strangle the Central Powers. In early 1915 Germany launched a counter-blockade using the new and deadly effective submarine. In May a German submarine sank the British passenger liner *Lusitania*. More than a thousand people died, including 139 U.S. citizens. President Woodrow Wilson protested vigorously. Germany was forced to restrict its submarine warfare for almost two years or face almost certain war with the United States.

Early in 1917 the German military command—confident that improved submarines could starve Britain into submission before the United States could come to its rescue—resumed unrestricted submarine warfare. This was a reckless gamble. The United States declared war on Germany and eventually tipped the balance in favor of the Triple Entente.

QUICK REVIEW <

What role did nationalism play in the outbreak of the First World War?

What factors led to the Russian Revolution, and what was its outcome?

What were the global consequences of the First World War?

How did leaders deal with the political dimensions of uncertainty in the interwar years?

In what ways were the anxieties of the postwar world expressed in new forms of communication?

☑ LearningCurve
Check what you know.

How did total war affect the home fronts of the major combatants?

> **PICTURING THE PAST**

ANALYZING THE IMAGE: How is neutral Belgium personified? What do you think the artist's purpose was?

CONNECTIONS: How did governments use propaganda and other means to unite people for the war effort?

THE WAR'S IMPACT ON CIVILIANS was no less massive than on the men crouched in trenches. Total war mobilized entire populations, led to increased state power, and promoted social equality. It also led to dissent and a growing antiwar movement.

Mobilizing for Total War

total war

▶ Practiced by countries fighting in World War I, a war in which the government plans and controls all aspects of economic and social life in order to make the greatest possible military effort.

Within months of the outbreak of the First World War, national unity governments began to plan and control economic and social life in order to wage **total war**. Governments imposed rationing, price and wage controls, and even restrictions on workers' freedom of movement. These total-war economies blurred the old distinction between soldiers on battlefields and civilians at home. The ability of central governments to manage and control highly complicated economies increased and strengthened their powers, often along socialist lines.

Germany went furthest in developing a planned economy to wage total war. Soon after war began, the Jewish industrialist Walter Rathenau convinced the

CHAPTER LOCATOR | What were the long-term and immediate causes of World War I, how did it become a global war? | How did total war affect the home fronts of the major combatants?

CHAPTER 28

854 WORLD WAR AND REVOLUTION

German government to set up the War Raw Materials Board to ration and distribute raw materials. Food was also rationed, and the board successfully produced substitutes, such as synthetic rubber and synthetic nitrates, for scarce war supplies. Following the terrible Battles of Verdun and the Somme in 1916, military leaders forced the Reichstag to accept the Auxiliary Service Law, which required all males between seventeen and sixty to work only at jobs considered critical to the war effort. Women also worked in war factories, mines, and steel mills.

France and Great Britain mobilized economically for total war less rapidly and less completely than Germany, as they could import materials from their colonies and from the United States. When it became apparent that the war was not going to end quickly, however, the Western Allies all passed laws giving their governments sweeping powers over all areas of the nation's daily life — including industrial and agricultural production, censorship, education, health and welfare, the curtailment of civil liberties, labor, and foreign aliens.

The Social Impact of War

The social impact of total war was no less profound than the economic impact, though again there were important national variations. The military's insatiable needs — nearly every belligerent power resorted to conscription to put soldiers in the field — created a tremendous demand for workers at home. This situation brought about momentous changes.

One such change was increased power and prestige for labor unions. Unions cooperated with war governments in return for real participation in important decisions. This entry of labor leaders into policymaking councils paralleled the entry of socialist leaders into the war governments.

Women's roles also changed dramatically. In every belligerent country, large numbers of women went to work in industry, transportation, and offices. Moreover, women became highly visible — not only as munitions workers but as bank tellers, mail carriers, and even police officers. Women also served as nurses and doctors at the front. (See "Individuals in Society: Vera Brittain," page 856.) In general, the war greatly expanded the range of women's activities and changed attitudes toward women. Although at war's end most women were quickly let go and their jobs were given back to the returning soldiers, their many-sided war effort caused Britain, Germany, and Austria to grant them the right to vote immediately after the war.

Recent scholarship has shown, however, that traditional views of gender — of male roles and female roles — remained remarkably resilient and that there was a significant conservative backlash in the postwar years. Even as the war progressed, many men, particularly soldiers, grew increasingly hostile toward women. Some were angry at mothers, wives, and girlfriends for urging them to enlist and fight in the horrible war. Soldiers with wives and girlfriends back home grew increasingly convinced that they were cheating on them. Others worried that factory or farm jobs had been taken by women and there would be no work when they returned home. Men were also concerned that if women received the vote at war's end, they would vote themselves into power.

War promoted social equality, blurring class distinctions and lessening the gap between rich and poor. Greater equality was reflected in full employment,

| What factors led to the Russian Revolution, and what was its outcome? | What were the global consequences of the First World War? | How did leaders deal with the political dimensions of uncertainty in the interwar years? | In what ways were the anxieties of the postwar world expressed in new forms of communication? | ☑ LearningCurve Check what you know. |

855

INDIVIDUALS IN SOCIETY
Vera Brittain

Although the Great War upended millions of lives, it struck Europe's young people with the greatest force. For Vera Brittain (1893–1970), as for so many in her generation, the war became life's defining experience, which she captured forever in her famous autobiography, *Testament of Youth* (1933).

Brittain grew up in a wealthy business family in northern England, bristling at small-town conventions and discrimination against women. Very close to her brother Edward, two years her junior, Brittain read voraciously and dreamed of being a successful writer. Finishing boarding school and beating down her father's objections, she prepared for Oxford's rigorous entry exams and won a scholarship to its women's college. Brittain also fell in love with Roland Leighton, an equally brilliant student from a literary family and her brother's best friend. All three, along with two more close friends, Victor Richardson and Geoffrey Thurlow, confidently prepared to enter Oxford in late 1914.

When war suddenly approached in July 1914, Brittain shared with millions of Europeans a thrilling surge of patriotic support for her government, a prowar enthusiasm she later played down in her published writings. She wrote in her diary that her "great fear" was that England would declare its neutrality and commit the "grossest treachery" toward France.* She seconded Roland's decision to enlist, agreeing with her sweetheart's glamorous view of war as "very ennobling and very beautiful." Later, exchanging anxious letters in 1915 with Roland in France, Vera began to see the conflict in personal, human terms. She wondered if any victory or defeat could be worth Roland's life.

Struggling to quell her doubts, Brittain redoubled her commitment to England's cause and volunteered

Vera Brittain was marked forever by her wartime experiences. (Hulton Archive/Getty Images)

as an army nurse. For the next three years she served with distinction in military hospitals in London, Malta, and northern France, repeatedly torn between the vision of noble sacrifice and the reality of human tragedy. She lost her sexual inhibitions caring for mangled male bodies, and she longed to consummate her love with Roland. Awaiting his return on leave on Christmas Day in 1915, she was greeted instead with a telegram: Roland had been killed two days before.

Roland's death was the first of the devastating blows that eventually overwhelmed Brittain's idealistic patriotism. In 1917 first Geoffrey and then Victor died from gruesome wounds. In early 1918, as the last great German offensive covered the floors of her war-zone hospital with maimed and dying German prisoners, the bone-weary Vera felt a common humanity and saw only more victims. A few weeks later brother Edward — her last hope — died in action. When the war ended, she was, she said, a "complete automaton," with "my deepest emotions paralyzed if not dead."

Returning to Oxford and finishing her studies, Brittain gradually recovered. She formed a deep, restorative friendship with another talented woman writer, Winifred Holtby, published novels and articles, and became a leader in the feminist campaign for gender equality. She also married and had children. But her wartime memories were always there. Finally, Brittain succeeded in coming to grips with them in *Testament of Youth*, her powerful antiwar autobiography. The unflinching narrative spoke to the experiences of an entire generation and became a runaway bestseller. Above all, perhaps, Brittain captured the ambivalent, contradictory character of the war, in which millions of young people found excitement, courage, and common purpose but succeeded only in destroying their lives with their superhuman efforts and futile sacrifices. Becoming ever more committed to pacifism, Brittain opposed England's entry into World War II.

*Quoted in the excellent study by P. Berry and M. Bostridge, *Vera Brittain: A Life* (London: Virago Press, 2001), p. 59; additional quotations are from pp. 80 and 136.

rationing according to physical needs, and a sharing of hardships. Society became more uniform and more egalitarian.

Growing Political Tensions

During the war's first two years, belief in a just cause and patriotic nationalism united soldiers and civilians behind their various national leaders. Each government employed censorship and propaganda to maintain popular support.

By spring 1916, however, cracks were appearing under the strain of total war. In April Irish nationalists in Dublin unsuccessfully rose up against British rule in the Easter Rebellion. Strikes and protest marches over inadequate food flared up on every home front. In April 1917 nearly half the French infantry divisions mutinied for two months after suffering enormous losses in the Second Battle of the Aisne. Later that year there was a massive mutiny of Russian soldiers supporting the revolution.

The Central Powers experienced the most strain. In October 1916 a young socialist assassinated Austria's chief minister. Conflicts among nationalities grew, and both Czech and Yugoslav leaders demanded autonomous democratic states for their peoples. By 1917 German political unity was also collapsing, and prewar social conflicts were re-emerging. A coalition of Socialists and Catholics in the Reichstag called for a compromise "peace without annexations or reparations." Thus Germany, like its ally Austria-Hungary and its enemy France, began to crack in 1917. But it was Russia that collapsed first and saved the Central Powers—for a time.

QUICK REVIEW

What steps did the major combatants take to harness the full power of their populations and economies?

What factors led to the Russian Revolution, and what was its outcome?

Lenin and His Supporters

Vladimir Lenin (center) with two other major figures of the Russian Revolution, Joseph Stalin (left) and Mikhail Kalinin (right). After Lenin's death in January 1924, Stalin moved to seize power and ruled the Soviet Union until his death in 1953. Kalinin was one of Lenin's earliest followers and then supported Stalin in the power struggle after Lenin's death. He was one of the few "old Bolsheviks" to survive Stalin's purges and received a large state funeral following his death from natural causes in 1946. (Photo by Keystone-France/Gamma-Keystone via Getty Images)

THE 1917 RUSSIAN REVOLUTION, directly related to the Great War, opened a new era with a radically new prototype of state and society that changed the course of the twentieth century.

The Fall of Imperial Russia

Imperial Russia in 1914 was still predominantly a rural and nonurbanized society. Russia came late to industrialization (see page 729), and, although rapidly expanding, industrialization was still in its early stages. Peasants made up perhaps 80 percent of the population. Besides the royal family and the nobility, the rest of Russian society consisted of the bourgeoisie (the elite, educated upper and middle classes, such as liberal politicians, propertied and professional classes, military officer corps, and landowners) and the proletariat (the popular masses, such as the urban working class, and rank-and-file soldiers and sailors). These two factions contended for power when the tsar abdicated in 1917.

Like their allies and their enemies, Russians embraced war with patriotic enthusiasm in 1914. For a moment Russia was united, but soon the war began to take its toll.

CHAPTER LOCATOR | What were the long-term and immediate causes of World War I, how did it become a global war? | How did total war affect the home fronts of the major combatants?

Russia quickly exhausted its supplies of shells and ammunition, and better-equipped German armies inflicted terrible losses—1.5 million casualties and nearly 1 million captured in 1915 alone. Russian soldiers were sent to the front without rifles. The Duma, Russia's lower house of parliament, and *zemstvos* (zemst-vohs), local governments, led the effort toward full mobilization on the home front. These efforts improved the military situation, but overall Russia mobilized less effectively for total war than did the other warring nations.

Although limited industrial capacity was a serious handicap in a war against highly industrialized Germany, Russia's real problem was leadership. A kindly, slightly dull-witted man, Tsar Nicholas II (r. 1894–1917) distrusted the moderate Duma and rejected popular involvement. As a result, the Duma, whose members came from the elite classes, and the popular masses became increasingly critical of the tsar's leadership and the appalling direction of the war. In response, Nicholas (who had no military background) traveled to the front in September 1915 to lead Russia's armies—and thereafter received all the blame for Russian losses.

His departure was a fatal turning point. His German-born wife, Tsarina Alexandra, took control of the government and the home front. She tried to rule absolutely in her husband's absence with an uneducated Siberian preacher, Rasputin, as her most trusted adviser. In a desperate attempt to right the situation, three members of the high aristocracy murdered Rasputin in December 1916. In this atmosphere of unreality, the government slid steadily toward revolution.

Large scale-strikes, demonstrations, and protest marches were now commonplace, as were bread shortages. On March 8, 1917, a women's bread march in Petrograd (formerly St. Petersburg) started riots, which spread throughout the city. While his ministers fled the city, the tsar ordered that peace be restored, but discipline broke down, and the soldiers and police joined the revolutionary crowd. The Duma declared a provisional government on March 12, 1917. Three days later, Nicholas abdicated.

"The Russian Ruling House"

This wartime cartoon captures the ominous, spellbinding power of Rasputin over Tsar Nicholas II and his wife, Alexandra. Rasputin's manipulations disgusted Russian public opinion and contributed to the monarchy's collapse. (© INTERFOTO/Alamy)

The Provisional Government

The March Revolution was joyfully accepted throughout the country. A new government formed in May 1917, with the understanding that an elected democratic government, ruling under a new constitution drafted by a future Constituent Assembly, would replace it when circumstances permitted. The provisional government established equality before the law; freedom of religion, speech, and assembly; the right of unions to organize and strike; and other classic liberal measures.

March Revolution
▶ The first phase of the Russian Revolution of 1917, in which unplanned uprisings led to the abdication of the tsar and the establishment of a transitional democratic government that was then overthrown in November by Lenin and the Bolsheviks.

| What factors led to the Russian Revolution, and what was its outcome? | What were the global consequences of the First World War? | How did leaders deal with the political dimensions of uncertainty in the interwar years? | In what ways were the anxieties of the postwar world expressed in new forms of communication? | ✓ LearningCurve Check what you know. |

The provisional government soon made two fatal decisions, however, that turned the people against the new government. First, it refused to confiscate large landholdings and give them to peasants, fearing that such drastic action in the countryside would only complete the disintegration of Russia's peasant army. Second, the government decided that the continuation of war was still the all-important national duty and that international alliances had to be honored. Neither decision was popular. The peasants believed that when the tsar's autocratic rule ended, so too did the nobles' title to the land, which was now theirs for the taking. The army believed that the March Revolution meant the end of the war.

From its first day, the provisional government had to share power (dual power) with a formidable rival that represented the popular masses—the **Petrograd Soviet** (or council) of Workers' and Soldiers' Deputies, an organization comprised of two to three thousand workers, soldiers, and socialist intellectuals. This counter-government, or half government, issued its own radical orders, further weakening the provisional government. Most famous of these was Army Order No. 1, issued in March 1917, which stripped officers of their authority and gave power to elected committees of common soldiers.

Order No. 1 led to a total collapse of army discipline. Soldiers began returning to their villages to get a share of the land that peasants were seizing from landowners, either through peasant soviets (councils) or by force, in a great agrarian upheaval. Through the summer of 1917, the provisional government, led from July by the socialist Alexander Kerensky, became increasingly more conservative and authoritarian as it tried to maintain law and order. The government was being threatened from one side by an advancing German army and from the other by proletarian forces, urban and rural alike, shouting "All power to the soviets!" and calling for an even more radical revolution.

Lenin and the Bolshevik Revolution

Among those leading the call for radical revolution was Vladimir Ilyich Lenin (1870–1924). Lenin became an enemy of imperial Russia when his older brother was executed for plotting to kill the tsar in 1887. As a law student Lenin studied Marxist doctrines with religious ferocity. Exiled to Siberia for three years because of socialist agitation, Lenin lived in western Europe after his release for seventeen years and developed his own revolutionary interpretations of Marxist thought (see page 716).

Three interrelated ideas were central for Lenin. First, he stressed that only violent revolution could destroy capitalism. Second, Lenin believed that a socialist revolution was possible even in an agrarian country like Russia. According to classical Marxist theory, a society must have reached the capitalist, industrial stage of development before its urban workers, the proletariat, can rise up and create a Communist society. Lenin thought that although Russia's industrial working class was small, the peasants, who made up the bulk of the army and navy, were also potential revolutionaries. Third, Lenin believed that at a given moment revolution was determined more by human leadership than by vast historical laws. He called for a highly disciplined workers' party, strictly controlled by a dedicated elite of intellectuals and full-time revolutionaries like him.

Petrograd Soviet

▶ A counter-government that was a huge, fluctuating mass meeting of two to three thousand workers, soldiers, and socialist intellectuals.

- The necessity of violent revolution
- The possibility of socialist revolution in Russia
- The importance of a disciplined workers' party led by committed revolutionaries

Lenin's ideas did not go unchallenged by other Russian Marxists. At a Social Democratic Labor Party congress in London in 1903, Lenin demanded a small, disciplined, elitist party; his opponents wanted a more democratic party with mass membership. The Russian Marxists split into two rival factions. Because his side won one crucial vote at the congress, Lenin's camp became known as **Bolsheviks**, or "majority group"; his opponents were Mensheviks, or "minority group."

In March 1917 Lenin and nearly all the other leading Bolsheviks were living in exile abroad or in Russia's remotest corners. After the March Revolution, the German government provided safe passage for Lenin across Germany and back into Russia, hoping he would undermine Russia's sagging war effort. They were not disappointed. Arriving in Petrograd on April 16, Lenin attacked at once, issuing his famous April Theses. To the Petrograd Bolsheviks' great astonishment, he rejected all cooperation with what he called the "bourgeois" provisional government, and instead called for exactly what the popular masses themselves were demanding: "All power to the soviets!" and "Peace, Land, Bread!" Bolshevik support increased through the summer, culminating in mass demonstrations in Petrograd on July 16–20 by soldiers, sailors, and workers. Lenin and the Bolshevik Central Committee had not planned these demonstrations and were completely unprepared to support them. Nonetheless, the provisional government labeled Lenin and other leading Bolsheviks traitors and ordered them arrested. Lenin had to flee to Finland.

Meanwhile, however, the provisional government itself was collapsing. The coalition between liberals and socialists was breaking apart as their respective power bases—bourgeoisie and proletariat—demanded they move further to the right or left. Prime Minister Kerensky's unwavering support for the war lost him all credit with the army, the only force that might have saved him and democratic government in Russia. In early September an attempted right-wing military coup failed as Petrograd workers organized themselves as Red Guards to defend the city and then convinced the coup's soldiers to join them. Although the workers' actions were organized by local unions and factories—the Bolshevik leaders had no hand in stopping the coup—the Bolsheviks gained more support nevertheless. Lenin, from his exile in Finland, now called for an armed Bolshevik insurrection before the Second All-Russian Congress of Soviets met in early November.

In October the Bolsheviks gained a fragile majority in the Petrograd Soviet. Lenin did not return to Russia until mid-October and even then remained in hiding. It was Lenin's supporter Leon Trotsky (1879–1940) who brilliantly executed the Bolshevik seizure of power. On November 6 militant Trotsky followers joined with trusted Bolshevik soldiers to seize government buildings and arrest provisional government members. That evening Lenin came out of hiding and took control of the revolution. The following day revolutionary forces seized the Winter Palace, and Kerensky capitulated. At the Congress of Soviets, a Bolshevik majority

Bolsheviks

▶ The majority group; this was Lenin's camp of the Russian party of Marxist socialism.

What factors led to the **Russian Revolution, and what was its outcome?** | What were the global consequences of the First World War? | How did leaders deal with the political dimensions of uncertainty in the interwar years? | In what ways were the anxieties of the postwar world expressed in new forms of communication? | ✓ LearningCurve Check what you know.

861

declared that all power had passed to the soviets and named Lenin head of the new government.

The Bolsheviks came to power for three key reasons. First, by late 1917 democracy had given way to anarchy as the popular masses no longer supported the provisional government. Second, in Lenin and Trotsky the Bolsheviks had a truly superior leadership who were utterly determined to provoke a Marxist revolution. Third, the Bolsheviks appealed to soldiers, urban workers, and peasants who were exhausted by war and eager for socialism.

Dictatorship and Civil War

The Bolsheviks' true accomplishment was not taking power but keeping it and conquering the chaos they had helped create. Once again, Lenin was able to profit from developments over which he and the Bolsheviks had no control. Since summer 1917 an unstoppable peasant revolution had swept across Russia, as peasants divided among themselves the estates of the landlords and the church. Thus Lenin's first law, which supposedly gave land to the peasants, actually merely approved what peasants were already doing. Lenin then met urban workers' greatest demand with a decree giving local workers' committees direct control of individual factories.

The Bolsheviks proclaimed their regime a "provisional workers' and peasants' government," promising that a freely elected Constituent Assembly would draw up a new constitution. However, when Bolshevik delegates won fewer than one-fourth of the seats in free elections in November, the Constituent Assembly was permanently disbanded by Bolshevik soldiers acting under Lenin's orders.

Lenin then moved to make peace with Germany, at any price. That price was very high. Germany demanded the Soviet government surrender all its western territories in the Treaty of Brest-Litovsk (BREHST lih-TAWFSK), in March 1918. With Germany's defeat eight months later, the treaty was nullified, but it allowed Lenin time to escape the disaster of continued war and pursue his goal of absolute political power for the Bolsheviks—now renamed Communists—within Russia.

The war's end and the demise of the democratically elected Constituent Assembly revealed Bolshevik rule as a dictatorship. Officers of the old army organized so-called White opposition to the Bolsheviks in southern Russia, Ukraine, Siberia, and west of Petrograd and plunged the country into civil war from November 1917 to October 1922. The Whites came from many political factions and were united only by their hatred of the Bolsheviks—the Reds. In almost five years of fighting, 125,000 Reds and 175,000 Whites and Poles were killed before the Red Army under Trotsky's command claimed final victory.

The Bolsheviks' Red Army won for several reasons. Strategically, they controlled the center, while the disunited Whites attacked from the fringes. Moreover, the Whites' poorly defined political program failed to unite all of the Bolsheviks' foes under a progressive democratic banner. Most important, the Communists developed a better army, against which the divided Whites were no match.

The Bolsheviks also mobilized the home front. Establishing War Communism— the application of the total-war concept to a civil conflict—they seized grain from peasants, introduced rationing, nationalized all banks and industry, and required everyone to work. Although these measures contributed to a breakdown of nor-

The Russian Civil War, 1917–1922

- Ceded after Treaty of Brest-Litovsk, 1918
- Bolshevik territory, 1919
- Occupied by Allies, 1919
- White Army forces
- Boundary of U.S.S.R., 1921

War Communism

▶ The application of the total-war concept to a civil conflict; the Bolsheviks seized grain from peasants, introduced rationing, nationalized all banks and industry, and required everyone to work.

CHAPTER LOCATOR | What were the long-term and immediate causes of World War I, how did it become a global war? | How did total war affect the home fronts of the major combatants?

CHAPTER 28
862 WORLD WAR AND REVOLUTION

mal economic activity, they also served to maintain labor discipline and to keep the Red Army supplied.

Revolutionary terror also contributed to the Communist victory. The old tsarist secret police was re-established as the Cheka, which hunted down and executed thousands of real or supposed foes. During the so-called Red Terror of 1918–1920, the Cheka sowed fear, silenced opposition, and executed an estimated 250,000 "class enemies."

KEY EVENTS OF THE RUSSIAN REVOLUTION

1914	Russia enters World War I
1916–1917	Tsarist government in crisis
March 1917	March Revolution; Duma declares a provisional government; tsar abdicates; Petrograd Soviet issues Army Order No. 1
April 1917	Lenin returns from exile
October 1917	Bolsheviks gain a majority in the Petrograd Soviet
November 7, 1917	Bolsheviks seize power; Lenin named head of new Communist government
March 1918	Treaty of Brest-Litovsk; Trotsky becomes head of the Red Army
1917–1922	Civil war
1922	Civil war ends; Lenin and the Bolshevik Communists take control of Russia

Finally, foreign military intervention in the civil war ended up helping the Communists. The Allies sent troops to prevent war materiel that they had sent to the provisional government from being captured by the Germans. After the Soviet government nationalized all foreign-owned factories without compensation and refused to pay foreign debts, Western governments began to support White armies. While these efforts did little to help the Whites' cause, they did permit the Communists to appeal to the ethnic Russians' patriotic nationalism.

QUICK REVIEW <

How were the Bolsheviks able to defeat their rivals and take control of Russia?

| **What factors led to the Russian Revolution, and what was its outcome?** | What were the global consequences of the First World War? | How did leaders deal with the political dimensions of uncertainty in the interwar years? | In what ways were the anxieties of the postwar world expressed in new forms of communication? | LearningCurve Check what you know. |

863

What were the global consequences of the First World War?

IN SPRING 1918 THE GERMANS LAUNCHED their last major attack against France. It failed, and Germany was defeated. The armistice came in November, and in January 1919, as civil war spread in Russia and chaos engulfed much of eastern Europe, the victorious Western Allies came together in Paris hoping to establish a lasting peace. The eventual peace settlement, however, failed to establish a lasting peace or to resolve the issues that had brought the world to war.

The End of the War

Peace and an end to the war did not come easily. Victory over revolutionary Russia had temporarily boosted sagging German morale, and in spring 1918 the German army attacked France once more. The German offensive was turned back in July at the Second Battle of the Marne, where 140,000 fresh American soldiers saw action. Adding 2 million men in arms to the war effort by August, the late but massive American intervention decisively tipped the scales in favor of Allied victory.

By September British, French, and American armies were advancing steadily on all fronts. On October 4 the German emperor formed a new, more liberal German government to sue for peace. As negotiations over an armistice dragged on, the frustrated German people rose up. On November 3 sailors in Kiel (keel) mutinied, and throughout northern Germany soldiers and workers established revolutionary councils on the Russian soviet model. Austria-Hungary surrendered to the Allies the same day. With army discipline collapsing, Kaiser William abdicated and fled to Holland. Socialist leaders in Berlin proclaimed a German republic on November 9 and agreed to tough Allied terms of surrender. The armistice went into effect on November 11, 1918.

The Paris Peace Treaties

Seventy delegates from twenty-seven nations attended the opening of the Paris Peace Conference at the Versailles Palace on January 18, 1919. The delegates met with great expectations. A young British diplomat later wrote that the victors

CHAPTER LOCATOR | What were the long-term and immediate causes of World War I, how did it become a global war? | How did total war affect the home fronts of the major combatants?

864 CHAPTER 28
WORLD WAR AND REVOLUTION

"were journeying to Paris . . . to found a new order in Europe. We were preparing not Peace only, but Eternal Peace."[1]

This idealism was strengthened by President Wilson's January 1918 peace proposal, the Fourteen Points. Wilson stressed national self-determination and the rights of small countries and called for the creation of a League of Nations, a permanent international organization designed to protect member states from aggression and avert future wars.

The real powers at the conference were the United States, Great Britain, and France. Germany and Russia were excluded, and Italy's role was limited. Almost immediately the three Allies began to quarrel. President Wilson insisted that the first order of business be the League of Nations. Wilson had his way, although Prime Ministers Lloyd George of Great Britain and, especially, Georges Clemenceau of France were unenthusiastic. They were primarily concerned with punishing Germany.

The "Big Three" were soon in a stalemate over Germany's fate. Although personally inclined to make a somewhat moderate peace with Germany, Lloyd George felt pressured for a victory worthy of the sacrifices of total war. Clemenceau also wanted revenge and lasting security for France, which, he believed, required the creation of a buffer state between France and Germany, Germany's permanent demilitarization, and vast German reparations. Wilson, supported by Lloyd George, would hear none of this.

In the end, Clemenceau agreed to a compromise. He gave up the French demand for a Rhineland buffer state in return for a formal defensive alliance with the United States and Great Britain. Both Wilson and Lloyd George also promised their countries would come to France's aid if it was attacked.

The Treaty of Versailles was the first step toward re-establishing international order, though it was an order that favored the victorious Allies. Germany's colonies were given to France, Britain, and Japan as League of Nations mandates. Germany's territorial losses within Europe were minor: Alsace-Lorraine was returned to France, and parts of Germany were ceded to the new Polish state (see Map 28.4). The treaty limited Germany's army to one hundred thousand men and allowed no new military fortifications in the Rhineland.

More harshly, the Allies declared that Germany (with Austria) was responsible for the war and therefore had to pay reparations equal to all civilian damages caused by the war. The actual reparations figure was not set, however, leaving open the possibility that it might be set at a reasonable level in the future when tempers had cooled.

Other agreements reached in Paris also had far-reaching consequences for the course of the twentieth century. In eastern Europe, Poland regained its independence (see Map 19.1, page 570), and the independent states of Austria, Hungary, Czechoslovakia, and a larger Romania were created out of the Austro-Hungarian Empire (see Map 28.4). A greatly expanded Serbian monarchy united Slavs in the western Balkans and took the name Yugoslavia.

Promises of independence made to Arab leaders were largely brushed aside, and Britain and France extended their power in the Middle East, taking advantage of the breakup of the Ottoman Empire. As League of Nations mandates, the French received Lebanon and Syria, and Britain took Iraq and Palestine. Palestine was to include a Jewish national homeland first promised by Britain in 1917 in the Balfour Declaration (see page 891). These Allied acquisitions, although officially

League of Nations
▶ A permanent international organization established during the 1919 Paris Peace Conference to protect member states from aggression and avert future wars.

Treaty of Versailles
▶ The 1919 peace settlement that ended World War I; it declared Germany responsible for the war, limited Germany's army to one hundred thousand men, and forced Germany to pay huge reparations.

What factors led to the Russian Revolution, and what was its outcome? | **What were the global consequences of the First World War?** | How did leaders deal with the political dimensions of uncertainty in the interwar years? | In what ways were the anxieties of the postwar world expressed in new forms of communication? | ✓ LearningCurve Check what you know.

865

Boundaries of German, Russian, and Austro-Hungarian Empires in 1914

New and reconstituted nations

Demilitarized or Allied occupation zone

MAP 28.4 ■ Territorial Changes in Europe After World War I

The Great War brought tremendous changes to eastern Europe. Empires were shattered, new nations were established, and a dangerous power vacuum was created by the relatively weak states established between Germany and Soviet Russia.

> MAPPING THE PAST

ANALYZING THE MAP: What territory did Germany lose, and to whom? What new independent states were formed from the old Russian empire?

CONNECTIONS: How were the principles of national self-determination applied to the redrawing of Europe after the war? Did this theory work out?

League of Nations mandates, were one of the most imperialistic elements of the peace settlement. Another was mandating Germany's holdings in China to Japan (see page 901). Germany's African colonies were mandated to Great Britain, France, South Africa, and Belgium. The mandates system left colonial peoples in the Middle East, Asia (see Chapter 29), and Africa bitterly disappointed and demonstrated that the age of Western and Eastern imperialism lived on.

CHAPTER LOCATOR | What were the long-term and immediate causes of World War I, how did it become a global war? | How did total war affect the home fronts of the major combatants?

866 CHAPTER 28 WORLD WAR AND REVOLUTION

American Rejection of the Versailles Treaty

The 1919 peace settlement was not perfect, but for war-shattered Europe it was an acceptable beginning. The remaining problems could be worked out in the future. Such hopes were dashed, however, when the United States quickly reverted to its prewar preferences for isolationism and the U.S. Senate, led by Republican Henry Cabot Lodge, rejected the Versailles treaty. Wilson rejected all attempts at compromise on the treaty, ensuring that it would never be ratified in any form and that the United States would never join the League of Nations. Moreover, the Senate refused to ratify Wilson's defensive alliance with France and Great Britain. Using U.S. action as an excuse, Great Britain also refused to ratify its defensive alliance with France. Betrayed by its allies, France stood alone, and the great hopes of early 1919 had turned to ashes by year's end.

QUICK REVIEW <

How did the American, British, and French visions
of the postwar peace differ?

| What factors led to the Russian Revolution, and what was its outcome? | **What were the global consequences of the First World War?** | How did leaders deal with the political dimensions of uncertainty in the interwar years? | In what ways were the anxieties of the postwar world expressed in new forms of communication? | ✔ LearningCurve Check what you know. |

867

How did leaders deal with the political dimensions of uncertainty and try to re-establish peace and prosperity in the interwar years?

THE PURSUIT OF REAL AND LASTING PEACE in the first half of the interwar years proved difficult for many reasons. Germany hated the Treaty of Versailles. France was fearful and isolated. Britain was undependable, and the United States had turned its back on Europe's problems. Eastern Europe was in ferment, and no one could predict Communist Russia's future. Moreover, the international economic situation was poor and was greatly complicated by war debts and disrupted patterns of trade. Yet for a time, from 1925 to late 1929, it appeared that peace and stability were within reach.

Germany and the Western Powers

Nearly all Germans and many other observers immediately and for decades after believed the Versailles treaty represented a harsh dictated peace and should be revised or repudiated as soon as possible. Many right-wing Germans believed there had been no defeat; instead they believed German soldiers had been betrayed by liberals, Marxists, Jews, and other "November criminals" who had surrendered in order to seize power.

Historians have recently begun to reassess the treaty's terms, however, and many scholars currently view them as relatively reasonable. They argue that much of the German anger toward the Allies was based more on perception than reality. With the collapse of Austria-Hungary, the dissolution of the Ottoman Empire, and the revolution in Russia, Germany emerged from the war an even stronger power in eastern Europe than before, and economically stronger and more populated than France or Great Britain. Moreover, when contrasted with

CHAPTER LOCATOR | What were the long-term and immediate causes of World War I, how did it become a global war? | How did total war affect the home fronts of the major combatants?

868 CHAPTER 28 WORLD WAR AND REVOLUTION

the extremely harsh Treaty of Brest-Litovsk that Germany had forced on Lenin's Russia, and the peace terms Germany intended to impose on the Allies if they won the war, the Versailles treaty was far from being a vindictive and crippling peace. Had it been, Germany could hardly have become the economic and military juggernaut that it was only twenty years later.

This is not to say, however, that France did not seek some degree of revenge on Germany for both the Franco-Prussian War (see page 726) and the Great War. Most of the war on the western front had been fought on French soil. The expected reconstruction costs and the amount of war debts owed to the United States were staggering. Thus the French believed that heavy German reparations were an economic necessity that could hold Germany down indefinitely and would enable France to realize its goal of security.

The British soon felt differently. Prewar Germany had been Great Britain's second-best market, and after the war a healthy, prosperous Germany appeared to be essential to the British economy. In addition, the British were suspicious of France's army—the largest in Europe—and the British and French were at odds over their League of Nations mandates in the Middle East.

While France and Britain drifted in different directions, the Allied reparations commission completed its work, and in 1921 the young German republic—known as the Weimar Republic—made its first reparations payment. Then in 1922, wracked by rapid inflation and political assassinations and motivated by hostility and arrogance as well, the Weimar Republic announced its inability to pay more and proposed a reparations moratorium for three years.

The British were willing to accept a moratorium, but the French were not. Led by their prime minister, Raymond Poincaré (1860–1934), they decided they had to either call Germany's bluff or see the entire peace settlement dissolve to France's great disadvantage. So in January 1923 French and Belgian armies occupied the Ruhr district, industrial Germany's heartland, creating the most serious international crisis of the 1920s.

Strengthened by a wave of patriotism, the German government ordered the people of the Ruhr to stop working and to resist French occupation nonviolently. The French responded by sealing off not only the Ruhr but also the entire Rhineland from the rest of Germany, letting in only enough food to prevent starvation.

By summer 1923 France and Germany were engaged in a great test of wills. French armies could not collect reparations from striking workers at gunpoint. But French occupation was paralyzing Germany and its economy, and the German government was soon forced to print money to pay its bills. Prices soared, and German money rapidly lost all value. Many retired and middle-class people saw their savings wiped out. Many Germans felt betrayed. They hated and blamed the Western governments, their own government, big business, the Jews, the workers, and the Communists for their misfortune.

In August 1923, as the mark's value fell and political unrest grew throughout Germany, Gustav Stresemann (1878–1929) became German chancellor. Stresemann adopted a compromising attitude. He called off the peaceful resistance campaign in the Ruhr and in October agreed in principle to pay reparations but asked for a re-examination of Germany's ability to pay. Poincaré accepted. Thus, after five years of hostility and tension, Germany and France, with British and American help, decided to try compromise and cooperation.

French Occupation of the Ruhr, 1923–1925

What factors led to the Russian Revolution, and what was its outcome?

What were the global consequences of the First World War?

How did leaders deal with the political dimensions of uncertainty in the interwar years?

In what ways were the anxieties of the postwar world expressed in new forms of communication?

LearningCurve
Check what you know.

869

Hope in Foreign Affairs

In 1924 an international committee of financial experts headed by American banker Charles G. Dawes met to re-examine reparations. Under the terms of the resulting **Dawes Plan** (1924), Germany's yearly reparations were reduced and linked to the level of German economic prosperity. Germany would also receive large loans from the United States to promote German recovery, as well as to pay reparations to France and Britain, thus enabling those countries to repay the large sums they owed the United States. This circular flow of international payments was complicated and risky, but it worked for a while, facilitating a worldwide economic recovery in the late 1920s.

This economic settlement was matched by a political settlement. In 1925 European leaders met in Locarno, Switzerland. Germany and France solemnly pledged to accept their common border, and both Britain and Italy agreed to fight either France or Germany if one invaded the other. Stresemann also agreed to settle boundary disputes with Poland and Czechoslovakia by peaceful means, and France promised those countries military aid if Germany attacked them.

Other developments also strengthened hopes for international peace. In 1926 Germany joined the League of Nations, and in 1928 fifteen countries signed the Kellogg-Briand Pact. The signing nations "condemned and renounced war as an instrument of national policy."

Hope in Democratic Government

European domestic politics also offered reason for hope. During the Ruhr occupation and the great inflation, Germany's republican government appeared ready to collapse. In 1923 Communists momentarily entered provincial governments. In November an obscure politician named Adolf Hitler proclaimed a "national socialist revolution" in a Munich beer hall. Hitler's plot to seize government control was poorly organized and easily crushed. Hitler was sentenced to prison, where he outlined his theories and program in his book *Mein Kampf* (*My Struggle*, 1925).

The moderate businessmen who tended to dominate the various German coalition governments believed that economic prosperity demanded good relations with the Western powers, and they supported parliamentary government at home. Elections were held regularly, and as the economy boomed in the aftermath of the Dawes Plan, republican democracy appeared to have growing support among a majority of Germans. There were, however, sharp political divisions in the country. Many unrepentant nationalists and monarchists populated the right and the army. Members of Germany's Communist Party received directions from Moscow, and they accused the Social Democrats of betraying the revolution.

France's situation was similar to Germany's. Communists and socialists battled for the workers' support. After 1924 the democratically elected government rested mainly in the hands of moderate coalitions, and business interests were well represented. France's great accomplishment was rapid rebuilding of its war-torn northern region, and good times prevailed until 1930.

Britain, too, faced challenges after 1920. The great problem was unemployment, which hovered around 12 percent throughout the 1920s. The state provided unemployment benefits and a range of additional social services. These and other

CHAPTER LOCATOR | What were the long-term and immediate causes of World War I, how did it become a global war? | How did total war affect the home fronts of the major combatants?

870 CHAPTER 28 WORLD WAR AND REVOLUTION

measures kept living standards from seriously declining, defused class tensions, and pointed the way to the welfare state Britain established after World War II.

The wartime trend toward greater social equality continued, however, helping maintain social harmony. Relative social harmony was accompanied by the rise of the Labour Party. Committed to moderate, "revisionist" socialism (see page 743), the Labour Party under Ramsay MacDonald (1866–1937) governed the country in 1924 and 1929–1935.

The British Conservatives under Stanley Baldwin (1867–1947) showed the same compromising spirit on social issues, and Britain experienced only limited social unrest in the 1920s and 1930s. In 1922 Britain granted southern, Catholic Ireland full autonomy after a bitter guerrilla war. Thus developments in both international relations and domestic politics gave the leading democracies cause for cautious optimism in the late 1920s.

QUICK REVIEW

What developments in the 1920s gave some observers
hope that lasting peace and stability were possible?

What factors led to the Russian Revolution, and what was its outcome? | What were the global consequences of the First World War? | **How did leaders deal with the political dimensions of uncertainty in the interwar years?** | In what ways were the anxieties of the postwar world expressed in new forms of communication? | LearningCurve Check what you know.

871

In what ways were the anxieties of the postwar world expressed or heightened by revolutionary ideas in modern thought, art, and science and in new forms of communication?

Unlocking the Power of the Atom

Many of the fanciful visions of science fiction came true in the twentieth century, although not exactly as first imagined. This 1927 cartoon satirizes a professor who has split the atom and has unwittingly destroyed his building and neighborhood in the process. In the Second World War scientists harnessed the atom in bombs and decimated faraway cities and their inhabitants. (© Mary Evans Picture Library/The Image Works)

MANY PEOPLE HOPED THAT HAPPIER TIMES would return after the war, along with the familiar prewar ideals of peace, prosperity, and progress. These hopes were in vain. Great numbers of men and women felt themselves increasingly adrift in an age of anxiety and continual crisis.

Uncertainty in Philosophy and Religion

Before 1914 most people in the West still believed in Enlightenment philosophies of progress, reason, and individual rights. As the century began, progress was a daily reality, apparent in the rising living standard, the taming of the city, the

CHAPTER LOCATOR | What were the long-term and immediate causes of World War I, how did it become a global war? | How did total war affect the home fronts of the major combatants?

CHAPTER 28
872 WORLD WAR AND REVOLUTION

spread of political rights to women and workers, and the growth of state-supported social programs.

Even before the war, however, the German philosopher Friedrich Nietzsche (NEE-chuh) (1844–1900) called such faith in reason into question. In the first of his *Untimely Meditations* (1873), he argued that Western civilization overemphasized rationality and stifled the passions and animal instincts that drive human activity and true creativity. Nietzsche believed that reason, democracy, progress, and respectability were outworn social and psychological constructs that suffocated self-realization and excellence. Rejecting religion, Nietzsche claimed that Christianity embodied a "slave morality" that glorified weakness, envy, and mediocrity. Little read during his lifetime, Nietzsche attracted growing attention in the early twentieth century.

The First World War accelerated the revolt against established philosophical certainties. Logical positivism, often associated with Austrian philosopher Ludwig Wittgenstein (VIHT-guhn-shtighn) (1889–1951), rejected most concerns of traditional philosophy as nonsense and argued that life must be based on facts and observation. Others looked to existentialism for answers. Highly diverse and even contradictory, existential thinkers were loosely united in a search for moral values in an anxious and uncertain world. Often inspired by Nietzsche, they did not believe that a supreme being had established humanity's fundamental nature and given life its meaning. In the words of the French existentialist Jean-Paul Sartre (ZHAWN-pawl SAHR-truh) (1905–1980), "Man's existence precedes his essence. . . . To begin with he is nothing. He will not be anything until later, and then he will be what he makes of himself."[2]

In contrast, the loss of faith in human reason and in continual progress led to a renewed interest in Christianity. After World War I several thinkers and theologians began to revitalize Christian fundamentals, and intellectuals increasingly turned to religion between about 1920 and 1950. Sometimes described as Christian existentialists because they shared the loneliness and despair of atheistic existentialists, these believers felt that religion was one meaningful answer to terror and anxiety.

existentialism

▶ The name given to a highly diverse and even contradictory philosophy that stresses the meaninglessness of existence and the search for moral values in a world of terror and uncertainty.

The New Physics

Starting at the turn of the century, a series of discoveries challenged the established certainties of Newtonian physics. An important first step toward the new physics was the British physicist J. J. Thomson's 1897 discovery of subatomic particles, which proved that atoms were not stable and unbreakable. The following year Polish-born physicist Marie Curie (1867–1934) and her French husband, Pierre (1859–1906), discovered radium and demonstrated that it constantly emits subatomic particles and thus does not have a constant atomic weight. Building on this, German physicist Max Planck (1858–1947) showed in 1900 that subatomic energy is emitted in uneven little spurts, which Planck called "quanta," and not in a steady stream, as previously believed.

In 1905 the German-Jewish genius Albert Einstein (1879–1955) further undermined Newtonian physics. His theory of special relativity postulated that time and space are relative to the observer's viewpoint and that only the speed of light is constant for all frames of reference in the universe. In addition, Einstein's theory

What factors led to the Russian Revolution, and what was its outcome?

What were the global consequences of the First World War?

How did leaders deal with the political dimensions of uncertainty in the interwar years?

In what ways were the anxieties of the postwar world expressed in new forms of communication?

✓ LearningCurve
Check what you know.

873

stated that matter and energy are interchangeable and that even a particle of matter contains enormous levels of potential energy.

In the 1920s breakthrough followed breakthrough, with some discoveries raising new doubts about reality. The implications of the new theories and discoveries were disturbing to millions of people in the 1920s and 1930s. The new universe was strange and troubling, and, moreover, science appeared distant from human experience and human problems.

Freudian Psychology

With physics presenting an uncertain universe so unrelated to ordinary human experience, questions about the power and potential of the human mind assumed special significance. The findings and speculations of psychologist Sigmund Freud (1856–1939) were particularly disturbing.

Before Freud, most psychologists assumed that human behavior resulted from rational thinking by the conscious mind. By analyzing dreams and hysteria, Freud developed a very different view of the human psyche. Freud concluded that human behavior was governed by three parts of the self: the id, ego, and superego. The irrational unconscious, which he called the id, was driven by sexual, aggressive, and pleasure-seeking desires and was locked in constant battle with the mind's two other parts: the rationalizing conscious—the ego—which mediates what a person can do, and ingrained moral values—the superego—which specify what a person should do. Thus for Freud human behavior was a product of a fragile compromise between instinctual drives and the controls of rational thinking and moral values.

id, ego, superego
▶ Freudian terms for the primitive, irrational unconscious (id), the rationalizing conscious that mediates what a person can do (ego), and the ingrained moral values that specify what a person should do (superego).

Twentieth-Century Literature

Western literature was also influenced by the general intellectual climate of pessimism, relativism, and alienation. Some novelists used the stream-of-consciousness technique with its reliance on internal monologues to explore the psyche. The most famous stream-of-consciousness novel is *Ulysses*, published by Irish novelist James Joyce (1882–1941) in 1922. Abandoning conventional grammar and blending foreign words, puns, bits of knowledge, and scraps of memory together in bewildering confusion, the language of *Ulysses* was intended to mirror modern life itself.

Creative writers rejected the idea of progress; some even described "anti-utopias," nightmare visions of things to come. In 1918 Oswald Spengler (1880–1936) published *The Decline of the West*, in which he argued that Western civilization was in its old age and would soon be conquered by East Asia. Likewise, T. S. Eliot (1888–1965) depicted a world of growing desolation in his famous poem *The Waste Land* (1922). Franz Kafka's (1883–1924) novels portrayed helpless individuals crushed by inexplicably hostile forces.

modernism
▶ A variety of cultural movements at the end of the nineteenth century and beginning of the twentieth that rebelled against traditional forms and conventions of the past.

Modern Architecture, Art, and Music

Like scientists and intellectuals, creative artists rejected old forms and old values after the war. Modernism in architecture, art, and music meant constant experimentation and a search for new kinds of expression.

CHAPTER LOCATOR | What were the long-term and immediate causes of World War I, how did it become a global war? | How did total war affect the home fronts of the major combatants?

874   CHAPTER 28
WORLD WAR AND REVOLUTION

The United States pioneered in the new architecture. In the 1890s the Chicago School of architects, led by Louis H. Sullivan (1856–1924), used cheap steel, reinforced concrete, and electric elevators to build skyscrapers and office buildings lacking almost any exterior ornamentation. The buildings of Frank Lloyd Wright (1867–1959) were renowned for their sometimes-radical design, their creative use of wide varieties of materials, and their appearance of being part of the landscape.

In Europe architectural leadership centered in German-speaking countries. In 1919 Walter Gropius (1883–1969) merged the schools of fine and applied arts at Weimar into a single interdisciplinary school, the Bauhaus. Throughout the 1920s the Bauhaus, with its stress on functionalism and good design for everyday life, attracted enthusiastic students from all over the world.

functionalism

▶ The principle that buildings, like industrial products, should serve the purpose for which they were made as well as possible.

Eiffel Tower, 1926

The works of the French artist Robert Delaunay (1885–1941) represent most of the major art styles of the early twentieth century, including modernism, abstraction, futurism, fauvism, cubism, and Orphism. His early renderings of the Eiffel Tower (1909–1912), the iconic symbol of urbanization, the machine age, and, as a radio tower, limitless communication, possess features drawn from several of these styles. His later paintings of the Eiffel Tower, such as the one shown here, draw on a much wider palette of brilliant colors, reflecting aspects of a style known as Orphism, with which he is most closely identified. (*Eiffel Tower*, 1926, oil on canvas by Robert Delaunay [1885–1941]/Private Collection/Photo © Christie's Images/The Bridgeman Art Library)

What factors led to the Russian Revolution, and what was its outcome?

What were the global consequences of the First World War?

How did leaders deal with the political dimensions of uncertainty in the interwar years?

In what ways were the anxieties of the postwar world expressed in new forms of communication?

☑ LearningCurve
Check what you know.

Art increasingly took on a nonrepresentational, abstract character. New artistic styles grew out of a revolt against French impressionism, which was characterized by an overall feeling, or impression, of light falling on a real-life scene before the artist's eyes, rather than an exact copy of objects. Though individualistic in their styles, "postimpressionists" and "expressionists" were united in their desire to depict unseen inner worlds of emotion and imagination.

In 1907 in Paris the famous Spanish painter Pablo Picasso (1881–1973), along with Georges Braque, Marcel Duchamp, and other artists, established cubism—an artistic approach concentrated on a complex geometry of zigzagging lines and sharply angled overlapping planes. Since the Renaissance, artists had represented objects from a single viewpoint and had created unified human forms. Cubism represented a radical new view of reality.

The ultimate stage in the development of abstract, nonrepresentational art occurred around 1910. Artists such as the Russian-born Wassily Kandinsky (1866–1944) turned away from nature completely.

Radicalization accelerated after World War I. The most notable new developments were New Objectivity, Dadaism, and surrealism. Paintings inspired by the New Objectivity were provocative, emotionally disturbing, and harshly satirical. Dadaism attacked all accepted standards of art and behavior, delighting in outrageous conduct. Surrealists painted fantastic worlds of wild dreams and complex symbols.

Developments in modern music were strikingly parallel to those in painting. Attracted by the emotional intensity of expressionism, composers depicted unseen inner worlds of emotion and imagination. Likewise, modernism in opera and ballet flourished. Led by Viennese composer Arnold Schönberg (SHUHN-buhrg) (1874–1951), some composers turned their backs on long-established musical conventions. As abstract painters arranged lines and color but did not draw identifiable objects, so modern composers arranged sounds without creating recognizable harmonies.

Movies and Radio

In the decades following the First World War, motion pictures became the main entertainment of the masses worldwide. Motion pictures offered ordinary people a temporary escape from the hard realities of international tensions, uncertainty, unemployment, and personal frustrations. Motion pictures also became powerful tools of indoctrination, especially in countries with dictatorial regimes.

Radio also dominated popular culture after the war. In 1920 the first major public broadcasts were made in Great Britain and the United States. Every major country quickly established national broadcasting networks. In the United States these were privately owned and financed by advertising. In Europe, China, Japan, India, and elsewhere the typical pattern was direct government control. By the late 1930s more than three-fourths of the households in both democratic Great Britain and dictatorial Germany had at least one radio. Radio was well suited for promoting patriotism and spreading political propaganda. Radios were revolutionary in that they were capable of reaching all of a nation's citizens at once, offering them a single perspective on current events, and teaching them a single national language and pronunciation.

CHAPTER LOCATOR | What were the long-term and immediate causes of World War I, how did it become a global war? | How did total war affect the home fronts of the major combatants?

876 CHAPTER 28 WORLD WAR AND REVOLUTION

The International Appeal of Cinema

A movie house in Havana, Cuba, in 1933 showing two American films made in 1932: *El Rey de la Plata* (*Silver Dollar*) starring Edward G. Robinson and *6 horas de Vida* (*Six Hours to Live*) featuring Warner Baxter. The partially visible poster in the upper right is advertising *El último varon sobre la Tierra* (*The Last Man on Earth*), an American-produced Spanish-language movie staring Raul Roulien, first released in Spain in January 1933. (Walker Evans [1903–1975]/© Copyright 1933. Cinema, 1933, printed ca. 1970. Gelatin silver print. Gift of Arnold H. Crane, 1971 [1971.646.12)] © Walker Evans Archive, Metropolitan Museum of Art, New York, NY, USA/Image copyright © The Metropolitan Museum of Art/Image source: Art Resource, NY)

QUICK REVIEW <

How did the new physics challenge Enlightenment certainties?

| What factors led to the Russian Revolution, and what was its outcome? | What were the global consequences of the First World War? | How did leaders deal with the political dimensions of uncertainty in the interwar years? | **In what ways were the anxieties of the postwar world expressed in new forms of communication?** | ✓ LearningCurve Check what you know. |

877

CHAPTER SUMMARY

Nationalism, militarism, imperialism, and the alliance system increased political tensions across Europe at the end of the nineteenth century. Franz Ferdinand's assassination in 1914 sparked a regional war that soon became global. Four years of stalemate and slaughter followed. Entire societies mobilized for total war, and government powers greatly increased. Women earned greater social equality, and labor unions grew. Many European countries adopted socialism as a realistic economic blueprint.

Horrible losses on the eastern front led to Russian tsar Nicholas II's abdication in March 1917. A provisional government controlled by moderate social democrats replaced him but refused to withdraw Russia from the war. A second Russian revolution followed in November 1917, led by Lenin and his Communist Bolshevik Party. The Bolsheviks established a radical regime, smashed existing capitalist institutions, and posed an ongoing challenge to Europe and its colonial empires.

The "war to end war" brought only a fragile truce. The Versailles treaty took away Germany's colonies, limited its military, and demanded admittance of war guilt and exorbitant war reparations. Separate treaties redrew the maps of Europe and the Middle East. Allied wartime solidarity faded, and Germany remained unrepentant, setting the stage for World War II. Globally, the European powers refused to extend self-determination to their colonies, instead creating a mandate system that sowed further discontent among colonized peoples.

In the 1920s moderate political leaders sought to create an enduring peace and rebuild prewar prosperity though compromise. By decade's end they seemed to have succeeded: Germany experienced an economic recovery, France rebuilt its war-torn regions, and Britain's Labour Party expanded social services. Ultimately, however, these measures were short-lived.

The war's horrors, particularly the industrialization of war that slaughtered millions, shattered Enlightenment ideals and caused widespread anxiety. In the interwar years philosophers, artists, and writers portrayed these anxieties in their work. Movies and the radio initially offered escape but soon became powerful tools of indoctrination and propaganda.

CHAPTER LOCATOR | What were the long-term and immediate causes of World War I, how did it become a global war? | How did total war affect the home fronts of the major combatants?

CHAPTER 28
878 WORLD WAR AND REVOLUTION

CONNECTIONS The Great War continues to influence global politics and societies. To understand the origins of many modern world conflicts, one must study first the intrigues and treaties and the revolutions and upheavals that were associated with this first truly world war.

In Chapter 30 we will see how the conflict contributed to a worldwide depression, the rise of totalitarian dictatorships, and a Second World War more global and destructive than the first. In the Middle East the Ottoman Empire came to an end, allowing France and England to carve out mandated territories—including modern Iraq, Palestine/Israel, and Lebanon—that remain flash points for violence and political instability in the twenty-first century. Nationalism, the nineteenth-century European ideology of change, took root in Asia, partly driven by Wilson's promise of self-determination. In Chapter 29 the efforts of various nationalist leaders—Atatürk in Turkey, Gandhi in India, Mao Zedong in China, Ho Chi Minh in Vietnam, and others—to throw off colonial domination will be examined, as well as the rise of ultranationalism in Japan, which led it into World War II and to ultimate defeat.

America's entry into the Great War placed it on the world stage, a place it has not relinquished as a superpower in the twentieth and twenty-first centuries. Russia, too, eventually became a superpower, but this outcome was not so clear in 1919 as its leaders fought for survival in a vicious civil war. By the outbreak of World War II Joseph Stalin had solidified Communist power, and the Soviet Union and the United Sates would play leading roles in defeating totalitarianism in Germany and Japan. But at war's end, as explained in Chapter 31, the two superpowers found themselves opponents in a Cold War that lasted for much of the rest of the twentieth century.

LaunchPad

ONLINE DOCUMENT PROJECT
Calling Young Women to War

What words and images did governments use to recruit women to serve in World War I?

Examine several recruitment posters aimed at women, and then complete a quiz and writing assignment based on the evidence and details from this chapter. *See inside the front cover to learn more.*

What factors led to the Russian Revolution, and what was its outcome?

What were the global consequences of the First World War?

How did leaders deal with the political dimensions of uncertainty in the interwar years?

In what ways were the anxieties of the postwar world expressed in new forms of communication?

✔ LearningCurve
Check what you know.

879

CHAPTER 28 STUDY GUIDE

STEP 1 GET STARTED ONLINE

 LearningCurve

Now that you've read the chapter, make it stick by completing the LearningCurve activity.

STEP 2 EXPLAIN WHY IT MATTERS

Put your reading into practice. Identify each term below, and then explain why it matters in world history.

TERM	WHO OR WHAT & WHEN	WHY IT MATTERS
militarism (p. 846)		
Triple Entente (p. 848)		
trench warfare (p. 850)		
total war (p. 854)		
March Revolution (p. 859)		
Petrograd Soviet (p. 860)		
Bolsheviks (p. 861)		
War Communism (p. 862)		
League of Nations (p. 865)		
Treaty of Versailles (p. 865)		
Dawes Plan (p. 870)		
Mein Kampf (p. 870)		
existentialism (p. 873)		
id, ego, superego (p. 874)		
modernism (p. 874)		
functionalism (p. 875)		

STEP 3 MOVE BEYOND THE BASICS

To demonstrate a more advanced understanding of the nature and consequences of "total war," fill in the chart below with descriptions of the military, political, social, and economic impact of total war. In what ways was total war a conflict between nations as opposed to armies?

	Military	Political	Social	Economic
Impact of Total War				

PUT IT ALL TOGETHER Now, take a step back and try to explain the big picture. Remember to use specific examples from the chapter in your answers.

WORLD WAR I

▶ What factors contributed to the division of Europe into two hostile blocs? Why did European leaders fail to resolve the tensions and conflicts that led to this situation?

▶ How did political leaders channel their nation's resources into the war effort? How did their policies affect European society and government?

THE RUSSIAN REVOLUTION

▶ How did the war undermine the tsarist regime in Russia? How did the tsar himself contribute to the collapse of his government?

▶ To what extent did Lenin dictate the course of events during the Russian Revolution? To what extent did he merely take advantage of opportunities as they presented themselves?

THE POSTWAR WORLD

▶ What steps did Western leaders take to repair the political and economic damage of World War I? Why were the new political and economic systems they created so fragile?

▶ How did the experience of World War I shape Western thought and culture in the 1920s?

LOOKING BACK, LOOKING AHEAD

▶ Compare and contrast the peace settlements that followed the Napoleonic wars and World War I. Which was more successful? Why?

▶ Argue for or against the following statement: "The roots of the economic crisis and global conflicts of the 1930s and 1940s can be found in the failures of the 1920s." What evidence can you present to support your position?

> **IN YOUR OWN WORDS**

Imagine that you must give an oral report to the class answering the following question: In what ways did the First World War represent a fundamental turning point in world history? What would be the most important points and why?

29
NATIONALISM IN ASIA
1914–1939

> How did nationalism shape developments across Asia in the decades following the First World War? Chapter 29 examines nationalist movements in Asia in the decades following the First World War. The First World War sped the development of modern Asian nationalism. Before 1914 the nationalist gospel of anti-imperialist political freedom and racial equality had already won converts among Asia's westernized, educated elites. In the 1920s and 1930s it increasingly won the allegiance of the masses. Between the outbreaks of the First and Second World Wars, each Asian country developed a distinctive national movement rooted in its own unique culture and history. And as in Europe, nationalist movements gave rise in Asia to conflict both within large, multiethnic states and between independent states.

LearningCurve

After reading the chapter, use LearningCurve to retain what you've read.

Kasturba Gandhi Wife of Indian political leader Mohandas Gandhi, Kasturba was barely fourteen years old and he thirteen when the marriage took place. Kasturba (1869–1944) supported Gandhi through decades of struggle for Indian independence. Here she spins cotton on a charkha, or spinning wheel, part of Gandhi's campaign for Indians to become self-sufficient by making their own cloth and freeing themselves from imported British goods. (© Dinodia Photo Library/The Image Works)

> Why did modern nationalism develop in Asia between the First and Second World Wars, and what was its appeal?

> How did the Ottoman Empire's collapse in World War I shape nationalist movements in the Middle East?

> What role did Gandhi and his campaign of militant nonviolence play in leading India to independence from the British?

> How did nationalism shape political developments in East and Southeast Asia?

Why did modern nationalism develop in Asia between the First and Second World Wars, and what was its appeal?

I**IN THE LATE NINETEENTH** and early twentieth centuries the peoples of Asia adapted the European ideology of nationalism to their own situations. The First World War profoundly affected Asian nationalist aspirations by altering relations between Asia and Europe. For four years Asians watched Europeans vilifying and destroying each other. Japan's defeat of imperial Russia in 1905 (see page 729) had shown that an Asian power could beat a European Great Power; now for the first time Asians saw the entire West as divided and vulnerable.

Asian Reaction to the War in Europe

The Great War was a global conflict, but some peoples were affected more significantly than others. The Japanese and Ottoman Turks were directly involved, fighting with the Allies and Central Powers, respectively. The Chinese, who overthrew their emperor in 1911, were more concerned with internal events and the threat from Japan than they were with war in Europe. In British India and French Indochina the war's impact was unavoidably greater. Total war required the British and the French to draft their colonial subjects into the conflict.

An Indian or Vietnamese soldier who fought in France and came in contact there with democratic and republican ideas, however, was less likely to accept foreign rule when he returned home. The British and the French therefore had to make rash promises to gain the support of these colonial peoples and other allies during the war, suggesting in many cases that colonial peoples would move toward self-rule once victory was achieved. After the war the nationalist genie the colonial powers had called on refused to slip meekly back into the bottle.

U.S. President Wilson's war aims also raised the hopes of peoples under imperial rule. In January 1918 Wilson proposed his Fourteen Points (see page 884), whose key idea was national self-determination for the peoples of Europe and the Ottoman Empire. Wilson recommended in Point 5 that in all colonial questions

| **Why did modern nationalism develop in Asia between the First and Second World Wars, and what was its appeal?** | How did the Ottoman Empire's collapse in World War I shape nationalist movements in the Middle East?

1904–1905
Russo-Japanese War ends in Russia's defeat

1916
Sykes-Picot Agreement divides Ottoman Empire; Lucknow Pact forms alliance between Hindus and Muslims in India; New Culture Movement in China begins

1917
Balfour Declaration establishes Jewish homeland in Palestine

1919
Amritsar Massacre in India; May Fourth Movement in China; Treaty of Versailles; Afghanistan achieves independence

1920
King of Syria deposed by French; Gandhi launches campaign of nonviolent resistance against British rule in India

1920s–1930s
Large numbers of European Jews immigrate to Palestine; Hebrew becomes common language

1923
Sun Yatsen allies Nationalist Party with Chinese Communists; Treaty of Lausanne ends war in Turkey; Mustafa Kemal begins to modernize and secularize Turkey

1925
Reza Shah Pahlavi proclaims himself shah of Persia and begins modernization campaign

1927
Jiang Jieshi, leader of Chinese Nationalist Party, purges his Communist allies

1930
Gandhi leads Indians on march to the sea to protest the British salt tax

1931
Japan occupies Manchuria

1932
Iraq gains independence in return for military alliance with Great Britain

1934
Mao Zedong leads Chinese Communists on Long March; Philippines gains self-governing commonwealth status from United States

1937
Japanese militarists launch attack on China; Rape of Nanjing

"the interests of native populations be given equal weight with the desires of European governments," and he seemed to call for national self-rule. This message had enormous appeal for educated Asians, fueling their hopes of freedom.

The Mandates System

After winning the war, the Allies tried to re-establish or increase their political and economic domination of their Asian and African colonies. Although fatally weakened, Western imperialism remained very much alive in 1918, partly because President Wilson was no revolutionary. At the Paris Peace Conference Wilson compromised on colonial questions in order to achieve some of his European goals and create the League of Nations.

The compromise at the Paris Peace Conference between Wilson's vague, moralistic idealism and the European determination to maintain control over colonial empires was a system of League of Nations mandates over Germany's former colonies and the old Ottoman Empire. Article 22 of the League of Nations Covenant, which was part of the Treaty of Versailles, assigned territories "inhabited by peoples incapable of governing themselves" to various "developed nations." "The well-being and development of such peoples" was declared "a sacred trust of civilization." The **Permanent Mandates Commission**, whose members came from European countries with colonies, was created to oversee the developed nations' fulfillment of their international responsibility. Thus the League elaborated a new

Permanent Mandates Commission
▶ A commission created by the League of Nations to oversee the developed nations' fulfillment of their international responsibility toward their mandates.

What role did Gandhi and his campaign of militant nonviolence play in leading India to independence from the British?

How did nationalism shape political developments in East and Southeast Asia?

 LearningCurve
Check what you know.

principle—development toward the eventual goal of self-government—but left its implementation to the colonial powers themselves.

The mandates system demonstrated that Europe was determined to maintain its imperial power and influence. Bitterly disappointed patriots throughout Asia saw the system as an expansion of the imperial order. Yet Asian patriots did not give up. They preached national self-determination and struggled to build mass movements capable of achieving freedom and independence.

In this struggle Asian nationalists were encouraged by Soviet communism. After seizing power in 1917, Lenin declared that the Asian inhabitants of the new Soviet Union were complete equals of the Russians with a right to their own development. The Communists also denounced European and American imperialism and pledged to support revolutionary movements in colonial countries. The example, ideology, and support of Soviet communism exerted a powerful influence in the 1920s and 1930s, particularly in China and French Indochina (see page 901).

Nationalism's Appeal

There were at least three reasons for the upsurge of nationalism in Asia. First and foremost, nationalism provided the most effective means of organizing anti-imperialist resistance both to direct foreign rule and to indirect Western domination. Second, nationalism called for fundamental changes and challenged old political and social practices and beliefs. As in Russia after the Crimean War, in Turkey after the Ottoman Empire's collapse, and in Japan after the Meiji Restoration, the nationalist creed after World War I went hand in hand with acceptance of modernization by the educated elites. Third, nationalism offered a vision of a free and prosperous future, and provided an ideology to ennoble the sacrifices the struggle would require.

Nationalism also had a dark side. As in Europe (see page 715), Asian nationalists developed a strong sense of "we" and "they." "They" were often the enemy. European imperialists were just such a "they," and nationalist feeling generated the will to challenge European domination. But, as in Europe, Asian nationalism also stimulated bitter conflicts and wars between peoples, in three different ways.

First, as when the ideology of nationalism first developed in Europe in the early 1800s (see pages 715–716), Asian (and African) elites were often forced to create a national identity in colonies that Europeans had artificially created, or in multiethnic countries held together by authoritarian leaders but without national identities based on shared ethnicities or histories. Second, nationalism stimulated conflicts between relatively homogeneous peoples in large states, rallying, for example, Chinese against Japanese and vice versa. Third, nationalism often heightened tensions between ethnic or religious groups within states. In nearly all countries there were ancient ethnic and religious differences and rivalries. Imperial rulers of colonial powers and local authoritarian rulers exploited these ethnic and religious differences to "divide and conquer" the peoples in their empires. When the rigid imperial rule ended, the different national, religious, or even ideological factions turned against each other, each seeking to either seize control of or divide the existing state, and to dominate the enemy "they" within its borders.

CHAPTER LOCATOR | Why did modern nationalism develop in Asia between the First and Second World Wars, and what was its appeal? | How did the Ottoman Empire's collapse in World War I shape nationalist movements in the Middle East?

886 CHAPTER 29 NATIONALISM IN ASIA

Nationalism's appeal in Asia was not confined to territories under direct European rule. Europe and the United States had forced even the most solid Asian states, China and Japan, to accept unequal treaties (see page 795) and humiliating limitations on their sovereignty. Thus the nationalist promise of genuine economic independence and true political equality with the West appealed as powerfully in old but weak states like China as in colonial territories like British India.

QUICK REVIEW

What was the mandates system, and how did it contribute to the intensification of Asian nationalism?

What role did Gandhi and his campaign of militant nonviolence play in leading India to independence from the British?

How did nationalism shape political developments in East and Southeast Asia?

LearningCurve
Check what you know.

How did the Ottoman Empire's collapse in World War I shape nationalist movements in the Middle East?

Mustafa Kemal

Surnamed Atatürk, meaning "father of the Turks," Mustafa Kemal and his supporters imposed revolutionary changes aimed at modernizing and westernizing Turkish society and the new Turkish government. Dancing here with his adopted daughter at her high-society wedding, Atatürk often appeared in public in elegant European dress — a vivid symbol for the Turkish people of his radical break with traditional Islamic teaching and custom. (Hulton Archive/Getty Images)

THE MOST FLAGRANT ATTEMPT TO EXPAND Western imperialism occurred in southwest Asia (Map 29.1). There the British and the French successfully encouraged an Arab revolt in 1916 and destroyed the Ottoman Empire. Europeans then sought to replace Turks as principal rulers throughout the region. Turkish, Arab, and Persian nationalists, as well as Jewish nationalists arriving from Europe, reacted violently. They struggled to win nationhood, and as the Europeans were forced to make concessions, they sometimes came into sharp conflict with each other, most notably in Palestine.

CHAPTER LOCATOR | Why did modern nationalism develop in Asia between the First and Second World Wars, and what was its appeal? | **How did the Ottoman Empire's collapse in World War I shape nationalist movements in the Middle East?**

CHAPTER 29
888 NATIONALISM IN ASIA

MAP 29.1 ■ The Partition of the Ottoman Empire, 1914–1923

By 1914 the Ottoman Turks had been pushed out of the Balkans, and their Arab provinces were on the edge of revolt. That revolt erupted in the First World War and contributed greatly to the Ottomans' defeat. When the Allies then attempted to implement their plans, including independence for the Armenian people, Mustafa Kemal arose to forge in battle the modern Turkish state.

> **MAPPING THE PAST**

ANALYZING THE MAP: What new countries were established as a result of the partition of the Ottoman Empire? Where were mandates established? What might you conclude about European views of the Middle East based on how Europe divided up the region?

CONNECTIONS: How might the collapse of the Ottoman Empire in World War I have contributed to the current situation in the Middle East?

What role did Gandhi and his campaign of militant nonviolence play in leading India to independence from the British?

How did nationalism shape political developments in East and Southeast Asia?

✓ LearningCurve
Check what you know.

The Arab Revolt

Long subject to European pressure, the Ottoman Empire failed to reform and modernize in the late nineteenth century (see pages 765–767). Declining international stature and domestic tyranny led to revolutionary activity among idealistic exiles and young army officers who wanted to seize power and save the Ottoman state. These patriots, the so-called Young Turks, succeeded in the 1908 revolution, and subsequently they were determined to hold together the remnants of the vast multi-ethnic empire. Defeated in the Balkan war of 1912 and stripped of practically all territory in Europe, the Young Turks redoubled their efforts in southwest Asia. The most important of their possessions were Syria—consisting of modern-day Lebanon, Syria, Israel, the West Bank, the Gaza Strip, and Jordan—and Iraq. The Ottoman Turks also claimed the Arabian peninsula but exercised only loose control there.

For centuries the largely Arab populations of Syria and Iraq had been tied to their Ottoman rulers by their common faith in Islam (though there were Christian Arabs as well). Yet beneath the surface, ethnic and linguistic tensions simmered between Turks and Arabs.

Young Turk actions after 1908 made the embryonic "Arab movement" a reality. The majority of Young Turks promoted a narrow Turkish nationalism. They further centralized the Ottoman Empire and extended the sway of Turkish language and culture. In 1909 the Turkish government brutally slaughtered thou-

The Armenian Atrocities

When in 1915 some Armenians welcomed Russian armies as liberators after years of persecution, the Ottoman government ordered a genocidal mass deportation of its Armenian citizens from their homeland in the empire's eastern provinces. American ambassador to Constantinople Henry Morgenthau included this photo in his 1918 autobiography, *Ambassador Morganthau's Story*, with this caption: "Scenes like this were common all over the Armenian provinces in the spring and summer months of 1915. Death in its several forms — massacres, starvation, exhaustion — destroyed the larger part of the refugees. The Turkish policy was that of extermination under the guise of deportation." (© Bettmann/Corbis)

CHAPTER LOCATOR | Why did modern nationalism develop in Asia between the First and Second World Wars, and what was its appeal? | How did the Ottoman Empire's collapse in World War I shape nationalist movements in the Middle East?

CHAPTER 29
890 NATIONALISM IN ASIA

sands of Armenian Christians, a prelude to the wholesale massacre of more than a million Armenians during the First World War. Meanwhile, Arab discontent grew.

During World War I the Turks aligned themselves with Germany and Austria-Hungary (see page 852). As a result, the Young Turks drew all of the Middle East into what had been up to that point a European war. Arabs opposed to Ottoman rule found themselves allied with the British, who encouraged the alliance with vague promises of an independent Arab kingdom. After British victories on the Arab peninsula in 1917 and 1918, many Arab patriots expected a large, unified Arab state to rise from the dust of the Ottoman collapse. Within two years, however, Arab nationalists felt bitterly betrayed by Great Britain and its allies.

Arab bitterness was partly directed at secret wartime treaties between Britain and France to divide and rule the old Ottoman Empire. In the 1916 Sykes-Picot Agreement, Britain and France secretly agreed that France would receive modern-day Lebanon, Syria, and much of southern Turkey, and Britain would receive Palestine, Jordan, and Iraq. The Sykes-Picot Agreement contradicted British promises concerning Arab independence after the war and left Arab nationalists feeling cheated and betrayed.

A related source of Arab frustration was Britain's wartime commitment to a Jewish homeland in Palestine. The Balfour Declaration of November 1917, made by the British foreign secretary Arthur Balfour, offered British support for the idea of a Jewish homeland in Palestine. Some British Cabinet members believed the Balfour Declaration would appeal to German, Austrian, and American Jews and thus help the British war effort. Others sincerely supported the Zionist vision of a Jewish homeland (see page 894), but also believed that Jews living in this homeland would be grateful to Britain and thus help maintain British control of the Suez Canal.

In 1914 Jews made up about 11 percent of the predominantly Arab population in the Ottoman territory that became, under British control, Palestine. The "national home for the Jewish People" mentioned in the Balfour Declaration implied to the Arabs — and to the Zionist Jews as well — some kind of Jewish state that would be incompatible with majority rule.

After failed efforts at the Paris Peace Conference to secure Arab independence, Arab nationalists met in Damascus at the General Syrian Congress in 1919 and unsuccessfully called again for political independence. Ignoring Arab opposition, the British mandate in Palestine formally incorporated the Balfour Declaration and its commitment to a Jewish national home. In March 1920 the Syrian National Congress proclaimed Syria independent, with Faisal bin Hussein as king. A similar congress declared Iraq an independent kingdom.

Western reaction to events in Syria and Iraq was swift and decisive. A French army stationed in Lebanon attacked Syria, taking Damascus in July 1920. Faisal fled, and the French took over. Meanwhile, the British put down an uprising in Iraq and established effective control there. Western imperialism appeared to have replaced Turkish rule in the Middle East (see Map 29.1).

The Turkish Revolution

Days after the end of the First World War, French and then British troops entered Constantinople to begin a five-year occupation of the Ottoman capital. A treaty forced on the helpless sultan dismembered Turkey and reduced it to a puppet

Sykes-Picot Agreement

▶ The 1916 secret agreement between Britain and France that divided up the Arab lands of Lebanon, Syria, southern Turkey, Palestine, Jordan, and Iraq.

Balfour Declaration

▶ A 1917 statement by British foreign secretary Arthur Balfour that supported the idea of a Jewish homeland in Palestine.

What role did Gandhi and his campaign of militant nonviolence play in leading India to independence from the British?

How did nationalism shape political developments in East and Southeast Asia?

☑ LearningCurve
Check what you know.

891

state. Great Britain and France occupied parts of Turkey, and Italy and Greece claimed shares as well. In 1919 Greek armies carried by British ships landed on the Turkish coast at Smyrna and advanced into the interior. Turkey seemed finished.

But Turkey produced a great leader and revived to become an inspiration to the entire Middle East. Mustafa Kemal (1881–1938), considered the father of modern Turkey, was a military man sympathetic to the Young Turk movement. After the armistice, he watched with anguish the Allies' aggression and the sultan's cowardice. In early 1919 he began working to unify Turkish resistance.

The sultan, bowing to Allied pressure, initially denounced Kemal, but the cause of national liberation proved more powerful. The catalyst was the Greek invasion and attempted annexation of much of western Turkey.

Refusing to acknowledge the Allied dismemberment of their country, the Turks battled on through 1920 despite staggering defeats. The next year the Greeks advanced almost to Ankara, the nationalist stronghold in central Turkey. There Mustafa Kemal's forces took the offensive and won a great victory. The Greeks and their British allies sued for peace. The resulting Treaty of Lausanne (1923) recognized a truly independent Turkey (see Map 29.1).

Mustafa Kemal believed Turkey should modernize and secularize along Western lines. His first moves, beginning in 1923, were political. Kemal called on the National Assembly to depose the sultan and establish a republic and had himself elected president. Kemal savagely crushed the demands for independence of ethnic minorities within Turkey like the Armenians and the Kurds, but he realistically abandoned all thought of winning back lost Arab territories. He then created a one-party system in order to work his will.

Kemal's most radical changes pertained to religion and culture. Profoundly influenced by the example of western Europe, Mustafa Kemal set out to limit religious influence in daily affairs. Kemal decreed a revolutionary separation of church and state. Secular law codes inspired by European models replaced religious courts. State schools replaced religious schools and taught such secular subjects as science, mathematics, and social sciences.

Mustafa Kemal also struck down many entrenched patterns of behavior. Women, traditionally secluded and inferior to males in Islamic society, received the right to vote. Civil law on a European model, rather than the Islamic code, now governed marriage. Women could seek divorces, and no man could have more than one wife at a time. Men were forbidden to wear the tall red fez of the Ottoman era. The old Arabic script was replaced with a new Turkish alphabet based on Roman letters, which facilitated massive government efforts to spread literacy after 1928. Finally, in 1935, surnames on the European model were introduced. The National Assembly granted Mustafa Kemal the surname Atatürk, which means "father of the Turks."

By his death in 1938, Atatürk and his supporters had consolidated their revolution. Government-sponsored industrialization was fostering urban growth and new attitudes, encouraging Turks to embrace business and science. Poverty persisted in rural areas, as did some religious discontent among devout Muslims. But like the Japanese after the Meiji Restoration, the Turkish people had rallied around the nationalist banner to repulse European imperialism and were building a modern secular nation-state.

Treaty of Lausanne
▶ The 1923 treaty that ended the Turkish war and recognized the territorial integrity of a truly independent Turkey.

CHAPTER LOCATOR | Why did modern nationalism develop in Asia between the First and Second World Wars, and what was its appeal? | How did the Ottoman Empire's collapse in World War I shape nationalist movements in the Middle East?

892 CHAPTER 29 NATIONALISM IN ASIA

Modernization Efforts in Persia and Afghanistan

In Persia (renamed Iran in 1935) strong-arm efforts to build a unified modern nation ultimately proved less successful than in Turkey. In the late nineteenth century Persia had also been subject to extreme foreign pressure, which stimulated efforts to reform the government as a means of reviving Islamic civilization. In 1906 a nationalistic coalition of merchants, religious leaders, and intellectuals revolted. The despotic shah was forced to grant a constitution and establish a national assembly, the Majlis.

Yet the 1906 Persian revolution was doomed to failure, largely because of European imperialism. In 1907 Britain and Russia divided the country into spheres of influence. Britain's sphere ran along the Persian Gulf; the Russian sphere encompassed the whole northern half of Persia (see Map 29.1). Thereafter Russia intervened constantly. It blocked reforms, occupied cities, and completely dominated the country by 1912. When Russian power collapsed in the Bolshevik Revolution, British armies rushed into the power vacuum. By bribing corrupt Persians, Great Britain in 1919 negotiated a treaty allowing the installation of British "advisers" in every government department.

The Majlis refused to ratify the treaty, and the blatant attempt to make Persia a British satellite aroused the national spirit. In 1921 reaction against the British brought to power a military dictator, Reza Shah Pahlavi (1877–1944), who proclaimed himself shah in 1925 and ruled until 1941.

Inspired by Turkey's Mustafa Kemal, Reza Shah had three basic goals: to build a modern nation, to free Persia from foreign domination, and to rule with an iron fist. The challenge was enormous. Persia was a vast, undeveloped country. The rural population was mostly poor and illiterate, and among the Persian majority were sizable ethnic minorities with their own aspirations. Furthermore, Iran's powerful religious leaders hated Western (Christian) domination but were equally opposed to a more secular, less Islamic society.

To realize his vision of a strong Persia, the shah created a modern army, built railroads, and encouraged commerce. He won control over ethnic minorities such as the Kurds in the north and Arab tribesmen on the Iraqi border. He reduced the privileges granted to foreigners and raised taxes on the powerful Anglo-Persian Oil Company. Yet Reza Shah was less successful than Atatürk.

Because the European-educated elite in Persia was smaller than the comparable group in Turkey, the idea of re-creating Persian greatness on the basis of a secularized society attracted relatively few determined supporters. Many powerful religious leaders turned against Reza Shah, and he became increasingly brutal, greedy, and tyrannical.

Afghanistan, meanwhile, was nominally independent in the nineteenth century, but the British imposed political restrictions and constantly meddled in the country's affairs. In 1919 emir Amanullah Khan (1892–1960) declared war on the British government in India and won complete independence for the first time. Amanullah then decreed revolutionary modernizing reforms designed to hurl his primitive country into the twentieth century. Amanullah pushed too hard and too fast, however, and the result was tribal and religious revolt, civil war, and retreat from reform. Islam remained both religion and law. A powerful but

Majlis

▶ The national assembly established by the despotic shah of Iran in 1906.

Afghanistan Under Amanullah Khan

What role did Gandhi and his campaign of militant nonviolence play in leading India to independence from the British?

How did nationalism shape political developments in East and Southeast Asia?

✓ LearningCurve
Check what you know.

primitive patriotism enabled Afghanistan to win political independence from the West, but not to build a modern society.

Gradual Independence in the Arab States

French and British mandates forced Arab nationalists to seek independence by gradual means after 1920. Arab nationalists were indirectly aided by Western tax-payers who wanted cheap—that is, peaceful—empires. As a result, Arabs won considerable control over local affairs in the mandated states, except Palestine, though the mandates remained European satellites in international and economic affairs.

In Iraq the British chose Faisal bin Hussein, whom the French had deposed in Syria, as king. Faisal obligingly gave British advisers broad behind-the-scenes control. The king also accepted British ownership of Iraq's oil fields. Given the severe limitations imposed on him, Faisal (r. 1921–1933) proved to be an able ruler, gaining his peoples' support and encouraging moderate reforms. In 1932 he secured Iraqi independence at the price of a restrictive long-term military alliance with Great Britain.

Egypt had been occupied by Great Britain since 1882 (see page 767) and had been a British protectorate since 1914. Following intense nationalist agitation after the Great War, Great Britain in 1922 proclaimed Egypt formally independent but continued to occupy the country militarily and control its politics. In 1936 the British agreed to restrict their troops to their bases in the Suez Canal Zone.

The French compromised less in their handling of their mandated Middle East territories. Following the Ottoman Empire's collapse after World War I, the French designated Lebanon as one of several ethnic enclaves within a larger area that became part of the French mandate of Syria. They practiced a policy of divide and rule and generally played off ethnic and religious minorities against each other. In 1926 Lebanon became a separate republic but remained under the control of the French mandate. Arab nationalists in Syria finally won promises of Syrian independence in 1936 in return for a friendship treaty with France.

In short, the Arab states gradually freed themselves from Western political mandates but not from Western military threats or from pervasive Western influence. Since large Arab landowners and urban merchants increased their wealth and political power after 1918, they often supported the Western hegemony. Radical nationalists, on the other hand, recognized that Western control of the newly discovered Arab oil fields was proof that economic independence and genuine freedom had not yet been achieved.

Arab-Jewish Tensions in Palestine

Relations between the Arabs and the West were complicated by the tense situation in the British mandate of Palestine, and that situation deteriorated in the interwar years. Both Arabs and Jews denounced the British, who tried unsuccessfully to compromise with both sides. Arab nationalist anger, however, was aimed primarily at Jewish settlers. The key issue was Jewish migration from Europe to Palestine.

Jewish nationalism, known as Zionism, took shape in Europe in the late nineteenth century. The Zionist movement encouraged some of the world's Jews to settle in Palestine, but until 1921 the great majority of Jewish emigrants preferred the United States.

After 1921 the situation changed radically. An isolationist United States drastically limited immigration from eastern Europe, where war and revolution had kindled anti-Semitism. Moreover, the British began honoring the Balfour Declaration despite Arab protests. Thus Jewish immigration to Palestine from turbulent Europe in the interwar years grew rapidly, particularly after Adolf Hitler became German chancellor in 1933. By 1939 Palestine's Jewish population had increased almost fivefold since 1914 and accounted for about 30 percent of all inhabitants.

Jewish settlers in Palestine faced formidable difficulties. Although much of the land purchased by the Jewish National Fund was productive, the sellers of such land were often wealthy absentee Arab landowners who cared little for their Arab tenants' welfare. When the Jewish settlers replaced those long-time Arab tenants, Arab farmers and intellectuals burned with a sense of injustice. Moreover, most Jewish immigrants came from urban backgrounds and preferred to establish new cities like Tel Aviv or to live in existing towns, where they competed with the Arabs. The land issue combined with economic and cultural friction to harden Arab protest into hatred.

The British gradually responded to Arab pressure and tried to slow Jewish immigration. This effort satisfied neither Jews nor Arabs, and by 1938 the two communities were engaged in an undeclared civil war.

On the eve of the Second World War, the frustrated British proposed an independent Palestine with the number of Jews permanently limited to only about one-third of the total population. Zionists felt themselves in grave danger of losing their dream of an independent Jewish state.

Nevertheless, in the face of adversity Jewish settlers gradually succeeded in forging a cohesive community in Palestine. Hebrew, for centuries used only in religious worship, was revived as a living language in the 1920s–1930s to bind the Jews in Palestine together. Despite its slow beginnings, rural development achieved often remarkable results. The key unit of agricultural organization was the **kibbutz** (kih-BOOTS), a collective farm on which each member shared equally in the work, rewards, and defense. An egalitarian socialist ideology also characterized industry, which grew rapidly. By 1939 a new but old nation was emerging in the Middle East.

kibbutz
▶ A Jewish collective farm on which each member shared equally in the work, rewards, and defense.

QUICK REVIEW

What kind of state did Mustafa Kemal build in Turkey? How did his accomplishments serve as a model for other nationalist leaders in the Middle East?

What role did Gandhi and his campaign of militant nonviolence play in leading India to independence from the British?

How did nationalism shape political developments in East and Southeast Asia?

✓ LearningCurve
Check what you know.

What role did Gandhi and his campaign of militant nonviolence play in leading India to independence from the British?

Gandhi on the Salt March, June 1930

A small, frail man, Gandhi possessed enormous courage and determination. His campaign of nonviolent resistance to British rule inspired the Indian masses and mobilized a nation. Here he is shown walking on his famous march to the sea to protest the English-Indian government's monopoly on salt production. (akg-images)

THE NATIONALIST MOVEMENT IN BRITISH INDIA grew out of two interconnected cultures, Hindu and Muslim. While the two joined together to challenge British rule, they also came to see themselves as fundamentally different. Nowhere has modern nationalism's power both to unify and to divide been more strikingly demonstrated than in India.

British Promises and Repression

When the First World War began, the British feared an Indian revolt. Instead Indians supported the war effort. About 1.2 million Indian soldiers and laborers voluntarily served in Europe, Africa, and the Middle East. The British government in India and the native Indian princes sent large supplies of food, money, and ammunition. In return, the British opened more good government jobs to Indians and made other minor concessions.

CHAPTER LOCATOR | Why did modern nationalism develop in Asia between the First and Second World Wars, and what was its appeal? | How did the Ottoman Empire's collapse in World War I shape nationalist movements in the Middle East?

As the war in distant Europe ground on, however, inflation, high taxes, food shortages, and a terrible influenza epidemic created widespread suffering and discontent. The prewar nationalist movement revived stronger than ever, and moderates and radicals in the Indian National Congress Party (see page 784) joined forces. Moreover, in 1916 Hindu leaders in the Congress Party hammered out an alliance—the **Lucknow Pact**—with India's Muslim League. The Lucknow Pact forged a powerful united front of Hindus and Muslims and called for putting India on equal footing with self-governing British dominions like Canada, Australia, and New Zealand.

The British response to the Lucknow Pact was mixed. In August 1917 the British called for the development of self-governing institutions in India, but the proposed self-government was much more limited than that granted the British dominions. In late 1919 the British established a dual administration: part Indian and elected, part British and authoritarian. Sensitive matters like taxes, police, and the courts remained solely in British hands.

Old-fashioned authoritarian rule also seriously undermined whatever positive impact this reform might have had. The 1919 Rowlatt Acts indefinitely extended wartime "emergency measures" designed to curb unrest and root out "conspiracy." The result was a wave of rioting across India.

Under these tense conditions a crowd of some ten thousand gathered to celebrate a Sikh religious festival in an enclosed square in the Sikh holy city of Amritsar in the northern Punjab province. Unknown to the crowd, the local English

Lucknow Pact

▶ A 1916 alliance between the Hindus leading the Indian National Congress and the Muslim League.

British Man Fishing in India

British colonial officials, such as this gentleman reposing in a wicker chair while fishing in India around 1925, enjoyed lifestyles that were often much more comfortable than would have been the case back in England. Gardeners, chauffeurs, maids, cooks, and other personal servants, like the three men helping the fisher, were commonly hired to wait on the colonists hand and foot. Some justified the lifestyle as demonstrating the refinements of civilization — part of the white man's burden. (Photograph by Ralph Ponsonby Watts/© Mary Evans Picture Library/The Images Works)

What role did Gandhi and his campaign of militant nonviolence play in leading India to independence from the British?

How did nationalism shape political developments in East and Southeast Asia?

☑ LearningCurve
Check what you know.

commander, General Reginald Dyer, had banned all public meetings that very day. Dyer marched his troops into the square and, without warning, ordered them to fire into the crowd until the ammunition ran out. Official British records of the Amritsar Massacre list 379 killed and 1,137 wounded, but these figures remain hotly contested as being too low. Tensions flared, and India stood on the verge of more violence and repression. That India took a different path to national liberation was due largely to Mohandas K. Gandhi (1869–1948), the most influential Indian leader of modern times.

The Roots of Militant Nonviolence

Gandhi grew up in a well-to-do family, and after his father's death, he went to study law in England, where he passed the English bar. Upon returning to India, he decided in 1893 to try a case for some wealthy Indian merchants in the British colony of Natal (part of modern South Africa).

In Natal Gandhi took up the plight of the expatriate Indian community. White plantation owners had been importing thousands of poor Indians as indentured laborers since the 1860s. Some of these Indians, after completing their period of indenture, remained in Natal as free persons and economic competitors. In response, the Afrikaner (of Dutch descent) and British settlers passed brutally discriminatory laws. Poor Indians had to work on plantations or return to India. Rich Indians, who had previously had the vote in Natal, lost that right in 1896. Gandhi undertook his countrymen's legal defense.

Meanwhile, Gandhi was searching for a spiritual theory of social action. He studied Hindu and Christian teachings and gradually developed a weapon for the poor and oppressed that he called satyagraha (suh-TYAH-gruh-huh). Gandhi conceived of satyagraha, loosely translated as "soul force," as a means of striving for truth and social justice through love and a willingness to suffer the oppressor's blows, while trying to convert him or her to one's views of what is true and just. Its tactic was active nonviolent resistance.

When South Africa's white government severely restricted Asian immigration and internal freedom of movement, Gandhi put his philosophy into action and organized a nonviolent mass resistance campaign. Thousands of Indian men and women marched in peaceful protest and withstood beatings, arrest, and imprisonment.

In 1914 South Africa's exasperated whites agreed to many of the Indians' demands. They passed a law abolishing discriminatory taxes on Indian traders, recognized the legality of non-Christian marriages, and permitted the continued immigration of free Indians.

Gandhi's Resistance Campaign in India

In 1915 Gandhi returned to India a hero. The masses hailed him as a mahatma, or "great soul"—a Hindu title of veneration for a man of great knowledge and humanity. In 1920 Gandhi launched a national campaign of nonviolent resistance to British rule. He urged his countrymen to boycott British goods, jobs, and honors and told peasants not to pay taxes.

The nationalist movement had previously touched only the tiny, prosperous, Western-educated elite. Now both the illiterate masses of village India and the

satyagraha
▶ Loosely translated as "soul force," which Gandhi believed was the means of striving for truth and social justice through love, suffering, and conversion of the oppressor.

CHAPTER LOCATOR | Why did modern nationalism develop in Asia between the First and Second World Wars, and what was its appeal? | How did the Ottoman Empire's collapse in World War I shape nationalist movements in the Middle East?

898 CHAPTER 29 NATIONALISM IN ASIA

educated classes heard Gandhi's call for militant nonviolent resistance. It particularly appealed to the masses of Hindus who were not members of the warrior caste or the so-called military races and who were traditionally passive and nonviolent. The British had regarded ordinary Hindus as cowards. Gandhi told them that they could be courageous and even morally superior. Under Gandhi's leadership, the Indian National Congress became a mass political party, welcoming members from every ethnic group and cooperating closely with the Muslim minority.

In 1922 some Indian resisters turned to violence, murdering twenty-two policemen. Savage riots broke out, and Gandhi abruptly called off his campaign. Arrested for fomenting rebellion, Gandhi served two years in prison. Upon his release Gandhi set up a commune, established a national newspaper, and set out to reform Indian society and improve the lot of the poor. For Gandhi moral improvement, social progress, and the national movement went hand in hand. Above all, Gandhi nurtured national identity and self-respect.

During Gandhi's time in prison the Indian National Congress had splintered into various factions, and Gandhi spent the years after his release quietly trying to reunite the organization. In 1929 the radical nationalists, led by Jawaharlal Nehru (1889–1964), pushed through the National Congress a resolution calling for virtual independence within a year. The British stiffened in their resolve against Indian independence, and Indian radicals talked of a bloody showdown.

Into this tense situation Gandhi masterfully reasserted his leadership, taking a hard line toward the British but insisting on nonviolent methods. He organized a massive resistance campaign against the tax on salt. From March 12 to April 6, 1930, Gandhi led fifty thousand people in a spectacular march to the sea, where he made salt in defiance of the law. A later demonstration at the British-run Dharasana salt works resulted in many of the 2,500 nonviolent marchers being beaten senseless by policemen in a brutal and well-publicized encounter. Over the next months the British arrested Gandhi and sixty thousand other protesters for making and distributing salt. But the protests continued, and in 1931 the frustrated and unnerved British released Gandhi from jail and sat down to negotiate with him over Indian self-rule. Negotiations resulted in a new constitution, the Government of India Act, in 1935, which greatly strengthened India's parliamentary representative institutions and gave Indians some voice in the administration of British India.

India, ca. 1930

Despite his best efforts, Gandhi failed to heal a widening split between Hindus and Muslims. Indian nationalism, based largely on Hindu symbols and customs, increasingly disturbed the Muslim minority. Tempers mounted, and both sides committed atrocities. By the late 1930s Muslim League leaders were calling for the creation of a Muslim nation in British India, a "Pakistan," or "land of the pure." As in Palestine, the rise of conflicting nationalisms in India based on religion would lead to tragedy (see pages 962–963).

QUICK REVIEW

Why did the British find it so difficult to suppress the Indian independence movement?

What role did Gandhi and his campaign of militant nonviolence play in leading India to independence from the British?	How did nationalism shape political developments in East and Southeast Asia?	LearningCurve Check what you know.

How did nationalism shape political developments in East and Southeast Asia?

The Fate of a Chinese Patriot

On May 30, 1925, Shanghai police opened fire on a group of Chinese demonstrators who were protesting unfair labor practices and wages and the foreign imperialist presence in their country. The police killed nine people and wounded many others, touching off nationwide and international protests and attacks on foreign offices and businesses. This political cartoon shows the fate of the Chinese patriots at the hands of warlords and foreign imperialists. (© Library of Congress, LC-USZ62-99451)

> PICTURING THE PAST

ANALYZING THE IMAGE: Which figures represent Chinese warlords, foreign imperialists, and Chinese patriots? What does the cartoon suggest about the fate of the Chinese demonstrators? What emotions are these images trying to evoke in the person viewing the cartoon?

CONNECTIONS: Why might foreign imperialists and Chinese warlords work together to put down the demonstrations?

BECAUSE OF THE EFFORTS OF THE MEIJI REFORMERS, nationalism and modernization were well developed in Japan by 1914 (see pages 796–797). Initially China lagged behind, but after 1912 the pace of nationalist development began to quicken.

In the 1920s the Chinese nationalist movement managed to reduce the power and influence both of the warlords who controlled large territories in the interior and of the imperialist West. These achievements were soon undermined, how-

CHAPTER LOCATOR | Why did modern nationalism develop in Asia between the First and Second World Wars, and what was its appeal? | How did the Ottoman Empire's collapse in World War I shape nationalist movements in the Middle East?

900 CHAPTER 29
NATIONALISM IN ASIA

ever, by an internal civil war followed by war with an expanding Japan. Nationalism also flourished elsewhere in Asia, scoring a major victory in the Philippines.

The Rise of Nationalist China

The 1911 Revolution led by Sun Yatsen (1866–1925) overthrew the Qing Dynasty, ending imperial rule in China. Sun Yatsen proclaimed China a republic and thereby opened an era of unprecedented change for Chinese society. In 1912 Sun Yatsen turned over leadership of the republican government to the other central figure in the revolution, Yuan Shigai (Yüan Shih-k'ai). Called out of retirement to save the dynasty, Yuan (1859–1916) betrayed the Qing Dynasty's Manchu leaders and convinced the revolutionaries that he could unite the country peacefully and prevent foreign intervention. Once elected president of the republic, however, Yuan concentrated on building his own power. In 1913 he used military force to dissolve China's parliament and ruled as a dictator. China's first modern revolution had failed.

The extent of the failure became apparent only after Yuan's death in 1916, when the central government in Beijing almost disintegrated. For more than a decade thereafter, power resided in a multitude of local military leaders, the so-called warlords. Their wars, taxes, and corruption created terrible suffering.

Foreign imperialism intensified the agony of warlordism. Japan's expansion into Shandong and southern Manchuria during World War I (see page 852) angered China's growing middle class and enraged China's young patriots (see Map 29.2, page 907). On May 4, 1919, five thousand students in Beijing exploded against the decision of the Paris Peace Conference to leave the Shandong Peninsula in Japanese hands. This famous incident launched the May Fourth Movement, which opposed both foreign domination and warlord government.

The May Fourth Movement, which was both strongly pro-Marxist and passionately anti-imperialist, looked to the October 1917 Bolshevik Revolution in Russia as a model for its own nationalist revolution. In 1923 Sun Yatsen decided to ally his Nationalist Party, or Guomindang, with Lenin's Communist Third International and the newly formed Chinese Communist Party. The result was the first of many so-called national liberation fronts.

Sun, however, was no Communist. In his *Three Principles of the People*, elaborating on the official Nationalist Party ideology — nationalism, democracy, and people's livelihood — nationalism remained of prime importance. Democracy, in contrast, had a less exalted meaning. Sun equated it with firm rule by the Nationalists, who would improve people's lives through land reform and welfare measures.

Sun planned to use the Nationalist Party's revolutionary army to crush the warlords and reunite China under a strong central government. When Sun unexpectedly died in 1925, Jiang Jieshi (traditionally called Chiang Kai-shek) (1887–1975) took his place. In 1926 and 1927 Jiang led Nationalist armies in a successful attack on warlord governments in central and northern China. In 1928 the Nationalists established a new capital at Nanjing.

In fact, national unification was only skin-deep. China remained a vast agricultural country plagued by foreign concessions, regional differences, and a lack of modern communications. Moreover, the uneasy alliance between the Nationalist Party and the Chinese Communist Party had turned into a bitter, deadly rivalry.

May Fourth Movement
▶ A Chinese nationalist movement against foreign imperialists; it began as a student protest against the decision of the Paris Peace Conference to leave the Shandong Peninsula in the hands of Japan.

What role did Gandhi and his campaign of militant nonviolence play in leading India to independence from the British?

How did nationalism shape political developments in East and Southeast Asia?

LearningCurve
Check what you know.

Fearful of Communist subversion of the Nationalist government, Jiang decided in April 1927 to liquidate his left-wing "allies" in a bloody purge. Chinese Communists went into hiding and vowed revenge.

China's Intellectual Revolution

Nationalism was the most powerful idea in China between 1911 and 1929, but it was only one aspect of a complex intellectual revolution, generally known as the **New Culture Movement**. The New Culture Movement was founded around 1916 by young Western-oriented intellectuals in Beijing. These intellectuals attacked Confucian ethics, which subordinated subjects to rulers, sons to fathers, and wives to husbands. As modernists, they advocated new and anti-Confucian virtues: individualism, democratic equality, and the critical scientific method. They also promoted the use of simple, understandable written language as a means to clear thinking and mass education. China, they said, needed a whole new culture, a radically different worldview.

New Culture Movement

▶ An intellectual revolution, sometimes called the Chinese Renaissance, that attacked traditional Chinese, particularly Confucian, culture and promoted Western ideas of science, democracy, and individualism, from around 1916 to 1923.

Many intellectuals thought the radical worldview China needed was Marxist socialism. Though undeniably Western, Marxism provided a means of criticizing Western dominance, thereby salving Chinese pride. Chinese Communists could blame China's pitiful weakness on rapacious foreign capitalistic imperialism. Thus Marxism, as modified by Lenin and applied by the Bolsheviks in the Soviet Union, appeared as a means of catching up with the hated but envied West. For Chinese believers, it promised salvation soon.

Chinese Communists could and did interpret Marxism-Leninism to appeal to the masses—the peasants. Mao Zedong (Mao Tse-tung) in particular quickly recognized the impoverished Chinese peasantry's enormous revolutionary potential. Mao's (1893–1976) first experiment in peasant revolt—the Autumn Harvest Uprising of September 1927—was not successful, but Mao learned quickly. He advocated equal distribution of land and broke up his forces into small guerrilla groups. After 1928 he and his supporters built up a self-governing Communist soviet, centered at Ruijin (Juichin) in southeastern China, and dug in against Nationalist attacks.

China's intellectual revolution also stimulated profound changes in popular culture and family life. After the 1911 Revolution Chinese women enjoyed increasingly greater freedom and equality and gradually gained unprecedented educational and economic opportunities. Thus rising nationalism and the intellectual revolution interacted with monumental changes in Chinese family life. (See "Individuals in Society: Ning Lao, a Chinese Working Woman," page 904.)

From Liberalism to Ultranationalism in Japan

The Meiji reformers' spectacular success deeply impressed Japan's fellow Asians. The Japanese, alone among Asia's peoples, had mastered modern industrial technology by 1910 and had fought victorious wars against both China and Russia. The First World War brought more triumphs. In 1915 Japan seized Germany's Asian holdings and retained most of them as League of Nations mandates. The Japanese economy expanded enormously. Profits soared as Japan won new markets that wartime Europe could no longer supply.

In the early 1920s Japan made further progress on all fronts. In 1922 Japan signed a naval arms limitation treaty with the Western powers and returned some of its control over the Shandong Peninsula to China. These conciliatory moves reduced tensions in East Asia. At home Japan seemed headed toward genuine democracy. The electorate expanded twelvefold between 1918 and 1925 as all males over twenty-five won the vote. Two-party competition was intense. Japanese living standards were the highest in Asia. Literacy was universal.

Japan's remarkable rise was accompanied by serious problems. Japan had a rapidly growing population but scarce natural resources. As early as the 1920s Japan was exporting manufactured goods in order to pay for imports of food and essential raw materials. Deeply enmeshed in world trade, Japan was vulnerable to every boom and bust. These economic realities broadened support for Japan's colonial empire. Before World War I Japanese leaders saw colonial expansion primarily in terms of international prestige and national defense. Now, in the 1920s, Japan's colonies also seemed essential for markets, raw materials, and economic growth.

Japan's rapid industrial development also created an imbalanced "dualistic" economy. The modern sector consisted of a handful of giant conglomerate firms, the **zaibatsu**, or "financial combines." Zaibatsu firms wielded enormous economic power and dominated the other sector of the economy, an unorganized multitude of peasant farmers and craftsmen. The result was financial oligarchy, corruption of government officials, and a weak middle class.

zaibatsu
▶ Giant conglomerate firms in Japan.

Behind the façade of party politics, Japanese elites jockeyed savagely for power. Cohesive leadership, which had played such an important role in Japan's modernization by the Meiji reformers, had ceased to exist. By far the most serious challenge to peaceful progress was fanatical nationalism. As in Europe, ultranationalism first emerged in Japan in the late nineteenth century but did not flower fully until the First World War and the 1930s.

Though their views were often vague, Japan's ultranationalists shared several fundamental beliefs. They were violently anti-Western. They rejected

What role did Gandhi and his campaign of militant nonviolence play in leading India to independence from the British?

How did nationalism shape political developments in East and Southeast Asia?

✓ LearningCurve
Check what you know.

Ning Lao, a Chinese Working Woman

The voice of the poor and uneducated is often muffled in history. Thus *A Daughter of Han*, a rare autobiography of an illiterate working woman as told to an American friend, Ida Pruitt, offers unforgettable insights into the evolution of ordinary Chinese life and family relations.

Ning Lao was born in 1867 to poor parents in the northern city of Penglai on the Shandong Peninsula. Her foot binding was delayed to age nine, since she "loved so much to run and play." She described the pain when the bandages were finally drawn tight: "My feet hurt so much that for two years I had to crawl on my knees."* Her arranged marriage at age fourteen was a disaster. She found that her husband was a drug addict ("in those days everyone took opium to some extent") who sold everything to pay for his habit. Yet "there was no freedom then for women," and "it was no light thing for a woman to leave her house" and husband. Thus Ning Lao endured her situation until her husband sold their four-year-old daughter to buy opium. Taking her remaining baby daughter, she fled.

Taking off her foot bandages, Ning Lao became a beggar. Her feet began to spread, quite improperly, but she walked without pain. And the beggar's life was "not the hardest one," she thought, for a beggar woman could go where she pleased. To better care for her child, Ning Lao became a servant and a cook in prosperous households. Some of her mistresses were concubines (secondary wives taken by rich men in middle age), and she concluded that concubinage resulted in nothing but quarrels and heartache. Hot

The tough and resilient Ning Lao (right) with Ida Pruitt.
(Reproduced with permission of Eileen Hsu-Balzer)

tempered and quick to take offense and leave an employer, the hard-working woman always found a new job quickly. In time she became a peddler of luxury goods to wealthy women confined to their homes.

The two unshakable values that buoyed Ning Lao were a tough, fatalistic acceptance of life — "Only fortune that comes of itself will come. There is no use to seek for it" — and devotion to her family. She eventually returned to her husband, who had mellowed, seldom took opium, and was "good" in those years. She reflected, "But I did not miss him when he died. I had my newborn son and I was happy. My house was established. . . . Truly all my life I spent thinking of my family." Her lifelong devotion was reciprocated by her son and granddaughter, who cared for her well in her old age.

Ning Lao's remarkable life story encompasses both old and new Chinese attitudes toward family life. Her son moved to the capital city of Beijing, worked in an office, and had only one wife. Her granddaughter, Su Teh, studied in missionary schools and became a college teacher and a determined foe of arranged marriages. She personified the trend toward greater freedom for Chinese women.

Generational differences also highlighted changing political attitudes. When the Japanese invaded China and occupied Beijing in 1937, Ning Lao thought that "perhaps the Mandate of Heaven had passed to the Japanese . . . and we should listen to them as our new masters." Her nationalistic granddaughter disagreed. She urged resistance and the creation of a new China, where the people governed themselves. Leaving to join the guerrillas in 1938, Su Teh gave her savings to her family and promised to continue to help them. One must be good to one's family, she said, but one must also work for the country.

*Ida Pruitt, *A Daughter of Han: The Autobiography of a Chinese Working Woman* (New Haven, Conn.: Yale University Press, 1945), p. 22. Other quotations are from pages 83, 62, 71, 182, 166, 235, and 246.

QUESTIONS FOR ANALYSIS

1. Compare the lives of Ning Lao and her granddaughter. In what ways were they different and similar?
2. In a broader historical perspective, what do you find most significant about Ning Lao's account of her life? Why?

ONLINE DOCUMENT PROJECT

How did China's conflicts with the Western powers and Japan affect its people? Read the excerpts from Ning Lao's autobiography, and then complete a quiz and writing assignment based on the evidence and details from this chapter. *See inside the front cover to learn more.*

democracy, big business, and Marxist socialism. Reviving old myths, they stressed the emperor's godlike qualities and the samurai warrior's code of honor, obedience, and responsibility. Despising party politics, they assassinated moderate leaders and plotted armed uprisings to achieve their goals. Above all else, the ultranationalists preached foreign expansion.

The ultranationalists were noisy and violent in the 1920s, but it took the Great Depression of the 1930s to tip the scales decisively in their favor. The worldwide depression hit Japan like a tidal wave in 1930. Exports and wages collapsed; unemployment and raw suffering soared. The ultranationalists blamed the system, and people listened.

Japan Against China

Among those who listened with particular care were young Japanese army officers in Manchuria, the underpopulated, resource-rich province of northeastern China controlled by the Japanese army since its victory over Russia in 1905. The rise of Chinese nationalism embodied in the Guomindang unification of China challenged Japanese control over Manchuria. In response, junior Japanese officers in Manchuria, in cooperation with top generals in Tokyo, secretly manufactured an excuse for aggression in late 1931. They blew up some Japanese-owned railroad tracks near the city of Shenyang (Mukden) and then, with reinforcements rushed in from Korea, quickly occupied all of Manchuria in "self-defense."

When the League of Nations condemned Japanese aggression in Manchuria, Japan resigned in protest. Japanese aggression in Manchuria proved that the army, though reporting directly to the Japanese emperor, was an independent force subject to no outside control.

For China the Japanese conquest of Manchuria was disastrous. Japanese aggression in Manchuria drew attention away from modernizing efforts. The Nationalist government promoted a massive boycott of Japanese goods but lost interest in social reform. Above all, the Nationalist government after 1931 completely neglected land reform and the Chinese peasants' grinding poverty.

Having abandoned land reform, partly because they themselves were often landowners, the Nationalists under Jiang Jieshi devoted their energies between 1930 and 1934 to great campaigns of encirclement and extermination of the Communists' rural power base in southeastern China. In 1934 they closed in for the kill, but, in one of the most incredible sagas of modern times, the main Communist army broke out, beat off attacks, and retreated 6,000 miles in twelve months to a remote region on the northwestern border (Map 29.2). Of the estimated 100,000 men and women who began the **Long March**, only 8,000 to 10,000 reached the final destination in Yan'an. There Mao built up his forces once again, established a new territorial base, and won local peasant support by taking aggressive action to improve peasant life.

Long March

▶ The 6,000-mile retreat of the Chinese Communist army to a remote region on the northwestern border of China, during which tens of thousands lost their lives.

> ### > Mao's Unprecedented Pro-Peasant Policies:

- Communist forces did not pillage and rape as imperialist and warlord armies had always done
- The Communists set up schools to teach illiterate peasants to read and write
- The Communists established health clinics to provide the peasants with basic medical care
- Communist armies helped the peasants plant and harvest their crops
- Communist courts tried the warlords and landlords for crimes against the peasants

In Japan politics became increasingly chaotic. In 1937 the Japanese military and the ultranationalists were in command. Unable to force China to cede more territory in northern China, they used a minor incident near Beijing as a pretext for a general attack. This marked the beginning of what became World War II in Asia. The Nationalist government, which had just formed a united front with the

Japanese Atrocities in China

In this August 1938 photograph, Japanese soldiers taunt their young Chinese prisoners before executing them. (Hulton Archive/Getty Images)

CHAPTER LOCATOR | Why did modern nationalism develop in Asia between the First and Second World Wars, and what was its appeal? | How did the Ottoman Empire's collapse in World War I shape nationalist movements in the Middle East?

CHAPTER 29
906 NATIONALISM IN ASIA

MAP 29.2 ■ The Chinese Communist Movement and the War with Japan, 1927–1938

After urban uprisings ordered by Stalin failed in 1927, Mao Zedong succeeded in forming a self-governing Communist soviet in mountainous southern China. Relentless Nationalist attacks between 1930 and 1934 finally forced the Long March to Yan'an, where the Communists were well positioned for guerrilla war against the Japanese.

Map legend:
- Areas under Communist control before Nov. 1934
- Area under Communist control, 1929–1938
- Areas occupied by Japan by end of 1938
- Route of the Long March, Oct. 1934–Oct. 1935: main forces from Jiangxi Soviet
- Other forces

Communists, fought hard, but Japanese troops quickly took Beijing and northern China. After taking the port of Shanghai, the Japanese launched an immediate attack up the Yangzi River.

Foretelling the horrors of World War II, the Japanese air force bombed Chinese cities and civilian populations with unrelenting fury. Nanjing, the capital, fell in December 1937. Entering the city, Japanese soldiers went berserk and committed dreadful atrocities over seven weeks. The "Rape of Nanjing" combined with other Japanese atrocities to outrage world opinion. The Western powers denounced Japanese aggression but, with tensions rising in Europe, took no action.

What role did Gandhi and his campaign of militant nonviolence play in leading India to independence from the British?

How did nationalism shape political developments in East and Southeast Asia?

 LearningCurve
Check what you know.

By late 1938 Japanese armies occupied sizable portions of coastal China (see Map 29.2). But the Nationalists and the Communists had retreated to the interior, and both refused to accept defeat. In 1939, as Europe edged toward another great war, China and Japan were bogged down in a savage stalemate, providing a spectacular example of conflicting nationalisms.

Striving for Independence in Southeast Asia

The tide of nationalism was also rising in Southeast Asia. Nationalists in French Indochina, the Dutch East Indies, and the Philippines urgently wanted genuine political independence and freedom from foreign rule. In both French Indochina and the Dutch East Indies they ran up against an imperialist stone wall. The obstacle to Filipino independence came from America and Japan.

The French in Indochina, as in all their colonies, resisted all efforts to move toward self-government. This uncompromising attitude stimulated the growth of an equally stubborn Communist opposition under Ho Chi Minh (1890–1969), which despite ruthless repression emerged as the dominant anti-French force in Indochina.

Uncle Sam as Schoolmaster

In this cartoon that first appeared on the cover of *Harper's Weekly* in August 1898, unruly students identified as a "Cuban Ex-patriot" and a "Guerilla" are being disciplined with a switch by a stern Uncle Sam as he tries to teach them self-government. The gentleman to the left reading a book is José Miguel Gómez, one of Cuba's revolutionary heroes, while the Filipino insurrectionist Emilio Aguinaldo is made to wear a dunce cap and stand in the corner. The two well-behaved girls to the right represent Hawaii and Puerto Rico. (The Granger Collection, NYC — All rights reserved.)

CHAPTER LOCATOR | Why did modern nationalism develop in Asia between the First and Second World Wars, and what was its appeal? | How did the Ottoman Empire's collapse in World War I shape nationalist movements in the Middle East?

CHAPTER 29
908 NATIONALISM IN ASIA

In the East Indies—modern Indonesia—the Dutch made some concessions after the First World War, establishing a people's council with very limited law-making power. But in the 1930s the Dutch cracked down hard, jailing all the important nationalist leaders. Like the French, the Dutch were determined to hold on.

In the Philippines, however, a well-established nationalist movement achieved greater success. By the late nineteenth century the Filipino population was 80 percent Catholic. Filipinos shared a common cultural heritage and a common racial origin. Education, especially for girls, was advanced for Southeast Asia. Economic development helped to create a westernized elite, which turned first to reform and then to revolution in the 1890s. As in Egypt and Turkey, long-standing intimate contact with Western civilization created a strong nationalist movement at an early date.

Filipino nationalists were bitterly disillusioned when the United States, having taken the Philippines from Spain in the Spanish-American War of 1898, ruthlessly beat down a patriotic revolt and denied the universal Filipino desire for independence. As the imperialist power in the Philippines, the United States encouraged education and promoted capitalistic economic development. And as in British India, an elected legislature was given some real powers.

As in India and French Indochina, demands for independence grew. One important contributing factor was American racial attitudes. Americans treated Filipinos as inferiors and introduced segregationist practices borrowed from the American South. American racism made passionate nationalists of many Filipinos. However, it was the Great Depression that had the most radical impact on the Philippines.

As the United States collapsed economically in the 1930s, the Philippines suddenly appeared to be a liability rather than an asset. American farm groups lobbied for protection from cheap Filipino sugar. To protect American jobs, labor unions demanded an end to Filipino immigration. Responding to public pressure, in 1934 Congress made the Philippines a self-governing commonwealth and scheduled independence for 1944. Sugar imports were reduced, and immigration was limited to only fifty Filipinos per year.

The Spanish-American War in the Philippines, 1898

QUICK REVIEW <

How did ideological conflicts shape the struggle to create a unified, genuinely independent nation in China?

What role did Gandhi and his campaign of militant nonviolence play in leading India to independence from the British?

How did nationalism shape political developments in East and Southeast Asia?

✓ LearningCurve
Check what you know.

CHAPTER SUMMARY

The Ottoman Empire's collapse in World War I left a power vacuum that both Western imperialists and Asian nationalists sought to fill. Strong leaders, such as Turkey's Mustafa Kemal led successful nationalist movements in Turkey, Persia, and Afghanistan. British and French influence over the League of Nations–mandated Arab states declined in the 1920s and 1930s as Arab nationalists pushed for complete independence. The situation in Palestine, where the British had promised both Palestinians and Jewish Zionists independent homelands, deteriorated in the interwar years as increasingly larger numbers of European Jews migrated there.

Gandhi's active, nonviolent resistance campaign, which he called satyagraha, convinced the British that colonial rule in India was over, and India won independence in 1947. Regrettably, following independence, extreme Muslim and Hindu religious nationalism threatened to tear India apart.

China's 1911 Revolution successfully ended the ancient dynastic system before the Great War, while the 1919 May Fourth Movement renewed nationalist hopes after it. Jiang Jieshi's Nationalist Party and Mao Zedong's Communists, however, would violently contest who would rule over a unified China. Japan, unlike China, industrialized early and by the 1920s seemed headed toward genuine democracy, but militarists and ultranationalists then launched an aggressive campaign of foreign expansion which contributed to the buildup to World War II. As the Great Depression took hold, Filipino nationalists achieved independence from the United States.

CONNECTIONS Just as nationalism drove politics and state-building in Europe in the nineteenth century, so it took root across Asia in the late nineteenth and early twentieth centuries. While nationalism in Europe developed out of a desire to turn cultural unity into political reality, in Asia nationalist sentiments drew their greatest energy from opposition to European imperialism and domination. Asian modernizers also pressed the nationalist cause by demanding an end to outdated conservative traditions that they argued only held back the development of modern, independent nations capable of throwing off Western domination and existing as equals with the West.

The nationalist cause in Asia took many forms and produced some of the twentieth century's most remarkable leaders. In Chapter 32 we will discuss how nationalist leaders across Asia shaped the freedom struggle and the resulting independence according to their own ideological and personal visions. China's Mao Zedong is the giant among the nationalist leaders who emerged in Asia, but he replaced imperialist rule with one-party Communist rule. Gandhi's dream of a unified India collapsed with the partition of British India into Hindu India and Muslim Pakistan and Bangladesh. India and Pakistan remain bitter, and nuclear-armed, enemies today, as we will see in Chapter 33. Egypt assumed a prominent position in the Arab world after World War II under Gamal Nasser's leadership and, after a series of wars with Israel, began to play a significant role in efforts to find a peaceful resolution to the Israeli-Palestinian conflict. That conflict, however,

CHAPTER LOCATOR | Why did modern nationalism develop in Asia between the First and Second World Wars, and what was its appeal? | How did the Ottoman Empire's collapse in World War I shape nationalist movements in the Middle East?

CHAPTER 29
910 NATIONALISM IN ASIA

continues unabated as nationalist and religious sentiments inflame feelings on both sides. Ho Chi Minh eventually forced the French colonizers out of Vietnam, only to face another Western power, the United States, in a long and deadly war. As described in Chapter 32, a unified Vietnam finally gained its independence in 1975, but, like China, the country was under one-party Communist control.

Japan remained an exception to much of what happened in the rest of Asia. After a long period of isolation, the Japanese implemented an unprecedented program of modernization and westernization in the late 1800s. Japan continued to model itself after the West when it took control of former German colonies as mandated territories after the Great War and occupied territory in China, Korea, Vietnam, Taiwan, and elsewhere. In the next chapter we will see how ultranationalism drove national policy in the 1930s, ultimately leading to Japan's defeat in World War II.

ONLINE DOCUMENT PROJECT

Foreign Intervention in China

How did China's conflicts with the Western powers and Japan affect its people?

Read the excerpts from Ning Lao's autobiography, and then complete a quiz and writing assignment based on the evidence and details from this chapter. *See inside the front cover to learn more.*

What role did Gandhi and his campaign of militant nonviolence play in leading India to independence from the British?

How did nationalism shape political developments in East and Southeast Asia?

☑ LearningCurve
Check what you know.

CHAPTER 29 STUDY GUIDE

GET STARTED ONLINE

 LearningCurve

Now that you've read the chapter, make it stick by completing the LearningCurve activity.

EXPLAIN WHY IT MATTERS

Put your reading into practice. Identify each term below, and then explain why it matters in world history.

TERM	WHO OR WHAT & WHEN	WHY IT MATTERS
Permanent Mandates Commission (p. 885)		
Sykes-Picot Agreement (p. 891)		
Balfour Declaration (p. 891)		
Treaty of Lausanne (p. 892)		
Majlis (p. 893)		
kibbutz (p. 895)		
Lucknow Pact (p. 897)		
satyagraha (p. 898)		
May Fourth Movement (p. 901)		
New Culture Movement (p. 902)		
zaibatsu (p. 903)		
Long March (p. 906)		

MOVE BEYOND THE BASICS

To demonstrate a more advanced understanding of nationalist movements in Turkey, India, China, and Japan, fill in the table below with descriptions of four key factors that shaped the development of nationalist movements in each country: political and social context, ideology, movement goals, and internal divisions. How did Western imperialism shape each movement?

	Political and Social Context	Ideology	Movement Goals	Internal Divisions
Turkey				
India				
China				
Japan				

PUT IT ALL TOGETHER

Now, take a step back and try to explain the big picture. Remember to use specific examples from the chapter in your answers.

NATIONALISM IN THE MIDDLE EAST

▶ What role did Western powers play in the Middle East after World War I? How did the Western presence shape Middle Eastern nationalist movements?

▶ What was the relationship between Islam and nationalism in the postwar Middle East?

NATIONALISM IN INDIA

▶ What was Gandhi's contribution to the Indian nationalist movement? In what ways did he transform the movement?

▶ Why did it prove so difficult for Hindus and Muslims to maintain a united front against the British?

NATIONALISM IN EAST AND SOUTHEAST ASIA

▶ Why did competing nationalist movements emerge in China? What common origins and beliefs did the movements share?

▶ How did nationalism contribute to Japan's rise to regional dominance? How did it undermine Japan's domestic political stability?

LOOKING BACK, LOOKING AHEAD

▶ How did Asian nationalism in the twentieth century differ from European nationalism in the nineteenth century? What explains the differences you note?

▶ World War I played a crucial role in stimulating Asian nationalism. Looking ahead, what role might you anticipate World War II playing in shaping the ongoing development of Asian nationalist movements?

> ## IN YOUR OWN WORDS

Imagine that you must give an oral report to the class answering the following question: **How did nationalism shape developments across Asia in the decades following the First World War?** What would be the most important points and why?

30

THE GREAT DEPRESSION AND WORLD WAR II

1929–1945

> **How did the economic suffering created by the Great Depression contribute to the outbreak of World War II?** Chapter 30 examines the Great Depression and World War II. In 1929 the interconnected global economy collapsed. In the wake of the Great Depression, people everywhere looked to new leaders for relief, some democratically elected, many not. A global trend toward dictatorship produced a particularly ruthless brand of totalitarianism that reached its fullest realization in the Soviet Union, Nazi Germany, and Japan in the 1930s. Germany's and Japan's aggressive expansion sparked World War II. By war's end, millions had died on the battlefields and in the bombed-out cities. Millions more died in the Holocaust, in Stalin's Soviet Union from purges and forced imposition of communism, and during Japan's quest to create an "Asia for Asians."

Jewish Boy in Nazi-Controlled France Israel Lichtenstein, wearing a Jewish star, was born in Paris in 1932. His father was one of an estimated 1 million Jews who died in the Auschwitz concentration camp. Israel and his mother were also sent to a concentration camp, but they escaped and survived the Holocaust by going into hiding until the end of the war. Israel later immigrated to the nation of Israel. (United States Holocaust Memorial Museum, courtesy of Israel Lichtenstein)

✓ LearningCurve
After reading the chapter, use LearningCurve to retain what you've read.

> What caused the Great Depression, and what were its consequences?

> What was the nature of the new totalitarian dictatorships, and how did they differ from conservative authoritarian states and from each other?

> How did Stalin and the Communist Party build a totalitarian order in the Soviet Union?

> How did Italian fascism develop?

> Why were Hitler and his Nazi regime initially so popular, and how did their actions lead to World War II?

> How did Germany and Japan build empires in Europe and Asia, and how did the Allies defeat them?

What caused the Great Depression, and what were its consequences?

Louisville Flood Victims, 1937

During the Great Depression, Louisville, Kentucky, was hit by the worst flood in its history. The famous documentary photographer Margaret Bourke-White captured this image of African American flood victims lining up for food. Not only does the billboard message mock the Depression-era conditions, but the smiling white family appears to be driving its car through the line of people, drawing attention to America's race and class differences. (Margaret Bourke-White/Time-Life Pictures/ Getty Images)

LIKE THE GREAT WAR, the Great Depression must be spelled with capital letters. Beginning in 1929 an exceptionally long and severe economic depression struck the entire world with ever-greater intensity, and recovery was uneven and slow. The social and political consequences of prolonged economic collapse were enormous and were felt worldwide.

The Economic Crisis

Though economic activity was already declining moderately in many countries by early 1929, the U.S. stock market crash in October of that year really started the Great Depression. The American stock market boom was built on borrowed money. Two factors explain why. First, the wealth gap (or income inequality) between America's rich and poor reached its greatest extent in the twentieth century in 1928–1929. One percent of Americans then held 70 percent of all America's wealth. Eventually, with not enough money to go around, the 99 percent had to

CHAPTER LOCATOR | What caused the Great Depression, and what were its consequences? | What was the nature of the new totalitarian dictatorships?

CHAPTER 30
916 THE GREAT DEPRESSION AND WORLD WAR II

1921
New Economic Policy in Soviet Union

1922
Mussolini seizes power in Italy

1924–1929
Buildup of Nazi Party in Germany

1925
Hitler, *Mein Kampf*

1927
Stalin comes to power in Soviet Union

1928
Stalin's first five-year plan

1929
Start of collectivization in Soviet Union; Lateran Agreement

1929–1939
Great Depression

1931
Japan invades Manchuria

1932–1933
Famine in Ukraine

1933
Hitler appointed chancellor in Germany; Nazis begin control of state and society

1935
Mussolini invades Ethiopia; creation of U.S. Works Progress Administration as part of New Deal

1936
Start of great purges under Stalin; Spanish Civil War begins

1936–1937
Popular Front government in France

1939
Germany occupies Czech lands and invades Poland; Britain and France declare war on Germany, starting World War II

1940
Japan signs formal alliance with Germany and Italy; Germany defeats France; Battle of Britain

1941
Germany invades Soviet Union; Japan attacks Pearl Harbor; United States enters war

1941–1945
The Holocaust

1944
Allied invasion at Normandy

1945
Atomic bombs dropped on Japan; World War II ends

borrow to make even basic purchases—as a result, the cost of farm credit, installment loans, and home mortgages skyrocketed. Then a point was reached where the 99 percent could borrow no more, so they stopped buying.

Second, wealthy investors and speculators took increasingly greater investment risks. One such popular risk was to buy stocks by paying only a small fraction of the total purchase price and borrowing the remainder from their stockbrokers or from banks. Such buying "on margin" was extremely dangerous. When prices started falling, the hard-pressed margin buyers started selling to pay their debts. The result was a financial panic. Countless investors and speculators were wiped out in a matter of days or weeks, and the New York stock market's crash started a domino effect that hit most of the world's major stock exchanges

The financial panic in the United States triggered a worldwide financial crisis. Throughout the 1920s American bankers and investors had lent large sums to many countries, and as panic spread, New York bankers began recalling their short-term loans. Frightened citizens around the world began to withdraw their bank savings, leading to general financial chaos. The recall of American loans also accelerated the collapse in world prices, as business people dumped goods in a frantic attempt to get cash to pay what they owed.

| How did Stalin and the Communist Party build a totalitarian order in the Soviet Union? | How did Italian fascism develop? | Why were Hitler and his Nazi regime initially so popular, how did their actions lead to WWII? | How did Germany and Japan build empires in Europe and Asia, how did the Allies defeat them? | ✓ LearningCurve Check what you know. |

The financial chaos led to a drastic decline in production in country after country. Countries now turned inward and tried to go it alone. Many followed the American example, in which protective tariffs were raised to their highest levels ever in 1930 to seal off shrinking national markets for American producers only.

Although historians' opinions differ, two factors probably best explain the relentless slide to the bottom from 1929 to early 1933. First, the international economy lacked leadership able to maintain stability when the crisis came. Neither the seriously weakened British nor the United States—the world's economic leaders—stabilized the international economic system in 1929. Instead Britain and the United States cut back international lending and erected high tariffs.

Second, in almost every country, governments cut their budgets and reduced spending instead of running large deficits to try to stimulate their economies. That is, governments needed to put large sums of money into the economy to stimulate job growth and spending. After World War II such a "counter-cyclical policy," advocated by the British economist John Maynard Keynes (1883–1946), became a well-established weapon against depression. But in the 1930s orthodox economists generally regarded Keynes's prescription with horror.

Mass Unemployment

The need for large-scale government spending was tied to mass unemployment. The 99 percent's halt in buying contributed to the financial crisis, which led to production cuts, which in turn caused workers to lose their jobs and have even less money to buy goods. This led to still more production cuts, and unemployment soared.

> **Mass Unemployment at Its Peak:**

- Britain: 18 percent
- Germany: 25 percent
- Australia: 32 percent
- The United States: 33 percent

Mass unemployment created great social problems. Poverty increased dramatically, although in most industrialized countries unemployed workers generally received some meager unemployment benefits or public aid that prevented starvation. Millions of unemployed people lost their spirit, and homes and ways of life were disrupted in countless personal tragedies. Only strong government action could deal with the social powder keg preparing to explode.

The New Deal in the United States

The Great Depression and the response to it marked a major turning point in American history. Herbert Hoover (U.S. pres. 1929–1933) and his administration initially reacted with limited action. When the financial crisis struck Europe with full force in summer 1931 and boomeranged back to the United States, banks failed and unemployment soared. In 1932 industrial production fell to about 50 percent of its 1929 level.

In these desperate circumstances Franklin Delano Roosevelt (U.S. pres. 1933–1945) won a landslide presidential victory in 1932 with promises of a "New Deal for the forgotten man." Roosevelt's basic goal was to preserve capitalism by reforming it. Rejecting socialism and government ownership of industry, Roosevelt advocated forceful federal government intervention in the economy. His commitment to national relief programs marked a profound shift from the traditional stress on family support and local community responsibility.

New Deal

▶ Franklin Delano Roosevelt's plan to reform capitalism through forceful government intervention in the economy.

CHAPTER LOCATOR | What caused the Great Depression, and what were its consequences? | What was the nature of the new totalitarian dictatorships?

918 CHAPTER 30
THE GREAT DEPRESSION AND WORLD WAR II

As in Asia, Africa, and Latin America, American farmers were hard hit by the Great Depression, and agricultural recovery became a top priority. Innovative programs, such as the 1933 Agricultural Adjustment Act, aimed to raise prices and farm income by limiting production.

Roosevelt then attacked mass unemployment. New federal agencies launched a vast range of public works projects so the federal government could directly employ as many people as financially possible. The Works Progress Administration (WPA), set up in 1935, employed one-fifth of the entire U.S. labor force at some point in the 1930s, and these workers constructed public buildings, bridges, and highways.

Following the path blazed by Germany's Bismarck in the 1880s (see page 740), the U.S. government in 1935 established a national social security system with old-age pensions and unemployment benefits. The 1935 National Labor Relations Act declared collective bargaining to be U.S. policy, and union membership more than doubled. In general, between 1935 and 1938 government rulings and social reforms chipped away at the privileges of the wealthy and tried to help ordinary people.

Despite undeniable accomplishments in social reform, the New Deal was only partly successful as a response to the Great Depression. Some economic progress was made, but the New Deal never did pull the United States out of the depression; only the Second World War did that.

The European Response to the Depression

The American stock market's collapse in October 1929 set off a chain of economic downturns that hit Europe, particularly Germany and Great Britain, the hardest. Postwar Europe had emerged from the Great War deeply in debt and in desperate need of investment capital to rebuild. The United States became the primary creditor and financier. Germany borrowed, for example, to pay Britain war reparations, and then Britain took that money and repaid its war debts and investment loans to America. When the American economy crashed, the whole circular system crashed with it.

Of all the Western democracies, the Scandinavian countries under socialist leadership responded most successfully to the challenge of the Great Depression. When the economic crisis struck in 1929, Sweden's socialist government pioneered the use of large-scale deficits to finance public works projects and thereby maintain production and employment. Scandinavian governments also increased social welfare benefits. All this spending required a large bureaucracy and high taxes. Yet both private and cooperative enterprise thrived, as did democracy. Some observers considered Scandinavia's welfare socialism an appealing middle way between what they considered to be sick capitalism and cruel communism or fascism.

In Britain, Ramsay MacDonald's Labour government (1929–1931) and, after 1931, the Conservative-dominated coalition government followed orthodox economic theory. The budget was balanced, but unemployed workers received barely enough welfare support to live. Nevertheless, the economy recovered considerably after 1932, reflecting the gradual reorientation of the British economy. Britain concentrated increasingly on the national, rather than the international, market. Old export industries, such as textiles and coal, continued to decline, but new

How did Stalin and the Communist Party build a totalitarian order in the Soviet Union?

How did Italian fascism develop?

Why were Hitler and his Nazi regime initially so popular, how did their actions lead to WWII?

How did Germany and Japan build empires in Europe and Asia, how did the Allies defeat them?

☑ LearningCurve
Check what you know.

919

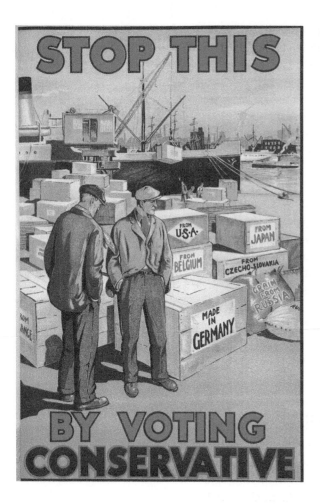

STOP THIS

FROM U.S.A.
FROM JAPAN
FROM BELGIUM
FROM CZECHO-SLOVAKIA
GRAIN FROM RUSSIA
MADE IN GERMANY
FROM FRANCE

BY VOTING CONSERVATIVE

British Conservative Party Poster, 1931

This campaign poster from the 1931 British general election portrays crates and bags of goods being unloaded on English docks. (Photo by The Conservative Party Archive/Getty Images)

> PICTURING THE PAST
ANALYZING THE IMAGE: Where are the goods on the dock from? What do the Conservatives want stopped? **CONNECTIONS:** Was this attitude toward foreign goods unique to England? What other countries held similar views? What effect did such attitudes have on the worldwide depression?

industries, such as automobiles and electrical appliances, grew. These developments encouraged British isolationism and often had devastating economic consequences for Britain's far-flung colonies and dominions, which depended heavily upon reciprocal trade with Great Britain and the United States.

The Great Depression came late to France as it was relatively less industrialized and more isolated from the world economy. But once the depression hit, it stayed. Economic stagnation both reflected and heightened an ongoing political crisis, as liberals, democratic socialists, and Communists fought for control of the French government with conservatives and the far right. The latter groups agitated against parliamentary democracy and turned to Mussolini's Italy and Hitler's Germany for inspiration. At the same time, the Communist Party and many workers looked to Stalin's Russia for guidance.

Frightened by the growing popularity of Hitler- and Mussolini-style right-wing dictatorships at home and abroad, the Communist, Socialist, and Radical Parties in France formed an alliance—the Popular Front—for the May 1936 national elections. Following its clear victory, the Popular Front government launched a far-reaching program of social and economic reform. Popular with workers and the lower middle class, these measures were quickly sabotaged by rapid inflation, rising wages, a decline in overseas exports, and cries of socialist revolution from frightened conservatives. Politically, the Popular Front lost many left-wing supporters when it failed to back the republican cause in the Spanish Civil War, while Hitler and Mussolini openly armed and supported Franco's nationalists (see page 936). In June 1937, with the country hopelessly divided, the Popular Front collapsed.

Popular Front

▶ A New Deal–inspired party in France that encouraged unions and launched a far-reaching program of social reform.

Worldwide Effects

The Great Depression's magnitude was unprecedented, and its effect rippled well beyond Europe and the United States. Because many countries and colonies in Africa, Asia, and Latin America were nearly totally dependent on one or two commodities for income, the implementation of protectionist trade policies by the leading industrial nations had devastating effects.

CHAPTER LOCATOR | What caused the Great Depression, and what were its consequences? | What was the nature of the new totalitarian dictatorships?

The Great Depression hit the vulnerable commodity economies of Latin America especially hard. With foreign sales plummeting, Latin American countries could not buy the industrial goods they needed from abroad. The global depression provoked a profound shift toward economic nationalism after 1930, as popularly based governments worked to reduce foreign influence and gain control of their own economies and natural resources. These efforts were fairly successful. By the late 1940s factories in Argentina, Brazil, and Chile could generally satisfy domestic consumer demand for the products of light industry. But as in Hitler's Germany, the deteriorating economic conditions in Latin America also gave rise to dictatorships, some of them modeled along European Fascist lines (pages 976–980).

The Great Depression marked a decisive turning point in the development of African nationalism. For the first time, educated Africans faced widespread unemployment. African peasants and small business people who had been drawn into world trade, and who sometimes profited from booms, also felt the economic pain, as did urban workers. In some areas the result was unprecedented mass protest.

While Asians were somewhat affected by the Great Depression, the consequences varied greatly by country or colony and were not as serious generally as they were elsewhere. That being said, where the depression did hit, it was often severe. The price of rice fell by two-thirds between 1929 and 1932. Also crippling to the region's economies was Asia's heavy dependence on raw material exports. With debts to local moneylenders fixed in value and taxes to colonial governments hardly ever reduced, many Asian peasants in the 1930s struggled under crushing debt and suffered terribly.

When the Great Depression reached China in the early 1930s, it hit the rural economy the hardest. China's economy depended heavily on cash-crop exports and these declined dramatically, while cheap foreign agricultural goods—such as rice and wheat—were dumped in China. Agricultural prices in 1932 were only 41 percent of 1921 prices, and rural incomes fell by over 50 percent between 1931 and 1934. While Chinese industrial production dropped off after 1931, it quickly recovered. Much of this growth was in the military sector, as China tried to catch up with the West and also prepare for war with Japan.

In Japan the terrible suffering caused by the Great Depression caused ultranationalists and militarists to call for less dependence on global markets and the expansion of a self-sufficient empire. Such expansion began in 1931 when Japan invaded Chinese Manchuria, which became a major source of the raw materials needed to feed Japanese industrial growth (see Chapter 29). Japan recovered more quickly from the Great Depression than any other major industrial power because of prompt action by the civilian democratic government, but the government and large corporations continued to be blamed for the economic downturn. By the mid-1930s this lack of confidence, combined with the collapsing international economic order, Europe's and America's increasingly isolationist and protectionist policies, and a growing admiration for Nazi Germany and its authoritarian, militaristic model of government, had led the Japanese military to topple the civilian authorities and dictate Japan's future.

QUICK REVIEW

How did the world's governments respond to challenges posed by the Great Depression?

How did Stalin and the Communist Party build a totalitarian order in the Soviet Union?

How did Italian fascism develop?

Why were Hitler and his Nazi regime initially so popular, how did their actions lead to WWII?

How did Germany and Japan build empires in Europe and Asia, how did the Allies defeat them?

 LearningCurve
Check what you know.

What was the nature of the new totalitarian dictatorships, and how did they differ from conservative authoritarian states and from each other?

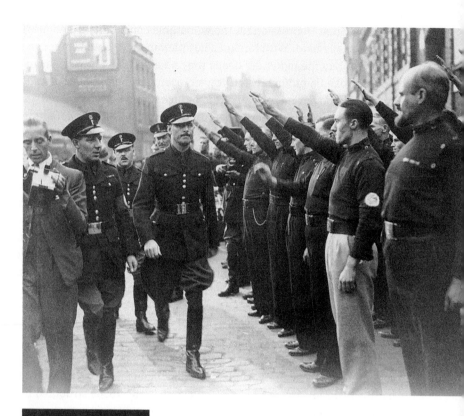

The Spread of Fascism

In the 1920s and 1930s most European countries had Fascist sympathizers. The British Union of Fascists, led by Sir Oswald Mosley, modeled itself on Mussolini's nationalist Fascist Party. Its members were highly visible in their black uniforms, but they never numbered more than a few thousand and never elected a member to Parliament. Here Mosley and his Black Shirts prepare to march through London's Jewish East End in October 1936. Antifascist demonstrators attacked Mosley's followers and stopped the march. (Central Press/Getty Images)

BOTH CONSERVATIVE AND RADICAL totalitarian dictatorships arose in Europe in the 1920s and the 1930s. Although they sometimes overlapped in character and practice, they were profoundly different in essence.

Conservative Authoritarianism

The traditional form of antidemocratic government in world history was conservative authoritarianism. Like Russia's tsars and China's emperors, the leaders of such governments relied on obedient bureaucracies, vigilant police departments, and trustworthy armies to control society. They forbade or limited popular participation in government and often jailed or exiled political opponents. Yet they had neither the ability nor the desire to control many aspects of their subjects' lives. As long as the people did not try to change the system, they often enjoyed considerable personal independence.

CHAPTER LOCATOR | What caused the Great Depression, and what were its consequences? | **What was the nature of the new totalitarian dictatorships?**

CHAPTER 30
922 THE GREAT DEPRESSION AND WORLD WAR II

After the First World War, conservative authoritarianism revived, especially in Latin America. Conservative dictators also seized power in Spain and Portugal, and in the less-developed eastern part of Europe. There were several reasons for this development. These lands lacked strong traditions of self-government, and many new states, such as Yugoslavia, were torn by ethnic conflicts. Dictatorship appealed to nationalists and military leaders as a way to repress such tensions and preserve national unity. Large landowners and the church were still powerful forces in these predominantly agrarian areas and often looked to dictators to protect them from progressive land reform or Communist agrarian upheaval. Conservative dictatorships were concerned more with maintaining the status quo than with mobilizing the masses or forcing society into rapid change or war.

Radical Totalitarian Dictatorships

By the mid-1930s a new kind of radical dictatorship—termed totalitarian—had emerged in the Soviet Union, Germany, and, to a lesser extent, Italy. It can be argued that totalitarianism began with the total war effort of 1914–1918 (see Chapter 28), as governments acquired total control over all areas of society in order to achieve one supreme objective: victory. This provided a model for future totalitarian states.

In 1956 American historians Carl Friedrich and Zbigniew Brzezinski identified at least six key features of modern totalitarian states.[1] The six features are (1) an official ideology that demanded adherence from everyone, that touched every aspect of a citizen's existence, and that promised to lead to a "perfect final stage of mankind"; (2) a single ruling party, whose "passionate and unquestionably-dedicated-to-the-ideology" members were drawn from a small percentage of the total population (following Lenin's "vanguard of the proletariat" model; see page 860), hierarchically organized, and led by one charismatic leader, the "dictator"; (3) complete control of "all weapons of armed combat"; (4) complete monopoly of all means of mass communication; (5) a system of terror, physical and psychic, enforced by the party and the secret police; and (6) central control and direction of the entire economy.

While all these features were present in Stalin's Communist Soviet Union and Hitler's Nazi Germany, there were some major differences. Most notably, Soviet communism seized private property for the state and sought to level society by crushing the middle classes. Nazi Germany also criticized big landowners and industrialists but, unlike the Communists, did not try to nationalize private property, so the middle classes survived. This difference in property and class relations led some scholars to speak of "totalitarianism of the left"—Stalinist Russia—and "totalitarianism of the right"—Nazi Germany.

Moreover, Soviet Communists ultimately had international aims: they sought to unite the workers of the world. Mussolini and Hitler claimed they were interested in changing state and society on a national level only. Both Mussolini and Hitler used the term fascism to describe their movements' supposedly "total" and revolutionary character. Orthodox Marxist Communists argued that the Fascists were powerful capitalists seeking to destroy the revolutionary working class and thus protect their enormous profits. So while Communists and Fascists both sought the overthrow of existing society, their ideologies clashed, and they were enemies.

totalitarianism
▶ A radical dictatorship that exercises complete political power and control over all aspects of society and seeks to mobilize the masses for action.

fascism
▶ A movement characterized by extreme, often expansionist nationalism, anti-socialism, a dynamic and violent leader, and glorification of war and the military.

| How did Stalin and the Communist Party build a totalitarian order in the Soviet Union? | How did Italian fascism develop? | Why were Hitler and his Nazi regime initially so popular, how did their actions lead to WWII? | How did Germany and Japan build empires in Europe and Asia, how did the Allies defeat them? | ✓ LearningCurve Check what you know. |

923

European Fascist movements shared many characteristics, including extreme nationalism; an anti-socialism aimed at destroying working-class movements; a crushing of human individualism; alliances with powerful capitalists and land-owners; and glorification of war and the military. Fascists, especially in Germany, also embraced racial homogeneity. Indeed, while class was the driving force in communist ideology, race and racial purity were profoundly important to Nazi ideology.

Although 1930s Japan has sometimes been called a Fascist society, most recent scholars disagree with this label. Some European Fascist ideas did appear attractive to Japanese political philosophers, such as nationalism, militarism, the corporatist economic model, and a single, all-powerful political party. However, there were also various ideologically unique forces at work in Japan, including ultranationalism, militarism (building on the historic role of samurai warriors in Japanese society), reverence for traditional ways, emperor worship, and the pro-found changes to Japanese society beginning with the Meiji Restoration in 1867 (see page 796). These also contributed to the rise of a totalitarian, but not Fascist, state before the Second World War.

> **QUICK REVIEW**

What were the most important differences between the totalitarian states established in Germany, the Soviet Union, and Japan?

CHAPTER LOCATOR | What caused the Great Depression, and what were its consequences? | What was the nature of the new totalitarian dictatorships?

CHAPTER 30
924   THE GREAT DEPRESSION AND WORLD WAR II

Soviet Collectivization Poster

Soviet leader Joseph Stalin ordered a nationwide forced collectivization campaign from 1929 to 1933. Following communist theory, the government created large-scale collective farms by seizing land and forcing peasants to work on it. In this idealized 1932 poster, farmers are encouraged to complete the five-year plan of collectivization, while Stalin looks on approvingly. The outcome instead was a disaster. Millions of people died in the resulting human-created famine. (Deutsches Plakat Museum, Essen, Germany/Archives Charmet/The Bridgeman Art Library)

How did Stalin and the Communist Party build a totalitarian order in the Soviet Union?

JOSEPH STALIN (1879–1953) cautiously consolidated his power and eliminated his enemies in the mid-1920s. Then in 1928 he launched the first **five-year plan**— a "revolution from above,"[2] as he so aptly termed it, to transform Soviet society along socialist lines. Stalin and the Communist Party used constant propaganda, enormous sacrifice, and unlimited violence and state control to establish a dynamic, modern totalitarian state in the 1930s.

five-year plan

▶ Launched by Stalin in 1928 and termed the "revolution from above," its goal was to modernize the Soviet Union and generate a Communist society with new attitudes, new loyalties, and a new socialist humanity.

| How did Stalin and the Communist Party build a totalitarian order in the Soviet Union? | How did Italian fascism develop? | Why were Hitler and his Nazi regime initially so popular, how did their actions lead to WWII? | How did Germany and Japan build empires in Europe and Asia, how did the Allies defeat them? | ✓ LearningCurve Check what you know. |

From Lenin to Stalin

By spring 1921 Lenin and the Bolsheviks had won the civil war, but they ruled a shattered and devastated land. Facing economic disintegration, the worst famine in generations, riots by peasants and workers, and an open rebellion by previously pro-Bolshevik sailors at Kronstadt, Lenin changed course. In March 1921 he announced the **New Economic Policy (NEP)**, which re-established limited economic freedom in an attempt to rebuild agriculture and industry. Peasant producers could sell their surpluses in free markets, as could private traders and small handicraft manufacturers. Heavy industry, railroads, and banks, however, remained wholly nationalized.

The NEP was successful both politically and economically. Politically, it was a necessary but temporary compromise with the Soviet Union's overwhelming peasant majority. Economically, the NEP brought rapid recovery. In 1926 industrial output surpassed prewar levels, and peasants were producing almost as much grain as before the war.

As the economy recovered, an intense power struggle began in the Communist Party's inner circles, for Lenin left no chosen successor when he died in 1924. The principal contenders were Stalin and Leon Trotsky. While Trotsky appeared to be the stronger of the two, in the end Stalin won because he gained the party's support, the only genuine source of power in the one-party state.

Stalin gradually achieved absolute power between 1922 and 1927. He used the moderates to crush Trotsky and then turned against the moderates and destroyed them as well. Stalin's final triumph came at the party congress of December 1927, which condemned all deviation from the general party line as formulated by Stalin.

The Five-Year Plans

The 1927 party congress marked the end of the NEP and the beginning of socialist five-year plans. The first five-year plan had staggering economic objectives. In just five years, total industrial output was to increase by 250 percent and agricultural production by 150 percent. By 1930 economic and social change was sweeping the country in a frenzied effort to modernize, much like the Industrial Revolution in Europe in the 1800s (see Chapter 23), and dramatically changing the lives of ordinary people, sometimes at great personal cost.

Stalin unleashed his "second revolution" because, like Lenin, Stalin and his militant supporters were deeply committed to socialism as they understood it. Stalin was also driven to catch up with the advanced and presumably hostile Western capitalist nations. Domestically, there was the peasant problem. For centuries peasants had wanted to own the land, and finally they had it. Sooner or later, the Communists reasoned, the peasants would become conservative capitalists and threaten the regime. Stalin therefore launched a preventive war against the peasantry to bring it under the state's absolute control.

That war was **collectivization**—the forcible consolidation of individual peasant farms into large, state-controlled enterprises. Beginning in 1929 peasants were ordered to give up their land and animals and become members of collective farms. As for the kulaks, the better-off peasants, Stalin instructed party workers to "break their resistance, to eliminate them as a class."[3] Stripped of land and

New Economic Policy (NEP)

▶ Lenin's 1921 policy re-establishing limited economic freedom in an attempt to rebuild agriculture and industry in the face of economic disintegration.

collectivization

▶ Stalin's forcible consolidation of individual peasant farms into large, state-controlled enterprises.

CHAPTER LOCATOR | What caused the Great Depression, and what were its consequences? | What was the nature of the new totalitarian dictatorships?

926 CHAPTER 30 THE GREAT DEPRESSION AND WORLD WAR II

livestock, many starved or were deported to forced-labor camps for "re-education." Because almost all peasants were poor, the term *kulak* soon meant any peasant who opposed the new system.

Forced collectivization led to disaster. Many peasants slaughtered their animals and burned their crops in protest. Nor were the state-controlled collective farms more productive. Grain output barely increased, and collectivized agriculture made no substantial financial contribution to Soviet industrial development during the first five-year plan.

In Ukraine Stalin instituted a policy of all-out collectivization with two goals: to destroy all expressions of Ukrainian nationalism, and to break the Ukrainian peasants' will so they would accept collectivization and Soviet rule. Stalin began by purging Ukraine of its intellectuals and political elite. He then set impossibly high grain quotas for the collectivized farms. This grain quota had to be turned over to the government before any peasant could receive a share. The result was a terrible man-made famine, called in Ukrainian the *Holodomor* (Hunger-extermination), in Ukraine in 1932 and 1933, which probably claimed 3 to 5 million lives. Many scholars and dozens of governments and international organizations have declared Stalin's and the Soviet government's policies a deliberate act of genocide.

Collectivization was a cruel but real victory for Communist ideologues who were looking to institute their brand of communism and to crush opposition as much as improve production. By 1938, 93 percent of peasant families had been herded onto collective farms at a horrendous cost in both human lives and resources. Regimented as state employees and dependent on the state-owned tractor stations, the collectivized peasants were no longer a political threat.

The industrial side of the five-year plans was more successful. Soviet industry produced about four times as much in 1937 as in 1928. No other major country had ever achieved such rapid industrial growth. Heavy industry led the way, and urban development accelerated: more than 25 million people migrated to cities to become industrial workers during the 1930s.

The sudden creation of dozens of new factories demanded tremendous resources. Funds for industrial expansion were collected from the people through heavy hidden sales taxes. Firm labor discipline also contributed to rapid industrialization. Trade unions lost most of their power, and individuals could not move without police permission. When factory managers needed more hands, they were sent "unneeded" peasants from collective farms.

Foreign engineers were hired to plan and construct many of the new factories. Highly skilled American engineers, hungry for work in the depression years, were particularly important until newly trained Soviet experts began to replace them after 1932. Thus Stalin's planners harnessed the skill and technology of capitalist countries to promote the surge of socialist industry.

Life and Culture in Soviet Society

Daily life was hard in Stalin's Soviet Union. There were constant shortages, and scarcity of housing was a particularly serious problem. A relatively lucky family received one room for all its members and shared both a kitchen and a toilet with others on the floor. Less fortunate people built scrap-lumber shacks in shantytowns. Despite these hardships, many Communists saw themselves as heroically

| How did Stalin and the Communist Party build a totalitarian order in the Soviet Union? | How did Italian fascism develop? | Why were Hitler and his Nazi regime initially so popular, how did their actions lead to WWII? | How did Germany and Japan build empires in Europe and Asia, how did the Allies defeat them? | ✓ LearningCurve Check what you know. |

927

building the world's first socialist society while capitalism crumbled and fascism rose in the West.

Offsetting the hardships were the important social benefits Soviet workers received, such as old-age pensions, free medical services and education, and day-care centers for children. Unemployment was almost unknown. Moreover, there was the possibility of personal advancement. Rapid industrialization required massive numbers of trained experts. Thus the Stalinist state broke with the egalitarian policies of the 1920s and provided tremendous incentives to those who acquired specialized skills. A growing technical and managerial elite joined the political and artistic elites in a new upper class, whose members were rich and powerful.

Soviet society's radical transformation profoundly affected women's lives. The Russian Bolshevik Revolution immediately proclaimed complete equality of rights for women. In the 1920s divorce and abortion were made easily available, and women were urged to work outside the home. After Stalin came to power, however, he encouraged a return to traditional family values.

The most lasting changes for women involved work and education. Peasant women continued to work on farms, and millions of women now toiled in factories and heavy construction. The more determined women entered the ranks of the better-paid specialists in industry and science. By 1950, 75 percent of all doctors in the Soviet Union were women.

Culture was thoroughly politicized through constant propaganda and indoctrination. Party activists lectured workers in factories and peasants on collective farms, while newspapers, films, and radio broadcasts recounted socialist achievements and warned of capitalist plots.

Stalinist Terror and the Great Purges

In the mid-1930s the push to build socialism and a new society culminated in ruthless police terror and a massive purging of the Communist Party. In late 1934 Stalin's number-two man, Sergei Kirov, was mysteriously murdered. Although Stalin himself probably ordered Kirov's murder, he used the incident to launch a reign of terror.

In August 1936 sixteen prominent "Old Bolsheviks" — party members before the 1917 revolution — confessed to all manner of plots against Stalin in spectacular public show trials in Moscow. Then in 1937 the secret police arrested a mass of lesser party officials and newer members, torturing them and extracting confessions for more show trials. In addition to the party faithful, union officials, managers, intellectuals, army officers, and countless ordinary citizens were struck down. In all, at least 8 million people were arrested, and millions of these were executed. Those not immediately executed were sent to gulags — labor camps from which few escaped. Many were simply worked to death as they provided convict labor for Stalin's industrialization drive in areas of low population.

Stalin's mass purges remain baffling, for most historians believe those purged posed no threat and confessed to crimes they had not committed. Some historians have challenged the long-standing interpretation that blames the great purges on Stalin's cruelty or madness. They argue that Stalin's fears were exaggerated but genuine and were shared by many in the party and in the general population.[4]

CHAPTER LOCATOR | What caused the Great Depression, and what were its consequences? | What was the nature of the new totalitarian dictatorships?

CHAPTER 30
928 THE GREAT DEPRESSION AND WORLD WAR II

Women and Children Prisoners

Millions of Soviet citizens were sent to forced-labor prison camps from 1929 to 1953, and over 1.5 million died. Ten to 20 percent of these prisoners were women, many of them found guilty of nothing more than being married to men considered enemies of the state. This photo, taken around 1932, shows a woman and possibly her two children performing hard manual labor in one of these camps. (© akg-images/The Image Works)

Historians who have accessed recently opened Soviet archives, however, continue to hold that Stalin was intimately involved and personally directed the purges, abetted by amenable informers, judges, and executioners. In short, a ruthless and paranoid Stalin found large numbers of willing collaborators for crime as well as for achievement.

QUICK REVIEW

What were the economic and ideological goals of the Soviet five-year plans? To what extent were those goals achieved?

| How did Stalin and the Communist Party build a totalitarian order in the Soviet Union? | How did Italian fascism develop? | Why were Hitler and his Nazi regime initially so popular, how did their actions lead to WWII? | How did Germany and Japan build empires in Europe and Asia, how did the Allies defeat them? | ✓ LearningCurve Check what you know. |

How did Italian fascism develop?

Mussolini Leading a Parade in Rome

Benito Mussolini was a master showman who drew on Rome's ancient heritage to promote Italian fascism. He wanted a grand avenue to stage triumphal marches with thousands of troops, so he had the Way of the Imperial Forums built through the old city. Here Mussolini rides at the head of a grand parade in 1932 to inaugurate the new road, passing the Roman Coliseum, one of the focal points along the route. (© Stefano Bianchetti/Corbis)

MUSSOLINI'S FASCIST MOVEMENT and his seizure of power in 1922 were important steps in the rise of dictatorships between the two world wars. Mussolini and his supporters were the first to call themselves "Fascists." His dictatorship was brutal and theatrical, and it contained elements of both conservative authoritarianism and modern totalitarianism.

The Seizure of Power

In the early twentieth century Italy was a liberal state with civil rights and a constitutional monarchy. On the eve of the First World War, the parliamentary regime granted universal male suffrage. But there were serious problems. Poverty was widespread, and many peasants were more attached to their villages and local interests than to the national state. Church-state relations were often tense. Class differences were also extreme, and by 1912 the Socialist Party's radical wing led the powerful revolutionary socialist movement.[5]

CHAPTER LOCATOR | What caused the Great Depression, and what were its consequences? | What was the nature of the new totalitarian dictatorships?

CHAPTER 30
930 THE GREAT DEPRESSION AND WORLD WAR II

World War I worsened the political situation. Having fought on the Allied side almost exclusively for purposes of territorial expansion, the parliamentary government disappointed Italian nationalists with Italy's modest gains at the Paris Peace Conference. Workers and peasants also felt cheated: to win their support during the war, the government had promised social and land reform, which it failed to deliver after the war.

The Russian Revolution inspired and energized Italy's revolutionary socialist movement, and radical workers and peasants began occupying factories and seizing land in 1920. These actions scared and mobilized the property-owning classes. Thus by 1921 revolutionary socialists, antiliberal conservatives, and frightened property owners were all opposed—though for different reasons—to the liberal parliamentary government.

Into these crosscurrents of unrest and fear stepped Benito Mussolini (1883–1945). Mussolini began his political career as a Socialist Party leader and radical newspaper editor before World War I. Expelled from the Italian Socialist Party for supporting the war, and wounded on the Italian front in 1917, Mussolini returned home and began organizing bitter war veterans into a band of Fascists—from the Italian word for "a union of forces."

At first Mussolini's program was a radical combination of nationalist and socialist demands. As such, it competed directly with the well-organized Socialist Party and failed to attract followers. When Mussolini realized his violent verbal assaults on rival Socialists won him growing support from conservatives and the frightened middle classes, he began to shift gears and to exalt nation over class.

Mussolini and his private army of **Black Shirts** also turned to physical violence. Few people were killed, but Socialist newspapers, union halls, and local Socialist Party headquarters were destroyed. A skillful politician, Mussolini convinced his followers they were opposing the "Reds" while also making a real revolution of the little people against the established interests.

With the government breaking down in 1922, partly because of the chaos created by his Black Shirt bands, Mussolini stepped forward as the savior of order and property. In October 1922 thirty thousand Fascists marched on Rome, threatening the king and demanding he appoint Mussolini prime minister. Victor Emmanuel III (r. 1900–1946) forced to choose between Fascists or Socialists, asked Mussolini to form a new cabinet. Thus, after widespread violence and a threat of armed uprising, Mussolini seized power "legally."

Black Shirts

▶ A private army under Mussolini that destroyed Socialist newspapers, union halls, and local Socialist Party headquarters, eventually pushing Socialists out of the city governments of northern Italy.

The Regime in Action

In 1924 Mussolini declared his desire to "make the nation Fascist"[6] and imposed a series of repressive measures. Press freedom was abolished, elections were fixed, and the government ruled by decree. Mussolini arrested his political opponents, disbanded all independent labor unions, and put dedicated Fascists in control of Italy's schools. He created a Fascist youth movement, Fascist labor unions, and many other Fascist organizations. By year's end Italy was a one-party dictatorship under Mussolini's unquestioned leadership.

Mussolini was only primarily interested, however, in personal power. Rather than destroy the old power structure, he remained content to compromise with the conservative classes that controlled the army, the economy, and the state.

| How did Stalin and the Communist Party build a totalitarian order in the Soviet Union? | How did Italian fascism develop? | Why were Hitler and his Nazi regime initially so popular, how did their actions lead to WWII? | How did Germany and Japan build empires in Europe and Asia, how did the Allies defeat them? | ☑ LearningCurve Check what you know. |

931

He controlled labor but left big business to regulate itself, profitably and securely. There was no land reform.

Mussolini also drew increasing support from the Catholic Church. In the Lateran Agreement of 1929, he recognized the Vatican as a tiny independent state and agreed to give the church heavy financial support. The pope in return urged Italians to support Mussolini's government.

Like Stalin and Hitler, Mussolini favored a return of traditional roles for women. He abolished divorce and told women to stay at home and produce children. In 1938 women were limited by law to a maximum of 10 percent of the better-paying jobs in industry and government.

Mussolini's government passed no racial laws until 1938 and did not persecute Jews savagely until late in the Second World War, when Italy was under Nazi control. Nor did Mussolini establish a truly ruthless police state. Only twenty-three political prisoners were condemned to death between 1926 and 1944. Mussolini's Fascist Italy, though repressive and undemocratic, was never really totalitarian.

Lateran Agreement

▶ A 1929 agreement that recognized the Vatican as an independent state, with Mussolini agreeing to give the church heavy financial support in return for the pope's public support.

> **QUICK REVIEW**

Why is it inaccurate to describe Mussolini's Fascist Italy as a totalitarian state?

CHAPTER LOCATOR | What caused the Great Depression, and what were its consequences? | What was the nature of the new totalitarian dictatorships?

CHAPTER 30
932   THE GREAT DEPRESSION AND WORLD WAR II

Why were Hitler and his Nazi regime initially so popular, and how did their actions lead to World War II?

THE MOST FRIGHTENING DICTATORSHIP developed in Nazi Germany. Nazism asserted an unlimited claim over German society and proclaimed the ultimate power of its aggressive leader, Adolf Hitler. Nazism's aspirations were truly totalitarian.

The Roots of Nazism

Nazism grew out of many complex concepts, of which the most influential were extreme nationalism and racism. These ideas captured the mind of the young Adolf Hitler (1889–1945) and evolved into Nazism.

The son of an Austrian customs official, Hitler did poorly in high school and dropped out at age sixteen. He then headed to Vienna, where he was exposed to extreme Austro-German nationalists who believed Germans to be a superior

Nazism

▶ A movement born of extreme nationalism and racism and dominated by Adolf Hitler from 1933 until the end of World War II in 1945.

How did Stalin and the Communist Party build a totalitarian order in the Soviet Union?

How did Italian fascism develop?

Why were Hitler and his Nazi regime initially so popular, how did their actions lead to WWII?

How did Germany and Japan build empires in Europe and Asia, how did the Allies defeat them?

 LearningCurve
Check what you know.

933

people and central Europe's natural rulers. They advocated union with Germany and violent expulsion of "inferior" peoples from the Austro-Hungarian Empire.

From these extremists Hitler eagerly absorbed virulent anti-Semitism, racism, and hatred of Slavs. He developed an unshakable belief in the crudest distortions of Social Darwinism (see page 736), the superiority of Germanic races, and the inevitability of racial conflict. Anti-Semitism and racism became Hitler's most passionate convictions.

Hitler greeted the Great War's outbreak as a salvation. The struggle and discipline of serving as a soldier in the war gave his life meaning, and when Germany suddenly surrendered in 1918, Hitler's world was shattered. Convinced that Jews and Marxists had "stabbed Germany in the back," he vowed to fight on.

In late 1919 Hitler joined a tiny extremist group in Munich called the German Workers' Party. By 1921 Hitler had gained absolute control of this small but growing party, now renamed the National Socialist German Worker's Party, or Nazi Party. A master of mass propaganda and political showmanship, Hitler worked his audiences into a frenzy with wild attacks on the Versailles treaty, the Jews, war profiteers, and Germany's Weimar Republic.

In late 1923 Germany under the Weimar Republic was experiencing unparalleled hyperinflation and seemed on the verge of collapse (see page 868). Hitler, inspired by Mussolini's recent victory, attempted an armed uprising in Munich. Despite the failure of the poorly organized plot and Hitler's arrest, Nazism had been born.

Hitler's Road to Power

At his trial Hitler violently denounced the Weimar Republic and attracted enormous publicity. From the unsuccessful revolt, Hitler concluded he had to gain power legally through electoral competition. During his brief prison term he dictated *Mein Kampf* (*My Struggle*), in which he expounded on his basic ideas on race and anti-Semitism, the notion of territorial expansion based on "living space" for Germans, and the role of the leader-dictator, called the *Führer* (FYOUR-uhr).

The Nazis remained a small splinter group until the 1929 Great Depression shattered economic prosperity. By the end of 1932 an incredible 43 percent of the labor force was unemployed. Industrial production fell by one-half between 1929 and 1932. No factor contributed more to Hitler's success than this economic crisis.

Hitler rejected free-market capitalism and advocated government programs to promote recovery. He pitched his speeches to middle- and lower-middle-class groups and to skilled workers. As the economy collapsed, great numbers of these people "voted their pocketbooks"[7] and deserted the conservative and moderate parties for the Nazis. In the 1930 election the Nazis won 6.5 million votes and 107 seats, and in July 1932 they gained 14.5 million votes—38 percent of the total—and became the largest party in the Reichstag.

Hitler and the Nazis appealed strongly to German youth. In 1931 almost 40 percent of Nazi Party members were under thirty, compared with 20 percent of Social Democrats. National recovery, exciting and rapid change, and personal advancement made Nazism appealing to millions of German youths.

Hitler also came to power because of the breakdown of democratic government. Germany's economic collapse in the Great Depression convinced many voters that the country's republican leaders were stupid and corrupt. Disunity on the left was another nail in the republic's coffin. The Communists refused to

CHAPTER LOCATOR | What caused the Great Depression, and what were its consequences? | What was the nature of the new totalitarian dictatorships?

cooperate with the Social Democrats, even though the two parties together out-numbered the Nazis in the Reichstag.

Finally, Hitler excelled in backroom politics. In 1932 he succeeded in gaining support from key people in the army and big business who thought they could use him to their own advantage. Many conservative and nationalistic politicians thought similarly. Thus in January 1933 President Paul von Hindenburg (1847–1934) legally appointed Hitler, leader of Germany's largest party, as German chancellor.

The Nazi State and Society

Hitler quickly established an unshakable dictatorship. When the Reichstag building was partly destroyed by fire in February 1933, Hitler blamed the Communist Party. He convinced President von Hindenburg to sign dictatorial emergency acts that abolished freedom of speech and assembly and most personal liberties. He also called for new elections in an effort to solidify his political power.

When the Nazis won only 44 percent of the votes, Hitler outlawed the Communist Party and arrested its parliamentary representatives. Then on March 23, 1933, the Nazis forced through the Reichstag the so-called **Enabling Act**, which gave Hitler absolute dictatorial power for four years.

Hitler and the Nazis took over the government bureaucracy, installing many Nazis in top positions. Hitler next outlawed strikes and abolished independent labor unions, which were replaced by the Nazi Labor Front. Professional people — doctors and lawyers, teachers and engineers — also saw their independent organizations swallowed up in Nazi associations. Publishing houses and universities were put under Nazi control, and students and professors publicly burned forbidden books. Modern art and architecture were ruthlessly prohibited. Life became violently anti-intellectual. By 1934 a brutal dictatorship characterized by frightening dynamism and total obedience to Hitler was already largely in place.

In June 1934 Hitler ordered his elite personal guard — the SS — to arrest and shoot without trial roughly a thousand long-time Nazi storm troopers. Shortly thereafter army leaders swore a binding oath of "unquestioning obedience" to Adolf Hitler. The SS grew rapidly. Under Heinrich Himmler (1900–1945), the SS took over the political police (the Gestapo) and expanded its network of concentration camps.

From the beginning, German Jews were a special object of Nazi persecution. By late 1934 most Jewish lawyers, doctors, professors, civil servants, and musicians had been banned from their professions. In 1935 the infamous Nuremberg Laws classified as Jewish anyone having three or more Jewish grandparents and deprived Jews of all rights of citizenship. By 1938 roughly one-quarter of Germany's half million Jews had emigrated, sacrificing almost all their property in order to leave Germany.

In late 1938 the attack on the Jews accelerated and grew more violent. On November 9 and 10, 1938, the Nazis initiated a series of well-organized attacks against Jews throughout Nazi Germany and some parts of Austria. This infamous event is known as Kristallnacht, or Night of Broken Glass, after the broken glass that littered the streets following the frenzied destruction of Jewish homes, shops, synagogues, and neighborhoods by German civilians and uniformed storm troopers. Many historians consider this night the beginning of Hitler's Final Solution against the Jews (see page 942), and after this event it became very difficult for Jews to leave Germany.

Enabling Act
▶ An act pushed through the Reichstag by the Nazis that gave Hitler absolute dictatorial power for four years.

| How did Stalin and the Communist Party build a totalitarian order in the Soviet Union? | How did Italian fascism develop? | **Why were Hitler and his Nazi regime initially so popular, how did their actions lead to WWII?** | How did Germany and Japan build empires in Europe and Asia, how did the Allies defeat them? | ☑ LearningCurve Check what you know. |

935

Some Germans privately opposed these outrages, but most went along or looked the other way. Although this lack of response reflected the individual's helplessness in a totalitarian state, it also reflected the strong popular support Hitler's government enjoyed.

Hitler's Popularity

Hitler had promised the masses economic recovery — "work and bread" — and he delivered. The Nazi Party launched a large public works program to pull Germany out of the depression. In 1935 Germany turned decisively toward rearmament. Unemployment dropped steadily, and by 1938 the Nazis boasted of nearly full employment. For millions of Germans economic recovery was tangible evidence that Nazi promises were more than show and propaganda.

For ordinary German citizens, in contrast to those deemed "undesirable," Hitler's government offered greater equality and more opportunities. In 1933 class barriers in Germany were generally high. Hitler's rule introduced changes that lowered these barriers. The new Nazi elite included many young and poorly educated dropouts, rootless lower-middle-class people like Hitler who rose to the top with breathtaking speed. More generally, however, the Nazis tolerated privilege and wealth only as long as they served party needs. The well-educated classes held on to most of their advantages, and only a modest social leveling occurred in the Nazi years

Not all Germans supported Hitler, and a number of German groups actively resisted him after 1933. Tens of thousands of political enemies were imprisoned, and thousands were executed. In the first years of Hitler's rule, the principal resisters were trade-union Communists and Socialists. Catholic and Protestant churches produced a second group of opponents. Their efforts were directed primarily at preserving genuine religious life, however, not at overthrowing Hitler. Finally, in 1938 and again during the war, some high-ranking army officers, who feared the consequences of Hitler's reckless aggression, plotted, unsuccessfully, against him.

Aggression and Appeasement, 1933–1939

After Germany's economic recovery and Hitler's success in establishing Nazi control of society, he turned to the next item on his agenda: aggressive territorial expansion. Germany's withdrawal from the League of Nations in October 1933 indicated its determination to rearm. When in March 1935 Hitler established a general military draft and declared the "unequal" Versailles treaty disarmament clauses null and void, leaders in Britain, France, and Italy issued a rather tepid joint protest and warned him against future aggressive actions.

But the emerging united front against Hitler quickly collapsed. Britain adopted a policy of appeasement, granting Hitler everything he could reasonably want (and more) in order to avoid war. British appeasement, which practically dictated French policy, had the support of many powerful British conservatives who, as in Germany, underestimated Hitler. The British people, still horrified by the memory, the costs, and the losses of the First World War, generally supported pacifism rather than war.

In March 1936 Hitler suddenly marched his armies into the demilitarized Rhineland, violating the Treaties of Versailles and Locarno. France would not move without British support, and Britain refused to act. As Britain and France opted for appeasement and the Soviet Union watched all developments suspiciously,

→ Italian campaigns, 1935–1936

Italy's Ethiopian Campaign, 1935–1936

Hitler found powerful allies. In October 1936 Italy and Germany established the so-called Rome-Berlin Axis. Japan, which wanted support for its occupation of Manchuria, also joined the Axis alliance (see page 905).

At the same time, Germany and Italy intervened in the Spanish Civil War (1936–1939), where their support helped General Francisco Franco's Fascist movement defeat republican Spain. Republican Spain's only official aid in the fight against Franco came from the Soviet Union.

In late 1937 Hitler moved forward with his plans to crush Austria and Czechoslovakia as the first step in his long-contemplated drive to the east for living space. By threatening Austria with invasion, Hitler forced the Austrian chancellor in March 1938 to put local Nazis in control of the government. The next day German armies moved in unopposed, and Austria became two provinces of Greater Germany (Map 30.1).

MAP 30.1 ■ The Growth of Nazi Germany, 1933–1939

Until March 1939 Hitler brought ethnic Germans into the Nazi state; then he turned on the Slavic peoples, whom he had always hated. He stripped Czechoslovakia of its independence and prepared for an attack on Poland in September 1939.

How did Stalin and the Communist Party build a totalitarian order in the Soviet Union?

How did Italian fascism develop?

Why were Hitler and his Nazi regime initially so popular, how did their actions lead to WWII?

How did Germany and Japan build empires in Europe and Asia, how did the Allies defeat them?

LearningCurve
Check what you know.

937

Simultaneously, Hitler demanded that the pro-Nazi, German-speaking territory of western Czechoslovakia—the Sudetenland—be turned over to Germany. Democratic Czechoslovakia was prepared to defend itself, but appeasement triumphed again. In September 1938 British prime minister Arthur Neville Chamberlain (1869–1940) flew to Germany three times in fourteen days. In these negotiations Chamberlain and the French agreed with Hitler that the Sudetenland should be ceded to Germany immediately. Sold out by the Western powers, Czechoslovakia gave in.

Hitler's armies occupied the remainder of Czechoslovakia in March 1939. This time, there was no possible rationale of self-determination for Nazi aggression. When Hitler used the question of German minorities in Danzig as a pretext to confront Poland, Chamberlain declared that Britain and France would fight if Hitler attacked his eastern neighbor. Hitler did not take these warnings seriously and pressed on.

Then, in an about-face that stunned the world, sworn enemies Hitler and Stalin signed a nonaggression pact in August 1939. Each dictator promised to remain neutral if the other became involved in war. An attached secret protocol divided eastern Europe into German and Soviet zones "in the event of a political and territorial reorganization."[8] Stalin agreed to the pact for three reasons: he distrusted Western intentions, he needed more time to build up Soviet industry and military reserves, and Hitler offered territorial gain.

For Hitler, everything was now set. On September 1, 1939, the Germans attacked Poland from three sides. Two days later, Britain and France, finally true to their word, declared war on Germany. The Second World War had begun.

> ## QUICK REVIEW

What role did economic factors play both in Hitler's rise to power and his popularity once in power?

CHAPTER LOCATOR | What caused the Great Depression, and what were its consequences? | What was the nature of the new totalitarian dictatorships?

CHAPTER 30
938 THE GREAT DEPRESSION AND WORLD WAR II

How did Germany and Japan build empires in Europe and Asia, and how did the Allies defeat them?

Prelude to Murder

This photo captures the terrible inhumanity of Nazi racism. Frightened and bewildered families from the soon-to-be-destroyed Warsaw Ghetto are being forced out of their homes by German soldiers for deportation to concentration camps. There they face murder in the gas chambers. (Keystone/Getty Images)

NAZI SOLDIERS SCORED ENORMOUS SUCCESSES in Europe until late 1942, establishing a vast empire of death and destruction. Japan attacked the United States in December 1941 and then moved to expand their empire throughout Asia and the Pacific Ocean. Eventually, the mighty coalition of Britain, the United States, and the Soviet Union overwhelmed the aggressors in manpower and military strength.

Hitler's Empire in Europe, 1939–1942

Using planes, tanks, and trucks in the first example of a blitzkrieg, or "lightning war," Hitler's armies crushed Poland in four weeks. The Soviet Union quickly took its share agreed to in the secret protocol—the eastern half of Poland and the Baltic states of Lithuania, Estonia, and Latvia. In the west French and British armies dug in; they expected another war of attrition and economic blockade. But in spring 1940 the Nazi lightning war struck again. After occupying Denmark, Norway, and Holland, German motorized columns broke through southern Belgium and into France.

blitzkrieg
▶ "Lightning war" using planes, tanks, and trucks, first used by Hitler to crush Poland in four weeks.

| How did Stalin and the Communist Party build a totalitarian order in the Soviet Union? | How did Italian fascism develop? | Why were Hitler and his Nazi regime initially so popular, how did their actions lead to WWII? | **How did Germany and Japan build empires in Europe and Asia, how did the Allies defeat them?** | ✔️ LearningCurve Check what you know. |

Vichy France, 1940

Occupied by Germany

Annexed by Germany

As Hitler's armies poured into France, aging marshal Henri-Philippe Pétain formed a new French government—the so-called Vichy (VIH-shee) government—and accepted defeat. By July 1940 Hitler ruled practically all of western continental Europe; Italy was an ally, the Soviet Union a friendly neutral (Map 30.2). Only Britain, led by Winston Churchill (1874–1965), remained unconquered.

To prepare for an invasion of Britain, Germany first needed to gain control of the air. In the Battle of Britain, which began in July 1940, German planes attacked British airfields and key factories. In September Hitler began indiscriminately bombing British cities to break British morale. British aircraft factories increased production, and Londoners defiantly dug in. By September Britain was winning the air war, and Hitler abandoned his plans for an immediate German invasion of Britain.

Hitler now allowed his lifetime obsession of creating a vast eastern European empire for the "master race" to dictate policy. In June 1941 Germany broke the Nazi-Soviet nonaggression pact and attacked the Soviet Union. By October Leningrad was practically surrounded, Moscow was besieged, and most of Ukraine had

EVENTS LEADING TO WORLD WAR II

1919	Treaty of Versailles is signed
1921	Hitler heads National Socialist German Worker's Party (Nazis)
1922	Mussolini seizes power in Italy
1927	Stalin takes control of the Soviet Union
1929–1939	Great Depression
1931	Japan invades Manchuria
January 1933	Hitler is appointed chancellor of Germany
March 1933	Reichstag passes the Enabling Act, granting Hitler absolute dictatorial power
October 1933	Germany withdraws from the League of Nations
1935	Nuremberg Laws deprive Jews of all rights of citizenship
March 1935	Hitler announces German rearmament
October 1935	Mussolini invades Ethiopia and receives Hitler's support
March 1936	German armies move unopposed into the demilitarized Rhineland
October 1936	Rome-Berlin Axis created
1936–1939	Spanish Civil War
1937	Japan invades China
March 1938	Germany annexes Austria
September 1938	Munich Conference: Britain and France agree to German seizure of the Sudetenland from Czechoslovakia
March 1939	Germany occupies the rest of Czechoslovakia; appeasement ends in Britain
August 1939	Nazi-Soviet nonaggression pact is signed
September 1, 1939	Germany invades Poland
September 3, 1939	Britain and France declare war on Germany

CHAPTER LOCATOR | What caused the Great Depression, and what were its consequences? | What was the nature of the new totalitarian dictatorships?

Legend:
- Axis powers and their allies
- Occupied by Germany and its allies
- Allied powers and their allies
- Neutral nations
- Boundary of Greater Germany
- Major battle

Siege of Leningrad, Sept. 1941–Jan. 1944

Germans repulsed, Dec. 1941

Moscow, Oct. 1941–Jan. 1942

Siege of Stalingrad, Aug. 21, 1942–Jan. 31, 1943

Siege, Sept. 1939 Uprising, Aug.–Sept. 1944

Germany surrenders, May 8, 1945

Battle of Britain, fall 1940

Invasion of Normandy June 6, 1944

Battle of the Bulge Dec. 1944

Axis troops occupy Vichy France, Nov. 10 and 11, 1942

Italian front Feb. 1945

Rome (Liberated June 1944)

Monte Cassino May 1944

Salerno Sept. 1943

Allies invade Sicily and Italy, July–Sept. 1943

Sicily July 1943

Battle for Crete, May 20–June 1, 1941

Axis troops evacuated, May 1943

Casablanca Nov. 1942

Joined Allies, Nov. 1942

El Alamein autumn 1942

Scale: 0 200 400 miles / 0 200 400 kilometers

MAP 30.2 ■ World War II in Europe and Africa, 1939–1945

The map shows the extent of Hitler's empire at its height, before the Battle of Stalingrad in late 1942 and the subsequent advances of the Allies until Germany surrendered on May 7, 1945.

been conquered. But the Soviets did not collapse, and when a severe winter struck German armies outfitted in summer uniforms, the invaders were stopped.

Although stalled in Russia, Hitler ruled an enormous European empire. He now began building a **New Order** based on the guiding principle of Nazi totalitarianism: racial imperialism. Hitler envisioned a vast eastern colonial empire where enslaved Poles, Ukrainians, and Russians would die or be killed off while Germanic peasants would resettle the abandoned lands. Himmler and the elite

New Order

▶ Hitler's program, based on the guiding principle of racial imperialism, which gave preferential treatment to the Nordic peoples above "inferior" Latin peoples and, at the bottom, "subhuman" Slavs and Jews.

| How did Stalin and the Communist Party build a totalitarian order in the Soviet Union? | How did Italian fascism develop? | Why were Hitler and his Nazi regime initially so popular, how did their actions lead to WWII? | **How did Germany and Japan build empires in Europe and Asia, how did the Allies defeat them?** | ✓ LearningCurve Check what you know. |

SS corps, supported by military commanders and German policemen, implemented a program of destruction in the occupied territories to create a "mass settlement space" for Germans.

The Holocaust

Finally, the Nazi state condemned all European Jews to extermination in the Holocaust. After Warsaw fell in 1939, the Nazis forced Jews in the occupied territories to move to urban ghettos, while German Jews were sent to occupied Poland. After Germany attacked Russia in June 1941, forced expulsion spiraled into extermination. In late 1941 Hitler and the Nazi leadership, in some still-debated combination, ordered the SS to speed up planning for "the final solution of the Jewish question."[9] Throughout the Nazi empire Jews were systematically arrested, packed like cattle onto freight trains, and dispatched to extermination camps.

Arriving at their destination, small numbers of Jews were sent to nearby slave labor camps, where they were starved and systematically worked to death. (See "Individuals in Society: Primo Levi," page 944.) Most victims were taken to "shower rooms," which were actually gas chambers. By 1945 about 6 million Jews had been murdered.

Who was responsible for this terrible crime? After the war historians laid the guilt on Hitler and the Nazi leadership. Beginning in the 1990s studies appeared revealing a much broader participation of German people in the Holocaust and popular indifference (or worse) to the Jews' fate.[10] In most occupied countries local non-German officials also cooperated in the arrest and deportation of Jews.

Japan's Asian Empire

By late 1938, 1.5 million Japanese troops were bogged down in China, holding a great swath of territory but unable to defeat the Nationalists and the Communists (see pages 905–908). In 1939, as war broke out in Europe, the Japanese redoubled their ruthless efforts. Implementing a savage policy of "kill all, burn all, destroy all," Japanese troops committed shocking atrocities, including the so-called Rape of Nanjing. During Japan's war in China—the second Sino-Japanese War (1937–1945)—the Japanese are estimated to have killed 4 million Chinese people.

In August 1940 the Japanese announced the formation of a self-sufficient Asian economic zone. Although they spoke of liberating Asia from Western imperialism and of "Asia for the Asians," their true intentions were to eventually rule over a vast Japanese empire. Ultranationalists moved to convince Japan's youth that Japan had a sacred liberating mission in Asia.

For the moment, however, Japan needed allies. In September 1940 Japan signed a formal alliance (the Axis alliance) with Germany and Italy, and Vichy France granted the Japanese domination over northern French Indochina. The United States, upset with Japan's occupation of Indochina and fearing embattled Britain would collapse if it lost its Asian colonies, froze scrap iron sales to Japan and applied further economic sanctions in October.

As 1941 opened, Japan's leaders faced a critical decision. In 1941 the United States was the world's largest oil producer and supplied over 90 percent of

Holocaust

▶ The attempted systematic extermination of all European Jews and other "undesirables" by the Nazi state during World War II.

Axis powers and their allies
Occupied by Germany and its allies
■ Extermination camp
● Major concentration camp
◆ Site of mass killing
✦ Ghetto

The Holocaust, 1941–1945

Japan's oil needs. Japan had only a year and a half's worth of military and economic oil reserves, which the war in China and the Japanese military and merchant navies were quickly drawing down. On July 26, 1941, President Roosevelt embargoed all oil exports to Japan and froze its assets in the United States. Japan now had to either recall its forces from China or go to war before running out of oil. It chose war.

On December 7, 1941, Japan launched a surprise attack on the U.S. fleet in Pearl Harbor in the Hawaiian Islands. Japan hoped to cripple its Pacific rival, gain time to build a defensible Asian empire, and eventually win an ill-defined compromise peace.

The Japanese attack was a limited success. The Japanese sank or crippled every American battleship, but by chance all the American aircraft carriers were at sea and escaped unharmed. Hours later the Japanese destroyed half of the American Far East Air Force stationed at Clark Air Base in the Philippines. Americans were humiliated by these unexpected defeats, which soon overwhelmed American isolationism and brought the United States into the war.

Hitler immediately declared war on the United States. Simultaneously, Japanese armies successfully attacked European and American colonies in Southeast Asia. After American forces surrendered the Philippines in May 1942, Japan held a vast empire in Southeast Asia and the western Pacific (Map 30.3).

The Japanese claimed they were freeing Asians from Western imperialism, and they called their empire the Greater East Asian Co-Prosperity Sphere. Most local populations were glad to see the Western powers go, but Asian faith in "co-prosperity" and support for Japan steadily declined as the war progressed. Although the Japanese set up anticolonial governments and promised genuine independence, real power always rested with Japanese military commanders and their superiors in Tokyo. Moreover, the Japanese never treated local populations as equals, and the occupiers exploited local peoples for Japan's wartime needs.

The Japanese often exhibited great cruelty toward prisoners of war and civilians. For example, Dutch, Indonesian, and perhaps as many as two hundred thousand Korean women were forced to provide sex for Japanese soldiers as "comfort women." Recurring cruel behavior aroused local populations against the invaders.

The Grand Alliance

While the Nazis and the Japanese built their empires, Great Britain, the United States, and the Soviet Union joined together in an unlikely military pact called the Grand Alliance. Grand Alliance leaders agreed to a Europe first policy. Only after defeating Hitler would the Allies mount an all-out attack on Japan. To encourage mutual trust, the Allies adopted the principle of the unconditional surrender of Germany and Japan, and no unilateral treaties. This policy cemented the Grand Alliance because it denied Germany and Japan any hope of dividing their foes.

The Grand Alliance's military resources were awesome. The United States possessed a unique capacity to wage global war with its large population and mighty industry. The British economy was totally and effectively mobilized, and the country became an important staging area for the war in Europe. As for the Soviet Union, so great was its economic strength that it might well have defeated Germany without Western help.

Europe first policy

▶ The military strategy, set forth by Churchill and adopted by Roosevelt, that called for the defeat of Hitler in Europe before the United States launched an all-out strike against Japan in the Pacific.

How did Stalin and the Communist Party build a totalitarian order in the Soviet Union?

How did Italian fascism develop?

Why were Hitler and his Nazi regime initially so popular, how did their actions lead to WWII?

How did Germany and Japan build empires in Europe and Asia, how did the Allies defeat them?

✓ LearningCurve
Check what you know.

943

Most Jews deported to Auschwitz were murdered as soon as they arrived, but the Nazis made some prisoners into slave laborers, and a few of these survived. Primo Levi (1919–1987), an Italian Jew, became one of the most influential witnesses to the Holocaust and its death camps.

Like many in Italy's small Jewish community, Levi's family belonged to the urban professional classes. The young Primo Levi graduated in 1941 from the University of Turin with highest honors in chemistry. Since 1938, when Italy introduced racial laws, he had faced growing discrimination, and two years after graduation he joined the antifascist resistance movement. Quickly captured, he was deported to Auschwitz with 650 Italian Jews in February 1944. Stone-faced SS men picked only ninety-six men and twenty-nine women to work in their respective labor camps. Levi was one of them.

Nothing had prepared Levi for what he encountered. The Jewish prisoners were kicked, punched, stripped, branded with tattoos, crammed into huts, and worked unmercifully. Hoping for some sign of prisoner solidarity in this terrible environment, Levi found only a desperate struggle of each against all and enormous status differences among prisoners. Many stunned and bewildered newcomers, beaten and demoralized by their bosses — the most privileged prisoners — collapsed and died. Others struggled to secure their own privileges, however small, because food rations and working conditions were so abominable that ordinary Jewish prisoners perished in two to three months.

Sensitive and noncombative, Levi found himself sinking into oblivion. But instead of joining the mass of the "drowned," he became one of the "saved" — a complicated surprise with moral implications that he would ponder all his life. As Levi explained in *Survival in Auschwitz* (1947), the usual road to salvation in the camps was some kind of collaboration with German power.* Savage German criminals were released from prison to become brutal camp guards; non-Jewish political prisoners competed for jobs entitling them to better conditions; and, especially troubling for Levi, a small number of Jewish men plotted and struggled for the power of life and death over other Jewish prison-

Primo Levi, who never stopped thinking, writing, and speaking about the Holocaust. (© Gianni Giansanti/Sygma/Corbis)

ers. Though not one of these Jewish bosses, Levi believed that he himself, like almost all survivors, had entered the "gray zone" of moral compromise. Only a very few superior individuals, "the stuff of saints and martyrs," survived the death camps without shifting their moral stance.

For Levi, compromise and salvation came from his profession. Interviewed by a German technocrat for the camp's synthetic rubber program, Levi performed brilliantly in scientific German and savored his triumph as a Jew over Nazi racism. Work in the warm camp laboratory offered Levi opportunities to pilfer equipment that could then be traded to other prisoners for food and necessities. Levi also gained critical support from three saintly prisoners who refused to do wicked and hateful acts. And he counted "luck" as essential for his survival: in the camp infirmary with scarlet fever in February 1945 as advancing Russian armies prepared to liberate the camp, Levi was not evacuated by the Nazis and shot to death like most Jewish prisoners.

After the war Primo Levi was forever haunted by the nightmare that the Holocaust would be ignored or forgotten. Always ashamed that so many people whom he considered better than himself had perished, he wrote and lectured tirelessly to preserve the

*Primo Levi, *Survival in Auschwitz: The Nazi Assault on Humanity*, rev. ed. 1958 (London: Collier Books, 1961), pp. 79–84, and *The Drowned and the Saved* (New York: Summit Books, 1988). These powerful testimonies are highly recommended.

memory of Jewish victims and guilty Nazis. Wanting the world to understand the Jewish genocide in all its complexity so that never again would people tolerate such atrocities, he grappled tirelessly with his vision of individual choice and moral compromise in a hell designed to make the victims collaborate and persecute each other.

QUESTIONS FOR ANALYSIS

1. Describe Levi's experience at Auschwitz. How did camp prisoners treat each other? Why?
2. What does Levi mean by the "gray zone"? How is this concept central to his thinking?
3. Will a vivid historical memory of the Holocaust help prevent future genocide? Why or why not?

ONLINE DOCUMENT PROJECT

What choices did Holocaust survivors face? Listen to testimonies from Holocaust survivors, and then complete a quiz and writing assignment based on the evidence and details from this chapter. *See inside the front cover to learn more.*

The War in Europe, 1942–1945

Halted at the gates of Moscow and Leningrad in 1941, the Germans renewed their offensive against the Soviet Union in 1942 and attacked Stalingrad in July. The Soviet armies counterattacked, quickly surrounding the entire German Sixth Army of 300,000 men. By late January 1943 only 123,000 soldiers were left to surrender. In summer 1943 the larger, better-equipped Soviet armies took the offensive and began to push the Germans back (see Map 30.2).

Not yet prepared to attack Germany directly through France, the Western Allies engaged in heavy fighting in North Africa (see Map 30.2). In autumn 1942 British forces defeated German and Italian armies at the Battle of El Alamein (el a-luh-MAYN) in Egypt. Shortly thereafter an Anglo-American force took control of the Vichy French colonies of Morocco and Algeria.

Having driven the Axis powers from North Africa by spring 1943, Allied forces invaded Italy. War-weary Italians deposed Mussolini, and the new Italian government accepted unconditional surrender in September 1943. But German commandos rescued Mussolini and made him head of a puppet government. German armies seized Rome and all of northern Italy. After almost two years of fighting, the German armies in Italy finally surrendered on April 29, 1945. Two days earlier Mussolini had been captured by partisan forces, and he was executed the next day.

On June 6, 1944, American and British forces under General Dwight Eisenhower landed on the beaches of Normandy, France. From there, they pushed inland and broke through the German lines. In March 1945 American troops crossed the Rhine and entered Germany.

The Soviets had been advancing steadily since July 1943, and on April 26, 1945, the Red Army met American forces on the Elbe River in Germany. As Soviet forces fought their way into Berlin, Hitler committed suicide in his bunker on April 30. On May 7 the remaining German commanders capitulated.

The War in the Pacific, 1942–1945

In April 1942 the Japanese devised a plan to take Port Moresby in New Guinea and also destroy U.S. aircraft carriers in an attack on Midway Island (see Map 30.3). Having broken the secret Japanese code, the Americans skillfully won a series of decisive naval victories. First, in the Battle of the Coral Sea in May 1942, an American carrier force halted the Japanese advance on Port Moresby. Then, in the Battle of Midway in June 1942, American pilots sank all four of the attacking Japanese aircraft carriers and established overall naval equality with Japan in the Pacific.

The United States gradually won control of the sea and air as it geared up its war industry. In July 1943 the Americans and their Australian allies opened an "island-hopping" campaign toward Japan. By 1944 hundreds of American submarines were hunting in "wolf packs," decimating shipping and destroying economic links in Japan's far-flung, overextended empire.

The Pacific war was brutal and atrocities were committed on both sides. Aware of Japanese atrocities in China and the Philippines, the U.S. forces seldom took Japanese prisoners after the Battle of Guadalcanal in August 1942, killing even those rare Japanese soldiers who offered to surrender. American forces moving across the central and western Pacific in 1943 and 1944 faced unyielding resistance, and this resistance hardened soldiers as American casualties kept rising. A product of spiraling violence, mutual hatred, and dehumanizing racial stereotypes, the war's brutality intensified as it moved toward Japan.

In June 1944 U.S. bombers began a relentless bombing campaign of the Japanese home islands. In October 1944 American forces under General Douglas MacArthur landed on Leyte Island in the Philippines. In the ensuing Battle of Leyte Gulf, the Japanese lost 13 large warships, including 4 aircraft carriers, while the Americans lost only 3 small ships. The Japanese navy was practically finished.

In spite of massive defeats, Japanese troops continued to fight on. Indeed, the bloodiest battles of the Pacific war took place on Iwo Jima in February 1945 and on Okinawa in June 1945. American commanders believed that an invasion of Japan might cost 1 million American casualties and possibly 10 to 20 million Japanese lives. In fact, Japan was almost helpless,

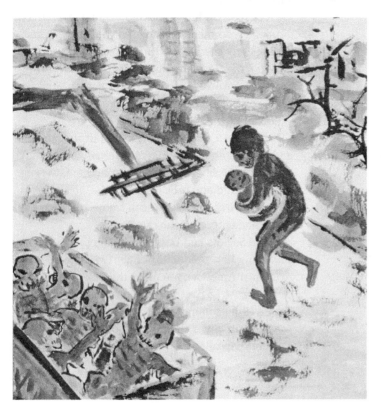

A Hiroshima Survivor Remembers

Yasuko Yamagata was seventeen when she saw the brilliant blue-white "lightning flash" that became a fiery orange ball consuming everything that would burn. Thirty years later Yamagata painted this scene, her most unforgettable memory of the atomic attack. An incinerated woman, poised as if running with her baby clutched to her breast, lies near a water tank piled high with charred corpses. (GE15-05 drawn by Yasuko Yamagata, Hiroshima Peace Memorial Museum)

CHAPTER LOCATOR | What caused the Great Depression, and what were its consequences? | What was the nature of the new totalitarian dictatorships?

CHAPTER 30
946 THE GREAT DEPRESSION AND WORLD WAR II

MAP 30.3 ■ World War II in the Pacific

Japanese forces overran an enormous amount of territory in 1942, which the Allies slowly recaptured in a long, bitter struggle.

> MAPPING THE PAST

ANALYZING THE MAP: Locate the extent of the Japanese empire in 1942, and compare it to the Japanese-controlled territory at surrender in 1945. Where was the fighting in the Pacific concentrated?

CONNECTIONS: How was the course of the war's end in Europe different from that of Asia, and what does this suggest about the difficulties that the Allies faced in fighting the Japanese?

its industry and cities largely destroyed by intense American bombing. As the war in Europe ended in April 1945, Japanese leaders were divided. Hardliners argued that surrender was unthinkable. A peace faction argued that Japan should seek a negotiated end to the war.

On July 26 Truman, Churchill, and Stalin issued the Potsdam Declaration, which demanded unconditional surrender. The declaration left unclear whether

How did Stalin and the Communist Party build a totalitarian order in the Soviet Union?

How did Italian fascism develop?

Why were Hitler and his Nazi regime initially so popular, how did their actions lead to WWII?

How did Germany and Japan build empires in Europe and Asia, how did the Allies defeat them?

✓ LearningCurve
Check what you know.

947

the Japanese emperor would be treated as a war criminal. The Japanese, who considered Emperor Hirohito a god, sought clarification and amnesty for him. The Allies remained adamant that the surrender be unconditional. The Japanese felt compelled to fight on.

On August 6 and 9, 1945, the United States dropped atomic bombs on Hiroshima and Nagasaki in Japan. Also on August 9, Soviet troops launched an invasion of the Japanese puppet state of Manchukuo (Manchuria, China). To avoid a Soviet invasion and further atomic bombing, the Japanese announced their surrender on August 14, 1945. The Second World War, which had claimed the lives of more than 50 million soldiers and civilians, was over.

> **QUICK REVIEW**

How did the Nazi's racial ideology shape German wartime policies and priorities?

CHAPTER SUMMARY

The 1929 American stock market crash triggered a Great Depression. Western democracies expanded their powers and responded with relief programs. Authoritarian and Fascist regimes arose to replace some capitalist democracies. Only World War II ended the depression.

The radical totalitarian dictatorships of the 1920s and 1930s were repressive, profoundly antiliberal, and exceedingly violent. Mussolini set up the first Fascist government, a one-party dictatorship, but it was never truly a totalitarian state on the order of Hitler's Germany or Stalin's Soviet Union.

In the Soviet Union Stalin launched a socialist "revolution from above" to modernize and industrialize the U.S.S.R. Mass purges of the Communist Party in the 1930s led to the imprisonment and deaths of millions.

Hitler and the Nazi elite rallied support with a totalitarian ideology that combined racism and extreme nationalism. The Great Depression caused German voters to turn to Adolph Hitler and the Nazis for relief. After Hitler declared the Versailles treaty disarmament clause null and void, British and French leaders tried appeasement. On September 1, 1939, his unprovoked attack on Poland forced the Allies to declare war, starting World War II.

Nazi armies first seized Poland and Germany's western neighbors and then turned east. Here Hitler planned to build a New Order based on racial imperialism. In the Holocaust that followed, millions of Jews and other "undesirables" were systematically exterminated. In Asia the Japanese created the Greater East Asian Co-Prosperity Sphere as a vehicle of Japanese domination and control. After Japan attacked Pearl Harbor, the United States entered the war. In 1945 the Grand Alliance of the United States, Britain, and the Soviet Union defeated Germany and Japan.

CHAPTER LOCATOR | What caused the Great Depression, and what were its consequences? | What was the nature of the new totalitarian dictatorships?

CHAPTER 30
948   THE GREAT DEPRESSION AND WORLD WAR II

CONNECTIONS If anyone still doubted the interconnectedness of all the world's inhabitants following the Great War, those doubts faded as events on a truly global scale touched everyone as never before. First a Great Depression shook the financial foundations of the wealthiest capitalist economies and the poorest producers of raw materials and minerals. Another world war followed, bringing global death and destruction. At war's end, as we shall see in Chapter 31, the world's leaders revived Woodrow Wilson's idea of a League of Nations and formed the United Nations in 1946 to prevent such tragedies from ever reoccurring.

Although the United Nations was an attempt to bring nations together, the postwar world became more divided than ever. Chapter 31 will describe how two new superpowers—the United States and the Soviet Union—emerged from World War II to engage one another in the Cold War for nearly the rest of the century. Then in Chapters 32 and 33 we will see how less developed nations in Asia, Africa, and Latin America emerged after the war. Many of them did so by turning the nineteenth-century European ideology of nationalism against its creators, breaking the bonds of colonialism.

ONLINE DOCUMENT PROJECT

Remembering the Holocaust

What choices did Holocaust survivors face?

Listen to testimonies from Holocaust survivors, and then complete a quiz and writing assignment based on the evidence and details from this chapter. *See inside the front cover to learn more.*

| How did Stalin and the Communist Party build a totalitarian order in the Soviet Union? | How did Italian fascism develop? | Why were Hitler and his Nazi regime initially so popular, how did their actions lead to WWII? | How did Germany and Japan build empires in Europe and Asia, how did the Allies defeat them? | ✓ LearningCurve Check what you know. |

CHAPTER 30 STUDY GUIDE

STEP 1 **GET STARTED ONLINE**

 LearningCurve

Now that you've read the chapter, make it stick by completing the LearningCurve activity.

STEP 2 **EXPLAIN WHY IT MATTERS**

Put your reading into practice. Identify each term below, and then explain why it matters in world history.

TERM	WHO OR WHAT & WHEN	WHY IT MATTERS
New Deal (p. 918)		
Popular Front (p. 920)		
totalitarianism (p. 923)		
fascism (p. 923)		
five-year plan (p. 925)		
New Economic Policy (NEP) (p. 926)		
collectivization (p. 926)		
Black Shirts (p. 931)		
Lateran Agreement (p. 932)		
Nazism (p. 933)		
Enabling Act (p. 935)		
blitzkrieg (p. 939)		
New Order (p. 941)		
Holocaust (p. 942)		
Europe first policy (p. 943)		

STEP 3 **MOVE BEYOND THE BASICS**

To demonstrate a more advanced understanding of the totalitarian regimes of the 1920s and 1930s, fill in the chart below with descriptions of the ideologies and policies of the governments of the Soviet Union, Italy, and Germany. How did ideology shape the policies of each government?

	Ideology	Social Policy	Economic Policy	Foreign Policy
The Soviet Union				
Italy				
Germany				

PUT IT ALL TOGETHER

Now, take a step back and try to explain the big picture. Remember to use specific examples from the chapter in your answers.

THE GREAT DEPRESSION

▶ Compare and contrast the response to the Great Depression in the United States, France, Britain, Germany, and the Scandinavian countries. How would you explain the similarities and differences you note?

▶ What light does the Great Depression shed on the nature of global economic connections in the 1920s and 1930s? How did an economic crisis that began in the United States and Europe spread to Asia, Africa, and Latin America?

THE AGE OF DICTATORS

▶ In your opinion, was Italy under Mussolini a totalitarian state? Why or why not?

▶ Compare and contrast Stalinism and Nazism. What were the most important differences between the two ideologies? How did both systems use the persecution of "outsiders" to promote loyalty and obedience to the regime?

THE SECOND WORLD WAR

▶ What role did race play in the German and Japanese drive for territorial expansion? Is it fair to describe World War II, in Europe and in the Pacific, as a racial war?

▶ In your opinion, why did the Allies win the war? What role did industrial production play in the Allied victory? What other factors were important?

LOOKING BACK, LOOKING AHEAD

▶ Argue for or against the following proposition: "World War II was the inevitable consequence of the destruction of World War I and the fatally flawed peace treaties produced at its conclusion." What evidence can you present to support your position?

▶ What similarities and differences do you see between the Great Depression of the 1930s and the global economic crisis of the early twenty-first century? Could the contemporary crisis lead to another "Age of Dictators"? Why or why not?

> IN YOUR OWN WORDS

Imagine that you must give an oral report to the class answering the following question: **How did the economic suffering created by the Great Depression contribute to the outbreak of World War II?** What would be the most important points and why?

31

DECOLONIZATION, REVOLUTION, AND THE COLD WAR

1945–1968

> How did decolonization and the Cold War shape global developments in the decades following World War II? Chapter 31 examines political and economic developments in the decades following World War II. In the aftermath of World War II, the immediate challenge was to repair the enormous damage done by the fighting. This challenge was complicated by rivalry between the United States and the Soviet Union that developed into a tense but nonviolent conflict known as the Cold War. Devastated by war, the nations of Europe could no longer hold onto their overseas empires, and nearly every colonial territory gained formal independence between 1945 and the early 1960s. A revolution in China consolidated Communist rule. At the same time, remarkable growth and economic prosperity occurred in the postwar era. There were, however, limits to postwar prosperity, and these decades of economic growth did not resolve underlying tensions and conflicts.

New Leadership in Africa Kwame Nkrumah, nationalist leader and first prime minister of Ghana after its independence in 1957. (Photo by Underwood Archives/Getty Images)

✓ **LearningCurve**

After reading the chapter, use LearningCurve to retain what you've read.

> How did the Cold War and decolonization shape the postwar world?

> How did religion and the legacies of colonialism affect the formation of new nations in South Asia and the Middle East after World War II?

> How did the Cold War shape reconstruction, revolution, and decolonization in East and Southeast Asia?

> What factors influenced decolonization in Africa after World War II?

> Why did populism emerge as such a powerful political force in Latin America?

> Why did the world face growing social unrest in the 1960s?

How did the Cold War and decolonization shape the postwar world?

United Nations Programs at Work, 1951

As part of a UN assistance program, the United Nations Children's Fund (UNICEF) provided milk to children in Greece in the aftermath of civil war in that country.
(© Amerika Haus/SZ Photo/The Image Works)

Cold War

▶ The postwar conflict between the United States and the Soviet Union.

THE BITTER RIVALRY BETWEEN the United States and the Soviet Union divided postwar Europe and became a **Cold War**—not an outright military confrontation between nations, but a long, tense standoff. As the Cold War took shape, activists and observers around the world debated the meaning of freedom and independence in a postcolonial world.

The Cold War and the Division of Europe

The Cold War originated in disputes over the political outcome of the war. During talks among the three major powers—the United States, Britain, and the Soviet Union—held toward the end of the war, Soviet leader Joseph Stalin insisted that control of eastern Europe was the best way to guarantee military security from Germany. When Harry Truman demanded free elections throughout eastern Europe, Stalin refused.

Truman's tough stance was bolstered by the fact that the United States was the only country that possessed atomic weapons at the end of the war. Just as the

CHAPTER LOCATOR | **How did the Cold War and decolonization shape the postwar world?** | How did religion and the legacies of colonialism affect the new nations in South Asia and the Middle East?

954 CHAPTER 31 DECOLONIZATION, REVOLUTION, AND THE COLD WAR

1945
United Nations established

1946–1955
Populist Juan Perón leads Argentina

1947
Independence of India

1948
Marshall Plan aid in Europe; independence of Israel

1949
Chinese Revolution; formation of NATO

1949–present
Harsh restrictions against religion and speech in China

1950–1953
Korean War

1953–1964
Khrushchev implements policy of de-Stalinization in the Soviet Union

1956
Nasser nationalizes Suez Canal Company; Soviet invasion of Hungary

1957
Formation of Common Market

1957–1964
Decolonization in sub-Saharan Africa

1957–1975
War between North and South Vientam

1959
Cuban Revolution

1960
Brazil's new capital, Brasília, inaugurated

1961
Building of Berlin Wall

1962
Cuban missile crisis

1964–1965
Civil Rights Act and Voting Rights Act passed in United States

1965
Great Proletarian Cultural Revolution in China

1967
Six-Day War in Israel

U.S. sense of security came from having a monopoly on the atomic bomb, Stalin pursued security for the Soviet Union by militarily occupying eastern Europe and imposing obedient governments that would provide a buffer against the threat of western European aggression.

President Harry Truman misread these occupations as a campaign for world domination. Communist movements beyond Stalin's occupation zone in Greece and China fed these fears. In October 1945 Truman issued the Truman Doctrine, aimed at "containing" communism to areas already occupied by the Soviet army by providing military and economic support to governments threatened by Communist control.

Truman asked Congress for military aid for Greece and Turkey to prevent the spread of communism. Soon after, Secretary of State George C. Marshall proposed a broader package of economic and food aid—the Marshall Plan—to help Europe rebuild. Stalin refused Marshall Plan assistance for all of eastern Europe, where he had established Soviet-style Communist dictatorships. The Soviet Union's aid and support for the overthrow of the democratically elected Czechoslovakian government in February 1948 shocked the U.S. Congress into action, and on April 2, 1948, it voted for the Marshall Plan.

On July 24, 1948, Stalin blocked all road traffic through the Soviet zone of Germany to Berlin. The Western allies responded with an airlift of provisions to the West Berliners. After 324 days the Soviets backed down. In 1949 the United States

Truman Doctrine
▶ American policy of preventing the spread of Communist rule.

Marshall Plan
▶ American plan for providing economic aid to Europe to help it rebuild.

How did the Cold War shape revolution and decolonization in East and Southeast Asia?

What factors influenced decolonization in Africa after World War II?

Why did populism emerge as such a powerful political force in Latin America?

Why did the world face growing social unrest in the 1960s?

LearningCurve
Check what you know.

NATO

▶ The North Atlantic Treaty Organization, an anti-Soviet military alliance of Western nations.

superpowers

▶ Countries whose military (or economic) might dwarfed that of other countries.

formed an anti-Soviet military alliance of Western governments: the North Atlantic Treaty Organization (**NATO**). Stalin countered by tightening his hold on his satellites, later united in the Warsaw Pact. Europe was divided into two hostile blocs. British prime minister Winston Churchill warned that an "iron curtain has descended across the Continent."[1]

The Soviet Union, with its massive army arrayed across eastern Europe, and the United States, with its industrial strength and atomic weapons, emerged from the war as **superpowers** whose might dwarfed that of other countries. Superpower status reached an awkward balance after the Soviet Union developed its own atomic weapons in 1949. Both nations pitched themselves into a military and geopolitical confrontation that stopped short of outright war: the Cold War (Map 31.1).

A deep ideological divide defined the rivalry between the United States and the Soviet Union. The United States saw itself as the defender of a "free world" governed by liberal principles such as free markets, private property, and individ-

MAP 31.1 ■ Cold War Europe in the 1950s

Europe was divided by an "iron curtain" during the Cold War. None of the Communist countries of eastern Europe were participants in the Marshall Plan.

CHAPTER LOCATOR | How did the Cold War and decolonization shape the postwar world?

How did religion and the legacies of colonialism affect the new nations in South Asia and the Middle East?

CHAPTER 31
956 DECOLONIZATION, REVOLUTION, AND THE COLD WAR

ual rights protected by democratic constitutions. The Soviet Union defined itself as the defender of the rights of workers and peasants against their exploiters, the rights of colonial peoples against their colonizers, and economic development based on rational production and equitable distribution. The Cold War sharpened the distinctions between these models, creating opposing paths that the superpowers pressured other countries to follow.

The United Nations

In 1945 representatives of fifty nations met in San Francisco to draft a charter for a new intergovernmental organization called the United Nations. Like that of its predecessor, the League of Nations (see Chapter 28), the immediate goal of the United Nations was to mediate international conflicts in order to preserve peace. But in 1945 the founders of the United Nations foresaw a more ambitious role for the new body than the League of Nations had played: beyond conflict resolution, the UN would support the decolonization of territories under foreign rule; promote economic development; and expand access to health care, protection for workers, environmental conservation, and gender equity.

The United Nations was divided into two bodies: a General Assembly that met annually and included all nations that signed the UN Charter; and a Security Council made up of the five main regional powers (the United States, the Soviet Union, the United Kingdom, China, and France), each of which held veto power over the council's decisions, making it a body that in effect only functioned through unanimous consent.

The UN gave critical support to decolonization efforts. Its charter defended the right of self-determination, and it served as a forum for liberation movements to advocate for their claims, negotiate the terms of independence, or define new national boundaries. In addition, UN member nations volunteered military forces to serve around the world as peacekeepers.

The Politics of Liberation

The term *Third World* emerged in the 1950s when many observers viewed Africa, Asia, and Latin America as a single entity, different from both the capitalist, industrialized "First World" and the Communist, industrialized "Second World." The Cold War rivalry between the United States and the Soviet Union reinforced this "three-bloc" perspective, which staked out separate camps for the superpowers, and created a third general category for everyone else. Despite differences in history and culture, most so-called Third World countries in Africa, Asia, and Latin America were poor and economically underdeveloped. They also shared many characteristics that encouraged the development of a common consciousness about their marginalization and ideologies for defining their future.

The roots of many liberation movements in these countries went back well before the Second World War and often as far back as the nineteenth century. After the Second World War weakened the colonial powers, nationalist movements in the colonies became more insistent. As nations fought against colonial rule, their quest for liberation took many forms. Economically, they pursued national industrialization and development to end dependence on industrialized

How did the Cold War shape revolution and decolonization in East and Southeast Asia? | What factors influenced decolonization in Africa after World War II? | Why did populism emerge as such a powerful political force in Latin America? | Why did the world face growing social unrest in the 1960s? | ✓ LearningCurve Check what you know.

957

nations. Politically, they sought alliances within the industrializing world to avoid the neocolonial influences of more powerful nations. Intellectually, they reacted against Western assumptions of white supremacy.

The former colonies faced intense pressure to align themselves ideologically and economically with either the United States or the Soviet Union, and few could resist the pressure or the incentives those powers brought to bear. Nonetheless, to varying degrees, they tried to operate independently from the two superpowers in a number of ways. In 1955 leaders of twenty-nine recently independent nations in Asia and Africa met in Bandung, Indonesia, to create a framework for political and economic cooperation to help them emerge from colonialism without having to resubordinate their nations either to their former colonizers or to pressures from the Cold War superpowers. The participants outlined principles for rejecting pressure from the superpowers and supporting decolonization. In 1961 nations participating in the Bandung Conference met in Yugoslavia to form a Non-Aligned Nations Movement.

Dependency and Development Theories

In 1948 the United Nations established the Economic Commission for Latin America (ECLA) in Santiago, Chile, to study economic development. Under the direction of Argentine economist Raúl Prebisch, ECLA produced one of Latin America's most influential intellectual contributions of the twentieth century: a diagnosis of reasons why Latin America, like other less industrialized regions of the world, remained economically and technologically dependent on Europe and the United States, along with prescriptions for remedying that dependency. These ideas formed what became known as dependency theory.

According to dependency theory, countries in Latin America, Africa, and Asia were trapped in the position of borrowers of capital and technology, and producers of primary commodities such as agricultural and mineral goods. Since western Europe and the United States industrialized in the nineteenth century, they secured a lasting economic advantage magnified by colonialism and neocolonialism, which reorganized production and consumption around the world for their benefit.

According to this analysis, the prosperity of Europe and the United States was built on the impoverishment of other regions of the world because the products that industrialized countries made were worth more than the agricultural or mineral exports of other nations. This inequality in the market value of goods increased over time as the relative value of commodities such as coffee or copper decreased relative to the value of manufactured goods like automobiles or technologically advanced goods like computer software.

How could this pattern be broken? One approach was modernization theory, championed by U.S. economist Walt Whitman Rostow. He suggested that societies passed through phases of development from primitive to modern, and that adopting the political, economic, or cultural practices of places like the United States was the best remedy for poverty. Modernization theory shaped foreign aid programs: the U.S. government deployed armies of experts around the world to advise governments and communities on how to modernize. These technicians

dependency theory
▶ The belief that development in some areas of the world locks other nations into underdevelopment.

modernization theory
▶ The belief that all countries evolved in a linear progression from traditional to mature.

CHAPTER LOCATOR | How did the Cold War and decolonization shape the postwar world? | How did religion and the legacies of colonialism affect the new nations in South Asia and the Middle East?

CHAPTER 31
958 DECOLONIZATION, REVOLUTION, AND THE COLD WAR

often did not understand local conditions, believing that the American way was the only way, and these projects were often riddled with unintended negative consequences. As a result, many people began to mistrust these experts.

To peoples emerging from colonialism, dependency theory offered a more appealing path. Dependency theorists rejected liberalism because they believed free-market capitalism reinforced social and economic problems by inhibiting the accumulation of wealth in dependent regions. Instead they favored state intervention to remake national economies so that resources would be distributed more equitably. Prebisch advocated a practice that became common in much of the world: import substitution industrialization (ISI). Under ISI policies, countries imposed trade barriers to keep certain foreign products out and provided subsidies to develop domestic industries that could make the same goods. Some dependency theorists suggested that even ISI was not enough, and that deeper social reforms were needed, such as the redistribution of farmlands from large landowners to rural workers, as well as state control of major industries and banks.

import substitution industrialization (ISI)
▶ The use of trade barriers to keep certain products out of one's country so that domestic industry can emerge and produce the same goods.

The governments that attempted land redistribution or the nationalization of foreign firms often faced a fierce backlash by landowners, foreign corporations, and political conservatives. In many cases, reformist governments were deposed in military coups supported by the United States. The U.S. reaction against reformers in countries like Guatemala, where the elected government was overthrown in a coup organized by the United States in 1954, pushed reformers in other countries into more radical and defiant approaches. In Cuba a revolutionary movement led by Fidel Castro took power in 1959. Castro's regime executed a deep social and economic transformation of Cuba, including the redistribution of land and urban properties. This pressure from the United States pushed revolutionary Cuba into an alliance with the Soviet Union. The Argentine military strategist who worked closely with Castro, Che Guevara, became an icon of radical revolutionary liberation. He built his ideas for social change into a revolutionary theory, Guevarism, which suggested that private property and wage labor were forms of exploitation that could be overthrown by free workers volunteering their labor to help liberate others.

One of the most influential areas where the idea of liberation crystallized was a movement within the Catholic Church called liberation theology. The movement emerged in Latin America amid reforms of church doctrine carried out by Pope John XXIII (pontificate 1958–1963), who called on clergy to engage more directly with the contemporary world. In 1968 the Latin American Council of Bishops gathered in Medellín, Colombia, and invoked dependency theory as it called on clergy to exercise a "preferential option for the poor," by working toward "social justice," including land redistribution, the recognition of peasants' and labor unions, and denouncing economic dependency and neocolonialism.

liberation theology
▶ A movement within the Catholic Church to support the poor in situations of exploitation that emerged with particular force in Latin America in the 1960s.

Drawing on dependency theory and sometimes verging on revolutionary Marxism, priests attracted to liberation theology often challenged governments and fought against landowners and business owners they saw as oppressors. After the 1970s, Popes John Paul II (pontificate 1978–2005) and Benedict XVI (pontificate 2005–2013) suppressed liberation theology and silenced its most outspoken thinkers. Advocates of liberation theology greeted the naming of a pope from Latin America, Francis, in 2013 as a return to the focus on fighting poverty and social exclusion within the Catholic Church.

How did the Cold War shape revolution and decolonization in East and Southeast Asia?

What factors influenced decolonization in Africa after World War II?

Why did populism emerge as such a powerful political force in Latin America?

Why did the world face growing social unrest in the 1960s?

☑ LearningCurve
Check what you know.

Interpreting the Postcolonial Experience

Many intellectuals who came of age during and after the struggle for political emancipation embraced a vision of solidarity among peoples oppressed by colonialism and racism. Some argued that genuine freedom required a total rejection of Western values in addition to an economic and political break with the former colonial powers. Frantz Fanon (1925–1961), a French-trained black psychiatrist from the Caribbean island of Martinique, argued that decolonization is always a violent and totally consuming process whereby one "species" of men, the colonizers, is completely replaced by an absolutely different species—the colonized. Fanon believed that throughout Africa and Asia the former imperialists and their local collaborators—the "white men with black faces"—remained the enemy.

As countries gained independence, some writers looked beyond wholesale rejection of the industrialized powers. They, too, were anti-imperialist, but they were often also activists and cultural nationalists who celebrated the rich histories and cultures of their peoples. Many did not hesitate to criticize their own leaders or fight oppression and corruption.

The Nigerian writer Chinua Achebe (1930–2013) rendered these themes with sharp insight. Achebe sought to restore his people's self-confidence by reinterpreting the past. For Achebe, the "writer in a new nation" had first to embrace the "fundamental theme" that Africans had their own culture before the Europeans came and that it was the duty of writers to help Africans reclaim their past. Achebe took up this task in his 1958 novel *Things Fall Apart*, which brings to life the men and women of an Ibo village at the beginning of the twentieth century, with all their virtues and frailties. In later novels Achebe portrayed the post-independence disillusionment of many writers and intellectuals, which reflected trends in many developing nations in the 1960s and 1970s: the rulers seemed increasingly corrupted by Western luxury and estranged from the rural masses. From the 1970s onward, Achebe was active in the struggle for democratic government in Nigeria.

Novelist V. S. Naipaul, born in Trinidad in 1932 of Indian parents, also castigated governments in the developing countries for corruption, ineptitude, and self-deception. Another of Naipaul's recurring themes is the poignant loneliness and homelessness of people uprooted by colonialism and Western expansion.

> **QUICK REVIEW**

What was dependency theory, and how did activists and reformers apply it to countries in Latin America, Africa, and Asia?

CHAPTER LOCATOR | How did the Cold War and decolonization shape the postwar world? | How did religion and the legacies of colonialism affect the new nations in South Asia and the Middle East?

CHAPTER 31
960 DECOLONIZATION, REVOLUTION, AND THE COLD WAR

Indira Gandhi, daughter of Jawaharlal Nehru, became prime minister of India in 1966. She is shown here at a 1966 meeting of the Non-Aligned Nations Movement, seated between Yugoslav president Josip Tito (left) and Egyptian president Gamal Abdel Nasser (right). (© Sueddeutsche Zeitung Photo/The Image Works)

How did religion and the legacies of colonialism affect the formation of new nations in South Asia and the Middle East after World War II?

AS EUROPE MOVED TOWARD GREATER economic unity in the postwar era, nationalist independence movements in former colonies dramatically reversed centuries of overseas imperial expansion. The three South Asian countries created through independence from Britain and subsequent partition, India, Pakistan, and Bangladesh, reflected the dominant themes of national renaissance and modernization that characterized the end of colonialism, but ethnic and religious rivalries greatly complicated their renewal and development.

The nationalists who guided the formation of modern states in the Arab world struggled to balance Cold War pressures from the United States and the Soviet Union, as well as the tension between secular modernization and Islam. In many cases, these pressures resulted in the formation of one-party dictatorships that became corrupt and failed to alleviate poverty. At the heart of this world, Jewish nationalists founded the state of Israel following the Second World War. The Zionist claim to a homeland came into sharp, and often violent, conflict with the rights and claims of the Palestinian people displaced by the creation of Israel.

| How did the Cold War shape revolution and decolonization in East and Southeast Asia? | What factors influenced decolonization in Africa after World War II? | Why did populism emerge as such a powerful political force in Latin America? | Why did the world face growing social unrest in the 1960s? | ☑ LearningCurve Check what you know. |

Independence in India, Pakistan, and Bangladesh

World War II accelerated the drive toward Indian independence begun by Mohandas Gandhi (see page 898). In 1942 Gandhi called on the British to "quit India" and threatened another civil disobedience campaign. He and the other Indian National Congress Party leaders were soon after arrested and were jailed for much of the war. Meanwhile, the Congress Party's prime rival skillfully seized the opportunity to increase its influence.

Muslim League

▶ Political party in colonial India that advocated for a separate Muslim homeland after independence.

The Congress Party's rival was the Muslim League, led by the English-educated lawyer Muhammad Ali Jinnah (1876–1948). Jinnah feared Hindu domination of an independent Indian state led by the Congress Party. Asserting the right of Muslim areas to separate from the Hindu majority, Jinnah called on the British government in March 1940 to grant the Muslim and Hindu peoples separate national states, in recognition of what he saw as their essentially separate national identities. Gandhi regarded Jinnah's two-nation theory as untrue and as promising the victory of hate over love.

Britain agreed to speedy independence for India after 1945, but conflicts between Hindu and Muslim nationalists led to murderous clashes in 1946. When it became clear that Jinnah and the Muslim League would accept nothing less than an independent state of Pakistan, the British mediated a partition that created a predominantly Hindu nation and a predominantly Muslim nation. On August 14, 1947, India and Pakistan gained political independence from Britain as two separate nations (Map 31.2).

Massacres and mass expulsions followed independence. Perhaps a hundred thousand Hindus and Muslims were slaughtered, and an estimated 5 million became refugees. Gandhi labored to ease tensions between Hindus and Muslims, but in the aftermath of riots in January 1948, he was killed by a Hindu gunman who resented what he saw as Gandhi's appeasement of Muslims.

Jawaharlal Nehru (1889–1964) and the Indian National Congress Party ruled India for a generation and introduced major social reforms. Hindu women gained legal equality, including the right to vote, to seek divorce, and to marry outside their castes. The constitution abolished the untouchable caste. In practice, less discriminatory atti-

MAP 31.2 ■ The Partition of British India, 1947

Violence and fighting were most intense where there were large Hindu and Muslim minorities — in Kashmir, the Punjab, and Bengal. The tragic result of partition, which occurred repeatedly throughout the world in the twentieth century, was a forced exchange of populations and greater homogeneity on both sides of the border.

CHAPTER LOCATOR | How did the Cold War and decolonization shape the postwar world? | **How did religion and the legacies of colonialism affect the new nations in South Asia and the Middle East?**

CHAPTER 31

962 DECOLONIZATION, REVOLUTION, AND THE COLD WAR

tudes toward women and untouchables evolved slowly—especially in rural villages, where 85 percent of the people lived.

The Congress Party leadership pursued nationalist, state-driven economic development, but population growth of about 2.4 percent per year consumed much of the increased output of economic expansion. The relocation of millions during the partition of Indian and Pakistan exacerbated poverty. The Congress Party maintained neutrality in the Cold War, distancing itself from both the United States and the Soviet Union. Instead India became one of the most avid advocates of a "third force" of nonaligned nations.

At independence, Pakistan was divided between eastern and western provinces separated by more than a thousand miles of Indian territory, as well as by language, ethnic background, and social custom. The Bengalis of East Pakistan were neglected by the central government, which remained in the hands of West Pakistan's elite after Jinnah's death. In 1971 the Bengalis revolted and won their independence as the new nation of Bangladesh after a violent civil war. Bangladesh, a secular parliamentary democracy, struggled to find political and economic stability amid famines and flooding.

Arab Socialism in the Middle East

In the postwar period, new Arab states in the Middle East emerged from long legacies of colonial rule. These new nations embraced Arab socialism, a modernizing, secular, and nationalist project of nation building aimed at economic development, a strong military and Pan-Arab unity that would deter imperial impulses from Europe or the superpowers. Arab socialism focused on modernization and state formation rather than ideological Marxism.

Arab socialism held particular significance for women in Middle Eastern societies. It cast aside religious restrictions on women's dress, education, occupations, and public activities. In countries like Egypt and Iraq, Western dress, the openness of education, and access to professions enjoyed by urban, typically affluent women symbolized an embrace of modernity.

In 1952 army officers overthrew Egypt's monarchy and expelled the British military force that the king had allowed to occupy the country. The movement's leader, Gamal Abdel Nasser (1918–1970), built a nationalist regime aimed at eradicating the vestiges of European colonialism, as well as creating an economic transformation through land redistribution and state support for industrialization. Applying the principles of Arab socialism, Nasser pursued the secularization of Egyptian society and equal opportunity for women and men, and created an extensive social welfare network.

Nasser's National Charter called for the nationalization of railroads, mines, ports, airports, dams, banks, utilities, insurance companies, and heavy industries. In the countryside the size of landholdings were limited and large estates broken up.

In 1956 Nasser took a symbolic and strategic step toward nationalizing Egypt's economy when he ordered the army to take control of the Suez Canal, still held by Britain and France. A coalition of British, French, and Israeli forces invaded to retake the canal. The Soviet Union offered support to Egypt. To prevent Soviet intervention and a Soviet-Egyptian alliance, the United States negotiated a cease-fire that granted Egypt control of the Suez Canal against the wishes

Arab socialism

▶ A modernizing, secular, and nationalist project of nation building aimed at economic development and the development of a strong military.

How did the Cold War shape revolution and decolonization in East and Southeast Asia?

What factors influenced decolonization in Africa after World War II?

Why did populism emerge as such a powerful political force in Latin America?

Why did the world face growing social unrest in the 1960s?

✓ LearningCurve
Check what you know.

963

of the British and French governments. Alongside control of the canal, Nasser's other main economic goal was the construction of a massive hydroelectric dam—the Aswan Dam—on the Nile River, which would provide electricity and control flooding to intensify agriculture. Nasser negotiated the funding and technical expertise for building the damn with both the United States and the Soviet Union, eventually settling on Soviet aid. The Suez crisis and the construction of the Aswan Dam were examples of a nationalist leader like Nasser successfully playing the superpowers against each other.

Nationalist military officers in other Arab countries emulated Nasser's public political profile and socialist developmental projects. In countries like Syria and Iraq, these nationalists formed the Pan-Arab socialist Ba'ath Party. Syria briefly merged with Egypt from 1958 until 1961, forming the United Arab Republic. Ba'athist military officers who resented Nasser's control of Syria revolted against Egypt and established a new national Syrian government dominated by the Ba'ath Party. In Iraq the Ba'ath Party formed part of the military movement that in 1958 overthrew the British-backed monarchy, leading to a long reign by Ba'athist leaders that ended when a U.S. military invasion toppled Saddam Hussein in 2003.

The Arab-Israeli Conflict

Palestinian Arabs, as well as Arabs in new states, strenuously opposed Jewish settlement in Palestine (see pages 894–895). The British announced in early 1947 their intention to withdraw from Palestine in 1948. The difficult problem of a Jewish homeland was dumped in the lap of the United Nations. In November 1947 the UN General Assembly passed a plan to partition Palestine into two separate states—one Arab and one Jewish (Map 31.3). The Jews accepted, and the Arabs rejected, the partition of Palestine.

By early 1948 an undeclared civil war raged in Palestine. When the British mandate ended on May 14, 1948, the Jews proclaimed the state of Israel. Arab countries immediately attacked, but Israeli forces drove off the invaders and conquered more territory. Roughly nine hundred thousand Palestinian refugees fled or were expelled from old Palestine. The war left an enormous legacy of Arab bitterness toward Israel and its political allies, Great Britain and the United States. In 1964 a loose union of Palestinian refugee groups opposed to Israel joined together, under the leadership of Yasir Arafat (1929–2004), to form the Palestine Liberation Organization (PLO).

Palestine Liberation Organization (PLO)

▶ Created in 1964, a loose union of Palestinian refugee groups opposed to Israel and united in the goal of gaining Palestinian home rule.

Nationalist leaders in neighboring Syria and Egypt cultivated political support at home through fierce opposition to Israel and threats to crush it militarily. This tension repeatedly erupted into war. On June 1, 1967, when Syrian and Egyptian armies massed on Israel's borders, the Israeli government launched surprise air strikes that destroyed most of the Egyptian, Syrian, and Jordanian air forces. Over the next five days Israeli armies took control of the Sinai Peninsula and the Gaza Strip from Egypt, the West Bank and East Jerusalem from Jordan, and the Golan Heights from Syria. In the Six-Day War (also known as the 1967 Arab-Israeli War), Israel proved itself to be the pre-eminent military force in the region, and it expanded the territory under its control threefold.

After the war Israel began to build large Jewish settlements in the Gaza Strip and the West Bank, home to millions of Palestinians. On November 22, 1967, the UN Security Council adopted Resolution 242, which contained a "land for peace"

CHAPTER LOCATOR | How did the Cold War and decolonization shape the postwar world? | How did religion and the legacies of colonialism affect the new nations in South Asia and the Middle East?

CHAPTER 31
964 DECOLONIZATION, REVOLUTION, AND THE COLD WAR

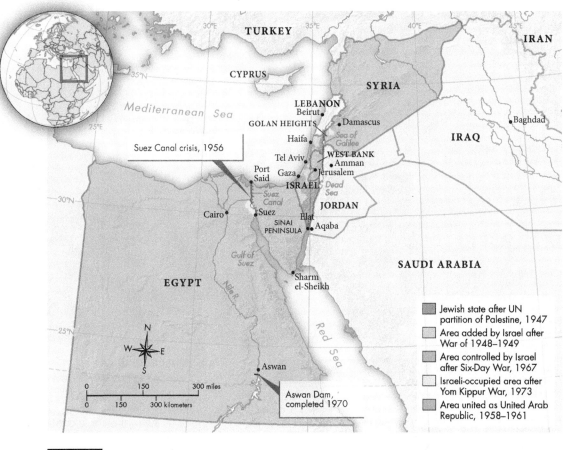

MAP 31.3 ■ The Middle East After 1947

The partition of Palestine by the United Nations resulted in the creation of Israel in 1948, which faced repeated conflicts with rival Arab states.

Map legend:
- Jewish state after UN partition of Palestine, 1947
- Area added by Israel after War of 1948–1949
- Area controlled by Israel after Six-Day War, 1967
- Israeli-occupied area after Yom Kippur War, 1973
- Area united as United Arab Republic, 1958–1961

formula by which Israel was called upon to withdraw from the occupied territories, and in return the Arab states were to withdraw all claims to Israeli territory, cease all hostilities, and recognize the sovereignty of the Israeli state. The tension between rival territorial claims persisted.

QUICK REVIEW

How did religious divisions complicate India's transition from colony to independent nation?

How did the Cold War shape revolution and decolonization in East and Southeast Asia?

What factors influenced decolonization in Africa after World War II?

Why did populism emerge as such a powerful political force in Latin America?

Why did the world face growing social unrest in the 1960s?

LearningCurve
Check what you know.

How did the Cold War shape reconstruction, revolution, and decolonization in East and Southeast Asia?

Communist China Poster Art

One of the most popular art forms in Communist China was poster art, millions of copies of which were printed to adorn the walls of homes, offices, factories, and businesses. This uniquely Chinese form contained neither abstract, modern, or bourgeois elements nor classical Chinese art styles. Such posters glorified the state, its leaders, and the heroes of the revolution. The two young women in this poster wear uniforms and caps bearing the Communist red star, the five points of which represent the five components of Communist society: the youth, the army, the peasants, the workers, and the intellectuals. (Courtesy, Chinese Poster Collection, University of Westminster, London)

> **PICTURING THE PAST**

ANALYZING THE IMAGE: Who is depicted, and what are they doing? What message do you think the artist seeks to convey with this image?

CONNECTIONS: What social function or application might posters such as this one have? Is this sort of expression unique to Communist societies, or can you think of examples of other types of art that promote public messages?

IN ASIA JAPAN'S DEFEAT ended the Second World War, but other conflicts continued: nationalists in territories colonized by European nations intensified their struggle for independence, and in China Nationalist and Communist armies confronted each other in a renewed civil war. In 1949 Communist forces under Mao Zedong triumphed and established the People's Republic of China. The Communist victory in China shaped the nature of Japan's reconstruction, as its U.S. occupiers determined that an industrially and economically strong Japan would serve as a counterweight to Mao. U.S. fear of the spread of communism drew the country into conflicts in Korea and Vietnam, intensifying the stakes in the decolonization struggle across East and Southeast Asia.

CHAPTER LOCATOR | How did the Cold War and decolonization shape the postwar world? | How did religion and the legacies of colonialism affect the new nations in South Asia and the Middle East?

966 CHAPTER 31 DECOLONIZATION, REVOLUTION, AND THE COLD WAR

The Communist Victory in China

When Japan surrendered to the Allies in August 1945, Communists and Nationalists both rushed to seize evacuated territory. Communists and Nationalists had fought each other before the Second World War, but had put aside their struggle to resist Japanese invasion. With the war over, the Nationalists and Communists resumed their conflict. By 1948 the Nationalist forces disintegrated before the better-led, more determined Communists. The following year Nationalist leader Jiang Jieshi and 2 million mainland Chinese fled to Taiwan, and in October 1949 Mao Zedong proclaimed the People's Republic of China (Map 31.4).

Communism triumphed in China for many reasons. Mao Zedong and the Communists had avoided pitched battles and concentrated on winning peasant support and forming a broad anti-Japanese coalition. By reducing rents, promising land redistribution, enticing intellectuals, and spreading propaganda, they emerged in peasant eyes as the true patriots, the genuine nationalists.

Between 1949 and 1954 the Communists consolidated their rule. They seized the vast landholdings of a minority of landlords and rich peasants and distributed the land to 300 million poor peasants. Meanwhile, as Mao admitted in 1957, mass arrests led to eight hundred thousand "class enemies" being summarily executed; the true figure is probably much higher. Millions more were deported to forced-labor camps.

Mao and the party looked to the Soviet Union for inspiration in the early 1950s. China adopted collective agriculture and Soviet-style five-year plans to promote rapid industrialization. Russian specialists built many Chinese factories, and the Soviets provided considerable economic aid. In the cultural and intellectual realms, too, the Chinese followed the Soviet example. Basic civil and political rights were abolished. Temples and churches were closed. They enthusiastically promoted Soviet Marxist ideas concerning women and the family. Full equality, work outside the home, and state-supported child care became primary goals.

In 1958 China broke from the Marxist-Leninist course of development and began to go its own way. Mao proclaimed a **Great Leap Forward** in which industrial growth would be based on small-scale backyard workshops and steel mills run by peasants living in gigantic self-contained communes. The intended great leap produced an economic disaster, as land in the countryside went untilled when peasants turned to industrial production. As many as 30 million people died in famines that swept the country in 1960–1961. When Soviet premier Nikita Khrushchev criticized Chinese policy in 1960, Mao condemned him and his

MAP 31.4 ■ Decolonization in Asia
After the Second World War, countries colonized by Britain, France, the Netherlands, and the United States gained their independence. In cases such as Vietnam and Indonesia, independence came through armed struggles against colonizers who were reluctant to leave.

Great Leap Forward
▶ Mao Zedong's acceleration of Chinese development in which industrial growth was to be based on small-scale backyard workshops run by peasants living in gigantic self-contained communes.

How did the Cold War shape revolution and decolonization in East and Southeast Asia?	What factors influenced decolonization in Africa after World War II?	Why did populism emerge as such a powerful political force in Latin America?	Why did the world face growing social unrest in the 1960s?	✓ LearningCurve Check what you know.

Great Proletarian Cultural Revolution

▶ A movement launched by Mao Zedong that attempted to purge the Chinese Communist Party of long-serving bureaucrats and recapture the revolutionary fervor of his guerrilla struggle.

Red Guards

▶ Radical cadres formed of Chinese youth who would attack anyone identified as an enemy of either the Chinese Communist Party or Chairman Mao.

Russian colleagues as detestable "modern revisionists." The Russians cut off economic and military aid, splitting the Communist world apart.

Mao lost influence in the party after the Great Leap Forward fiasco and the Sino-Soviet split, but in 1965 he staged a dramatic comeback, launching the Great Proletarian Cultural Revolution. He sought to purge the party and to recapture the revolutionary fervor of the guerrilla struggle (see page 902). The army and the nation's young people responded enthusiastically, organizing themselves into radical cadres called Red Guards. Students denounced their teachers and practiced rebellion in the name of revolution. Mao's thoughts, through his speeches and writings, were collected in the *Little Red Book*, which became scripture to the Red Guards.

The Red Guards sought to erase all traces of "feudal" and "bourgeois" culture and thought. Ancient monuments and countless works of art, antiques, and books were destroyed. Party officials, professors, and intellectuals were exiled to remote villages to purify themselves with heavy labor. Universities were shut down for years. Thousands of people died, many of them executed, and millions more were sent to rural forced-labor camps.

Conflict in Korea

As tensions rose in Europe, the Cold War spread to Asia. In 1945 Korea was divided into Soviet and American zones of occupation, which in 1948 became Communist North Korea and anticommunist South Korea. When the Russian-backed Communist forces of North Korea invaded South Korea in spring 1950, President Truman sent U.S. troops to lead a UN coalition force to stop what he interpreted as a coordinated Communist effort to dominate Asia.

The Korean War (1950–1953) was bitterly fought, but ended in a stalemate. The well-equipped North Koreans conquered most of the peninsula, but the South Korean, American, and UN troops rallied and drove their foes north to the Chinese border. At that point China intervened and pushed the South Koreans and Americans back south. In 1953 a fragile truce was negotiated, and the fighting stopped. Thus the United States extended its policy of containing communism to Asia, but drew back from invading Communist China and possibly provoking nuclear war.

The Korean War

- → North Korean invasion, June–Sept. 1950
- → UN offensive, Sept.–Nov. 1950
- → Communist Chinese offensive, Nov. 1950–Jan. 1951

Japan's American Reconstruction

Japan, like Germany, was formally occupied by all the Allies, but real power resided in American hands. U.S. general Douglas MacArthur exercised almost absolute authority. MacArthur and the Americans had a revolutionary plan for defeated Japan, introducing reforms designed to make Japan a free, democratic society along American lines.

Japan's sweeping American revolution began with demilitarization and a systematic purge of convicted war criminals and wartime collaborators. The American-dictated constitution of 1946 allowed the emperor to remain the "symbol of the State." Real power resided in the Japanese Diet, whose members were popularly elected. A bill of rights granted basic civil liberties and freed all political prisoners. Article 9 of the new constitution abolished the Japanese armed forces and renounced war. The American occupation left Japan's powerful bureaucracy

CHAPTER LOCATOR | How did the Cold War and decolonization shape the postwar world? | How did religion and the legacies of colonialism affect the new nations in South Asia and the Middle East?

largely intact and used it to implement fundamental social and economic reforms. The occupation promoted the Japanese labor movement, introduced antitrust laws, and granted Japanese women equality before the law. The occupation also imposed revolutionary land reform that strengthened the small independent farmers who became staunch defenders of postwar democracy.

America's efforts to remake Japan in its own image were powerful but short-lived. As Mao's forces prevailed in China, however, American leaders began to see Japan as a potential ally, not as an object of social reform. The American command began purging leftists and rehabilitating prewar nationalists. When the occupation ended in 1952, Japan regained independence, and the United States retained its vast military complex in Japan. Japan became the chief Asian ally of the United States in its efforts to contain the spread of communism in East Asia.

Baseball in Japan

Though baseball arrived in Japan in the late nineteenth century, it increased in popularity during U.S. occupation. This photo from 1950 shows children in their baseball uniforms, with a U.S. Jeep in the background. (Courtesy: CSU Archives/The Everett Collection)

The Vietnam War

French Indochina experienced the bitterest struggle for independence in Southeast Asia. With financial backing from the United States, France tried to reimpose imperial rule there after the Communist and nationalist guerrilla leader Ho Chi Minh (1890–1969) declared an independent republic in 1945. French forces were decisively defeated in the 1954 Battle of Dien Bien Phu. At the subsequent international peace conference, French Indochina gained independence. Laos and Cambodia became separate states, and Vietnam was temporarily divided into separately governed northern and southern regions pending elections to select a single unified government within two years. The South Vietnamese government refused to hold the elections, and civil war between it and the Communist Democratic Republic of Vietnam, or North Vietnam, broke out.

Cold War fears and U.S. commitment to the ideology of containment drove the United States to get involved in Vietnam. President Dwight D. Eisenhower (elected in 1952) refused to sign the Geneva Accords that temporarily divided the country, and provided military aid to help the south resist North Vietnam. Eisenhower's successor, John F. Kennedy, increased the number of American "military advisers." In 1964 President Lyndon Johnson greatly expanded America's role in the Vietnam conflict.

The American strategy was to "escalate" the war sufficiently to break the will of the North Vietnamese and their southern allies without resorting to "overkill," which might risk war with the entire Communist bloc. South Vietnam received massive military aid. Large numbers of American forces joined in

| How did the Cold War shape revolution and decolonization in East and Southeast Asia? | What factors influenced decolonization in Africa after World War II? | Why did populism emerge as such a powerful political force in Latin America? | Why did the world face growing social unrest in the 1960s? | ✓ LearningCurve Check what you know. |

969

combat. The United States bombed North Vietnam with ever-greater intensity. But there was no invasion of North Vietnam or naval blockade of its ports.

Most Americans initially saw the war as part of a legitimate defense against communism, but the combined effect of watching the results of the violent conflict on the nightly television news and experiencing the widening dragnet of a military draft spurred a growing antiwar movement. By 1967 a growing number of critics had denounced the American presence in Vietnam as an intrusion into a complex and distant civil war. The north's Tet Offensive in January 1968, a major attack on South Vietnamese cities, failed militarily but shook Americans' confidence in their government's ability to manage the conflict. Within months President Johnson announced he would not stand for re-election, and he called for negotiations with North Vietnam.

Elected in 1968, President Richard Nixon sought to disengage America gradually from Vietnam. He intensified the continuous bombardment of the enemy while simultaneously pursuing peace talks with the North Vietnamese. He also began a slow process of transferring the burden of the war to the South Vietnamese army, cutting American forces there from 550,000 to 24,000 in four years. Nixon finally reached a peace agreement with North Vietnam in 1973 that allowed the remaining American forces to complete their withdrawal in 1975.

The Vietnamese Communists unified their country in 1975 and began the process of nation building. Millions of Vietnamese civilians faced reprisals for aligning with the United States, including Hmong and Degar peoples (such as the Mnong) and other ethnic minorities. They first fled to refugee camps elsewhere in Southeast Asia and later settled as refugees in the United States. (See "Individuals in Society: Sieng, a Mnong Refugee in an American High School," page 1038.)

> ## QUICK REVIEW

How did the Communist victory in China shape U.S. policy toward Japan and Vietnam?

CHAPTER LOCATOR | How did the Cold War and decolonization shape the postwar world? | How did religion and the legacies of colonialism affect the new nations in South Asia and the Middle East?

CHAPTER 31
970   DECOLONIZATION, REVOLUTION, AND THE COLD WAR

The Opening of Parliament in Ghana

As part of an ancient ritual, two medicine men pour out sacred oil and call on the gods to bless the work of the Second Parliament and President Kwame Nkrumah, standing on the right. The combination of time-honored customs and modern political institutions was characteristic of African states after they secured independence. (AP Photo)

BY 1964 MOST OF AFRICA had gained independence (Map 31.5). Only Portugal's colonies and white-dominated southern Africa remained beyond the reach of African nationalists. The rise of independent states in sub-Saharan Africa came about as a reaction against Western imperialism and through the growth of African nationalism.

The Growth of African Nationalism

African nationalism resembled similar movements in Asia and the Middle East in its reaction against European colonialism, but there were two important differences. First, because the imperial system and Western education did not solidify in Africa until after 1900 (see pages 758–759), national movements came of age in the 1920s and reached maturity after 1945. Second, Africa's multiplicity of ethnic groups, coupled with colonial boundaries that often bore no resemblance to

| How did the Cold War shape revolution and decolonization in East and Southeast Asia? | **What factors influenced decolonization in Africa after World War II?** | Why did populism emerge as such a powerful political force in Latin America? | Why did the world face growing social unrest in the 1960s? | ☑ LearningCurve Check what you know. |

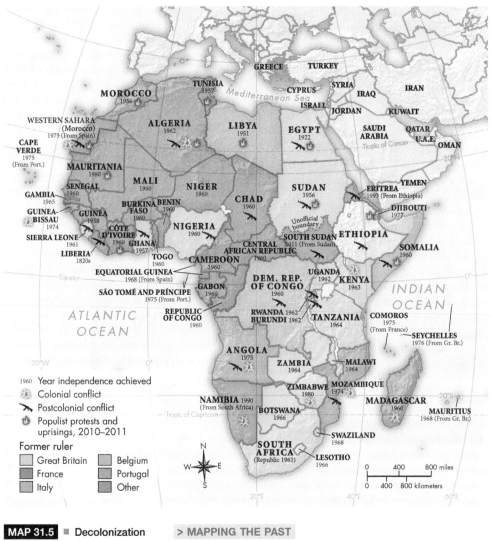

MAP 31.5 ■ Decolonization in Africa, 1947 to the Present

Most African territories achieved statehood by the mid-1960s, as European empires passed away, unlamented.

Map legend:
1960 Year independence achieved
Colonial conflict
Postcolonial conflict
Populist protests and uprisings, 2010–2011
Former ruler
Great Britain
France
Italy
Belgium
Portugal
Other

> MAPPING THE PAST

ANALYZING THE MAP: How many African states achieved independence after 1945? How many experienced some sort of postcolonial conflict?
CONNECTIONS: How did the imperialist legacy serve to complicate the transition to stable, independent nations in Africa and Latin America?

existing ethnic geography, greatly complicated the development of political—as distinct from cultural—nationalism. Was a modern national state based on ethnic or clan loyalties? Was it to be a continent-wide union of all African peoples? Would the multiethnic territories carved out by European empires become the new African nations? Such questions were not fully addressed until after 1945.

The first nationalist impetus came from the United States and the Caribbean. The most renowned participant in this "black nationalism" was W. E. B. Du Bois (1868–1963). The cofounder of the National Association for the Advancement of Colored People (NAACP) in the United States, Du Bois organized Pan-African congresses in Paris during the Paris Peace Conference in 1919 and in Brussels in 1921. **Pan-Africanists** sought black solidarity and, eventually, a vast self-governing union of all African peoples. Jamaican-born Marcus Garvey (1887–1940) was the most influential Pan-Africanist, rallying young, educated Africans to his call of "Africa for the Africans."

In the 1920s a surge of anticolonial nationalism swept educated Africans in French and British colonies. African intellectuals in Europe formulated and articulated *négritude*, or blackness: racial pride, self-confidence, and joy in black creativity and the black spirit. This westernized African elite pressed for better access to government jobs, modest steps toward self-government, and an end to humiliating discrimination.

The mass protests that accompanied the deprivations of the Great Depression, in particular the cocoa holdups of 1930–1931 and 1937–1938, fueled the new nationalism. Cocoa dominated the British colonial economy in the Gold Coast (which became Ghana). As prices plummeted after 1929, cocoa farmers refused to sell their beans to the British firms that fixed prices and monopolized exports. Now farmers organized cooperatives to cut back production and sell their crops directly to European and American chocolate manufacturers. The cocoa holdups mobilized the population against the foreign companies and demonstrated the power of mass organization and protest.

The repercussions of the Second World War in Africa greatly accelerated the changes begun in the 1930s. Many African soldiers who served in India had been powerfully impressed by Indian nationalism. As African mines and plantations strained to meet wartime demands, towns mushroomed into cities, which became centers of discontent and hardship.

Western imperialism also changed. The principle of self-government was written into the United Nations charter and was supported by Great Britain's postwar Labour government. Thus the key issue for Great Britain's various African colonies was their rate of progress toward self-government. The British and the French were in no rush, but an emerging group of African nationalist leaders was less patient. These postwar African leaders formed an elite by virtue of their advanced Western education, and they were profoundly influenced by Western thought. But compared with the interwar generation of educated Africans, they were more radical and had humbler social origins.

Postwar African nationalists pragmatically accepted prevailing colonial boundaries to avoid border disputes and achieve freedom as soon as possible. Sensing a loss of power, traditional rulers sometimes became the new leaders' worst political enemies. Skillfully, the new leaders channeled postwar hope and discontent into support for mass political organizations that offset this traditional authority. These organizations staged gigantic protests and became political parties.

Ghana Shows the Way

The most charismatic of this generation of African leaders was Kwame Nkrumah (KWA-may ihn-CROO-mah) (1909–1972). Nkrumah spent ten years studying in the United States, where he was influenced by European socialists and Marcus Garvey. Under his leadership the Gold Coast—which he renamed "Ghana"—became the first sub-Saharan state to emerge from colonialism.

Nkrumah came to power by building a radical party that appealed particularly to modern groups—veterans, merchant women, union members, urban toughs,

Pan-Africanists

▶ People who sought black solidarity and envisioned a vast self-governing union of all African peoples.

cocoa holdups

▶ Mass protests in the 1930s by Gold Coast producers of cocoa who refused to sell their beans to British firms and instead sold them directly to European and American chocolate manufacturers.

How did the Cold War shape revolution and decolonization in East and Southeast Asia?

What factors influenced decolonization in Africa after World War II?

Why did populism emerge as such a powerful political force in Latin America?

Why did the world face growing social unrest in the 1960s?

☑ LearningCurve
Check what you know.

973

and cocoa farmers. Rejecting halfway measures, Nkrumah and his Convention People's Party staged strikes and riots.

After he was arrested in 1950, Nkrumah campaigned from jail and saw his party win a smashing victory in the 1951 national elections. Called from prison to head the transitional government, Nkrumah and his nationalist party defeated westernized moderates and more traditional political rivals in free elections. In 1957 Ghana became independent. After Ghana's breakthrough, independence for other African colonies followed rapidly. The main problem in some colonies was the permanent white settlers, not the colonial officials. Wherever white settlers were numerous, as in Kenya, Algeria, and Rhodesia, they fought to preserve their privileged position.

French-Speaking Regions

Decolonization took a different course in French-speaking Africa. The events in the French North African colony of Algeria in the 1950s and early 1960s help clarify France's attitude toward its sub-Saharan African colonies.

Algeria's large, and mostly Catholic, European population—known as the pieds-noirs (black feet) because its members wore black shoes instead of sandals—was determined to keep Algeria part of France. In November 1954 Algeria's anticolonial movement, the **National Liberation Front** (FLN), began a bitter war for independence. After the FLN won and created an independent Algerian state in 1962, an estimated 900,000 of the 1.25 million Europeans and indigenous Jews fled.

The long and violent anticolonial war in Algeria, following Indochina's military victory, sharply divided France and undermined its political stability. As a result, it was difficult for France to respond to nationalists in its other African colonies until Charles de Gaulle returned to power in 1958. Seeking to maximize France's influence over the future independent nations, de Gaulle devised a divide-and-rule strategy. He divided the French West Africa and French Equatorial Africa federations into thirteen separate governments. Plebiscites were called in each territory to ratify the new arrangement. An affirmative vote meant continued ties with France; a negative vote signified immediate independence and a complete break with France.

De Gaulle's gamble was shrewd. The educated black elite identified with France and dreaded an abrupt separation. They also wanted French aid to continue. France had given the vote to its educated colonial elite after the Second World War, and about forty Africans held French parliamentary seats after 1946. For these reasons, French Africa's leaders tended to be moderate in their pursuit of independence.

In Guinea, however, a young nationalist named Sékou Touré (1922–1984) led his people to overwhelmingly reject the new constitution in 1958. Inspired by Ghana's Nkrumah, Touré laid it out to de Gaulle face-to-face: "We have one prime and essential need: our dignity. But there is no dignity without freedom. . . . We prefer freedom in poverty to opulence in slavery."[2]

Though peoples that had been colonized by France and Britain often found paths for independence, those of other regions of Africa struggled with the colonial policies of other European nations less prepared to acknowledge the wave of decolonization. Portugal's dictatorship hoped to keep its colonies in perpetuity.

pieds-noirs
▶ The predominantly Catholic French population in the French colony of Algeria, called "black feet" because they wore black shoes instead of sandals.

National Liberation Front
▶ The victorious anticolonial movement in Algeria.

CHAPTER LOCATOR | How did the Cold War and decolonization shape the postwar world? | How did religion and the legacies of colonialism affect the new nations in South Asia and the Middle East?

974 CHAPTER 31 DECOLONIZATION, REVOLUTION, AND THE COLD WAR

To ensure this, the Portuguese regime intensified white settlement and repression of nationalist groups in its colonies of Angola and Mozambique.

Belgium, a long-time practitioner of colonial paternalism coupled with harsh, selfish rule in its enormous Congo colony (see page 754), had always discouraged the development of an educated elite. When Belgium abruptly decided to grant independence in 1959 after intense riots, the fabric of Congo's government and society broke down. The mineral-rich nation stabilized under the U.S.-backed dictatorship of Mobutu Sese Seko, who renamed the country Zaire. Mobutu's corruption deepened poverty as the tremendous wealth generated from mining went into the hands of foreign companies and Mobutu's family and cronies.

QUICK REVIEW <

Why was the process of decolonization more difficult and tumultuous in some African colonies than in others?

How did the Cold War shape revolution and decolonization in East and Southeast Asia?

What factors influenced decolonization in Africa after World War II?

Why did populism emerge as such a powerful political force in Latin America?

Why did the world face growing social unrest in the 1960s?

✔ LearningCurve
Check what you know.

> Why did populism emerge as such a powerful political force in Latin America?

Revolutionaries in Cuba

Che Guevara (left) and Fidel Castro (right), whose successful revolution in Cuba inspired armed movements across Latin America. (© United Archives/Topfoto/The Image Works)

I**N THE DECADES AFTER THE SECOND WORLD WAR**, Latin American nations struggled to find a political balance that integrated long-excluded groups such as women, workers, and peasants in the face of growing anxiety and resistance by liberal oligarchs. Populist politicians rose to power by building a base of support among the urban and rural poor. They often combined charisma with promises of social change, particularly through national economic development that would create more and better job opportunities. Revolutionary leader Fidel Castro carved an alternative path in Cuba. Castro went beyond the reforms advocated by populists and sought an outright revolutionary transformation of Cuban society.

Economic Nationalism in Mexico

Although Spain's Central and South American colonies and Portuguese Brazil won political independence in the early nineteenth century, the new nations struggled to achieve genuine economic independence. Latin American countries had developed as producers of foodstuffs and raw materials exported to Europe and the United States in return for manufactured goods and capital investment. This exchange brought considerable economic development but exacted a heavy price: neocolonialism (see page 819). The Great Depression further hampered development and provoked a shift toward economic nationalism, a systematic effort by nationalists to end neocolonialism and to free their national economies from U.S. and western European influences.

Economic nationalism and industrialization were especially successful in the largest countries in Latin America: Mexico, Brazil, and Argentina. In Mexico, Lázaro Cárdenas, elected president in 1934, carried out sweeping economic reforms. Millions of acres of large estates were divided among small farmers or were returned undivided to Indian communities. State-supported Mexican businessmen built many small factories to meet domestic needs. In 1938 Cárdenas nationalized the petroleum industry. The 1930s also saw the flowering of a distinctive Mexican culture that proudly celebrated cultural mixture and intermarriage between Indians, Africans, and Europeans.

The presidents who followed Cárdenas used the state's power to promote industrialization, and the Mexican economy grew consistently through the 1970s. While the country's economic health improved, social inequities remained. The upper and middle classes reaped the lion's share of the benefits of this economic growth.

economic nationalism

▶ A systematic effort by Latin American nationalists to end neocolonialism and to free their national economies from American and western European influences.

The Plaza of the Three Cultures in Tlatelolco, Mexico City

Modern apartment buildings rise behind Aztec ruins and a Spanish church built in 1536. Mexican authorities massacred student protesters at this plaza to suppress unrest before the 1968 Summer Olympics in the city. (© Macduff Everton/The Image Works)

How did the Cold War shape revolution and decolonization in East and Southeast Asia?

What factors influenced decolonization in Africa after World War II?

Why did populism emerge as such a powerful political force in Latin America?

Why did the world face growing social unrest in the 1960s?

LearningCurve Check what you know.

Populism in Argentina and Brazil

populists

▶ Politicians who appealed to the working class and poor with appeals to nationalism and to social justice.

Argentina and Brazil's postwar economic development was shaped by a rising cadre of **populist** politicians. Earlier liberal politicians had dismissed the electoral potential of the working class and denied it the right to vote. But as pressure for universal voting rights intensified, first for men and then for women, large numbers of Latin Americans who had never been given a political voice gained it, beginning with universal male suffrage in Argentina in 1912 and Mexico in 1917. Women gained the right to vote across Latin America in the decades that followed. To appeal to new voters, populist candidates promised schools and hospitals, higher wages, and nationalist projects that would create more industrial jobs.

At the turn of the century Argentina's economy prospered through its liberal export boom (see Chapter 27), but industrialization followed only haltingly and the economy faltered. Populist Juan Perón, an army colonel, was elected president in 1946 with support of Argentina's unions. Juan Perón's charismatic wife Eva, known by her nickname Evita, played a vital role in promoting Perón. Once in power, Perón embarked on an ambitious scheme to transform Argentina's economy: the government would purchase all of the country's agricultural exports in order to negotiate their sale abroad at a higher price. He would reinvest the profits in industry and raise worker wages to stimulate demand.

Perón's scheme worked in the immediate postwar period, when European agricultural production had not yet recovered and the international price of Argentina's exports was high. But when commodity prices declined, Perón reduced government payments to farmers, who ceased to bring their harvests to market. In the coming decades Argentina never returned to the high rates of economic growth it enjoyed at the beginning of the century. Despite these economic setbacks, Perón initially remained highly popular, buoyed by the popular appeals made by Evita. (See "Individuals in Society: Eva Perón," page 979.)

After Evita died of cancer in 1952, much of the magic slipped away. Amid the stagnating economy even Perón's union supporters faltered, and he responded harshly to press criticism. In 1955 the armed forces deposed Perón, and he fled to exile in Spain. The military ruled Argentina for the next three years. Nonetheless, Perón remained the most popular politician in the country. Presidential candidates could not win without discreetly winning the exiled Perón's endorsement, and this veiled support for Perón by civilian leaders prompted repeated military interventions. The 1955–1958 military government was the first of several, including a dictatorship that ruled from 1966 to 1973.

In Brazil, reacting against the economic and political liberalism through which coffee planters dominated the country, the armed forces installed a state governor, Getúlio Vargas, as president in 1930. Vargas initiated democratic reforms, but veered into a nationalist dictatorship known as the "New State" (1937–1945), inspired by European fascism. Despite his harsh treatment of opponents, he was popular with the masses and was elected to a new term as president in 1950, now reinvented as a populist who promised nationalist economic reforms that would favor industrial workers. The armed forces and conservatives mistrusted Vargas's appeals to workers and organized to depose him in 1954. Before they could act, Vargas killed himself.

Juscelino Kubitschek, elected in 1955, continued to build upon Vargas's populism and nationalism. Between 1956 and 1960 Kubitschek's government borrowed

CHAPTER LOCATOR | How did the Cold War and decolonization shape the postwar world? | How did religion and the legacies of colonialism affect the new nations in South Asia and the Middle East?

978 CHAPTER 31 DECOLONIZATION, REVOLUTION, AND THE COLD WAR

INDIVIDUALS IN SOCIETY
Eva Perón

When Eva Perón died of cancer at age thirty-three on July 26, 1952, the state radio broadcaster sadly announced that "today at 20:25 Eva Perón, Spiritual Leader of the Nation, entered immortality." Argentina went into official mourning; although Perón had never held an official political office, she was accorded a state funeral. Immediately after her death her corpse was embalmed, with the intention of putting it on public display forever in a planned memorial larger than the Statue of Liberty.

Often called Evita (the Spanish diminutive of Eva), she was one of five illegitimate children born near Buenos Aires to Juan Duarte and Juana Ibarguren. Duarte returned to his legitimate wife and children when Eva was a year old, leaving Juana and her children destitute and dependent on Juana's sewing for their existence. As they grew older all the children had to work, but Eva apparently also dreamed of becoming an actress.

At fifteen Eva Duarte moved to the cosmopolitan city of Buenos Aires. Although she had little formal education and no connections, she possessed beauty and charisma, and soon she joined a professional theater group with which she toured nationally. She also modeled, appeared in a few movies, and then obtained regular employment as a character on a radio series. By 1943, although only twenty-three years old, she was one of the highest-paid actresses in the country.

In 1943 Eva met widowed Colonel Juan Perón, then secretary of labor and social welfare in the military government that had seized power that year. Juan Perón had grand ambitions, intending to run for president. Eva Duarte became his partner and confidante, and she won him support among the Argentine masses. In 1945 Juan Perón and Eva Duarte married.

A year later Perón won the presidency. Eva had gone out on the campaign trail and organized support for her husband from *los descamisados* (the shirtless ones), her name for Argentina's poor. When Perón assumed the presidency, Eva, though not officially appointed, became the secretary of labor. Having come from a childhood of poverty herself, she now worked tirelessly for the poor, for the working classes, and with organized labor. She instituted a number of social welfare measures and promoted a new Ministry of Health, which resulted in the creation of new hospitals and disease-treatment programs. In 1948 she established the Eva Perón Welfare Foundation, which grew into an immense semiofficial welfare agency, helping the poor throughout Argentina and even contributing to victims of natural disasters in other countries.

Eva Perón waves to supporters from the balcony of the presidential palace, Casa Rosada, in Buenos Aires, on October 17, 1951. (Archivo Clarin/AP Photo)

From early on, Eva Perón had supported women's suffrage, and in September 1947 Argentine women won the right to vote. Eva then formed the Female Perónist Party, which by 1951 had five hundred thousand members. Thousands of Argentine women have credited Eva's example as a reason for their involvement in politics. In 1951 she seemed ready to run for vice president beside her husband. The huge base of women, the poor, and workers assured them victory. Her declining health, however, forced her to turn down the nomination. Juan Perón won the election by over 30 percent, but when Eva died the following year, his authoritarian rule and bad economic policies lost him support, and a military junta forced him into exile.

Eva Perón's life story is an amazing one, but what happened following her death is just as extraordinary. Before the massive monument intended to hold her embalmed body could be built, the military seized power, and her body disappeared. Seventeen years later the generals finally revealed that it was in a tomb in Milan, Italy. Juan Perón, living in Spain with his third wife, had the body exhumed and brought to Spain, where he kept it in his house. Perón returned to Argentina in 1973 and won the presidential election, but died the following year. His wife, Isabelita Perón, succeeded him as president. Juan and Eva's bodies were briefly displayed together at his funeral and then, finally, buried.

Source: Nicholas Fraser and Marysa Navarro, *Evita: The Real Life of Eva Perón* (New York: Norton, 1976).

QUESTIONS FOR ANALYSIS

1. Why do you think Eva Perón was adored by the Argentine people when she died?
2. What were some of the welfare and government programs that Eva Perón promoted?

ONLINE DOCUMENT PROJECT

What were the political implications of Eva Perón's public presentation of herself? Examine photos of Eva Perón, and then complete a quiz and writing assignment based on the evidence and details from this chapter. *See inside the front cover to learn more.*

heavily from abroad to promote industry and build the futuristic new capital of Brasília in the midst of a wilderness.

In 1961 leftist populist João Goulart became Brazil's president. Goulart sought social and economic reforms, including the redistribution of land and limits on the profits multinational corporations could take out of the country. In 1964 a military coup backed by the United States deposed Goulart. The armed forces held power for the next twenty-one years.

Communist Revolution in Cuba

Cuba remained practically an American colony until the 1930s, when a series of rulers with socialist and Communist leanings seized and lost power. Cuba's political institutions were weak and its politicians corrupt. In March 1952 Fulgencio Batista (1901–1973) staged a coup with American support and instituted a repressive authoritarian regime that favored wealthy Cubans and multinational corporations.

The Cuban Revolution led by Fidel Castro (b. 1927) began in 1953 and finally overthrew the Cuban government on New Year's Day 1959. Castro had not come to power as a Communist: his main aim had been to regain control of Cuba's economy and politics from the United States. But U.S. efforts to overthrow him and to starve the Cuban economy drove him to form an alliance with the Soviet Union, which agreed to place nuclear missiles in Cuba to protect against another U.S. invasion. When President John F. Kennedy demanded the missiles be removed, the military and diplomatic brinksmanship of the 1962 Cuban missile crisis ensued. In 1963 the United States placed a complete commercial and diplomatic embargo on Cuba that has remained in place ever since.

Castro now declared himself a Marxist-Leninist and relied on Soviet military and economic support. Under Castro, medical attention and education became free and widely accessible. But such reforms were achieved at great cost and through the suppression of political dissent. Political opponents were jailed or exiled. Meanwhile, economic reforms were improvised with ideological objectives rather than economic logic, which often resulted in productive inefficiency and scarcity of foodstuffs and other goods.

Cuba

> **QUICK REVIEW**

What groups in Latin American society found the populist message appealing? What groups were most actively opposed to the implementation of the populist agenda?

CHAPTER LOCATOR | How did the Cold War and decolonization shape the postwar world? | How did religion and the legacies of colonialism affect the new nations in South Asia and the Middle East?

980 CHAPTER 31 DECOLONIZATION, REVOLUTION, AND THE COLD WAR

Why did the world face growing social unrest in the 1960s?

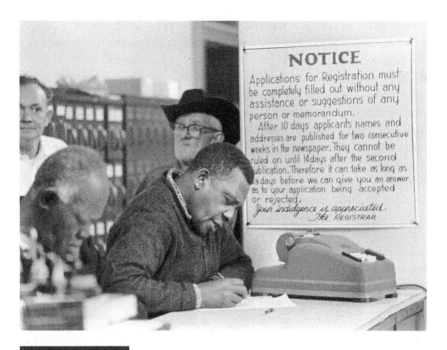

Registering to Vote

African American residents of Hattiesburg, Mississippi, register to vote in 1964. The sign on the wall indicates that their names will be published in the newspaper for two consecutive weeks, making African Americans vulnerable to violent reprisals for registering to vote. (© 1976 Matt Herron/ Take Stock/The Image Works)

IN THE 1950S AND 1960S the United States and the Soviet Union, as well as both western and eastern Europe, rebounded economically from the combined strains of the Great Depression and the Second World War. But these decades of economic growth did not resolve underlying tensions and conflicts.

The Soviet Union Struggles to Move Beyond Stalin

Though the "Great Patriotic War of the Fatherland" had fostered Russian nationalism and a relaxation of totalitarian terror, Stalin's new rivalry with the United States provided him with an excuse to re-establish a harsh dictatorship. Stalin reasserted control of the government and society through the reintroduction of five-year plans. Once again, Soviet central planners favored heavy and military industry over consumer goods, housing, and collectivized agriculture. Stalin exported this system to eastern Europe. Rigid ideological indoctrination, attacks

| How did the Cold War shape revolution and decolonization in East and Southeast Asia? | What factors influenced decolonization in Africa after World War II? | Why did populism emerge as such a powerful political force in Latin America? | **Why did the world face growing social unrest in the 1960s?** | ✔️ LearningCurve Check what you know. |

on religion, and a lack of civil liberties were soon facts of life in the region's one-party states. Only Yugoslavia's Josip Tito (1892–1980) could resist Soviet domination successfully because there was no Russian army in Yugoslavia.

In 1953 the aging Stalin died. Even as his heirs struggled for power, they realized that reforms were necessary because of the widespread fear and hatred of Stalin's political terrorism. They curbed secret police powers and gradually closed many forced-labor camps. Change was also necessary for economic reasons. Agriculture was in bad shape, and shortages of consumer goods discouraged hard work. Moreover, Stalin's foreign policy had led directly to a strong Western alliance, isolating the Soviet Union.

The Communist Party leadership was badly split on just how much change to permit. Reformers, led by Nikita Khrushchev (1894–1971), argued for major innovations and won. Khrushchev spoke out in a "secret speech" against Stalin and his crimes and initiated a series of reforms known as de-Stalinization in the West. Khrushchev eased foreign policy, declaring that "peaceful coexistence" with capitalism was possible. The government relaxed controls over heavy industry and the military and shifted some resources from these areas to consumer goods, improving standards of living substantially throughout the 1960s.

De-Stalinization stimulated rebelliousness in the eastern European satellites. Poland won greater autonomy in 1956 after extensive protests forced the Soviets to allow a new Communist government. The people of Budapest, Hungary, installed a liberal Communist reformer as their new chief in October 1956. The rebellion was short-lived. After the new government promised free elections and renounced Hungary's military alliance with Moscow, the Soviet Army invaded and crushed the revolution, killing around 2,700 protesters. When the United States did not come to their aid, Hungarians and most eastern Europeans concluded that their only hope was to strive for small domestic gains while obediently following Russia in foreign affairs.

In August 1961, amid concerns about growing defections to the West, the East German government began construction of a wall between East and West Berlin. It also built a ninety-mile-long barrier between the three allied sectors of West Berlin and East Germany, thereby completely cutting off West Berlin.

By late 1962 party opposition to Khrushchev's policies had gained momentum. De-Stalinization was seen as a dangerous threat to party authority. Moreover, Khrushchev's policy toward the West was erratic and ultimately unsuccessful. In 1962 Khrushchev ordered the installation of nuclear missiles in Cuba, triggering the military standoff known as the Cuban missile crisis. After a tense diplomatic crisis Khrushchev backed down and removed the missiles. Two years later, Communist Party leaders removed Khrushchev in a bloodless coup. After Leonid Brezhnev (1906–1982) and his supporters took over in 1964, they talked quietly of Stalin's "good points," stopped further liberalization, and launched a massive arms buildup.

de-Stalinization

▶ The liberalization of the post-Stalin Soviet Union, led by reformer Nikita Khrushchev during his years as the head of the Soviet Union (1953–1964).

Western Europe's Postwar Challenge

In 1945 much of western Europe was devastated by the war, and prospects for a swift recovery looked bleak. Nonetheless, in the decades that followed, demo-

CHAPTER LOCATOR | How did the Cold War and decolonization shape the postwar world? | How did religion and the legacies of colonialism affect the new nations in South Asia and the Middle East?

CHAPTER 31
982 DECOLONIZATION, REVOLUTION, AND THE COLD WAR

cratic governments took root throughout western Europe and thrived in an atmosphere of civil liberties and individual freedom. Progressive Catholics and their Christian Democratic political parties were particularly influential. In Italy and Germany Christian Democrats took power, rejecting fascism and putting their faith in democracy. Socialists and Communists active in the resistance against Hitler returned with renewed prestige, especially in France and Italy. In the immediate postwar years welfare measures such as family allowances, health insurance, and increased public housing were enacted throughout much of Europe.

The Cold War prevented the allies occupying Germany from finding a political settlement, resulting in a partition between a Soviet-controlled German Democratic Republic (East Germany) and a Federal Republic of Germany (West Germany). Under its first postwar chancellor, Konrad Adenauer, West Germany recovered from near total devastation in World War II and became the leading economic power in Europe. A fierce opponent of communism, Adenauer forged close ties with the United States and fully supported efforts at European unity. He also initiated dialogues with leaders of Europe's Jewish community and with Israel to encourage a reconciliation of the Jewish and German peoples following the Holocaust.

European nations followed different paths to postwar recovery. West Germany balanced a free-market economy with an extensive social welfare network, while France resorted to central planning. But amid the destruction and uncertainty brought by two world wars caused by Europeans and fought in Europe, many Europeans believed that only unity could forestall future European conflicts.

The experience of close cooperation among European states for Marshall Plan aid led European leaders to pursue economic unity. France, West Germany, Italy, Belgium, the Netherlands, and Luxembourg joined together in 1952 to control and integrate their steel and coal production. In 1957 the six nations of the Coal and Steel Community signed the Treaty of Rome, creating the European Economic Community, popularly known as the **Common Market**. The treaty's primary goal was a gradual reduction of all tariffs among the six in order to create a single market.

Common Market

▶ The European Economic Community created in 1957.

The Common Market was a great success, encouraging hopes of rapid progress toward political as well as economic union. In the 1960s, however, a resurgence of more traditional nationalism in France led by Charles de Gaulle, French president from 1958 to 1969, frustrated these hopes. Viewing the United States as the main threat to genuine French independence, he withdrew all French military forces from NATO and developed France's own nuclear weapons. De Gaulle also thwarted initial efforts of Denmark, Ireland, Norway, and the United Kingdom to join the Common Market.

Migrant laborers, mainly from southern Italy, North Africa, Turkey, Greece, and Yugoslavia, also shaped western European societies and drove their economic recovery. Tens of millions of migrant workers made it possible for western European economies to continue to grow beyond their postwar labor capacity. Governments at first labeled the migrants as "guest workers" to signal their temporary status, though in practice many chose to remain in their new homes. As their communities became more settled, migrants faced a backlash from majority populations.

How did the Cold War shape revolution and decolonization in East and Southeast Asia?

What factors influenced decolonization in Africa after World War II?

Why did populism emerge as such a powerful political force in Latin America?

Why did the world face growing social unrest in the 1960s?

☑ LearningCurve
Check what you know.

983

America's Economic Boom and Civil Rights Revolution

The Second World War ended the Great Depression in the United States, bringing about a great economic boom. By the end of the war, the United States had the strongest economy and held several advantages over its past commercial rivals: its industry and infrastructure had not been damaged by war. In the first decades following the war, U.S. manufactured goods saturated markets around the world.

Postwar America experienced a genuine social revolution as well: after a long struggle African Americans began to experience major victories against the deeply entrenched system of segregation and discrimination. In 1954 the NAACP won a landmark decision in the Supreme Court, which ruled in *Brown v. Board of Education* that "separate educational facilities are inherently unequal." Civil rights leader Martin Luther King, Jr. (1929–1968) challenged inequality by using Gandhian methods of nonviolent peaceful resistance.

Civil Rights Act

▶ The 1964 U.S. act that prohibited discrimination in public services and on the job.

With African American support in key Northern states, Democrat Lyndon Johnson won the 1964 presidential election. Johnson secured enactment of the 1964 Civil Rights Act, which prohibited discrimination in public services and on the job, and the 1965 Voting Rights Act, which prohibited discrimination in voting. In the mid-1960s President Johnson began an "unconditional war on poverty" that promised the kind of fundamental social reform that had succeeded in western Europe after the Second World War.

The World in 1968

In 1968 pressures for social change boiled over into protests worldwide. Students across Latin America and western Europe, Czechoslovaks weary of the harshness of Soviet domination, activists for civil rights and women's rights in the United States along with opponents of the U.S. war in Vietnam all took loudly to the streets. The world seemed to be at a tipping point between the goals of conservative defenders of the existing social and political order and those of a young generation energized by the possibility of radical and swift change.

In Czechoslovakia the "Prague Spring"—a brief period of liberal reform and loosening of political controls—unfolded as reformers in the Czechoslovakian Communist Party gained a majority and replaced a long-time Stalinist leader with Alexander Dubček (DOOB-chehk), whose new government launched dramatic reforms. Dubček and his allies called for "socialism with a human face." Communist leaders in the Soviet Union and other eastern European states feared that they would face similar demands for reform from their own citizens. Protests against the excesses of Communist rule erupted in Poland and Yugoslavia.

In France, students went on strike over poor university conditions. When government forces punished those protesters harshly, a much larger and more radical wave of student protests erupted. The students were soon joined by a general strike carried out by France's labor unions. Similar student movements erupted across western Europe.

In Latin America students rose in protest as well. In Argentina students in the industrial city of Córdoba went on strike against the military dictatorship that had been in place since 1966. Joined by factory workers, the protesters took control of the city in an event known as the Cordobazo. In Brazil a national student

CHAPTER LOCATOR | How did the Cold War and decolonization shape the postwar world? | How did religion and the legacies of colonialism affect the new nations in South Asia and the Middle East?

CHAPTER 31
984 DECOLONIZATION, REVOLUTION, AND THE COLD WAR

strike challenged the military dictatorship that had been in power since 1964. In Mexico City, where the Olympic games were scheduled to be held, students used the international visibility of the event to protest the heavy-handed government. In each case the students challenged the authoritarian excesses of their regimes, but they were also animated by the example offered by revolutionary Cuba, which suggested that directly confronting the political regime could bring revolutionaries to power, and that once in power, they could quickly transform their societies.

In the United States protests against the Vietnam War and against the military draft erupted on college campuses nationwide. These protests marked an increase in popular mobilization in a country where civil rights marches in the South now extended to protests against discrimination and police violence in cities like Boston and Chicago. Protesters around the world were aware of each other, and their sense that they participated in a worldwide movement against the abuses of the established order empowered them.

Protesters and reformers faced violent reactions from the powerful political and economic groups they challenged. If 1968 seemed to be the peak of young radicals' aspirations for social transformation, this was because it also marked the intensification of the reaction against their efforts. Conservatives reacted against more than the protests of 1968: they sought to slow or sometimes reverse the dramatic changes that had taken place in the postwar era.

In October 1968 Soviet troops and tanks flooded into Czechoslovakia, crushing the Prague Spring and unseating Dubček. Supporters of the Prague Spring faced harsh persecution. In Cuba, where revolutionary dreams of liberation were increasingly subsidized by the Soviet Union, Castro was obligated to support the Soviet crackdown.

Around the world, protests were followed by violent crackdowns. The Mexican government massacred protesters, many of them students in Tlatelolco. The Argentine army and paramilitary groups launched a violent campaign to retake the city of Córdoba from protesters. In Brazil, the military regime reacted to protests by imposing a harsh new national security law that made criticizing the government an offense punishable by imprisonment. Around the world, revolutionary violence met with increasingly violent repression.

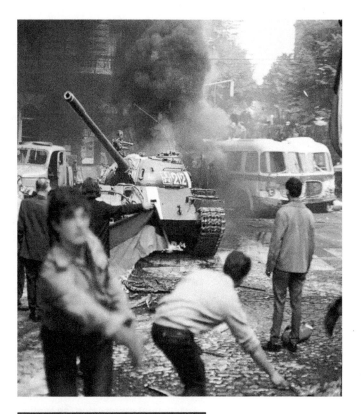

The Soviet Invasion of Prague, 1968

Czech demonstrators throw torches and wave flags in an attempt to stop a tank as the Soviet army crushes the protests of the Prague Spring in 1968. (© Libor Hajsky/epa/Corbis)

QUICK REVIEW <

What tensions and conflicts fueled the protest movements of the late 1960s?

How did the Cold War shape revolution and decolonization in East and Southeast Asia?

What factors influenced decolonization in Africa after World War II?

Why did populism emerge as such a powerful political force in Latin America?

Why did the world face growing social unrest in the 1960s?

✓ LearningCurve
Check what you know.

985

CHAPTER SUMMARY

The decades after the Second World War were an era of rebuilding after the destruction caused by years of war. In Germany and Japan in particular, rebuilding also meant charting a new political and economic path.

For the United States and the Soviet Union rebuilding had other meanings. For both countries, it meant building a military and ideological complex with which to confront each other in the Cold War. This involved building rival networks of military and economic alliances. In each country individually, rebuilding took other forms: in the Soviet Union it meant seeking the means to reform the system of political terror and coercion through which Stalin had ruled; in the United States it meant struggling to overcome the structures of white supremacism and other forms of racial discrimination that divided society and oppressed millions of citizens.

In Asia, Africa, and the Middle East rebuilding meant dismantling European colonialism to reconstitute independent states or to build new independent states. Here the idea of rebuilding took on its deepest meaning: learning how to replace not just colonial institutions but colonial mentalities, patterns of production, forms of education, and ways of relating to each other with new versions that were not dictated by colonizers.

In Latin America rebuilding meant finding the means to overcome patterns of social exclusion—especially of rural workers—that were legacies of its colonial experience, as well as finding a political formula that could integrate long-excluded groups. It also meant finding the means to build industry and develop economically, overcoming patterns of dependency. In the end, the decades after 1945 showed how much was possible through mass movements, advancing industrialization, and political self-determination. But the balance of these years also showed how much more work remained to overcome poverty, underdevelopment, and neocolonialism.

 CONNECTIONS The great transformations experienced by peoples around the world following the Second World War can best be compared to the age of revolution in the late eighteenth and early nineteenth centuries (see Chapter 22). In both eras peoples rose up to undertake the political, economic, social, and cultural transformation of their societies, and in both eras history seemed to accelerate as a quick succession of events had impacts across the globe.

Liberation movements spanning the globe sought not only to end imperial domination and remove social boundaries imposed by white racism, but also to make deeper changes in how peoples perceived themselves and their societies. As radical and new as these ideas were, they nonetheless owed much to the Enlightenment ideals about liberal individual rights.

Though the social revolutions in countries like China and Cuba and the independence movements across Africa, Asia, and the Middle East brought unprecedented

CHAPTER LOCATOR | How did the Cold War and decolonization shape the postwar world? | How did religion and the legacies of colonialism affect the new nations in South Asia and the Middle East?

986 CHAPTER 31
DECOLONIZATION, REVOLUTION, AND THE COLD WAR

deep and fast changes, they were only the first steps in remaking societies that had been created by centuries of colonialism. Uprooting the legacies of colonialism—in the form of poverty, continued domination of economies by foreign powers, limited industrialization, and weak states—remained a daunting challenge that societies continued to face in the future.

ONLINE DOCUMENT PROJECT
Gender Roles and Populism in Argentina

What were the political implications of Eva Perón's public presentation of herself?

Examine photos of Eva Perón, and then complete a quiz and writing assignment based on the evidence and details from this chapter. *See inside the front cover to learn more.*

How did the Cold War shape revolution and decolonization in East and Southeast Asia?

What factors influenced decolonization in Africa after World War II?

Why did populism emerge as such a powerful political force in Latin America?

Why did the world face growing social unrest in the 1960s?

LearningCurve
Check what you know.

CHAPTER 31 STUDY GUIDE

STEP 1 · GET STARTED ONLINE

✓ LearningCurve

Now that you've read the chapter, make it stick by completing the LearningCurve activity.

STEP 2 · EXPLAIN WHY IT MATTERS

Put your reading into practice. Identify each term below, and then explain why it matters in world history.

TERM	WHO OR WHAT & WHEN	WHY IT MATTERS
Cold War (p. 954)		
Truman Doctrine (p. 955)		
Marshall Plan (p. 955)		
NATO (p. 956)		
superpowers (p. 956)		
dependency theory (p. 958)		
modernization theory (p. 958)		
import substitution industrialization (ISI) (p. 959)		
liberation theology (p. 959)		
Muslim League (p. 962)		
Arab socialism (p. 963)		
Palestine Liberation Organization (PLO) (p. 964)		
Great Leap Forward (p. 967)		
Great Proletarian Cultural Revolution (p. 968)		
Red Guards (p. 968)		
Pan-Africanists (p. 973)		
cocoa holdups (p. 973)		
pieds-noirs (p. 974)		
National Liberation Front (p. 974)		
economic nationalism (p. 977)		
populists (p. 978)		
de-Stalinization (p. 978)		
Common Market (p. 982)		
Civil Rights Act (p. 982)		

> IN YOUR OWN WORDS

Imagine that you must give an oral report to the class answering the following question: **How did decolonization and the Cold War shape global developments in the decades following World War II?** What would be the most important points and why?

MOVE BEYOND THE BASICS

To demonstrate a more advanced understanding of postwar decolonization, fill in the chart below with descriptions of the decolonization process and its aftermath in the Middle East, Africa, and South Asia. What are the most important differences in the decolonization experience in each region? How would you explain the differences you note?

	Decolonization Process	Post-Independence Developments
The Middle East		
Africa		
South Asia		

PUT IT ALL TOGETHER

Now, take a step back and try to explain the big picture. Remember to use specific examples from the chapter in your answers.

ASIA AND THE MIDDLE EAST

▶ How did Asian and Middle Eastern nationalists drawn on Western ideas and models during the struggle for independence?

▶ What explains the dominant role the Israeli/Palestinian issue has played in Middle Eastern politics since 1945?

AFRICA AND LATIN AMERICA

▶ How did the circumstances under which Latin American and sub-Saharan African nations gained independence shape their subsequent development?

▶ Why was the Cuban Revolution such an important turning point in Latin American history?

THE LIMITS OF POSTWAR PROSPERITY

▶ To what extent were the protest movements of the 1960s a product of postwar affluence? What other factors contributed to their emergence?

▶ What were the most important forces for change in the postwar era? What important continuities were there between the pre- and postwar periods?

LOOKING BACK, LOOKING AHEAD

▶ Argue for or against the following proposition: "The European wars of the first half of the twentieth century made decolonization possible. Without them, the Western imperial system might still be in existence." What evidence can you present to support your position?

▶ In your opinion, in the next several decades will South and East Asia overtake Europe and North America as the dominant regions in the global economy? Why or why not?

32
LIBERALIZATION
1968–2000S

> **Why did liberalization emerge as a such a powerful force in the second half of the twentieth century, and what were the consequences of this development?** Chapter 32 examines the impact of liberalization in the late twentieth century. In the 1970s two currents ran against each other in much of the world. The radicalism of liberation in decolonization, revolutions, and mass social movements continued. But alongside this current ran a different one whose influence was undeniable by the 1990s: liberalization. After the Second World War, the United States had championed liberal economic policies, but this objective ran against the desires of other countries to protect and promote their own industrialization and economic development. But in the last decades of the century, the U.S. drive for global liberalization of trade experienced greater success, while reform movements in the Eastern bloc and in Latin America pursued human rights and political liberalization.

Sandinista Soldier in Nicaragua Street art in Jinotega, Nicaragua, shows an armed female soldier of the Sandinista National Liberation Front picking coffee beans in her military camouflage. The Sandinistas overthrew the U.S.-backed dictator Anastasio Somoza in 1979. After their victory, the Socialist Sandinistas ruled Nicaragua until 1990 and then returned to power in 2006. (© Thalia Watmough/aliki image library/Alamy)

> What were the short-term and long-term consequences of the OPEC oil embargo?

> How did war and revolution reshape the Middle East?

> What effect did the Cold War and debt crisis have on Latin America?

> How did white-minority rule end in southern Africa?

> How have East and South Asian nations pursued economic development, and how have political regimes shaped those efforts?

> How did decolonization and the end of the Cold War change Europe?

✓ **LearningCurve**

After reading the chapter, use LearningCurve to retain what you've read.

> What were the short-term and long-term consequences of the OPEC oil embargo?

Oil in Nigeria

A Nigerian woman ferries fuel drums across Warri Harbor, near an abandoned oil tanker. Nigeria's oil has brought great profits to some, but boom-and-bust cycles and corruption keep wealth out of the hands of most Nigerians. (© George Steinmetz/Corbis)

IN 1973 WAR ERUPTED AGAIN between Israel and its neighbors Egypt and Syria. The conflict became known as the Yom Kippur War. Armed with advanced weapons from the Soviet Union, Egyptian and Syrian armies came close to defeating Israel before the U.S. government airlifted sophisticated arms to Israel. Israel counterattacked, reaching the outskirts of both Cairo and Damascus before the fighting ended. Arab oil-exporting countries retaliated against U.S. support for Israel by imposing an embargo on oil sales to countries that had supported Israel during the war.

Amid the oil embargo, the war in Vietnam, and political conflict within the United States, U.S. political and economic influence as a global superpower seemed to decline.

The OPEC Oil Embargo

In 1960 oil-exporting countries formed a cartel called OPEC (the Organization of the Petroleum Exporting Countries) in order to coordinate production and raise prices. In 1973 OPEC countries agreed to an embargo, withholding oil sales to

CHAPTER LOCATOR | What were the short-term and long-term consequences of the OPEC oil embargo? | How did war and revolution reshape the Middle East?

992 CHAPTER 32 LIBERALIZATION

1973
Yom Kippur War; OPEC oil embargo

1979
Islamic revolution in Iran; second oil shock

1980
Rhodesian white minority rulers surrender power and the nation is renamed Zimbabwe

1980–1988
Iran-Iraq War

1982
Falklands (or Malvinas) War leads to the collapse of the Argentine junta

1985
Glasnost leads to greater freedom of speech and expression in the Soviet Union

1987
Palestinian intifada

1989
Collapse of Berlin Wall; "NO" campaign in Chile; Tiananmen Square protests suppressed in China

1989–1991
Fall of communism in Soviet Union and eastern Europe

1990–1991
Persian Gulf War

1991
Congress Party in India embraces Western capitalist reforms

1991–2001
Civil war in Yugoslavia

1993
Formation of European Union

1994
North American Free Trade Agreement goes into effect between Canada, Mexico, and the United States

1994
Nelson Mandela elected president of South Africa

2003–2011
Second Persian Gulf War

2007
Hamas seizes control of Gaza Strip from Palestinian Authority

2009–2014
Popular uprisings and protests across the Middle East

the United States and western Europe in response to U.S. support for Israel in the Yom Kippur War. As a result of the embargo, the price of oil increased almost overnight from $3 to $12 per barrel, quadrupling energy costs.

OPEC's ability to disrupt the world economy, and the U.S. government's powerlessness to reverse the disruption, suggested a new world order. Brazil's military leaders, for example, distanced themselves from their traditional alliance with the United States and built relations with OPEC countries.

Oil prices remained high and peaked again in the second oil shock of 1979 as a result of the Iranian revolution, which ousted the secular government and brought religious leaders to power. In the United States soaring energy costs sapped economic growth and also triggered inflation, making prices rise at a time when earning power was diminished, a combination dubbed stagflation. Europe and Japan, heavily dependent on oil imports, resorted to bicycle and mass transit use to reduce their energy needs, as well as intense development of nuclear power generation.

In the decade after the first oil shock, OPEC countries such as Saudi Arabia deposited their huge profits in large international banks. This money, which began as oil profits and circulated the world as bank loans, was known as petrodollars. In this economic cycle, the higher prices that consumers around the world paid for fuel generated profits for oil exporters that they invested in large banks. In turn,

petrodollars
▶ The global recirculation by international banks of profits from the higher price of oil.

What effect did the Cold War and debt crisis have on Latin America?   How did white-minority rule end in southern Africa?   How have East and South Asian nations pursued economic development?   How did decolonization and the end of the Cold War change Europe?   ✓ LearningCurve Check what you know.

993

these banks loaned this capital out to foreign governments. Many industrializing countries faced both high energy costs and heavy debts amassed through petro-dollar loans.

In the United States, as stagflation and the 1979 second oil shock drove rising inflation, the Federal Reserve Bank raised interest rates. Increased interest rates in the United States made it more expensive to borrow money, which slowed economic activity and led to an economic recession. The United States was not the only country to experience this recession: countries that exported goods to the United States faced reduced demand for their goods, and countries that borrowed from U.S. banks found that the interest on their debts increased as well. In industrializing nations the rapid increase in interest on their heavy debts became a crippling burden, triggering a global crisis. Debtor nations became dependent on U.S. assistance to restructure unsustainable loans; the U.S. government was able to impose neoliberal free-market reforms for the first time.

Beginning in the 1980s neoliberal policies increasingly shaped the world economy. Neoliberalism promoted free-market policies and the free circulation of capital across national borders. Debtor countries needed to continue to borrow in order to pay the interest on the debts they held, and their ability to secure loans now depended on their adherence to a set of liberal principles known as the Washington Consensus: policies that restricted public spending, lowered import barriers, privatized state enterprises, and deregulated markets.

The forces unleashed by the Yom Kippur War and the OPEC oil embargo of 1973 at first tipped the scale in favor of less industrialized nations, but by the 1980s the scale had swung back as debt and liberalization shifted power back to the most economically powerful countries, in particular the United States. The experiences of Mexico and Nigeria reflect the effects of the boom-and-bust cycle ignited by the oil embargo.

neoliberalism
▶ A return to policies intended to promote free markets and the free circulation of capital across national borders.

Washington Consensus
▶ Policies restricting public spending, lowering import barriers, privatizing state enterprises, and deregulating markets.

Mexico Under the PRI

By the 1960s Mexico was a democracy that functioned like a dictatorship. The Institutional Revolutionary Party (PRI) held nearly every public office. The PRI controlled both labor unions and federations of businessmen. More than a party, it was a vast system of patronage. Even at the landfills where the most desperately poor scavenged through trash, a PRI official collected a cut of their meager earnings. Mexico's road from the nationalist economic project that emerged from the 1910 revolution to the liberal reforms of the 1960s and 1970s is also the story of the PRI.

The PRI claimed the reform legacy of the Mexican Revolution. But these claims were undermined when PRI politicians ordered the deadly crackdown on student protesters in 1968 (see page 984). The party that had defined itself as the agent of progress and change became the reactionary party preserving a corrupt order.

In 1970 the PRI chose and elected as president populist Luis Echeverría, who sought to reclaim the mantle of reform by nationalizing utilities and increasing social spending. Echeverría and his successor, José López Portillo, embarked on massive development projects financed through projected future earnings of the state oil monopoly PEMEX. Amid inflation, corruption, and the decline of oil prices

CHAPTER LOCATOR | What were the short-term and long-term consequences of the OPEC oil embargo? | How did war and revolution reshape the Middle East?

994 CHAPTER 32 LIBERALIZATION

and demand during the global recession of the 1980s, the Mexican government fell into the debt crisis, and was compelled to embrace the Washington Consensus, which meant restricted spending, opening trade borders, and privatization.

The PRI was further undermined by its inept and corrupt response to a devastating earthquake that struck Mexico City in 1986. Two years later the PRI faced its first real presidential election challenge. Cuauhtémoc Cárdenas, who was the son of populist Lázaro Cárdenas, ran against PRI candidate Carlos Salinas de Gortari. On election night, as the vote counting favored Cárdenas, the government declared that the computers tabulating the votes had crashed and declared Gortari the winner. The PRI-controlled congress ordered the ballots burned afterward. The PRI now governed through simple fraud. In its last years holding power, the PRI pursued liberalization of the economy, negotiating a free-trade agreement with the United States and Canada, the North American Free Trade Agreement (NAFTA), which went into effect in 1994.

The debt crisis forced the PRI government to abandon the nationalist development project created in the decades after the 1910 revolution and to embrace economic liberalism, but the experience with neoliberalism proved equally corrupt. Mexico continued to face economic crises such as a 1994 financial panic. As the PRI's power slipped and as Mexico's trade with the United States intensified, violent drug cartels proliferated, especially in Mexico's northern border states, and competed for the lucrative drug trade into the United States.

Nigeria, Africa's Giant

After Nigeria gained independence from Britain in 1960, its key constitutional question was the relationship between the central government and its ethnically distinct regions (see Map 31.5, page 972). Under the federal system created after independence, each region had a dominant ethnic group and a corresponding political party. After independence Nigeria's ethnic rivalries intensified, and in 1967 they erupted in the Biafran war in which the Igbo ethnic group in southeastern Nigeria fought unsuccessfully to form a separate nation. The war lasted three years and resulted in famine that left millions dead.

The wealth generated by oil exports in the 1970s had contradictory effects on Nigerian society. On one hand, a succession of military leaders who held power after a 1966 coup grew increasingly corrupt throughout the 1970s. On the other hand, oil wealth allowed the country to rebuild after the Biafran war. By the mid-1970s Nigeria had the largest middle and professional classes on the continent outside of South Africa. Nigeria's oil boom in the 1970s resembled Mexico's experience: the expectation of future riches led to growing indebtedness, and when global demand and oil prices collapsed amid the global recession of the early 1980s, Nigeria faced a corrosive debt crisis.

Oil wealth allowed Nigeria to develop one innovative solution to its ethnic divisions: the construction of a modernist new capital, Abuja, modeled on Brazil's project in Brasília (see page 978). Located in the center of the country at the confluence of major regional and ethnic boundaries, Abuja symbolized equal representation in government. Residential areas in the new city were divided by ethnicity, but shopping and services were located between them to encourage commingling.

| What effect did the Cold War and debt crisis have on Latin America? | How did white-minority rule end in southern Africa? | How have East and South Asian nations pursued economic development? | How did decolonization and the end of the Cold War change Europe? | ✓ LearningCurve Check what you know. |

995

Except for an early period of civilian rule, Muslim army officers ruled Nigeria until 1998, when the brutal military dictator General Sani Abacha suddenly died. Nigerians adopted a new constitution in 1999, and that same year they voted in free elections and re-established civilian rule. Elections in 2003 ended thirty-three years of military rule. Nonetheless, ethnic tensions remained. Since 2000 ethnic riots have left thousands dead in the predominantly Muslim northern Nigerian states.

> **QUICK REVIEW**

How did the oil shocks of the 1970s contribute to the growing influence of neoliberal economic policies on the global economy in subsequent decades?

CHAPTER LOCATOR | What were the short-term and long-term consequences of the OPEC oil embargo? | How did war and revolution reshape the Middle East?

996 CHAPTER 32 LIBERALIZATION

How did war and revolution reshape the Middle East?

Israel's Wall of Separation

Protest messages along with images of Che Guevara and peace doves adorn the wall separating the Palestinian West Bank from Jerusalem, in the background. (SIPA/Sipa USA)

THE 1973 YOM KIPPUR WAR had a lasting effect across the Middle East. Egypt and Syria had again been defeated, but Israelis also felt more vulnerable after the war. The oil embargo empowered oil-exporting nations like Saudi Arabia, Libya, and Iraq. The Middle East faced deepening divisions, which added to the conflict between Israel and its neighbors. Rising Islamic militancy led to revolution in Iran, as well as a spreading religious challenge to the rule of secular, modernizing dictatorships in countries like Egypt.

The Palestinian-Israeli Conflict

After the 1973 war, the United States recognized the need to become more actively involved in the Middle East. Peacemaking efforts by U.S. president Jimmy Carter led to the Camp David Accords in 1979, which normalized relations between Israel and its neighbors Egypt and Jordan. With the prospect of border wars between Israel and its neighbors diminished, political attention turned to the conflict between Israel and Palestinian nationalist organizations. Tensions between

What effect did the Cold War and debt crisis have on Latin America?

How did white-minority rule end in southern Africa?

How have East and South Asian nations pursued economic development?

How did decolonization and the end of the Cold War change Europe?

✓ LearningCurve
Check what you know.

997

Syria and Israel shifted from their border into Lebanon, where Syria backed the militia Hezbollah. Hezbollah condemned the 1978 and 1982 Israeli invasions of Lebanon aimed at eradicating the Palestine Liberation Organization's control of southern Lebanon, and had as one of its stated objectives the complete destruction of the state of Israel.

In 1987 young Palestinians in the occupied territories of the Gaza Strip and the West Bank began the intifada, a prolonged campaign of civil disobedience against Israeli soldiers. Inspired increasingly by Islamic fundamentalists, the Palestinian uprising eventually posed a serious challenge not only to Israel but also to the secular Palestine Liberation Organization (PLO), long led from abroad by Yasir Arafat. The result was an unexpected and mutually beneficial agreement in 1993 between Israel and the PLO. Israel agreed to recognize Arafat's organization and start a peace process that granted Palestinian self-rule in Gaza and called for self-rule throughout the West Bank in five years. In return, Arafat renounced violence and abandoned the demand that Israel must withdraw from all land occupied in the 1967 war.

The peace process increasingly divided Israel. In 1995 a right-wing Jewish extremist assassinated Prime Minister Yitzhak Rabin. In 1996 a coalition of opposition parties won a slender majority, charging the Palestinian leadership with condoning anti-Jewish terrorism. The new Israeli government limited Palestinian self-rule where it existed and expanded Jewish settlements in the West Bank. On the Palestinian side, dissatisfaction with the peace process grew.

Failed negotiations between Arafat and Israel in 2000 unleashed an explosion of violence between Israelis and Palestinians known as the Second Intifada. In 2003 the Israeli government began to build a barrier around the West Bank, which met with opposition from Israelis and Palestinians alike.

The death of Yasir Arafat, the PLO's long-time leader, in November 2004 marked a turning point in the Israeli-Palestinian conflict. Mahmoud Abbas, Arafat's pragmatic successor, found little room for negotiation. In January 2006 Hamas, a Sunni Muslim political party, won a majority in the Palestinian legislature. Considered by Israel to be a terrorist organization, Hamas had gained widespread support from many Palestinians for the welfare programs it established in the West Bank and Gaza Strip.

Immediately after the Hamas victory, Israel, the United States, and the European Union suspended aid to the Palestinian Authority, the governing body of the West Bank and Gaza Strip established by the 1994 peace agreement. Since then, economic and humanitarian conditions for Palestinians living in the Gaza Strip have deteriorated.

Egypt: Arab World Leader

In 1977 Egypt's president, Anwar Sadat (1918–1981), negotiated a peace settlement with Israel known as the Camp David Accords. Each country gained: Egypt got back the Sinai Peninsula, which Israel had taken in the 1967 Six-Day War (see Map 31.3, page 965), and Israel obtained peace and normal relations with Egypt. Israel also kept the Gaza Strip. Some Arab leaders denounced Sadat's initiative as treason.

After Sadat was assassinated by Islamic radicals in 1981, Egyptian relations with Israel deteriorated, but Egypt and Israel maintained their fragile peace as

CHAPTER LOCATOR | What were the short-term and long-term consequences of the OPEC oil embargo? | **How did war and revolution reshape the Middle East?**

998 CHAPTER 32 LIBERALIZATION

Sadat's successor, Hosni Mubarak, took office. In return for helping to stabilize the region, the United States gave Egypt billions of dollars in development, humanitarian, and military aid. This aid failed to yield economic development, and Mubarak ruled with an increasingly dictatorial hand, silencing all opposition and punishing, torturing, and killing anyone perceived as a threat to his rule.

In December 2010 demonstrations broke out in Tunisia against the twenty-three-year authoritarian rule of President Zine Ben Ali, leading to his downfall on January 14, 2011. This populist revolt soon spread across North Africa and the Middle East, including Egypt. After three weeks of increasingly large demonstrations, coordinated through social media, Mubarak stepped down as president in 2011 and was arrested soon after. Libya, located between Tunisia and Egypt, also witnessed an uprising against its dictatorial leader of forty-two years, Muammar Gaddafi. Gaddafi struggled violently to remain in power, but was deposed and killed amid European and U.S. air strikes. That same year, a lengthy and intense civil war erupted in Syria.

The "Arab Spring" uprisings that swept the Middle East shook a political order that had rested in the hands of the armed forces and pursued secular, nationalist objectives. The reaction against these regimes was often religious and culturally conservative. The political transitions resulting from this upheaval tended to pit secular and religious factions against each other amid debates over the nature of government and social reform.

Revolution and War in Iran and Iraq

In oil-rich Iran foreign powers competed for political influence in the decades after the Second World War, and the influence of the United States in particular helped trigger a revolutionary backlash. In 1953 Iran's prime minister, Muhammad Mossadegh (1882–1967), tried to nationalize the British-owned Anglo-Iranian Oil Company, forcing the pro-Western shah Muhammad Reza Pahlavi (r. 1941–1979) to flee to Europe. However, loyal army officers, with the help of the American CIA, quickly restored the shah to his throne.

Pahlavi set out to build a powerful modern nation to ensure his rule. The shah undermined the power bases of the traditional politicians—large landowners and religious leaders—by means of land reform, secular education, and increased power for the central government. Modernization surged forward, accompanied by widespread corruption and harsh dictatorship. The result was a violent reaction against modernization and secular values. Led by the Islamic cleric Ayatollah Ruholla Khomeini, the fundamentalists deposed the shah in 1979 and tried to build their vision of a true Islamic state.

Iran's Islamic republic frightened its neighbors. Iraq, especially, feared that Iran—a nation of Shi'ite Muslims—would succeed in getting Iraq's Shi'ite majority to revolt against its Sunni leaders (Map 32.1). In September 1980 Iraq's ruler, Saddam Hussein (1937–2006), launched a surprise attack against Iran. The Iran-Iraq War last eight years and resulted in the death of hundreds of thousands of soldiers on both sides before ending in a modest victory for Iran in 1988.

Saddled with the costs of war, Hussein eyed Kuwait's great oil wealth. In August 1990 he ordered his forces to overrun his tiny southern neighbor and proclaimed its annexation to Iraq. To Saddam's surprise, his troops were driven out of Kuwait by an American-led, United Nations–sanctioned military coalition.

What effect did the Cold War and debt crisis have on Latin America?

How did white-minority rule end in southern Africa?

How have East and South Asian nations pursued economic development?

How did decolonization and the end of the Cold War change Europe?

LearningCurve
Check what you know.

999

MAP 32.1 ■ **Abrahamic Religions in the Middle East and Surrounding Regions**

Islam, Judaism, and Christianity, which all trace their origins back to the patriarch Abraham, have significant populations in the Middle East. Since the 1979 Iranian revolution, Shi'ites throughout the region have become more vocal in their demands for equality and power. One of the largest stateless ethnic groups, the Kurds, who follow various religions, has become a major player in the politics of the region, especially in Iraq and Turkey, where the group seeks Kurdish independence.

Map legend:

- Sunni Muslim
- Shi'ite Muslim
- Christian
- Large Christian minority
- Jewish
- Hindu or other
- Area of Kurdish predominance

> **MAPPING THE PAST**

ANALYZING THE MAP: Which religion dominates? Where are the largest concentrations of Jews and Christians in the Middle East located?

CONNECTIONS: How have divisions between Shi'ite and Sunni Muslims contributed to war in the region?

The United Nations Security Council imposed economic sanctions on Iraq as soon as it invaded Kuwait, and these sanctions continued after the Persian Gulf War to force Iraq to destroy its stockpiles of chemical and biological weapons. Sparked by allegations that Iraq still had such weapons, an American-led invasion of Iraq in 2003 began the Second Persian Gulf War and overthrew Saddam Hussein's regime. The invasion led to a lengthy U.S. occupation and a violent insurgency against U.S. military forces, which remained in Iraq until 2011.

As secular Iraq staggered, the Iran revolutionary regime seemed to moderate. Executive power in Iran was divided between a Supreme Leader and twelve-member Guardian Council selected by high Islamic clerics, and a popularly elected president and parliament. A reform movement pressed for relaxation of strict Islamic decrees and elected a moderate, Muhammad Khatami (b. 1943), as presi-

CHAPTER LOCATOR | What were the short-term and long-term consequences of the OPEC oil embargo? | How did war and revolution reshape the Middle East?

1000 CHAPTER 32 LIBERALIZATION

dent in 1997 and again in 2001. The Supreme Leader, controlling the army and the courts, vetoed Khatami's reforms and jailed some of the religious leadership's most vocal opponents.

In 2005 dubious election returns gave the presidency to conservative populist Mahmoud Ahmadinejad (b. 1956). Ahmadinejad won re-election in 2009 after a bitterly contested challenge from moderates. The government suppressed a "green revolution" of protests that broke out after news of the election results. In 2013 opposition groups came together to support the election of Hassan Rouhani, a centrist cleric who promised civil rights reforms and has made overtures to the West in the hopes of relieving economic sanctions in return for negotiating an end to Iran's nuclear weapons program.

QUICK REVIEW <

What role has the United States played in Middle Eastern politics since the 1973 Yom Kippur War? What impact have U.S. policies and interventions had on the region?

| What effect did the Cold War and debt crisis have on Latin America? | How did white-minority rule end in southern Africa? | How have East and South Asian nations pursued economic development? | How did decolonization and the end of the Cold War change Europe? | ✓ LearningCurve Check what you know. |

What effect did the Cold War and debt crisis have on Latin America?

The Mothers of the Plaza de Mayo

Mothers and grandmothers demand information about their children and grandchildren who were "disappeared" by the Argentine military junta in a protest in Buenos Aires. (Eduardo Di Baia/AP Photo)

AFTER THE CUBAN REVOLUTION IN 1959, the United States financed and armed military dictatorships to suppress any dissent that might lead to communism and to secure U.S. influence in the region. Many elected governments were toppled in military coups that brought right-wing military dictatorships to power with U.S. military and financial support.

Civil Wars in Central America

Central America experienced the greatest violence in Latin America during the Cold War. In the second half of the twentieth century nationalists in Central America sought economic development that was less dependent on the United States and U.S. corporations, and groups of peasants and urban workers began to press for political rights and improved living standards. Through the lens of the Cold War, Central American conservatives and the United States government saw these groups as Communists who should be suppressed. In turn, many workers and peasants radicalized and formed Marxist revolutionary movements. The

CHAPTER LOCATOR | What were the short-term and long-term consequences of the OPEC oil embargo? | How did war and revolution reshape the Middle East?

result of this conflict, and of U.S. support for right-wing governments and forces was hundreds of thousands of deaths.

In Guatemala reformist president Jacobo Arbenz was deposed in a military coup organized by the CIA in 1954. Subsequent Guatemalan leaders backed by the U.S. government violently suppressed peasant movements, resulting in the likely death of over two hundred thousand mostly indigenous people.

El Salvador and Nicaragua, too, faced civil wars. In 1979 the Sandinista movement overthrew dictator Anastasio Somoza Debayle. The Sandinistas, who conducted a revolutionary transformation of Nicaragua inspired by Communist rule in Cuba, were undermined by war with a U.S.-trained and U.S.-financed insurgent army called the Contras. In El Salvador a right-wing death squad killed Archbishop Oscar Romero in 1980 for speaking out against their violence.

U.S. policies that encouraged one faction to fight against the other deepened political instability and repression and intensified these civil wars. Acting against U.S. wishes, in 1986 Costa Rican president Oscar Arias mediated peace talks among the warring factions in Nicaragua, El Salvador, and Guatemala, which ended the wars and initiated open elections in each country, with former armed rivals competing instead at the ballot box.

Boom and Bust in Chile

In the 1960s Chilean voters pushed for greater social reforms, culminating in the election of the Marxist candidate Salvador Allende as president in 1970. Allende redistributed land and nationalized foreign businesses including copper mines, drawing fiery opposition from conservative Chileans, foreign businesses, and the U.S. government. U.S. president Richard Nixon created a clandestine task force to organize an "invisible blockade" to disrupt the Chilean economy by withholding economic aid and quietly instructing U.S. companies not to trade with or invest in Chile.

In 1973 Chile's armed forces deposed Allende, who killed himself rather than surrender as the military stormed the palace. A **junta**, or council of commanders of the branches of the armed forces, took power. Its leader, General Augusto Pinochet (1915–2006), instituted radical economic reforms, giving neoliberal economists a free hand to remake Chile into a showcase of free-market economics. Schools, health care, pensions, and public services were turned over to private companies. Regulatory protections for industry were slashed, and land was concentrated into the hands of large agricultural corporations. Pinochet's economic program was supported by lavish U.S. economic aid.

The reforms created a boom-and-bust cycle in which Chile became especially vulnerable to global economic changes. At its peak, Chile's economy grew at 8 percent per year. The costs of the reforms were just as intense. Income inequality soared: a handful of Chileans tied to big business conglomerates and banks made

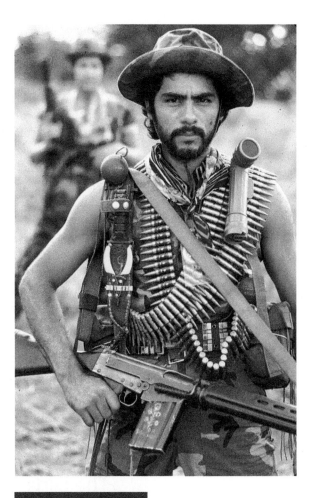

A Contra Rebel

A member of the Contra paramilitary force, which was armed and trained by the United States to fight against the socialist Sandinista government in Nicaragua. (© Bill Gentile/ZUMAPRESS.com)

junta

▶ A government headed by a council of commanders of the branches of the armed forces.

| What effect did the Cold War and debt crisis have on Latin America? | How did white-minority rule end in southern Africa? | How have East and South Asian nations pursued economic development? | How did decolonization and the end of the Cold War change Europe? | ✓ LearningCurve Check what you know. |

1003

fortunes, while workers faced job loss and an increasing cost of living. In 1975 the implementation of reforms that cut social programs and caused mass unemployment left half of the country's children malnourished. The 1982 recession in Chile put one-third of Chileans out of work.

Pinochet dealt violently with his critics. Thousands disappeared, and tens of thousands were tortured. These human rights abuses brought international condemnation and resistance within Chile. Groups of women who had lost children or spouses banded together with the protection of the Catholic Church and embroidered quilts known as *arpilleras*, rendering images of their missing relatives or other experiences with repression. Catholic leaders investigated human rights abuses, uncovering mass graves that served as proof of the dictatorship's violence.

Amid the excesses of Pinochet's dictatorship, opponents and even many allies looked for ways to curb his power and find the path for redemocratization. After the 1982 economic crisis, businessmen began to join with opposition groups to press for liberalization. Opposition groups proposed a return to democracy that maintained the major elements of free-market reforms. These groups banded together and called for Chileans to vote "NO" in the 1989 referendum on whether Pinochet would remain in power. The "NO" prevailed, and Chile held its first democratic elections in two decades.

The opposition alliance in Chile resembled many other alliances around the world that sought transitions from authoritarian rule: political opponents who advocated for human rights joined forces with business groups that sought markets in order to produce a postdictatorship democracy founded on free-market principles and support for human rights.

The Dirty War in Argentina

The Argentine military either held power or set the political rules for decades after it deposed populist Juan Perón in 1955 (see page 978). By 1973 the armed forces conceded that their efforts to "de-Perónize" the country had failed. They allowed Perón to return, and he was again elected president, with his third wife, María Estela, known as Isabelita, as vice president. Soon after the election, Juan Perón died and Isabelita Perón become president, She faced daunting circumstances: Marxist groups waged a guerrilla war against the regime, while the armed forces and death squads waged war on them.

In March 1976 a military junta took power and announced a Process of National Reorganization. The generals waged a "dirty war," seeking to kill and "disappear" people whom they considered a destructive "cancer" on the nation. Argentine military forces killed between fourteen thousand and thirty thousand of their fellow citizens during the dirty war.

A handful of mothers whose children had disappeared began appearing in the Plaza de Mayo in front of the presidential palace holding pictures of their missing children and carrying signs reading "Where are they?" A growing organization of the Mothers of the Plaza de Mayo was soon joined by the Grandmothers, who demanded the whereabouts of children born to women who were detained and disappeared while pregnant. These mothers were only kept alive until they gave birth. Their children were placed with adoptive families tied to the police or armed forces. Unlike in Chile and Brazil, in Argentina senior Catholic clergy did

CHAPTER LOCATOR | What were the short-term and long-term consequences of the OPEC oil embargo? | How did war and revolution reshape the Middle East?

CHAPTER 32
1004 LIBERALIZATION

not advocate for human rights or the protection of dissidents. Instead Argentine bishops praised the coup and defended the military regime until it ended in 1983.

In 1982, emboldened by its success in eradicating its opposition, the Argentine junta occupied a set of islands off of its southern coast that were claimed by Britain. Known in Britain as the Falklands and in Argentina as the Malvinas, the islands were home to a small British settlement. Britain resisted the invasion and the Falklands/Malvinas War resulted in a humiliating defeat for the Argentine junta. After the war the junta abruptly called for elections, and a civilian president took office in 1983.

The new president, Raúl Alfonsín, faced a debt crisis similar to Mexico's. He also had to figure out how to mete out justice for the crimes committed by the junta, whose members were tried and convicted. Their convictions created a backlash in the armed forces, which forced the government to halt prosecutions. Alfonsín was succeeded by Carlos Menem, who tried a different approach. Menem pardoned the junta members and embarked on free-market reforms, privatizing businesses and utilities and reducing trade barriers. Investment flooded in, and Argentina seemingly put the past to rest.

As the capacity to attract foreign investment through privatization ran out by the end of the century, Argentina faced economic crisis again. In 2001, amid a run on banks and a collapse of the Argentine peso, the country had five different presidents in a single month. Eventually, the economy stabilized during the presidency of Néstor Kirchner, succeeded by his wife, Cristina Fernández de Kirchner. Cristina Fernández de Kirchner resumed the prosecution of those responsible for violence during the dirty war.

Development and Dictatorship in Brazil

Brazil's military dictatorship, in power since 1964, pursued a different economic model than Chile's and Argentina's. Though Brazil's generals began with liberal reforms, they moved to a nationalist project of increased state control of industry, restrictions on imports, and heavy investments in energy and transportation infrastructure. They initially experienced great success, with annual growth rates averaging 11 percent between 1968 and 1973. This growth depended on cheap imported oil and harsh political repression. When the oil embargo threatened to cripple the country's accelerating industrialization, the generals borrowed heavily from abroad to subsidize fuel costs and conduct costly alternative energy projects.

The Brazilian cycle of borrowing petrodollars to subsidize oil imports and development projects was ruinous for the country. By the end of the 1970s Brazil had the largest foreign debt in the developing world. When the second oil shock hit in 1979, and as the U.S. government raised interest rates, making Brazil's debt more expensive to manage, the country entered what became known as a "lost decade" of recession and inflation. In the 1980s the economic crisis set the tone for a transition to democracy: as the generals made painful cuts to public services and as Brazilians faced crippling inflation and recession, people overwhelmingly turned against military rule and supported redemocratization.

As in Chile, Brazil's transition to democracy was shaped by liberalization. Business groups, which had grown uneasy with the dictatorship's borrowing and central planning, joined forces with human rights advocates to return the "rule of law," rather than arbitrary rule by generals. Unlike in Chile, the debt left behind

| What effect did the Cold War and debt crisis have on Latin America? | How did white-minority rule end in southern Africa? | How have East and South Asian nations pursued economic development? | How did decolonization and the end of the Cold War change Europe? | ✓ LearningCurve Check what you know. |

1005

by Brazil's military leaders drove liberal economic reforms. In order to sustain its debt payments, the Brazilian government accepted the Washington Consensus, reducing public spending and opening the economy to imports and foreign investment. Within this changed climate, in 1994 Brazilians elected Fernando Henrique Cardoso. Cardoso carried out the deepest and most sustained liberal reforms Brazil had seen since the 1930s.

> **QUICK REVIEW**

What explains the rise of authoritarian governments throughout Latin America during this period?

CHAPTER LOCATOR | What were the short-term and long-term consequences of the OPEC oil embargo? | How did war and revolution reshape the Middle East?

CHAPTER 32
1006 LIBERALIZATION

How did white-minority rule end in southern Africa?

Student Demonstrations Against Apartheid

Police fire tear gas at anti-apartheid protesters in 1989 at Witwatersrand University in Johannesburg. (Ulli Michel/Reuters/Landov)

THE RACIALLY SEGREGATED SYSTEM OF APARTHEID in South Africa was part of a larger system of white-minority rule that included Portuguese Angola and Mozambique, the government of Ian Smith in Rhodesia, and South African control of the former German colony of Namibia. In the 1970s the buffer of neighboring white-minority governments around South Africa crumbled. Domestic and foreign pressure brought a political transition to majority rule in Namibia and South Africa in the 1990s.

Portuguese Decolonization and Rhodesia

At the end of World War II Portugal was the poorest country in western Europe and was ruled by a dictatorship, but it still claimed an immense overseas empire that included Angola, Mozambique, Guinea-Bissau,and Cape Verde. Unlike other European colonial leaders, the Portuguese dictator António Salazar (1889–1970) refused to consider ending colonial rule. Without government support for independence, nationalists in Portugal's colonies resorted to armed insurrections. By the

What effect did the Cold War and debt crisis have on Latin America?

How did white-minority rule end in southern Africa?

How have East and South Asian nations pursued economic development?

How did decolonization and the end of the Cold War change Europe?

✓ LearningCurve
Check what you know.

early 1970s independence movements in Angola, Cape Verde, Guinea-Bissau, and Mozambique all fought guerrilla wars against the Portuguese army and colonial militias. The human toll was immense, and Portuguese officers returning from the colonies deposed the dictator in 1974. Guinea-Bissau and Cape Verde became independent that same year; Angola and Mozambique gained independence a year later. The nationalist movements that took power were all Marxist. Their radicalism was a product of their long struggle against oppression, inequality, and lack of access to their countries' resources.

The end of colonialism in Angola and Mozambique shifted the political landscape of southern Africa. Mozambique helped rebels fighting white-minority rule in Rhodesia, while the South African government saw independent Angola as a threat to apartheid and to its control over Namibia. The block of white-minority rule had been shattered, but neither Angola nor Mozambique would soon find peace.

The new government of Mozambique faced a guerrilla movement financed by Rhodesia. As Angola became independent, it faced immediate invasions from Zaire (encouraged by the United States) and South Africa. The new president of Angola, Agostinho Neto (1922–1978), requested military aid from Cuba. Until the late 1980s tens of thousands of Cuban troops faced off with the South African Defense Forces and mercenary armies to defend the government of Angola.

In the British colony of Rhodesia white settlers were a small minority of the population who declared independence on their own in order to avoid sharing power with the black majority. In 1965 they established a white-minority government under Ian Smith. The new Rhodesian state faced international condemnation for its treatment of black citizens, including the first economic sanctions imposed by the United Nations.

The Zimbabwe African People's Union (ZAPU) fought a guerrilla war against Rhodesia's white regime. Rebuffed by the United States and Britain, ZAPU turned to China and the Soviet Union for support. When Mozambique gained independence in 1974, its government allowed ZAPU and other guerrilla groups to use neighboring Mozambican territory as a staging ground to launch attacks on Rhodesia, making it impossible for the Ian Smith government to endure. Negotiations led to an open election in 1980 that ZAPU leader Robert Mugabe won easily. The new Mugabe government renamed the country Zimbabwe after an ancient city-state that predated colonial rule.

South Africa Under Apartheid

In 1948 the ruling South African National Party created a racist and segregationist system of discrimination known as apartheid, meaning "apartness" or "separation." The population was divided into four legally unequal racial groups: whites, blacks, Asians, and racially mixed "coloureds." South Africa was the most highly industrialized country in Africa at this time. Good jobs in the cities were reserved for whites. Blacks were restricted to outlying townships plagued by poverty, crime, and mistreatment from white policemen.

By the 1950s black South Africans and their allies mounted peaceful protests. A turning point came in 1960, when police in the township of Sharpeville fired at demonstrators and killed sixty-nine black demonstrators. The main black nationalist organization—the **African National Congress (ANC)**—was outlawed but sent

apartheid
▶ The system of racial segregation and discrimination that was supported by the Afrikaner government in South Africa.

African National Congress (ANC)
▶ The main black nationalist organization in South Africa, led by Nelson Mandela.

CHAPTER LOCATOR | What were the short-term and long-term consequences of the OPEC oil embargo? | How did war and revolution reshape the Middle East?

CHAPTER 32
1008 LIBERALIZATION

some of its leaders abroad. Other ANC members, led by a young lawyer, Nelson Mandela (1918–2013), stayed in South Africa to mount armed resistance. In 1962 Mandela was captured and sentenced to life imprisonment.

In the 1970s the South African government fell into the hands of "securocrats," military and intelligence officers who directed the state's resources into policing apartheid and dominating South Africa's neighbors by force. They adopted a policy known as the "total strategy," which intensified repression of black activists at home and launched military strikes against ANC and South West Africa People's Organization (SWAPO) camps operating in neighboring countries. At the United Nations, African leaders denounced the South African government, and activists in countries around the world pressured their governments to impose economic sanctions against the South African regime. South Africa's white leaders responded with a program of cosmetic reforms in 1984 to improve their international standing.

The reforms provoked a backlash. In the segregated townships young black militants took to the streets, clashing with heavily armed white security forces. Across the border with Angola, South African troops engaged in escalating conflicts with Angolan, ANC, SWAPO, and Cuban forces. Mounting casualties and defeat in major battles shook white South Africans' confidence.

Isolated politically, besieged by economic sanctions, and defeated on the battlefield, South African president Frederik W. de Klerk opened a dialogue with ANC leaders in 1989. He lifted the state of emergency imposed in 1985, legalized the ANC, and freed Mandela in February 1990. Mandela suspended the ANC's armed struggle and negotiated an agreement with de Klerk calling for universal suffrage, which meant black-majority rule.

In May 1994 Mandela was elected president of South Africa. Heading the new "government of national unity," which included de Klerk as vice president, Mandela and the South African people set about building a multiracial democracy. Seeking to sustain the economy built through South Africa's industrialization and to avoid white flight, Mandela repudiated his Marxist beliefs and reassured domestic and foreign investors of his commitment to liberalization.

Political Change in Africa Since 1990

Democracy's rise in South Africa was part of a trend toward elected civilian rule that swept through sub-Saharan Africa after 1990. The end of the Cold War that followed the breakup of the Soviet Union in 1990 transformed Africa's relations with Russia and the United States. Communism's collapse in Europe brought an abrupt end to Communist aid to Russia's African clients. U.S. support for pro-Western dictators, no matter how corrupt or repressive, declined as well. But the decrease in support for dictators left a power vacuum in which ethnic conflicts intensified, with often-disastrous results.

For instance, in the early 1990s the United States cut off decades of support for the anticommunist General Mobutu Sese Seko (1930–1997), who seized power in 1965 in Zaire (the former Belgian Congo, renamed the Democratic Republic of the Congo in 1997) and looted the country. Opposition groups toppled the tyrant in 1997, and a civil war ensued that left an estimated 5.4 million dead by 2007.

The agreement by national independence leaders across the continent to respect colonial borders prevented one kind of violence, but resulted in another.

What effect did the Cold War and debt crisis have on Latin America? | **How did white-minority rule end in southern Africa?** | How have East and South Asian nations pursued economic development? | How did decolonization and the end of the Cold War change Europe? | LearningCurve Check what you know.

1009

In countries whose national boundaries had been created by colonial powers irrespective of historic divisions, ethnic strife sometimes boiled over into deep violence, such as the genocides of ethnic Hutus by Tutsis in Burundi in 1972 and by Tutsis of Hutus in 1993 and 1994 in Rwanda, which left hundreds of thousands dead. A test of the alternative to preserving national boundaries came amid efforts to ease tensions that had created famine and hardship in Sudan. In 2011, 98 percent of the electorate in southern Sudan voted to break away and form a new country, South Sudan. The early promise of peace after separation has been challenged by increased ethnic and political violence in South Sudan.

Amid these conflicts, political and economic reform has occurred in other African nations where years of mismanagement and repression had delegitimized one-party rule. Above all, the strength of the democratic opposition rested on a growing class of educated urban Africans. Postindependence governments enthusiastically expanded opportunities in education, especially higher education. The result was a growing middle class of educated professionals who chafed at the ostentatious privilege of tiny closed elites and pressed for political reforms that would democratize social and economic opportunities. Thus after 1990 sub-Saharan Africa accompanied the global trend toward liberalization and human rights.

> QUICK REVIEW

Why did South Africa's white-minority government agree to end apartheid?

CHAPTER LOCATOR | What were the short-term and long-term consequences of the OPEC oil embargo? | How did war and revolution reshape the Middle East?

CHAPTER 32
1010 LIBERALIZATION

How have East and South Asian nations pursued economic development, and how have political regimes shaped those efforts?

The Election of Benazir Bhutto

Pakistan's Benazir Bhutto became the first female prime minister of a Muslim nation in 1988. (SIPA/Spa USA)

CHINA, JAPAN, AND THE COUNTRIES that became known as the "Asian Tigers" (South Korea, Hong Kong, Singapore, and Taiwan) experienced fantastic economic growth in the last decades of the twentieth century. The Chinese Communist Party maintained tight political control amid liberalization and economic growth. Japan's economy stagnated in the 1990s and struggled to recover amid growing competition from its neighbors. In South Asia tensions between India and Pakistan remained.

China's Economic Resurgence

Mao's Cultural Revolution of 1965–1969 created chaos and a general crisis of confidence, especially in the cities (see page 967). Intellectuals, technicians, and purged party officials launched a counterattack on the radicals and regained much of their influence by 1969. This shift opened the door to a limited but lasting reconciliation between China and the United States in 1972.

After Mao's death in 1976, Chinese leader Deng Xiaoping (1904–1997) and his supporters initiated the "Four Modernizations": agriculture, industry, science and

What effect did the Cold War and debt crisis have on Latin America?

How did white-minority rule end in southern Africa?

How have East and South Asian nations pursued economic development?

How did decolonization and the end of the Cold War change Europe?

✓ LearningCurve
Check what you know.

technology, and national defense. China's 800 million peasants were allowed to farm in small family units rather than in large collectives and to "dare to be rich" by producing crops of their choice. Peasants responded enthusiastically, increasing food production by more than 50 percent by 1984.

The successful use of free markets in agriculture encouraged further experimentation. Foreign capitalists were allowed to open factories in southern China and to export their products around the world. Private enterprise was permitted in cities. China's Communist Party also drew on the business talent of "overseas" Chinese in Hong Kong and Taiwan who understood world markets and sought cheap labor. The Chinese economy grew rapidly between 1978 and 1987, and per capita income doubled in these years.

Most large-scale industry remained state owned, however, and the Communist Party zealously preserved its monopoly on political power. When the worldwide movement for political liberalization took root in China in the 1980s, the government banned demonstrations and slowed economic liberalization. Inflation soared to more than 30 percent a year. The economic reversal, the continued lack of political freedom, and the conviction that Chinese society was becoming more corrupt led idealistic university students to spearhead demonstrations in 1989.

More than a million people streamed into Beijing's central **Tiananmen Square** in support of the students' demands. The government declared martial law and ordered the army to clear the students. Masses of courageous citizens blocked the

Tiananmen Square

▶ The site of a Chinese student revolt in 1989 at which Communists imposed martial law and arrested, injured, or killed hundreds of students.

Tiananmen Square, 1989

Protesters in Tiananmen Square surround a towering figure of the Goddess of Democracy built by Chinese art students. The statue was eventually destroyed by Chinese soldiers. (© Peter Turnley/Corbis)

> PICTURING THE PAST

ANALYZING THE IMAGE: What do you think this statue symbolized for demonstrators in Tiananmen Square?

CONNECTIONS: Why has the Goddess of Democracy become a lasting symbol of the 1989 student movement?

CHAPTER LOCATOR | What were the short-term and long-term consequences of the OPEC oil embargo? | How did war and revolution reshape the Middle East?

CHAPTER 32
1012 LIBERALIZATION

soldiers' entry into the city for two weeks, but in the early hours of June 4, 1989, tanks rolled into Tiananmen Square. At least seven hundred students died as a wave of repression, arrests, and executions descended on China.

As communism fell in eastern Europe and the Soviet Union broke apart, China's rulers felt vindicated. They believed their action had preserved Communist power, prevented chaos, and demonstrated the limits of reform. China became politically Communist and economically capitalist. In 2001 China joined the World Trade Organization, completing its immersion in the liberal global economy.

> ## The Chinese Economy (1978–2012)

- Nine percent average annual rate of growth and 16 percent average annual growth of foreign trade
- Average per capita income in China doubled every ten years
- March 2011 China replaced Japan as the world's second-largest economy

"Japan, Inc." and the "Asian Tigers"

Japan's postwar economic recovery, like Germany's, proceeded slowly at first. But during the Korean War, the Japanese economy took off and grew with spectacular speed. Between 1950 and 1970 Japan's economic growth averaged a breathtaking 10 percent a year.

Japan's emergence as an economic superpower fascinated outsiders. Many Asians and Africans looked to Japan for the secrets of successful modernization, but some of Japan's Asian neighbors again feared Japanese exploitation. In the 1970s and 1980s some Americans and Europeans accused "Japan, Inc." of an unfair alliance between government and business and urged their own governments to retaliate.

In Japan's system of managed capitalism, the government protected its industry from foreign competition, decided which industries were important, and then made loans and encouraged mergers to create powerful firms in those industries. The government rewarded large corporations and encouraged them to develop extensive industrial and financial activities. But the 1990s saw Japan's economy stagnate amid the bursting of a speculative bubble that crippled banks and led to record postwar unemployment as the country faced competition from industrializing neighbors in Asia.

The "Asian Tigers," named for their economic development, replicated the rapid industrialization that characterized Japan. Both South Korea and Taiwan were underdeveloped countries in the early postwar years—poor, small, agricultural, densely populated, and lacking natural resources.

They each pursued development through a similar series of reforms. First, land reform allowed small farmers to become competitive producers as well as consumers. Second, governments stimulated business through lending, import barriers, and control of labor. Third, nationalist leaders (Park Chung Hee in South Korea and Jiang Jieshi in Taiwan) maintained stability at the expense of democracy. When Park was assassinated in 1979, South Korea faced an even more authoritarian regime until democracy was established at the end of the 1980s. By the late 1990s South Korea had one of the largest economies in the world.

"Japan, Inc."

▶ A nickname from the 1980s used to describe the intricate relationship of Japan's business world and government.

Asian "Economic Tigers"

What effect did the Cold War and debt crisis have on Latin America?

How did white-minority rule end in southern Africa?

How have East and South Asian nations pursued economic development?

How did decolonization and the end of the Cold War change Europe?

✓ LearningCurve
Check what you know.

1013

In 1949, after Jiang Jieshi had fled to Taiwan with his Nationalist troops and around 2 million refugees, he re-established the Republic of China (ROC) in exile. Over the next fifty years Taiwan created one of the world's most industrialized economies, becoming a leader in electronic manufacturing and design. Mainland China continued to claim Taiwan, considering it part of "One China."

Development Versus Democracy in India and Pakistan

Jawaharlal Nehru's daughter, Indira Gandhi (no relation to Mohandas Gandhi) (1917–1984), became prime minister of India in 1966. She dominated Indian political life for a generation. In 1975 she subverted parliamentary democracy and proclaimed a state of emergency. Gandhi applied her emergency powers across a broad range of areas, including combating corruption, quelling labor unrest, and jailing political opponents. She also initiated a campaign of mass sterilization to reduce population growth. More than 7 million men were forcibly sterilized in 1976. Many believed that Gandhi's emergency measures marked the end of liberal democracy, but in 1977 Gandhi called for free elections in which she suffered a spectacular electoral defeat. Her successors fell to fighting among themselves, and in 1980 she returned to power in an equally stunning electoral victory.

Separatist ethnic nationalism plagued Indira Gandhi's last years in office. India remained a patchwork of religions, languages, and peoples, always threatening to further divide the country along ethnic or religious lines. Most notable were the 15 million Sikhs of the Punjab in northern India (see Map 31.2, page 962), with their own religion, distinctive culture, and aspirations for greater autonomy for the Punjab. By 1984 some Sikh radicals were fighting for independence. Gandhi cracked down hard and was assassinated by Sikhs in retaliation. Violence followed as Hindu mobs slaughtered over a thousand Sikhs throughout India.

One of Indira Gandhi's sons, Rajiv Gandhi, was elected prime minister in 1984 by a landslide sympathy vote. Rajiv Gandhi departed from the Congress Party's socialism and prepared the way for Finance Minister Manmohan Singh to introduce market reforms, capitalist development, and Western technology and investment from 1991 onward. These reforms were successful, and since the 1990s India's economy has experienced explosive growth.

Though the Congress Party held power in India almost continuously after 1947, in the 1990s Hindu nationalists increasingly challenged the party's grip on power. These nationalists argued that India was based, above all, on Hindu culture and religion. The Hindu nationalist party, known as the BJP, finally gained power in 1998. The new government immediately tested nuclear devices, asserting its vision of a militant Hindu nationalism. In 2004 the United Progressive Alliance (UPA), a center-left coalition dominated by the Congress Party, regained control of the government and elected Manmohan Singh as prime minister. Under Narendra Modi, credited with the rapid economic growth of Gujarat state, the BJP returned to power after a sweeping electoral victory in 2014.

After Pakistan announced that it had developed nuclear weapons in 1998, relations between Pakistan and India worsened. In 2001 the two nuclear powers seemed poised for conflict until intense diplomatic pressure from the United States and other nations brought them back from the abyss of nuclear war. Tensions

CHAPTER LOCATOR | What were the short-term and long-term consequences of the OPEC oil embargo? | How did war and revolution reshape the Middle East?

CHAPTER 32
1014 LIBERALIZATION

again increased in 2008 when a Pakistan-based terrorist organization carried out a terrorist attack in Mumbai, India's largest city, killing 164 and wounding over 300.

In the decades following the separation of Bangladesh, Pakistan alternated between civilian and military rule. General Muhammad Zia-ul-Haq, who ruled from 1977 to 1988, drew Pakistan into a close alliance with the United States, but relations with the United States chilled as Pakistan pursued its nuclear weapons program. In 1996 a fundamentalist Muslim group, the Taliban, seized power in Afghanistan, Pakistan's neighbor to the west. The Taliban's leadership allowed al-Qaeda to use Afghanistan as a base for launching acts of terrorism like the attack on the U.S. World Trade Center and the Pentagon in 2001. Following that attack, the United States invaded Afghanistan, driving the Taliban from power.

When the United States invaded Afghanistan in 2001, Pakistani dictator General Pervez Musharraf (b. 1943) renewed the alliance with the United States, and Pakistan received billions of dollars in U.S. military aid. But U.S. combat against radical terrorist groups drove militants into regions of northwest Pakistan, where they undermined the government's already-tenuous control. Cooperation between Pakistan and the United States in the war was often strained.

In 2007 Musharraf attempted to reshape the country's Supreme Court by replacing the chief justice with one of his close allies, bringing about calls for his impeachment. Former prime minister Benazir Bhutto (1953–2007) returned from exile to challenge Musharraf's increasingly repressive military rule. She was assassinated while campaigning. After being defeated at the polls in 2008, Musharraf resigned and went into exile in London. Asif Ali Zardari (b. 1955), Benazir Bhutto's husband, won the presidency by a landslide in the elections that followed.

QUICK REVIEW

What challenges do China and India face as they attempt to sustain the spectacular economic growth of recent decades?

What effect did the Cold War and debt crisis have on Latin America?

How did white-minority rule end in southern Africa?

How have East and South Asian nations pursued economic development?

How did decolonization and the end of the Cold War change Europe?

LearningCurve
Check what you know.

1015

> How did decolonization and the end of the Cold War change Europe?

Fall of the Berlin Wall

A man stands atop the partially destroyed Berlin Wall flashing the *V* for victory sign as he and thousands of other Berliners celebrate the opening of the Berlin Wall in November 1989. Within a year the wall was torn down, communism collapsed, and the Cold War ended. (Lionel Cironneau/AP Photo)

détente

▶ The progressive relaxation of Cold War tensions.

IN THE LATE 1960S AND EARLY 1970S the United States and the Soviet Union pursued a relaxation of Cold War tensions that became known as détente (day-TAHNT). Détente stalled when Brezhnev's Soviet Union invaded Afghanistan to save an unpopular Marxist regime. President Jimmy Carter reacted with alarm at the spread of Soviet influence.

Carter's successor, Ronald Reagan (U.S. pres. 1981–1989), further re-ignited the Cold War by calling the Soviet Union the "evil empire" and deploying nuclear arms in western Europe. Reagan found conservative allies in British prime minister Margaret Thatcher and German chancellor Helmut Kohl. But as Reagan, Thatcher, and Kohl rekindled the Cold War, the Soviet Union underwent a cycle of reform that culminated in the release of Soviet control over eastern Europe and the dismantling of the Soviet Union.

CHAPTER LOCATOR | What were the short-term and long-term consequences of the OPEC oil embargo? | How did war and revolution reshape the Middle East?

1016 CHAPTER 32 LIBERALIZATION

The Limits of Reform in the Soviet Union and Eastern Europe

After their 1968 military intervention in Czechoslovakia, Soviet leaders worked to restore order and stability. Free expression and open protest disappeared throughout their satellite nations. Dissidents were blacklisted or imprisoned in jails or mental institutions. A rising standard of living helped ensure stability as well. The privileges enjoyed by the Communist Party elite also served as incentives for such elites to do as the state wished. Beneath this appearance of stability, however, the Soviet Union underwent a social revolution. The urban population expanded rapidly, as did the number of highly trained scientists, managers, and specialists. These educated people read, discussed, and formed definite ideas about social questions ranging from pollution to urban transportation, fostering the growth of Soviet public opinion.

When Mikhail Gorbachev (b. 1931) became premier in 1985, he set out to reform the Soviet system with policies he called democratic socialism. The first set of reforms was intended to transform and restructure the economy. This limited economic restructuring, perestroika, permitted freer prices, more autonomy for state enterprises, and the establishment of some profit-seeking private cooperatives. Gorbachev also launched a campaign of openness, or glasnost, introduced in 1985. Where censorship and uniformity had long characterized public discourse, the new frankness approached free speech and marked a significant shift.

Democratization under Gorbachev led to the first free elections in the Soviet Union since 1917. Gorbachev and the party remained in control, but an independent minority was elected in 1989 to a revitalized Congress of People's Deputies. Democratization encouraged demands for greater autonomy from non-Russian minorities, especially in the Baltic region and in the Caucasus.

Finally, Gorbachev brought "new political thinking" to foreign affairs. He withdrew Soviet troops from Afghanistan in 1989 and sought to reduce Cold War tensions. Gorbachev pledged to respect the political choices of eastern Europe's peoples. Soon after, a wave of peaceful revolutions swept across eastern Europe, overturning Communist regimes.

Poland led the way. In August 1980 strikes grew into a working-class revolt. Led by Lech Wałęsa (lehk vah-LEHN-suh) (b. 1943), workers organized the independent trade union Solidarity. Communist leaders responded by imposing martial law in December 1981 and arresting Solidarity's leaders. Though outlawed, Solidarity maintained its organization and strong popular support. By 1988 labor unrest and inflation had brought Poland to the brink of economic collapse. Solidarity pressured Poland's Communist Party leaders into legalizing Solidarity and allowing free elections in 1989 for some seats in the Polish parliament. Solidarity won every contested seat. A month later Solidarity member Tadeusz Mazowiecki (1927–2013) was sworn in as prime minister.

Czechoslovakia's Velvet Revolution followed the dramatic changes in Poland and led to the peaceful ouster of Communist leaders. The Czech movement for democracy grew out of massive street protests led by students and intellectuals and resulted in the election of Václav Havel (VAH-slahf HAH-vuhl) as president in 1989. (See "Individuals in Society: Václav Havel," page 1018.)

Only in Romania was revolution violent. Communist dictator Nicolae Ceauşescu (chow-SHEHS-koo) (1918–1989) unleashed his security forces on

perestroika
▶ Economic restructuring and reform implemented by Soviet premier Mikhail Gorbachev that permitted an easing of government price controls on some goods, more independence for state enterprises, and the establishment of profit-seeking private cooperatives to provide personal services for consumers.

glasnost
▶ Soviet premier Mikhail Gorbachev's popular campaign for openness in the government and the media.

Solidarity
▶ Led by Lech Wałęsa, a free and democratic Polish trade union that worked for the rights of workers and political reform.

| What effect did the Cold War and debt crisis have on Latin America? | How did white-minority rule end in southern Africa? | How have East and South Asian nations pursued economic development? | **How did decolonization and the end of the Cold War change Europe?** | ☑ LearningCurve Check what you know. |

1017

Václav Havel

On the night of November 24, 1989, the revolution in Czechoslovakia reached its climax. Three hundred thousand people had poured into Prague's historic Wenceslas Square to continue the massive protests that had erupted a week earlier after the police savagely beat student demonstrators. Now all eyes were focused on a high balcony. There an elderly man with a gentle smile and a middle-aged intellectual wearing jeans and a sports jacket stood arm in arm and acknowledged the cheers of the crowd. "Dubček-Havel," the people roared. "Dubček-Havel!" Alexander Dubček, who represented the failed promise of reform communism in the 1960s (see page 984), was symbolically passing the torch to Václav Havel, who embodied the uncompromising opposition to communism that was sweeping the country. That very evening, the hard-line Communist government resigned, and soon Havel was the unanimous choice to head a new democratic Czechoslovakia. Who was this man to whom the nation turned in 1989?

Born in 1936 into a prosperous, cultured, upper-middle-class family, the young Havel was denied admission to the university because of his class origins. Loving literature and philosophy, he gravitated to the theater, became a stagehand, and emerged in the 1960s as a leading playwright. His plays were set in vague settings, developed existential themes, and poked fun at the absurdities of life and the pretensions of communism. In his private life, Havel thrived on good talk, Prague's lively bar scene, and officially forbidden rock 'n' roll.

In 1968 the Soviets rolled into Czechoslovakia, and Havel watched in horror as a tank commander opened fire on a crowd of peaceful protesters in a small town. "That week," he recorded, "was an experience I shall never forget."[*] The free-spirited artist threw himself into the intellectual opposition to communism and became its leading figure for the next twenty years. The costs of defiance were enormous. Purged and blacklisted, Havel lifted barrels in a brewery and wrote bitter satires that could not be staged. In 1977 he and a few other dissidents publicly protested Czechoslovakian violations of the Helsinki Accords on human rights, and in 1989 this Charter '77 group became the inspiration for Civic Forum, the democratic coalition that toppled communism. Havel spent five years in prison and was constantly harassed by the police.

Havel's thoughts and actions focused on truth, decency, and moral regeneration. In 1975, in a famous open letter to Czechoslovakia's Communist boss, Havel wrote that the people were indeed quiet, but

Václav Havel, playwright, dissident leader, and the first postcommunist president of the Czech Republic. (Chris Niedenthal/Black Star)

only because they were "driven by fear. . . . Everyone has something to lose and so everyone has reason to be afraid." Havel saw lies, hypocrisy, and apathy undermining and poisoning all human relations in his country: "Order has been established — at the price of a paralysis of the spirit, a deadening of the heart, and a spiritual and moral crisis in society."[†]

Yet Havel saw a way out of the Communist quagmire. He argued that a profound but peaceful revolution in human values was possible. Such a revolution could lead to the moral reconstruction of Czech and Slovak society, where, in his words, "values like trust, openness, responsibility, solidarity and love" might again flourish and nurture the human spirit. Havel was a voice of hope and humanity who inspired his compatriots with a lofty vision of a moral postcommunist society. As president of his country from 1989 to 2003, Havel continued to speak eloquently on the great questions of our time.

QUESTIONS FOR ANALYSIS

1. Why did Havel oppose Communist rule? How did his goals differ from those of Dubček and other advocates of reform communism?
2. Havel has been called a "moralist in politics." Is this a good description of him? Why or why not?

[†]Quoted ibid., p. 110.

ONLINE DOCUMENT PROJECT

How did people in Czechoslovakia overturn the existing social and political order? Explore the efforts of dissidents to produce a peaceful revolution, and then complete a quiz and writing assignment based on the evidence and details from this chapter. *See inside the front cover to learn more.*

[*]Quoted in M. Simmons, *The Reluctant President: A Political Life of Václav Havel* (London: Methuen, 1991), p. 91.

protesters, sparking an armed uprising. After Ceauşescu's forces were defeated, he and his wife were captured and executed.

Amid growing resistance, the Hungarian Communist Party scheduled free elections for early 1990. Hungarians tore down the barbed wire that separated Hungary and Austria (see Map 31.1, page 956) and opened their border to refugees from East Germany. As thousands of East Germans passed through Czechoslovakia and Hungary on their way to West Germany, a protest movement arose in East Germany. East Germany's leaders relented and opened the Berlin Wall in November 1989, before being swept aside. An "Alliance for Germany" won general elections and negotiated an economic union with West Germany.

Two factors contributed to the rapid reunification of East and West Germany. First, in the first week after the Berlin Wall opened, almost 9 million East Germans poured across the border into West Germany. Almost all returned home, but their experiences in the West aroused long-dormant hopes of unity and change. Second, West German chancellor Helmut Kohl was successful in convincing American, Soviet, and European leaders that they need not fear a reunified Germany. In 1991 East and West Germany merged into a single nation under West Germany's constitution and laws.

The great postcommunist tragedy was Yugoslavia, whose federation of republics and regions had been held together under Josip Tito's Communist rule. After Tito's death in 1980, power passed increasingly to the republics. Rising territorial and ethnic tensions were intensified by economic decline and charges of ethnically inspired massacres during World War II. The revolutions of 1989 accelerated the breakup of Yugoslavia. Serbian president Slobodan Milošević (SLOH-buh-dayn muh-LOH-suh-vihch) (1941–2006) attempted to grab land from other republics and unite all Serbs in a "greater Serbia." His ambitions led to civil wars that between 1991 and 2001 engulfed Kosovo, Slovenia, Croatia, and Bosnia-Herzegovina (Map 32.2). In 1999 Serbian aggression prompted NATO air strikes, led by the United States, against the Serbian capital of Belgrade as well as against Serbian military forces until Milošević relented. Milošević was voted out of office in 2000. The new Serbian government extradited him to a United Nations war crimes tribunal in the Netherlands to stand trial for crimes against humanity.

Recasting Russia Without Communism

Amid anticommunist upheavals in eastern Europe, the Soviet Union itself transitioned away from Communist Party rule. In February 1990 the Soviet Communist Party was defeated in local elections throughout the country. Gorbachev responded by asking Soviet citizens to ratify a new constitution that abolished the Communist Party's monopoly on political power and expanded the power of the Congress of People's Deputies. Gorbachev's eroding power and unwillingness to risk a popular election for the presidency strengthened his rival, Boris Yeltsin (1931–2007), the former mayor of Moscow. In May 1990, as leader of the Russian parliament, Yeltsin announced that Russia would declare its independence from the Soviet Union. In June 1991 Yeltsin was elected president of the Russian Federation within the Soviet Union, placing him in direct confrontation with Gorbachev, who wanted to keep the Soviet Union together amid carefully managed reforms.

In August 1991 Gorbachev survived an attempted coup by Communist Party hardliners and their allies in the armed forces. Not only did their coup attempt fail,

What effect did the Cold War and debt crisis have on Latin America?

How did white-minority rule end in southern Africa?

How have East and South Asian nations pursued economic development?

How did decolonization and the end of the Cold War change Europe?

LearningCurve
Check what you know.

1019

MAP 32.2 ■ The Breakup of Yugoslavia

Yugoslavia had the most ethnically diverse population in eastern Europe. The Republic of Croatia had substantial Serbian and Muslim minorities, and Bosnia-Herzegovina had large Muslim, Serbian, and Croatian populations, none of which had a majority. In June 1991 Serbia's brutal effort to seize territory and unite all Serbs in a single state brought a tragic civil war to the region.

but it also hastened the end of the Soviet Union. Yeltsin emerged as a popular hero for his dramatic resistance to the coup attempt.

In the aftermath of the attempted military takeover, an anticommunist revolution swept the Russian Federation as the Communist Party was outlawed and its property confiscated. Yeltsin and his liberal allies declared Russia independent and withdrew from the Soviet Union. All the other Soviet republics followed suit. Gorbachev agreed to their independence, and the Soviet Union ceased to exist on December 25, 1991 (Map 32.3).

As Boris Yeltsin presided over newly independent Russia, he sought to create economic conditions that would prevent a return to communism. Yeltsin opted for breakneck liberalization. This shock therapy, which followed methods similar to radical free-market policies in Chile and other parts of Latin America, freed prices on 90 percent of all Russian goods. The government also launched a rapid privatization of industry and turned thousands of factories and mines over to new private companies. However, instead of producing the hoped for prosperity, prices soared and production collapsed.

CHAPTER LOCATOR | What were the short-term and long-term consequences of the OPEC oil embargo? | How did war and revolution reshape the Middle East?

MAP 32.3 ■ **Russia and the Successor States**

After the attempt in August 1991 to depose Gorbachev failed, an anticommunist revolution swept the Soviet Union. Led by Russia and Boris Yeltsin, the republics that formed the Soviet Union declared their sovereignty and independence. Eleven of the fifteen republics then formed a loose confederation called the Commonwealth of Independent States, but the integrated economy of the Soviet Union dissolved into separate national economies, each with its own goals and policies.

Rapid economic liberalization had harsh consequences for Russia. Powerful state industrial monopolies became powerful private monopolies that cut production and raised prices in order to maximize profits. The managerial elite worked with organized crime to prevent the formation of would-be competitors. A new capitalist elite acquired great wealth and power, while the vast majority of people fell into poverty. As the quality of public services and health care declined, life expectancies fell. In 2003 Russia's per capita income was lower than at any time since 1978, essentially erasing the economic progress gained over the past twenty-five years.

The election of Yeltsin's handpicked successor, President Vladimir Putin (b. 1952), in 2000 ushered in a new era of "managed democracy." Putin's stress on public order and economic reform was popular, even as he became progressively

What effect did the Cold War and debt crisis have on Latin America?

How did white-minority rule end in southern Africa?

How have East and South Asian nations pursued economic development?

How did decolonization and the end of the Cold War change Europe?

☑ LearningCurve
Check what you know.

1021

more authoritarian. Putin consolidated the power and authority of the state around himself and his closest advisers, closing off the development of democratic pluralism and an independent legal system in Russia.

Putin carried out a brutal military campaign against the primarily Muslim republic Chechnya (CHEHCH-nyuh) (see Map 32.3, inset) that in 1991 declared its independence. Up to two hundred thousand Chechen civilians are estimated to have been killed between 1994 and 2011. Many more became refugees. Chechen resistance to Russian domination continued, often in the form of attacks such as a suicide bombing at Moscow's airport in 2011.

Unable to run for re-election in 2008, Putin handpicked a successor, Dmitry Medvedev, to be president, and took the position of Russian prime minister for himself. He remained the main power broker and returned to the presidency in 2012. Liberal reforms doomed much of Russia's industry, and its economy depended increasingly on oil and natural gas exports.

Political and ethnic divisions threatened peace and stability among the post-Soviet republics. Rival claims between the Republic of Georgia and the Russian Federation over the territory of South Ossetia led to war in 2008 in which Russian forces quickly defeated their Georgian rivals and established the pro-Russian autonomy of the region. In Ukraine, in 2014 pro-Western protesters toppled a president who refused to sign agreements with the European Union. In the aftermath of the uprising, Russian forces occupied Ukrainian province of Crimea along the Black Sea and backed secessionist movements in ethnically Russian regions of the Ukraine.

Integration and Reform in Europe

Building on integration efforts in the 1940s and 1950s established through NATO and the Common Market (see page 982), at the end of the twentieth century European nations moved toward greater unity. France and Germany took the lead in pushing for a monetary union among Common Market members. The European Union (EU), established in 1993, allowed for the free movement of people and goods among its original twelve member countries; created a common currency, the euro (2002); and formed a European Parliament.

The loss by western European countries of their colonies in Africa and Asia was a major incentive to unify within Europe because it dramatically shifted their access to markets and resources. For five centuries overseas empires not only provided the engine for economic development at home but also shaped international relations. As the cycle of colonialism ended, nations that had related to each other with the crutch of overseas empires now needed to forge new relationships directly with one another—the first time they had ever done so since the cycle of colonialism accompanied the process of nation-state formation. The result was an unprecedentedly close degree of economic and political integration.

European leaders embraced, or at least accepted, a neoliberal, free-market vision of capitalism. The most radical economic changes had been implemented in the 1980s by Margaret Thatcher (1925–2013) in Britain, who drew inspiration from Pinochet's Chile. Other governments also introduced austerity measures to slow the growth of public spending and the welfare state. Many individuals suffered under the impact of these reductions in public spending and social welfare, and the threat of unemployment shaped the outlook of a whole generation. Harder

European Union (EU)

▶ An economic and political alliance of twelve European nations formed in 1993 that has since grown to include twenty-seven European nations.

CHAPTER LOCATOR | What were the short-term and long-term consequences of the OPEC oil embargo? | How did war and revolution reshape the Middle East?

1022 CHAPTER 32 LIBERALIZATION

times meant that more women entered or remained in the workforce after they married.

In the 1990s Germany and France continued to lead the push for integration. French president François Mitterrand (1916–1996) and German chancellor Helmut Kohl (b. 1930) pursued a monetary union of European Community members, and the Maastricht Treaty of 1992 created a single EU currency, the euro. In 1993 the European Community rechristened itself the European Union (EU).

The success of the euro encouraged the EU to accelerate plans for an ambitious enlargement to the east. On May 1, 2004, the EU started admitting eastern European countries. By 2007 the EU had twenty-seven member states. Future candidates for membership include Croatia, Macedonia, former parts of the Soviet Union, and Turkey (Map 32.4).

MAP 32.4 ■ The European Union, 2014

No longer divided by ideological competition and the Cold War, much of today's Europe has banded together in a European Union.

The European Union
- Original members, 1951
- New members, 1973
- New members, 1981
- New members, 1986
- German reunification, 1990
- New members, 1995
- New members, 2004
- New members, 2007
- New members, 2013
- Candidate countries, 2014
- € Eurozone countries, 2014

What effect did the Cold War and debt crisis have on Latin America?

How did white-minority rule end in southern Africa?

How have East and South Asian nations pursued economic development?

How did decolonization and the end of the Cold War change Europe?

LearningCurve
Check what you know.

1023

A proposed EU constitution binding EU member states even closer together was scheduled to go into effect in 2007. First, however, it needed to be approved by voters in all member countries. In 2005 voters in France and Holland voted overwhelmingly against the constitution and threw the entire process into confusion. The rejected constitution was replaced with the Treaty of Lisbon in 2007. The new treaty kept most of the reforms contained in the original European constitution, but it revised the political structure of the EU bureaucracy. By November 2009 all members had approved it, and the Lisbon treaty came into force on December 1, 2009.

The economic crisis that began in 2008 tested the European Union and the euro. Countries that had adopted the euro currency had to meet stringent fiscal standards and imposed budget cuts and financial austerity. The resulting reductions in health care and social benefits hit ordinary citizens hard. A global economic recession magnified these difficulties. National governments could no longer manage their own currencies to promote recovery, and governments were forced to slash budgets to meet debt obligations. Economic austerity brought ruinous economic cycles that crippled Greece, Portugal, Spain, and Italy. The consequences of liberalization in Europe resembled the consequences elsewhere: economic growth was greater, but economic hardships were deeper.

> **QUICK REVIEW**

How did economic developments in the aftermath of the collapse of the Soviet Union shape subsequent political developments in Russia?

CHAPTER SUMMARY

In 1976 most of the world was governed by undemocratic regimes. These regimes came in many different types: some were controlled by Communist parties and others by right-wing military officers loyal to the United States. There were dictatorships ruled by nationalist leaders, strongmen who unseated independence leaders, and by members of families that owned much of a nation's resources. Some of these dictators created an illusion of governing democratically, but they restricted opposition or required one-party rule.

Some dictatorships created the space to engage in utopian projects to remake nations. Even when such dictatorships succeeded in their goals, they did so at enormous costs measured in debt and inflation, famine and malnutrition, the tattering of public institutions, and the reliance on repression to maintain order.

By the mid-1980s dictatorships around the world had begun to fall, and democratic transitions followed. During the 1980s most of Latin America returned to democracy, and in 1989 the fall of the Berlin Wall began a wave of political and economic change in the Soviet Union and eastern Europe. The end of the Cold War division of Europe accelerated a process of integration and unification that

CHAPTER LOCATOR | What were the short-term and long-term consequences of the OPEC oil embargo? | How did war and revolution reshape the Middle East?

CHAPTER 32
1024 LIBERALIZATION

had its roots in reconstruction after the Second World War and the process of decolonization that dismantled European empires. Alongside political transitions, a wave of economic liberalization, often promoted by the United States, swept the world. Trade and economic activity increased as a result of liberalization, but it also created growing gaps between rich and poor.

CONNECTIONS The experiences of people living under authoritarian regimes varied greatly. Many supported the regimes from which they drew privileges or found a reassuring sense of order. Others avoided political questions and stayed out of trouble.

Many, however, resisted the regimes. For some, a closed political system meant the only tools available were armed resistance. Guerrilla movements against authoritarian regimes were common, though the imbalance in their resources meant they mostly met with violent ends at the hands of security forces. Another form of resistance proved more effective: nonviolent, and ostensibly nonpolitical, resistance was harder for regimes to repress. Mothers asking for the whereabouts of missing children or quilting the scenes of their grief in Argentina and Chile, or workers organizing an independent union in Poland, found ways to challenge their regimes.

The most successful resistance was often opposition that was not explicitly ideological, such as the defense of human rights, or the establishment of the rule of law that would restrict a regime's arbitrary power. These pressures had a similar effect when applied to right-wing or socialist dictatorships alike: they were liberalizing. As dictatorships in Latin America, East Asia, and eastern Europe moved toward multiparty democracy, and as the Soviet bloc disintegrated, those countries shared a historical moment in which liberal economic and political reforms swept the world.

ONLINE DOCUMENT PROJECT

Václav Havel: Planning a Nonviolent Revolution

How did people in Czechoslovakia overturn the existing social and political order?

Explore the efforts of dissidents to produce a peaceful revolution, and then complete a quiz and writing assignment based on the evidence and details from this chapter. *See inside the front cover to learn more.*

What effect did the Cold War and debt crisis have on Latin America?

How did white-minority rule end in southern Africa?

How have East and South Asian nations pursued economic development?

How did decolonization and the end of the Cold War change Europe?

✔ LearningCurve
Check what you know.

STEP 1   **GET STARTED ONLINE**

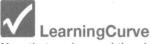 LearningCurve

Now that you've read the chapter, make it stick by completing the LearningCurve activity.

STEP 2   **EXPLAIN WHY IT MATTERS**

Put your reading into practice. Identify each term below, and then explain why it matters in world history.

TERM	WHO OR WHAT & WHEN	WHY IT MATTERS
petrodollars (p. 993)		
neoliberalism (p. 994)		
Washington Consensus (p. 994)		
intifada (p. 998)		
junta (p. 1003)		
apartheid (p. 1008)		
African National Congress (ANC) (p. 1008)		
Tiananmen Square (p. 1012)		
"Japan, Inc." (p. 1013)		
détente (p. 1016)		
perestroika (p. 1017)		
glasnost (p. 1017)		
Solidarity (p. 1017)		
European Union (EU) (p. 1022)		

STEP 3   **MOVE BEYOND THE BASICS**

To demonstrate a more advanced understanding of the impact of economic developments and policies on recent world history, fill in the chart below with descriptions of key economic events and their consequences. In your opinion, has liberalization had an overall positive impact on global economic development in the last fifty years? Why or why not?

	Description	Consequences
OPEC Oil Embargo		
Economic Liberalization in Latin America		
Economic Liberalization in China		
Economic Liberalization in the Aftermath of the Collapse of the Soviet Union		
The 2008 Financial Crisis		

PUT IT ALL TOGETHER Now, take a step back and try to explain the big picture. Remember to use specific examples from the chapter in your answers.

THE MIDDLE EAST AND ASIA

► What are the most important *internal* divisions within the Islamic societies of the Middle East?

► In your opinion, how stable is China's combination of economic liberalism and political authoritarianism? What does China's history since 1945 tell us about the likelihood of political liberalization in China in coming decades?

LATIN AMERICA AND AFRICA

► What policies and practices did Latin American authoritarian leaders employ to maintain their hold on power? Why did so many dictatorships give way to democracy in the late twentieth century?

► What light do the recent histories of Nigeria and South Africa shed on the challenges facing sub-Saharan Africa as the region enters the twenty-first century?

THE END OF THE COLD WAR

► How would you explain the pattern of post–Cold War development in Eastern Europe? Why were some states more successful than others?

► What forces were behind the push toward greater European unity in the late twentieth century? What might explain the increasing reluctance of ordinary Europeans to support further steps toward unification?

LOOKING BACK, LOOKING AHEAD

► Compare and contrast the economic relationship between the West and the rest of the world in 1900 and in 2000. What changed? What stayed the same?

► In your opinion, will liberal economic policies continue to dominate global economic activity in the next several decades? Why or why not?

> **IN YOUR OWN WORDS**

Imagine that you must give an oral report to the class answering the following question: **Why did liberalization emerge as a such a powerful force in the second half of the twentieth century, and what were the consequences of this development?** What would be the most important points and why?

33

THE CONTEMPORARY WORLD IN HISTORICAL PERSPECTIVE

> ## How is our understanding of the present shaped by our understanding of the past?

Chapter 33 examines the contemporary world in historical perspective. Since the end of the Cold War, many nations around the world have undergone transitions from dictatorship to democracy, and a growing number of nations have pursued free trade. These new experiences have been shaped by past struggles, and they have intensified global connections, aided by revolutions in communications and information technology. Amid these changes, stubborn regional and political conflicts remain in many parts of the world, and the experiences of poverty and marginalization continue to be widespread. But this is also a world in which, as in the past, humans have had the ability to shape, adapt, and transform the problems they confront.

> Does the contemporary world reflect the "end of history"?

> How have migration and the circulation of capital and technology continued to shape the world?

> What challenges did social reformers address at the turn of the twenty-first century?

> How have science and technology kept pace with population change?

The Digital Revolution People throughout the world have embraced the ease and convenience of mobile phone technology, which has increased dramatically since the introduction of the first cellular phone in 1985. (Masterfile/Royalty-Free)

LearningCurve
After reading the chapter, use LearningCurve to retain what you've read.

> Does the contemporary world reflect the "end of history"?

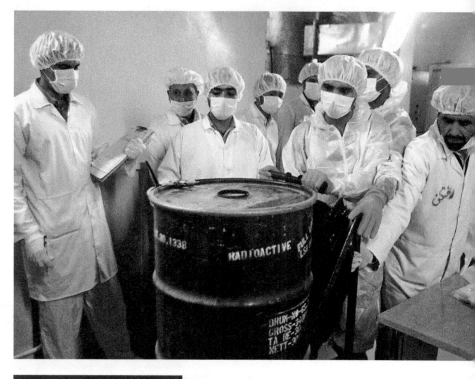

Iranian Nuclear Energy Program

Despite threats of sanctions from the United States, France, Germany, Great Britain, and Russia, Iran continues to develop its nuclear energy program. Here Iranian scientists move a container of radioactive uranium. (Behrouz Mehri/AFP/Getty Images)

I**N 1989, AS THE BERLIN WALL FELL** and the Soviet system disintegrated, a historian wrote a provocative article called "The End of History?" in which he argued that the collapse of the Soviet system meant the triumph of liberalism as a political and economic philosophy. The argument, and the essay's title, begged an interesting question. Was liberalism the ultimate stage of human political and economic development?

Around the world at the turn of the twenty-first century, liberalism certainly emerged as the dominant political and economic philosophy. But there have been limits to liberalism's reach and its effectiveness as a solution to political and economic problems. For instance, economic liberalism has tended to increase social inequality and the disparity of wealth between nations and regions in ways that are not sustainable. As a result, the rise of liberalism has been met by a growing range of social activism aimed at reducing social inequality; gender, ethnic, and racial marginalization; and the environmental costs of economic development.

The tension between liberalism and activism is one example of the kinds of contradictory and competing pressures that shape the contemporary world. For instance, the earth's growing population has increased demands for food produc-

CHAPTER LOCATOR | **Does the contemporary world reflect the "end of history"?** | How have migration and the circulation of capital and technology shaped the world?

CHAPTER 33
1030 THE CONTEMPORARY WORLD IN HISTORICAL PERSPECTIVE

1950s
Beginning of green revolution

1969–1979
Strategic Arms Limitation Talks (SALT) between the Soviet Union and United States

1970
Treaty on the Non-Proliferation of Nuclear Weapons

1981
UN World Health Organization International Code of Marketing of Breast-Milk Substitutes

1989
United Nations Convention on the Rights of the Child

1994
Zapatista Army for National Liberation insurrection in Chiapas, Mexico

1997
Chemical Weapons Convention goes into effect, banning the production of chemical weapons; Kyoto Protocol on global warming

2000–2010
Warmest decade in recorded history

2001
Al-Qaeda attacks on World Trade Center and U.S. Pentagon

2001
U.S. invasion and occupation of Afghanistan

2003
U.S.-led coalition invades Iraq; Human Genome Project completes sequencing of human genome

tion, prompting a revolution in agricultural sciences. Although new technologies have helped meet the world's demand for food, the diversion of water resources and the expansion of farming at the expense of forests remind us that new technologies often bring unintended costs. Similarly, the end of the Cold War has been met not with peace but with regional conflicts around the world. And with the intensification of communications, increase in travel, and the spread of technology, capital and liberal ideology have been met with conservative, often religious reactions in different regions of the world. Increasingly, those reactions have had a global impact as militants pursue their causes in the United States and Europe.

Complexity and Violence in a Multipolar World

When the Cold War ended, the existing global political alignment yielded to new regional relationships in which many middle powers exerted increased influence. Increasingly assertive middle powers, countries with significant economic influence either in relation to their neighbors or in broader trade networks, jockeyed for regional leadership.

middle powers
▶ Countries with significant economic influence that became increasingly assertive regional leaders after the Cold War.

> Middle Powers:

- South America: Brazil
- The Spanish-speaking Americas: Mexico
- Europe: France and Germany
- Sub-Saharan Africa: Nigeria and South Africa
- The Middle East: Turkey, Egypt, Iran, and Israel
- Asia: China, India, and Japan

What challenges did social reformers address at the turn of the twenty-first century?

How have science and technology kept pace with population change?

 LearningCurve
Check what you know.

While the end of the Cold War reduced superpower pressures that intensified regional conflicts, other factors continued to feed conflicts around the world. In the 1990s civil wars in Bosnia, Kosovo, Rwanda, and Afghanistan killed over a million people and created hundreds of thousands of refugees. Since 2000 new and continuing wars have caused millions more deaths and new refugees. Rivalries between ethnic groups often lay at the heart of these wars.

An Expanding Atomic Age

After the bombing of Hiroshima and Nagasaki in 1945 (see page 946), the United States briefly held a monopoly on atomic weapons. Since then, a growing number of nations have developed nuclear arms.

The Cold War arms race resulted in intense competition for the development of increasingly powerful atomic weapons, and it also meant massive spending in the United States, the Soviet Union, and Europe on the development of other military technology. While the superpowers and their closest allies sought to restrict access to nuclear weapons, they sold huge numbers of conventional arms to other nations.

Amid the Cold War arms race, atomic tests brought fear that radiation would enter the food chain. Concerned scientists called for a ban on atomic bomb testing. In 1963 the United States, Great Britain, and the Soviet Union reached an agreement, eventually joined by more than 150 countries, to ban nuclear tests in the atmosphere. In 1970 more than sixty countries signed the Treaty on the Non-Proliferation of Nuclear Weapons, designed to halt the spread of nuclear weapons to states that did not yet have them and to reduce stockpiles of existing bombs held by the nuclear powers. It seemed that the nuclear arms race might yet be reversed.

This outcome did not come to pass. French and Chinese leaders disregarded the test ban and by 1968 had developed their own nuclear weapons, although they later signed the nonproliferation treaty. India also developed nuclear weapons and in 1974 exploded an atomic device. Meanwhile, the nuclear arms race between the Soviet Union and the United States was so intense that after the 1960s both sides sought ways of slowing it and negotiated shared limits to their nuclear arsenals. A series of treaties between 1969 and 2010 have brought substantial reductions in nuclear weapons stockpiles.

India's nuclear test in 1974 in turn frightened Pakistan, which pursued its own nuclear weapons. In 1998 both India and Pakistan tested nuclear devices within weeks of each other. Other nations discreetly pursued nuclear arms without publicly stating that they possessed them.

In the 1950s Israel began developing nuclear weapons, and it is generally believed to have had an arsenal of nuclear weapons since the 1970s. Israel's apparent nuclear superiority was threatening to Arab states that for decades had tried to vanquish Israel. When Iraq attempted, with help from France, to develop nuclear capability in the 1980s, Israel responded by attacking and destroying the Iraqi nuclear reactor in June 1981.

The risks associated with the proliferation of nuclear weapons helped mobilize the international community and contributed to positive developments through the 1980s and 1990s. Between 1983 and 2003 Argentina, Romania, Brazil, South Africa, and Libya all agreed to abandon their nuclear weapons programs. Several

CHAPTER LOCATOR | Does the contemporary world reflect the "end of history"? | How have migration and the circulation of capital and technology shaped the world?

CHAPTER 33
1032 THE CONTEMPORARY WORLD IN HISTORICAL PERSPECTIVE

of the former Soviet republics that possessed nuclear arsenals returned their nuclear weapons to Russia. International agencies monitored exports of nuclear material, technology, and missiles that could carry atomic bombs. These measures encouraged confidence in global cooperation and in the nonproliferation treaty, which was extended indefinitely in 1995.

Despite these efforts, nuclear proliferation has continued. In 2003 the United States accused Iran of seeking to build nuclear weapons, and ongoing diplomatic efforts, sanctions, and other punitive measures have failed to induce Iran to limit its nuclear program. There is also the threat that enriched nuclear materials will fall into the hands of terrorist organizations or that countries possessing nuclear weapons technology would share it with other nations.

In the new century, long-standing tensions between North Korea and the United States, which had never signed a peace treaty to end the 1950–1953 Korean War, intensified over North Korea's pursuit of nuclear weapons and ballistic missile technology. As each side accused the other of failing to live up to its agreements, North Korea tested its first nuclear device in 2006. A year later, North Korea agreed to shut down its major nuclear facility at Yŏngbyŏn in exchange for thousands of tons of fuel oil from the West and the release of $25 million in frozen North Korean funds. In 2009, however, North Korea ended all diplomatic talks, expelled all nuclear inspectors, and conducted a nuclear test. In the years that followed, North Korean authorities have engaged in nuclear brinksmanship.

Al-Qaeda and Afghanistan

In the Middle East and Central Asia, conflicts that had involved the superpowers continued beyond the Cold War. The 1979 Soviet invasion of Afghanistan, as well as the Iranian revolution, which was followed by the Iran-Iraq War, led to enduring political upheaval that continued to draw the United States into violent conflicts in the twenty-first century.

In Afghanistan rebel groups supported by the United States fought the Soviet armed forces occupying the country, and forced a Soviet withdrawal in 1989. In 1996, after years of civil war, a puritanical Islamic movement called the Taliban filled the military and political vacuum left by the Soviet Union. The Taliban pursued a radical religious transformation of Afghan society, in particular by imposing harsh restrictions on women. The Taliban government provided safe haven in Afghanistan for a terrorist organization called al-Qaeda. In the 1990s, led by Osama bin Laden (1957–2011), al-Qaeda attacked U.S. diplomatic and military targets in Africa and the Middle East.

On September 11, 2001, al-Qaeda militants hijacked four passenger planes in the United States. They flew two of them into the World Trade Center buildings in New York City and a third into the Pentagon in Washington, D.C. A fourth, believed to be targeting the White House or the U.S. Capitol, crashed into a field in rural Pennsylvania. These terrorist attacks killed almost three thousand people. In response, the U.S. government demanded that the Taliban government in Afghanistan surrender the al-Qaeda leadership it hosted. When the Taliban refused, the United States formed a military coalition including NATO members as well as Russia, Pakistan, and rebel groups in Afghanistan. The coalition mounted an invasion, deposed the Taliban, and pursued al-Qaeda.

What challenges did social reformers address at the turn of the twenty-first century?

How have science and technology kept pace with population change?

✓ LearningCurve
Check what you know.

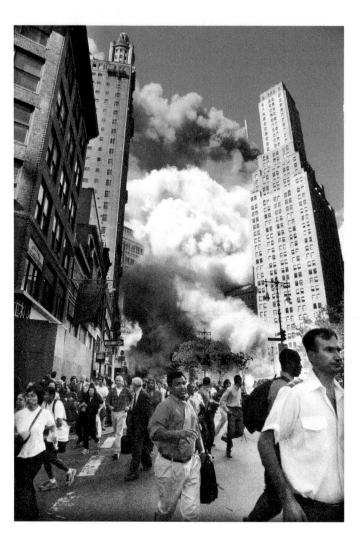

New York, September 11, 2001

Pedestrians race for safety as the World Trade Center towers collapse after being hit by jet airliners. (Amy Sanetta/AP Photo)

After the U.S.-led coalition deposed the Taliban in 2001 and installed a new government in Afghanistan, it faced a protracted guerrilla war against Taliban forces that controlled rural areas. The conflict in Afghanistan spread to Pakistan, where some members of al-Qaeda found refuge, and acts of terrorism increased around the world in the years following the invasion of Afghanistan.

Through years of war, the United States and allied governments devastated al-Qaeda's leadership and reduced its reach, but local groups acting in conflicts in the Middle East and Africa continued to act under al-Qaeda's name. Militants with loose ties to al-Qaeda set off multiple bombs in a Madrid train station on March 11, 2004, killing 191 and wounding over 1,800. In London on July 7, 2005, terrorist bombs killed 56 people and injured more than 700. At least three of the bombers were British citizens of Pakistani descent with unclear links to al-Qaeda. A suicide bomber who may have had links to al-Qaeda has also been blamed for the 2007 assassination of Pakistani presidential candidate Benazir Bhutto. In 2011 U.S. intelligence services identified bin Laden's hideout in Pakistan in a compound located near the country's main military academy in Abbottabad. In a night raid, U.S. forces killed bin Laden.

U.S. military action against al-Qaeda and the Taliban spilled over into another conflict in the Middle East when the U.S. government invaded Iraq in 2003. In the decade following the conclusion of the Persian Gulf War (1990–1991), Iraq faced international economic sanctions along with constant political and military pressure from the United States to surrender its chemical and biological weapons stockpiles. After 2001, amid the U.S. invasion of Afghanistan, U.S. president George W. Bush accused Iraq of rebuilding its nuclear, chemical, and biological weapons programs. To build domestic support for an invasion, the U.S. government also falsely implied that there were connections between Iraq and al-Qaeda. In 2002 UN inspectors found no weapons of mass destruction. France, Russia, China, Germany, and a majority of the smaller states argued for continued weapons monitoring, and France threatened to veto any resolution authorizing an invasion of Iraq. Rather than risk this veto, the United States and Britain claimed that earlier Security Council resolutions provided sufficient authorization and invaded Iraq in 2003.

CHAPTER LOCATOR | Does the contemporary world reflect the "end of history"? | How have migration and the circulation of capital and technology shaped the world?

A coalition of U.S.-led forces quickly defeated the Iraqi military, and in the power vacuum that ensued, armed groups representing all three main factions in Iraq—Sunni Muslims, Shi'ite Muslims, and Kurds—carried out daily attacks on Iraqi military and police, government officials, religious leaders, and civilians. Estimates of Iraqi deaths since the beginning of the war in 2003 and the U.S. withdrawal in 2011 ranged from 100,000 to over 1 million. Though the U.S. military occupation ended in 2011, the violence continued. Paradoxically, though the connection between al-Qaeda and the government of Saddam Hussein implied by President Bush did not exist, postwar Iraq became a place where militant groups that identified with al-Qaeda proliferated.

Iraq, ca. 2010

Areas that are predominantly
☐ Sunni (ca. 36%)
☐ Shi'ite (ca. 60%)
▨ Mixed
— Kurdish

QUICK REVIEW <

What contemporary trends and developments demonstrate some of the limits of liberalism?

What challenges did social reformers address at the turn of the twenty-first century?

How have science and technology kept pace with population change?

✔ LearningCurve
Check what you know.

1035

How have migration and the circulation of capital and technology continued to shape the world?

The Bazaar Economy

These merchant women selling vegetables in Pisac, Peru, form part of an informal economy. (© Juergen Ritterbach/vario Images RM/age fotostock)

MUCH OF THE HISTORY IN THIS TEXTBOOK is driven by the circulation of peoples over great distances. Migration continues to be one of the great engines of history, though its experience exposes one of the major contradictions in the way liberalization has been conducted: governments have pressed for the free circulation of goods and capital, but have sought to limit the movement of people across borders.

Migration

National immigration policies vary considerably. In Europe the process of integration has meant that European Union member countries permit the free movement of citizens from other EU nations. But in many other cases, restrictions on migration have increased even as barriers to trade and investment have fallen.

The border between the United States and Mexico reflects many of the challenges of contemporary migrations. As the United States conquered land that had belonged to Mexico in the nineteenth century (see Chapter 27), it restricted the movement of migrants northward across the border. At the beginning of the twenty-first century the U.S. government began building a wall at its border with

CHAPTER LOCATOR | Does the contemporary world reflect the "end of history"? | How have migration and the circulation of capital and technology shaped the world?

CHAPTER 33
1036 THE CONTEMPORARY WORLD IN HISTORICAL PERSPECTIVE

Mexico, further restricting the circulation of people even as the United States and Mexico negotiated a free-trade agreement that made it easier for goods and capital to cross the border.

Similar trade agreements, coupled with similar restrictions on migration, exist between the United States and many Central American and Caribbean nations. The United States is by far the leading source of foreign investment in those countries. And the United States has participated in military conflicts in all of those countries over the past century. Still, within the United States, the most intense public discussions about Latin America surround the restriction of migration.

In many cases, restrictions on immigration have increased in countries where national economic growth has slowed. For instance, as Japanese industry boomed in the 1980s, the country welcomed descendants of Japanese emigrants who had settled in South America in the first half of the century to come to Japan as guest workers. As manufacturing and economic growth stagnated in the 1990s, this circuit of migration to Japan dwindled. During the same period millions of people, first from South Korea and then Vietnam, Cambodia, and Laos, whose countries had experienced great upheavals in conflicts involving the United States, found legal refuge in the United States. (See "Individuals in Society: Sieng, a Mnong Refugee in an American High School," page 1038.)

Though pursuit of economic opportunity and flight from persecution are the major factors that drive international migration, other factors shape the creation of migratory circuits. A migratory circuit is a deep connection created between two regions through an initial experience of migration that results in a greater circulation of people. These migratory circuits have often followed experiences of violence. For instance, circuits of migration to the United States have often followed U.S. military actions, such as wars in Southeast Asia and Korea or military interventions in Latin America.

Migrants usually become ethnic, religious, or linguistic minorities in the countries where they settle, and they commonly face discrimination. Sometimes this discrimination is expressed in violence and oppression. In turn, discrimination and social pressures have also triggered violent reactions from ethnic minorities, such as riots in the Paris suburbs in 2007 and Stockholm in 2013 to protest discrimination experienced by Middle Eastern and North African migrants. When migrants lack legal standing, as is the case for millions in the United States, they can fall prey to criminal organizations or be exploited by employers.

Urbanization

Cities in Africa, Asia, and Latin America expanded at an astonishing pace after 1945. Many doubled or even tripled in size in a single decade (Table 33.1). In 1950 there were only eight **megacities** (5 million or more inhabitants), and only two were in developing countries. Of the fifty-nine megacities anticipated to exist by 2015, forty-eight will be outside North America and Europe.

megacities
▶ Cities with populations of 5 million people or more.

What caused this urban explosion? First, the overall population growth in the developing nations was critical. Urban residents gained substantially from a medical revolution that provided improved health care but only gradually began to reduce the size of their families. Second, more than half of all urban growth comes from rural migration. Manufacturing jobs in the developing nations were concentrated in cities.

What challenges did social reformers address at the turn of the twenty-first century?

How have science and technology kept pace with population change?

✓ LearningCurve
Check what you know.

INDIVIDUALS IN SOCIETY
Sieng, a Mnong Refugee in an American High School

In 2008, at a large urban high school in the U.S. South, Sieng, a seventeen-year-old Mnong refugee, recited the Pledge of Allegiance in his JROTC class. His aspiration to join the U.S. Marine Corps was an act of belonging that bridged both his life in the United States and his sense of his family and its history.

The Mnong are among a diverse group of ethnic minorities, known broadly as Montagnards, whose communities stretch across the central highlands of Vietnam. They are also a religious minority in Vietnam — many had converted to Christianity. During the Vietnam War, many Mnong provided military service alongside the United States, particularly with the U.S. Army Special Forces. After the war ended in 1975, the Mnong faced persecution and over time many fled the country, joining the current of refugees who resettled in camps in Thailand, Malaysia, the Philippines, and later Cambodia. Sieng's family left Vietnam when he was a child in the late 1990s. He recalled his journey:

> We had a hard time in Vietnam, so we had to leave. We didn't have no choice because we had no food, and no land. And [the Vietnamese government] wanted my dad and took my grandpa. So we left in the night and went through the jungle. We walked and walked and got lost. So me and my dad tried to find the way and we found a house. Some people let us sleep there and also gave us food. Then we got to a [refugee] camp in Cambodia and stayed there for a year. I didn't have school in Vietnam, and I didn't have school at the camp. Then we came here.

Arriving in the United States at the age of sixteen, Sieng was not literate in Mnong, Vietnamese, or English, the language of his new school. Sieng aspired to become a Marine so he could help other refugees and his family. He explained, "A man needs to take care of the family too, and that's what I want to do. The Marines will help me take care of my family."

For Sieng, being a refugee instilled a sense of pride, a sense of what he and his family had overcome in coming to the United States, and a sense of what he desired for the future. As the oldest male child, Sieng was, in his words, "second in command" in the home while his father worked the third shift at a shipping facility. In the United States Sieng was an ethnic minority and a refugee with limited English skills. He was misunderstood. A classmate in a world history class asked him where he was from in Mexico, and the question made him indignant:

Hmong students and their teaching assistant at a high school in Wisconsin recite the Pledge of Allegiance. (Morry Gash/AP Photo)

I am a *refugee*, not an immigrant! I am *Mnong*, not Vietnamese! But people call me Spanish. Some kids once asked me to say something in Spanish. . . . And Mexican students think I'm Chinese. They say, *"Hey Chino! Hey Chino!"* I get mad when they do this because I am more like American. My grandpa worked with Americans [in the war].

In a diverse school, amid other immigrants and ethnic minorities, Sieng found comfort in his identity as a refugee, reflecting on his family's past, its connection to the United States, and his role facilitating its journey, as he confronted a new environment, struggling to be understood.

Source: Liv T. Dávila, "Performing Allegiance: An Adolescent Refugee's Construction of Patriotism in JROTC," *Educational Studies* 39.5 (2014), in press. Reprinted by permission of Taylor & Francis LLC (http://www.tandfonline.com).

QUESTIONS FOR ANALYSIS

1. What aspects of Sieng's experience reflect broader patterns of migration?
2. How does Sieng's experience as a refugee shape his identity?
3. What role does JROTC play in Sieng's sense of belonging?

ONLINE DOCUMENT PROJECT

What are the key issues surrounding immigration reform? Examine documents related to the debate over U.S. immigration reform, and then complete a quiz and writing assignment based on the evidence and details from this chapter. *See inside the front cover to learn more.*

TABLE 33.1 ■ Urban Population as a Percentage of Total Population in the World and in Eight Major Areas, 1925–2025

Area	1925	1950	1975	2000	2025 (est.)
World Total	21%	28%	39%	50%	63%
North America	54	64	77	86	93
Europe	48	55	67	79	88
Soviet Union	18	39	61	76	87
East Asia	10	15	30	46	63
Latin America	25	41	60	74	85
Africa	8	13	24	37	54

Note: Little more than one-fifth of the world's population was urban in 1925. In 2000 the total urban proportion in the world was about 50 percent. According to United Nations experts, the proportion should reach two-thirds by about 2025. The most rapid urban growth will occur in Africa and Asia, where the move to cities is still in its early stages.

Newcomers have streamed to the cities even when industrial jobs have been scarce, seeking any type of employment. Many migrants were pushed into cities. As large landowners found it more profitable to produce export crops, their increasingly mechanized operations reduced the need for agricultural laborers. Ethnic or political unrest in the countryside can also push migrants into cities. These push factors have been particularly strong in Latin America, with its neocolonial pattern of large landowners and foreign companies that exported food and raw materials.

Most of the exploding numbers of urban poor earned precarious livings in a bazaar economy comprised of petty traders and unskilled labor. In the bazaar economy, which echoed early preindustrial markets, regular salaried jobs were rare and highly prized, and a complex world of tiny, unregulated businesses and service occupations predominated. Peddlers and pushcart operators hawked their wares, and sweatshops and home-based workers manufactured cheap goods for popular consumption. This bazaar economy grew prodigiously as migrants streamed to the cities.

bazaar economy
► An economy with few salaried jobs and an abundance of tiny, unregulated businesses such as peddlers and pushcart operators.

After 1945 large-scale urban migration profoundly affected traditional family patterns in developing countries, just as it had during the Industrial Revolution. Particularly in Africa and Asia, the great majority of migrants to cities were young men. There were several reasons for this pattern. Much of the movement to cities was temporary or seasonal. Moreover, the cities were expensive, and prospects there were uncertain. Only after a man secured a genuine foothold did he marry or send for his wife and children.

For rural women, the consequences of male out-migration to cities were mixed. Asian and African women found themselves heads of households, faced with managing the farm, feeding the children, and running their own lives. African and Asian village women had to become unprecedentedly self-reliant and independent. As a result, rural women in Africa and Asia began to gain some rights and opportunities, but they faced limitations as well.

Migration patterns in Latin America differed from this model. Whole families generally migrated, often to squatter settlements, much more commonly than in Asia and Africa. These families frequently belonged to the class of landless

What challenges did social reformers address at the turn of the twenty-first century?

How have science and technology kept pace with population change?

☑ LearningCurve
Check what you know.

laborers, which was generally larger in Latin America than in Africa and Asia. Migration was also more likely to be permanent. Another difference was that single women were as likely as single men to move to the cities, in part because women were in high demand as domestic servants. Even so, in Latin America urban migration seems to have had less of an impact on family patterns and on women's attitudes than it did in Asia and Africa.

In cities the concentration of wealth in few hands has resulted in unequal consumption, education, health care, and employment. The gap between rich and poor around the world can be measured both between the city and the country-side, and within cities (Map 33.1). Wealthy city dwellers in developing countries

MAP 33.1 ■ The Global Distribution of Wealth, ca. 2010

This size-comparison map, arranged according to global wealth distribution, vividly illustrates the gap in wealth between the Northern and Southern Hemispheres. The two small island nations of Japan and the United Kingdom have more wealth than all the nations of the Southern Hemisphere combined, although wealth creation in India and Brazil has advanced significantly. The wealthiest countries are also the most highly urbanized. As market capitalism expands in China, Vietnam, and other Asian countries and in Latin America and Africa, the relative-size ratios on the map will continue to change and evolve. Tiny Iceland, whose GDP is less than $20 billion, nevertheless has one of the highest per capita GDPs in the world.

> MAPPING THE PAST

ANALYZING THE MAP: Which three countries are the wealthiest? Where are the poorest countries concentrated?
CONNECTIONS: How were the two small nations of Japan and the United Kingdom able to acquire such enormous wealth?

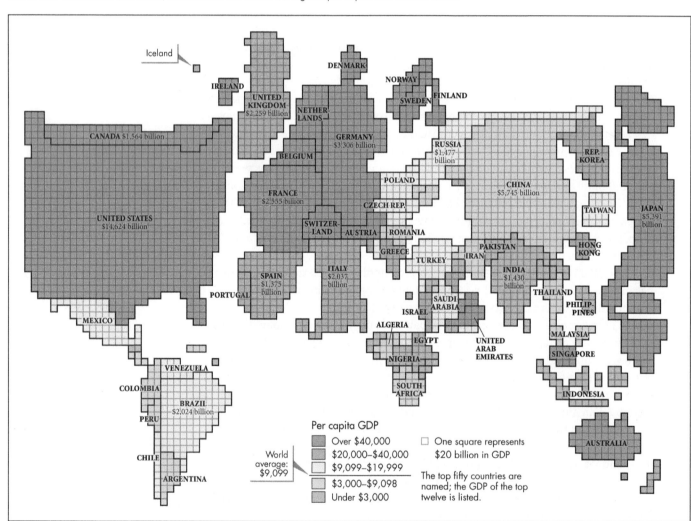

CHAPTER LOCATOR | Does the contemporary world reflect the "end of history"? | How have migration and the circulation of capital and technology shaped the world?

CHAPTER 33
1040 THE CONTEMPORARY WORLD IN HISTORICAL PERSPECTIVE

often had more in common with each other than with their poorer urban and rural people in their own country. As a result, the elites have often favored globalization that connects them with wealthier nations.

Multinational Corporations

A striking feature of global interdependence beginning in the early 1950s was the rapid emergence of **multinational corporations**, or multinationals, which are business firms that operate in a number of different countries and tend to adopt a global rather than a national perspective. Their rise was partly due to the revival of capitalism after the Second World War, increasingly free international economic relations, and the worldwide drive for rapid industrialization. Multinationals treated the world as one big market, coordinating complex activities across political boundaries and escaping political controls and national policies.

The impact of multinational corporations, especially on less industrialized countries, has been mixed. The presence of multinationals helped spread the products and values of consumer society to elites in the developing world. Critics considered this part of the process of neocolonialism, whereby local elites abandoned their nation's interests and contributed to continued foreign domination.

Multinational corporations are among the main beneficiaries of economic liberalism: growing openness of national markets and growing economic integration allow corporations to move goods, capital, and technology more fluidly and more intensely. But the growing interconnectedness of world markets comes with

multinational corporations

▶ Business firms that operate in a number of different countries and tend to adopt a global rather than a national perspective.

Multinational Companies in China

A Gap clothing store is reflected in the windows of an Apple store in Shanghai, China.
(© Jeffrey Greenberg/The Image Works)

What challenges did social reformers address at the turn of the twenty-first century?

How have science and technology kept pace with population change?

 LearningCurve
Check what you know.

costs. In particular, it has meant increased economic volatility such as the banking crisis that swept the United States and Europe in 2008 and plunged countries into deep and long recessions.

The recession created particular hardship in Greece, Italy, Spain, and Portugal. Monetary policy for the euro was set for the currency zone as a whole and was strongly influenced by its most powerful economies, Germany and France, which resisted expanding the monetary supply to relieve the most afflicted economies in the Eurozone. The tension between the economic policymaking of Germany and France and the deep economic crisis in southern Europe threatened European economic unity.

> **QUICK REVIEW**

What are the most important factors driving contemporary migration patterns? What steps have states taken to shape or limit the movement of people across borders?

CHAPTER LOCATOR | Does the contemporary world reflect the "end of history"? | How have migration and the circulation of capital and technology shaped the world?

CHAPTER 33
1042 THE CONTEMPORARY WORLD IN HISTORICAL PERSPECTIVE

Equal Marriage in Argentina

Latin America's first same-sex marriage occurred in Tierra del Fuego, Argentina, in 2009. (Tierra del Fuego Government/Reuters/Landov)

What challenges did social reformers address at the turn of the twenty-first century?

AS MOVEMENTS FOR HUMAN RIGHTS and social reform gained ground in the 1960s and 1970s, activists increasingly looked beyond national borders to form alliances. Movements for women's rights, nuclear disarmament, environmental protection, and addressing climate change all became both local and global efforts. For example, the global anti-apartheid movement kept pressure on nations to apply economic and political sanctions on the white minority regime in South Africa. But at the same time, the anti-apartheid movement served as a means to address local problems. For instance, in Brazil anti-apartheid activism helped draw attention to the country's own racial inequalities.

The 1977 Nestlé boycott exemplified the kinds of success such movements could achieve as well as their limitations. Critics charged that the Swiss company's intense marketing of powdered baby formula in poor countries or regions with little access to clean water posed a risk to children. Activists called on consumers around the world to boycott Nestlé products.

At first, Nestlé dismissed the boycott and sought to discredit the movement. However, widespread condemnation of Nestlé continued to mount, and in 1981 the UN World Health Organization responded to the campaign by developing a

What challenges did social reformers address at the turn of the twenty-first century?

How have science and technology kept pace with population change?

 LearningCurve
Check what you know.

1043

set of voluntary standards regulating the marketing of infant formula in poorer countries where access to clean water was precarious. In 1984 Nestlé agreed to follow the standards. The movement succeeded, but its success raised questions: multinational corporations operate beyond the reach of single governments and often operate in regions with weak regulatory or investigatory structures or in countries where repressive political systems shield them from scrutiny. As a result, it is hard to hold them accountable when their conduct is unethical. At the same time, social movements and nongovernmental organizations also acted outside the realm of public accountability.

Environmentalism

The modern environmental movement began with concerns about chemical waste, rapid consumption of energy and food supplies, global deforestation, and threats to wildlife. By the 1970s citizens had begun joining together in nongovernmental organizations to pursue preservation or restoration of the natural environment.

The environmental movement is actually several different movements, each with its own agenda. American biologist and writer Rachel Carson was an early proponent of the environmental health movement. In *Silent Spring* (1962), she warned of the dangers of pesticides and pollution. Environmentalists like Carson acted out of concern that all living things were connected and that damage to one part of an ecological system could have consequences across that ecosystem.

The conservation movement, represented in the United States by the Sierra Club and the Audubon Society, seeks to protect the biodiversity of the planet and emphasizes the spiritual and aesthetic qualities of nature. The ecology movement consists of different groups with somewhat similar agendas, ranging from politically active green parties to the nongovernmental organization Greenpeace. These organizations are concerned about a wide range of environmental issues, and they often highlight the connections between the environment, on the one hand, and social, economic, and political developments, on the other.

Environmentalists today are especially concerned about **global warming**, the increase of global temperatures over time caused by the buildup of carbon in the atmosphere that captures heat. As a result of global warming, average temperatures have increased worldwide in recent decades, a trend that most scientists expect will intensify without curbs on carbon emissions. Scientists believe that man-made climate change began with the Industrial Revolution in the eighteenth century. The subsequent release of hydrocarbons produced through the burning of fossil fuels—coal, oil, natural gas—have caused a greenhouse effect that traps these gases and heats up earth's atmosphere. Paradoxically, industrialization and increased consumption in the developing world meant diminished global inequalities but intensified global carbon emissions.

International concerns over the potentially catastrophic consequences of global warming resulted in a 1997 agreement, the Kyoto Protocol, which amended the United Nations Framework Convention on Climate Change. Countries that ratify the Kyoto Protocol agree to reduce their emissions of carbon dioxide and five other greenhouse gases. As of April 2014, 191 countries had ratified it. The most

global warming

▶ The belief of the majority of the world's scientists that hydrocarbons produced through the burning of fossil fuels have caused a greenhouse effect that has increased global temperatures over time.

Global Warming

In the twenty-first century development pressures meet growing concern about climate change. (Joel Pett Editorial Cartoon used with the permission of Joel Pett and the Cartoonist Group)

notable exception was the United States. The United Nations and environmental activists have continued to pursue an international environmental accord that can bring all nations into a shared effort to combat climate change.

Lesbian, Gay, and Transgender Rights

By the early 1970s a global gay rights movement championed the human rights of lesbian, gay, and transgendered people. The movement intensified in the 1980s as it became clear that governments neglected medical research and treatment for people sick with AIDS, which they dismissed as a "gay disease." The organization Act Up's advocacy campaign for AIDS research created a powerful symbol using the words "Silence = Death" inside a pink triangle to represent the AIDS crisis.

By the 1990s gay rights activists had broadened their efforts to challenge discrimination in employment, education, and public life. In 1995 Canada became the first country to allow same-sex marriage. In the ensuing years many European countries followed suit. But the legalization of same-sex marriage was not only a Western achievement: by 2013 Argentina, South Africa, Ecuador, and Uruguay had legalized same-sex marriage, while many other nations provided legal protections for families that stopped shy of marriage. Argentina led the way in legal support for transgendered people and made sexual reassignment surgery a legal right in 2012.

Women's Right to Equality

The 1995 United Nations Fourth World Conference on Women, held in Beijing, China, called on the world community to take action in twelve areas of critical concern to women: poverty, access to education and training, access to health

What challenges did social reformers address at the turn of the twenty-first century?

How have science and technology kept pace with population change?

LearningCurve
Check what you know.

care, violence against women, women and war, economic inequality with men, political inequality with men, creation of institutions for women's advancement, lack of respect for women's rights, stereotyping of women, gender inequalities and the environment, and violation of girl children's rights.[1] These are concerns that all women share, although degrees of inequality vary greatly from one country to another.

feminization of poverty

▶ The issue that those living in extreme poverty are disproportionately women.

The feminization of poverty, the disproportionate number of women living in extreme poverty, applies to even the wealthiest countries, where two out of every three poor adults are women. There are many causes for this phenomenon. Because women are primarily responsible for child care in many cultures, they have less time and opportunity for work. Male labor migration increases the number of households headed by women and thus the number of families living in poverty. Job restrictions, discrimination, and limited access to education reduce women's employment options. Birthrates are higher among poor women, particularly among adolescents. The poorest women usually suffer most from government policies, usually legislated by men, which restrict their access to reproductive health care and family planning.

Women have made gains in the workplace, making up 38 percent of the non-farm-sector global workforce in the early 2000s, as compared to 35 percent in 1990. But segregated labor markets remain the rule, with higher-paying jobs reserved for men. In the farm sector, women produce more than half of all the food and up to 80 percent of subsistence crops grown in Africa. Because this is informal labor and often unpaid, these women laborers are denied access to loans, and many cannot own the land they farm.

Social class continues to be a major divider of women's opportunities. Over the course of the twentieth century women from more affluent backgrounds experienced far greater gains in access to education, employment, and political representation than women in poverty did.

Children: The Right to Childhood

In 1989 the United Nations General Assembly adopted the Convention on the Rights of the Child, which spelled out a number of rights that are due every child. These include civil and human rights and economic, social, and cultural rights. It is not difficult to see why such a document was necessary. Globally, a billion children live in poverty—one in every two children in the world. The convention also addresses other concerns, including the fact that children make up half the world's refugees, and the problems of child labor and exploitation, sexual violence and sex trafficking, police abuse of street children, HIV/AIDS orphans, lack of access to education, and lack of access to adequate health care. The United States and Somalia remain the only two United Nations member nations that have not ratified the treaty.

As the twenty-first century began, nearly a billion people—mostly women denied equitable access to education—were illiterate. Increasing economic globalization has put pressure on all governments to improve literacy rates and educational opportunities; the result has been reduced gender inequalities in education. The greatest gains in literacy have occurred in South Asia and the Middle East.

CHAPTER LOCATOR | Does the contemporary world reflect the "end of history"? | How have migration and the circulation of capital and technology shaped the world?

CHAPTER 33
1046 THE CONTEMPORARY WORLD IN HISTORICAL PERSPECTIVE

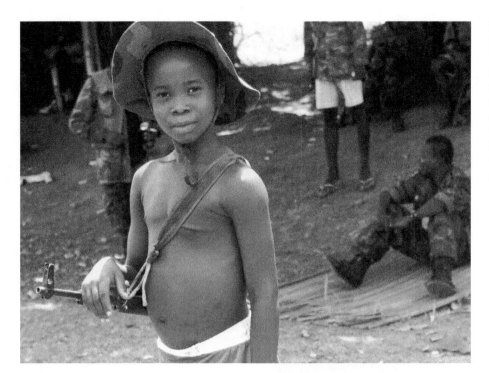

Mexico pioneered a new approach to combating poverty that has been implemented in a growing number of countries. Conditional cash transfer, or CCT, provides a stipend to families who meet certain goals, such as keeping their children in school. This approach addresses poverty directly, while enlisting families to work toward its long-term solution by increasing education levels, which will broaden opportunities for new generations. Versions of the program have been introduced across Latin America, Asia, and the Middle East.

QUICK REVIEW ◄

What global trends have led to the feminization of poverty?

What challenges did social reformers address at the turn of the twenty-first century?

How have science and technology kept pace with population change?

☑ LearningCurve
Check what you know.

1047

How have science and technology kept pace with population change?

Protest Against Genetically Modified Foods

Chilean demonstrators oppose the introduction of genetically modified crops. The banner reads, "I do not want transgenic crops in Chile: Movement for Food Sovereignty." (Eliseo Fernandez/Reuters/Landov)

> **PICTURING THE PAST**

ANALYZING THE IMAGE: What do the costumes suggest about the protesters' views about the effects of genetically modified foods?

CONNECTIONS: What are some of the advantages and disadvantages of the scientific engineering of food crops?

SINCE 1950 THE WORLD'S POPULATION has increased from 2.5 billion people to over 7 billion. This population growth has been matched by increasing demand for food and has placed growing strains on natural resources. Advances in agriculture and medicine have helped offset this challenge, while technological innovations in areas such as transportation and communications have increased the complexity of interactions among the world's growing number of people.

Intensified Agriculture and the Green Revolution

As the world's population grew in the second half of the twentieth century, food production strained to keep pace, prompting a greater emphasis on rural development and agricultural sciences. Before 1939 the countries of Asia, Africa, and Latin America had collectively produced more grain than they consumed. After 1945, as their populations soared, they began importing food from countries like

CHAPTER LOCATOR | Does the contemporary world reflect the "end of history"? | How have migration and the circulation of capital and technology shaped the world?

CHAPTER 33
1048 THE CONTEMPORARY WORLD IN HISTORICAL PERSPECTIVE

the United States. Although crops might fail in poor countries, starvation seemed a thing of the past.

Then, in 1966 and 1967, India was hit with a devastating famine. That close brush with mass starvation created widespread alarm that population growth was outpacing food production. The American scientist Paul Ehrlich envisioned a grim future in his 1968 bestseller *The Population Bomb*, which warned of a population crisis. Ehrlich was not the first scientist to make such dire predictions, and like Thomas Malthus before him (see page 689), he failed to understand the adaptability of farmers and agricultural technology to keep pace with population growth.

Technological improvements countered such nightmarish visions and offered hope. Plant scientists set out to develop new genetically engineered seeds. The first breakthrough came in Mexico in the 1950s when an American-led team developed new strains of high-yield wheat. These varieties enabled farmers to double their yields, though the plants demanded greater amounts of fertilizer and water for irrigation. Mexican wheat production soared. Thus began the transformation of agriculture in some poor countries—the so-called green revolution.

In the 1960s American-backed scientists in the Philippines developed a new hybrid "miracle rice" that required more fertilizer and water but yielded more and grew much faster than ordinary rice. Asian scientists developed similar hybrid strains of rice to meet local conditions.

As they applied green revolution technologies, many Asian countries experienced rapid increases in grain production. Farmers in India increased production more than 60 percent in fifteen years. China followed with its own highly successful version of the green revolution.

The green revolution offered new hope to industrializing nations, though its benefits often flowed to large landowners and export farms that could afford the necessary investments in irrigation and fertilizer. Experiences in China and other Asian countries showed, however, that even peasant families with tiny farms could gain substantially. Indeed, the green revolution's greatest successes occurred in Asian countries with broad-based peasant ownership of land. Conversely, the green revolution spread most slowly in regions with low rates of peasant landownership.

As the practice of planting genetically engineered crops to increase production grew in the late twentieth and early twenty-first centuries, many feared that such foods would have still-unknown harmful effects on the human body. The loss of biodiversity was also of growing concern. When one or two genetically engineered seeds replaced all the naturally occurring local seeds in an area, food security was threatened. With a shrinking diversity of plants and animals, farmers find it more difficult to find alternatives if the dominant hybrid seed in use becomes susceptible to a particular disease or pest or if a significant climate change occurs.

green revolution

▶ The increase in food production stemming from the introduction of high-yielding wheat, hybrid seeds, and other advancements.

Slowing Population Growth

By the 1970s and 1980s population growth in the industrialized countries had begun to fall significantly. By the 1990s some European leaders were expressing concern that low birthrates threatened national economies by reducing the labor force, the tax base, and the number of consumers. Between 1970 and 1975 China registered the fastest five-year birthrate decline in recorded history. Other

What challenges did social reformers address at the turn of the twenty-first century?

How have science and technology kept pace with population change?

LearningCurve
Check what you know.

countries, especially in Latin America and East Asia, experienced declines in fertility. Fertility in most of the developing world could fall below the replacement level (2.1 children per woman) before 2100.

There were several reasons for this decline in fertility among women in the developing world. As fewer babies died of disease or malnutrition, families needed fewer births to guarantee the survival of the number of children they wanted. Better living conditions, urbanization, and more education encouraged women to have fewer children.

In the early 1960s the introduction of the birth control pill allowed women to take control of their own fertility. Family planning was now truly possible. In the early twenty-first century, more than half of the world's couples practiced some form of birth control, up from one in eight just forty years earlier.

The Medical Revolution

The medical revolution began in the late 1800s with the development of the germ theory of disease (see page 731) and continued rapidly after World War II. Scientists discovered vaccines for many of the most deadly diseases. According to the United Nations World Health Organization, medical advances reduced deaths from smallpox, cholera, and plague by more than 95 percent worldwide between 1951 and 1966.

Medical advances significantly lowered death rates and lengthened life expectancies worldwide. Children became increasingly likely to survive their early years, although infant and juvenile mortality remained far higher in poor countries than in rich ones. By 1980 the average inhabitant of the developing countries could expect to live about fifty-four years, although life expectancy at birth varied from forty to sixty-four years depending on the country. In industrialized countries, life expectancy at birth averaged seventy-one years.

The medical benefits of scientific advances have been limited by unequal access to health care, which is more readily available to the wealthy than the poor. Between 1980 and 2000 the number of children under the age of five dying annually of diarrhea dropped by 60 percent through the global distribution of a cheap sugar-salt solution mixed in water. Still, over 1.5 million children worldwide continue to die each year from diarrhea, primarily in poorer nations. Deaths worldwide from HIV/AIDS, malaria, and tuberculosis were concentrated in the world's poorest regions, while tuberculosis remained the leading killer of women worldwide.

In 2007 the United Nations calculated that 36 million persons globally were infected with HIV, the virus that causes AIDS, and that AIDS was the world's fourth-leading cause of death. About 90 percent of all persons who die from AIDS and 86 percent of those currently infected with HIV live in sub-Saharan Africa (Map 33.2). In Africa HIV/AIDS is most commonly spread through heterosexual sex. Widespread disease and poverty are also significant factors in that Africans already suffering from other illnesses such as malaria or tuberculosis are less resistant to HIV and have less access to health care for treatment.

Another critical factor contributing to the spread of AIDS in Africa is the continued political instability of many countries—particularly those in the corridor running from Uganda to South Africa. This region was the scene of brutal civil and liberation wars that resulted in massive numbers of refugees, a breakdown

CHAPTER LOCATOR | Does the contemporary world reflect the "end of history"? | How have migration and the circulation of capital and technology shaped the world?

CHAPTER 33
1050 THE CONTEMPORARY WORLD IN HISTORICAL PERSPECTIVE

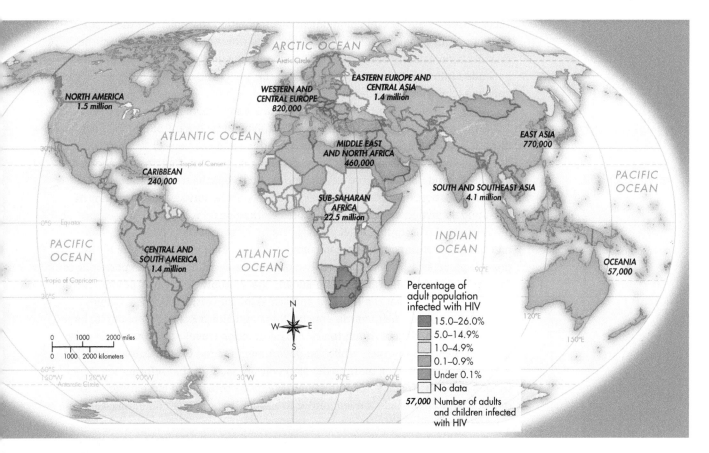

MAP 33.2 ■ People Living with HIV/AIDS Worldwide, ca. 2010

As this map illustrates, Africa has been hit the hardest by the HIV/AIDS epidemic. It currently has fifteen to twenty times more identified cases than any other region of the world. AIDS researchers expect that in the coming decade, however, Russia and South and East Asia will overtake and then far surpass Africa in the number of infected people. (Source: Data from World Health Organization, www.whosea.org)

in basic health-care services, and the destruction of family and cultural networks. The people living in this area in the countries of Uganda, Rwanda, Burundi, Zaire/Congo, Angola, Zimbabwe, Mozambique, and South Africa have been decimated by HIV/AIDS. Since 2001 relatively inexpensive AIDS drugs that are widely available in the West have been dispensed freely to many of those infected in Africa and Asia, but the availability of these drugs has generally failed to keep up with the need.

A Digital Revolution

The invention of moving pictures, the telephone, and other communications technologies between 1875 and 1900 prepared the way for a twentieth-century era of mass communications. In parallel, new information-processing technologies began with development of adding and calculating machines and culminated in the development of the first computers during the Second World War. As computing and communications technologies converged, they created the "information age." The global availability and affordability of radios and television sets in the

What challenges did social reformers address at the turn of the twenty-first century?

How have science and technology kept pace with population change?

LearningCurve
Check what you know.

1950s introduced a second communications revolution that followed the first revolution brought by telegraph and telephone. The transistor radio penetrated the most isolated hamlets of the world. Though initially less common, television use expanded into nearly every country during the 1960s and 1970s, even if there was only one television in a village.

The third, and perhaps greatest, communications revolution occurred with the first Apple personal computers in 1976, followed by the introduction of cell phones in 1985. The use of mass communications and the pace of technological development in communications have exploded since then. Cell phones allowed individuals and nations in the developing world to bypass traditional telephone lines, installation, and other obstacles, and cell phones have become among the most widely owned communications tools worldwide.

Despite the ubiquity of cell phones, the Internet, or World Wide Web, has had the greatest impact on human communication. First made available to the general public in 1994, the Internet has opened up seemingly infinite possibilities for global access to information and knowledge. Authoritarian governments have realized the threat that the Internet and social media platforms pose to their power and control. The governments of China and North Korea, for example, have spent millions of dollars trying to restrict information traveling in and out of their countries over the Internet, while the governments of the United States and other nations have spent even more to develop ways to monitor that information. Even as expanding means of communication have made censorship more difficult to enforce, they have made it even harder to keep information or communications private.

The intensity of innovation in communications and information technology created new business giants. Apple, Microsoft, Google, and IBM are entities that stand at the forefront of the contemporary world, and they absorb and distribute enormous amounts of capital. The success of these technology companies and the proliferation of computer, cellular telephone and Internet use are remarkable changes, but they also deepen a stubborn continuity: deep socioeconomic inequalities between countries and within countries. The unevenness of both the production and consumption of computer technology has resulted in a digital divide, meaning the gap in access to Internet and computer and telecommunications resources. This gap is the greatest between nations like the United States, western European countries, and Japan and nations in Africa and South or Southeast Asia. The digital divide also exists between the wealthy and poor, as well as between urban and rural areas within countries.

digital divide

▶ The gap between levels of access to computing, Internet, and telecommunications between rich and poor regions and populations.

> **QUICK REVIEW**

What challenges and opportunities have been created by the third communications revolution?

CHAPTER LOCATOR | Does the contemporary world reflect the "end of history"? | How have migration and the circulation of capital and technology shaped the world?

CHAPTER 33
1052 THE CONTEMPORARY WORLD IN HISTORICAL PERSPECTIVE

CHAPTER SUMMARY

The end of the Cold War confrontation between superpowers has resulted in a world in which regional tensions endure and sometimes become international conflicts. Consequently, in a way similar to its actions in the Cold War era, the United States after 1990 continued to be involved in military conflicts far from home in regions ranging from the Balkans to Libya, Iraq, and Afghanistan. These conflicts have also spurred arms races that have led to the emergence of new nuclear powers in South Asia and East Asia.

The transitions to economic and political liberalism in the former Soviet bloc and in Latin America were particularly dramatic expressions of the rise of liberalism worldwide, which included the economic and political integration of Europe and the emergence of China as an economic superpower. Growing interconnectedness of world markets has meant increased economic volatility, such as the global financial market crisis of 2008. Cycles of economic growth and crisis, as well as contradictory experiences of integration and regional conflict, are tensions of the modern world rooted in historical experiences.

 CONNECTIONS The present shapes the ways we ask questions about the past. Understanding of the past also shapes our questions about the present and the future. Our history of world societies shows that the forces that shape the world we live in have deep roots: Globalization reaches back for centuries. Current armed conflicts are based on historic tensions often rooted in ethnic differences or legacies of colonialism. The gaps between rich and poor countries, and between the rich and poor within countries, have sometimes been diminished by advances in science and technology or by reforms in social policy. But science, technology, and public policy also deepen those inequalities, as uneven industrialization and the digital divide reflect.

We find these competing tensions throughout history, and we find them often recurring over time and place: our relationship with the past is one of continuity and change. The study of history allows us to frame questions about complex, competing, and often-contradictory experiences. Asking these questions sharpens our focus on not only the past but also the present. We are shaped by history. But we also make it.

ONLINE DOCUMENT PROJECT

The Immigration Debate

What are the key issues surrounding immigration reform?

Examine documents related to the debate over U.S. immigration reform, and then complete a quiz and writing assignment based on the evidence and details from this chapter. *See inside the front cover to learn more.*

What challenges did social reformers address at the turn of the twenty-first century?

How have science and technology kept pace with population change?

 LearningCurve
Check what you know.

CHAPTER 33 STUDY GUIDE

STEP 1

GET STARTED ONLINE

 LearningCurve

Now that you've read the chapter, make it stick by completing the LearningCurve activity.

STEP 2

EXPLAIN WHY IT MATTERS

Put your reading into practice. Identify each term below, and then explain why it matters in world history.

TERM	WHO OR WHAT & WHEN	WHY IT MATTERS
middle powers (p. 1031)		
megacities (p. 1037)		
bazaar economy (p. 1039)		
multinational corporations (p. 1041)		
global warming (p. 1044)		
feminization of poverty (p. 1046)		
green revolution (p. 1049)		
digital divide (p. 1052)		

STEP 3

MOVE BEYOND THE BASICS

To demonstrate a more advanced understanding of the impact of global trends on Asia, Africa, and Latin America, fill in the chart below with descriptions of the impact in the following key areas: urbanization, population growth, and technology and science. In what ways has the social and economic history of these three regions converged in recent decades? In what ways has it diverged?

	Urbanization	Population Growth	Technological and Scientific Developments
Asia			
Africa			
Latin America			

PUT IT ALL TOGETHER

Now, take a step back and try to explain the big picture. Remember to use specific examples from the chapter in your answers.

LIBERALISM AND GLOBALIZATION

▶ What particular challenges do multinational corporations pose to developing nations?

▶ How would you explain the tendency of governments around the world to remove barriers to the circulation of goods and capital and at the same time that they erect new barriers to cross-border migration?

SOCIAL MOVEMENTS

▶ What are the most important obstacles to the formulation and implementation of a coordinated global response to climate change?

▶ Why do women and children remain the most vulnerable populations on the planet?

SCIENCE AND TECHNOLOGY

▶ In your opinion, will recent advances in communication technology lead to more or less political and individual freedom? Why?

▶ What challenges and opportunities have been created by recent advances in science and technology?

LOOKING BACK, LOOKING AHEAD

▶ In what ways does the current era of globalization differ from earlier period of accelerating global contacts?

▶ A hundred years from now, will the nation-state still be the basic unit of social and political organization? Why or why not?

> ## IN YOUR OWN WORDS

Imagine that you must give an oral report to the class answering the following question: **Why did liberalization emerge as a such a powerful force in the second half of the twentieth century, and what were the consequences of this development? What would be the most important points and why?**

ENDNOTES

Chapter 4

1. Patricia Buckley Ebrey, ed., *Chinese Civilization: A Sourcebook*, 2d ed., revised and expanded (New York: Free Press, 1993), p. 33. All quotations from this work reprinted and edited with the permission of The Free Press, a Division of Simon & Schuster, Inc. Copyright © 1993 by Patricia Buckley Ebrey. Copyright © 1981 by The Free Press. All rights reserved.

Chapter 9

1. Quoted in B. F. Stowasser, "The Status of Women in Early Islam," in *Muslim Women*, ed. F. Hussain (New York: St. Martin's Press, 1984), p. 25.
2. F. E. Peters, *A Reader on Classical Islam* (Princeton, N.J.: Princeton University Press, 1994), p. 250.
3. R. Hillenbrand, "Cordoba," in *Dictionary of the Middle Ages*, vol. 3, ed. J. R. Strayer (New York: Scribner's, 1983), pp. 597–601.

Chapter 10

1. T. Spear, "Bantu Migrations," in *Problems in African History: The Precolonial Centuries*, ed. R. O. Collins et al. (New York: Markus Weiner Publishing, 1994), p. 98.
2. J. S. Trimingham, *Islam in West Africa* (Oxford: Oxford University Press, 1959), pp. 6–9.
3. R. A. Austen, "The Trans-Saharan Slave Trade: A Tentative Census," in *The Uncommon Market: Essays in the Economic History of the Atlantic Slave Trade*, ed. H. A. Gemery and J. S. Hogendorn (New York: Academic Press, 1979), pp. 1–71, esp. p. 66.
4. Pekka Masonen and Humphrey J. Fisher, "Not Quite Venus from the Waves: The Almoravid Conquest of Ghana in the Modern Historiography of Western Africa," *History in Africa* 23 (1996): 197–232.
5. See H. G. Marcus, *A History of Ethiopia*, updated ed. (Berkeley: University of California Press, 2002), pp. 17–20.
6. Ibn Battuta, *The Travels of Ibn Battuta, A.D. 1325–1354*, vol. 1, ed. H. A. R. Gibb (London: University Press, 1972), pp. 379–380.
7. Austen, "The Trans-Saharan Slave Trade," p. 65; J. H. Harris, *The African Presence in Asia* (Evanston, Ill.: Northwestern University Press, 1971), pp. 3–6, 27–30; P. Wheatley, "Analecta Sino-Africana Recensa," in Neville Chittick and Robert Rotberg, *East Africa and the Orient* (New York: Africana Publishing, 1975), p. 109.

Chapter 11

1. Ross Hassig, *War and Society in Ancient Mesoamerica* (Berkeley: University of California Press, 1992), p. 81, 85.
2. Ross Hassig, *Aztec Warfare* (Norman: University of Oklahoma Press, 1988), p. 143.

Chapter 16

1. Thomas Benjamin, *The Atlantic World: Europeans, Africans, Indians and Their Shared History, 1400–1900* (Cambridge: Cambridge University Press, 2009), p. 141.
2. Herbert S. Klein, "Profits and the Causes of Mortality," in *The Atlantic Slave Trade*, ed. David Northrup (Lexington, Mass.: D. C. Heath, 1994), p. 116.

Chapter 19

1. Quoted in G. L. Mosse et al., eds., *Europe in Review* (Chicago: Rand McNally, 1964), p. 156.
2. Orlando Patterson, *Slavery and Social Death* (Cambridge, Mass.: Harvard University Press, 1982), p. 255.

Chapter 20

1. P. D. Curtin, *Economic Change in Precolonial Africa: Senegambia in the Era of the Slave Trade* (Madison: University of Wisconsin Press, 1975), pp. 34–35; J. A. Rawley, *The Transatlantic Slave Trade: A History* (Lincoln: University of Nebraska Press, 2005).
2. Quoted in R. Hallett, *Africa to 1875* (Ann Arbor: University of Michigan Press, 1970), p. 151.
3. Ibid., pp. 35–38.
4. P. E. Lovejoy, *Transformations in Slavery: A History of Slavery in Africa* (Cambridge: Cambridge University Press, 1992), p. 25, Table 2.1, "Trans-Saharan Slave Trade, 650–1600."
5. J. Iliffe, *Africans: The History of a Continent* (Cambridge: Cambridge University Press, 1995), p. 77.
6. R. Shell, *Children of Bondage: A Social History of the Slave Society at the Cape of Good Hope, 1652–1838* (Hanover, N.H.: University Press of New England, 1994), pp. 285–289.
7. R. Blackburn, *The Making of New World Slavery: From the Baroque to the Modern, 1492–1800* (New York: Verso, 1998), pp. 79–80.
8. *Equiano's Travels: The Interesting Narrative of the Life of Olaudah Equiano*, ed. P. Edwards (Portsmouth, N.H.: Heinemann, 1996), p. 23–26.
9. Rawley, *The Transatlantic Slave Trade*, pp. 45–47.
10. Robert W. July, *A History of the African People* (Prospect Heights, Ill.: Waveland Press, 1998), p. 171.
11. Robert W. July, *Precolonial Africa: An Economic and Social History* (New York: Scribner's, 1975), pp. 269–270.
12. A. G. Hopkins, *An Economic History of West Africa* (New York: Columbia University Press, 1973), p. 119.
13. P. Manning, *Slavery and African Life: Occidental, Oriental, and African Slave Trades* (New York: Cambridge University Press, 1990), pp. 22–23 and chap. 3, pp. 38–59.

Chapter 23

1. N. F. R. Crafts, *British Economic Growth During the Industrial Revolution* (Oxford: Oxford University Press, 1985), p. 32.
2. See especially J. Brenner and M. Rama, "Rethinking Women's Oppression," *New Left Review* 144 (March–April 1984): 33–71, and sources cited there.
3. Joel Mokyr, *The Enlightened Economy: An Economic History of Britain, 1700–1850* (New Haven, Conn.: Yale University Press, 2009), pp. 460–461.
4. Ibid., p. 455.
5. Quoted in D. Geary, ed., *Labour and Socialist Movements in Europe Before 1914* (Oxford: Berg, 1989), p. 29.

Chapter 24

1. Jonathan Sperber, *The European Revolutions, 1848–1851*, 2d ed. (Cambridge: Cambridge University Press, 2005), pp. 40–47.
2. J. McKay, *Tramways and Trolleys: The Rise of Urban Mass Transport in Europe* (Princeton, N.J.: Princeton University Press, 1976), p. 81.

Chapter 25

1. Iliffe, *Africans*, p. 169.
2. Lovejoy, *Transformations in Slavery*, p. 15.
3. R. Oliver, *The African Experience* (New York: Icon Editions, 1991), pp. 164–166.

Chapter 27

1. Jürgen Buchenau, *Mexican Mosaic: A Brief History of Mexico* (Wheeling, Ill.: Harlan-Davidson, 2008), p. 2
2. David Rock, *Argentina, 1516–1987: From Spanish Colonization to Alfonsín* (Berkeley: University of California Press, 1987), p. 154; Emilia Viotti da Costa, *The Brazilian Empire: Myths and Histories* (Chapel Hill: University of North Carolina Press, 2000), p. 78.

Chapter 28

1. Quoted in H. Nicolson, *Peacemaking 1919* (New York: Grosset & Dunlap Universal Library, 1965), pp. 8, 31–32.
2. Quoted in John Macquarrie, *Existentialism* (New York: Penguin Books, 1972), p. 15.

Chapter 30

1. Carl J. Friedrich and Zbigniew K. Brzezinski, *Totalitarian Dictatorship and Autocracy*, 2d ed. (Cambridge, Mass.: Harvard University Press, 1965), pp. 21–23.

2. See Robert C. Tucker, *Stalin in Power: The Revolution from Above, 1928–1941* (New York: W. W. Norton, 1992).

3. Robert Service, *Stalin: A Biography* (Cambridge, Mass.: Harvard University Press, 2005), p. 266.

4. M. Malia, *The Soviet Tragedy: A History of Socialism in Russia, 1917–1991* (New York: Free Press, 1995), pp. 227–270; see also the controversial work by historian John Archibald Getty, *Origins of the Great Purges: The Soviet Communist Party Reconsidered, 1933–1938* (New York: Cambridge University Press, 1985).

5. R. Vivarelli, "Interpretations on the Origins of Fascism," *Journal of Modern History* 63 (March 1991): 41.

6. Christopher Seton-Watson, *Italy from Liberalism to Fascism, 1870–1925* (London: Methuen, 1967), p. 661.

7. W. Brustein, *The Logic of Evil: The Social Origins of the Nazi Party, 1925–1933* (New Haven, Conn.: Yale University Press, 1996), pp. 52, 182.

8. Izidors Vizulis, *The Molotov-Ribbentrop Pact of 1939: The Baltic Case* (New York: Praeger, 1990), p. 16.

9. Jeremy Noakes and Geoffrey Pridham, eds., "Message from Hermann Göring to Reinhard Heydrich, 31 July, 1941," in *Documents on Nazism, 1919–1945* (New York: Viking Press, 1974), p. 486.

10. See, for example, Christopher Browning, *Ordinary Men: Reserve Police Battalion 101 and the Final Solution in Poland* (New York: HarperCollins, 1992); Robert Gellately, *Backing Hitler: Consent and Coercion in Nazi Germany* (Oxford: Oxford University Press, 2001); Ian Kershaw, *Hitler, the Germans, and the Final Solution* (New Haven, Conn.: Yale University Press, 2008).

Chapter 31

1. Winston Churchill, "Sinews of Peace" (the Iron Curtain Speech), delivered at Westminster College in Fulton, Missouri, March 5, 1946, in Robert Rhodes James, ed., *Winston S. Churchill: His Complete Speeches, 1897–1963*. Vol. 7: *1943–1949* (New York: Chelsea House, 1974), p. 7509.

2. Quoted in R. Hallett, *Africa Since 1875: A Modern History* (Ann Arbor: University of Michigan Press, 1974), pp. 378–379.

Chapter 33

1. United Nations, "Critical Areas of Concern," *Report of the Fourth World Conference on Women* (New York: United Nations Department for Policy Coordination and Sustainable Development, 1995), ch. 1, annex II, ch. 3, pp. 41–44, http://www.un.org/esa/gopher-data /conf/fwcw/off/a--20.en. See also Population Reference Bureau, *Women of Our World 2005* (Washington, D.C.: Population Reference Bureau, 2005) for the latest data and ten-year follow-up to the Beijing meeting.

INDEX

indulgences and, 436(i)
Jesus and, 165
Mandate of Heaven, **98**, 110–111, 904
the Marys at Jesus's Tomb, 214(i)
Old Kingdom tombs, 45
purgatory, 437
Qur'an and, 236
On the Revolutions of the Heavenly Spheres, 553, 557(t)
rulers and heaven, Shōtoku (prince), 197(t)
sacrifices to heaven, Zhou Dynasty, 98
sati practice, **351**, 500
Heavenly Kingdom of Great Peace (Taiping), 793
Heaven/Sky (god), 334
Hebrew Bible, 52–53, 134. *See also* Old Testament
Hebrew people. *See also* Jerusalem; Jews; Judaism
  Ark of the Covenant, 286, 287
  Babylonian Captivity, 53
  covenant, Yahweh and Hebrew people, 53
  described, 52–54
  Exodus, 53(m)
  family life, 54
  Judah (kingdom), 35(t), 53, 53(m)
  marriage, 54
  prophets
    Abraham, 53, 234(i), 236, 1000(i)
    Isaiah, 54, 600
    Moses, 53, 165, 236
  State (ca. 1250–800 B.C.E.), 53(m)
  stone seal (Jerusalem, ca. 600–700 B.C.E.), 52(i)
  Ten Commandments, 53–54, 216, 287
Hedwig of Silesia, Saint, 389(i)
Heian period, 378–381
  aristocratic culture, 379–380
  in chronology, 363(t)
  Esoteric Buddhism, 380
  Fujiwara family, 378–379, 381, 384
  Fujiwara Michinaga, 363(t), 380
  The Tale of Genji, 363(t), **379**, 380(i)
Helena (mother of Constantine the Great), sarcophagus of, 210(i)
Heliocentrism, 139, 559
Helladic period (ca. 3000–1200 B.C.E.), 116–118
  in chronology, 117(t)
  periodization, 114
Hellas, 116
Hellenic Greece (ca. 1200–323 B.C.E.)
  in chronology, 117(t)
  civil wars (323–ca. 300 B.C.E.), 117(t), 125, 132
  colonization (ca. 750–550 B.C.E.), 121, 122(m), 146
  origins, 114, 143
  Persian Wars (499–479 B.C.E.), 117(t), 125(m), 126(i)
  polis (plural *poleis*)
    Acropolis of Athens, 125, 126(i)
    democracy, **121**
    described, **120**–123
    development of (ca. 800–500 B.C.E.), 117(t), 120
    hoplites, 120(i), **121**, 124, 132

oligarchy, **121**
organization, 120–121
overseas expansion, 121, 122(m)
religious procession, 124(i)
Hellenistic period, **131**–141
  Alexander the Great
    conquests, 133(m)
    control of Gandhara kingdom, 78(i)
    death, 114, 131, 132
    debates, with Indian philosophers, 79
    enters Indus Valley (326 B.C.E.), 62, 65(t), 79
    Hellenization, 133–134
    military campaigns (336–324 B.C.E.), 117(t)
    Persian Empire conquest, 57, 79, 80(m), 131
    Philip II of Macedonia (father), 131, 132, 140
  Delos (island), 131(i)
  Gandhara art, 78(i)
  mystery religions, 128, 136, 137, 141
  philosophy, 137, 139
  polis to monarchy (404–200 B.C.E.), 132
  religion, 136–137
  Roman Republic and, 153
  sciences, 139–140
  terra-cotta figurine, Myrina (200 B.C.E.), 136(i)
  trade, 134–135
Hellenization, **133**–134
Helmet, Anglo-Saxon, 221(i)
Helots, 122
Henry (prince), 463–464
Henry III, 448
Henry II of England, 393, 394
Henry II of France, 489
Henry IV (Holy Roman emperor), 396
Henry IV of France, 448, 515(t), 524
Henry of Navarre, 448, 518
Henry VII, 433
Henry VIII, 423(t), 442, 516
Hera (goddess), 128(t)
Heraclius (emperor), 207
Herding. *See* Pastoralism
Hereditary groups. *See* Caste system
Heresy
  defined, **211**, **398**
  Galileo, 559
  Inquisition, 398, 434, 444, 516, 559
  witch-hunts, 449
Herodotus, 59
Herzl, Theodor, 743
Hetaerae and young man (drinking cup, Athens), 127(i)
Hideyoshi, Toyotomi, 610, 624(i), 626(m), 626–627, 634, 638
Hierarchical arrangements. *See* Social hierarchies
Hieroglyphics
  Aztecs, 299
  Egyptian civilization, 46, 50, 51, 51(t)
High Middle Ages, 401, 407, 409, 416, 550(i), 551. *See also* Middle Ages
hijra, 237. *See also* Muhammad
Hildegard of Bingen, 397, 397(i)
Himmler, Heinrich, 935, 941–942
Hindenburg, Paul von, 935

Hinduism
  Agni (god), 69
  Bhagavad Gita, 75, 77
  Brahmanic religion evolves to Hinduism (ca. 400 B.C.E.–200 C.E.), 65(t)
  Brahmanism, 65(t), 69–70, 74, 87
  cows and, 349
  dharma, **75**, 77, 80
  karma, **70**, 72, 84, 104, 188
  Krishna (god), 75, 77
  Mahabharata, 75, 77, 85
  Marathas (Hindu militant group), 503(m), 507, 508
  Ottoman Empire and Hindus, 500
  protected people, 248, **346**
  Puranas, 77
  Ramayana, 69, 77, 85, 119
  Upanishads, 65(t), 70, 785
  Vedas
    Bhaskara's mastery of, 348
    Buddha and, 74
    described, 67, 69, 75, 84
    Rig Veda, 65(t), **68**
  Vishnu (god), 71(i), 348, 354
Hippocrates, 129, 140
Hiroshima and Nagasaki, atomic bombs, 917(t), 946(i), 947(m), 948, 1032
Historical and Critical Dictionary (Bayle), 562, 564(t)
Histories (Herodotus), 59
History of the Former Han Dynasty (Ban Biao), 181
The History of the Wars of Justinian (Procopius), 208
History of the World (Rashid al-Din), 335(i)
Hitler, Adolf
  appeasement, 936–937, 940(t), 948
  as chancellor of Germany, 917(t), 935, 940(t)
  empire in Europe, 939–942
  Enabling Act, **935**, 940(t)
  Final Solution, 935, 942
  Mein Kampf, **870**, 917(t), 934
  Nazism and, 933–934
  New Order program, **941**, 948
  popularity, 936
  road to power, 934–935
  SS corps, 935, 941–942, 944
Hittite Empire
  expansion (ca. 1600 B.C.E.), 35(t), 48
  fall of, 48, 118
  Hattusili III-Ramesses II peace treaty, 48
  map, 47(m)
  Sea Peoples, 48
HIV/AIDS
  ACT UP organization, 1045
  deaths from, 1050
  orphans, 1046
  sub-Saharan Africa, 1050
  worldwide (ca. 2010), 1051(m)
Hobson, J. A., 751(t), 762–763
Hohokam people, 303–304, 304(m)
Hōjō family, 382
Holocaust
  Auschwitz, 915(i), 944, 945
  in chronology, 917(t)
  concentration camps, 758, 915(i), 935, 939(i), 942(m)

La Salle, René-Robert Cavelier, 537
Las Casas, Bartolomé de, 479
Lascaux Cave paintings, 15*(i)*
Late antiquity, 202, 231
Late Horizon, Andean culture, 305
Late Intermediate Period (Inca Empire), 306
Lateran Agreement of 1929, 917*(t)*, **932**
Lateran Council of 1059, 396
Latifundios, 154, *829*, 832
Latin America
    conservative authoritarianism in, 923
    Great Depression, 920–921
    immigration to (late nineteenth century), 832–833
    populism, 976–980
    rebuilding era (after World War II), 986
    re-entry into world economy (nineteenth century), 828–829
    revolutions, 671–676
        key events, 675*(t)*
        map (ca. 1780 and 1830), 674*(m)*
        origins of, 671–673
        resistance, rebellion, independence, 673–675, 674*(m)*
    urban population (1925–2025), 1039*(t)*
    U.S. intervention, 837–838
    Wars of Independence (1810–1825), 815*(t)*, 818, 828
Latium, 149
Laud, William, 530
Laura de Dianti (Titian), 428*(i)*
Lausanne, Treaty of, 885*(t)*, **892**
Law of inertia, **553**, 557*(t)*
Law of universal gravitation, **554**, 557*(t)*
Lawrence, T. E. (Lawrence of Arabia), 852
Laws
    barbarian groups, 220
    canon law
        Buddhist texts, 81, 375*(i)*, 376, 622
        Christianity, 170, 287
    Code of Manu (ca. 200 C.E.), 65*(t)*, **84**
    codes of conduct
        Bushido, **382**
        chivalry, 382, **405**
        Eightfold Path, **74**
    Combination Acts, 683(t), **705**
    Corpus Juris Civilis, 206–207
    dharma, **75**, 77, 80
    great white walls, **775**
    Hammurabi's law code, 42*(i)*, **42**–43
    Justinian's *Code*, **206**, 207*(t)*, 407–408
    laws, states, social hierarchies (3200–500 B.C.E.), 36–37
    lex Hortensia, 151
    Licinian-Sextian laws, 151
    Magna Carta, 391*(t)*, **394**
    Middle Ages, 394
    Mines Act of 1842, 683*(t)*, **700**
    Navigation Acts, 537*(m)*, 515*(t)*, **537**, 684
    shari'a, **243**, 248, 257, 258
    Ten Commandments, 53–54, 216, 287
    wergeld system, **220**
Laws of the Twelve Tables, 147*(t)*, 151
Lay followers. *See also* Buddhism; Jainism
    lay Buddhists, 74, 76–77
    lay Jains, 72
    Sudatta, and family, 76–77

League of Nations
    defined, **865**
    Germany in, 847*(t)*
    Mandates system, 885–886
Leakey, Mary, 4*(i)*
Lebanon, Phoenicians
    alphabet, 51, 51*(i)*, 59
    Carthage, 152
    described, **50**–51
    North Africa and, 270, 272
    settlements in Mediterranean, 51*(m)*
    trade in Mediterranean, 35*(t)*, 51*(m)*, 55*(t)*
Leclerc, Charles-Victor-Emmanuel, 667*(m)*, 668*(t)*
Legalism
    Daoism-Confucianism-Legalism comparison, 110*(t)*
    described, **108**–109
    Hans Feizi, 109
    Qin Dynasty, 109, 178, 201
Legends. *See* Epic poems; Myths
Legislative Assembly, 656, 658*(t)*
Leibniz, Gottfried Wilhelm von, 562, 564*(t)*
Lenin, Vladimir Ilyich
    New Economic Policy, 917*(t)*, **926**
    photo, 858*(i)*
Leo III (pope), 216, 227
Leopards
    leopard skins, East African coastal cities (late fifteenth century), 102*(i)*
    warrior fighting leopard, bronze mirror (Warring States Period), 102*(i)*
Leopold II (Habsburg Empire), 569
Leopold II of Belgium, 750*(i)*, 754, 756
Leo X (pope), 433, 437
Lepanto, Ottoman Empire, 487*(t)*, 489, 506
Lerdo Law, **819**
Lesbian, gay, and transgendered people, 1045
Lever, Archimedes, 138
Levi, Primo, 944–945
lex Hortensia, 151
Leyte Gulf, Battle of, 946
Liao Dynasty, 366, 367*(m)*, 367–368, 376
Liberalism
    defined, **715**, **814**
    in Spanish America, 814–816
Liberalization (1968–2000s), 990–1027
    apartheid
        described, 758, 1007, **1008**–1009
        global anti-apartheid movements, 1043
        student demonstrations, 1007*(i)*
    big picture, 1027*(i)*
    chronology, 993*(t)*
    CONNECTIONS, 1025
    European Union, 993*(t)*, 998, **1022**–1024, 1023*(m)*
    glasnost, 993*(t)*, **1017**
    "Japan, Inc.," **1013**–1014
    junta, 979, 993*(t)*, 1002*(i)*, **1003**–1005
    neoliberalism, **994**–995, 1003, 1022
    overview, 990
    perestroika, **1017**
    Solidarity, **1017**
    summary, 1024–1025
    Tiananmen Square, 993*(t)*, 1012*(i)*, **1012**–1013
    Washington Consensus, **994**–995, 1006

Liberation, 72, 84. *See also* Enlightenment (spiritual)
Liberation movements, 677, 957–958, 986
Liberation theology, **959**
Libya, OPEC oil embargo and, 997
Lichtenstein, Israel, 915*(i)*
Licinian-Sextian laws, 151
Life energy *(qi)*, 369, 370, 617
Limestone pillars, Göbekli Tepe site, 20, 20*(i)*
Lincoln, Abraham, 824
Linear A writing, 116
Linear B writing, 117
Li Si, 176–177, 178
Literacy
    Heian period, 379
    High Middle Ages, 409
    printing (invention) and, 368
    Shang society, 95
Literature, **717**, 858, 860, 861, 923. *See also* Bible; Epic poems; Myths; Plays; Poetry; Qur'an
    The Beautiful (Bhaskara), 348
    Bhagavad Gita, 75, 77
    Book of Changes, 91*(t)*, **109**
    Book of Documents, 91*(t)*, **97**–98, 110
    Enheduana's hymns, 42
    The Journey to the West (novel, Ming China), 618*(t)*
    khipus, 298*(i)*, **299**, 308, 324, 469
    Laozi (Daoist book and author's name), 91*(t)*, 108, 111
    Latin literature (reign of Augustus), 158
    Mahabharata, 75, 77, 85
    Periplus of the Erythraean Sea, 288–289
    Puranas, 77
    Ramayana, 69, 77, 85, 119
    realism, 713*(t)*, 738, 744
    Records of the Grand Historian (Sima Qian), 177*(t)*, **180**, 181
    "Rhapsody on the Two Capitals" (Ban Gu), 181
    romanticism, **717**, 858, 860, 861, 923
    The Tale of Genji, 363*(t)*, **379**, 380*(i)*
    Travels (Marco Polo), 255, 341*(i)*, 342
    Upanishads, 65*(t)*, 70, 785
    vernacular literature
        High Middle Ages, **409**, 416
        Ming Dynasty, 618, 638
        Renaissance, 426
    Zhuangzi (Daoist book and author's name), 91*(t)*, 108, 111
"Little ice age," 410, 508, 520, 619
Liu Bang, 178
Li Yuan, 190
Locke, John, 531, 559*(i)*, 562–563, 564*(t)*, 567, 646
Locomotive, *Rocket*, 683*(t)*, **688**
Loess soil, **90**–91, 92*(m)*
Logical positivism, 873
Logographic writing, 85, **95**–96, 95*(t)*
London, Crystal Palace, 683*(t)*, 689
Longbows, Hundred Years' War, 412
Long Count solar calendar, 303
Long March, 885*(t)*, **906**, 907*(m)*
Lord's Supper, Eucharist, 166, 216, 446
Lothair I, 227
Lotto, Lorenzo, 422
Louis IX, 392, 402*(m)*

About the Authors

John P. McKay (Ph.D., University of California, Berkeley) is professor emeritus at the University of Illinois. He has written or edited numerous works, including the Herbert Baxter Adams Prize-winning book *Pioneers for Profit: Foreign Entrepreneurship and Russian Industrialization, 1885–1913*.

Patricia Buckley Ebrey (Ph.D., Columbia University), professor of history at the University of Washington in Seattle, specializes in China. She has published numerous journal articles and *The Cambridge Illustrated History of China*, as well as several monographs. In 2010 she won the Shimada Prize for outstanding work of East Asian Art History for *Accumulating Culture: The Collections of Emperor Huizong*.

Roger B. Beck (Ph.D., Indiana University) is Distinguished Professor of African and twentieth-century world history at Eastern Illinois University. His publications include *The History of South Africa*, a translation of P. J. van der Merwe's *The Migrant Farmer in the History of the Cape Colony, 1657–1842*, and more than a hundred articles, book chapters, and reviews. He is a former treasurer and Executive Council member of the World History Association.

Clare Haru Crowston (Ph.D., Cornell University) teaches at the University of Illinois, where she is currently associate professor of history. She is the author of *Fabricating Women: The Seamstresses of Old Regime France, 1675–1791*, which won the Berkshire and Hagley Prizes. She edited two special issues of the *Journal of Women's History*, has published numerous journal articles and reviews, and is a past president of the Society for French Historical Studies.

Merry E. Wiesner-Hanks (Ph.D., University of Wisconsin-Madison) taught first at Augustana College in Illinois, and since 1985 at the University of Wisconsin-Milwaukee, where she is currently UWM Distinguished Professor in the department of history. She is the coeditor of the *Sixteenth Century Journal* and the author or editor of more than twenty books, most recently *The Marvelous Hairy Girls: The Gonzales Sisters and Their Worlds* and *Gender in History*. She is the former Chief Reader for Advanced Placement World History.

Jerry Dávila (Ph.D., Brown University) is Jorge Paulo Lemann Professor of Brazilian History at the University of Illinois. He is the author of *Dictatorship in South America*; *Hotel Trópico: Brazil and the Challenge of African Decolonization*, winner of the Latin Studies Association Brazil Section Book prize; and *Diploma of Whiteness: Race and Social Policy in Brazil, 1917–1945*. He has served as president of the Conference on Latin American History.